PennyPress

PUZZLER'S GIANT BOOK OF CROSSWORDS™ 61

Penny Press is the publisher of a fine family of puzzle magazines and books renowned for their editorial excellence.

This delightful collection has been carefully selected by the editors of Penny Press for your special enjoyment and entertainment.

Puzzler's Giant Book of Crosswords, No. 61, February 2017. Published four times a year by Penny Press, Inc., 6 Prowitt Street, Norwalk, CT 06855-1220. On the web at PennyDellPuzzles.com.

ISBN-13: 978-1-59238-106-7

ISBN-10: 1-59238-106-5

Printed by LSC Communications, Dwight, IL, U.S.A. 1/10/17

ENNY PRESS PUZZLE PUBLICATIONS

✦ PUZZLE MAGAZINES ✦

-Star Word Seeks
pproved Variety Puzzles
Classic Variety Puzzles Plus Crosswords
Easy & Fun Variety Puzzles
Easy Crossword Express
Family Variety Puzzles & Games
Famous Fill-In Puzzles
Fast & Easy Crosswords
Favorite Easy Crosswords
Favorite Fill-In
Favorite Variety Puzzles
Fill-In Puzzles
Garfield's Word Seeks
Good Time Crosswords
Good Time Easy Crosswords
Good Time Variety Puzzles
Large-Print Word Seek Puzzles
Master's Variety Puzzles
Merit Variety Puzzles & Games
Original Logic Problems
Penny's Finest Favorite Word Seeks
Penny's Finest Good Time Word Seeks
Penny's Finest Super Word Seeks
Quick & Easy Crosswords
Spotlight Celebrity Word Seek
Spotlight Movie & TV Word Seek
Spotlight Remember When Word Seek
Tournament Variety Puzzles
Variety Puzzles and Games
Variety Puzzles and Games Special Issue
Word Seek Puzzles
World's Finest Variety Puzzles

✦ SPECIAL SELECTED COLLECTIONS ✦

Alphabet Soup
Anagram Magic Square
Brick by Brick
Codewords
Cross Pairs Word Seeks
Crostics
Crypto-Families
Cryptograms
Diagramless
Double Trouble
England's Best Logic Puzzles
Flower Power
Frameworks
Large-Print Crosswords
Large-Print Cryptograms
Large-Print Missing Vowels
Letterboxes
Match-Up
Missing List Word Seeks
Missing Vowels
Number Fill-In
Number Seek
Patchwords
Places, Please
Quotefalls
Share-A-Letter
Simon Says
Stretch Letters
Syllacrostics
The Shadow
Three's Company
What's Left?
Word Games Puzzles
Zigzag

✦ PUZZLER'S GIANT BOOKS ✦

Crosswords
Sudoku
Word Games
Word Seeks

PUZZLE 1

• BOATS AFLOAT •

ACROSS

1. Robert or Alan
5. Friends
9. Ways and ____
11. Parcel out
12. Basil sauce
13. Showy flower
14. Nation
18. Lived
21. Singer Zadora
22. Campfire remnant
23. Forsake
27. Timid
30. Orchid necklace
31. Young woman
32. Freshly
34. Tint
35. Hit lightly
36. Fitzgerald of jazz
37. Airline letters
38. Lodging place
39. Change location
41. Tones down
44. Formal solo
45. Sketch
46. Biblical verse
47. Suggestive look
48. "____ Ballou"
49. Humpty Dumpty, for example
52. Fido's bane
54. Concerns for Freud
57. Pub fare
58. Spanish lady
60. Southeast Asian country
61. Golly!
62. Part of MPG
63. Small towers
65. Jinx
66. Nicholas ____ of "The Commish"
67. "____ to Remember"
68. Katherine Anne Porter novel
76. Clam's case
77. Cooked in oil
79. Premature
80. Beat
81. Self-conceits
82. Coll. entrance exams

DOWN

1. Current unit
2. Trevino and Marvin
3. Hundred-yard ____
4. Against
5. Not guilty, e.g.
6. Scads
7. The ____ Ranger
8. Messy place
10. Dunk
11. Rented res.
15. Semiprecious stone
16. Snorkeler's need
17. Ms. Thompson of "Family"
18. Cartoonist Disney
19. Addled
20. Captain
23. Feel poorly
24. Lingerie item
25. Single unit
26. Mesh fabric
27. Boat builder
28. Barbarians
29. Tokyo currency
31. Sparkled
33. Walks like a duck
36. Sermon topic
40. Man ____ mouse
42. Sector
43. Capp's Daisy ____
46. "____ Rider"
48. Bottle top
50. "I ____ You Babe"
51. Large African antelope
52. Mrs. Sprat's diet
53. ____ Angeles
55. Whitetail
56. Alluring
59. Woody's son
60. Fall faller
64. Game official, for short
68. Rug style
69. Villain's foe
70. Misfortunes
71. Wield
72. Frequently, in poems
73. Valuable lodes
74. Succotash bean
75. After Aug.
76. Comprehend
78. Uno, ____, tres . . .

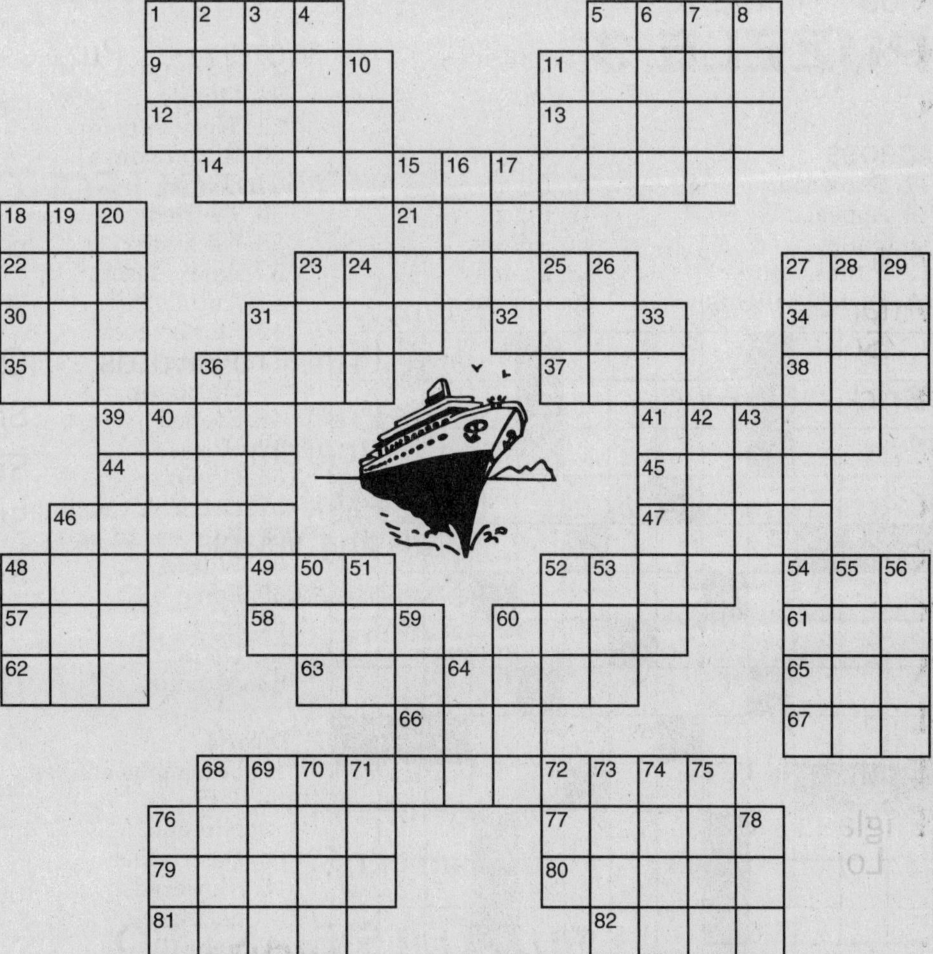

PUZZLE 2

ACROSS
1. Social grace
5. ERA or RBI
9. Bikini top
12. Sore
13. Ashen
14. Fit out
15. Cinch
16. Destroy
17. Unclose, to Keats
18. Lantern fuel
20. Unite
21. Aromatic mint plants
24. Grinned
28. Gesundheit preceder
31. Fiery felony
32. Taxi fees
33. Reimbursed
35. Falls short
36. Gnawing tooth
38. Transgress
40. Tripped
45. Luau dish
46. Ostrichlike birds
47. Molten rock
48. Long time
49. Cash rolls
50. Bakery worker
51. Printers' measures
52. Differently
53. Confined

DOWN
1. Chore
2. Skin woe
3. Singe
4. Input mistake
5. Widen
6. Tease
7. Outsiders
8. Knockout count
9. Window shoppers
10. Primed
11. Elderly
19. Picturesque
22. Sickly
23. Green vegetables
24. Cheers, e.g.
25. Sooner, to Browning
26. Headache remedies
27. Complain
29. Final letter
30. Snakelike curve
34. Dreary
35. Rich dessert
37. Author Terkel
38. En-garde blade
39. Hotel unit
41. Radar spot
42. Delicate fabric
43. ____-steven
44. Pub missile
46. Female bleater

PUZZLE 3

ACROSS
1. Bat wood
4. Appeal
8. Ballot
12. Fitness center
13. Poets' twilights
14. Matinee star
15. Buddy
16. Place
17. Allows
18. Chunky
20. Banister
22. ____ pop
24. Adventure yarns
28. Pang
31. Whitish gem
33. Bygone days
34. Sealed
36. Twirled
38. Neckwear
39. Asian desert
41. Automobiles
42. Small shoot
44. Apiece
46. Harmony
48. Seeped
52. Hazes
55. Deserve
57. Ostrich's cousin
58. Polynesian party
59. Within
60. Perch
61. Prod
62. Update
63. Attempt

DOWN
1. Venomous snakes
2. Tiff
3. Nimbus
4. Basil sauce
5. Flowered necklace
6. Snag
7. Voyaging
8. Country house
9. "____ on Melancholy"
10. Tyke
11. Chicago transports
19. Purposes
21. Emerald ____
23. Extinct bird
25. Joyous bash
26. Curing chemical
27. Lays down the lawn
28. New Testament book
29. Crop
30. Weeder
32. Cantata air
35. Like an omelet
37. Canyon sound
40. Suited
43. Publish
45. Housing unit
47. Within range
49. Gusto
50. Arabian prince
51. Tax
52. Winter illness
53. "____ Town"
54. Joke
56. Expel

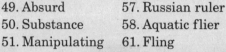

PUZZLE 4

ACROSS
1. Hone
5. Intervals
9. Switch positions
13. Per
14. Oahu greeting
16. Golfer's shout
17. Capri cash, of old
18. Maui geese
19. Stew
20. Nonsense
22. Dinnerware
24. Newt
25. Texas fare
26. Flits about
29. Shut hard
30. Cry noisily
33. Grief
35. Huge
37. Brass horn
38. Unfitting
40. Dieter's word
41. Provoker
43. Embarrassed
45. Track transaction
46. Kitchen boss
47. Aware of
48. Orange peels
50. Canine coat
52. Temporary replacement
54. County
59. James of jazz
60. Defense
62. Trickle
63. British prep school
64. Made on a loom
65. Julie Andrews film
66. Bruised
67. Foe of the "Titanic"
68. Gain income

DOWN
1. Swelling
2. Barber's concern
3. Pale brown
4. Those guys
5. Swindler
6. Quick-witted
7. Child's mount
8. "Murder, ____ Wrote"
9. Garbage
10. Very loud
11. Complimentary
12. Adjusts
15. Paving materials
21. Chihuahua currency
23. Chauffeured car
25. Hoof sound
26. Rounded chisel
27. Moderator
28. Phooey!
29. Muffler
31. Like a hot cereal
32. Seeped
33. Thrust
34. Retract
36. Hockey shot
39. Refusals
42. Skin problem
44. Damage
49. Absurd
50. Substance
51. Manipulating
52. Dregs
53. Director Preminger
54. Plunge headfirst
55. Fragrant bloom
56. Tiny amount
57. Russian ruler
58. Aquatic flier
61. Fling

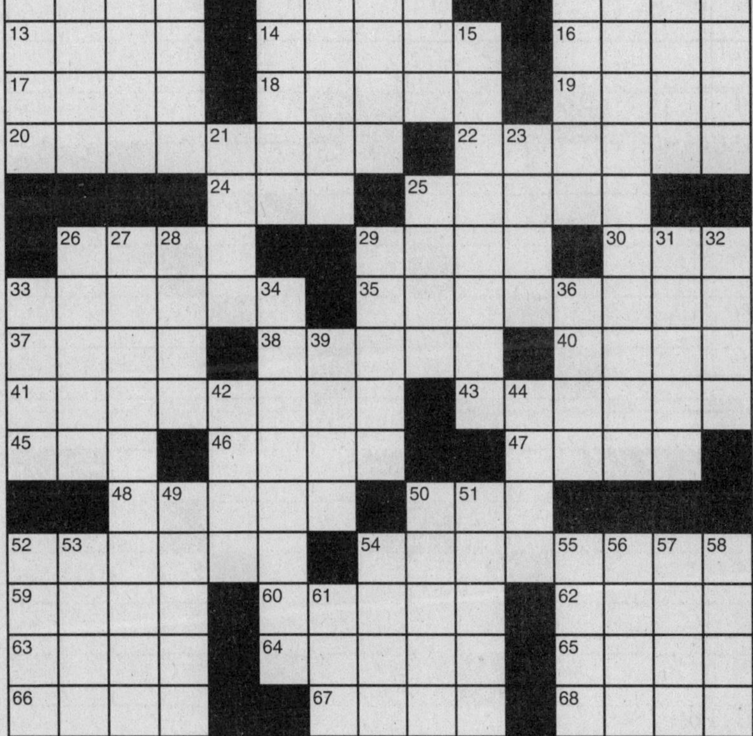

Quotagram PUZZLE 5

Fill in the answers to the clues. Then transfer the letters to the correspondingly numbered squares in the diagram. Each letter will be used only once. The completed diagram will contain a quotation.

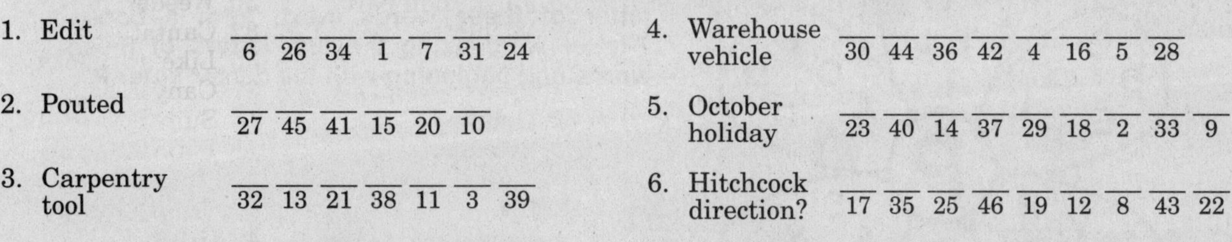

1. Edit ___ ___ ___ ___ ___ ___ ___ 6 26 34 1 7 31 24
2. Pouted ___ ___ ___ ___ ___ ___ 27 45 41 15 20 10
3. Carpentry tool ___ ___ ___ ___ ___ ___ ___ 32 13 21 38 11 3 39
4. Warehouse vehicle ___ ___ ___ ___ ___ ___ ___ ___ 30 44 36 42 4 16 5 28
5. October holiday ___ ___ ___ ___ ___ ___ ___ ___ ___ 23 40 14 37 29 18 2 33 9
6. Hitchcock direction? ___ ___ ___ ___ ___ ___ ___ ___ ___ 17 35 25 46 19 12 8 43 22

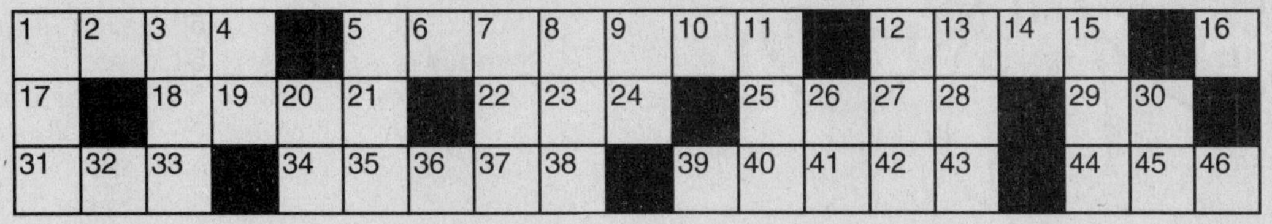

PUZZLE 6

ACROSS

1. Pinnacle
5. Jest
8. Liberal ____
12. Part of speech
13. Arm of water
15. Chime
16. Throw lightly
17. Distance runner
18. Ready to eat
19. Snow runner
20. Cookie fruit
21. Pressed
23. Fabric
25. "____ the Roof"
26. Pilot's assistant
29. Horned vipers
32. Coldest
33. Matured
35. List ending: abbr.
37. Food fishes
38. Beginning
40. Diva's solo
41. Bard's before
42. Chestnut, e.g.
43. Waning
45. PBS science series
47. Zodiac study
49. Formerly, formerly
51. Single
52. Screenplay
55. Naught
56. Author Fleming
59. Jack's tote
60. Planet's path
63. Farmland unit
64. Chip in a chip
65. Showy flower
66. Current fad
67. Clarinetist's insert
68. Poodle, e.g.
69. Lump of dirt

1	2	3	4	■	■	5	6	7	■	■	8	9	10	11
12				■	13				14	■	15			
16				■	17					■	18			
19			■	20			■	■	21	22				
■	■	23	24				■	25				■	■	■
26	27						28		■	29		30	31	■
32						■	33		34		■	35		36
37				■	38	39				■	40			
41			■	42				■	43	44				
■	45		46		■	47	48							
■	■	■	49		50		■	51					■	■
52	53	54				■	■	55			■	56	57	58
59				■	60	61	62			■	63			
64				■	65					■	66			
67				■	■	68			■	■	69			

DOWN

1. Aardvarks' tidbits
2. Restaurant employee
3. MTV offering
4. Printers' measures
5. Round Table member
6. Bedridden
7. Poor grade
8. Chefs' garments
9. Bridle control
10. Adhesive substance
11. Winter transport
13. Copycat
14. Expedition
20. Clouds
22. Highway
24. ____ down (reclines)
25. Spur on
26. Pleasant
27. Future oak
28. Desert springs
30. Magazine
31. Hornet's infliction
34. Timeless state
36. Shrewd
39. Well-groomed
40. Talented
42. Waterproof cover
44. Soup dish
46. Concealed
48. Adjusting
50. Whoa!
52. Boxers do it
53. Sugar source
54. Ceremony
57. Jason's ship
58. Must have
61. Sunburned
62. Shout of disapproval
63. Bow

PUZZLE 7

Daisy

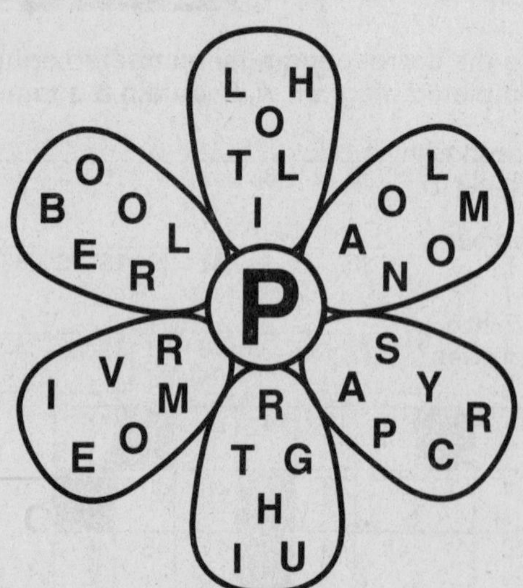

Form six 7-letter words using the letters in each Daisy petal PLUS the letter in the Daisy center, P. The P may not be used as the first letter of these words. Next, form a bonus 7-letter word using the first letters of these words and beginning with the center letter P.

PUZZLE 8

ACROSS
1. Killer whale
5. Comic-strip orphan
10. Colonial taxable
13. Temporary gift
14. Kitchen appliance
16. VCR button
17. Thrown missile
18. Harsh
19. Horror-film street
20. Violet blue
22. Surrounded by
23. Positive response
24. Initial for a superhero
25. Uttered
27. Goes wrong
29. Barker and Hope
30. Auditions
33. Dull pain
36. Notice
38. Devoted
39. Doubtful
40. Darlings
42. Camper's cover
43. Oven glove
44. Streetcar, in London
45. Periods in history
46. Insults
49. Lunch hour
51. Garlic feature
52. Load
53. Took a pew
56. In support of
58. Sudsy cleaner
60. Cut molars
62. Rodent pest
63. Improve
65. Elk
66. Native metal
67. Judge's decision
68. Baggage
69. Supplied
70. Like some hosiery
71. Crosscurrent

DOWN
1. Dated ditty
2. Speckled horses
3. Hallmark greetings
4. Person opposed
5. Soaked up
6. Born as
7. Maritime
8. Detail
9. More mysterious
10. Financial officer
11. Slippery
12. High point
15. Wipe again
21. Messy stuff
26. Available resources
28. Decayed
29. Wagered
30. Autocrat
31. Salad fish
32. Stage furnishings
33. BBs, e.g.
34. Hairdo
35. Left hastily
37. Golf goal
41. Silkier
47. Nuzzled
48. Some bees
50. Have a debt
52. Church feature
53. War horse
54. In front
55. Quarterback Bradshaw
56. Univ. teacher
57. Burger order
59. Bend
61. Border
64. Average grade

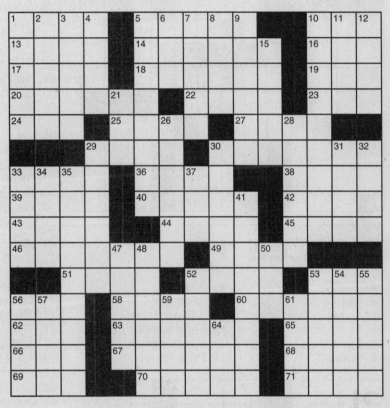

1	2	3	4	■	5	6	7	8	9	■	■	10	11	12
13				■	14					15	■	16		
17				■	18						■	19		
20				21		■	22				■	23		
24			■	25		26		■	27		28		■	■
■	■	■	29				■	30					31	32
33	34	35		■	36	37			■	■	38			
39				■	40				41	■	42			
43				■	■	44				■	45			
46				47	48		■	49		50		■	■	■
■	■	51				■	52				■	53	54	55
56	57		■	58		59		■	60		61			
62			■	63				64		■	65			
66			■	67						■	68			
69			■	■	70					■	71			

Bits and Pieces

PUZZLE 9

Can you identify these sports and activities from the Bits and Pieces shown in the boxes? The first words are always on the top and the second words on the bottom.

1. I E L / O C K

2. A B L / E N N

3. N G E / M P I

4. E L A / A C E

5. A T E / O L O

6. U L L / I D I

7. E A C / L E Y

8. M O L / E R B

PUZZLE 10

ACROSS

1. Tiny taste
4. Tibetan priest
8. Guitar's forerunner
12. Garden tool
13. Where to worship from
14. Alike
15. Breakfasted
16. Kettle or snare
17. Dandelion, e.g.
18. More ____ than good
20. Adjust
22. Out of bed
24. Totally cool!
27. Moved quickly
30. Silky
32. Departs
33. Inscribed
34. School assignment
36. Mixer part
37. Type
38. Healing agent
40. Pigpens
41. Wound covering
45. Nuisance
48. Grating
50. Have debts
51. Region
52. Conceal
53. Knee's site
54. Dull and colorless
55. Hearty dish
56. Newspaper items

DOWN

1. Persian king
2. Smidgen
3. Gaze
4. Young man
5. Feeling fear
6. Handles roughly
7. Legions
8. Patch of grass
9. Luau instrument
10. Even score
11. Result
19. Dillon and Lauer
21. Nibbled
23. St. Tropez, e.g.
24. Rampage
25. Pay to play
26. Tinter
27. Cold-cuts shop
28. Figure-skating jump
29. Venture
31. Waiters' needs
35. Stable sounds
36. Next to
39. Worthiness
40. Pierce
42. Soda flavor
43. Struck with wonder
44. Pleads
45. Bachelor's home
46. Mess up
47. Aegean, e.g.
49. Morning moisture

PUZZLE 11

ACROSS

1. Bursts
5. At once, to a doctor
9. Short farewell
12. Car's wheel shaft
13. Instep
14. Shad ____
15. Look like
16. Extinct reptile
18. Slow-moving mollusk
20. Confined
21. Busy activity
23. Mom's parent
27. Dog's foot
30. Rogues
32. Finished
33. Ran wild
35. Intrude
37. Skunk's defense
38. Seaweed
40. For what reason?
41. Brawl
43. "____ Wednesday"
44. Detect
46. Deed holder
51. Flourishes
55. Wriggly
56. Still, in verse
57. Fencing blade
58. Bottom support
59. Craps cube
60. Transported
61. Fitness clubs

DOWN

1. Mountain route
2. Cattle
3. Guilty, e.g.
4. Teamster's rig
5. Pathetic
6. Camera stand
7. Pimples
8. Sandal
9. Bathing-suit part
10. "I Got ____ Babe"
11. Eternity, in poetry
17. Sharpener
19. Delicate trim
22. Word from a crib
24. Affirm
25. Netting
26. Hunter's quarry
27. High-school dance
28. Nurse's ____
29. Mohair or cashmere
31. Autograph
34. Shade givers
36. BLT dressing
39. Ordinary churchgoers
42. Curvy letters
45. Vatican figure
47. Spiders' snares
48. Kind of tide
49. Movie lioness
50. Dark breads
51. Bunk
52. Necklace of flowers
53. Single unit
54. Matched group

CODEWORD

PUZZLE 12

Codeword is a special crossword puzzle in which conventional clues are omitted. Instead, answer words in the diagram are represented by numbers. Each number represents a different letter of the alphabet, and all of the letters of the alphabet are used. When you are sure of a letter, put it in the code key chart and cross it off in the alphabet box. A group of letters has been inserted to start you off.

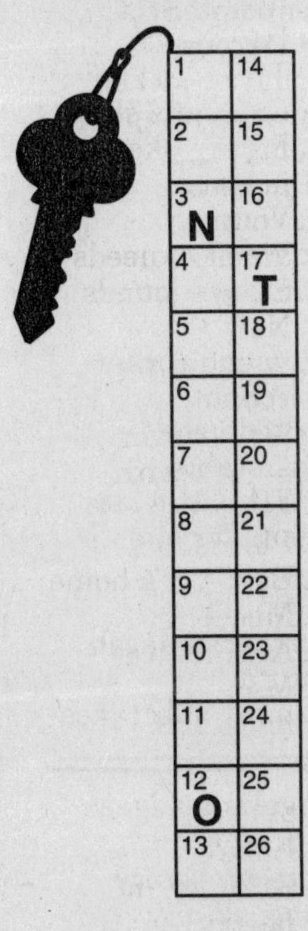

1	14
2	15
3 N	16
4	17 T
5	18
6	19
7	20
8	21
9	22
10	23
11	24
12 O	25
13	26

23	16	13	■	16	26	25	■	1	16	22	■	5	19	25
16	22	16	■	18	5	17	■	25	19	19	■	21	5	6
22	12	19	5	6	6	16	■	18	12	16	■	26	16	6
■	■	■	2	25	16	■	7	14	16	4	25	19	■	■
12	26	16	6	■	8	6	14	■	19	25	21	12	19	16
4	5	15	25	12	■	16	5	15	■	6	5	4	25	19
16	3	15	■	15	5	2	26	25	6	■	19	25	17	25
■	■	■	■	25	2	2	■	18	14	11	■	■	■	■
24	1	16	19	■	21	5	19	16	22	25	■	2	16	22
12	16	17	25	3 N	■	25	16	17	■	26	19	12	10	11
12	26	17	5	12 O	3	■	20	25	16	■	5	15	25	21
■	■	25	3	17 T	5	24	25	■	25	6	8	■	■	■
12	9	21	■	5	24	25	■	26	19	12	8	8	25	19
19	5	26	■	24	9	5	■	16	5	19	■	16	13	25
16	26	17	■	25	25	6	■	13	25	25	■	2	25	24

A	~~N~~
B	~~O~~
C	P
D	Q
E	R
F	S
G	~~T~~
H	U
I	V
J	W
K	X
L	Y
M	Z

Three From Nine

PUZZLE 13

Place the letters of the 9-letter words on the dashes, one letter per dash, to spell a 7-letter word, a 5-letter word, and a 3-letter word. Each letter of a 9-letter word will be used once.

1. WOEBEGONE

___ Y ___ S ___ R ___

___ A J ___

___ I ___

2. DISCHARGE

___ I ___ E ___ A ___

___ M ___ G ___

___ U ___

3. PIECEMEAL

___ O ___ L ___ G ___

___ X ___ O ___

___ I ___

4. ADVERSELY

___ I ___ P ___ A ___

___ G ___ E ___

___ E ___

5. TRUMPETED

___ I ___ Y ___ A ___

___ H ___ F ___

___ M ___

6. PENINSULA

___ A ___ S ___ G ___

___ A ___ E ___

___ N ___

PUZZLE 14

• SOME ARE RIGHT •

ACROSS

1. What's the big ____?
5. Barker and Bell
8. Sulk
12. Ringing sound
13. Strike decider
14. Pelvic bones
15. Division word
16. Sequins
18. Straphanger
20. Rub out
21. "Bill ____, the Science Guy"
22. Singer McEntire
24. Crone
26. Be in turmoil
28. Taunt
32. Flattened at the poles
34. Merle ____ of movies
36. Pare
37. Poet St. Vincent Millay
39. Industrious insect
40. Lay down the law
42. Transgress
44. More prudent
47. Retaliates
51. Percussion instrument
53. To boot
54. Fat for frying
55. Above, in verse
56. Bartlett or Bosc
57. Follow directions
58. Anatomical openings
59. Trustworthy

DOWN

1. Nile wader
2. "____ Be Cruel"
3. Involve in complications
4. Intense pain
5. Ruminate
6. Electrical unit
7. Bad Ems or Bath
8. Move seasonally
9. Spanish cooking pot
10. Baked desserts
11. Alleviate
17. Penpoint: Scot.
19. Dexterous
23. Collar or jacket
24. Bunny's jump
25. Honest ____
27. Film spool
29. Cowboy
30. Charged atom
31. Explosive letters
33. By now
35. Diamond corner
38. Merchant
41. Footed vase
43. Unsuitable
44. WWII battle site
45. Saudi, for one
46. Flame
48. Aloe ____
49. Brother of Jacob
50. Painful
52. Gummy substance

PUZZLE 15

• TELL ME A STORY •

ACROSS

1. Small devil
4. Tooth ailment
8. Big boys
11. Tidy
13. Linen source
14. "____, though I walk . . ."
15. Grimm story
17. Slick
18. Classic song
19. In the ____ way
21. Feed one's face
23. Dentists' concerns
26. Pharmacy offering
28. Poplar or pine, e.g.
29. Not secondhand
32. "Me and My ____"
34. Starchy root
35. Field of study
37. Fountain beverage
40. Fundamental
42. ____ diem
43. Craft
46. Fragrance
50. "____ Stoops to Conquer"
52. Cheap adventure story
54. "____ House"
55. Wickedness
56. Used to be
57. Inky implement
58. Period of time
59. Once known as

DOWN

1. Facts, briefly
2. Supper, e.g.
3. Remitted
4. Behind
5. Scratch
6. Angel's headgear
7. Strain
8. Detective story
9. Long, skinny fish
10. Vote against
12. True's partner
16. 52 weeks
20. Establish
22. Harbor ship
24. Alice's party
25. Skirt edge
27. Step on the ____
29. Snare
30. Age
31. Louis L'Amour story
33. Sever
36. Tire input
38. University official
39. Cupid's dart
41. Space ____
44. Jump into water
45. Asian ruler
47. Baker's chamber
48. No more than
49. Toward shelter
50. Soak up
51. Color
53. Nightmare street of film

BRICK BY BRICK

PUZZLE 16

Rearrange this stack of bricks to form a crossword puzzle. The clues will help you fit the bricks into their correct places. Row 1 has been filled in for you. Use the bricks to fill in the remaining spaces.

ACROSS

1. Farm yield
   Young horse
   Tiny particle
2. Inheritor
   Trademarks
   Casino city
3. Friendly nation
   Atmosphere gas
   Mexican sandwich
4. Hollywood's West
   Previous to, poetically
   Lobe locale
   Gave lunch to
5. Egyptian sight
   Dorothy's dog
6. Flop
   Bothers
7. Place for a Hula-Hoop
   Citric ____
   Surplus
8. Strong anger
   Adam's lady
   Combat
9. Molds
   Darling
   Type of exercise
10. Trespassed
    ____ out (barely make)
11. On a boat
    Smudged
12. Boxing great
    Foil metal
    Machine's tooth
    Confusion
13. Finance
    Recommend
    Prod
14. Not aweather
    Tall tales
    Singe
15. Impolite
    Handbag
    Makes mistakes

DOWN

1. Victor
   Music system
   At a distance
2. Type of race
   Press clothes
   Humdinger
3. Petroleum transporter
   Related
4. Force open
   TV spots
   "____ Miniver"
   4th letter
5. Ostrich's kin
   Fat
6. Sunshine State
   Milk factory
7. Seeped
   Hand over
   Tidy
8. Back in time
   Plunged
   To's partner
9. Sole
   Notion
   Fragrance
10. Chairs
    Guilt
11. Fixed routine
    Beer barrel
12. Gallery display
    Monkey suit
    Nay's opposite
    Function
13. Soft-shoe song
    More uncommon
14. A single time
    Boast
    ____ Allan Poe
15. Frame of mind
    Ms. Gilbert of "Roseanne"
    Active ones

BRICKS

E		Y	N		C	R		L	O	G		S		S
E			E	F	E	Y		O	R		U	E		E
A	D	O	A	L	I				R	U	D	E	K	E
R	G	E	F	U	N	R		Y	S	E	A	M	E	A
R	B	S				E	N	O	A	R	N	E	D	
T	R	A	M	S		A	C	O	T	O	T			S
E	A	R					T	I	E		E	E	V	E
R	R	S	R	E	D	D		R	D			D	E	A
S		R		D	I	F	E	D	H	E	I	W	A	R
E		T	C	I	D	O			A	L	L	O	G	A
I	R	E	S	T	U		E	R	A	L	E	I	N	T
F	O	R		E	X	A	M	I	R	U	D			A
D	U	D	M	A	E	A	R					O	G	O
S		A	P	Y	R	T	O	T	H	I	P	Z	O	N

DIAGRAM

	1	2	3	4	5	6	7	8	9	10	11	12	13	14	15
1	C	R	O	P		F	O	A	L			A	T	O	M
2															
3															
4															
5															
6															
7															
8															
9															
10															
11															
12															
13															
14															
15															

PUZZLE 17

ACROSS

1. Ripens, as cheese
5. Boyfriend
9. Build on
12. Fizzy drink
13. Auto pioneer
14. Hive-dwelling insect
15. Bean curd
16. Burn reliever
17. Nightmare street of film
18. Young louse
20. Ham operator's item
22. Pale purple
25. Asking price
27. Certain poem
28. Short cry
30. Clearly outline
34. Pub order
35. Fawn's mom
36. Anguish
37. Flowerless plant
39. Sticky stuff
41. Metal-containing rock
42. Watched
44. Slackened
46. Specialty
49. It might have come first
50. "Tarzan, the ___ Man"
51. On a cruise
54. Audition prize
58. Faucet
59. Stocking mishaps
60. Flock mothers
61. Subways' kin
62. Robin's home
63. Split ___

DOWN

1. Feat
2. Infant's sound
3. Legendary toymaker
4. Finnish bath
5. Ship
6. Plumbing joint
7. Stir
8. Consumers
9. On a cot
10. Pastrami vendor
11. Dealer's car
19. Frozen
21. Had a snack
22. Bread quantity
23. Lazy
24. Look suggestively
25. Rain source
26. Uncovered
29. Brim
31. Deuces
32. Center
33. Obey
38. Clear
40. Beer barrel
43. Wish
45. Come to terms
46. Doom
47. Milky gem
48. Agts.
49. Direction
52. Bring to court
53. Printers' concerns
55. "My ___ Private Idaho"
56. Governed
57. Tee's preceder

PUZZLE 18

ACROSS

1. Ladder rung
5. Inner hand
9. Go down the slope
12. Bridge charge
13. Opera tune
14. Towel monogram
15. Ox's harness
16. Consider
17. Pipe type
18. Public notices
20. Stitch loosely
22. Desert plants
25. Rules to follow
26. Cinder
27. Yearn
30. Opinion survey
34. Orchid necklace
35. Pirate's drink
36. Twins
37. Nation
39. Be informed about
41. Pop
42. Naturally!
44. Distribute
46. Blazer feature
49. Large antelope
50. Prior to, in verse
51. Rim
54. Restless desire
58. Admission charge
59. Dime or penny
60. Correct
61. Road surface
62. Campground home
63. Views

DOWN

1. Porky's abode
2. Likewise
3. Lodge member
4. Skirt feature
5. Tablets
6. "Bells ___ Ringing"
7. Tall tale
8. Caribbean dance
9. "___ So Cold"
10. Scot's skirt
11. Florida Key, e.g.
19. Chip enhancer
21. Cleo's snake
22. Beckon
23. Voyaging
24. Jaw part
25. Salesman's model
28. Ticks off
29. Sister
31. Gambling numbers
32. Hawaiian party
33. Rich deposit
38. Change locks?
40. Take first place
43. Choose
45. Hotel offering
46. Not right
47. Telephone code
48. Social equal
49. Lady's guy
52. Bambi's mom, e.g.
53. Card game
55. Endeavor
56. Feed lines to
57. "___ So Shy"

PUZZLE 19

ACROSS

1. Square of butter
4. Nocturnal insect
8. Make do
12. Top fighter pilot
13. What's the big ___?
14. Intimidates
15. That girl
16. Coin
17. Bookie's concerns
18. Placido Domingo, e.g.
20. Electric ___
22. Cook in water
25. "Bad, Bad ___ Brown"
29. Salami vendor
32. Sleeve or pant part
34. Kind of maniac
35. Departure
36. Lobe place
37. Smooth cloth
38. "Cheers," e.g.
39. Faithful
40. ___-jerk reaction
41. Blur
43. Trucker's vehicle
45. Brief farewell
47. Give pleasure
51. BLT spread
54. On the pinnacle
57. Depressed
58. Observer
59. Eternal spirit
60. ___ foo yung
61. Certain amphibian
62. Backpack
63. Beam

DOWN

1. Time gone by
2. Tooth-ailment symptom
3. Young adult
4. Extremely small
5. Keats poem
6. Perfect number?
7. Detest
8. Strong rope
9. Be in debt
10. Canary or cat
11. Dangerous curve
19. Newspaper item
21. North Pole worker
23. Bakery employee
24. Hawaiian feasts
26. Harness strap
27. Leer at
28. Ox's harness
29. Young society entrants
30. College final
31. Italian money, once
33. Provided at no charge
37. Remove from the surface
39. "___ to Remember"
42. Cancel a space launch
44. Syrup flavor
46. Atlantic coast region
48. Customer
49. Adventure story
50. Tense
51. "A Few Good ___"
52. OK, to Popeye
53. Evergreen shrub
55. Overly
56. Inning ender

PUZZLE 20

ACROSS

1. Dazzle
4. Cave dwellers
8. Over
12. Reporter's question
13. Section
14. Trademark
15. Lobster eggs
16. "Quantum ___"
17. Do a laundry chore
18. Lengths of fabric
20. Hot spring
22. Deserve, as a reward
25. Piece of prose
29. Adore to excess
32. Tiny particle
34. Before, in verse
35. Quiz
36. Stage reminder
37. Send by post
38. Gender
39. Stockades
40. Type of history
41. Blade
43. Arouse
45. Bother
47. Postpone
51. Admiral or guard
54. Carpenter's spike
57. Cherry-tree chopper
58. Sins
59. Gawk at
60. By means of
61. Actuality
62. Adventurous
63. Powdery residue

DOWN

1. Crooked
2. Halt, to a horse
3. Watcher
4. Hobby wood
5. "Roses ___ red . . ."
6. Herbal drink
7. Drains
8. Assumed name
9. Likewise not
10. Kind of maniac
11. Gained victory
19. Think
21. "The Princess and the ___"
23. Wedding toss
24. Verbs' colleagues
26. Scorch
27. Vocal solo
28. Shout
29. Student's furniture
30. Yoked animals
31. Judd Hirsch series
33. Trial run
37. Oliver's request
39. According to
42. Stop before second base
44. Lounged
46. Round handle
48. Liquid rock
49. Rotation center
50. Slangy assent
51. TKO caller
52. Notable timespan
53. Curve
55. In the past
56. Ailing

1	2	3	■	4	5	6	7	■	8	9	10	11
12			■	13				■	14			
15			■	16				■	17			
18			19		■	■	20	21		■	■	■
■	■	■	22		23	24	■	25		26	27	28
29	30	31		■	32		33		■	34		
35				■	36			■	37			
38			■	39				■	40			
41			42		■	43		44		■	■	■
■	■	■	45		46	■	■	47		48	49	50
51	52	53		■	54	55	56		■	57		
58				■	59				■	60		
61				■	62				■	63		

PUZZLE 21

ACROSS

1. Volcano's dust
4. Not at home
8. Hundred-yard ___
12. This girl
13. Just fair
14. Notion
15. Lend an ___ (listen)
16. Very black
17. Pulls
18. Before
20. Frequently, to Keats
22. Darling
25. Mechanical man
29. Punching tools
32. Note
34. Act like
35. Luau garland
36. Ostrichlike bird
37. Sought office
38. Hoover, e.g.
39. Military division
40. Firms up
41. Verbal exams
43. Gull-like bird
45. Longing
47. Small weight
51. Two of a kind
54. "Do ___ others . . ."
57. Strong brew
58. Farmland measure
59. Unhappy destiny
60. "For Me and My ___"
61. Casual pullovers
62. Pasture moms
63. CIA agent

DOWN

1. Confused
2. Persian ruler
3. At this location
4. Put ___ (reserve)
5. Hit the jackpot
6. Request
7. Spool-like toy
8. Duplicate
9. Hoopla
10. Make a blouse
11. Holds title to
19. Notices
21. To's partner
23. Blessing close
24. Pay
26. Stark
27. Milky jewel
28. 7 + 3, 1 + 9, etc.
29. Actor Ray
30. Don
31. Certain bean
33. Silent
39. Hire
40. Type of antelope
42. Harplike instruments
44. Chambers
46. Without a stitch on
48. Pesters
49. Thunder noise
50. Slippery
51. Stroke
52. Honored fighter pilot
53. Anger
55. ___ or never
56. Type of dancing

PUZZLE 22

ACROSS

1. Pants border
4. Dog docs
8. Off
12. Mock
13. Branding tool
14. Behind schedule
15. Scale notes
16. Grandmother
17. Inkling
18. Like a snake
20. Lump
22. French peak
24. Provided relief
28. "___ in the Clowns"
31. Santa's paperwork
34. Sunbeam
35. Bunyan's tool
36. Dry land
37. Exercise
38. Place to get fit
39. Jeans patch site
40. Ripened
41. Crowd
43. Central
45. Question
47. Backbone
51. Animal's home
54. Scamps
57. Wiggly fish
58. Peer
59. Couldn't ___ less
60. Shadowy
61. Midas's metal
62. Granny, for one
63. Light-switch positions

DOWN

1. ___ off to you!
2. Grand
3. Flat-topped hill
4. Plastic material
5. Historic epoch
6. Coal measure
7. Hosiery problem
8. Legal excuse
9. Mass
10. Had supper
11. Vote type
19. Tyke
21. Formal promise
23. Intend
25. Pharmacy offering
26. Comfort
27. Hid the gray
28. Kimono tie
29. World's fair, e.g.
30. ___ and dear
32. Rage
33. Daisy part
36. Just manages to earn
40. Picnic drink
42. Chanced
44. Map graphic
46. Punt
48. Remodel
49. Blood vessel
50. Graceful trees
51. Sea captain's book
52. Before now
53. Not well
55. ___ the lifeboats!
56. Golf instructor

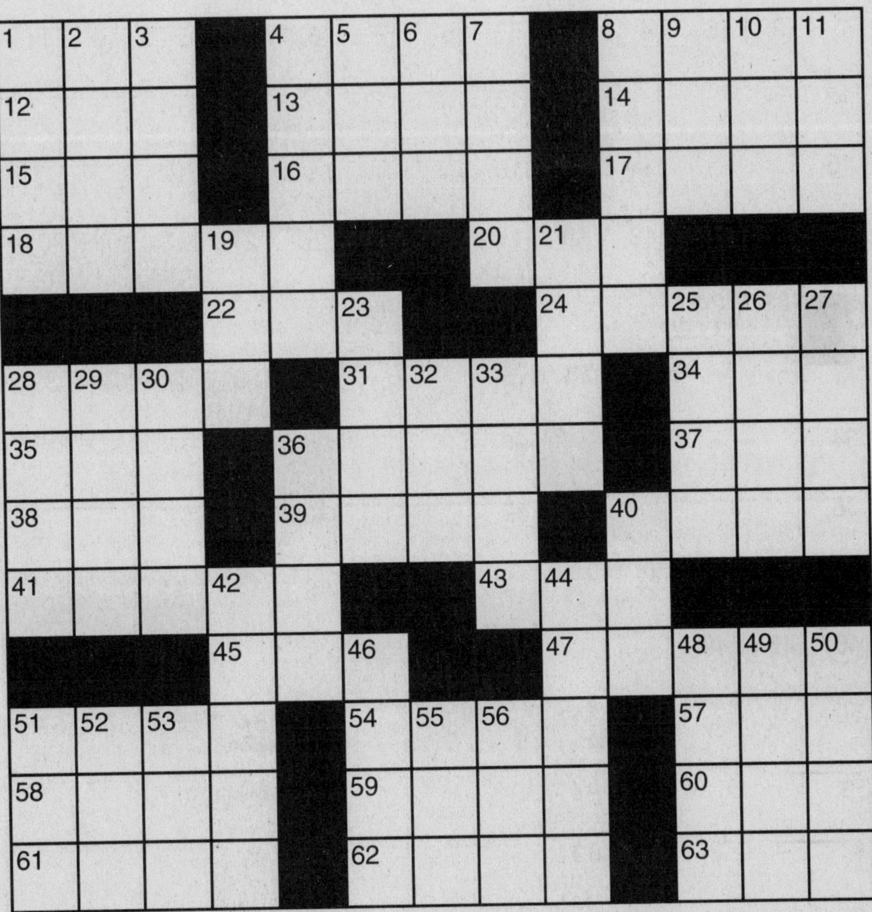

PUZZLE 23

ACROSS

1. Rush
5. Small particle
9. Pussyfoot?
12. World's fair, e.g.
13. Had on
14. Bartender's rocks
15. Boyfriend
16. Marsh stalk
17. Browning's before
18. Pig's place
20. Ventilated
22. Threaded fastener
25. Drop
27. Falsehood
28. Almost round
30. Vitality
34. List entry
36. Bad humor
37. Realtor's sign
38. Take out, in printing
39. Like some cheese
41. Label
42. Recital piece
44. Portrayal
46. Fish delicacy
49. In the past
50. United
51. Slant
54. "Do ___ others . . ."
58. Summer thirst-quencher
59. Radiate
60. Finger feature
61. Angler's need
62. Fellow
63. Colorized

DOWN

1. Society gal
2. Bunyan's tool
3. Fitness resort
4. Dwelling
5. Askew
6. Foot feature
7. Raw mineral
8. Olympic prize
9. Dock
10. Farm unit
11. Gardener's bane
19. Duo
21. Ailments
22. Glided
23. Refer to
24. Movie spool
25. North Dakota city
26. Out of the wind
29. Small liquid container
31. Minute amount
32. Jolly Roger, e.g.
33. Verge
35. Interlock
40. Unearth
43. Lubricated
45. Heap
46. Float aloft
47. Free
48. Sow
49. Stake
52. Ostrichlike animal
53. Assistance
55. Thumbs-down vote
56. Draw
57. Elderly

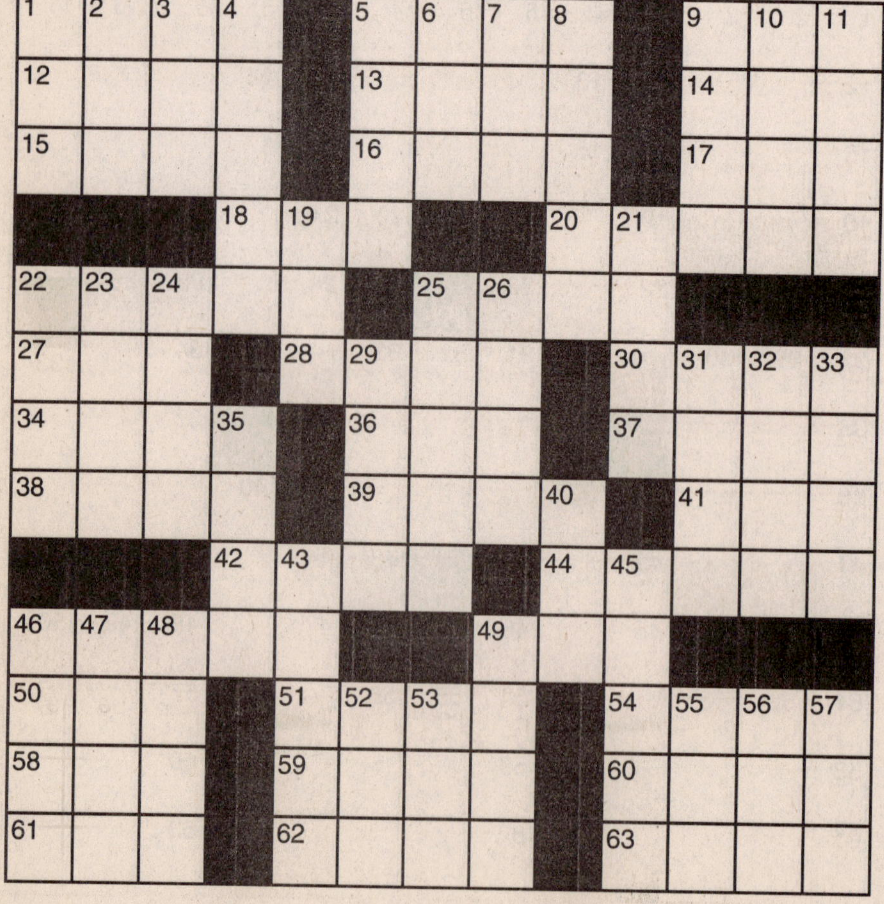

PUZZLE 24

ACROSS

1. Computer input
5. Has title to
9. Wild donkey
12. Etching fluid
13. Spike
14. Whirlpool bath
15. Art ___
16. Mistake in print
17. Sow or boar
18. Paid player
20. Stickum
22. Christmas visitor
25. Squirt
27. Pursue
28. Father
30. Every one
34. Picnic crasher
35. Folk dance
36. Rightful
37. Look intently
39. Over
41. "Look ___ ye leap"
42. Grimm heavy
44. Tripod
46. TV host
49. Decrease
50. Bill and ___
51. Blushing
54. More or ___
58. Weeding tool
59. Assemble
60. Throw off
61. Kooky
62. Provoke
63. Precious stone

DOWN

1. June honoree
2. Crack pilot
3. Twitch
4. Take for oneself
5. Conscious of
6. Path
7. Small bite
8. Incline
9. Certain vipers
10. Roast holder
11. Scholar
19. Kind of music
21. Dread
22. Switch
23. Tiptop
24. Observe
25. Cactus's defense
26. Book leaf
29. Partially closed
31. Sweet drinks
32. Heal
33. Shoe part
38. Fish eggs
40. Spider's parlor
43. Bacteria
45. More competent
46. Bouncing sound
47. Spirits
48. Like most colleges
49. Ogler
52. Type of bran
53. Tackle moguls
55. Australian bird
56. Bro or sis
57. Oinker's home

1	2	3	4	■	5	6	7	8	■	9	10	11
12				■	13				■	14		
15				■	16				■	17		
■	■	■	18	19		■	■	20	21			
22	23	24			■	25	26			■	■	■
27			■	28	29			■	30	31	32	33
34			■	■	35			■	■	36		
37			38	■	39			40	■	41		
■	■	■	42	43			■	44	45			
46	47	48			■	■	49			■	■	■
50			■	51	52	53		■	54	55	56	57
58			■	59				■	60			
61			■	62				■	63			

PUZZLE 25

ACROSS

1. Fresh talk
5. Likewise
8. "Dracula" author Stoker
12. Thunder sound
13. Durango dad
15. TV's Jay ___
16. With competence
17. Terminated
18. Devours
19. Commuter vehicle
20. Excess
21. Embroidery trim
23. Dress size
25. Restrained
28. Hair color
30. In a separate place
34. Sums
37. Alters
39. Damp and cold
40. Nap, in Mexico
42. Clothing
44. Cloud's locale
45. Animal horn
49. Probes
50. Tree dwellings
52. Breadwinner
54. Canadian city
56. Hurdle
60. Tropical fruit
63. That maiden
65. Scary sound
66. Manipulates
67. Edition
70. Burglar's goods
71. Fluff
72. Cautious
73. Soothe
74. Bridge ploy
75. Amaze
76. Piece of news

DOWN

1. Strikebreakers
2. Photograph book
3. Tijuana topping
4. Agent
5. Temper display
6. Uncanny
7. Rocky mineral
8. Seeps out
9. Authentic
10. Pot donation
11. The majority
13. Green soup
14. Adam's place
20. Common ailment
22. It's uplifting
24. Maiden
26. Poetic palindrome
27. Roadside hotel
29. Kidney or lima
31. Pupil site
32. Somber
33. Flock members
34. Org.
35. Embankment
36. Algerian governors
38. Drat!
41. Savory
43. Fictional plantation
46. Pekoe or oolong
47. Ordinance
48. Deletion
51. Browns bread
53. Nightfall
55. Dog's wagger
57. WWII craft
58. Unbound
59. Tribal symbol
60. Wood product
61. India's locale
62. Ink writers
64. "___ Look Me Over"
68. Mako's milieu
69. Do needlework
70. Luau souvenir

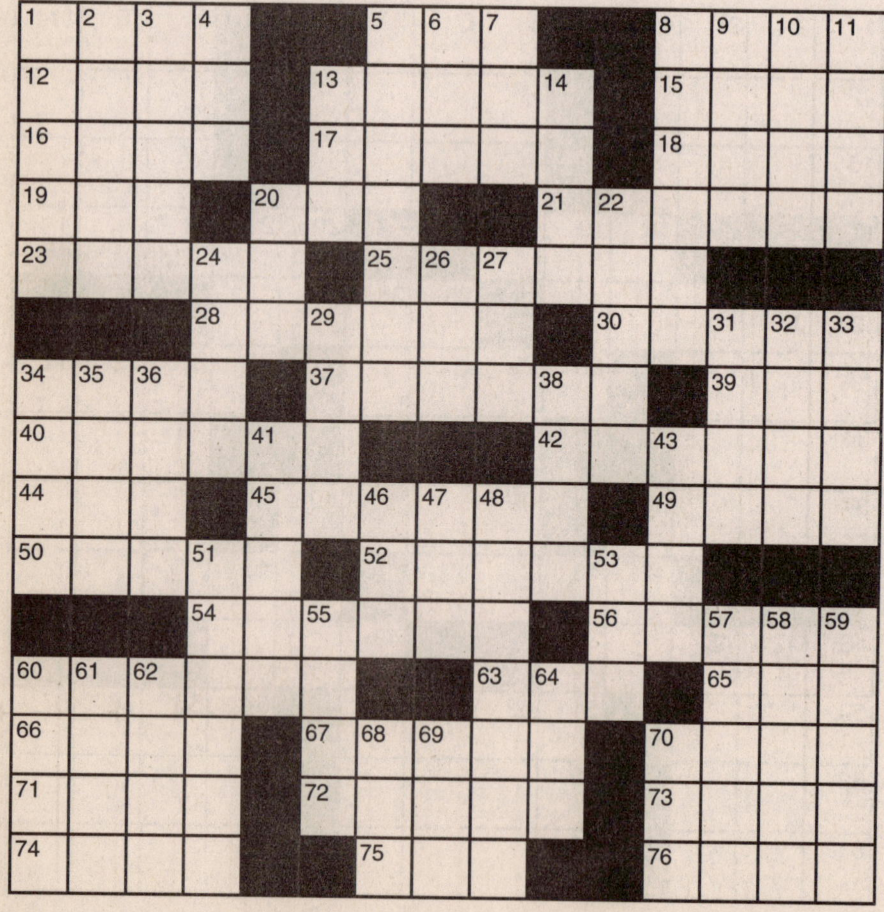

PUZZLE 26

ACROSS

1. Incline
6. Gator's relative
10. In one's bunk
14. Lemur's cousin
15. Steep
16. Nitwit
17. Teen woes
18. Bread topping
19. Medicinal plant
20. Tropical serpent
21. Look to be
22. Inhale sharply
23. Antlered animal
27. 23rd Greek letter
29. Glades
33. Hubbub
36. Yearn
37. Salty hello
39. Mule's kin
41. Befitting
42. Like most roofs
44. Bark sharply
45. Inlet, in Spain
46. Baseless
47. Tremble
50. Shut noisily
52. Cobbler fruit
54. WWII agency: abbr.
56. Threefold
57. Luminary
60. Skinny
63. Type of snake
66. Formal order
67. Hawaiian city
68. Grandma's brooch
70. Nimbus
71. Wapitis
72. Broker
73. Untidy situation
74. Network: abbr.
75. Bakery items

DOWN

1. Bacon portion
2. Loony
3. For adornment
4. Dessert pastry
5. Winding curve
6. Elected
7. Nettle
8. Double curve
9. Chew
10. Slow, in music
11. Gaucho's weapon
12. Heroic poem
13. Low in pitch
24. Kind of paneling
25. Mine product
26. Fathered
28. Boar's home
29. Burn
30. Azure
31. Judge's mallet
32. "Ain't ___ Sweet"
34. Wishful thinker
35. Willow tree
38. Weirder
40. Peppy
43. Priest's robe
46. Brat
48. Japanese belt
49. Bear's lair
51. Main arteries
53. Extreme
55. Cinders
57. Did the breaststroke
58. Real
59. Affectations
61. Mrs. Munster
62. Kinds
64. Had delivered
65. Plant holders
68. Siamese, e.g.
69. Muslim leader

PUZZLE 27

ACROSS

1. Painful
5. Out of danger
9. Learn's partner
13. "How do I love ___?"
14. Tumble
15. Wickedness
16. Merry tune
17. Celtic land
18. Affirmatives
19. Mountainous
21. Me
23. Sibling
24. Globe
27. ___-de-camp
30. Anecdote
31. Removes rind from
33. Pull with effort
36. Sort
37. Lingerie garment
38. Reed instruments
40. Have a meal
42. Condition
43. Hatched
44. Foot covering
46. Certain evergreen
47. Bald or golden
49. Express grief
50. Furniture wood
51. Opened
52. No longer is
55. Umps' kin
57. Accompany
59. Banner
62. Tree seed
65. Bullets and bombs
66. Marathon
67. Metal plate
68. Reserve
69. Had an obligation
70. Duration
71. Pass catchers

DOWN

1. Volume of maps
2. Texas fare
3. Assists
4. Himalayan creature
5. Luxurious resort
6. Feel under the weather
7. Meaty
8. Or ___ (threat)
9. Greenest
10. Kind of league
11. Struggle (for)
12. Raised trains
14. Perspiring
20. Airy dwellings
22. Fold
25. Rigging line
26. Betrayal
28. Impede
29. Cream of society
32. Spout
33. Earring site
34. WWII craft
35. Ravine
39. Made bigger
41. Dull sound
42. Transports
45. Adjust to surroundings
48. ___ out (barely make)
49. Brawn
52. Ladies
53. Ready to fight
54. Pauses
56. Truth
58. Wedding dessert
59. To and ___
60. Regulation
61. Head of a suit
63. Opposite of neath
64. Pound

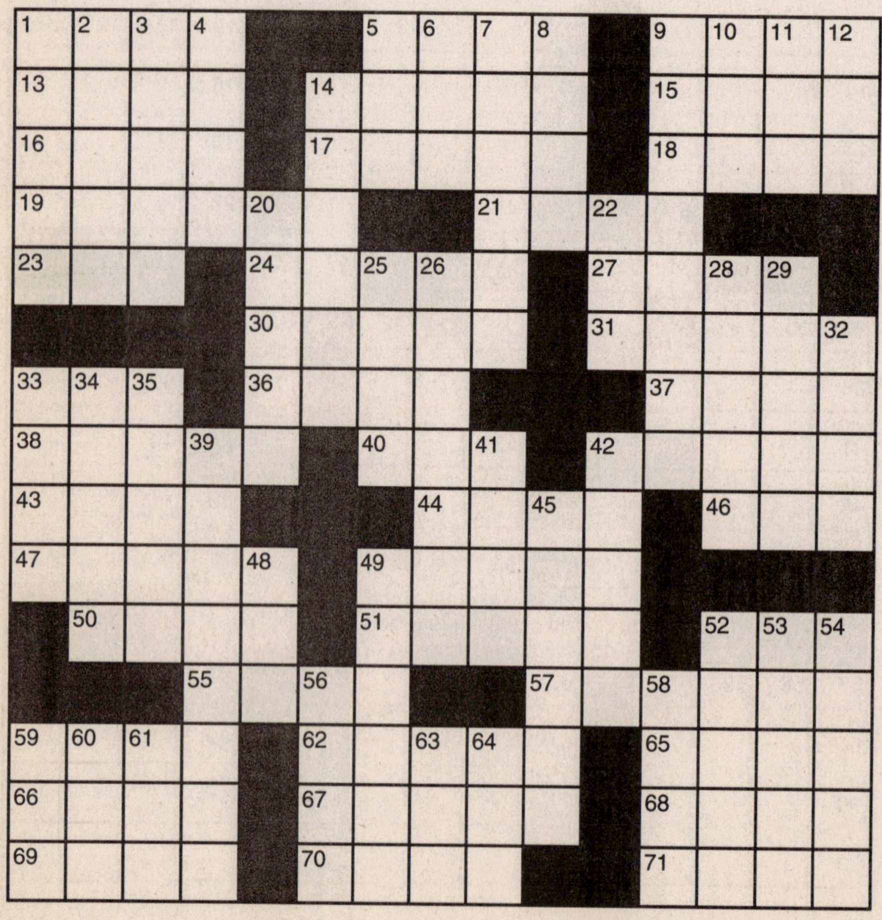

PUZZLE 28

ACROSS

1. Musical symbol
5. Opposite of hawed
9. Food additive
13. Mobile starter
14. Take advantage of
16. Norse poem
17. Comedian Mort ___
18. Even
19. Mild oath
20. Boar's tooth
21. Byron's before
22. Excite
24. Moral error
26. Roadside cafe
28. Card game
31. Joke
33. Yule drink
34. Last of the log
37. Synthetic fabric
39. Wide of the mark
41. Icy abode
43. Spokes
44. Oahu meal
45. Big shot
46. Slanted
47. That woman
48. Day's march
49. Previously named
50. Frozen dessert
52. Grown boys
54. Hazardous curve
55. Anchors a boat
57. Enjoyed lunch
59. Game tile with dots
62. Elevator directions
64. Polish copy
68. Final notice
69. Hawaiian porch
71. Relay event
72. Maui goose
73. Because
74. Heavy metal
75. Ogler
76. Clothing colorer
77. Bards' twilights

DOWN

1. Play players
2. Island feast
3. Ordinal suffixes
4. People
5. Lead ore
6. By any chance
7. Like a mansard roof
8. Casino cube
9. Zeal
10. Mentor
11. Collections
12. Neural network
15. Treeless plain
23. Army unit
25. Car-starting system
27. Sickly
28. Navigational device
29. Give a speech
30. Classic song
32. Burrowing rodent
34. Water plants
35. Broths
36. Punctures
38. Corn or olive
40. Rival
42. Picked up
51. Chills
53. More lenient
55. Bishop's headgear
56. Bright
58. Mysterious
59. Completed
60. Abide by
61. Unearth
63. Walk the floor
65. Risk
66. Image
67. Certain bills
70. Succor

1	2	3	4	■	5	6	7	8	■	■	9	10	11	12
13				■	14				15	■	16			
17				■	18					■	19			
20				■	21			■	22	23				
■	■	■	24	25		■	26	27				■	■	■
28	29	30	■	31		32	■	33			■	34	35	36
37			38		■	39	40		■	41	42			
43					■	44			■	45				
46					■	47			■	48				
49			■	50	51		■	52	53		■	54		
■	■	■	55				56	■	57		58	■	■	■
59	60	61				■	62	63		■	64	65	66	67
68				■	69	70				■	71			
72				■	73					■	74			
75				■	■	76				■	77			

PUZZLE 29

ACROSS

1. Light wood
6. Make the scene
10. Scoop
14. Pen name
15. Whitish gem
16. Approach
17. Weightlifter's feat
19. Indefinite number
20. So far
21. Motels
22. Sandy hills
23. Rate of speed
25. Goose egg
26. Basmati and wild
29. Fireproof fabric
34. Care for an orphan
35. Albacore
36. Tree part
38. Soup or coat
39. Riots
42. Proper
43. Make lace
44. Labor
45. The items here
47. Release
50. Auriculate
51. Antlered animal
52. Geek
54. Piece of prose
57. Long tale
59. Animal park
62. Darn it!
63. Contemplating
66. Pluck
67. Not fer
68. Library stamp
69. Rowers' needs
70. Fixed routine
71. Steeple part

DOWN

1. Infant
2. Sailor's direction
3. Fluff
4. Baglike structure
5. Hardwood tree
6. Eye part
7. Outspoken
8. Church observance
9. Subways' kin
10. Offensive remark
11. Blinking sign
12. Status
13. Minerals
18. Movie, for short
22. Calamity
23. Zip
24. With shrewdness
25. Pacific goose
26. Deeply engrossed
27. Perfect example
28. Raccoon's cousin
30. Leg extension
31. Student transport
32. Not as young
33. Drench
37. Opposite of hawed
40. Ham, e.g.
41. Estuary
46. Owned
48. Animals
49. Motor
53. Wear away
54. Consequently
55. Ms. Gilbert
56. Rouse
57. Utah lily
58. Mine entrance
59. Tubular pasta
60. Lollapalooza
61. Fiend
63. Scratch
64. Radio spots
65. Knock lightly

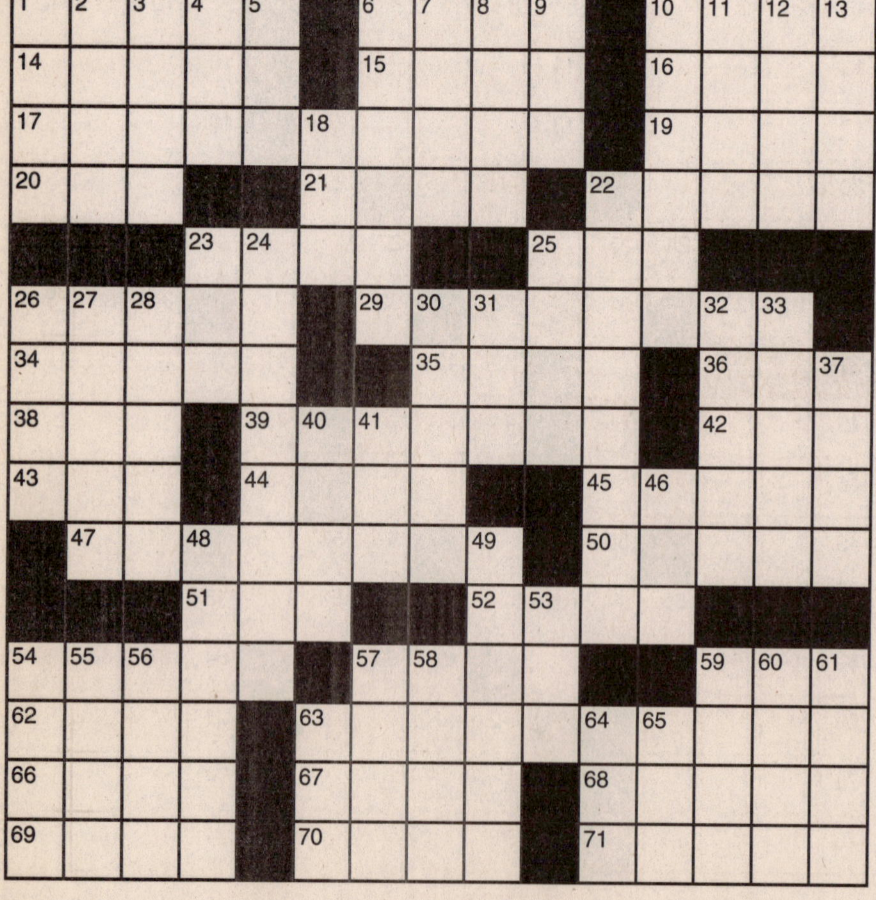

PUZZLE 30

ACROSS

1. Stuff full
5. Heavy weights
9. Skin on the head
14. Tax
15. Come again?
16. Sound
17. Warning
18. Islamic chief
19. Soot
20. Auto shelter
22. Adjective for Abner
24. Flower part
25. Relative, for short
26. TV commercials
28. Smoker's tool
30. Tennis barriers
32. Social class
34. Not happy
37. Horrify
39. Papeete's locale
41. Measure of time
44. Act the part
46. Beasts of burden
47. Take in
49. Large wading bird
51. Mold
52. Crosswise
54. "___ Again"
57. Look suggestively
58. Con's counterpart
60. Zig's partner
62. Thyme, e.g.
65. Energy unit
67. Decree
69. Earth pigment
71. Pelvic bones
73. Further
74. Uneven
75. Bards' sunsets
76. Swarm
77. Tricks
78. Sit a spell
79. Reduce

DOWN

1. Impedes
2. Stay
3. Recalcitrant
4. Wordy bird
5. Blazer material
6. Electric unit
7. Ply a hammer
8. Removes
9. Downturn
10. Hex
11. Cave access
12. Lemon's kin
13. Browning work
21. Shocked response
23. Rubbish
27. Swindle
29. Coat or soup
31. Polynesian plant
33. Hilo hello
34. Five's follower
35. Dined
36. Confused noise
38. Small rock
40. Sharpen
41. Held
42. Ginza belt
43. Exploit
45. Substitute worker
48. Waste cloth
50. Repute
53. Creepier
55. Flowering shrub
56. Speakers' platforms
57. Portly
59. Sunday meat
61. Elf
62. Weeder
63. Beige
64. Greek consonants
66. Mirth
68. Go out with
70. Scale notes
72. Officeholders

1	2	3	4	■	5	6	7	8	■	9	10	11	12	13
14				■	15				■	16				
17				■	18				■	19				
20				21		■	22		23	■	24			
25			■	26		27	■	28		29		■	■	■
■	30		31		■	32	33				■	34	35	36
■	■	■	37		38			■	39		40			
41	42	43		■	44			45		■	46			
47				48		■	49			50		■	■	■
51			■	52		53			■	54		55	56	■
■	■	■	57				■	58	59		■	60		61
62	63	64		■	65		66	■	67		68			
69				70	■	71		72		■	73			
74					■	75				■	76			
77					■	78				■	79			

PUZZLE 31

ACROSS

1. Smear
5. Fall on ___ ears
9. Reading lights
14. In addition to
15. Lofty hairstyle
16. Poet Dickinson
17. Root or birch
18. Fawn's mother
19. Hosiery fabric
20. Church recess
22. Unit of energy
24. Have bills
25. Hack
27. Obtains
29. Old French coin
30. Transparent wrap
36. Sphere
37. Site
38. Accompany
40. Longtime squabble
42. Major artery
44. Not all
45. Robin Hood's missiles
47. Audacity
49. Misdeed
50. Free
52. To the bitter ___
53. Irritated
54. Flower vessel
56. Cinder
59. Tire inflation inits.
60. Jet black
62. Ice-cream portion
64. Glory
66. Symbol
70. Lustrous velvet
71. Peepers
72. Scruff of the neck
73. Smirk scornfully
74. Tenant's fee
75. Increased in size

DOWN

1. Small quantity
2. Bar potable
3. Capitalize on
4. Cleanser ingredient
5. Flops
6. Fencing equipment
7. Thirst quencher
8. Give up
9. Distance measures
10. Singer Grant
11. Venus de ___
12. Snow remover
13. "Auld Lang ___"
21. Type size
23. Cancels
25. Matador
26. Shade of brown
28. Biological pouches
29. Couch
31. Pencil parts
32. Zodiac lion
33. Key ___
34. Lassos
35. Royal fur
39. Baby-sit
41. Speckles
43. Greek letter
46. Big lie
48. Tariff
51. Young cow
55. Chopping
56. Deadly serpents
57. Flip through
58. Sharpen
60. Warning sign
61. Bird home
63. Individual
65. Vote of assent
67. Coupe, e.g.
68. Unlock, in poems
69. Jersey or York

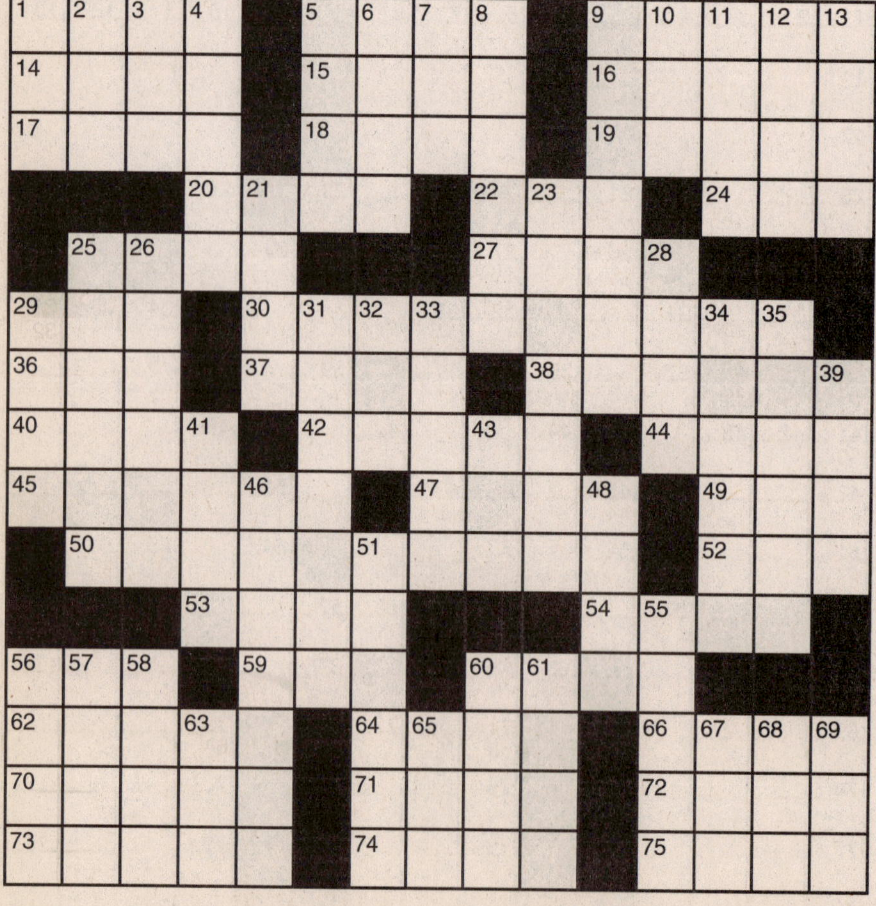

PUZZLE 32

ACROSS

1. Chicken cage
5. Nail
9. Basil sauce
14. Southern veggie
15. Ruth's foil
16. Nobelist Sadat
17. Rogues
18. Field mouse
19. Ascend
20. Ajar, to a bard
21. Way off
22. Electrical measures
23. Delta and United
26. Baglike structure
28. Hill builders
29. Not level
33. Pretend
36. Hot
39. Ostrich's kin
40. Rowboat need
41. Freshwater fish
42. Can metal
43. Application
44. Tint again
45. Letter drops
47. Landlord
49. Suspension
51. Cut off
52. Like shish kebab
56. Trailer truck
59. Glance
60. Above, poetically
61. Rise, as dough
63. Guitar's ancestor
64. Competently
65. Daisylike flower
66. Aid a felon
67. Totter
68. Cordwood measure
69. Earn a "C"
70. Rafter's peril

DOWN

1. Chocolate drink
2. Giraffe's kin
3. Direct
4. Mas' mates
5. Scholar
6. Declared
7. Map collection
8. Bucks
9. Inner shoe
10. Intertwine
11. Do the backstroke
12. Pat down
13. Spheres
24. Dally
25. Roadside hotel
26. Similar
27. "___ Day Now"
30. Presidential rejection
31. Spew
32. Religious sisters
33. Ump's call
34. Let up on
35. Enrages
37. Interfere
38. Witt's shoes
41. Criminal, slangily
44. Milne marsupial
45. Wood cutter
46. Caustic liquid
48. Thin slice
50. Doctrines
52. Diving equipment
53. Wearing clothes
54. Caught congers
55. Aridly
56. Baths
57. Formerly
58. Speck of dust
59. Wallop
62. "Look ___ ye leap"
64. "Chances ___"

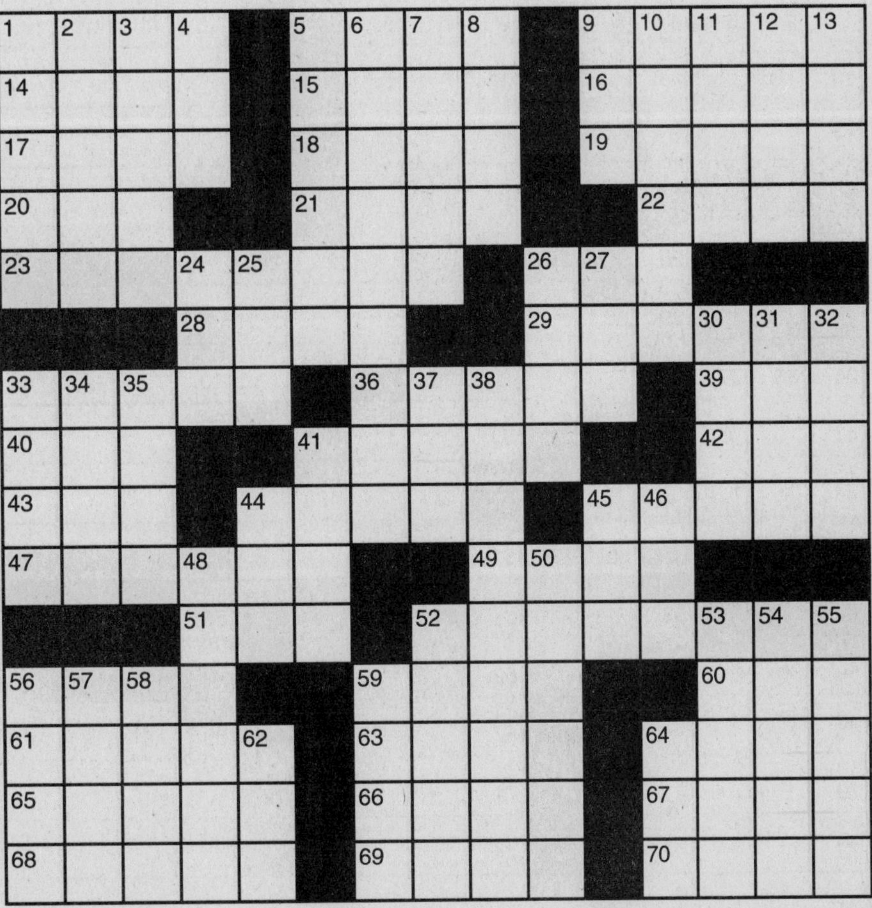

PUZZLE 33

ACROSS

1. Musty
6. Comrade
9. Garnish
14. Reef material
15. Tell a fib
16. Granny's brooch
17. Potent particles
18. "You ___ Sixteen"
19. Cornered
20. Lamb's father
21. Star flower
23. Winds up
24. Loose flesh
26. Broadened
29. Demolish
31. Uproar
32. Moose's relative
35. Pie topping
39. Forgive
41. Invasions
42. Pop's mate
44. Chop finely
45. Value
47. Junior, e.g.
49. Sandra or Ruby
50. Chow down
52. Nettle
53. Firedog
55. Moans
59. Applaud
62. Slide
64. Ms. Peeples
65. Tracking device
67. Foil metal
68. ___ statistics
70. Tusk material
71. Small bill
72. Happening
73. Sew loosely
74. Pea container
75. Takes a load off

DOWN

1. Winter neckwear
2. Demolish
3. Fragrance
4. On the ___ (in flight)
5. "Born Free" cat
6. ___ blonde
7. Made public
8. Looked slyly
9. Appear on stage
10. Braved
11. Harbinger
12. Critic Rex ___
13. Bows the head
22. Gulp
25. Spouse
27. Bite
28. Glossy paint
30. Unobserved
32. Ferber or Best
33. Secure
34. Place for a patch
35. Wilbur's steed
36. Alleviate
37. Church ceremony
38. Long time span
40. Gotten up
43. Stranded
46. Peeved
48. Brand-new
51. Highest point
53. Not together
54. Horned animal
56. Stakes
57. Ogre
58. Table and sea
59. Cattle stall
60. Volcano's liquid
61. Stirs
63. Kaput
66. Pastrami bread
69. "___ Gotta Be Me"

CAMOUFLAGE

PUZZLE 34

The answers to the clues can be found in the diagram, but they have been camouflaged. Their letters are in correct order, but sometimes they are separated by extra letters that have been inserted throughout the diagram. You must black out all the extra Camouflage letters. The remaining letters will be used in words reading across and down. Solve ACROSS and DOWN together to determine the correct letters where there is a choice. The number of answer words in a row or column is indicated by the number of clues.

	1	2	3	4	5	6	7	8	9	10	11	12	13
1	L	F	R	U	O	M	T	H	U	I	L	N	A
2	D	I	W	N	B	E	R	A	S	H	P	E	N
3	W	A	V	I	R	T	E	R	J	O	L	A	T
4	S	K	A	C	Y	E	K	D	H	I	E	R	D
5	E	N	D	G	U	R	E	N	E	R	H	S	E
6	D	C	I	H	S	V	T	E	R	N	E	B	B
7	L	C	O	A	T	N	I	N	O	N	D	Y	G
8	L	E	Z	E	W	A	U	Y	C	A	K	R	E
9	H	E	R	M	A	L	D	L	I	G	S	L	E
10	R	B	A	L	V	L	C	A	D	R	O	O	T
11	A	E	R	I	S	A	K	L	E	R	I	R	B
12	L	E	H	E	R	I	Y	H	A	O	W	D	L
13	T	D	E	W	M	P	C	E	R	W	V	E	E

ACROSS

1. Foam • Arm bone
2. Eatery • Pale
3. Table server • Cereal grain
4. Served perfectly • That girl
5. Last • Before, before
6. Tank • Recede
7. Parking site • Fool
8. Elbowroom • Wedding dessert
9. Royal messenger • Capri, for one
10. Love song • Source
11. Antenna • Blunder
12. Suspicious • Night bird
13. Disposition • Tiny

DOWN

1. Reside • Stop
2. Future wife • Hive insect
3. Wireless • Uncommon
4. Agreeable • Fib
5. Eject • Tepid
6. Everlasting • Track circuit
7. Oak, e.g. • Neat
8. Set • Harvard's rival
9. Theater aide • Autumn drink
10. Trumpet, e.g. • Not broad
11. Scallion • Plant
12. Close • Folk tales
13. Poker wager • Ladybug, e.g.

PUZZLE 35

ACROSS
1. Clumsy person
4. Long cut
8. Masking ___
12. Deceive
13. Old stringed instrument
14. Arena shape
15. Raises
17. Containers
18. Press clothes
19. Verge
20. Native of Stockholm
23. Compress
26. Certain parasites
27. Lean-to
28. Lobster eggs
31. Not at sea
33. Running in neutral
35. Reporter's question
36. Forewarning
38. Crazy
39. Hubbub
40. Partners
41. Powder mineral
44. Nuclear particle
46. Opera highlight
47. Keeps apart
51. Fruit rind
52. Repair
53. Prospector's quest
54. Beach covering
55. Hunted animal
56. Modern

DOWN
1. Bravo!
2. Feel awful
3. Payment for service
4. Angry look
5. Motorcar
6. Foul smell
7. "___ So Fine"
8. Carved pole
9. Raring to go
10. Ache
11. Besides
16. Movie rental
20. Cabbage salad
21. Dream
22. Resound
24. Restraint
25. Remark further
27. Trucker's rig
28. Civil uprising
29. Earlier
30. Self-images
32. Disintegrate
34. Andes animal
37. Pencil feature
39. Burn with water
40. Stale
41. Faucets
42. Place
43. Debtor's burden
45. Coloring
47. Rascal
48. Heavy weight
49. Previous to, poetically
50. Alter a skirt

PUZZLE 36

ACROSS
1. Hole punchers
5. Chicago transports
8. Cut, as a lawn
12. Gator's relative
13. Nope
14. Vibes
15. Mistake in print
16. By way of
17. Booby ___
18. Peculiar
20. Certain vipers
21. Eat late
24. Marketed again
26. Camera stand
28. Outdoorsy
32. Stared at
33. Inscribed
34. Hoed
36. Abate
37. Text reviser
39. 911 letters
40. Hits
43. Miss Spacek
45. Share a boundary
46. More, to Juan
47. Mind ___ matter
51. Gaucho's tool
52. "Diamonds ___ Forever"
53. Volcanic flow
54. Scream
55. Vegas preceder
56. Was aware of

DOWN
1. Perform onstage
2. Twisted, as a grin
3. Sever
4. Barge
5. Was jealous of
6. Hideouts
7. Secretly follow
8. Bullfighters
9. Not theirs
10. Cover
11. Dozes off
19. Wore away
21. Put on cargo
22. Coax
23. Heap
25. Decreases
27. Statue base
29. Medicine portion
30. Flower stalk
31. Cravings
35. Bleak
36. Profits' opposites
38. Jeweled crown
40. Newborn
41. Reed instrument
42. Tug
44. Yellow center
48. Moving vehicle
49. Woman of Eden
50. Uncooked

DOUBLE TROUBLE

PUZZLE 37

Not really double trouble, but double fun! Solve this puzzle as you would a regular crossword, except place one, two, or three letters in each box. The number of letters in each answer is shown in parentheses after its clue.

ACROSS

1. Without sound (6)
4. Consume text (4)
6. Unduly quick (5)
9. Waver (6)
10. Metaphor's cousin (6)
12. Shady porch (7)
13. Parade-ground order (4)
14. Coercion (6)
15. Spouseless (6)
16. Cinema path (5)
18. Follow closely (5)
19. Daytime show (7)
21. Disburden (6)
23. Surrounded by (4)
25. Look after (4)
26. Trite remark (9)
28. "____ of Frankenstein" (5)
29. Oboe, e.g. (4)
30. Suspicious (5)
31. Jot (7)
33. Iron (5)
34. TV frequency (7)
35. Class divisions (6)
37. Crushing tooth (5)
39. On the peak (4)
41. Recreational vehicle (6)
42. Emit vapor (5)
43. Dotted pattern (7)
45. Earn (7)
46. Outbuilding (4)
47. Soccer shoe (5)

DOWN

1. Location (4)
2. Deadly (6)
3. Play host (9)
4. Dregs (7)
5. Look up to (6)
6. Shoulder satchel (9)
7. Social rank (8)
8. Harvard's rival (4)
11. Fewer (4)
17. Wakeful (9)
18. Storekeeper, e.g. (9)
19. Physical substance (6)
20. Truly (6)
21. Solidarity (5)
22. Deafening (4)
23. Condense, as text (7)
24. Refuse heap (6)
27. Future time (5)
32. Not flexible (9)
33. Keep safe (8)
34. Enchanted (7)
35. Waterfalls (8)
36. Moderate (6)
37. Lion's share (4)
38. Fido's cord (5)
40. Fall over (6)
44. Fabric fold (5)

Ramble

PUZZLE 38

Fill in the diagram with the 5-letter answers to the clues. The numbers before the clues tell you where each word begins and ends. Note that some of the words read left to right and some read right to left. When completed, the line across the center of the diagram will spell out the title of an Oscar-winning song.

3-1. Lamp, e.g.
4-2. Australian animal
4-6. Musical toy
7-5. Seared bread
9-7. Cairo's locale
8-10. Laughing beast
10-12. Legal excuse
13-11. Honeydew, e.g.
13-15. Mock-up
16-14. Steam bath

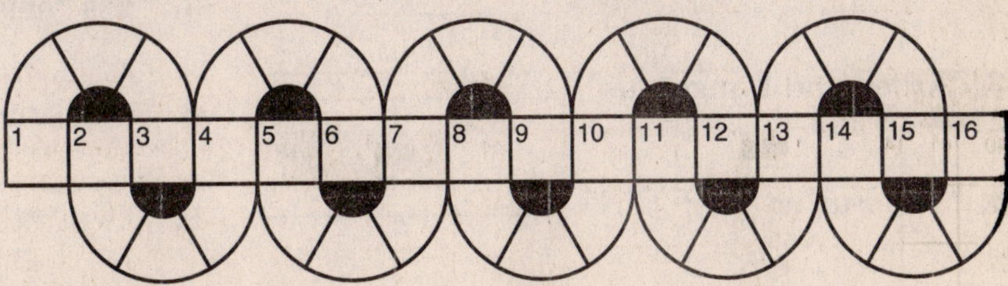

PUZZLE 39

ACROSS

1. Season
5. Toward the back, matey
8. Highest point
12. Out of the wind
13. Idolize
15. Halt, to a horse
16. Lend
17. Satchmo
18. Facial features
19. Ice-cream dessert
21. Not yup
23. Letter before dee
24. Yellow-pages fillers
25. Network
27. Pull suddenly
29. Places a wager
30. Leave off
33. Certain mineral
36. Different
39. Concealer
40. Garlic feature
41. Regards
43. Tackle
44. Start over
46. Taunt
47. His-and-____
48. Large bird of prey
49. Social gatherings
51. Watched
53. "____ It Romantic?"
54. Dessert option
57. Period
59. Dunks
61. Granting
63. Bull or ram
65. Raw-fish dish
67. Behind
68. Outrages
69. Merciless
70. Pimples
71. 1981 Beatty film
72. Sales agent, for short
73. Borscht ingredient

1	2	3	4	■	■	5	6	7	■	■	8	9	10	11
12				■	13				14	■	15			
16				■	17					■	18			
19				20		■	21			22	■	23		
24			■	25		26		■	27	28			■	■
■	■	■	29				■	■	■	30			31	32
33	34	35		■	36		37	38	■	39				
40				■	41				42	■	43			
44				45	■	46				■	47			
48					■	■	■	49		50		■	■	■
■	■	51			52	■	53				■	54	55	56
57	58		■	59		60		■	61		62			
63			64	■	65			66		■	67			
68				■	69					■	70			
71				■	■	72			■	■	73			

DOWN

1. Mexican condiment
2. Spoken
3. Slopes
4. Wait on
5. Stir
6. Located
7. The Kingston ____
8. Shoemaker's tool
9. Black-capped bird
10. Pine
11. Leisure
13. Cautioned
14. Spot
20. Mature, as wine
22. Every individual
26. Small landmass
28. Whinnies
29. Scarcely
31. Dry up
32. Makes mistakes
33. Greater number
34. Thought
35. Set
37. Embroider
38. Sends forth
42. Cutout used for drawing
45. Garden growth
50. Gulped down
52. Phonograph record
53. Distribute
54. Fragment
55. Absurd
56. Wading bird
57. Arab chieftain
58. Few and far between
60. Feline sound
62. Dull and colorless
64. Snakelike curve
66. With it

PUZZLE 40

Drop-Outs

The answer to each clue is the name of a famous person whose initials in the clue have been replaced with asterisks. In this case, each clue is a movie title and the initials are those of someone who appeared in the movie. For example, "Me*n *irls" ("MeAn Girls," initials AG) is Ana Gasteyer.

1. "Wayne's Wo**d" ____________
2. "*he *olor of Money" ____________
3. "Ar*ed and Dange*ous" ____________
4. "The Ful*er *rush Girl" ____________
5. "The **ack Cat" ____________
6. "A *idsummer Night's D*eam" ____________
7. "*iss *ongeniality" ____________
8. "**e Terminal" ____________
9. "Twili**t" ____________
10. "Ell* Enc*anted" ____________

PUZZLE 41

ACROSS
1. Newborn cow
5. Data
9. "Carmen," e.g.
14. ____-Hoop
15. Las Vegas light
16. Bobby Unser, e.g.
17. Turkish generals
18. Taxi charge
19. Moral
20. Big boys
21. Dissent
23. Ages and ages
24. Investigator
26. Vaselike vessel
28. To each his ____
29. Bar of soap
31. Wilt
34. Potent particle
37. Milky jewel
39. Tropical fish
41. Caribbean dance
43. "____ of Africa"
44. Swords
45. Invigorating
46. Plod
48. Colorful swimmer
49. Solidified
50. Smell bad
52. Get ____ of
54. Tail movement
55. In a fair manner
59. Baseballer Ruth
62. Large bird of prey
66. Nay's opposite
67. Dodge
69. Ditch of defense
70. Capri cash, once
71. Pungent flavors
72. Strong desire
73. Declare
74. Poker bets
75. Drive or reverse
76. GI's supper

DOWN
1. Victor
2. Hole-boring tool
3. Treeless plain
4. Scale notes
5. Raging fire
6. Close at hand
7. Golfer's warning
8. Change for a five
9. Metallic rock
10. Church plate
11. Bouncing sound
12. Harness strap
13. Curves
21. Use an axe
22. Loud, hearty laugh
25. Explosives
27. Nerve network
29. Fill seams
30. Choir voice
31. Pace
32. Neighborhood
33. Deep wound
34. Priests' garments
35. Bore
36. Pass over
38. Model's stance
40. Lyrical poem
42. Southern vegetable
47. Welcomer
51. Kind of trip
53. ____ League school
54. Splitting device
56. Innocent
57. Harplike instruments
58. "The Wonder ____"
59. Alpha's follower
60. Ladd or Thicke
61. Short hit
63. Arrogant
64. Skin opening
65. Sitar music
68. Half a figure eight
70. Fugitive's flight

Combos

PUZZLE 42

Form 16 longer words by joining pairs of short words and adding the letter P at the beginning. For example, P plus LOWS and HARE form PLOWSHARE.

A	HER	OR	ROOF	P ____	P ____
ABLE	ITCH	PIES	ROSE	P ____	P ____
AGE	LAIN	READ	SURE	P ____	P ____
AND	LANK	REST	TIFF	P ____	P ____
ANT	LEA	RICE	TON	P ____	P ____
ART	LESS	RIDGE	TOR	P ____	P ____
AS	MAN	RIM	TRAIT	P ____	P ____
BOY	O	ROB	UP	P ____	P ____

PUZZLE 43

BRICK BY BRICK

Rearrange this stack of bricks to form a crossword puzzle. The clues will help you fit the bricks into their correct places. Row 1 has been filled in for you. Use the bricks to fill in the remaining spaces.

BRICKS

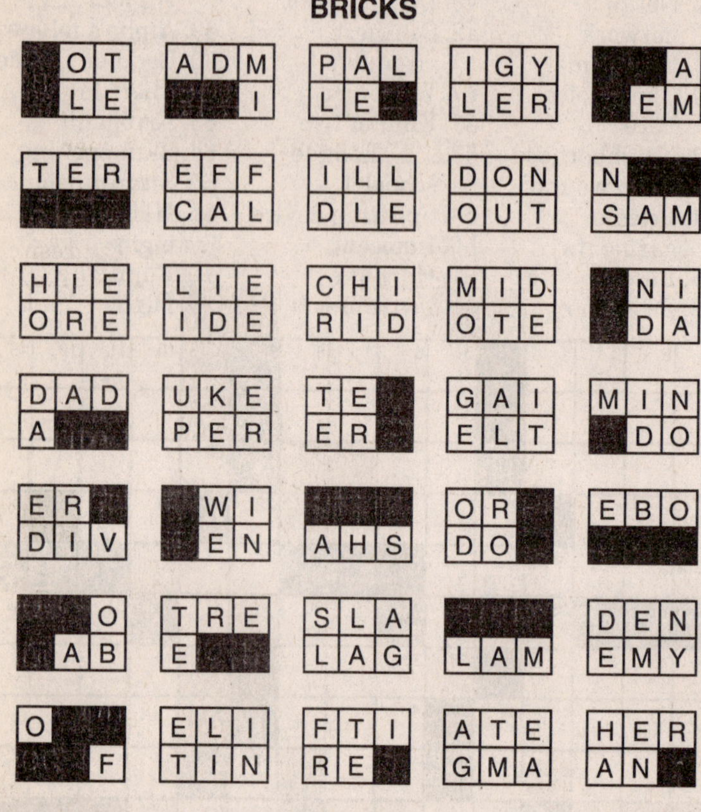

DIAGRAM

	1	2	3	4	5	6	7	8	9	10	11	12	13	14	15
1	I	S	S	U	E	■	■	H	A	S	P	■	A	S	S
2															
3															
4															
5															
6															
7															
8															
9															
10															
11															
12															
13															
14															
15															

ACROSS

1. Put forth
Fastener
Stubborn animal
2. Writing tablet
Gift giver
Greek letter
3. Tavern treat
Best
Clear of
4. Black, to a poet
Exercise machine
5. Bar reorder
Out of work
6. Image
Semiprecious gem
7. TV's "Mid-night ____"
Up to it
Exclamations
8. Hurry
Keener
Fib
9. Mine product
Be venture-some
Separate
10. Wall section
Shoe cover
11. Buddhist monk
Touched
12. Remove
Among
13. Can metal
Belief
Express feeling
14. Tiny Tim's instrument
Additional
Extend
15. ____ your request
Lanky
Friend's opposite

DOWN

1. Wight or Man
Repeating sound
Ease off
2. Thick slice
Weather forecast
Similar
3. Palm starch
Run off
Prospector
4. Tool
Grand Coulee, for one
5. Eternally, to a poet
Program
Folk hero
6. Countless
Chit
7. Love to excess
Back
Muslim leader
8. Clock division
Noshed
Gov. agents
9. Part of a.m.
Sash
Anxiety
10. Cream or baking
Solemn promise
11. Nudge
____ photo-graph
Ram's partner
12. Unit of length
Essential nutrient
13. Pungent
Came to rest
Way
14. Carnival worker
Conceal
Ingredient
15. Edge along
Prophet
Turn down

PUZZLE 44

ACROSS
1. Discard
5. Kitten sound
8. Foot part
12. Great affection
13. Truckers' rigs
15. Paid players
16. Diva's tune
17. Hang around
18. Med. course
19. Spanish treasure ship
21. Covered walkway
23. Oriental legume
25. Abound
26. American poet
29. Traveler's permit
31. Lobe place
34. Joust
35. Rotate
37. Fox trot, e.g.
39. Incite
40. Dunderhead
41. Ticket receipt
42. Quiver item
44. Put
46. Strokes lightly
47. Hide the gray
48. Yodeling sound
50. Cinema path
52. Skier's lift
54. Mesmerized
56. Certain cylinder valve
58. Desirous
63. Train's track
64. Brilliance
67. Plus
68. Hr. parts
69. Uniform cloth
70. Caviars
71. Pond growth
72. Skater's need
73. Only

DOWN
1. Mine refuse
2. Spanish hour
3. Diabolic
4. Wheel's partner
5. Malicious person
6. Large bird
7. Gain a victory
8. Room
9. Decorative
10. Burden
11. Villa d'____
13. Bamboo plants
14. RBIs, e.g.
20. Superman's letter
22. Scan a book
24. Pilot
26. Woolly
27. Feeling sorry about
28. Toast spread
30. Facts, briefly
32. Serious
33. Confed. soldiers
34. Pair
36. Fashionable
38. Deadly serpents
43. Frail
45. Elk
49. Stream
51. "____ a Gift"
53. Model material
55. Come to
56. Marie Wilson role
57. Finger tip
59. Damage
60. Arctic Ocean site
61. Customer
62. Give up
65. Fraternity letter
66. Natural resin

Face to Face

PUZZLE 45

Place the eight squares on the left into the diagram so that each number will match the number in the adjacent square. Do not turn the squares or rearrange the numbers within each square.

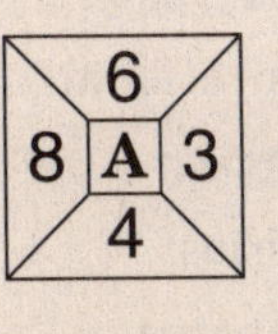

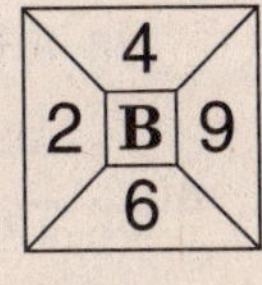

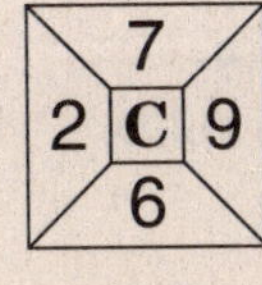

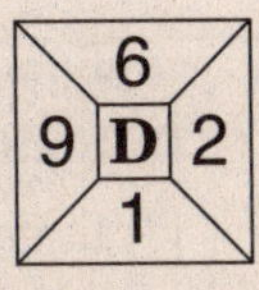

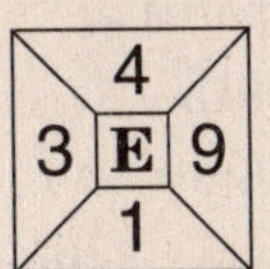

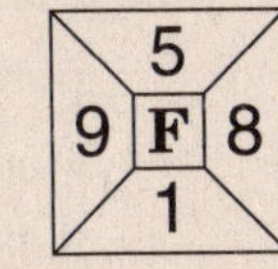

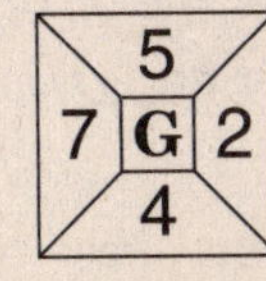

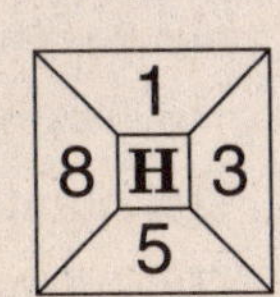

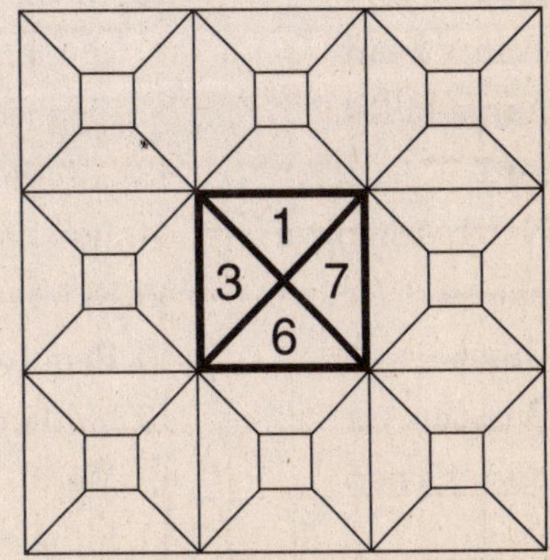

PUZZLE 46

OVERLAPS

Place the answer to each clue into the diagram beginning at the corresponding number. Words will overlap with other words.

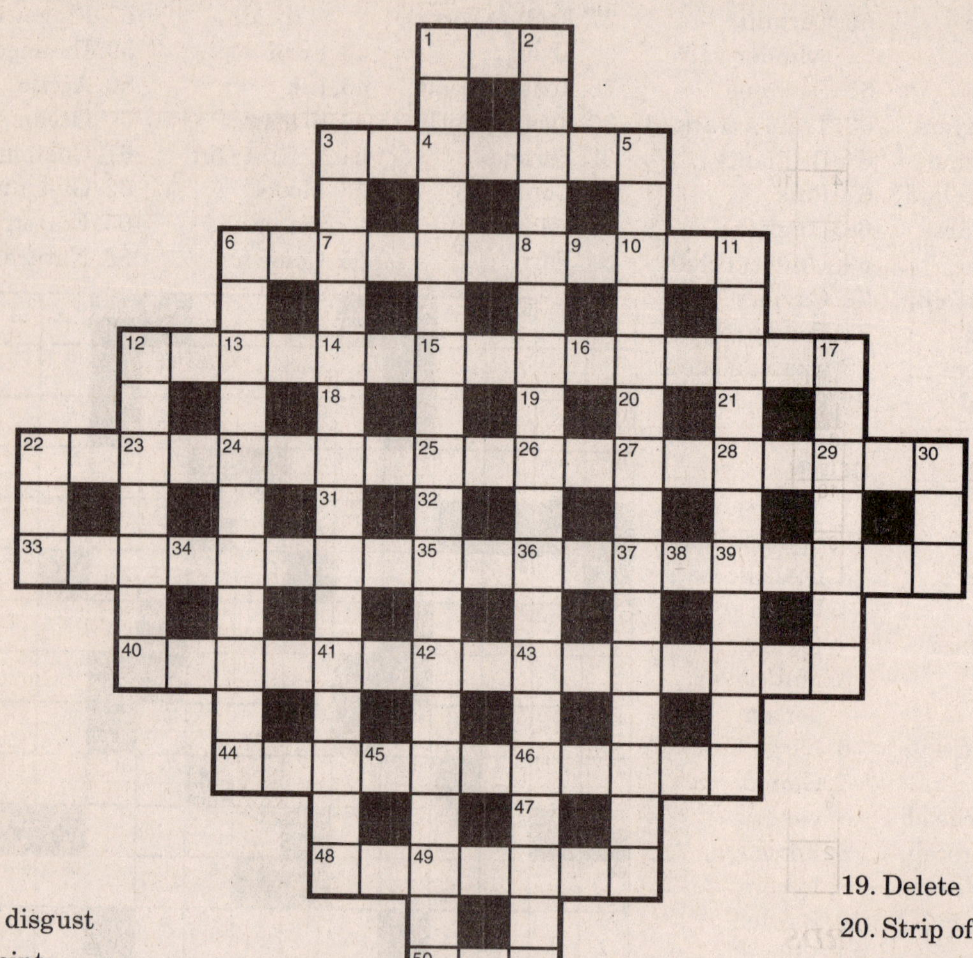

ACROSS

1. Cry of disgust
3. Viewpoint
4. Learn
6. Moment
7. Pardon
9. Cool!
12. Spain's capital
14. Running in neutral
15. Jargon
16. Pointy beard
22. Large-billed bird
24. North American nation
25. Gamble
26. Bassoon, e.g.
27. Rafter's peril
28. Pairs
33. Good for farming
34. Consecrated
35. Ford failure
36. Individualities
38. Evening star
40. Of Indian groups
41. Egg white
43. Allude to
44. Iron or tin
45. Skirt style
46. Requirements
48. Mother of Zeus
49. Merits
50. Fitness center

DOWN

1. Pressing
2. Barn dance
3. Public sale
4. Docile
5. Dramatist Coward
6. Flank
8. Landlord, e.g.
10. Split to splice
11. Lugged
12. Distance unit
13. Transfer design
15. Mantel
17. Important ages
18. Burden
19. Delete
20. Strip of skin
21. Sharpened
22. Sweet or chick
23. Slightest
24. Bone-building nutrient
27. Sniggling
29. Colorado resort
30. Knight's title
31. Customary
32. Furry pet
36. Educational meeting
37. Tarries
39. Prepares to publish
41. Modify
42. Soldiers' lodgings
47. Territory

CODEWORD

PUZZLE 47

Codeword is a special crossword puzzle in which conventional clues are omitted. Instead, answer words in the diagram are represented by numbers. Each number represents a different letter of the alphabet, and all of the letters of the alphabet are used. When you are sure of a letter, put it in the code key chart and cross it off in the alphabet box. A group of letters has been inserted to start you off.

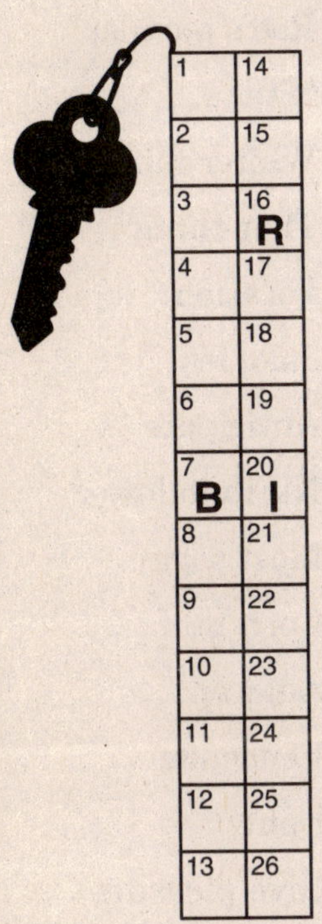

1	14
2	15
3	16 R
4	17
5	18
6	19
7 B	20 I
8	21
9	22
10	23
11	24
12	25
13	26

9	3	23	■	13	9	7	■	9	20	22	■	20	25	10
4	10	20	■	10	15	10	■	11	21	21	■	5	21	2
21	9	24	■	15	10	11	■	10	5	2	■	24	9	2
11	16 R	20 I	7 B	10	■	■	■	■	■	10	26	21	8	6
■	■	■	10	4	2	10	16	■	20	16	10	■	■	■
■	1	9	12	■	9	8	10	■	5	9	11	11	6	■
3	20	4	21	■	2	10	25	9	5	11	■	16	21	11
10	4	9	11	10	■	16	10	2	■	10	16	21	2	10
9	25	11	■	4	21	11	20	21	5	■	21	14	10	5
■	23	10	22	10	5	■	26	16	21	■	12	10	4	■
■	■	■	9	25	10	■	11	10	16	3	10	■	■	■
19	18	9	16	11	■	■	■	■	■	11	16	20	25	17
18	16	5	■	16	21	10	■	14	20	9	■	24	9	5
9	12	10	■	20	16	17	■	10	4	4	■	24	16	21
2	10	15	■	25	10	10	■	10	4	17	■	6	10	11

A	N
~~B~~	O
C	P
D	Q
E	~~R~~
F	S
G	T
H	U
~~I~~	V
J	W
K	X
L	Y
M	Z

***LOVE CODEWORDS?** Enjoy hours of fun with our special collections of Selected Codewords!* *See page 159 for details.*

Quotation Puzzle

PUZZLE 48

Place each word onto a set of dashes. Then transfer the letters into the correspondingly numbered squares. When each word has been placed on the correct set of dashes, a quotation will be revealed by reading across the diagram.

BRIEF
CRATE

DINE
HORSE

STOP
TROT

VITAL

1. ___ ___ ___ ___ ___ (28 2 19 23 30)
2. ___ ___ ___ ___ (13 5 9 25)
3. ___ ___ ___ ___ ___ (14 26 32 3 20)
4. ___ ___ ___ ___ ___ (4 21 29 18 15)
5. ___ ___ ___ ___ (1 8 10 17)
6. ___ ___ ___ ___ ___ (16 24 11 6 27)
7. ___ ___ ___ ___ (12 7 31 22)

1	2	3	4	5	6	7	8	9	10	■	11	12
■	13	14	15	■	16	17	18	19	20	21	■	22
23	24	25	■	26	27	■	28	29	30	31	32	■

PUZZLE 49

ACROSS

1. College teacher, briefly
5. Deep cut
9. Brief
14. Fluid rock
15. ___ of passage
16. Steamship
17. Not new
18. Region
19. TV host
20. Clever
22. Raring to go
24. Moose's kin
25. Exit
27. Felix, e.g.
30. Paddle
31. Pledge
36. Amaze
37. Andean animal
40. Painter's tripod
42. Extent
44. Water blockade
45. Sioux, e.g.
46. Squelch
47. Explode
49. Bear's cave
50. The things there
52. Female
53. Chicago trains
54. Hay bundlers
57. Harmful
60. Competently
61. Apparel
66. Unlocking, in poetry
68. Angers
70. Matinee ___
71. Variety show
72. Motorcycle
73. Annexes
74. Exalted
75. Glazes
76. Editor's comment

DOWN

1. +
2. Hives
3. Kaput
4. Decrease
5. Continual
6. Broadcast
7. Rob
8. ___ ho!
9. Husky's load
10. That boy
11. Single time
12. Rod's partner
13. "Star ___"
21. Winter fabrics
23. That thing's
26. Vocation
27. Jalopies
28. Anticipate
29. Ninth follower
32. Most soggy
33. Corn unit
34. Adjacent
35. Renegade
38. Dent
39. Give pleasure
41. Glasses part
43. Sticky glop
48. Expressions
51. Kind of tide
55. Excuse
56. Verse
57. Tennis's Bjorn ___
58. Impersonator
59. Opera star
60. ___ on the vine
62. Knotted
63. At leisure
64. Bun
65. Otherwise
67. Catholic sister
69. Get by

PUZZLE 50

ACROSS

1. Play
5. Butter serving
8. Pocket bread
12. Elaborate solo
13. Shoulder gesture
15. Press pleats
16. Shopping plaza
17. Jazz band
18. Bronze coin
19. Argument
20. Whatever
21. Washes
23. Yanked
25. Skirt type
26. Scold
28. Putter, e.g.
32. In the lead
33. Stringed instrument
34. Undivided
35. Small bottle
36. Chinese mammal
37. ___ weevil
38. Feeling awful
39. Essence
40. Iris's center
41. Aversion
43. Winner's place
44. Successes
45. Reared
46. Mashed veggie
49. Attention-getting word
50. Make corrections to
54. Like
55. Cheek reddener
57. Agreeable
58. Songbird
59. Glucose
60. Fifty-fifty
61. "Lyin' ___"
62. Perfect score
63. Pointed projectile

DOWN

1. Sloped walkway
2. Taken by mouth
3. Road distance
4. Magnificent
5. Call up
6. Land force
7. Bath place
8. Easy task
9. Enrages
10. Manner
11. Hill-builders
13. Startle
14. Magilla, e.g.
22. Data
24. Offbeat
25. Sculpts
26. ___ con carne
27. Recuperates
28. Aladdin's pal
29. Coils
30. Dark
31. Dinner chime
32. Eager
33. Flings
36. Ministers
37. Loaded
39. Fishing necessity
40. Filled pastry
42. Shows gratitude
43. Young chicken
45. Initiated
46. Ashen
47. Approval
48. Get bored
49. Very large
51. Opera star
52. Frosting user
53. Portable shelter
56. Absent

PUZZLE 51

ACROSS

1. Enjoy a pool
5. Deep voice
9. Things
14. Fancy edging
15. Withdraw
16. New
17. Microwave appliance
18. "___ in the Money"
19. Digging tool
20. Egyptian sight
22. Youngster
24. Downturn
25. Incision
26. Notice
28. Fragrance
32. Clothesline
33. Badge metal
34. Follower
36. Behaves
40. Fabric
42. Baltic or Bering
43. Luau greeting
44. Tramp
45. Tentacle
47. Pull with effort
48. Prewinter season
50. Rubdown
52. Vienna's river
55. Argument
56. Be in the red
57. Paddle
59. Baseball units
63. Immature insect stage
65. Camp worker
67. Soccer legend
68. Iron-rich dish
69. Opposing votes
70. Flat
71. Horse
72. Tiny fly
73. Smooth, as wood

DOWN

1. Animal feed
2. Squiggly
3. Cake froster
4. Peril
5. Enchant
6. Given the boot
7. Respectful form of address
8. Editor's term
9. Foot's arch
10. Cover
11. Elude
12. Doc
13. Got some shuteye
21. Chomp
23. Bloodhound's clue
27. Small duck
28. Engrave with acid
29. Barn's neighbor
30. Haughty person
31. Painter's stand
32. Empire
35. Watch
37. Soft drink
38. Hoodlum
39. Wise one
41. Bean curd
43. Fiery crime
45. Dog's pest
46. Serious
49. On (a ship)
51. Steals
52. Toy figures
53. Expect
54. Boldness
58. Clanged
59. Inkling
60. Russian river
61. Secluded valley
62. "You ___ Me"
64. Type of neckline
66. Charged atom

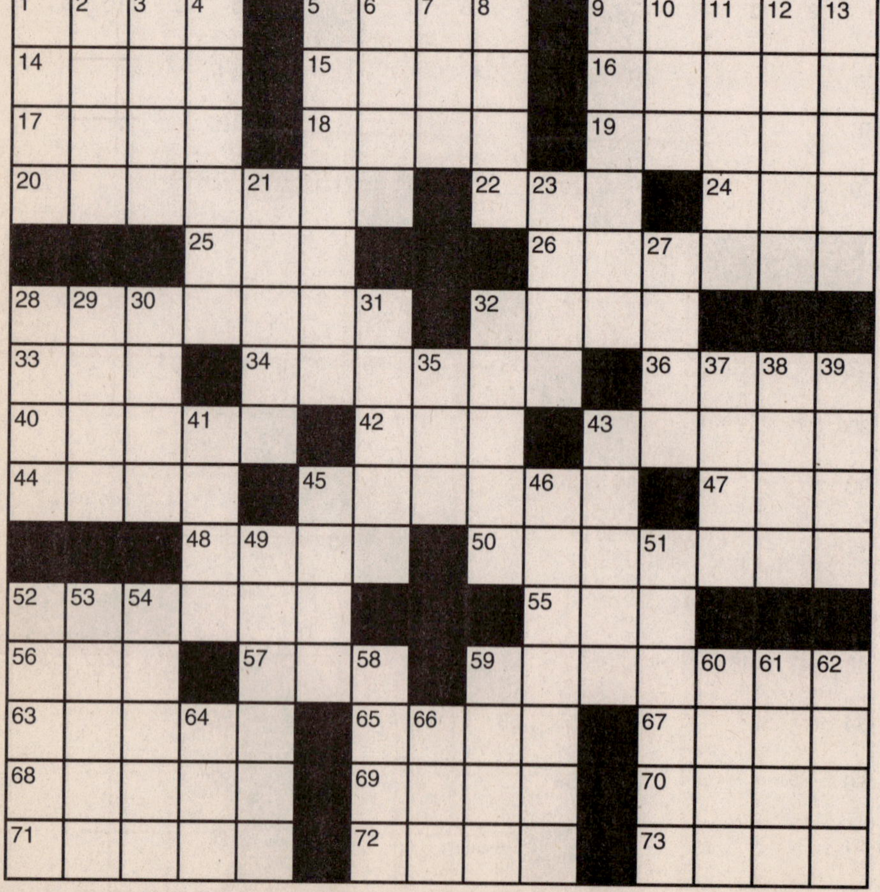

PUZZLE 52

ACROSS

1. Powerful dunk
5. Watering hole
8. Minor quarrel
12. New Zealand fruit
13. Works hard
15. Per
16. Outrages
17. Modify
18. Dogwood or pine
19. Gnat, e.g.
20. Is able to
21. Cafeteria
23. Solicit
25. Huge
27. Hooded jacket
30. Request
33. Stay attached
35. Type of bread
36. Overalls feature
38. Tissue layer
39. Stalemate
42. Australian bird
43. Focus
44. Cook's vessel
45. Fish sauce
47. Small hound
50. Coward
51. Cubicle
53. Vroom the engine
54. Certain snowman
57. "___ Send Me"
59. Give off
63. Abide
64. Big deal
66. Hubbub
67. Sign of the future
68. Sups
69. Dueling blade
70. Exited
71. Deface
72. End or heat

DOWN

1. Leave out
2. Italian money, once
3. Amazes
4. Error
5. Fizzy beverage
6. Steinway, e.g.
7. French peak
8. Love seat
9. Carve
10. Serving scorer
11. Those people
13. Fasten
14. Most costly
22. Certain snake
24. Indian robe
26. Coves
27. Father
28. Improvise
29. Reason's partner
31. Helps a crook
32. Flat beans
34. Hired
35. Squealer
37. Hide underground
40. Browning, e.g.
41. Alleviate
46. Held firmly
48. Not in class
49. Acquired
52. Laughing animal
53. Deep grooves
54. Gush
55. Icy coating
56. Kitchen hot box
58. Unique being
60. Pout
61. Suggestion
62. Two-___ sloth
65. Energy

PUZZLE 53

ACROSS

1. Leer
5. Hidden supply
10. Largest amount
14. Agitate
15. Beige and off-white
16. Earthen vessel
17. Quilts
19. Jazz or Magic
20. Lemon quaff
21. Laser's kin
22. Form
23. Method
25. Gasps for air
27. Division
29. Coloration
30. Polish
33. Outside pitch
36. Limousine, e.g.
38. Turn into
40. Exams
42. Liveliness
44. Reindeer herders
45. Put up with
47. Snakelike fish
49. Ending for slug or song
50. Old pronoun
51. Always, to a bard
53. ___-de-camp
55. Wimp
57. Sewed loosely
61. Novices
64. Breed of cat
66. Back in time
67. Cheaper spread
68. Poetry and prose
70. Put on the ___
71. "La Boheme," e.g.
72. Rich Little, e.g.
73. Uncomplicated
74. Emerald
75. Circus safeguards

DOWN

1. Killer whales
2. Something pleasing
3. Tropical fruits
4. Shoemaker's helper
5. Potter's clay
6. Bible book
7. Crawl
8. Cheer
9. Serpentine curve
10. Cloth eaters
11. Olive genus
12. Hockey shot
13. Subdue
18. Harbinger
22. Iron alloy
24. Sheer fabric
26. Knob
28. Dance like Hines
30. Line
31. Strike callers
32. Of the highest quality
33. Vessel
34. Curvature
35. Like some lingerie
37. Female ruff
39. Coffee shops
41. Emits
43. Certain legume
46. Peg for Lopez
48. Generous
52. Chef's instruction
54. Statistics
55. Humdinger
56. Nibbler
58. Brownish gray
59. Wading bird
60. Go-getters
61. Shredded
62. Hipbones
63. Soaks flax
65. Really
68. Tennis shot
69. Poolside pursuit

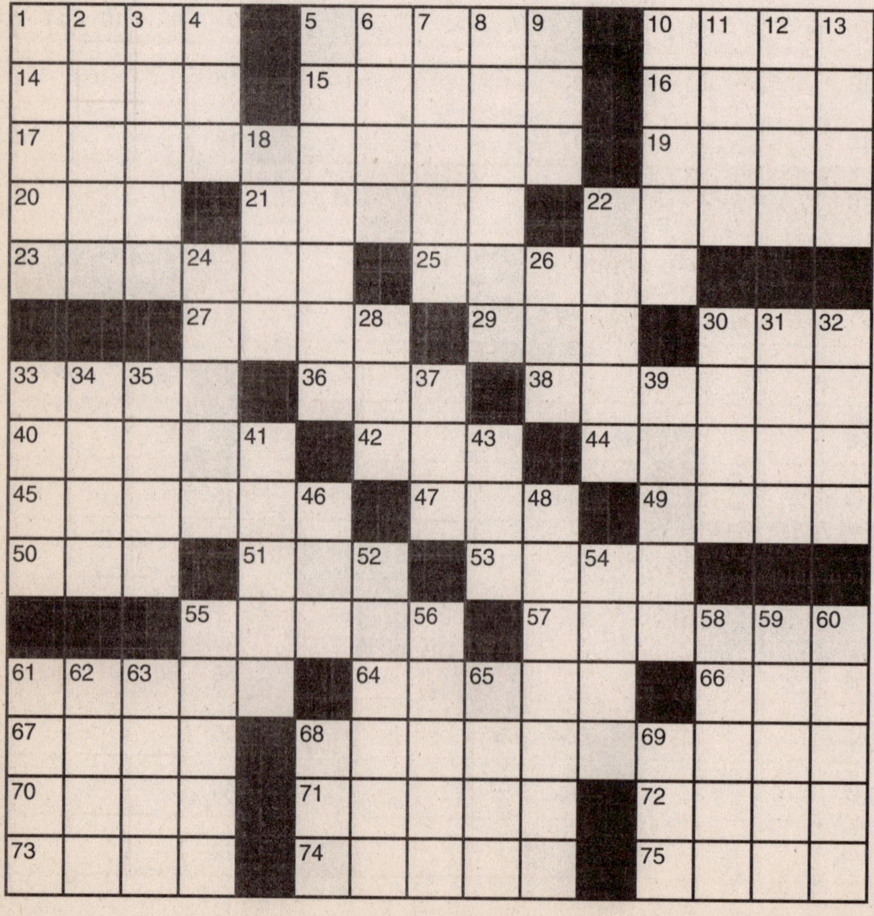

PUZZLE 54

ACROSS

1. Goatee, e.g.
6. Anatomy's concern
10. EMT's word
14. Debate
15. Rose's love
16. Bitter vetch
17. Lariat
18. Palm drink
19. Climax
20. Be suitable for
22. Territory
24. Rogues
28. Beach shelter
31. Sample
32. Seed coat
33. Breakfast order
34. Plan
36. Viewpoint
37. Period
40. Right-hand page
41. Dripping
42. Fair attractions
44. High rails
45. Wingtip, e.g.
47. Dictator
48. Pedro's cloak
50. Grimm monster
51. By route of
54. One of two
55. At no time, in poetry
56. Backers
58. Dawn drops
60. Store news
61. Branch offshoot
64. Rose oil
69. Organic compound
70. Chalet feature
71. Not tight
72. Makes a dress
73. Color changer
74. Loamy deposit

DOWN

1. Pub
2. Earlier than, in verse
3. Turkish title
4. Dull routine
5. Turn a ___ ear
6. Rooster type
7. Tokyo waistband
8. Submerge
9. Hungered
10. Forest dweller
11. Implied
12. Suit of mail
13. Very little
21. Sacred image
23. Burger joint
24. Key personnel
25. Staggering
26. LPs' successors
27. Slash
29. Beg
30. Came to ground
35. Spiritual music
37. Saying
38. Category of art
39. Chemical compound
41. Accustomed
43. Fe, to a chemist
46. Raised
47. Went like mad
49. Equivocator
51. Flower jars
52. Senseless
53. Aflame
57. Wiggly ones
59. Barricade
62. Route
63. "___ Got You Under My Skin"
65. Furthermore
66. Foot appendage
67. Donkey
68. Thing, in law

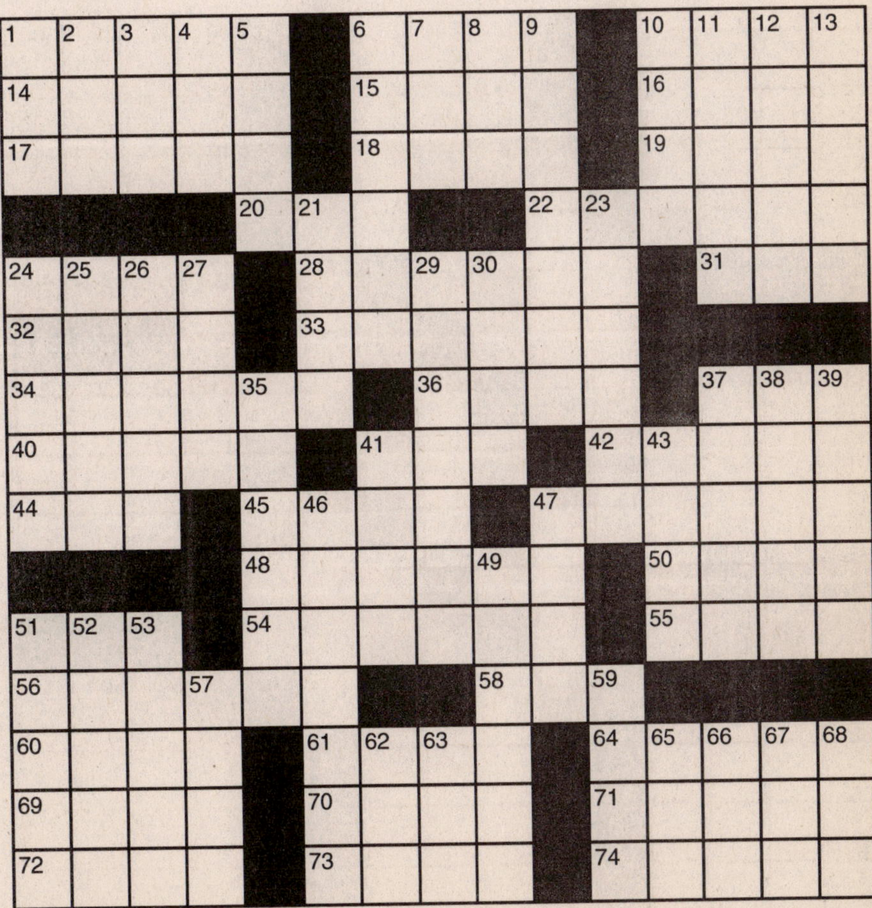

PUZZLE 55

ACROSS
1. Hidden supply
6. Nile biters
10. Pod member
14. Admixture
15. Stylish
16. Yard section
17. Gawk
18. Albacore, e.g.
19. Tex-Mex fare
20. Long periods
21. Inn
22. The sun
23. Jugs
25. Entrance door
28. Do wrong
31. High railroads
32. Appetizing store
33. Mated
35. Aquarium occupant
39. Land amid water
40. Chef's formula: abbr.
41. Easy gait
42. Yule snack
45. Calorie counter
47. Look-alike
48. Brethren
49. Reverent dread
50. Redeem
53. Listens
55. Time past
56. Babble
58. Conspiracy
62. Cup of joe
64. Shangri-la official
65. Without an escort
66. Made like
67. Expel
68. Thrifty person
69. Cuddled
70. Magenta and cerise
71. Strict

DOWN
1. Container
2. Voice range
3. Social group
4. Equine
5. Chart or contact
6. Role players
7. Closes
8. Yearn
9. Surgical knife
10. Opposite of seld
11. Sunday meat
12. Hot chocolate
13. Coral island
21. Blend
24. Teeny
26. Timeworn
27. Infantry weapon
28. Adventure tale
29. Too hasty
30. Annoy
32. Grumpy associate?
34. Pauses
35. "___ Smart"
36. Tiny amount
37. Pour forth
38. Roll-call response
40. Sprint
43. Duo
44. More agile
45. Earth
46. Printer's fluid
48. Jewelers' measures
50. Hindu prince
51. Yawning
52. New
53. Muggy
54. Slapping noise
57. Feeble, as an excuse
59. Passion
60. Unique chap
61. Gull's cousin
63. Append
65. Pack animal

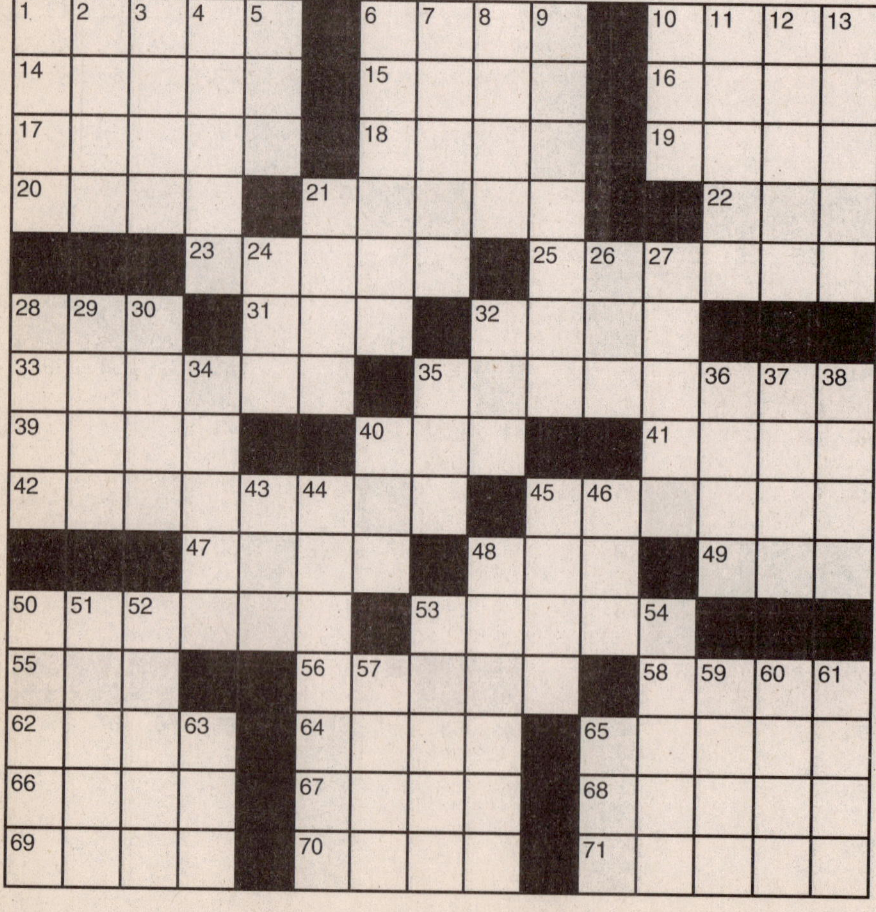

PUZZLE 56

ACROSS

1. "True ___"
5. EMT's word
9. Suspends
14. Highway division
15. Haul
16. Supply
17. Letter holders
19. Watery
20. Period of life
21. Freddy's street
22. Band instrument
24. Crew
25. Stuns with noise
27. Used to be
30. Antlered creature
32. Indian dress
33. Cartoon panther color
34. Wins
36. Skimpy
38. Attempts
41. Chin beards
42. Woman's shirt
43. Chaps
44. Leather strap
45. Chamber
47. Not nays
50. Unhappy
51. Kind of spray can
53. Knob
55. Urban blight
56. Tango number
57. Stylist's goop
58. Canadian peninsula
61. Near
64. Pacific or Arctic
65. Niblick number
66. Wallet fillers
67. Writings
68. Observer
69. Hornet's home

DOWN

1. Glitter
2. Stoves
3. Create
4. Plumbing joint
5. Woman's wrap
6. Sail supports
7. Had a snack
8. Experimenter
9. Basil and thyme, e.g.
10. Bluish green
11. Convent sister
12. Bathtub ___
13. Snoop
18. Accountants' books
23. In ___ (exactly)
26. Fourth notes
27. Grape juice
28. Initial wager
29. The ___ the limit!
31. Roughly
33. Sucker
35. Hi-fi, today
37. Mail-order ___
38. ___ and flows
39. Dog's bane
40. Crease
41. Diamond, e.g.
43. Sticky substance
46. Church instruments
48. Motor
49. Napped leathers
51. Hymn closers
52. Possessor
54. Hallowed
55. Minor quarrel
58. Obtained
59. Head of a suit
60. Gender
62. Falsify
63. Beau, to Lloyd

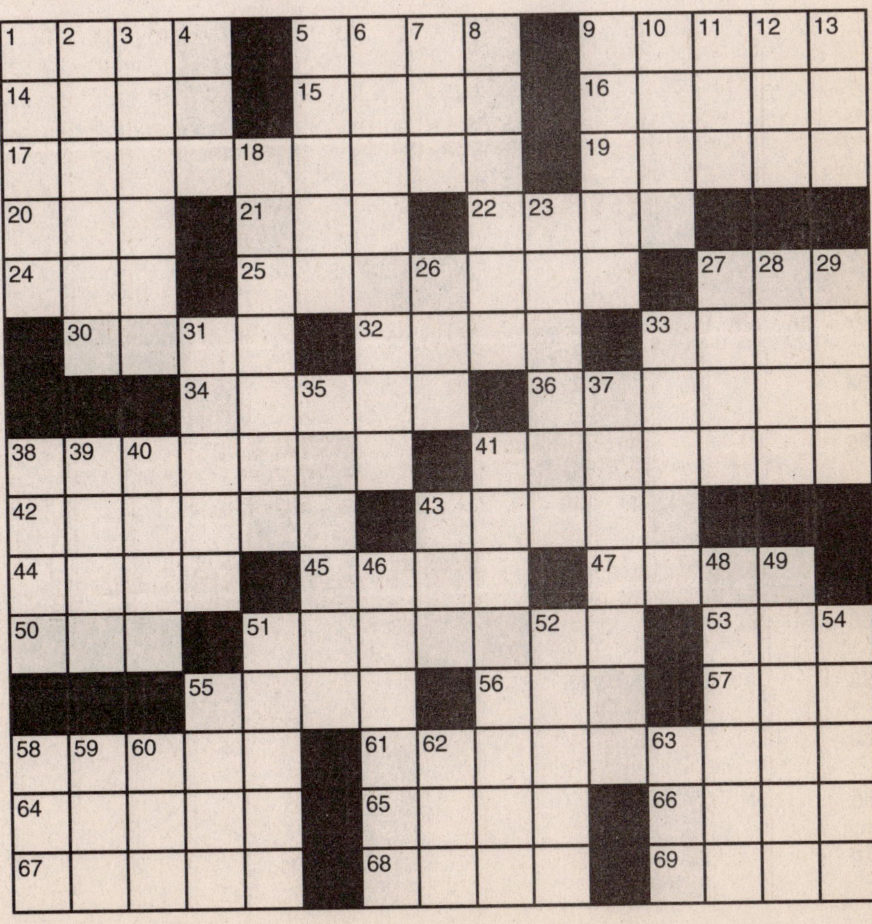

PUZZLE 57

ACROSS

1. Daytime TV fare
6. Short reminder
10. Morsel
13. Guardian spirits
15. Copied
16. Ostrich's kin
17. Sound system
18. Predicaments
20. Clump of turf
21. Influence
23. Trickle
24. Russian emperor
25. Pressed
27. Full of gaps
30. Season beginner
33. Already retired
34. Kitchen herb
35. Roll tightly
38. Thorny flowers
40. Large container
41. Sprite
43. Assembled
44. Sob
46. Jeans patch site
47. Spicy lunchmeat
49. Groucho's prop
50. Kind
53. Advance
55. By the mouth
56. Facial feature
59. Owl's question
62. Tag incorrectly
64. Foreign ___
66. Atlas entry
67. Squeeze
68. Basic food item
69. Beast of burden
70. Roofing substances
71. Winter toys

DOWN

1. Back talk
2. Atop
3. Seasoned
4. Apiece
5. Trashy
6. Built
7. Saga
8. Thawing
9. Poem of praise
10. Evil spirit
11. Astound
12. Cleared tables
14. Settee
19. Anchor
22. To's mate
24. Admit defeat
26. Great Barrier ___
27. Injure
28. Wind instrument
29. "___ we forget . . ."
31. Biblical song
32. Swallow
35. Aircraft part
36. Place
37. Colorer
39. Mute bird
40. Through
42. Comparable
45. Branch of math
47. Window bottom
48. Sickly
49. Military students
50. Pause mark
51. Vocal solos
52. Grates
54. Corn and canola
57. Century unit
58. Tall shade trees
59. Clean
60. Clutch
61. Wallet bills
63. Ham it up
65. Lass

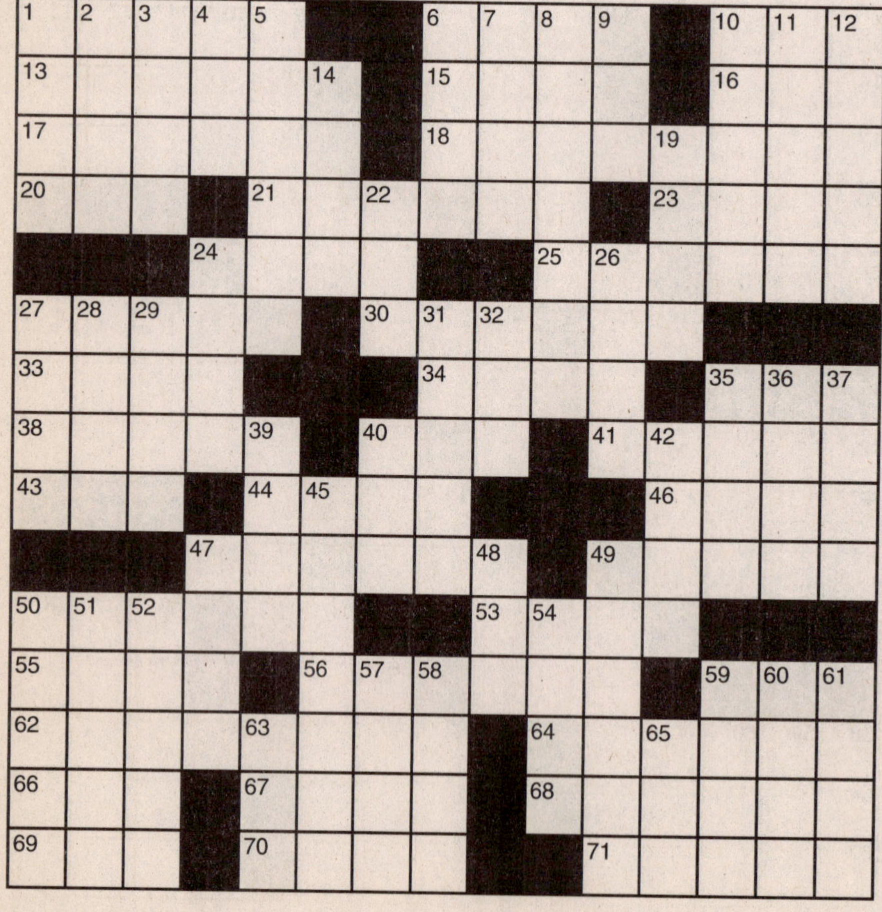

PUZZLE 58

ACROSS

1. Kind of hurrah
5. Legendary birds
9. Detester
14. Mixture
15. Of a time
16. Doddering
17. Frequent attender
18. Guitar device
19. Articles
20. Consume
22. Lap pup
24. Bee's follower
25. Craggy hills
28. Less polite
31. Sharp crests
33. Ump's kin
35. Billiard shot
39. Act
42. Compound of oxygen
43. Limb
44. Type measures
45. Wary of attack
47. Botanist's specimen
48. Entirely
49. Magician's word
51. Brown pigment
54. "___ So Cold"
55. Female ruff
58. Fairy-tale villain
60. Study
62. Terrible
65. Truck sections
68. Cartographer's speck
69. Horned animal
70. Engage
71. Sideways glance
72. Apartment
73. Bloodhound's trail
74. Pass catchers

DOWN

1. Reason
2. Isolated
3. Blockade
4. Raced
5. Headmaster
6. ___ pro nobis
7. Beanie
8. Splash
9. Japanese verse
10. Paid to play
11. Lace
12. Hackberry, e.g.
13. Legal thing
21. Flower part
23. Once
26. Mend
27. Deprives
29. Writer Jong
30. Staff again
32. Tangle
34. Suffix with slug or song
35. Musical finale
36. Skating jumps
37. Ransack
38. Love song
40. Take a stand against
41. Wire measure
46. Boxers do it
50. More succinct
52. ___ the pavement
53. Arctic abode
55. Gone aloft
56. Caught congers
57. Pitchers
59. Yodeling sound
61. Despicable
62. Bend
63. He's on first
64. Fish flipper
66. Financial assistance
67. Slangy chum

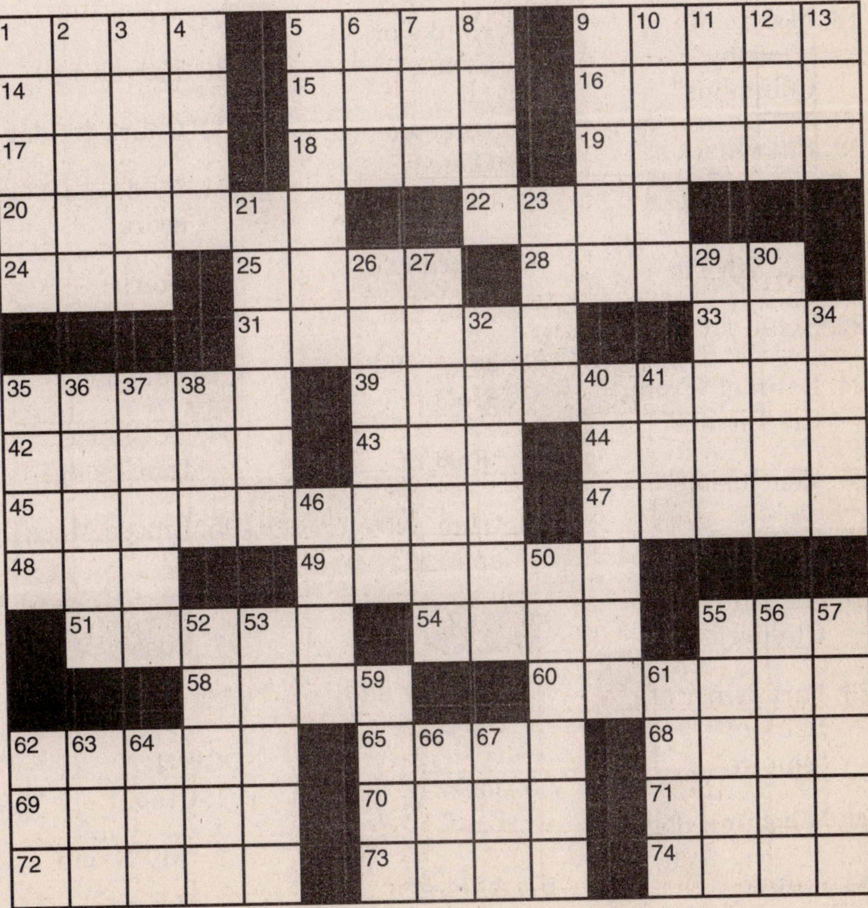

PUZZLE 59

MOVIES & TELEVISION

ACROSS

1. "___ Degrees of Separation"
4. "What's Happening!!" character
7. "___ Na Na"
10. "The Night We Never ___"
13. "___ Got a Secret"
14. Musical composition
16. Hastened
17. "Peyton Place" role
18. Martin of "Goodbye, Columbus"
19. Entwine
20. Safeguard
21. ___ Tin Tin
22. Small fly
24. Balin of "From the Terrace"
25. Conclusion
26. Grows older
27. "___ My Children"
29. Part owner of Sanford's "empire"
31. Whodunit dog
33. A Judd
36. Summers of "Gilligan's Island"
38. Pentateuch
41. Costar of "Kaz"
42. Star of "Aaron's Way"
43. "The ___ Man"
44. "Tootsie" actress
45. Actor Thinnes
46. "The Seven ___ Itch"
48. Hanks or Cruise
49. Director Gance ("J'Accuse")
51. Soprano Eames
53. 30-second spots
56. "East of ___"
58. "Hue and ___"
59. Geek
63. "Beauty and the ___"
65. Jones of "L.A. Law"
67. A Bergen
68. Principal on "It's Your Move"
69. Surrender
70. Plummets
71. Pastoral poem
73. Beaver's expletive
74. Verse of praise
75. "___ Connection"
77. "___ Wednesday"
79. Tree juice
81. Magician's stick
85. Lisa on "Green Acres"
86. Leg joint
87. Wear out
89. Farrah's ex
90. Court divider
91. Made a perfect score
92. Spirit
93. Ms. Sue ___ Langdon
94. "A Chorus Line" song
95. Emcee Mack
96. "___-Devil"
97. Beatty of films

DOWN

1. Croon
2. "My Name Is ___"
3. Lawless role
4. "Cannery ___"
5. "The ___ Fools"
6. Argentina's Peron
7. Marty's pal
8. "___ Gabler"
9. Sapara of "Crusoe"
10. Houlihan of "M*A*S*H"
11. Peter Gunn's girl
12. Turns brown
15. "The Jetsons" boss
16. Duvall or Long
23. Tunie of "As the World Turns"
26. Source of energy
28. Reta Shaw on "Mr. Peepers"
30. Jolson and Pacino
32. "My Little Margie" star
33. Egg drink
34. Melissa on "Falcon Crest"
35. Opposite of neath
36. Host of "Scrabble"
37. Smiled scornfully
39. "Long ___ Tomorrow"

PUZZLE 59

40. Overzealous actor

45. "___ Rock West"

47. March sister

50. Ms. Palmer

52. "The Remarkable ___"

53. Actor Vigoda

54. Dolores ___ Rio

55. Slobber

57. Sighed like Mr. Ed

58. Actress Holm

60. Freudian topic

61. Talk session

62. Welby and Kildare, e.g.

64. "The West ___ Waltz"

66. Society-page word

67. Actor Byrnes

72. Kerwin of films

74. First name of talk shows

75. Host Jay ___

76. Prop for Emeril

78. "The Bad ___"

80. Feels bad

82. Either Hale

83. Pacific honker

84. Feat

86. "Krazy ___"

88. Compass heading

PUZZLE 60

ACROSS

1. Way off
5. Women
9. Dory sticks
13. Painful
14. Flee to wed
16. Flavorless
17. Teamster's rig
18. Friendlier
19. Fuss
20. Receive
22. Was indebted to
24. Type of evergreen
25. Argue
29. Habit
31. "For ___ a jolly . . ."
32. Opposite of neath
33. Spin like ___
34. Upon
36. Highbrow
38. Miscalculate
41. Source of energy
42. Jest with
44. Booty
46. Live
47. Flower support
48. Olympic sled
49. Salamander
52. Mesh fabric
54. Shining star
55. Strife
58. Had faith
60. ___ cube
61. Young goats
64. Vigoda of "Fish"
65. Spring event
67. Snarl
69. Slack
73. Center
74. Muggy
75. ___-in-the-wool
76. Emcee
77. New York athletes
78. Evergreens

DOWN

1. Burro
2. Rival
3. Kind of wrestling
4. Ruler's term
5. Least rough
6. Boxing legend
7. Insane
8. Spout
9. Many times, poetically
10. In the air
11. Marconi's medium
12. Gale
15. Put up
21. Power trip
23. Twins
25. Horse command
26. "___-Cop"
27. Mary or John Jacob
28. Actor Borgnine
30. Magic formula
33. Not present
35. Forewarnings
37. Bread variety
39. Drive out
40. Scoundrel
43. Precious stones
45. Look after
50. Forest creature
51. Consider
53. Bathroom feature
55. Tether
56. Sneeze sound
57. Scorches
59. Run-down
62. Bongo or snare
63. Several
66. Soak
68. Cleverness
70. Popeye's yes
71. Ply the needle
72. Newspaper execs

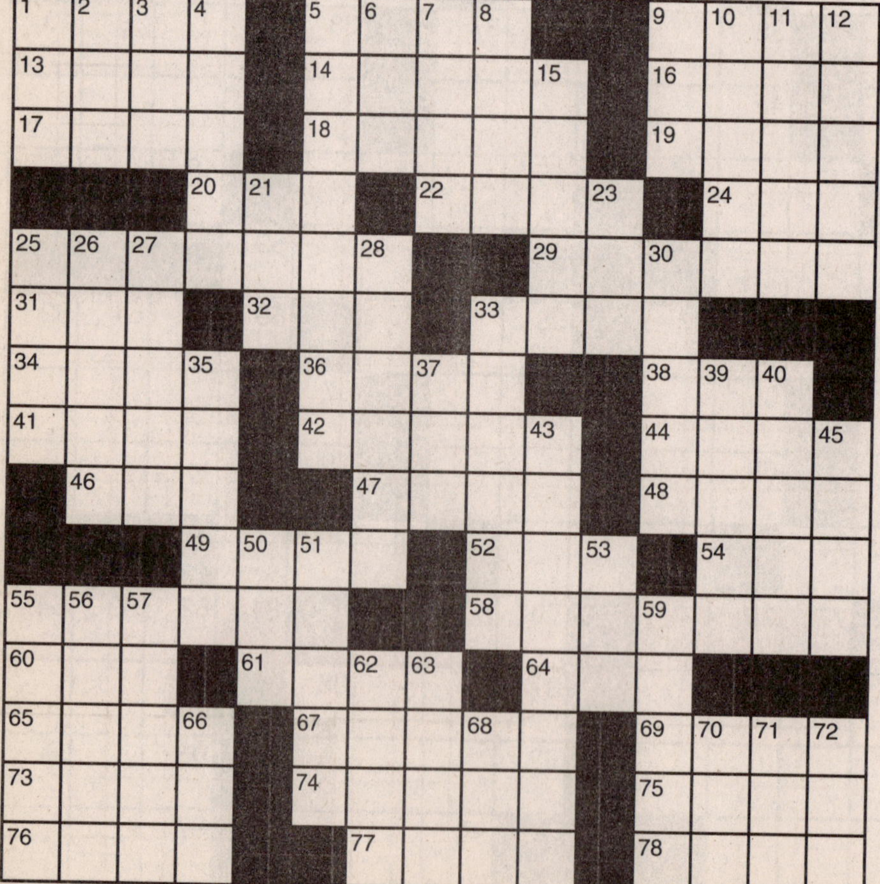

PUZZLE 61

ACROSS
1. Flower leaf
6. Unattractive
10. Has a mortgage
14. Creamy white
15. Ballet exercise
16. Perky
17. Present
18. Dagger handle
19. Pond organism
20. Ho's strings
21. Mart
23. Fusion
24. Acapulco coin
26. Makes aware
28. Moistens, poetically
30. Season beginner
35. Residence
38. Comparison word
41. Bossa ___
42. Library motto?
45. School wings
46. Food morsels
47. Demon
48. Winged
50. Newts
52. "___ Bovary"
55. Objective
59. Foul-up
63. Shaped like a ball
65. Press for payment
66. Collaborator
67. Stringed instrument
68. Dated ditty
70. Rotisserie part
71. In some other way
72. Lariat
73. Strong emotion
74. Saw
75. Assorted

DOWN
1. GI's wall decor?
2. Call to mind
3. Musical pitches
4. Circle segment
5. Soap-making substances
6. Cover with fabric
7. Fierce look
8. Type of prisoner
9. Nonetheless
10. October gemstone
11. Watering hole
12. Thus
13. Corset feature
22. Playing marble
23. Horned viper
25. Most bizarre
27. Chinese association
29. Yet, in verse
31. Sign up
32. Lymph ___
33. Exact
34. African coin
35. Totally confused
36. Beak
37. Spanish stew
39. ___ or miss
40. Put together
43. Musical ending
44. Frequently, to Byron
49. Grounded bird
51. Lawyer's charge
53. Lace mat
54. Got up
56. African antelope
57. Posh digs
58. Work clay
59. Waistband
60. Indian palm
61. Miner's way in
62. Celebration
64. Campus quarters
67. Neckline shape
69. Waikiki wreath

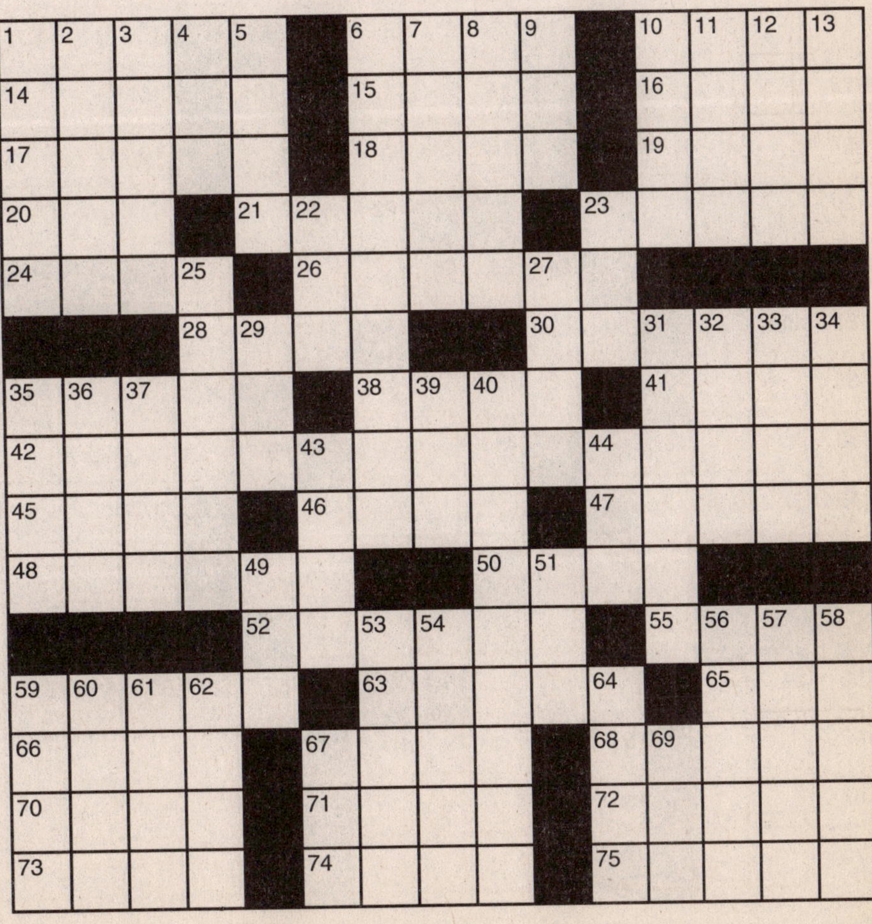

PUZZLE 62

ACROSS

1. Prank
6. Shirt protectors
10. Feminine pronoun
13. Uncanny
14. Not rented
16. Desk wood
17. Nobility
18. Scornful look
19. Enjoyed dinner
20. Me, ___, and I
22. Took the helm
24. Deerskin
27. Bell and Barker
30. Rajah's mate
31. Pressroom employee
35. Sign
36. Crowd actors
38. Scruff of the neck
39. Inflexible
41. Building annex
42. Small landmass
43. Stadium part
44. Faultfinder
46. Screw up
47. Scribble
49. Lose brightness
50. Utter
51. Eminent conductor
53. Swift cat
56. Instruction
62. Slack
63. Dodge
66. Implicate
67. High mountain
68. Variety show
69. Pastry chef
70. Flirt
71. Fishing-pole part
72. Use up

DOWN

1. Swarm
2. Bank (on)
3. Flower
4. Quote
5. Hull bottom
6. Student's vehicle
7. Motel
8. Made holy
9. Simmers
10. Glide high
11. Dislike
12. ___ out (barely managed)
15. Cornered
21. Linen source
23. Gray and Moran
25. Door sign
26. Emergency transportation by plane
27. Hazes
28. Caper
29. Downhill athlete
30. Game official
32. Falsehoods
33. Gluck's forte
34. Attempt again
37. Rite site?
40. Picture border
42. Diamonds
44. Butcher's tool
45. Effigy
48. "Like ___ for Chocolate"
52. Remove whiskers
53. Crab's appendage
54. Crown of light
55. World's fair, e.g.
57. Declines
58. Strike
59. Benefit
60. Warning sign
61. Dweeb
64. Appropriate
65. Scaleless fish

PUZZLE 63

ACROSS
1. Farce
5. Russian ruler
9. Intense rage
12. For takeout
13. ___ of Capricorn
15. Dent
16. Hymn-ending word
17. Apartment, e.g.
18. Playing marble
19. "Titanic" foe
20. Have a debt
21. Family cars
23. Gun a motor
25. Circle portion
26. Sound systems
30. "Eight Is ___"
33. Australian "bear"
34. Apparel
36. Request
37. Those elected
38. Bedtime song
41. Whichever
42. Comedians
44. Beef
45. Pays to play
47. Glacial cover
49. Units of heat
51. Enjoyable
52. Aardvark's tidbit
53. Dodged
56. Atlas item
58. "Less ___ Zero"
62. Harden
63. Detect
65. Ancient instrument
66. "Me and My ___"
67. Hard worker
68. Dueling tool
69. Secret watcher
70. Merge
71. "___ Poets Society"

DOWN
1. Random try
2. Catcher's plate
3. Ripening agent
4. Mutt
5. Ship's staff
6. Region
7. Fitting
8. Inlets
9. Impeccable
10. Downpour
11. Units of work
13. Treasure stash
14. Not dirty
22. Hard candy
24. Epochal
26. ___ boom
27. With refinement
28. Gawk
29. Waldorf, e.g.
30. "___ Tide"
31. Autry and Hackman
32. Ride and wire
33. Green fruit
35. Value
39. Ref's kin
40. Knitter's purchase
43. Skim
46. Provoked
48. Concerning
50. One who stares
53. Easter edibles
54. Bound
55. Terrible fate
56. Paper factory
57. Did well on
59. Exaggeration
60. Sector
61. Must have
64. Connection

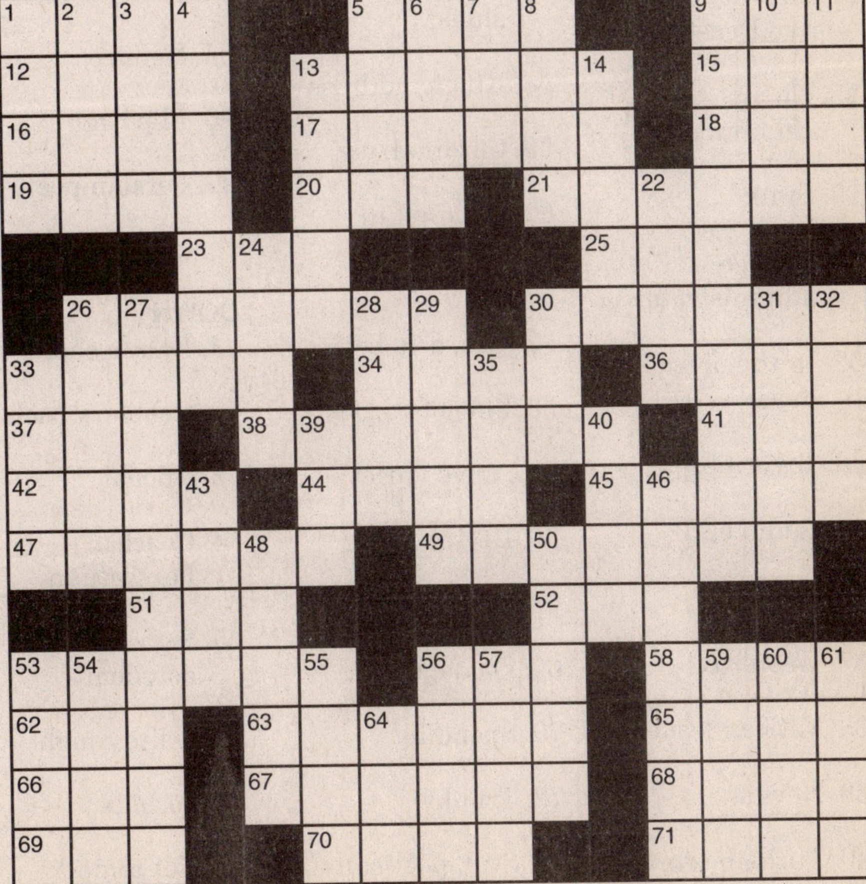

PUZZLE 64

ACROSS

1. Ali ___
5. Nun's wear
10. Rationing out
16. Fan
18. Scarlett's surname
19. Channel
20. Daydreamer
22. French dance
23. Performs on stage
24. Bustles
25. Thug
27. "Beauty ___ the Beast"
28. No, in Edinburgh
29. Stalk
31. College administrator
32. In the olden days
33. Tavern brew
34. Radio buff
35. Honks
37. Western
38. Vatican leader
39. Newts
40. Turkish coin
41. Palms off
44. Makes edging
45. Computer in ""2001"
46. Flap
49. Hostels
50. Actor Saviano
51. Yaks
52. Polar abundance
53. Careen
54. Roy Rogers's wife
56. Hassock
57. Medieval shield
58. Kingly address
59. Cardinal, e.g.
60. Opposed to
61. Mil. concern
62. "___ a Rebel"
63. Side of bacon
64. Apple variety
66. Decree
68. Carry
69. Damage
70. Spending
72. Trunks
73. Still, poetically
74. H.S. football site
77. Arrow notch
78. Drift
79. Offers
80. Above, to a poet
81. Day of the wk.
82. Melville's captain
83. Congers
85. ___ mater
86. Verdi opera
88. Important occasion
92. Straight
93. Oriental
94. Foreigners
95. Itemize
96. Flip over
97. Persian poet

DOWN

1. Baby's shoe
2. Cobblers' tools
3. Appeal
4. Coach Parseghian
5. Sigh of boredom
6. Polite cough
7. Forbids
8. Hot temper
9. Bull's-eyes
10. Georgia city
11. Author Hunter
12. Decade number
13. Magic spells
14. Slight variation
15. Sex
16. Safari boss
17. Not the express
21. Topic
26. Hemisphere gp.
29. Filmed
30. Knocks
31. Stipples
32. Dory stick
35. Twit
36. Suddenly
37. Artists' media
38. Furtive whisper
40. Chemists' lairs
41. Put away neatly
42. Ready
43. Not enough
44. Painted tinware
45. Lend a ___
47. Keen
48. Suit
50. Pickle holders
51. Outfit

PUZZLE 64

54. Doctor's menu

55. Glass bottles

56. Not present

58. Thick carpet

63. Popcorn seasoning

64. Deplored

65. Large vases

67. Pen's fluid

68. German-style restaurant

69. Robbery

70. Develop

71. Foray

72. Sheepish sound

74. Portfolio

75. Sweetheart of yore

76. Carts

78. Fingerprint ridge

79. Combine

82. Turkish regiment

83. Actress Adams

84. Spirit

85. Song for Sills

87. Grazing ground

89. Sixth sense: abbr.

90. Confucian way

91. Graceful tree

PUZZLE 65

ACROSS

1. Dermal dilemma
5. Hubbubs
9. Geographer's volume
14. Tibia
15. Bright green
16. Blame
17. Is located
18. Cultivated
19. Settle
20. Miscue
21. Bunch
22. Huff and puff
23. Rot
25. Linger
29. ___ cutlet
31. Obeying
35. More agile
38. Dump
39. Fire
40. Hot drink
41. Trend
43. Roe
44. Light-switch positions
45. Locomotive sound
46. Leather maker
49. Holds fast
51. Withered
52. Method
54. Scratchy
58. Hit
61. Yank
63. Work on the garden
64. Nerve
66. Harassed
67. Certain star
68. Sporting blades
69. Perimeter
70. ___-friendly
71. Fuses together
72. Quick look
73. Gull-like bird

DOWN

1. Beasts of burden
2. Peep
3. Safecracker's soup
4. Some dash widths
5. Pond organism
6. Square-dance attire
7. End of a series
8. Alter slacks
9. Muslim official
10. Yanked
11. Milan money, formerly
12. Pub offerings
13. Big first for baby
21. Merriment
24. Climbing vine
26. ___ kid
27. Remove
28. Give permission
30. Bows
32. Religious symbol
33. Hub
34. Snarl
35. Greek portico
36. Remain unsettled
37. Reckless
38. Binge
42. Corrosion
45. Call out
47. Nutmeg covering
48. Lacrosse goal
50. Caught sight of
51. Dirty spot
53. Lyric poem
55. Opted for
56. Hang around
57. Desire
58. Small duck
59. Steady gait
60. Skating maneuver
62. Onion's kin
65. Tee's preceder
66. Ribbed fabric
67. Bolt's mate

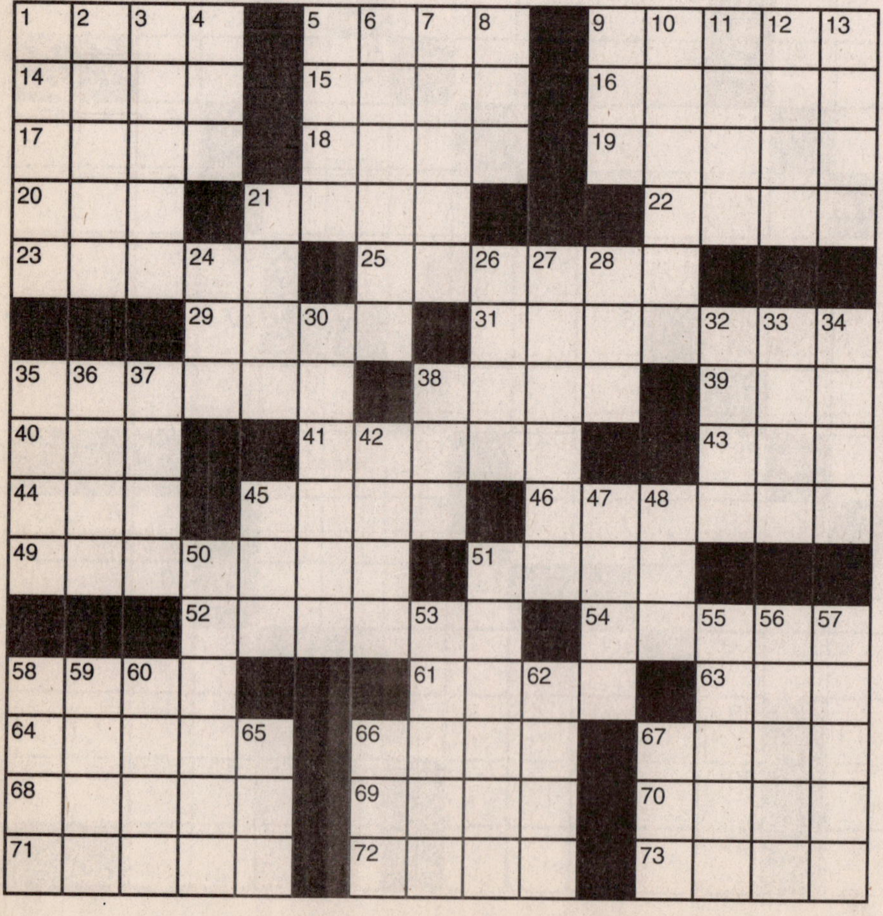

PUZZLE 66

ACROSS

1. Complacent
5. Bawls
9. Blue dye
13. Up to
14. Kingdom
15. Green fruit
16. Not pro
17. Follow in order
18. College final
19. Pet rodent
21. Booby ___
23. The self
24. Notable period
25. Big truck
27. Expand
29. Praise too highly
31. Harem chamber
34. Hawaiian goose
35. Explorer Vasco ___
39. Pew
41. Label
43. Rajahs' wives
44. Form of soccer
46. Grouchy one
48. Freud's concerns
49. Importance
51. Elegance
54. Cozy or towel
55. That fellow's
58. Ms. Gardner
59. Impress clearly
61. Acquaint
63. Hoarfrost
65. Coral island
67. "___ Fear"
68. Turns right
69. Hauled
70. Egg cell
71. Gambling numbers
72. Hitherto
73. Racks up

DOWN

1. Show business
2. Prospector
3. Very, very
4. Talkative
5. Old Japanese money
6. Malt kiln
7. Book-jacket ads
8. Slandered
9. Beerlike beverage
10. Vetoed
11. Portrayal
12. Fish garnish
14. Experience again
20. Locomotive
22. Arctic animal
26. Fellow
28. Aquatic plant
30. Respond
31. Kimono sash
32. Cave
33. Also
36. Black cuckoo
37. In-between
38. Horse's relative
40. Deal with
42. Moxie
45. Reiterate
47. From time immemorial
50. Zone
51. City east of Bismarck
52. Covered with vines
53. Titled
55. Throw
56. Data
57. Goblet stalks
60. Words of inquiry
62. Holy picture
64. Road turn
66. Tennis call

PUZZLE 67

ACROSS

1. TV and jet
5. Table seasoning
9. "___ It Be"
12. Pearly gem
13. Attraction
15. Native metal
16. "If I ___ King"
17. Tater
18. Engine component
19. ABC, NBC, or CBS
21. Complain
22. Cleo's snake
23. Jane or John
24. Bit of land
26. Blush
30. Proclamation
33. In excess of
34. Paper amount
35. Slumbering
39. Unit of length
40. Holland export
41. Jungle sound
42. Court argument
43. Stouts
44. Traveler's permit
45. Allotted
47. Brunch dish
49. Hold firmly
52. Authority
53. Outskirts
54. "___ Magic"
57. Criminal
62. Lemon drink
63. Neckwear
65. Depart
66. Cozy place
67. Contacts solution
68. Black-tie event
69. Road turn
70. Encounter
71. Urban blight

DOWN

1. Scattered seed
2. Three-sided blade
3. Little pie
4. Destroyed
5. Wheel part
6. Quick to learn
7. Slender
8. Cheerio
9. Not widespread
10. Wipe out
11. Attract
13. Kitchen garb
14. Reason
20. Poetic work
25. Withhold food
26. Frolic
27. Hateful
28. Remove from print
29. Fantasies
30. Caught congers
31. Platform
32. Demon
34. Regulation
36. Bubble
37. Reduce
38. Phooey!
40. Tit for ___
46. Long poems
47. Speak in public
48. Trim the lawn
49. A+ or C-
50. Takes the bus
51. Prayer enders
52. Factory
55. British trolley
56. Tag ___
58. Desk supports
59. Important test
60. Grain tower
61. Men-only party
64. Contend

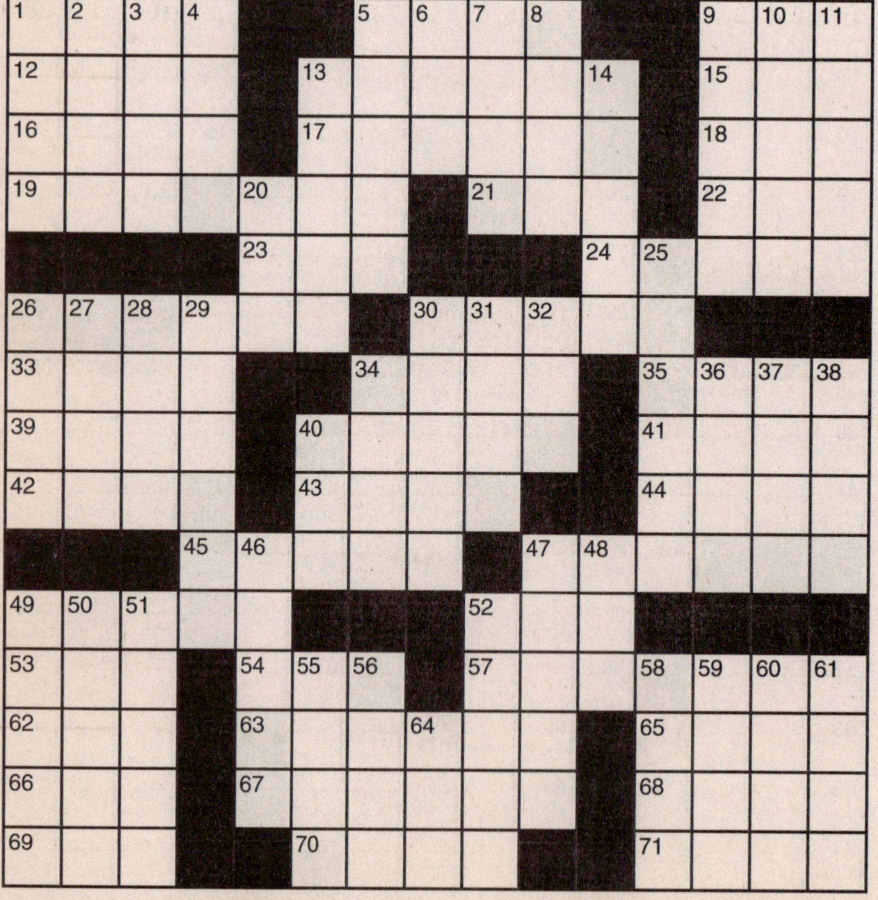

PUZZLE 68

ACROSS

1. Spill liquid
5. Coffee
9. Ribbed fabric
12. Monk's hood
13. Pick out
15. Prior to, in verse
16. Location
17. Conjurer's command
18. Slash
19. Frenzied
21. Make lace
22. Likely
23. Baseball's Willie ___
24. Void
26. Pseudonym
29. Trucker's rig
31. Shallow pan
32. Paint
36. Melt
40. Solemn promise
42. S-shaped moldings
43. Clay square
44. Malayan boat
45. Leather maker
47. Chop off
48. Bringer of a court action
50. Tiny landmass
52. Tub soakings
55. Sodden
57. Unclosed, in poems
58. Purpose
61. Very large
65. Fish's wing
66. Plunder
68. Dreadful
69. Lard
70. Spectrums
71. Organic compound
72. Light-switch positions
73. Actress Chase
74. Hibernates

DOWN

1. Nature's Band-Aid
2. Ancient knowledge
3. Debtor
4. Blood part
5. Pulls suddenly
6. Pub fare
7. Waistcoat
8. Official records
9. Summarize
10. Gush lava
11. Picayune
13. Peppy
14. ___ pole
20. Freedom
25. Catcher's catcher
26. At the peak
27. False witness
28. Hooked on
29. Recognized
30. Otherwise
33. Jot down
34. Chinese gelatin
35. Stag guests
37. Road incline
38. Soothing plant
39. Sobbed
41. ___ browns
46. Frost
49. Take by force
51. Dug up
52. Popular
53. Of bees
54. Nylon shelters
55. Belief
56. Sleeve lurkers
59. New Delhi dress
60. Dreadful
62. IX
63. Treat pleats
64. Cartoon transparencies
67. Solicit

1	2	3	4	■	■	5	6	7	8	■	■	9	10	11
12				■	13					14	■	15		
16				■	17						■	18		
19				20			■	21			■	22		
■	■	■	23				■	■	■	24	25			
26	27	28			■	■	■	29	30			■	■	■
31			■	32	33	34	35			■	36	37	38	39
40			41	■	42					■	43			
44				■	45					46	■	47		
■	■	■	48	49			■	■	■	50	51			
52	53	54			■	■	■	55	56			■	■	■
57			■	58	59	60	■	61				62	63	64
65			■	66			67			■	68			
69			■	70						■	71			
72			■	■	73				■	■	74			

PUZZLE 69

ACROSS

1. Feather adhesive
4. Southern nut
9. Partly open
13. Be obligated to
14. Cuban cigar
15. Goofy
16. Draw off
17. Available power
18. Gambler's wager
19. Prior to, in poems
20. Backbone
21. "___ Than Zero"
22. Large fruit
24. Upper crust
27. Grind
30. Mortified
34. High heel, e.g.
37. Cheer from a bullring
39. Live
40. House location
41. Useful legume
43. Zilch
44. Military unit
46. Toodle-oo!
47. Quote
48. Carried
50. You're something ___!
52. Go secretly
54. Golf club
58. Health spots
61. Florida city
64. Notable time span
65. Doorman's call
66. Use a sieve
67. Jaguar, e.g.
68. Flirty look
69. Warns
70. Poem of praise
71. Look searchingly
72. Fender blemishes
73. Urge

DOWN

1. Indian pole
2. Mindful
3. Drive off
4. Plate of glass
5. Ceaselessly
6. Slice
7. Ms. Lansbury
8. Vote against
9. Flowery shrubs
10. Tarzan's mate
11. Pismires
12. Whiskeys
14. Red hair-dye
23. Mine rock
25. A.k.a. Jacob
26. At that time
28. Relieve
29. Tissue layer
31. Tiny
32. Fix copy
33. Strike from print
34. Untidy person
35. Time division
36. ___ von Bismarck
38. Wane
41. Warning
42. Organ of sight
45. Choosier
47. Third letter
49. Tell a secret
51. Mute birds
53. Black or Carpenter
55. Phony duck
56. School mark
57. Ingested
58. Hold it!
59. Summon
60. Shaft
62. Retail store
63. Fruit stones
66. Sorrowful

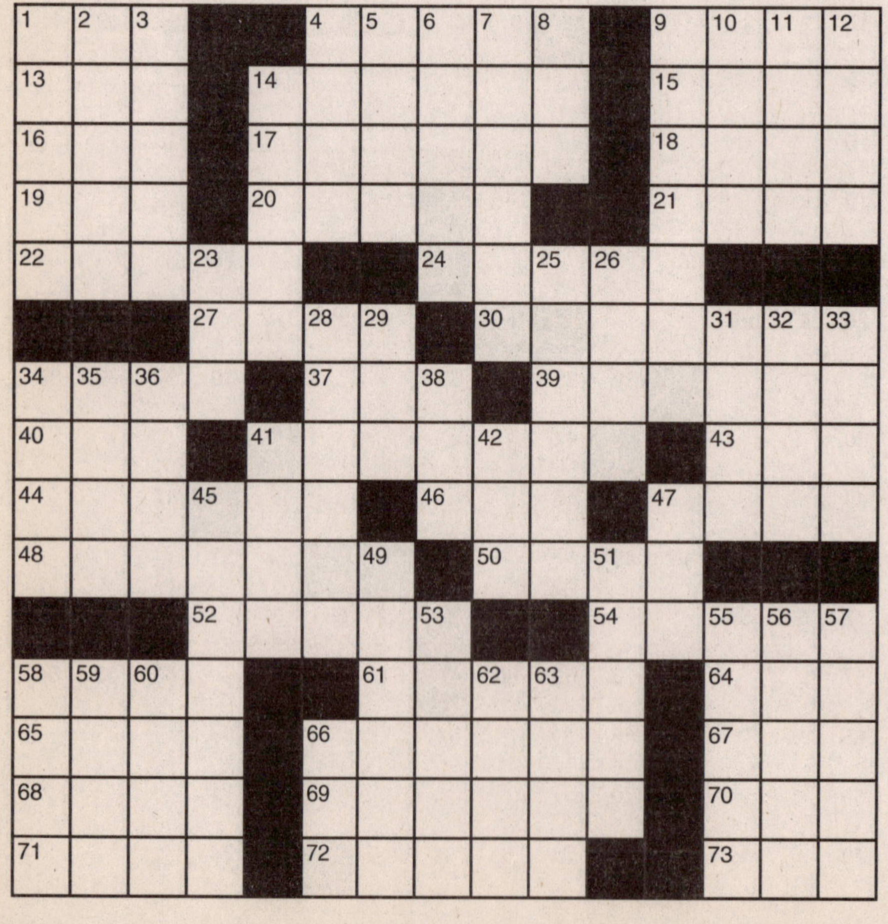

DOUBLE CROSSER

PUZZLE 70

Fill in the correct missing letters in the crossword diagram, making sure that no word is repeated. Then transfer those letters to the correspondingly numbered dashes below the diagram to reveal a quotation.

H	A	S	P			A	2	A	R		O	9	T	S
38	N	T	20	L		16	O	S	E		D	R	O	P
B	E	I	G	34		E	27	T	14	A	D	I	4	E
	12	R	E	N		S	Y	37	U	P		D	E	W
			O	D	29			A	N	35	S			
W	E	A	39		V	A	R	19			T	22	D	E
6	X	E		C	E	D	E		H	13	Y	D	E	N
S	I	R		A	N	D	1	R	25	N		E	V	26
P	10	I	E	R	5		G	O	R	E		A	32	M
31	E	E	K			E	30	D	S		A	11	L	Y
			E	E	L	S			E	L	8			
A	F	23		F	A	C	T	S		A	P	21	E	
C	36	U	R	T	24	H	3	P		33	E	N	A	L
18	O	B	O		S	E	R	E		A	R	I	7	E
E	15	S	E		O	17	E	D			E	28	E	E

1 2   3 4 5   6   7 8 9 10 11

12 13 14 15 16,   17 18 19   20 21

22 23   24 25   26 27 28 29 30 31 32 33 34

35 36   37 38 39?

PUZZLE 71

ACROSS

1. Honshu mountain
5. Islamic prince
9. Fedoras
13. Ages
17. Imitated
18. Beguile
19. Spiny houseplant
20. Coffee grind
21. Nat or Natalie
22. Intricate
24. Blow
25. Swell
27. Arabian port
28. Grimy
30. Deposit, as eggs
31. Watch part
32. Copenhagen native
33. Perplex
36. Enemies
37. Cringing
41. Implore
42. Moves up and down
43. Neck areas
44. Meadow
45. Pouch
46. Debtors' letters
47. Intertwined
48. Loose flesh
49. Moral
51. ___-gritty
52. Secret plans
53. Gael
54. ___ Lama
55. Residue
56. Pallid
58. Huge wave
59. Paying attention to
62. Lasting conflict
63. Doubting person
64. Mound
65. Pool player's need
66. Operated
67. Los Angeles cager
68. Domestic
69. Cease!
70. Predestined
72. ___ dire
73. Singles out
74. Ranch sounds
75. Spike
76. Astrological symbol
77. Foolish old person
80. Buddies
81. Most melancholy
85. Actor Baldwin
86. Like some exercises
89. Playboy
90. Food list
91. Peak
92. Irish republic
93. Secondhand
94. Affirmative gestures
95. Little bites
96. Unfavorable replies
97. Kitten sounds

DOWN

1. Confront
2. "Once ___ a midnight dreary..."
3. Congeal
4. In principle
5. Mournful poem
6. Backless shoe
7. Tax shelter: abbr.
8. Partial refunds
9. Sultan's wives
10. Shepard or Arkin
11. Preschooler
12. Vacillated
13. More nervous
14. Voiced
15. Longest river
16. Disobeyed highway signs
23. Keats's outputs
26. Actress Charlotte ___
29. Individuals
31. Wails
32. Snow White's roomie
33. Church recess
34. Confound it!
35. German canine
36. Vile
37. Succulents
38. Unreasonable
39. Shipshape
40. Chatters
42. Gravy holder
43. Of birth
46. Religious picture
47. Fragrant bloom
48. Got away
50. Chilled
51. Lowest point
52. ___ school
54. Broke bread

PUZZLE 71

55. ___ Sea Scrolls

56. Hair style

57. Scorch

58. Small children

59. Beneficiary

60. Zero

61. Acquires

63. Trudeau's nationality

64. Ave!

67. Perjurer

68. Make damp

69. Monotonous

71. Calculating device

72. Glen

73. Bounder

75. Tom, Dick, and Harry, e.g.

76. Tribes

77. "___ Yankees"

78. Margarine

79. Look after

80. Splendid display

81. Beget

82. Slacken

83. Slant

84. Knight and Danson

87. ___-fi

88. Brazilian seaport, for short

1	2	3	4	■	5	6	7	8	■	9	10	11	12	■	13	14	15	16
17				■	18				■	19				■	20			
21				■	22				23					■	24			
25				26			■	27				■	28	29				
■	■	■	30			■	31				■	32				■	■	■
33	34	35			■	36				■	37					38	39	40
41				■	42				■	43					■	44		
45			■	46				■	47					■	48			
49			50				■	51					■	52				
■	■	53					■	54				■	55				■	■
56	57				■	58					■	59					60	61
62				■	63					■	64				■	65		
66			■	67					■	68					■	69		
70			71					■	72					■	73			
■	■	■	74				■	75				■	76			■	■	■
77	78	79				■	80				■	81				82	83	84
85				■	86	87					88			■	89			
90				■	91				■	92				■	93			
94				■	95				■	96				■	97			

PUZZLE 72

CLUES IN TWOS

Some of the Clues in this crossword are In Twos. Fill in two different answers to the same clue in the squares indicated.

ACROSS
1. Speedy pace
5.] Rage
9.]
13. First name in architecture
14. Jason's ship
15. Type
16.] Pine
18.]
19. Quantity
20. Branch
22. "Crocodile Rock" singer John
25. Skillful
27. ___ Alto
31. Pasture
32. Woman of Eden
33.] Chicken
35.]
37. Apple of one's eye
38. Use a soapbox
39. Yonder
41. Bigfoot's kin
43. ___ blanche
46. Piglet's mother
47.] Wind
51.]
53. Captain's yes
54. ___ Annie of "Oklahoma!"
55. River of Hades
56. Corporate symbol
58. Wood nymph
60. Zero in on
61. Old card game
62.] Cool
66.]
72. Otic
73. Secluded valley
74. The Andrews Sisters, e.g.
75.] Top
76.]
77. Remitted

1	2	3	4	■	5	6	7	8	■	■	9	10	11	12
13				■	14				■	15				
16				17					■	18				
■	■	■	19			■	■	20	21		■	■	■	■
22	23	24			■	25	26			■	27	28	29	30
31			■	■	32			■	33	34				
35			36	■	37			■	■	38				
■	■	■	39	40			■	41	42			■	■	■
43	44	45			■	■	46			■	47	48	49	50
51					52	■	53			■	■	54		
55				■	56	57			■	58	59			
■	■	■	■	60			■	■	61			■	■	■
62	63	64	65		■	66	67	68				69	70	71
72					■	73				■	74			
75				■	■	76				■	77			

DOWN
1. Ess follower
2. Race at idle
3. Lode's load
4. Chest
5. Mar
6. Prior to, in poetry
7. Ripen
8. Of sound
9. Female ruff
10. Tempest ___ ___ teapot
11. Bruin great
12. Decimal base
15. Phys ed
17. Western's prop
21. Scale notes
22. Gnome
23. Astrological feline
24. Shooter
25. Proclaim aloud
26. Put a fin on a filly
27. European capital
28. Blue-and-yellow macaw
29. Charter
30. Keatsian composition
32. Ecological org.
34. Crude bed
36. Glove material
40. Tasseled hat
41. Fluctuate
42. Ram's dam
43. Rival of NBC
44. Knack
45. Spanish king
46.] Settle
48.]
49. Ms. Lupino
50. Doze off
52. Actor Wallach
57. 24th Greek letter
58. Something of poor quality
59. Haley epic
60. Totally
61. Wildcat
62. Tractor part
63. Cry's companion
64. Roth savings pl.
65. Cicero's lang.
67. Heidi's home
68. Glimpse
69. Strong resentment
70. Diarist Anais ___
71. Understood

PUZZLE 73

Connections

Place the 7-letter answers to the clues into the diagram, each answer starting at the top with the letter I and ending at the bottom with the letter E. When the diagram is filled, a 10-letter word will read across the outlined row of the diagram.

1	2	3	4	5	6	7	8	9	10
I	I	I	I	I	I	I	I	I	I
E	E	E	E	E	E	E	E	E	E

1. List
2. Huge
3. Mimic
4. Progress
5. Bill
6. Motivate
7. Entail
8. Slant
9. Encroach
10. Perturbing

PUZZLE 74

ACROSS
1. Greek cheese
5. Flock male
8. Lyric poems
12. Removed summarily
13. Add to
14. Courageous one
15. Cartoonist Addams, shortly
16. Vigor's partner
17. Brunch, e.g.
18. Account
19. Organic compound
21. Fraternity letter
22. Roofer
25. Moved crosswise
27. Self-centered person
29. Some votes
30. Thought
32. Barber's sign
34. Egged on
37. Hay bundlers
39. Laundromat appliances
41. Pub order
42. Shack
44. Talk session
45. Bridge feat
47. Hooter
48. Prom-night wheels
49. Pinch
50. Born as
51. 1968, e.g.
52. Ship's staff
53. Take a wrong turn
54. Hitherto

DOWN
1. Truths
2. Breathe out
3. Pekoe portion
4. Sales pitches
5. Car gear
6. Related
7. Office notes
8. Electrical unit
9. In a profound way
10. Eliminates
11. Reliable
20. One-dimensional
23. Sheer linen
24. Large ducks
26. Mommy's partner
28. Touch lightly
31. Young child
32. Whiteness
33. Acid salt
35. Creepier
36. Stage offerings
37. Simple
38. Was radiant
40. Soccer or volleyball
43. Wide-spouted pitcher
46. Animal's throat
48. Caustic stuff

PUZZLE 75

ACROSS
1. Had a cupcake
4. Pillow cover
8. Float through the air
12. Hang down
13. Palm drink
14. Automobile part
15. Embrace
16. News story
17. Unskilled worker
18. Plums' stones
20. Posted
22. Punching tools
24. Baptism receptacle
25. Muscle spasm
27. Dressed
31. Barnyard female
32. Raw-fish dish
34. Ostrichlike animal
35. Competitor
37. Scientist Marie ____
39. Ailments
40. Spoils
41. Revenue
44. Waiter's offering
46. Plant's anchor
47. On the road
49. Foil metal
52. Medieval slave
53. Boot bottom
54. Geological period
55. Hair colorist
56. Weeded
57. Height limit?

DOWN
1. Inferno residue
2. Greek letter
3. Purple vegetable
4. Fit of anger
5. Successes
6. Big monkey
7. Prehistoric beast
8. Elk
9. Skating maneuver
10. Frozen water mass
11. Be inclined
19. Belief
21. Caper
22. Workout aftermath
23. Brown songbird
24. Goes without food
26. Sacred song
28. Sends on a new course
29. Exude
30. Club payments
33. Free a dog
36. Disturber of the peace
38. Large vase
41. Infuriated
42. Snoopy
43. Traffic barrier
44. Fellow
45. Looked at
48. Romance
50. Annoy
51. Refusal

PUZZLE 76

CODEWORD

Codeword is a special crossword puzzle in which conventional clues are omitted. Instead, answer words in the diagram are represented by numbers. Each number represents a different letter of the alphabet, and all of the letters of the alphabet are used. When you are sure of a letter, put it in the code key chart and cross it off in the alphabet box. A group of letters has been inserted to start you off.

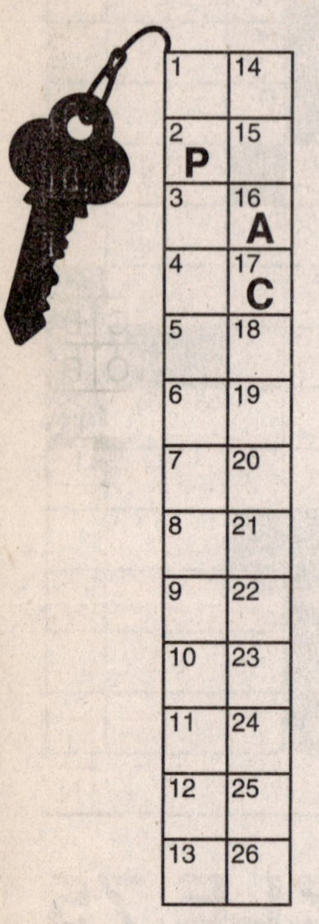

1	14
2 P	15
3	16 A
4	17 C
5	18
6	19
7	20
8	21
9	22
10	23
11	24
12	25
13	26

18	11	2	■	12	20	9	■	16	2	8	■	21	8	9
11	22	8	■	8	7	8	■	18	16	19	■	8	26	8
12	3	8	■	18	3	8	■	11	26	8	■	19	16	26
8	10	2	8	18	■	■	■	6	16	26	22	8	24	24
■	■	■	26	8	15	6	8	16	15	■	16	18	8	8
2	18	23	24	■	11	16	26	■	8	11	22	■	■	■
26	23	22	9	■	17	4	16	26	■	2	16	24	9	16
11	18	15	■	23	13	8	■	16	19	8	■	11	19	22
25	18	11	24	24	■	18	16	9	8	■	1	23	20	9
■	■	■	19	8	12	■	26	20	2	■	23	26	5	8
24	11	25	16	■	26	20	17	11	9	9	16	■	■	■
17 C	26	20	14	24	11	22	■	■	■	16	15	14	16	22
16 A	5	8	■	16	22	15	■	26	8	25	■	16	26	8
2 P	16	18	■	20	17	8	■	8	18	25	■	24	20	10
8	22	15	■	18	11	10	■	2	18	3	■	24	16	9

~~A~~	N
B	O
~~C~~	~~P~~
D	Q
E	R
F	S
G	T
H	U
I	V
J	W
K	X
L	Y
M	Z

PUZZLE 77

Suspended Sentence

The words in each vertical column go into the spaces directly below them, but not necessarily in the order they appear. When you have placed all the words in their correct spaces, you will be able to read a quotation across the diagram from left to right.

RATHER OR TO LOVE	IS NECESSARILY A OTHERS	WITHOUT A WILLINGNESS A	RATIONAL PRETENSE TO CHOICE	BE CHOICE OR NOT	GUILE BUT SIMPLY PRESENT

BRICK BY BRICK

PUZZLE 78

Rearrange this stack of bricks to form a crossword puzzle. The clues will help you fit the bricks into their correct places. Row 1 has been filled in for you. Use the bricks to fill in the remaining spaces.

ACROSS

1. Boutonniere spot
   Servant, in Asia
   Overhead curve
2. Giraffe's kin
   Warangal wear
   Pastrami palace
3. Sponsorship
   Pierce
   Baker's need
4. Greens charge
   Quaker pronoun
   Untethered
5. So-so grade
   Modern
6. Former French coin
   "____ Wore a Yellow Ribbon"
   Busy activity
7. Somersault
   Military uniforms
   Sass
8. Highway division
   Frozen water
   On cloud ____
9. Energy measure
   Hindu incantation
   Call to prayer
10. Moray or electric
    Humpty Dumpty, e.g.
    "____ Say Die"
11. Repute
    Strive
12. Flower part
    Showy bloom
    Use a bench
13. Watercourse
    Judith Anderson's title
    Let up
14. Maple genus
    Fixed quantity
    Wiping cloth
15. Type of meat
    Rodents
    Of a region

DOWN

1. Package of bread
   Skedaddle
   Substitute
2. Soapberry tree
   Flash of light
   Filled tortilla
3. Book part
   Instigator
4. Roof finial
   Sleeveless garment
   Simper
5. Pay attention
   Dole
6. What the ____!
   Schedule
7. African fox
   Door fixture
   Cuckoo
8. Mother
   Drama division
   Ape
9. Macaw
   Glacial ridge
   Network
10. Japanese grill
    Not pro
11. TV host Rick ____
    Synthetic
12. Embellish
    Nation's sea power
    Sound of disapproval
13. Modernize
    Cut wood
14. Musical staff sign
    Mideast money
    Willow genus
15. Tip
    Unrestricted
    Spill the beans

BRICKS

WEL NAL	NEV TRY	SIT ATE	INE ZAN	■■S HAK
LAN ERG	I■D B■O	ADR CEN	IS■ ■AB	PI■ IS■
■TO ■ZO	ANC P■K	OKA AEG	R■U K■M	■EG STE
MEN I■D	ADO LIP	STA WAD	ICE NTR	ACE POR
IFT T■■	SAR STA	■IR AME	HE■ IS■	■■N A■A
ER■ ■■■	G■■ EM■	■TH CEE	E■■ ■MA	EE■ ■RE
FEE ■■■	EEL ■■E	NIT ICE	■FR FLI	ELI VEN

DIAGRAM

	1	2	3	4	5	6	7	8	9	10	11	12	13	14	15
1	L	A	P	E	L	■	A	M	A	H	■	A	R	C	H
2															
3															
4															
5															
6															
7															
8															
9															
10															
11															
12															
13															
14															
15															

PUZZLE 79

ACROSS

1. Minor quarrel
5. Likely
8. Muscle strain
12. Celebrity's transport
13. "The Pelican ____"
15. Lower jaw
16. List entry
17. Patch the roof again
18. Wait on
19. Energetic person
21. Too bad!
23. ____ of Reason
24. Tight
26. Clipped
28. Felt at home
32. Passing grade
33. Self-esteem
34. At this place
36. Mealtime prayer
40. Before now
41. Embassy official
43. Merry month
44. Legends
46. Employ
47. Earlier than, in poems
48. Inquire
50. Helped to grow
53. Component
57. By and by
58. Garden buzzer
59. Celtics, e.g.
61. Moved slowly
65. Uncovered
67. Foreigner
69. Hawaiian party
70. Immoral
71. Thickly populated
72. Grimm villain
73. Regard
74. Brother's sib
75. Well-mannered guy

1	2	3	4	■	■	5	6	7	■	■	8	9	10	11
12				■	13				14	■	15			
16				■	17					■	18			
19				20		■	21			22	■	23		
■	■	■	24			25	■	26			27			
28	29	30					31	■	32			■	■	■
33			■	■	34			35	■	36		37	38	39
40			■	41					42		■	43		
44			45		■	46				■	■	47		
■	■	■	48		49	■	50			51	52			
53	54	55				56	■	57				■	■	■
58			■	59			60	■	61			62	63	64
65			66	■	67			68		■	69			
70				■	71					■	72			
73				■	■	74			■	■	75			

DOWN

1. Coasted
2. Compassion
3. Hymn closer
4. Burger garnish
5. "We ____ Not Alone"
6. Flat bread
7. Wild ducks
8. Deed
9. Chintzy
10. Door joint
11. Open-____
13. Carried
14. French money, once
20. ____ the lifeboats!
22. Blockade
25. Incisors, e.g.
27. Miles ____ hour
28. Smile broadly
29. Like an omelet
30. Booty
31. Sink feature
35. Beige and off-white
37. U.S.
38. Feel concern
39. Ogled
41. Thing of worth
42. Leading lady
45. Glazed ____
49. Massage
51. Shipping weight
52. Free of an obstruction
53. Subsided
54. "____ It to Beaver"
55. Creepy
56. Yarns
60. Tiny
62. Immense
63. Deserve
64. Tune for two
66. Tall tree
68. 19th letter

PUZZLE 80

Domino Theory

Arrange the four dominoes on the right into the pattern on the left so that a correct multiplication problem is formed. The number of dots on each half-domino is considered a one-digit number; for example, a half with six dots represents the number 6.

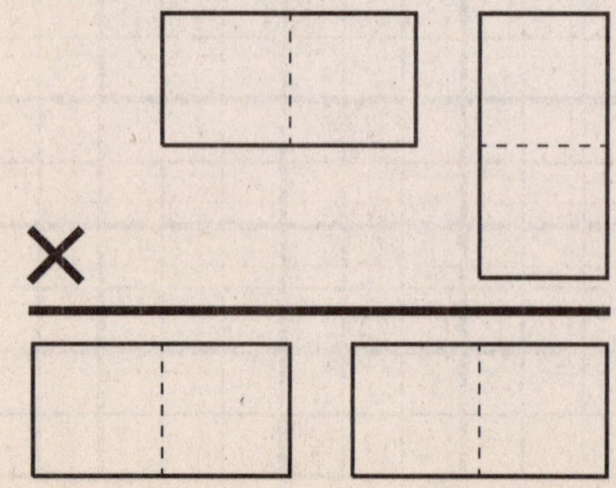

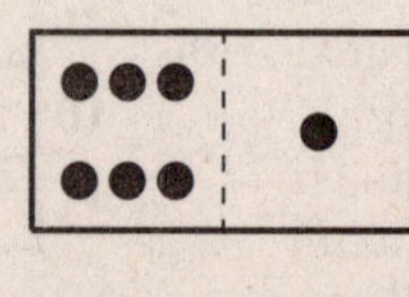

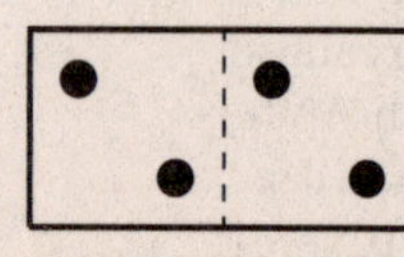

PUZZLE 81

ACROSS

1. Ponder
5. Japanese wrestling
9. Vicinities
14. Grimm beginning
15. Away from port
16. Okra dish
17. Russian emperor
18. Soft mattress
20. That boy
21. Unpretentious
22. Handicrafts
23. Seems
25. Horseback sport
27. Tycoon Onassis
28. Pain
30. Mont. neighbor
33. Oak source
36. Distance runner
37. Cozy place
38. Transport
39. Punctuation mark
40. Marsh plant
41. Food scrap
42. Went astray
43. Senator Goldwater
44. Evergreen shrub
45. Disembark
46. Photo
47. Not certain
49. Garden insect
53. Assess
55. Take a stand against
58. Flightless bird
59. Unnecessary
61. Record on cassette
62. Bright-eyed
63. Nah!
64. Valuable rocks
65. Change color again
66. Zoomed
67. ____ and ends

DOWN

1. Cafe order
2. Unfasten
3. Rascal
4. Always, in poems
5. Hunting expedition
6. Employers
7. Lion's diet
8. Formal promise
9. Span in years
10. Rustic
11. Embellish
12. Help a heist
13. Puts down turf
19. Word connector
21. Make a living
24. Aristocrat
26. "____ the fields we go . . ."
28. Felt poorly
29. Dolt
31. Bambi, e.g.
32. Garcia of "Ocean's Twelve"
33. Sailor's hail
34. Give a hoot
35. Got the better of
36. "September ____"
39. Kindergarten stick
40. Risque
42. Gremlin's kin
43. ____ one's time
46. Elapsed
48. River shuttle
49. Jeweler's glass
50. Vandyke, e.g.
51. Called the game
52. Estimate
53. Bring up the ____
54. Car's wheel shaft
56. Zoo cages
57. ____ deck
60. Partook of
61. As well

Rhyme Time

PUZZLE 82

The answers to the clues below are pairs of rhyming words. For example: "Plump feline" would be FAT CAT.

1. Ancient crease
2. Grin collection
3. City jester
4. Close to this place
5. Skinny branch
6. Corn fad

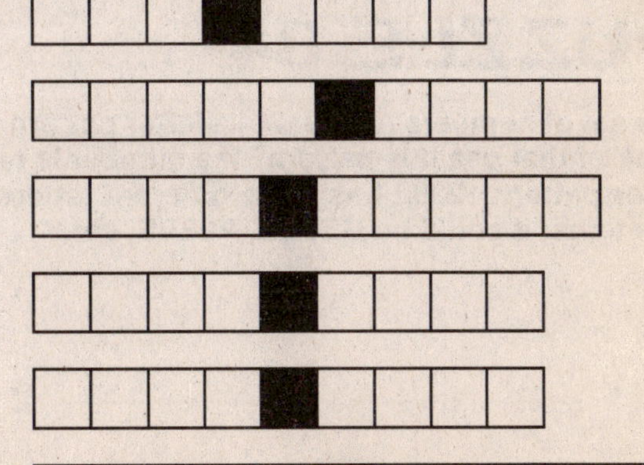

PUZZLE 83 DOUBLE TROUBLE

Not really double trouble, but double fun! Solve this puzzle as you would a regular crossword, except place one, two, or three letters in each box. The number of letters in each answer is shown in parentheses after its clue.

ACROSS

1. Tent occupant (6)
4. Edict (6)
7. Magic word (6)
10. Contralto Marian ____ (8)
11. Skulk (5)
12. Dining nook (6)
13. Luau wreath (3)
14. Moved quickly (6)
15. In any amount (8)
16. Appetizers (7)
18. Reveal (6)
19. Neighbor of India (8)
22. Memorize (5)
25. Taste (6)
27. North Sea feeder (6)
28. Map graphic (5)
29. Tenant (8)
30. Wind-flower (7)
32. Brittle silicate (4)
33. Felt hat (5)
35. Mixed (8)
37. Banish (5)
39. Basic food item (6)
41. Sermon response (4)
42. Other-worldly (3)
43. Motorcycle name (5)
44. Predica-ment (8)
45. Changed (7)
46. Concise (5)

DOWN

1. Taper (6)
2. "____ Idol" (8)
3. Human being (6)
4. Leave (6)
5. Bragged (6)
6. Sway (4)
7. Mouth section (6)
8. Convalesce (7)
9. Range (5)
14. Office fixture (4)
15. Possessive pronoun (5)
17. Obvious (8)
18. Breadth (7)
20. Ulysses' home (6)
21. Pollen-bearing part (6)
22. Ocean cruiser (5)
23. Gets paid (5)
24. Ping-Pong need (3)
25. Solar events (6)
26. Emptiness (4)
31. Paragon (5)
32. Pros-pected (5)
34. Spectator (9)
35. Approve (7)
36. Doubled (6)
37. Deplete (6)
38. Ogled (4)
40. Satisfy (6)
41. Greenish blue (4)
42. Renown (4)
43. Fiery (3)

1	2	3	■	4	5	6	■	7	8	9
10			■	11			■	12		
13		■	14			■	15			■
■	16	17		■	■	18		■	■	■
■	■	19		20	21		■	22	23	24
25	26		■	27			■	28		
29			■	30			31		■	■
■	■	■	32		■	■	33		34	■
■	35	36		■	37	38		■	39	40
41			■	42			■	43		
44			■	45			■	46		

PUZZLE 84 Common Code

The set of numbers represents a letter pattern for certain words. How many common words can you think of that use this pattern? If a number is repeated, the same letter is repeated. For example, the letter pattern 12232 has three different letters, with the same letter in the second, third, and fifth positions; it could be GEESE, PEEVE, etc.

1 2 2 3 4

PUZZLE 85

• ADHERENCE •

ACROSS
1. Squabble
5. Mr. Holm
8. Excuse me!
12. Vibes
13. Once ____ blue moon
14. Cocktail fruit
15. Old fogy
18. Spot
19. ____ Lingus
20. Alley denizen
22. Mine section
27. Invite
30. Jam ingredient?
32. St. Thomas, e.g.
33. Remain faithful
37. ____ cracker
38. TV's Maude
39. Thanksgiving side
40. Brackish
42. Mil. ranks
44. "____ Maria"
47. Open shoelaces
51. Impasse cause
56. Normandy river
57. Cain's mother
58. Church calendar
59. Soft wood
60. Hide the gray
61. Mexican worker

DOWN
1. Lip
2. Careful shot
3. "Nessun dorma," e.g.
4. Suggested
5. "Richard ____" (Shakespeare)
6. Dancer Pavlova
7. Basketball's Archibald
8. Bitter brew
9. That dude
10. It'll never fly
11. Club ____
16. Find fault
17. "48 ____"
21. Key hider, often
23. Clout
24. Pallid
25. Kennel pest
26. Period
27. Professional soc.
28. Plato's porch
29. Youngsters
31. Carry off
34. House pet
35. Hair stuff
36. Devour
41. Shaggy ox
43. Investigate
45. Competed
46. Jealousy
48. Tree swing
49. European leader?
50. Thames school
51. Weak one
52. ____-state area
53. Lodging house
54. Piano key
55. I didn't know that!

PUZZLE 86

• SOMETHING'S FISHY •

ACROSS
1. Chicago district
5. Phooey!
9. Capture
12. Buckeye State
13. Was a passenger
14. Salt Lake City student
15. Perform with ceremony
17. Wish otherwise
18. Also
19. Bankrupt
20. "Being ____" (Bening film)
23. Allot
26. With, in France
27. Arranged in a collection
31. Alcott heroine
32. Formal gown
33. Worthless coin
34. Baby basket
36. Tresses
37. Biblical brother
38. Perch
39. Campus spot
42. Bern's river
43. Web address
44. Maybe
50. In the past
51. First person
52. Circus performer
53. But
54. Goose egg
55. ____-evident

DOWN
1. ____ Lonely Boys
2. Gotcha!
3. Driveway blotch
4. ____ justice
5. Bond film
6. Louis XIV, e.g.
7. Hand-held tool
8. Duffer's aid
9. Expert
10. Place for a thimble
11. Babysitter, often
16. Extinct New Zealand bird
19. Game official
20. Doorway part
21. Eye part
22. Staying power
23. Bates, for one
24. Drop a line?
25. Ceiling material
27. Staff
28. Japanese golfer Aoki
29. Years and years
30. Tune for two
32. Bro, e.g.
35. Blue
36. Quagmire
38. Hooray!
39. Wharf
40. Encourage
41. Thanks ____!
42. Peak
44. Piping god
45. Ancient Tokyo
46. Operated
47. Miss-named?
48. Nev. neighbor
49. Tiny toymaker

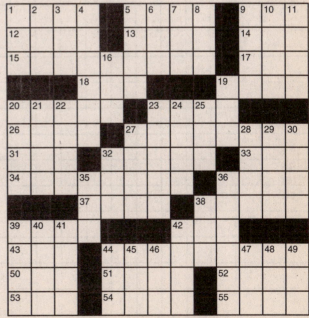

PUZZLE 87

Diagramless crosswords are solved by using the clues and their numbers to fill in the answer words and the arrangement of black squares. Insert the number of each clue with the first letter of its answer, across and down. Fill in a black square at the end of each answer. Every black square must have a corresponding black square on the opposite side of the diagram to form a diagonally symmetrical pattern. Puzzles 87 and 88 have been started for you.

ACROSS
1. Hound
4. Hide ___ hair
7. Stitch

1 D 2 O 3 G

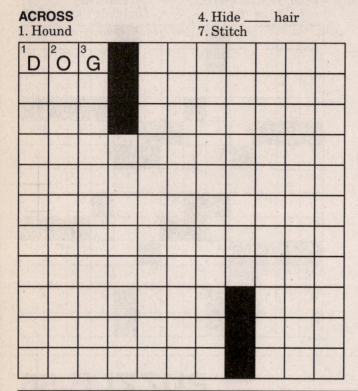

10. Sick
11. Amazement
12. Crossed letter
13. Fruit drink
14. Ballpoint
15. Lode's load
16. Fibber
18. Bypass
20. Trucker's rig
21. Grins
22. Snooped
24. Ditchdigger's tool
27. Simple
31. Stockpile
32. A single time
33. Soup tin
34. Bit of advice
37. Pot or cart
38. Kind of maniac
39. Browning's before
40. ___ and outs
41. Low grade
42. Morning mist
43. Matched pair

DOWN
1. Watch faces
2. Classic song
3. Shimmer
4. Brief sleep
5. Be in hock
6. Retitle
7. Backless seat
8. Ghostly
9. Garden invaders
17. Chances
19. Home movie
21. Half-dozen
23. Glued
24. Walked the floor
25. Mental picture
26. Kayak's cousin
28. Nonsupporters
29. Public argument
30. Bread ingredient
35. Great wrath
36. Church bench

PUZZLE 88

ACROSS
1. Crusted dessert
4. Chemist's room
7. Penny
8. Farm measure
10. Filtrate

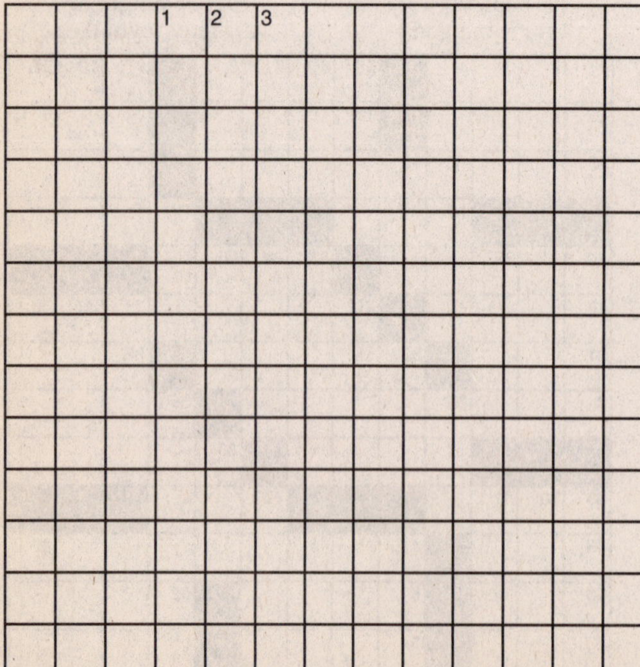

11. Light rays
13. Assistance
14. Residence
16. Swindle
18. Precede
20. Fa's follower
21. Lamb's mom
22. Mr. Goldfinger
24. Stairway down
27. Rascal
29. Couple
30. Czech region
34. Acted out
38. "Give ___ Try"
39. Pixie
41. Dalai ___
42. Band bookings
44. Miami team
46. Curry or Conway
47. ___ Claus
49. Manservant
51. Jungle sound
52. Approve
53. Auction action
54. Reed or Harrison

DOWN
1. Pod veggie
2. Ruler marking
3. Group spirit
4. Designated
5. Top card
6. Some lingerie
7. Aromatic evergreen
9. Game-show host
10. In ___ of
12. Cut
13. Chicken ___ king
15. Trendy
17. Came across
19. Gambling cubes
23. Type of shaft
25. Total
26. Curl
28. Willis film
30. Huge
31. Elevator inventor
32. Comic-strip Viking
33. Ginger ___
35. British buddy
36. Give off
37. Beaver project
40. Kind act
43. Snooty person
45. Accept
48. Mai ___ (cocktail)
50. Careless

PUZZLE 89

ACROSS
1. Facts and figures
5. Level
6. Relies
9. Everyone
10. Asian beast of burden
12. ____ de Janeiro
13. Peach seed
15. "Lend me your ____"
17. ____ and feather
19. Consume
21. "I ____ Rhythm"
23. Young child
25. Snakelike fish
27. Cushion
29. Be under the weather
31. Waiter's bonus
33. Canvas shelter
36. Swab
38. Born as
39. Cruise or Hanks
41. Charged particle
42. Come down
45. Lacking fat
46. Small pie

DOWN
1. Lament
2. "____ Maria"
3. Hamilton bill
4. Actor Griffith
6. Challenge
7. Charles Lamb's pseudonym
8. Foolish one
11. Hobby-store purchase
14. Label
16. Took a chair
18. Shad delicacy
20. Highest point
22. Pekoe, e.g.
24. Make lace
26. Illuminated
28. Not very bright
30. Merciful
32. Saucepan
34. Sign gas
35. Look after
37. Group of whales
40. Sandwich with broiled cheese
43. Ocean
44. Auto

Starting box on page 562

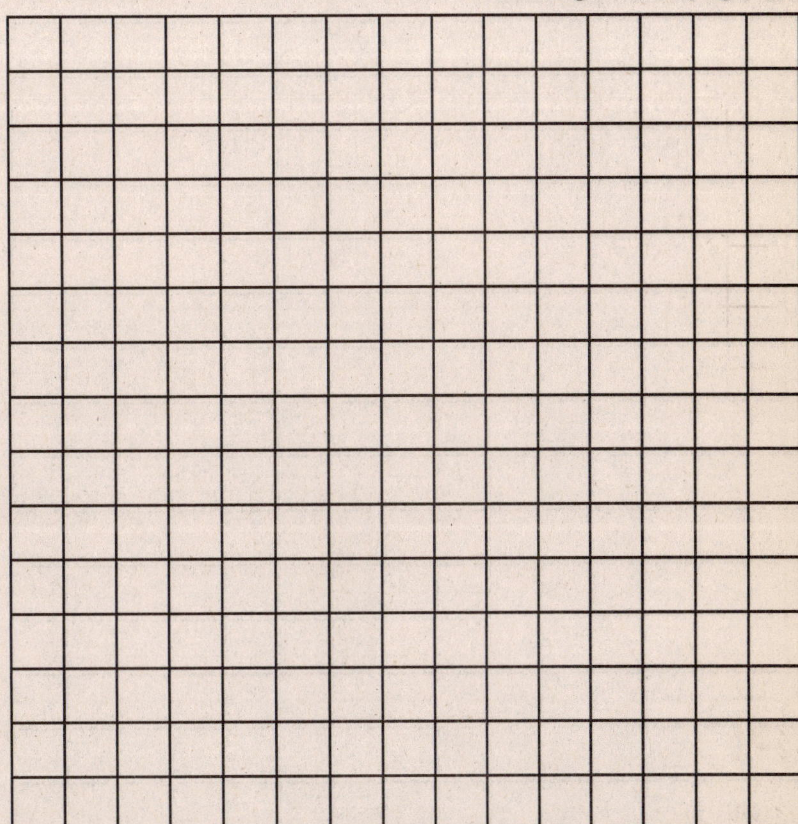

To the Nines

PUZZLE 90

Place a number in each empty box so that each row, column, and nine-box square contains the numbers 1 to 9.

1.

	4			7	8		6	
	5		1			7	2	
8		1		6				3
7			4		9	8		
	8		7			3		
4		3		5			7	2
	6	8			4		5	
			6	8		4	3	
9		4			7		8	

2.

		8	7	9		6		
9						8	7	
		6	8	3				5
5	9	1						
			5		3	7		
		7			1		8	6
4	5							8
			4	6	2			
	6					9	4	2

PUZZLE 91

ACROSS

1. Western actor Jack ____
5. Pianist Tatum
8. Carry on, as war
9. Study hard
13. Contend
14. Happening
16. Hawser
17. Pacifist
18. Kitty litter?
19. Always
20. High cards
21. Faucet
22. Military fugitive
24. Citrus fruit
26. Consume
27. Indicated
31. Beat it!
32. Ta ta
34. Sigma's follower
36. Bleak
38. Penitent
42. Shear
44. Fat for frying
45. Give off
46. Level
48. Colony insects
49. Oven setting
50. Hinder
52. Piggy
53. Among
54. Exceptional
55. "For ____ a jolly . . ."
56. Casino machine

DOWN

1. Sheepish female
2. Etna outpouring
3. FBI employee
4. Pertaining to thought
5. Long-legged shorebird
6. Watercourse
7. Golf pegs
9. Air of truth
10. Roam
11. Copies
12. No more than
15. Lukewarm
17. Info
23. Crimson
25. Screen
28. Crude copper
29. Aimed at
30. Islamic leader
32. Slice
33. Lubricated
34. Viennese pastries
35. Ampersands
37. Shakers' partner
38. Narrow boat
39. Country's McEntire
40. Mosque official
41. Polynesian idol
43. Flower segment
44. Wood slat
47. Roman emperor
51. Soak, as flax

Starting box on page 562

PUZZLE 92

Cancellations

There are thirteen presidents and a saying hidden in the diagram. Taking one letter from each box, cross off the 7-letter words from the across rows. Then cross off the 6-letter words from the down columns. The leftover letters, one in each box, will reveal the saying, reading left to right, row by row.

ACROSS

1. ____________
2. ____________
3. ____________
4. ____________
5. ____________
6. ____________

DOWN

1. ____________
2. ____________
3. ____________
4. ____________
5. ____________
6. ____________
7. ____________

	1	2	3	4	5	6	7
1	I L T	H D I	A N E	C A P	W S O	A L T	R C N
2	K A E	O E A	R L N	O I N	E T I	D L R	I Y A
3	K Y M	A O E	D C T	H I E	S L I	U O L	N D R
4	R H L	V E A	H N R	O R D	U I S	N M R	O T G
5	C O W	E N L	A I U	N R C	T E O	W O A	E O N
6	J N R	D R A	R E C	R K E	N S F	U N O	N L R

PUZZLE 93

ACROSS
1. Profound
5. In this place
9. Violent anger
10. Zone
11. Compulsion
12. Wharf
13. Song of praise
15. Tux features
17. Courts
18. Chilled
19. Debt letters
20. I
21. Tear
24. Inhale audibly
27. Droop
28. Employ
29. Conceal
30. Antlered animal
31. Peevishness
32. U.S. state
33. Body of water
34. Stratego piece
35. Born: Fr.
36. Crystl Bustos's stick
37. Pop
38. Joke
39. 28-pound units
40. Thespian's job
43. Mickey, Minnie et al.
44. Obscure
45. At the summit of
47. Farmer's asset
48. Precious stones
49. Peepers
50. Facile

DOWN
1. Bodhrans
2. Merit
3. Hen product
4. Opening, as bananas
5. Grumpy roommate?
6. Part of HOMES
7. Angler's item
8. Pinnae
13. Part of a horse
14. Pronoun
16. King topper
17. Spouse
20. Majestic tree
21. Destroy
22. Key
23. Equal
24. Part of the leg
25. African river
26. Laze
27. Crafty
30. Chow down
31. Offers
33. Porter's charge
34. Created
36. Prohibit
37. Another Grumpy roommate?
38. Encircles
39. Unsteady
40. Qualified
41. Singer Aiken
42. Melody
43. Comic Mabley
46. Steeped drink

Starting box on page 562

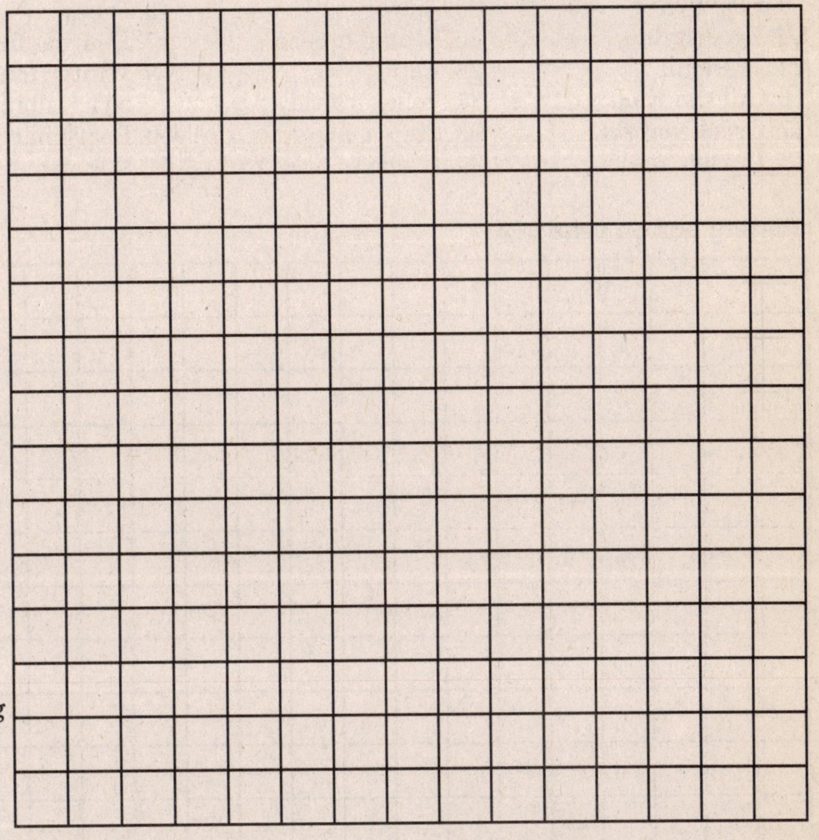

In and Around

PUZZLE 94

Place the 4-letter answers to the clues into the diagram, from the outside to the inside. When you have finished, two 12-letter words will be revealed, reading from 1 to 12 on both the outermost ring and the third ring from the outside.

1. Sommelier's coworker
2. Teen woe
3. Mediterranean resort
4. Part of the face
5. Shade of brown
6. Netlike fabric
7. Mrs. Munster
8. Prayer ender
9. Heavy volume
10. Thing
11. Possesses
12. Fa, e.g.

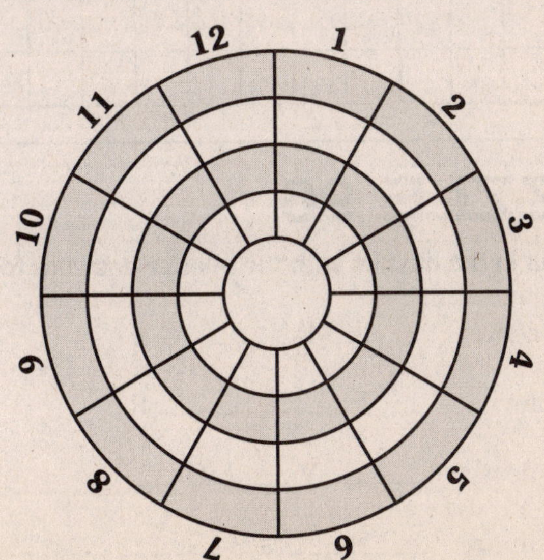

PUZZLE 95

ACROSS

1. Drains
5. Tropical bird
8. Judicious
9. Lion's cave
10. Type style
12. Tranquil
16. "All the King's ____"
17. Greek vowels
18. Luxury resort
19. High tennis shots
20. Bird no more
22. Defeat soundly
24. Flightless bird
25. Smear
26. Strong breeze
28. Eerie
31. Follow closely
33. Step heavily
34. A side of New York
37. Distance traveled
39. Astute
41. Feminine salutation
42. Type of jacket
43. Indisposed
44. Rock-concert blaster
45. Dump
47. Heating fuel
49. White House office shape
50. Boot liner
51. Wigwams' kin
54. Sheriff's assistant
57. Indian title
58. Mined minerals
59. Baglike structure
60. Physics measures

DOWN

1. "____ Lake"
2. Feel awful
3. Fraternity letter
4. Dry, as wine
5. Classified ____
6. Previously named
7. Permanent
10. Mischievous child
11. Afternoon meal
13. Over
14. Soda-can top popper
15. Curvy shape
18. Finnish bath
20. Kitten sound
21. Forget
22. Stinging insect
23. Bungalow
25. Vaulted roof
27. Not bright
28. Metric weight
29. Old witch
30. Chatty ox?
32. Infinite
33. Shipwright's lumber
35. Calyx leaf
36. Abound
38. Natural resin
40. Day break?
43. Hockey shot
45. Write down
46. "____ Got Sixpence"
47. Cereal grain
48. Freezing
50. Cat
52. Cenozoic, e.g.
53. Attack!
54. Bambi's mother
55. Gum up the works
56. Wooden pin

Starting box on page 562

PUZZLE 96

Complete-A-Word

Fill in the dashes with the 4-letter answers to the clues to complete 7-letter words.

1. Apple center ___ ___ R ___ ___ C T
2. Sensible ___ P ___ N ___ ___ R
3. Bottomless ___ ___ V ___ L O ___
4. Floor square ___ H ___ M B ___ ___
5. Faction R E ___ P ___ ___ ___
6. Large pond B ___ ___ N ___ ___ T
7. Soap form ___ R ___ C ___ ___ R
8. Slender ___ U B ___ ___ ___ E

PUZZLE 97

ACROSS

1. Bias
5. Duffer's goal
8. Circle of light
9. Be in the red
10. Outdoor area
11. Bargains
14. Earth's center
15. Greek walkway
16. Stacked bed
17. Chip in a chip
19. Actor Hagman
21. Murmur
24. Swallow
26. Matured
27. Individual
28. Writer Bombeck
29. Mama pig
30. Cleverness
31. Band instrument
33. Platform
35. Lot's wife, ultimately
37. Use a straw
38. Chasing game
39. "Casablanca" role
41. Zsa Zsa's sister
42. Mineral deposit
43. Indian gown
44. Slippery fish
45. Country house
46. Disney's clownfish
48. Chief
49. Skillfully
51. Formal solo
52. Paragon
54. Like a rock
56. LAX posting
57. Arabian gulf
58. Big truck
59. Fill a suitcase

DOWN

1. Hammer-head, e.g.
2. "Kiss Me, ____"
3. Inventor Whitney
4. Romance
5. Shell
6. Stuns
7. Roper's need
10. Small horse
12. More protracted
13. Ringed planet
14. Bean ____
16. Milwaukee nine
18. Graceful tree
19. Cheesy dish
20. Very eager
21. Canine sound
22. Division
23. Ran into
25. Easter shades
31. Busy place
32. Milky gem
34. Comet feature
35. Holler
36. With hands on hips
37. Date
40. Singer Janis ____
42. Traveler's permit
45. Not valid
47. Not as new
48. Verge
50. Abominable snowman
51. A Baldwin brother
53. Fall behind
54. Tree juice
55. Harem room

Starting box on page 562

Block Letters

PUZZLE 98

A single letter is on each of the six sides of four toy blocks. No letter is repeated. Any side of a block can be faceup, and the blocks can be in any order. The twelve words listed can be spelled faceup using the four blocks. What are the six letters on each block?

BRIM	HANK	HOME	QUIT	STOW	WIFE
CLIP	HOAX	PUNY	RUDE	VEIN	ZEAL

PUZZLE 99

ACROSS

1. Takes off
6. Clock dial
10. Fanatic
11. Grief
12. Book size
13. Difficult time
14. Cook's vessel
15. Bowling number
16. Straw storage
17. Brit's baby buggy
19. Previously, in poetry
20. Air
21. Bringer of a civil action
22. Be stuck (on)
24. New days
29. Very dry
30. Melded
31. Make raw
32. Lily type
33. On a single occasion
36. Copper rust
38. Red hair-dye
40. Biblical verb
41. Family member
42. Marine, informally
46. Thought
50. Sailor's greeting
51. Theft
56. Minister's helper
57. Load cargo
58. Person opposed
59. Bind securely
60. Animal facility
62. Finish
63. Enroll
65. Austrian peaks
67. Garden bloom
68. Back
70. Toy gun ammo
73. Allied nations
74. Spryness
78. Hatchet
79. Jamie Foxx film
80. Pie nuts
81. Soap remover
83. TV-replay method
84. Dog
85. Medieval serf
86. Long-horned antelope

DOWN

1. Denomination
2. Fedora, e.g.
3. Please
4. Delaware's capital
5. Threw rocks at
6. Aluminum wrap
7. Likewise
8. Hairdo
9. Previously, formerly
10. Speed
11. Wood nymph
13. Maserati, e.g.
14. Excuse
16. Colored
17. Blend to a pulp
18. Royal rule
20. Broke a fast
21. Waist accessory
23. Feel obligated to
25. Drama divisions
26. Impulse
27. Zola novel
28. Bridge length
33. Bread variety
34. Utmost degree
35. Swindle
36. Photo
37. Egyptian symbol
39. Choral voice
40. Owned
41. Lock's partner
43. Bard's twilight
44. Greek letter
45. At present
46. Loiter
47. College head
48. New England coast
49. Throb
52. Without trouble
53. Emcee's speech, for short
54. Impassive
55. Points
57. Soak in gravy
60. Wacky
61. Stale
64. Horned mammal, briefly
66. In short supply
69. ____ a living!
71. Along the middle
72. Contour feather
73. Unclad
74. Church recess
75. Firms up
76. Religious symbol
77. Fancy fabric
79. Split
82. Do wrong

Starting box on page 562

PUZZLE 100

ACROSS

1. Hamlet and Gertrude
6. Assemble
7. Moth-repellent wood
12. Too ___ by half
13. In isolation
14. Type of force
15. Horsemanship
17. ___-on-Hudson
18. Texas college
19. Moss or potato
20. Ancient Troy
23. Signals silently
24. In the middle of the boards
27. Olympics participant
28. Tart and tangy
29. Magda's little sis
31. Course ender
34. Popular soap-opera malady
37. At the same remoteness
41. Georgia senator
42. Disconnect
43. "The Secret War of Harry ___"
44. Actor Tom ___
47. Panay port
49. Thrusting sword
51. Spanish dramatist
52. Botanical helmet
53. City northeast of Lisbon
55. Journal passage
56. Mideast peninsula
57. Young and Penn

DOWN

1. Minnesota port
2. Pico de ___
3. "The Moon's a Balloon" author
4. Guy's summer
5. Sun. lect.
7. Wheel projection
8. Israeli airline
9. Lady of Spain
10. Lackluster
11. Entertain lavishly
12. La ___, Wisconsin
14. Trestle
16. The Emerald Isle
17. Zagreb native
19. Mediating
21. Actress Hagen
22. New York nine
25. Greek letter
26. Deviate
30. Canceled, as a TV show
32. "___ Lay Dying"
33. Maiden
34. Italian province
35. ___ Jerry (vintage pop group)
36. Corroded
37. Caruso or Fermi
38. Claim as true
39. Trendy movement
40. Surgical saw
43. Opposite of lenis
45. Cadence
46. Goggle
47. Massey of the movies
48. Navigation system
50. Light shaft
53. CIA's predecessor
54. Cobbler

Starting box on page 562

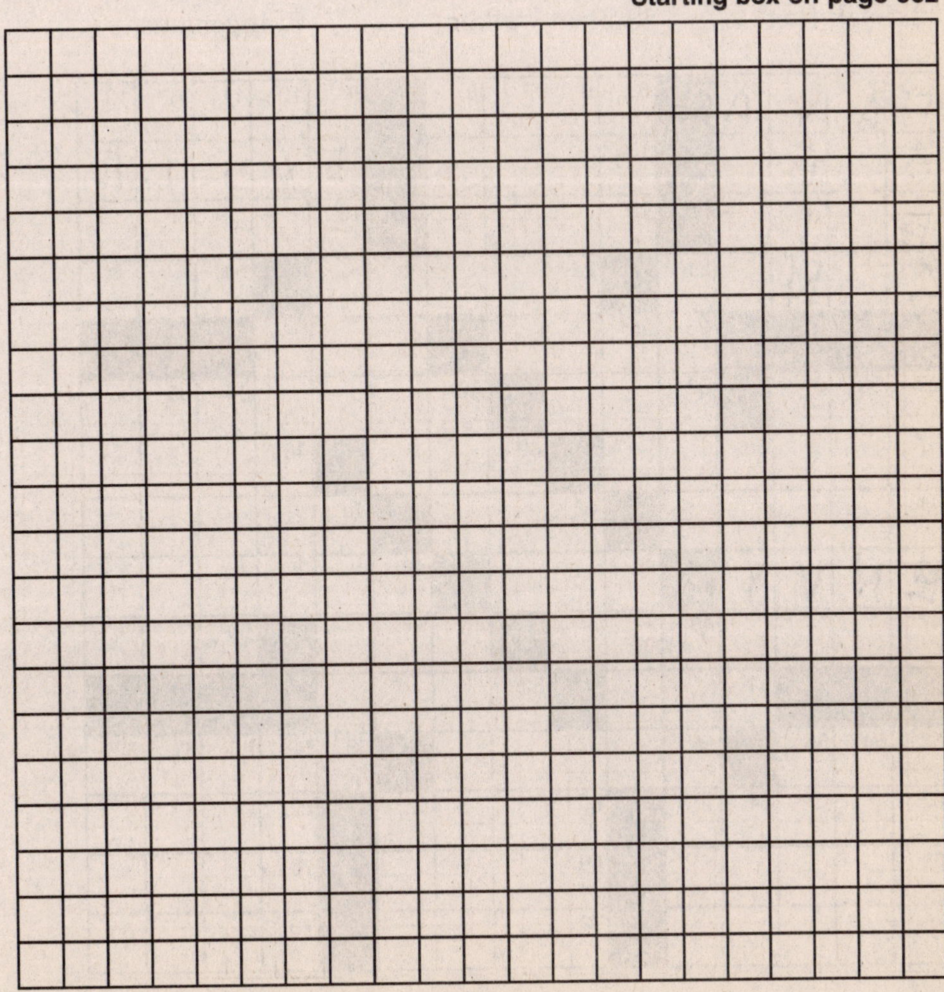

PUZZLE 101

ACROSS

1. Kind of bean
5. Tale
9. Heroism
14. Augury
15. Lyrical
16. Deport
17. Send out
18. Imp
19. Hawaiian honkers
20. Of sound
22. Beginning
24. Kid
25. Single entity
27. Barrel
29. Plant fluid
32. Soak flax
33. Marriage
37. Hit town
39. Atlantic fish
40. Reeded instrument
41. Hollow stone
42. Twosome
43. "___ Little Kiss"
44. Jealousy
45. First-aid ___
46. Glacial epoch
47. German bread
49. Totality
50. Stashed
51. Fold over
52. Gaucho's gear
53. Beat walker
56. Speak
58. Entice
63. Keep away from
65. Observance
67. Heap
68. Species
69. Turkish officials
70. Hipbone sections
71. Culminated
72. Jumble
73. High notes

DOWN

1. Rivals
2. Caisson's contents
3. Blood vessel
4. One opposed
5. Shed tears
6. Ingenious
7. Titan
8. Bible book
9. Expressed
10. Woodcutter's tool
11. Dryer leavings
12. Bagel topper
13. Surplus
21. Arc
23. Supplemented
26. Previously known as
28. Hand warmer
29. Philosophers
30. Kin of ain't
31. City in Utah
33. Pursue
34. Fetish
35. Welsh herder
36. Typed (in)
38. Pastoral poem
39. Incision
42. Confused noise
43. Elaborate display
45. Saved
46. Home with the flu
48. Praised
49. Main arteries
52. Light brown
53. Canary's home
54. Kitchen cooker
55. Small lake
57. Streetcar
59. Spectacular
60. Runner's distance
61. Ballet exercise
62. Pouched brews
64. Hard feelings
66. Santa has one

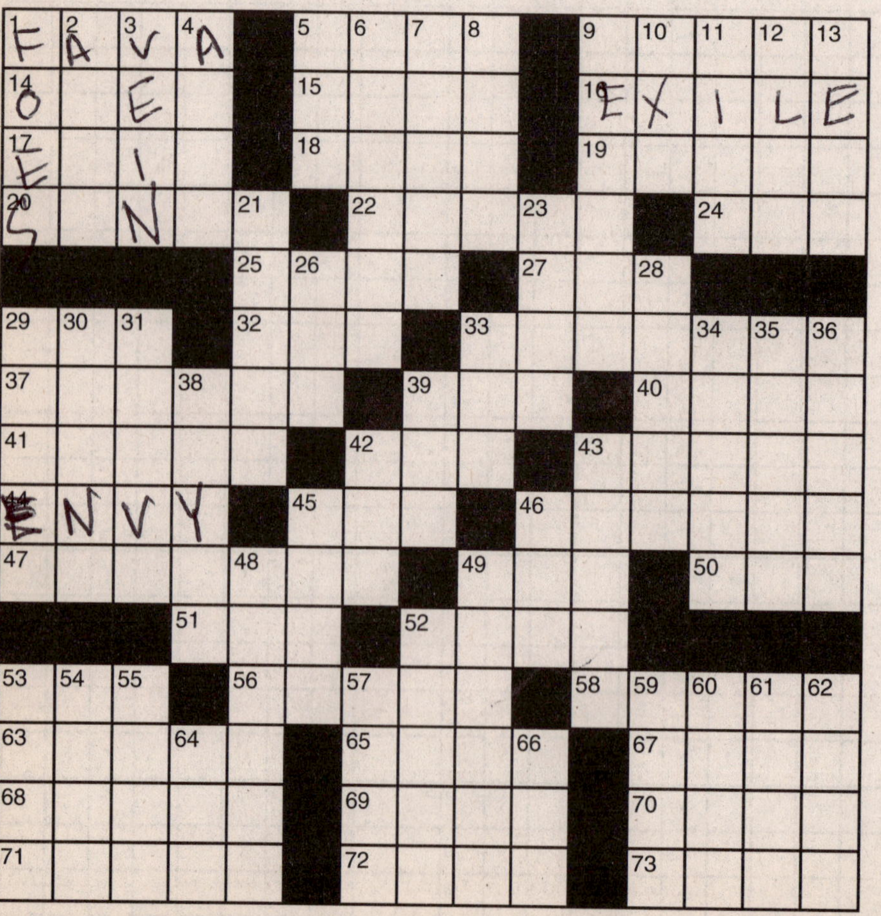

PUZZLE 102

ACROSS

1. Soggy
5. Butterfly catcher
8. Kind of brick
13. Brainchild
14. Eggs
15. First bidder
16. Sports figures?
17. Nettle
18. More soaked
19. Platform
20. Agreeable
22. Ages
23. Do well
25. Killer whales
27. Mariner
31. Frisky swimmer
35. Snare
38. Peeked
40. Primo pilot
41. Unity
42. Willow
43. Greek letter
44. Llama doc
45. Lean back
47. Male delivery?
48. Conscious
50. Aft
52. At all
54. Vaporous
58. Mall unit
61. Stretch wide
64. Mound
65. Make bubbly
67. "___ So Shy"
69. Toll
70. Plea
71. Chatter
72. See no ___
73. Mexican sauce
74. Messy place
75. Cub groups

DOWN

1. Electronic device
2. Large antelope
3. Intern
4. Relays
5. Election mo.
6. Fair
7. Doorman's cry
8. Large primate
9. Loathe
10. Wise about
11. "I've ___ This Way Before"
12. Proves human
15. Debtor
21. Vanity
24. Part of a trip
26. Atlantic fish
28. Burn soother
29. Lash enhancer
30. Blue dyes
32. Lights out signal
33. Yodeler's feedback
34. Control strap
35. PBS science series
36. Over again
37. VHS alternative
39. Marine eagle
45. Gun a motor
46. Unit of energy
49. Reimburses
51. Snoozed
53. Watcher
55. Strainer
56. Overwhelmed by humor
57. Shouts
58. Exhausts
59. Zeus's wife
60. Not injected
62. Motives
63. Orderly
66. Afternoon brew
68. Wiretap

PUZZLE 103

ACROSS

1. Haze
5. Festive
9. Charity
13. Corn bread
14. Equestrian
15. Like a pin
16. ___ and found
17. Avoid
18. Toodle-oo
19. Brewery beverage
20. Footfall
21. More exquisite
22. Skin decoration
24. Shade
27. Annex shape
28. Earthenware container
29. Little
32. Bent
35. Scolding
37. Volcano output
38. Recreation
39. Hairstyle
40. Tools
43. Except
45. Still, in poems
46. In addition
47. Luau offering
48. Unique being
50. Provide
54. Plant again
58. Chef's need
60. Gardening device
61. Frankly declare
62. Glass bottle
64. Cup of joe
65. Yield
66. Desert springs
67. Purchaser
68. Historical periods
69. Selects
70. Coastal flier

DOWN

1. Slapping noise
2. Bucks
3. Start
4. Fetch
5. Contribute
6. Modify
7. Preceded
8. "Chances ___"
9. Person opposed
10. Incline
11. Spouse
12. Sky light
14. Related again
20. Dover or lemon
21. Greek cheese
23. Austin native
25. Candid
26. Neither's partner
29. Rub with a cloth
30. Closes
31. Freudian topics
32. Chimney vent
33. Not punctual
34. Tied, as a score
35. ___ stop
36. Holland export
38. Berg
41. Store away
42. Charged atom
43. Disturbs
44. Name word
49. Drive out
51. Stage
52. Sweetheart
53. Hanker
54. Marathon
55. Constantly
56. Fizzy drink
57. Is beholden to
59. Victory symbols
62. Murmur amorously
63. Take the ___
64. Stick out

PUZZLE 104

ACROSS

1. Antitoxins
5. On a cot
9. Rapidly
14. Had money problems
15. Congestive sound
16. Math ratios
17. Labor's Eugene ___
18. Talon
19. Genuflected
20. Have being
21. Female chickens
22. Ginger drink
23. Nonwinners
26. Imitate
29. Join metal
31. Powdery
32. Put up with
33. Eliminate
38. Murmur amorously
39. Misconduct mark
41. Mad Hatter's party
42. Touchy
44. Smidgens
46. Passion
47. Not often
48. Snakes
51. Made from fleece
53. Prickly case
54. Rosary segment
55. Twice five
58. Positive electrode
61. Garden tool
62. Collaborator
63. Search over
64. Flush
65. Pork cut
66. Conger catcher
67. Traveled
68. Place your bet

DOWN

1. Fountain treat
2. Water jug
3. Defiant uprising
4. Sales pitches
5. Sagittarius
6. Cotton bundler
7. Lively spirits
8. Moistens, poetically
9. Question
10. Clip
11. Close by
12. Orchestra member
13. Chemical compound
24. Eccentric
25. More dilapidated
26. Type of skirt
27. J, F, or K
28. Kind of room
29. Pouches
30. Bassoon's cousin
31. Cab tab
33. Give out
34. Race in neutral
35. Concentration
36. Duck
37. Simple
40. Greek vowels
43. Feminine pronoun
45. Galena or ferrite
47. Mouse, e.g.
48. Mock
49. Ninny
50. Slobber
51. Use a loom
52. Made of a hardwood
54. Percolate
56. Alter copy
57. Hawaiian goose
59. Payable
60. Be incorrect
62. Wing

PUZZLE 105

ACROSS

1. Ranis' garments
6. "___ So Fine"
9. Marsh bird
13. Mountain ridges
15. Theory
16. Diabolic
17. Flop
18. Wildebeest
19. Push in
20. House wing
21. Hurried
23. Open
24. Critic Roger ___
26. Sapphire
28. Not solidified
30. Snared
33. Soft food
36. Fill up
37. Great rage
38. Stage production
40. Not suitable
42. Lend support
43. Barks
44. Restless
45. Londoner's brew
46. Earthy deposit
47. Soap-making substance
48. Mournful sound
50. Longs for
51. Hive denizen
52. Large antelope
54. Health food
57. Mexican lizard
60. Unit of radiation
63. Came to rest
64. Keats's container
65. Dry creek bed
67. Thaw
68. Youngster
69. Appeared
70. Apple or pear
71. Beast of burden
72. Cordwood measure

DOWN

1. Diamond decision
2. Nutmeg coat
3. Land
4. "___ De-lovely"
5. Hidden
6. Lofty
7. Anglo-Saxon peon
8. Smear
9. Stonecrop
10. Baking appliance
11. Fruit covering
12. Type of saxophone
14. Rotten
22. Furrow
25. Horn sounds
27. Vortex
28. Ordinary
29. Au pair
31. Bay window
32. Rode a bike
33. "Madam, I'm Adam," e.g.
34. Plenty
35. Personal histories
39. Plastic ingredient
41. Tot
49. Interstellar cloud
50. Durango dads
51. Isolated hill
53. Grazing grounds
54. Pack down
55. Fridge tub
56. Movie
58. Important ages
59. Ifs, ___, or buts
61. Ogler
62. Vogue
66. Steep flax

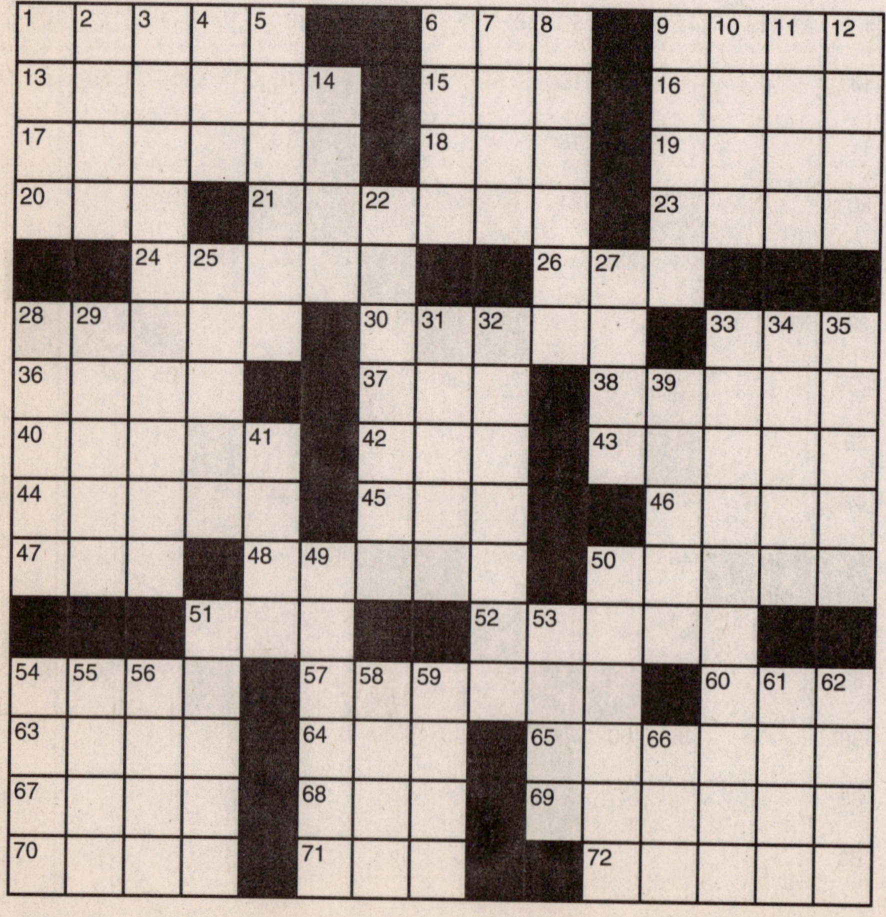

PUZZLE 106

ACROSS

1. Russian emperor
5. The Red Planet
9. Pigment
14. Molten rock
15. Perception
16. Boredom
17. Dill seed
18. Sheet, as of paper
19. Long gun
20. 10,000
22. Vehicles
24. Like a centenarian
25. Ajar, to a bard
26. Quality
28. Suitability
32. Bugs
36. Conflict
37. Exceed
39. Type type
40. Coral reef
43. Command
45. Playground chute
46. Fill again
48. Movie, briefly
50. Guy
51. Binder
53. Fit to consume
56. Releases
58. Decrepit horse
59. City on the Danube
62. Colorful swimmer
63. On fire
67. Mansard and gambrel
69. ___ deck
71. Islamic leader
72. Fish features
73. Sea eagle
74. Current measures
75. Put on
76. Female ruffs
77. The greatest amount

DOWN

1. Bivalve
2. Wacky
3. Declare
4. Allotment
5. Blandest
6. Orange cooler
7. Respond
8. African expedition
9. Lasts
10. Cuckoo species
11. Data
12. Void's partner
13. Even
21. Simian
23. Royal Indian
27. Wild duck
28. Knowledgeable
29. Eucharistic plate
30. Fairy-tale creature
31. Weep
33. Ascend
34. ___ wave
35. Part of an act
38. Domino spot
41. Take it easy
42. School sport
44. Stamping tool
47. Abstruse
49. Hors d'oeuvres
52. Harvester
54. Name
55. Shining
57. Coastline
59. Impel with force
60. Meat cut
61. Cast
64. Bullets, to a GI
65. Rushes
66. Previously
68. Winter ailment
70. Single's order

PUZZLE 107

CODEWORD

Codeword is a special crossword puzzle in which conventional clues are omitted. Instead, answer words in the diagram are represented by numbers. Each number represents a different letter of the alphabet, and all of the letters of the alphabet are used. When you are sure of a letter, put it in the code key chart and cross it off in the Alphabet Box. A group of letters has been inserted to start you off.

1 T	2	3	4	5	6	7	8	9	10	11 R	12	13
14	15	16	17	18	19	20	21	22	23 E	24	25	26

3	2	16	24	11	■	■	8	18	2	15	■	9	4	22
2	4	17	25	17	■	26	22	23	11	5	■	4	2	19
11	23	25	17	21	■	22	19	19	23	11	■	2	21	8
■	■	■	■	23	1	2	■	■	■	24	9	1	■	■
6	2	19	8	■	17	21	8	■	22	8	2	25	4	23
17	1	2	4	17	14	■	12	23	6	■	21	23	2	11
25	23	11	5	4	■	3	17	21	17	■	■	21	5	23
■	■	■	■	12	23	2	■	17	1	8	■	■	■	■
1	23	6	■	■	4	17	9	1	■	2	13	2	11	21
2	10	17	21	■	2	21	23	■	1	13	17	6	23	11
11 R	23 E	1 T	22	11	6	■	20	24	24	■	1	17	21	5
■	■	19	24	17	■	■	■	25	24	2	■	■	■	■
19	18	17	■	9	24	4	17	24	■	4	4	2	3	2
8	23	14	■	4	17	2	6	23	■	25	24	7	23	11
17	11	12	■	23	4	3	8	■	■	8	19	23	6	1

Alphabet Box

A B C D ~~E~~ F G H I J K L M N O P Q ~~R~~ S ~~T~~ U V W X Y Z

PUZZLE 108

ACROSS

1. Embarrass
6. Sums
10. Snooze
14. Musical pace
15. Has-___
16. Canyon's answer
17. Public
18. Tibetan priest
19. Golf club
20. Talking bird
21. Surrenderer
22. Undressed
23. Armed conflict
25. Woeful cry
27. News flash
31. Close
34. Atlas part
35. Mower's pride
36. "Sesame ___"
38. Horned serpents
40. Roadside inn
42. Dogwood, e.g.
43. Firmly placed
45. Make muddy
47. "___ Got No Strings"
48. Crosscurrent
49. Nectar gatherer
51. Dealer's car
53. Get the picture
54. Place a bet
57. Quick-witted
60. Loafer
64. Withdraw gradually
65. Stage drama
66. Smelled bad
67. Feeble, as an excuse
68. World spinner
69. Therefore
70. Hied
71. Woolly bleaters
72. Sidled

DOWN

1. Small particle
2. Bunch
3. Last word in prayer
4. Spread out awkwardly
5. Torrid
6. Apt
7. Inactive
8. Dishonor
9. Get tangled
10. Include again
11. Unbleached color
12. Not barefoot
13. Dial sound
21. Soft and smooth
24. "___ Night Long"
26. Hill dweller
27. Sew loosely
28. Increased
29. Duo
30. Beginning part
32. Cliff home
33. "Superman" star
34. Bell and Kettle
36. Most foxy
37. Peg
39. Made woeful
41. Years and years
44. Fabric tinter
46. Caustic material
49. Empty inside
50. Overcame
52. Syrup source
54. Hole punchers
55. Kind of tide
56. Calm
58. Roof detail
59. Whiskeys
61. Suspend
62. Earlier
63. ___ out (barely earned)
66. That girl

PUZZLE 109

ACROSS

1. Shoemaker's device
4. Frenzied
8. Parson's house
13. Life story, for short
14. Drive out
15. Air a view
16. 19th letter
17. Fasten again
18. Field goal, to Shaq
19. Actress Bara
21. Spinning toy
22. Spending limits
23. Skin cream additive
25. Gratify
28. Evergreen type
30. Mad
32. Awful
35. Narrow vision
37. Alike
38. Expert flier
39. Bounds
40. Haphazard
42. "___-Devil"
43. Important time
44. Drinks with scones
45. Creepier
47. Blend
48. Flee
50. Ampersand
51. Pilaster
52. Bloodhound's trail
54. Three-foot unit
57. Wharf rodent
59. "___ Science"
63. Plant swelling
65. Bulb vegetable
67. Gooey liquid
68. Make broader
69. Zeniths
70. Easily bruised thing?
71. Full of rocks
72. Motels
73. Street finder

DOWN

1. Help a hood
2. Desire
3. Surrender
4. Wood chopper
5. Winter glove
6. Medley
7. Remembrance
8. Clever remark
9. Swiftly
10. Indian palm
11. Crop
12. Poetic twilights
14. Of a historic time
20. "That ___ Cat"
24. Slickest
26. Biscotti flavoring
27. High-strung
28. Mushrooms
29. Directory
31. Spicy dip
32. Washbowl
33. Pined
34. Antelope's pal
35. Bears or Raiders
36. Corroded
41. Pasta tubes
46. Hard to come by
49. Love tonic
51. Promo producers
53. Has title to
54. Evergreen shrubs
55. Miner's entrance
56. Decorate anew
58. In a short time
60. News article
61. Sitar music
62. Fall
64. At least one
66. Switch positions

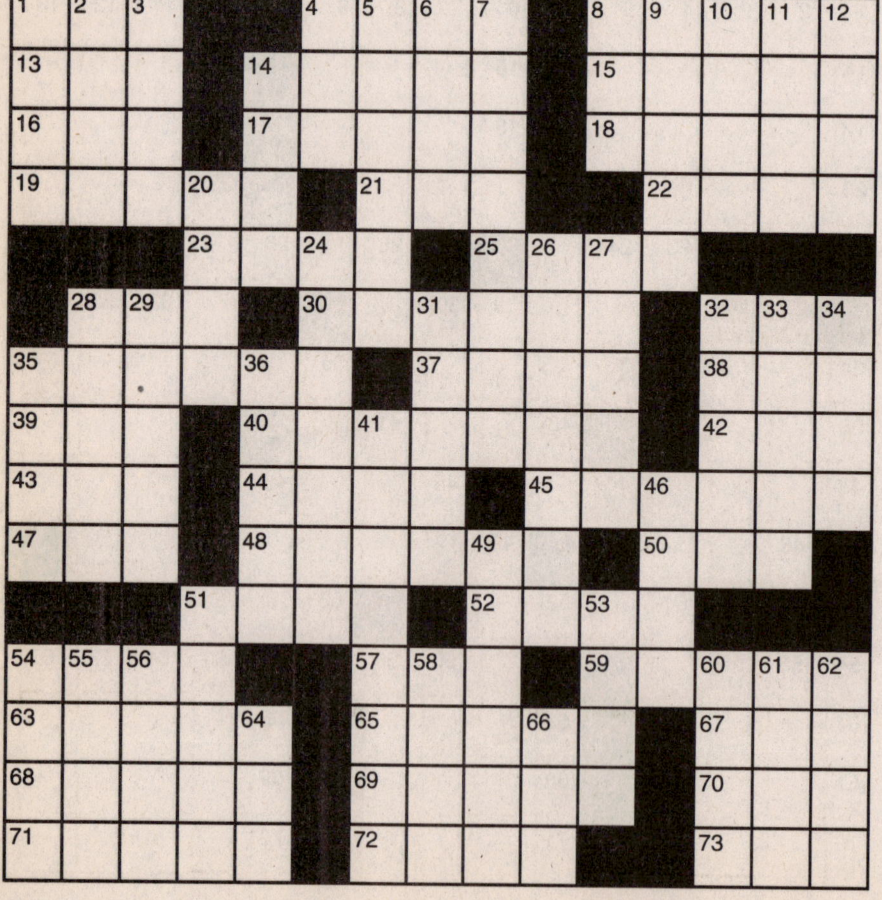

PUZZLE 110

ACROSS

1. Shop turner
6. Slangy assent
10. Pale brown
14. Love, in France
15. Wheel shaft
16. Cows' calls
17. One who watches
18. Tricky
19. Word in a threat
20. House shape
21. "___ It Romantic?"
23. Moved quickly
25. Feel indignant about
27. Shocking art style
28. Highly excited
30. By an ___ (barely)
34. Crack
37. Pay
39. Chop finely
40. Stylish
41. Faucet
42. Uncooked
43. Leer at
45. More retiring
47. Religious song
48. Behaves like King Kong
50. Rajah's mate
52. Cat's sound
53. Sofa
57. Pet
60. Retained
62. Smart blow
63. In ___ of
64. Enthusiastic
66. Poke fun at
68. Sonnets' kin
69. Pastrami purveyor
70. Host
71. Tot
72. Had conveyed
73. Sword fights

DOWN

1. Type of beam
2. Plentiful
3. Labors
4. ___ and cry
5. Going astray
6. Stretch wide
7. Way out
8. Entirely
9. Primes
10. Green gem
11. Indianapolis player
12. American Beauty, e.g.
13. Secondhand
22. Stash
24. Citrus cooler
26. Enjoy dinner
27. More profound
29. Collect
31. Drafty
32. Swindle
33. Cut down
34. Urban problem
35. NBC's peacock, e.g.
36. Meaningless
38. The ___ Nineties
44. Embrace, as a cause
45. Extends
46. Coarse file
47. Smack
49. Northern bird
51. Gained as a clear profit
54. Hint
55. Picasso's prop
56. Certain rapiers
57. Vegas machine
58. Orderly
59. Stench
60. Oven
61. Correct, as copy
65. Flying formation
67. Ostrichlike animal

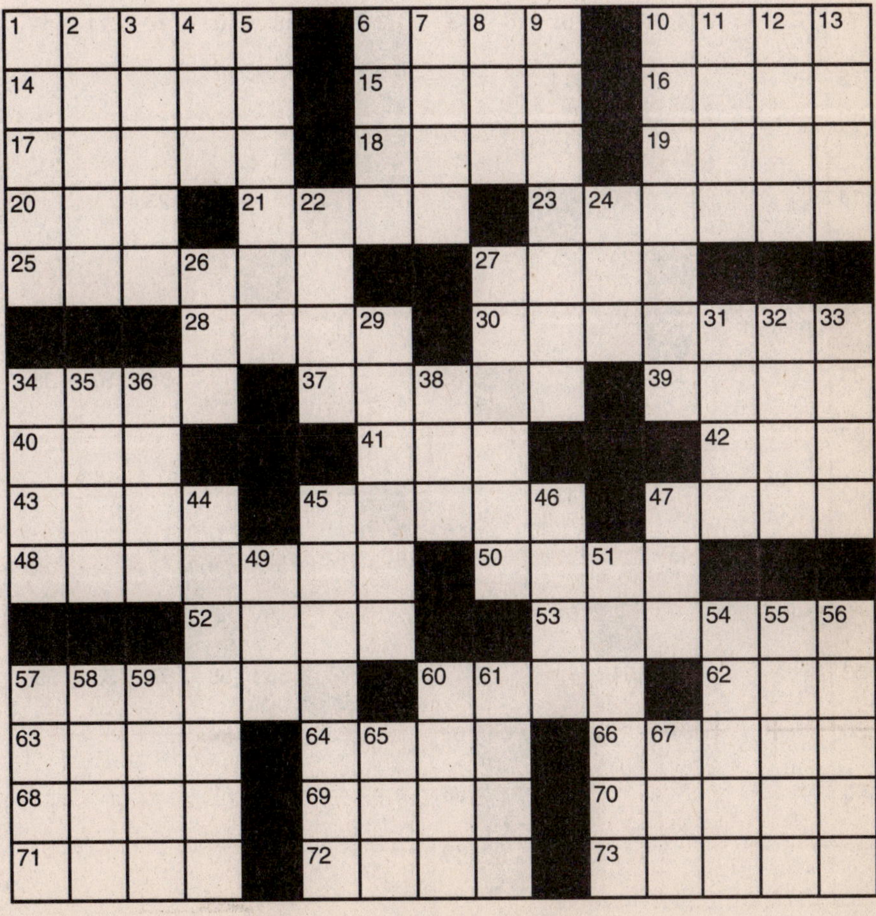

PUZZLE 111

ACROSS

1. Strikebreaker
5. Sash
8. Individuals
13. Ear piece
14. Scamper
15. Prayer
16. Spanish jar
17. Floating menagerie
18. Ecstatic
19. Plant disease
21. Caught congers
23. Solidify
24. Drunk
26. Devout
27. Piercing tool
30. African antelope
31. And
33. Rope loops
35. Skin spots
39. Bread morsel
40. Ashen
41. Cowboy's rope
42. Promoted
44. When wages are disbursed
45. Londoner's so long
46. Chat
47. Curvy road turn
48. French I word
51. Straighten out
53. Greek letter
54. Burning crime
55. Disdain
60. Raunchy
62. Unit of length
64. Sickness
65. Kind of street
66. Extinct bird
67. Camera eye
68. Witness again
69. Bow
70. Athletic event

DOWN

1. Purple plum
2. Winter ailment
3. Gifted
4. Two-by-four
5. Mouths
6. Dresser
7. Signed
8. Throw in the cards
9. Roe
10. Dismiss
11. Genuflect
12. Unhappily
15. Pin's cousin
20. Branch of mathematics
22. Come to know
25. Switch positions
26. Corny
27. Noun suffix
28. Shabby
29. Shrill
32. Writes illegibly
34. Struck
35. Fashion
36. Put a burden on
37. Greek vowels
38. States
40. Detaches
43. Hardy
44. Golfer's goal
46. Of lower rank
48. Slip-up
49. Biblical your
50. Gowns
52. Pause mark
54. Wings
56. Composed
57. Curved molding
58. Old Norse inscription
59. Robin's retreat
61. Fearful reverence
63. Varnish ingredient

1	2	3	4	■	5	6	7	■	■	8	9	10	11	12
13				■	14			■	15					
16				■	17			■	18					
19				20	■	21		22			■	23		
■	■	■	■	24	25					■	26			
27	28	29	■	30			■	31		32		■	■	■
33			34			■	35					36	37	38
39					■	40			■	41				
42					43			■	44					
■	■	■	45				■	46			■	47		
48	49	50		■	51		52				■	■	■	■
53			■	54					■	55	56	57	58	59
60			61			■	62		63	■	64			
65						■	66			■	67			
68					■	■	69			■	70			

PUZZLE 112

ACROSS

1. To ___ it may concern
5. Rainbow shape
8. Pod member
12. Fine-tune
13. Blue dyes
15. Stable baby
16. Incensed
17. Breed of cat
18. Certainty
19. Boat basin
21. Not home
23. That female
24. Beany's friend
26. Tidier
28. Molded dessert
31. Jolt suddenly
32. Superstar
33. Greek letter
36. Thus
40. Bird bill
41. Generation
42. "Stand ___ Deliver"
43. Watch part
45. Impassive
47. Winglike parts
48. Arctic abundance
50. Street fighters
52. Doctor's hammer
55. Magi gift
56. Intend
57. Wait
59. Dial on the phone
63. Gawk
65. Of the ear
67. Freedom
68. Colony insects
69. Sizable
70. Wedding-cake layer
71. Senate votes
72. Concentrated solution
73. Formerly

DOWN

1. Fancy
2. Kibbutz dance
3. Unique person
4. Type of insurance
5. Black cuckoo
6. Adversary
7. Ball of yarn
8. On's opposite
9. Broil
10. Hidden supply
11. Vary
13. Locust shrub
14. Poem division
20. Fishing tool
22. Type of vote
25. Cove
27. Mock
28. Mill and rummy
29. Make ready to publish
30. Earring site
34. Specialist
35. Crinite
37. Chest sound
38. Snarl
39. Emotional poems
44. Be sociable
45. Done in installments
46. Hoop
47. Sports figure
49. Male swan
51. Feast ___ famine
52. Heathen
53. Woody vine
54. Vacant
55. Festive
58. ___ citizenship
60. Hideout
61. Functions
62. Brash
64. Sharp curve
66. Years of life

PUZZLE 113 FLOWER POWER

The answers to this petaled puzzle will go in a curve from the number on the outside to the center of the flower. Each number in the flower will have two 5-letter answers. One goes in a clockwise direction and the second in a counterclockwise direction. We have entered two answers to help you begin.

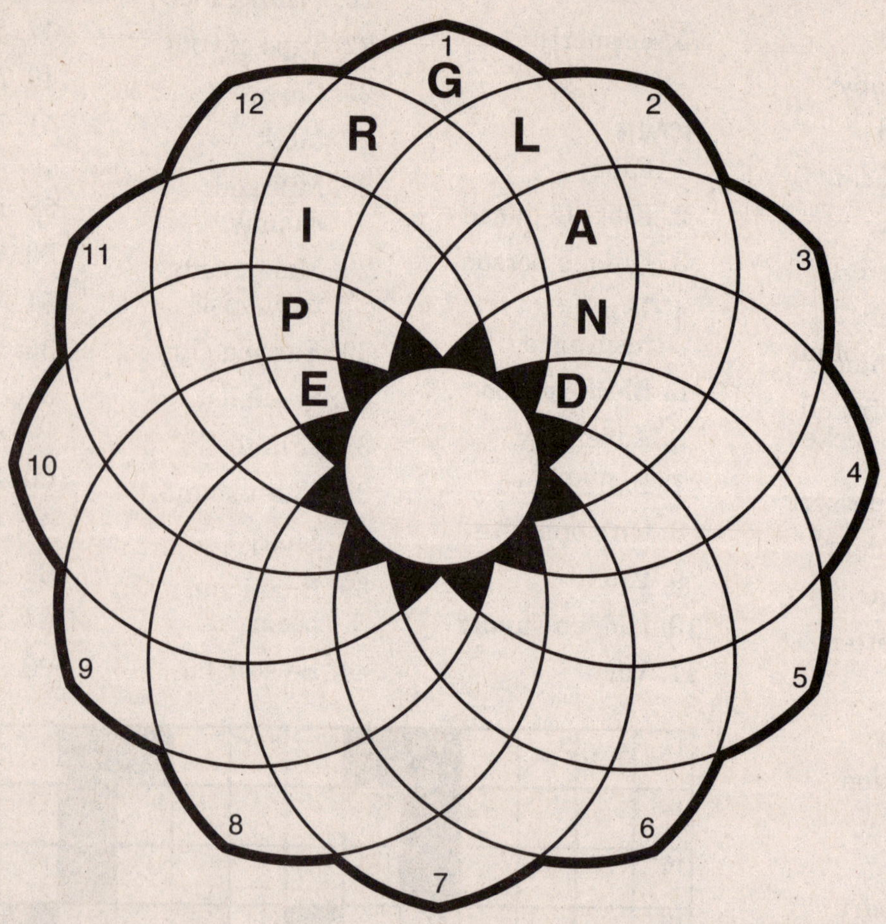

CLOCKWISE

1. Secreting organ
2. Bunch
3. Sudsy
4. Ogre
5. Spark producer
6. Fuzzy fruit
7. Arrange in folds
8. Trend
9. Indian group
10. Feel about
11. Honor
12. Essential

COUNTERCLOCKWISE

1. Complain
2. Move quietly
3. Bowling division
4. Pat or Daniel
5. Impostor
6. Stout
7. Divinity
8. Construction machine
9. Piece of land
10. Chart
11. Trophy
12. Explore

FLOWER POWER FANS! *Fun is always in full bloom with every volume of Selected Flower Power. To order, see page 159.*

PUZZLE 114

ACROSS

1. Current measures
5. Prudish
9. On an ___ keel
13. Decoy
14. Vanity
15. Denver's distance
16. Alliance
17. Washer cycle
18. ___ moss
19. Venetian-blind part
20. Future chicken
21. Prickles
23. Electrical unit
25. Make a seam
26. Alien
30. Bring up
33. Back talk
34. Predinner reading
35. Alliance
37. Period of life
38. Cuban dance
40. Thirst quencher
41. Expression
44. Military prison
46. Postal code
47. Diamond protector
48. Praised
50. Bath site
52. Downed lunch
53. Game tile with dots
56. Mock
58. Tall spar
62. Luau instruments
63. Seat
65. Toll road
66. Fountain drink
67. Harangue
68. Black stone
69. Group of computer bits
70. Talking bird
71. Don't strike

DOWN

1. Priestly robes
2. Ruminate
3. Malayan boat
4. Division
5. Puritan
6. Wedding symbol
7. Freud's concerns
8. Assembles
9. Authorize
10. Challenger
11. Ardor
12. Captures
14. First showing
22. Present!
24. Stitched edge
26. Argument
27. Verdi composition
28. African antelope
29. Deadens
31. Staring intently
32. Repeated
33. Racing circuit
35. Possible to post
36. Corded fabric
39. Car protector
42. Performer
43. Whirled
45. Belly
49. Rates of speed
51. "___ Buddies"
53. Dimwitted
54. All right!
55. Defrost
56. Chestnut horse
57. Small amount
59. "___ No Sunshine"
60. Kind of terrier
61. Writing
64. Struggle

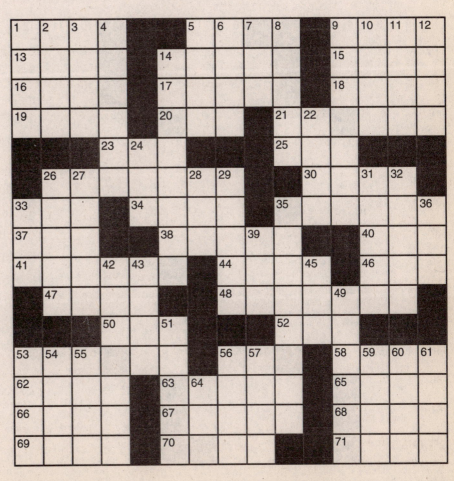

1	2	3	4	■	■	5	6	7	8	■	9	10	11	12
13				■	14					■	15			
16				■	17					■	18			
19				■	20			■	21	22				
■	■	■	23	24		■	■	■	25			■	■	■
■	26	27				28	29	■	■	30		31	32	■
33			■	34				■	35					36
37			■	■	38			39		■	■	40		
41			42	43		■	44			45	■	46		
■	47				■	■	48				49			■
■	■	■	50		51	■	■	■	52			■	■	■
53	54	55				■	56	57		■	58	59	60	61
62				■	63	64				■	65			
66				■	67					■	68			
69				■	70				■	■	71			

PUZZLE 115

ACROSS

1. Flavor
6. Athenian vowels
10. Speck
13. Residence
14. Tilting
15. ___ out a living
16. Soar
17. Vicar's residence
18. Half of a bikini
19. Yet, in verse
20. Fern leaf
22. Of birth
24. Glossy
26. Certain amphibians
28. Pilots
30. Storm or state
33. Flat breads
34. Bower
35. Knee's locale
37. Works onstage
38. Deluge
39. Chance
40. Go down the slope
41. Sepals
42. First appearance
43. Expeditions
45. Cantaloupes
46. Astonished
47. Authority
48. Raccoon's kin
51. In the lead
53. Rearward, nautically
56. Guy who stays at home?
57. Diner patron
59. Percentage
61. Pullover
62. Grunt
63. Sea
64. Call it quits
65. Wear down
66. Nuisances

DOWN

1. Herb
2. Up to it
3. Christmas plant
4. Curious
5. Short jackets
6. Spunk
7. Highly volatile thing
8. Burro
9. Loudmouth
10. IOU
11. Southern veggie
12. River duck
14. On a rampage
21. Legal thing
23. Nile biter
25. Meadows
27. Vittles
28. Baths
29. Clock sounds
30. Aikman et al.
31. Embellishes
32. Broadcast again
34. Swamp dweller
36. Acquires
38. Card game
39. Printer's term
41. Most crafty
42. Bead of condensation
44. Plump
45. Ostrichlike bird
47. Sassy
48. Irresistible
49. Portent
50. Impersonated
52. ___ and now
54. Command
55. Weighty units
58. Cuckoo
60. Master

PUZZLE 116

ACROSS

1. Celebration
5. Venomous vipers
9. Impersonated
13. Catch sight of
14. Lance
16. ___ the fat
17. Gather a crop
18. Prolonged attack
19. Lacquered metal
20. Swindler
22. Theatrical work
24. Football holder
25. Lemon drinks
27. Hold in a condensed coating
29. Sleeping furniture
32. Mongrel
33. Facial feature
34. Called forth
36. Diving bird
37. Longing
41. Twice four
42. Snoop
43. Stare
44. Court response
45. Irritate
46. Small bill
47. Casino game
49. Court
50. Fade away
51. Assistance
54. Salary
55. Big bird
56. Daily darkness
58. Harnessed
63. Made an exit
65. Pay hike
67. Remove from print
68. Therefore
69. Youth
70. Basilica part
71. Tinter
72. Kauai goose
73. Stalk

DOWN

1. Wayward ice
2. On a boat
3. Bridge
4. Exaggeration
5. Donkey
6. Muffet's startler
7. Social equals
8. Epic
9. Tread the boards
10. Album entry
11. Sniggler
12. Wimp
15. Comment
21. Side
23. Ruckus
26. Flop
28. Hog's dinner
29. Horn noise
30. Sermon topic
31. Venetian magistrate
33. Purchase
35. Uniform color
36. Floating zoo
38. Anecdote
39. Grouchy person
40. Basil, e.g.
42. Supportive of
43. Sticky
45. Sickly
46. Pooch
48. Yet, poetically
49. Holmes's sidekick
51. Marry again
52. Coarse abrasive
53. Forward thrust
54. Complain
57. Advancement
59. Harem rooms
60. Retained
61. Choice word
62. Consider
64. Rocky hill
66. Prior to, in poems

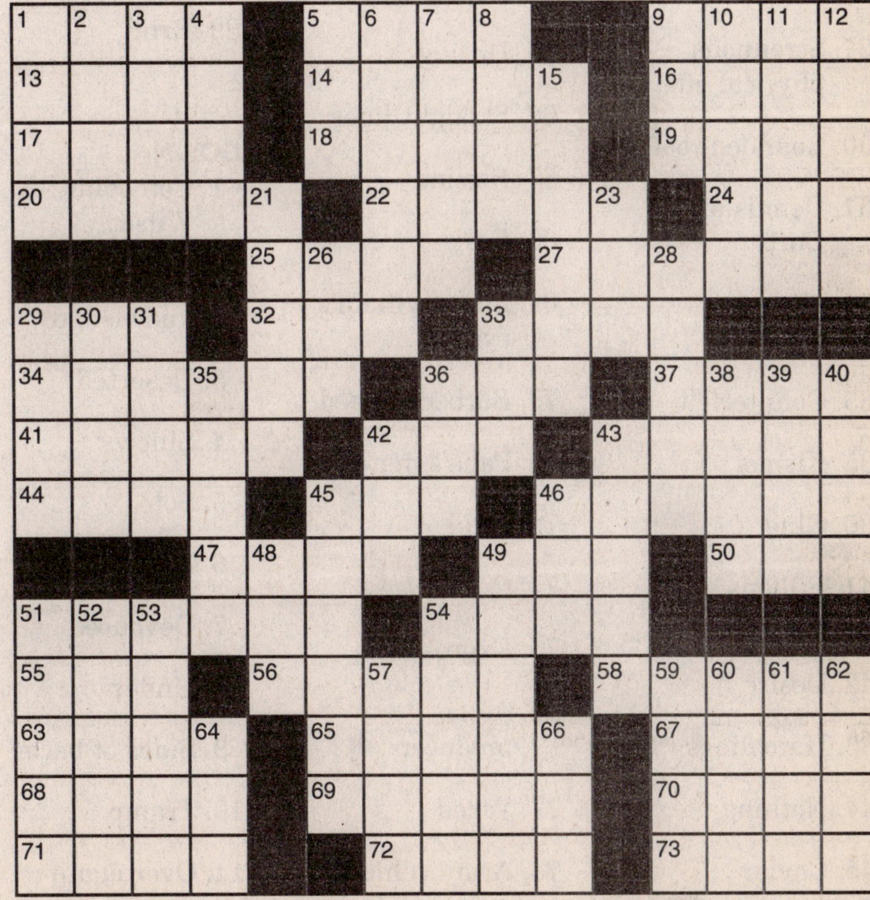

PUZZLE 117

ACROSS
1. Lady's shoe
5. Fast steed
9. Persian ruler
13. Earth
17. Ear part
18. Tardy
19. Solitary
20. Of the mouth
21. OPEC member
22. Undo
23. Still asleep
24. Spiders' spinnings
25. Locket
27. Strenuous physical effort
30. Rounded roof
31. Dennis and Doris
32. Slithery swimmer
33. Counterfeit
35. Kismet
36. Glue
41. Billions of years
42. Desire
43. Hatchlings
44. Nothing
45. Caviar
46. Poet Ogden ___
47. Tine
48. Short article
49. Glider's need
51. Soot
52. "The Getaway" actor
53. Inclined
54. Finnish bath
55. Up to now
56. Selected
59. Hold fast
60. Chiefly
64. Rope fiber
65. During
66. Straight lines
67. Recline
68. Fury
69. Like a villain's eyes
70. Barbecue need
71. Papa's mate
72. Solid
74. Quiet
75. Expressions
76. Acorn producer
77. Vexed
78. Army vehicle
79. Exotic entertainer
84. Most embarrassed
87. Moistureless
88. State confidently
89. Orangutans
91. "___ Karenina"
92. Husband's mate
93. Past years
94. Like Felix Unger
95. Nautical wood
96. Sly gaze
97. Winter forecast
98. Old salts
99. Brim

DOWN
1. Comedian Wilson
2. Folk knowledge
3. Deserted
4. Sinews
5. Solo
6. Entranced
7. Devoured
8. Under
9. Sides of bacon
10. Tramp
11. Over again
12. Porcupine
13. U and I
14. Domain
15. Hunting dogs, for short
16. If not
26. Actress Irving
28. Soap-making ingredient
29. Cattail kin
31. Smidgen
33. South American nation
34. Bird's target
35. Tyson's weapon
36. Smell
37. Completed
38. Penetrating preposition
39. Fought
40. New Haven trees
42. Drift
43. Carry
46. Scruff of the neck
47. Breakfast fruit
48. Pinch
50. File
51. Merrily
52. Sprinkles
54. Playground apparatus

PUZZLE 117

55. Caterwaul

56. Smart

57. Wedge

58. Sign

59. Gab

60. Lexicographer Webster

61. Covered with soot

62. Green fruit

63. Positive votes

65. Work period

66. Went up

69. Donkey's cry

70. Seedless raisin

71. Decree

73. Less friendly

74. Toolshed implement

75. Trend

77. Metal fastener

78. Quizzes

79. Sob

80. Lake that sounds weird

81. Duration

82. Shakespeare's river

83. Roman emperor

84. "___ Window"

85. Catch

86. Seize

90. Jacket or soup

PUZZLE 118

ACROSS

1. At the center
6. Fake
10. Arabian garments
14. Eaten away
15. Head flankers
16. Taboo
17. Skating areas
18. Untruths
19. Metric weight unit
20. Court barrier
21. Brood
23. Rent
24. Toils
26. "___ They Sail"
29. Film
30. Greasiest
34. Be overfond
36. Backbone
39. Wedding dessert
40. Cuckoo
41. Ogre
42. Moral offense
43. Cub Scout groups
45. Primp
47. Workout locales
48. Carbon-based
50. Citrus drinks
52. French spa
54. Dull finishes
57. Showy flower
60. Microwave, e.g.
62. Estuary
63. Bring up
64. Constructed
66. Campus people
68. Icicle holder
69. Is in the red
70. Fencers' choices
71. Appealed
72. Pummel
73. Attempt again

DOWN

1. Woodland plants
2. Bay window
3. Touching
4. Request
5. Reduce
6. Vend
7. Japanese verse
8. "We ___ the World"
9. Unset texts: abbr.
10. Saintly
11. Violent wind
12. Collections
13. Not all
22. Employs
23. Diamond girl
25. Struggle (for)
27. Present
28. Fasten
31. Place of leisure
32. Browse
33. Decade numbers
34. Carpentry joint
35. Unique being
37. Veranda
38. Strong anger
44. Relished
45. Photo
46. Moniker
47. Comprehend
49. Veto
51. Hoofer
53. Alpine song
55. Downy duck
56. Impudent
57. Type of school
58. Cure
59. Wash
61. Suit item
64. Cleaning implement
65. Fill with reverence
67. Unclose, poetically

1	2	3	4	5	■	6	7	8	9	■	10	11	12	13
14					■	15				■	16			
17					■	18				■	19			
20			■	21	22			■	■	23				
24			25			■	26	27	28			■	■	■
■	■	29				■	■	30				31	32	33
34	35			■	36	37	38			■	39			
40			■	■	■	41			■	■	■	42		
43			44	■	45				46	■	47			
48				49			■	■	50	51			■	■
■	■	■	52				53	■	54				55	56
57	58	59			■	■	60	61			■	62		
63				■	64	65			■	66	67			
68				■	69				■	70				
71				■	72				■	73				

PUZZLE 119

ACROSS

1. Harem rooms
5. Law ___ order
8. Field mouse
12. Round projection
13. Utter words
15. Eager
16. Widemouthed pitcher
17. Lyric poem
18. Tantrum
19. Opponent
20. Catch as catch ___
21. Musical beat
23. Trick
25. Cuckoo
26. Greek vowel
27. Snitch
30. Not ruled
32. Ahead
34. Cabbage dish
39. Crazy bird
40. Cotton ___
41. South American rodent
42. Barkeep's announcement
45. Expression
47. Complying
49. So-so grade
50. Syrup source
53. Game cube
54. Crucifix
56. Longed for
58. Evergreen
59. Shankar's music
63. Enrage
64. Jagged
66. Jai ___
67. Distinctive theories
68. Had supper
69. Delay
70. Vermin
71. Commercials
72. Court calls

DOWN

1. Olive genus
2. Unhappy
3. Aid in a felony
4. Letter stroke
5. Horrify
6. Night sign
7. Male parent
8. Diversify
9. Egglike
10. Not heavy
11. Plant disease
13. Minute part
14. Central part
22. Stash away
24. "___ Town"
25. Before long
27. Capsize
28. Wild ox
29. Pairs
31. Coldly
33. Tiny colonist
35. Undercover agent
36. Secular
37. Dermal dilemma
38. Employee's take
40. Happiness
43. Secret language
44. Remained
45. Slept noisily
46. Before this time
48. Purple flowers
50. Paper currency
51. Get out of bed
52. Tropical trees
55. Talk in a slow manner
57. Waistcoat
58. Enamored
60. Wings
61. Pace
62. River islands
65. Estuary

1	2	3	4	■	■	5	6	7	■	■	8	9	10	11
12				■	13				14	■	15			
16				■	17					■	18			
19				■	20			■	21	22				
■	■	■	23	24			■	25			■	26		
27	28	29	■	30			31				■	■	■	■
32			33			■	34				35	36	37	38
39				■	■	40			■	■	41			
42				43	44			■	45	46				
■	■	■	■	47				48			■	49		
50	51	52	■	53			■	54			55	■	■	■
56			57			■	58			■	59	60	61	62
63				■	64	65				■	66			
67				■	68					■	69			
70				■	■	71			■	■	72			

PUZZLE 120

ACROSS

1. Garden pest
6. Aid a hood
10. Inn drinks
14. Lariat
15. Economize
16. Celebration
17. Baseball's Rod ___
18. Leg warmers
20. Dam up
21. Poker starter
22. Road turn
23. Onion feature
27. That woman's
29. Apple kernel
32. Animosity
33. Defensive position
37. Before, to Byron
38. Furor
40. Mimic
41. Down-under animal
43. Type of rummy
44. Suggest
45. ___ in a lifetime
46. Capsize
48. Loop trains
49. Ugly thing
52. Hair goo
53. Steep hemp
54. Furthermore
55. Chopped
57. Omelet need
60. Tubular pasta
62. Rapier
66. Wondering
69. Oak offspring
70. Pelvic bones
71. Tense
72. African river
73. Landlord's fee
74. Think
75. Curl

DOWN

1. Circle segments
2. Swamp fuel
3. ___ and hounds
4. Short articles
5. Small crow
6. Solicit
7. Boring
8. Break ___
9. Cut one's choppers
10. Past
11. Open fabric
12. Part of BPOE
13. Fresh talk
19. Plant
24. Layered mineral
25. Do wrong
26. Alliance
28. Meander
29. Black tea
30. Sarcasm
31. Hippie's concern
33. Misplay, at cards
34. Higher
35. Miss Scarlett, e.g.
36. Romantic rendezvous
39. Hurry along
42. For fear that
44. Doing nothing
47. Brand-___
50. Flow out slowly
51. Stirred up
55. Door joint
56. Ornamentation
57. Arab ruler
58. Storm
59. Smirk
61. Current
63. Corn cake
64. Work units
65. Mr. Slaughter
67. Large vessel
68. Health club
69. Shtick

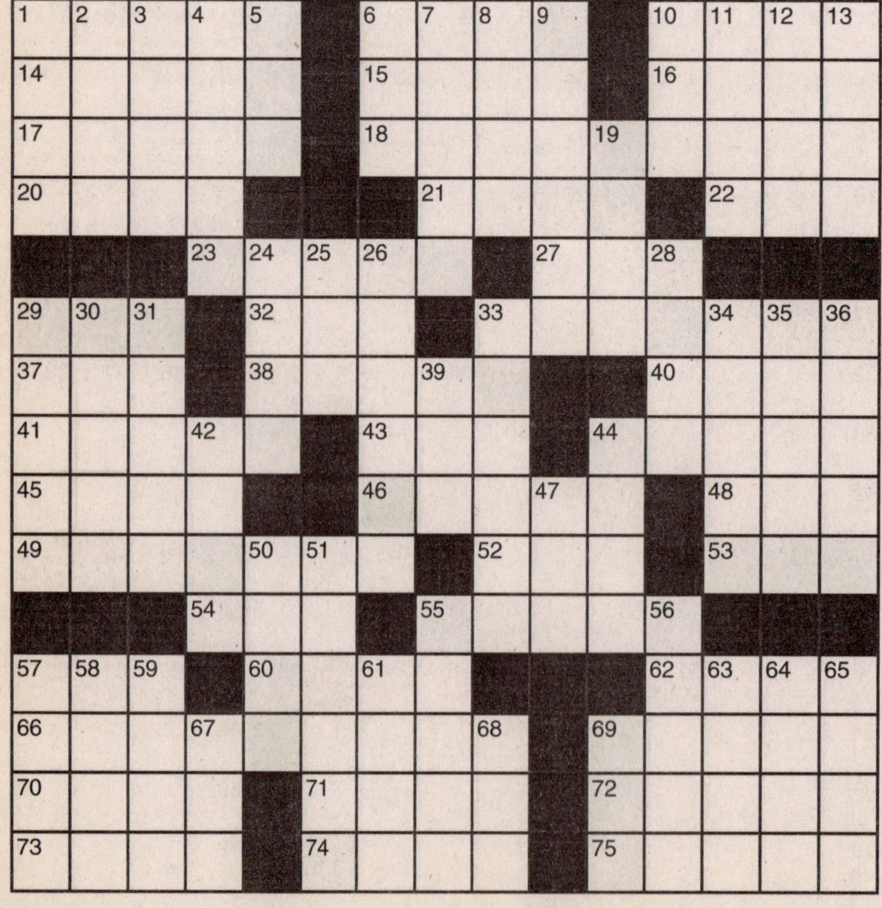

PUZZLE 121

ACROSS

1. Chest muscles
5. Collections
9. ___ profundo
14. Helm position
15. Very small amount
16. Square
17. Horrid
18. Gateway
19. Lariat
20. Plant disease
22. Cut
24. Actor Kilmer
25. Society miss
26. Intuit
28. Some beers
30. Rosters
32. Quartet
33. More unkind
35. Patriarch
36. Slightly open
40. Tailor
41. Bomb
42. Disgrace
43. Swerve
44. Fake hair
45. Postal items
46. Snoozing
48. Hitchhike
49. Attorney
52. Aquatic ridge
53. Whatever
56. Mining extract
57. Chopper
59. Folded sheet of paper
61. Yucca's kin
63. Cathedral section
65. African coin
66. New
67. Deuce topper
68. Eight bits
69. Charger
70. Sped
71. Comedian Mort ___

DOWN

1. Surfaced (a road)
2. Omit, as a vowel
3. Have a party
4. Look to be
5. Help
6. Rope loops
7. Coral island
8. Rani's raiment
9. Dresser
10. Kind of cuckoo
11. Use a razor
12. Shankar's instrument
13. Milky gems
21. Subsequent to
23. Dolt
27. Hearing apparatus
29. Author Greene
31. Type of street
32. Rage
33. Bell and Kettle
34. Wapiti
35. Burrowed
37. Creole dish
38. Stereo component
39. Legal thing
41. Completed
42. Cram
44. Once existed
45. "Murder, ___ Wrote"
47. Witnessed
48. Shorter
49. Borrowed sums
50. Specialized jargon
51. Loom
52. Printer's proof
54. Tenth's predecessor
55. Alpine song
58. Power unit
60. Spheres
62. Neckline shape
64. Catch someone's ___

PUZZLE 122

ACROSS

1. Small fights
6. Roster
10. Chop
14. Charmer's snake
15. Feel pain
16. Worshiped one
17. Let
18. Salon treatment
19. Briny expanses
20. Sound a horn
21. Rich
23. Bird of prey
27. Believe it or ___!
28. Wages
31. Pleasure boat
36. Canopy ___
37. Taboo
38. Hightail it
39. Clay brick
41. Light-switch positions
43. Packs away
44. Lightly cooked
45. Present
47. Actual profit
48. Winter forecast
50. Rode at full speed
52. Seek the affection of
54. Classify
55. Thick fog
59. Antlered animals
63. Freeway exit
64. The thing there
67. Maui howdy
68. Finished
69. Sandwich shop
70. Sticker
71. Turn down
72. Miners' quests
73. Monotonous hum

DOWN

1. Wound covering
2. Barber's sign
3. Skilled
4. Award
5. Woodcutting tool
6. Racetrack circuit
7. Hockey surface
8. Reduced
9. Beat
10. Record
11. Mental light-bulb
12. Black fuel
13. Threat word
22. Pig's home
24. Skin problem
25. Owl's question
26. Game of chance
28. Gas or brake, e.g.
29. Dote on
30. Cuban line dance
32. Ship's stern
33. Duplication
34. Cut down
35. Quiz
36. Hinders
40. Winged insect
42. Fine sand
43. Cease
46. Outfielder's catch
49. Tango number
50. Ground squirrel
51. Kitchen tool
53. Exceed
55. Push
56. Roof edge
57. Hemsley series
58. Peppy
60. Daft
61. Genghis or Kublai
62. Transaction
65. Bubbly brew
66. "___ the season . . ."
67. Remark further

PUZZLE 123

ACROSS

1. Loot
5. Spouse
9. At that time
13. Guided journey
14. Wash
15. Roof overhang
16. Gumbo necessity
17. Devoured
18. Always
19. Free from dependence
20. Utter
21. Lean
22. Not at work
24. Ensnare
27. Unfasten
31. In the lead
34. Wrapping film
35. Lasso
38. Hobo
40. Ostrich kin
41. Bouquet seller
43. Hustle and bustle
44. Thing, at law
45. Pointer
46. Painter's stand
48. Typhoon, e.g.
50. Least fresh
52. Showy bloom
55. Molasses spirit
56. Mast
59. Slick
61. Unit of matter
65. Forearm bone
66. Antique weapons
67. Main church section
68. Sweater fancier
69. Brilliance of success
70. Toward shelter
71. Is in the red
72. Bonds
73. Lincoln's coin

DOWN

1. Put on (cargo)
2. Roused from sleep
3. Atmosphere
4. Breakfast fare
5. Title of respect
6. Storage area
7. Greek letter
8. Poetic dusk
9. Cut one's choppers
10. Own
11. Constant
12. Geek
14. Complaints
23. Pomp
25. Makes lace
26. French manor
27. Employer
28. Monikers
29. Bread's edge
30. Formal teen dance
32. Degrade
33. Ranch guests
36. Palindromic preposition
37. Pretense
39. Shed, as feathers
42. Star's car
47. Annual reference book
49. TV's Winfrey et al.
51. Rendezvous
53. Present
54. Crop
56. Japanese wrestling
57. Turn the soil
58. Chip in
60. Grazing grounds
62. Fable, e.g.
63. Baking site
64. Join
66. Darn

1	2	3	4	■	■	5	6	7	8	■	9	10	11	12
13				■	14					■	15			
16				■	17					■	18			
19				■	20				■	■	21			
■	■	■	22	23		■	24		25	26		■	■	■
27	28	29				30	■	■	31			32	33	■
34					■	35	36	37			■	38		39
40			■	41	42						■	43		
44			■	45					■	46	47			
■	48		49			■	■	50	51					
■	■	■	52			53	54	■	55			■	■	■
56	57	58		■	■	59		60		■	61	62	63	64
65				■	66					■	67			
68				■	69					■	70			
71				■	72				■	■	73			

PUZZLE 124

ACROSS

1. Food fish
5. "___ It a Pity"
9. Promising individual
14. Bow
15. Poetic contraction
16. Alpine ridge
17. In the vicinity of
18. Mexican "sandwich"
19. Wash up
20. Appetizer
22. Soda-flavoring nut
24. Hazardous curve
25. Likewise not
26. Hockey, e.g.
28. Early Scandinavian
31. Ticked off
35. Edge
36. Rested
38. Endeavor
39. Greek vowel
42. Life story, briefly
44. Disperse
45. Hibernates
47. Badger
49. Effort
50. Artist's board
52. Meaty
55. African felines
57. Horse's morsel
58. Beast of burden
61. Double
62. Dry creek bed
66. Confused situation
68. Nanny or billy
70. Footless creature
71. Summoned
72. Beauty spot
73. Mr. Cleaver
74. Digging tool
75. Impersonated
76. "___ So Cold"

DOWN

1. Judge's bench
2. Field of study
3. Look over
4. Became smaller
5. Resident doctors
6. Baltic or Red
7. Bottle parts
8. Army groups
9. Nightclubs
10. Danish money
11. Dole
12. Old English letters
13. Female ruffs
21. Luau offering
23. Batches
27. Small pastry
28. Country house
29. Force
30. Chitchat
32. Merriment
33. Inclusive word
34. Damp
35. Coarse file
37. Malleable metal
40. Shoe feature
41. Skill
43. Klutz
46. Put on board
48. Crowed
51. Puzzle
53. Lend an ___
54. Drinking tubes
56. Pry into
58. Snakes
59. Clothing fastener
60. Epic
63. Colorful fish
64. Time past
65. Evens' opposites
67. Gave lunch to
69. Brewery product

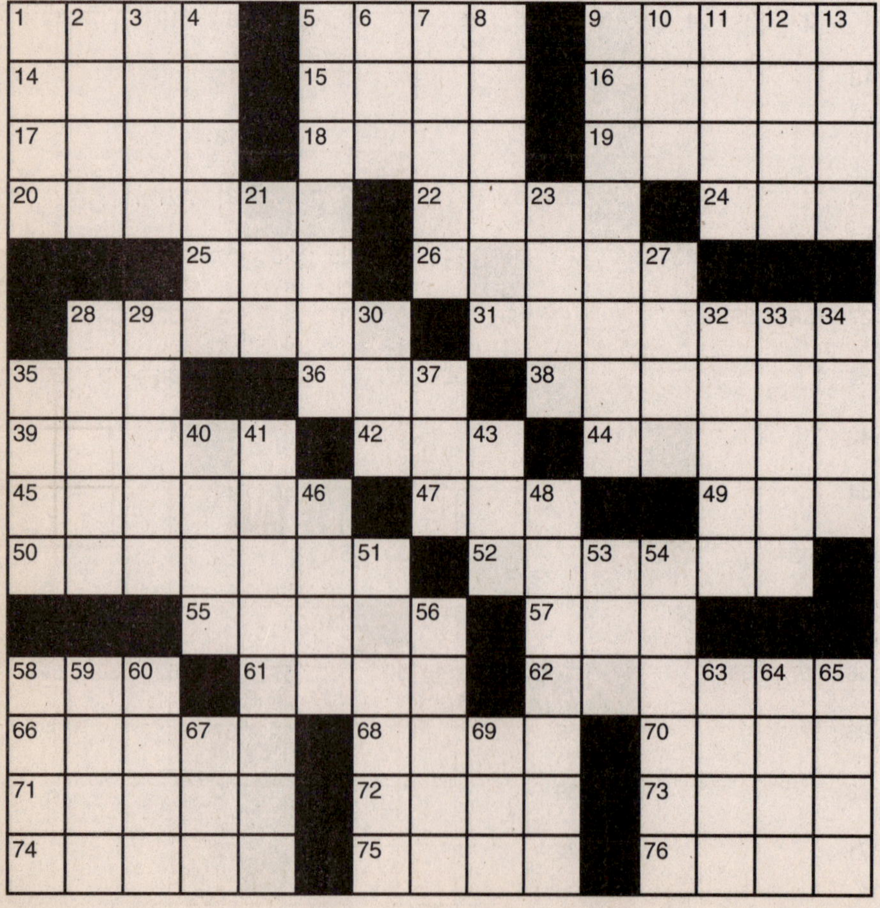

PUZZLE 125

ACROSS

1. Hoopla
4. Turn
8. At a distance
12. Shooter pellet
13. Radio noise
15. Not a soul
16. BPOE member
17. Bother
18. Londoner's farewell
19. Twist awry
21. Carpenter, at times
23. Chowed down
24. Caravan's stopover
26. Camel feature
29. ___ salts
30. Males
33. Reed instrument
34. Hit the hay
35. Chopping tool
36. Infantry member
38. Subtracts
40. Young boy
41. Cut
43. Bakery item
44. Porky's home
45. Looks suggestively
46. "___ the night before . . ."
47. Exhausted
48. Hair tint
50. Entry
53. Bravery
57. Sandal, e.g.
58. Involve
61. Machine's tooth
62. Seaweed
63. Draw
64. Bug
65. Persuade
66. Pink
67. Raised RRs

DOWN

1. Imitated
2. Cold-cuts shop
3. Acorn trees
4. Gaze intently
5. Previous
6. That thing's
7. Zero
8. Nonsupporters
9. Young horse
10. Initial bet
11. Raise
13. Scotch serving
14. Inhibited
20. Sealed
22. Aspired
24. Choose
25. Stage lines
26. Emcees
27. WWII craft
28. Like old cheese
29. More uncanny
30. Large parrot
31. Spare
32. Cozy abodes
34. Freed
37. The British ___
39. Express
42. Shout
47. Tearful
48. Bureau mat
49. Holiday season
50. Begs
51. Gnaw
52. Soda type
53. Creeps
54. Skin problem
55. Motive
56. Hens' grenades?
59. Negative connector
60. In addition

PUZZLE 126

ACROSS

1. Fellows
4. Pastrami seller
8. Owl's call
12. Affirmative response
13. College final
14. Longing
15. Teacher's ____
16. Relaxed
17. Unadorned
18. Light-bulb word
20. Mom's brothers
22. Fragrance
24. Fido's bane
25. Complain
26. Travel document
30. Tick off
31. Attack
32. Campus cheer
33. Sweet endings
35. Middle Eastern bread
36. Disarray
37. Envy's color
38. African tour
41. Diving bird
42. Computer operator
43. Bridge length
45. "A Tale of ____ Cities"
48. Tournament
49. In the nick of ____
50. Eternity
51. Back talk
52. Burn
53. Buck's mate

DOWN

1. Motorist's aid
2. Seeing organ
3. Television companies
4. "____ Dawn" (Reddy song)
5. Door sign
6. On the ____ (fleeing)
7. Overpowering drives
8. Shiny wheel accessory
9. Given by mouth
10. Folklore giant
11. Summer shirts
19. Electrical unit
21. Twiggy home
22. Sulfuric ____
23. Certain steak order
24. Goes without food
26. Keeps on
27. Familiarized
28. Speed
29. By comparison with
31. Brewed drink
34. Hurts
35. Specialist
37. Hopeless case
38. Quantities
39. Totally confused
40. Service charges
41. Tibetan priest
44. Cherry or mince
46. Court romantically
47. Dollar bill

PUZZLE 127

ACROSS

1. Chowder mollusk
5. Wanes
9. Sunday seat
12. Yard-care tool
13. Terrible smell
14. Ill temper
15. Zealous
16. Came back
18. Excessive excitement
20. Light-hued
21. Tooth pain
23. Andean animal
27. Clumsy one
30. Gives silent assent
32. Computer symbol
33. Humiliates
35. Receive
37. "Swan Lake" costume
38. Fashion shade
40. Below-average grade
41. Rob
43. Italian money, once
45. Presidential "no"
47. Fire
51. Practice for a play
55. Prima donna's solo
56. In times past
57. Repents of
58. Hire
59. Dad
60. Gains
61. Certain apples, for short

DOWN

1. Study at the last minute
2. Liquid rock
3. Similar
4. Newspapers and radio
5. Goof
6. Honked
7. Alpha's follower
8. ____ and crossbones
9. Bobby or cotter
10. Sooner than, in poems
11. Join in matrimony
17. Antique
19. Skin woe
22. Flexible tube
24. Did better than a B on
25. Pout
26. Chip in a chip
27. Mare's meal
28. Be adjacent to
29. Fortune
31. India attire
34. Gracious
36. Restrain
39. Storage space
42. Become educated
44. Startle
46. Actual
48. Surface measure
49. White metal
50. Grub
51. Emulate Ice-T
52. Conceit
53. Sock or bunny
54. Superhero's chest letter

ACROSS

1. Arkin or Rich
5. Door catch
9. "Brother ___"
12. Jon Hall TV role
14. Actress Burke
15. "Queen of the ___"
16. Cara or Dunne
17. Margaret Cho TV series, with "Girl"
20. Study
21. Comedienne Phyllis ___
23. Claire ___ of "My So-Called Life"
24. "Nana" actress
25. Humor
26. "I ___ What You Did"
29. Hebrew harp
30. Dapper
34. Ms. Dolenz of "She's Out of Control"
35. "The Flying ___"
36. Clayton ___ (Lone Ranger portrayer)
38. Pinch
39. Dorothy ___ of "Peyton Place"
41. Bullied
42. Summer quaffs
43. Ms. Jackson of "Harris and Company"
44. "Barnaby ___"
45. Dernier ___
46. "___ and the Detectives"
48. Comedian Soupy ___
49. "To ___ a Lady"
52. Dennis Quaid film
53. "___ Island"
54. "Norma ___"
55. Zilch
56. Director Cecil B. ___
58. "Animal ___"
59. "Much ___ About Nothing"
60. ___-Darwinism
61. Ms. Loughlin of "Full House"
62. "___—The Story of Michelangelo"
64. Fondle
66. "___ Hudson Street"
69. "Mission: Impossible" actor
71. Agent Kuryakin from U.N.C.L.E.
73. German industrial area
74. Certain poet
75. Iranians, of old
76. "___ Cry Tomorrow"
77. "Callaway ___ Thataway"
78. Ted ___ of "Blossom"

DOWN

1. Dry
2. "Double ___"
3. Hemsley series
4. "Cadillac ___"
5. "___ in Pink Tights"
6. Tim ___ of "Home Improvement"
7. "___ Wars"
8. Actress Dawber
9. Gigi ___ of "The John Larrouqette Show"
10. Wellaway!
11. "The ___ Commandments"
13. Comedian Skelton
14. Abby ___ of "Falcon Crest"
15. "The ___ Configuration"
18. Newscaster Murrow
19. "___ the Titanic"
22. Put forth
26. "Cheers" bartender
27. Group for Dr. Welby
28. Shatner or Devane
29. Actress Chlumsky
30. "Nobody ___ It Better" (Bond film theme)
31. "Eerie, ___"
32. Dundee negative
33. "Pygmalion" playwright's monogram
36. "Easy ___"
37. Has obligations
40. "Lorenzo's ___"
41. Dennis ___ of "Bearcats"
42. "Butterflies ___ Free"
44. Fonda or Russell
45. Comic character Kadiddlehopper
46. Byrnes of "77 Sunset Strip"
47. "Izzy and ___"
48. "___ at the Fair"
49. "___ When It Sizzles"
50. Comedian Caesar
51. "Xanadu" gp.
53. "___ and Present Danger"
54. Most unusual
57. Bury
58. "Another Part of the ___"
61. Linda ___ of "Alice"
62. Common duck
63. Romance lang.
64. Sheriff ___ (Glenn Ford role)
65. British actor Alistair ___
66. "M*A*S*H" actor
67. "___ of Laura Mars"
68. Lip
69. Greek letter
70. "Kings ___"
72. Actor Ayres

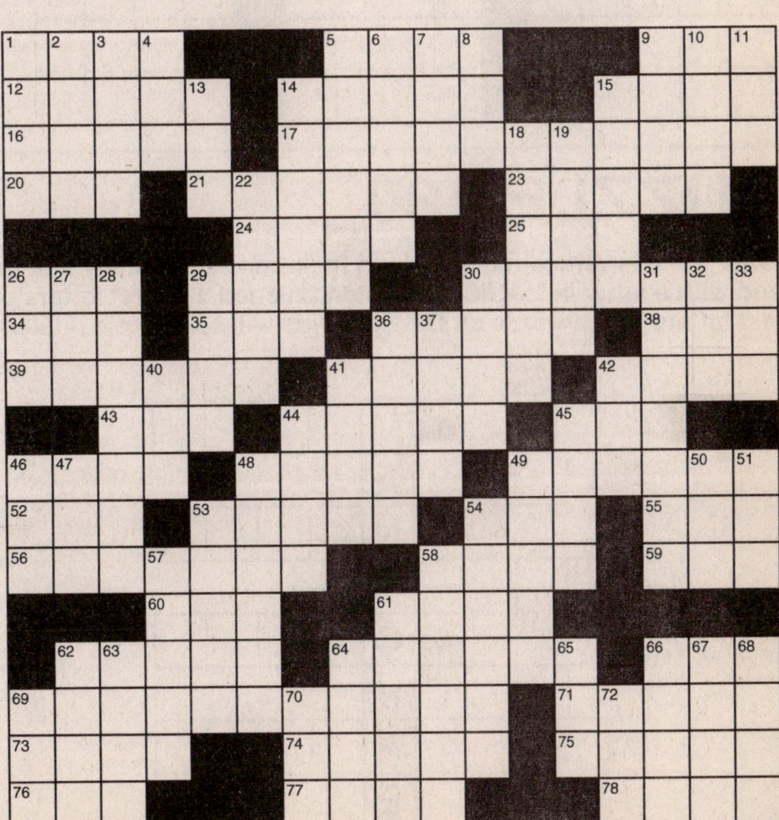

PUZZLE 129

ACROSS
1. Manuscript mark
5. Chowder mollusk
9. Backsides
14. A pop
15. Helper
16. In-box contents
17. Building lot
18. Victory gestures
19. Lark
20. Overfed
22. Had a little lamb
24. Calculate
25. Coal product
26. Stable fare
28. Knock on wood
31. Sign
33. Magazine piece
36. Detest
38. Zeros
40. Comparison word
41. Anchor
42. Kin of a violin
43. Filter clogger
44. Places
45. Healthy
46. Lawn barrier
47. Slumped
49. Personal pronoun
51. Above, in poems
52. Munch
53. Loud call
55. Large primate
57. Workout site
59. Tuneful
63. Forward thrust
65. October's gem
67. Chop finely
68. Previous
69. Letterhead graphic
70. Fifty-fifty
71. Religious factions
72. Ninny
73. Ultimate

DOWN
1. Black and Caspian
2. Diplomacy
3. Hosiery hue
4. Burglary
5. Underground area
6. Committed perjury
7. Juice drink
8. Phoenix neighbor
9. Elect again
10. Ballpark judge
11. Sweet cordial
12. Splotched
13. Snow slider
21. Just
23. Trunk
27. Championship
28. Highway exits
29. Regarding
30. Suited for pictures
32. Baker's instruction
33. Back street
34. Jousting weapon
35. Walk in
37. Director Welles
39. Feeling rotten
42. Like taffy
46. Roll up
48. Beepers
50. Spotted cat
54. Swiss warble
55. Italian peaks
56. Sheer
58. Shed
59. Biblical visitors
60. Opera star
61. Cold desserts
62. Dollar division
64. Obtained
66. Explosive noise

1	2	3	4	■	5	6	7	8	■	9	10	11	12	13
14				■	15				■	16				
17				■	18				■	19				
20				21			■	22	23		■	24		
■	■	■	25			■	■	■	26	27			■	■
28	29	30	■	31		32	■	33					34	35
36			37		■	38	39			■	40			
41				■	42					■	43			
44				■	45				■	46				
47				48			■	49	50		■	51		
■	■	52				■	■	■	53		54	■	■	■
55	56		■	57		58	■	59				60	61	62
63			64		■	65	66			■	67			
68					■	69				■	70			
71					■	72				■	73			

PUZZLE 130

Fore 'n' Aft

Enter the answers to the clues into their correspondingly numbered boxes. The words will begin or end with a letter in MANICURE. When finished, the first letters of the words on the left side and the last letters of the words on the right side will spell out a related answer.

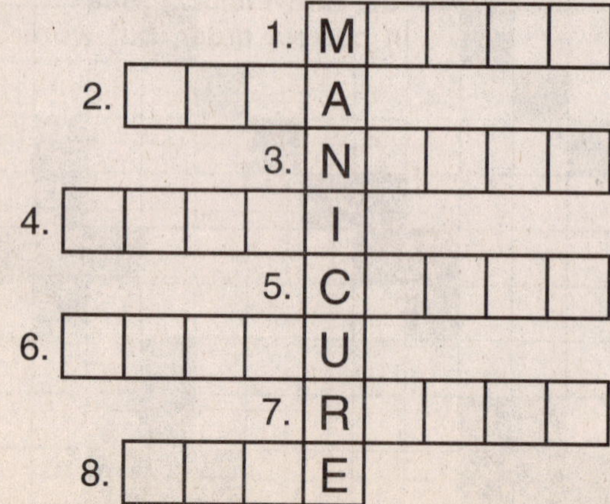

1. Theme
2. Granny
3. Ruth's relative
4. Fine fiddle
5. Sahara transport
6. Japanese auto company
7. Limerick, e.g.
8. Sales pitch

DOUBLE TROUBLE

PUZZLE 131

Not really double trouble, but double fun! Solve this puzzle as you would a regular crossword, except place one, two, or three letters in each box. The number of letters in each answer is shown in parentheses after its clue.

ACROSS

1. Upper House (6)
4. Victory (8)
7. Immature (8)
8. Cave in (8)
10. Synagogue official (5)
11. Account book (6)
13. Acclaim (5)
15. Parboil (6)
17. Muzzler loader (6)
18. Irish singer (4)
19. Not to mention (8)
21. Actress Durbin (6)
23. Coin factory (4)
24. Piano piece (5)
26. Core (6)
28. One of a flight (5)
30. Moldable (6)
32. Windstorms (8)
35. Caveat ___ (6)
37. "My Antonia" author (6)
39. Overjoy (5)
40. Smack (4)
41. Flow (7)
43. Nourished (3)
44. Unnecessary (8)
46. Dancer's pal (6)
48. Frequently (5)
49. Back street (5)

DOWN

1. Lucky number (5)
2. Did perfectly (6)
3. Wire (8)
4. Agreement (11)
5. Squelch (5)
6. Tent peg (5)
7. Joyful (8)
9. Alias (9)
10. Riffraff (6)
12. Eat away (5)
14. Peter or Paul (5)
16. Alpine home (6)
20. Outdo (5)
22. Sleuth Drew (5)
25. Food shop (12)
27. Male hawk (6)
28. Stalks (5)
29. Boeing craft (8)
31. National song (6)
33. Type of shoe (6)
34. Like Russian dolls (6)
36. Sub missile (7)
38. Actor Tony ___ (7)
42. Military command (6)
45. Departed (4)
47. "___ Jude" (3)

■	■	1	2	3	■	4	5	6	■	■
■	7				■	8			9	■
10		■	11		12		■	13		14
15		16	■	17			■	18		
19			20	■	21		22	■	23	
■	■	24		25	■	26		27	■	■
28	29	■	30		31	■	32		33	34
35		36	■	37		38	■	39		
40			■	41			42	■	43	
■	44		45		■	46		47		■
■	■	48			■	49			■	■

It's Your Move

PUZZLE 132

Start at the outlined box and move from box to box across, up, down, or diagonally to reveal a message. Every box will be used once. All the letters are in correct order, but words are run together. The solution path cannot cross itself.

1.

AT	R	**YO**	U
IO	PI	AS	R
NS	AR	ES	TI
Y	E	BI	LI
OU	RP	OS	SI

2.

B	ST	Y	**IF**
EB	LU	MU	OU
E	AT	AS	T
UE	L	LE	BE
B	HT	IG	BR

PUZZLE 133

BRICK BY BRICK

Rearrange this stack of bricks to form a crossword puzzle. The clues will help you fit the bricks into their correct places. Row 1 has been filled in for you. Use the bricks to fill in the remaining spaces.

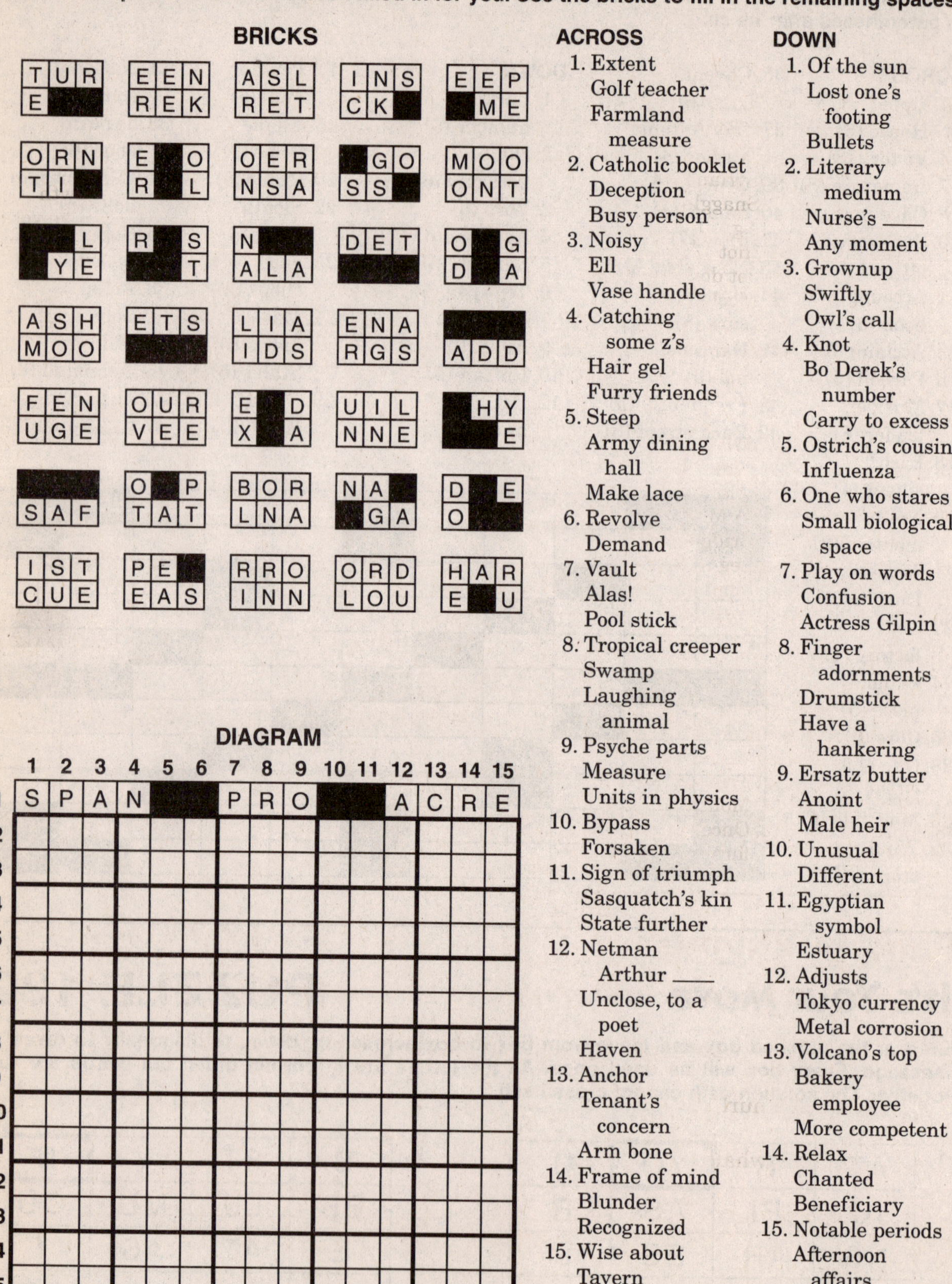

ACROSS

1. Extent
Golf teacher
Farmland measure
2. Catholic booklet
Deception
Busy person
3. Noisy
Ell
Vase handle
4. Catching some z's
Hair gel
Furry friends
5. Steep
Army dining hall
Make lace
6. Revolve
Demand
7. Vault
Alas!
Pool stick
8. Tropical creeper
Swamp
Laughing animal
9. Psyche parts
Measure
Units in physics
10. Bypass
Forsaken
11. Sign of triumph
Sasquatch's kin
State further
12. Netman Arthur ____
Unclose, to a poet
Haven
13. Anchor
Tenant's concern
Arm bone
14. Frame of mind
Blunder
Recognized
15. Wise about
Tavern
Long journey

DOWN

1. Of the sun
Lost one's footing
Bullets
2. Literary medium
Nurse's ____
Any moment
3. Grownup
Swiftly
Owl's call
4. Knot
Bo Derek's number
Carry to excess
5. Ostrich's cousin
Influenza
6. One who stares
Small biological space
7. Play on words
Confusion
Actress Gilpin
8. Finger adornments
Drumstick
Have a hankering
9. Ersatz butter
Anoint
Male heir
10. Unusual
Different
11. Egyptian symbol
Estuary
12. Adjusts
Tokyo currency
Metal corrosion
13. Volcano's top
Bakery employee
More competent
14. Relax
Chanted
Beneficiary
15. Notable periods
Afternoon affairs
Guzzled

BRICK BY BRICK FANS! Get a ton of Brick by Bricks—over 50 fun puzzles in each of our special collections! To order, see page 159.

PUZZLE 134

ACROSS

1. Spice-jar holder
5. Actor Stephen et al.
9. Jonathan, e.g.
14. Zip
15. Scoop
16. Style
17. Nil
18. Doodle
19. Canvas sheets
20. Poker payment
21. Bill Clinton's VP
22. Enthusiasm
23. Island gift
24. Hairstyling aid
25. Indian melody
28. Card game of old
30. Hearty
32. Ticket
35. Windflowers
38. African mammal
40. Inhabit
41. Flawless
43. Gemstone
44. Picturesque
46. Unmerciful
48. Aloft, poetically
49. Small cabinet
51. Aboveground trains
52. Scoff
53. Rower's tool
55. Game marble
58. Cognizant of
61. Gambol
63. Solo for Caruso
64. Truancy
66. Syrian fabrics
67. Snagglepuss, e.g.
68. Riot
69. Jot down
70. Moolah
71. Snow vehicles
72. Ruby and Joey
73. Sale caveat

DOWN

1. Kidney-related
2. "A Man ____"
3. Bridge variety
4. Leg middle
5. Mountain crest
6. Signed up
7. From a distance
8. Planters
9. Fore's partner
10. "____ Suite"
11. Trim down
12. Mouth parts
13. Once, formerly
24. Sticky mess
26. Awry
27. School wing
29. Harbinger
31. Consumers
32. Cloth wall hangings
33. Poet's plaint
34. Guys' dates
35. Furthermore
36. Amiable
37. Habitat
39. Sample of voters
42. Mechanize
45. Arctic abundance
47. Female pronoun
50. Mission
52. Jested
54. Church parts
56. Garlic-flavored mayo
57. Desires
58. Units of resistance
59. Director Coward
60. Painted metalware
62. Woodwind instrument
63. Pond growth
65. Affirmative vote

Pairs in Rhyme

PUZZLE 135

Each of these pairs of words is a rhyme for a familiar phrase.

Example: Car and ride (**Answer:** Far and wide)

1. Snit and hurl ______________________
2. Mill and whale ______________________
3. Bits and carts ______________________
4. Hog and tony ______________________
5. Toddy and bowl ______________________
6. Hangers and sash ______________________

PUZZLE 136

CODEWORD

Codeword is a special crossword puzzle in which conventional clues are omitted. Instead, answer words in the diagram are represented by numbers. Each number represents a different letter of the alphabet, and all of the letters of the alphabet are used. When you are sure of a letter, put it in the code key chart and cross it off in the alphabet box. A group of letters has been inserted to start you off.

18	9	15	■	■	7	6	6	■	■	6	20	11	17	15
7	24	24	■	6	15	9	9	19	■	10	26	9	15	17
15	7	7	■	20	13	9	8	7	■	26	15	15	7	24
■	■	17	3	17	1	15	■	22	11	17	15	■	■	■
5	17	6	13	■	23	13	7	24	26	14	■	6	17	3
17	11	9	9	22	■	7	4	17	25	■	22	1	6	13
20	7	8	20	17	11	■	15 T	26	14	■	1	23	2	12
■	■	■	20	24	7	6	1 I	19	7	8	15	■	■	■
1	6	11	7	■	5	1	8 N	■	24	1	8	6	7	24
16	7	7	24	■	1	8	23	13	■	14	7	11	11	7
12	7	15	■	19	9	23	15	9	24	■	6	7	11	22
■	■	■	21	9	8	7	■	20	13	17	6	7	■	■
17	24	24	9	3	■	24	17	20	1	19	■	20	17	19
24	17	12	9	8	■	7	25	7	8	19	■	7	5	9
7	8	7	25	12	■	■	20	24	9	■	■	24	9	15

A	~~N~~
B	O
C	P
D	Q
E	R
F	S
G	~~T~~
H	U
~~I~~	V
J	W
K	X
L	Y
M	Z

PUZZLE 137

Partners

Unscramble the words and match up the Partners.

1. SUBSITIC	______	&	______	a. INAGA
2. SWANOT	______	&	______	b. VINTESILEO
3. EFRA	______	&	______	c. PRESSIT
4. HOCE	______	&	______	d. GYVAR
5. IDOAR	______	&	______	e. KURGALFEN
6. CRYTA	______	&	______	f. MIBL
7. FEIL	______	&	______	g. SNICSURSA
8. EMIT	______	&	______	h. ANOLIGHT
9. MOINS	______	&	______	i. KRCIC
10. TRASS	______	&	______	j. UNPHERB

PUZZLE 138

ACROSS

1. Peel
6. Footwear item
10. Yearning
14. Laughing animal
15. Newscaster Roger ___
16. Do in, as a dragon
17. Copying
18. Fascinated
19. Sensitive
20. Female fowl
21. Night hooter
23. Rosie the ___
25. Religious statues
27. Young bug
28. Submarine detector
30. Winter Olympics event
32. Mom's man
35. Shucks!
36. Freighter
38. Madden
39. Uncivil
40. Mexican treats
42. Ids' counterparts
43. Bakery employee
44. Ivy
45. Expensive fur
46. Apiece
47. Prayer ending
49. Betty or Vanna
51. Certain poem
52. Encounter
54. Shyly
58. "Chances ___"
59. Lobster eggs
62. Spoken
63. Oaf
65. Operate a car
67. Classify
68. Fairy-tale monster
69. Painter's stand
70. Secondhand
71. Magician's prop
72. Color changers

DOWN

1. Persian ruler
2. Variety
3. Leash
4. Resting place
5. Chinese temple
6. Tiny
7. Embrace
8. Smell
9. Sidling
10. Investment
11. Thicken
12. Bunny's kin
13. Observer
22. Most unsatisfactory
24. Compete
25. Circle or city
26. Cutting
28. Gravy, e.g.
29. Succession
31. Atop
32. Number
33. "Home ___"
34. Writing surface
35. Leak
37. Own
38. Make payment
41. Waste conduit
47. Find the sum
48. Soft
50. Obeyed
51. Lubricated
53. Evaluated
54. Bean curd
55. Spring bloom
56. Gander or stag
57. Eastern exercise
59. Get up
60. Concluded
61. Morays
64. Large vase
66. Actor Milland

PUZZLE 139

ACROSS

1. ___ Mahal
4. Epic
8. Aggressive
13. Emma Peel portrayer
17. Tokyo, formerly
18. Composer Markevitch
19. Ancient Roman port
20. Soprano Moffo
21. "Blue Bayou" singer
23. Gorge
24. Nature's Band-Aid
25. Tackle
26. Phony
28. Parrots
30. More capable
32. More certain
33. Greek cheese
34. Onion's kin
35. Separate
36. Radio, in London
40. ___ de Cologne
41. Orr's scores
42. Australian shout
43. Cash dispenser: abbr.
44. Moola
46. Musical sound
47. Sycamore, e.g.
48. Hankering
49. Bundled hay
50. Singer Reese
51. Domains
54. Turmoil
55. Pencil top
56. French priests
57. Recipient of a gift
58. Kimono sashes
59. Blue-dye herb
60. Intimidate
61. Peer
65. Naval off.
66. Comedian Hill
67. Eye color
68. Cream or cube
69. Part of a Reuben
71. Distributed
72. Irritated state
73. Ventilates
74. Suggestions
75. Tall flowers
76. Eastwood and Walker
79. Billiards shot
80. Author Heyerdahl
81. ___ avis
82. Football coach Rockne
84. Vaguely
88. "___ for All Seasons"
89. ___ alia
90. Gabor and Peron
91. Skater Babilonia
92. Supernatural power
93. Destitute
94. Bump
95. Drench

DOWN

1. Thrice: pref.
2. Bustle
3. Medieval entertainer
4. Hindu lute
5. Seaweed
6. Deity
7. Slyly
8. Pouch
9. Escort
10. Asterisk
11. Belonging to John
12. Talked on and on
13. Alfalfa or Spanky, e.g.
14. Andes empire
15. Nibble
16. Chews the fat
22. Look for
27. Onassis and namesakes
29. Suit to ___
30. Guinness of films
31. Admirer
32. Gap
33. Inlet
35. Ballads
36. Suitor
37. Holliman and Weaver
38. Stone monument
39. Blur
41. Unfriendly bacteria
42. Actress Webb
45. Lined
46. Printer's insert
47. Twit
49. Easter pet
50. Workshop tool

PUZZLE 139

51. Rarer

52. Blackest black

53. Put down

54. Discovered

55. Receded

57. Ivey and Delaney

58. Seeps

60. Soft leather

61. Chatted

62. Mosque's towers

63. Etching fluid

64. Seines

66. Young herring

67. Cacklers

70. Chimp's treat

71. It loves company

72. Atlantic City machine

74. Detested

75. Apparition

76. Study for finals

77. Dalai ___

78. Turkey's neighbor

79. Silent

80. Govt. agent

83. Opposite of SSW

85. Eden exile

86. Thai language

87. Puppy plaint

PUZZLE 140

ACROSS

1. Fundamental
6. Machines' parts
10. Midas's metal
14. Pretentious
15. Sulawesi ox
16. Muffin topping
17. Apiculture
19. Swerve
20. Large parrot
21. Electrical unit
22. Exhausted
23. Refer (to)
26. Blacksmith, at times
28. Talking starling
30. Redeem
34. Leave by ladder
37. Shade of green
40. Pair
41. Prisoner
42. Culture mediums
43. Know the ___ and outs
44. Fish delicacy
45. Confusion
46. Pop
48. Pull weeds
50. Rude person
52. Old-floor sound
55. Kindle
59. Quartet doubled
62. Laboratory bottle
64. Be sociable
65. Ram's coat
66. Largest portion
69. Hence
70. ___ India Company
71. Hole-boring tool
72. Sofa or bench
73. Readies the presses
74. Smallest

DOWN

1. Rum-soaked cake
2. Staggering
3. Be a thief
4. Interrogate
5. Soap ingredient
6. Guitar device
7. Indigo shrubs
8. June, e.g.
9. Slump
10. Rule
11. Olive genus
12. Nasty look
13. Small boat
18. Fairly matched
22. Withdraw
24. Ref
25. Coloring agent
27. Mine shipments
29. Aquatic plant
31. Provoke
32. Holds the deed to
33. Greatest
34. Light beige
35. Airshow maneuver
36. Rare person
38. Galoot
39. Defeat decisively
42. Pay to play
45. Ilk
46. Marsh
47. Vase
49. Wildcat
51. Motor fluids
53. Of birds
54. Newsstand
56. Picture
57. Car needs
58. Put forth
59. Has unpaid bills
60. Heart
61. Roman garment
63. Hill builders
66. Oahu necklace
67. Viewed
68. Shade

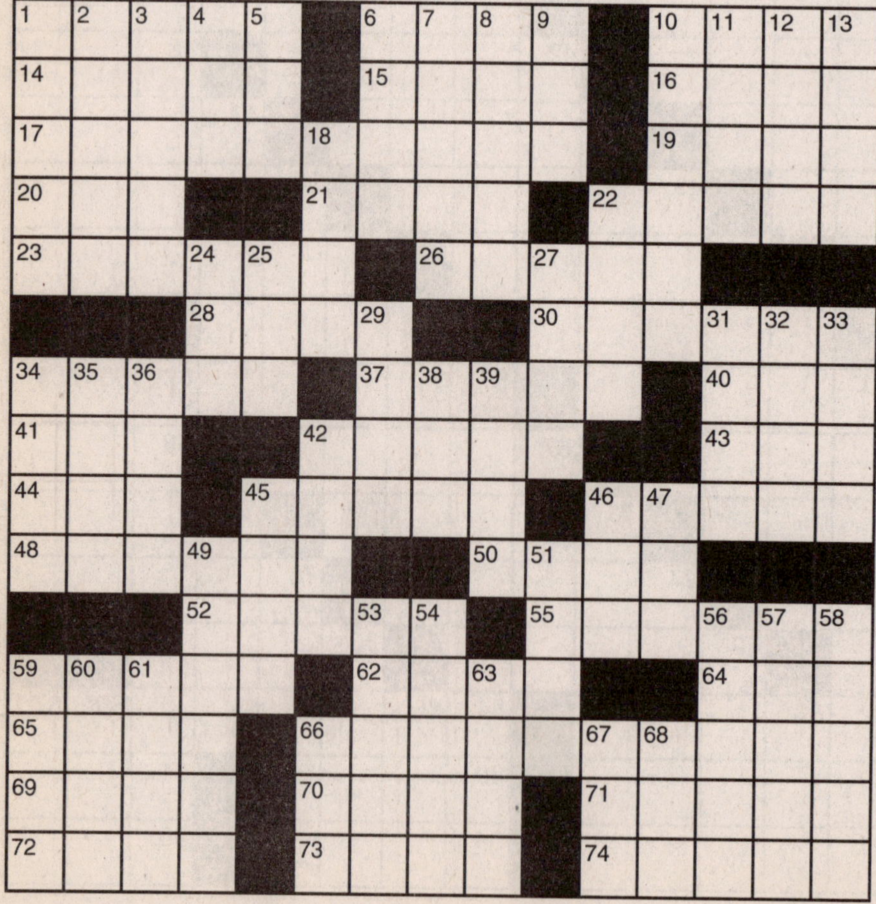

PUZZLE 141

ACROSS

1. Drudge
5. Assist nefariously
9. Faux pas
14. Arm bone
15. Winter Olympics event
16. Antipathy
17. Closed hand
18. Slight advantage
19. Stanza
20. Tlingit pole
22. Category of art
24. Twilight, in poems
25. One who presses
27. Eaten away
29. Kind of doll
31. Cook's vessel
32. Drape
33. Pencil utensil
35. Empty interval
36. Gone
40. Meaty
41. Cumshaw
42. Printer's proof
43. Butter's alternative
44. Have property
45. In the middle
46. Dismantle
48. Cow chow
49. Change color
50. Ate nothing
53. Feast or ___
55. Everything
56. Colorless
58. Curl producers
61. Place for tennis
63. Back then
65. Spew
66. Conductor Lehman ___
67. Glance over
68. Small fish
69. Cranky
70. Watch over
71. Piece of wood

DOWN

1. Clump of hair
2. Potpourri
3. Incite
4. At some future time
5. Tavern beverage
6. Allowance
7. Tent caterpillar
8. New driver
9. Rule
10. Summer quencher
11. Canned
12. Signal flare
13. Edit
21. Glum
23. Sow's opposite
26. Neither's mate
28. Eyed
29. "___ Man"
30. Nutmeg coat
32. General Arnold
34. Yell
35. Juniper liquor
37. Of the skin
38. Altercation
39. Musical quality
41. Pair
42. Immerse again
44. Chances
45. It's the word!
47. In a tidy way
48. French dance
50. Gem surface
51. Secluded
52. Garden pests
53. Barrier
54. Craves
57. Give a party
59. Isinglass
60. Don't strike
62. Leave work behind: abbr.
64. Final bit

1	2	3	4	■	5	6	7	8	■	9	10	11	12	13
14				■	15				■	16				
17				■	18				■	19				
20				21	■	22			23		■	24		
■	■	25			26			■	27		28			
29	30		■	31			■	32				■	■	■
33			34			■	35			■	36	37	38	39
40					■	41			■	42				
43				■	44			■	45					
■	■	■	46	47			■	48			■	49		
50	51	52				■	53				54		■	■
55			■	56		57			■	58			59	60
61			62		■	63			64	■	65			
66					■	67				■	68			
69					■	70				■	71			

PUZZLE 142

ACROSS

1. One of the deck
5. Reveal
9. The majority
13. Muffin topper
14. Light rings
16. Needle case
17. Prudence
19. Extreme
20. Japanese mushroom
21. Harem chamber
22. Top-grade recipient
23. Morning drop
24. Tumbler volume
28. Those people
29. Slangy yes
30. Varnish ingredient
33. Formal request
37. Digger
39. Heavy metal
40. Baby fox
42. During
43. White heron
45. Free
48. Two, in Madrid
49. Frequently, to a poet
52. Sandy mound
53. Plumpest
55. Linen robe
58. Computer info
61. Mouths
62. Uncanny
64. Algerian seaport
65. Delicacy
68. Filth
69. Musical transition
70. Wise about
71. Olive genus
72. Midday
73. Final

DOWN

1. Encrypted
2. Dress cut
3. Plant again
4. Landing pier
5. Female
6. Stetson or bowler
7. Stews
8. Sylvan
9. Award
10. Of the ear
11. Positive
12. Stratum
15. Predicament
18. Not wrong
25. Oahu wreath
26. On a rampage
27. Downs' partner
28. Fork section
30. Buddhist priest
31. Miner's portal
32. Formally yield
33. ___ Piper
34. Therefore
35. Craggy peaks
36. Not a bit
38. Slice off
41. Ocean motion
44. Small fry
46. Kramden's vehicle
47. Come in
50. ___ the bill (pays)
51. Soup container
53. Mr. Claus
54. Romantic dance
55. Field of action
56. Rosters
57. Stupefy
58. Extinct bird
59. Nutmeg coating
60. Weight allowance
63. Organic compound
66. Pair
67. Yet, to a bard

PUZZLE 143

ACROSS

1. Killer whale
5. Wrestling maneuver
9. Central and Hyde
14. ___-do-well
15. Forest sight
16. Atmosphere layer
17. Make merry
19. Dinghy support
20. Angled annex
21. Aha!
23. Rents
24. Chef's utensil
25. Caustic stuff
27. Stimulated
31. Fido's strap
34. Puts to sea
35. Cupid's dart
37. "___ So Fine"
39. Verbal test
40. Deviate
41. Forbidden thing
42. Neither hide ___ hair
43. Freezing rain
44. Impertinent
45. Well-groomed
47. Regardless
49. Bar drink
50. Need aspirin
51. Teen's woe
54. Modernized
58. Classified notices
61. Colorful language
63. Desk item
65. Chinese "bear"
66. Makes furious
67. Employer
68. Influences
69. Penny, e.g.
70. Flushed

DOWN

1. In the past
2. Rod's partner
3. Monastery room
4. "Bells ___ Ringing"
5. Leapt
6. Impostor
7. Pay to play
8. Gentle
9. Pea container
10. Southern shrub
11. Wander about
12. Weave yarn
13. Matched groups
18. Pork and ___
22. Mix of two or more metals
24. Capsule
26. Spreading evergreen
27. Hammerin' Hank ___
28. Jeweled headpiece
29. Not on time
30. Fouled up
32. Yell
33. Therefore
34. Dad's boy
36. Fare
38. Milk alternative
40. Slicker
41. Screw's cousin
43. Pen
44. One who watches
46. Chic
48. Most rational
51. Deadly serpents
52. Scratch
53. Granny
55. Spectacular
56. Venture
57. Unlocked
58. To boot
59. Engraved stamps
60. Peppy
62. Engine fuel
64. Nasty mutt

1	2	3	4	■	5	6	7	8	■	9	10	11	12	13
14				■	15				■	16				
17				18					■	19				
20			■	21					22	■	23			
■	■	■	24			■	■	■	25	26		■	■	■
■	27	28				29	30	■	31			32	33	■
34					■	35		36			■	37		38
39				■	40					■	41			
42			■	43					■	44				
■	45		46			■	47		48					■
■	■	■	49			■	■	■	50			■	■	■
51	52	53		■	54	55	56	57			■	58	59	60
61				62	■	63					64			
65					■	66				■	67			
68					■	69				■	70			

PUZZLE 144

FLOWER POWER

The answers to this petaled puzzle will go in a curve from the number on the outside to the center of the flower. Each number in the flower will have two 5-letter answers. One goes in a clockwise direction and the second in a counterclockwise direction. We have entered two answers to help you begin.

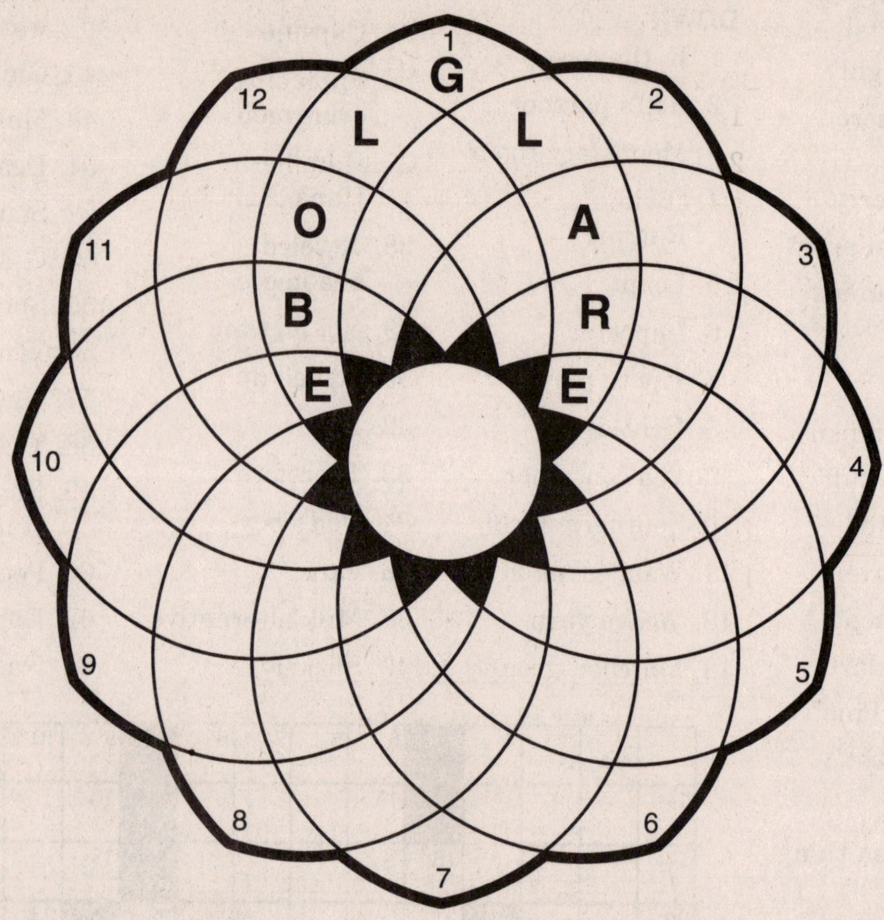

CLOCKWISE

1. Fierce look
2. Speckle
3. Cent
4. Milk factory
5. Float aimlessly
6. Loony
7. Dim
8. Rose spike
9. Type of net
10. First-year cadet
11. Plants
12. Polish

COUNTERCLOCKWISE

1. Orb
2. Ignite
3. "___ Suite"
4. Plow name
5. Waltz, e.g.
6. Enjoy a martini
7. Pixie
8. Chewy candy
9. Capital-letter key
10. Showy flower
11. Tease
12. Actress Close

PUZZLE 145

ACROSS

1. Coral ___
5. Yearned
10. Arrange
14. Morally bad
15. Male duck
16. Three voices
17. Frenzy
18. Labyrinths
19. Evaluate
20. Sticky stuff
22. Slaved
24. Angler's tool
25. Metal sources
26. Sharp knock
27. Covered
28. Woodlands
32. Yale, e.g.
35. Go by plane
36. Garden tool
37. Bank transactions
38. Not me
39. Burst of flame
41. Sunflower product
42. Price label
43. Felonies
44. Flourish
47. Barnyard animal
48. Above, in poems
49. Liquid measure
50. Observed
53. Snare
56. Flowering shrub
58. Animal's home
59. Treasury agent Ness
61. Gather leaves
62. Prom car
63. Investigate in depth
64. For keeps
65. Large amount
66. Flirted
67. Existed

DOWN

1. Played over
2. Avoid
3. Twice four
4. Scamper away
5. Halsey, for one
6. Desired strongly
7. Mists
8. ___ out a living
9. Ruin
10. Wide streak
11. Spoken
12. Church ceremony
13. Like some stockings
21. Performs alone
23. Rowing blade
27. Trick
28. Cold-weather ailment
29. Counterfeit
30. Yanked
31. Comprehends
32. Messy fellow
33. Spring
34. Angelic headwear
35. Thick mist
38. Colorful tuber
39. Border
40. Fired up
42. Underwater missile
43. Glided
45. Distress
46. Baltic or Bering
47. Channel
49. Dentist's tool
50. Gracious
51. Inquisitive one
52. What place?
53. House additions
54. Hammer's target
55. Clock a race
57. Witch's concoction
60. Journey section

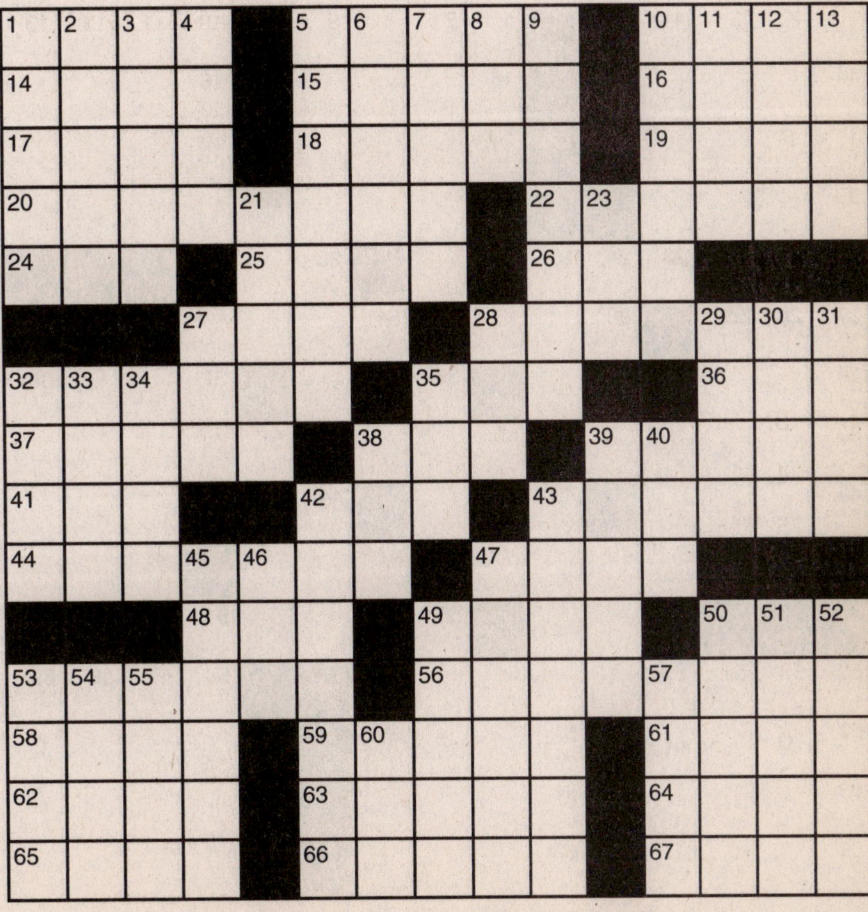

PUZZLE 146

ACROSS

1. Clam's case
6. Disagreement
10. Mouth parts
14. Tree marsupial
15. Lake, in Scotland
16. Neutral color
17. Analysis
18. Opposer
19. Invalid
20. Empty out
21. Instructions
23. Fire's remains
26. New Zealand parrot
27. "I ___ a Teenage Zombie"
30. Pea abode
31. Soup legume
34. Amass
36. Persian or Siamese
37. Cow's foot
39. Tatter
40. Cuddle
41. Paint finish
42. Summit
43. Pet rock, e.g.
44. Upper house
45. Staircase shape
47. Through
48. Drunkard
49. Clear
50. Masculine
52. Mushroom
56. Brilliant fish
60. Seed cover
61. Malicious
62. Giraffe's kin
63. Assembled
64. Withered
65. Poet's product
66. Beseeched
67. Deuce topper
68. Did arithmetic

DOWN

1. Card game
2. Garden tube
3. Freedom from difficulty
4. South American animal
5. "Now I ___ me . . ."
6. Scheduled
7. Cornmeal cakes
8. Official records
9. Clump of bushes
10. Biblical beast
11. Holy image
12. Prudish one
13. Soap bubbles
22. Chick's mama
24. Potato
25. Soil-breaking tool
27. Stinger
28. Pains
29. Leftover piece
31. Dawdle
32. Small quantities
33. Gambling game
35. Reignited
36. Chew the ___ (ponder)
38. Distance measures
40. Actor Linden
41. Ground grain
43. Most plump
44. Moral lapse
46. Legal thing
47. Hollow
50. Watered silk
51. Harnessed
52. Pack down
53. Not injected
54. Camp assistant
55. "___ There"
57. Oater friend
58. Church part
59. Hurried
62. Reproductive cells

PUZZLE 147

ACROSS

1. Lacking hair
5. Rapid
10. Usually, to a poet
13. Molding curve
14. Errands
16. By means of
17. Nonsense
18. Custom
19. Tissue thickness
20. Stiff hair
21. Generations
22. Noblemen
24. Beast of Borden
26. In that place
28. More unusual
31. Mexican shawls
33. Prospector's find
34. Neither good nor bad
36. Bro's sibling
39. Lawn material
40. Restricted
42. Sort
43. Female bighorn
44. Go backward
45. Latin way
46. Photo takers
49. Deceive
51. Declare
53. Enemy
54. Male deer
55. Crest
58. Hang loosely
62. Brutus's breakfast?
63. Charm
65. Ballet bend
66. Fish catcher
67. Greet
68. Bards' sunsets
69. Sooner than, in poems
70. Charger
71. Spoils

DOWN

1. Swamps
2. Fever and chills
3. Not right
4. Mar
5. Threaded fastener
6. Hum
7. Bit
8. Confounds
9. Social drink
10. Burdensome
11. "The Most Happy ___"
12. Secret meeting
15. Snooze
23. "You ___ My Love"
25. Exam format
27. Pulled
28. Increased
29. Lined up
30. Do over
31. Forward roll
32. Writer Jong
35. Swamps
37. Pelvic bones
38. Card game
41. Art ___
47. Astern
48. Flat-topped hills
50. Assistant
51. Ring
52. Critic, at times
53. Honored
56. Indication
57. Apportion
59. Biscuit topper
60. Bits of fiber
61. Fewer
64. Bell and Barker

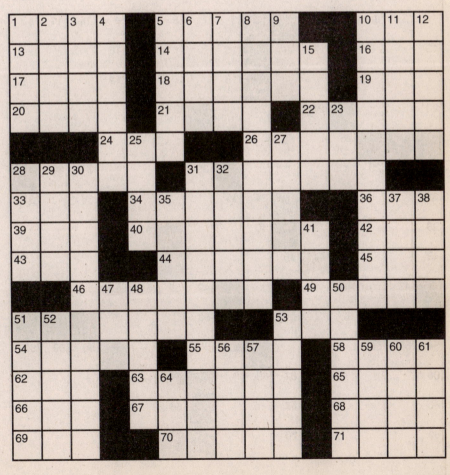

PUZZLE 148

ACROSS

1. Type of tie
6. Spigot
9. Bullets and bombs
13. French wine
15. Make haste
16. Hoodlum
17. Compassionate
18. Notable span
19. Roof overhang
20. Certainly!
21. Chess piece
23. Lope
25. Former Italian money
26. Highest medal
27. Next to
30. Group of eight
33. Gator's relative
34. Summon
36. Gorilla
38. Dim
40. Make free of
41. Monarch
43. Tolkien creature
44. Dwindled
46. Deplores
47. Tijuana dish
49. Heartfelt
52. Made angry
53. Wood splitters
54. Decorates
57. Hipbones
58. Large cask
61. Metamorphic stage
62. Unfavorable
64. Challenge
66. Wallop
67. Have bills
68. Combines
69. Or ___
70. Large parrot
71. Ridicule severely

DOWN

1. In need of a massage
2. Turn around
3. Machines' parts
4. Danish money
5. Alley item
6. Now and ___
7. Diver's necessity
8. Proud bird
9. Outline
10. Castle defense
11. Budge
12. Humdinger
14. Shreds
22. Liquid-filled mattress
24. Transform
25. Thrash
26. Large quantity
27. Summit
28. Hog's sound
29. Main blood vessel
31. Worth
32. Thrusting weapons
35. Struggle
37. Once, once
39. Crave
42. Coffeepots
45. Large antelope
48. Optical illusion
50. Basic tenet
51. Harvester
54. Church recess
55. Boring
56. Composition
57. Notion
58. Galba's garb
59. Capitalizes on
60. Tree home
63. Respect
65. Con's foe

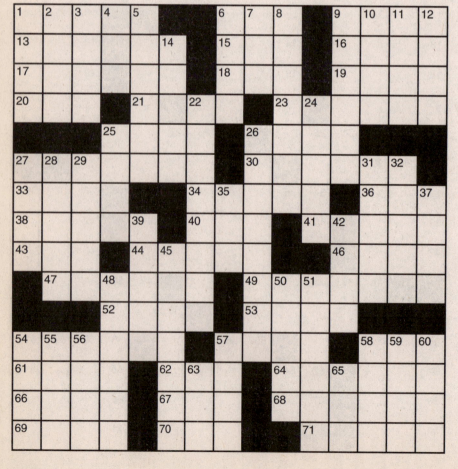

PUZZLE 149

ACROSS

1. Golfing pegs
5. Cobbler's utensil
8. Hiker's trail
12. Possess
13. Groom's attendant
15. Feel great pity
16. Cooled
17. Album entry
18. Look rudely
19. Small woody plants
21. Taunted
23. Peak
26. Circle segment
27. Inhale and exhale
29. Goodies
33. Raised, as rabbits
34. Army noncom
36. Coin opening
37. Three strikes
38. To's associate
39. Single thing
40. Agitated state
42. Fixed gaze
44. Guy
45. Audio system
47. Main
49. Rower's need
50. Literary work
51. Guarantee
54. Job or story
58. Tattle
59. Informal talk
63. Wrench, e.g.
64. Lounge
65. Eagle's claw
66. Molecule part
67. Fencing sword
68. Track action
69. Unlawful flights

DOWN

1. "___ Old Man"
2. Apiece
3. At any time
4. Won over
5. Cigarette residue
6. Reporter's question
7. Say yes to
8. Queens' houses
9. Certain air heroes
10. "How do I love ___?"
11. Cattle group
13. Unexpected results
14. Spin
20. Swimsuit top
22. Foul up
24. Long pole
25. Apartment balcony
27. Full force
28. Fasten again
30. Hawaiian hello
31. Of sound
32. Phase
33. Employer
35. Vidal et al.
41. Distress
42. Most tender
43. "___ Pulver" (film)
44. Fine glassware
46. Corn serving
48. Hosiery shade
51. Competent
52. Spill, as liquid
53. Bargain
55. Tad
56. Condemn
57. "Desire Under the ___"
60. Site for scientists
61. Tavern brew
62. Negative word

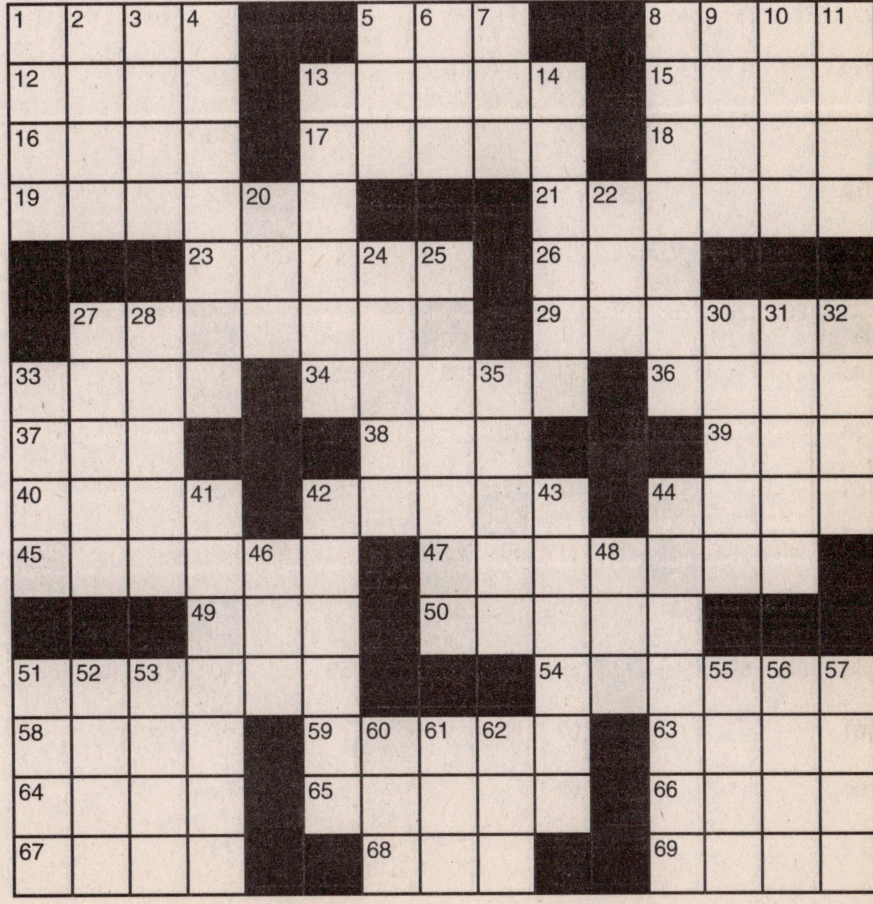

PUZZLE 150

ACROSS

1. Hunk
5. Endorse
9. Dice
13. Insect stage
14. Squabble
15. Untruthful one
16. Periods
17. Frothy
18. Golden Rule word
19. Glowing
21. Skier's line
22. Ordinal suffixes
23. Mooch
26. Made beforehand
29. Circle section
30. Request
33. Char
34. Truncate
36. Nth ___
38. Marine
40. Yuletide drink
42. Prolonged attack
43. Wildcat
45. Block
47. Watch your ___!
48. Unite in marriage
49. Chinese tea
51. A or Z
53. Smoked sausage
55. Tubular pasta
58. Infirm
59. Boggy
64. Repeat
65. Leather
67. Milan money, once
68. Catches sight of
69. Platters
70. Adequate, to a bard
71. Odyssey
72. Very dry
73. Basted

DOWN

1. Practice boxing
2. Olympic event
3. Imitated
4. Clobber
5. Slangy chum
6. Quartz variety
7. Roof topper
8. Significant term
9. Like this puzzle
10. Covert suggestion
11. Pledge
12. Masters
14. Celestial
20. On holiday
24. Black, to poets
25. Super serves
26. Serenity
27. Talked wildly
28. Epochal
30. Alpine ridge
31. Rocker Bob ___
32. Reserve
33. December forecast
35. Whale group
37. Essence
39. Places
41. Showy
44. Christians, e.g.
46. Mixes up
50. Entice
52. Shooter
53. Newsstand
54. Dim
55. Enthusiasm
56. Bakery employee
57. "Of ___ I Sing"
60. Strong brews
61. Quarry
62. Ship's front
63. Bored reaction
66. Color

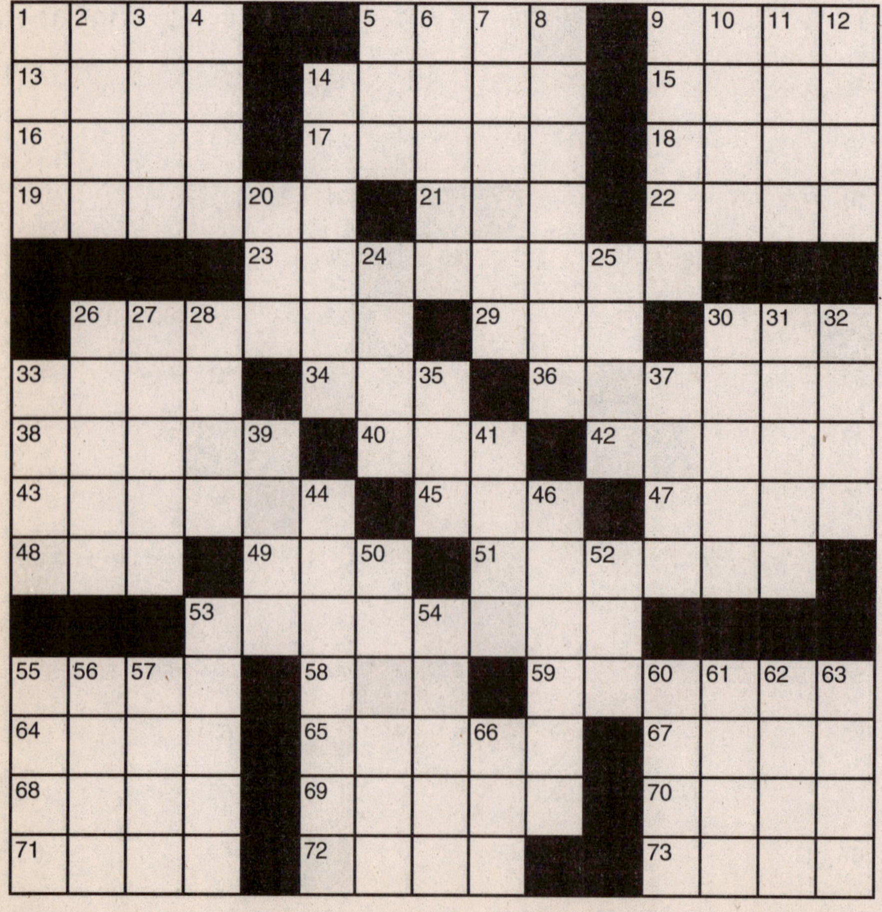

PUZZLE 151

ACROSS

1. Scrub a space mission
6. Turkish titles
10. Sleeping place
14. Electrician, often
15. Love seat
16. Bouncing sound
17. Grassy plain
18. Eucalyptus eater
20. Almost never
22. Baby buggy
23. Andy Capp's drink
24. Vigor
26. Nastier
28. Umbrella
32. Airplane part
33. Final
34. Use a towel
36. Check
40. Scoundrel
42. ___ whiz!
43. Pitfall
44. Mournful sound
45. Hold title to
47. Phone feature, sometimes
48. Wrong way for Greeley
50. In theory
52. Cave
55. Ignited
56. Green
57. Salamanders
60. Roofing straw
65. Pardons
68. Banishment
69. Deviate
70. Fringe
71. Showed once more
72. Conclusions
73. Sign type
74. Tundra vehicles

DOWN

1. Shoemaking tools
2. Ill temper
3. By word of mouth
4. Rip up
5. Scout units
6. Query
7. Gooey stuff
8. Distantly
9. Deli meat
10. Society entrant
11. Atlantic or Arctic
12. Fissile rock
13. More painful
19. Modifies
21. Cat call
25. Dilemma
27. Things to be done
28. Benefit
29. Nerve-cell part
30. Boil over
31. Protective charm
32. Boll ___
35. Soup veggie
37. Dog's wagger
38. Of an age
39. Put trust (in)
41. Makes jubilant
46. Ready for print
49. Relent
51. Airs
52. Somber
53. Curly noodles
54. Had as property
58. Time and ___ wait . . .
59. Utah lily
61. Skating maneuver
62. Fatigue
63. Attired
64. Female birds
66. Sets for med. dramas
67. Old Japanese coin

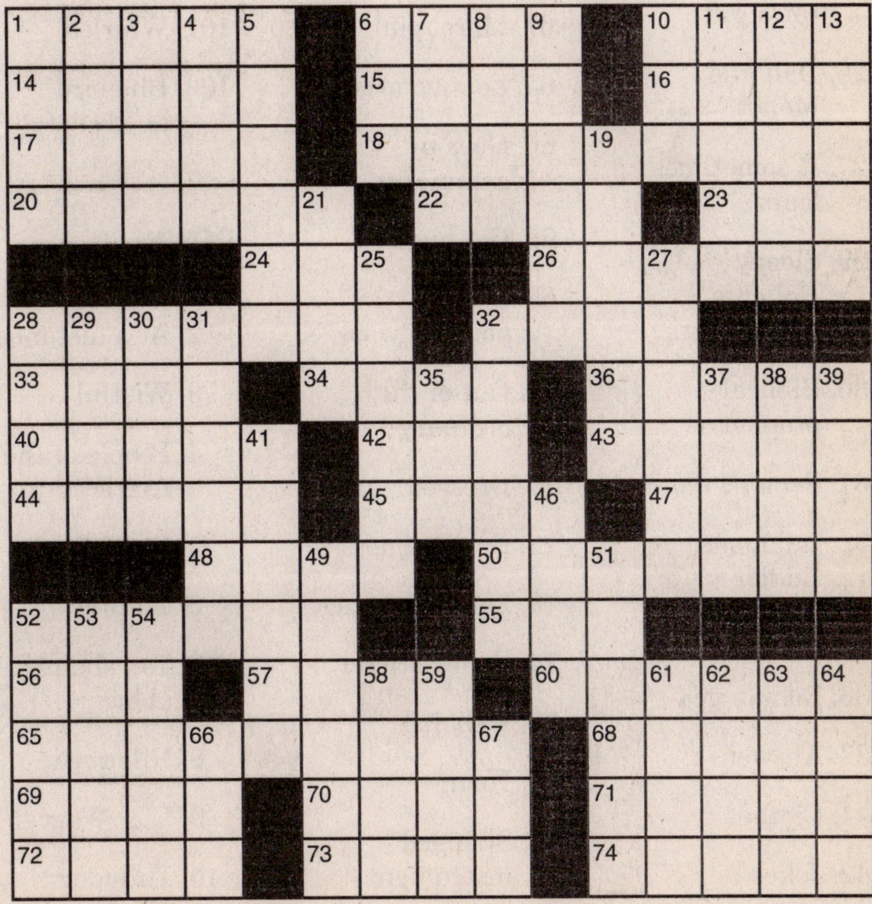

PUZZLE 152

ACROSS

1. Window section
5. Potato ___
9. Quick on the ___
13. Furlough
17. Sky sightings: abbr.
18. Halo
19. Thorny blossom
20. Highlighted song
21. Cher film
22. Bring in a crop
23. Peter Cottontail's gift
25. Dali and Monet
27. It sometimes leaps
29. Sleepy Hollow's Ichabod ___
30. Biblical prophet
31. Senior's dance
32. Infamous fiddler
34. Radiant
36. Roman god
37. Answer
41. Clothes
42. Jokes
43. Walks quietly
44. Caviar source
45. "Mikado" costume item
46. Basketball side
47. Cad
48. Magnitude
49. Small flute
51. Fairy godmother's stick
52. Founded
53. Unusual
57. Rough, like a snake
60. Beer, slangily
61. Marsupial
65. Lounge around
66. Goes by catamaran
68. Got bigger
69. "...have you ___ wool?"
70. Out of the ordinary
71. Dressed
72. Fruit stones
73. Leave the stage
74. Coffee stirrer
77. Webbing
78. Foam
79. Stringed instrument
80. Toad bump
81. Noose
82. Author Wilde
85. Polite cough
86. Matt Dillon, e.g.
89. Tall hat
92. Chilled
94. Des Moines's state
95. Flimsy, as an excuse
96. ___ Major
97. Shade of color
98. Units
99. Unrefined metals
100. Sugar source
101. Whirled
102. Bluebird's abode

DOWN

1. Cougar
2. At a distance
3. Wistful
4. People of the Arctic
5. Carries
6. Tints
7. Tax shelter: abbr.
8. Nile reed
9. "___ Weaver"
10. Thunder
11. Beast of burden
12. Damp
13. Brightly-colored bird
14. Territory
15. Omen
16. Kitchen herb
24. Beige
26. Plant
28. Eternity
31. Use a loudspeaker
32. Indicates agreement
33. If not
34. At the peak of
35. Mongolian desert
36. Prefer
37. Riyadh resident
38. Eye part
39. Trickle
40. Want
42. Gold leaf
43. Bodies of water
46. Pretty
47. Rendered fats
48. Speaks
50. Nun's room
51. Was willing
52. Part of the face
54. Chinese or Korean
55. Sheree or Jay

PUZZLE 152

56. Tarzan's companions
57. Piggy-bank opening
58. Secret writing
59. "The Four Seasons" actor
62. Jazz instrument
63. Squadron
64. Legend
66. Native of Glasgow
67. Sunbather's pain reliever
68. Heart of the matter
72. Lets
73. Natural force
75. Works hard
76. Not polluted
77. Daisy ___
78. "___ he's a jolly..."
80. Cake or germ
81. Loaded
82. City near Lillehammer
83. Leading actress
84. Show up
85. Church part
86. Food list
87. Astonishes
88. Survive
90. Tavern
91. Rage
93. Dirty Harry, e.g.

PUZZLE 153

ACROSS

1. One-edged sword
6. Substitute worker
10. Pinnacle
14. Treeless plain
15. Leaf's angle
16. Malayan boat
17. Caravan stop
18. Railings
20. Phases
22. Office note
23. Several
24. Sulu's station
25. Mushroom top
27. Soothing salve
29. Small biological space
32. Old-fashioned
35. Northern toymaker
38. Turmoil
40. Actor Richard ___
41. Welsh cheese dish
43. Buzzing insects
45. Cinch
46. Bathhouse
48. Sailor's response
49. Dogma
51. Excellent
53. High notes
55. Abundance
56. Tea choice
60. Last of the log
62. Corrode
64. Caster
66. Customers
69. Renown
70. Pitch
71. Teeter
72. Secure again
73. Impresses
74. Inserts
75. Anesthetic of old

DOWN

1. Wade
2. Like Pegasus
3. Fundamental
4. Puzzlement
5. Ascended
6. Account
7. Specimen
8. Road distance
9. Probe
10. Quick to learn
11. Soft drink
12. Poet's dawn
13. Not hard
19. Sudsy stuff
21. Picturesque
26. Pathways from hearts
28. Tibetan monk
30. Polish
31. Breakout
33. Make laugh
34. Or ___!
35. Formerly
36. Bowler's path
37. Right to vote
39. Lack of musical ability
42. Foil's relative
44. Jeep
47. Hurried about
50. Arctic or sooty
52. Soldier's lodging
54. Collection of Hindu aphorisms
57. Fabric
58. Creepy
59. Laundromat item
60. Deeds
61. Snail's pace
63. Plant
65. Brute
67. Hazardous curve
68. Certain trains

1	2	3	4	5	■	6	7	8	9	■	10	11	12	13
14					■	15				■	16			
17					■	18				19				
20					21	■	22				■	23		
24				■	25	26		■	27		28		■	■
■	■	■	29	30				31	■	32			33	34
35	36	37	■	38					39	■	40			
41			42				■	43		44				
45				■	46		47				■	48		
49				50	■	51					52	■	■	■
■	■	53			54	■	55			■	56	57	58	59
60	61		■	62		63		■	64	65				
66			67					68	■	69				
70				■	71				■	72				
73				■	74				■	75				

PUZZLE 154

ACROSS

1. Cup of joe
5. Trim excess from
9. Figure
14. Water buffaloes
15. Imitator
16. Not as old
17. Do in, as a dragon
18. Bridge section
19. Seasons
20. Steersman's place
21. Pointed
23. October birthstone
25. Potent particles
28. Radiance
30. Gentle animal
33. Rub off
35. Wrinkle-prone fabric
36. Touches lightly
38. Clump of turf
39. Pitcher's stat
40. Sediment
43. Cuddle
44. Flow back
45. Golden ___ (retiree)
46. Remove
48. Cabbage's kin
50. Posse
52. Back of the neck
53. Category
55. At the summit
57. Kermit, once
60. Throw lightly
64. Cupid's target
67. Heavy metal
68. "Do ___ others . . ."
69. Game-show host
70. Convertibles
71. Hearty breads
72. Like pale colors
73. Captain's direction
74. World's fair, e.g.

DOWN

1. Tease
2. Wheel rod
3. ___ cutlet
4. From now on
5. Italian staple
6. Horrify
7. Gather in
8. Coastal eagle
9. Map feature
10. Field
11. Carpenter's tool
12. Capture
13. Hesitant sounds
22. Jewish cleric
24. Chinese mammal
26. Accident
27. Mate
28. Auto safety device
29. No can do
31. Bedeck
32. Pas' mates
34. Threshold
35. Onion relative
37. Office writer
41. ___ on (urged)
42. Soup or coat
47. Ecstatic joy
49. Meal course
51. Abundant
54. Gave a PG to
56. Taut
58. Type type
59. Aloud
61. Black stone
62. Stair
63. Ho-hum
64. Fashion line
65. Australian bird
66. False front

1	2	3	4	■	5	6	7	8	■	9	10	11	12	13
14				■	15				■	16				
17				■	18				■	19				
20				■	21				22			■	■	■
■	■	■	23	24			■	■	25			26	27	■
■	28	29			■	30	31	32		■	33			34
35					■	■	36			37	■	38		
39			■	40	41	42					■	43		
44			■	45				■	■	46	47			
48			49	■	50			51	■	52				■
■	53			54		■	■	55	56			■	■	■
■	■	■	57			58	59			■	60	61	62	63
64	65	66			■	67				■	68			
69					■	70				■	71			
72					■	73				■	74			

PUZZLE 155

BEES IN YOUR BONNET

ACROSS

1. Harry's lady
5. Door part
9. Descartes word
13. Make beer
17. Leave off
18. Cleveland Indian?
19. Trickle
20. Took transportation
21. Marathon segment
22. Ell
23. Greenhouse square
24. Mrs. Chaplin
25. Bully
28. Front
30. Suffer
31. For takeout
33. Columnist Landers
34. Most vertically challenged
39. Firecracker sound
41. Habitation
45. Incline
46. AAA suggestion
47. Game-preserve herd
49. Geometry calculation
50. Rolled item
51. Oblation
54. Arctic explorer
55. Pesky insect
56. Building block
59. Friendship 7 astronaut
61. Texas nine
63. The works
65. Snob
67. Golfer Trevino
68. Caught off-guard
72. Haggard
74. Upright
78. Stroll
79. A cry for help
81. You, once
82. Bashful
83. Mecca man
84. Fume
86. Roaring Twenties, e.g.
88. Prune
89. Category
91. Disagreement
93. Bushy-tailed rodent
95. Lyrical before
97. First person
99. Scratch the surface
100. New kid in town
104. Fortysome-thing
110. Long haul
111. Pronto, initially
113. Passport stamp
114. Miniature missive
115. Staff member
116. Calendar entry
117. Paradise
118. Arkansas town
119. Country bumpkin
120. Bird treat
121. Unlikely prom king
122. Caterpillar kind

DOWN

1. Failure
2. Saudi prince
3. Grain elevator
4. Flight attendant
5. Ring bearer?
6. Italian song
7. Brand-new
8. Sire
9. Second sight
10. "60 Minutes" name, once
11. Chap
12. "Don Giovanni," e.g.
13. Frugal gourmet?
14. Space
15. Novelist Ferber
16. Withdraw gradually
26. Drill attachment
27. Rip off
29. Quotable collection
32. Meander
34. Greek portico
35. Principal
36. Not fooled by
37. Bachelor party
38. Lets the cat out of the bag
40. Rotary Club symbol
42. Normandy river
43. Sugar substitute?
44. Grub
48. No joke
52. Recover
53. Toro retort
57. Tortuous task
58. Forest dweller

PUZZLE 155

60. Wyle of "ER"

62. Born in France

64. Without

66. Scottish river

68. Festoon

69. Fleet beast

70. Buck heroine

71. Ellipsis marks

73. Caligula's nephew

75. Neutral tone

76. Cote sounds

77. Sort

80. Split up

85. Bankroll

87. Fabric strip

88. King topper

90. East ender?

92. Bar bill

94. Cultural Revolution leader

96. Zounds!

98. Guru

100. Pierce

101. ZZ Top, e.g.

102. Improve

103. Jacob's twin

105. Wait

106. Belgian flower

107. Seconds

108. Harrow's rival

109. Leftovers

112. Apple of one's eye

PUZZLE 156

ACROSS

1. Ids' counter-parts
5. Gossip
9. Greek finale
14. Certain Scandinavian
15. Again
16. British title
17. Culture medium
18. Talking bird
19. Silver bar
20. Deli sausage
22. Pointer
24. Slangy negative
25. Looking at
27. Chantilly
29. Two, in Madrid
31. Recital piece
33. Campus buildings
36. Large dolphins
38. Dislikes
41. Raw metals
42. Rub clean
43. ERA or RBI
44. Troubadours
46. Puff away
47. Ranch animal
48. Dried up
50. Soak, as flax
51. Cat call?
53. Battery type
55. Active word
58. Rubbish
60. Hardy
63. Seed coats
65. Windmill blade
67. Reprobate
68. Opening
69. Islamic chief
70. So be it
71. Poor
72. Butterfly catchers
73. Minus

DOWN

1. Guido's high notes
2. Excessively enthusiastic
3. Having a milky iridescence
4. Mist
5. Spotted game tile
6. Poison ___
7. Lease money
8. Woodland path
9. Kimono sash
10. Affectation
11. Hence
12. Gooey stuff
13. Poker play
21. Young lady
23. Father
26. Stare
28. Romaine
29. Condemn
30. Gold braid
32. Egg shapes
34. Racetrack
35. Python, e.g.
37. Put together
39. German city
40. Editor's term
42. Slip-up
45. Kicker's aid
46. Denomination
49. Staircase parts
52. Intermingled
54. Of the ears
55. Too proud
56. Fish-eating eagle
57. Madden
59. Docile
61. Membership fees
62. Desires
64. Swine's abode
66. Young bug

PUZZLE 157

ACROSS

1. Analyze a sentence
6. Flees
10. Suit item
14. 2nd President
15. Mosque official
16. Imprint firmly
17. Fusses
18. Place
19. Polynesian feast
20. Legendary story
21. Honorable
23. Supplies with fuel
25. Antitoxins
26. Attach a button
28. Swamps
33. Rascal
37. Spike of corn
40. Wash away
41. Stationery
42. Freudian term
43. Rushlike plant
44. Mountain ridge
45. Computer operating syst.
46. Donkeys
47. Genders
48. Shaggy ox
50. TV serial
54. Heaviness
59. Cushion cover
64. Blackthorn
65. Medicinal herb
66. Half-moon shape
67. Not fresh
68. Big cat
69. Alcohol lamp
70. Bygone
71. Come down to earth
72. Swarm
73. Poor

DOWN

1. Heads
2. Pass a bill
3. Ham operator's item
4. Protective garment
5. Road turn
6. Slur
7. Improper
8. Varnish finish
9. Daub
10. African plain
11. Needle case
12. Look at briefly
13. Vicious criminal
21. Consume
22. Junior, e.g.
24. Post-pasta drink
27. Gardener's nemesis
29. Rages
30. Batons
31. Perimeter
32. Beholds
33. Hot tubs
34. Worry
35. Acme
36. Give out
38. Way back when
39. Hopeful
49. Deep respect
51. Baby hooter
52. Intense, as pain
53. Lustrous satin
55. Yucca fiber
56. Forest clearing
57. Punctured
58. Very small
59. Satiate
60. Pelvic bones
61. "On Golden Pond" bird
62. Extend credit
63. Fabric joint
67. Father's boy

1	2	3	4	5	■	6	7	8	9	■	10	11	12	13
14					■	15				■	16			
17					■	18				■	19			
20				■	21					22				
23				24		■	25				■	■	■	■
■	■	■	■	26		27	■	■	■	28	29	30	31	32
33	34	35	36		■	37	38	39	■	40				
41					■	42			■	43				
44					■	45			■	46				
47					■	■	■	48	49		■	■	■	■
■	■	■	■	50	51	52	53	■	54		55	56	57	58
59	60	61	62					63		■	64			
65				■	66				■	67				
68				■	69				■	70				
71				■	72				■	73				

PUZZLE 158

ACROSS

1. Slides
6. Stitched
10. Dispute
14. Dark
15. Gumbo pod
16. Knitting rib
17. Dignity
18. Dam
19. Fervor
20. Boggy
22. Planned
24. Confused
26. Advertise
27. Wall clinger
29. Ampersands
31. Lead or zinc
35. Difficulties
36. Future fish
37. Angry outburst
38. Outfit
39. Popped
41. Feathery scarf
42. Kissers
44. Danish money
45. Nee
46. Daub
47. Above
48. Chunk of eternity
49. Cruel
51. Stable baby
53. Scraggly
56. Court cases
60. Of a historic time
61. The other guys
64. Tint again
65. Long hair
66. Pinch
67. Prevent
68. Large wading bird
69. Hit
70. Oui and ja

DOWN

1. Takes food
2. Be informed
3. Pelvic bones
4. Discourages
5. Stages
6. Piglet's mother
7. Increase
8. Bracelet locales
9. T-man
10. More sugary
11. Tropical tree
12. Wings
13. Tear
21. Craves
23. Muggy
25. Small buffalo
27. Vernacular
28. Fashion
30. Station
32. Forbidden
33. Decorate
34. Slender
35. "A Farewell to ___"
37. Brewing kettle
39. Mouselike animal
40. College teacher, shortly
43. Tacos' cousins
45. Accept
47. Haphazardly
50. Nonsupporters
52. Lineup
53. Interstate hauler
54. Seafood item
55. Hindu princess
57. Summer drinks
58. Small harp
59. Movie backdrops
62. Greek vowel
63. Doily

1	2	3	4	5	■	6	7	8	9	■	10	11	12	13
14					■	15				■	16			
17					■	18				■	19			
20					21	■	■	22		23				
■	■	■	24			25	■	26				■	■	■
■	27	28		■	29		30		■	31		32	33	34
35				■	36			■	37					
38			■	39				40			■	41		
42			43			■	44			■	45			
46					■	47				■	48			■
■	■	■	49		50		■	51		52		■	■	■
53	54	55					■	■	56			57	58	59
60				■	61		62	63	■	64				
65				■	66				■	67				
68				■	69				■	70				

PUZZLE 159

ACROSS

1. Nutmeg spice
5. Bachelors' homes
9. Honkers
14. Winglike parts
15. Flu symptom
16. Inquirer
17. Tale
18. Hang
19. Stalks
20. Slangy chum
21. Vicinity
22. Revise
23. Personify
26. Neck back
29. Suitors
32. Madagascar mammals
36. Tomato ___
39. Walking pole
41. Birth-name word
42. Raccoon relation
43. Geologic period
44. Cow's milk gland
46. Joule's kin
47. Doc
49. Rope loop
50. Playground item
52. Vocal group
54. Olive genus
56. Jacquard-weave fabric
60. Sub shop
63. Hastened
66. Corrosive liquid
67. Mimicry
69. Cab
70. Southern bread
71. Gift recipient
72. Decorates, as a cake
73. Presently
74. Thing of worth
75. Impulsive
76. Surrender

DOWN

1. Possibly
2. Apprehension
3. Chocolate substitute
4. Yet, in verse
5. Tropical fruit
6. Maturing agent
7. Sand ridge
8. Auto style
9. Pump purchase
10. Value
11. ___ out (made do)
12. Large trailer
13. Formerly
24. Final notice
25. Based on ten
27. Everybody
28. Funnel-shaped flower
30. Consumed
31. Impassive
33. Take apart
34. Female ruffs
35. Parched
36. Holes in one
37. Irritated
38. Book leaf
40. Go slowly
45. Student's residence
48. Flock female
51. Party
53. Queer
55. Lively
57. Apart
58. Church council
59. New Hampshire town
60. Art movement
61. Heroic poem
62. Camera feature
64. South American rodent
65. 24th letters
68. Thus far
70. Inner shoe

PUZZLE 160

ACROSS
1. Stereo
5. Big bag
9. Uninteresting
13. Spunk
14. Wiping cloth
15. Former Milan money
16. Julep herb
17. Tennis tournaments
18. Exclude
19. Court attendant
20. Cool, man!
21. Aesopian offering
22. "Puttin' On the ___"
24. Horn's sound
26. Faux pas
28. Coordination
29. Mass
32. Wealthy group
33. Kitchen expense
35. Unique item
36. Wander
37. Comment
38. Everlasting
40. Females
41. Newt
42. Slick
43. Attorney General Reno
44. Golfer's tap
45. Goofy
46. Many times
49. Male swan
50. Spar
54. Pastoral settings
55. Elton's ivories
57. Capri or Royale
58. Escapade
59. Map feature
60. Sign of pathos
61. Affected
62. ___ out (barely made)
63. Stretch wide

DOWN
1. Asian plant
2. Hipbone sections
3. Tusk
4. Meddle
5. November's gem
6. Had a debt
7. X
8. City trains
9. Swell
10. Tree part
11. Testa
12. Dislike strongly
14. Viennese pastry
21. Centers
23. No ___, ands, or buts
24. Representative
25. Solely
26. Swindler
27. Ward off
28. Flower arrangement
29. Elflike being
30. Eight musicians
31. "I've ___ Lonely Too Long"
32. Aspiration
33. Leaning
34. Namelessness
36. Fit of pique
39. Parser's word
40. Pallid
43. Blouse ruffle
44. Bothersome
45. Divided into areas
46. Water jug
47. Anxiety
48. Fruit dessert
49. Lawyer's challenge
51. Adrift
52. Cabbage dish
53. Gull's kin
55. Jack Horner's fare
56. Writing fluid

PUZZLE 161

ACROSS

1. Boric and citric
6. Units in physics
10. Stillness
14. Nettle's kin
15. Crazy sort
16. Hodgepodge
17. Muscle spasm
18. Island feast
19. Shed
20. Shorten
21. Pronoun
23. Beef or veal
24. Injure
25. Flop
27. Dummy
30. Barked
34. Prevent
36. Hide-and-seek word
37. Switch positions
40. Radio's Kasem
41. Wharf rodent
42. Rabbit fur
44. Large deer
45. Aggravate
47. Treeless plain
48. Eager
50. Defrost
51. "American ___"
55. Time gone by
57. Awestruck
58. Senility
62. Cut a lawn
65. Insulting remark
66. African goat
67. Not o'er
69. Ponder intently
70. Scents organ
71. Fasten again
72. Puts in grass
73. Receives
74. Build

DOWN

1. Eyebrow shape
2. Handle with ___
3. Mosque priest
4. Not very bright
5. Dark brown
6. House wings
7. Libertine
8. Objective
9. Put out, as a candle
10. Period's partner
11. Healing plants
12. Reddish purple
13. Slogan
22. Endeavor
24. Additional
26. Pastoral poem
27. Small fish
28. Roundish
29. Writing table
31. Did wrong
32. Say good-bye
33. Altar plate
35. Representative
37. Brilliant fish
38. Young senorita
39. Skier's thought
43. Chorister
46. Washing away
49. Ticket
51. Shocked responses
52. Inuit abode
53. Out of one's ___
54. Monsters
56. Family
59. Orchestra member
60. Pop quiz
61. Fires
62. Partner
63. Of the ear
64. Hone
68. Auction ending

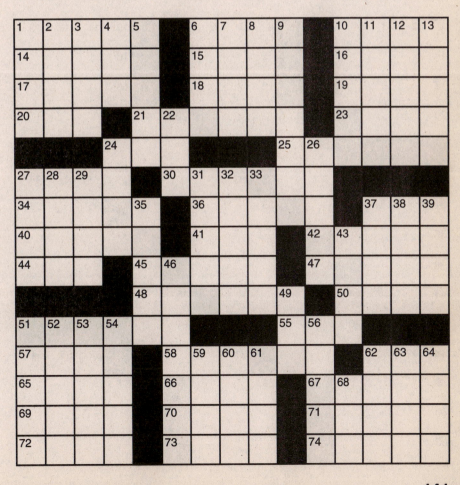

1	2	3	4	5	■	6	7	8	9	■	10	11	12	13
14					■	15				■	16			
17					■	18				■	19			
20			■	21	22					■	23			
■	■	■	24			■	■	■	25	26				
27	28	29		■	30	31	32	33			■	■	■	■
34				35	■	36					■	37	38	39
40					■	41			■	42	43			
44			■	45	46				■	47				
■	■	■	■	48					49	■	50			
51	52	53	54			■	■	■	55	56		■	■	■
57				■	58	59	60	61			■	62	63	64
65				■	66				■	67	68			
69				■	70				■	71				
72				■	73				■	74				

PUZZLE 162

ACROSS

1. Lieu
6. Take suddenly
10. Quote
14. Desert plants
15. Empty
16. In a line
17. Hurts
18. On the water
19. Royal title
20. As well
21. Trig, e.g.
23. Predicaments
25. ___ and outs
26. Surface layer
27. Impudent
30. Raw
34. Volume of maps
35. Wonderful
36. Horse food
37. Faucet problem
38. Father
39. Scarce
40. Morsel
41. More sensible
42. Toll roads
43. Coiled
45. Muggy
46. Building annexes
47. Lived
48. Market owner
51. Each of two
52. Spanish aunt
55. Italian money, once
56. Skunk feature
58. Oneness
60. Sincere
61. Unseat
62. Blender setting
63. Finest
64. Net
65. Flower stalks

DOWN

1. Shoo!
2. Mexican mouthful
3. Canyon's answer
4. Grazed
5. Lay off
6. Tiny pests
7. Hurry
8. Beerlike drink
9. Bad-luck symbol
10. Gambling house
11. Spring bloom
12. Ripped
13. Meadow moms
22. Some
24. Civil strife
26. Show contempt
27. Shoulder band
28. Excuse
29. Syrup source
30. Egged on
31. Uniform color
32. Having handles
33. Fabric tints
34. Says further
35. Heredity carriers
38. Place to dance
39. Wheel's edge
41. Discount event
42. Workout exercises
44. Up-to-date
45. Derby, e.g.
47. Value
48. Droplet
49. Ready for picking
50. Native metals
51. Job supervisor
52. Car's spare
53. Gossipy bit
54. Yes votes
57. Rightful
59. Pistachio or cashew

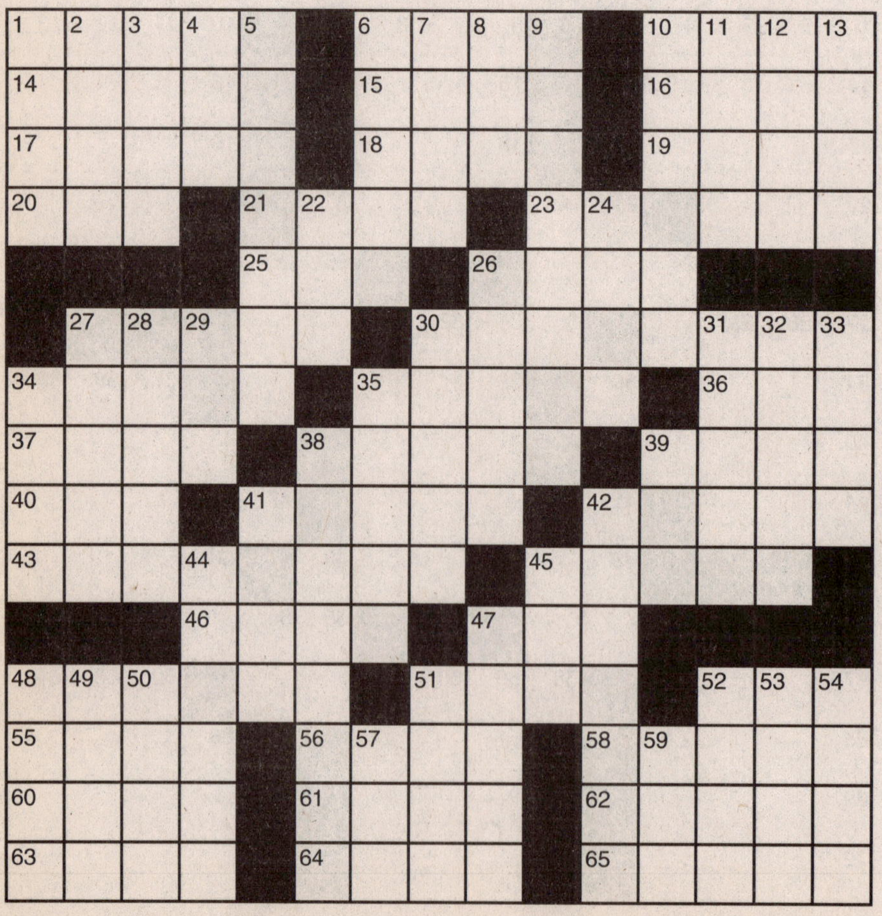

CODEWORD

PUZZLE 163

Codeword is a special crossword puzzle in which conventional clues are omitted. Instead, answer words in the diagram are represented by numbers. Each number represents a different letter of the alphabet, and all of the letters of the alphabet are used. When you are sure of a letter, put it in the code key chart and cross it off in the Alphabet Box. A group of letters has been inserted to start you off.

1	2	3	4	5	6	7	8	9	10	11	12	13
		E		A								

14	15	16	17	18	19	20	21	22	23	24	25	26
					D							

12	26	5	■	7	8	3	■	18	5	19	■	26	3	23
21	14	23	■	8	21	1	■	8	11	3	■	5	26	3
5	4	23	■	19	14	21	■	9	3	10	■	15	3	13
26	4	8	6	3	■	18	21	18	■	23	18	3	3	23
12	3	4	3	■	■	■	4	5	22	5	7	■	■	■
■	19	3	3	26	■	17	5	24	3	■	3	4	12	23
■	■	■	12	5	4	5	1	■	5	12	23	14	23	3
3	5	4	■	26	14	1	9	3	1	23	■	20	16	3
9	4	5	7	5	24	■	3	5	12	3	10	■	■	■
9	3	1	3	■	20	4	5 A	23	■	18	8	12	7	■
■	■	■	17	4	5	14	19 D	■	■	■	5	25	14	5
15	8	12	23	5	■	24	3 E	23	■	11	4	14	24	20
5	19	21	■	24	5	26	■	5	9	21	■	3	20	20
8	10	10	■	26	5	10	■	26	5	1	■	5	10	3
1	3	3	■	12	7	3	■	3	10	2	■	2	3	16

Alphabet Box

A B C D E F G H I J K L M N O P Q R S T U V W X Y Z

PUZZLE 164

ACROSS

1. Oxidation
5. Scram!
9. Corner
13. Bicycle part
17. Ruler mark
18. ____ mater
19. Second of a series
20. Adolescent's bane
21. Terrible
22. Official decree
23. Did away with
25. Letter from Athens
26. Shoe fillers
27. Gift paper
28. Gushes
29. Flower leaf
31. Approaching
33. Pressure meas.
34. Banish
36. Wavelet
40. Family chart
44. ____ or false
45. Clamors
47. Provide guns
48. Light-switch positions
51. Impromptu
53. UFO pilot
54. Ballet step
55. Showy display
57. Dusk, in verse
58. Washstand item
59. Make a choice
61. Vital fluid
63. French bread, once
65. Injury
68. Baked taro
69. Bland
70. Pretend
73. Say a rosary
74. Toto's bark
76. Boringly proper
78. Singer Merman
80. Scrutinize
81. Flock member
82. Key
84. Sailor's direction
86. School semester
88. Lauds
89. Pack animals
92. Perfect
94. Knell
96. Ninny
98. Made in Dublin
101. Podium
104. Risks money
106. Rocky peak
107. Endorse
109. Flintstones' pet
110. Hit hard
111. Available
112. African lily
113. Advantage
114. Good guy
115. Gives silent consent
116. A Sinatra daughter
117. Garden buzzers
118. Hitherto

DOWN

1. Travels by horse
2. Joined
3. Scuff
4. "Woman of ____ Year"
5. Umpire's call
6. Customers
7. Italian violinmaker
8. Create a doily
9. Aspen lift
10. Country's McEntire
11. Above
12. Chum
13. Like old streetlamps
14. Yodeler's feedback
15. Freshly
16. Cerise and scarlet
24. Conditions
26. Roman goddess of spring
27. Flog
30. Appropriate
32. Scrounge
33. Pierre's papa
35. Unmannerly
37. Shrimp
38. European weasel
39. Burrow
41. Ecstatic joy
42. Epoch
43. Certain dashes
46. Skiing surface
48. Sphere
49. None
50. Plug
52. Impose
56. Bronx attraction
58. Devour
60. Burst
62. Type of jockey
64. Boom box
66. Anti's answer
67. Apply henna to
69. Artificial
71. Difficult job
72. Reveal
74. Although
75. Dumbfound
77. Journey, for Shatner
78. You're something ____!
79. Is winning
83. Matterhorn's location
85. Fast-running bird
87. Bricklayers
90. Buck adornment
91. Searches thoroughly
93. Electrical unit
95. Linger
97. Rye fungus
98. Monopoly token
99. Repurchase agreement
100. Glazed
101. Cold-cuts seller
102. Without a bk.'s author listed
103. Brainchild
105. Little piggies
108. Tangled mass
109. Society gal
110. Ship's pronoun

PUZZLE 165

ACROSS
1. Reality
5. Amazed
9. Zip
13. Continental prefix
14. Explore
15. Church section
16. Ireland, in verse
17. "____ With a View"
18. Chew steadily
19. Dormant
21. Cozy home
23. Suffer
24. Falco or Adams
25. Coldly
27. Rocky peak
29. County tax advisor
34. Nom de plume
36. Cedar, e.g.
37. Slender jug
41. Bright sign
42. Short journey
43. Begone!
44. Flat bell
45. Deadly serpents
46. Work shift
47. Twice nine
50. Mao ____-tung
51. Strike a ____
54. Method
56. KO counter
57. Trim
61. Wading birds
64. Can. province
66. Pass
68. Wine center
69. Snuffed Puff?
70. Farm measures
71. Small valley
72. Polish
73. "Of ____ I Sing"
74. Canary food

DOWN
1. Touch
2. Atmosphere
3. Guideline
4. Mixed paint
5. LAX posting
6. Thug
7. Band instrument
8. Sparklers
9. School subj.
10. Kauai porch
11. Benefit
12. Recently
14. Meat spreads
20. Long and Vardalos
22. Spanish uncle
26. Summit
27. Flavor
28. Dairy-case choice
30. Stow
31. Burst
32. Perceive
33. Establish
35. Infuriate
38. Linen offering
39. Eternities
40. Fixed routine
42. Spree
46. High-hatter
48. Freud's concerns
49. Radiates
51. Wreck
52. Greeting
53. Many times
55. Fender flaws
58. Cool!
59. Unit of length
60. Cut back
62. Dueling blade
63. Desert dirt
65. Astound
67. 2.0 GPA

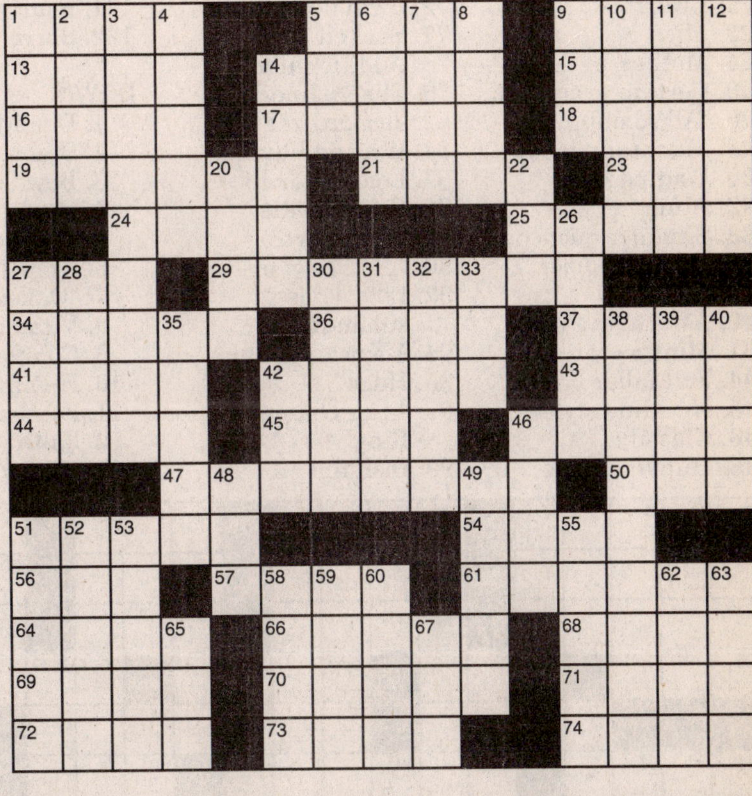

One and Only

PUZZLE 166

The word WEEKEND is hidden in the diagram One and Only one time. It will read in a straight line forward, backward, up, down, or diagonally.

E W D N N N D N E W E E K K W D K W W N K W N N E
D N E E W K N N D W E D N E N D N D K E D K E K D
D N W W W W E N E W D E N D W W N N E K E E W E N
D E E E D K K N W K W D K K N W E K N D E N N E W
N K N D N E E N W W E D N D E W K E N D E E D W N
W D W W N N W W N E N E K N E E D N N E E E W W D
D N K D W E E K N E D D W N E W E D D K W K N N W

PUZZLE 167

ACROSS

1. Incite
6. Tuna containers
10. Lessen
13. Just fair
17. Wells ____
18. Hodgepodge
19. Common alias
20. Washstand item
21. Amphibians
22. Breakfast, e.g.
23. Miss
24. Mother, in Paris
25. Certain evergreen
26. "All About ____"
28. Mountain hollow
30. Wading birds
32. Alum
33. Summer quencher
35. Choir member
38. Finch
40. Astern, to Pulver
41. Mink's coat
44. Fall faller
45. Neckline style
46. Classify
48. Human trunk
50. Monotony
52. Airport abbr.
54. Cover charges
55. "The Phantom of the ____"
56. Temperature gauges
61. Pal of Pooh
64. Division of history
65. Choose
66. Paper storage
72. Swindler
77. Spoken
78. Additionally
79. Sluggishness
82. Jeopardizes
84. Writing liquids
87. Lemony drink
88. Crisp cookie
89. Slow start?
90. "____ Now or Never"
92. Like some submarines
94. Mexican dollar
95. Huge
97. "____ Diamond Ring"
99. Insignia
103. Strap
104. Theory
105. Trumpeter Severinsen
108. Chest noise
109. Med subject
111. Filled tortilla
113. Protozoan
115. Flabbergast
116. Slip
117. Level
118. Urchin
119. ____ off (angry)
120. Steep (flax)
121. Fourth letters
122. Serrated

DOWN

1. Doubtful
2. Stable dweller
3. Bow
4. Coop product
5. Failure
6. Amusing movies
7. "Cakes and ____"
8. Vitamin B component
9. Comforts
10. Hemmed
11. Feather wrap
12. Faith
13. Highway vehicle
14. Is obliged to
15. Withered
16. Metal sources
27. Stopcock
29. Overrule
31. Sheet of cotton
32. Errand runner
34. Lasting impression?
35. Part of a.k.a.
36. Spring
37. Domesticate
39. "Empty ____"
41. At no cost
42. Customer
43. Famous flagmaker
47. Michael Stipe's band
49. Many times, to a poet
51. G-man
53. Elec. measure
57. Cackler
58. Sooner than, to bards
59. Deserter
60. Engrave
62. Bread variety
63. Woodwind player
66. Links warning
67. Showy flower
68. Lad's girl
69. Forest creature
70. Negative particle
71. Shut loudly
73. Hinged fasteners
74. Bald eagle's kin
75. Turkish officials
76. Misprint
80. Versions
81. Mechanics, for short
83. Area
85. "Citizen ____"
86. Pompous
91. Logger's cry
93. Series of eight
96. Cancel a space launch
98. Reflection
99. Formerly
100. Better half
101. Indigo
102. Allow to borrow
105. Trial
106. Tokyo sashes
107. Walking stick
110. St. Pat's land
112. Average mark
114. Dent

DOUBLE TROUBLE

PUZZLE 168

Not really double trouble, but double fun! Solve this puzzle as you would a regular crossword, except place one, two, or three letters in each box. The number of letters in each answer is shown in parentheses after its clue.

ACROSS

1. Wide-mouthed bottle (6)
4. Rock (5)
6. Garlic piece (5)
8. Southern beauty (5)
10. Tiny (6)
11. Let (6)
12. Component (10)
14. Junior (3)
15. Artifact (5)
16. Mob (4)
18. Pen (4)
19. Loyalty (10)
22. Hardy (6)
24. Farm tract (4)
26. Formerly (4)
27. Loss (9)
29. Nice (6)
30. Gnash (5)
32. Impulsive (4)
34. Moth repellent (5)
35. Changeable (6)
36. Against (4)
37. Bath item (5)
39. Ache (5)
41. Scarce (4)
43. Care (7)
45. Sprite (3)
47. Comparison word (4)
48. Instruct (5)
49. Trash (6)
50. Represent pictorially (9)
52. Mention (4)
54. Edible bulb (5)
55. Admonition (6)
56. Intensify (8)
59. Hindu god (5)
60. Before (3)
62. Depend (4)
63. Lip (3)
65. One who abets (10)
68. Pants part (6)
70. Shawl (6)
71. Intersect (4)
72. Delete (5)
73. Timespan (3)
74. Ebb (6)

DOWN

1. Horn and Cod (5)
2. Sane (8)
3. Holiday (4)
4. Rage (5)
5. Nor's partner (7)
6. Adhere (5)
7. Cloudy (8)
8. Contradict (5)
9. Advanced (4)
11. "The ____ Brief" (7)
13. Frontier (4)
15. Enrollment (12)
17. Camel type (9)
20. Smirk (4)
21. Yield (4)
23. Diamond move (4)
24. Gain speed (10)
25. Lease (4)
28. Instant (5)
29. Patio (4)
30. Award (5)
31. Sign (10)
33. Reveal (4)
35. Pecuniarily (11)
38. Remove (9)
40. Soil (5)
42. Attain (5)
44. Say (5)
46. Podded vegetable (3)
49. Tawny cat (4)
50. Dig (5)
51. Ball holder (3)
53. Afternoon social (3)
55. Knight (8)
57. Bellow (6)
58. Raised level (7)
59. Send (4)
61. Carl or Rob (6)
64. Obstruct (6)
65. Peak (4)
66. Halley's discovery (5)
67. Stop (5)
69. Ocean (3)
70. Dry (4)

LOOKING FOR DOUBLE TROUBLE? You've found it! Treat yourself to special collections of your favorite puzzles—over 50 in each! To order, see page 159.

PUZZLE 169 — BRICK BY BRICK

Rearrange this stack of bricks to form a crossword puzzle. The clues will help you fit the bricks into their correct places. Row 1 has been filled in for you. Use the bricks to fill in the remaining spaces.

BRICKS

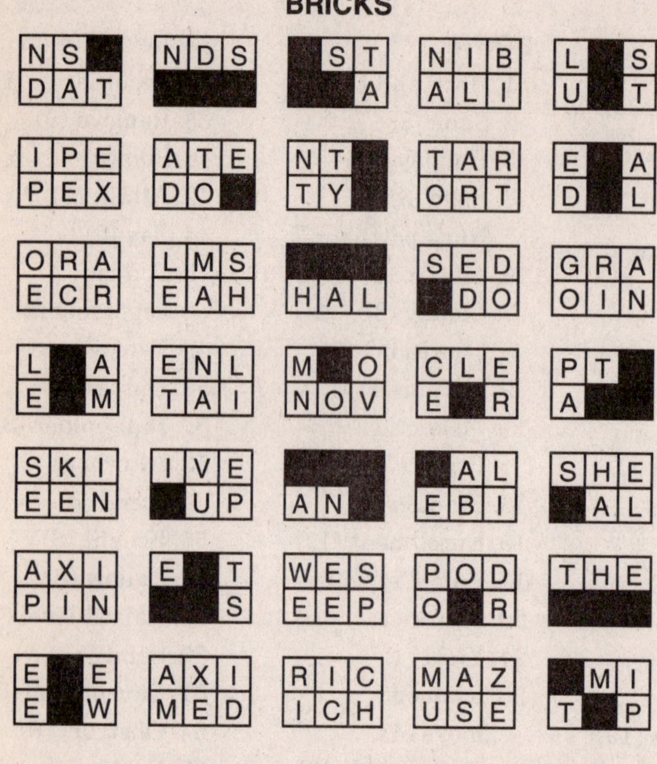

DIAGRAM

	1	2	3	4	5	6	7	8	9	10	11	12	13	14	15
1	P	A	P	A			S	C	A	B		J	A	V	A
2															
3															
4															
5															
6															
7															
8															
9															
10															
11															
12															
13															
14															
15															

ACROSS

1. Daddy
   Wound cover
   Slangy coffee
2. Uttered
   Steady gaze
   Rams' mates
3. Hosiery hue
   Flourless cake
   Shed tears
4. Those guys
   Choose
   Ship's pronoun
5. ____ Scotia
   TV's Thicke
6. Adds spice to
   Minister
7. Skater Babilonia
   Keep current
   Wealthy
8. Pen section
   ____ worker
   Alpine slider
9. Touched ground
   Sharp
   Night, in verse
10. Calm
    Periodic payments
11. Fuddy-duddy
    Acme
12. Pea packet
    Ginger ____
    Charity
13. Ring of light
    Make another offer
    Jacob's wife
14. Leaf angle
    Astound
    Cab
15. Ancient Persian
    Ponder
    Rotate

DOWN

1. Odist
   Alcohol burners
   Cured pork
2. Curved support
   Pinned
   Hatchet
3. Peel
   Topic for Freud
   Hinged top
4. Graduates
   Polliwog
5. Egg cell
   As well
6. Hat like Lincoln's
   Small portion
7. Slow, as traffic
   Flightless bird
8. Wheelbarrow
   Indian robes
   Arab garments
9. Picasso's forte
   Tease
10. Hive dwellers
    Many-legged bug
11. "Shallow ____"
    Variety
12. Gem vendor
    Ennobles
13. Great respect
    Awakened
    Hurdle
14. Sign of triumph
    Chipped
    Skirt style
15. Egyptian cobra
    Jaws' projections
    Tibia

PUZZLE 170

• PEOPLE & PLACES •

ACROSS

1. Caffeinated drink
5. Performs
9. Phooey!
13. Ding
17. On the crest of
18. Scottish Gaelic
19. Lamb, literarily
20. Toast topper
21. Heavenly body
22. Actress Patricia ____
23. Weaving need
24. Social group
25. Jan & Dean song
28. Bistro
30. Signal yes
31. Schedule letters
32. To boot
33. Baseball stick
36. Go to bed
39. Barbed-missile shooter
43. Unaccompanied
45. Dawn deity
46. Water bodies
47. Flintstones' pet
48. Mona ____
49. Ms. Sothern
50. Endures
51. Wallach et al.
52. Dinner course
54. Cupid's target
55. Declare
56. Dress bottom
57. Fountain treats
58. Pro
59. "Staying ____"
62. Violin's kin
63. Fail to heed
67. Asian desert
68. Pub game
69. Retrieve
70. Minute amount
71. Corrupt
72. Elevator inventor
73. Barbara ____ Geddes
74. Bar seat
75. Warning
77. Liking
79. Vane letters
80. Glimpse
81. Shannon of song
82. Yang's mate
84. "Man of La ____"
87. Elvis film
93. Territory
94. At that time
96. Sharp-tasting
97. Colorado resort
98. Mail drop
99. Essence
100. Diminutive suffix
101. Raison d'____
102. Oodles
103. Listen to
104. Judge
105. Coarse grass

DOWN

1. Handy money
2. Mr. Preminger
3. Shark type?
4. Chef's smock
5. Strip
6. Baseballer Hershiser
7. Jacob's twin
8. Vendors
9. Ms. Reese
10. Jesus or Matty
11. Pedro's river
12. Lacking a moniker
13. Aykroyd film
14. Fashion magazine
15. Pretty close
16. Singer Orlando
26. Folk tales
27. Colorado Indian
29. Botanist Gray
32. Into pieces
33. Uncovered
34. "I cannot tell ____"
35. Pitch
37. Hiker's shelter
38. Positive atom
39. Browns quickly
40. ____ monster
41. Module
42. Snout
44. Lovin' Spoonful song
46. Eastern-pact letters
49. Give grenades to
50. ____ and whistles
53. Shoe width
54. Ceases
55. Distress code
57. Deserve
58. Tantrum
59. Golden ____
60. Tennis score
61. In the same place mentioned: abbr.
62. Gymnast Rigby
63. Snack store
64. Blessing
65. Jacket style
66. New Haven school
68. Li'l Abner's home
69. Harden
73. Delayed
74. Slangy knife
76. Like: suff.
77. Gun in neutral
78. Procedure
81. Greasy spoon
83. Not once
84. Upright pole
85. Woody's son
86. Store sign
87. Aloe ____
88. Past curfew
89. Museo display
90. Fence door
91. Million ending
92. Musher's vehicle
95. Tilling tool

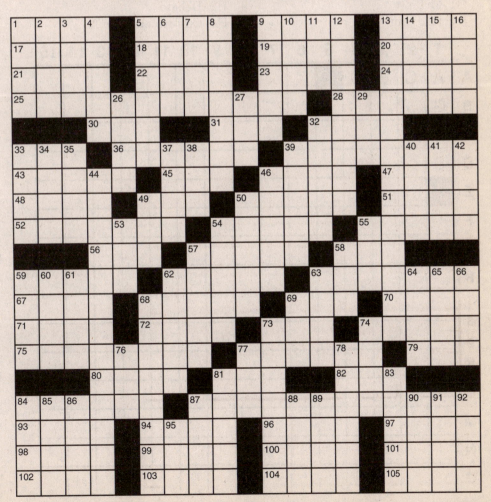

PUZZLE 171 BATTLESHIPS

The diagram represents the sea, which contains a crossword puzzle; the answer words are Battleships. The letter-number combination to the left of each clue indicates the location in the diagram where a Battleship has been hit (for example, A2 is in the first row, second column). A hit is any one of the letters in the answer word. Using this clue, you must determine the exact location of each answer and whether it is an across or a down word. Fill in black squares to separate words as in a regular crossword. We have filled in the answers to clues A2 and D1.

A2 Scored well on
A4 Military runaway
A7 Somewhat
A9 Minute amount
A12 Office note
A13 Utter
B1 Amusement
B3 Muslim prince
B7 Sonar's kin
B9 Metal containers
B14 During
C2 Wagon
C3 Goddess of discord
C6 Expiate
C8 Fuss
C10 Upright
C13 Storage tower
C15 Fragrance
D1 Mellows
D4 Pull taut
D6 Expanse of land
D10 Disperse widely
D12 Ship's captain
D14 5,280 feet
E5 Evaluates
E11 Cravat
F1 Rascal
F3 Seasons, in a way
F8 Crimson
F9 Ditto's sister
F13 Curtain
F14 Puzzler
G2 Streams
G5 Chore
G6 Droop
G9 Cast a ballot
G11 Attendant
G15 This instant
H2 Debate
H4 Culture medium
H6 Glacial ridge
H7 Fracas
H8 Cut off
H13 Doddering
H14 Float upward
I1 Mire
I7 Composer Stravinsky
I10 Summer shirt
I12 More wicked
I15 Wide-mouthed jugs
J3 Goes first
J4 Vermin
J9 Woven network
J11 Mimickers
K4 Walk unsteadily
K5 Mexican cheer
K10 Closely packed
K12 Maturity accelerators
L1 Wading bird
L3 As a substitute
L5 Bit of land
L7 Knight's wife
L11 Flower vessel
L13 Go in again
M2 Watercraft
M3 Store event
M8 Colorful parrot
M10 More recent
M14 Other
M15 Director Kenton
N2 Protuberance
N4 Doing nothing
N6 Designer Charles ____
N7 Ham it up
N9 Scold
N14 Demolish, in London
N15 Oboist's need
O1 Fortuneteller
O6 Waste pipe
O8 Heifer
O13 Ensnare
O14 Hurried

	1	2	3	4	5	6	7	8	9	10	11	12	13	14	15
A	A	C	E	D	■										
B	G														
C	E														
D	S														
E	■														
F															
G															
H															
I															
J															
K															
L															
M															
N															
O															

PUZZLE 172

• HOOPS ACTION •

ACROSS

1. Go up and down
7. Dispenser green
11. Guitarist's location
15. ___ serif
19. Suit bigwig
20. Teen breakout
21. Bound
22. Ninny
23. Chicago sub?
25. Rose's beloved
26. Excellent
27. Guys, but not dolls
28. Excellence
29. Orlando chit?
32. Tar
34. Put on
35. Honkers
36. Circus performer
39. Adherent's suffix
40. Deprive of strength
42. Emperor
44. Utah gala?
47. Tennis subtlety
51. Element 8 compounds
52. Roasting rod
53. Brown rival
54. Avis output
55. Nephric
56. Bottom line
58. Tear
59. "That's right!"
60. Rap's Dr. ___
61. Press
63. Pine
66. Some sibs
68. San Antonio spontaneity?
71. Destroy
74. Come down
75. Pisa dough, once
76. Saw
79. Turkish title
80. Sledge
82. Lab, maybe
83. Land in France
85. MCAT's kin
86. Firstborn, maybe
87. Shawm, updated
90. Filled treat
91. Coastal havens
93. Phoenix tanner?
96. "No big deal"
97. Play people
98. Rapa ___
99. Links locale
100. Extra, usually
103. Yan's pan
104. Cleats' place
107. Oklahoma City boss?
111. Liking
112. Madras mister
115. Small monkey
116. Row
117. Houston old-timer?
120. Thought of Paris
121. Writer Waugh
122. ___ Shan (Chinese peak)
123. Water spirit
124. Average grades
125. Graph starter
126. Copter predecessor
127. Bed canopy

DOWN

1. Door frame
2. Cleveland Indian
3. CPR experts
4. Convened
5. Soul
6. Napa Valley draws
7. File site
8. Sharp
9. Weekend TV staple
10. Tiller
11. Wine holder
12. Spring sign
13. Huge
14. Swarm
15. Rubberneckers
16. Came to
17. Ball teams
18. Cubic measure
24. South side
30. Mature
31. Yawning
32. Miata maker
33. Invitation initials
36. Norwegian arm
37. More careless
38. Modern mag
41. Lao language
42. Post
43. Trooper
45. Mr. Calderon
46. Practice
47. Hide the gray
48. Runner's goal
49. In excess of
50. Gets darker
56. University clan
57. Half dos
58. "Stand" band
59. ABA member
62. Nautical directors
63. ___ loss
64. Phi's follower
65. Rural layer
67. Grab
68. Bath bath
69. Potato piece
70. Spanish cheer
71. License plates
72. Grimm meanie
73. Three-toed bird
76. Incipient raisin
77. Window type
78. Ms. Garber
81. ___ Nova
82. Flock's perch
84. Slur
86. Stash
87. Honshu port
88. Commuter's option
89. Aware of
90. Roald Dahl book
92. Brilliant blooms
94. Canadian province
95. "Big Trouble" star
97. Intimidate
100. Topmost floor
101. Castigate
102. He learns
103. Hotshot
105. Total
106. Sierra ___
108. French state
109. Tee off
110. Tiny bit
112. Sketch
113. Painter Magritte
114. Road to Rome
118. Start to grate
119. LP successors

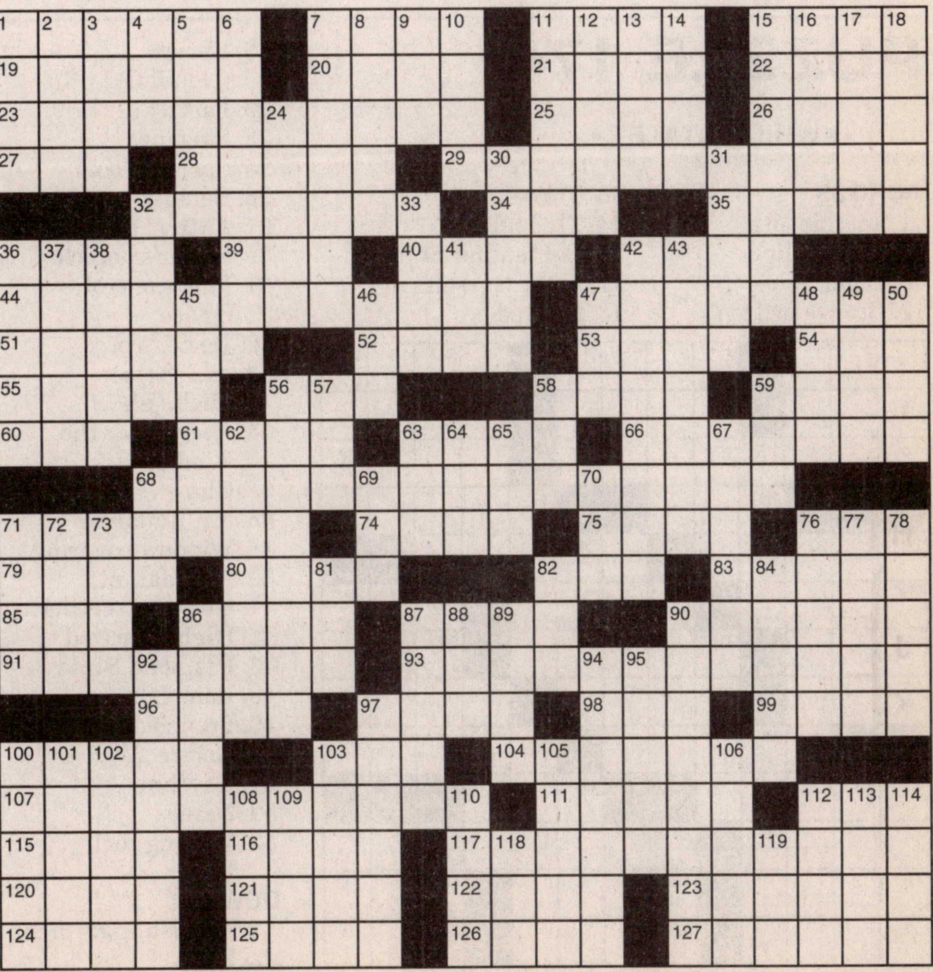

PUZZLE 173

• IT BURNS ME UP! •

ACROSS
1. Prophetic sign
5. Tableland
9. Lard
12. Million ender
13. Like ___ of bricks
14. Climbing vine
15. Troublemaker
17. Tear
18. Payable
19. "Superman" star
21. Bistros
24. Hunt
26. Eager
27. Mink, e.g.
28. Mine car
31. Neither's partner
32. Fall behind
33. Rubber tree
34. Water jug
36. Watch closely
37. Highlander
38. Tiny bits
40. Jabs
41. ___ Gras
43. Four qts.
44. The self
45. Liquor
51. Light source
52. Lather
53. Cautious
54. Owns
55. Totals
56. Rim

1	2	3	4	■	5	6	7	8	■	9	10	11
12				■	13				■	14		
15				16					■	17		
■	■	■	18			■	■	19	20			
21	22	23			■	24	25				■	■
26				■	27			■	28		29	30
31			■	■	32			■	■	33		
34			35	■	36			■	37			
■	■	38		39			■	40				
41	42				■	■	43			■	■	■
44			■	45	46	47				48	49	50
51			■	52				■	53			
54			■	55				■	56			

DOWN
1. Lout
2. 1002, to Caesar
3. Make a mistake
4. Required
5. Foal's mom
6. JFK info
7. Male offspring
8. Agassi of tennis
9. It carries hoses
10. Tel ___
11. Variety
16. Kramden drove one
20. Superlative suffix
21. Walking stick
22. Swear to
23. Hearth tools
24. Docks
25. Sudden impulse
27. Dog's nemesis
29. Lotion ingredient
30. New York team
35. Fishing pole
37. Comfort
39. Spats
40. Animal's foot
41. Netting
42. Water, to Pedro
43. Precious stones
46. Debtor's letters
47. Flock father
48. Tyke
49. Omelet item
50. Dark bread

PUZZLE 174

• WHICH STATE? •

ACROSS
1. Testing site
4. Tailor's line
8. Choir voice
12. Bronze or Iron
13. Threesome
14. Fly high
15. Centennial State
17. Actor Russell
18. Existed
19. Ehrich ___ (Houdini)
20. Faintly
23. Sketches
25. Spring bloom
26. Benefit
27. Author Fleming
30. Mover's vehicle
31. Flow-control device
32. Doctor's org.
33. ___ Arbor, Michigan
34. Away from the wind
35. Clip
36. Mr. Kefauver
38. Window covering
39. Foundation
41. Ghost's greeting
42. Highly excited
43. Diamond State
48. Babe ___
49. Frenzied
50. Deface
51. Rhythm
52. Names
53. Writing tool

1	2	3	■	4	5	6	7	■	8	9	10	11
12			■	13				■	14			
15			16					■	17			
■	■	■	18			■	■	19				
20	21	22			■	23	24				■	■
25				■	26				■	27	28	29
30			■	31					■	32		
33			■	34				■	35			
■	■	36	37				■	38				
39	40				■	■	41			■	■	■
42				■	43	44				45	46	47
48				■	49				■	50		
51				■	52				■	53		

DOWN
1. Varnish ingredient
2. Past
3. Barbara ___ Geddes
4. Get sidetracked
5. Epochs
6. Assistance
7. Cow's sound
8. Lopsided
9. Pelican State
10. Coal products
11. Table scraps
16. Night creatures
19. Decline
20. Prima donna
21. Persia, today
22. Gopher State
23. Gives sparingly
24. Wander
26. Cotton bundle
28. Surrounded by
29. Neck part
31. Tanks
35. Display
37. Vision
38. Drenches
39. Nasty remark
40. Chills and fever
41. Shapeless lump
43. June honoree
44. Flightless bird
45. Current measure
46. "Norma ___"
47. Sea eagle

CODEWORD

PUZZLE 175

Instructions for solving Codeword puzzles are given on page 11.

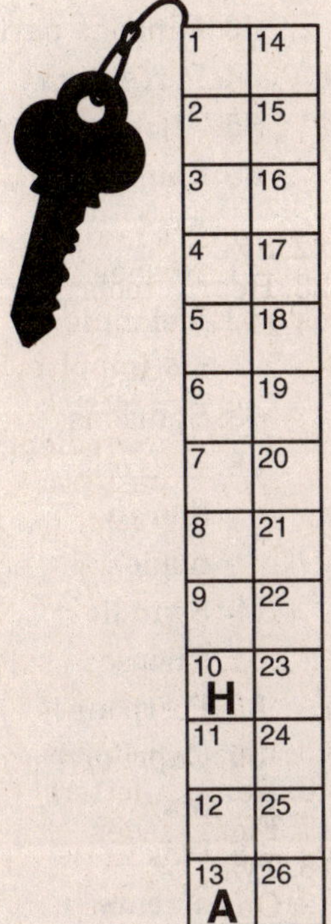

1	14
2	15
3	16
4	17
5	18
6	19
7	20
8	21
9	22
10 H	23
11	24
12	25
13 A	26

24	23	10 H	13 A	22	7	26			13	7	24	13
15		13		15		13		13		26		7
13	12	7	24	21	13	15		11	22	13	2	18
21		26		13		22		22		14		24
19	12	24	13	12		7	3	13	12	12	25	1
	13		15		4		13		22		16	
13	19	20	25	14	21		7	26	12	14	16	24
	14		25		13		26		13		24	
2	25	5	16	25	12	26		13	15	24	12	26
12		13		21		13		15		9		10
24	21	20	25	8		17	13	3	26	14	6	24
24		25		23		15		10		2		14
15	25	12	19			24	21	13	2	26	25	12

~~A~~	N
B	O
C	P
D	Q
E	R
F	S
G	T
~~H~~	U
I	V
J	W
K	X
L	Y
M	Z

CODEWORD

PUZZLE 176

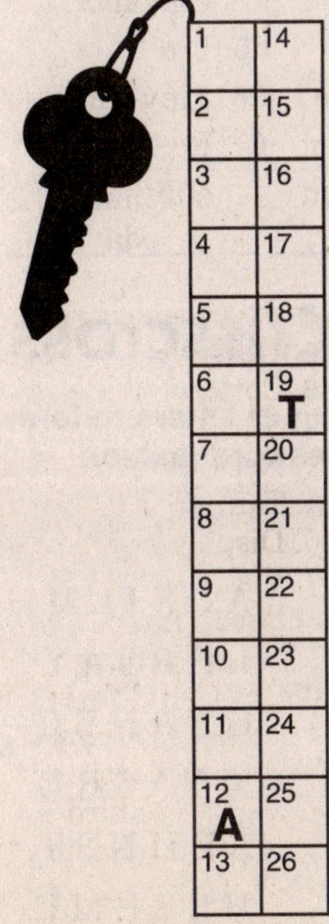

1	14
2	15
3	16
4	17
5	18
6	19 T
7	20
8	21
9	22
10	23
11	24
12 A	25
13	26

24	20	8	8	12				10	12	19	20	7
20		16		2	12	19	19	16		21		16
6	17	16	16	13		9		23	21	9	14	15
17				16	24	21	18	15		16		9
16	19	4	21	1				11	12	23	22	21
		17		19	12	7	16					23
12	13	22	23	15		21		25	20	25	20	14
14					7	20	9	20		12		
3	20	5	5	15				13	12 A	19 T	12	11
17		17		12	22	12	8	16				21
13	21	19	26	4		18		22	23	20	16	5
26		21		21	24	16	23	12		11		19
19	12	13	22	21				23	16	11	12	15

~~A~~	N
B	O
C	P
D	Q
E	R
F	S
G	~~T~~
H	U
I	V
J	W
K	X
L	Y
M	Z

PUZZLE 177

• ARMED WITH IDIOMS •

ACROSS

1. Small nail
5. Harvests
10. Singer Billy ____
14. Berne's river
15. Confess
16. Loosen
17. Stand firm
20. Family-style car
21. Ragout
22. Perched
23. Specks
26. Thin board
28. Director Spheeris
32. Self-centeredness
36. Notable period
37. Diving birds
39. Mirth
40. Is direct
44. Voyaging
45. City in England
46. Purpose
47. Homesteader
50. Made up for
52. Slide sideways
54. Actor Newman
55. Charged particle
58. Rapier
60. Achievements
64. Impending danger
68. Son of Jacob
69. Ruse
70. Pale color
71. Dutch cheese
72. Worries
73. Back talk

DOWN

1. Game fish
2. Pace
3. Desertlike
4. Ten years
5. Ship deserter
6. Tokyo, formerly
7. Renowned cookie-maker
8. Liquid measures
9. TV's "Remington ____"
10. Water container
11. Blame
12. Poet St. Vincent Millay
13. Gone astray
18. Hills
19. Festoon
24. Play a piccolo
25. Thread holder
27. African nation
28. Smooth-shelled nut
29. Jagged
30. Monikers
31. Join
33. Hipbone part
34. Perception
35. Allotted
38. Source of wool
41. Noshes
42. Icelandic work
43. Spurious
48. ____ out (barely made)
49. Swindle
51. Chooses
53. Postpone
55. Capri or Man
56. Was in arrears
57. Suddenly bright star
59. Singer Adams
61. Lamb's alias
62. Hideouts
63. Concordes, e.g.: abbr.
65. Lip
66. Tiny colonist
67. Rockies, e.g.: abbr.

1	2	3	4	■	5	6	7	8	9	■	10	11	12	13
14				■	15					■	16			
17				18						19				
20					■	■	21				■	22		
■	■	■	23		24	25	■	26			27	■	■	■
28	29	30					31	■	32			33	34	35
36			■	37				38	■	■	39			
40			41						42	43				
44				■	■	45					■	46		
47				48	49	■	50				51			
■	■	■	52			53	■	54				■	■	■
55	56	57	■	58			59	■	■	60		61	62	63
64			65					66	67					
68				■	69					■	70			
71				■	72					■	73			

PUZZLE 178

Crisscross

Beside each diagram are six groups of scrambled letters. Rearrange each group of letters to form a word, and then fit the words into the diagram to read across and down in crossword fashion.

1.

AENRTU
ILNOOT
LADORL
NEDRAC
CEIOTX
RAOTID

2.

ACEILM
LHRSAY
GYANEC
MTASRE
AEHNST
HESEMC

PUZZLE 179

• SEA WORLD •

ACROSS

1. Pedometer unit
5. Stash
9. Sample
13. Lummox
17. Hemingway's nickname
18. Own
19. Unhitching post?
20. Love of Radames
21. Mideast mogul
22. Hyalite
23. Oft
24. Ness, et al.
25. Cirrocumulus clouds
28. Good
30. Mars, in Athens
31. Hart's mate
33. Who, me?
34. Jungfrau, e.g.
37. Hammett hound
39. Mrs. Copperfield
41. Wedding worker
45. Bumpkins
47. Edge
49. Butts
51. Where the heart is
52. Eggshell
53. Inventor McCormick
55. Imagine that!
56. Cronyn of "Cocoon"
57. Tree
59. Detect
61. Untouched
63. Versatile verb
64. Circe, for one
66. Took off
67. Whitewash
71. Showed up
72. Dish
76. Brainchild
77. Took a load off
79. Unenthusiastic
81. Wild West name
82. Alley yowlers
83. Work on text
85. "Emerald Point ____"
86. Pen
87. Like some leaves
89. He did the lord's work
91. Shake
93. Fourth grade
94. Canal site
96. Brusque
98. Squad
100. The Beatles, e.g.
104. Snake feeder
109. Golden Rule word
110. Where to keep a spare tyre
112. Comedian Carvey
113. Kiri Te Kanawa, e.g.
114. Golden calf
115. Ohio lake
116. Transmit
117. Declaim
118. Dummy
119. Julia's ex
120. Campaign
121. All there

DOWN

1. Unwanted e-mail
2. Novelist Janowitz
3. It's a long story
4. Warm jacket
5. Banks
6. Bayeux embroidery
7. Pimlico's layout
8. Like Richard Burton
9. Pie of the Pirates
10. Sushi, often
11. Bamboozle
12. Sitka symbol
13. 1974 Cy Young winner
14. Green bean
15. Baltic tributary
16. Copenhagen native
26. You were, to Caesar
27. Nanny's charge
29. Bud's buddy
32. Tow
34. A Guinness
35. Cuckoo
36. Engine sound
38. Buenos ____
40. Sunday sign-off
42. Day division
43. Madame Bovary
44. Theater spool
46. Potluck staple
48. Grammy field
50. Branded
53. Fold
54. Nursery-rhyme dieter
58. Sooner than
60. Sana's locale
62. Summer shade
65. Gurkha's country
67. Quote
68. Bouquet
69. Nautilus skipper
70. Cub Scouts
73. Sortie
74. Art Deco artist
75. Foil's kin
78. Layer
80. Strength-building exercise
84. Board member
86. Corrode
88. Do lunch
90. Government org.
92. Upper house
95. Rise up
97. Mormon missionary
99. Phrygian king
100. Cockney cash
101. Release
102. Perched on
103. Loyalist
105. Doll's cry
106. "____ Zapata!"
107. Flush
108. Like a triple play
111. Texas tea

PUZZLE 180

• STATE FLOWERS •

ACROSS

1. Sunset color
4. Vigor
7. Foal producer
11. Cold wind
15. Commensurate
17. Stout
18. Middleman
20. "White Wedding" performer
21. Alabama's bloom
23. Cassia plant
24. Odds-displaying board
25. Hacienda brick
26. Faulty serve
28. Cask
29. Lineage chart
30. Write
31. Gorilla
34. Lamb cut
36. Small landmass
38. Vessel's stout pole
39. Spoken
41. Knitting needs
44. Carson's successor
47. Stumble
49. Balderdash
51. Fumble
53. Angry
55. Fix up
58. Elliptical
59. License plate
60. Aquatic growth
63. Corolla segment
64. Feed-bag fillers
65. Tolkien village
66. Military response word
67. Playbill info
69. Adam's son
72. Ranch animal
74. Baby boy, to Juan
75. Slalom
78. South African archbishop
79. Reckon
81. Like TV shows
83. Cosmetician Lauder
85. Quarry
86. Part of QED
89. Paroxysm
90. Multiplication ____
92. Deed over
94. Castle, in chess
96. Pass by
98. Gob
99. Swab
100. Kilmer or Avery
103. Legume type
106. ____ whillikers!
108. Wyo. clock zone
110. Eradicate
112. Bring home the bacon
113. Sheol
115. Louisiana's blossom
118. Laborer of old
119. Ruminant's stomach
120. Zsa Zsa's sister
121. Offers
122. Printer's direction
123. Sea mammal
124. Catch
125. Scottish river

DOWN

1. Kind of tire
2. Bypass
3. Fiend
4. Crony
5. Teacher of Samuel
6. Bell sequence
7. Overcome
8. Bronze or Iron
9. "La Boheme" update
10. Lethargy
11. Montana's flower
12. Redolence
13. Sound of surf
14. Toward shelter
16. Beak
19. Old World herb
22. Vault
27. Go to Gretna Green
32. Dab
33. Be wrong
35. Sox supporter
37. ____ b'Omer
38. Tippler
40. Pillage
42. Fluctuating star
43. Petty quarrel
44. Illuminated
45. Eventful time
46. Harangue
48. Savings-plan inits.
50. Nuance
52. Loop trains
54. Auricle
56. Vice President Agnew
57. ____ vital
61. Without
62. Costume
65. Texas's efflorescence
66. Snow White's friends, e.g.
68. Put
69. Downed
70. Fail
71. Singer James
73. Of great extent
74. Grandfather of Saul
75. Baden-Baden, for example
76. Beer holder
77. Carp-family fish
80. Psychics
82. Ararat lander
84. Shade provider
87. Equip
88. In addition
91. "____ Is Enough"
93. Lass
95. Door sign
97. Binges
100. Cogent
101. Private remark
102. Landlord's contract
103. Comb creators
104. Orient
105. "Judith" composer
107. Adams or Brickell
109. Revenuers
111. Purloin
114. Monitoring gp.
116. Roman salutation
117. Hood's heater

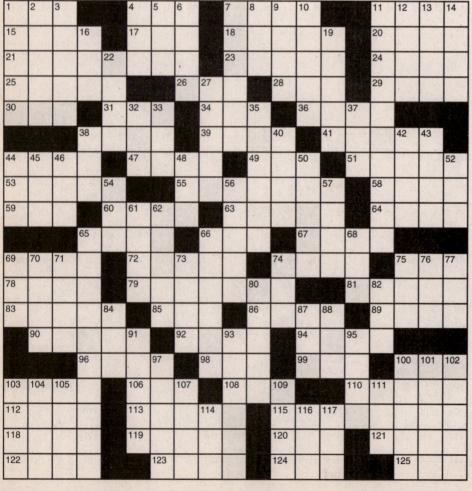

PUZZLE 181

• LEADER OF THE BAND •

ACROSS

1. Pulls
5. Ooze
9. Request
12. Stalk
16. He loves, a la Ovid
17. Couple
18. Secular
20. Present!
21. Comedian Martha ____
22. Teen bane
23. Sailing
24. Outlet
25. Seabird
26. Bandleader
29. Andy's aunt
30. Biblical kingdom
32. Scot's "own"
33. Feminine suffix
35. Farm basket
36. Renoir's forte
37. Remembers
40. English county
41. Humph!
42. Beseech
43. Tenet
45. Dowel
46. Stale
47. Cloth scrap
48. Encrusted
49. More annoyed
53. Swab
54. Angler's boots
55. Radio spots
56. Tumbler
58. Did lunch
59. Lags
62. Tennis call
63. Intersected
67. Song part
68. Dismiss
69. Cong. helper
71. Earlier
72. Gown fabric
73. Perform
74. Sass
75. Novarro of film
77. Kitchen area
79. Loco
80. Charity
81. Virgil's "existence"
82. Dejected
83. Exclusively
84. Faux ____
86. Bandleader
91. Card game
94. Feel sore
96. Nebraska Indian
97. Billions of years
98. Gentle
99. Iraq's neighbor
100. Church section
101. Location
102. Nautical "yeses"
103. Bawdy
104. Caress
105. Job opening
106. Charter

DOWN

1. Vetch
2. Poet Khayyam
3. Bandleader
4. Pittsburgh player
5. Twitch
6. Apiece
7. One, in Emden
8. Made
9. Mr. Delon
10. Letter enc.
11. German port
12. Andress film
13. Bandleader
14. Part of HOMES
15. Allot
19. Citadel student
27. Healthy
28. Punctuated
31. Mock
34. Diatribes
35. Tibia front
36. Suffer
37. Gains
38. Early bird?
39. Prophet
40. Hot tub
41. Pro
42. Some buds
44. Tooth-mender's deg.
50. Sultanas
51. Inertia
52. Curvy turn
53. Small rug
54. "____ and Peace"
56. Candied
57. Advanced
59. Boob tubes
60. Thumb through
61. Bandleader
63. Flatfoot
64. Bandleader
65. Self-images
66. Mr. Rickles
68. Puma, e.g.
69. Exuberance
70. Rescue
75. Scampered
76. Like some teams
78. Lakota
79. Fannie ____
82. Trapshooting
83. Start
84. Jack's tote
85. Farm unit
87. Roofing thatch
88. PBS science series
89. Work hard
90. Aware of
92. So be it!
93. Trial
95. Objective

PUZZLE 182 CRYPTIC CROSSWORD

British-style or Cryptic Crosswords are a great challenge for crossword fans. Each clue contains either a definition or direct reference to the answer as well as a play on words. The numbers in parentheses indicate the number of letters in the answer words.

ACROSS

1. Dog food (4)
3. Case copper cracked for federal agency (5,5)
10. Places in California packing liquid cosmetics (9)
11. Smoldering wood bits from explosion must be extinguished rapidly (5)
12. What engravers do inside Heaven is ill-defined (7)
13. A game may offer nine payoffs at the casino after the 1st (7)
14. Choir section lost a beat (5)
15. Fought and broke up (8)
18. Just naughty, hiding knight's weapon (8)
20. Search inside mosques, tabernacles (5)
22. Olive-stuffer worked in tempo (7)
24. Toot while circling street (7)
25. Enlisted men don't open hot dogs (5)
26. Collect marble split by Greg (9)
27. Some very thin gauze covers whole ball of wax (10)
28. Burden is on us (4)

DOWN

1. Huge financial reverse taken in fossil fuel (8)
2. Rector has rearranged symphony (9)
4. Sheep, ox, yak, bears bond (5)
5. Was a checkout clerk fired? (9)
6. Wash a drinking vessel, receiving tip (5,2)
7. Superhero sidekick's too-short clothing (5)
8. Most distressed, struggling stores (6)
9. Branches of rumored mythological river (6)
15. Such tacos, prepared for corn-and-bean dish (9)
16. Ocular discomfort finally made Roger exercise (9)
17. We hear they rip off Pittsburgh players (8)
19. General pardon set many free (7)
20. Shake an arrow-holder (6)
21. Thin boxes bulge on the right side (6)
23. Finely chop aromatic herbs, I'm told (5)
24. Joker riding a child's toy (5)

*To receive a free copy of our guide, "**How to Solve Cryptic Crosswords**," send a self-addressed, business-sized, stamped envelope to Cryptic Clues, Penny Press, 6 Prowitt Street, Norwalk, CT 06855-1220 or visit the Puzzler's Corner section of our website at **PennyDellPuzzles.com**.*

PUZZLE 183

• PRESIDENTIAL MAKEUP •

ACROSS

1. Interpret
5. Med. course
9. Greek letters
14. Pins
18. Dugout
19. Las ____
21. Molder
22. "____ a man . . ."
23. Phyllis and Denzel
26. Blue or White
27. Clio's sister
28. Big guy
29. Blood parts
30. Raft
31. Series
33. Guts
35. Impartial
38. Finland's Saarinen
40. Pinnae
42. Alluring
43. Earl and Ann
48. Put up
52. Shooter
53. Stocky
54. Eleve's site
56. Peachy
57. From the beginning
59. Trade lingo
61. Dwelling
63. Oxford surface
64. Turn back to zero
66. Irrational
68. Police protection?
70. Insidious
71. Dylan and Joseph
78. Stable bit
81. Of an age
82. Dove's bane
83. Germanic god
87. Slice
89. Globe bearer
92. Jeweled coronet
96. Marry
97. Baited
99. Buccaneer's port?
101. Separated
103. Set the pace
104. Series ending
105. Victor and J. Edgar
108. Bard's lament
111. Singer Lofgren
112. Math ratio
113. Turtles and such
117. Stowe character
120. Exclude, legally
124. Ms. Peron
125. Hipbone sections
127. Mountain nymph
129. Technical piece
130. Glide
132. Richard and Peter
135. Dormant
136. Old Peruvians
137. "A Confederacy of Dunces" author
138. "Sommersby" star
139. Catbird seat?
140. Prescient ones
141. Some deer
142. Feudal serf

DOWN

1. Crazes
2. Noted critic
3. Bellowing
4. Less sanitary
5. Latin salutation
6. Colorful amphibian
7. Over
8. Discrimination
9. Playwright Jonson
10. Work units
11. Carried
12. Really likes
13. Roman council
14. Much of a martini
15. Simple sect
16. Battle royal
17. Place
20. Generous person
24. Lost cases
25. Intrude upon
32. Ms. Scacchi
34. Heath
36. Cans
37. Persian king
39. ____ about
41. Disdainful type
43. Bate
44. Floors
45. Embrace
46. Wee particles
47. Ball catcher
49. Epic poetry
50. Walled structure
51. Three-spot
52. Pitch
55. Hessian river
58. Dampen
60. ____ Mahal
62. Serpentine shape
65. French brew
67. Drops in the morning
69. AAA offering
72. Anatomical openings
73. Actor Damon
74. Muslim deity
75. Adipose
76. Tuck's title
77. Today
78. Northern capital
79. Styptic agent
80. Biblical weed
84. Tessera
85. State
86. Composer Rorem
88. Sired
90. Grace period?
91. Small spar
93. Disposed
94. Stadium cries
95. Calla lily, e.g.
98. Mustachioed painter
100. Flowering
102. More stylish
106. Lively wit
107. Hint
109. Court defenses
110. Moon goddess
113. Pine secretion
114. Escape
115. Buckets
116. Because
118. Man of La Mancha
119. Swift brute
121. Clears, in a way
122. Garnish
123. Zellweger of films
126. Cracked
128. Hill's partner
131. Rent
133. Beast of burden
134. In medias ____

PUZZLE 184

• NOVEMBER BIRTHDAYS •

ACROSS

1. Chihuahua bites
6. Tinker with, in a way
10. Goatee's place
14. Neck of mutton
19. Bouquet
20. Unusual, for Caesar
21. Bulgarian coins
22. Maya pet
23. Singer born 11/26/1939
25. Like Pegasus
26. Boring tool
27. Miss America's accessory
28. Au contraire!
29. Composer born 11/14/1900
32. Jackson or Johnson
35. Fetch
36. Actress Wallace
37. Removed
40. Ouija board word
41. Sentry's cry
43. Tire meas.
45. Villa d'____
49. Wild ass
51. "Utopia" author
52. Water carriers
54. Spain's El ____
55. U.S. poet
56. Writer born 11/30/1835
58. Tine
60. Shoppe adjective
61. Little lady
62. Capek drama
63. Loquacious
64. Take the Concorde
65. Sothern and Jillian
66. Replica
68. Got some shuteye
69. Fiver
70. President born 11/24/1784
73. Poke
76. Pump up
78. Thailand neighbor
79. Adjutant
80. Ajar
81. Sauna wear
83. ____ chi ch'uan
84. Has
85. Sacred cow?
86. Actress Anouk ____
87. Musician born 11/12/1945
90. Vacancy sign
91. Gulf st.
92. "Babylon 5" regular
94. They might be in your pants
95. Gabby Hayes's horse
96. Newcastle-upon-____
98. "Then what?"
99. "Time Machine" people
100. Actress Dawber
101. Hot off the presses
102. Japanese drama
104. "____ Lay Dying"
105. Canine's coat
108. Singer born 11/5/1941
114. United
115. Trip takers?
119. Gilbert and Teasdale
120. Wine region
121. Singer born 11/1/1957
124. Wild West transport
125. Regard
126. Transaction
127. "The Wreck of the Mary ____"
128. Dick and Jane, e.g.
129. Poi ingredient
130. ____ souci
131. Dart

DOWN

1. Makes a doily
2. "La Donna e mobile," e.g.
3. Dupes
4. Gerald Ford's city
5. Gained a lap
6. Comedy components?
7. Florentine exile
8. Pique
9. Seat of Irish kings
10. Bordeaux wine
11. Spartan slave
12. Netman Lendl
13. DEA agent
14. Land's end
15. Grand ____ Dam
16. Sitar song
17. Egyptian god
18. Prepare for action
24. Lower
30. Shoelace ornament
31. Frigg's husband
33. Minsk no
34. Fingerprint feature
37. Deceive
38. Ring-shaped pasta
39. Singer born 11/28/1943
42. Noah's command
43. Make a yoke
44. Go astray
46. Composer born 11/24/1868
47. Hue
48. Nervous
50. To the right
51. Swamp
52. ____ Loa
53. Realm
56. Chop
57. Habeus corpus et al.
59. Seance sound
61. Pesky insects
63. Lumps
65. Rhododendron's kin
66. Beaten path
67. Equality St.
68. David's weapon
71. Hockey's Chevrier
72. Gapes
74. Per
75. Award
77. Spike or Brenda
81. 27th president
82. Slick
83. On a peg
84. Bellybutton type
85. Web provider
87. Noted diarist
88. 81-Down, notably
89. Lennon's lady
90. Break, in a way
93. Lionized actor?
95. Skater's spin
97. Keep busy
99. Northern native
100. Discussion groups
103. Caravan stops
104. Paid to play
106. Pitcher Ryan
107. Jack
108. Org.
109. Pro ____
110. Streetcar
111. Emulate the Cheshire Cat
112. Exploited
113. Attorneys' degs.
116. Tackle
117. Another, senor
118. Cold comfort?
122. Vote for
123. Harem room

PUZZLE 185 CLAPBOARD

In this crossword puzzle all words in the same row or column overlap by one or two letters.

ACROSS

1. Twisted snack
6. Expressive
14. Rex Reed, e.g.
15. Marathon entrant
16. Discomfort
18. Tender
20. Indicated
23. Peace symbols
24. ___ Diego
26. Water pitcher
28. Covers the inside of again
31. Narrow cut
32. Tidiest
35. Rich cake
36. Tokyo, once
38. O'Hara's home
40. ___ you kidding?
41. Bert's pal
42. Early garden
45. Metric land measures
46. ___ boom
47. Aromatic trees
50. "Frasier" character
51. Take the helm
53. Remove soap from
54. In reserve
55. Downy duck
57. Bowler's button
61. State official
62. Ostrich or emu
63. Came forth
64. Kitchen alcove
65. Cincinnati nine
66. Performed alone
67. Reverie

DOWN

1. Careful
2. Begin again
3. Fifty-fifty
4. Acapulco aunt
5. Gusto
6. Wool grower
7. Allow to be borrowed
8. Director Welles
9. Tremble
10. Green
11. Isolated
12. St. Petersburg's river
13. New Jersey's capital
17. Heart parts
19. Wiggly swimmers
21. Close by
22. Golfer's peg
23. Morse-code signal
25. Assistant
27. Tedious
29. Present occasion
30. Great Lake
33. Notched
34. Watchman
35. Attempted
37. Beginning
38. Scarlet songbird
39. Experienced again
43. Quayle and Rather
44. Celtic
46. Passover feasts
48. Chore
49. Calorie counter
52. Uncanny
55. Consequently
56. Dummy
58. Location
59. Singer James
60. Abound

1	2	3	4	5	6	7	8	9	10	11	12	13
14							15					
16			17	18	19							
20		21		22		23				24	25	
26	27		28				29	30	31			
32				33	34	35				36		37
38		39	40		41				42	43	44	
45			46				47	48	49			
50				51			52	53				
54				55		56		57		58	59	60
61							62					
63						64						
65			66					67				

PUZZLE 186

• PRESIDENTS 27-38 •

ACROSS

1. Turquoise
5. Go huskies!
9. Cry for attention
13. Articles
18. Road warning
19. Hooked on
20. Fast car
22. Lawful
23. Circuits
24. Glasgow gal
25. Maine campus
26. Bogart's key
27. 1953-61; 1913-21
31. Lincoln coin
32. Isolate
33. Test model
34. Four Corners state
35. Best
39. Decimal place
42. Split
44. Tennessee battle site
45. Tree house?
47. Shells
49. ___ Palmas
52. Connection
53. 1969-74; 1945-53; 1909-13
56. Corrida cry
57. Wake up
59. Arabian gulf
60. Hibernia
61. A simple question
62. Raccoon kin
65. British peer
66. 1929-33; 1963-1969; 1974-77
71. Corundum
73. Ohio city
74. Unctuous
75. Newcastle export
76. Usher
78. Stand for something
80. Bombay bread
83. 1921-23; 1923-29
88. Nor'easter
89. Giant slugger
90. Gas
91. Flush
92. Rules of order?
94. Blue
95. Stats
96. Uniform trimming
97. Willing
100. French I word
103. He deposed Faruk
106. Auricular
107. 1933-45; 1961-63
114. Assembly
116. Rancor
117. Like the Gobi
118. Vibes
119. Ano starter
120. Transition
121. Broadway auntie
122. Sprouted
123. Make zero, perhaps
124. Cut short
125. Funk
126. Spread

DOWN

1. Up to it
2. ___ d'Orsay
3. Diamond officials
4. Altar locale
5. Talmud part
6. Open, in a way
7. Puts away
8. Lodge
9. Figurehead's spot
10. Eastern dress
11. Chastises
12. Keyed up
13. Sickly
14. China piece
15. Graceful wader
16. ___ Carta
17. Ai or unau
21. Leeway
28. Verne hero
29. Going back
30. "Psycho" psycho
35. Cold capital
36. Mr. Donahue
37. Point
38. Sort
40. German one
41. Take-home amount
43. It's charged
45. Tune
46. Tel. no.
47. Soundtrack
48. Marseilles Mrs.
49. Highland noble
50. "Hair" do
51. Uzi's kin
53. Island bird
54. Shoot!
55. Maudlin
57. Tar's call
58. Bulgarian coin
61. Cup or Series
62. Portable bed
63. Interjection
64. Ms. Miller
65. Cotton pod
66. Core
67. Mix chemically
68. Rocket launch
69. Proboscis
70. Tut, tut!
71. Parrot
72. Trench
76. Duke of baseball
77. Trip taker
78. Magazine execs
79. Mature
80. Fed.
81. Side petals
82. Coming up
84. Saver's fund
85. Mouths
86. Fired up
87. Vapid
88. Veldt beast
92. Ticket taker?
93. It's spun
94. Obtain
95. Form
96. Yupik speaker
97. Intern, often
98. Make amends
99. Swamps
101. Pitch
102. Lassos
104. Memorable mission
105. Amati's kin
108. Vanity case
109. Quayle, once
110. Emulates Xanthippe
111. Continental currency
112. Doodled
113. Open
115. Word for word?

PUZZLE 187

THE DICK VAN DYKE SHOW

ACROSS

1. Tortilla snack
5. Weakens
9. Caustic liquid
13. Shopping plaza
17. Hurry-up abbr.
18. Maple or oak
19. Marine bird
20. Elaborate melody
21. Former Italian money
22. Collar style
23. Paper or pudding
24. Enjoy a book
25. Alan Brady
28. Livestock hangout
30. Spanish cheer
31. Brush's kin
33. Nosh
34. Served ablaze
38. Wichita's locale
40. Marking post
44. Luxury auto
45. Scurried
47. Unsightly
49. Easy gait
50. Love, in Madrid
51. Talk
54. Dawn goddess
55. Famous canal
56. Giver's opposite
58. Under
60. Skye or Boston
62. Sweet spud
64. Actress Sophia ___
66. Goblet edge
67. Cooked with vapor
71. Pavarotti, for one
73. Crow
77. Tranquil
78. TV unit
80. Top story
82. Comply
83. Singer Redding
84. Brave one
86. Pollution-control dept.
87. Gather crops
88. Sample
90. Copies
93. Sewing need
95. N.Y. clock zone
97. Bather's bar
98. Asner and Harris
99. Outer garment
103. Jerry Helper
109. Untamed
110. Nick's wife
112. Motel offering
113. Trademark
114. Tra-___
115. Chew on
116. "M*A*S*H" star
117. Hammer, e.g.
118. Bridge feat
119. Ornamental pattern
120. Glimpsed
121. Director Preminger

DOWN

1. Powder ingredient
2. China's continent
3. Singer Vicki ___
4. Milky stone
5. Pittsburgh athletes
6. Bandleader Shaw
7. Drudge
8. New York Indian
9. Aviation prefix
10. Pegboard game
11. Ancient Peruvian
12. Plow inventor
13. Laura Petrie
14. Domain
15. Fibber
16. Diane or Cheryl
26. Steal
27. Reagan's nickname
29. Afternoon sleep
32. E. Lansing school
34. Level
35. Kind of bean
36. Berserk
37. Buddy Sorrell
38. Prepare to pray
39. Mail drop
41. Actress Loughlin
42. Mayberry tot
43. ___-do-well
46. P.D. alert
48. Belgian river
52. Much
53. Seoul, South ___
57. Butt into
59. Exited
61. "Adam's ___"

PUZZLE 187

63. Netting

65. Short letters

67. Highlander

68. So long

69. Yale students

70. Feat

72. Split

74. In the sack

75. Aquarium attraction

76. Sort

79. Knight of the Round Table

81. Sammy Davis, Jr. song, with "The"

85. Sioux Indian

89. Keyboard key

91. ___ Mahal

92. Musical dramas

94. Sixth sense

96. Serving utensil

98. Wear away

99. Wise birds

100. Small bottle

101. Jazz's Fitzgerald

102. Topnotch

104. Play part

105. Choir voice

106. ___ beer

107. "___ You Babe"

108. Unaccompanied

111. Dumbfound

PUZZLE 188

ACROSS

1. Clubs and spades, e.g.
6. Cheat
10. ___ the last laugh
14. City near Cleveland
15. '50s hoop
16. Maturing agent
17. Type of tea
18. Black, as pen-fluid
19. Macadamias
20. Attract
22. Most bizarre
24. Manicure board
26. Fellows
27. Defected
28. Talk wildly
31. Powerful person
35. Stool pigeon
36. Metropolitan
37. Got up
38. Appropriate
39. "___ of the Opera"
41. Duffel ___
42. Capri and Wight
44. Violin's kin
45. See you later!
46. Parasite
47. Pre-owned
48. Way to lose
49. Tosses
51. Fix text
53. Arouse
56. Stallions' mates
58. Capture
59. Secular
61. Reason
65. Vehicles
66. Half-moon shape
67. Staggering
68. Exaggeration
69. ___ out (barely managed)
70. Frets

DOWN

1. Tree exudate
2. Ho's instrument
3. Annoy
4. Honked
5. Elvis's expression
6. China's flaw
7. Smallest pup
8. Kind
9. Marshy inlet
10. Cutting tool
11. Chills and fever
12. Docs for Durocs
13. Formerly
21. Incense ingredient
23. Forceful person
24. Expire, as time
25. Valor
26. Peaceful
27. Fragile
29. Asian calculator
30. Weathercocks
32. Thread holder
33. Approved
34. Sire
36. Outcome
40. Not as young
43. Overshadow
48. Mojave, e.g.
50. Beautiful lady
52. Tablelands
53. Imprint with acid
54. Medical photo
55. Freshwater fish
56. Not yours
57. Scored on a serve
60. North Sea bird
62. Barbara Bush, ___ Pierce
63. Do a tailor's job
64. High train lines

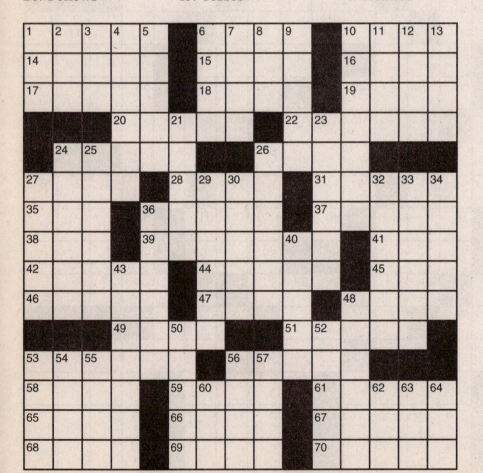

1	2	3	4	5	■	6	7	8	9	■	10	11	12	13
14					■	15				■	16			
17					■	18				■	19			
■	■	■	20		21			■	22	23				
■	24	25				■	■	26				■	■	■
27				■	28	29	30		■	31		32	33	34
35			■	36					■	37				
38			■	39					40		■	41		
42			43		■	44					■	45		
46					■	47				■	48			
■	■	■	49		50		■	■	51	52				■
53	54	55				■	56	57				■	■	■
58				■	59	60			■	61		62	63	64
65				■	66				■	67				
68				■	69				■	70				

PUZZLE 189

ACROSS

1. Some adders
5. Like an omelet
9. Hems and ___
13. Come again?
14. Rice and Sexton
16. Wicked
17. Volcanic overflow
18. Very thin
19. Stand up
20. Frozen dessert
22. Disposed (of)
24. Arms depot
27. Incantation
30. Labor
31. Manner
34. Thanksgiving fare
35. Keats's twilight
36. Restaurant list
37. Prickly stem
38. Hesitant sounds
39. Flat-bottomed boat
40. Seasoned
41. Guy
42. Punctuation mark
43. Ruby-colored
44. Type type
45. Valuable holding
46. Olympian
48. Disparaging remark
52. Try
57. Gentle creature
58. Show feeling
61. Soft drink
62. Slender
63. More fresh
64. Car part
65. Messes up
66. Aquatic bird
67. ___ and ends

DOWN

1. Hole-making tools
2. Persian ruler
3. Blacktop
4. "___ Search"
5. Earnestly
6. Small flies
7. Stocky antelope
8. Craving
9. Cattle group
10. Keen
11. Knowing
12. Toboggan's cousin
15. Exert
21. Hay bundler
23. Not well
25. Everlasting
26. Refusals
27. Upwelling
28. Used a crowbar
29. ___ out (barely earned)
31. Cliff home
32. Metal bar
33. Was sorry for
34. Aspen lift
36. Disfigures
38. Every
39. Attack
41. Winter hand warmer
42. Blueprint
44. Sidekick
47. Nosher
48. At leisure
49. Poetic contraction
50. Burn
51. Decorative vases
53. Yodeler's feedback
54. Disposition
55. Proceed slowly
56. Little boys
59. Gathered
60. Have bills

PUZZLE 190

ACROSS

1. Sheep's fleece
5. Infatuated
9. Work units
13. Rajah's mate
14. Black
16. Vault
17. Ledger entry
18. Preference
19. Cabbage's relative
20. Toss
22. Inexpensive
24. Male child
25. Puffin's kin
27. Dash
29. Fish features
32. Encloses
35. Pet birds
38. Collection of Hindu aphorisms
39. Caliph
40. Urge
41. Garment of India
42. Actor Murphy
44. Devitalized
47. Soft-shell clam
49. Lubricated
50. Move slightly
51. Greek letter
52. Movie, for short
54. Private instructor
57. Southpaw
62. Captain's direction
64. Less colorful
66. Former Italian currency
67. Color
68. Thrice minus once
69. Flexible armor
70. Despise
71. Topers
72. Whoa!

DOWN

1. Formal decree
2. Solemn statement
3. Lollapalooza
4. Exec's wheels
5. Understand
6. Toward the rear
7. Golly's kin
8. Poker offering
9. Broad-antlered deer
10. Land
11. Colorful
12. Went over the limit
15. Pine
21. Hike
23. Shoe liners
26. Take advantage of
28. Pertaining to a reason
29. Entire range
30. Like an opal
31. Cowboy's rope
32. Laborer of yore
33. Made a mistake
34. Declared
35. Edible seeds
36. Watcher
37. Decimal unit
43. Exude
45. Decay
46. Small bottle
48. Explode
51. Upright
52. Narrow trail
53. Pelvic bones
55. Playing marbles
56. Hodgepodge
58. Shade providers
59. Formal order
60. Threesome
61. Shrill bark
63. Summer, on the Seine
65. Legal matter

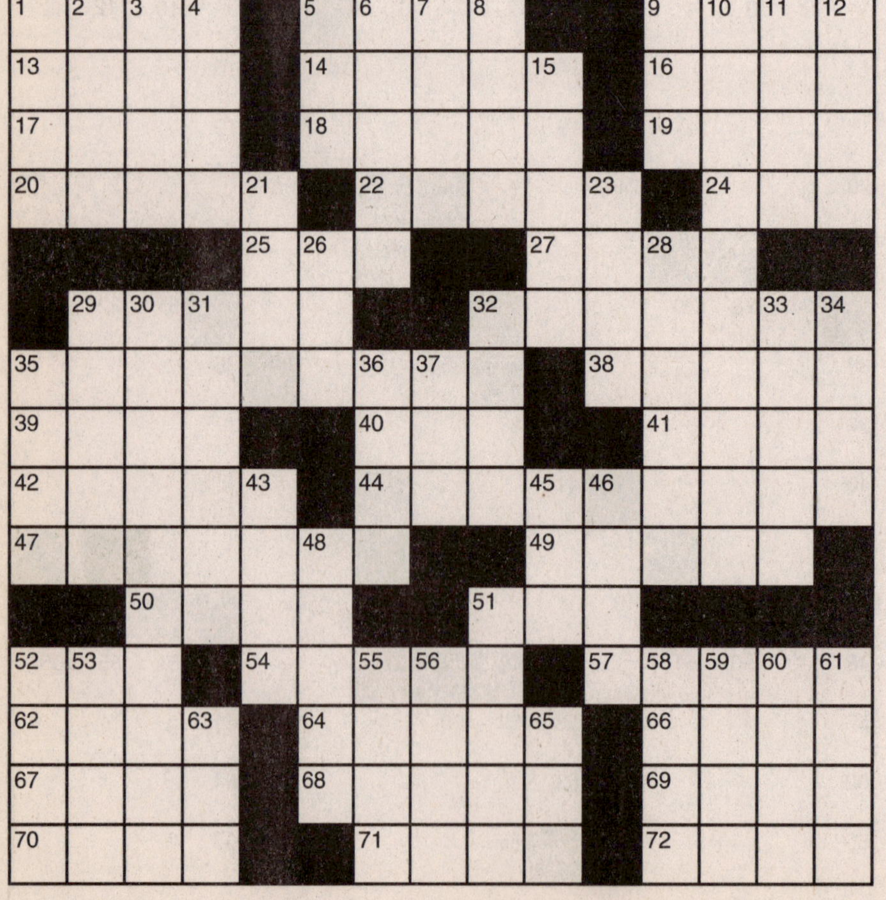

PUZZLE 191

ACROSS

1. Study for finals
5. Shopper's help
9. Liquid measure
14. Brave-deed doer
15. Atop
16. ___ board
17. Bronze and Stone
18. Stocking mishap
19. Bowling term
20. Cope
22. Largemouth ___
24. Ordinary
25. Emcees
29. Scoundrel
31. Quite beautiful
34. Mule's cousin
37. Hoped
39. Suggestion
40. Garden or hound
42. Noise
43. Matched pair
44. Wrought ___
45. Colored
47. Cloud's location
48. Some spray cans
50. Jogged
52. Patch the roof
53. Ways
57. Seven-year ___
60. Cornflakes, e.g.
61. Take by theft
65. Cure
67. Speechless
68. Greetings!
69. Man Friday
70. Received a high grade on
71. Moray fisherman
72. College figure, for short
73. Eyepiece

DOWN

1. Victor
2. Grand
3. Boxing site
4. Inlay
5. ___ one's temper
6. Traveler's stop
7. Take a ___ at (try)
8. Caesar's garb
9. Assignment
10. Mischievous being
11. English beverage
12. Blow it
13. Pastrami on ___
21. Nibble
23. Tremble
26. Temper tantrum
27. Ocean movements
28. Slink
30. Twist awry
31. Avoids
32. Campground item
33. Strong, as meat
34. Operatic melody
35. More achy
36. Make a run
38. Earth
41. Tangle
46. Notre ___
49. Seafarer
51. Average
54. Tennis term
55. Consumed
56. Snow coasters
58. Fellow
59. Inheritor
60. Musical staff sign
61. That girl
62. Follows ess
63. House wing
64. Pub beverage
66. Flurry

PUZZLE 192

ACROSS

1. Brusque
5. Deteriorates
9. Like the Sahara
13. Butter substitute
14. Lessen
16. Overcurious
17. Structural
19. Parable
20. Burdened
21. Veteran
23. Clergy mem.
25. Multitude
26. Gallivant
29. "The ___" (Diana Ross film)
31. Fixed a shoe
35. Dined
36. Surrounded by
39. Adequate, to a bard
41. Bluish gray
43. Convent dweller
44. '70s nightclub
45. Crown of light
46. Glacial epoch
48. Guitar's kin
49. Typhoon
51. Diamond, e.g.
52. Letter before tee
53. Cathedral section
56. Conducted
58. Fast felines
62. Heart vessel
66. Chauffeured car
67. Poplar variety
70. Like
71. Cornered, as a raccoon
72. Indian dress
73. Captures
74. Coastal bird
75. Previously

DOWN

1. Black fuel
2. Arm bone
3. Devour a book
4. Carrier
5. Bump into
6. Ginza belt
7. Filled tortillas
8. Delay
9. Not pro
10. Meander
11. Florida Key, e.g.
12. Color changer
15. Most mature
18. Kind of street
22. Couple
24. Vitality
26. Cut
27. Map collection
28. Dispensed
30. Metallic element
32. Flower necklace
33. Result
34. Wharves
37. Proper
38. Catch
40. Miseries
42. Also
44. Dishonor
46. Collision
47. Mousse alternative
50. Squealer
54. Singer Dinah ___
55. Chemical compound
57. Hunt with a divining rod
58. Tribe
59. Wilderness walk
60. Discharge
61. Geologic divisions
63. Crowd noise
64. Rocky peaks
65. Miner's portal
68. Hamilton bill
69. Keats work

FLOWER POWER

PUZZLE 193

The answers to this petaled puzzle will go in a curve from the number on the outside to the center of the flower. Each number in the flower will have two 5-letter answers. One goes in a clockwise direction and the second in a counterclockwise direction. We have entered two answers to help you begin.

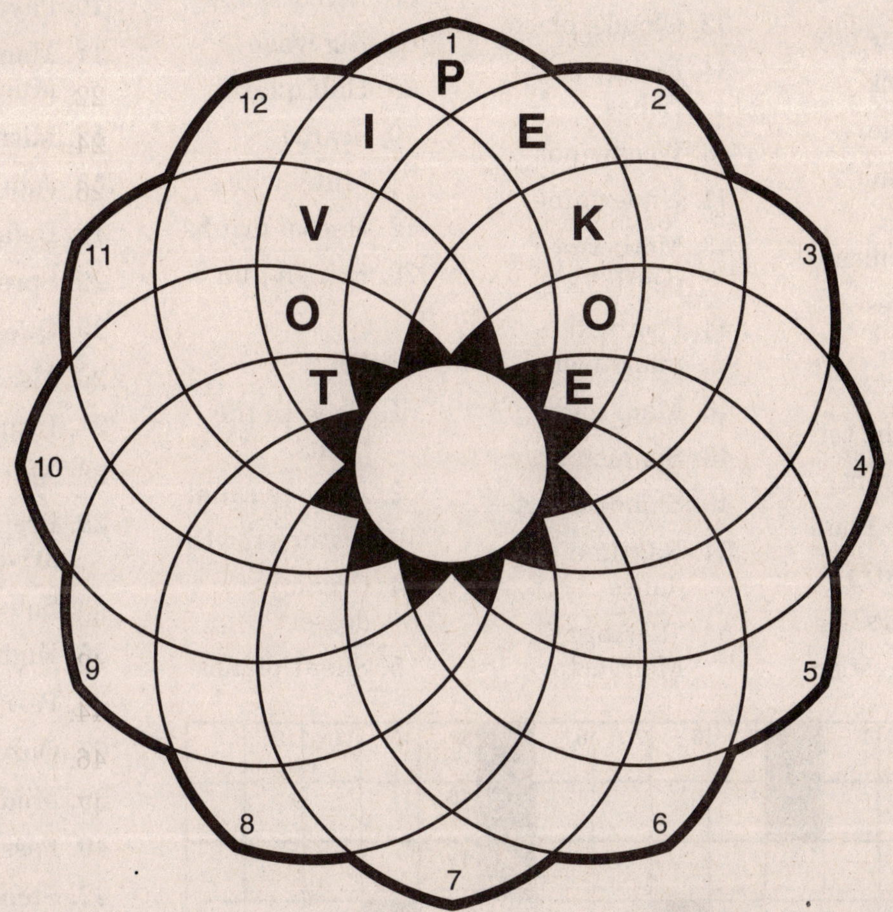

CLOCKWISE

1. Kind of tea
2. Cut a rug
3. Entices
4. Disorderly
5. Type of newspaper
6. Fabric weave
7. Pertaining to the sun
8. Sofa
9. Biased one
10. Hearsay
11. Detach
12. Metric liquid measure

COUNTERCLOCKWISE

1. Swivel
2. Dissuade
3. Pastry chef
4. Landed property
5. Thaw
6. Sample, as food
7. Chard or cheese
8. Lacy mat
9. "___ the Kid"
10. Challenger
11. Sweetener
12. Yellow citrus fruit

PUZZLE 194

HIDDEN TREES

ACROSS

1. Drill
5. Robin or Andy
9. Clay brick
14. A Guthrie
15. Ms. Falana
16. Light measurement
17. Statuettes
19. Cut and shuffled
20. Poufed the coif
21. Staff member
23. Never, in Bonn
24. Opera extra
27. Rock stars?
30. Hefty wrestler
31. Holiday forerunner
32. Cloud's place
34. Freshwater fishes
38. Woodwinds
41. Undermine
43. Mother-of-pearl
44. Football maneuver
46. Maui meal
48. Spanish bravo
49. Samoan port
51. Ragtime dance
54. "12 Angry Men" actor
58. Id's kin
59. Norse goddess of fate
60. Glacial epoch
64. Harpoon
66. Remorseless
68. Big wave
69. Half quart
70. Scarce
71. Milky white
72. Herbal drinks
73. British gun

DOWN

1. Go with the float
2. Famous canal
3. Water growth
4. Creamy dessert
5. Silent planes
6. Charged particle
7. Indistinct
8. Essentials
9. Council member
10. Payable
11. Man from Muscat
12. Misrepresent
13. Join
18. Default result
22. Spread
25. Questions
26. Ms. Ponselle
27. Insignificant
28. All tied up
29. Prepared to drive
33. Squeal
35. Highlander
36. Perry's creator
37. Ooze
39. Mild expletive
40. Passively
42. Steno's milieu
45. Yucatan youth
47. Stands firm
50. Precipitous
52. Individually
53. Blackens
54. Softens
55. Another time
56. Musical piece
57. Singer Lennox
61. Latin I lesson word
62. Crawford's ex
63. Utopia
65. Crow's call
67. Literary olio

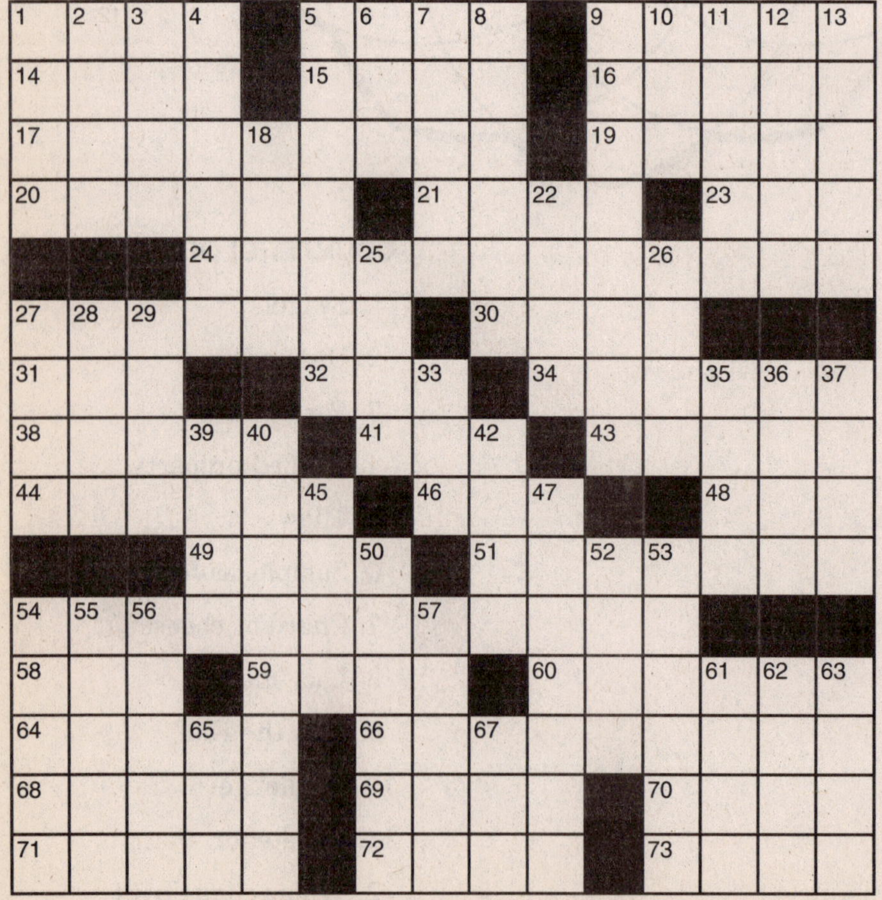

PUZZLE 195

JEWELRY SHOP

ACROSS

1. Phantom's domain
6. Cracked open
10. Clockmaker Thomas
14. Say yes to
15. Command
16. "Casablanca" role
17. Al Jolson's ex
19. Half a Carrey film
20. Columbus-Savannah dir.
21. Actress Fay ___
22. Painter Munch
24. Raised platform
25. Rural unit
26. Pointed roof
28. Prosper
32. Troy story
33. Prize preceder
34. Arkin movie
35. Paper measure
36. Skinned
37. Space chimp
38. Game of chance
39. Clears
40. Wedding bands?
41. Advocates
43. Nearby
44. Obligation
45. Piglet's pal
46. Snicker sound
49. Theatrical bunch
50. Gossiper's question
53. Demolish
54. Buttercup's kin
57. Battle song?
58. Constantly
59. Mysterious
60. Trudge
61. Protected
62. Tinters

DOWN

1. Crews' controls?
2. Asset
3. European river
4. Singer Acuff
5. Ungraceful
6. Zones
7. Month named for Caesar
8. Shandy ingredient
9. Tape again
10. Australian fish
11. Mr. Kazan
12. Despot
13. Arduous
18. Famous canal
23. Actress Joanne ___
24. Oahu attraction
25. Healing plants
26. Hit the hay
27. Elton's ivories
28. Crosses over
29. Ancient Greek colony
30. Bobbin
31. Boo!
32. Vexes
33. Cow farm
36. Mentors' charges
40. Having molars
42. Bring action against
43. Forgotten
45. Man with a mission?
46. Pitfall
47. Aristocrat
48. Singer Pinza
49. Musical symbol
50. "The Way We ___"
51. Rapunzel's pride
52. Works by Keats
55. Caesar's breakfast
56. Spanish king

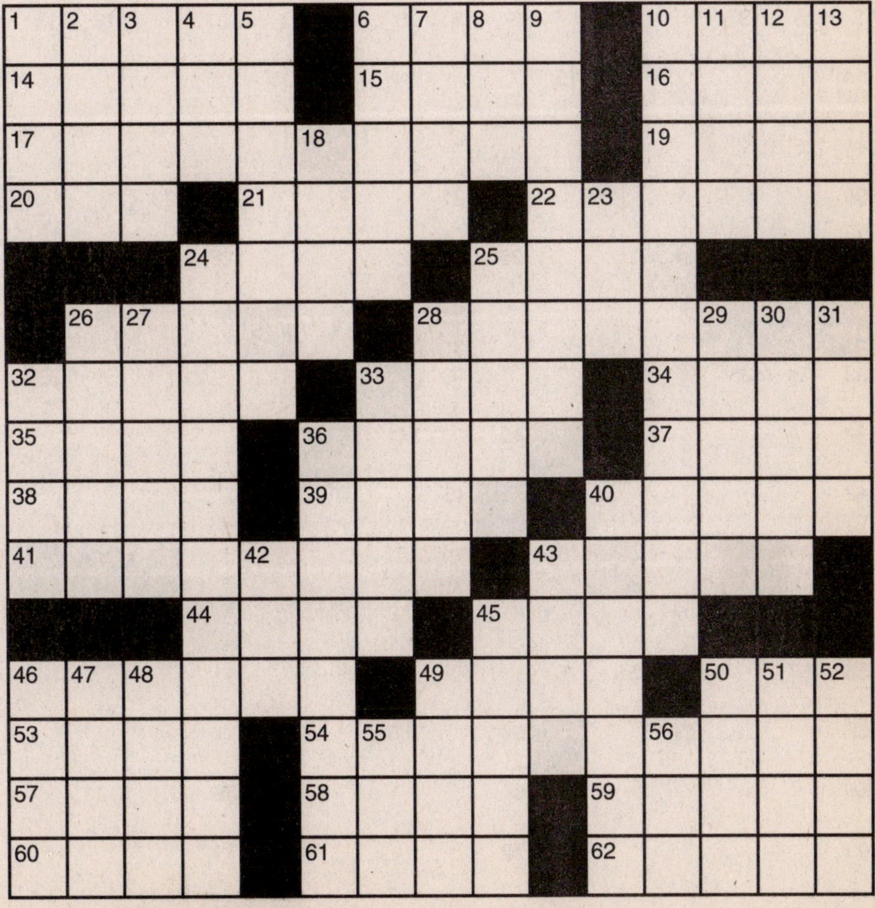

PUZZLE 196

WHAT'S IN A NAME?

ACROSS

1. English resort
5. Tra followers
9. Trod the boards
14. Nobelist Wiesel
15. Cupid
16. Wallace of early flicks
17. Rapid-fire weapons
19. Nostalgic piece
20. "Plenty of fish in ___"
21. Mentor
23. German article
24. Musical aptitude
25. From ___ Z
27. Full of holes, maybe
29. Makes
31. Arab garb
33. Cupboards
36. City on the Somme
39. Straighten
40. Possessed
42. Speechify
43. Holy place?
45. Gave
47. Type of wood
48. Did a cowboy's job
50. Deviated
52. "___ Not Unusual"
53. Go gray
56. Alphabet start
58. "The Heat ___"
60. Made amends
62. Bundled hay
64. Tress holders
66. Toughen
67. Diabolic
68. "I cannot tell ___"
69. Exclude
70. All there
71. Cad

DOWN

1. Ms. Davis
2. Hi from Ho
3. Track official
4. Edges
5. Heir, often
6. Islands off New Guinea
7. Pine for
8. Take for granted
9. Circa
10. Animation frame
11. Cuddly toy
12. Canal or lake
13. Vat man
18. Hungered (for)
22. Bus rider Parks
26. Pledge
28. Fair-___ (blond)
29. Movie house
30. Despots
32. Feed the kitty
33. Feline
34. Natural balm
35. Police baton
37. Shyness
38. But, to Brutus
41. TV's Ricky
44. Corrida shouts
46. Distinguished
49. Sun-dried bricks
51. More expansive
53. Feeble
54. Lamp dweller
55. Ford dud
56. Snoozing
57. Curse
59. PBS show
61. Colorful fish
63. Historic chapter
65. Container

1	2	3	4	■	5	6	7	8	■	9	10	11	12	13
14				■	15				■	16				
17				18					■	19				
20						■	21		22		■	23		
24			■	25		26	■	27			28		■	■
■	■	■	29				30			■	31		32	■
33	34	35						■	36	37				38
39					■	40		41	■	42				
43					44	■	45		46					
■	47			■	48	49						■	■	■
■	■	50		51			■	52			■	53	54	55
56	57		■	58			59	■	60		61			
62			63		■	64		65						
66					■	67				■	68			
69					■	70				■	71			

PUZZLE 197

A HAIRY QUOTATION

ACROSS

1. Driving-safety group: abbr.
5. Essence
9. Denomination
13. Writer Wiesel
14. Ms. Osmond
15. Sapling
16. Folk stories
17. Guam's capital
18. Take away
19. Start of quote
22. Animal pouch
23. Container top
24. Pig's home
25. At the time
27. Tightly pulled
29. Avenues: abbr.
32. Coloring
34. More of quote
37. Turn aside
39. "Ben-___"
40. Sideshow
41. More of quote
44. Broil
45. Printing measures
46. Move quickly
47. Molding curve
49. Portable bed
50. Cops' group: abbr.
51. Song syllable
54. End of quote
59. Molten flow
60. Defense group: abbr.
61. Channel changer
62. French seasons
63. Dirty
64. This, to Pedro
65. Gunfighter Wyatt ___
66. Arranges
67. In order

DOWN

1. Defrosts
2. Maui greeting
3. Candor
4. Judge
5. Beeped
6. Oil-producing land
7. Singer Turner
8. Prepares leftovers
9. Narration
10. Ms. Bombeck
11. Work overhead
12. Asian holiday
14. Boat basin
20. Bullfight cry
21. Say
26. That woman's
27. Feel
28. Atmosphere
29. Savvy, in a way
30. Vidale sitcom
31. Prophet
32. Yarn
33. Bakery hot spot
35. Therefore
36. Relaxation
38. Alps region
42. Vacations
43. Nary a soul
48. Leg, in slang
49. Hold tightly
50. Baby carriages
52. Lasso
53. Lace tag
54. So long, in Liverpool
55. By any chance
56. Raced
57. Fried, in France
58. Yemeni port
59. Grant's foe

PUZZLE 198

• IN A STATE •

ACROSS

1. Shadowbox
5. Pie ___ mode
8. Identical
12. Nuclear bit
16. ___ Krishna
17. Chalice cloth
19. Now's mate
20. Test model
21. Enthusiastic
22. Norwegian seaport
23. Nevada city
24. Freeway sign
25. Gin cocktail
29. Lawyer: abbr.
30. Chemical suffix
31. Pontiac model
32. "The Raven" writer's monogram
33. Swiss peaks
35. Sun, to Miguel
36. Entertainer John ___
39. By and by
42. Invent
46. Detergent
48. Persuade
49. Sicilian peak
52. Portion out
54. Blackthorn fruit
56. Miner's goal
57. Pasture
59. Ring-shaped reef
61. Throw
63. ___ of Babel
64. Pesters
67. Private teacher
70. French waterway
72. Industrialist Cyrus ___
73. Indy 500 champion
74. In past days
76. Humorist Rogers
79. Caesar, e.g.
81. Minor quarrel
82. Separate
84. Shoddy
86. Nullify
88. Draw or stud
90. Fat
92. Make lace
93. Tangle
95. Earth: pref.
97. Corn or safflower
98. Testing center
101. Abel, to Adam
103. Rocky Mountain school
108. Desertlike
110. Large book
111. Verve
112. Shaped like an egg
113. Mexican morsel
114. Help a criminal
115. Ms. Ward
116. Singer Young
117. Forest creatures
118. Eyepiece
119. Actor Mineo
120. Heredity factor

DOWN

1. Embarrass
2. Golfer Corey ___
3. Develop
4. Blushing colors
5. Disciples
6. Cowboy's tool
7. "___ Need"
8. Streaks
9. Throat clearer
10. List of dishes
11. ___ Gay (plane)
12. Picnic drink
13. Southern dance
14. Fail to include
15. Rock's ___ the Hoople
18. Saunter
26. Frankenstein's aide
27. Butter serving
28. Part of a house
34. Ballet move
35. Weighing devices
37. Distress letters
38. Actor Holbrook
40. Maize spike
41. Canadian whiskey
43. Melville captain
44. So long, in Liverpool
45. Gnaw away
47. Burst open
49. Salamander
50. Uncle, in Salamanca
51. Allan Houston, e.g.
53. British composer
55. Diner offering
58. Ms. Barrymore

60. Pretend

62. Nightfall

65. Type of apple

66. Difficulty

68. Egg cells

69. Squealer

71. ___ Van Winkle

74. Venomous snake

75. Infant's sound

77. ___ Alamos

78. Mr. Gehrig

80. Patriotic

83. Bowling-frame count

85. Rues

87. Like a beanpole

89. Charles S. Dutton series

91. Brewed drink

PUZZLE 198

94. Complete

96. Some Keats poems

97. Florida city

98. Embankment

99. Encore!

100. Southern beauty

101. Glut

102. Certain exam

104. Earring's place

105. Peck film, with "The"

106. Corrida cries

107. Hanker

109. John ___ Passos

PUZZLE 199

FINALLY

ACROSS

1. Decomposes
5. Lincoln and Fortas
9. Hunt for bargains
13. Kibbutz dance
17. Rock-guitarist Clapton
18. Actress Carter
19. Robin Cook novel
20. Attention-getter
21. U2's principal singer
22. Celebration
23. Poet's Ireland
24. Hemingway's sobriquet
25. To stop
28. Veep's superior
29. Ballet step
30. London gallery
31. Kansas City nine
33. Rooster's comb, e.g.
36. Vertical pole
38. Burden
39. Rya, e.g.
40. Follow closely
42. Plains Indian
46. Yoko ___
47. Immigrants' island
49. Medic or trooper preceder
50. The way in
51. Upper limb
52. Ms. Helmsley
54. Mosque priest
55. Coin factory
58. Unable to cope
62. "Thin Man" role
63. Exam type
64. Mosquito genus
65. Drilling equipment
67. Neophyte
68. "Graf ___"
69. Actress Barkin
72. Box
75. Convoyed
77. Stated
78. Colorado Indian
79. Scorch
80. Ship deserters
82. Bullion
84. Respect
87. Daze
89. Sault ___ Marie
90. Feel concern
91. Earn enough to live on
96. Pizzeria chamber
97. Verve
98. German article
99. Flight impediment
102. Show the way
103. Sunday newspaper section
104. Sector
105. Shoestring
106. Mechanics' guesses: abbr.
107. Crystal gazer
108. Sly look
109. Dueling sword

DOWN

1. Southern soldier, once
2. Spanish gold
3. Lightly color
4. Hot news items
5. Black ___ (cattle type)
6. Metronome info
7. Her, to Juan
8. Leans to one side
9. Bloodhound's clue
10. Nomadic group
11. Elide
12. Wide view
13. Filmgoer's delight
14. Tara surname
15. Drive back
16. Accumulate moola
26. Pitter follower
27. Devour
32. ___ Mae Brown ("Ghost" role)
33. ___-Magnon
34. Seek office
35. It's often inflated
36. Wire-diameter measure
37. Mr. Baba
38. Navigational device
41. Soprano Gluck
42. Walking stick
43. Lombardy lake
44. Frost
45. Author Bombeck
48. Coast
49. Wild West law group
51. Unsettled

53. Parisian summer

55. Speck

56. Eye feature

57. DEA agent

59. Candle

60. Root (out)

61. Berliner's three

66. Put into writing

68. Hems and haws

70. Anzio lander: abbr.

71. Cruces preceder

72. Hidden mike

73. Jurist Lance ____

74. Court divider

76. Female sandpiper

80. Regret

PUZZLE 199

81. Temper with heat

83. Haystack find?

84. French school

85. Copies to disk

86. Pick up the tab

87. Ray

88. Purport

89. Besmirch

92. Lotion ingredient

93. Desperate

94. Dirk

95. Snare

100. Red Baron, e.g.

101. Turn right

PUZZLE 200

GET INTO YOUR STRIDE

ACROSS

1. At the center
5. Doctrines
9. Competent
12. Talon
16. Wise men
17. Scat!
18. Market decline
20. Bonheur or Ponselle
21. Love god
22. Gull cousin
23. Dynamic lead-in
24. College credit
25. Doodling
27. Brit's jail
28. Without ice
29. Garlic cousin
30. Float
32. Thus
34. Syrup source
37. ___ light
39. A crowd?
43. Golfer Aoki
44. Island of New York
46. Vientiane natives
48. "Star Wars" surname
50. Discounter's boast
51. Sister of Ares
52. Former draft org.
53. Escalation
54. Strike
55. Notorious Marquis
56. Mad reversal
57. Preserve
58. Balderdash
60. Part of TLC
63. Fancy fossil resin
66. Undergarment
68. Half a dance?
71. Norse monarch
72. Biblical weed
73. Martian craft
75. List ender
77. Soaked by the sea
78. Peel
79. Sir Arthur Conan ___
80. Tasty dessert
82. Ceremonies
83. Lennon's love
85. Bring home the bacon
86. Solar disk
88. Lantern
91. Calamities
93. Car part
98. Not aweather
99. Duffer's concerns
100. Dieter's word
101. Dog's bane?
102. Needy
103. Sherpa sighting
104. Eve's grandson
105. Move swiftly
106. Sermon seats
107. Take advantage of
108. Certain
109. Auld lang ___

DOWN

1. Singer Ed ___
2. Writer Connelly
3. Mr. Stravinsky
4. Reject a tax deduction
5. Yucca fiber
6. Arab leader
7. Poet's sunup
8. Crooner
9. Slow, in music
10. Forewords
11. Spanish bull
12. Most crisp
13. Singular
14. Katmandu's place
15. Light-bulb word
19. Aldermen
26. Diminutive
31. Dryly humorous
33. Addams family cousin
34. Muffet's title
35. Pops the question
36. Remits
37. Koko's dagger
38. Relaxation
40. ___ avis
41. Writer Bagnold
42. Latin being
44. Environment
45. Approves
47. Flightless bird
49. Coach Parseghian
50. Dykstra of baseball
54. Grill's go-with
56. Darkroom workers

PUZZLE 200

57. Average grade

59. Uncover, poetically

60. Sorority member

61. Choir section

62. Risque

64. Stable denizen

65. Handcuffs

66. Mast

67. Vegas or Cruces

68. Shoot the breeze

69. Take on

70. Simians

73. Scams

74. Corporate children?

76. Perfect score, for some

77. Swiss stream

81. Movie dog

82. Director Reiner

84. Greasy

86. John Jacob ___

87. Not those

88. Sami

89. Medicinal plant

90. Cat's comment

92. Stead

94. Hokkaido aborigine

95. Compatriot

96. Hold back

97. See socially

PUZZLE 201

KITCHEN COUPLES

ACROSS

1. Footwear item
5. Computer's fodder
9. Nixon's successor
13. ___ of Man
17. Cash drawer
18. Flightless birds
19. Nobelist Wiesel
20. Combat of honor
21. Brink
22. Humdinger
23. Former Steeler coach
24. Stone and Iron
25. Complexion ingredients
29. Alias letters
30. "Bewitched" boss Larry ___
31. Jane or John
32. Erode
34. Mine find
35. Entreat
36. Glaring
40. Luigi's love
43. Bruin Bobby ___
44. Having wings
45. Son of Seth
46. Luau neckwear
47. "Surfin' ___"
48. Copperhead, e.g.
49. Genetic abbr.
50. Malady
53. Soho fellow
54. Tightwad
56. Leeds's river
57. Politician Gorton
58. Heavenly instrument
59. Singer Summer
61. Tend a furnace
62. ___ lot
65. Total
66. Skyline sight
67. Rotating disk
68. Dove's comment
69. Rend
71. Prong
72. Week unit
73. Queen of ___
75. ___ needle
77. Wager
78. "The ___ Sanction"
79. Beat-icon Cassady
80. Pod dweller
81. Flits about
82. "___-Devil"
84. Basic ingredients
91. Theater section
93. ___ bien
94. Piglet's pal
95. This, in Madrid
96. Egg-shaped
97. Pinball foul
98. South African fox
99. Bridge feat
100. Bonus
101. Widemouthed pot
102. In no event, to Keats
103. Lone

DOWN

1. Stride
2. Secrete
3. Gymnast Korbut
4. Voter
5. Erase
6. Entertain
7. Russian city
8. Into pieces
9. Yard barrier
10. Swan genus
11. Enrage
12. Dover's locale
13. Muckraker Tarbell
14. Little girls' ingredients
15. Onion's cousin
16. "Born Free" lioness
26. Fabled race loser
27. Faithful companion
28. Ryan of films
33. "Chances ___"
35. Bikini top
36. Offbeat person
37. Fisherman's haunt
38. "___ but the Brave"
39. Autocrat
40. Liston opponent
41. Gibson or Blanc
42. Salad-dressing ingredients
43. WWII spy org.
44. Battery terminal
47. Utilize
48. Quench
51. Anais ___
52. Seaver's stat
53. Actor Eric ___
54. Blemish

55. Provoke

57. Wasp's vengeance

58. ___ radio

59. Sinister

60. Thor's father

61. Laundry cycle

62. Salary

63. San Francisco's ___ Hill

64. Indian state

66. Short dagger

67. Feline

70. Hot time in France

72. Showing no emotion

73. Fizzy drink

74. Party giver

76. Flat cap

PUZZLE 201

77. Gentle bear

78. Soap suds

80. Italian staple

81. Silly fowl

82. Sty fare

83. Moved in a certain direction, nautically

85. Seed coat

86. Relate

87. Sit

88. Norwegian port

89. List ender

90. Alike

92. Large deer

PUZZLE 202

FOILED AGAIN!

ACROSS

1. Reunion attendee
5. Wistful word
9. Iowa town
13. Steel-mill leftover
17. Staff member
18. Go bad
19. Lively tune
20. Sundowner
21. Boxer's bane
22. Informed of
23. Diva Gluck
24. Finito
25. Foil
28. Hardly ever
30. Poetic tribute
31. Tight-lipped
32. Farr's costar
33. Duplicate
36. Cover completely
38. Bloodhound, e.g.
42. Abner's radio partner
43. From the top
45. Prepare for a fight
46. Letter from Athens
47. There are lodes of these
49. House shape
50. Borscht base
51. Part of RBI
52. Unspecific
54. Wanted-poster word
55. Remnant
56. Traffic ingredient?
57. Grouch
58. Ed Asner role
59. Seer's card
62. Bootblack's offering
63. China closet
67. Press agent?
68. Glass bottle
69. ___ choy
70. Foyer flooring
71. Pencil center
72. Loosen
73. The Ram
75. Flesh and blood
76. Berate
78. Vitality
79. Pick up the tab
81. "Hamlet" has five
82. Gp. for internists
83. Bad start
84. Borneo sultanate
87. Foil
93. Ms. Bonheur
94. Reject, as a bill
96. City on the Oka
97. Tip-top
98. Indeed!
99. Actor Kincaid
100. Indicator
101. Assess
102. Ms. Lipinski
103. Metallic fabric
104. Catch sight of
105. Paint like Pollock

DOWN

1. Fishing tool
2. Agitate
3. Yemen port
4. Football's Jones
5. Expiate
6. Oxygen tank?
7. Humanities
8. Abominable guy?
9. Eye opener?
10. Salsa temperature
11. Freddy's street
12. Strategic Defense Initiative
13. Foil
14. World spinner
15. Fourth person
16. Like "Halloween"
26. Sneaking suspicion
27. Ballpark verdict
29. Cause of inflation?
32. Buick buckets
33. Noisy shoe
34. Enticement
35. Premonition
36. Social visit
37. Dipstick covering
38. Directive to Lassie
39. One of 24
40. Sicilian peak
41. Grate
44. Reverse, e.g.
45. Left Bank river
48. Foil
50. Empty
53. Betrayer
54. Emerge

PUZZLE 202

55. Have a bawl

57. Pursue

58. Winfrey rival

59. Cash drawer

60. Sector

61. Meander

62. Narrow boards

63. Jukebox food

64. Winged goddess

65. Essayist's pen name

66. RV alternative

68. Fiesta

69. Burning issue of the '70s

73. Topped with ice cream

74. Cherry leftover

77. Good service?

78. Big bird

80. Incentive

82. Dateless

83. Playground ruffian

84. Unruly child

85. "Arrivederci" city

86. Opportunist

87. Cyclotron fodder

88. Garden bloomer

89. Spring tide

90. Pride remark

91. Naysayer

92. Brooder remark

95. History-book chapter

PUZZLE 203

ACROSS

1. Ski resort feature
6. "The Merry Widow" composer
11. Wooden shoe
15. Hoosegow
19. Painter Winslow ___
20. Foe
21. Mend
22. Unctuous
23. Sacred images
24. Figaro's occupation
27. Where Heather grows
28. Obstruct
29. City in Japan
30. One, in Munich
31. Ballpark event
34. Anthem poet
35. Actor Romero
39. Light scent
44. Arrow poison
45. Groove
46. "Prince Valiant" character
47. "Cry ___ River"
48. Of a grain
51. Peak: abbr.
52. Like sandpaper
54. Bean Town dessert?
57. Oregon's capital
58. Part of a shoe
59. "Love at First ___"
60. Opposed to aweather
61. Malaga miss
63. Hamster or rabbit, e.g.
64. Chess champ
67. Sotto voce
68. Salary
69. 1988 Olympics site
70. Horse-drawn cab
72. Circle part
73. Bullring hero
76. Variety
77. Munitions
79. Greek consonants
80. Roused
82. Artist's gypsum
86. Shrew
87. Church vestment
88. Moslem physician
89. According to
90. Morse code sound
91. Standard
92. Beautician's tool
94. Fine porcelain
97. Charming
98. Psychology topic
100. Irritable
101. Tire input
103. Hitchcock's subjects
106. Retainer
107. Yo, Mac!
111. Belgian youths?
116. Actress Ekberg
117. Garment piece
118. Judge
119. ___ of Langerhans
120. Tooth for grinding
121. Bleaters
122. Fred's four-legged friend
123. Serves
124. Houston ballplayer

DOWN

1. Wedge
2. Loony
3. Melville novel
4. Booth Tarkington book
5. Sounds of hesitation
6. Land north of Israel
7. Glossy paint
8. "Leave ___ to Heaven"
9. Pulpit of old
10. Blended whiskeys
11. Throttle
12. Morgan ___ (Arthur's half sister)
13. Hemisphere gp.
14. Mirth
15. Gregarious one
16. Feel bad
17. St. south of Wisconsin
18. Soap-making ingredient
25. Lawn tool
26. Guanaco's kin
28. Disparage
32. Gardener's mulch
33. George Eliot heroine
36. Taste
37. More affected
38. Actress Adoree
39. Units of energy
40. Psychics' stock in trade
41. Useful
42. Tale of derring-do
43. King of a singer
44. High note
48. Sleep ___
49. Behave
50. Small quakes
53. Occupants
54. ___ noire
55. Heed
56. El Cordobes, for one
58. "Madigan" lead
62. Spanish river
63. Boot liner
65. "Blessed ___ the meek"
66. Alistair MacLean novel
68. Brace
69. Colorful carps
70. Like some chocolate bunnies

PUZZLE 203

71. Loamy
72. Kind of radio
73. Craving
74. Giraffe's kin
75. King Lear's daughter
76. A boxer does it
78. Me, to Marcel
79. Canadian Indian
81. Mrs. Charles
83. Achilles's mother
84. Auricle
85. Spring mo.
86. Coach Lombardi
90. Abhors
93. Rents
94. Hamlet
95. More skillful
96. God of sleep
98. Actor Buddy ___
99. Thingamajig
102. Salmon's spawning ground
104. Drizzle
105. Middling
108. Mississippi mud
109. Hesperus, e.g.
110. Tropical food plant
111. Ciao
112. "Cannery ___"
113. Small guitar, for short
114. Orchid necklace
115. Director Grosbard
116. Physicians' org.

PUZZLE 204

ACROSS

1. Ready to pick
5. Pribilof dweller
9. Coral island
14. Greek cheese
18. Again
19. Shells
20. Southern shrub
21. Foray
22. Move to Easy Street
24. Succeed wildly
26. Lennon's wife
27. Dappled
28. Bodies of knowledge
29. Minstrels' instruments
30. Born
31. Forever, in verse
32. Kitchen tool
33. Crush
34. Ham it up
35. Connects
36. Antique photographs
40. What forty-niners did
44. Glowing
45. ___ Baba
46. Special committee
47. Sort
48. Senorita
49. Popular gem
50. Antique auto
51. Chicago hrs.
52. Win a lottery
56. Sets aside
59. Takes a nap
60. Succumbs
61. Redding the singer
62. Hot chocolate
63. Exceedingly
64. Stings
67. Creak
68. Paragon
72. Get lucky
74. Chicken ___ king
75. Tennis expert
76. Aurochs
77. Airwave buffs
78. Qty.
79. Former Hungarian leader Janos ___
81. Catch
82. Level
84. Comes on like gangbusters
86. Sunday best
88. Use up
90. "To Autumn," e.g.
91. Delivery trucks
92. Emergency signal
93. Luau fare
94. Express
97. Spoils
99. Deliver a speech
100. Bristle
101. Computer's brain: abbr.
102. Roll merrily along
104. Get rich quick
106. Neighborhood
107. Unusual thing
108. By and by
109. Old Norse inscription
110. Gentle
111. Special menus
112. Punch
113. Units of work

DOWN

1. Actor Novarro
2. Silly
3. Black tea
4. Palindromic female
5. Glut
6. Coal
7. Inside of
8. Captain's diary
9. North Atlantic islands
10. Not as wild
11. Bullfighter's cheers
12. Bucharest coin
13. Arctic region
14. Bubbly
15. "___ on down the Road"
16. Knots
17. Mags' bread and butter
20. Squirrel staple
23. Old-fashioned remedy
25. Corroded
28. Cafe au ___
32. Ham
33. Within
34. Highest peak in the Philippines
35. Throws over
36. Elephants' ivories
37. Pertaining to John Paul II
38. Spiral-horned antelope
39. Jockey's attire
40. Rabbit
41. Viewpoint
42. Explorer Heyerdahl
43. Circles
44. Lasso
48. Atomic particles
49. Minds
51. Brisk
52. Witches' conveyances
53. Summarize
54. Doglike scavenger
55. Ireland, to an Irishman
57. Early times

PUZZLE 204

58. Westernmost of the Aleutian Islands
62. Morsel
63. Electrical units
64. Overcharged
65. Wall painting
66. Island off Venezuela
67. Chemists' weights
68. Christened
69. Hairstyle
70. Gizzard
71. Cornucopia
73. Hoodlums
78. Welk's start
79. Alaskan bear
80. Dined
82. Chatter
83. Ship's rope
84. "Sommersby" actor
85. Honking
87. Czech composer
88. Tilts
89. Pushover
92. Pie filler
93. Eva or Juan
94. Search high and low
95. Imitating
96. Winter festivals
97. Dig
98. Molding
99. Bugbear
100. Portico
102. Lower limb
103. Mai ___ cocktail
104. Giant jet
105. Afore

PUZZLE 205

ACROSS

1. Platters
6. Thick slice
10. Emulated a certain wolf
16. Chou ___
17. English counties
19. Big ape
20. Linebacker's leap
22. Sweet
23. Kermit's color
24. Romances
25. Indian nurses
27. Freezer abundance
28. Healthy grains
29. Father
30. Prince Valiant's wife
31. It's a blast!: abbr.
32. Witness
34. Bowser's banes
35. Comic
36. Votes against
37. Rugged country
38. Pyromaniac's crime
41. Manage
44. Temple
45. 40 cubic feet
47. How: Sp.
48. Propeller's arm
49. Wrestling maneuver
52. Colorado Indian
53. Dr. Brothers
54. Chili ingredients
55. Mince
56. Make golden
57. Clinging plants
58. Whim
59. Escapade
60. Of the ear
61. Male
62. Crooner Perry ___
63. Cousins' mothers
64. Analyze a sentence
65. Rule or order
66. Constellation Volans
68. Envy
69. Attorney's deg.
70. Fleur-de-___
71. Gamble
72. Cycles
73. Dodge
75. Daunt
77. Soft drink
78. Plaything
79. Gov. bond
80. Swindle
85. FDR's youth org.
86. Actress Adams
87. Nibbles
88. Hoss's brother
89. Quiet!
90. Famed deer
91. Singer Lopez
93. Dental thread
94. Compunction
96. Great success
99. Cozies' places
100. Shout of glee
101. Fruit pulp
102. Actor James ___
103. Shaker and mover
104. Pod's contents

DOWN

1. Help pay
2. Bays
3. Most crafty
4. Raise ___
5. Peccadillo
6. Tot
7. Parasites
8. Mississippi flatboats
9. "___ and the Dragon"
10. Uproarious commotion
11. Flower holders
12. For shame!
13. Nocturnal rodent
14. Choose
15. Miami's county
17. Emporiums
18. Closed
19. Mountain passes
21. Slid
23. Sailor
26. Qty.
29. Saw logs
30. TV host Funt
31. Frigate hand
33. Battery posts
34. End
35. Diminish
37. Gretzky of the rink
39. Endures
40. Pine leaf
41. Principally
42. Ghost ship
43. Aspect
44. Wine bottle
45. Small nails
46. Bauxite, for one
49. Physicist Enrico ___
50. Baltic port
51. Gaiety

PUZZLE 205

53. Shake
54. Floats
56. Jelly fruit
59. Actress Rainer
60. Footless
62. Caesar's 151
63. Excited
66. Terrify, in Dumfries
67. Lattice
68. Dry and voltaic
72. Lyrical
74. Dopey's roomie
75. Slight
76. Classify
77. Nickels and dimes
79. Gentles
80. Net fisherman
81. Abounding
82. Worshiped
83. Bulks
84. Type sizes
85. Comfort
86. Spars
89. Mexican miss: abbr.
90. Slangy pals
91. Spelling error
92. Mellow
93. Chimney part
95. Unlatch, poetically
97. Cover
98. Roman goddess of plenty

PUZZLE 206

ACROSS

1. Come again?
5. Swiss range
9. Actress Conn and others
14. Early man
18. Bee's home
19. Nolte movie, with "The"
20. European river
21. Glen
22. Locomotive
24. Hinged appliance
26. Meditation room
27. Foursome
30. Connected
31. Catholic booklet
34. Food plan
35. Romanian region
36. "I'll Be Around" group
40. Poet Torquato ___
42. India's neighbor
46. Popeye is one
47. Governor Grasso
48. Meryl Streep film
51. ___, dos, tres
52. Ancient Near East country
54. Settee
56. Boisterous
57. Russian jet
58. Sea eagles
60. Of ships
63. Pepper plant
65. "The Gold Bug" author
66. New
68. Type of race
70. Menu phrase
71. ___ and outs
72. Beehive State
73. Historical period
76. Persia, today
78. Hockey great
80. Stood for office
82. Nail
83. Stiletto
86. Ship deserter
87. Keep an ___ (watch)
90. 1954 pact: abbr.
92. Group of rooms
93. "___ Believer"
94. Goofed
96. Actual
98. Comic Johnson
99. Kimono sash
100. Raymond Burr role
103. Lawyers: abbr.
105. 1948 Western alliance: abbr.
106. Roman date
108. Edition
109. Masquerade
111. "Amo, amas, I love ___"
114. Graceful creature
116. Son of Isaac
117. Corrupt
120. Saint Elizabeth and Ernest Thompson
122. Lacking sense
126. Heavy-metal band
128. Golf club
131. Otherwise
132. Civil-rights activist Roy ___
133. And elsewhere
134. Manager Gaston's nickname
135. Observer
136. Rental contract
137. Armored vehicle
138. Genesis spot

DOWN

1. ___ kid
2. Employ
3. Bard's river
4. Sinew
5. Furor
6. Irish mythological figure
7. Pain in the neck
8. Keanu Reeves film
9. Holmes's partner
10. "If ___ a Million"
11. Not similar: abbr.
12. Below
13. Moon: pref.
14. Fly
15. Move swiftly
16. ___ vera
17. Heal
23. Singer Lena ___
25. Antelope
28. Small monkey
29. Type of admiral
32. Singer Shannon and others
33. Acrylic fiber
35. Alamo hero
36. Guide
37. Military chaplain
38. Cold War barrier
39. African expedition
41. Stuffed shirt
43. Lifting weights
44. Negatively charged atom
45. Theater boxes
49. Bugsy Siegel's wife
50. Facial feature
53. Convene
55. Declare
59. Capture
61. Much
62. Turner and Wood
64. "___ Theme" ("Dr. Zhivago")
67. "Casey at the Bat" author
69. New Haven university

74. Billy or nanny
75. Capture
77. Water, in Madrid
78. Heavenly hunter
79. Stallone role
81. Fiddling emperor
84. Jones and James
85. Pee Wee ___
88. Birds of a region
89. Famous loch
91. Bizarre
95. Hand out
97. Summers, in Paris
100. Muslim religion
101. Song for two
102. Architect Saarinen
104. Soil
107. Breadwinner

PUZZLE 206

110. ___ Kennedy Shriver
112. Profit
113. Type of net
115. Embed
117. Engraved stamps
118. Perry's creator
119. Model's stance
120. Six, in Seville
121. ___ good example
123. Parched
124. Musical symbol
125. Pennsylvania valley
127. Double-helix molecule
129. Singer Morrison
130. BPOE member

PUZZLE 207

Diagramless crosswords are solved by using the clues and their numbers to fill in the answer words and the arrangement of black squares. Insert the number of each clue with the first letter of its answer, across and down. Fill in a black square at the end of each answer. Every black square must have a corresponding black square on the opposite side of the diagram to form a diagonally symmetrical pattern. Puzzles 207 and 208 have been started for you.

ACROSS
1. Haul
4. Ms. ___-Man
7. Carte

8. Teheran's land
10. Act of goodwill
11. Large jib
13. Caustic stuff
14. Manipulate
16. Hockey great
17. Albumen's neighbor
19. French brandy
21. Durable wood
23. Team member
26. Atlas contents
30. Unctuous stuff
31. Precious stone
33. "Norma ___"
34. MC's speech
36. On the qui vive
38. Acute
39. Become submerged
40. 66, e.g.
41. Steeped drink

DOWN
1. Even
2. Oaxaca one
3. Hindu preceptor
4. Skyscraper squatter?
5. How ___ you?
6. Body of rules
7. Deli dressing
9. Asta's mistress
10. Soar
12. Rainbow segment
15. 20
18. Islet
20. Workout site
22. Shoo!
23. Taro dish
24. Chain part
25. Change
27. Stadium
28. Urban oasis
29. Collection
32. Part of a sailboat
35. Soak, as flax
37. Fib

PUZZLE 208

ACROSS
1. School of whales
4. Far
7. Steals from

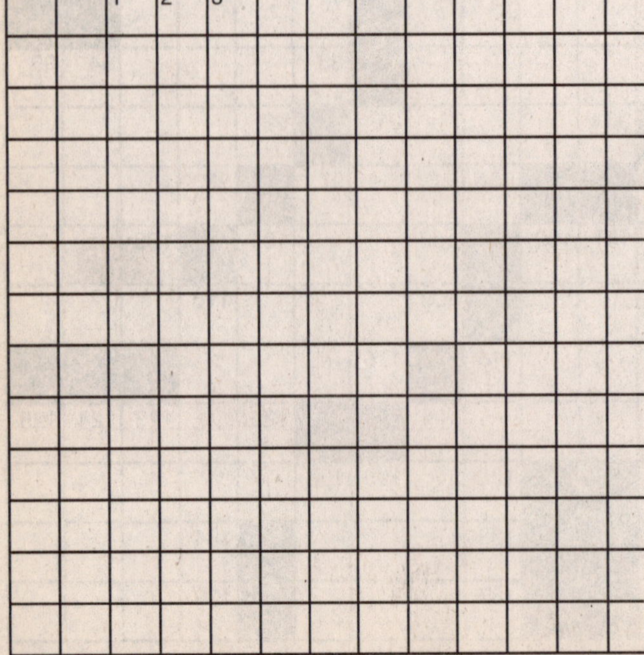

11. Political sanctuary
12. Malevolent
13. Use a chair
14. WWII theater
15. Place for a beret
16. The jig ___!
18. Said
20. Eva or Juan
22. Conger
23. Car style
25. Andean beast
29. Legume
31. Metamorphic rock
33. Dining-table accessories
37. Can. province
38. Mata ___
39. Doorstep item
41. "___ the ramparts . . ."
42. Algerian seaport
43. Garden bulbs
45. Spider-Man's weapons
46. Milk curdler
47. Aye

DOWN
1. Hand movement
2. Presidential daughter
3. Backyard pest
4. Poker actions
5. 1984 Nobelist
6. Ham it up
7. Spreads verbally
8. Above
9. Nip
10. Rosebud, e.g.
13. Small drink
17. Seed vessel
19. Part of AT&T
21. Table-linen items
24. Born named
26. ___ carte
27. Kin of Danson's character
28. Swear
30. Knightshirt?
32. Pinna
33. Demonstrate
34. Fabled loser
35. Graceful steed
36. Rational
40. Wee
44. Unit

PUZZLE 209

ACROSS

1. Girl o' my heart
4. Raring to go
6. Married ladies
8. Perfectly flat
10. Positions
12. Type of eclipse
14. Snoopy, in his imagination
16. Jimmy Carter's award
18. Himalayan monarchy
20. What partisans take
22. ____ Decimal System
24. Curtain material
26. Fountain orders
28. Truckee River city
29. Research room

DOWN

1. Furry foot
2. No good
3. Imparts
5. Imp
7. Frame
9. Red Square honoree
11. Permanent location?
13. Vestments
15. Not so hot
17. Burdened
19. Clive Staples ____
21. Man of La Mancha
23. High-pitched song?
25. "Peter Pan" dog
27. Story or sister

Starting box on page 562

Word Play

PUZZLE 210

For each puzzle, rearrange each 5-letter word and place it into the corresponding row in the diagram so that it forms a 6-letter word with the addition of the letter shown in the diagram. The outlined column reading down will reveal a bonus word.

A.
1. TRAMP ✓
2. SPARE
3. ALERT
4. STRIP
5. EDSEL
6. TINGE
7. UNCLE
8. ASSET

1.	I	M	P	A	R	T
2.				I		
3.					I	
4.					I	
5.		I				
6.	I					
7.						I
8.		I				

B.
1. BLAME ✓
2. POSIT
3. RERAN
4. SIREN
5. TRAIN
6. EARED
7. ERASE
8. NOBLE

1.	G	A	M	B	L	E
2.				G		
3.				G		
4.					G	
5.						G
6.		G				
7.	G					
8.						G

PUZZLE 211

ACROSS

1. Stun
4. Far from hirsute
6. Apian-caste member
8. Noisy
9. Born: Fr.
11. Plant anchor
12. 2004, e.g.
14. In the lead
16. Colorless person
18. Leg part
19. Environmental concern
21. Numerical prefix
22. Devour
24. Screen
27. Hubbub
28. Rotten
30. Trite
31. Spill the beans
33. Go against
34. Cooling quaff
35. Game fish
36. Clandestine
38. Guitar part
39. Aye

Starting box on page 562

DOWN

1. Roughly
2. TV's Robin
3. BPOE member
5. Contradict
6. Teak, e.g.
7. Henderson's TV hubby
8. Meat ____
10. Jug handles
11. Abatement
13. Edge
14. Deed
15. Injure
17. Verse
20. Benefit
23. Essay
25. Bawl
26. Luau dance
27. Divan
29. Boys
30. Penny
32. Veal + time
33. Musical twosomes
35. Genealogy chart
37. Weep

PUZZLE 212

Mathboxes

Fill in the missing numbers across and down using only the digits given above the diagrams. Each of the given digits will be used only once. Always perform the mathematical operations in order from left to right and from top to bottom.

1 2 2 3 4 6 8 9

A.

2 2 3 3 4 5 6 7 8

B.

PUZZLE 213

ACROSS

1. Trial
5. Smash
8. Music halls
9. Great service?
10. Fraud
11. Loan
13. Stroked
15. Second son
18. Cong. member
21. Roman ruler
22. Optimism
23. Robin's residence
24. Level
25. Lots
28. Forest dweller
29. Label
30. Donated
33. Angered
34. Profess
35. Golfer Hogan
36. Wharf denizens
37. Jeopardy
42. Watches closely
46. Onus
47. Life span
48. Pot sweetener
49. Groom the grass
50. Spotted

DOWN

1. Lacquered metal
2. Doctor the books
3. Bench
4. Weight allowance
5. Linden of "Barney Miller"
6. Cooler coolers
7. Sawbuck
12. Actor Glover
13. Story line
14. Herd
16. Quilting session
17. Hosp. sections
19. Fencing blade
20. Inky implement
22. That girl
25. Oat eater
26. Adjust
27. Composer Rorem
28. Succinct
29. Bird's bill
30. Actress Teri ____
31. Frank's ex
32. Former soldier
38. Too bad!
39. Nary a one
40. Airport exit
41. Fabulous garden
43. Starchy root
44. Freudian concern
45. Ply needle and thread

Starting box on page 562

Word Spiral

PUZZLE 214

Fill in the spiral diagram in a clockwise direction with the 4-letter answer words. The last letter of each word will be the first letter of the next word. When the diagram is completed, a 7-letter word will read down the center column.

1. Door directive
2. Cut of pork
3. Brown seaweed
4. Brace
5. Gad about
6. Trumpet insert
7. Back talk?
8. Load
9. Tater
10. Lackluster
11. Brazen
12. Twilight
13. Tough problem
14. Weighty volume
15. Islamic prince
16. Peel

1			2			3
	9			10		
	14			15		
8					11	4
			16			
	13			12		
7			6			5

PUZZLE 215

ACROSS

1. Cleopatra's serpent
4. Sorrow
6. E.R. workers
9. Spans
11. Songs for two
13. Let up
14. Listen secretly
17. Fabric tint
18. Lexicographer Webster
19. Central Asia's ____ Sea
21. Pickling spice
22. Salary
24. Power unit
25. Slippery fish
26. Land force
27. Gentlewoman
28. Run away
29. Freight weights
30. Autograph
31. Type of sculpture
32. ____-de-France
33. Dimple
34. Chocolate substitute
37. Elm or ash
38. Vex
39. Usher's offering
40. Rock's ____ Na Na
43. Versatile
46. Ale alternative
47. Smudge
48. Sooner
50. ____ Diego
51. Circular
52. Busy insect

DOWN

1. Awaken
2. Facet
3. Small dowel
4. Battleship's color
5. Attorney's charge
6. Hurry
7. Composer Rorem
8. Sipping tube
9. Crib or cot
10. Soundness of judgment
11. Agreement
12. Marsh rail
15. Potential-difference measure
16. Elaborate parade
20. West Yorkshire city
21. English title
23. Foxy
24. Brown songbird
26. Libya neighbor
27. Misplaced
28. Threadlike
29. Melody
30. Attack!
31. June bug, e.g.
33. Dingy
35. Automobile pioneer
36. Smiles radiantly
37. Rend
39. Comedian Laurel
40. Paris's river
41. Pay attention to
42. Airport abbr.
44. Pod dweller
45. Corn serving
46. Sad
49. Steal from

Starting box on page 562

PUZZLE 216

Building Blocks

Using only the letters in the word BIG, complete the words in the Building Blocks. Words read across only. Every word contains each letter of BIG at least once.

PUZZLE 217

ACROSS

1. Car for hire
4. Prepared fruit
6. Flower holder
10. ____ ego
11. Catchall abbr.
12. Soft shade
14. Fads
16. Tired
18. Appear
20. Enzyme ending
21. Collect
23. A Gabor
24. Ship part
26. Historic starter
27. Gypsy Rose ____
28. Floor square
30. Baseball glove
31. Hymn of praise
32. Commotion
33. Mets or Jets
35. Levy
36. ERA or RBI
38. Do wrong
39. Attempt
41. Twists
43. Mum
45. Marries in haste
50. Finish last
51. Not together
52. Goulash
53. Cent
54. Once known as

DOWN

1. Dark drink
2. ____ and crafts
3. Edible root
4. Limit
5. Attracted
6. Really
7. Downed dinner
8. Without
9. Church leader
13. Take off
14. Italian three
15. Permeate
17. Busy ____ bee
19. Game fish
22. Bard
23. Afore
25. Moist
26. Kilt feature
28. Kid
29. ____ of March
30. Stir
32. Fraulein's thank you
34. Gym pads
35. Cookie box
37. Formal wear
38. Park it
40. Ink stain
41. Understood
42. Hockey shot
44. Language suffix
46. Doing business
47. Window unit
48. Marine flier
49. Farm enclosure

Starting box on page 562

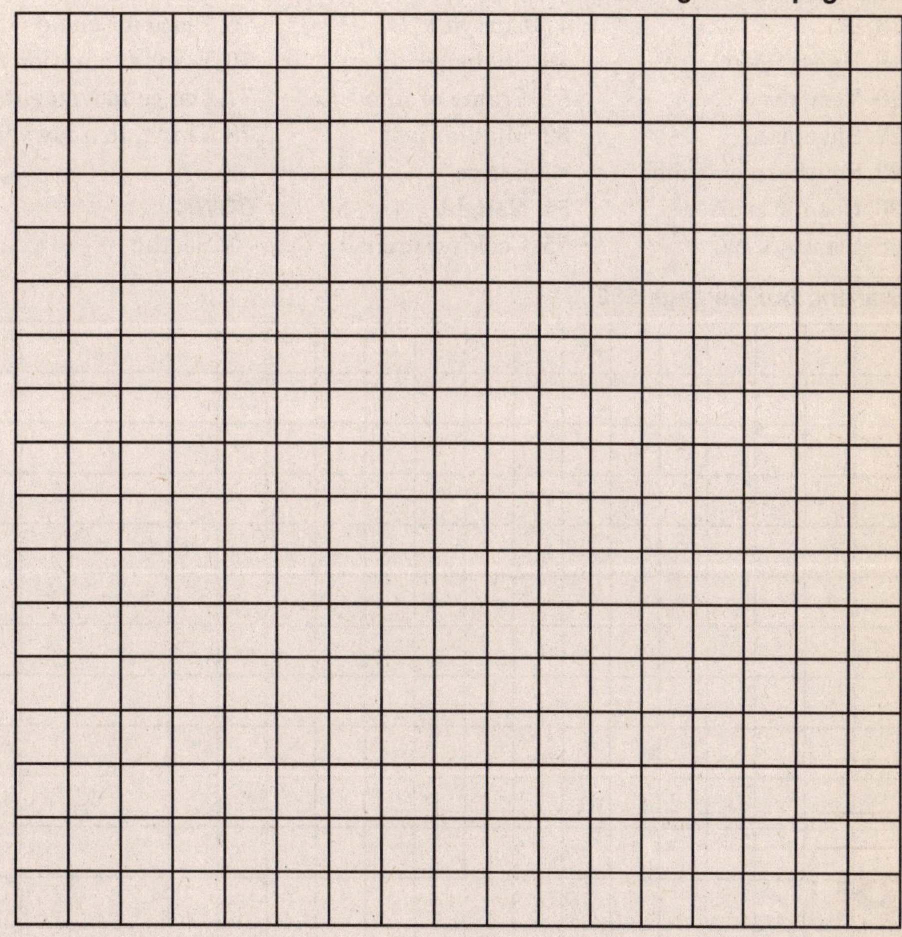

Roll of the Dice

PUZZLE 218

The six dice are actually the same die shown in six different positions. What 6-letter word is formed by the letters on the six bottom faces, reading from left to right?

PUZZLE 219

ACROSS

1. Slangy "marvelous"
4. Fertilizer compounds
7. Joy
8. Combat
11. Roster
15. Plant swelling
16. Margarine
18. Doc
19. Heavy mist
20. Very very
22. Sheepish?
23. Southern side dish
26. Cosmic cruiser
28. Stimpy's pal
29. Walk heavily
31. Cancel
32. Autumn mon.
33. Hard row to ____
34. Seed protection
35. Barked
37. So far
38. Impersonator
42. Humor forms
44. Alpine vocalist
47. Carryall
48. Shake, as a tail
51. Frame of mind
52. Middle East native
54. Naught
55. Cooking utensil
56. Latin quarter
58. ____ of passage
59. Hold a session
60. Competitive advantage
64. Snow vehicles
66. Analyze (a sentence)
67. Toadies' replies
68. ____-fi
69. Attach
70. Set of cards
71. Retains
74. Damsel
75. Place for clouds
76. Bombay's nation
77. Dance movements
78. Thing, to a lawyer

DOWN

1. Seethe
2. Saharan
3. Deprived
5. Mood
6. Rug style
8. "If Ever I ____ Leave You"
9. Cohort
10. Eye part
11. Variety show
12. Lyrical
13. Fork point
14. Top-grade recipient
17. Cantankerous
18. Ditch of defense
21. Prized marble
23. Multiplies
24. Paint again
25. Entirely
26. Rival
27. Briny
30. Valuable vein
36. Tantrum
38. Immature
39. By means of
40. Pass, as time
41. Modernized a road
43. Throng
45. Exclude
46. Leases
49. Assortment
50. Profited
53. Foremen
54. Quick drink
56. School transports
57. Summit
58. Reckless
60. Iridescent sparkler
61. Granny
62. Avian predators
63. Mild oath
65. German art songs
68. Hits the slopes
72. Plumbing tube
73. Back talk

Starting box on page 562

PUZZLE 220

• UNLIKELY COUPLES •

ACROSS
1. Sleuth Spade
4. Dine late
7. Cart brace
9. Puccini product
11. ___ Nevada
13. Former
15. Mastered
17. Striped-wing flier
20. Sooner than, to a bard
22. Response to a joke
24. Prestige
26. Eastern European
27. "Famous ___"
28. Director Howard
29. Made a getaway
30. Sheathe
32. Summer diversion
34. Jenny Gago series
36. Fulda feeder
37. Bedlam
38. Ocean predator
42. Put on
43. Alternatively
44. Daily delivery
48. Jauntily
50. A Siamese twin
53. Arena take
54. French resort city
56. Common Market abbr.
57. Aegean island
59. Soda, for some
60. Building additions
62. Hanker
66. "That's Life" singer
69. Polishes
71. Certain fowl
74. Furthermore
75. Poultry predator
78. Colony insect
79. Clerical vestments
80. Infomercials
81. Gym shoe
85. Earns an F
88. Douglas pine
90. In shape
91. Adolescent
92. Classify
93. Burr TV role
96. Sicilian volcano
97. Have a malady
98. North American constrictor
101. Inventory
103. Candidate
105. Detroit pro
107. River carrier
108. Instruction units
109. Glove material
110. Lunched

DOWN
1. Long-tailed climber
2. ___ you kidding?
3. Sheen or Short
4. Son of Adam
5. Mr. Geller
6. Actress Tiffin
7. Wind dir.
8. Smile
9. Lennon's love
10. Touch tenderly
12. Ripen
13. Portent
14. Important times
15. Nautical greeting
16. Waterfall
18. Fascinated
19. Nipper's co.
21. Christmas ___
22. Possessed
23. Gp. for Ben Casey
25. Swab
26. Remnant
30. Ames and Begley
31. Birth name word
33. Revere
34. Repudiate
35. Dawn goddess
36. Icelandic saga
38. "Diamond ___"
39. NRC predecessor
40. Fan's cry
41. Fall behind
45. ___ Haydn
46. DDE's command
47. Agt.
48. Fruit flesh
49. Break the ___
51. Diarist Anais ___
52. Chamois
54. Church seat
55. The Greatest
58. Pebble
61. Dry, as wine
63. Torah closets
64. Lobster eggs
65. Diva Merriman
66. Bastes
67. Peeve
68. Spins
70. Golf blunder
72. Rose of ___
73. Small boy
76. Sort
77. ABC rival
81. Funnyman Caesar
82. Etta ___ of comics
83. Dusk, to Donne
84. Genetic initials
85. Italian monk
86. Reclined
87. Open
88. Nail shaper
89. Apr. org.
90. Mexican party
94. Forty winks
95. Aspen equipment
98. Fasten
99. Card game
100. Peggy or Pinky
102. November winners
104. ___ tai
106. Vietnamese holiday

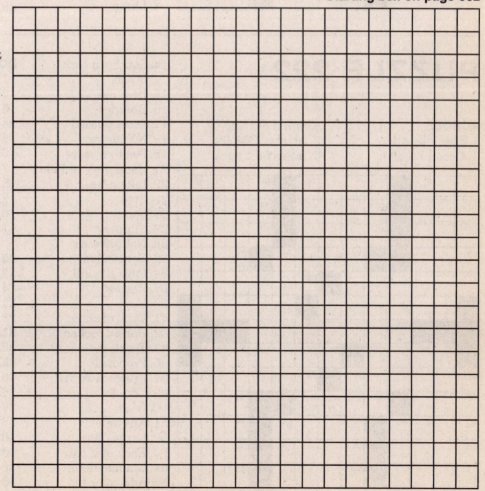

Starting box on page 562

PUZZLE 221

ACROSS
1. "Adam's ____"
4. Gets hitched
8. Smack
12. Excitement
13. Opera tune
14. Handy money
15. Large number
17. Location
18. If not
19. Mail carrier
21. Peaceful
24. Educational meeting
27. Championship
32. Like some handshakes
33. Reach
34. Come in
35. Coated with crumbs
36. Paint
38. Spanish treasure ship
42. Bothers
46. Away from the wind
47. Not guilty
50. RBI, e.g.
51. Broil
52. By means of
53. Short jumps
54. Outskirts
55. Pig's digs

DOWN
1. Anger
2. Adored one
3. Hisses
4. Lump
5. Poet's before
6. Infant's attire
7. Boutique
8. Begone, cat!
9. Slightly hot
10. On the briny
11. Comparative word
16. Wish
20. Sofa
22. Main course
23. Beam of light
24. "Ain't ____ Sweet"
25. Hallow follower
26. Thick pad
28. Type style
29. Tiny bit
30. Recline
31. Discontinue
33. Furnish with weapons
35. Censored
37. Roar
38. Deep cut
39. Choir voice
40. Hurdle
41. Allows
43. Guns the engine
44. Purl's opposite
45. Linger
48. Henpeck
49. Miner's quest

PUZZLE 222

ACROSS
1. Fore's partner
4. Ocean breaker
8. Small earring
12. Actress Peeples
13. Important ages
14. Southern corn bread
15. Last mo.
16. Bungles
17. One opposed
18. NY hours
19. Positive votes
21. Command to Fido
22. Like glue
25. Step
27. Sorer
29. Slippery
30. Not alfresco
32. Contended
34. Pays the bill
37. Bestow
39. Rods
41. Type of cabin
42. Barely cooked
44. Touch-me-____
45. Proposal
47. Freshwater fish
49. Couple
50. Irish ____
51. Anytime
52. Large deer
53. Each of a pair
54. Change decor
55. Add color to

DOWN
1. Peru's mountains
2. Spanish party
3. Plan
4. Tiny
5. Displayed
6. Differ
7. Road curves
8. Health resort
9. Throat part
10. Messy
11. Remove the frost from
20. Hi-fi
23. Tribal head
24. More humane
26. Recut wood
28. Decompose
31. Bought by mail
32. Sorcery
33. Eat
35. Camped
36. Gradually
37. Ascend
38. Runner
40. Feed (the fire)
43. Talk wildly
46. Hearth residue
48. Golf teacher, shortly

PUZZLE 223

• CIRCLET •

ACROSS

1. Emulate Eminem
4. Stomach muscles, for short
7. Buddhist monument
9. Coral ledge
11. Listen to again
12. Concepts
14. Backpack
15. Students' jewelry
19. "___ will be done . . ."
20. Pakistani city
22. Wanders
24. Reverence
25. Open to view
26. Swiss song
27. Stylist's goo
28. Have being
29. Trading center
31. Toss
33. Send back
35. Tropical cuckoo
36. Pasture
37. Slow, in music
38. Sicilian spouter
40. Retirees' org.
41. Santa's worker
42. Clock std.
44. Ultimate
47. Draw with acid
50. South African corn
54. Eureka!
55. Garden tool
56. German subs
57. Prickly seedcase
58. Cry for assistance
59. Cable network
60. Pabulum
61. Man with a van
63. Cut severely
66. Pesky insect
67. Buckwheat pancake
68. Sightseer
69. Purchase
70. Showy bauble
73. Old Greek coin
75. Concur
76. Golden
78. Flank
79. Sports groups
80. Food fish
81. Id ___

DOWN

1. Regret
2. Geronimo, for one
3. Living room
4. Get up
5. Sleeping spots
6. Prophet
7. Place
8. Tolkien trilogy
10. Meadow fungus
11. Orbison or Rogers
13. Nose
14. "___ & Louise"
16. Gallery display
17. Gallivant
18. Stinks
19. Woolen fabric
21. "___ Maria"
23. Wild plums
24. Taj Mahal site
28. Doddering
29. Ms. West
30. Adam ___ of "Trust Me"
32. Ewe said it
34. Candle count
39. Single-celled creature
43. Chinese philosophy
44. Arrest
45. Hand digit
46. "___ and Maude"
48. Mil. rank
49. Cool
51. Big baby, maybe
52. Europe's "boot"
53. Notice
58. Hair rinse
59. Manipulate
62. Seven, to Nero
63. ___-disant
64. Crescent-shaped
65. Debates
68. Cornered
69. Derek and Diddley
71. ___ the Red
72. Make over
74. Clear, as tables
77. Rodent

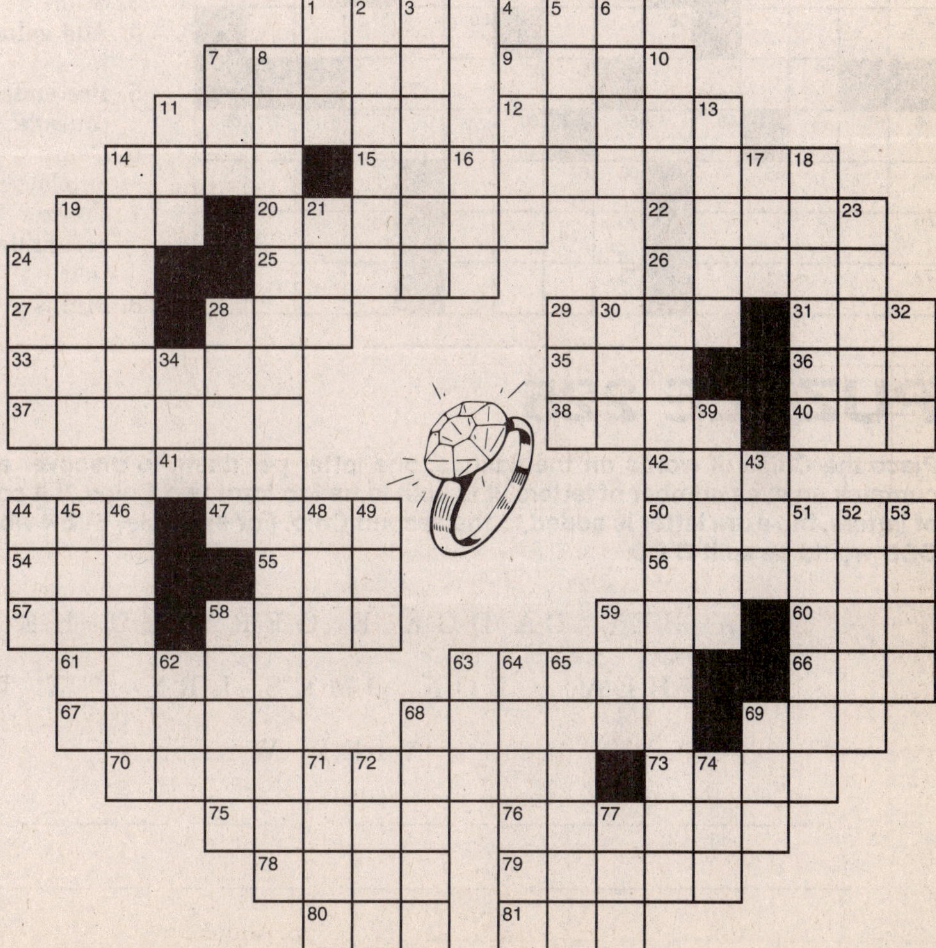

PUZZLE 224

ACROSS

1. Flower holder
5. Pitch water
9. Religious factions
14. Saint's image
15. Cereal grain
16. House of ice
17. Arab chieftain
18. Fruit coolers
19. Frogs' cousins
20. Alleviate
22. This woman
24. As well
25. Clinch
27. "____ It Romantic?"
29. Despaired
31. Highest card
33. Slippery fellows
36. Amateur's opposite
37. Venomous snake
39. "La Boheme" solo
40. White-plumed bird
42. Coolio's medium
43. Stench
44. Atmosphere
45. Perfect example
47. Surnamed at birth
48. Golf gadgets
49. Notable time period
50. Ruler's term
52. Harmony
54. Falls
56. Soak (up)
58. Possessive pronoun
60. Bandits
64. Residence
66. Lids
68. Got down
69. ____ boom
70. Toward the sheltered side
71. Zilch
72. Line of shrubs
73. Dull person
74. Regard

DOWN

1. Challenger
2. Pinnacle
3. Stain
4. Add value to
5. Pretended courage
6. Camp employees
7. Freezer accumulation
8. Minus
9. Locations
10. Psyche part
11. Rattling
12. Commotion
13. Fair
21. Choose by ballot
23. Speed
26. Walked in a procession
28. Well-groomed
29. Dispute
30. Be in agreement
32. Superman's garment
34. Summer fabric
35. For Pete's ____!
36. Organic fuel
38. Ship's clink
41. Effortless
43. Dozed off
46. Awakened
49. Accomplishment
51. Crete, e.g.
53. Brother's girl
55. Cowboy, at times
56. Obi
57. Double-reed instrument
59. Scrutinize
61. Burn-soothing plant
62. Chablis, e.g.
63. Goblet feature
65. Get
67. Pub beverage

PUZZLE 225

Chips

Place the Chips of words on the dashes, one letter per dash, to discover a saying. When a word contains an even number of letters, it is split in half to form two Chips. If it contains an odd number of letters, the extra letter is added to the second Chip. For example, EVEN would be split EV EN and ODD would be split O DD.

A BEC CA DGE E GER GRU HE HE

HEA I LON OMES RRY T T T

VIER W

_ _ _   _ _ _ _ _ _   _ _   _ _ _ _ _   _

_ _ _ _ _ _,   _ _ _   _ _ _ _ _ _ _   _ _

_ _ _ _ _ _ _.

PUZZLE 226

ACROSS

1. Soul
6. Circle parts
10. Slackens
14. Musical divisions
15. Totem ____
16. Decline
17. Ties
18. Sham
19. Foolish
20. Window frame
21. Rests
22. Moisten again
23. Zealous
25. Health resort
27. Corrosive stuff
28. Cultural
31. Los Angeles woe
32. Bara of films
33. Aura
38. Jail room
39. Privileged few
40. Laughing sound
41. Exaggeration
43. Send payment
44. Back of the neck
45. Certain engines
46. Crow's sound
49. Popeye's yes
50. Fork point
51. Aids a felon
53. Heavy hammer
55. Hard evidence
59. Cairo's river
60. Oil source
61. Coffeehouse request
62. Includes
63. Dissenter
64. Blooper
65. In case
66. Interrupt
67. Sheds tears

DOWN

1. High cards
2. ____ Scotia
3. Caesar's fateful date
4. Treat roughly
5. Horse's cousin
6. Plant pest
7. Tooth part
8. School friend
9. Gender
10. Verge
11. Barroom fight
12. Golf count
13. Large outpouring
21. Attack, Fido!
22. Sitar music
24. Through
26. Corn bread
28. Clearly outline
29. Those guys
30. Assist
31. Beam
33. Secret wedding
34. Hence
35. Poetic part
36. Buckeye State
37. Cole and Turner
39. Internet auction site
42. Genetic molecules
43. Manage
45. "____ We Meet Again"
46. Waterway
47. Remain
48. Fuses
50. Dutch flower
52. Experiment
54. Low voice
56. Estate unit
57. Karate blow
58. Old salts
60. Had been
61. Kitten's cry

1	2	3	4	5	■	6	7	8	9	■	10	11	12	13
14					■	15				■	16			
17					■	18				■	19			
20				■	21				■	22				
■	■	■	23	24			■	25	26		■	27		
28	29	30				■	31				■	■	■	■
32					■	33					34	35	36	37
38				■	39					■	40			
41				42					■	43				
■	■	■	■	44				■	45					
46	47	48	■	49			■	50				■	■	■
51			52		■	53	54			■	55	56	57	58
59				■	60				■	61				
62				■	63				■	64				
65				■	66				■	67				

Blips PUZZLE 227

Place one of the given letters in each circle to form nine 3-letter words reading from top to bottom. Use each letter only as many times as it is listed. Do not repeat a word in your solution.

A B D E G I N R S T T W X

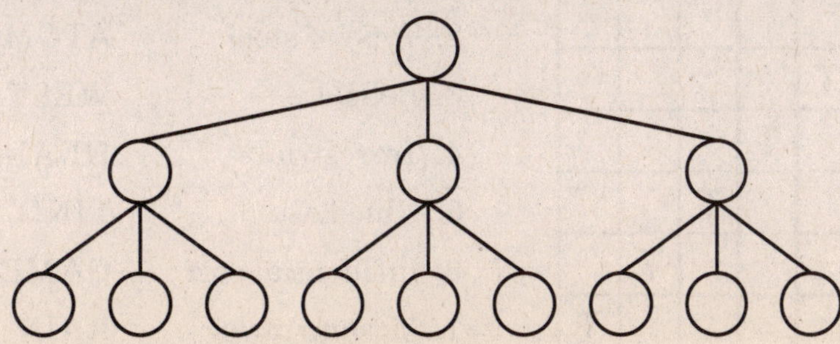

PUZZLE 228

ACROSS

1. Remain
6. Sutures
10. Audacity
14. Musical form
15. Classroom questions
16. Nobelist Wiesel
17. Cardinal feature
18. Kind of skirt
19. Horne of song
20. Chop
21. Prepared for print
23. Neuron appendage
24. Grounded bird
25. Gangster's gun
27. Chime
30. Befitting
33. Abridge
36. Small charges?
37. In the course of
39. Fab
41. Punctures
43. Hurried
44. Subside
46. DDE's arena
47. Floating
50. Dueling device
51. He's against you
53. Excessively
54. Twilights, in verse
55. Boggy land
56. Ile's place
58. Glacier piece
61. Missing links
65. Drag
68. Reed instrument
69. BLT spread
70. Electronic component
72. Political coalition
73. Glazed
74. Rye fungus
75. Propelled
76. Turn over
77. Brings up

DOWN

1. Curve
2. Had on
3. Freshly
4. Topics for Freud
5. Clan symbol
6. Highway hauler
7. Withdraw
8. Fade
9. Jot
10. Italian dessert
11. Writer Haley
12. Brit's flooring
13. Slender
22. Pair
24. Extra
26. Pond-scum ingredient
27. Future knight
28. Ham it up
29. Chef's attire
31. Cat sound
32. Characteristic
34. Fall in folds
35. Eroded
38. Facts, shortly
40. Odd couple?
42. Identical
45. Brewed drink
48. Peppy
49. Heavy reading
52. Consequence
57. Finisher
58. Corn units
59. Competent
60. Diving fowl
62. Speed
63. Looked at
64. Manner
65. Roman garment
66. Nose wrinkler
67. Douses
71. Bad humor

PUZZLE 229

Anacross

There are three clues for each 7-letter answer word to be entered across in the diagram: a definition, a pair of words that are an anagram of the answer, and the letter T already in its correct place in the diagram. When all the answers have been filled in correctly, the center column reading down will reveal the name of a place.

1	T						
2		T					
3			T				
4				T			
5					T		
6						T	
7							T

DEFINITIONS	ANAGRAMS
1. Stamp	PELT + RAM
2. Type of stool	ATOM + NOT
3. Behold	WEST + SIN
4. Terrestrial	HEAL + TRY
5. Glue base	TING + ALE
6. Influential sort	GAME + TAN
7. Mosque tower	RAIN + MET

BRICK BY BRICK

PUZZLE 230

Rearrange this stack of bricks to form a crossword puzzle. The clues will help you fit the bricks into their correct places. Row 1 has been filled in for you. Use the bricks to fill in the remaining spaces.

ACROSS

1. Blood parts
   Black cuckoos
   Atlantic fish
2. Declare
   Sarcastic
   Tokyo, of old
3. Shifting device
   Folk-dance attire
   Big truck
4. With a protective covering
   Lay eyes on
   Wind dir.
5. Verily
   Stuff full
6. Swells
   Rocket's departure
7. Black-eyed ____
   Basement
   Unique chap
8. Monastery head
   Babble
   Doddering
9. Airshow maneuver
   Having more morning moisture
   Elev.
10. Misting mechanism
    Cosmic cloud
11. Soothing succulent
    Actor Chaney
12. Behind
    Good times
    Veranda
13. Marsupial Aussie
    Audition again
    Pot for paella
14. Belonging to us
    Expresses scorn
    Put up with
15. Twisted
    D.C. denizens
    Bards' sunsets

DOWN

1. Heroic narrative
   Companions
   In line
2. At any time
   Form of jazz
   Quartet
3. Paper quantity
   Scientist's workplace
4. Dry creek bed
   Milky stone
5. Answer
   Not mine
6. Think
   Intensifies
7. Parched
   Wilier
   Footwear
8. Follower of neither
   Attorney's concern
   Ocean bird
9. Rustic hotels
   Short basketball goal
   Creates lace
10. Motorcycle adjunct
    Conger fishermen
11. Office worker
    Bower
12. Many millennia
    Make bare
13. Ritual
    Toward shelter, nautically
14. Norse deity
    "The Most Happy ____"
    Family
15. Venetian magistrate
    Worry
    Sense organs

BRICKS

YAP EWI	AYE LOE	IC■ DL■	AVE GEA	OT■ P■D
EAR ENS	R■I R■D	■BL PEA	EBU LON	R■N ■■■
S■B ■■E	ACE LLA	AKE R■O	EDO RIG	ABB LOO
OFF NER	D■S ■■■	ILE ALT	OUR WRY	LA■ ■■■
EE■ CRA	ARM ■■■	ERR R■O	ORE YEA	ENE M■■
S■T HEA	OAT ■CE	ORT ENS	■SN ■■S	RON IRN
■UP ■RE	AFT ROO	SPR ■■A	■AN ER■	S■T LLA

DIAGRAM

	1	2	3	4	5	6	7	8	9	10	11	12	13	14	15
1	S	E	R	A	■	■	A	N	I	S	■	■	C	O	D
2															
3															
4															
5															
6															
7															
8															
9															
10															
11															
12															
13															
14															
15															

PUZZLE 231

ACROSS

1. Stain
5. Dry, as wine
8. Dew time
12. Motorcar
13. Scour
15. Canyon sound
16. Metal bar
17. Kitchen utensil
18. Flower garlands
19. Reactor or energy
21. Gasoline number
23. Voter
26. Agree wordlessly
27. High voice
31. Admired
33. Long ago
34. Polluted air
36. Detaches
40. Fear
42. Bat wood
43. Tendon
44. Last Greek letter
45. Sasquatch's cousin
47. Plato's portico
48. Rye fungus
50. Designating
52. Dirt-road hazard
55. Insist
57. Energy or weight
59. Teased
64. Softball team
65. Greek letter
68. Outing
69. Faction
70. Theater
71. Suggest strongly
72. Retained
73. Decide
74. Inlets

DOWN

1. Horse house
2. Hawaiian feast
3. Auricular
4. Bridge booth
5. Make a run
6. Stray
7. Actor's hint
8. Go soft
9. View from the beach
10. African mammal
11. Meddled
13. Prepares fish
14. Stream
20. Electric fish
22. Ships' hands
24. Storage rooms
25. With no slack
27. Spelling blunder
28. Ramble
29. Bald eagle's kin
30. Neutral color
32. Belief in God
35. City official
37. Not pro
38. Rare gas
39. Loot
41. Wrist bones
46. Trouser length
49. Small lizard
51. Had for lunch
52. Creamy dressing
53. Useful
54. Of musical pitch
56. Data
58. Fix
60. Defeat decisively
61. Money in Milan, once
62. Irritable
63. Low grades
66. Activity
67. ___ rally

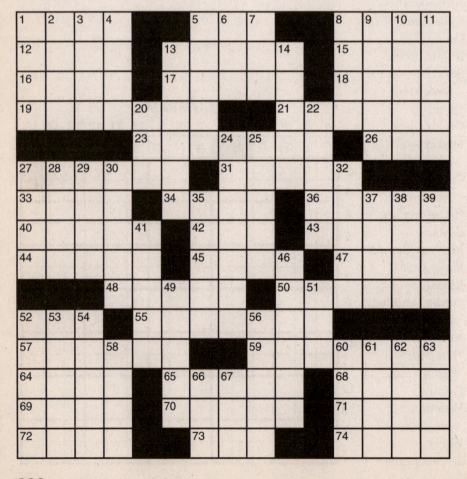

1	2	3	4	■	■	5	6	7	■	■	8	9	10	11
12				■	13				14	■	15			
16				■	17					■	18			
19				20			■	■	21	22				
■	■	■	■	23			24	25			■	26		
27	28	29	30			■	31				32	■	■	■
33				■	34	35			■	36		37	38	39
40				41	■	42			■	43				
44					■	45			46	■	47			
■	■	■	48		49			■	50	51				
52	53	54	■	55				56			■	■	■	■
57			58			■	■	59			60	61	62	63
64				■	65	66	67			■	68			
69				■	70					■	71			
72				■	■	73			■	■	74			

PUZZLE 232

ACROSS

1. Beat walkers
5. On the peak
9. Greek letters
14. Cockeyed
15. Frayed
16. Flee, romantically
17. Malicious
18. So be it!
19. Exact copy
20. Clairvoyant
22. Fall bloomer
23. Airport letters
24. Electric unit
26. Contains
27. Villain
31. Indian abodes
34. List of chores
36. Needlefish
37. ___ over heels
41. Hit with an open hand
42. Vision
44. Israeli statesman Eban
45. Roll-call response
46. Sock part
47. ___ in on (aimed for)
49. Crushes
52. Curves
53. Enjoin
56. Conjunctions
57. Crowd
59. Frighten
61. Notice
66. Floor exercise
67. Excite
69. Lascivious look
70. Escape from
71. Poems by Keats
72. Floor pads
73. Erased
74. Lymph ___
75. Pay-phone feature

DOWN

1. Tenting grounds
2. Is obligated to
3. Offer thanks devoutly
4. Out of ___
5. Be ready for
6. Male feline
7. Assayers' concerns
8. Coop
9. Changed into
10. Building wings
11. Fang
12. Sleep disorder
13. Clairvoyants
21. Listen
24. Colorful fish
25. Frequency measure
27. Impetuous
28. Stare at
29. Shifting device
30. Remove pins from
32. Urged (on)
33. Portion out
35. Moving
38. Black, in poems
39. Slumbering
40. Papas
43. Atomic particles
48. Declines
50. Frolicked
51. Cured, as meat
53. Located
54. Vital
55. Pertaining to birth
58. Fat
60. Obnoxious
62. Shade sources
63. "___ People"
64. Congressional rejection
65. Formerly, of old
67. Finished first
68. Big fuss

PUZZLE 233

ACROSS

1. Attempt
5. Like a horror film
9. Wearing pumps
13. Old Italian bread
14. Fencing blades
16. Daiquiri ingredient
17. Below
19. Not fer
20. The self
21. Grammar-class no-no
22. LXXX
24. Composed
26. Help a robber
28. Part of D.J.
30. Weapon storage site
35. Naysayer
38. Skin problem
40. Fly unaccompanied
41. Kind
42. Besmirch
43. Formal wear
44. Lower joint
45. "Soul Train" watcher
46. Emmets
47. More dingy
49. "___ Breaky Heart"
52. Dig for mollusks
54. Rile
58. Kowtow
62. Out of range
64. Prom wear
65. Zhivago's love
66. Mood
69. Alack!
70. Refute
71. Rarity
72. Pressroom word
73. Time long ago
74. Wrongful act

DOWN

1. Swings around
2. Color slightly
3. Passion
4. Hive resident
5. Bottled spirits
6. Unfold
7. Lariat
8. At any rate
9. Metal refining dregs
10. Towering
11. Eliminate
12. Not accept
15. Less opaque
18. Rajah's wife
23. Part of TGIF
25. Corrected copy
27. Monkey treat
29. Photog's need
31. School themes
32. Part of speech
33. Deplaned
34. Much
35. Solicits
36. A little piggy's share
37. Maple or elm
39. It makes Ross cross
42. Celestial
48. Decorate a cake
50. Pure and modest
51. Earless seal
53. Caribbean dance
55. Office worker, for short
56. Tempter
57. Exercise
58. Elated
59. Breath sound
60. Certain exam
61. Florist's buy
63. Twice two
67. Scottish novelist
68. Very warm

1	2	3	4	■	5	6	7	8	■	■	9	10	11	12
13				■	14				15	■	16			
17				18						■	19			
20			■	21				■	22	23				
24			25			■	26	27			■	■	■	■
■	■	■	28			29	■	30			31	32	33	34
35	36	37		■	■	38	39			■	40			
41				■	42					■	43			
44				■	45				■	■	46			
47				48			■	49	50	51		■	■	■
■	■	■	■	52			53	■	54			55	56	57
58	59	60	61			■	62	63			■	64		
65				■	66	67					68			
69				■	70					■	71			
72				■	■	73				■	74			

PUZZLE 234

ACROSS

1. Footless creature
5. The sun
8. Deli side order
12. Advertising symbol
13. Case or crust
15. Religious leader
16. Quiet town
17. "Under ___"
18. Popular bloom
19. More expensive
21. Tranquilized
23. Broadcast
25. Convent member
26. Sneer
29. Forbidden by law
33. Knowledge
34. Become involved
37. Atlantic fish
39. Keats's container
40. Tiny bits
41. Be obliged to pay
42. Stone or Bronze
43. Consecrates
45. Ump's kin
46. Hermit
48. Halloween treat
50. Society gal
51. Cover the roof again
54. Funnel-shaped flower
58. Catching
62. Lyrical
63. Newsstand
65. Fragrance
66. Stare flirtatiously
67. Clothe
68. Boxer's boundary
69. Corrosive liquids
70. ___ kwon do
71. Destroyed

DOWN

1. Priests' robes
2. Mope
3. Monster
4. Mark a page
5. Church feature
6. Unclose, to a poet
7. Table features
8. Pounced
9. Ransack
10. Church recess
11. Garden growth
13. Employer
14. Volunteer again
20. Diving position
22. Conflict for two
24. More filthy
26. Ocean bird
27. Join
28. Circle or tube
30. Borrowed sum
31. Oak's nut
32. Mooed
35. Small motorcycle
36. Cowboy's shoe
38. Challenge
43. Minister's word
44. Strikebreaker
47. Extracts
49. Trellises
52. Develop
53. Appropriate
54. Billiards' kin
55. Fidgety
56. Domino piece
57. "___ That a Shame"
59. Effigy
60. Not yep
61. Developed
64. "Ghost" role

PUZZLE 235

ACROSS

1. Debate side
4. Nervous twitches
8. On top of
12. Went before
13. Make bubbly
15. Uh-uh
16. Aged
17. Gazed slyly
18. Team
19. Man's jewelry item
21. Practical joke
22. Allowed to borrow
23. Cancel
24. Short jacket
26. Stead
28. Hit with hen grenades?
32. Caspian feeder
35. Blood part
39. Act like
40. Galahad's title
41. Type of watch display
42. Ump's kin
43. Lodge member
44. He cometh
45. Conform to
46. Lecterns
48. Twerp
50. Repeated
54. ___ down (washed)
58. Stop marching
61. Samara maker
62. Ring
63. Settled
64. County-fair prize
66. Massage
67. Tight closure
68. Go to extremes
69. Cider girl
70. This place
71. Important periods
72. According to

DOWN

1. Schemes
2. Artifact
3. More unusual
4. High schooler
5. Strong rage
6. Ship's load
7. Bargain
8. Unblock a pipe
9. Ponder
10. Dentist's command
11. Certain amphibian
13. Legal excuse
14. Border
20. Yank
24. Protrude
25. Not imaginary
27. Legend
29. Mode of dress
30. Fleche weapon
31. Resist
32. Applied
33. Madden
34. Boats like Noah's
36. Draw a bead
37. Be upright
38. Hair apparent
41. Part of CD
45. Stink-bomb's discharge
47. ___ of fish
49. Horned mammal, briefly
51. Sub sandwich
52. Green shade
53. Fire's remnant
55. Paper money
56. Slip away from
57. Exclude
58. Breakfast dish
59. Helm position
60. Falsifier
62. Grand Banks catch
65. Undies item

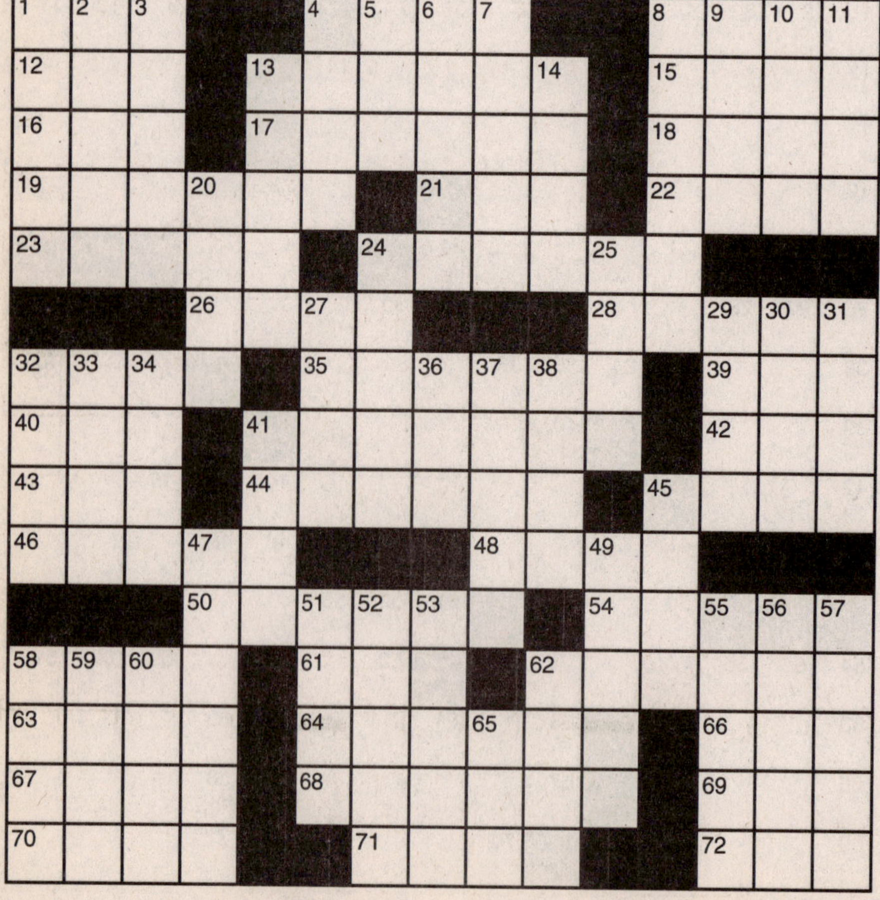

PUZZLE 236

ACROSS

1. Lock of hair
6. Requests
10. Finds the sum of
14. Prevention measure
15. Browning, e.g.
16. Legal paper
17. Deck out
18. On a voyage
19. Hot rock
20. Salami vendor
21. Quickly!
23. Scratch
24. Conveyor ___
26. Suave
28. Cry of discovery
31. Whirlybird blade
33. Cuckoo
34. Hire
36. Very black
40. Checked with a stopwatch
42. Motor lubricant
43. Acid type
44. Fret
45. Struggles
47. Church seat
48. Witnesses
50. Spread out awkwardly
52. Flushed
55. Church recess
56. Keats's output
57. Pleasantly
60. Dark red wine
64. Windy
66. Shout
67. Furor
68. Wander about
69. Shells
70. Tie type
71. Merganser
72. "___ we forget . . ."
73. Lets it stand

DOWN

1. Warty critter
2. Not polite
3. Organic compound
4. Copyist
5. Old Japanese coin
6. Into pieces
7. Not bad
8. Excited
9. Law
10. Hole piercer
11. Playwright's offering
12. Couch
13. Look hard
21. Strategy
22. Galleon's loot
25. ___ out (barely made)
27. Hat part
28. Gobbles up
29. Individual
30. Frost
31. Train tracks
32. Look nastily
35. Frequent attendee
37. Palm drink
38. Understood
39. Wail
41. Meadow munchers
43. Egyptian snakes
45. Therapeutic
46. View
49. Currency, in Osaka
51. Dinner, e.g.
52. Laughs loudly
53. Set phrase
54. Brass
55. Mete
58. Showed up
59. Shade givers
61. ___ upon a . . .
62. Civil disorder
63. Makes lace
65. Tree type
67. Bell and Kettle

1	2	3	4	5	■	6	7	8	9	■	10	11	12	13
14					■	15				■	16			
17					■	18				■	19			
20				■	21					22	■	23		
■	■	■	24	25			■	■	26		27			
28	29	30				■	31	32				■	■	■
33			■	34		35				■	36	37	38	39
40			41		■	42			■	43				
44				■	45				46		■	47		
■	■	■	48	49				■	50		51			
52	53	54				■	■	55				■	■	■
56			■	57		58	59			■	60	61	62	63
64			65	■	66				■	67				
68				■	69				■	70				
71				■	72				■	73				

PUZZLE 237

ACROSS

1. Long tale
5. Insects
9. One plus one
12. Kitchen cooker
13. Limited
15. Old witch
16. Soft material
17. Shun
18. Feel sick
19. Appoint
21. Grapple
23. Gang
25. Spelling error
26. Traveler's permit
28. Charcoal residue
30. Resort, of a sort
33. Drumstick
34. Seagoing vessel
36. Scares
39. Vinegar's partner
40. Funnel-shaped flower
42. Exasperate
43. Shiny
45. Telephoned
46. Nutritious bean
47. Dunk
48. Pig's place
49. Warning sign
51. Urge
54. Baking ___
56. Tangle up
59. Prison leader
63. Broom's wet cousin
64. Lot
67. Thick cord
68. Function
69. Anxiety
70. Newsroom word
71. Alter a skirt
72. Looks over
73. Physicians, for short

DOWN

1. Couch
2. Sts.
3. Hair goops
4. Pranks
5. Grocery holder
6. Coffee container
7. Enlargement
8. Remorseful
9. "___ Girl"
10. Sob
11. Gape
13. Ten minus one
14. Shed tears
20. Understands
22. Average
24. Postpone
26. Covers
27. Eskimo's dwelling
29. Gush suddenly
31. Composure
32. Ohio city
33. Jam ingredient?
35. ___, you!
36. Wrongdoing
37. Chinese temple
38. Heavens
41. Some votes
44. Rotate
48. Wine
50. Impaired
52. Evening bugle call
53. Jalopy
55. Night people
56. Australian birds
57. News finder
58. Erupt
60. Dull-witted one
61. Legend
62. Court dividers
65. Charlie, in code
66. Pluralizing letter

PUZZLE 238

ACROSS

1. Opposed to
5. Molten rock
9. Gladiator's domain
14. Burn
15. Like the Gobi
16. Jogger
17. Submerge
18. Walked
19. On guard
20. Yolk holder
21. Ship's spine
22. Thin
23. The things there
25. Capital of Oregon
28. Create a sweater
30. Loosen by turning
35. Selection
38. Leaders
39. Frost
40. British noblewoman
41. Mushrooms, e.g.
43. Burning substance
44. For keeps
45. Deluge refuge
46. Donors
48. Feeling
50. In the past
51. Shorthand pro
53. Decree
57. Hushed
61. Gambling term
63. Crop
64. Winter drink
65. Carbonated beverage
66. Garment of India
67. Bedeck
68. ___-friendly
69. Becomes older
70. Filleted
71. Sleep
72. Nuisance

DOWN

1. Object of value
2. Horse sound
3. Latin-American dance
4. Exasperate
5. Overdue
6. Stop
7. String instrument
8. Supplement
9. Sirens
10. Film part
11. Duel tool
12. Dull person
13. Affectedly bohemian
21. Gambling game
24. Snow lovers
26. Breathing organ
27. "___ Pulver"
29. Baby
31. Longed for
32. Eastern staple
33. Arab chieftain
34. Joins in matrimony
35. Ballads
36. Surface a road
37. Fed. agents
38. Squid's fluid
42. Longing
47. Glazes
49. Oahu, e.g.
50. Heaps
52. Lasso
54. Vision
55. Apple centers
56. Wring
57. Union pariah
58. Hubbub
59. Church picture
60. Body of knowledge
62. Projectile
65. Nasty mutt
66. Maple-syrup source

1	2	3	4	■	5	6	7	8	■	9	10	11	12	13
14				■	15				■	16				
17				■	18				■	19				
20			■	21				■	■	22				
23			24		■	25		26	27		■	■	■	■
■	■	■	28		29		■	30			31	32	33	34
35	36	37				■	38			■	39			
40				■	41	42				■	43			
44				■	45			■	46	47				
48				49			■	50				■	■	■
■	■	■	■	51			52		■	53		54	55	56
57	58	59	60		■	■	61		62		■	63		
64					■	65				■	66			
67					■	68				■	69			
70					■	71				■	72			

PUZZLE 239

ACROSS

1. That girl
4. Doorway side
8. Removed leaves
13. Wood chopper
14. Fragrances
16. Cook's oil
17. Large truck
18. Small body of land
19. Quitter's toss
20. Destroyed
22. Little pie
24. Dismiss
25. Batter's hat
27. Measure of gold
29. Bolster
31. Tussaud's medium
32. Strong coffee
35. Spassky's turn
38. Word game
40. Bates film
42. Tolerate
44. Muscle spasm
46. Scorch
47. Pry bars
49. Mama's ___
51. Jogged one's memory
52. Caustic stuff
53. Kind of doll
55. All the cards
57. Matter
59. Hero meat
63. Leading
66. ___ the last laugh
68. Less dated
69. Farmland units
71. MTV feature
73. Bedlam
74. Weasel out of
75. Water plants
76. Go wrong
77. Peevish
78. Matched groups
79. Fodder

DOWN

1. Severe
2. Banishment
3. Grand
4. Connector
5. Sale notices
6. Shed feathers
7. Snap
8. Decay
9. Overhead
10. Salad bar fruit
11. In any way
12. Editor's word
15. Drinking aid
21. Hinder
23. Trolley
26. Apex
28. Pivot point
30. Place
32. Entree listing
33. Try to persuade
34. Made a hue turn
35. Shopping place
36. Mind
37. ___ la France!
39. Pen part
41. Hooklike blade
43. Proves human
45. Atlantic fish
48. Waistband
50. Oui or ja
54. Tropical jelly
56. Light boats
57. Inactive
58. Ills
60. Covered with water
61. TV and radio, e.g.
62. Satire
63. Sloop's pole
64. Anguish
65. Pupil site
67. Sidle
70. Heavens
72. Gobble up

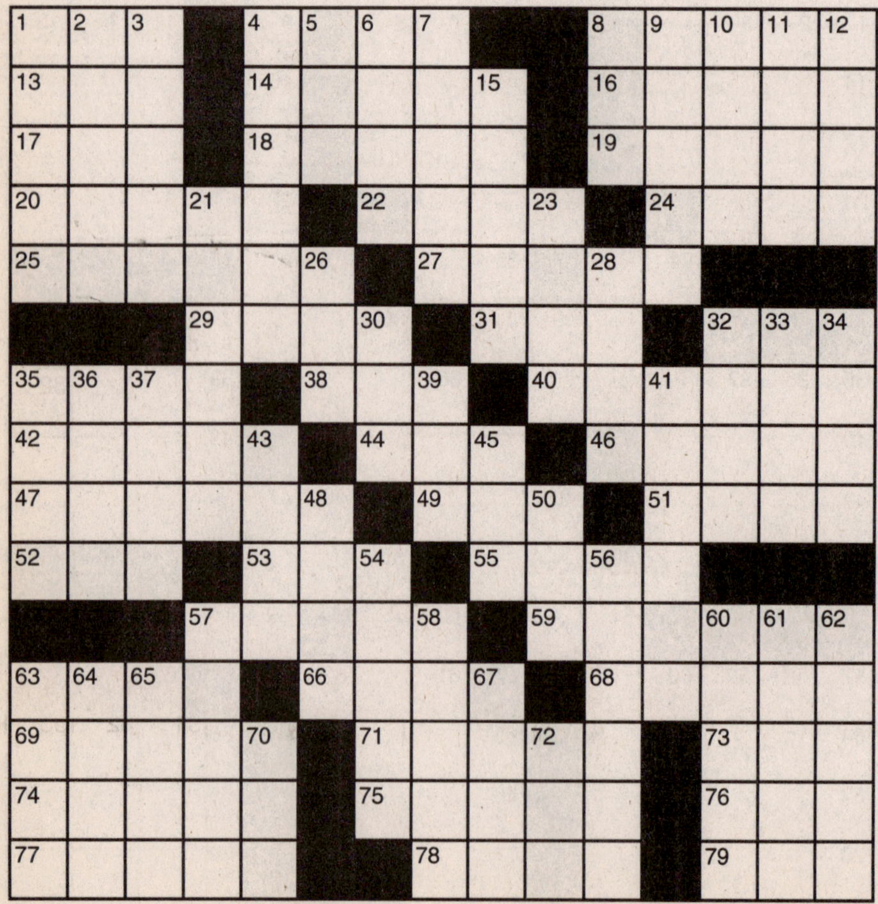

FOUR-MOST

PUZZLE 240

All of the 4-letter entries in this crossword puzzle are listed separately and are in alphabetical order. Use the numbered clues as solving aids to help you determine where each 4-letter entry goes in the diagram.

4 LETTERS

AFAR
CROC
DELE
DRAG
EARL
EARN
EDIE
ENDS
EVIL
EZRA
NE'ER
OVAL
OWED
PARE
PATH
PLED
PLOW
POTS
RARE
REAL
RODE
RYES
SLED
SOLO
THAI
TIME
TIRE
UNIT
X-RAY
ZERO

ACROSS

5. ___ your request
13. Lime refresher
16. Suggestion
18. Theater employee
21. Surplus
24. Wintry
26. Mr. Onassis
27. Rope
30. Master
33. Male bighorn
34. Fictitious name
35. Bill, eventually
36. Caustic material
37. Sugar tree
38. Gold source
39. Tell a lie
40. Mooed
45. Mature
49. Restroom door sign
55. Boxing legend
58. Actual profit

DOWN

1. Eyebrow shape
2. Tit ___ tat
3. Ruckus
4. Repeat
7. Revenge
8. Energetic
19. Deli meat
25. Sportscaster Howard ___
28. Mobile native
29. Short drink
39. Wells ___
41. Playful swimmer
51. Nag's nosh
52. Exist
53. Leaders

1	2	3	4	■	5	6	7	■	8	9	10	11
12				■	13			■	14			
15				■	16			■	17			
■	■	■	18	19				■	20			
21	22	23			■	■	24	25		■	■	■
26			■	27	28	29			■	30	31	32
33			■	34					■	35		
36			■	37					■	38		
■	■	■	39			■	■	40	41			
42	43	44		■	45	46	47			■	■	■
48				■	49			■	50	51	52	53
54				■	55			■	56			
57				■	58			■	59			

PUZZLE 241

ACROSS

1. Snaky shape
4. Urgent request
8. Dismounted
12. Luau necklace
13. British title
14. Mineral vein
15. Australian leaper
17. Florida Key, e.g.
18. Black-____ pea
19. Consumed
20. Went by horse
23. Slippery swimmers
25. Self-images
26. Does sums
27. Curve
30. Most senior
32. Pet rodent
34. Astrological Lion
35. Earring's site
37. Plus
38. Checkers, e.g.
39. Changed the color
40. Disrobe
43. Stereo system
46. Opera highlight
47. Part of NFL
51. Placard
52. Hot spot
53. Birthday number
54. Party thrower
55. Precious stones
56. Lobster ____

DOWN

1. Antlered animal
2. Baltic or Bering
3. Preacher's topic
4. Frolic
5. Folk knowledge
6. Worn down
7. Fuss
8. Assumed name
9. Misplaced
10. Loiter
11. Young adult
16. Ganders' mates
19. Other than that
20. Lively dance
21. Gape
22. Extinct bird
24. Brink
26. Nuclear particle
27. Skillfully
28. Come up
29. Blockhead
31. Openhanded blow
33. Audio medium
36. Act
38. Goliath was one
40. Cloth belt
41. Musical combo
42. Big trucks
44. Bit of info
45. Fish appendages
47. Seasonal beverage
48. Brief snooze
49. "Long, Long ____"
50. Allowed

PUZZLE 242

ACROSS

1. Majestic
6. Shoreline
11. Coliseums
13. Small sword
14. Cease
15. Main course
16. Plaster type
18. Cloud's locale
19. Fail to win
22. Shouted disapproval
24. Lodging place
25. Certain baby blossom
29. Whoa!
31. Biblical vessel
32. Rover's treat
33. Cigarette filling
35. Lemon drink
36. Sitcom's Morgenstern
38. At the summit of
39. Slender fish
42. Assembles
44. Bumpy
46. Ups the bet
50. Sirloins
51. Withstand
52. Sizable
53. Category

DOWN

1. Great, slangily
2. Neighbor of Nev.
3. Absolutely!
4. Licorice-tasting seed
5. Survive
6. River craft
7. Select
8. Ventilates
9. Search for
10. Three, in cards
12. Puny pencil
13. Bake again
17. Deteriorate
19. Shopper's aid
20. Informed of
21. Snooty one
23. Society miss
26. Sloop, e.g.
27. Erase
28. Bottomless
30. Strokes standard
31. Future oaks
34. Fresh
37. Farm unit
38. Actor's remark
39. Flood
40. Initial stake
41. Coral shelf
43. Zest
45. Receptacle
47. Bask
48. Miscalculate
49. Envision

DOUBLE TROUBLE

PUZZLE 243

Not really double trouble, but double fun! Solve this puzzle as you would a regular crossword, except place one, two, or three letters in each box. The number of letters in each answer is shown in parentheses after its clue.

ACROSS

1. Hidden loot (5)
3. Worth (5)
6. Look over (4)
8. Saddle horn (6)
9. Elongate (7)
10. Plant shoot (6)
11. Step in (9)
13. Alienate (8)
15. Gladly receive (7)
18. Assistant (4)
19. Most recent (6)
22. Be the star of (8)
24. Personnel (5)
26. Napless (10)
28. Consequently (9)
30. Blooper (5)
31. Guard (8)
33. Establish (5)
34. Show up (4)
35. Entrance hall (5)
37. Impetus (8)
39. David rocked his world (7)
43. Overcast (6)
44. Bombast (7)
47. Burning (6)
48. Dispatch (4)
49. Heredity factors (5)
50. Grazing grounds (4)

DOWN

1. Hem and haw (7)
2. Postpone (6)
3. Immense (4)
4. Attract (4)
5. Clearly outlines (6)
6. Forage (8)
7. Army member (3)
8. Main idea (5)
10. Shovel's kin (5)
12. Handrail support (5)
14. Apprentice (7)
16. Lucid (8)
17. Honey beverage (4)
19. Suds (6)
20. Severe fright (6)
21. Lieu (5)
23. In a supple way (7)
24. Market (5)
25. Influence (6)
27. Cellar (8)
29. Allude (5)
32. Facts, briefly (4)
34. Shakespearean genre (6)
36. Word for Descartes (4)
37. Pitcher's perch (5)
38. Offense (7)
40. Likely (6)
41. Book of maps (5)
42. Smog (4)
43. Shut (5)
45. Mover's ride (3)
46. Performs (4)

■	1	2	■	3	4	5	■	■	6	7
8			■	9			■	10		
11			12	■	■	13	14			■
■	■	■	15	16	17	■	18		■	■
19	20	21	■	22		23		■	24	25
26			27		■	28		29		
30		■	31		32		■	33		
■	■	34		■	35		36	■	■	■
■	37			38	■	■	39	40	41	42
43			■	44	45	46	■	47		
48		■	■	49			■	50		■

Mind Tickler

PUZZLE 244

If a country's population consists of 125 men for every 100 women, how many women are there for every 100 men?

PUZZLE 245

ACROSS

1. Command to Lassie
5. Steam
10. Goldfish, e.g.
14. Tortoise's foe
15. Vital
16. Descendant
17. Infrequent
19. White-tailed flier
20. Exclamation of awe
21. Aware of
22. Image
24. Ocean oasis
26. Innings number
28. Serpentine curve
29. Most rotund
32. Lyric poem
33. Bright thought
34. ____ off (angry)
36. Savor
41. Collar site
42. Slalom
43. Sneaker
44. Organic compound
46. Circus shelter
48. Earth
49. Be in hock
51. With enthusiasm
53. Dry, as wine
56. Feudal bigwig
58. Bard's instrument
59. Lurch
61. Complete
63. Escape
66. Out of port
67. Petite
70. Danson and Koppel
71. Competition
72. Dill, formerly
73. Casino machine
74. Remodelings
75. Mother, in Calais

DOWN

1. "Go away!"
2. Filled tortilla
3. Frank Lloyd Wright, e.g.
4. Senate vote
5. Most conceited
6. Plenty
7. Mexican tree
8. Future chicks
9. Let borrow again
10. Kitchen boss
11. Lofty pad
12. Hoops
13. Quarries
18. Flounder
23. Sock fillers
25. Pointed stick
27. Antiseptic
29. Dandy
30. Lemony drinks
31. Free lipstick
35. Stretch
37. Valuable
38. Beach location
39. Labor
40. Elusive
45. Actor's pursuit
47. Natural abilities
50. Speculate
52. Spiritual leader
53. Leaves hurriedly
54. Artist's stand
55. Motto
57. Having a rounded roof
60. Compass point
62. Grappa's cousin
64. Claim
65. Dole
68. "____ Got a Secret"
69. Highland hat

PUZZLE 246

Step by Step

In five steps change each word one letter at a time into a new 5-letter word so that by the fifth step each letter has been changed. Do not rearrange the order of the letters. You do not have to change the letters in order.

Example: Rouge, Rough, Cough, Couch, Conch, Cinch

1. PASTY
2. HOMER
3. DROOP
4. FORTY

PUZZLE 247

ACROSS

1. Give a PG to
5. Weight allowance
9. Nocturnal hooters
13. Nutmeg covering
14. Fowl for food
15. Bride's wear
16. Blubbers
17. Start
18. Roof projection
19. Fraternity letter
20. Baseball's Boggs
21. Made money
23. Nautical distance
25. Hot and dry
26. "The ____ Cometh"
28. Navigational system
32. Hunts
35. Chief
37. Hurry
38. Cow's chew
39. Metallic sound
41. "____ to Joy"
42. Black bird
43. Herbal drinks
44. Chalkboard need
47. Proportion
49. Ate heartily
51. Too inquisitive
53. Stockpile
57. Affluence
60. Deer
61. Geologic age
62. Indy event
63. Quickly
65. Young woman
66. "____ It Romantic?"
67. Globe
68. Dormant
69. Casual pullovers
70. Bright green
71. Tinter

DOWN

1. Grates
2. Obeyed reveille
3. Leg bone
4. Chicago trains
5. Bicycle built for two
6. Basilica recess
7. Lobster eggs
8. Diner sign
9. Carry to excess
10. Withdraw gradually
11. Not taped
12. Snow glider
14. Join together
20. Candle part
22. Is unwell
24. Wire measurement
25. Erelong
27. Embarrass
29. Greek consonants
30. Man Friday
31. At no time, in poetry
32. Burn mark
33. "____ Clipper"
34. Miner's way in
36. Like shish kebab
40. Frilly
43. Honk
45. Kick back
46. Thirst quencher
48. Coastal features
50. Ancient seer
52. Serape
54. Prepared
55. Silk fabric
56. Finisher
57. Legal document
58. Loosen
59. Complexion woe
60. Injure
64. Luau offering
65. Halfway

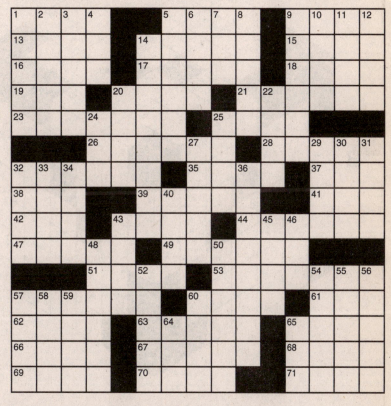

Letter Tiles

PUZZLE 248

Form four words reading across and five words reading down by placing the eight Letter Tiles into the diagram. Horizontal tiles go into horizontal spaces, vertical tiles into vertical spaces. In the example, three tiles fit together to form the words SAW, ONE, SO, AN, and WE.

Example:

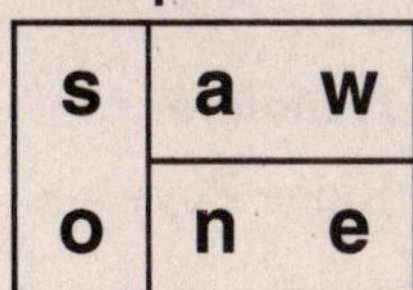

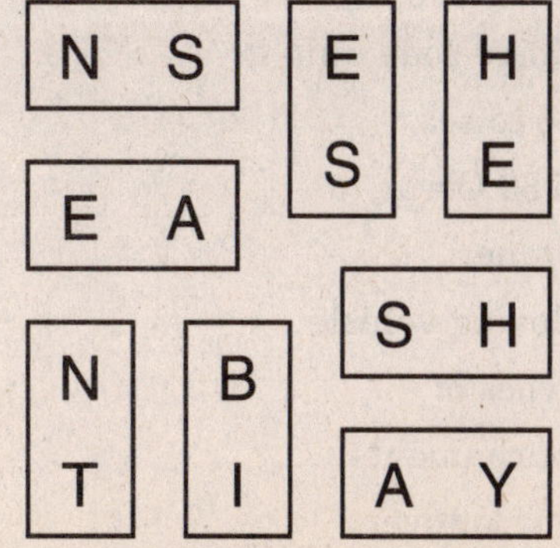

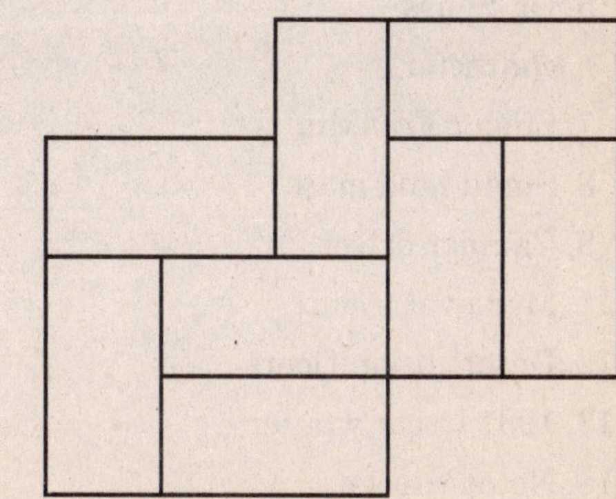

PUZZLE 249 THREE-D CROSSWORD

Here's a crossword with a third dimension! Each of the three faces (A, B, and C) is a crossword with words reading across and down. As you solve this puzzle, you'll see that some of the answers from one face continue on another face of the cube. Watch your ABCs, and you'll find that this is a real blockbuster.

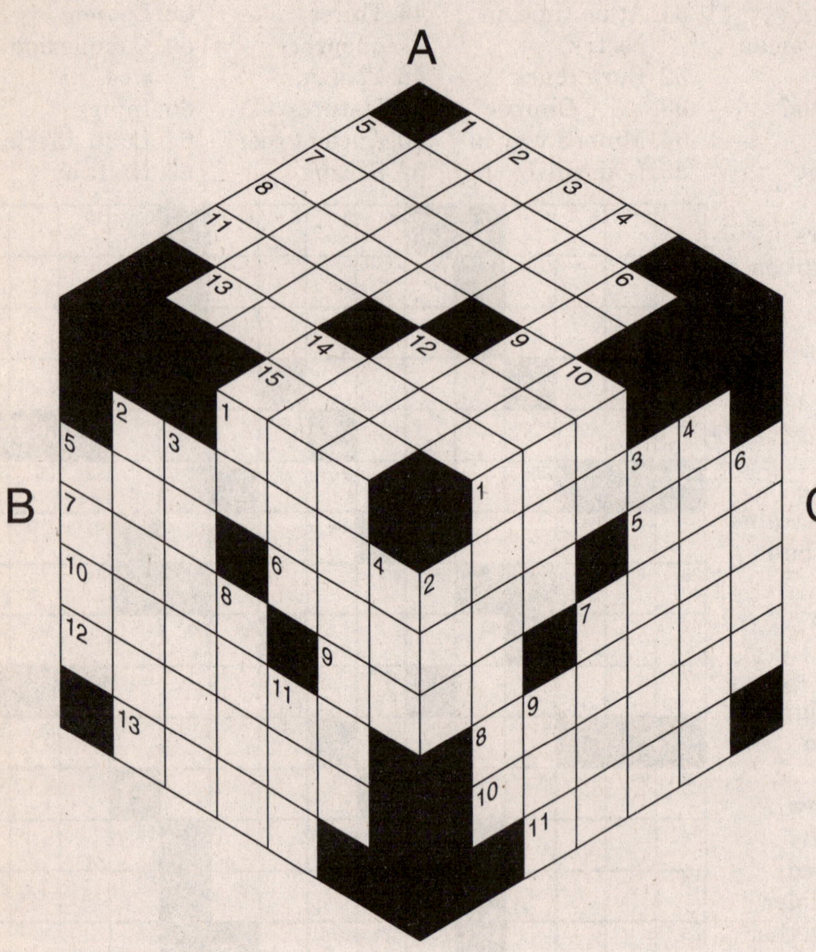

A CLUES

ACROSS

1. District
5. Dr. Seuss character
7. Singer Franklin
8. Small land mass
9. Camper driver
11. Medieval poem
12. Desert basin floors
13. 1981 Oscar winner
15. Noted Stooge

DOWN

1. Poland's capital
2. Aviatrix Earhart
3. Ceremony
4. Morse code unit
5. Go to sea
6. 1986 Oscar winner
10. Moving vehicle
12. Types of tournaments
14. Div. leftover

B CLUES

ACROSS

1. Water barrier
2. 1930 Oscar winner
5. Slicker
6. Leaf pores
7. Client
9. Mislaid
10. Deli meat
12. Motto
13. Cadence

DOWN

2. Schnoz protectors
3. Spotted cat
4. ____ Canals
5. Rumple
8. Craze
11. Plot

C CLUES

ACROSS

1. "So long!"
5. Meadow
7. Egg-shaped
8. Delight
10. Annual
11. Stage show

DOWN

2. "____ Pinafore"
3. Oak Ridge Boys song
4. Truly
6. Actress Sheedy
7. Spoken
9. Wise to

CODEWORD

PUZZLE 250

Instructions for solving Codeword puzzles are given on page 11.

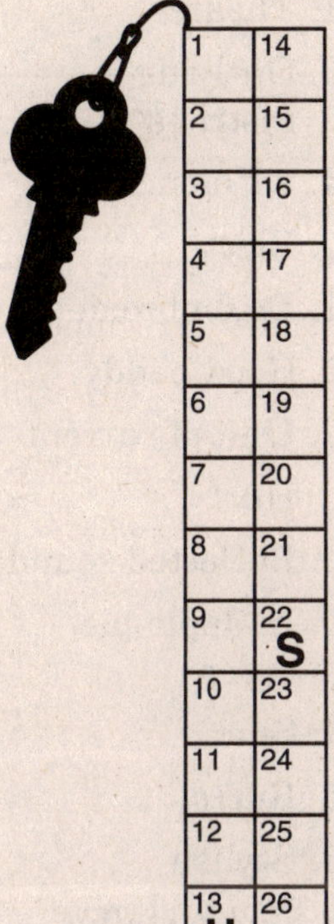

1	14
2	15
3	16
4	17
5	18
6	19
7	20
8	21
9	22 S
10	23
11	24
12	25
13 U	26

10	4	18	14	13 U	■	21	■	20	13	17	12	4
6	■	19	■	22 S	19	4	2	13	■	1	■	19
4	5	5	15	6	■	9	■	18	19	6	23	12
23	■	6	■	■	11	6	15	12	■	23	■	18
12	17	26	18	25	■	■	■	■	22	15	4	21
■	■	■	■	13	19	18	2	7	■	4	■	6
14	4	16	17	16	■	5	■	13	19	24	18	19
18	■	17	■	6	4	22	6	15	■	■	■	■
15	17	23	6	■	■	■	■	6	20	13	18	24
15	■	6	■	16	4	11	15	■	■	16	■	4
3	13	5	21	6	■	18	■	24	23	17	26	7
17	■	17	■	1	18	15	15	4	■	4	■	6
7	13	8	8	7	■	5	■	15	18	12	10	6

A	N
B	O
C	P
D	Q
E	R
F	~~S~~
G	T
H	~~U~~
I	V
J	W
K	X
L	Y
M	Z

CODEWORD

PUZZLE 251

1	14
2	15
3	16
4	17
5	18
6	19 Y
7	20
8	21 O
9	22
10	23
11	24
12	25
13	26

7	8	16	21	5	■	23	■	23	13	21	7	1
11	■	11	■	14	23	13	21	1	■	12	■	21
25	21	2	7	8	■	8	■	8	22	8	20	10
■	■	■	■	25	14	22	8	5	■	■	■	14
16	11	10	14	■	■	■	■	10	14	26	3	5
3	■	8	■	18	11	3	17	17	■	5	■	■
22	8	19 Y	21 O	11	■	20	■	14	9	3	17	14
■	■	8	■	8	4	14	8	5	■	6	■	14
24	8	10	14	4	■	■	■	■	20	6	8	5
8	■	■	■	13	21	13	14	7	■	■	■	■
23	11	23	15	3	■	3	■	8	25	17	3	22
13	■	3	■	13	14	17	14	9	■	3	■	11
14	7	1	13	19	■	13	■	3	7	1	17	19

A	N
B	~~O~~
C	P
D	Q
E	R
F	S
G	T
H	U
I	V
J	W
K	X
L	~~Y~~
M	Z

PUZZLE 252

ACROSS

1. June honoree
4. Personality parts
8. Performs
12. Blunder
13. Distress
15. Reporter's question
16. Baltic or Bering
17. No can do
18. Certain bean
19. Skewered meat
21. Opera stars
23. Lower limb
24. Kind of tent
26. Broadcast
28. Main
32. Tango number
33. King's superior
34. Whiten
37. Running circuits
41. Hoaxes
43. Volcanic dust
44. Motionless
45. Handbag
46. Naval rank
48. Pair
49. Half-dozen
51. Most chilly
53. Bill makers
58. Be obliged to pay
59. Con's foe
60. Lieu
62. Young girl
66. Forfeit
68. Large lizard
70. More than should be
71. Hunch
72. Mounted gun
73. Broad-antlered deer
74. Examination
75. Kind of hurrah
76. Gloom

DOWN

1. Computer perch
2. Telephone code
3. Dull
4. Chunk of eternity
5. Alum
6. Planet's path
7. Crack, as a case
8. Hole-punching tool
9. ___ con carne
10. Subdues
11. Theater
13. Outlying districts
14. Affluence
20. Elect
22. Do embroidery
25. Good buddy
27. Unit of current
28. Hurl
29. Reflected sound
30. In apple-pie order
31. Slim
35. Burro
36. Stylish
38. Camp staffer
39. Additionally
40. Mailbox opening
42. Tableland
44. Frosty, e.g.
46. Strange
47. Sticky stuff
50. "___ a Living"
52. Kauai keepsake
53. Bowler's bane
54. Wear down
55. Snouts
56. Royal
57. Health club feature
61. Fogelberg et al.
63. Irish ___
64. Fly unaccompanied
65. Oxen neckwear
67. Have breakfast
69. Commandment word

1	2	3	■	■	4	5	6	7	■	■	8	9	10	11
12			■	13					14	■	15			
16			■	17						■	18			
19			20		■	21				22	■	23		
■	■	■	24		25	■	26				27			
28	29	30				31	■	■	32			■	■	■
33			■	34			35	36		■	37	38	39	40
41			42		■	43			■	44				
45				■	46				47		■	48		
■	■	■	49	50		■	■	51			52			
53	54	55				56	57	■	58			■	■	■
59			■	60				61	■	62		63	64	65
66			67	■	68				69		■	70		
71				■	72						■	73		
74				■	■	75				■	■	76		

PUZZLE 253

ACROSS
1. Extension
4. Undiluted
8. In the sack
12. Opponent
13. Come
15. Skirt panel
16. Pipe joint
17. Anger
18. Steers
19. Realize
21. Harass
23. Unattached
25. Eggnog spice
29. Wyeth's field
32. Elevated
34. Pastry dessert
35. Result
37. Select
38. Say
41. Unwrap
42. Chronicle
43. Cast
45. Send away
48. Tropical fruit
50. TKO caller
53. Red hair-dye
55. Luau welcome
56. Reside
58. Feminine sheep
59. Constant
62. Friend in need
63. Tiny Tim's instrument
64. Rest
66. Lead actor
69. Motto
73. What to give it
76. Hooligan
77. In the direction of
78. Coral or Dead
79. Harness part
80. Coastal flier
81. Deer's kin

DOWN
1. Rear
2. Potential pike
3. Most humble
4. Shrimp
5. Footed vase
6. Get ___ of
7. Nightfall
8. Full of excitement
9. Emulate Ali
10. Shelley's before
11. Cozy retreat
13. Excitement
14. Marine eagle
20. Born as
22. Generation
23. To's associate
24. Split
26. Rich
27. Make a knot
28. Ariel, e.g.
29. It bit Cleo
30. Be repentant
31. Half a score
33. Doze off
36. Auction signal
39. Drink slowly
40. Playpen item
42. Longer than an era
44. Lass's friend
45. That woman
46. Cut down
47. Single item
49. Sweet or chick
50. Set loose
51. Architectural add-on
52. Pesky insect
54. Pose a question
57. Lived
60. Examine
61. Hanker
63. Egg on
65. Ampersand
66. Sloppy home
67. Even if, poetically
68. Northern bird
70. Land tract
71. Be in debt
72. Needlefish
74. Toothpaste form
75. Desk wood

PUZZLE 254

ACROSS

1. Hawaiian dance
5. Did the butterfly
9. Applauds
14. Lyrical poems
15. La Scala solo
16. Rascal
17. Missing
18. Bronze coin
19. Gloat
20. Computer key
22. Band
24. Chicago Loop trains
25. Relax
27. Aboard
29. Ship's ramp
32. Compel
36. Price label
37. Ogled
38. Risk
40. Wading bird
42. Dispute
44. Mil. defense alliance
45. Acid salt
47. Frat letters
49. Spanish queen
50. ___-friendly
51. Later
54. Collect
56. Stench
57. Befitting
60. Combine
62. Elevated
66. Chocolate substitute
68. Carry on
70. Plus
71. Court case
72. Rapier's kin
73. Sculptor's product
74. Tend a fire
75. Web-footed bird
76. Selects

DOWN

1. Bagel feature
2. Japanese noodles
3. For fear that
4. Rearward
5. Animal pouch
6. Grappler
7. "It ___ Me Babe"
8. ___ of honor
9. Moved stealthily
10. Bagel topper
11. Chills and fever
12. Opposite of push
13. Tennis match divisions
21. King's stand-in
23. Egyptian symbol
26. Agent
28. Greek liqueur
29. Celts
30. Coincide
31. Pass a bill
33. Scarcer
34. Noble
35. Norse poetry collection
36. Biblical pronoun
39. Response
41. Paddles
43. Anyplace
46. Chalet feature
48. Ill will
52. Polecat
53. Crooked
55. Stroll
57. Biblical book
58. Hair divider
59. Quartet with an absentee
61. Show astonishment
63. Won ton or split pea
64. Once, once
65. Catches
67. Mighty tree
69. Morn plus 12 hours

1	2	3	4	■	5	6	7	8	■	9	10	11	12	13
14				■	15				■	16				
17				■	18				■	19				
20				21	■	22			23		■	24		
■	■	■	25		26		■	27			28	■	■	■
■	29	30					31			■	32	33	34	35
36			■	37				■	38	39				
40			41		■	42	43		■	44				
45					46	■	47		48		■	49		
50				■	51	52					53			■
■	■	■	54	55			■	56				■	■	■
57	58	59	■	60			61		■	62		63	64	65
66			67		■	68			69	■	70			
71					■	72				■	73			
74					■	75				■	76			

PUZZLE 255

ACROSS

1. Cherry leftover
5. Serpent's song
9. Finch food
13. Insane
14. Improvise
16. Ship direction
17. Distinctive air
18. Jeweled headpiece
19. Ceiling block
20. Twisted
22. Command to a child
23. Piece of news
24. Biblical book
26. Proprietors
28. Walk leisurely
32. Cast
33. Garden soil
34. Throb with pain
37. Pitched
42. Poker beginning
43. Dock
45. Time long past
46. Itty-bitty
48. On the briny
49. Desert hill
50. Erode
52. Gave up seconds
54. Clever
58. Part of a ship's hull
60. Finely sharpened
61. Aloud
63. Trusty
68. Military helper
69. Summer viewing
71. Prohibit
72. Lean
73. Steer clear of
74. Sitting above
75. View
76. Editor's mark
77. Citrus fruit

DOWN

1. Cabbage dish
2. Sightsee
3. Neutral shade
4. Complain
5. Derby, e.g.
6. Foolish person
7. Marble slices
8. Title of respect
9. Glossy fabric
10. First-class
11. Sniggler
12. Believes
15. Louisiana marsh
21. Lassie
25. Hammer part
27. Moisten
28. Wood strip
29. Sound quality
30. Value
31. Forewarning
32. Not there
35. Informal talk
36. Hath, presently
38. Jekyll's other self
39. Decisive defeat
40. Coastal eagle
41. Tidy a garden
44. Become dim
47. Certain evergreen
51. Love
53. Unwell
54. Use a rink
55. Inheritors
56. Immerse again
57. Opponent
58. Fineness unit
59. Avoid
62. Vrooms the engine
64. Circle's kin
65. Bigfoot's kin
66. Source of energy
67. Easy gait
70. Clear

PUZZLE 256

ACROSS

1. Aids a felon
6. Fancy event
10. Pilsner
14. Baste again
15. Work
16. Spanish jar
17. Social level
18. Pinball foul
19. Up against
20. Hi-fi
22. Radiance
24. "___ to a Nightingale"
25. Diner's cloth
27. Solution
29. Barrel
31. Pouchlike part
32. Came to earth
33. Give off
35. 1994, e.g.
37. Deviation
41. Laughs loudly
43. Horse's mouthpiece
44. Nod off
45. Subsidiary statute
46. Imitation butter
48. ___-jerk reaction
49. Cajole
51. Buff
53. ___ out (make do)
54. Loony
57. Dictator
59. Bonfire residue
60. Ship's front
62. Expresses scorn
65. Informal talk
67. No-win situations
69. Regal headpiece
70. Doer of brave deeds
71. Aweather's opposite
72. Bar legally
73. Formerly
74. Harmony
75. Clarinets, e.g.

DOWN

1. Curves
2. Thrash
3. Necessary
4. Aquarium denizen
5. Pushes a broom
6. Acquired
7. Of bees
8. Dilly
9. Celestial
10. Long scarf
11. Push aside
12. Evade
13. Appraiser
21. All right!
23. Blue dyes
26. Antique refrigerator
28. Plant stem
29. Active word
30. Chinese port
32. Major roadway
34. Follow
36. Be indisposed
38. Pass through
39. Go in quest of
40. Fencer's sword
42. In one fell ___
47. Belongs to us
50. Pathways from hearts
52. Repartee
54. Hidden reserve
55. Friend of the groom
56. Blackens
57. 'Twixt partner
58. Library no-no
61. Like suntan lotion
63. Walked on
64. Maple drippings
66. Preschooler
68. Dry, as wine

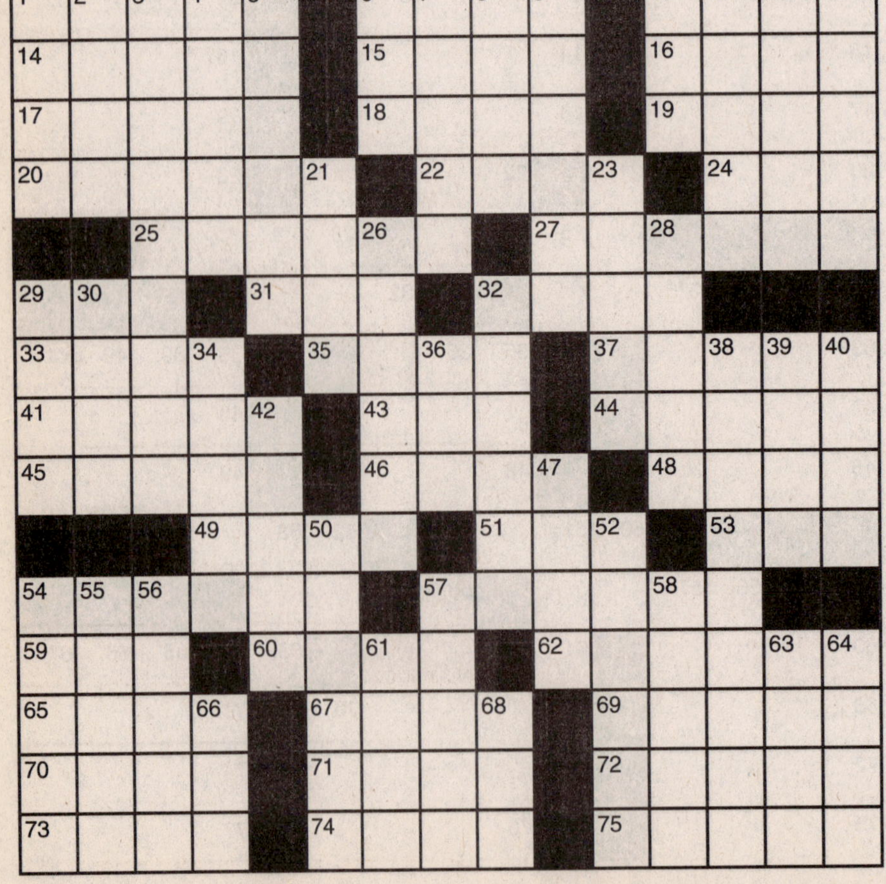

PUZZLE 257

ACROSS

1. Sail-holding pole
5. Wrinkle-faced dogs
9. Tops
14. Arm bone
15. On the main
16. Horned beast
17. Float
18. Merchandise
19. Benefactor
20. Writing fluid jar
22. Last Supper diner
24. Bee's follower
25. Place
27. Bog down
28. Potter's clay
30. Cold and rainy
33. Completely
36. Blazing
39. Lariat
40. Bobble the ball
42. Hermit
43. Pluckiest
45. Clarify again
47. Unlatch, in poems
48. Palest
50. Song sung singly
52. Utmost
53. Fitting
56. Connect for service
59. Pearl source
61. Back tooth
62. Off-white
65. Elbow
66. Proverb
67. Barren wasteland
68. In a minute
69. Handed out
70. Facts
71. Document of ownership

DOWN

1. Box or video
2. "Home ___"
3. Python
4. Canvas cover
5. Meadow
6. Employ
7. Hairstyling goo
8. Sandwich meat
9. Gusto
10. Selected
11. Unused
12. Organic compound
13. Achy
21. Met offerings
23. Type type
26. Narrative
28. Refer to
29. Incense ingredient
30. Indian princess
31. Let it be so!
32. Had been
33. Consequently
34. ___ tide
35. Gentle
37. Meaty
38. Place for hay
41. Leash for Dobbin
44. "Walking ___"
46. Slow routes
49. Long-faced
50. Platform
51. Paddled
53. Make amends
54. Black tea
55. Craze
56. Mosque official
57. Bump
58. Narrow board
60. Nail
63. Cedar Rapids college
64. Straight line

PUZZLE 258 CRISS-CROSSWORD

The answer words for Criss-Crossword are entered diagonally, reading downward, from upper left to lower right or from upper right to lower left. We have entered the words FUN and DUD as examples.

TO THE RIGHT

1. Amusing
2. Family room
3. Rio ___
4. Employ
5. Colorado Indian
6. Serious
7. Haze
9. "Mask" actress
11. Turns brown
13. Avers
14. Mrs. Chaplin
16. Microbes
17. "Norma ___"
19. Kind of boom
22. Engrave
24. Give off
25. Sweet potato
28. Chemical compound
30. Upon
31. Foot lanes
33. Spring month
35. Famous uncle
36. Witty saying
38. Hamilton's bill
39. Route

TO THE LEFT

2. Bomb
3. French playwright
4. Vase
5. "Born in the ___"
6. Office workers
7. Rival
8. Tennis shot
10. "Pretty Woman" star
12. ___ Shamra
13. Bother
15. Medicine amount
16. Pertaining to DNA
18. Unusual
20. Samms and others
21. Cinch
23. Circle parts
26. Pose
27. Muslim leader
29. Doubting guy
32. Tall building
34. Kiltie's beret
35. Bashful
37. Mother
38. Asian holiday
40. Pot

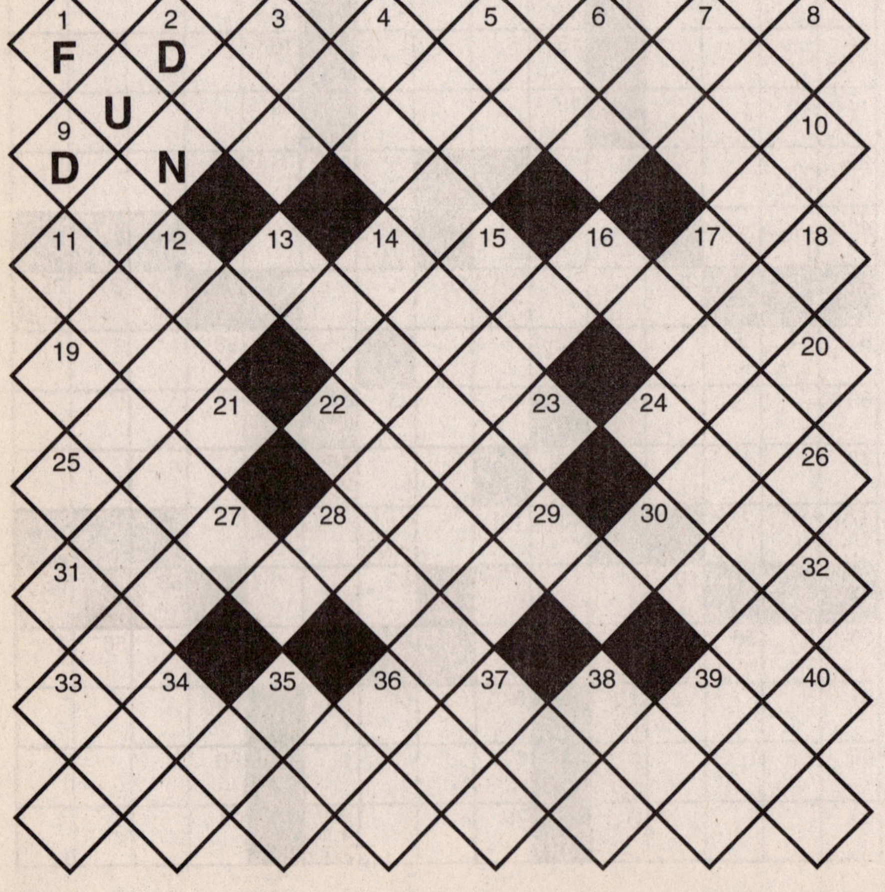

PUZZLE 259

ACROSS

1. Guy
5. Greek letter
8. Card game
12. Hang loosely
13. Sports complex
15. Erase
16. Car
17. Civilian clothes
18. Apollo landing site
19. Shop owner
21. Measure of farmland
22. Aardvark's morsel
23. Chose
25. Slow, in music
29. Gator's cousin
31. Nitwit
32. Consequently
37. Appeal
38. Bread surface
39. Wild goat
40. Siamese cat
42. Banal
43. Out of control
44. Talks back
45. Hold in a condensed coating
49. Leather-working tool
50. Cry
51. Pretty
58. Perched
59. Rosebush prickle
60. Biting
61. Level
62. Heroic tales
63. Bargain price?
64. Went auburn
65. Pale
66. ___-jerk reaction

DOWN

1. Clean erasers
2. Time of day
3. Woman's choir voice
4. Ketchup splash
5. Glass bottle
6. Weight
7. "___ the Night"
8. Poison ___
9. Start of kid's riddle
10. Place on a pedestal
11. Muted, with down
13. Chemical prefix
14. Plane station
20. Parade spoiler
24. Break the ___
25. Electrical units, for short
26. Charity
27. Section
28. Target
29. Thick lump
30. Kick back
32. The Stooges, e.g.
33. Evergreen trees
34. Kimono sashes
35. Neural network
36. 24th letters
38. Battles
41. Golf score
42. Bath powder
44. Graceful birds
45. Academy ___
46. Stall
47. Nab
48. Chose
49. Scottish island
52. Dissolve
53. Roman robe
54. Objective
55. Religious symbol
56. Liana
57. Selvage

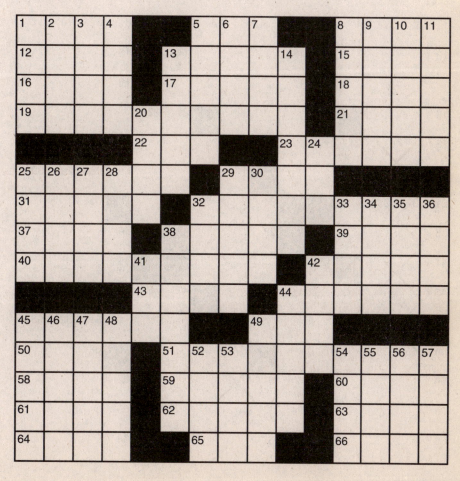

1	2	3	4	■	■	5	6	7	■	■	8	9	10	11
12				■	13				14	■	15			
16				■	17					■	18			
19				20						■	21			
■	■	■	■	22			■	■	23	24				
25	26	27	28			■	29	30			■	■	■	■
31					■	32					33	34	35	36
37				■	38					■	39			
40				41					■	42				
■	■	■	■	43				■	44					
45	46	47	48			■	■	49			■	■	■	■
50				■	51	52	53				54	55	56	57
58				■	59					■	60			
61				■	62					■	63			
64				■	■	65			■	■	66			

PUZZLE 260

ACROSS

1. Uncertain
5. Duo
8. Ladder rung
12. Globule
13. "Evening ___"
15. Baseball base
16. Wise about
17. Subway-fare coin
18. Curb
19. Function
20. Whittle down
21. Turns
23. Land
25. Smirk
26. Prove human
27. Afghans
31. Having talent
34. Run off to wed
35. Large tart
36. Dentist's tool
38. Ruin
39. Happy face
41. Beaver creation
42. Tingly
44. Got a top grade on
45. Grabs
47. Indicate yes
49. Engage
50. High-___ (forceful)
54. Salad ingredient
57. Self-centered
58. Summer cooler
59. Similar
60. Arouses
62. Breakfast offerings
63. Shortcoming
64. Crazy
65. Eccentric one
66. Corrosive liquids
67. Nursery item
68. Gambler's concern

DOWN

1. Concerning
2. Meaning
3. Bistro patron
4. Hoopla
5. Rosebush prickle
6. Rouse
7. Shelley poem
8. Get smaller
9. ___ the line (obeys)
10. Give out
11. Writing implements
13. One of a flight
14. Snare
20. Average
22. Chardonnay and Chianti
24. Totter
25. Fame
27. Blues
28. Heroic story
29. Piece of linoleum
30. Source
31. Takes on
32. Fiber source
33. Certain bean
34. Host
37. Lawful
40. Crafted
43. Hurled
46. Gratitude
47. Loud
48. To each his ___
50. Hamburger serving
51. Blew up
52. Moved gradually
53. Students' tables
54. Like a beanpole
55. Fine
56. Furry rodents
57. Presidential "no"
61. Simple shelter
62. ___ trip

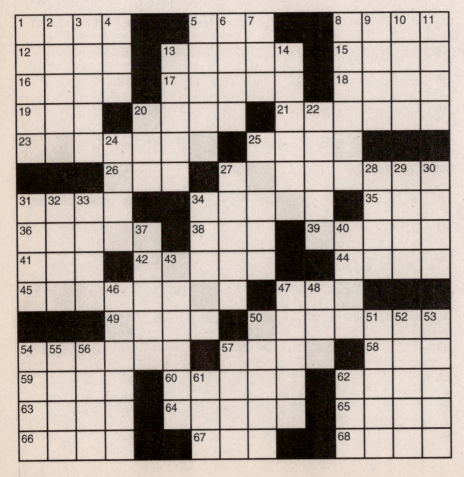

PUZZLE 261

ACROSS

1. Fraudulent scheme
5. Bullets
9. Merchandise holders
14. Dry watercourse
15. Low poker hand
16. Brilliance
17. King toppers
18. Trident feature
19. Trite
20. Small candle
22. Dance club
24. Do basting
25. Fast cars
27. Ins and ___
29. Card game
30. French toast spice
34. Indefinite subject
37. Lyrical
39. Musician Eddy
40. Billion years
41. Fire-breathers
43. ___ off (make angry)
44. Charm
46. Lion's ruff
47. Blockhead
48. Term
50. "We ___ Not Alone"
52. World's fair, e.g.
53. Pierced
57. "Tell ___ About It"
59. Tingly
62. Baseball deal
63. Collect
65. Put an edge on
67. Needle case
68. Agile
69. Heroic poetry
70. Religious order
71. Released
72. Ties the knot
73. Playing card

DOWN

1. Mower's width
2. Chocolate source
3. Highly skilled
4. Stingy
5. Skillful
6. Housecleaners
7. Tiny
8. Valuable lodes
9. Reverberates
10. Play part
11. Peer
12. Curly greens
13. Worry
21. Pal of Pooh
23. Bilk
26. Room opening
28. Greek letter
30. Groucho's prop
31. Image
32. Lollapalooza
33. A friend in ___ . . .
34. Oolong and pekoe
35. Kansas, to Dorothy
36. Count
38. British noblewoman
41. Hated
42. Tide phase
45. Gender
47. Immediate
49. Bambino
51. Soak flax
53. Church council
54. Assessor
55. Draw forth
56. Divinity
57. 50 percent
58. Arab prince
60. Gnaw
61. Aspiration
64. Ship's pronoun
66. Serpentine curve

PUZZLE 262

ACROSS

1. In that place
6. Client
10. Physicians, for short
14. Sanctuary
15. Stubborn animal
16. Saint's image
17. Upright
18. College teacher, for short
19. Short reminder
20. Spooky
21. Chronicle
23. Balloon filler
24. Baby buggy
27. Increase
29. Roof feature
32. Recycled tire
34. Shinier
36. Bear or cap
40. Hair tamer
41. Afternoon show
44. Unlatch, in poems
45. Brawl
47. Sheets and pillowcases
49. Titanic's obstacle
52. Barber's word
53. Drip
56. Hero store
58. Deary
59. Majestic address
61. Piano composition
65. Rude look
67. Superman's garment
69. Important exam
70. Regrets
71. Bit of news
72. Ms. O'Neal
73. Fishing tools
74. Golfing pegs
75. Sloppy people

DOWN

1. Biblical pronoun
2. Bunny's kin
3. At all times
4. Cookbook contents
5. Computer command
6. Ref's cousin
7. Convinced
8. Runaway groom
9. Purify
10. Not bright
11. Arctic, e.g.
12. Amusing
13. Saw logs
22. "___ of Love"
25. Operatic melody
26. Athletic event
28. Uproar
29. Omelet needs
30. Opposed to aweather
31. Electrical unit
33. Band
35. Artists' garments
37. Only
38. Acme
39. Lease payment
42. Geek
43. Verge
46. Personal quirk
48. First
50. Call forth
51. Scold
53. Rose spike
54. Rascal
55. Bay
57. Bank and field
60. Duel weapon
62. Biblical preposition
63. Paint
64. Shade trees
66. Santa has one
68. Printers' measures

1	2	3	4	5	■	6	7	8	9	■	10	11	12	13
14					■	15				■	16			
17					■	18				■	19			
20					■	■	21			22	■	23		
■	■	■	24		25	26	■	27			28			
29	30	31		■	32		33					■	■	■
34				35				■	■	36		37	38	39
40			■	41				42	43		■	44		
45			46		■	■	47				48			
■	■	■	49		50	51				■	52			
53	54	55					■	56		57		■	■	■
58			■	59			60	■	■	61		62	63	64
65			66	■	67			68	■	69				
70				■	71				■	72				
73				■	74				■	75				

PUZZLE 263

ACROSS

1. Unmatched
4. Arab chieftain
8. Fire alarm
13. Short life story
14. Took a train
15. Scratch
16. Tavern
17. Hit a hole in one
18. Arranged in advance
19. Prepared to drive
21. Dispute
23. "___ So Fine"
24. Milky stone
26. New Zealand bird
28. Type of gin
30. Hazardous
33. Female college grad
35. Aardvark's prey
36. Brokaw's delivery
38. Habit wearer
39. Railroad nail
41. Oahu garland
42. Dreary
44. Fashion line
45. Helicopter blades
48. Quickly
50. Gets the gold
51. Mend
52. Dirt
54. State further
57. Remitting funds
59. 2000, e.g.
63. Eerie
65. Racket
67. Big bird
68. Angels' headgear
69. Minute amount
70. Tennis shot
71. Rectify
72. Sprinted
73. Height limit?

DOWN

1. Final bio.
2. Have a meal
3. Performed
4. Dynasty
5. Brown color
6. Perfect example
7. Roulette bets
8. Metal fasteners
9. Outrage
10. Headstrong
11. Fencing sword
12. Fish snares
15. Sliver
20. Condemn
22. Pepe Le Pew
25. Mighty tool
27. Golfer Woosnam
28. Lap
29. Of the moon
31. Outlaw
32. Water pitchers
33. Also
34. Places for butts
35. Strive
37. Fam. member
40. Large bloom
43. Torso, for short
46. Have
47. Orderly
49. Snoozed
52. Pry into
53. Marble
54. Tooth problem
55. Small portion
56. Expunge
58. Bearded flower
60. Shocking fishes
61. Frenzied
62. Expensive gem
64. Eternity
66. Cool!

PUZZLE 264

FLOWER POWER

The answers to this petaled puzzle will go in a curve from the number on the outside to the center of the flower. Each number in the flower will have two 5-letter answers. One goes in a clockwise direction and the second in a counterclockwise direction. We have entered two answers to help you begin.

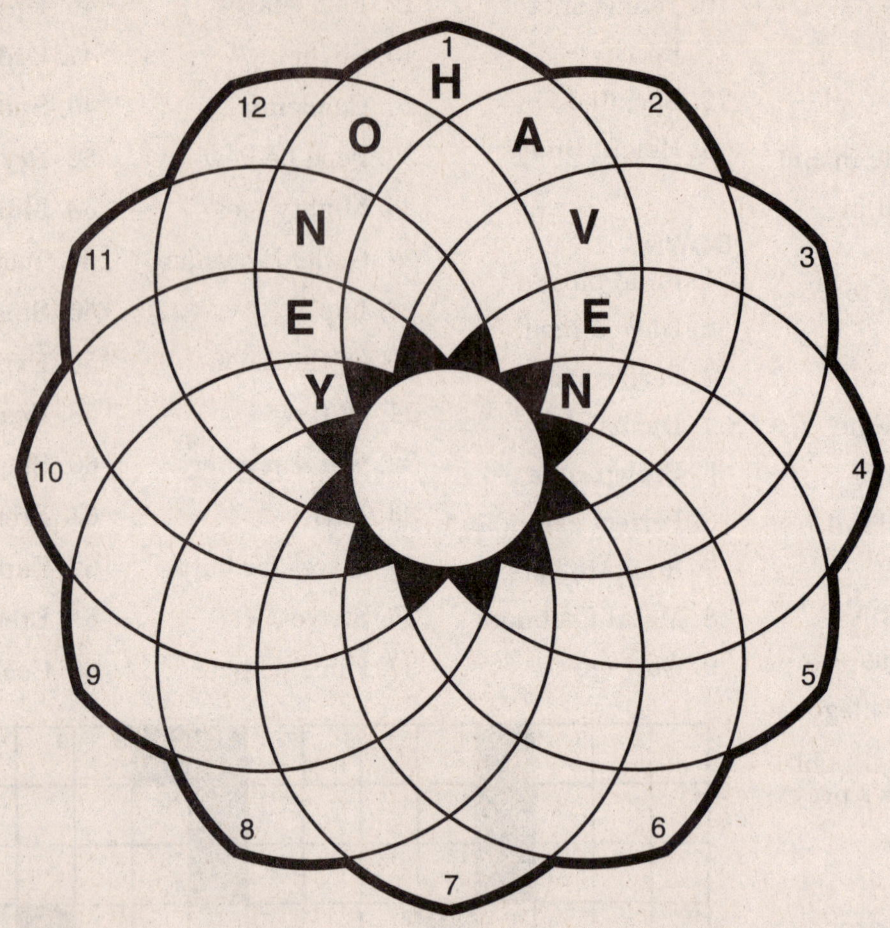

CLOCKWISE

1. Port
2. Style
3. Cook slightly in oil
4. Sheriff's men
5. Swamp
6. Sack
7. Emerge from an egg
8. Type of bean
9. Cheerful
10. Ward off
11. Barry Levinson film
12. Shanty

COUNTERCLOCKWISE

1. Sweetheart
2. Courtroom rapper
3. Cut apart
4. Board
5. Express grief
6. Starchy adhesive
7. Mustang, e.g.
8. Short stop
9. Fasten
10. Kind of dressing
11. Thickness
12. African animal, for short

PUZZLE 265

ACROSS

1. Facial's targets
6. It precedes beauty
9. Blot
12. "Carmen," e.g.
13. Exact duplicate
15. Previously, in verse
16. Stick-on transfer
17. All systems go
18. Large vase
19. Grain holder
21. Football gadget
22. Rascal
23. Home utility
26. Salamander
28. Monasteries
30. Aromatic spice
32. Rustic
34. Diva's highlight
35. Witnessed
37. More or ___
40. Building partitions
42. Rent out
43. Turning tool
45. Skirt feature
46. Load
48. Campus figure
49. Minor role
51. Resounded
53. Movie
56. Feline sigh
58. Meddle
59. Tilling tool
60. Central
62. Drip
64. ___ a boy!
65. Wed on the run
67. Leafy bower
71. Porch welcomer
72. Decorated again
73. Ogre
74. Curve
75. Despicable guy
76. Berlin river

DOWN

1. Seed coat
2. Unlatch, in poems
3. Kind of room
4. Historic times
5. Lens cleanser
6. Hops beverage
7. Sheep's kin
8. Make esteemed
9. Tennis term
10. Assortment
11. Kneels
13. Gloat
14. Look at
20. Appendages
23. Bite
24. Halos
25. Not moving
27. Rock-a-bye site
29. Laundry bottle
31. Harmful intent
33. Till
36. Choice word
38. Crouch
39. Utter
41. Hem and haw
44. Circular current
47. Had being
50. Sent a letter
52. Lotions
53. Ring out
54. Small bits
55. Hives
57. Like some cars
61. Dimwit
63. Private school
66. Ham on the hoof
68. Soap unit
69. Buck
70. Grain

PUZZLE 266

ACROSS

1. Postage mark
6. Elsie's offspring
10. Behind
13. Debated
15. Soothing plant
16. ___ detector
17. Midday nap
18. Soccer star
19. Know the ___ and outs
20. Gardening aid
21. Bicycle part
23. Vampire ___
24. Flightless bird
26. Without effort
29. Rules to follow
32. ___ aboard!
33. Revise
34. Hobbies
37. Went crazy
41. Flower part
42. Comment
44. Yielded
45. Managed
47. Dynamic
49. Admiral or guard
51. Time period
52. Cervid
53. More agile
56. Baseball's Willie ___
58. Luau garland
59. Glide
62. Tortilla dish
66. Electrified particle
67. Cry like a baby
68. "The ___ Cometh"
70. Printers' concerns
71. Notion
72. Dog
73. Kind of bread
74. Water and bunk
75. Omens

DOWN

1. Waist accessory
2. Three voices
3. A long time
4. Ruminated
5. Canary or cat
6. Item for Superman
7. Out of the weather
8. Lingered
9. Fixed charge
10. Ike's excuse
11. Ultimate
12. Touchy
14. Wastes time
22. Pistol sheath
25. Rowing implement
27. Atmosphere
28. Phase
29. Compact ___
30. Aware of
31. Short distance
33. Honors
35. Filing board
36. Beach shade
38. Corral opening
39. Nastiness
40. Adorn
43. Variable
46. Cee's follower
48. Lively
50. Gallery
53. Craftier
54. Showy flower
55. Cleanse
57. Shorthand pro
60. Unpaid
61. Woeful exclamation
63. In the company of
64. Candy ___
65. Till smallies
67. Lobster-eater's shield
69. Vehicle for hire

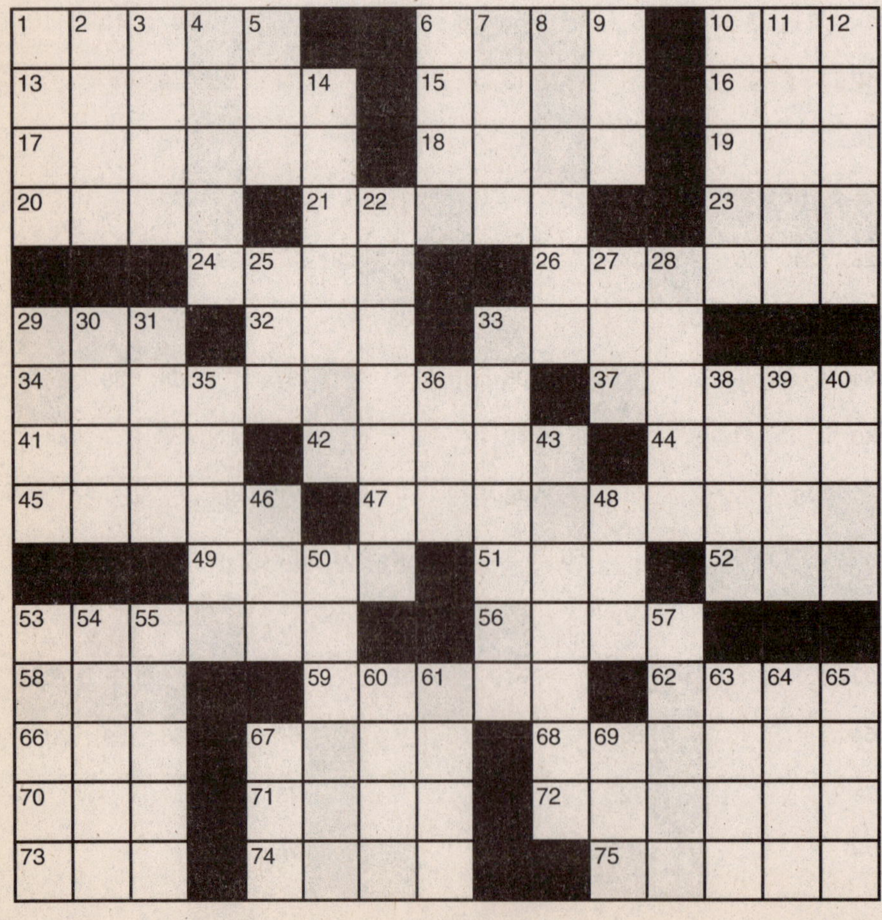

PUZZLE 267

ACROSS

1. Used a computer
6. Clearance
10. Money drawer
14. Termite, e.g.
15. Zip
16. Winglike parts
17. Plato's market
18. Make (one's way)
19. Dye
20. Knock lightly
21. Dwarfed tree
23. Little boys
24. Scrape
26. Facts, briefly
28. Auricular
30. City railroads
33. Sheen
36. Hone
37. Coat or hat
39. Escort
41. Fishing device
42. Roman rooms
44. Natural mineral
45. Ermine
48. Student-pilot's goal
49. Simmer
50. Tell's missile
52. June bug
53. Doubtful
54. Lip
56. Hammer or drill
58. Centers
61. Astrology diagram
64. Sweet-potato's kin
67. Be adjacent
68. Center of rotation
69. Nile animal, for short
71. Allot
72. Stream
73. Iroquoian Indians
74. Watcher
75. Take out, as text
76. Marsh plants

DOWN

1. Aspen lift
2. Kind of exercise
3. Store manager, perhaps
4. Always, to Keats
5. Brownish gray fabrics
6. Sutured
7. Brews
8. Hawaiian porch
9. Bringing to a close
10. Skin designs
11. Pelvic bones
12. Alight
13. "___ Start All Over Again"
22. Verdi work
25. Emulate a thespian
27. Common ailment
28. Has title to
29. Greek letter
31. Back muscles, for short
32. Food fish
34. Molasses dessert
35. Letter stroke
38. Metric pound
40. Count (on)
43. Way to the heart
46. Mediator
47. Rocky hill
49. Life story, briefly
51. Magician
55. Nerve
57. Pale yellow
58. Celebrity
59. Yield to commands
60. Pretty
62. Pickle variety
63. Florida Key, e.g.
65. Made like
66. Bryophytic growth
70. Indignation

1	2	3	4	5	■	6	7	8	9	■	10	11	12	13
14					■	15				■	16			
17					■	18				■	19			
20			■	21	22					■	23			
■	■	24	25			■	■	26		27		■	■	■
28	29			■	30	31	32	■	33			34	35	■
36				■	37			38	■	39				40
41			■	■	42				43	■	■	44		
45			46	47	■	48				■	49			
■	50				51	■	52			■	53			
■	■	■	54			55	■	■	56	57			■	■
58	59	60		■	61		62	63			■	64	65	66
67				■	68				■	69	70			
71				■	72				■	73				
74				■	75				■	76				

PUZZLE 268

A QUICK STUDY

ACROSS

1. Tub ritual
5. Labrador litter
9. Legend
13. Bacon ration
17. Debate exchange
18. Victorious
19. Larger-life link
20. Gefilte fish fish
21. Young voter
22. Shuttle letters
23. Green, on a weather map
24. "___ from Muskogee"
25. Quickly
28. Flat payment
29. Hebrew prophet
32. Actor Byrnes
33. ___ butter
35. Composer Ayer
36. Converge
39. Talented
42. Friend of the groom
45. For shame!
46. Goofed
48. Slightest
50. Pay or gran ending
51. Reverberate
53. ___ City, North Carolina
55. Dermis or center start
56. Dismiss
57. A.k.a. Superman
59. Fudd of cartoons
61. Slips by
63. Met star
65. Cotton candy content
67. Reflex site
68. Sincere
71. It's Orion's left foot
73. Expanse
76. Shaving cream additive
77. Hear here
79. Nogales guy
81. Not nigh
82. Easy mark
83. Worries
85. Divide
87. Bad humor
88. Father of Methuselah
90. Heroic poem
92. Wriggly
93. Salmon eggs
94. Stunt
96. Oahu strings
98. Studio props
100. Twofold
102. Posthaste
107. Tennis star Arthur ___
108. Intellect
109. North of Santa Fe
110. Olive genus
114. Sad drop
115. Ms. Sommer
116. She, in Paris
117. Folk dance
118. Pretentious
119. Bring up
120. Papyrus, e.g.
121. Cling to

DOWN

1. Mite
2. Cooling drink
3. Last of Lent?
4. Asian capital
5. Black cats
6. Provo's state
7. Watch the birdie
8. Shovel
9. Flaky dessert
10. Mighty whaler
11. Author Sheehy
12. Queen ___ lace
13. Fern seeds
14. Speedily
15. Cognate
16. Red root
26. Census info
27. Puzzling
29. Bury
30. Gravy
31. Fast
34. Shack
37. Huron neighbor
38. Snitches
40. Retainer
41. Record
43. What ___ is new?
44. Phooey!
47. Criticize
49. Kimono material
52. Woolly
54. Host Philbin
56. Phantom's domain
58. Threshold

PUZZLE 268

60. Goes ballistic
62. Pismire
64. Unanchored
66. Comic Taylor
68. Dexterity
69. Ladd or Rickman
70. Bible weed
72. Passion
74. Mrs. Brady
75. Paper sources
78. Ribbed fabric
80. Circulated
83. Half of a dance
84. Cicely Tyson film
86. Robert or Meg
89. Dieter's stick
91. Snowmobile part
95. Hourglass, e.g.
97. Rush in
99. Baby bird?
100. Evidence
101. Cable subscriber
103. Rosetta's river
104. Singer Paul ___
105. Clearance event
106. Painted metalware
111. Dreg
112. Shoebox trio
113. Yodeler's perch

PUZZLE 269

COMMAND PERFORMANCE

ACROSS

1. Guzzle
5. Speed
9. Disrobe
14. Early man
15. Exclude
16. Almond or tomato
17. Business org.
18. Judge's bench
19. Workers' collective
20. Bailiff's cry
23. Rive
24. Gel
25. Gambler's games
28. Dill
31. Wound trace
35. Stop the mission
36. Befuddled
38. Dark brew
39. Basic training exercise
43. Some MIT grads
44. Three, in Bonn
45. Eagle's nest
46. Sp. lady
48. Concerning
50. Specter
51. "A Boy Named ___"
53. 1052, to Cato
55. Shipshape
63. Holland export
64. Freshwater plant
65. Pinch
66. "That's ___"
67. Craggy peaks
68. Goose egg
69. Tavern treat
70. Let it stand!
71. Mardi ___

DOWN

1. Filled tortilla
2. Stink
3. Cowpoke's chum
4. Nero and Augustus
5. Batman's sidekick
6. Blake of "Gunsmoke"
7. Hue
8. Clearly outline
9. The final frontier
10. Palm reader's cards
11. Q-V connection
12. Roman way
13. Hide
21. Took it easy
22. Fragrant chemical
25. Stares down
26. More qualified
27. Rule the ___
29. Rock bottom
30. Compass pt.
32. Nile city
33. ". . . ___ well"
34. Find a new tenant
37. Slowly, in music
40. Bay window
41. Cartoon cat
42. Employing again
47. Hope
49. Refugee
52. Higher
54. Smallest
55. Euro. nation
56. Legendary Roman king
57. Sleep like ___
58. Devours
59. Storyline
60. Way in
61. Alcohol lamp
62. Norma and Charlotte

1	2	3	4	■	5	6	7	8	■	9	10	11	12	13
14				■	15				■	16				
17				■	18				■	19				
20				21					22					
■	■	■	23				■	■	24			■	■	■
25	26	27			■	28	29	30		■	31	32	33	34
35					■	■	36			37	■	38		
39					40	41					42			
43			■	44				■	■	45				
46			47	■	48			49	■	50				
■	■	■	51	52		■	■	53	54			■	■	■
55	56	57				58	59					60	61	62
63					■	64				■	65			
66					■	67				■	68			
69					■	70				■	71			

PUZZLE 270

GAME BIRDS

ACROSS

1. Pedro's mouth
5. Steep slope
10. Shoulder burden?
14. State
15. Prophet
16. Took Amtrak
17. Maryland bird
20. Elev.
21. Cook book
22. Fool with
23. Italian bye
24. Jab
25. Hare haven
28. Smog
29. Prince of Broadway
32. Vocal solos
33. Deli directive
34. "___ fan tutte"
35. Washington birds
38. Potter work
39. Singles
40. Russian co-op
41. Self starter?
42. Did well on
43. Took long steps
44. Shoo!
45. Farm unit
46. Make sea water drinkable
49. ___ gin fizz
50. Candle count
53. Missouri bird
56. ___ even keel
57. Speechify
58. Spoils
59. Collect
60. Dubbed
61. Reflex site

DOWN

1. Ali ___
2. Football shape
3. Irishman
4. Craft
5. Polynesian
6. Former New York governor
7. Taj Mahal city
8. Mourn
9. Unicellular group
10. Felony
11. Earring style
12. Not working
13. Equal
18. Least cordial
19. Shed tool
23. Pack
24. Uses a beeper
25. Squander
26. Clearings
27. Irani coins
28. Wet down
29. Instructive book
30. Was curious
31. Thread material
33. Creed
34. Novelist John Le ___
36. Site
37. Bitterness
42. Rights advocacy org.
43. Tallied
44. French river
45. Winged
46. Brit. military honors
47. Sicily's Mount ___
48. Croat
49. Trick
50. Soon
51. Garden door
52. If not
54. Madrid Mrs.
55. Bother

PUZZLE 271

• GRIDIRON EVENT •

ACROSS

1. Spider's creation
4. Immediately
7. Glass container
10. Paul Bunyan's tool
11. Revises text
14. One, in Madrid
15. Take a chair
16. ____-washy
17. Singer Shannon
18. Annual inter-conference event
21. Exercise spot
22. Suitable
23. Venus de ____
26. Steadfast
30. Crusty dessert
31. Lettuce variety
32. Chimp, e.g.
33. Tall chest of drawers
36. Pitcher Nolan ____
37. One billion years
38. Beame or Lincoln
40. Events leading to 18A
46. Leap
47. Roebuck's partner
48. Bark shrilly
50. Tax agcy.
51. Strives
52. Compass dir.
53. Ms. Remick
54. Baseball's Durocher
55. Lair

DOWN

1. Existed
2. Way out
3. "Little Women" role
4. Full of gossip
5. Abomination
6. Thin streak
7. Martial art
8. Once again
9. Hamburger holder
12. Larcenies
13. Turkey's neighbor
19. It's often inflated
20. AC letters
23. Speed meas.
24. Three, to Caesar
25. Lower limb
26. Bean or sauce
27. Negative vote
28. Auditor's inits.
29. Egg layer
31. Consult
34. Exclamation
35. Raise
36. Unit of radiation
38. Concur
39. Opera voice
40. TV's Donahue
41. Folk knowledge
42. Church recess
43. Flunk
44. Watched closely
45. Rational
49. Writing implement

PUZZLE 272

• HOMING BIRD •

ACROSS

1. Casual greetings
4. Consumed
7. Woe is me!
11. DDE's command
12. Messy person
13. Cairo's river
14. Kiwi's kin
15. Low female voice
16. Mock
17. Dovecote
20. State
21. Debtor's letters
22. Fossil fuel
25. Greek vowel
26. Overhead trains
29. Pokeweeds
33. Bullring cheer
34. Arced toss
35. Pot builder
36. Juan's uncle
37. Came in first
39. Fancy dance steps
44. Diva's solo
45. Raggedy Ann, e.g.
46. Squid squirt
49. Hacks
50. Affectedly bohemian
51. Meadow
52. It's often scraped
53. Of course!
54. 2,000 pounds

DOWN

1. Alter for length
2. Judge Lance ____
3. Cleansing bar
4. Back street
5. Dorothy's dog
6. Polished rubber
7. Type of pear
8. In ____ of
9. Pub beverages
10. Withered
12. Epic tale
18. Capri, e.g.
19. Frost
22. Nav. rank
23. Lubricate
24. Grow older
25. Subside
26. One, in Bonn
27. Allow
28. Opposite of NNW
30. Mixture
31. Relating to lunchtime
32. Pealed
36. Pester
37. Droops
38. Exclusively
39. Cram
40. Islamic nation
41. Deride
42. Sported
43. River's deposit
47. Classic starter
48. Neb.'s neighbor

DILEMMA

PUZZLE 273

Except for 1 Across, there are two clues for each number and two identical sides in the diagram. Your Dilemma is to discover which answer goes on the right side and which answer goes on the left. Note: The heavy lines indicate the ends of words as black squares do in regular crosswords.

ACROSS

1. First-grader's place
9. Negligent
   Break bread
10. Multitude
    Romance
11. Liberate
    Initial bet
12. Heart
    Set down
13. Flawless
    Succinct
14. Understanding
    Bonfire fuel
15. Cold
    Angry
17. Hint
    Grassland
18. Eventful time
    Buffoon
20. Circular
    Wipe away
23. Excavate
    Nothing
24. Of the nose
    Show up
26. Bungle
    Capri, e.g.
28. Fuse, in a way
    Pore over
29. Dearth
    Minor planet
32. Waste pipe
    Feudal lord
34. Function
    "How the West ___ Won"
35. Crisp cookie
    Golden Rule word
38. Atlantic Coast area
    Nova
40. Rim
    Revise
41. Isinglass
    Ship's company
43. Mangy dog
    Center
44. Aggregate
    Coronet
45. Bay window
    Body of water
46. Tonic's partner
    Shade tree
47. Expensive
    Pare
48. Exploit
    Probability

DOWN

1. Genteel
   Great joy
2. Country road
   Three feet
3. Surplus
   Precipitous
4. Make inferior
   Conductor
5. Master of ceremonies
   Christmas sprig
6. Spoken
   Cozy corner
7. Soup dish
   Repugnant
8. Shelf
   Coliseum
16. Native of Dublin
    Train tracks
17. Guitar holder
    Sitar, e.g.
19. Lit up
    Piccolo's cousin
21. Inexperienced
    "___ Gang"
22. Most senior
    Walk unsteadily
25. Raised platform
    Seaweed
26. Spurious
    Debate topic
27. Poet's before
    Plead
30. Vocal vibrato
    Take back
31. Insult
    Anticipated
33. Put up with
    Persuade
36. Concur
    Shinbone
37. River mammal
    Daisy ray
39. Parboil
    Lofty nest
42. Scepter
    Charity
43. Brick carrier
    Policeman

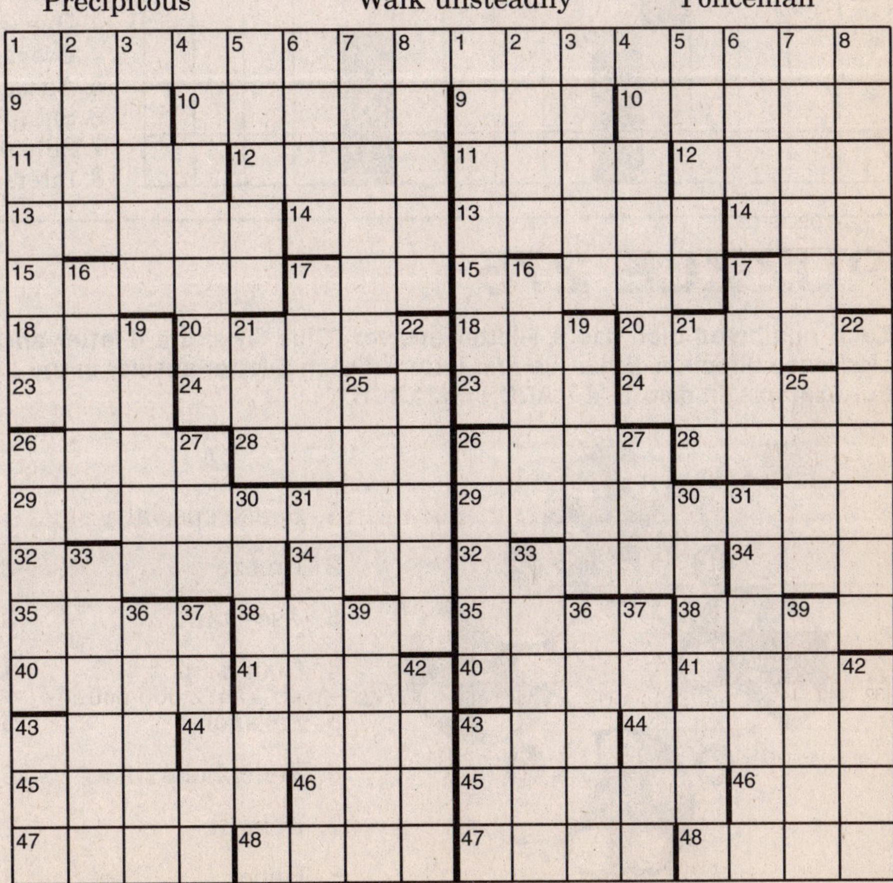

PUZZLE 274

• MOVEMENTS •

ACROSS

1. Bible book
5. He loves, to Cato
9. Feints
14. Obligation
15. Andes nation
16. ____ nous
17. Bouquet
18. Duet
19. Blemish
20. Military rank
23. Signs
24. Binds
25. Whittled
27. Small bit
28. Runner's distance
29. Hi-fi item
32. Coals
35. ____ out
36. Actor Stephen ____
37. Portal
38. Actor J. Cobb
39. WWII offensive
40. Pronto
41. Borscht ingredient
43. Grabs
45. Develop
46. Anglo-Saxon coins
47. Decay
48. Cellulose fabric
50. Peach State
54. Baby aprons
56. Circumstances
58. ____ acid
60. Blue jay's abode
61. Singer Tennille
62. Reveals
63. Puncture
64. Spent
65. Mr. Previn
66. Actress Ione ____
67. Desertlike

DOWN

1. Scientist von Baeyer
2. TV and radio
3. Orchestra members
4. One who swaggers
5. Affixes
6. Signifies
7. Sills solo
8. Interstate
9. Legal term
10. Loosen
11. Exemplars
12. Ponch, on "CHiPs"
13. D.C. denizens
21. Binge
22. Yarn
26. Crimson
28. Encounters
30. Beef, e.g.
31. Remits
32. Writer Ferber
33. Synthesizer inventor
34. Famous Australian builder
38. Slants
39. Loose rock fragments
41. Lad
42. Cupid
43. Form by twining
44. Basis
49. "Lou Grant" star
50. Embellish
51. Honker
52. Private
53. Stage comment
54. Ali ____
55. Bowie's wife
57. Ship wood
59. Simple sugar suffix

PUZZLE 275

Disco

Each numbered disc has a 5-letter answer (Clue A) and a 4-letter answer (Clue B) reading in a clockwise direction. Enter the first letter of each 5-letter answer in the circle in the preceding disc. For example, in disc 1: M + ARCH = MARCH.

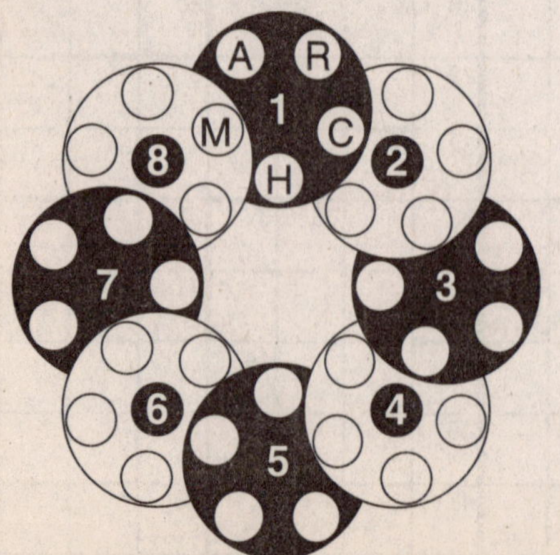

A	B
1. Sousa specialty	1. Curved doorway
2. Freeze	2. Mound
3. Ascertain	3. Merit
4. Cough up	4. Throw off
5. Paragon	5. Bargain
6. Xenophobe's fear	6. Legal hold
7. Delight	7. Delayed
8. Hobo	8. Freeway entrance

DOUBLE TROUBLE

PUZZLE 276

Not really double trouble, but double fun! Solve this puzzle as you would a regular crossword, except place one, two, or three letters in each box. The number of letters in each answer is shown in parentheses after its clue.

ACROSS

1. Lattice (4)
3. Enthusiasm (5)
5. Meal (6)
8. Pardon (7)
10. Bewilder (6)
11. Straight (6)
12. Minaret (5)
14. Impertinent (5)
15. Artful dodge (4)
17. Plan B (11)
20. Varnish ingredient (5)
22. Vigor (8)
24. Pep (3)
25. Self-satisfied (4)
26. Ominous (4)
27. Keen (5)
28. Prospector (5)
29. Motorbike (5)
30. Theater space (4)
31. Associate (9)
33. Divinity (5)
34. Intensely hued (8)
36. Exam (4)
37. Brief burst (5)
38. Diadem (5)
40. Portion (5)
42. Undivided (5)
44. Treasure (7)
47. As a substitute (7)
48. Metal bar (5)
49. Depart (5)

DOWN

1. Seizes (5)
2. Object of adoration (4)
3. Baloney (4)
4. Fur piece (5)
5. Savor (6)
6. Sheet of glass (4)
7. Lead (4)
9. Quash (4)
10. Swap (6)
13. Affluence (6)
14. Fearless (5)
15. Iron oxidation (4)
16. Good fortune (11)
18. Sailing master (9)
19. Stopwatch (5)
20. Make payment to (10)
21. Spill the beans (4)
23. Cupidity (5)
25. Grin (5)
27. Painter's stand (5)
29. Style (4)
31. Shirt part (6)
32. Hotel customer (5)
34. Judicial assembly (5)
35. Ineffective (6)
37. Stretch out (6)
39. Workout result (4)
40. Transgress (3)
41. Celerity (5)
42. Building extension (4)
43. Catcall (4)
45. Stir up (4)
46. Come close (5)

1	2	■	■	■	3	4	■	5	6	7
8		9	■	10			■	11		
■	■	12	13		■	■	14		■	■
15	16	■	17		18	19		■	20	21
22		23		■	24		■	25		
■	26		■	27			■	28		■
29			■	30		■	31			32
33		■	34			35		■	36	
■	■	37		■	■	38		39	■	■
40	41		■	42	43		■	44	45	46
47			■	48		■	■	■	49	

Chain Words

PUZZLE 277

Join these twelve words into a chain. Pick one word to start. The word that follows will do at least one of the following: 1. rhyme with it, 2. have the same meaning, 3. be an anagram of it, or 4. have one different letter. Work forward and backward to complete the chain. The first and last words will not connect. For example, the following is a chain: State, Great, Large, Lager, Later.

Allot	Agree	Alloy	Swear
Royal	Lager	Regal	Loyal
Share	Verse	Eager	Curse

PUZZLE 278

BRICK BY BRICK

Rearrange this stack of bricks to form a crossword puzzle. The clues will help you fit the bricks into their correct places. Row 1 has been filled in for you. Use the bricks to fill in the remaining spaces.

BRICKS

DIAGRAM

	1	2	3	4	5	6	7	8	9	10	11	12	13	14	15
1	P	A	S	T			S	C	A	R		V	A	L	E
2															
3															
4															
5															
6															
7															
8															
9															
10															
11															
12															
13															
14															
15															

ACROSS

1. Beyond
   Disney villain
   Glen
2. Associate
   Garlic mayo
   Fin. funds
3. ____ d'etat
   Most noted
4. Emphasized
   Apartment
5. Reproach
   Deadly snake
6. Mexican dip
   Unclothed
7. Miner's take
   Black fuel
   Dazzled
8. Not fer
   Passenger car
   Indian outfit
9. Unadorned
   Wagner TV role
   Golf club
10. Courts
    Short roster
11. Beg
    Nervous
12. Young horses
    Maritime
13. Efface
    Marsh bird
14. Whirl
    Church council
    Trounce
15. Formerly
    Equal
    Additional

DOWN

1. Shoe liners
   Strikebreaker
   Ere
2. Like crazy
   Seaweed, e.g.
   Not drunk
3. Mumble
   Burrow
   Garden greens
4. Do data entry
   Tendon
   Bouncy tune
5. Rip-off
   Expel
6. Church niche
   Use an ax
   6th sense
7. Ambulance horn
   Seashore
   Tavern drink
8. Female students
   "____ House"
   Idiotic
9. Bar order
   Not suitable
   Croc's kin
10. Hoop part
    Principle
    Tinted
11. Glazed
    Light-bulb word
12. Grappa's cousin
    Studio item
    Capri, e.g.
13. Coliseum
    Watercourse
    Wind up
14. Nations
    Work units
    Circle segments
15. Prevent, in law
    Slim down
    "Swan ____"

PUZZLE 279

• SOUNDS THE SAME •

ACROSS

1. Former host
5. It's beyond your control
10. Spring event
14. Earthen jug
15. Kemo Sabe's pal
16. Deception
17. Correct, Ceremony, Craftsman
20. Greek vowel
21. Court order
22. Heeds
23. Cellophane
24. Confront
26. Give it all
29. Barnyard sound
30. Truncate
33. Speechify
34. Yemen port
35. Author Jaffe
36. Soft fabric, Sort, Small container
39. Teen's woe
40. He-man
41. Bone-chilling
42. The blue above
43. News flash
44. Main line
45. Pete Sampras, often
46. Drop
47. Wild West transport
50. Major work
51. Green shade
54. Filaments, Fast animals, Frankfort fellows
58. Merrie ____ England
59. Yonder
60. Johnnycake
61. "Waiting for the Robert ____"
62. Diet dish
63. Scheme

DOWN

1. Stoma
2. Touched down
3. Pond growth
4. Go, team!
5. Flag feature
6. Composure
7. Money to play with
8. Sault ____ Marie
9. Trim the lawn
10. Chief concern?
11. Very large
12. Pallid
13. Soaks
18. Hit the road
19. Stone
23. Name
24. Diamond
25. Mrs. Shakespeare
26. Davenports
27. Follow
28. Dreary
29. Antipathy
30. Longest river in France
31. Studio sign
32. Short-story writer Grace ____
34. Subsequently
35. Scarlett's Butler
37. Italian family
38. ____ the thought
43. Cools down
44. Entertained
45. See eye to eye
46. Met musical
47. Oxford, e.g.
48. Lanky
49. Man Friday
50. Pitcher Hershiser
51. Urge on
52. Marine bird
53. Lost
55. Alts.
56. Eureka!
57. Center starter

Throwbacks

PUZZLE 280

You have to throw your mental gears into reverse to play this game. Reading backward there are at least three 4-letter words to be found in each of the longer words. You can skip over letters, but don't change the order of the letters. For example, in the word DECLARE you can find the word RACE reading backward by starting with the next-to-last letter and skipping over the L, but you can't find the word READ without changing the order of the letters.

1. ESTIVAL ________ ________ ________
2. COGNATES ________ ________ ________
3. RECEPTOR ________ ________ ________
4. BELOMANCY ________ ________ ________
5. HOMEGROWN ________ ________ ________
6. OUTLASTED ________ ________ ________
7. JUVENALIAN ________ ________ ________
8. LOVELINESS ________ ________ ________

PUZZLE 281

CODEWORD

Codeword is a special crossword puzzle in which conventional clues are omitted. Instead, answer words in the diagram are represented by numbers. Each number represents a different letter of the alphabet, and all of the letters of the alphabet are used. When you are sure of a letter, put it in the code key chart and cross it off in the alphabet box. A group of letters has been inserted to start you off.

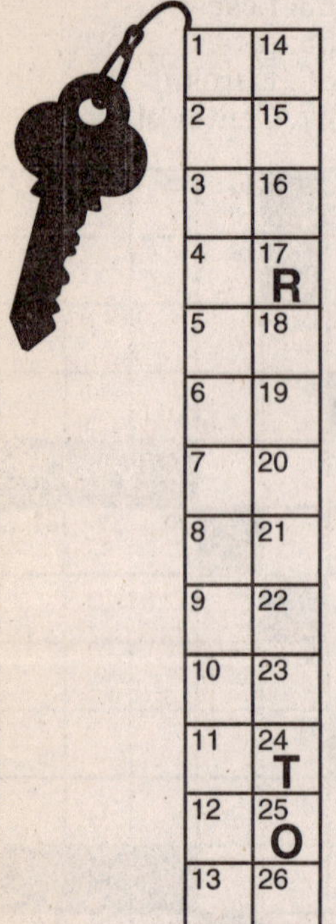

1	14
2	15
3	16
4	17 R
5	18
6	19
7	20
8	21
9	22
10	23
11	24 T
12	25 O
13	26

11	13	10	■	16	1	13	■	15	24 T	25 O	17 R	13
4	13	16	■	24	18	21	■	13	17	17	25	17
13	1	15	■	25	16	24	■	8	18	13	13	6
6	13	24	■	23	18	17	15	18	13	■	■	■
16	17	13	16	■	■	16	24	13	■	2	20	13
■	■	■	1	13	15	15	25	6	■	20	6	15
16	9	16	1	13	16	■	25	7	13	16	6	15
17	20	3	■	17	18	26	26	13	17	■	■	■
13	3	25	■	20	7	13	■	■	13	22	22	15
■	■	■	19	6	13	13	1	15	■	16	1	16
25	1	26	20	13	■	26	20	5	■	6	25	17
14	13	16	24	15	■	13	5	18	■	12	25	3
24	20	5	13	15	■	26	25	3	■	25	26	13

A	N
B	~~O~~
C	P
D	Q
E	~~R~~
F	S
G	~~T~~
H	U
I	V
J	W
K	X
L	Y
M	Z

PUZZLE 282

CODEWORD

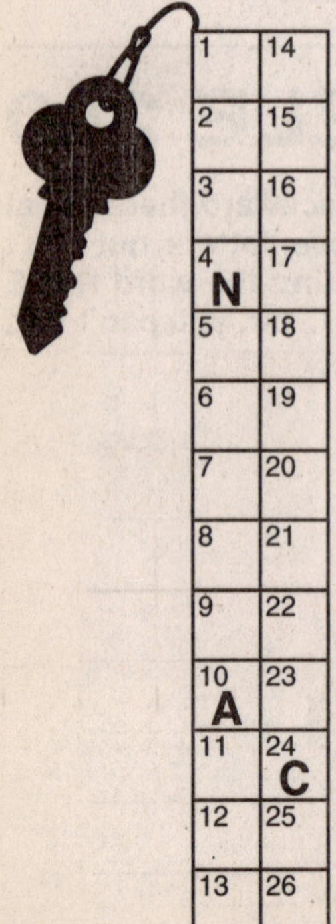

1	14
2	15
3	16
4 N	17
5	18
6	19
7	20
8	21
9	22
10 A	23
11	24 C
12	25
13	26

14	10	17	■	5	2	14	25	■	26	22	26	14
17	8	22	■	2	10	8	9	■	10	21	14	15
17	2	22	1	8	7	2	22	■	24	22	3	22
■	■	■	9	22	5	■	10	5	6	■	■	■
■	5	22	10	9	■	22	5	24 C	14	9	25	■
2	10	24	20	■	10	11	23	10 A	■	22	9	10
14	23	9	■	5	13	23	9	4 N	■	25	14	4
19	4	23	■	25	9	10	20	■	5	10	2	25
■	10	5	5	10	8	2	■	22	10	9	2	■
■	■	■	10	9	24	■	16	10	15	■	■	■
18	10	13	5	■	14	13	14	5	5	23	26	5
8	3	22	5	■	25	10	12	22	■	26	10	13
13	14	4	20	■	5	2	22	3	■	13	9	20

~~A~~	~~N~~
B	O
~~C~~	P
D	Q
E	R
F	S
G	T
H	U
I	V
J	W
K	X
L	Y
M	Z

PUZZLE 283

ACROSS

1. Punt
5. Data
9. Daisy part
14. Wings
15. Regard
16. Roman rooms
17. Cod's kin
18. Having a milky iridescence
20. Made angry
21. Stool pigeon
22. Bed linens
23. Dwarfed shrub
25. Occupied a chair
26. Seville coin
30. Generations
34. Electrical measure
37. Fish hawk
38. "Casablanca" role
39. Room and ___
41. Electron-deficient atom
42. Mother-of-pearl
43. Border
44. Remodeled
46. Chop
47. ___ off (angry)
48. Sports venues
49. Electric unit
51. Ideal place
56. Net protector
59. Ship's record
61. Grate
62. Below
64. Deep grooves
65. Play's setting
66. Discharge
67. Key
68. Quizzes
69. Having fancy trim
70. Takes in

DOWN

1. Hindu title
2. Mild cigar
3. Old bucket of song
4. Unwanted plants
5. Piano keys
6. Palm drink
7. Noteworthy act
8. Pussycat's pal
9. Turkish title
10. And so forth
11. Shade source
12. Nonstandard contraction
13. Back muscles
19. Literary composition
24. Footless animal
27. One who watches
28. Disintegrate
29. Mortise filler
31. Affluent
32. Land measurement
33. Distort
34. Assist Capone
35. Fashion
36. Book part
40. Fragrant
42. Vespiary
44. Japanese noodles
45. Misbehaving
50. Employs
52. Gold braid
53. Interruption
54. Yucca fiber
55. Church sections
56. Outburst
57. ___ upon a time . . .
58. Summer quenchers
59. Dalai ___
60. Of the ear
63. It's a moray

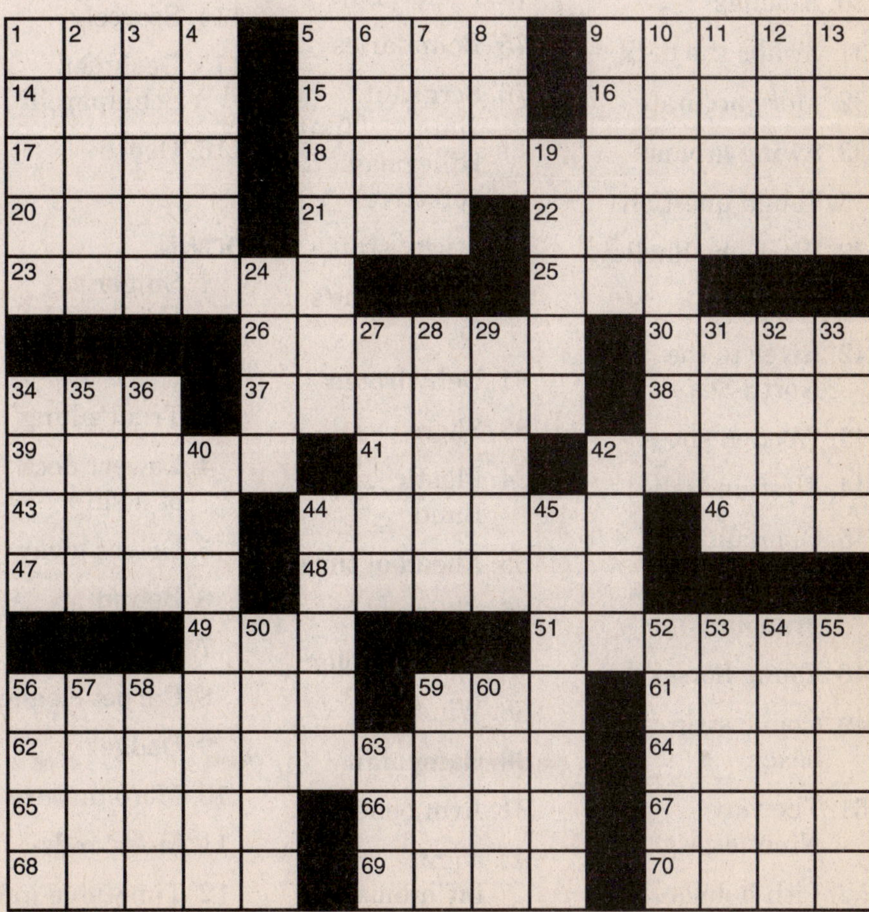

PUZZLE 284

ACROSS

1. Incipient omelet
4. Cold capital
8. Margins
14. Passageway
18. Secular
20. Mother of Zeus
21. Fly
22. Literary Lamb
23. Relax
24. Stack of slices
25. Roy Crane's comic-strip hero
27. Dinny's master
29. Fops
30. Amends
31. Swabs the deck
32. More accurate
33. Swing around
35. Tough question
38. Works by Shelley
39. Granted
42. River to the North Sea
43. Wooden shoes
44. First, in Italy
45. Operculum
47. Grains of granola
48. Young horses
49. Comic-strip boxer
51. The Gay Nineties, e.g.
52. Pith helmet
53. Cocoons
54. Hurried
55. Comic-strip matron
58. Venomous vipers
59. Get to
61. Opera set in Egypt
62. Join
64. Polo ground?
65. Conforms
68. Soon
69. Sam Catchem's partner
74. Prefer: Lat.
75. Boundaries
76. Sergeant Jim ___ (Tony Hillerman detective)
77. Sticky stuff
78. Killer Kane's foe
81. Dehydrated
83. Shore
84. Plastic ___ Band
85. Ahead of time
86. Chimes
87. Neutral color
88. Windpipe
90. Campaign
91. Arm bones
92. Joint inflammation
93. French menu
94. Chichen ___ (Mayan ruins)
96. Darkroom solution
99. Latches
100. Ignatz Mouse's friend
104. Comic-strip reporter
107. King Leonardo, e.g.
108. Begrudge
109. Did better than a B
110. Flowering shrub
111. Counting-out word
112. Fashion's Christian ___
113. Incarnation of Vishnu
114. Scarcely
115. Designer Schiaparelli
116. Deuce

DOWN

1. Singer Fitzgerald
2. British poky
3. Trout's lung
4. Lowest deck of a ship
5. Drives away
6. Bound
7. Lummox
8. Carpet cleaners
9. Dodges
10. More mature
11. Mobs' rods
12. Timetable info
13. Rorqual
14. Listened
15. Kirghiz mountains
16. Enumerate
17. Places
19. Aka Twain
26. Of the nervous system
28. Time past
29. Remains
32. Gadget
33. Critical remark
34. Lhasa leader
35. Introduction
36. "Butterfield 8" author
37. Indian lute
38. Braid
39. Regions
40. Wed secretly
41. Levees
43. Coconut meat
44. Snapped
46. Male parents
48. Provisions
49. Merely
50. Grouchy muppet
52. Taunt
53. Special attention
56. Water opossum
57. Ambitious
59. Inquired
60. Summon to court
63. Denials
64. Feels sympathy
65. Pulpit, of old

PUZZLE 284

66. Intimidate
67. Star in Big Dipper's handle
68. Miss Quested ("A Passage to India")
70. Coldly
71. Once more
72. Line dance
73. Garment pieces
75. Wading bird
79. Write down
80. Hawaiian island
81. Loans
82. Clayburgh's hubby
83. Fastened a rope
86. Describe graphically
87. Telephone
89. Schedule
90. Hardy's partner
93. Garden green
94. Chain gang restriction
95. Singer Tucker
96. Ski lift
97. Whale of a movie
98. Natural insecticide
99. Mix
100. German seaport
101. Woven
102. State
103. Amateur
105. Volcano's dust
106. Hot tub
107. Farrah's ex

PUZZLE 285

IT'S A CIRCUS!

ACROSS

1. Jupiter
5. Nitwits
10. Way off
14. Enthusiastic
15. Jagged
16. Nursemaid
17. Legal term
18. Uncoupling
20. Pedaling performer
22. Bird dog
23. Bering or Ross
24. Thou, now
27. Jibs and genoas
30. Petite sizes
32. Sauna locale
35. Olympics site
37. Extensive
38. High-wire performer
42. Rotation spot
43. Six Degrees of ___ Bacon
44. Ems' cousins
45. "Sling Blade" actor
48. A Starr
50. Green parrot
51. College off.
53. Rubble
57. Swaying performer
61. Silencing
63. One against
64. Marched
65. Becker of "L.A. Law"
66. Bali H'ai, e.g.
67. Transgressions
68. City on the Aire
69. Shortcoming

DOWN

1. Two-faced deity
2. Sheepish
3. Drop in on
4. Proclamations
5. Observer
6. City south of Moscow
7. Bound
8. Russian despots
9. Chain
10. Feed the kitty
11. Like a nymph
12. Author Beattie
13. Tatter
19. He was "Little Nicky"
21. Fermenter
25. Timeworn
26. Manipulators
28. Appear
29. Building manager
31. Pointed tool
32. Unadorned
33. Mischief-maker
34. Tumult
36. Son of Leah
39. FDR successor
40. Air disturbances
41. Madden
46. He was, to Brutus
47. Rescind
49. Procure
52. Class
54. Sluice
55. Yucca fiber
56. Penned
58. Ruby and cerise
59. Desktop publication
60. Ms. Markey
61. Milk amts.
62. Psychic Geller

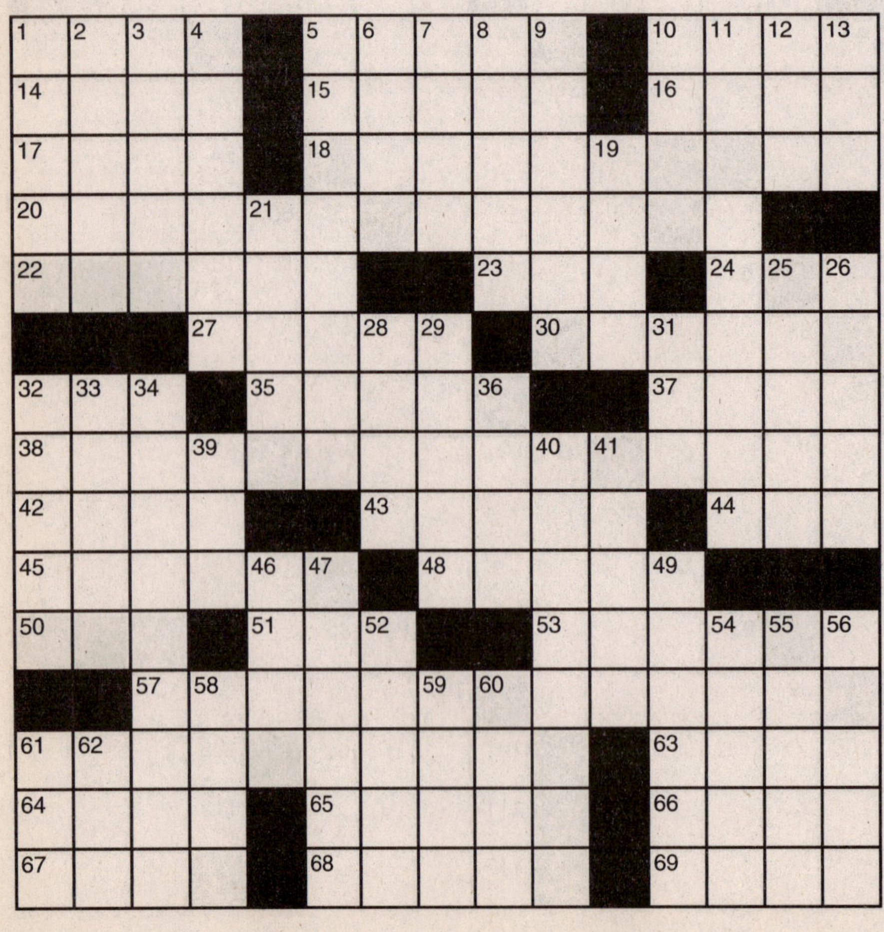

PUZZLE 286

HEAR, HERE!

ACROSS

1. Hemingway's nickname
5. Deep gulf
10. Staff
14. ___ Bator
15. Averse
16. Trickle
17. Town
18. Prohibited poet
20. Sensed, in a way
22. Nasty smile
23. Barker and Bell
24. Mr. Connery
26. Meat dish
28. Roadie's responsibility
30. Comes down
33. Faux pas
37. Line outside a pool hall
39. Showy flower
40. Kringle's alias
41. Penpoint
43. Leaning
44. Like hen's teeth
45. Boat-shop event
47. Goose genus
49. Wee
50. Pumpernickel ingredient
51. Do, e.g.
53. Lounge lazily
55. Black or Red
58. Eclipse variety
61. Mongol dwellings
64. Admiral's umbilicus
67. Type of sandwich
68. Roman poet
69. Expiate
70. William, to Charles
71. Plots or cots
72. Sutured
73. Jog

DOWN

1. Taverns
2. Astringent
3. Peels fruit
4. You may be right?
5. White vestment
6. Certain snakes
7. Narrative
8. Emphasize
9. 1/500 ream
10. Ear part
11. Gad
12. Poet Pound
13. Gets hitched
19. Tiny remnant
21. Ankle bone
25. Roybridge refusal
27. Bides time
28. Ghana's capital
29. Disney warrior
31. "Sister Act" extra
32. Belief system
34. Short-order cook at the monastery
35. Ed's girlfriend?
36. ___ Lauder
38. Mercury's orbit?
42. Cote call
43. Brass, e.g.
46. Under the weather
48. Tumble
49. Upper House
52. Albacores
54. Cipher
55. Condescending one
56. Icicle's spot
57. Enthusiastic
59. Declare frankly
60. M. Descartes
62. Half a sextet
63. Classify
65. Classified information?
66. Was in charge

1	2	3	4	■	5	6	7	8	9	■	10	11	12	13
14				■	15					■	16			
17				■	18					19				
20				21	■	22					■	23		
■	■	24			25	■	■	26			27	■	■	■
28	29		■	30		31	32		■	33		34	35	36
37			38					■	■	■	39			
40					■	41		42	■	43				
44				■	■	■	45		46					
47				48	■	49					■	50		
■	■	■	51		52		■	■	53		54		■	■
55	56	57	■	58			59	60	■	61			62	63
64			65						66	■	67			
68				■	69					■	70			
71				■	72					■	73			

PUZZLE 287

MY HEAVENS

ACROSS

1. Online activity
5. Huck's transport
9. Barn adjunct
13. Carson's heir
14. Foil's kin
15. Poke
16. Mr. Rubik
17. Competed
18. Nightwear item
19. Climbing plant
21. Estate
22. Semicircle
23. Lipid
24. ___-Magnon
27. No-win contest
28. German article
29. Food fish
32. Save
34. Feldspar variety
36. Happen
37. Famous ref. work
38. Ordinary
39. Kind of mole
41. Coins
42. Title of respect
43. Anger
44. Half a drink?
45. "48 ___"
46. Tiny colonist
47. ___ glance
48. Stood
51. Ceiling opening
56. Not clerical
57. Actor Will ___
58. Cart
59. A Guthrie
60. Needle case
61. OK Corral name
62. Aerie
63. Sgt. Friday's employer
64. Pierre's girlfriend

DOWN

1. One of Red's aliases
2. Leander's love
3. Part of AD
4. Animated short, shortly
5. Daydream
6. Each
7. Nourish
8. Bill's film buddy
9. Lean eater of rhyme
10. Steel source
11. Timber wolf
12. Polish river
20. Morose
21. Dasyure or wombat
23. Marsh
24. Traverse
25. Straight muscles
26. Emmy and Tony's kin
28. Failure
29. Sofa
30. Where the lovestruck walk
31. Strikes out
33. Mongrel
34. Get it?
35. Literary monogram
37. Sugary suffix
40. Morsel
41. Brownish butterfly
44. Rouge et al.
46. Neck scarf
48. He played Hawkeye
49. Hard to come by
50. Corn and peanut
51. Bristle
52. Light bulb?
53. Chemist's weight
54. Spy Mata ___
55. Sort
57. Congeal

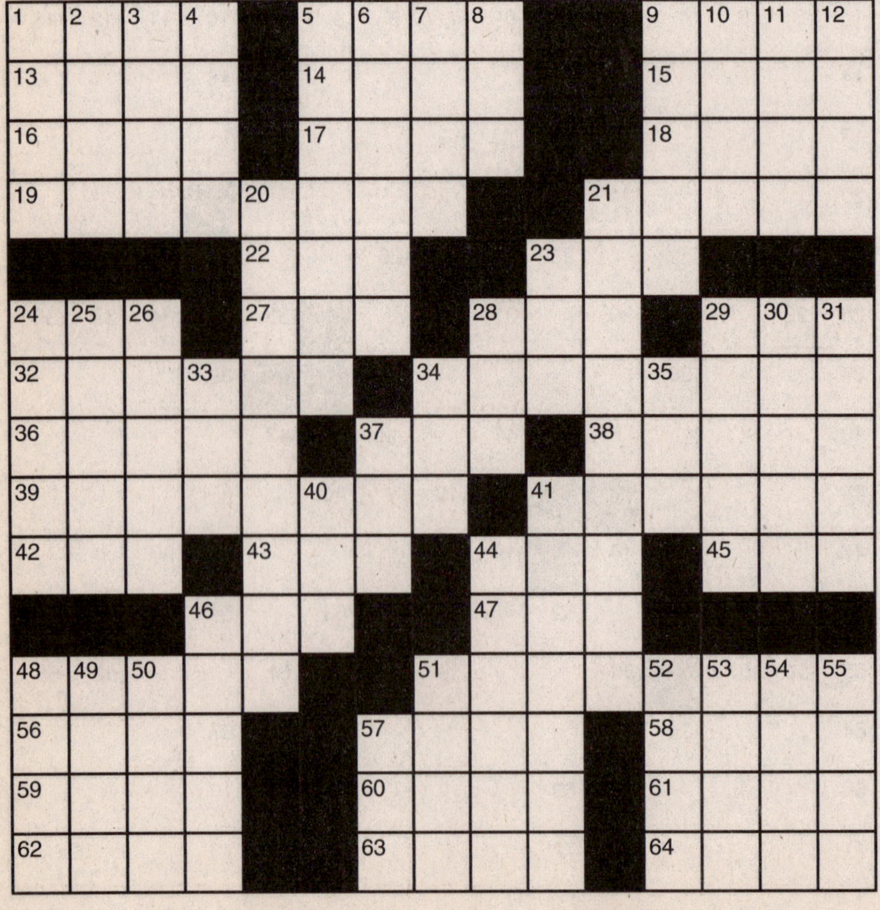

PUZZLE 288

FINGER FOOD

ACROSS

1. Heavy ___
6. ___ butter
10. Gold fabric
14. Clay brick
15. Attila's invaders
16. Terrible ruler
17. Recipe holders
19. Tangy
20. Vientiane voter
21. Soup cracker
23. Personnel
25. "Old ___"
26. Cell body
30. Short shortstop
32. Mountainous
33. Certain Fellow
34. "Star Wars" returnees
38. Blake's black
39. Groove
40. Adoring words
41. Harmonized
42. Mo. before Sep.
43. Break
45. Great Redskin
47. Praying ___
48. Turn from sin
51. Sandy area
53. Earth's waistline
55. Malice
60. Speak cattily
61. Medieval time
63. Origin
64. Burn balm
65. Delicacy
66. "___ There"
67. Refs' counts
68. Clockmaker's namesakes

DOWN

1. Flexible armor
2. Novelist Ferber
3. List heading
4. Prime a crime
5. Repertoire
6. Ladd movie
7. "Ben-___"
8. Some are tight
9. Appraised
10. One of Hood's hoods?
11. Use
12. Seine feeder
13. Pierce
18. Meat, in Malaga
22. Guitarist Paul
24. Type of iron
26. Scottish denials
27. Exile island
28. ___ my soul!
29. Wedding wee one
31. NY hours
35. Run the news room
36. TV's Ricky
37. Doctrines
39. Bad toupee
42. Coin-operated eatery
43. Compact
44. Medicine form
46. Picnic pooper
48. Printer's term
49. Sub.
50. Track prize
52. Gets a lift
54. Vex
56. Pottery
57. "___ a kick out . . ."
58. Rachel's sister
59. D-Day vessels
62. Spanish sir

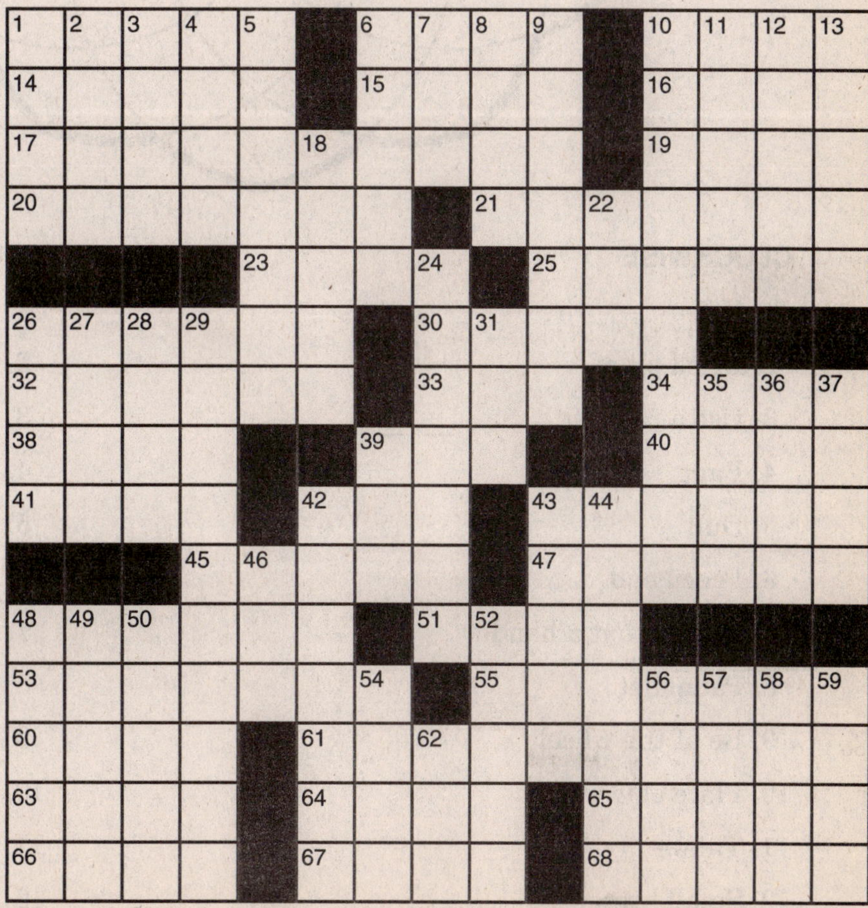

PUZZLE 289

FLOWER POWER

The answers to this petaled puzzle will go in a curve from the number on the outside to the center of the flower. Each number in the flower will have two 5-letter answers. One goes in a clockwise direction and the second in a counterclockwise direction. We have entered two answers to help you begin.

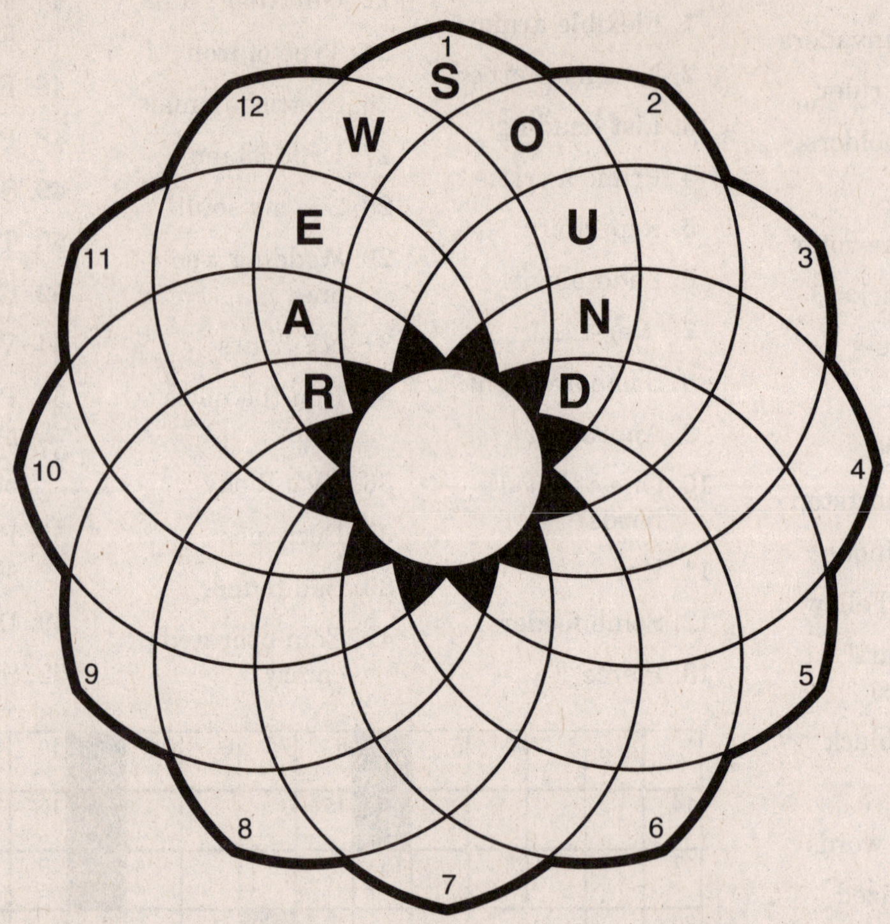

CLOCKWISE

1. Noise
2. Dried plum
3. Use a rasp
4. Bang
5. Dull
6. Pencil end
7. Handed out a hand
8. Pamphlet
9. Be at the wheel
10. Place of worship
11. Thieve
12. Small hooter

COUNTERCLOCKWISE

1. Pledge an oath
2. Arctic bear
3. Thin cereal
4. Full force
5. Dull
6. Batter's place
7. Pour water over
8. False move
9. Prejudice
10. Inclined
11. Ice pellets
12. Marine mammal

PUZZLE 290

• MONEY MATTERS •

ACROSS

1. Pry
6. Fictional sleuth
10. Fitness center
13. Spain and Portugal
15. Enthralled
17. Be perplexed
19. Biblical pronoun
20. Fertilizer component
21. The lowdown
24. Escritoire
26. Adult insect
30. Approaches
32. Albanian currency
34. Fido's friend
35. Doorway shelter
37. Julia of films
39. Pan's kin
40. Be neologistic
43. Hebrew judge
45. Macadamize
46. Conclusion
49. Falsehoods
51. Shade
53. Prescribed portions
54. Russian ballet city
56. Proton's place
58. Cowboy country
59. Frost, e.g.
61. Amount of matter
63. Settle accounts
70. Get more points than
71. Fan's shout
72. Alphabet trio
73. Further
74. Exhausted

DOWN

1. Certain sib
2. CBS rival
3. Done, to Donne
4. Handel opus
5. Essence
6. ____-Magnon
7. Feast of Lights
8. Declare
9. Japanese-American
10. That woman
11. Green veggie
12. Tack on
14. Did perfectly on
16. Hoaxes
18. Cad
21. Pig ____ poke
22. Fresh
23. Enthusiast
25. Snake
27. Pacify
28. Glop
29. Giant legend
31. Quick slash
33. Waves
36. Bugging bug
38. Put down
41. Pilots
42. Arctic footwear
43. Large deer
44. 52, to Gaius
47. Guitarist Paul
48. Ballpark fig.
50. Frosh, next year
52. Heavy volume
55. Utter
57. Crush
60. Chemical compound
62. Barge
63. Cud chewer
64. Type of vb.
65. Farm enclosure
66. Named at birth
67. Author Levin
68. Norm
69. Bashful

Split Personalities

PUZZLE 291

The names of six conductors have been split into 2-letter segments. The letters in each segment are in order, but the segments have been scrambled. For each group, can you put the pieces together to identify the conductor?

1. IN AR LE NS ER ON DB TE ____________
2. TA BI ZU EH NM ____________
3. WI IA JO MS HN LL ____________
4. TO KI OP DS LE WS OL KO ____________
5. ZA IO WA IJ SE ____________
6. RT BE AW RO SH ____________

PUZZLE 292

• NEW YORK, NEW YORK •

ACROSS

1. Clear the decks?
5. Snatch
9. Small charges?
13. Dutch export
17. 1000 grams
18. Only
19. Reckon
20. Steady gait
21. Molecule part
22. Trace
23. Theaters
24. Fewer
25. Manhattan's tip
28. Plays the Muse
30. MOMA offering
31. Gamble
33. Towel word
34. Moon phase
39. Do road work
41. Was ill
45. Merry tune
46. Hard to come by
48. Ripple
50. One and only
51. Olympics chant
52. Secretarial course
54. Kareem, once
55. Meet defeat
56. Sideline
58. All gone
60. Gave back
62. Attention
64. Table
66. A Silver
67. Computer attachment
71. Torn asunder
73. Make fit
77. Deal
78. Baby bug
80. Go AWOL
82. Pierre's life
83. Attest
84. Neutral tone
86. Light fabric
87. Traffic marker
88. Victoria Cross, e.g.
90. Diminish
92. Teetered
94. Grassy place
96. Start of something big
98. Pinch
99. Rubbish
103. Part of a trick question
109. Atmosphere
110. Shot
112. Wash. neighbor
113. Mind
114. Get moving
115. Dunker, possibly
116. Encore!
117. It may have lines
118. Expensive wood
119. Teased
120. Directly
121. Collections

DOWN

1. Card game
2. Accompanying
3. Skin softener
4. Pretentious words
5. Shiny
6. Horseradish, e.g.
7. Pay to play
8. Goat's tuft
9. Flurry
10. Middle aged?
11. Hammer end
12. SRO show
13. Immigration station
14. Mover and shaker
15. St. Peter's feature
16. Chow hall
26. Curvature
27. Bark
29. Ms. Zadora
32. Untried
34. Members-only group
35. Court order?
36. Gusto
37. Mane line?
38. Musical chord
40. For keeps
42. Bounty
43. Otherwise
44. Exploit
47. Come in!
49. Oinochoe
52. Comparison word
53. Icy
57. Manhattan's 840 acres
59. Orange variety
61. Bathtub amusement
63. Painter Magritte
65. Si and oui
67. Unwanted messages
68. It may be batty
69. Got an A
70. Sake ingredient
72. State bird of Hawaii
74. Swear
75. Soft wood
76. Sat on a peg
79. Squashed
81. X-ray unit
85. Hire
87. Jailors
89. Allow
91. Ovum
93. Family member
95. Trellis
97. Bouquet
99. Playbill listing
100. Troubadour's instrument
101. Opera excerpt
102. Plane prefix
104. Graceland name
105. Caligula's nephew
106. Double reed
107. Change states
108. Unopposed rounds
111. Ballerina's prop

PUZZLE 293

• PAUL'S PICKS •

ACROSS

1. Candle part
5. Fat
9. Cleanser
13. Performs
17. Indian tourist site
18. "I cannot tell ___"
19. Brink
20. Origin
21. Mail drop
22. Gopher State: abbr.
23. Legal hold
24. Manner
25. Newman/ McQueen thriller, with "The"
29. Humble
30. Vast time span
31. Sole
32. ___ tai
33. Slangy assent
35. Health facility
36. Autocrat
39. Wanders
42. Bridle
46. Head growth
48. Leg joint
49. Ancient Peruvian
52. Anxious
54. Prayer ender
56. Genetic initials
57. Fleecy fabrics
59. Makes gentle
61. Chime
63. Baby hooter
64. Version
67. Course
70. Crude metals
72. Nervous
73. Nobles
74. Golfer's average
76. Muck
79. Stubborn beasts
81. Gore, to Clinton
82. God of love
84. Camp dwelling
86. Classifier
88. Winchester, e.g.
90. Laura or Bruce
92. French season
93. "___ Breckenridge"
95. Go astray
97. Stable morsel
98. Building site
101. Lennon's mate
103. Newman/Field mystery
108. "___ Lisa"
110. Leave out
111. Nibble
112. Completed
113. Streets: abbr.
114. Gambling town
115. Manipulator
116. Grizzly
117. Milland and Charles
118. Youth
119. Sawbucks
120. Caen's river

DOWN

1. Rubbish
2. Snow hut
3. King's headgear
4. Capshaw or Jackson
5. Cover with layers
6. Dress shape
7. Finger ornament
8. Jeans material
9. Greedy
10. Garfield's friend
11. Ripener
12. Cent
13. Limb
14. Newman/Kennedy film
15. Hoopla
16. Goulash
26. Hemp product
27. Turner or Cole
28. Above, to Blake
34. Thumbs up!
35. Less fresh
37. Drivers' club: abbr.
38. Lip
40. Males
41. Black or Baltic
43. Despise
44. Mild oath
45. Send payment
47. Confederate soldier, to a Yank
49. ___ Jima
50. Immediately
51. Newman/Cruise blockbuster, with "The"
53. Biblical tree
55. Dweeb
58. Stalk
60. Nasal cavity
62. Paris museum
65. Norwegian port
66. At no time, to poets
68. Summer shirt
69. Sixth sense
71. Pose
74. Each
75. Jackie's second husband
77. Comic Buttons
78. Opposite of WSW
80. Freighters
83. Crafty
85. New Jersey city
87. Singer James
89. Significant time
91. AEC's successor
94. Stop the launch
96. Contradict
97. Frequently
98. Internal organ
99. Atlantic, e.g.
100. ___ Haute, Indiana
101. General Bradley
102. Bossa ___
104. Hook's mate
105. Berlin article
106. Seine feeder
107. Claude Akins series
109. Pack animal

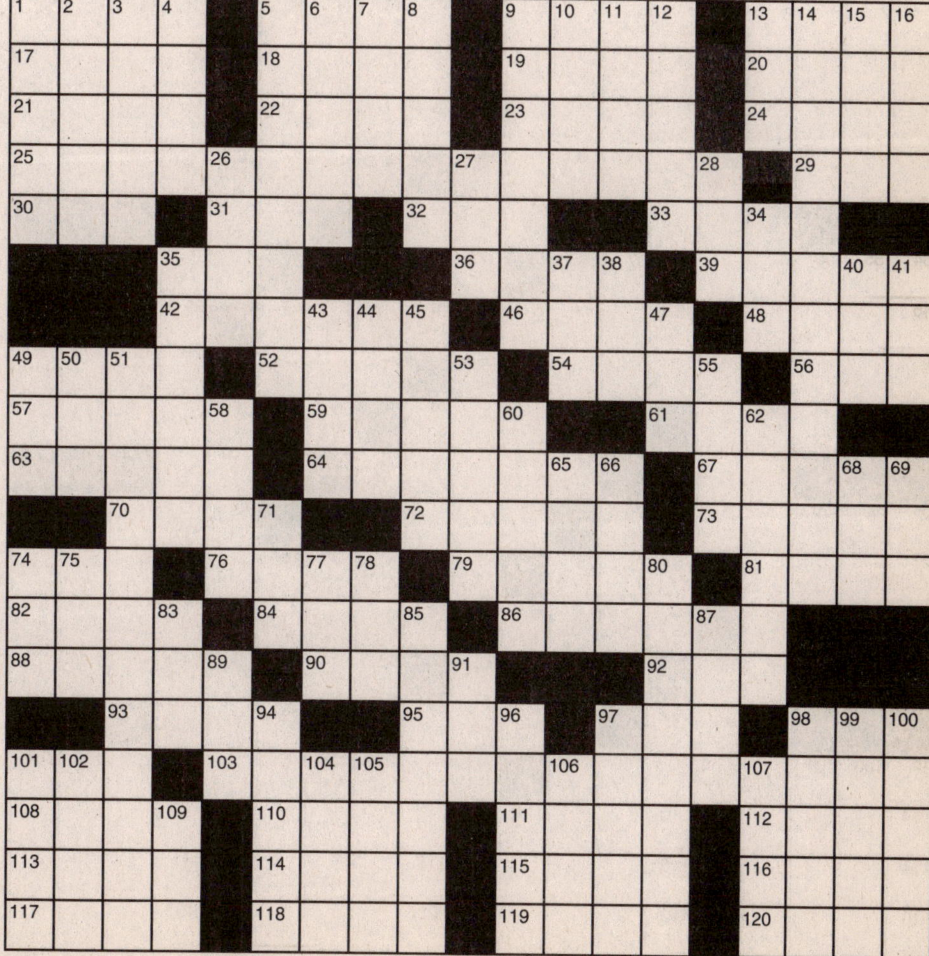

PUZZLE 294

• WHO GIVES TLC? •

ACROSS

1. Marathon
5. Some tennis shots
9. Like Pindar's poems
13. Floor cleaners
17. Earthen pot
18. Sailor's cry
19. Volcanic flow
20. Ersatz butter
21. Culture medium
22. Fashion house
23. Nip
24. Cake layer
25. Dogpatch resident
28. Desk's leg space
30. Popular ISP
31. Senate gofer
33. Metal source
34. Perpetuate
39. Actor Carvey
41. Incendiarism
45. Benefit
46. Iodine source
48. Change decor
50. Olympic sled
51. Actor Holm
52. Rouse
54. Excavate
55. Popular cookie
56. ____ de menthe
58. Copier's need
60. Trampled
62. Dolt
64. Nuzzled
66. Lamb's dam
67. Feigned
71. Approaches
73. Aromatic compound
77. Rich soil
78. Heavy weight
80. Groups of three
82. "____ Got a Secret"
83. Wrong
84. They're often inflated
86. Dole
87. Paradise
88. Fangs
90. Slaughter of baseball
92. Morally degenerate
94. Relieve (of)
96. Break sharply
98. "The Greatest"
99. Adventure
103. "Amazing Grace" star
109. Special alliance
110. Pealed
112. Broth
113. Folk tales
114. ____ beer
115. Film lioness
116. To be, in Paris
117. Wicked
118. There are seven
119. Act
120. Oboist's need
121. Trickle

DOWN

1. Wander
2. Pond-scum ingredient
3. Quahog or coquina
4. Reserve
5. Feminine
6. Buckeye State
7. Novel, e.g.
8. Maple product
9. Stale
10. Made gloomy
11. Terrible tsar
12. Small role
13. Profitable sources
14. Hodgepodge
15. Rind
16. Achy
26. Over there
27. Angry
29. Epoch
32. Needlefish
34. Long poem
35. Spree
36. Marine eagle
37. Gusto
38. Singer John
40. Mine passage
42. Irrational, in math
43. Curved molding
44. Bright, as colors
47. Pine nut
49. Cruel person
52. Joist
53. Adjust again
57. Career paths for the maternal
59. Equip for war again
61. Is obligated to
63. Gala
65. Like some fruit
67. Bed board
68. Inventor Elias ____
69. Swiss river
70. Venetian magistrate
72. Glut
74. Ocean surge
75. Tied
76. Tenant's expense
79. Falderal
81. Left hastily
85. Michael, to Kirk
87. Food
89. Haunch
91. "Cheers" bartender
93. ____ carte
95. Challenged
97. Riddle
99. Recedes
100. Blackthorn
101. "Your Show of Shows" costar
102. Valley
104. Speck
105. Certain
106. Strong emotion
107. A Great Lake
108. Yip
111. Gallivant

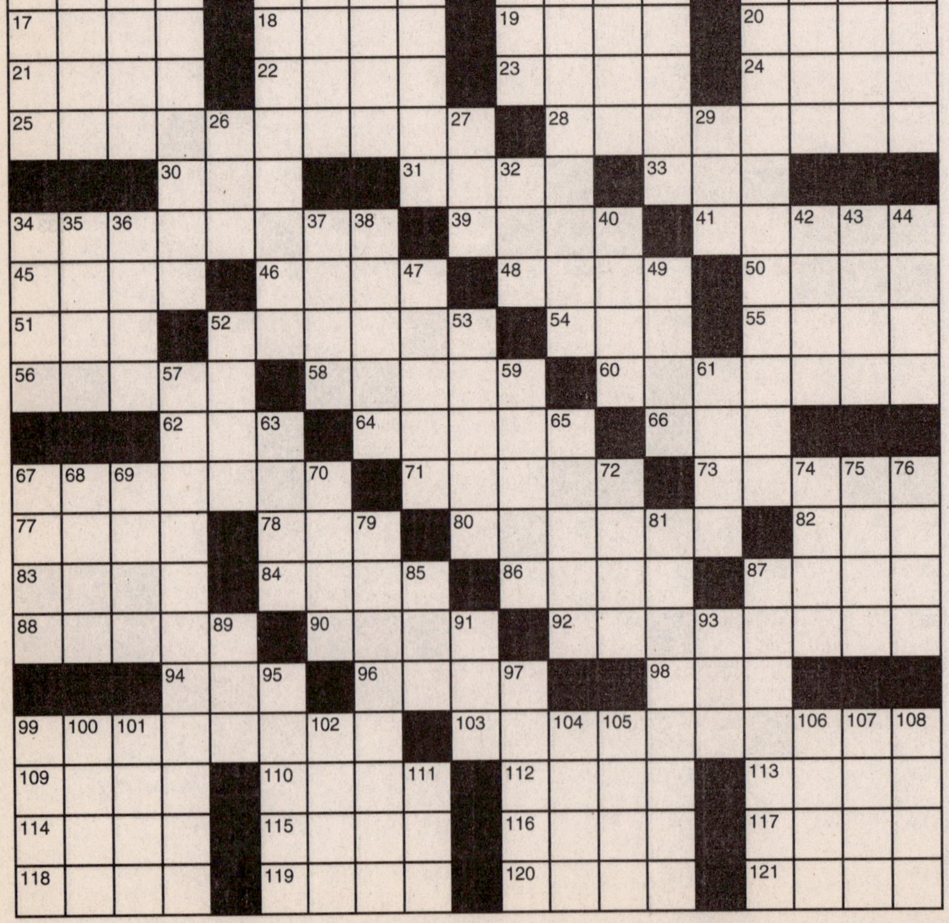

PUZZLE 295

• GATHERINGS •

ACROSS

1. Boot liner
4. Ribbed fabric
7. Daze
10. Brave
13. Swindle
14. Join
15. Possessive pronoun
16. Guitarist Paul
18. Skill
19. Creek
20. Oxlike beast
21. Fine sand
22. College head
24. Pearl diver
26. Lawn material
27. Luau instrument, briefly
28. Silkworm
30. Trim
32. Purchase
34. Too proper
36. Shoe width
37. Medicinal amount
39. Prize marble
40. Lavish meal
44. Call
45. Hazardous curve
46. Madras mister
47. Young bug
49. ____ diem
50. Belonging to him
51. Old English letter
52. Wing
55. Sniggler's catch
56. Sunbeam
57. Eye, in Madrid
60. Cease-fire
62. Alumni gathering
66. Tropical jelly
68. Stubborn
70. "____ Don't Leave"
71. Minister's speech
72. Fabulous bird
73. Slender fish
75. Speculate
76. Slapstick prop
77. Declare, in bridge
78. "____ Will Buy?"
80. Advise, to a Brit
82. You ____ what you sow
84. Food fish
85. Goad
87. Deface
88. Row
89. Pine
90. Eloquent speaker
92. Part of the legislature
94. Annul
95. Meal course
96. Sooner than
97. Even if, poetically

DOWN

1. Cat
2. Talented
3. Lassie's breed
4. Apartment, e.g.
5. Misjudge
6. "Rich Man, ____ Man"
7. Parties
8. "Swan Lake" costume
9. Teeter
10. ____ and now
11. Hipbone sections
12. Beach picnic
17. Actress Jessica ____
18. Good-bye
20. Small canyon
21. Cloud's place
23. Silent greeting
25. Hole-boring tool
26. Bottled water source
27. Exploit
29. Needed: abbr.
31. Sound of a blow
33. Appetite
35. Family member, for short
38. Tree's juice
40. Thorny plant
41. Bride's way
42. First month, to Pedro
43. Giant
46. "Ain't ____ Sweet"
48. "____ kingdom come . . ."
52. Pointed marker
53. Noon feast
54. An ____ up one's sleeve
57. "____ Miss Brooks"
58. Scout gathering
59. Elliptical
60. Rocky pinnacle
61. Work unit
63. Brown pigment
64. By birth
65. Emcee's speech, for short
66. Golly's partner
67. Likewise
69. Agile, nautically
71. Taste
74. Distant
76. Dad, e.g.
79. Fictional monster
81. Take a gamble
83. Lessen
84. Refer to
86. Knight's challenge
89. Gambling game
91. Mariner
93. Utmost

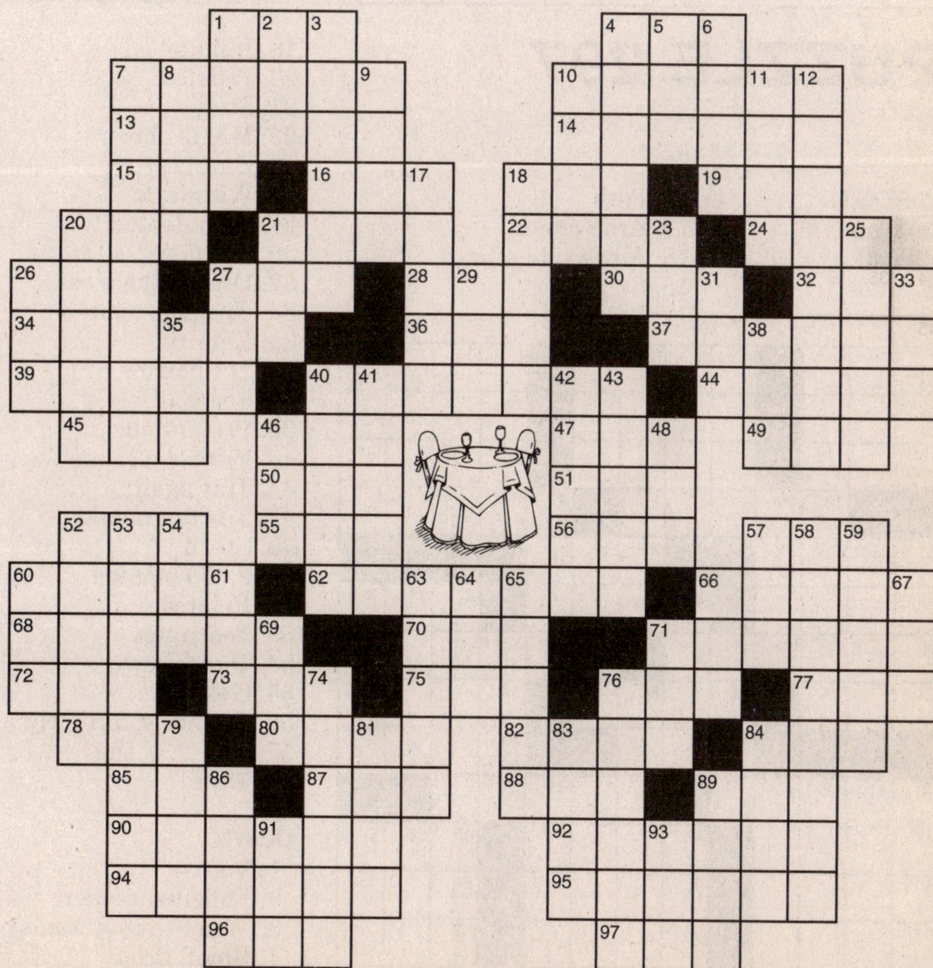

PUZZLE 296

ACROSS

1. Cook
5. Kind
9. Pa
12. Sole
13. Tuba, e.g.
14. Stray
15. Poker play
16. Psyche components
17. Age
18. Negative connector
19. Grouch
20. Gab
21. ____ cracker
23. Expositions
26. Helix
28. Playthings
29. "The ____ Brief"
31. Blockhead
33. Latke ingredient
36. Felt hat
38. Wall paintings
40. Totally awesome!
41. Hordes
43. Wire-diameter measure
44. Previous to, to a poet
45. "Waterloo" group
46. Handed over
47. McCourt book
48. Aperture
49. To shelter
50. Clique
51. Favorites
52. Writing table

DOWN

1. Resound
2. Esteems
3. Corner
4. Charge
5. Relating to heat
6. Indian discipline
7. Investigation
8. Printers' measures
9. Radio personality
10. Places in order
11. Sketches
19. Occupation
22. African mammal, for short
24. Standing
25. Underwater radar
27. Sass
30. Fights
31. Sweetie
32. Most peculiar
34. Mexican food
35. Green fruits
36. Fusses
37. Stroll
39. Glossy
42. Last word?
45. Egyptian snake
46. Move about

PUZZLE 297

ACROSS

1. Wane
4. Sad
8. Moist
12. Not nay
13. Path
14. Arab chief
15. Always, to a bard
16. Skip
17. Loony
18. Infants
20. Pedaled
21. Stuns
23. Mama sheep
25. Enrage
26. Withdraw
27. Be indebted to
30. Oahu, e.g.
32. Drank like a cat
34. Checkup sounds
35. Elderly
37. Let borrow
38. See you!
39. Pretentious
40. Primes a crime
44. Tint again
47. Tibetan monk
48. Stead
49. 2,000 pounds
52. Related
53. Yearnings
54. Due follower
55. Gels
56. Formerly, formerly
57. "We ____ the World"

DOWN

1. Watch
2. Pollen-spreader
3. Weight-room items
4. Small drop
5. Fancy fabric
6. For men and women
7. Greeted
8. Lunchtime stop
9. Frenzied
10. Pantry pests
11. Exhort
19. On the water
20. Greek letter
21. Cantata air
22. Aspire
24. Uncivilized
26. Nervous
27. Musical comedy
28. Departed
29. Circular current
31. Seizes
33. Merriment
36. Spookier
40. Woe!
41. Roast
42. Send forth
43. Cures leather
45. Poetic twilights
46. Powder
48. Concentrated solution
50. Bobby ____ of hockey
51. First named

PUZZLE 298

ACROSS
1. Slur
5. Snatch
9. Reprimand
14. Italian town
15. Grandma
16. Comedy
17. Temper tantrum
18. "____ the Roof"
19. "Tosca," e.g.
20. Play a guitar
22. Rd.
24. Fresh
25. Scruff of the neck
28. Sleep time, to some
30. Bleach
32. Radio antenna
35. Stop!
36. Arden and Plumb
38. Bestow
40. Charged particle
41. Spot
43. French "me"
44. Loop of rope
46. Regulation
47. Throw a fishing line
48. Right now!
50. Protected
52. Hammerhead
53. Cake layer
54. Droop
57. Battering ____
58. Take a hike
62. Australian marsupial
64. Correct copy
68. Arab chieftain
69. Bayou
70. Moniker
71. Brief message
72. "____ porridge hot . . ."
73. Variety
74. Low card

DOWN
1. More or ____
2. "____ It a Pity"
3. Mix
4. Funnel-shaped flower
5. African animal
6. Knock sharply
7. Mexican year
8. Fountain treat
9. Wingtip saver
10. Drinking vessel
11. Peck film, with "The"
12. Folk knowledge
13. Sketch
21. Tangle
23. Struggle (for)
26. Fruit cover
27. Surroundings
29. One, to Dietrich
30. Yell
31. Deep respect
33. Commercial producer
34. Baggy
35. Prevail
37. Ostrichlike animal
39. Cleverness
41. Make
42. Large truck
45. Soak in gravy
47. Most recent
49. Iced drink
51. Congregated
54. Pass over
55. Tiptop
56. Showy
59. Love, in Madrid
60. Widow's ____ (small amount)
61. Predator's quest
63. "____ Girls"
65. Part of a week
66. Scamp
67. Summer shirt

Riddle Me This

PUZZLE 299

Here are 5 riddles and their mixed-up answers! Unscramble each group of letters to form a word. Use those words to fill in the answer blanks.

SPNSA EH THWI SGDI PAFYPREL TI RANDEG ELENDES SOEH SIT

1. Why is a shovel the miner's favorite tool?
   __ __   __ __ __ __   __ __
2. What socks are found in the backyard?
   __ __ __ __ __ __   __ __ __ __
3. How does a pine tree sew?
   __ __ __ __   __ __ __   __ __ __ __ __ __ __
4. What do pilots write letters on?
   __ __ __ __ __ __ __ __
5. What kinds of cookies do turtles like?
   __ __ __ __ __

PUZZLE 300

ACROSS

1. Strikebreaker
5. Obi, e.g.
9. Test drive
13. Nimbus
14. Channel
16. Disguise
17. Like
18. Loud
19. Spanish pot
20. Acquires
21. Angora or calico
22. Kitchen gadget
24. Broke bread
26. Jab
28. Connecting words
29. Less troublesome
32. Jostle
34. Dull brown
35. Sum up
38. Teen woe
41. Complain
43. Hasten
44. Way up
45. Sailboat
46. Microscopic organism
48. Massage place
49. Sanctify
52. Toughen
54. Greek vowel
56. Senseless
58. Once named
59. Greens dishes
61. Also
63. Benefit
67. Cultivate
68. Long sandwiches
70. Golden Rule word
71. Double curve
72. Actress Massey
73. Hawaiian necklaces
74. Mats
75. Recognize
76. Building curve

DOWN

1. Carpet style
2. Baked dessert
3. Dismounted
4. Dwarfed tree
5. Heartfelt
6. Wild ox
7. Skirt features
8. "____ So Shy"
9. Clog, e.g.
10. Linen item
11. Loafer
12. Draws in on
15. Representative
23. Recede
25. Gull's kin
27. Plains abode
29. Nervous
30. Radiance
31. Got out of hand
33. Stable bit
36. Ravine
37. Intend
39. Palm drink
40. Epochal
42. 100%
44. Lucid
47. Wood cutter
50. Cease
51. Japanese specialty
53. Space dust
54. Bar legally
55. Eurasian forest
57. Feudal title
60. Tavern stock
62. Forbidden thing
64. Lulu
65. Auditory
66. Snack
69. Moose kin

PUZZLE 301

Blockbuilders

Fit the letter blocks into the diagram to spell out the name of a famous person.

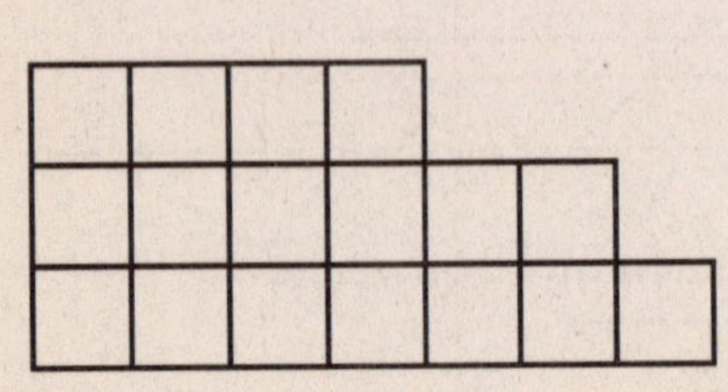

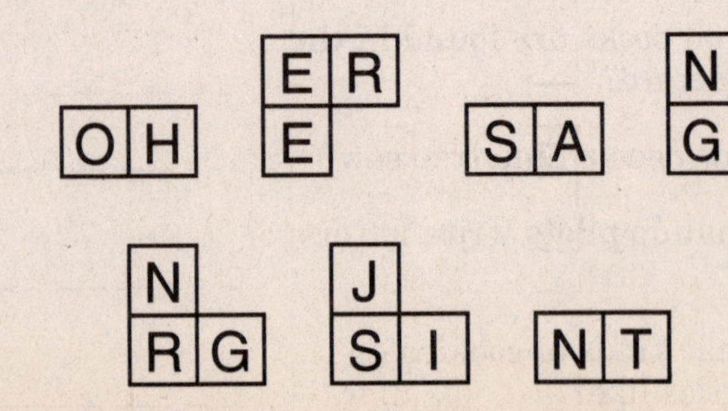

PUZZLE 302

ACROSS
1. Michigan city
6. Nest contents
10. Requests
14. Circle parts
15. Suitor
16. Applaud
17. Show feeling
18. Cattle shed
19. Healthy
20. Snakelike swimmer
21. Sailor's landing
23. Studio couch
25. Citrus peel
26. Attack!
27. Trick
29. Read quickly
30. Lower limb
33. Track down
34. Trite
35. A few
36. Type of orange
38. Beret
39. Postal machine
41. "Stroker ___"
42. Strange
44. Office message
45. Become firmer
46. TV's Nanny
47. Wisconsin farm
49. Dundee lid
50. Affectionate
51. Monasteries
55. Ailing
56. Not NNE
59. Actress Sorvino
60. Colorado tribe
62. Camel's kin
64. Scent
65. Litter's littlest
66. Artist's stand
67. Patched
68. Concludes
69. Chirp

DOWN
1. Unconfined
2. Gold-threaded fabric
3. Admired person
4. Young insect
5. Man's jewelry
6. Dwindled
7. Cogwheel
8. Slender fish
9. Early clock
10. Sore
11. Hunk
12. Curly greens
13. Went quickly
22. Sign
24. With blemishes
25. Lawn broom
26. View
27. Harmony
28. Frolic
29. Blot
30. Subsequent
31. Adversary
32. Greek sandwich
33. Unexpected problem
34. Beat it!
37. Southpaw
40. At the center of
43. Manuscript smudge
47. Sawbones
48. Short sock
50. Clenched hands
51. Cookie man
52. Stick around
53. Head front
54. Merit
55. Ship off
56. Query letter enc.
57. Hook's mate
58. Poet Whitman
61. Beer cask
63. Legal code

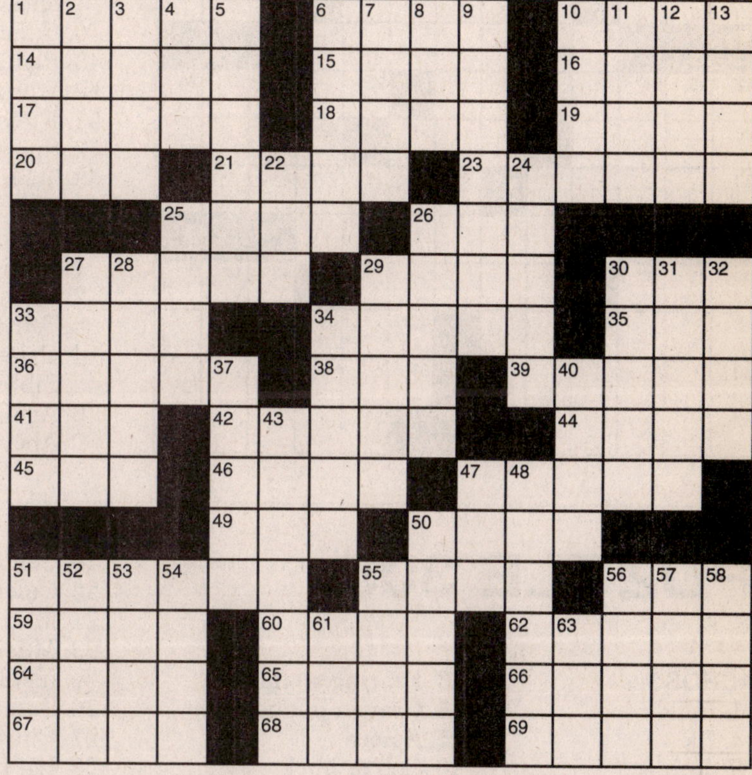

Triangle Sums

PUZZLE 303

The two diagonals divide the diagram on the right into four large triangles. Place the nine squares on the left into the diagram so that the sums of the four numbers in those triangles are equal. If a square is divided, place it in the diagram in a square that is divided the same way.

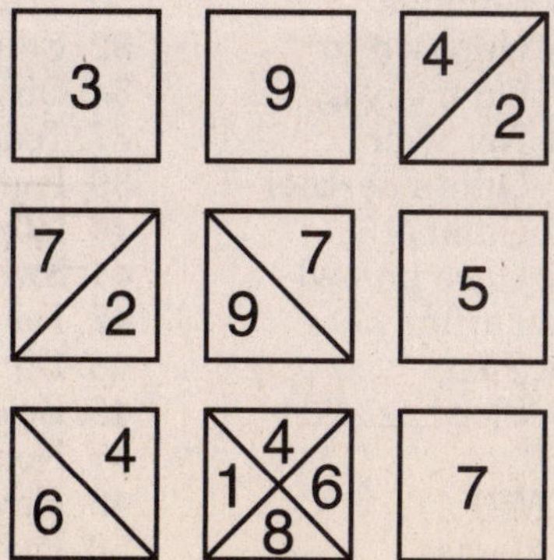

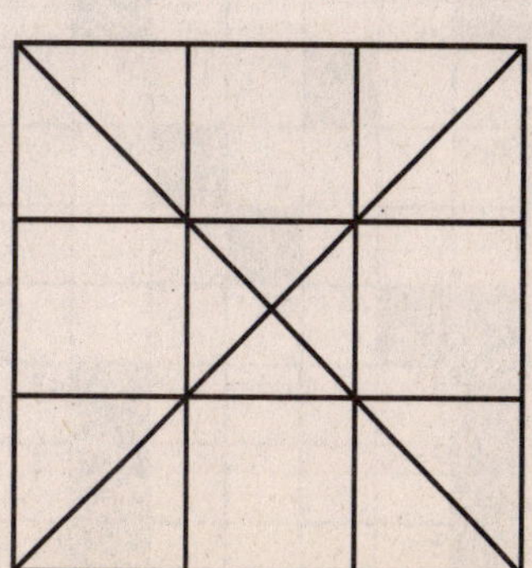

PUZZLE 304

ACROSS

1. Defrosts
6. Soprano, e.g.
11. Courageous
13. Went off course
14. Tangle
15. Slipping
16. Hazardous curve
17. Exams
19. Farm pen
20. Somber
22. Fit
25. Cast about
29. Burn soother
30. Drill need
32. Exceptional
33. Microbes
35. Restricted
37. Soft drink
39. Bikini part
42. Primary artery
43. Sports enthusiast
46. Cancel
48. Reduced
50. Worshiper
51. Kitchen tool
52. Spire
53. Took out

DOWN

1. Biblical pronoun
2. Barnyard birds
3. Tentacles
4. Grief
5. Sibling
6. Against
7. Above, in poems
8. Pupil place
9. Bronze coin
10. Irritable
12. Winged tot
13. Presidential rejection
18. Alike
20. Plant stalks
21. Divest
22. Recess game
23. Stout brew
24. Hide ____ hair
26. Scoundrel
27. Before
28. Get hitched
31. Grade-A
34. Super ____ (water gun brand)
36. Complained
38. Activist
39. Imp
40. Make over
41. Swear
43. Topple
44. Away from a storm
45. Twerp
47. Miner's goal
49. Consult

PUZZLE 305

ACROSS

1. Belly
4. Ilk
8. Jumps
12. Blond shade
13. Fencing weapon
14. Graven image, e.g.
15. Apiece
16. Cob or buck
17. Facial feature
18. Coldly
20. Cultivated
21. Map collection
23. Musical instrument
26. Summon
27. Cinch
28. Hit the slopes
31. Excused
33. Whipped
35. Lancelot's title
36. Slippery
38. Smell
39. Hatteras or Canaveral
40. Mortgages
41. Bass, e.g.
44. Smudge
46. Opposed to
47. On a voyage
48. Not well
51. Ollie's partner
52. Gambol
53. Once named
54. Forum wear
55. Snag
56. Sloe ____ fizz

DOWN

1. Lapse
2. Employ
3. Exciting movie
4. Highway sights
5. Milky jewel
6. Put trust in
7. Suit to a ____
8. Door fixture
9. Fragrance
10. Sit
11. Large quantity
19. Storm preceder
21. Masters
22. Hack
24. Newborn
25. Unlatch
27. Watch your ____!
28. Guiding
29. Eager
30. Printing fluids
32. Edible seed
34. Diva's highlight
37. Teaching unit
39. Populous land
40. Hurdled
41. Swiftly
42. Fascinated by
43. Dateless
45. Brief note
47. Noah's transport
49. Hawaiian garland
50. Football's Dawson

CODEWORD

PUZZLE 306

Codeword is a special crossword puzzle in which conventional clues are omitted. Instead, answer words in the diagram are represented by numbers. Each number represents a different letter of the alphabet, and all of the letters of the alphabet are used. When you are sure of a letter, put it in the code key chart and cross it off in the alphabet box. A group of letters has been inserted to start you off.

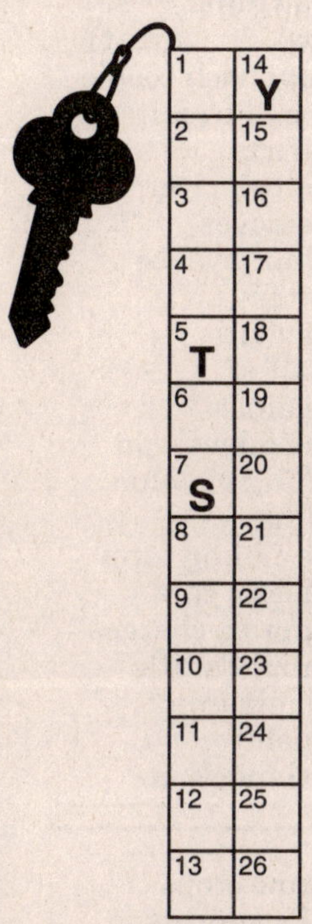

1	14 Y
2	15
3	16
4	17
5 T	18
6	19
7 S	20
8	21
9	22
10	23
11	24
12	25
13	26

12	2	11	■	22	23	10	■	7	9	11	■	20	26	5
20	16	9	■	20	19	9	■	26	2	23	■	5	22	14
2	21	21	■	5	9	25	■	23	17	16	■	21	2	26
21	23	20	7	23	■	26	18	10	15	■	21	20	24	23
■	■	■	5	22	9	21	21	7	■	26	9	7	23	16
20	6	18	20	■	25	23	5	■	3	9	8	■	■	■
21	18	22	15	■	23	1	2	5	23	16	■	20	7	26
7	20	19	23	■	21	23	25	9	17	■	13	9	20	21
9	16	23	■	22	23	7	20	21	23	■	2	17	13	9
■	■	■	12	23	5	■	5	23	23	■	7	23	23	16
26	2	21	20	13	■	4	18	22	22	20	4	■	■	■
20	22	9	8	■	21	20	25	20	■	21	14	22	2	10
7	15	2	■	7	2	7 S	■	5	8	9	■	2	22	23
5	23	17	■	9	20	5 T	■	23	9	17	■	5	9	23
20	16	7	■	26	22	14 Y	■	16	9	23	■	23	17	7

A	N
B	O
C	P
D	Q
E	R
F	~~S~~
G	~~T~~
H	U
I	V
J	W
K	X
L	~~Y~~
M	Z

LOVE CODEWORDS? *Enjoy hours of fun with our special collections of Selected Codewords! See page 159 for details.*

Slide-O-Gram

PUZZLE 307

Place the seven words into the diagram, one word for each row, so that one of the columns reading down will spell out a seven-letter word that is related to the others. Each given letter is part of one word.

Composer

Melody

Orchestra

Rhapsody

Scale

Score

Symphony

									L		
				A							
				P							
									R		
						M					
	O										
									A		

PUZZLE 308

• OUT OF TUNE •

ACROSS

1. Entirely
4. Vision starter
8. Hopper
11. Seven, to Caesar
12. Bring up
13. Choir member
14. In poor taste
16. Final
17. How baby kisses
18. Health farms
20. Function
22. "____ of Old Smokey"
25. Initial bet
28. Onionlike veggie
31. Raw metal
32. By way of
33. Analyze
34. Fixed charge
35. Moose's kin
36. Gov. division
37. Get an ____ effort
38. Superman portrayer
40. ____ Diego
42. Mailed
44. Retail outlet
48. Chimney grime
50. Football violation
53. Data
54. Shoe bottom
55. Period
56. Ump's kin
57. Chair
58. Mil. registration org.

DOWN

1. Admit openly
2. Existence
3. British elevator
4. Aikman and Donahue
5. Snakelike fish
6. ____-tzu
7. Transgresses
8. Countdown event
9. Part of TGIF
10. Negative word
13. Actor Arkin
15. Hint
19. Dawdling
21. Or ____ (threat)
23. Sandwich cookie
24. Social equal
25. Affirm
26. Cairo's river
27. Removes
29. Clairvoyance letters
30. Devours
33. Gulf of ____
37. Against
39. President's no
41. Thing of value
43. Fling
45. Gambling term
46. Classic cars
47. Approx. charges
48. Knight's title
49. Single unit
51. Enemy
52. Orlando's st.

PUZZLE 309

• EMERALD CITY QUEST •

ACROSS

1. Beef, e.g.
5. Admirer
8. Small fry
11. A Musketeer
13. Gorilla
14. Questioning grunt
15. He wanted a brain
17. Opposite of WNW
18. Dog-paddled
19. ABA member
20. Praline nut
23. Cab
25. Debtor's letters
26. Black birds
28. Part of an hr.
29. Book's back
31. Atlas item
33. Fun-house shout
35. Actress Alicia
36. Weeded
37. Improves
40. Phony
42. Opera song
43. Ms. MacGraw
44. Dorothy's kind of path
49. Chaney of film
50. Rower's tool
51. Slur over
52. Bandleader Brown
53. Morning hrs.
54. Large quantity

DOWN

1. More, in Mexico
2. Et al.'s kin
3. Cry of triumph
4. Trunk
5. Grow crops
6. GI's address
7. Recent
8. He wanted a heart
9. Unseat
10. Those people
12. Stitched
16. Rogue
19. Hewing tool
20. Goal
21. Reporter Lane
22. Dorothy's greeters
23. Sun-bronzed
24. Wide st.
26. Edge
27. Dune material
29. Observe
30. Cushion
32. Ballet step
34. Fish eggs
37. Rainbow's shape
38. Actor Connors
39. British nobles
40. Topple
41. Lotion ingredient
42. Ventilates
44. Squeezing snake
45. Male sheep
46. Olive or canola
47. Citrus drink
48. Morning moisture

BRICK BY BRICK

PUZZLE 310

Rearrange this stack of bricks to form a crossword puzzle. The clues will help you fit the bricks into their correct places. Row 1 has been filled in for you. Use the bricks to fill in the remaining spaces.

ACROSS

1. Spanish pot
   Key letter
   Divert
2. Red horse
   Grad
   Fend off
3. Homeric tale
   English river
   Timepiece
4. Letter stroke
   Oprah's gift?
   Picnic pests
5. Actress Raines
   Final word
6. Ravine
   Mine accesses
7. Batter's ploy
   Head of a suit
   Light
8. Joule's kin
   In theory
   Shelter
9. Italian ice creams
   Adam's loss
   Rowboat items
10. Prime number
    Turkey's cry
11. Therefore
    Leaf part
12. Shock
    June, to Wally
    Australian critter
13. Yearns
    Flock females
    Ball
14. Window type
    Chap
    Arden and Plumb
15. Vestibule
    Affected
    Ding

DOWN

1. Metals
   Grovel
   Blackthorn
2. Canter
   Heals
   Ripped
3. Lion's pad
   Aspect
   Troop group
4. Very old
   Retaliator
5. Go by plane
   Road for Cato
   Cagey
6. Outlaw
   Filling
7. Refinement
   At the end
8. Bluefin
   Corn serving
   Debtor
9. Protozoan
   Sinew
10. Letter bin
    Porky's abode
11. Lob's path
    Jumpy
    Auction word
12. Skin pigment
    Grateful
13. Informed of
    Kind of wave
    Hub
14. Faction
    Cordwood amount
    Dell
15. Large deer
    Certain dashes
    Kiln

BRICKS

NTS ■■■	LUM ENE	LY■ B■O	■CA BUN	ERG GEL
VES ENT	SER ■■■	NYO T■A	N■A C■N	GAB A■A
■■G O■A	VEN ERG	EAL ■RI	PEL OCK	OBB XIL
ADI IGN	MOM EWE	NGO ALA	STU LON	N■■ CE■
EL■ RY■	IF■ ELL	LE■ ■■■	ROA EPI	■DI S■G
T■E Y■D	DEN ARS	■ID ATI	GEN ART	■SE ■■■
TS■ ITE	ORI ENT	N■■ GS■	■RE ■CL	■■A MEN

DIAGRAM

	1	2	3	4	5	6	7	8	9	10	11	12	13	14	15
1	O	L	L	A	■	B	E	T	A	■	A	M	U	S	E
2															
3															
4															
5															
6															
7															
8															
9															
10															
11															
12															
13															
14															
15															

PUZZLE 311

ACROSS

1. Cure
5. Hole punch
8. Bubble
12. Land measure
13. Delta, in code
14. Con
15. Stop, Dobbin!
16. Matched pair
17. Gusto
18. Female pigs
19. Cougar
21. Kind of tide
24. Ivory keyboards
28. Soft toss
31. Charged atom
33. Sooty dirt
34. Rowing need
35. Fang
37. So-so grade
38. Begin
40. Wheel track
41. Finish
42. Repute
44. See you!
46. Ship prison
48. Sketch
52. Food list
55. Brewery brew
57. Chess, e.g.
58. Berserk
59. Chaps
60. Made do
61. Guy
62. Winners
63. Cozy rooms

DOWN

1. Turns left
2. Second saying?
3. In a line
4. Charter
5. TV spots
6. Blubber
7. Ease off
8. Church fair
9. Single unit
10. ___ a living!
11. Aglow
20. Very strong
22. Fierce
23. Ghost's cry
25. Pleasing
26. Warning
27. Bird food
28. Mislay
29. Stable grains
30. Spoiled kid
32. Scand. land
36. Lard container
39. Criticism
43. Florida city
45. Hemmed
47. Narrow valley
49. Garden tool
50. Pulpit word
51. Marries
52. Crazy
53. Australian bird
54. Agree silently
56. Type spaces

<table>
<tr><td>1</td><td>2</td><td>3</td><td>4</td><td>■</td><td>5</td><td>6</td><td>7</td><td>■</td><td>8</td><td>9</td><td>10</td><td>11</td></tr>
<tr><td>12</td><td></td><td></td><td></td><td>■</td><td>13</td><td></td><td></td><td>■</td><td>14</td><td></td><td></td><td></td></tr>
<tr><td>15</td><td></td><td></td><td></td><td>■</td><td>16</td><td></td><td></td><td>■</td><td>17</td><td></td><td></td><td></td></tr>
<tr><td>18</td><td></td><td></td><td></td><td>■</td><td>■</td><td>19</td><td></td><td>20</td><td></td><td>■</td><td>■</td><td>■</td></tr>
<tr><td>■</td><td>■</td><td>■</td><td>21</td><td>22</td><td>23</td><td>■</td><td>24</td><td></td><td></td><td>25</td><td>26</td><td>27</td></tr>
<tr><td>28</td><td>29</td><td>30</td><td>■</td><td>31</td><td></td><td>32</td><td>■</td><td>33</td><td></td><td></td><td></td><td></td></tr>
<tr><td>34</td><td></td><td></td><td>■</td><td>35</td><td></td><td></td><td>36</td><td></td><td>■</td><td>37</td><td></td><td></td></tr>
<tr><td>38</td><td></td><td></td><td>39</td><td></td><td>■</td><td>40</td><td></td><td></td><td>■</td><td>41</td><td></td><td></td></tr>
<tr><td>42</td><td></td><td></td><td></td><td></td><td>43</td><td>■</td><td>44</td><td></td><td>45</td><td>■</td><td>■</td><td>■</td></tr>
<tr><td>■</td><td>■</td><td>■</td><td>46</td><td></td><td></td><td>47</td><td>■</td><td>■</td><td>48</td><td>49</td><td>50</td><td>51</td></tr>
<tr><td>52</td><td>53</td><td>54</td><td></td><td>■</td><td>55</td><td></td><td>56</td><td>■</td><td>57</td><td></td><td></td><td></td></tr>
<tr><td>58</td><td></td><td></td><td></td><td>■</td><td>59</td><td></td><td></td><td>■</td><td>60</td><td></td><td></td><td></td></tr>
<tr><td>61</td><td></td><td></td><td></td><td>■</td><td>62</td><td></td><td></td><td>■</td><td>63</td><td></td><td></td><td></td></tr>
</table>

PUZZLE 312

ACROSS

1. Frequently, to Keats
4. Cavort
8. Epic tale
12. Pub beverage
13. Unwritten
14. Frosting user
15. Social drink
16. Scant
17. Nerd
18. Mexican sauce
20. Volcano's dust
22. Whatever
24. Tingly
28. Feet of ___
31. Fragrance
34. Tint
35. Deep
36. Topper
37. Bedridden
38. Tangy refresher
39. ___ out (barely made)
40. October gem
41. The press, etc.
43. Nearest star
45. Swine home
47. Oyster's product
51. Sonnets' kin
54. Sorrowful word
57. Pod vegetable
58. Dilly
59. Fair feature
60. Nightmare street
61. Take out, as text
62. Bird's home
63. Change the color of

DOWN

1. Cereal grains
2. Pet pest
3. Wild duck
4. Ancient Italian
5. Mine rock
6. Harm
7. Urgent request
8. Love at first ___
9. Top card
10. Golly ___
11. Noah's ship
19. Vocalize
21. British title
23. Egg center
25. Flake
26. Maui dance
27. Scream
28. Silent type
29. Mother ___
30. Stunned
32. "___ Hard"
33. Racetrack numbers
39. Chow down
40. ___-man band
42. Distribute
44. Surprise win
46. Knitter's need
48. Parodied
49. Depend
50. Gold-threaded fabric
51. ___ Glory
52. Payable now
53. Building wing
55. Falsify
56. Radio promos

1	2	3	■	4	5	6	7	■	8	9	10	11
12			■	13				■	14			
15			■	16				■	17			
18			19		■	■	20	21		■	■	■
■	■	■	22		23	■	■	24		25	26	27
28	29	30		■	31	32	33		■	34		
35			■	■	36			■	■	37		
38			■	39				■	40			
41			42		■	■	43	44		■	■	■
■	■	■	45		46	■	■	47		48	49	50
51	52	53		■	54	55	56		■	57		
58				■	59				■	60		
61				■	62				■	63		

PUZZLE 313

ACROSS

1. Sky light
5. Pig's place
8. Auction
12. Duct
13. Before, in a poem
14. VCR button
15. Abominable Snowman
16. Big boy
17. Food staple
18. Dismal
20. Nibbler
21. Laughing ___
24. Haul
25. Above, in poems
26. Mothers
29. Perform
32. Scratch
33. Pep
34. Rage
35. Snake shape
36. Passenger
38. Uno plus uno
39. Atlantic fish
40. Kick out
42. Disturbed
45. Couch
47. Tack
48. Mister
49. Young dogs
53. Pickle herb
54. Distinct period
55. Sailing
56. Conscious of
57. It's a moray
58. Geek

DOWN

1. Foreign agent
2. Gift for Dad
3. Skillful
4. Royal rule
5. Highway vehicle
6. Streetcar
7. Desire
8. Parsley piece
9. Came to ground
10. Frilly fabric
11. Ogler
19. Pound
20. Motor coach
21. House
22. Team cheers
23. Bungles
24. Gold fabric
27. Eager
28. Halfway
29. Helper
30. Gator's kin
31. Exam
36. Decompose
37. KO counter
39. Violin's kin
41. Tokyo's land
42. Reverse
43. Ache
44. River deposit
45. Kingly address
46. Not written
48. Spot
50. Employ
51. By means of
52. Downcast

1	2	3	4	■	5	6	7	■	8	9	10	11
12				■	13			■	14			
15				■	16			■	17			
■	■	■	18	19			■	20				
21	22	23			■	■	24			■	■	■
25			■	26	27	28			■	29	30	31
32			■	■	33			■	■	34		
35			■	36				37	■	38		
■	■	■	39			■	■	40	41			
42	43	44			■	45	46			■	■	■
47				■	48			■	49	50	51	52
53				■	54			■	55			
56				■	57			■	58			

PUZZLE 314

ACROSS

1. Reed instrument
5. Luxury hotels
9. Casual top
12. Orderly
13. Shed tears
14. Sunbeam
15. Powder ingredient
16. Poker beginning
17. "___ Got Sixpence"
18. Fade away
20. Title giver
22. Juliet's love
25. Doll or kite
26. Browning's before
27. Pale
30. Very bad
34. Truck
35. Railroad nail
37. Exist
38. Snail's kin
40. Like some cars
41. ___ of a gun
42. Corn piece
44. Valleys
46. Skin on the head
49. Second letter
50. Crow's sound
51. Hunch
54. Soothe
58. Generation
59. Sisters
60. Family group
61. Danger color
62. Eros and Zeus
63. Chops

DOWN

1. Pick
2. Bikini part
3. Motor lubricant
4. Host
5. Mop
6. Corral
7. Clever
8. Shorthand, shortly
9. Cut to size
10. Roof part
11. Ogler
19. Tropical snakes
21. Sailor's response
22. Guns the engine
23. ___ hygiene
24. Bill of fare
25. Toddler
28. Horse goad
29. ___-and-hers
31. Urn
32. Press
33. Contact ___
36. Verge
39. Stylist's goop
43. Imitating
45. Parasite
46. Wound's mark
47. Shut in
48. Deeply impressed
49. Low voice
52. Couple
53. Purpose
55. Brewery brew
56. Viewed
57. Printers' concerns

1	2	3	4	■	5	6	7	8	■	9	10	11
12				■	13				■	14		
15				■	16				■	17		
■	■	■	18	19		■	■	20	21			
22	23	24			■	■	25			■	■	■
26			■	27	28	29		■	30	31	32	33
34			■	35				36	■	37		
38			39	■	40				■	41		
■	■	■	42	43		■	■	44	45			
46	47	48			■	■	49			■	■	■
50			■	51	52	53		■	54	55	56	57
58			■	59				■	60			
61			■	62				■	63			

PUZZLE 315

ACROSS

1. Instructor, for short
5. Inspires with fear
9. Not even
12. Not taped
13. Single-person song
14. Fish eggs
15. October stone
16. ___-esteem
17. Go ___ over
18. River-mouth plain
20. More qualified
22. Elegant
26. Morning wetness
29. Landlord's fee
30. Atlantic-coast region
34. ___ and aah
35. Avid
37. Third letter
38. Stuck-up person
40. Request
41. Fleecy female
42. Trainee
44. Ship's load
47. Pulverize
52. ___-man band
53. Eagle type
57. Fragrance
58. Directed
59. Stead
60. Musical quality
61. Tango requirement
62. Trim
63. Large amount

DOWN

1. Proceed slowly
2. Full-grown
3. Egg-shaped
4. Experienced
5. Burro
6. Anguish
7. Addition to a house
8. Couches
9. Type of surgeon
10. Dummy
11. Fawn's mother
19. Land unit
21. See ya!
23. Vaulted
24. Right, acute, or obtuse
25. Take the wheel
26. Rules to follow
27. Geologic age
28. Reporter's question
31. Playing card
32. Stitch
33. ___ off (anger)
36. Resounded
39. "The ___ Chill"
43. Honorable
44. Stable youth
45. Once again
46. Accomplish again
48. Deteriorates
49. False god
50. Nil
51. Attracted
54. Join forces with
55. Part of a trip
56. Payable now

1	2	3	4	■	5	6	7	8	■	9	10	11
12				■	13				■	14		
15				■	16				■	17		
18				19	■	■	■	20	21			
■	■	■	■	22	23	24	25			■	■	■
26	27	28	■	29				■	30	31	32	33
34			■	35				36	■	37		
38			39	■	40				■	41		
■	■	■	42	43					■	■	■	■
44	45	46			■	■	■	47	48	49	50	51
52			■	53	54	55	56	■	57			
58			■	59				■	60			
61			■	62				■	63			

PUZZLE 316

ACROSS

1. Deeds
5. Rip
9. With it
12. Throw for a ___
13. Soprano's solo
14. Pinna
15. Penniless
16. Meadow baby
17. Prior to, in verse
18. Printer's need
20. Harshly
22. Church-hall game
25. Slap
26. Shad ___
27. Bean curd
30. Bridge seat
34. "___ Your Move"
35. Unwell
36. Score to beat
37. Arithmetic
39. Humdinger
41. Kind of maniac
42. Frosty
44. Jack of nursery-rhyme fame
46. Subject
49. Above, in poems
50. Direction
51. From a distance
54. Clarinet's relative
58. Beer's cousin
59. Cobbler's concern
60. Verbal test
61. Piece of turf
62. Squiggly swimmers
63. Henhouse site

DOWN

1. Swiss peak
2. Bird cry
3. Likewise
4. Parsley branch
5. Chatter
6. Important span
7. Intention
8. Synagogue figure
9. Pay attention to
10. Nobleman
11. Mice, to cats
19. Negative
21. Had popcorn
22. Edge
23. Tiny bit
24. Eagle's dwelling
25. Ship's bottom
28. Slick
29. Winter ailment
31. Imitator
32. Legend
33. Colt's gait
38. That guy
40. Consume
43. Quit
45. Affirmation
46. "___ the night before . . ."
47. Saint's headgear
48. Saw
49. Metal-bearing rocks
52. Rival
53. Entirely
55. Bathing-suit part
56. Rowboat tool
57. Popular street name

1	2	3	4	■	5	6	7	8	■	9	10	11
12				■	13				■	14		
15				■	16				■	17		
■	■	■	18	19		■	■	20	21			
22	23	24			■	■	25			■	■	■
26			■	27	28	29		■	30	31	32	33
34			■	■	35			■	■	36		
37			38	■	39			40	■	41		
■	■	■	42	43		■	■	44	45			
46	47	48			■	■	49			■	■	■
50			■	51	52	53		■	54	55	56	57
58			■	59				■	60			
61			■	62				■	63			

PUZZLE 317

ACROSS

1. Science room
4. Invalid
8. Existed
12. Pitcher's stat
13. Toward the middle of
14. Egg shape
15. Reception
16. Lofty home
17. Agts.
18. Fresh
20. Moray, e.g.
22. ___-advised
24. Peculiarly
28. Confound
31. Unlocked
34. Not me
35. Possesses
36. Express
37. House addition
38. Wood-chopping tool
39. Bit of land
40. Doing nothing
41. '70s nightclub
43. Physician
45. Connecting word
47. Memorize
51. Unhealthy air
54. Surrounded by
57. Luau necklace
58. Clean
59. Yanked
60. Poolside pursuit
61. Ancient
62. Impersonator
63. Lyric poem

DOWN

1. Allows
2. Field of study
3. Bleats
4. Plastic material
5. United
6. "___ Impossible"
7. Love too much
8. Planet
9. December 31, e.g.
10. Quick blow
11. Subways' cousins
19. Moral lapse
21. Timespan
23. At a ___ (puzzled)
25. Colorized
26. Lounge
27. Santa's time
28. Roe source
29. Cab
30. Exploits
32. Sidekick
33. Gazed upon
39. Electrified atom
40. Cold cubes
42. Penned in
44. More mature
46. Statistics
48. Singing voice
49. Interpret writing
50. Almost ten
51. Fitness center
52. Cocoa cup
53. Crude mineral
55. Janitor's tool
56. Strong anger

1	2	3	■	4	5	6	7	■	8	9	10	11
12			■	13				■	14			
15			■	16				■	17			
18			19		■	■	20	21		■	■	■
■	■	■	22		23	■	■	24		25	26	27
28	29	30		■	31	32	33		■	34		
35			■	■	36			■	■	37		
38			■	39				■	40			
41			42		■	■	43	44		■	■	■
■	■	■	45		46	■	■	47		48	49	50
51	52	53		■	54	55	56		■	57		
58				■	59				■	60		
61				■	62				■	63		

PUZZLE 318

ACROSS

1. Light-bulb word
5. Auto trouble
9. False front
12. Spiny houseplant
13. Camp staffer
14. Shad ___
15. Gooey stuff
16. Consider
17. Sound receiver
18. ___ out (make do)
20. Sunday song
22. Approve
25. Clean the floor
26. Tropical serpent
27. Mate for mama
30. Dull pain
34. Large vase
35. Hepburn's love
37. Race in neutral
38. Tot
40. Brainchild
41. Before, to Shelley
42. Faulty
44. Not as old
46. Legal excuse
49. Cloud's locale
50. Shark feature
51. Bowling alley
54. Like some tea
58. Genesis ship
59. Modify copy
60. Designate
61. Manta ___
62. Seurat trademarks
63. Scrounge

DOWN

1. Tail movement
2. Everybody
3. Moreover
4. Plains dwelling
5. Dissolve
6. One of a pack?
7. Fruit drink
8. Musical pace
9. Expanse
10. Furnace fuel
11. Duration
19. Maintained
21. Hot spring
22. Border on
23. Like some King films
24. Military status
25. Certain spice
28. Lacking moisture
29. Mat
31. Personnel
32. Present!
33. Perpetually
36. Tug
39. Decline
43. Suffered
45. Looking at
46. Long way off
47. Old Italian bread?
48. Very black
49. Related groups
52. Confusion
53. Young louse
55. Caboose, e.g.
56. Australian bird
57. Society miss

1	2	3	4	■	5	6	7	8	■	9	10	11
12				■	13				■	14		
15				■	16				■	17		
■	■	■	18	19		■	■	20	21			
22	23	24			■	■	25			■	■	■
26			■	27	28	29		■	30	31	32	33
34			■	35				36	■	37		
38			39	■	40				■	41		
■	■	■	42	43		■	■	44	45			
46	47	48			■	■	49			■	■	■
50			■	51	52	53		■	54	55	56	57
58			■	59				■	60			
61			■	62				■	63			

PUZZLE 319

ACROSS

1. Subsequently
5. Suitor
9. Ill will
14. Stringed toy
15. Spring flower
16. Having handles
17. Get ready
18. Ranch novice
19. "___ Comes Mary"
20. Concluded
22. Salon treatment
24. Opening bet
25. Quick to learn
27. Sup
29. Way up
32. Quiet
37. Pass
38. Stare rudely
39. Dollar bill
40. Holland sight
41. Gypsy's card
43. Pivot point
44. Bartender's rocks
45. Bonus
46. Coves
48. Trend
50. Like old bread
51. Possessive pronoun
52. Urge
53. Streetcar
56. World's fair, e.g.
59. School paper
64. Silent Marx
66. Carnival attraction
68. Heavenly circle
69. Lower-leg joint
70. Downwind
71. Face shape
72. More prudent
73. Call out
74. Classroom furnishing

DOWN

1. Hunt-and-peck
2. Bugle
3. Looked at
4. Not yep
5. Auction action
6. Blow up
7. Military assistant
8. Employer
9. Red or Black
10. Mouth part
11. Clothes presser
12. Circus shelter
13. Outskirts
21. Raised platform
23. Noon, to some
26. Sham
28. Sampras serve, often
29. Orange portion
30. Stolen
31. Mimic
32. Cartoon pig
33. ___ trip
34. Tricked
35. Harmony
36. Fewer
37. Blue-pencil
42. Rainbow shape
43. Full amount
45. Fluffy or Fido
47. Not a soul
49. Golf ball feature
52. Swiss song
53. Melt
54. Hindu princess
55. Clumsy vessels
57. Doctor's picture
58. Mound
60. Not barefoot
61. Put aside
62. Ah, me!
63. Egg center
65. Not 'neath
67. Wiggly fish

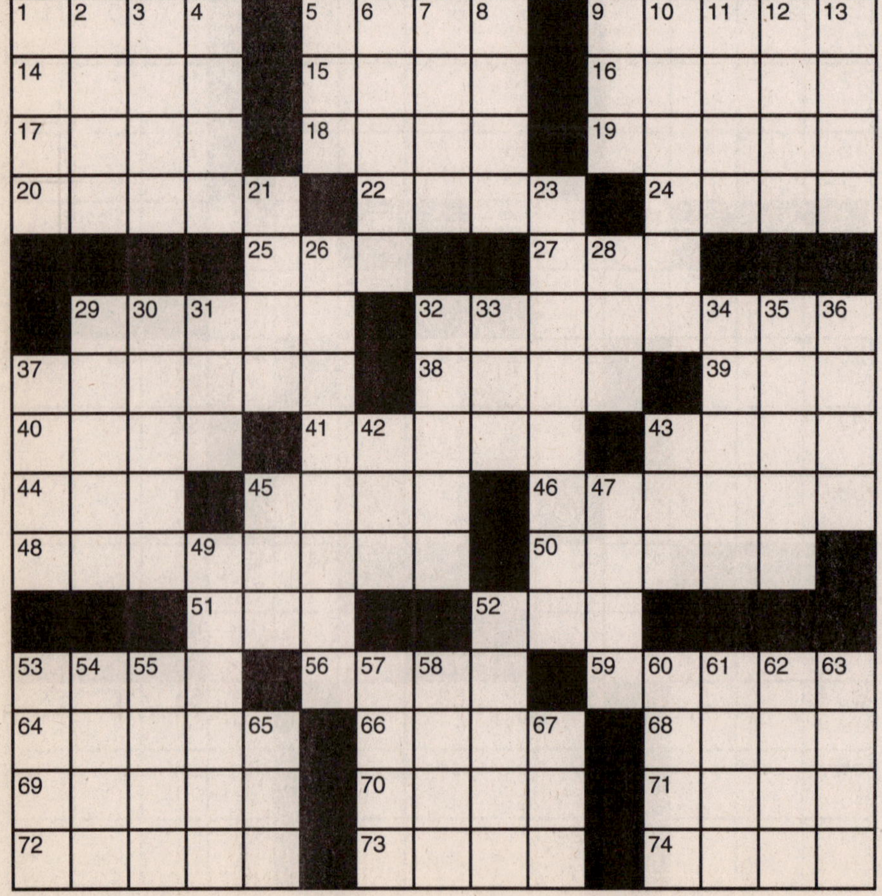

PUZZLE 320

ACROSS
1. Round dance
5. Farm unit
9. Sagas
14. Dark
15. Ridge above the eye
16. Reason
17. Trial period
19. Saluting gunfire
20. Behold
21. Grammar word
23. Spring
24. Maple, e.g.
25. Support
27. In progress
30. Carter and Gwyn
33. Champagne cocktail
35. Food outlet
36. Switch positions
39. "___ Always Loved You"
40. Pale brown
42. Wipe
43. Informal room
44. Gator's kin
45. Sesame paste
48. Searches
50. Squelch
51. Zany
55. Modify
57. Asian ruler
58. Toppled
61. Greek letter
64. Shy
66. Geometric figure
68. Plant swelling
69. Foal
70. Qualified
71. Baste again
72. Jumble
73. Dogs and cats

DOWN
1. Chicks' mamas
2. Wind instrument
3. Gallivant
4. Black bird
5. Continue
6. Cowardly
7. Fixed routine
8. Ornate pitcher
9. Chicago trains
10. Cook just to boiling
11. Arctic house
12. Polite
13. Reprimand
18. Fruit pastries
22. Lead missile
24. Furthermore
26. Omega's preceder
27. Among
28. Basketball team
29. Forewarning
31. Judgment
32. Cut of lamb
34. Sudden
36. Skip
37. Forbidden thing
38. Turn
41. Billion years
44. Chinese tea
46. Stage direction
47. Success
49. Calyx parts
51. Gauge
52. Organic compound
53. Thin coins
54. Larceny, e.g.
56. Profundity
59. Restless desire
60. Malayan boat
61. Toga
62. Sword handle
63. Ballads
65. Small crow
67. Microwave

1	2	3	4	■	5	6	7	8	■	9	10	11	12	13
14				■	15				■	16				
17				18					■	19				
20			■	21					22	■	23			
■	■	■	24				■	■	25	26				
27	28	29			■	30	31	32			■	■	■	■
33					34	■	35				■	36	37	38
39			■	■	40	41				■	■	42		
43			■	44				■	45	46	47			
■	■	■	■	48				49	■	50				
51	52	53	54			■	■	55	56			■	■	■
57				■	58	59	60				■	61	62	63
64				65	■	66					67			
68					■	69				■	70			
71					■	72				■	73			

PUZZLE 321

ACROSS

1. Weak person
5. Jazz type
8. Portend
12. Domain
13. Pond flocks
15. Golf-bag item
16. Fish lung
17. Long-legged bird
18. Beach soil
19. Will subject
21. Mobile home owners?
23. Tent sites
26. Taproom
27. Battle of rivals
29. Electrified atom
31. Bates, for one
35. Quick swim
36. Frank
39. Highway vehicle
40. "___ a Small World"
41. Make a lap
42. Cow's chew
44. Moray or electric
45. Tread
47. Granny's chair
49. "___ to Remember"
50. Traveler's stop
52. Bring legal action
53. Sore
55. Snatch
57. Put it on Mame
59. Embarrassed
63. Disgraced
67. Virginia dance
68. Tropical jelly
71. Strong affection
72. Beef or veal
73. Woodcutter
74. Lincoln and Vigoda
75. Peppy
76. Lease
77. Take five

DOWN

1. Salary
2. Colored eye-part
3. Defrost
4. King's house
5. Honey source
6. Rowing implement
7. Secret plan
8. Cafes
9. Certain exam
10. Fully cooked
11. Last bits
13. Not us
14. Ignore
20. Powders
22. Lamb's dad
24. Spotted ponies
25. Grassy layer
27. Duplicate
28. Topple
30. Coin
32. Fangs
33. Grinding material
34. ___ of the valley
35. Spoon's companion
37. Walking on ___
38. Unpaid
43. Stage production
46. Fine
48. Chicago baseballer
51. Take it on the ___
54. Wine locale
56. Entreats
58. Remotely
59. Venus de Milo's lack
60. Dribble
61. Find out
62. ___ citizenship
64. Earring's site
65. Preholiday nights
66. Cozy home
69. Fill with wonder
70. Former GI

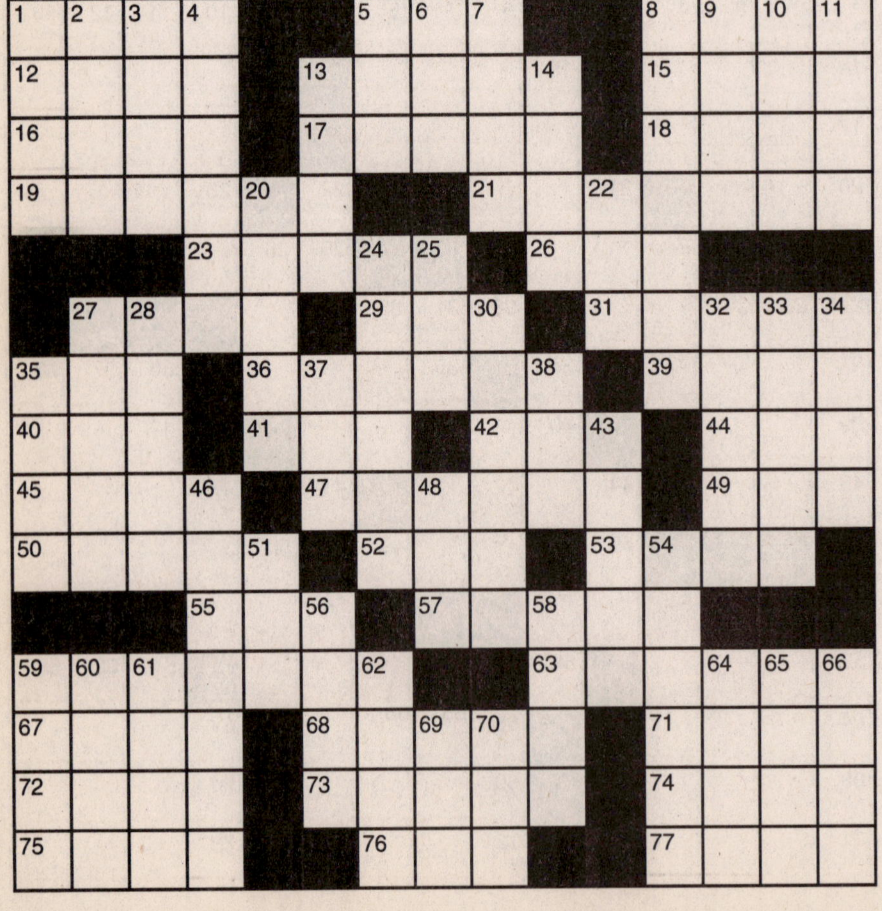

PUZZLE 322

ACROSS

1. Came to ground
5. Harmful insect
9. Lighthearted
13. Taboo
14. Therefore
15. Leisure
16. Bean curd
17. Fire crime
18. Feel pain
19. Turbulent
21. Fisher birds
23. Fugitive
26. Gawk at
29. Attempt
30. At a distance
34. Butt into
35. Strenuous
36. Boxed
38. Champs
40. Fabric
42. PBS science series
43. Reduced
45. Breakfast, e.g.
47. Sludge
48. Memo error
49. World's fair, e.g.
50. Baltic or Bering
51. Angled
54. Cooking herb
58. Say from memory
63. District
64. Extremely small
67. Unwritten
68. Cover with gold
69. Boston skater
70. Connection
71. Depletes
72. Look
73. Requests

DOWN

1. Red, army, and carpenter
2. Winnings
3. Data
4. See the sights
5. Through
6. Printers' concerns
7. Ladle
8. Uptight
9. Equipment
10. Bridal-gown trim
11. Pale
12. Below-average grades
14. Needle's place?
20. Interlock
22. Bartlett, e.g.
24. Poet Sandburg
25. Belly
26. Significant periods
27. Luxurious boat
28. Fingernail-filing material
31. Devotee
32. Potent particles
33. Variety show
36. Party supervisor
37. 20th-century art movement
39. Dine in the evening
41. Body of printing
44. Nuzzle
46. Metallic vein
52. Young sheep
53. In flames
54. Captures
55. Elaborate melody
56. Canine cry
57. Children
59. Soda
60. Pupil's site
61. Gas container
62. Antlered animals
65. Stage signal
66. Wheel part

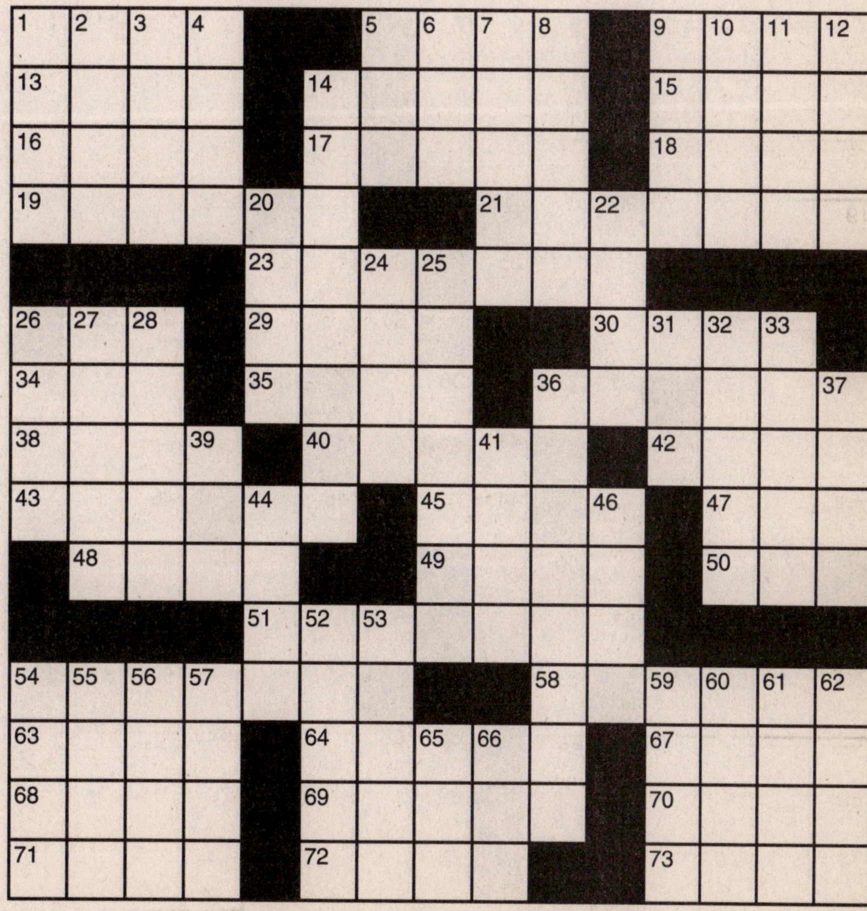

PUZZLE 323

ACROSS

1. Hot springs
5. Provided lunch for
8. Long gun
13. Sprightly tune
14. Be in hock
15. ___ worker
16. Unique being
17. KO counter
18. Boll ___
19. Next to
21. Snead's gizmo
23. Beatty film
24. Fighting hand
26. Catch
28. Lower in pitch
30. Creates
34. Cookie holder
35. Fido's lead
37. Movie-rental choice
39. Preface
41. ___ soup
42. ___ Pyle
43. Vaccine
44. Cut a rug
46. Cervid
47. Energetic person
49. Lunge
51. More than should be
52. Spotted
53. Dunce
57. Great fury
59. Floating
63. Unwinds
65. Garfield, e.g.
67. Inspiration
68. Western or cheese
69. Rush
70. Appealed
71. Inverted vee
72. Strange
73. Snakelike fish

DOWN

1. Oscar Madison, e.g.
2. Evergreen variety
3. Ginger drinks
4. Discord
5. Predict
6. Female bighorn
7. Adept
8. Fish beginnings
9. Cake froster
10. Cinco
11. Set down
12. Angled additions
15. Promise
20. Tactful person
22. Mesmerizes
25. Secret opening
27. Vexed
28. Ate
29. Access
31. To's counterpart
32. Domesticates
33. Small silver fish
34. "___ the season . . ."
36. Where whales wallow
38. Biblical vessel
40. Scamper
45. Swindled
48. Damp
50. Immature
53. Gator's kin
54. Shangri-la official
55. Kaput
56. Editor's comment
58. Canyon sound
60. Not utilized
61. Sense
62. Little bits
64. "___ It Be"
66. Help

PUZZLE 324

ACROSS

1. Farmland units
6. Baseball arbiters
10. Religious leader
14. Young pig
15. Carpenter's need
16. "Far and ___"
17. Spaghetti
18. Hunted animal
19. Solar plexus, for one
20. Dump
21. African insect
23. Fruit quaffs
24. Mushrooms, e.g.
25. Poignant
27. Mexican sauce
29. PBS and NBC
34. Properly
35. Flop
37. Expend
38. Cereal plant
39. Not nope
40. Jest with
42. Digger
43. Steer clear of
45. Bard's black
47. It may be red
48. Moonlight music?
50. Plant swelling
52. Curvy turn
53. Eagle's loft
55. Prance
58. Gem weights
60. Hot spring
63. Sport blade
64. Mine rocks
65. Take place
67. Caps
68. Car spare
69. Hit
70. Scotch serving
71. Brashness
72. Nostrils

DOWN

1. Venomous snakes
2. Small talk
3. Optimistic
4. Have a bagel
5. Rank
6. Remove pins from
7. Bond's drink
8. Slapstick props
9. Craftiest
10. Contradiction
11. Was in arrears
12. Party spread
13. Storm centers
22. Glitch
24. Take wing
26. Dazzled
27. Smooth
28. Bachelor's last stand?
30. Nevada town
31. Alter slacks
32. Swedish money
33. Don't strike!
34. Deer daughters
36. Emulated
39. Appetites
41. Unmoving
44. Farthest down
46. Carriers
47. Passing grade
49. Scarves
51. Cast out
54. Comforts
55. Soaks flax
56. Brilliant fish
57. Short note
59. Domingo solo
60. Battle mark
61. Dark purple
62. Scroll closets
66. Chinese tea

PUZZLE 325

ACROSS

1. Kind of bean
5. Mart
9. Mock
13. In ___ of (instead of)
14. Slogged
16. Opposed to, for Li'l Abner
17. Mine access
18. Closer
19. Holiday drinks
20. Granted a permanent job
22. Watercourse
24. Witty remark
25. Ham
28. Card game
32. Green stuff
34. Declare taboo
35. Rotten
36. Admonish
37. Jar covering
38. Cowboy's rope
40. Wire measurement
41. In ___ (together)
44. Isinglass
46. Electric ___
47. Majestic
48. Gas quantities
50. Singer Fats ___
52. Clash
53. Shower
54. Haircutters
58. Holy statue
61. Postpone
63. Locale
64. "The ___ Is High"
65. Goofed
66. Tack
67. Origin
68. Dropper's word
69. Medieval laborer

DOWN

1. Smooth
2. Military helper
3. Blood vessel
4. Fall
5. Farmer's crop
6. Round of applause
7. Kooky
8. Runt
9. Custodian
10. In the past
11. Porky, e.g.
12. Nanny has three
15. Small portion
21. Housetop
23. Circular vault
26. Molar's coating
27. Binds again
28. Caused suffering to
29. Blue dye
30. Tinge
31. Andean animal
33. Shriek
34. Smudge
36. In reverse
39. Soft metal
42. Tasted
43. Mixture
45. Distantly
48. Matador
49. Sophisticated
51. Bare
54. Honk
55. Periods
56. Harness piece
57. Clearance
58. "___ a Wonderful Life"
59. Casino cube
60. Certain poem
62. To's mate

PUZZLE 326

ACROSS

1. Less cordial
6. Wedge
10. Friendly talk
14. Majestic
15. Camp helper, e.g.
16. Violent anger
17. Extravagance
18. "Empty ___"
19. Tavern orders
20. Switch positions
21. Inquire
23. Struggle
25. King Kong, e.g.
26. Boxing match
27. Dwarfed tree
30. Coffee container
31. NBA player, e.g.
34. Talk idly
35. Dent
37. Imperfection
38. Removed leaves
39. Peach, for one
40. Signal light
41. Got a hole in one
42. Pitcher's stat
43. Flowed out slowly
44. Desire
45. Faulty item
47. Clamor
49. X marks this spot
50. Above, to Keats
51. Stitching
54. Photo
55. Vane initials
58. Almost round
59. Resounding sound
62. Pallid
64. Peddle
65. ___-do-well
66. Recoiled
67. Solely
68. Wording
69. Looks after

DOWN

1. News
2. Toe woe
3. Spoonbill's kin
4. Building section
5. Slipped back
6. Plunged
7. Make haste
8. Freud's concerns
9. Shooting star
10. Skill
11. Saint's headgear
12. Golden ___ (retiree)
13. Big quiz
22. Shark's home
24. Enjoyment
25. Fed the kitty
26. Agency
27. Support
28. Made of a hardwood
29. Obstruct
31. "___ Suite"
32. Fewer
33. Felt obligated
34. Say a rosary
36. Cushion or pocket
37. Dumbfound
40. Weather report
45. Lion's lair
46. Immediate
48. Luau fare
49. Not flat
51. Mediocre
52. Steady
53. Room divider
54. ___ of entry
55. Tibia
56. Acorn, e.g.
57. Terminates
60. Bee chaser
61. Jinx
63. "___ Drives Me Crazy"

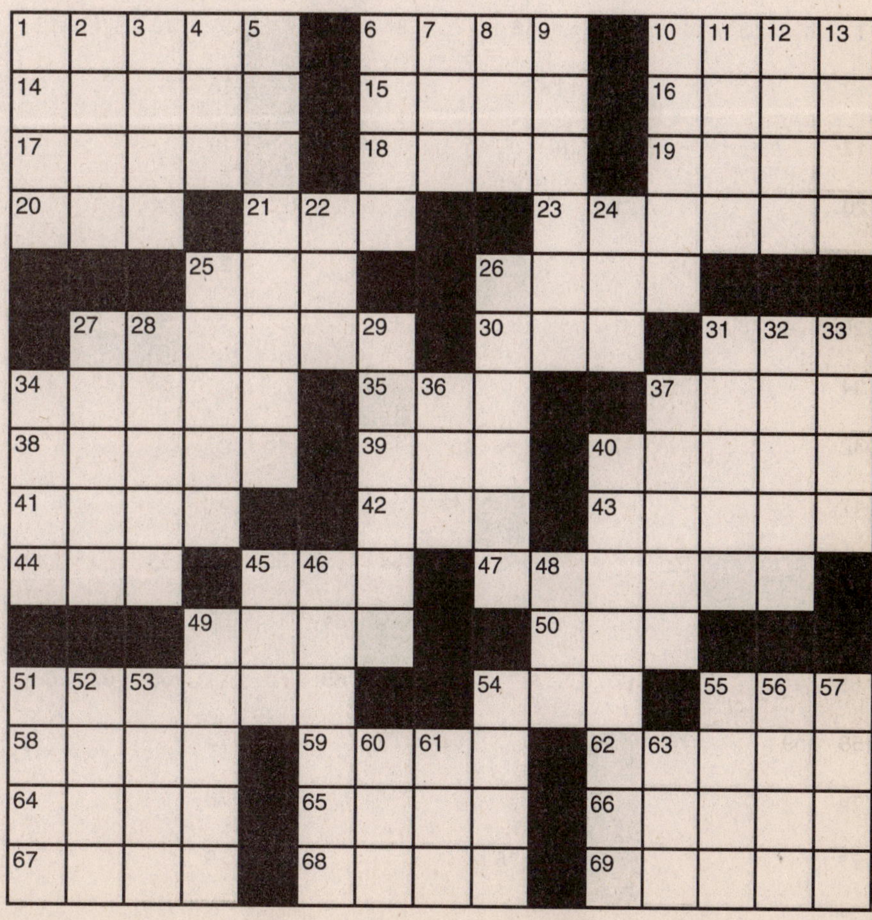

PUZZLE 327

ACROSS

1. Ran, as colors
5. Corridor
9. Bakery item
13. Not taped
14. Unsociable
16. Hound's trail
17. Soprano's solo
18. Utilize again
19. Salary
20. Sentimental song
22. Window bottom
24. Wordplay
25. Pose for a portrait
26. Signed up
28. Elope
31. Diary
33. Lady's guy
34. Preholiday nights
36. Dads
38. Transferred, as land
42. Kingdom
44. Chump
46. Blown liquid
47. Make beloved
49. Not nay
51. Put aside
52. Personality parts
54. Do sums
56. Crib or cot
57. "General ___"
61. Smash
63. Hill-building insect
64. Soft drink
65. Went over copy
69. Fibbed
71. Assessor
73. Dam
74. Musical quality
75. Happy face
76. Preacher's word
77. Snoot
78. Pens
79. Without

DOWN

1. Talk too much
2. Italian money unit, once
3. "___ Woman"
4. Distributes cards
5. Car style
6. Brewery brew
7. Scoundrel
8. Behind
9. Draw along
10. Change to fit
11. Rascal
12. Fashion
15. Cut down
21. Be sick
23. Ropes
27. Dance movements
28. "You ___ Meant for Me"
29. Flat
30. The Grateful ___
32. Cooking fuel
35. Slumber
37. Announce
39. Colorless
40. Overhang
41. Colored, as hair
43. Art of illusion
45. Black-eyed ___
48. Helicopter parts
50. Holds fast
53. Deli sausage
55. Achieved
57. Stops
58. Leek's cousin
59. Office worker
60. Caesar's language
62. Kind of wave
66. Tempo
67. ___ out (barely manages)
68. Fox shelters
70. Society newcomer
72. Moose's cousin

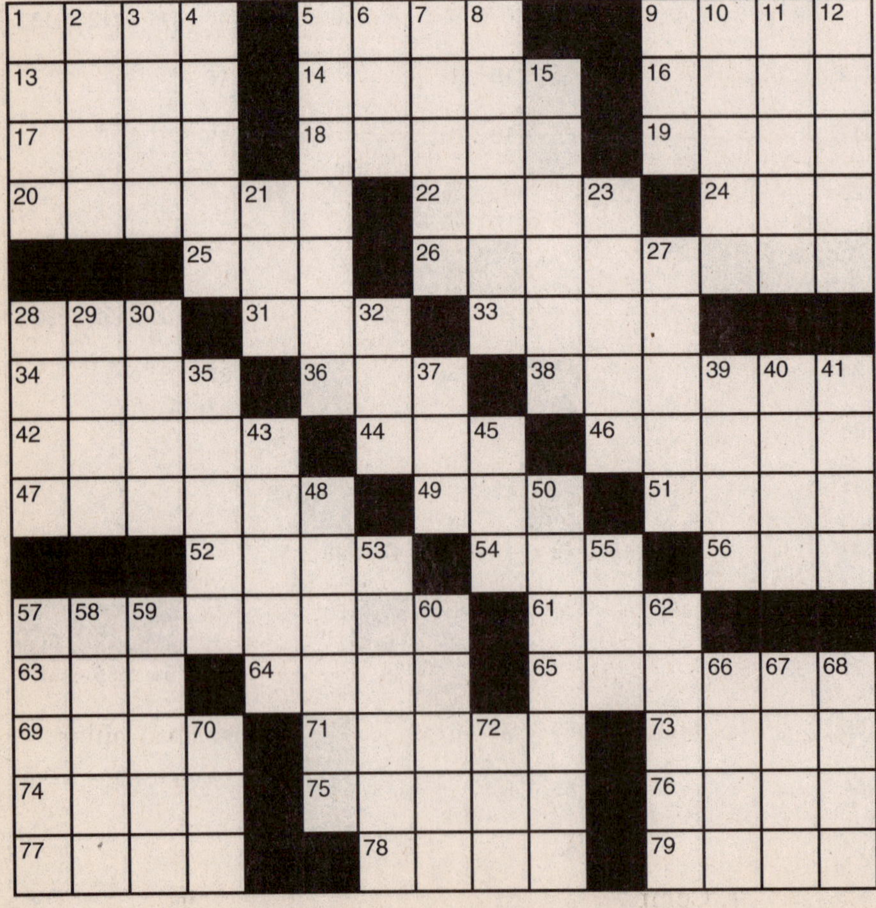

FULL CIRCLE

PUZZLE 328

To complete this circular puzzle fill in the answers to the AROUND clues in a clockwise direction. For the RADIAL clues move from the outside to the inside.

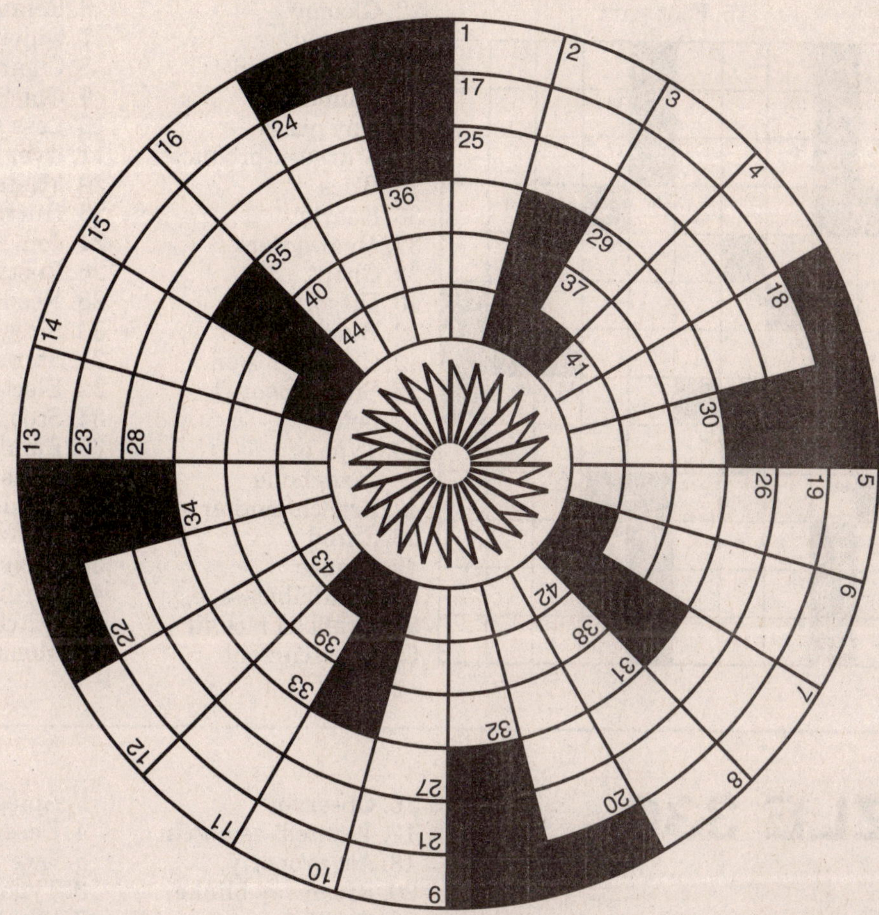

AROUND (Clockwise)

1. Honeymooner's look
5. European landmark site
9. Potential royalty?
13. Talk down about
17. Graven images
19. Objects
21. Knave
23. Bee colonies
25. He played Mr. Chips
26. Honey badger
27. Girder type
28. Conspicuous
29. Unkeyed, musically
31. Biscuits
33. Change over time
35. Honey, fermented
37. Mirth
38. Without self-control
39. Lustrous fabric
40. Pond growth
41. Take out, as text
42. Limber
43. Aquatic mammal
44. Tide type

RADIAL (Out to in)

1. Hurry, Dobbin!
2. Hoopla
3. Of an area
4. Joyful
5. Hook, for one
6. Where to find Bologna
7. Complete collection
8. Wee critters
9. Playful
10. Pilfer
11. S-shaped moldings
12. Tropical fruit
13. Garden tool
14. Rouse
15. Blvd.
16. Legendary Broadway belter
18. Heat source
20. Downturn
22. Ham it up
24. Inscribed pillar
30. Spades bid
32. And not
34. Meadow
36. Turkish official

PUZZLE 329

ACROSS
1. Castro's country
5. Road covering
8. High point
12. Oil gp.
13. Guitar's kin
14. Leg front
15. Foot part
16. "____ the season . . ."
17. Retain
18. Besides
19. Wise about
21. Lyric verse
22. Gloomy
25. Fretted
27. Aquatic bird
28. Rain drain
29. Hay grass
31. Sturgeon product
33. Woes
36. Nearly
37. Meat orders
39. Chop
40. Dissolve
42. Barrier
43. Capitalizes on
45. Shakespeare's before
46. Type of saxophone
47. French mother
48. Shred
49. Glance
50. Bouillabaisse, e.g.
51. Grabbed a chair
52. Crosscurrent

DOWN
1. Jackets
2. Pull weeds
3. Flatter
4. Bonn complaint
5. Private instructor
6. Related
7. Quiet
8. Cigar residue
9. Opt for
10. Less spicy
11. Over
20. Military unit
23. Hurrah
24. Join
26. Rusty
28. Needlefish
30. Sires
31. Storage space
32. Electrical unit
34. Scooped soup
35. Emulated Boitano
36. Grads
37. Cleaned the stoop
38. Hazy
41. Verdi melody
44. Stitch
46. Monkey's cousin

PUZZLE 330

ACROSS
1. "____ So Cold"
5. Pack away
9. Uno and uno
12. Mortgage
13. Keep the faith
14. Ump's call
15. Fairy-tale starter
16. Observer
17. Twisted, as a grin
18. Act properly
20. Broadway blinker
22. Phi Beta ____
24. Still sleeping
27. Plastic material
30. Shaky
32. "Much ____ About Nothing"
33. Verdi work
35. Honored fighter pilot
36. Gravely
38. Some tubs
40. Extensions
41. Savory jelly
43. View
45. Straighten
49. Pork
51. Miles off
53. Famous canal
54. Have unpaid bills
55. Pulls
56. Heroic tale
57. Mighty tool
58. Type of gin
59. Rebuff

DOWN
1. Untidy one
2. Sharpen
3. Apiece
4. Deceptive
5. Ewe
6. Type of poodle
7. Like an outdoor concert
8. "____ in the Money"
9. Pessimistic
10. Plural pronoun
11. Oinker's home
19. Heroism
21. Furniture wood
23. Quarries
25. Engrave
26. Changes color
27. Florist's container
28. Sacred cow
29. Lords
31. Rustic house
34. Frolicsome
37. Snaky curve
39. Entry
42. Bag
44. Taps lightly
46. Caspian Sea feeder
47. Latvian city
48. Dancer's jump
49. Short flight
50. Reverent dread
52. In the past

DOUBLE TROUBLE

PUZZLE 331

Not really double trouble, but double fun! Solve this puzzle as you would a regular crossword, except place one, two, or three letters in each box. The number of letters in each answer is shown in parentheses after its clue.

ACROSS

1. Orate (7)
5. Assistants (5)
9. Darling (8)
11. Going aimlessly (10)
12. Facial fuzz (5)
13. Payment (10)
15. Ruff's mate (3)
16. Fancy headpiece (5)
18. Marine hazards (6)
19. Guy's title (6)
20. Most luxurious (7)
22. Drudgery (5)
23. Covers completely (5)
24. Shorten, as a sail (4)
25. Sitting Bull foe (6)
26. Ship loader (9)
28. Prickly greenery (5)
29. Fierce look (5)
30. Croix de Guerre, e.g. (5)
32. Lowest tide (4)
33. Purplish red (7)
35. Sift (5)
36. Exerted (8)
38. Go someplace (6)
40. Opened a keg (6)
41. Sampled (6)

DOWN

1. Welsher (8)
2. Liqueur (7)
3. Hideaway (4)
4. Paddock parent (4)
5. Bearing (6)
6. Likewise (3)
7. Searched about (8)
8. Snitch on (6)
10. Imperfections (9)
11. Sodium and lithium (6)
14. Breakfast food (5)
17. Rowdily (9)
19. Deceived (11)
21. Splinter (7)
22. Avarice (5)
24. Very respectful (8)
25. Bunkum (8)
26. Put on (5)
27. Most facile (7)
28. Upright (6)
29. Mirthful (4)
31. Razed (7)
33. Burrowed (5)
34. Acidic (4)
37. Emulate (3)
39. Ms. Haddad (3)

1	2	3	4				5	6	7	8
9				10		11				
12			13		14				15	
16		17		18				19		
	20		21				22			
		23				24				
	25				26				27	
28				29				30		31
32			33				34		35	
36		37				38		39		
40							41			

Foursomes

PUZZLE 332

In each puzzle the letters have a different numerical value from 1 to 9. Four sums of combinations of four letters are indicated by the arrows. For example, in the first puzzle, 17 is the sum of the values of the letters I, T, U, and E. Find the values of the letters and place them on the correspondingly numbered blanks to spell a word or phrase. The center letter is entered to start you off.

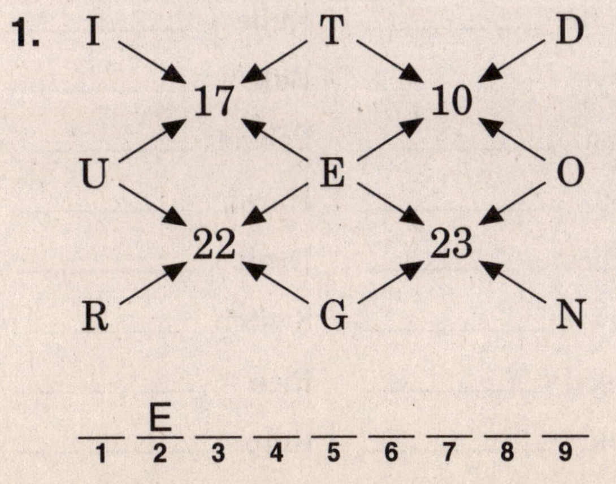

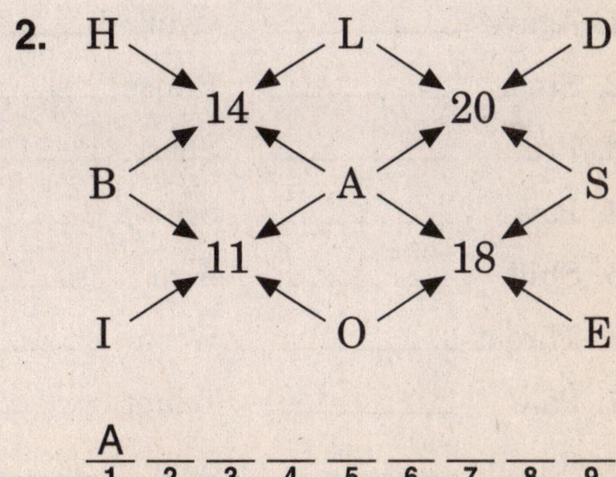

PUZZLE 333

ACROSS

1. Covers with turf
5. Reed instrument
9. Window feature
13. Came to ground
14. Tropical trees
16. Pay to play
17. Hawaiian goose
18. Hogwash
19. Quartet
20. Doctrine
22. Hot streak
23. Last bits
24. Slangy chum
26. Louts
28. Subtraction phrase
32. Up, in baseball
36. Jollity
37. Interpret
39. Fleecy mama
40. Outline
41. Muslim ruler
43. Wings
44. Generation
45. Hunch
46. Not well
48. Venture-some one
50. Seques-tered
52. Screen
54. Abundance
55. Corn bin
58. Cease
60. Western event
65. Protag-onist
66. Doddering
68. Aria singer
69. Limbless animal
70. Electri-cian, often
71. Unrefined metals
72. Small horse
73. Caution
74. Lease payment

1	2	3	4	■	5	6	7	8	■	■	9	10	11	12
13				■	14				15	■	16			
17				■	18					■	19			
20				21	■	22				■	23			
■	■	■	■	24	25		■	26		27		■	■	■
■	28	29	30				31		■	32		33	34	35
36						■	37		38		■	39		
40				■	41	42				■	43			
44			■	45				■	46	47				
48			49		■	50		51						■
■	■	■	52		53		■	54			■	■	■	■
55	56	57		■	58		59		■	60	61	62	63	64
65				■	66				67	■	68			
69				■	70					■	71			
72				■	■	73				■	74			

DOWN

1. Beach blanket?
2. Surrogate butter
3. Dent
4. Bloom holder
5. Make a selection
6. Brit's pushcart
7. Mixture
8. Boss's underling
9. Most secure
10. Soon
11. Wall support
12. For the lady
15. Ward of Hollywood
21. Help
25. Spoked
27. Craze
28. Subarctic forest
29. Pointer
30. Knowledge
31. Of a region
33. Disprove
34. Accolade
35. Abound
36. Lighthearted
38. Get up
42. Engine expert
43. Sternward
45. Dudgeon
47. Close
49. Express tangibly
51. Worker at an inn
53. "Pygmalion" author
55. Fellow
56. Default result
57. Symbol of strength
59. Milano money, once
61. Nose wrinkler
62. Drastic
63. Fairly matched
64. Grain oven
67. Prior to, in verse

PUZZLE 334

Family Ties

Each group contains four unrelated words. Without rearranging the letters, change one letter in each of the words to form four related words.

Example: Rise, Lilt, Patsy, Ires (**Answer:** Rose, Lily, Pansy, Iris)

1. Agave	________	Oval	________	Wade	________	Rube	________
2. Stem	________	Praise	________	Pry	________	Bale	________
3. Press	________	Short	________	Vast	________	Packet	________
4. Poor	________	Scamp	________	Fez	________	Harsh	________
5. Shill	________	Arm	________	Trace	________	Draft	________
6. Threat	________	Waste	________	Saw	________	Switch	________
7. Pale	________	Tempt	________	Steed	________	Rice	________
8. Retail	________	Sane	________	Bold	________	Kelp	________

PUZZLE 335

ACROSS

1. Seaweed extract
5. Vocal
9. Crosswise
14. Dominion
15. Krupa of jazz
16. Film genre
17. Female dancer
19. Cote dwellers
20. Reproductive cells
21. Strip
23. Left
24. Spoked
26. Dud
28. Harmony
31. Regret
32. Sternward
35. Arrest
38. Angers
40. Sprinter
42. Natural emollient
43. Hades river
45. Take out text
46. Bizarre
48. Bucket
49. Unused
50. Knowledge
51. Bard's work
53. Knee bend
55. Game bird
57. Strikes
61. Fall
64. "____ Bovary"
67. Luau necklace
68. Squirted
70. Urn holders
72. Gawker
73. Muslim prince
74. Bearded bloom
75. Overgrown
76. Fare
77. Alluring

DOWN

1. Vine frame
2. Jelly fruit
3. Soothe
4. Electric unit
5. Shrek or Fiona
6. Harness part
7. Cancel
8. Chair's job
9. Total up
10. Tanned
11. Roof edge
12. Preacher's word
13. Tall spar
18. Vortex
22. Ratite bird
25. Organic compound
27. Above, in verse
29. Nothing
30. Party decoration
32. Passed easily
33. Tripped
34. Cherry, e.g.
35. Falcon
36. Downwind
37. Meat cut
39. Greek vowel
41. Sayonara
44. Pipe type
47. Wear
52. Lusterless
54. Frosts
55. Zoom
56. Plant disease
58. Blaze
59. Cartoon cat
60. Coward
61. Reveal
62. Opera box
63. Man, e.g.
65. Mine entrance
66. Only
69. Evaporate
71. McCourt book

1	2	3	4	■	5	6	7	8	■	9	10	11	12	13
14				■	15				■	16				
17				18					■	19				
20			■	21					22	■	23			
24			25		■	■	26			27		■	■	■
■	■	■	28		29	30	■	31			■	32	33	34
35	36	37		■	38		39		■	40	41			
42				■	43				44	■	45			
46				47	■	48				■	49			
50			■	51	52		■	53		54		■	■	■
■	■	■	55				56	■	■	57		58	59	60
61	62	63		■	64			65	66		■	67		
68				69	■	70					71			
72					■	73				■	74			
75					■	76				■	77			

Wacky Words

PUZZLE 336

Rearrange each group of letters to form a word with one letter left over. When done correctly, these words form a wacky definition of the word formed by the leftover letters when read from top to bottom.

	DEFINITION	WORD
ETHA	☐☐☐	☐
ELPCOPE	☐☐☐☐☐☐	☐
CHWO	☐☐☐	☐
NRRU	☐☐☐	☐
UA	☐	☐
EPSIH	☐☐☐☐	☐

PUZZLE 337 BRICK BY BRICK

Rearrange this stack of bricks to form a crossword puzzle. The clues will help you fit the bricks into their correct places. Row 1 has been filled in for you. Use the bricks to fill in the remaining spaces.

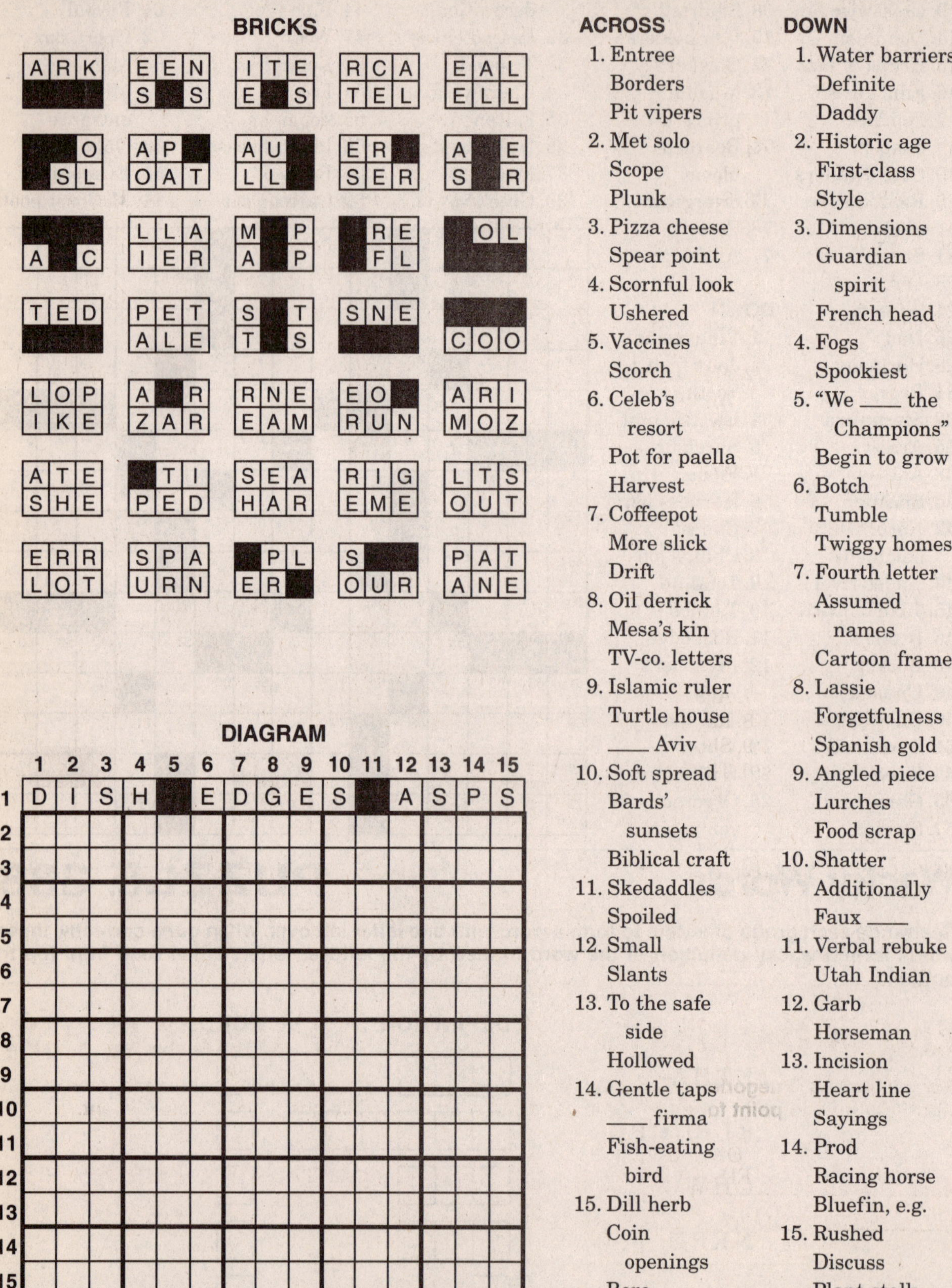

ACROSS

1. Entree
Borders
Pit vipers
2. Met solo
Scope
Plunk
3. Pizza cheese
Spear point
4. Scornful look
Ushered
5. Vaccines
Scorch
6. Celeb's resort
Pot for paella
Harvest
7. Coffeepot
More slick
Drift
8. Oil derrick
Mesa's kin
TV-co. letters
9. Islamic ruler
Turtle house
____ Aviv
10. Soft spread
Bards' sunsets
Biblical craft
11. Skedaddles
Spoiled
12. Small
Slants
13. To the safe side
Hollowed
14. Gentle taps
____ firma
Fish-eating bird
15. Dill herb
Coin openings
Bore

DOWN

1. Water barriers
Definite
Daddy
2. Historic age
First-class
Style
3. Dimensions
Guardian spirit
French head
4. Fogs
Spookiest
5. "We ____ the Champions"
Begin to grow
6. Botch
Tumble
Twiggy homes
7. Fourth letter
Assumed names
Cartoon frame
8. Lassie
Forgetfulness
Spanish gold
9. Angled piece
Lurches
Food scrap
10. Shatter
Additionally
Faux ____
11. Verbal rebuke
Utah Indian
12. Garb
Horseman
13. Incision
Heart line
Sayings
14. Prod
Racing horse
Bluefin, e.g.
15. Rushed
Discuss
Plant stalk

PUZZLE 338

ACROSS

1. Sponge
6. Jail-cell components
10. Cold War letters
14. Inuit's abode
15. Got down
16. Type of shark
17. Kate Nelligan film
18. Undermined
20. Las Vegas sign
21. Secondhand
22. Have bills
23. "____ Always Loved You"
25. Confederate general
26. Eat at another's expense
30. Removes a hat
35. Service expense
36. Observer
37. Escape from
38. Birch variety
40. Paddle
42. Accumulate
43. Skirt feature
44. Congressional assistant
46. Totally awesome!
47. Reduce gradually
49. Of a major blood vessel
51. Different
53. Immature amphibian
54. Messy dwelling
57. Chaos
60. Farmer's harvest
64. Airplane device
66. Seacoast
67. Luminous radiation
68. Knicks, e.g.
69. Calmness
70. Convene
71. Serpents
72. Madison Avenue employee

DOWN

1. Demeanor
2. Stare at
3. Margarine
4. Stevens of "Susan Slade"
5. ____ polloi
6. Foundation
7. Alack!
8. Raunchy
9. Shoplifted
10. Thurman of "Prime"
11. Palm starch
12. Depict unfairly
13. Traveled by bus
19. ____ off (furious)
21. Put faith (in)
24. Change direction
26. "The Most Happy ____"
27. Immerse again
28. Tennyson's atop
29. Bellowing
31. Repeatedly, to Keats
32. Fauna's partner
33. Untamed
34. Begonia's beginning
35. Swift
39. Parisian season
41. Clever humor
42. Peasant
45. Consider
48. Kimono, e.g.
49. Confuses
50. Yearned
52. "____ Dawn" (Reddy song)
54. Junk e-mail
55. Proven
56. Olden days
58. Hurdle
59. "A Farewell to ____"
61. Wander
62. "Jaws" boat
63. Hammerhead part
65. Butter square
66. Luxury hotel

End of the Line

PUZZLE 339

For each of the categories listed, can you think of a word or phrase ending with each letter on the right? Count one point for each correct answer. A score of 15 is good, and 21 is excellent.

COLORS	ONE-WORD FILM TITLES	LIQUIDS	WORLD CAPITALS	BIRDS	
					S
					H
					A
					R
					K

PUZZLE 340 AT 6'S AND 7'S

Clues to all the 6- and 7-letter entries in this crossword are listed first, and they are in scrambled order. Use the numbered clues as solving hints to help you determine where each one belongs in the diagram.

6-LETTER ENTRIES
Lowers
Calyx parts
Close up again
Give the cold shoulder
Small apartment
Hindu chant
Counsel
Pas de deux duet
Island wear
Finishes a salad
Family cars
Bitsy biter
Nomad
Classify
Rents again
Intrinsic
Meal
Mad as a hatter, e.g.

7-LETTER ENTRIES
____ store
Lobster, e.g.
Romantic one
Blessing
Bitter derision
Contrition
Adjusts
German pastry
Like some volcanoes
Twiddles one's thumbs
Religious hermit
Margarita maker
Posh
Vague discomfort
Sound systems
Home of the brave

ACROSS
13. Long in the tooth
18. Nuptial word
21. Boxing count
24. Glut
25. Left at sea
28. Bronze or Iron
30. Hollywood gp.
33. Strict
38. Church corner
40. Vortex
42. Cherish
43. Biggest Little City
44. Workout site
46. Pitcher
48. "Stand" band
49. Hands
50. Purpose
51. Mimic a crow
52. Clip contents
53. Mood
54. Fencing foil
55. Vote for
56. '60s musical
57. Top of the head
59. Cut short
61. Uninvited picnickers
64. Bellows
68. Links prop
69. Chill
72. Battle mark
75. Expunge
81. Sum total
85. Xenon, e.g.
88. Brouhaha

DOWN
1. Part of amu
2. Assist
3. Scruff
4. Ivan and Peter
7. Investment plan
9. Maritime
10. Skip
12. Poetic before
13. Hip about
14. Nasty look
15. Make an impression?
23. Take to court
25. Hang
29. Paraphernalia
34. Alternate route
39. This second!
44. Dupe
45. Cake serving
47. Farm mom
52. Gotcha!
54. DeMille work
58. Den
65. In the past
70. Parade unit
71. Attacks
72. Adventure
73. Outfitted
74. To boot
76. Sea bird
78. Auspices
79. Green shade
80. Pedal pushers?
82. Finish a lap
83. Golly!

1	2	3	4	5	6	■	7	8	9	10	11	12	■	13	14	15
16						■	17						■	18		
19						■	20						■	21		
22						23	■	24				■	25			
■	■	■	26				27			■	28	29		■	■	■
30	31	32	■	33					■	34				35	36	37
38			39	■	■	■	40		41		■	42				
43				■	44	45		■	46		47		■	48		
49				■	50			■	51			■	52			
53			■	54					55			■	56			
57			58		■	59		60		■	■	■	61			
62					63		■	64		65	66	67	■	68		
■	■	■	69			■	70						71	■	■	■
72	73	74		■	75	76			■	77				78	79	80
81			■	82					83	■	84					
85			■	86						■	87					
88			■	89						■	90					

CODEWORD

PUZZLE 341

Codeword is a special crossword puzzle in which conventional clues are omitted. Instead, answer words in the diagram are represented by numbers. Each number represents a different letter of the alphabet, and all of the letters of the alphabet are used. When you are sure of a letter, put it in the code key chart and cross it off in the alphabet box. A group of letters has been inserted to start you off.

1	14	
2	15	
3	16	
4	17	
5	18	
6	19 P	
7	20	
8	21	
9	22	
10	23	
11	24	
12 O	25	
13 T	26	

3	6	13	■	2	8	9	■	22	25	13	■	13 T	25	23
25	21	12	■	12	25	7	■	25	5	12	■	12 O	22	6
26	12	18	19	9	13	6	■	11	3	24	■	19 P	12	14
■	■	■	12	23	6	■	9	17	6	■	17	25	18	6
2	16	12	22	5	17	■	19	6	22	■	26	20	25	22
22	25	22	6	■	10	11	5	■	1	22	25	■	■	■
12	5	5	17	■	12	5	12	22	■	6	22	22	17	■
21	6	6	■	25	14	8	■	25	5	5	■	12	23	17
■	5	22	25	18	■	6	5	21	24	■	4	9	11	19
■	■	■	17	19	25	■	24	6	23	■	9	23	13	12
10	25	26	7	■	5	6	6	■	25	18	11	5	17	13
12	14	6	17	■	16	25	22	■	18	11	8	■	■	■
13	25	5	■	2	12	22	■	17	11	15	13	6	6	23
6	7	6	■	12	11	8	■	25	13	6	■	6	22	25
8	6	5	■	6	23	17	■	14	6	5	■	8	6	21

A	N
B	~~O~~
C	~~P~~
D	Q
E	R
F	S
G	~~T~~
H	U
I	V
J	W
K	X
L	Y
M	Z

Anagram Quotes

PUZZLE 342

Unscramble the set of letters below each blank to complete the quotations.

1. ________ is a ______ and _____ a _______ .
IITTNAROD DUGEI TON LIJARE

2. If ________ is the ______ ________ of _____ , ____________
ARDEB TRSIF YESNICEST FLEI INTOCAREER

is a ______ ________ .
SOCEL DONCES

PUZZLE 343

ACROSS

1. Weakens
5. Command to Lassie
9. Football bomb
13. ___ vera
14. Farm gate
15. Light rhythm
16. Auditioner's goal
17. Uproar
19. Pen fluid
20. Shipped
21. Remove stitches
22. Harbors
24. Shoe front
25. Not theirs
26. Total of salaries
30. Snort
33. Triangular sail
34. Call of disapproval
35. ___ down (washed)
36. Witch
37. Splotches
39. Have title to
40. Mission
41. Most melancholy
42. Shooting stars
45. Particles of sand
46. Grand Coulee, e.g.
47. Caves
51. Divide evenly
54. Dang!
55. Strike suddenly
56. Dental tool
59. Ho-hum
60. Hairstyle
61. Backsides
62. Unique being
63. Saloon brew
64. Electrical units
65. Troublesome thing

DOWN

1. Indian garments
2. Without company
3. Lively dance
4. Glimpse
5. Feats
6. Tips slightly
7. The whole amount
8. "___, though I . . ."
9. Surfacing machine
10. Needs aspirin
11. Type of gin
12. Stash away
14. Wine
18. Navigational marker
20. Noise
23. Corn cake
24. Account
26. Porky of cartoons
27. Slender woodwind
28. Plenty
29. Preoccupied
30. To ___ it may concern
31. Gordie or Elias
32. "___ It Romantic?"
33. Pack tightly
36. Belonging to him
37. Narrow cuts
38. Golfer's tap
40. Twist someone's ___
41. Consommes
43. Magazine VIP
44. Sworn promise
45. Clutches
47. Sourpuss
48. Atmosphere layer
49. Comforts
50. Hockey or golf
51. Cigar remnant
52. John XXIII, e.g.
53. Valuable vein
57. Bathing-suit part
58. Liquor from molasses
59. Dunk

PUZZLE 344

ACROSS

1. Nudge
5. Least adequate
10. Idle chatter
14. NBC's peacock, e.g.
15. Rapidly
16. Lounging wear
17. Boat blades
18. Container
20. "I ___ of Jeannie"
22. Reflex-test joint
23. Lady lobster
24. Hindu teacher
27. Look after
29. Obeying
32. Makes it?
35. Sly one
36. By way of
37. Blouses
39. An inning has six
41. Inclined
43. Bouillon
44. Sign up
46. Maui garland
47. "___ Which Way You Can"
48. Baby's father
49. Shouting
52. Bends
55. Sharp
56. Noisy dispute
59. Courage
61. A tiny Tom
65. Fair
69. Voyaging
70. "Spenser: For ___"
71. Oversight
72. Star performer
73. Editor's direction
74. Goddess, e.g.
75. Sea eagle

DOWN

1. Walk heavily
2. Din
3. Fiend
4. Medicine amount
5. Military conflict
6. Unclose, in verse
7. Luggage holder
8. Perfume
9. Indian home
10. Lingerie item
11. Lake, in Scotland
12. Skillful
13. "I've ___ Lonely Too Long"
19. Tin anniversary
21. Sludge
25. Competitor
26. Army group
28. Podium
29. Annoy relentlessly
30. Additional
31. Merrily
33. Mournful sound
34. Bitten by a bee
35. Opponent
37. Fence step
38. Agent
40. Fountain beverage
42. Onion's kin
45. Enormous
50. Court call
51. Breathe in
53. Diced
54. Inventory
56. Bowl cheers
57. Final notice
58. Became frayed
60. Eastern garment
62. Consumer
63. Cruel
64. Commanded
66. Old soldier
67. Disintegrate
68. Without water

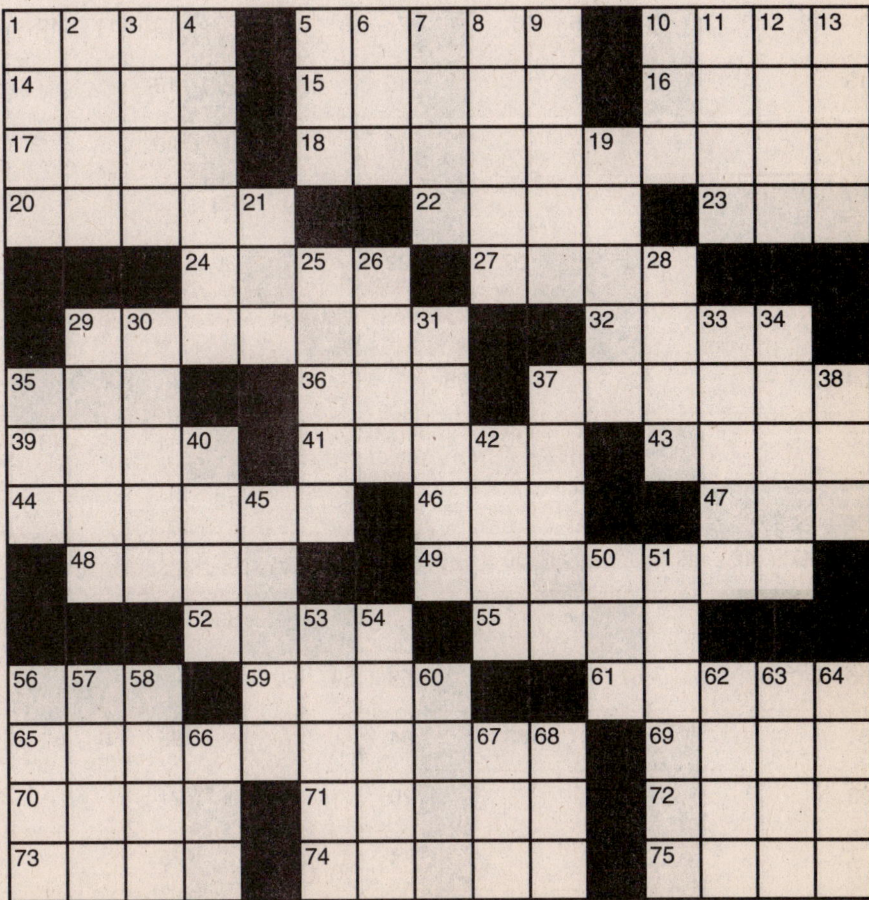

PUZZLE 345

ACROSS

1. To some extent
4. Elec. unit
7. Get older
10. Monkey's uncle
13. Rightful
14. Polite address
15. Burst open
16. Call loudly
17. Vulgar
19. Fasten, as a shoe
20. Average grade
21. Fedoras, e.g.
22. Closer
24. Froster
27. Zip
30. Sisters
31. Skirt type
32. Cord necktie
33. Picnic drinks
34. Too proper
36. Constantly
38. Movie locale
39. Repel's opposite
41. Pair
44. Noteworthy act
45. Word connector
47. Projecting roof edge
50. Game of chance
52. Strong cord
53. Hold onto
54. Give up
55. On the ___ (quarreling)
56. Author
58. Shoulder burden?
61. Football player
62. Captured
64. Fez danglers
68. It's a moray
69. Thick stuff
70. Tutto
71. Solicit
72. Urger's word
73. Cloud's place
74. Shad product
75. Wane

DOWN

1. Chaos
2. Knob
3. Oui
4. Sailing
5. After-dinner candy
6. Immediately
7. Fitting
8. Leaving
9. Parrier's blade
10. Amass
11. Spruces up
12. Observers
18. Tennis's Evert
23. Furthermore
24. Wild kids
25. Be concerned
26. Leave the stage
28. Forewarned
29. Bossa ___
32. Group of computer bits
33. Mannered
35. Strongbox
37. Parrot
40. Confiscate
41. Ten C-notes
42. Bawled
43. Single units
46. Braces
47. Moneymaker
48. Eagerly
49. Dobbin's doc
51. Bee's drink
53. Hardly sour
54. Swindler
57. Hen grenades
59. Heavenly headwear
60. Bit of land
63. Squirt gun, e.g.
65. Meadow mower
66. Toss
67. Shed a tear

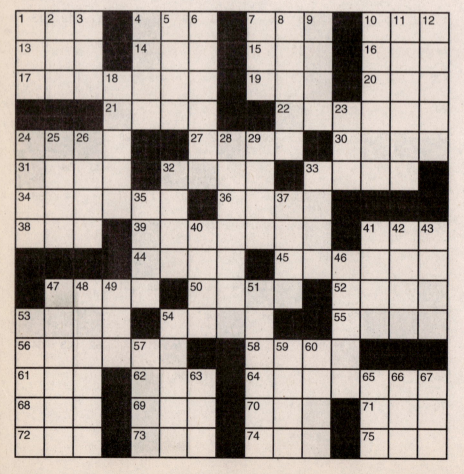

1	2	3	■	4	5	6	■	7	8	9	■	10	11	12
13			■	14			■	15			■	16		
17			18				■	19			■	20		
■	■	■	21				■	■	22		23			
24	25	26		■	■	27	28	29		■	30			
31				■	32				■	33				■
34				35		■	36		37		■	■	■	■
38			■	39		40					■	41	42	43
■	■	■	■	44				■	45		46			
■	47	48	49		■	50		51		■	52			
53			■	54					■	■	55			
56				57		■	■	58	59	60		■	■	■
61			■	62		63	■	64				65	66	67
68			■	69			■	70			■	71		
72			■	73			■	74			■	75		

PUZZLE 346

ACROSS
1. Thickens
5. Animal pouch
8. Thick slice
12. Sincere appeal
13. Rub clean
15. Stream
16. Swinging cadence
17. Babe Ruth specialty
18. Very light beige
19. Dined
20. That lady
21. Unanchored
23. Nope's opposite
24. On the Atlantic
26. Unwell
27. Cackler
29. Ho-hum
31. Large vessel
34. Berate
36. Cast
37. Self-image
38. Gas containers
39. Rush
40. Moves gradually
42. Tiny Tim's instrument
43. Elms and oaks
45. Sorry people
46. Rose plot
47. Zeroes in
48. Favorite
49. Hostel
50. Barcelona bull
53. Fitting
56. Medals
59. "Never ___ Me Go"
60. Paving liquid
61. Lean and ___
62. Wash away
65. Ocean cycle
66. Widow's ___ (small sum)
67. Wooden pin
68. Business
69. Slipped
70. Decimal base
71. Dollar bills

DOWN
1. Spread out
2. Nobility
3. Called
4. Posed for a picture
5. Tally
6. Body part
7. Hint
8. Magic words
9. Daft
10. Halo
11. Very dry champagne
13. "___ So Cold"
14. Cook slowly
20. Tumbler's feat
22. Bloom holder
25. Palest
28. Large deer
30. Mine finds
31. Plant life
32. Golden ___ (retiree)
33. Pitch lightly
34. Pencil remainder
35. Bar of soap
36. Those folks
41. Payable
44. Washed
49. Irritated
51. Of the past
52. Angler's tool
54. Father
55. Difficult journeys
56. Gifts to charity
57. Lament
58. Opposed to
63. Decompose
64. Be beholden to
65. Noah's number

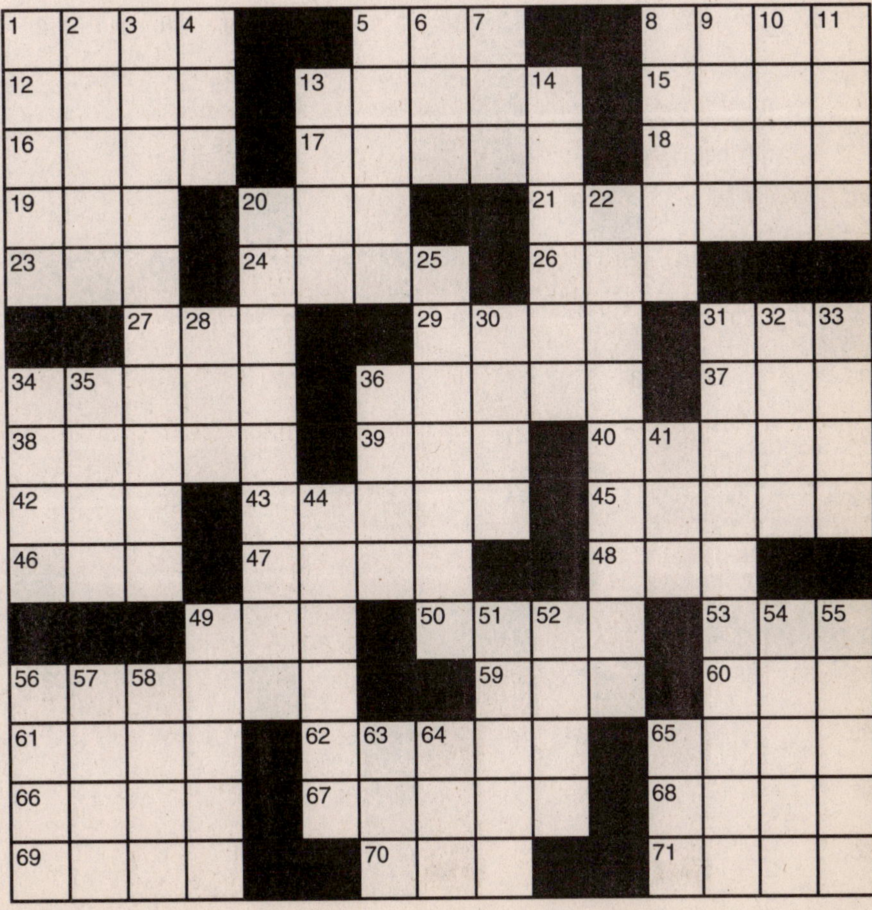

PUZZLE 347

ACROSS

1. Sand bar
6. Draw upon
9. Legendary tale
13. American birds
15. Athens vowel
16. TV's "Miami ___"
17. List of corrections
18. Clever remark
19. Duel tool
20. Associate
21. Reindeer herders
23. Beatty film
24. Cat call
26. Southern potato
28. Reply
32. Makeshift bed
35. Charged particle
36. Tizzies
37. Moved in a curve
39. Hindu pundit
41. Puppy's bite
42. Showy flower
43. Tin or iron
44. Crow
46. Certain poem
47. Art ___
48. Pupils
50. "___ Day Now"
52. Irritated
53. Leave a mark
56. More ancient
59. Hot tubs
63. Angelic headlight
64. Colorful carp
65. Tempt
67. Biblical preposition
68. Hen's product
69. Calorie counter
70. Electric sign gas
71. Rules to follow
72. Shop

DOWN

1. Trickle
2. Aesop racer
3. Fairy-tale heavy
4. Warnings
5. Said yes to
6. Substitute worker
7. On
8. Fall guy
9. Always
10. Cleaner or dream
11. Frozen
12. So-so grades
14. Pub
22. Rooflike shelters
25. Greek E
27. Converter
28. Oared
29. Growing out
30. Walking pole
31. Embrace, as a cause
33. Move quickly
34. Forwards
35. Doctrine
38. Hair tint
40. Coconut cookie
45. Worshiped
49. Empty ___
51. Harnessed
53. Keep away from
54. Wickerwork material
55. Choir voice
57. Symbol
58. Leakey sites
60. Flat bread
61. Made a hole in one
62. Shriveled
66. Critic's pick?

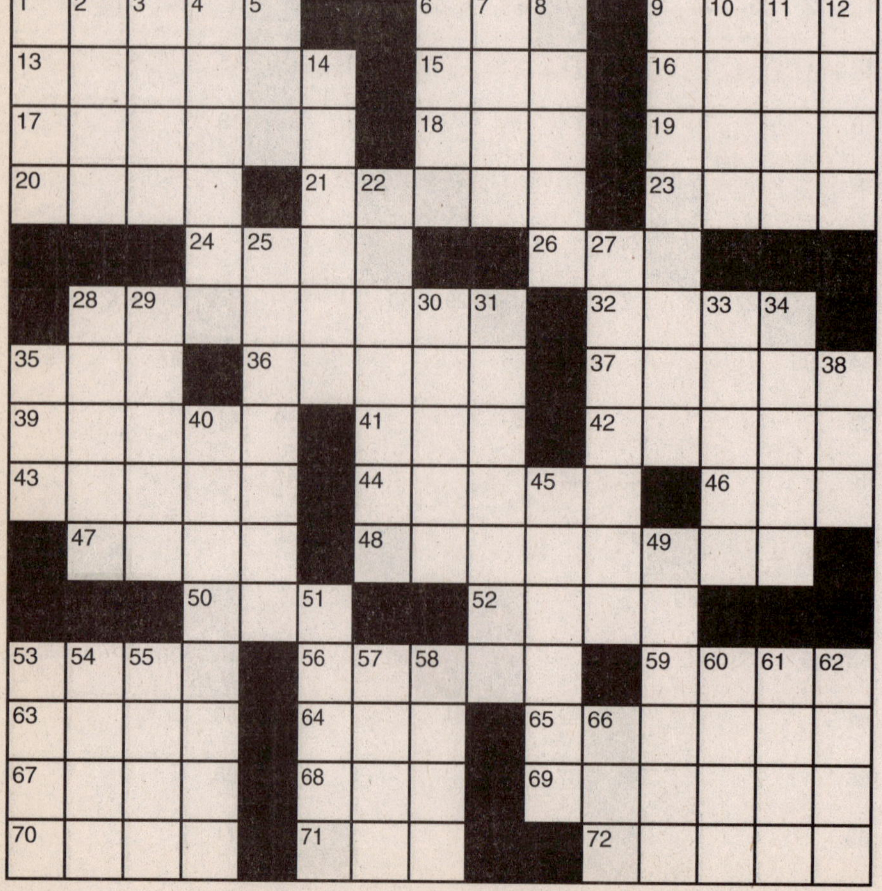

PUZZLE 348

ACROSS

1. Openings
5. Alcoholic brew
9. Not he
12. Defeat soundly
13. Strengthened
15. Bo Derek's number
16. Opponent
17. Writer
18. Totally awesome!
19. Divert
21. Miner's find
22. "___ Always Loved You"
23. Guitar's kin
24. Natty
26. Black birds
30. Subject
32. CIA employee
33. Active one
34. Head gestures
38. Memory joggers
39. Night animal
40. Discard
41. Mr. Stravinsky
42. Snow glider
43. Royal headwear
44. Epoxy user, e.g.
46. Rudder handle
47. Drawing stick
50. Feel unwell
51. Always, to a poet
52. Everything
54. Water bird
59. Musical twosome
60. Carpenter, often
62. Industrial fuel
63. 19th letter
64. Smudges
65. Fix text
66. Understand
67. Baby collies
68. Animals' shelters

DOWN

1. Alum
2. Tiptop
3. Strike a golf ball
4. Rustle
5. Beast
6. Gobble up
7. Canyon's answer
8. Request again
9. Runway
10. ___ ho!
11. Closer
13. Supports
14. Nighttime vision
20. Em and Bee
25. Writing tool
26. Rajah's mate
27. Fascinated
28. Prohibit
29. Available power
30. Bell's site, often
31. Gripped
33. Disburse in parts
35. Spoken
36. Be bold
37. Dispute
40. Yet
42. Indoor ray-deliverer
45. Lends
46. Rows
47. Relinquishes
48. Recycle
49. Materialized
50. Imitators
53. In ___ of
55. Like summertime tea
56. Morse or ZIP
57. Comparable
58. Hair protectors
61. Drink like a cat

PUZZLE 349

ACROSS

1. Whirlpool, e.g.
4. Baby's protector
7. Hi-fi item
10. I topper
13. Hosiery color
14. "People ___ Funny"
15. Notice
16. Self-esteem
17. Performance
18. Permitted
19. Tree's juice
20. Winter virus
21. Complaints
23. In one's bunk
25. Watcher
26. Flight
28. Coral islands
30. Toro's lure
33. ___ a living!
35. ___ up (enlightened)
38. Nautical term
39. Medicine measure
41. Moray catcher
43. Main squeeze?
44. Removable cover
45. Troops
47. King beater
48. Penitent
50. Skip
52. Halt!
53. Plants
55. Sun's path
56. Not his
57. Heavens to ___!
59. Color tone
61. Silver coin
64. Hammer, e.g.
66. Biblical song
70. Tangy drink
71. Attack command
72. Shelley poem
74. Through
75. Itch
76. First mobile home?
77. Sardine container
78. Rascal
79. Depressed
80. Certainly
81. Uncanny
82. Mayday!

DOWN

1. Pierce
2. Measured tread
3. Up-front bid
4. Model wood
5. Fury
6. Greek letter
7. Valuable thing
8. Field
9. Verve
10. Disobey
11. Gawk
12. Journey
22. Run off
24. Fiddle or drum
25. You're something ___!
27. South of France
29. Right to property
30. Vehicles for hire
31. Reserved
32. Sea jewel
34. Hubbub
36. Overjoy
37. Room design
40. Top sheik
42. Agents, for short
44. Small harp
46. Imprint firmly
49. Kimono
51. BLT dressing
52. "___ So Cold"
54. Apparel
58. Anklets
60. Capsize
61. 24-hour periods
62. Scheme
63. Heal
65. Like a crazy hombre
67. Latin warbler
68. Exec's auto
69. Atlas contents
71. Utter
73. Father

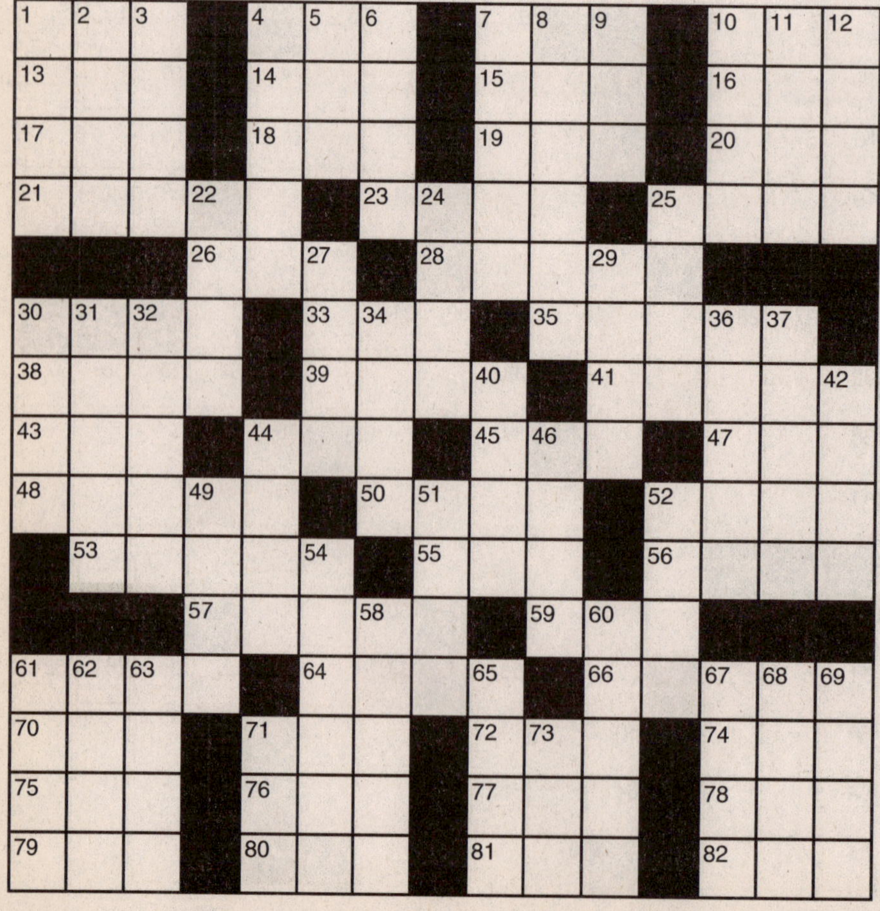

PUZZLE 350

ACROSS

1. Fore-and-___
4. Beach toy
8. Social class
13. Life story
14. Marshy inlet
15. Not of this planet
16. Shade tree
17. Sporting facility
18. Distributed
19. Go ashore
21. Make ___ of
23. Type measures
24. Place in office
26. Cap-gun sound
28. Grate
31. Mexican sauce
34. Curves
38. Select
39. Short skirt
40. Bend out of shape
41. Glacial mass
43. Made of a hardwood
44. "___ Wars"
45. Aloud
46. Musical club
47. Bartender's rocks
48. Spelling error
49. Wipe again
51. Wisecrack
52. Unhappiness
54. Couch
56. Certain sprite
59. Pose a question
61. Turkey's comment
65. More wretched
67. Develop
70. Feel poorly
71. Summon
72. Social equals
73. Those elected
74. Married again
75. Course book
76. Game prop

DOWN

1. Slumbering
2. Manicure item
3. Pyramid, for some
4. Winter jackets
5. Sailor's yes
6. Positive atom
7. Hawaiian cookout
8. Brief film role
9. Capp's drink
10. Location
11. Abound
12. Comes to a close
14. Vacant
20. Certain adder
22. Barcelona's nation
25. Mexican food
27. Bears' feet
28. R2D2, e.g.
29. Mimicry
30. Shoulder band
32. Found agreeable
33. Shows contempt
35. Proportion
36. Crevice
37. Binge
42. Flush
43. Fairy-tale monsters
50. Custardlike food
51. Poke sharply
53. Propelled
55. Enemies
56. Eternally
57. Abide
58. Ebb and ___
60. Maintained
62. Enticement
63. Border
64. In a different way
66. ___ out (barely make)
68. Born
69. Gender

1	2	3	■	■	4	5	6	7	■	8	9	10	11	12
13			■	14					■	15				
16			■	17					■	18				
19			20			■	■	21	22		■	23		
■	■	■	24			25	■	■	26		27	■	■	■
28	29	30		■	31		32	33		■	34	35	36	37
38			■	■	■	39				■	40			
41			42	■	43					■	44			
45				■	46				■	■	■	47		
48				■	49				50	■	51			
■	■	■	52	53		■	■	54		55		■	■	■
56	57	58	■	59		60	■	■	61			62	63	64
65			66		■	67	68	69			■	70		
71					■	72					■	73		
74					■	75				■	■	76		

PUZZLE 351

ACROSS

1. As well
5. Auctioned off
9. Angered
13. Overly proud
14. Amalgam
15. London trolley
16. Makes like
17. Duck
18. Breakfast order
19. Part of TGIF
20. Trim
21. Bathing-suit part
22. City property
23. Exploits
25. Preacher's target
28. Bucket
30. Popular seafood
32. Climbing vine
33. Cuts off
36. Last letter
37. Aesop racer
40. Takes home
41. Stockades
42. "Blessed ___ the meek . . ."
43. Water
45. Join
46. Deceive
47. Speak wildly
50. Make glum
52. Full-grown
55. Army enlister?
57. Period of note
58. Dawn to dawn
59. Bill, finally
60. Plate of glass
62. "Blue ___"
65. Correspond
66. Mellows
67. Lagoon's boundary
68. Land amid water
69. Fishing sticks
70. Perfect numbers?
71. Root vegetable

DOWN

1. Profit
2. Compact computer
3. Midday nap
4. Light-switch settings
5. Skier's topography
6. Elderly
7. Tree part
8. Color fabric
9. Firm
10. Arrange
11. Waste cloth
12. Ambulance letters
14. Flurries
20. Dilly
21. Shirt protectors
24. More frightening
25. Nacho sauce
26. Odd's opposite
27. Cereal grains
29. Bar rocks
31. Circle
34. Summer TV fare
35. Field cover
37. Commands to horses
38. Section
39. Flushed
41. Garden veggie
43. Plan
44. Deuce beater
48. Suitcase
49. Make possible
51. Doll up a window
53. Worshiped objects
54. Actor Newman
56. Peep
60. Links figure
61. Back in time
62. Fly swatter?
63. Gulped down
64. Over there
65. Triangular sail

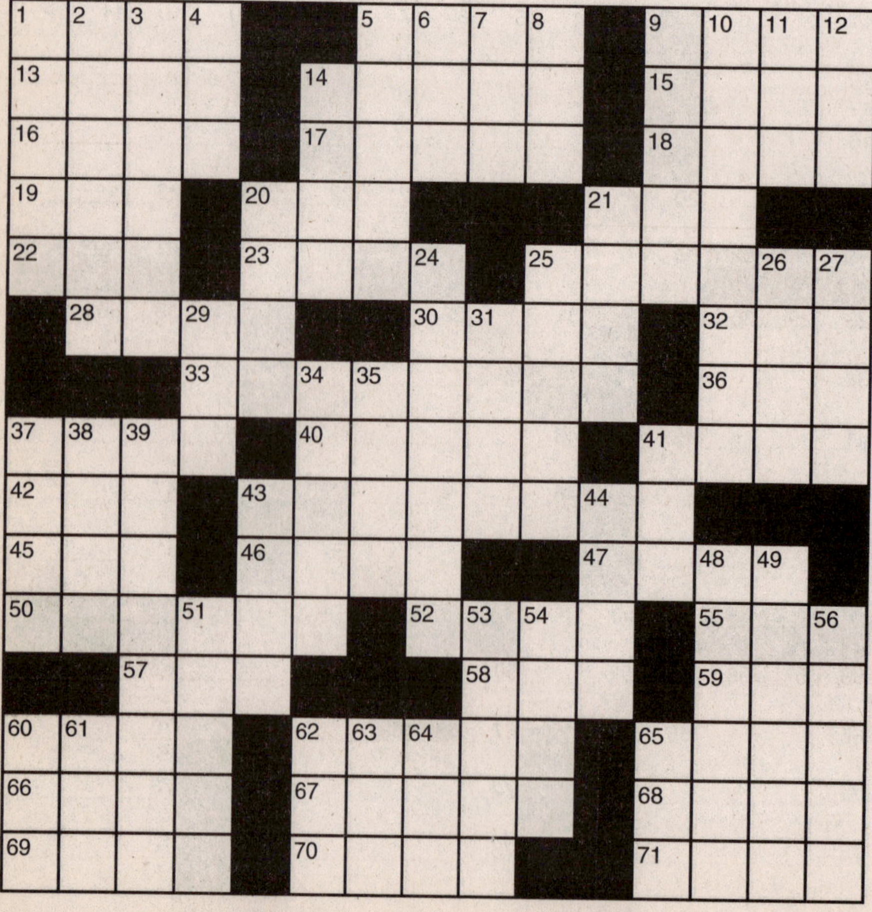

PUZZLE 352

ACROSS

1. Chinese pan
4. The Grateful ___
8. Resonate
12. ___ out (barely make)
13. Authorize
15. Lunchtime
16. Previous to, in verse
17. Transpire
18. Actress Fonda
19. Queens' houses
21. Yuletide singer
23. Pens
25. ___ sauce
26. Ring
28. Poise
33. Bikini top
34. Group of three
36. Common phrase
37. Large decorative vase
38. Cheer
40. Type of antelope
41. Belief
43. Vapor
44. Males
45. Most sugary
47. Radiates
50. Gender
51. More achy
53. Gathered
57. Passionate
61. Calcutta dress
62. Sheepherding dog
64. Luau instrument, briefly
65. Lower joint
66. Rains ice
67. None
68. Broil
69. Crosscurrent
70. Secret watcher

DOWN

1. Sob
2. Soup vegetable
3. Ship bottom
4. Agent
5. Cancel
6. Stereo component
7. Record
8. Relished
9. Fuel source
10. Sharpen
11. Unique chap
13. Pie nut
14. Razz
20. Pro
22. Violinist's need
24. Feelings
26. Cupid's dart
27. Scope
29. Decomposes
30. Opposite of day
31. Traffic barriers
32. Flightless birds
33. Blossoms
35. Drives into
38. Despises
39. Endless time
42. Sloppier
46. Managers, for short
48. Allots
49. Great anger
52. Lubricated
53. Inquires
54. Lion's ruff
55. Realm
56. Dispense
58. Convent residents
59. Pass over
60. Wriggly
63. Escorted

PUZZLE 353

MOVIES & TELEVISION

ACROSS

1. A Maverick
5. Sauna locale
8. Luxury's seat?
11. "___ Wolf McQuade"
15. Slender woodwind
16. Sesame
17. Chemical suffix
18. Inside of
19. Up to it
20. Opposing
22. Mister Ed's neck hair
23. Rock to and fro
25. Maj. Nelson's agcy.
26. Eileen on "It's Your Move"
27. Fez and bowler
29. Courage
31. "The ___ Inferno"
35. Uttered
36. "The ___ Hawk"
39. Actor Wallach
40. Sow's nose
42. Fleets
44. Carter on "Gimme a Break"
46. Part of "GWTW"
47. Melodic sounds
48. Matlock's profession
50. Bible hymn
53. Witness
54. Cracker type
57. "___ Miner's Daughter"
59. Obstacle
62. Inclined
63. "The ___ Hand"
65. Spy org.
66. Take it on the ___
67. Assignment
70. Brad Pitt film
72. Of the skin
74. Glad eye
75. "Look Back In ___"
78. Locality
80. Tex or John
84. Make mad
85. "Family Matters" character
87. Soprano Mills
88. Frosted
89. Cousin on "The Addams Family"
90. Mr. Ameche
91. "A ___ Breed"
92. Sandra and Ruby
93. Comic Louis ___
94. "Desk ___"
95. Hurried away

DOWN

1. "The Love ___"
2. Xavier's ex
3. Miss Daisy, e.g.
4. Grow molars
5. "___ From Scratch"
6. Arnold Ziffel, e.g.
7. Thicke on "Growing Pains"
8. Camera parts
9. Cochise on "Broken Arrow"
10. Dino, Astro or Spot
11. "Falcon Crest" actor
12. Actor Sharif
13. Niblick number
14. "East of ___"
21. Ziering on "Beverly Hills 90210"
24. "Up to His ___"
26. Cone-bearing trees
28. "The ___ Sisters"
30. Mama Harper's son
31. Rating for Bo
32. Chico's cheer
33. Alec and Stephen's bro
34. "The ___ of Navarone"
36. Suppress
37. Marine shocker
38. Donkey
41. Educate
43. Contends
45. Garrison on "It's Your Move"

PUZZLE 353

49. Trout in "On Golden Pond"

51. Margot in " Superman"

52. Thomas on "That Girl"

54. "___ in the Family"

55. Ms. Peeples

56. TV producer

58. "Fay" star

60. Tire filler

61. Fuel for KITT

64. Lunch place

68. Wiseacre

69. "The ___ Kid"

71. "The Jerk" actress

72. "Mr. ___ Goes to Town"

73. Author Deighton

75. Without rain

76. Pleasant

77. Club for singers

79. Subjoins

81. "The Parent ___"

82. Irish land

83. Donna or Rex

85. Tonic go-with

86. A Stooge

PUZZLE 354

ACROSS

1. Curves
5. Courageous
9. Sew loosely
14. Dump
15. "Far and ___"
16. Halt legally
17. Top-grade recipient
18. Horse strap
19. Horned mammal, briefly
20. Revise
22. Neck area
24. Thing, in law
25. Onion's relative
27. Clever remark
28. Yellow wildflower
31. Realty unit
35. Coal size
36. Dueling weapon
37. Popeye, e.g.
39. Foot-leg joint
41. False hair
43. Boasts
44. Had aspirations
46. Midge
48. Dripping
49. Order to go
50. "___ Sue"
53. Apple seed
54. Exhausted
55. Possessive pronoun
58. Choir gown
60. Employable
64. South American animal
66. Athenian vowels
68. Exits
69. Lab burners
70. Pimples
71. Ardor
72. Stonecrop
73. The one here
74. Medicine portion

DOWN

1. Partially open
2. Asian staple
3. Ball of yarn
4. Walk
5. Drink maker
6. Be in debt
7. Reposed
8. Powerhouse
9. Artist's hat
10. Volcanic output
11. Paint-can direction
12. Musical sound
13. Epic poetry
21. Recover
23. Hulls
26. Understood
28. Style
29. Like the old bucket of song
30. Royal rule
31. Walking on ___
32. Bozo, e.g.
33. Paddled
34. Formerly
35. Writing tablets
38. Role players
40. Young boy
42. Chew steadily
45. Threesome
47. Wakens
51. Cheerful
52. Not matured
53. Refracting crystal
55. Sorbets
56. Carryall
57. Desert covering
59. Imprint with acid
61. ___ tie
62. Grazing grounds
63. Anglo-Saxon peon
65. St. Anthony's cross
67. Black cuckoo

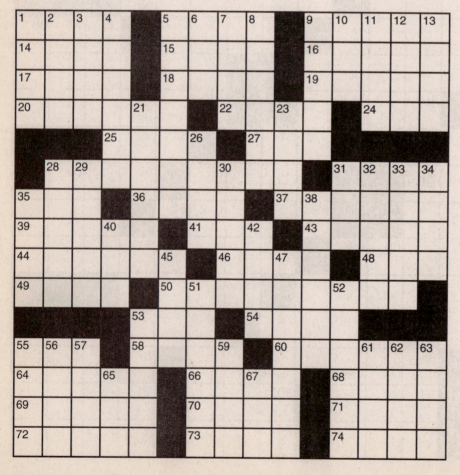

1	2	3	4	█	5	6	7	8	█	9	10	11	12	13
14				█	15				█	16				
17				█	18				█	19				
20				21		█	22		23		█	24		
█	█	█	25			26	█	27			█	█	█	█
█	28	29					30			█	31	32	33	34
35			█	36				█	37	38				
39			40		█	41		42	█	43				
44					45	█	46		47		█	48		
49				█	50	51					52			█
█	█	█	█	53			█	54				█	█	█
55	56	57	█	58			59	█	60			61	62	63
64			65		█	66		67		█	68			
69					█	70				█	71			
72					█	73				█	74			

PUZZLE 355

ACROSS

1. Mother's little yelper?
5. Faucets
9. Fireplace fuel
12. Clarinet's kin
13. Menace
15. Kind of maniac
16. "I ___ Forget You"
17. Kind of beehive
18. Entirely
19. Haul
20. Computer food
21. ___ down (softened)
23. Taken illegally
25. Fastener
28. Writing liquids
30. Haphazard
34. Cuddly bear
37. Peach leftovers
39. Clearance event
40. Rower's blade
41. By oneself
42. Take to court
43. Alum
45. Skirt length
46. Fabric colorers
48. Saintly
50. Cut
52. Fall drink
54. Rambled
58. Female voices
61. Camel feature
63. Lumberjack's tool
64. Couple
65. Applaud
68. Variety
69. Corn portion
70. Wrote one's name on
71. Sleeping
72. Bask
73. Cattle calls
74. Solidifies

DOWN

1. Stadiums
2. Concerning
3. Small drum
4. Thus far
5. The thing there
6. Vocal solos
7. As ___ your request
8. Somber
9. Slender
10. Eyeball
11. Precious metal
13. Say gracias
14. Carved pole
20. Hold back
22. Big-eyed birds
24. Topper
26. Tabby treat
27. Increase
29. Interlace
31. Lighten
32. Garble
33. Notices
34. Cato's clothing
35. Gain income
36. Lag behind
38. Electrified particle
41. Among
44. Art ___
46. Decline
47. Positive vote
49. Speech impediments
51. Equipped with weapons
53. Hippo's acquaintance
55. Perhaps
56. Throw out
57. Homeowners' papers
58. Citrus drinks
59. Hilo party
60. Shredded
62. Functions
66. Border
67. Before now
68. Touch game

PUZZLE 356

ACROSS

1. Take the series
6. Heel
9. Rascal
14. Split in two
15. The Greatest
16. Stand for something
17. Common viper
18. FBI kin
19. Enough
20. House of Lords members
21. Mexican food
23. Make a boo-boo
24. Heronlike birds
26. Defeat
30. Compass dir.
31. Cook's amt.
33. Song gal
34. Taste
37. Kill a bill
38. Stage signal
39. Talked a blue streak?
40. "Leave ___ to Heaven"
41. Silly
43. Shakespeare's luck
44. Uncluttered
46. Winter wear
47. Common verb
48. Hear legally
49. Food additive: abbr.
50. Adam or Mae
52. Riverdale native
55. Wail
58. Salty solution
60. Spin
62. Lively dance
65. Put on
66. Shade
67. Actress Garson
68. Catchall abbr.
69. Peru Indians
70. Stomach
71. Observe
72. Salesman

DOWN

1. Form
2. Fisherman, sometimes
3. Church official
4. Perpetually
5. Tenacious
6. Prickly plants
7. Assumed name
8. Circle dimension
9. Secure
10. Desert dweller
11. Nile viper
12. Singer Torme
13. Thickness
22. Rank of prof.
25. Busy one
27. Green grouch
28. Hot spot
29. Shiny
30. Musical sense
32. Christmas plant
34. Oh, go on!
35. Mindful
36. Bounds
37. Llama doc
40. Fall fun
42. Yuletide drink
45. Of an age
46. French friend
51. Showed disapproval
53. Big bill
54. Therefore
55. Because
56. Liver, e.g.
57. Fortunate
59. Rhine feeder
61. Airplane feature
62. Woods's org.
63. Sphere
64. Wreath

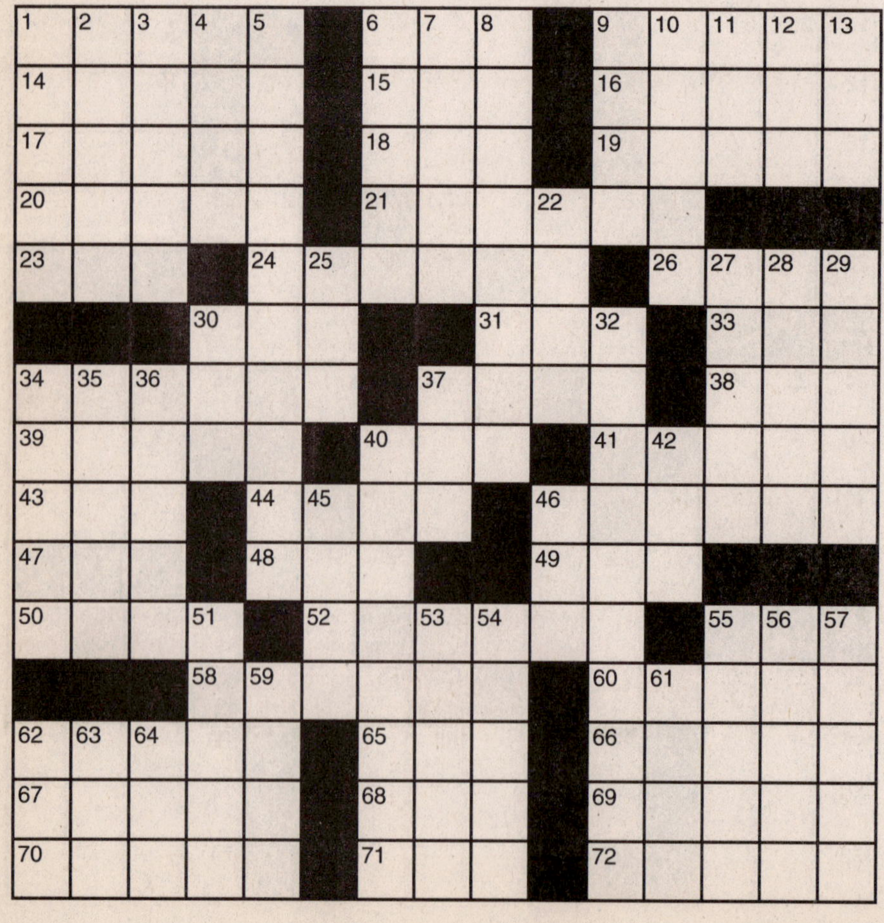

PUZZLE 357

ACROSS

1. Resell, as tickets
6. Large horn
10. Nuisance
14. Cold-weather treat
15. Taken by mouth
16. Female voice
17. Straighten
18. Till
19. Cheeky
20. Young boy
21. Patrolman
23. Egg producer
25. Average mark
26. Prepare for traffic
27. Pretended
29. Pet birds
34. Maximum
35. Pencil part
36. External
38. Cried
39. Challenger
41. Places to rejuvenate
45. Smells
47. "Anchors ___"
49. Limber
51. Appointed group
53. Picked
54. Decides between
55. Be sickly
56. Ridicule
59. Fire remnant
60. Old witch
63. Bank (on)
65. MTV viewer
67. Black
69. Musical club
70. Feel concern
71. Alter slacks
72. "Against All ___"
73. Tinted
74. Packs

DOWN

1. Shoo!
2. Caffeinated drink
3. Vinegar, e.g.
4. Tree-trunk bit
5. Breakfast food
6. Hairpiece
7. Coffeepot
8. Basin
9. Sunburn soother
10. Baby food
11. Picks a leader
12. Lane
13. Hauled
22. Carry to excess
24. Title
26. Ministers
28. Girdles
29. Cathedral bench
30. "You ___ My Lucky Star"
31. Make like Coolio
32. Chest
33. Prosecute
37. Hobos
40. Circle portion
42. Hollow
43. Length of life
44. This girl
46. Colorist
48. Dries up
49. Protect
50. Surveyed
52. Uttered a low wail
53. Freight
57. Seven-year ___
58. Suitor
60. Santa's comment
61. Once again
62. Sports facilities
64. Affirmative
66. Before, to Shelley
68. Risk cash

1	2	3	4	5	■	6	7	8	9	■	10	11	12	13
14					■	15				■	16			
17					■	18				■	19			
20			■	21	22		■	23		24	■	25		
■	■	■	26				■	■	■	27	28			
29	30	31					32	33	■	34				■
35						■	36		37			■	■	■
38				■	39	40				■	41	42	43	44
■	■	■	45	46				■	47	48				
■	49	50			■	51		52						
53					■	■	■	54				■	■	■
55			■	56	57	58	■	59			■	60	61	62
63			64	■	65		66		■	67	68			
69				■	70				■	71				
72				■	73				■	74				

PUZZLE 358

ACROSS

1. Relay section
4. Spanish abode
8. Went over 55
12. Ali ___
16. Nevada town
17. Rental props.
18. Mata ___
19. "East of Eden" role
20. In the know about
21. Chirp
22. Poor box donations
23. Teheran's nation
24. Purpose
25. Sooner than, to Byron
26. Halsey's rank
28. Waiter
31. ___ for the course
33. Louder
37. Composition
38. Dutch ___ disease
39. Confederate men
40. No, in Scotland
41. Fishing boat item
43. Digging tool
45. Chooses by vote
47. Game-show member
51. Ten-year units
53. Altar words
54. Tarzan portrayer
55. Tokyo's land
56. Resort in New Mexico
60. Gypsy's card
62. Actress Charlotte ___
64. Make a choice
65. Quiz choice
66. Bullets, for short
67. Agitated
69. Actress Balin
71. Cheer for a matador
72. Suggest
75. Inure
77. Type of columnist
80. Showed again
82. Halloween's mo.
83. Response, briefly
84. Pain in the neck
86. ___-de-France
87. National bird
91. Model
93. Catchall abbr.
94. Made fashionable
95. Tennis shoe
98. Batman and Robin, e.g.
100. Freud's concerns
101. Festival
104. Three musicians
105. Spanish lady
106. Border
107. Ripener
108. Knoxville's st.
109. Slanted
110. Ship bottom
111. "Gidget ___ to Rome"
112. Writes a p.s.
113. Risks money
114. Botch

DOWN

1. Telescope parts
2. Comes in
3. Gunk
4. Escapade
5. Copycat
6. Most costly
7. Venomous snake
8. Roe source
9. Part of the hand
10. Royal fur
11. Stripped down
12. Scoops
13. Timetable abbr.
14. Tropical constrictor
15. Author Beattie
16. Awaken
26. Naval fleet
27. Passageway
29. Weathercock
30. Shoelace hole
32. Swiss peak
34. Business abbr.
35. Have a hot dog
36. Home: abbr.
39. Summarize
42. Sesame
44. Train stop
46. This, to Juanita
47. Middle Eastern bread
48. Eve's partner
49. "Cheers" barfly
50. Pancake topping
52. Adventure
55. Outlaw James
57. Thanks ___!
58. Scandinavian capital

PUZZLE 358

59. Look like

61. Dropper's word

63. On a ship's left side

65. Spigot

68. Spookier

70. Sgt. or cpl.

73. Develop

74. Light dramatic work

75. Interesting story

76. Command to Lassie

77. Space

78. Stop ___ dime

79. Speedy plane

81. High, in music

85. Trapped

88. Powerless flier

89. Accounts book

90. A Ford

92. Russian rulers, once

94. Lathers

96. Gentle

97. Vast periods of time

99. Entity

101. Wisecrack

102. Yore

103. Majors or Remick

105. Wipe gently

106. Squeak by

■	1	2	3	■	4	5	6	7	■	8	9	10	11	■	12	13	14	15
16				■	17				■	18				■	19			
20				■	21				■	22				■	23			
24			■	■	25			■	26					27		■	■	■
28			29	30		■	31	32		■	■	33				34	35	36
37					■	■	38			■	39				■	40		
■	■	■	41		42	■	43			44		■	45		46			
47	48	49				50		■	51			52				■	■	■
53			■	54			■	55					■	■	56	57	58	59
60			61		■	62	63		■	64			■	65				
66				■	■	67			68		■	69	70		■	71		
■	■	■	72	73	74					■	75				76			
77	78	79				■	80			81		■	82			■	■	■
83			■	84		85		■	86			■	■	87		88	89	90
91			92				■	■	93			■	94					
■	■	■	95				96	97		■	98	99		■	■	100		
101	102	103		■	104				■	105				■	106			
107				■	108				■	109				■	110			
111				■	112				■	113				■	114			■

PUZZLE 359

ACROSS

1. Running behind
5. Appealed
9. Villages
14. Rich Little, e.g.
15. Military employee
16. Edible bulb
17. Mast
18. Pork cut
19. Pace
20. Addition to a house
21. Tempt
23. Chapel seat
24. Outcome
27. Coat sleeve
28. Particularly
31. "___ Smile Without You"
35. Good-bye
38. Kitchen gadget
39. "Staying ___"
40. Snaky fish
42. Grow
43. Managed
44. Detach
46. Youngster
47. Countries
49. Scatter
50. Doodle
54. Bend
57. Scents
60. Deep suffering
61. Running tracks
63. Garden green
64. Prima donna
65. Artist Edgar ___
66. Love deity
67. Cake decorator
68. Opponent
69. Hair holders
70. Blockhead

DOWN

1. Surgical beam
2. Orchard product
3. Wild ducks
4. Drop the ball
5. Artist's board
6. Big cat
7. Fix copy
8. Refusal
9. Kind of pole
10. "Still the ___"
11. Weak person
12. Uh-uh
13. Frozen precipitation
22. "___ Baby"
25. Irregular
26. Mooed
29. Saloon order
30. Made holy
31. Not fine
32. Opera highlight
33. Wasp's home
34. Forest plant
35. Statistic
36. Hand-cream ingredient
37. Ready to eat
38. Model T starter
41. Hawaiian necklace
45. Have as property
47. Neither's partner
48. Roused
49. Fresh
51. "You Only Live ___"
52. Protect
53. Understood
54. Foreshadow
55. Roasting chamber
56. Pay
58. Filly's mom
59. Much
62. Getaway
64. Commotion

1	2	3	4	■	5	6	7	8	■	9	10	11	12	13
14				■	15				■	16				
17				■	18				■	19				
20			■	■	21				22		■	23		
24			25	26		■	■	27			■	■	■	■
■	■	■	28			29	30			■	31	32	33	34
35	36	37						■	■	38				
39					■	40		41	■	42				
43					■	■	44		45					
46				■	47	48						■	■	■
■	■	■	■	49			■	■	50			51	52	53
54	55	56	■	57			58	59		■	■	60		
61			62		■	63				■	64			
65					■	66				■	67			
68					■	69				■	70			

PUZZLE 360

ACROSS

1. Covers with grass
5. Witches
9. Scheme
13. Aid a wrongdoer
14. Bad BMW
15. Like a black olive
16. Fly unaccompanied
17. Embellishes
19. Predictor
20. Young bug
21. Route
22. Distribute
24. Broccoli shoot
27. What a relief!
29. A lot
31. Pull
33. Ascended
34. Base
36. Bawl
37. Mutt
38. Leather punch
41. Green veggie
42. Haw's partner
43. Hostelry
44. Scanned
46. Hair lock
48. Judge
50. Long timespans
52. A side of New York
53. Hunt
55. Back of a ship
57. None
58. Small dog
59. Applaud
63. Wintry frosting?
67. Lug
68. Guideline
69. Wacky
70. Fashion shade
71. Bellow
72. Turns to the right
73. Quantity of paper

DOWN

1. Brashness
2. Orchestra instrument
3. Take out, as text
4. Tales
5. Dirigible's filler
6. Novice
7. Sailor
8. Yukon footwear
9. Said the rosary
10. Aglow
11. Unlock, in poems
12. Affirmative word
14. Contact ___
18. Criticize
23. Cuss
25. Bows
26. Hardest to find
27. Trims twigs
28. Wasp
30. Dirty Harry, e.g.
32. School wings
33. Biting
35. Spud
39. Wimp
40. Delay
45. Regardless of
47. Cattle farmer
49. Fireplace shelf
51. Tricks
54. Kind of detector
56. Like an omelet
60. Lingerie trim
61. Personal atmosphere
62. Tomato variety
63. Crooked
64. Cast
65. Has the bug
66. Actor's hint

PUZZLE 361

ACROSS

1. Wild horse
7. Gallivant
10. Couch
14. ___ algebra
15. Dog-day drink
16. Wading bird
17. Group of eight
18. Bashful
20. Task
21. Religious leader
22. Commandment pronoun
23. Stool pigeon
26. Jail chamber
28. Date chart
33. Pass along
36. Fiery gem
37. Literary work
39. Colorless gas
41. Female fox
43. Roadside lodging
44. Chimney output
45. Adversary
46. Laugh-a-minute
48. Expanse
49. Barbecue
51. Most grating
53. Chimney residue
55. Tennis expert
56. Have bills
59. Metal fastener
61. Sport-shoe feature
66. Demurely
68. Crooked
69. Corrupt
70. Not him
71. String
72. Captures
73. Bard's before
74. Begins

DOWN

1. Alliance
2. Affluent
3. Conscious of
4. At hand
5. Underground area
6. Miner's rock
7. Short breath
8. Kind of committee
9. Lower in pitch
10. Quick drink
11. Newspaper notice
12. Trout, e.g.
13. Pale
19. Lamprey catchers
24. Hoopla
25. Rhino's kin
27. Andean animals
28. Sheltered bay
29. Doing an impression
30. Not as strict
31. Resins
32. Mystical
34. Venerate
35. Teams of oxen
38. Busybody
40. Shipshape
42. Hose
47. Roofing goo
50. Detest
52. Spacecraft
54. Floor installer
56. Portent
57. Used a loom
58. Rewrite
60. Stringed instrument
62. Turkish coin
63. Eastern ruler
64. Assist a felon
65. Pitch
67. Certain railways
68. Horse's relative

PUZZLE 362

ACROSS

1. Newt
4. Bean shell
7. Sib
10. Winter ailment
13. Fish beginnings
14. Eggs
15. Strike caller
16. Legal matter
17. Noted period
18. Mare's morsel
19. Occurrence
21. Rudder handle
24. Red or carpenter
25. British title
27. Boat paddle
29. Roster
33. Makeup locale
36. Select
37. Heckelphone
38. Grant's foe
39. Belief
41. Defense
42. Clinton's VP
43. Small stream
45. Bay window
48. Collection of Hindu aphorisms
50. Gained a lap
53. Persian fairy
54. Cleo's killer
55. Pot
57. Arden and Plumb
58. Trendy
59. Desire
60. With it
62. Big talker
66. Not as dirty
70. Exist
71. In the past
74. Motor fluid
75. Lode yield
76. Clear liquor
77. Billfish
78. Sapphire, e.g.
79. ___ off steam
80. Not subtract
81. Flow back

DOWN

1. Before, to a bard
2. Gift-tag word
3. Chinese plant
4. Billiards game
5. Oblong
6. Palm fruit
7. Bring legal action
8. Communicate
9. Revolve
10. '60s coif
11. Taken
12. Purpose
20. Amble
22. Sickly
23. Motel unit
25. Grown grig
26. Skipper's OK
28. Separate
30. Sash
31. Tennis toss
32. Floral garland
34. Matinee star
35. June bug
40. Painter's plaster
41. Wings
42. Japanese entertainer
44. Tick off
45. Unclose, to a poet
46. Ser. deliverer
47. Great rage
49. High hairstyle
50. Computer memory
51. Swiss mountain
52. Casual shirt
54. Current measure
56. However, in verse
61. Organic compound
63. Sitar music
64. Parched
65. Nurse
66. Metal tooth
67. Fib
68. Shade giver
69. Soak flax
72. Talker's gift?
73. Circle

PUZZLE 363

ACROSS

1. Defies
6. Name
9. Lump of dirt
13. Sports palaces
15. Increase
16. Nature walk
17. Pry
18. Tennis call
19. Land measurement
20. Dads
21. Large truck
23. Beg
24. Concocted
25. Dainty
26. Facts
29. Bewitched
34. Speechmaker
36. Plucked strings
37. Nog liquor
39. Entertained with drink
40. Batter's goal
41. Demean
43. Senate vote
44. Monty's transaction
46. Great gusts
47. Moon, e.g.
50. "___ Than Zero"
51. Onager
52. Spent
54. Rendezvous
57. Like fine cheese
58. Wary
61. Party giver
62. Flower wreath
64. Walk cautiously
66. Sport blade
67. ___ up to (admit)
68. Roster
69. Dweeb
70. Earn
71. Quitter's prop

DOWN

1. Soggy
2. Region
3. Blushing colors
4. Stop
5. Mexican sauce
6. Snack shop
7. Luau instrument
8. Gambling stake
9. Skier's retreat
10. Certain parasites
11. Soup veggie
12. Exploit
14. Planter
22. Troops
23. Mail friend
24. Partner
25. Fighting
26. Pillow filler
27. Melodies
28. Singer Tucker
30. Tex-Mex dish
31. Pass the ___
32. Wipe out
33. Cleans
35. Most strange
38. Muddle
40. Mr. Linden
42. Uncovered
45. Subways' cousins
46. Attacks
48. Sampled
49. Yank
53. Decree
54. Formerly
55. Cord
56. French river
57. "___ Misbehavin'"
58. Put on cargo
59. Gap
60. Cheer
62. Fire fuel
63. Woolly female
65. Expert

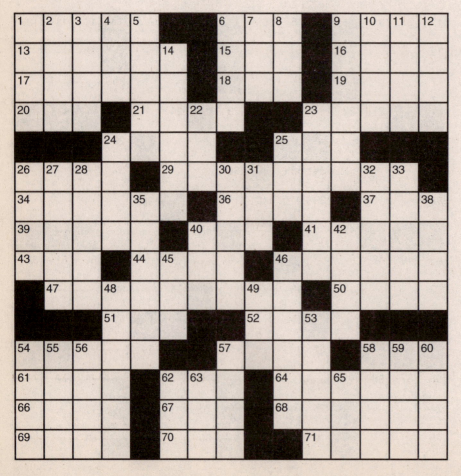

1	2	3	4	5	■	■	6	7	8	■	9	10	11	12
13					14	■	15			■	16			
17						■	18			■	19			
20			■	21		22		■	■	23				
■	■	■	24				■	■	25			■	■	■
26	27	28		■	29		30	31				32	33	■
34				35		■	36				■	37		38
39					■	40			■	41	42			
43			■	44	45			■	46					
■	47		48					49		■	50			
■	■	■	51			■	■	52		53		■	■	■
54	55	56			■	■	57				■	58	59	60
61				■	62	63		■	64		65			
66				■	67			■	68					
69				■	70			■	■	71				

HEADHUNTING

PUZZLE 364

Don't lose your head as you fill in the diagram. The first letter of each answer word will go somewhere within the word itself; all the other letters appear in order. For example, CART might be aCrt, arCt, or artC. (NOTE: The second letter of the answer word is always first.) Look for the letters which are shared by across and down words.

ACROSS

1. Prim
5. Infiltrate
10. Ms. Gilpin
14. Winged
15. Fess up
16. Dill herb
17. Past curfew
18. Disguises
19. French seasons
20. Harassment
22. Danson sitcom
24. Comes closer
25. Herbal drink
26. Cooked with vapor
29. Eric the ___
30. Spanish queen
33. Slow down
34. Abridge
36. Dish carrier
37. Peg for Palmer
38. Contends
39. Abandoned
42. Bird of prey
44. Snaky curve
45. Chicken-to-be
46. Free of germs
47. Had brunch
48. Brusque
49. Wanders
52. Occupant
56. Ms. Pavlova
57. Mushroom seed
59. Swipe
60. Head, to Yves
61. Dental string
62. News flash
63. Life of Riley
64. Untidy
65. Soup veggies

DOWN

1. Shakespearean king
2. Game stake
3. Maize spikes
4. Impasse
5. Tolerated
6. Nudge
7. Subway gate, briefly
8. Dog's doc
9. Collided
10. Principle
11. Impersonator
12. Ms. Summer
13. Poses
21. Practice boxing
23. Enjoy a novel
26. Cubic meter
27. Taunt
28. Playgrounds
29. After taxes
30. Private
31. Lariat
32. "Superman" actor
34. Fawn's mama
35. Say again
37. Gosh!
40. Overcast
41. Church feature
42. Please
43. Went like mad
46. Anxiety
47. Utah, e.g.
48. Psychics
49. Sicilian peak
50. Museo offering
51. Reasonable
53. Maintain
54. Not favoring
55. Goblet part
58. Bossy's call

PUZZLE 365

ACROSS

1. Mellows
5. Small lake
9. Hired vehicles
13. Wildlife protection agcy.
17. Lose brightness
18. Medicinal plant
19. Dash
20. Stage item
21. Lt. metal
22. Cancel
24. Landlord's income
25. Tells from memory
27. Drama sections
28. Gets up
30. Soon
31. Wallet items
32. Glide on ice
33. Sacrificial table
35. Covers
36. Slyly
39. Impoverished
40. Defeat
41. Portion
42. Struggle
43. ___ Galahad
44. Uncommon
45. Failures
46. Houseplant
47. Take into bondage
49. Bosc and Bartlett
50. Golden-touch king
51. Muslim official
52. Wading bird
53. Large
54. Strong point
57. Damp
58. Persevere
62. Servant, in Asia
63. Train station
64. Car
65. Recent: pref.
66. Unhappy
67. Fonda or Falk
68. Declines
69. Look over
70. Compliments
72. Coloring agents
73. Tiny fruit
74. Publicized
75. Be distressed
76. Bad habit
77. Names
79. Take suddenly
80. Subordinate rulers
83. Sheep's coat
84. Morse-code messages
87. Jacob's brother
88. Concerning
89. New York canal
90. Woodwind
91. Dist.
92. Bird's home
93. Pats gently
94. Shakes
95. Northern Italian city

DOWN

1. A long way off
2. Tempest
3. Teachers
4. Informational meeting
5. Communion plate
6. Mexican cheers
7. Neither's companion
8. Insists
9. Pennies
10. Cry of dismay
11. Flying mammal
12. Tennis shoes
13. Fairy
14. Safeguarded
15. Traffic barrier
16. Leased props.
23. Sherbets
26. Rocky pinnacle
29. Speak wildly
31. French river
32. Openhanded blows
33. Church section
34. Cut of meat
35. Folk legends
36. Task
37. Former Roman money
38. Cravings
40. Molten rock
41. Slope
44. Violent anger
45. Banquet
46. Pear-shaped fruits
48. Narrow wooden strip
49. Earlier
50. French painter

PUZZLE 365

52. Contends

53. Wagers

54. Quick

55. Poet Khayyam

56. Heating devices

57. Rationed

58. Saloons

59. Grows larger

60. Scorch

61. Curtis or Danza

63. Abhorred

64. Assist a felon

67. Unmixed

68. Facial fringe

69. Exude

71. Soldier's lodging

72. Tow

73. Small piece

75. Releases

76. Flower holders

77. Look-alike

78. Actress Skye

79. Talkative

80. Haze

81. Section

82. Certain

85. Significant period

86. Lawyers' gp.

PUZZLE 366

DOUBLE CROSSER

When you fill in the correct missing letters in the crossword diagram, those letters, transferred to the correspondingly numbered dashes below the diagram, will reveal a quotation. Make sure no word is repeated in the diagram. Proper names, abbreviations, contractions, and foreign words are not allowed. There are different possibilities to fill the diagram, but only one way will give you the correct quotation.

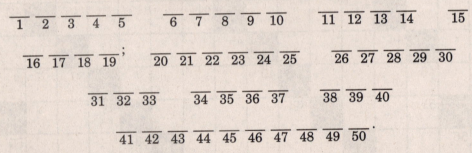

_ _ _ _ _ (1 2 3 4 5) _ _ _ _ _ (6 7 8 9 10) _ _ _ _ (11 12 13 14) _ (15)

_ _ _ _ (16 17 18 19); _ _ _ _ _ _ (20 21 22 23 24 25) _ _ _ _ _ (26 27 28 29 30)

_ _ _ (31 32 33) _ _ _ _ (34 35 36 37) _ _ _ (38 39 40)

_ _ _ _ _ _ _ _ _ _ (41 42 43 44 45 46 47 48 49 50).

PUZZLE 367

Crackerjacks

Find the answer to the riddle by filling in the center boxes with the letters needed to complete the words across and down. When you have filled in the Crackerjacks, the letters reading across the center boxes from left to right will spell out the riddle answer.

RIDDLE: What come at night without being called, and are lost in the day without being stolen?

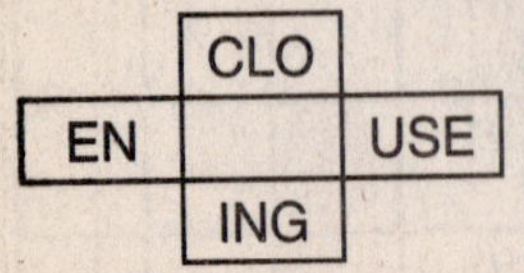

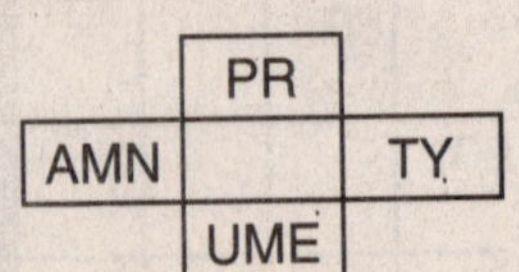

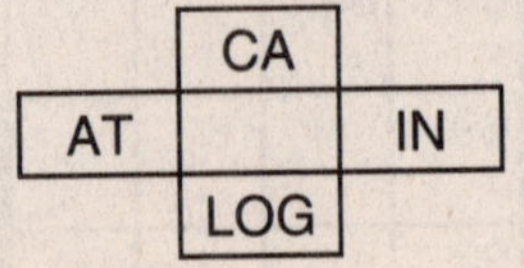

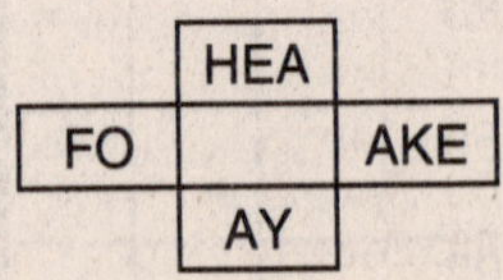

ANSWER: ________________

PUZZLE 368

ACROSS

1. Division term
5. Bashful
8. Deli side order
12. Harvest
13. Anguish
14. Apiece
15. Boundary
16. Lawyer
18. Author Ayn ____
20. Wharves
21. Flower petal
24. Sandwich cookie
26. "Look ____ ye leap"
27. Epic
29. ____-friendly
33. Christmas drink
35. King's home
37. Medicinal amount
38. Sonnets' kin
40. Cobra's cousin
41. Salary
43. Rutherford B. ____
45. Coward
48. In ____ of
50. Lacquered
52. Violent wind
56. Skin problem
57. Noshed
58. Daredevil Knievel
59. At that time
60. Green vegetable
61. Coral ridge

DOWN

1. Bitter anger
2. Actor Beatty
3. Price label
4. Musical drama
5. Graceful water bird
6. Frankfurter
7. Thus far
8. Weighty
9. Bowler's path
10. High scorer
11. Motives
17. Ajar, to a poet
19. Too
21. Type of catalog
22. Consequently
23. Pins down
25. Marathon, e.g.
28. Eagerly expectant
30. Linger
31. Word in a threat
32. Agts.
34. Correspondents
36. Tennis's Arthur ____
39. Remove
42. Skipper's OK
44. Boring tool
45. Chair
46. Ruler mark
47. Not loony
49. Inkling
51. Sip like a cat
53. St. crosser
54. Grant's foe
55. Gnome

PUZZLE 369

ACROSS

1. "____ to Joy"
4. Nude
8. Summit
12. Jest
13. Afresh
14. Wild hog
15. Find a sum
16. Reside
17. "The ____ from Brazil"
18. Stringed toys
20. Coastal eagle
22. Fox's home
24. Yucca fiber
28. Capri, for one
31. Honk
33. Bump hard
34. Pawn
36. Papeete's locale
38. Periodical, for short
39. Nerve-cell part
41. Imitator
42. Show scorn
44. Angler's throw
46. Church niche
48. Housing contract
52. Spring peeper
55. Female singer
57. Damp dirt
58. Competent
59. "Gidget ____ to Rome"
60. Porker
61. Cake layer
62. Clearly outline
63. Messy place

DOWN

1. Fine
2. Bauble
3. Circular current
4. Hobby wood
5. Tropical cuckoo
6. Worship
7. Washstand item
8. French clergy
9. Pigeon's purr
10. Merry month
11. Hesitant sounds
19. Toast topper
21. Indian palm
23. African goat
25. Stumble
26. Tardy
27. Arab chief
28. Theories
29. Laurel or Musial
30. Theater box
32. Sicilian volcano
35. "The World According to ____"
37. Detest
40. Spotted cat
43. Gung-ho
45. Splash
47. Wise seasoning?
49. Electrical units
50. Clubs or hearts, e.g.
51. Irritable
52. Suet
53. Baseball stat
54. Spanish hooray
56. Gumshoe

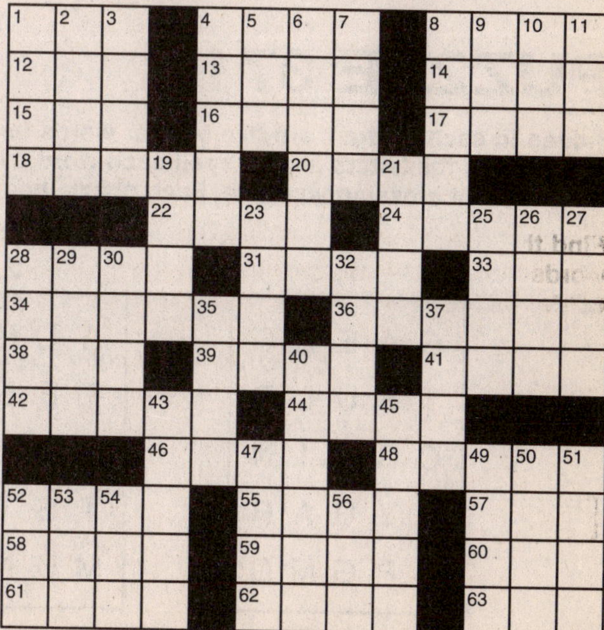

PUZZLE 370

CODEWORD

Codeword is a special crossword puzzle in which conventional clues are omitted. Instead, answer words in the diagram are represented by numbers. Each number represents a different letter of the alphabet, and all of the letters of the alphabet are used. When you are sure of a letter, put it in the code key chart and cross it off in the alphabet box. A group of letters has been inserted to start you off.

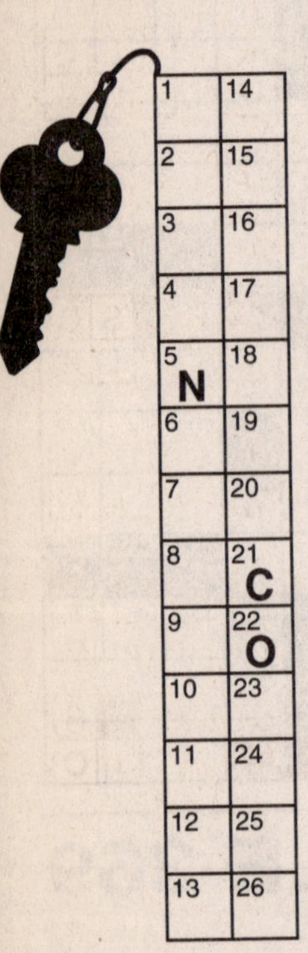

1	14
2	15
3	16
4	17
5 N	18
6	19
7	20
8	21 C
9	22 O
10	23
11	24
12	25
13	26

20	16	17	■	11	8	24	■	3	16	17	■	24	16	1
16	24	16	■	8	14	14	■	18	7	19	■	16	5	16
12	22	2	■	16	5	18	■	24	8	9	■	10	22	14
18	14	8	■	21 C	8	8	■	■	5	22	5	10	16	2
11	16	5	26	22 O	■	10	9	16	4	5	2	■	■	■
■	■	■	16	5 N	2	■	16	17	8	■	12	16	10	2
9	16	18	1	■	16	13	4	16	■	■	■	24	16	14
16	21	14	8	■	23	4	5	21	12	■	25	22	9	16
14	12	22	■	■	■	18	1	8	16	■	4	24	9	19
25	8	5	22	■	10	8	8	■	6	8	1	■	■	■
■	■	■	17	22	8	2	14	19	■	20	4	17	8	14
16	2	2	8	5	1	■	■	22	16	2	■	9	8	16
23	16	14	■	20	22	6	■	4	20	8	■	4	14	5
16	15	8	■	8	14	16	■	5	8	8	■	24	18	24
12	18	2	■	2	16	15	■	24	16	23	■	20	8	8

A	~~N~~
B	~~O~~
~~C~~	P
D	Q
E	R
F	S
G	T
H	U
I	V
J	W
K	X
L	Y
M	Z

PUZZLE 371

Word Ways

Hidden in each diagram are five 5-letter words beginning with the same letter. Draw a continuous line through the letters as you spell each word by moving in any direction from letter to adjoining letter without crossing your line. Each puzzle has a different starting letter.

1.

G	A	E	Z	G
T	S	U	L	D
O	G	E	I	N
H	Y	U	A	R
P	P	G	M	G

2.

A	L	M	U	N
T	E	S	E	I
M	O	L	P	M
T	S	I	C	A
M	U	N	H	M

3.

T	S	P	S	E
R	N	M	H	L
O	S	A	S	F
K	W	T	W	C
C	I	S	L	O

BRICK BY BRICK

PUZZLE 372

Rearrange this stack of bricks to form a crossword puzzle. The clues will help you fit the bricks into their correct places. Row 1 has been filled in for you. Use the bricks to fill in the remaining spaces.

ACROSS

1. Eastern title
   Fight
   Ink stain
2. Jamaican beverage
   Wig
   Lira replacement
3. Prior to, in verse
   Shabby
   Banner
4. Like a greenhouse
   Evil demons
5. Of birds
   Harpy
6. Neural network
   Less green
   Domino spot
7. Encumbered
   Vanilla-flavored drink
8. Australian birds
   Ranted
   Hungarian sheepdog
9. Imaginary
   Steve or Tim
10. Duffer's stand
    Tableau
    Puts up the farm
11. Sort
    Love dearly
12. Social event
    Having property
13. Earthen vessel
    Spoiled
    Positive vote
14. Hide
    Record holder
    Catty comment
15. Gardening aid
    Blazer material
    Interfere

DOWN

1. War god
   Exited
   Frosh's senior
2. Spiritual instructor
   Type of nettle
   Butter substitute
3. Grace closer
   Draw forth
   Calamities
4. Most recent
   Seeing red
5. Tried hard
   Map dot
6. Raccoon relative
   Relaxing chairs
7. Bearskin item
   Esoteric
   High, in music
8. Disposed
   State of bliss
   Novel
9. Wee legume
   Skinned
   EPCOT center?
10. Thinker
    Drab color
11. Injure
    Roughened
12. Obfuscate
    Anger
13. Humdinger
    Young fowl
    Humid
14. Vocal
    Runs in neutral
    Rubbernecker
15. Clothing
    Agony
    Fresh

BRICKS

MEW	URO	■BE	REE	TE■
PRY	LAG	ORE	A■R	EN■
■■■	PIP	ENE	RIP	LEE
AN■	ODA	■AD	CRE	TWE
LIT	GHO	D■P	TEE	PEL
AVI	HAG	■AL	■■■	HOS
VE■	ULS	DED	■■■	■SC
ED■	■■■	AYE	ANC	ILK
SOI	■RE	T■S	LAN	EMU
OLL	LAD	E■■	ID■	FIC
■TO	UPE	E■E	TS■	AVE
■RA	GTA	G■F	■■■	NAL
RUM	ULI	ER■	SUN	S■R
ERE	LEN	AMS	■■■	TIO

DIAGRAM

	1	2	3	4	5	6	7	8	9	10	11	12	13	14	15
1	A	G	A	■	S	C	R	A	P	■	■	B	L	O	T
2															
3															
4															
5															
6															
7															
8															
9															
10															
11															
12															
13															
14															
15															

PUZZLE 373

ACROSS

1. Hourglass filler
5. Daisylike plant
10. Halt!
14. Double-reed instrument
15. String instrument
16. Mama's mate
17. Jungle
19. Figure-skating jump
20. Road bend
21. Passed with flying colors
22. Salt additive, sometimes
24. Bashful
25. Sun-bronzed
26. Catholic leader
27. Ushered
28. Rapid
29. Pot cover
32. Modernize
35. Submit to
37. Paprika, e.g.
39. Heroic story
40. Tavern order
41. Sign
42. Snake's poison
44. Gaiety
46. "___ in Yonkers"
47. Lay eyes on
48. Bewildered
50. Likewise
52. Pull along
53. Stitch together
54. Aglow
57. Earnest
60. Land measurement
61. Ripen, as cheese
62. ___ out (barely made)
63. Trustworthy
66. Rocky mass
67. Madison Square Garden, e.g.
68. Waterfowl
69. Select
70. Monet's stand
71. ___ and cons

DOWN

1. Tender spots
2. Embarrass
3. Rowdy
4. Burrow
5. Guacamole ingredient
6. Ambulance sound
7. Having foot digits
8. Overhead trains
9. Proportions
10. Black card
11. Hired vehicle
12. Honest
13. Ashy
18. Destiny
23. Picks
26. Check endorser
27. Crazy
28. "The Most Happy ___"
29. Luxury auto
30. Freezes
31. Fender damage
32. Guns, as an engine
33. Fencing weapon
34. Wine and ___
36. Doughnut-shaped roll
38. Adventurer Marco ___
43. Title of respect
45. Everlasting
49. Hot fudge or strawberry
51. Had creditors
52. Shrub wall
53. Spectacle
54. Union group
55. Snowy abode
56. Young adults
57. Denomination
58. Soup vegetable
59. Ooze
60. Copycats
64. Historic time
65. European peak

PUZZLE 374

Start and Finish

Form words which Start and Finish with the same letter. For example, ___ O A S ___ becomes TOAST when a T is placed at the beginning and end of that set of letters. Use a different letter for each set.

1. ___ I G O ___
2. ___ E G A ___
3. ___ I D O ___
4. ___ U N C ___
5. ___ A G L ___
6. ___ U T D ___
7. ___ O I N ___
8. ___ I V I ___
9. ___ U M M ___
10. ___ A C I ___
11. ___ R U I ___
12. ___ I O S ___

PUZZLE 375

ACROSS

1. "___ of Fools"
5. Verve
8. Covering
12. Lounge around
13. Fundamental
15. Relinquish
16. Skillfully
17. Higher of two
18. Unique being
19. Not me
20. Brawl
21. Overseas
23. Prickly
25. Orchestra member
26. Performer
28. Question
30. ___ and drabs
34. Edible crustacean
36. Say a rosary
38. Sawbones
39. Aegean or North
40. In the lead
42. Generation
43. Graze
44. Circus insect
45. Black eye
48. Incredible bargain
50. To's mate
52. Diary item
53. Faction
55. Uniform color
57. Flowering shrub
60. Hideout
61. Evergreen tree
64. Cameo, e.g.
65. Makes a mule's sound
67. Majestic address
68. ___-jerk reaction
69. Keeps
70. Command to Fido
71. Drip
72. Flit (about)
73. Circular current

DOWN

1. Do in
2. Vagrant
3. Draw pictures for
4. Thickness, as of lumber
5. Tropical fruit
6. Glimpse from afar
7. Apple or pumpkin
8. Record keeper
9. Gambling game
10. Inspiration
11. Geek
13. Char
14. Fiddler or horseshoe, e.g.
20. Solid
22. Torso
24. Luau dish
25. Gumbo necessity
26. Burros
27. Defraud
29. Asparagus unit
31. Recognized
32. Hole driller
33. Frightening
35. Best friend
37. Sale notices
41. Weight
44. Hightail it
46. Listen to
47. Printer's need
49. Gone to bed
51. Approved
54. Truck sections
56. Cobra's comment
57. Clumsy vessels
58. Sector
59. Away from the wind
60. Volcano's overflow
62. Seeing red
63. Depend
66. Cloth shred
67. Personal pronoun

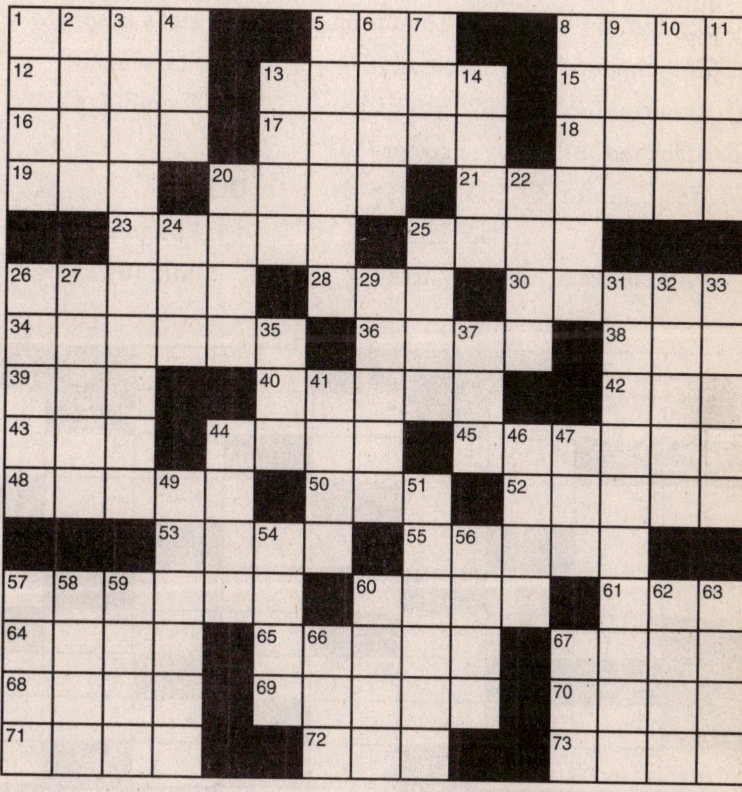

Hubcaps

PUZZLE 376

Insert two letters into the center of each circle below to form three 6-letter words reading across and diagonally (top to bottom). When you are finished, the letters you have entered, reading across, will spell a bonus word.

1.

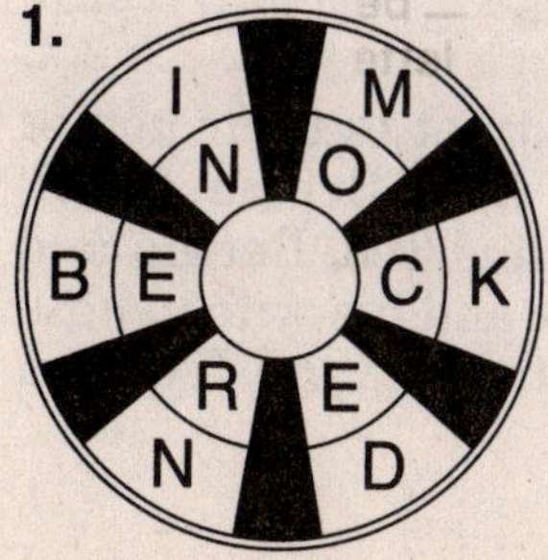

2.

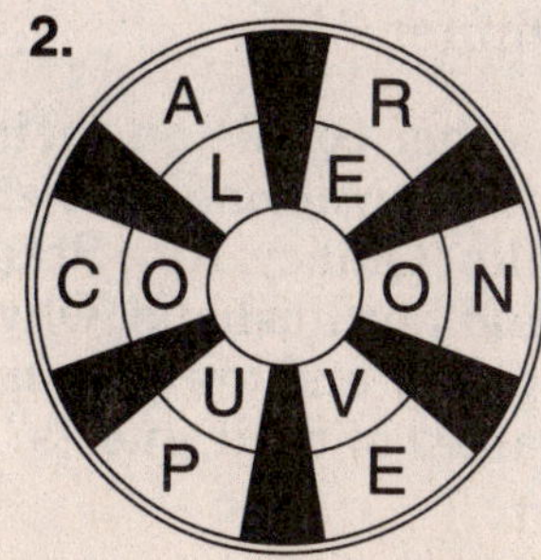

3.

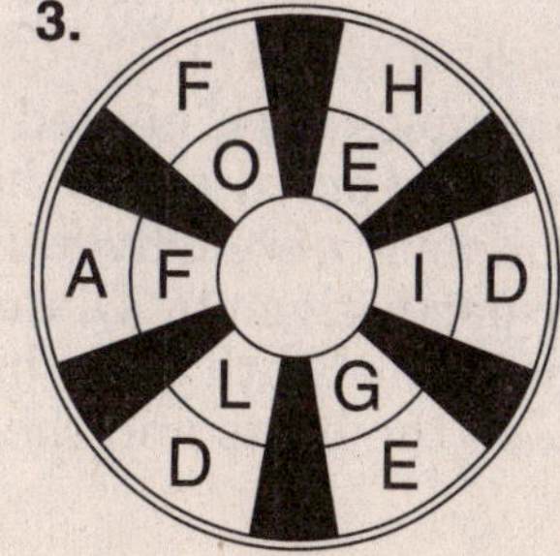

4.

BONUS WORD: ______________

PUZZLE 377 DOUBLE TROUBLE

Not really double trouble, but double fun! Solve this puzzle as you would a regular crossword, except place one, two, or three letters in each box. The number of letters in each answer is shown in parentheses after its clue.

ACROSS

1. Wayne's buddy (5)
3. Part of BLT (5)
5. Film ____ (4)
7. Authorized (8)
9. Jelly fruit (6)
10. Say again (7)
11. Detached (5)
13. Removal (8)
15. Affirmed (8)
17. West Pointer (5)
18. Musical syllables (4)
19. Within a vehicle (7)
21. Wood-eater (7)
24. Burn with steam (5)
26. Work shift (5)
28. Smallest (5)
30. Edmonton team (6)
32. Attention getters (5)
34. Caviar (3)
35. Throat parts (7)
37. Titling error (8)
39. Fathered (8)
41. Merry (6)
42. Sailor (7)
43. Thyroid, e.g. (5)
45. Expunge (5)
48. Mel's place (5)
49. Stare at (3)
50. Tremble (6)

DOWN

1. Pungent bulb (6)
2. Formerly (4)
3. Embargo (3)
4. Surrendered (8)
5. Vague idea (6)
6. Furious (5)
8. Composed (6)
9. Give up (4)
10. Adjust again (5)
12. Excuse (6)
14. Mailbox find (6)
15. Map book (5)
16. Electrical transformer (9)
17. Red birds (9)
20. Crow (5)
22. Road measure (4)
23. Small cafe (7)
25. Birch tree (5)
27. Not us (4)
29. Pilot (5)
31. Rock (5)
33. Kate or Adam (5)
36. Sole (6)
38. Smirk (5)
39. Novice (8)
40. Sea mammal (5)
41. Window shade (5)
42. ____ Gras (5)
44. Pro vote (3)
46. Greenish blue (4)
47. Detach (5)

1	2	■	■	■	3	4	■	■	5	6
7		8	■	9			■	10		
■	■	11	12		■	13	14			■
15	16			■	17			■	■	■
18		■	19	20		■	21	22	23	■
24		25	■	26		27	■	28		29
■	30		31	■	32		33	■	34	
■	■	■	35	36		■	37	38		
■	39	40			■	41			■	■
42			■	43	44		■	45	46	47
48		■	■	49		■	■	■	50	

PUZZLE 378 Deduction Problem

Two for Dinner

Three husband-and-wife couples each invited another couple on their street to their homes for dinner. The names of the women either hosting or attending were Amy, Bertha, Carol, Diane, Edith, and Fay. The men were Oliver, Philip, Quincy, Ray, Stan, and Ted. Bertha and Stan attended the dinner party given by Diane and her husband. Oliver and his wife (whose name isn't Amy) were invited by Edith and Philip. Ray and his wife invited Fay and Ted. Can you determine the names of the hosts and the names of their guests?

PUZZLE 379

• CIRCULAR MOTION •

ACROSS

1. Inquires
5. Tokyo sash
8. Boxing official: abbr.
11. Egyptian deity
12. Rotate
13. Madrid cheer
14. Consort with
16. Operate
17. Yaks
18. Had
20. Golf scores
23. Streets
24. Lager's cousin
25. Incense ingredient
26. Cole and Turner
28. Unhappiness
29. Collars
32. Fable teller
34. Forget-me-____
35. Railroad rail
36. Workweek starter
39. String instrument
40. Chest noise
41. Big bird
42. Completes
47. Soft metal
48. Handicrafts
49. Brass horn
50. Peculiar
51. Derek of film et al.
52. Rustle

DOWN

1. Swiss river
2. Actor Erwin
3. Scope of knowledge
4. Kind of drum
5. Musical work
6. Storage unit
7. Interior
8. Stylish penmanship
9. "Someone ____ Baby"
10. Nourish
12. Saturates
15. Singer Charles
19. Alert
20. Forbid
21. Pay suffix
22. Be active
23. Grain
25. Floor cleaner
27. Make airtight
28. Chinese skillet
30. Constrictor
31. Farm enclosure
33. Beetle
35. Fearful
36. Supplies with people
37. Stale
38. Twiggy homes
39. Reject, as a bill
40. Grooves
43. Cancun gold
44. Away
45. National police: abbr.
46. Distant

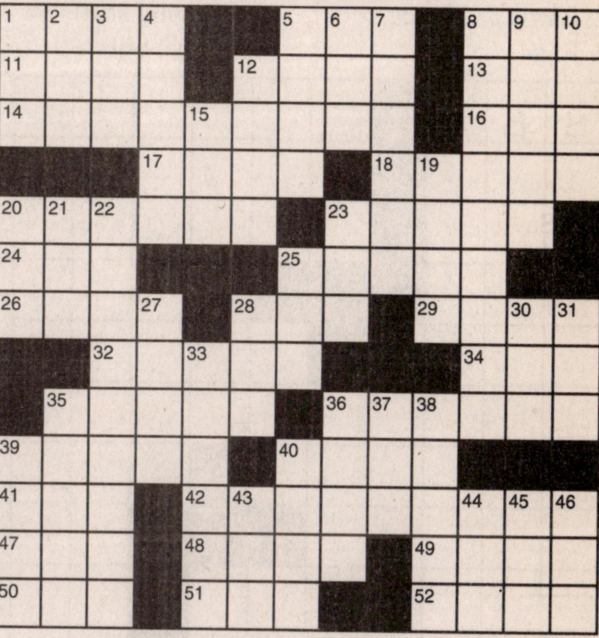

PUZZLE 380

• MISSING "LIST" •

ACROSS

1. Stop
4. Major network: abbr.
7. Actor Bert ____
11. Gunk
12. Bunny's motion
13. Narrow boat
14. Roster of food
16. Ghost towns
17. Group: abbr.
18. Start
19. Louisiana marsh
22. Came ashore
24. Billfold item
25. Milwaukee player
27. Nibble
29. Previously
30. "This Is ____ Life"
34. ____ the Hun
37. Browning's before
38. Most foxy
40. Expose
42. Comment
43. Cost-of-living directory: abbr.
44. Bungalow
45. Roster of addresses
49. Torment
50. Basketball's contents
51. Flower wreath
52. Ice mass, for short
53. Chemical suffix
54. Mr. Cariou

DOWN

1. Quiche base
2. And not
3. Scooby-____
4. Little angel
5. Tennis's Bjorn ____
6. Have a look-see
7. Roster of random items
8. Flavoring seed
9. Sharpened
10. Coffee break
13. Witch
15. Pigeon's purr
19. Swampy place
20. Raggedy-doll name
21. Vote for
22. Lawful
23. Army truancy: abbr.
26. Squealers
28. Roster of potential candidates
31. Above, to a poet
32. Psychic Geller
33. Congressman: abbr.
35. Itty-bitty
36. Strive
38. Play platform
39. Work
41. Sesame plant
42. Nature's bandage
43. Eve's son
45. Sheep's cry
46. Bedridden
47. First named
48. Clear liquor

PUZZLE 381

Diagramless crosswords are solved by using the clues and their numbers to fill in the answer words and the arrangement of black squares. Insert the number of each clue with the first letter of its answer, across and down. Fill in a black square at the end of each answer. Every black square must have a corresponding black square on the opposite side of the diagram to form a diagonally symmetrical pattern. Puzzles 381 and 382 have been started for you.

ACROSS

1. Baltic or Bering
4. Rage
7. Except
10. Paving stuff
11. Have bills
12. Bonfire residue
13. ____ trip
14. Gremlin's kin
15. Bring to court
16. Shade tree
17. Vocal solos
19. Vault
21. Frozen formation
22. Consumed
24. Collards, e.g.
27. Radiate
31. Pep party
32. Period of note
33. Black gold
34. Had being
37. Total
38. Function
39. Commotion
40. Neckline shape
41. Write
42. Certain evergreen
43. Be incorrect

DOWN

1. Sword
2. Golf coup
3. Fragrance
4. Rival
5. Hole punch
6. Mar
7. Simple
8. Typical
9. This and this
18. Circle
20. Pare
21. Common contraction
23. Nevertheless
24. Bunch
25. Rear
26. Columnist Goodman
28. Abandon
29. Direct
30. She walks in water
35. Refreshing drink
36. Spread

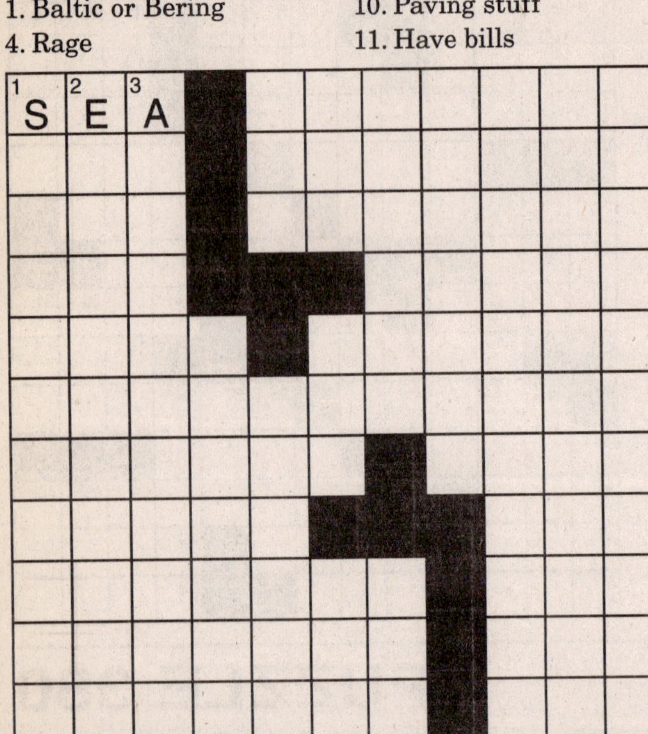

PUZZLE 382

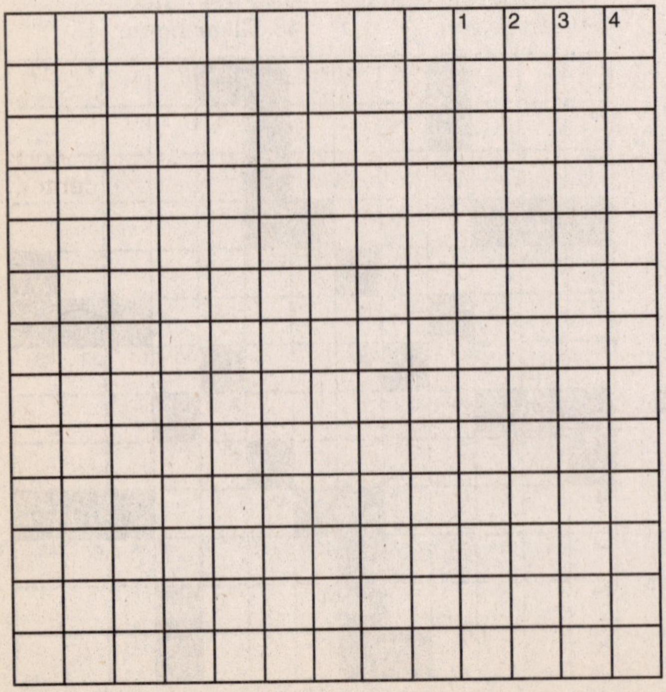

ACROSS

1. Touch down
5. Walkway
9. Mishmash
10. Lamb's pseudonym
11. Public argument
12. Stories
13. Hounds' quarries
14. Unity
15. Cardiff native
16. Kisser
17. Route
19. Financial management
24. Mavens
25. Exultant work
26. Chess defeat
28. Hanoi holiday
29. Forest clearing
31. Zones
33. Whisker remover
34. Respite
35. Affirm
36. Not as much
37. Low

DOWN

1. Union chapter
2. Watchful
3. Baseball side
4. Deer daughters
5. Goober
6. Assert
7. Cravat
8. Possesses
11. Outbuildings
12. Male turkeys
15. Bounders
17. Rush
18. Crude copper
20. Hose down
21. Inns
22. Principles
23. Family favorites
26. Labyrinths
27. Venerate
29. Snatch
30. Igneous flow
31. Everyone
32. Parisian street

PUZZLE 383

ACROSS
1. Dude
5. Wed in secret
6. Sucker
9. Accused
10. Color
11. Pond scum
12. Cake topper
14. Red veggies
15. Broker
16. Solitary
17. Brawny
18. Audibly
19. Lodge
20. Golly!
23. Pagan god
24. Indian craft
25. Dingy
26. Dad's lady
27. "____ in Toyland"
28. Gander's mate
29. City of Light
30. Bread's edge
31. Type of parking
32. Pennants
33. Balanced
34. Pie piece
35. Had a bite
36. Run away
38. Put down turf
39. Cloth joints
40. Alike

DOWN
1. Some shellfish
2. Where the heart is
3. Monkey's cousin
4. Ancestry
5. Upper class
6. Glistening
7. Polly, to Tom
8. Tent stake
9. Combine
11. Asian capital
13. Prison room
14. Flower
15. Vehicles
16. Actor Ray
17. Dog treats
18. Purpose
19. Nun's garb
20. Dozen dozen
21. Direction
22. Tiger's-____
24. Negligent
25. Dig out
27. Bundle of hay
28. Elegance
29. Surfaced a road
30. Snips
31. President's no
32. Blaze
33. Song syllables
34. Ripoff
37. Ocean

Starting box on page 562

Satellites

PUZZLE 384

Form ten words by placing one syllable in each circle. The center circle will contain the first syllable for each of the ten words. Each syllable will be used once. Words read outward from the center. If you need help getting started, you will find the first syllable on page 545.

AL ATE BEL BUS CA CAL
CIP CUS GAN IZE JU
LATE LION MU NA NER
NEW OR PER PIT RE RO
SAL SION TION U VE VER

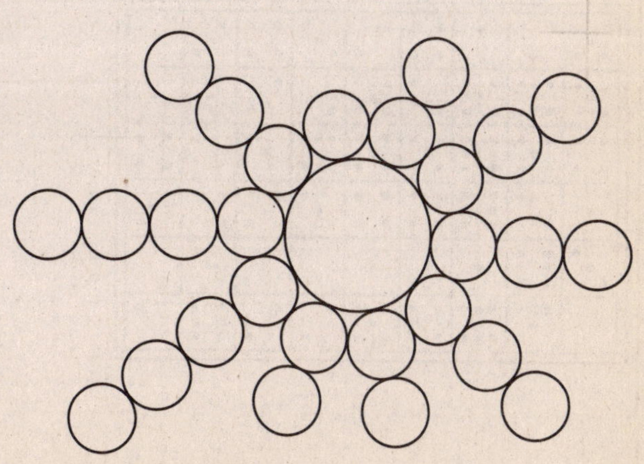

PUZZLE 385

ACROSS

1. Existence
5. Branch
8. Actress Linda ____
10. She, objectively
13. Ocean
14. Zone
16. Mine find
17. Wood shaper
19. Pakistani language
20. Director Craven
21. Repeat
22. Sheep's comment
23. Versifier
25. Civil uprising
27. Inexpensive
29. Theme
30. Confucian basis of conduct
33. Stone
34. Skating maneuvers
35. Care for
36. Choose
37. Consecrate
38. Dog variety
39. Per person
40. Primary
41. Church official
44. Exclude
46. Gallery offering
49. Bridal wear
50. Animal
51. Gunk
52. Motor
54. Actress Grant
55. Ram's mate
56. Fork prongs
57. Be mistaken
58. Afternoon socials

Starting box on page 562

DOWN

1. ____ majesty
2. "____ Got Sixpence"
3. Teaching staff
4. ____ nous
5. Snoozing
6. Respond
7. School subject
9. Soft drink
10. In what way?
11. Before, to a bard
12. Aretha Franklin hit
15. Furrow
18. Ringer game
22. Feathery wraps
24. Mighty tree
26. Fla. Keys
27. ____-Magnon
28. Bunny's jump
29. CEO, e.g.
30. Adolescent
31. Scottish one
32. Peculiar
34. Winged
35. Angle or cycle starter
37. Direct course
38. Coat before frying
40. Skinflint
41. "All About ____"
42. Loaned
43. Numeral
45. Guy
47. Argument
48. Boot tip
50. Porgy's love
53. Educators' gp.

PUZZLE 386

Loose Tile

The tray on the left seemed the ideal place to store the set of loose dominoes. Unfortunately, when the tray was full, one domino was left over. Determine the arrangement of the dominoes in the tray and which is the Loose Tile.

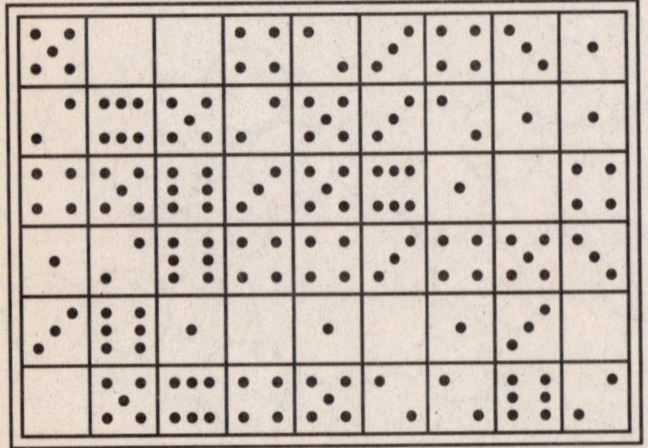

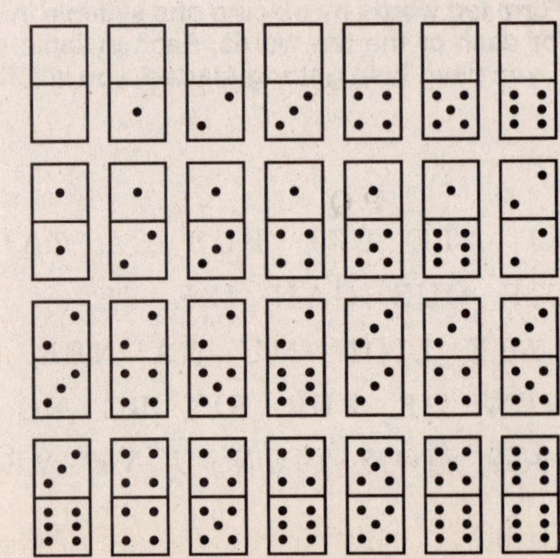

PUZZLE 387

ACROSS

1. Ship's mast
5. Disfigure
8. Met song
9. Washington bills
11. Bass bait
12. One of the Barrymores
14. Weep noisily
15. Inventor Whitney
16. Raise crops
19. Past its prime
21. Command to a mule
22. Picasso's specialty
23. Examiner
26. Carpet
27. Elect
30. Jail fugitive
34. Boat propeller
35. Nightmare street?
37. Barren
39. Deep purple color
41. Golf standard
42. Food for dipping
44. Nimble
47. Kind of gin
48. Snooty person
49. Pottery oven
50. Talk idly
51. Balin and Claire

DOWN

1. Cuts lumber
2. Evidence of truth
3. Auto safety device
4. Flock leader
5. "Izzy and ____"
6. Colony insect
7. Fixes leftovers
10. Find a buyer
13. Recline
17. Posterior
18. List of activities
19. "My Gal ____"
20. Endeavor
24. Become mature
25. "____ Gun" (Cruise film)
28. Look quickly
29. Narrate
31. Flying high
32. Passenger vehicle
33. Noah's craft
36. Cotton fabric
37. Fitness facility
38. License plates
40. Slangy cash
43. Enclosures
45. Mauna ____
46. Taper off
47. Alpine slider

Starting box on page 562

Crypto-Verse

PUZZLE 388

To read this verse, you must first solve this simple substitution code.

PJR OEPQ HEYZD PDXLX VJQJQJH MLEP,

J MLJHHDEUUXL HZXUUXO EQ JQ XAXUDJQZ'H ZEX.

ZDX XAXUDJQZ HJBO, PBZD ZXJLH BQ DBH XRXH,

"UBNW EQ HEFXVEOR REYL EPQ HBGX."

PUZZLE 389

ACROSS

1. Lid
4. Mecca man
6. Rotund
7. Show piece?
10. Expand
11. Finish
13. Choler
14. Palm fruit
16. Lad's lady
17. Power tool
19. Set
20. Shortening
21. Tree trim
24. Haul
25. Owned
26. Suffer
28. Instigates
30. Niche
32. Gallery offering
33. Pleasure craft
35. Weaponry
37. Holiday tune
39. Yard units
40. Ms. Olin
41. Sacred texts
44. Spider's snare
45. Paragon
46. Two-by-four
47. Bard's before

DOWN

1. Telegrams
2. Length times width
3. Grammatical tense
5. Quilting party
6. Lubricates
7. Calculate
8. Bad child's lump
9. Wreck completely
10. Makes the call
12. It may be heavy
13. Some consonant sounds
15. Small bush
18. Margin
19. Titan
21. Craving
22. A snap
23. Fragrant flower
27. Not express
29. Fun's companion
31. Cast
34. Pitch
35. Glowing
36. Lively dance
38. Hunting dog
41. Overalls part
42. Nice notion
43. Grizzly

Starting box on page 562

PUZZLE 390

Number Square

Fill in answers to the clues with 2- and 4-digit numbers, one digit per square. The heavy lines separate the answers.

1	2	3	4
5		6	
7	8	9	
10			

ACROSS

1. Four odd digits
5. The first digit is three times greater than the second digit
6. Perfect square
7. Two consecutive digits in reverse order
9. Two identical digits
10. The sum of the first two digits is equal to the sum of the second two digits

DOWN

1. Four different digits totaling 18
2. Less than 9 Down but more than 6 Across
3. Perfect square
4. 3 Down multiplied by 5 Across
8. 6 Across reversed
9. Perfect square

PUZZLE 391

ACROSS
1. Bro or sis
4. Taxi
7. Assist in crime
9. ___ Lanka
12. Rush
13. French impressionist
15. Author Fleming
16. European capital
17. Copy by machine
19. Evader
21. Lacquered metal
22. Stage drama
23. Hwy.
24. Food wrap
26. Broadcast
27. Fawns' moms
28. Sign before Virgo
29. Decree ___
31. Flawed
32. Of the cheek
34. Sweet roll
36. ___ gin fizz
38. Lettuce variety
39. Gaucho's gear
41. Circle segment
42. Shake with fear
45. Santa ___
46. Rich soil
47. Musician Clapton
49. Ornamental shrub
51. Competitor
53. Dull pain
55. Rearward, nautically
56. Ghostly
58. Thai's NE neighbor
59. Pig's digs
60. Ms. Downey
61. Blunder
62. Building space

DOWN
1. Downcast
2. Mountain goat
3. Father
4. Routine task
5. Objective
6. Garden buzzer
8. Gypsy's card
9. Rope fiber
10. Suggestive
11. ___ nutshell
14. Dense
16. Active starter
18. Inert gas
19. Inventor Whitney
20. Jimmied
22. Sheriff's squad
25. Pretend
26. ___ carte
30. ___ and outs
31. Vital fluid
33. Scrapbook
34. Cleanser ingredient
35. L.A. college
37. Born first
38. Kayak's cousin
40. Eagle's abode
42. Grimy
43. "If I ___ a Million"
44. Snake or Gila, e.g.
45. Loathe
46. Storage spot
48. Yuletide tune
50. "How the West ___ Won"
52. Luxury auto
53. Hops beverage
54. Jalopy
57. Swallow

Starting box on page 562

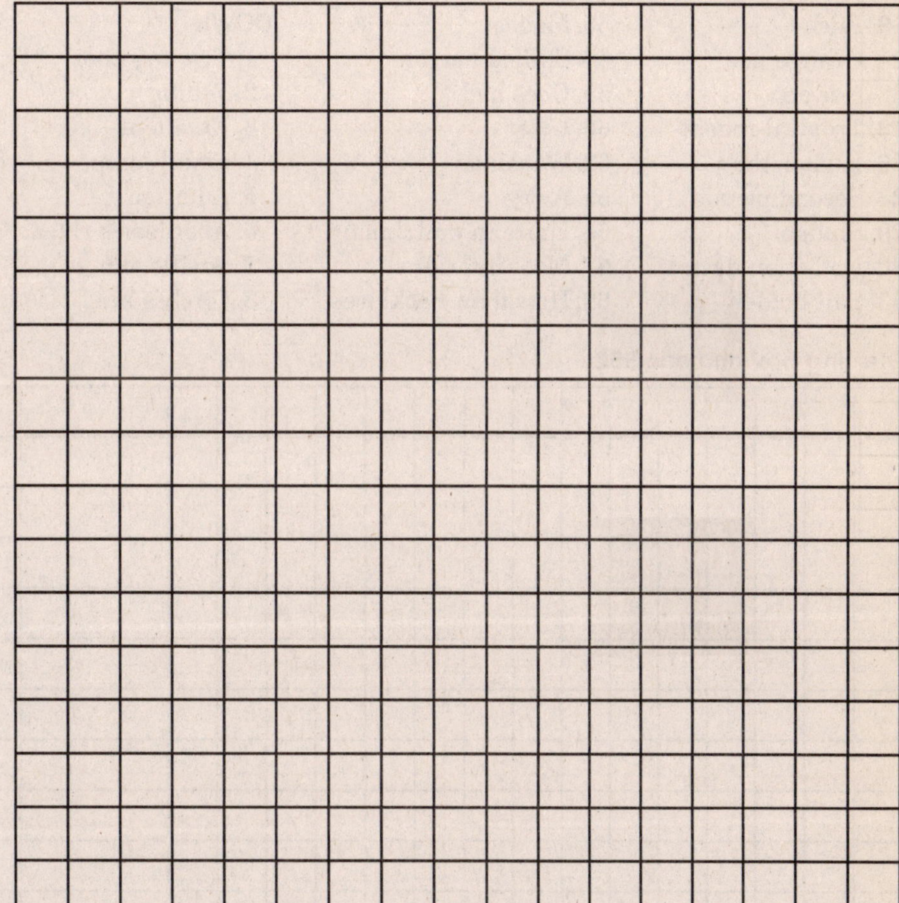

Double Up

PUZZLE 392

Each puzzle consists of four 5-letter words that use ten different letters exactly twice apiece. Thus, since there are already two E's in the first puzzle, you cannot use another E. There is only one V in that puzzle; think of a word using the second V.

1.

2.

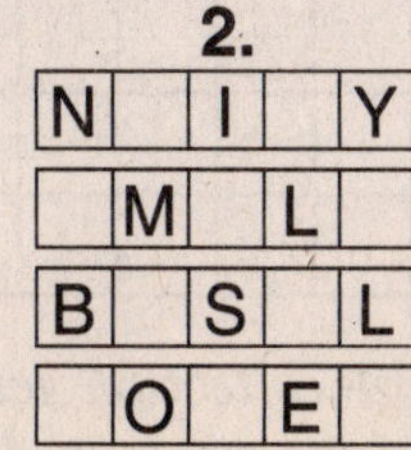

3.

4.

C _ I _ A
_ P _ E _
S _ I _ E
_ A _ N _

PUZZLE 393

ACROSS

1. Washed
7. Mom's boy
10. Baltimore ____
11. Beginner
14. Tumble
15. Storyteller
16. Fedora, for example
17. Spat
18. Tennis calls
19. Filch
21. Orange peel
22. Not act.
23. Tropical rodent
26. Higher than
28. Second person
29. Sludge
30. Detection device
33. Sail holder
35. Sped
39. Apple pastry
40. Hole punch
42. Costume
44. Iranian money unit
45. Proverb
48. Feminine pronoun
50. Mongrel dog
51. More mature
53. Greek vowels
54. Debtor
56. Modest
58. Skilled person
59. Goes bad
60. Utter
62. Warnings
65. Awry
66. Unite in matrimony
67. Most inferior
69. Hawaiian necklaces
71. Skilled
74. Stooped
75. Marble
77. Congeal
79. Mining product
80. Lassie's doc
82. Prop for Col. Klink
84. Chafe
87. Extensive view
88. Kind of chair
89. U-boat
90. Made a doily

DOWN

1. Two together
2. Yelling
3. Excellent
4. Small jump
5. Addition
6. Aberdeen's river
7. Seville sun
8. Circle's kin
9. Saltpeter
11. Politician Gingrich
12. Dove's home
13. Formerly
15. Got up
17. Gun a motor
20. Howls
21. Astrologer's chart
24. Pigeon's call
25. Ambience
26. Stereo-system part
27. Small town
30. Hot tub
31. Diving duck
32. Peachy-keen!
33. Oodles
34. Pickup
35. Three, in Turin
36. Canola product
37. Plane spotter
38. Choose
41. "____ Done It?"
43. Slangy chum
46. Piece
47. Superman's initial
49. Bulletin
52. Legal matter
55. Game callers
57. Small vessel
61. Rearward, nautically
63. Actress Meriwether
64. Change copy
67. Had being
68. "____ Day at a Time"
70. Scholar
71. Crest
72. Stratagem
73. Pitches
74. Cotton pod
76. Hoagie
78. Vegetarian staple
81. Placed on a peg
83. Baby tiger
84. PC key
85. ____ constrictor
86. Groove

Starting box on page 562

PUZZLE 394

ACROSS

1. Came down
5. Vipers
9. Bouquet
10. Undiluted
11. Large salamander
14. Skulk
16. Shortening
17. Commonplace
19. Genetic initials
20. Commit to memory
22. Bro., for one
24. Ukraine city
26. Like sashimi
29. Genesis vessel
30. Minister's residence
32. "TV Guide" abbr.
33. Former Pisa dough
34. Bagel topper
38. Empties the truck
40. Dried fruit
41. Conspiracy
43. Concerning
44. Hockey great
45. Destinies
47. Hold up
50. Entree selection
55. Kennedy and Koppel
56. Card game
58. Woodwind
59. Bend
61. Agitate
63. Actress Ward
64. Delve
65. Clark's cohort
67. Butcher's hanger
69. Pouchlike structure
71. Wood shapers
73. Australian hopper
74. Mighty particle
77. Final letters
79. Classic car
80. USA component
82. Type of clam
89. Hawaiian goose
90. Simian
92. Middle Eastern chiefs
93. Ruby or Sandra
94. Coal measure
95. Flit
97. Dance step
98. Make broader
100. Letter from Athens
103. Worker's request
105. Units of electric resistance
106. Disentangle
108. Dinner offering
111. Dorothy's pet
112. Jungle sounds
113. Decorative jug
114. Bohemian

DOWN

1. Klee contemporary
2. Bud's pal
3. Drive
4. Emulates Hines
5. Bread spread
6. California's Big ____
7. Goad
8. Basted
9. Insert
11. Spoil
12. Coffee server
13. Hearty laugh
15. Riata
16. Superior, e.g.
18. River island
20. Resin
21. Behave humanly
22. College cheer
23. Compass pt.
25. Moving vehicle
27. Fervor
28. Existed
30. Tim or Tug
31. 6th sense
33. Part of L.A.
35. Previously
36. Surrealist Joan ____
37. Gremlin's kin
39. Young girl
42. Cereal grain
46. Old Testament land
48. Biscuit topper
49. String tie
50. Peas' container
51. Sashes
52. Forum wear
53. Deli delight
54. Walked heavily
57. Shade provider
60. Place to get a slice
62. King and Hagman
63. Record on film
66. Espy
68. Digits
70. Sort of role
72. Dry, as wine
75. Billfold note
76. Galena or bauxite
78. Haggard heroine
80. Picnic problem
81. Bounder
83. Monarch
84. Small inlet
85. Monopoly props.
86. 2 to 1, e.g.
87. Born as
88. Poetic contraction
91. Epoch
96. Gratuity
98. Reporter's query
99. Little devil
101. London gallery
102. Declare
104. Marsh bird
105. Exclamations
107. Nice summer
109. Krazy ____
110. Weep

Starting box on page 562

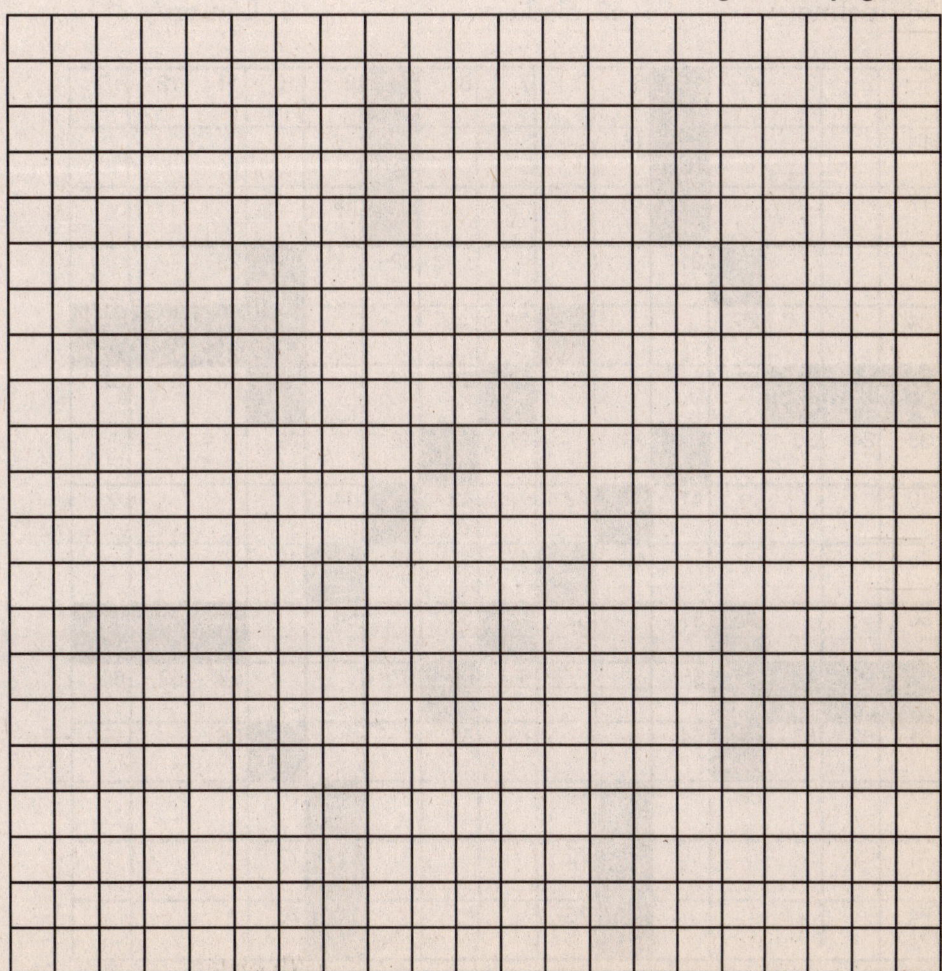

PUZZLE 395

ACROSS

1. Welfare
5. Do the butterfly
9. Strong
14. Lullaby
15. "___, Nanette"
16. Ancient language
17. Image of worship
18. Mined minerals
19. Father's brother
20. Baby bug
21. Boy Scout item
23. "___ About You?"
24. Even chance
26. Incline
27. Poems
29. Stage prompt
30. Child's game
33. Reach
36. Name
38. Lubricate
40. Purple flower
42. Previously named
44. Luxurious boat
45. Sung dramas
47. House extension
49. Yo-yos, e.g.
50. Small
51. Cook's vessel
53. Show anger
55. Sad cry
57. Summer TV fare
61. Entreat
64. ___ disc player
66. On the contrary
67. Excuse
69. Overhead curve
70. Time long past
71. Small body of land
72. Bowling channel
73. Let up on
74. Lingerie item
75. Needle openings
76. Stair

DOWN

1. Work shift
2. Sound track
3. Hair tangles
4. Lamprey
5. Pried
6. Bass lure
7. Incompetent
8. Decorative inlay
9. Gusty
10. Kurosawa film
11. Restless desire
12. Barn's neighbor
13. Recognized
21. Chew one's ___ (meditate)
22. Snail's kin
25. Navigation device
28. Brightest star
30. Mexican treat
31. Pale
32. Attains
33. Not busy
34. Conduit
35. Not windward
37. Spelling event
39. Restaurant patron
41. Volume
43. Santa's staffer
46. Alone
48. Sways suddenly
52. Mexican dish
54. Came across
56. Flower arrangement
58. WWII craft
59. Care for
60. Expensive
61. Load the hook
62. Alternative
63. Coat with gold
65. Skin affliction
68. Floral plot
70. No's opposite

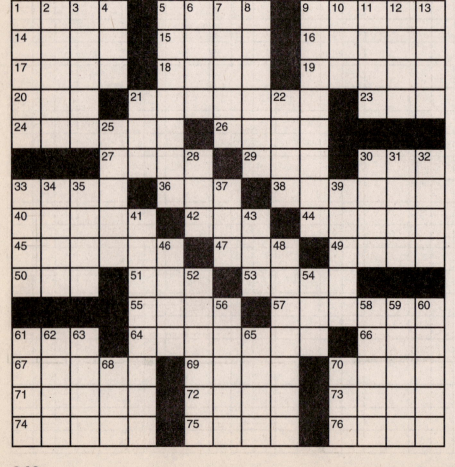

1	2	3	4	■	5	6	7	8	■	9	10	11	12	13
14				■	15				■	16				
17				■	18				■	19				
20			■	21					22		■	23		
24			25			■	26				■	■	■	■
■	■	■	27			28	■	29			■	30	31	32
33	34	35		■	36		37	■	38		39			
40				41	■	42		43	■	44				
45					46	■	47		48	■	49			
50			■	51		52	■	53		54		■	■	■
■	■	■	■	55			56	■	57			58	59	60
61	62	63	■	64				65			■	66		
67			68		■	69				■	70			
71					■	72				■	73			
74					■	75				■	76			

PUZZLE 396

ACROSS

1. Way in
5. "The ___ Must Be Crazy"
9. Implored
13. Up to it
14. Dressing dispenser
15. Sitar music
16. Coyote's kin
17. Hosiery thread
18. Nervous
19. Get close
20. Endeavor
22. Rabbit feature
24. Caught wind of
28. Donna Summer's genre
30. Sliver
33. Airy
34. Burn-soothing plant
35. Dobbin's burden
36. "Ode on a Grecian ___"
37. Live it up
40. Ailing
41. Overlay
43. Kiln
44. Feathered
46. Amaze
48. Drifts
49. Dictation taker
50. Deadly snake
51. Eyelet
56. Boys
60. Nature's bandage
63. Wavelike fabric
64. Yoked animals
65. Limo, e.g.
66. Best
67. Type size
68. Ship's gang
69. Hamilton bills
70. Toil

DOWN

1. Sunup
2. Slender woodwind
3. Earthen pot
4. Revitalize
5. Fortitude
6. Depose
7. Remove, to a printer
8. Bloom holder
9. Make believe
10. Fellow
11. Nog ingredient
12. 24 hours
14. Mild cigar
21. ___ Beta Kappa
23. Behaves
25. Livy's reception room
26. Kingdoms
27. Aridly
28. Most desperate
29. Set on fire
30. Melting snow
31. Any ___ in a storm
32. Lower limb
33. "___ Tanner"
34. Woe is me!
38. Luau favorite
39. Majestic poetry
42. Robin Hood's weapon
45. Small computers
47. Hide ___ hair
48. Badger's kin
52. Skip
53. Pie a la ___
54. Demeanor
55. Notable times
57. Leaf's angle
58. Art ___
59. Glitch
60. Anatomical pouch
61. Unfriendly dog
62. Dined

PUZZLE 397

ACROSS

1. Wrathful
4. Noblewoman
8. Chiefs
13. On thin ___
14. Cruising
15. Net tender
16. Faintly lit
17. Moo juice
18. Wicker material
19. Matinee ___
21. Expel
23. Not new
24. Summer in Paris
26. Loosen
28. CIA operatives
30. "O Sole ___"
31. Downs' partners
34. Possessive pronoun
35. Totally
36. Housetop
38. Snaky fish
39. Lunchtime
43. Hot temper
44. Talk too much
46. Con's foe
47. Relaxed
49. To's mate
50. Score to beat
51. Specifier
52. Warm fabric
54. Shirt sleeve
55. Gremlin's kin
58. Lend a hand
61. Scent
65. In abundance
67. Skid
69. Wood chopper
70. Nibbled
71. Liquid rock
72. Five and five
73. Did a tailor's job
74. Spotted
75. Fire or carpenter

DOWN

1. Skirt type
2. Etching liquid
3. Salesman's car
4. On the ___
5. Stage lines
6. Pastrami shop
7. Chatters
8. Stash
9. Graze
10. Choir voice
11. TV knob
12. Convey
15. Breakfast food
20. Flowery wreaths
22. Construct
25. Bubblegummer
27. "___ Gang"
28. Ledge
29. ___ bear
30. Landed property
32. Composure
33. More achy
34. Woven network
37. Nourished
40. Was against
41. Some exams
42. 365-day period
45. Fiddler's necessity
48. Bullets, for short
51. "___ Son"
53. Propelled
55. Nest contents
56. Bowling alley, e.g.
57. Fault
59. Bit of land
60. Do in, as a dragon
62. Facts
63. Yoked animals
64. Landlord's concern
66. Be obliged to pay
68. Lily leaf

PUZZLE 398

ACROSS

1. Sick
4. Pear-shaped fruit
7. Lively
12. As well
13. Island greeting
15. Serenity
16. Selfish trip
17. Private teacher
18. Multiplication term
19. Byword
21. Radiance
23. Gusto
24. Building shape
26. Serving scoop
28. Love song
31. "___ Send Me"
32. Night hooter
35. Nerve
36. Couple
38. ___-eyed (romantic)
40. Express
42. Christmas toymaker
44. Gardening tool
45. Divided equally
47. Faintly lit
49. Actress Fonda
50. That girl
51. Intense fury
53. English titles
55. Not fitting
57. Luau fare
58. Serene
61. Unkind
63. Unfasten
67. Vocal solos
69. Create
71. Fruity beverage
72. Drum type
73. Bowling term
74. Formerly known as
75. Clean house
76. Eavesdrop
77. Shaggy ox

DOWN

1. Think piece
2. Advertising emblem
3. Winnings
4. Winter ailment
5. Tad
6. Demon
7. Condo's kin: abbr.
8. Grasp
9. Unexciting
10. Decorates a cake
11. Take a break
13. Coral-island chain
14. Assortment
20. Bank employee
22. Uproars
25. Youngster
27. Guitar's ancestor
28. Wash up
29. Marriage site
30. Appropriate
32. Kidney, e.g.
33. Small birds
34. Ancient instrument
35. Pour
37. "___ Yeller"
39. Be next to
41. Restraint
43. Falsehood
46. Liquid measure
48. Atlas part
52. Sporting blades
54. Travel course
55. Mental picture
56. Canvas covers
58. Autos for hire
59. Queued up
60. Toe the ___
62. Kind of tide
64. Wacky
65. Hunch
66. Quick look
68. Dunk
70. Blubber

PUZZLE 399

ACROSS

1. Wearing boots
5. "Swan Lake" costume
9. Vatican head
13. Cassette, e.g.
14. Pay up
15. Impersonated
16. Word of woe
17. Winesap, e.g.
18. For men only
19. Alleviate
21. Inn has two
23. Cooler cubes
24. Trickier
26. Cup's mate
28. Egg box
31. Radiates
33. Speak falsely
34. Writing tool
36. Odds and ___
40. Obey reveille
42. Electrified particle
43. TV's "F ___"
44. Wordy birdie
45. Fortify
47. "My ___ and Only"
48. Typed (in)
50. Chanced
52. Orb
55. Be miserly
57. Historic age
58. Recede, as the tide
60. Confident
64. Forest-floor plant
66. Jewish cleric
68. Blue or bean
69. Division word
70. Some exams
71. Logger's target
72. Beginning
73. "If I ___ a Rich Man"
74. Fax

DOWN

1. Night light
2. ___ and hearty
3. October gem
4. Cease
5. Plains dwelling
6. Ref's cousin
7. Floor square
8. Tool
9. Mas' mates
10. Of sight
11. Calm
12. Garden tool
14. Steep-sided valley
20. Leave by ladder
22. Posed
25. Archives
27. Client
28. ___ chowder
29. Breezy
30. Harness part
32. Skirt length
35. Four plus five
37. Recess
38. Fully cooked
39. Went lickety-split
41. Rice wine
43. Waters down
45. Facial fringe
46. Difficult time
49. Sooner than, in poems
51. Feats
52. Highway vehicles
53. Likely
54. ___ makes waste
56. Suspend
59. Without clothing
61. Seldom seen
62. Fifty-fifty
63. Changed colors
65. Instant grass
67. Forbid

PUZZLE 400

ACROSS

1. Picks
5. Distantly
9. Receded
14. Radiance
15. Actress Lillian ___
16. Andean climber
17. Trattoria offering
19. Alma ___
20. Beer spigot
21. Red dyes
23. Region
24. Lass
25. Kanga's kid
26. Closes
27. Dangers
31. Prompted
33. Part of BTU
34. Frosters
36. Flat hat
39. Made into fillets
41. Needlefish
42. Stagnant
44. Animal pouch
45. Musical piece
47. Epochal
48. Talking pet
49. Removed paint from
52. Mexican treat
55. Greek vowel
57. Diving bird
58. Within
59. Not obvious
61. Maui dish
64. Extend a subscription
66. Union Pacific and Amtrak
68. Fat
69. Laborer of yore
70. Architect Christopher ___
71. Preference
72. Origin
73. For fear that

DOWN

1. Malt kiln
2. Metamorphic stage
3. Box in
4. Sink downward
5. Dating from time immemorial
6. Suits
7. Moving
8. African mammal
9. Freddy's street
10. Burned brightly
11. Wand
12. Edit
13. Ventures
18. Listen to
22. Like a lemon
24. Fence opening
27. Centers
28. Wild ox of Sulawesi
29. Galvanizing metal
30. John Hancocks
32. Snaky shape
35. Rogue
36. Field cover
37. Wings
38. Fuse
40. Waterless
43. Tropical wood
46. "The Defiant ___"
48. Humble
50. Telephoned
51. Person who regrets
52. Mystical cards
53. Protozoan
54. Motion pictures
56. Degrade
60. Fork prong
61. Cut back
62. Lyric poems
63. "___ It Romantic?"
65. Itty-bitty
67. It gives a hoot

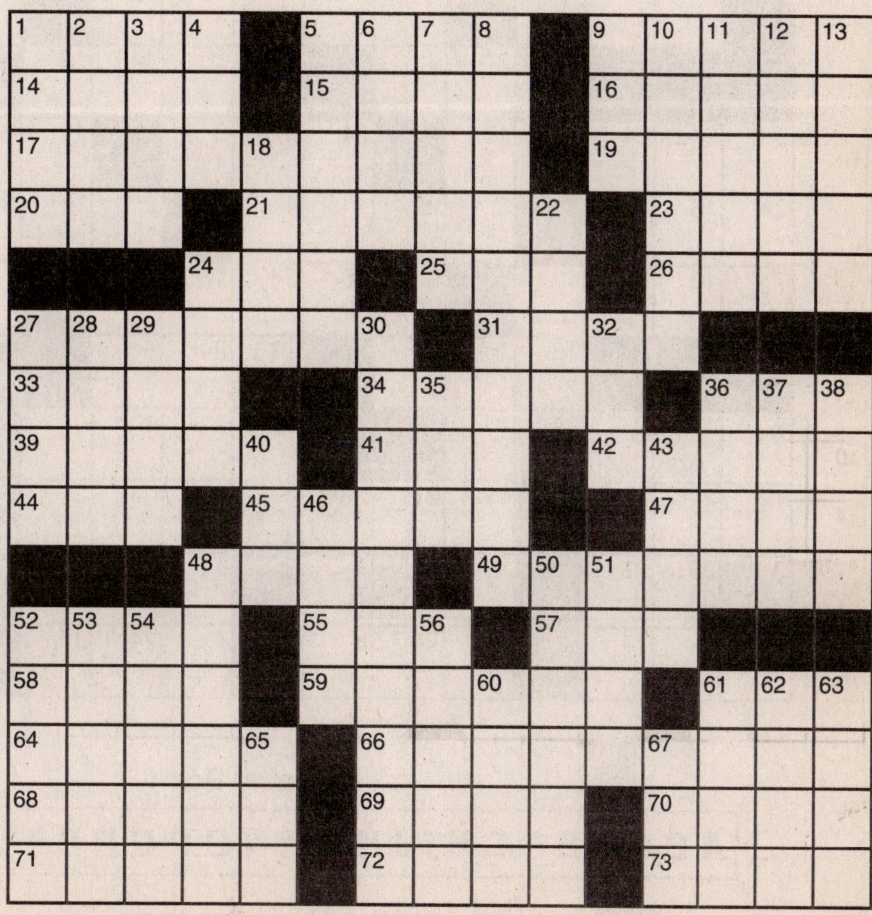

PUZZLE 401 CODEWORD

Codeword is a special crossword puzzle in which conventional clues are omitted. Instead, answer words in the diagram are represented by numbers. Each number represents a different letter of the alphabet, and all of the letters of the alphabet are used. When you are sure of a letter, put it in the code key chart and cross it off in the Alphabet Box. A group of letters has been inserted to start you off.

1	2	3	4	5	6	7	8	9	10	11	12	13
										H		
14	15	16	17	18	19	20	21	22	23	24	25	26
E			M									

17	24	5	■	11 H	24	9	■	1	24	13	■	24	23	12
12	5	14	■	14 E	16	14	■	12	1	14	■	6	24	17
20	12	3	■	17 M	26	25	■	8	14	24	■	24	23	14
24	23	24	■	5	24	7	14	■	■	4	14	4	24	20
3	14	20	■	■	7	14	20	■	26	20	8	■	■	■
■	14	7	24	■	12	7	7	14	4	■	14	24	9	14
■	■	■	1	24	4	■	12	18	14	12	■	3	2	14
5	9	24	18	17	■	24	2	8	■	11	24	22	14	18
24	18	18	■	5	2	4	4	■	2	17	5	■	■	■
7	13	5	12	■	9	10	24	17	5	■	7	24	7	■
■	■	■	16	14	14	■	23	24	9	■	■	9	24	3
9	19	2	24	21	■	■	14	7	10	11	■	5	26	14
12	2	4	■	12	21	26	■	7	24	2	■	26	18	18
3	26	23	■	20	12	4	■	14	18	15	■	4	12	7
24	5	14	■	13	24	8	■	4	14	15	■	14	4	24

Alphabet Box

A B C D E F G H I J K L M N O P Q R S T U V W X Y Z

PUZZLE 402

ACROSS

1. Metric weight
5. Egyptian snake
8. Untidy one
12. Principle
13. Church feature
15. Maui feast
16. Certain exam
17. Cook's wear
18. "B.C." insects
19. Tiny bit
21. Dismount
23. Shade tree
24. Rooks and pawns
26. Poor grades
27. Novel
28. Dollop
31. Self-centered person
34. Uncontrolled blaze
36. Seethe
37. Surpass
38. Spirited
39. Wrigley Field, for one
42. Caesar and Cobb
44. Pig's home
45. Hoopla
46. Knit one, ___ one
47. Clothes collection
49. Joan of ___
52. African trip
55. Hawaiian native, e.g.
57. In the thick of
58. Quiz response
60. Pinch
61. Oliver's wish
62. Robin's sound
63. Clutch
64. ___ out (barely earned)
65. Curvy letter
66. Towel word

DOWN

1. Feel one's way
2. Rustic
3. Warning signal
4. Defrost
5. Granny Smiths
6. Fathers
7. Not amateur
8. Destroyed
9. Respiratory organ
10. Solemn vow
11. Type of sculpture
13. Scented bag
14. Tooth coating
20. Frozen treats
22. Bawdy
25. Quick cut
26. Pickle flavor
28. Met star
29. Hot and dry
30. Garden plots
31. Recedes
32. Bearded animal
33. Greasy
34. Stir-fry vessel
35. Autumn
37. Trampled
40. Carson's predecessor
41. Floating
42. Rent to another
43. Locale
46. Groups of searchers
47. Sloshed in water
48. Aggravates
49. Cherish
50. Cover the roof again
51. Horseshoe and fiddler
52. Matching
53. In a frenzy
54. Inferno
56. Near
59. Astonishment

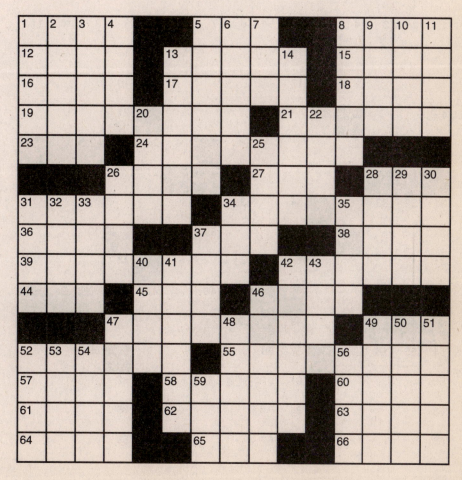

1	2	3	4			5	6	7			8	9	10	11
12					13				14		15			
16					17						18			
19				20					21	22				
23				24				25						
			26					27				28	29	30
31	32	33					34				35			
36						37					38			
39				40	41				42	43				
44				45				46						
			47				48					49	50	51
52	53	54					55				56			
57					58	59					60			
61					62						63			
64						65					66			

PUZZLE 403

ACROSS

1. Substitute worker
5. Jeweler's sale
8. Close forcefully
12. Track
13. Forbidden
15. Minute amount
16. Far from attractive
17. Citified
18. Questionable
19. Addition shape
20. Eager
21. Unruly kids
22. Quit
24. Liquid gold
26. Sheriff Kane's deadline
27. Make happen
31. "Less ___ Zero"
34. By way of
36. Corn piece
37. Babble
38. Figured out
40. Flood control
41. Before a conflict
43. Actress Lenz
44. Speckles
45. More peculiar
46. "___ Might Be Giants"
48. Radio spots
50. Trailblazers
54. Frenzied
57. Holiday songs
59. Hula necklace
60. Label
61. How to leave Garbo
62. Male elephant
63. Needles' holes
64. Plateaus
65. Ready for print
66. "I ___ Forget You"
67. Electric or moray
68. Acquires

DOWN

1. More loyal
2. Majestic bird
3. Factories
4. Tissue thickness
5. White flower
6. Receded
7. Whine
8. Alike
9. Threaten
10. Surmounting
11. Bath rugs
13. Flaky dessert
14. Informed of
20. "Long ___ and Far Away"
23. Hostel
25. Glazed
28. Pull strings?
29. Usher
30. Stately trees
31. Mistake in print
32. Not soft
33. Impersonated
35. Two-by-two structure?
36. Door slots
38. Fat
39. Part of NFL
42. Least powerful
44. Tinting agent
47. Naval off.
49. Hoax
50. Not poetry
51. Escape
52. Ignited again
53. Bank deposits
54. Fresh
55. BLT topping
56. Prophetic sign
58. Opposite of aweather
62. Beseech

PUZZLE 404

ACROSS

1. Statutes
5. Brainchild
9. Dangle
13. Canyon feedback
14. Three-note chord
15. Wild ox
16. One billion years
17. Party givers
18. Vitality
19. Piece
21. Burn remedy
22. Busy insect
23. Theater escort
27. Narrow cut
29. Request again
32. Winged
33. Decreasing
35. Luau necklace
37. Canal transport
39. Lively
41. Athens vowel
42. Stroked lightly
44. Danger
45. Japanese grill
47. Fido's treat
48. Transform
49. Sass
50. Slalom runners
53. Versions
58. Remains
59. Stonecrop
61. Cluster
62. Doing nothing
63. Low ship deck
64. Staffer
65. Necessity
66. Customs
67. Confused

DOWN

1. Plant part
2. Top-grade recipient
3. Stop, Flicka!
4. It gives you a trill
5. Wrought ___
6. Bother
7. Graze
8. Radio spots
9. Danger
10. Indigo plant
11. Banned
12. Green plum
14. "Of ___ I Sing"
20. Assembled
24. Nab
25. Wielded a strop
26. Units in physics
27. Laziness
28. Hawaiian porch
30. Small and sprightly
31. Apply again
32. Mature
33. Appoint
34. Scrub in the tub
36. Type
38. Iridescent gem
40. Certain storm
43. With fatigue
46. Egg collector
47. Drill need
49. Not stiff
50. Wedge
51. African antelope
52. Woes
54. Pairs
55. Hodgepodge
56. Bows the head
57. Proofreader's word
59. Plant
60. Big Band, e.g.

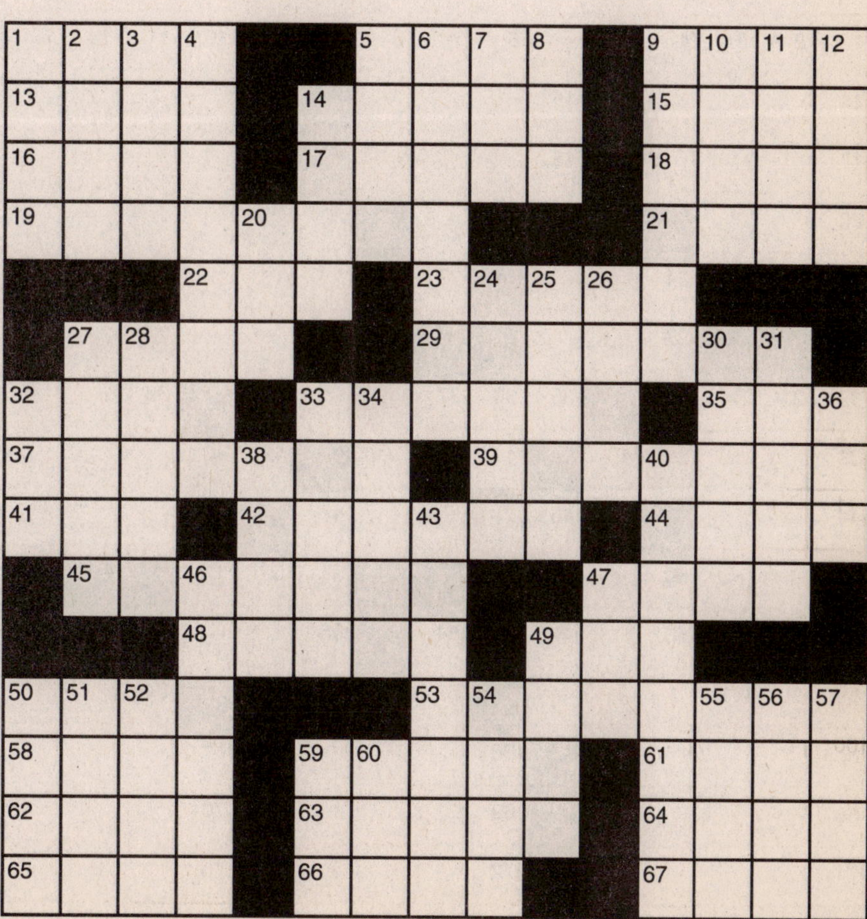

PUZZLE 405

ACROSS

1. Certain amphibians
5. Rumple
9. "Angel ___"
14. Burn reliever
15. Ruler mark
16. Aquatic plants
17. Cajun soup thickener
18. Remain
19. Terrier type
20. Unit of energy
21. Potent particle
22. Fastened
23. Showy bloom
25. Became ashen
27. Exasperate
28. Washing off
32. Smoker's device
35. Resounded
38. Loud noise
39. Adjust
41. Part of the sleep cycle
42. Protozoan
44. Bark sharply
45. "The ___ Cometh"
48. Hops kiln
49. Smudged
51. Skinny fish
53. Criminal
55. Diluted
59. Fundamentals
62. Formerly, once
64. Scheduled
65. Eight-piece ensemble
66. Title of respect
67. Insect stage
68. Mythical cave-dweller
69. Alcohol lamp
70. Maple genus
71. Exciting
72. Slender
73. Hammer end

DOWN

1. Like many seals
2. Fauna's partner
3. ___ act to follow
4. Gender
5. Error
6. Till
7. Rascal
8. Bashful
9. Spanish ranch
10. Large antelopes
11. Not fer
12. Infrequent
13. Look after
21. Balloon input
22. Ballet movement
24. Hold on property
26. Fragrance
29. Concept
30. Penpoints
31. Biting fly
32. Foots the bill
33. Muslim chief
34. "___ Le Moko"
36. Motto
37. Dress bottom
40. Shortly
43. Shed
46. Cartoon transparencies
47. Dan Rather, e.g.
50. Away from home
52. Sup
54. Under, in poems
56. Draw out
57. Calcutta coin
58. Wish for
59. "___ Sides Now"
60. Land parcel
61. Plato's porch
63. Rajah's wife
66. Confronted
67. Baby's food

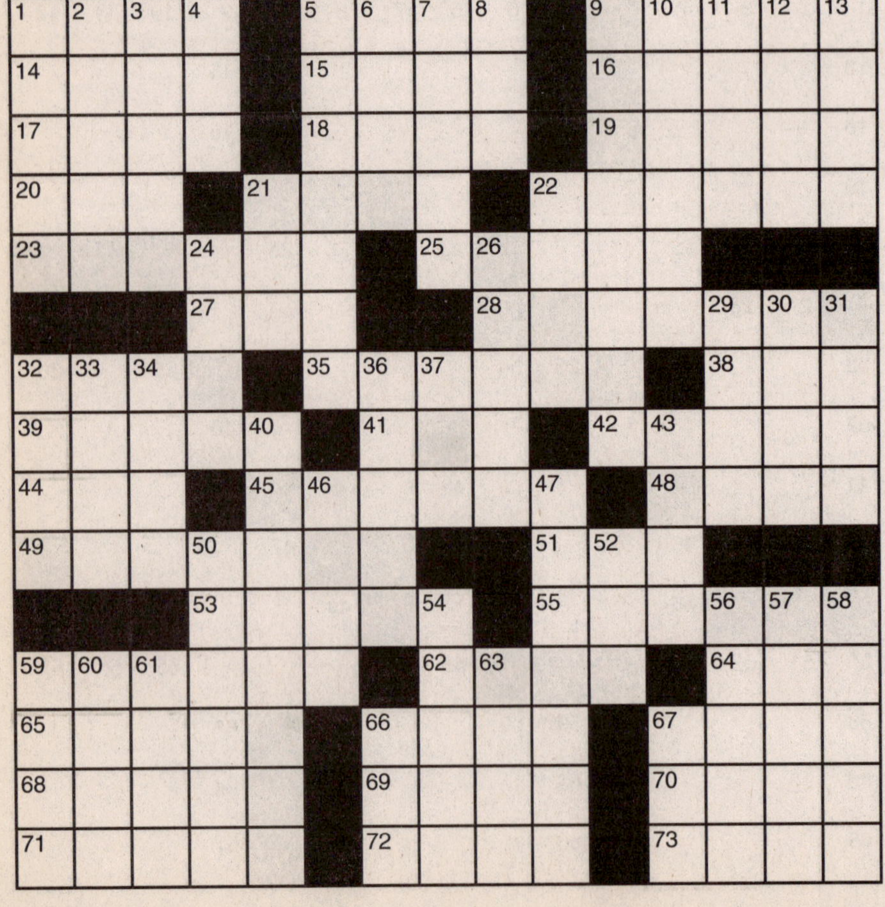

PUZZLE 406

ACROSS

1. Bargain event
5. Not at home
9. Monastery head
14. Scheme
15. Labyrinth
16. Top quality
17. Or ___ (threat)
18. Unruly tyke
19. Consumed
20. Colors
21. Wiggly fish
22. Immediate
23. Rowing blade
25. Road bend
27. Muffler
30. Hidden supply
32. Switch positions
35. Burglar
36. Pale
37. Companion
38. Dowel
39. Frequently, to Keats
41. Mine yield
42. Flightless bird
43. ___ out a living
44. Mr. Starr
46. More uncommon
48. Joined
49. Power tool
50. Clutch
51. Health club
52. Workout room
53. Archer's aim
58. Game piece
60. Milky jewel
64. Sea
65. Soft drink
66. Judge's wear
67. Opened
68. Unseat
69. Extensions
70. Breathers
71. Sis's sibs
72. Low grades

DOWN

1. Ran fast
2. Comrade
3. Meet defeat
4. Unpleasant sight
5. Yellowish fossil resin
6. Silver or glass follower
7. Flowering bushes
8. Thus far
9. Impersonator
10. Boast
11. Chomp
12. Warning sign
13. Pup ___
22. Escort
24. Have the means
26. Pupil's place
27. Scatter
28. Strangle
29. Helped
30. Tabby's treat
31. Vitality
32. Verdi work
33. Monikers
34. Drink noisily
40. Foremost
45. Alluring charm
47. ___ car
52. Small flies
53. ___ of duty
54. Skin woe
55. Scarlet hues
56. Pace
57. Halts
59. As well
61. Totem ___
62. Competent
63. Not so much
65. Corn core

PUZZLE 407

FLOWER POWER

The answers to this petaled puzzle will go in a curve from the number on the outside to the center of the flower. Each number in the flower will have two 5-letter answers. One goes in a clockwise direction and the second in a counterclockwise direction. We have entered two answers to help you begin.

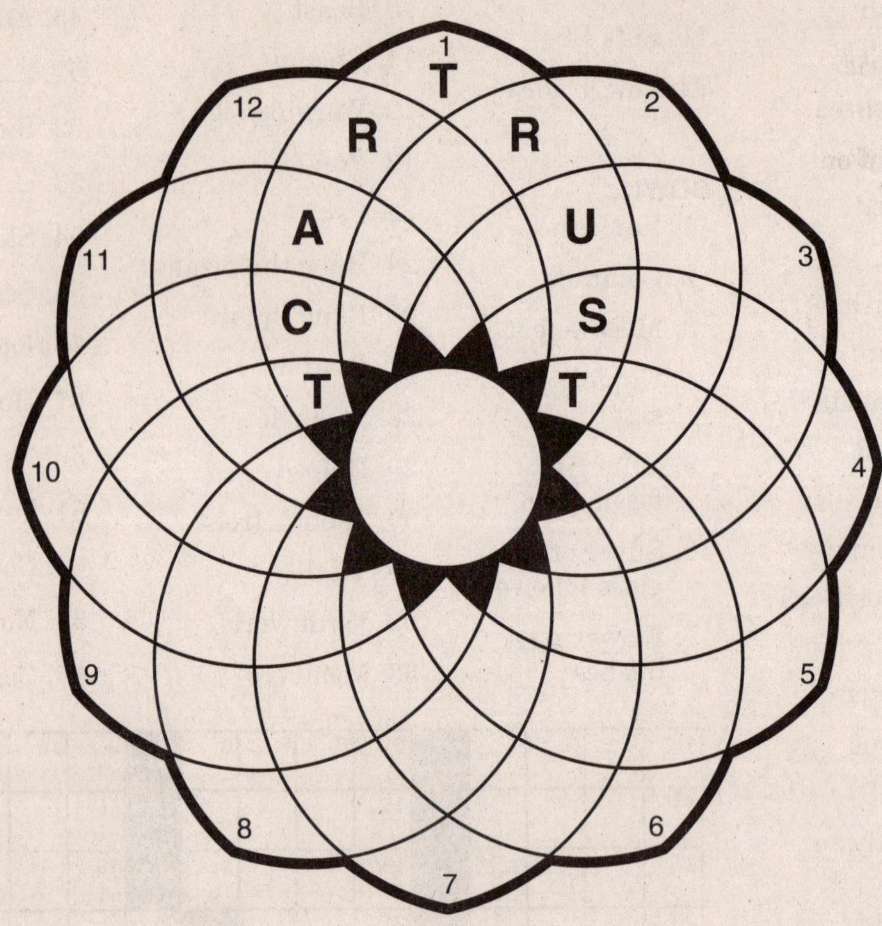

CLOCKWISE

1. Depend
2. Violet variety
3. Valentine shape
4. Chest
5. Spoils
6. Submarine finder
7. Kitchen gadget
8. ___ out (dwindle)
9. Bus station
10. Tango, e.g.
11. Breakfast bread
12. Dull buzz

COUNTERCLOCKWISE

1. Piece of land
2. Not poetry
3. Visit frequently
4. Uneasy
5. Brag
6. Regretful
7. Hennery
8. Spotted horse
9. Rot
10. Thwart
11. Thin candle
12. Gift giver

PUZZLE 408

ACROSS

1. Shish ___
6. Of the congregation
10. Doe's beau
14. Fight site
15. Killer whale
16. Doily fabric
17. Steamship
18. Legal hold on property
19. Radiance
20. Have a burger
21. Prospector's quest
23. Meddle (with)
25. Infant food
26. Dustcloth
27. Snaky letter
28. Humors
32. Athenian vowels
34. Lawbreaker
35. Prized
40. Minor
41. Praises
42. Ascended
43. Trattoria treat
45. Dull buzz
46. Conserve
47. Chirped
49. Cry
52. Guided
53. Poison ___
54. Shudder
56. Sherpa's sighting
58. Twosome
61. Spanish stewpot
62. So be it!
64. Covered with water
66. Disquiet
67. Drive
68. ___ pole
69. Leg joint
70. Lobe locales
71. Decorative vessels

DOWN

1. Wrinkly vegetable
2. Solo at the Met
3. Bowed
4. Wallet item
5. Steal
6. Lounge around
7. Parched
8. Skater's surface
9. Choral compositions
10. Shut loudly
11. Brownish gray
12. TV's "Green ___"
13. Motor parts
22. Select
24. Turkish officials
25. Fork tines
26. Revise again
28. Newts
29. Ooze
30. Defendant's answer
31. Spoken
33. Four-wheeled carriage
36. Road groove
37. Tree anchor
38. Laborer of yore
39. Accomplishment
41. Power to influence
44. Angel's headdress
45. Stray
48. Comedian
49. Baby deliverer
50. Acrylic fiber
51. Contradict
55. Ram or bull
56. Leap ___
57. Concludes
58. Palm fruit
59. Patron
60. Resistance units
63. Extinct bird
65. Amaze

1	2	3	4	5		6	7	8	9		10	11	12	13
14						15					16			
17						18					19			
20				21	22				23	24				
			25					26				27		
28	29	30				31		32			33			
34						35	36					37	38	39
40					41						42			
43				44						45				
			46					47	48					
49	50	51		52					53					
54			55				56	57				58	59	60
61					62	63				64	65			
66					67					68				
69					70					71				

PUZZLE 409

ACROSS

1. Fodder
6. Den
10. Wearing boots
14. Dog
15. Teen's problem
16. Company symbol
17. Playing marble
18. Darn
19. Mine and yours
20. Likewise not
21. Taper off
23. Give consent
24. Unhealthy
25. A mother's boy
27. Resound
30. Concur
33. Broke a fast
36. Grime
37. Divides
38. Drilling tool
39. Poison ___
41. Get it?
42. Adolescent
44. Tarzan's friend
45. Not us
48. Wight, e.g.
49. Absolutely!
50. Emerge from sleep
51. Poetic contraction
52. Artfully shy
53. Bible craft
55. Reality
59. Important time
60. Amigo
63. Rajah's mate
64. Persuade
67. Showy
69. Battery liquid
70. Amazed
71. Metal suit
72. Dole out
73. Caesar's garb
74. Rental document

DOWN

1. Bridge section
2. Fast-food order
3. Thunder
4. Play division
5. Steering device
6. Baby ram
7. Perfect shot
8. Lodging
9. "The Hunt for ___ October"
10. Walk heavily
11. Time measure
12. Bogeyman
13. Portion
22. Uninteresting
23. Restless
24. Small amount
25. Drastic
26. United
27. Thesis
28. Auto model
29. Residences
31. Strut
32. Finely contoured
33. Mistreat
34. Caption
35. Anesthetic
40. Bus
43. Pig sound
46. Duo number
47. Catch
54. Imperial
55. Streetcar
56. Campaign
57. Group
58. Spring or neap
59. Seaweed
60. Cougar
61. Stirs
62. Apollo's music maker
64. Used a bench
65. Self-importance
66. Fireplace item
68. How ___ you?

PUZZLE 410

ACROSS
1. Crinkly cloth
6. Slips up
10. Eager
14. Make merry
15. Bounty
16. Type of cone
17. Sleep interrupter
18. Mother's little yelper?
19. Alleviate
20. Center
21. Patterned
23. Look at
24. Dawn droplets
25. Make a quilt
26. Rules to follow
29. Impostor
31. Century part
33. Library no-nos
37. Boutique
38. Eagerly expectant
41. Gobi transport
43. Dull person
44. Freshen
46. Dinner jacket
48. Stringed instruments
50. Barnyard fowl
53. Diver's territory
54. Light-switch positions
56. Cousins, e.g.
57. Moreover
59. Flagrant
61. Winter illness
62. Paper repairer
65. Dog in Oz
66. Wheat seed
68. Draft animals
69. Black bird
70. Caregiver
71. Be inclined
72. Psalm
73. Army groups

DOWN
1. Stuffs
2. Comfort
3. One who dodges
4. ___ se
5. Type of wood
6. Push aside
7. Highway
8. Lounging garments
9. Made fashionable
10. Acted like
11. By means of
12. Outs' opposites
13. Door opener?
21. Doc
22. Flock mamas
24. Pair
26. Broad valley
27. Skunk's defense
28. Transmit
30. One with a halo
32. Outrigger
34. Was located
35. Australian bird
36. Gender
38. Parts of a circle
39. Eccentric person
40. Lone
42. Legal
45. Sheep fleece
47. Cozy retreat
49. Grab
51. African trip
52. Sign up
55. Anecdote
56. Part of a.k.a.
58. Sand hills
59. Curve
60. Part of a molecule
62. Tyke
63. Wood chopper
64. Writing implement
66. Type of antelope
67. Gallop

1	2	3	4	5	■	6	7	8	9	■	10	11	12	13
14					■	15				■	16			
17					■	18				■	19			
20			■	■	21					22		■	■	■
23			■	24			■	25			■	26	27	28
■	29		30			■	■	■	31		32			
■	■	■	33			34	35	36	■	37				
38	39	40		■	41				42	■	43			
44				45	■	46				47		■	■	■
48					49	■	■	■	50			51	52	■
53			■	54		55	■	56			■	57		58
■	■	■	59				60			■	■	61		
62	63	64		■	65				■	66	67			
68				■	69				■	70				
71				■	72				■	73				

PUZZLE 411

ACROSS

1. Stew
5. Small nail
9. Fishhook part
13. Within
17. False witness
18. Atop
19. ___ vera
20. Ore deposit
21. Unit of land
22. Casino city
23. Weep
24. Burrowing mammal
25. Dweller
27. Rocks back and forth
29. Did a pressing job
31. Roof piece
33. Zip
34. Kickers' stands
35. Roll shape
39. Encouragement
44. Paddle's cousin
45. Massage
47. Famous
48. Caviar
49. Threesome
51. Set
53. Moth-eaten
54. Demolish
55. Privacy
57. Sheer fabric
59. Dwindled
60. Floating refuge
61. Rugged country
62. Actor Selleck
63. Viewpoint
66. Musical instrument
67. Went to the market
71. Trevino and Greenwood
72. Nourished
73. Quench
75. Heroic tale
76. Goof
77. Target practice locale
79. Eddy
81. Skillet
82. Quilts
85. Citrus drink
87. Poems of praise
88. Chess piece
90. Noah's scout
91. Mr. Carnegie
94. Waited
96. Situate
100. Roast
101. Uniform
103. Kind of moss
105. Football's Aikman
106. Docile
107. Point connector
108. TV's Hawkeye
109. Simplicity
110. Molt
111. Allows
112. Inventory
113. Changed color

DOWN

1. Bland
2. Paddy harvest
3. Deserve
4. Takes out to dinner
5. Sweater style
6. Tarzan's friend
7. Bilks
8. Recognized
9. Ancient city on the Euphrates
10. Too bad!
11. Squabble
12. Thought
13. Nearly
14. Earth's satellite
15. At rest
16. Achievement
26. Chip
28. Focus
30. Scan
32. Foe
34. Championship
35. Camp beds
36. Unusual
37. Newsman Sevareid
38. Check
40. Implements
41. Persia, today
42. Dribble
43. Lack
46. Lucifer
50. Some exams
52. Tots' toys
54. Boat runways
56. Before, in poems
58. Pedestal occupiers
59. Romance
61. Grinder
62. Furnace control

PUZZLE 411

63. Actor McCowen

64. Pianist Peter ___

65. Heart of the wheat

66. Piggy-bank fillers

67. Took to the slopes

68. Baby's father

69. Gosh!

70. Copenhagen resident

72. So long

74. Punching tool

77. Went by horse

78. Weasels

80. Cherish

83. Branched off

84. Blue

86. Caught

89. Katmandu's locale

91. Play parts

92. Biblical boatman

93. Curved roof

94. Stooped

95. Fast food shop

97. Platter

98. Misplace

99. Gazed at

102. Struggle

104. TV commercials

1	2	3	4	■	5	6	7	8	■	9	10	11	12	■	13	14	15	16
17				■	18				■	19				■	20			
21				■	22				■	23				■	24			
25				26		■	27		28			■	29	30				
■	■	■	31			32	■	33			■	34				■	■	■
35	36	37					38	■	39		40					41	42	43
44			■	45				46	■	47					■	48		
49			50	■	51				52	■	53			■	54			
55				56			■	57	58				■	59				
■	■	■	60			■	61					■	62			■	■	■
63	64	65			■	66					■	67				68	69	70
71				■	72			■	73		74			■	75			
76			■	77				78	■	79				80	■	81		
82			83						84	■	85				86			
■	■	■	87				■	88		89	■	90				■	■	■
91	92	93				■	94				95	■	96			97	98	99
100				■	101	102			■	103		104		■	105			
106				■	107				■	108				■	109			
110				■	111				■	112				■	113			

PUZZLE 412

ACROSS
1. Open-mouthed
6. Old English letters
10. Cracked
14. Fax's ancestor
15. Meticulous
16. Silent jester
17. Japanese city
18. Scruff
19. Sashes
20. Bell and Kettle
21. Romanian currency
23. Part of PTA
25. Junket
27. Glenn Ford's "___ County"
28. Suave
32. Insurgent
35. Elliptical
36. Nonconformist
37. Darlin'
40. Bounding gait
41. Nettle's cousin
42. Derby, e.g.
43. Female merino
44. Clear
45. Femme fatale
46. Rows
47. Mousetrap bait
48. Sky streaker
51. Needle case
53. Geronimo, e.g.
55. Steep hemp
56. Criticism
59. Nerve network
60. Pedestal part
63. Hogwash
65. Infuriated
66. Pharmacist's weight
67. Surgeon's beam
68. No frills
69. Harsh cry
70. Discharge

DOWN
1. Iota
2. Asian clog
3. Lamenting cry
4. ___ annum
5. Triumphed
6. Boredom
7. Londoner's libation
8. One's luck
9. Degree
10. Neither good nor bad
11. Agreed
12. Chemical compound
13. Hiatuses
22. Make a boner
24. Maple genus
26. Oath
28. Charity
29. Admit
30. Religious leader
31. Soupy's missile
33. City in Oklahoma
34. Orthography contest
36. Dearth
37. Harness part
38. Wood sorrels
39. Pacific goose
41. Dart
42. Shad's output
44. Wood strip
45. Reduce gradually
46. Regress
47. Stage prompt
48. Venezuelan Indian
49. Sung drama
50. Mother, to a Brit
52. Walk noisily
54. Swirl
56. Ascend
57. Gibbons
58. Brazen
61. Sky altar
62. Small crow
64. Tease

PUZZLE 413

ACROSS

1. Auto's path
5. Gator's cousin
9. Primer pooch
13. Reverse
14. Intend to
15. Taboo
16. Silent jester
17. Chinese "bear"
18. Friendly nation
19. Long scarf
20. Flat Asian bell
21. Wanders off
23. Broadcast
25. Use the keyhole
26. Pay
27. Intersected
28. Quick farewell
31. Yearn for
34. Pathetic
35. Aquarium clown
36. Make right
37. Tend a baby
38. Throng
39. Breathing organ
40. Semiformal wear
41. Knights' weapons
42. Curvy letter
43. Summit
44. Ship's mast
45. A ways off
47. Striking
51. To the rear of a ship
53. TV alien
54. Stylist's goop
55. ___ forest
56. Detached
58. In addition
59. Dimwit
60. Dells
61. Lobster traps
62. Coop troop
63. Birds of prey
64. Sleep restlessly

DOWN

1. Latin dance
2. Edible bulb
3. Madison Avenue employee
4. Fawn's mother
5. Possibility
6. Extent
7. No spring chicken
8. Embraced
9. Pitfall
10. Arctic predator
11. Solely
12. Attic collection
14. Sink item
20. Security officer
22. Hue holiday
24. Being obligated to
27. Gym pad
29. Lawn
30. Graceful trees
31. Remove from print
32. Outback birds
33. Feeling
34. Five's follower
35. Pledged
37. Dine in the evening
38. Elegant
40. Windstorm
41. Surges
43. Gooey stuff
44. Mall units
46. Wards off
47. Pint-size
48. Icicle built for two
49. Birds' homes
50. Shine
51. Curved opening
52. Buyer's attraction
57. Fluffy's foot
58. Likely

PUZZLE 414

ACROSS

1. Central points
5. Throb
9. "___ in Heaven"
13. Crystalline tanning solid
14. Salesman's pitch
15. Female sheep
16. Profound
17. Add up
18. "All ___ Jazz"
19. Fizzy water
20. Angered
21. Adjutant
22. Editor's direction
24. Bee entrant
27. Cowboy's nooses
30. Do knot work
31. Printing measures
32. More frosty
33. Extra
35. Knockout count
36. Wall-covering hanger
38. Slithery slayer
41. Burst forth
42. Recess
44. Dry, as wine
47. Bear's hideout
48. Wild talker
49. Washer setting
51. Motion picture
52. Breathing rattle
53. Computer image
55. Clerical vestments
59. Key
60. Chars
61. Grow fatigued
62. Celtics or Cardinals
63. Point in question
64. Eastern ruler
65. Goofs
66. Plant stalk
67. "___ Enchanted Evening"

DOWN

1. Crazes
2. Kind of spread
3. Helped with a prompt
4. Stalemate
5. To the left, at sea
6. Refer to
7. Advantage
8. House wing
9. Heavy ___
10. For a time
11. Make numb
12. Chemical compounds
14. Pigs' pads
23. Sub's weapon
25. Trim
26. Perpetual
27. Kindled
28. Perfect serve
29. Sermon topic
33. Most spirited
34. Vim
37. Length x width
38. Go on stage
39. "___ Done Him Wrong"
40. Part of rpm
43. Prisoners
44. Elf
45. Pencil topper
46. Cyclone shelter
48. Shower off
50. Appears
51. Ancient marketplace
54. Judge's concern
56. Exec's car
57. Hat edge
58. Dried up
60. Family mem.

PUZZLE 415

ACROSS

1. Played a part
6. Spy's message form
10. Tibetan ox
13. Bellow
14. "___ We All"
16. ___ out (barely make)
17. Shiny fabrics
18. All systems go
19. Nib
20. Meadow mother
21. Baby beagle
23. Color again
25. Booster
26. The ___ of March
27. Endorse
31. Ice or roller
35. Tubular pasta
36. Horse or gull
37. Divisions
38. Small bit
40. Palm fruits
42. Played the first card
43. Clarify again
45. School paper
48. Free from dirt
49. Religious faction
51. For every
52. Fix
55. Stubborn animal
56. '60s do
59. Electric fish
60. More painful
62. Like bathroom floors
64. Subways' kin
65. Pinch playfully
66. Wipe out
67. Soap ingredient
68. Specks
69. Financial obligations

DOWN

1. Fit
2. Talon
3. Subdue
4. Prior to, in verse
5. Loses hope
6. Freshwater fish
7. Mine material
8. Sweetie
9. Completed
10. Abominable Snowman
11. Related
12. Retained
15. Kinds
22. Unfasten
24. Solicit
25. Apartment
27. Windmill blades
28. Sour compounds
29. Red or carpenter
30. Jeweled crown
32. Out of bed
33. Quite small
34. At ___! (army command)
35. Pack animal
39. Animal shelter
40. Hated
41. Not nearby
44. Party foods
46. What bit Cleopatra
47. Bread ingredient
48. Hi-fi
50. Gang
52. Pare
53. Put faith in
54. Other than
55. Boats like Noah's
56. Fat
57. Doze
58. Some poems
61. Ingest
63. Strong anger

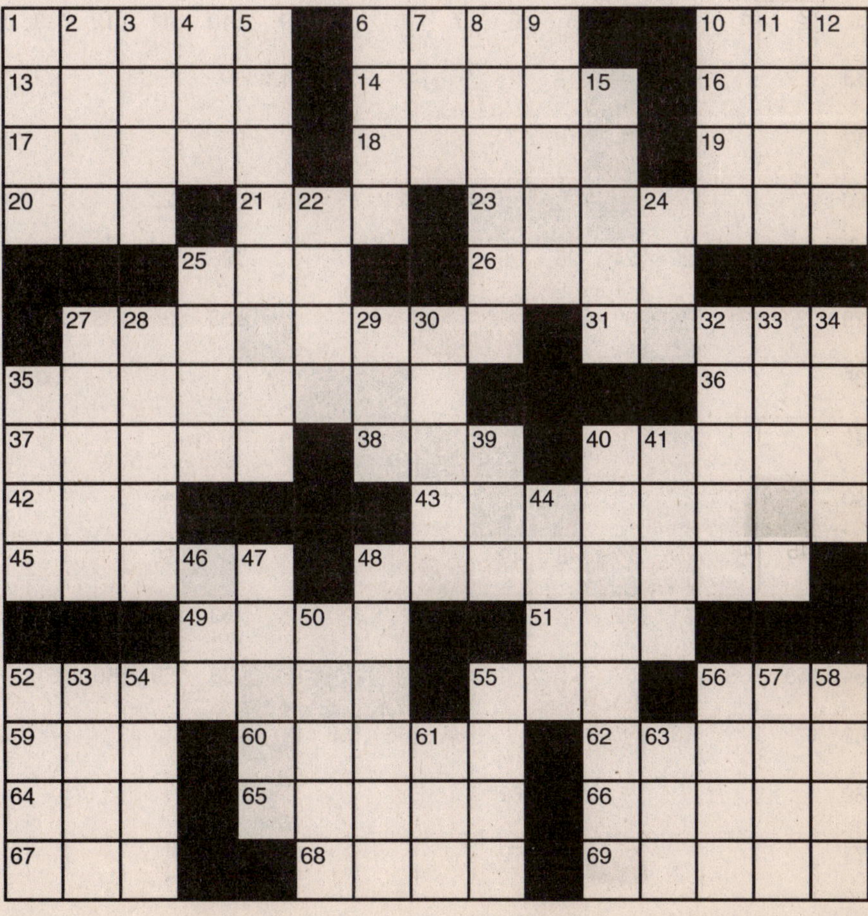

PUZZLE 416

ACROSS

1. Like some lingerie
5. Gaucho gear
9. Salesmen's cars
14. Atmosphere
15. Metal bar
16. "___ We All"
17. Goulash, e.g.
18. Flavor remainder
20. "Our ___"
21. Shad delicacy
22. Fiery
23. Sacred writings
29. Apprehend
32. Sincere
33. Impair
36. Citrus refresher
37. Atlantic coast area
38. Instructor
40. Shoplifted
42. Dwell
43. Ghost
44. What's the big ___?
46. Ushered
47. Tango requirement
48. Over
50. Excessively
51. Was sorry
54. Health club
57. Teensy
58. Mountain feedback
62. Shrewdness
67. Diving bird
68. Inquisitive person
69. Chime
70. Flower container
71. Flat hills
72. Evergreens
73. 24th letters

DOWN

1. Survive
2. Mobile starter
3. Ship's gang
4. Shows boredom
5. Swimsuit top
6. Clod
7. Illuminated
8. Makes aware
9. Library stamp
10. Important period
11. Intertwine
12. Knowledgeable about
13. Editor's word
19. Decisive defeat
24. Face part
25. "The ___ to Rio"
26. Winners
27. Stroke gently
28. Flightless birds
29. Snoozes
30. Conform
31. Underneath
34. Leaning
35. Beverly Hills drive
38. Taunt
39. Change over
41. Anchor
42. Musical symbol
44. Ill will
45. Morse code symbol
48. Periods in history
49. Eerie
52. Decorative jugs
53. Dig
54. Fraud
55. Posture
56. Clumsy boats
59. Persuade
60. Nylons
61. Washington bills
63. Baltic or Bering
64. Maiden-name word
65. Carpentry tool
66. Subways' kin

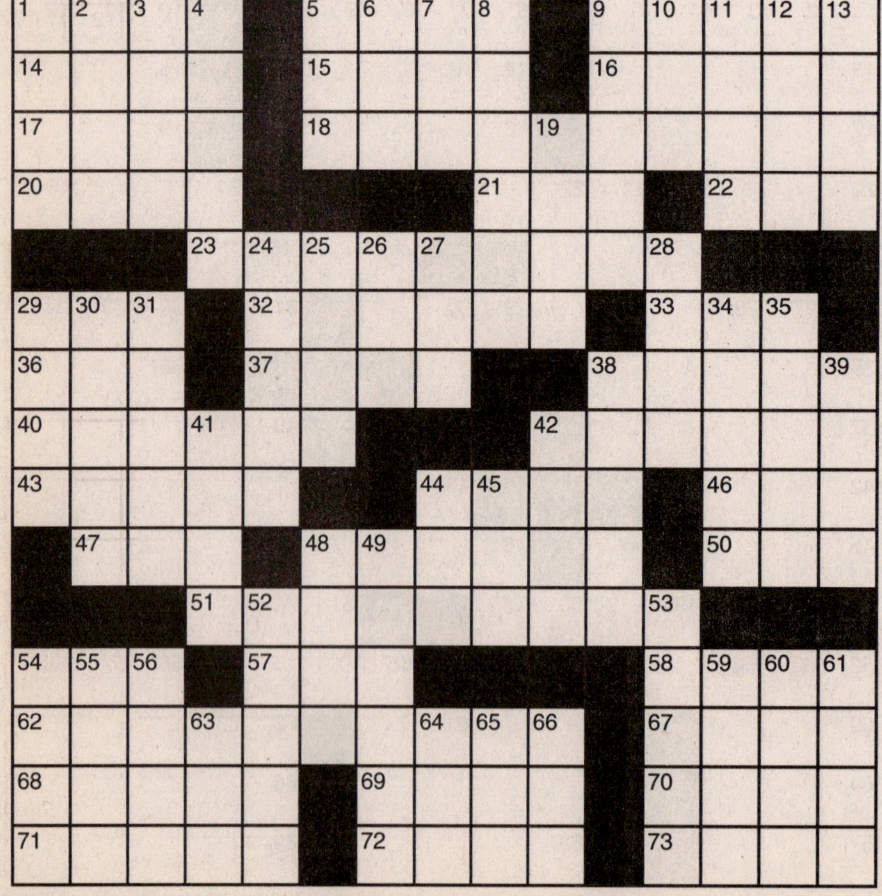

PUZZLE 417

ACROSS

1. ___ diver
6. Imitates
10. Fly alone
14. Relaxes
15. Foot bottom
16. Dumbstruck
17. Jerk
18. Island dance
19. Weighty metal
20. Edward's nickname
21. Cake decorator
23. Whiskey bottles
25. Clothes presser
26. Title of respect
27. Audio medium
29. Lobe ornaments
33. Cantaloupe, e.g.
34. Signed
35. Fierce anger
36. Almost round
37. Playful animal
38. Has-___
39. "___ Miss Brooks"
40. Practices boxing
41. Walked
42. Vaguely
44. Planted
45. Not any
46. Threshold
47. Tourist's must
50. Pudding or paper
51. Physique, for short
54. Lined up
55. Neat, to a Brit
57. Shipment
59. Italian money, once
60. Pledge
61. Dote on
62. Oodles
63. Deli breads
64. Steeple

DOWN

1. Faction
2. Part of TLC
3. Employed
4. Honeycomb builder
5. Headache reliever
6. Pale
7. Rain heavily
8. Plumbing joint
9. Sailor
10. Spiced sausage
11. Is obligated to
12. Drip
13. Betting numbers
22. Bill and ___
24. Pork fat
25. Matinee ___
26. Constructs
27. Variety show
28. Frighten
29. Door
30. Dorothy, to Em
31. Selfishness
32. Cause to go
33. Anchor
34. Rome's land
37. Telephone employee
38. Sob
40. Sky light
41. Skunk
43. Kind of street
44. Attack!
46. Expresses relief
47. Tranquil
48. Elaborate melody
49. Dawn, in verse
50. Ceremony
51. Facial feature
52. Meanie
53. Performer
56. Manta ___
58. Excitement

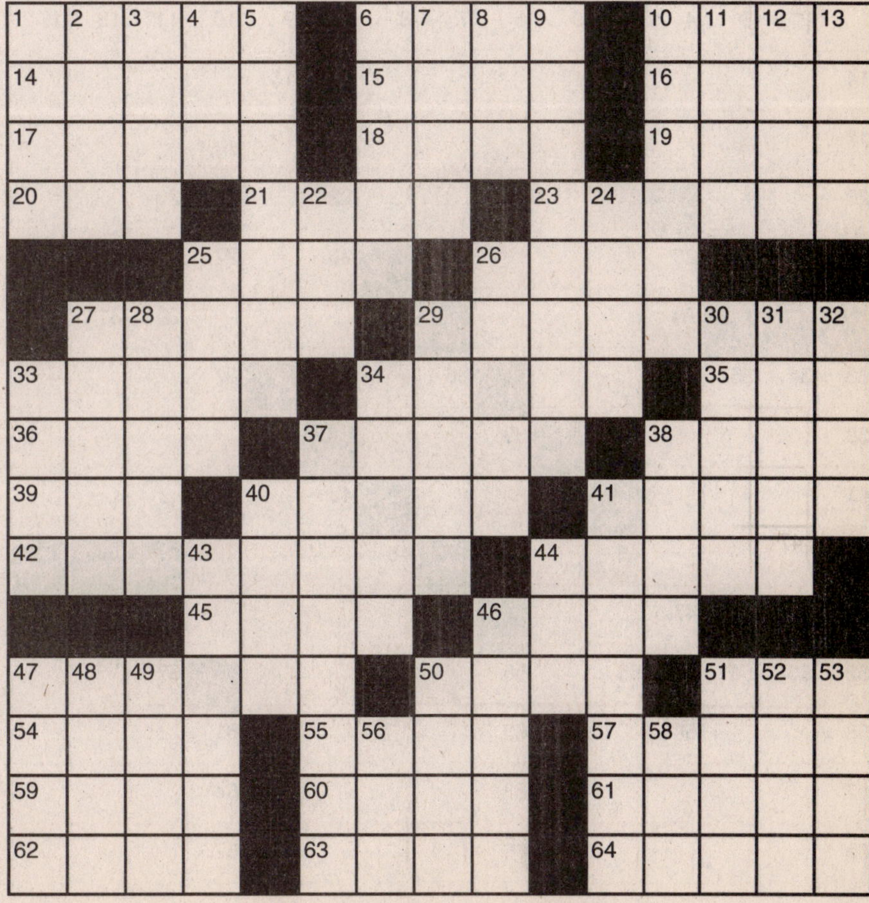

PUZZLE 418

ACROSS

1. Diamond corner
5. Smile radiantly
9. "___ Away"
14. Selects
15. Hence
16. Best
17. Heavy burden
18. Small ensemble
19. Violin's cousin
20. Old Japanese coin
21. Painter Moses
23. Society miss
24. Follow closely
26. Curve
28. Sheet of cotton
29. Train trailer
33. Hanks movie
36. Topaz, e.g.
37. Vista
38. Lively spirits
39. Ham on ___
40. Category
41. Indecent
42. Chewing stick
43. Laborer
44. Lotion ingredient
46. Arrived
47. Capture
48. Ripped
52. Toothed tool
55. Loss of hope
57. Rowboat need
58. Folklore figure
60. Airplane front
61. Burlap fiber
62. Creepy
63. Makes angry
64. Utilizes
65. Subdued
66. Annoying person
67. Wallet bills

DOWN

1. Helping hand
2. Sleep disorder
3. Bit
4. Snaky shape
5. Promise in marriage
6. Off course
7. Maturing
8. Frame of mind
9. Baking soda, briefly
10. Hymn of praise
11. Merge
12. Hay bundle
13. Messy fellow
21. Drinking vessel
22. Form of address
25. ___ ship!
27. Like some wagons
29. So-so grade
30. Pig's comment
31. Desiccated
32. Jug
33. Retail
34. Court response
35. Yard
36. Health club
39. Seek office
40. "___ Pyle, U.S.M.C."
42. Taunt
43. Most cautious
45. Dished out
46. Pursues
48. Fern seed
49. Extinguish
50. Moth-___
51. Garb
52. Galley direction
53. Environs
54. Fish bait
56. Cut short
59. Fib
61. Protrude

PUZZLE 419

ACROSS

1. Curd's companion
5. 45 player
9. Second saying
13. Acclaim
14. Fiedler stick
15. Hairy ridge
16. Came to rest
17. Jugs
18. Nee
19. Buff
21. Matched
22. Certain poem
23. Mistletoe payoff
25. Roused
28. Color again
32. Short snooze
33. Baking chamber
34. Lemon
36. Excellent
40. Parks and Lahr
42. Society miss
44. Baby insect
45. Tempt
47. Sense of humor
49. Legal hold
50. Container
51. Clothing workers
53. Twinges
56. Feathery plant
57. Hat
58. Word with neither
60. Nibbled
65. Bohr's particle
67. Ease up
69. Shout
70. Italian bread?
71. Make payment
72. Southern veggie
73. Plant holders
74. Windows of the soul
75. Made an exit

DOWN

1. Shawl
2. Corona
3. See no ___
4. Sherpa sighting
5. Hem's partner
6. Elements
7. Tiger's warning
8. Moment
9. Wane
10. Criminal
11. Swarm
12. Had as property
14. In back of
20. Use snow runners
24. Seven-card ___
26. Cry
27. Horrify
28. Wapner's attire
29. Smooth
30. Sassy
31. Playful acts
35. Lawn moisture
37. Wedding band?
38. Again
39. Prospects for gold
41. Ripoff
43. Nip
46. Trap
48. Focal point
52. Lodging
53. Resell at a high price
54. Urban outback?
55. To the left, at sea
56. Picture holder
59. Comply
61. In line
62. Came to
63. Qualify for
64. Doggone it!
66. Second degrees: abbr.
68. Third word of "America"

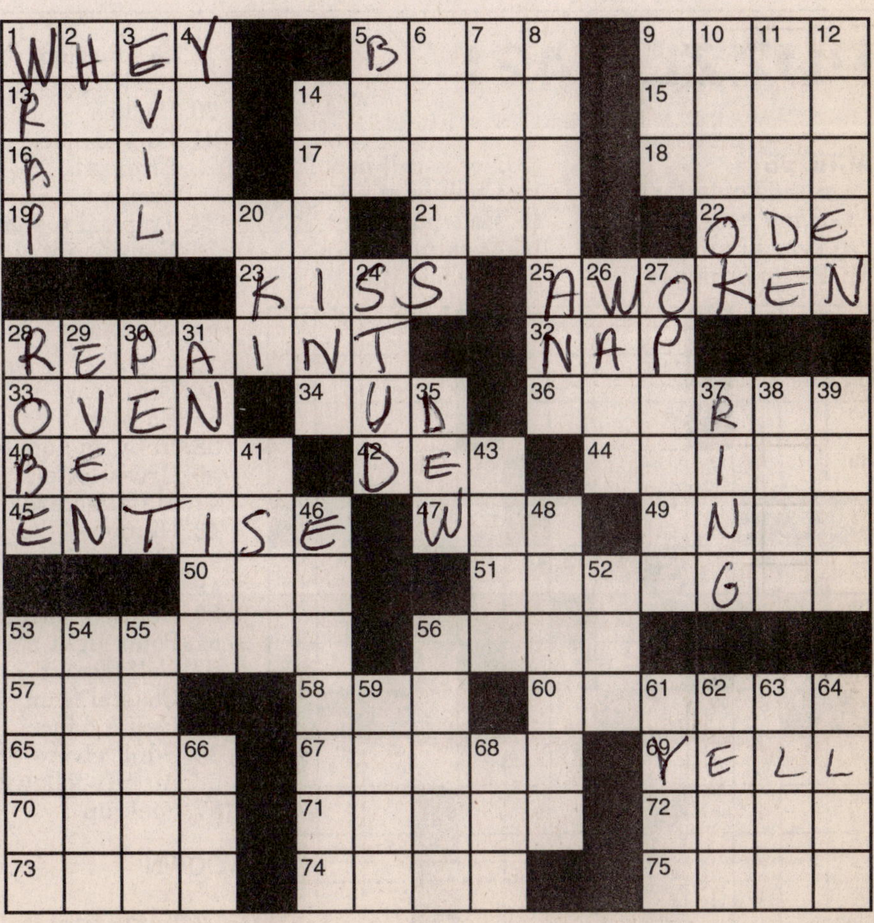

PUZZLE 420

ACROSS

1. Building extensions
5. Strikebreaker
9. Flit about
12. Drip
13. Burrito's kin
14. Nibbled
15. Agitate
16. Biblical preposition
17. Hamlet, to Gertrude
18. "____ It Romantic?"
20. Lively
22. Flat boat
25. Warning sign
27. Brit. rock group
28. Waiter's offering
30. Folding beds
34. Fix
36. Summer top
38. Golf pegs
39. On the ocean
41. State falsely
42. Emerald ____
44. Plant again
46. Seeming
49. Math course
51. Coffee vessel
52. Defense gp.
54. Glitzy party
58. Back in time
59. Author Zane ____
60. Spunk
61. Japanese money unit
62. ____ out (barely manages)
63. Wet, as grass

DOWN

1. Hazardous curve
2. Rent out
3. Orchid necklace
4. Shoot
5. Bewilder
6. Swiss state
7. Statute
8. Alcohol
9. Huff and puff
10. At the peak of
11. Refuse to accept
19. 18-wheeler
21. Part of a foot
22. Ernie's pal
23. Opposed to aweather
24. Thick cord
26. Muffle
29. Of a historic time
31. Certain paints
32. The Stooges, e.g.
33. Hearty dish
35. Tag-sale phrase
37. Indira's robe
40. Sofa
43. Burn, in a way
45. ____ on (encouraged)
46. Wharf
47. Craving
48. Soon, to Shakespeare
50. Rogers and Orbison
53. Bible craft
55. Tavern brew
56. Attorney's concern
57. To some extent

PUZZLE 421

ACROSS

1. Shade of blue
4. Hand over
8. Type of milk
12. Pecan or mince
13. Nerve-cell part
14. Champion
15. Hole puncher
16. Cooking items
17. Precinct
18. Graduation certificate
20. Pushes
21. Part of a set
22. Economic booms
23. Tropical rodent
26. Not distant
28. Cenozoic, e.g.
31. Incite
33. Smoothed with a tool
35. For every
36. Enclose
38. Ruby and opal
39. Greek letter
41. Manufacture
43. Dimness
45. Thrive
49. Emanation
50. Gentle creature
51. Polar sight
52. Golf hazard
53. Coastal flier
54. Half a dance?
55. Adult elvers
56. Alpha's follower
57. Soak up

DOWN

1. Nail
2. Fuzzy fruit
3. Shrill bark
4. Tender chicken
5. Inspector
6. Bestow
7. Some dash widths
8. Pointy
9. Lantern fuel
10. Infuriated
11. Extinct birds
19. Island feast
20. Knit one, ____ one
23. Baby's food
24. Exist
25. Klinger's rank
27. Obvious
29. Dream letters
30. Classified ____
32. Dog-paddle
34. Matures
37. Current measure
40. Daytime TV fare
42. 1988 Olympics site
43. Corral opening
44. Attract
46. Movies
47. Bouncing sound
48. Harvest
50. Society girl

MOVIES & TELEVISION

PUZZLE 422

ACROSS

1. "Soap" family name
5. "Honeymoon in ___"
9. Social reformer Jacob ___
13. Miscalculates
14. Israeli Abba ___
15. "Return to ___"
17. "___ in Seattle"
19. "The Long, Long ___"
21. ___ the mark
22. "___ That Jazz"
23. Adah's husband
25. Tommy ___ Jones
26. Actress Storm
28. Future oaks
30. Ms. Arden
31. '85 Spacek film
33. Film of algae
34. "Green ___"
36. Dr. Frankenstein's assistant
37. Metric measures
39. Actor Parker
40. "___ Orleans"
41. Harass
42. Enrages
44. Actress Rolle
46. Like certain peanuts
49. Charter
50. Bumppo of "The Leatherstocking Tales"
52. "Major ___"
54. '60s musical, then film
56. "___ of a Summer Night"
58. Actor Paul ___
59. Paddle one's own ___
60. Lollapalooza
61. Kevin ___ of "Footloose"
62. Plant holder
63. Actress North
66. Actress Rowlands
67. Prefix for before
68. "___ a Kick out of You"
69. Shakespearean actor Aldridge
70. Three, in Roma
73. "___ Pretty"
76. Aim
79. "United ___" (TV series)
80. "At ___" (Jimmie Walker series)
81. "Long Day's Journey ___ Night"
82. Greek love god
83. Box lightly
84. "Rock of ___"

DOWN

1. "___ Pilot"
2. "___ & Janis" (comic strip)
3. "A ___ in Brooklyn"
4. Language suffix
5. "___ Starr"
6. Director Gance
7. ___ Vegas
8. Anxious
9. Fred Berry role on "What's Happening!!"
10. Actress Balin
11. Ugandan Amin
12. Actor Peter ___
15. "___ Trek"
16. Superman portrayer
18. "___ Rider"
20. Roger ___ of "Cheers"
24. "___ Like It Hot"
27. "The Fresh Prince of Bel ___"
28. "___ High"
29. In a prudent manner
31. "___ and Bill"
32. Critic James ___
33. Begins
35. "___ la Vie"
37. "Remains to Be ___"
38. "___ Act"
41. "___ Always Tomorrow"
43. Willard et al.
45. '50 Jean Simmons film
47. "___ Rita"
48. Linda ___ of soap operas
50. "The Naughty ___"
51. Toward shelter
53. "Gunga ___"
54. Mel ___ of "thirtysomething"
55. Mouseketeer Funicello
57. "The ___ the Merrier"
58. "The Six Million Dollar ___"
59. Coffee holders
61. Actor Orson ___
64. Gregory ___ of "Tap"
65. Henhouse output
66. Actress Garson
69. "___ Wonderful World"
71. Footballer Kyle ___
72. Sonny Shroyer series
74. Sailor
75. Robert ___ of "Quincy, M.E."
77. Snooze
78. Spanish aunt

PUZZLE 423

ACROSS

1. ___ out (barely made)
5. Cider source
10. Scoundrels
14. Precious
15. Unclouded
16. Like crazy
17. Urgency
19. Fodder storage
20. Clan symbol
21. Implore
22. Fret
23. Agts.
25. Strongbox
28. Cured pork
31. Extol
33. Compass point
36. Opening
38. Mason's tool
40. Ore deposit
41. Stillness
43. Singles-bar patter
44. Food box, briefly
46. Camp lights
48. Become narrower
49. Sushi favorite
50. Spanish article
51. In case
53. Torch
55. Columnist Bombeck
58. Defective
60. Winter coat
64. Campus bigwig
65. Be in agreement
67. Entrance barrier
68. Scallion's cousin
69. Spirited
70. Formerly, formerly
71. Legumes
72. Leases

1	2	3	4	■	5	6	7	8	9	■	10	11	12	13
14				■	15					■	16			
17				18						■	19			
20					■	21			■	■	22			
■	■	■	23		24		■	25	26	27		■	■	■
28	29	30	■	31			32	■	33			34	35	■
36			37					■	38					39
40				■	41			42		■	43			
44				45		■	46			47				
■	48					■	49				■	50		
■	■	■	51			52	■	53			54	■	■	■
55	56	57		■	■	58	59		■	60		61	62	63
64				■	65				66					
67				■	68					■	69			
70				■	71					■	72			

DOWN

1. Rewrite
2. Casino game
3. Far or Middle
4. More parched
5. Pretend
6. Gratification
7. Coops
8. Falls short of
9. Afore
10. Baking dish
11. Landed
12. Allot
13. Pack
18. Silvery fish
24. Poor folk
26. Insect's feeler
27. In favor of
28. 50%
29. Helm direction
30. Press
32. Did business
34. Spin
35. Salon coloring
37. Mars
39. Minus
42. Large kettle
45. Golly
47. Pats down
52. Steak choice
54. Of the Vatican
55. Rim
56. Back part
57. Gym pads
59. Diva's number
61. Wander about
62. Purl's reverse
63. States further
65. Corn holder
66. Printer's measures

PUZZLE 424

Guess Who

Change one letter in each word to form ten names of famous people.

Example: CLERK TABLE (**Answer:** Clark Gable)

1. BARE RUTS ____________
2. SALTY RICE ____________
3. ERA HERON ____________
4. MICE DAGGER ____________
5. JOIN BROWS ____________
6. ANY CASTER ____________
7. GLENS COULD ____________
8. MARK LEAKER ____________
9. MOAN MIRE ____________
10. MARINE TATERS ____________

DOUBLE TROUBLE PUZZLE 425

Not really double trouble, but double fun! Solve this puzzle as you would a regular crossword, EXCEPT place one, two, or three letters in each box. The number of letters in each answer is shown in parentheses after its clue.

ACROSS

1. Flat bottle (5)
3. Contaminated (7)
7. Athlete's trainer (5)
10. Coarse sand (4)
11. Spread throughout (7)
12. Festive occasion (6)
13. Ancestor (10)
15. Give no attention to (7)
17. Racecourse (5)
18. Said aloud (4)
20. Citrus beverage (3)
21. Tree outgrowth (4)
23. Movable bar (5)
25. Royal rod (7)
28. Sample, as food (5)
30. Having creative abilities (8)
33. Rental contract (5)
34. Fortress (7)
36. Concept (4)
37. Metal bar (5)
39. Wicked (4)
41. Examination (4)
43. Group of cattle (4)
46. Physically well (7)
48. Attribute (to) (7)
50. Commence (5)
51. Grown-up (6)
53. Wild hog (4)
54. Fervor (5)
55. Obvious (7)
56. Sparrow's home (4)

DOWN

1. Shockingly noticeable (8)
2. Move rapidly and lightly (7)
3. Narrowed (7)
4. Applicant for a patent (8)
5. Tiny amount (3)
6. Genesis garden (4)
7. Blend (8)
8. Influence (6)
9. Seat (5)
14. Hen's call (6)
16. Mild oath (4)
19. Relieve (9)
22. At a distance (4)
24. Formerly, formerly (4)
26. Urgent request (4)
27. Concise (5)
28. Unspoken (5)
29. Lieu (5)
31. Ocean motion (4)
32. Frosting (5)
35. Alternative to stairs (8)
38. Different (5)
40. Sick (3)
42. Height (7)
44. Ornamental cloth strip (6)
45. Most precious (7)
46. Got word (5)
47. Aromatic herb (5)
49. Fragrance (5)
50. Play the lead (4)
52. Enthusiastic (4)

1	2	■	3	4	5	6	■	7	8	9
10		■	11				■	12		
13		14			■	15	16			■
17			■	18	19	■	20		■	■
■	■	21	22	■	23	24	■	25	26	27
28	29	■	30	31			32	■	33	
34		35	■	36		■	37	38	■	■
■	■	39	40	■	41	42	■	43	44	45
■	46			47	■	48	49			
50			■	51	52			■	53	
54			■	55				■	56	

Piece by Piece PUZZLE 426

We have eliminated the spaces between the words in a quotation and divided all the letters into 3-letter pieces. Rearrange the pieces to reconstruct the message. The dashes indicate the number of letters in each word.

EIS ENT FEE FEE GYO GYO HAT HOP LIN LIN
MAN PER SNT THE THE UHA UHA VEI VET

_ _ _ _   _ _   _ _ _   _ _ _ _ _ _ _   _ _ _

_ _ _ _   _ _ _ _   _ _ _   _ _ _ _ _ _ _   _ _ _

_ _ _ _   _ _ _'_   _ _ _ _ _ _ _ _ _.

PUZZLE 427

BRICK BY BRICK

Rearrange this stack of bricks to form a crossword puzzle. The clues will help you fit the bricks into their correct places. Row 1 has been filled in for you. Use the bricks to fill in the remaining spaces.

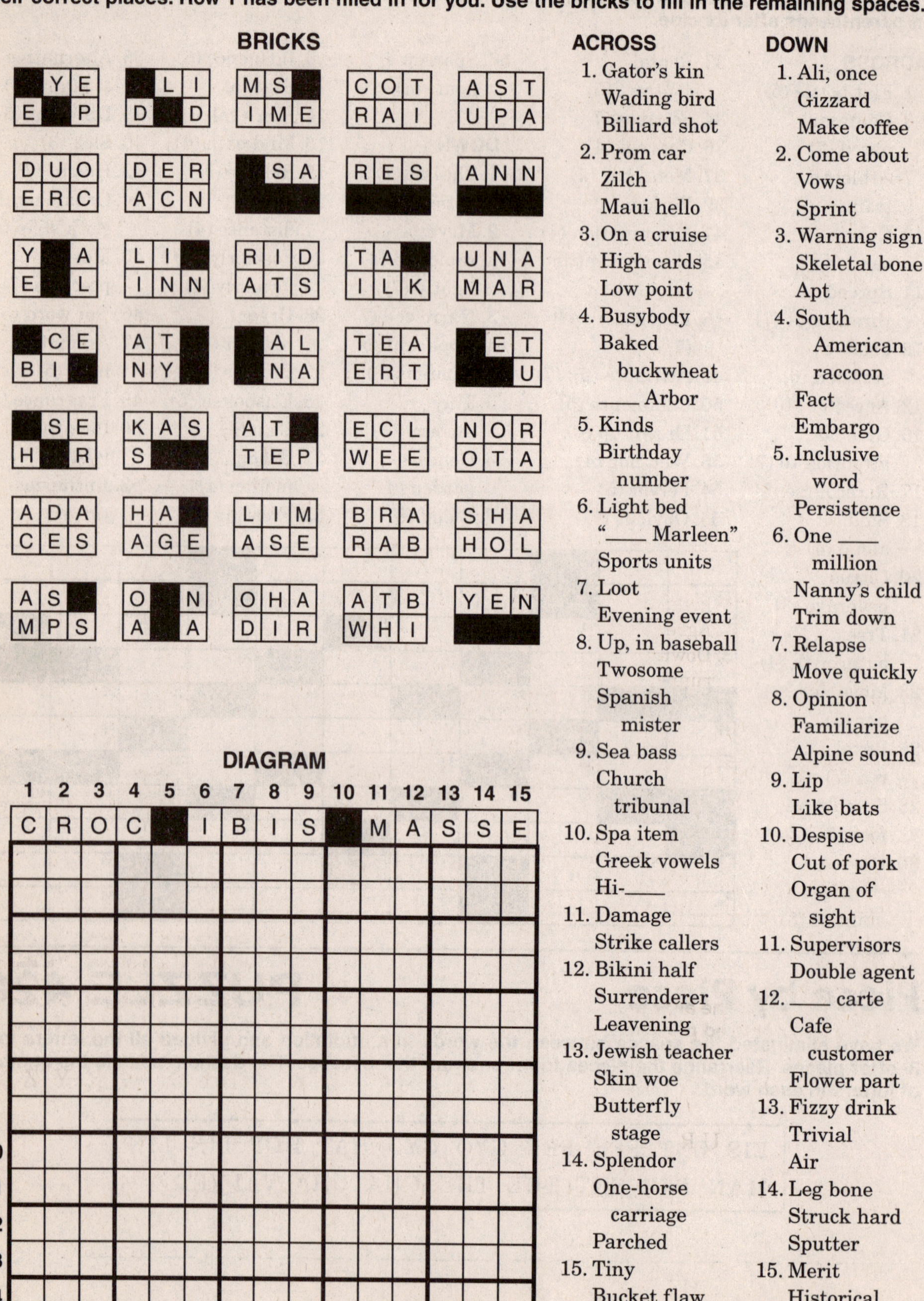

ACROSS

1. Gator's kin
   Wading bird
   Billiard shot
2. Prom car
   Zilch
   Maui hello
3. On a cruise
   High cards
   Low point
4. Busybody
   Baked buckwheat
   ____ Arbor
5. Kinds
   Birthday number
6. Light bed
   "____ Marleen"
   Sports units
7. Loot
   Evening event
8. Up, in baseball
   Twosome
   Spanish mister
9. Sea bass
   Church tribunal
10. Spa item
    Greek vowels
    Hi-____
11. Damage
    Strike callers
12. Bikini half
    Surrenderer
    Leavening
13. Jewish teacher
    Skin woe
    Butterfly stage
14. Splendor
    One-horse carriage
    Parched
15. Tiny
    Bucket flaw
    Broad muscles, shortly

DOWN

1. Ali, once
   Gizzard
   Make coffee
2. Come about
   Vows
   Sprint
3. Warning sign
   Skeletal bone
   Apt
4. South American raccoon
   Fact
   Embargo
5. Inclusive word
   Persistence
6. One ____ million
   Nanny's child
   Trim down
7. Relapse
   Move quickly
8. Opinion
   Familiarize
   Alpine sound
9. Lip
   Like bats
10. Despise
    Cut of pork
    Organ of sight
11. Supervisors
    Double agent
12. ____ carte
    Cafe customer
    Flower part
13. Fizzy drink
    Trivial
    Air
14. Leg bone
    Struck hard
    Sputter
15. Merit
    Historical epochs
    Boys

PUZZLE 428

ACROSS
1. Fight
5. European snakes
9. Type of catalog
13. At any ____
14. Gossip columnists' sources
16. Trim material
17. Overhead
18. Lawful
19. Tooth woe
20. None
21. Tenant's concern
22. Writer
24. Vassar, e.g.
26. Ill-humor
27. "____ Got No Strings"
28. Popular plant
30. Baseball club
33. Berserk
36. Come to a halt
38. Slit
40. Checkers or chess
41. Sturgeon delicacy
42. In ____ of
43. Regarding
45. Theory
47. Alack!
48. Spoil
49. Excitements
51. Vagrant
53. Self-respect
54. Baked pasta dish
58. Part of FBI
61. Unconnected
62. Pina colada liquor
63. Exam type
64. Vampire's craving
66. Flightless bird
67. Monster
68. Trunk
69. Decorative jug
70. Clairvoyant
71. Prom attendee
72. Differently

DOWN
1. Swiss coin
2. Proportion
3. Ring-shaped reef
4. Not nope
5. Claims
6. Fishing net
7. Agreement
8. Downhill runner
9. Roster
10. Per
11. Mimic
12. Forest creature
15. Step
21. Race in neutral
23. Large vases
25. Compare
28. Things to eat
29. Fencer's sword
30. Jail money
31. Dazed
32. In this way
33. Golden ____ (retiree)
34. Deli spread
35. Pass over
37. Musical group
39. South American animal
44. Overly enthusiastic
46. Forsake
50. Be skeptical
52. Operate
53. Conger catcher
54. Slack
55. Dog's warning
56. Art subjects
57. Fondness, in Florence
58. Hisses
59. Strong impulse
60. Burger order
61. Folk wisdom
65. Portion
66. Below-average grade

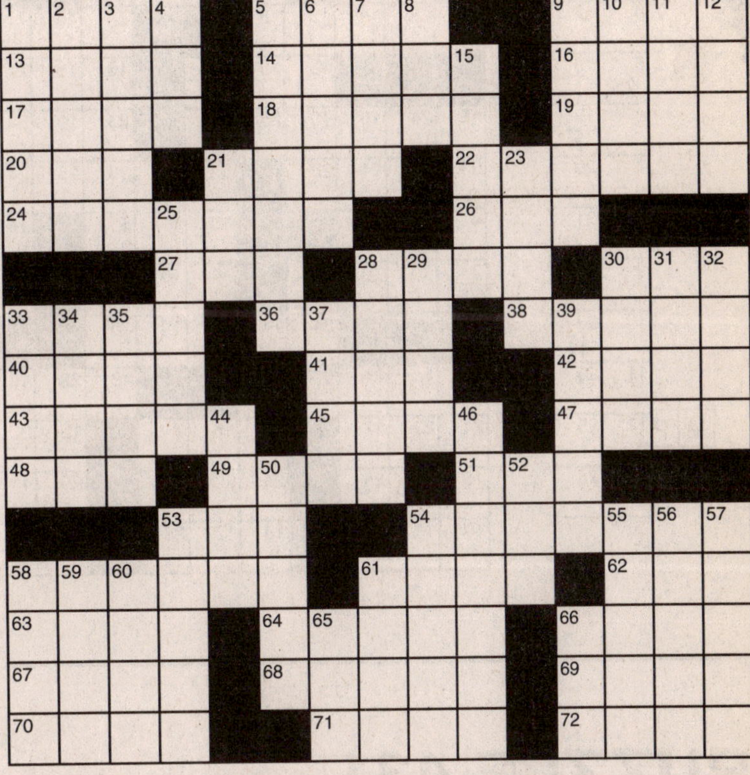

ABC's

PUZZLE 429

Use all 26 letters of the alphabet to complete the ten words. Each letter is to be used only once, and only one letter is used per dash.

A B C D E F G H I J K L M N O P Q R S T U V W X Y Z

1. C U R ___ ___ ___
2. E ___ O ___ ___ C
3. ___ ___ N ___ E T
4. ___ U I ___ H E
5. O ___ T I ___ ___
6. ___ O T ___ N ___
7. ___ E A ___ O T
8. ___ R O O ___ E
9. ___ A ___ I S ___
10. E ___ T E E ___

PUZZLE 430

CODEWORD

Codeword is a special crossword puzzle in which conventional clues are omitted. Instead, answer words in the diagram are represented by numbers. Each number represents a different letter of the alphabet, and all of the letters of the alphabet are used. When you are sure of a letter, put it in the code key chart and cross it off in the alphabet box. A group of letters has been inserted to start you off.

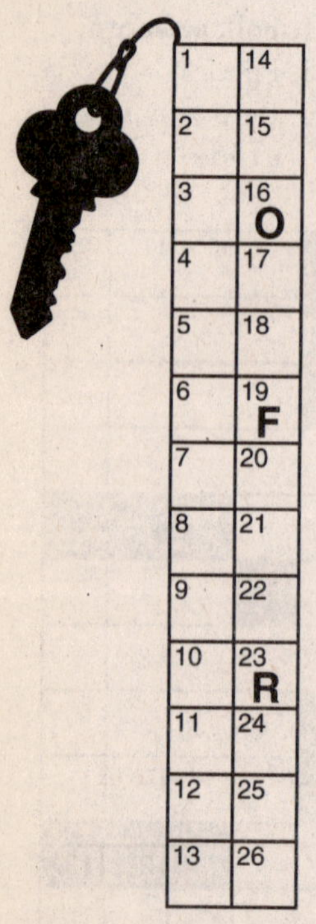

1	14
2	15
3	16 O
4	17
5	18
6	19 F
7	20
8	21
9	22
10	23 R
11	24
12	25
13	26

26	16	7	■	2	24	2	■	17	16	26	■	14	24	12
24	17	10	■	6	4	10	■	16	23	10	■	16	13	10
25	10	10	■	24	7	10	■	16	24	19	■	7	24	5
21	24	5	■	14	10	23	24	■	■	16	8	24	11	14
16	25	14	10	18	■	■	7	16	7	12	10	■	■	■
■	■	■	13	10	10	■	16	15	24	■	12	11	23	16
18	24	15	10	23	25	■	23	10	5	■	■	16	24	23
23	16	24	23	■	5	24	25	25	24	■	26	20	3	3
4	25	25	■	■	10	6	5	■	14	18	10	23	10	16
2	10	10	2	■	14	10	10	■	8	10	24	■	■	■
■	■	■	24	14	22	10	25	■	■	9	20	24	19	19 F
10	1	24	6	18	■	■	18	22	16	20	■	2	23	16 O
24	23	17	■	23	16	7	■	16	26	4	■	2	10	23 R
15	24	25	■	24	2	10	■	25	4	6	■	6	24	12
10	11	10	■	13	10	26	■	10	18	24	■	10	8	10

A	N
B	~~O~~
C	P
D	Q
E	~~R~~
~~F~~	S
G	T
H	U
I	V
J	W
K	X
L	Y
M	Z

PUZZLE 431

Exchange Boards

Form common 4- and 6-letter words by exchanging the 2-letter groups from one set of boards to the other. Start by taking all the pieces from the LEFT BOARDS and adding them to the RIGHT BOARDS to complete 4-letter words. Then take all the pieces that were given in the RIGHT BOARDS and add them to the LEFT BOARDS to complete 6-letter words. Proper names, contractions, and foreign words are not allowed.

LEFT BOARDS (6-Letter Words)

TO	NG	
	LO	
	PO	RT

		ON
SW		CH
GL		CE
GA		GE

RIGHT BOARDS (4-Letter Words)

	RD
	IT
AN	
VE	

	IM
	UE
RA	
	OW

UR	
WI	
	LL
PA	

PUZZLE 432

ACROSS

1. Part of USMC
6. Speech imperfection
10. Cloak
14. Of a fatty acid
15. Islamic ruler
16. Off yonder
17. Property
19. Baseball's Petrocelli
20. Spotted playing tile
21. Assembled for battle
23. Eft
25. Apiece
26. Before, in verse
27. Arrogant
30. Anatomical pouch
32. Gist
34. Eternity
35. Located behind
40. Damp
43. "___ Got a Secret"
44. Musical piece
45. Translate
47. Fueled
48. Broadcast
49. Bath site
51. Soft throw
52. Classified ___
55. Dickens character
57. Vatican head
59. Place for a bossy passenger?
62. Made an incision in
66. Land tract
67. At a ___ (very slowly)
69. One-horse carriage
70. Semester
71. Jeweled coronet
72. Stage hogs
73. Swill
74. Declare void

DOWN

1. Strong twine
2. Margarine
3. Paper amount
4. Stacking
5. Public spat
6. Permit
7. Mosque official
8. Stomach-flattening exercise
9. Here!
10. Feel concern
11. Like a house ___
12. Indianapolis player
13. Gnaw away
18. Scatters seeds
22. More genuine
24. Piglike mammal
27. Trailer truck
28. Lunar body
29. Single entity
31. Desire wrongly
33. Sis's sibling
36. Contrived situation
37. Facts, briefly
38. Poems
39. Serling and Steiger
41. Abundance
42. Stumbles
46. Clerics
50. Cotton pod
51. Alley item
52. Make embarrassed
53. Country cottage, to Yeltsin
54. Shoo!
56. Committee
58. Ziti or penne
60. Lock openers
61. Poi source
63. Actor James ___
64. Hose shade
65. Transaction
68. Little demon

PUZZLE 433

ACROSS

1. Type of truck
4. General Bradley
8. Baseballer Tommie ___
12. New England cape
15. Cotton unit
16. Meander
17. Outbuilding
18. Track shape
20. Range
21. Help in holdups
22. ___ d'oeuvres
23. Surrender, as territory
24. Speed up
26. Ceremonies
28. Ponders intently
29. Swine
30. Prefix for three
31. Seamstress's need
34. Became mature
38. Go off the deep ___
40. Wilder's "___ Town"
41. Hammer's music
44. Aroma
45. Pal
47. Key
49. "___ Believer"
50. Entirety
51. Beast's neck gear
52. Eager
53. Declare openly
54. More relaxed
56. Sprinted
57. Rows
58. Olive ___
59. Frosting
61. Current fashion
62. Snow building
65. By route of
66. Mimicked
71. Liquid measure
72. Wooden pins
73. Author Ephron
74. Brewery product
75. ___ de Cologne
76. March King
78. Vapor
79. ___ monster
80. Author Rand
81. Corn unit
82. Salesman: abbr.
85. Pittsburgh athlete
87. Weight watcher
90. Small flap
92. Stockade
93. Revise
95. "Carmen," e.g.
97. Mailman's concern
101. Gossip
102. State north of Missouri
104. Voyaging
106. Run easily
107. Unique being
108. Baseball's Hershiser
109. Phonograph record
110. Football's Dickerson
111. Nuptial response
112. Bump
113. Or ___!
114. Charles Dutton TV series

DOWN

1. Woody vine
2. Bullfight cheers
3. Withstand
4. Old Miami stadium
5. Horde
6. Prevent
7. Go to bed
8. Tennis star
9. Casper, e.g.
10. Always, in poems
11. Koch and Begley
12. Wintertime drink
13. Bachman-Turner ___
14. Miami's county
15. Scrooge's word
19. Brown or Paul
25. Geologic age
27. Pie pan
28. Boldly forward
32. Retain
33. Weep over
34. Prowl
35. Run in neutral
36. Survey
37. Actress Patty ___
39. Sofa
42. Cupid
43. Dogs' feet
46. Develops
48. Voicing a tune
51. Toy that comes and goes
52. Met melodies
53. Actress Turturro of "Angie"
55. Weaver's machine

PUZZLE 433

57. So long, in London
60. Havana export
61. Gold medal position
62. Notion
63. Elephant hue
64. Cleaned
67. Extinct birds
68. Turn ___ (flee)
69. Fashion magazine
70. Precious
72. Full-strength
76. Bird food
77. Breakfast grain
79. Softer
83. Summer, to Pierre
84. Procession
86. A foot wide?
88. Emcee's speech, for short
89. Sculled
91. Aromatic herb
93. Bother
94. Skirt type
96. Colorless
98. Matador's foe
99. Heroic poem
100. Kind of room
102. Atom
103. Spanish gold
105. Superhero's chest letter

PUZZLE 434

ACROSS

1. Carve
5. Do in, as a dragon
9. Angelic instrument
13. Printer's term
14. Mindful
15. Clarinet's relative
16. Chew
17. Citrus fruits
18. Different
19. Curve shape
20. Heathen
21. Laundry machine
22. Fix
24. Had a burger
26. Teamster's rig
28. Solution
33. Footwear without heels
36. Compact ___
39. Auto for hire
40. Fables
41. Deal out
42. Like the Mojave
43. Client
44. Offer for cash
45. Shades
46. Freshman's cap
48. Skunk feature
50. Tub
52. Soothing
56. Ineptly
60. Revise
63. Neither here ___ there
64. Approve
65. Dueling swords
66. In the know about
67. Money, in Turkey
68. Beautiful lady
69. Below-average grades
70. Individuals
71. Plays the horses
72. Goes wrong

DOWN

1. Lawn tool
2. Nervous
3. Grip
4. Chop down
5. Guzzle
6. Tibetan monk
7. Sports field
8. Affirmative response
9. Weeder
10. With competence
11. Ascended
12. Equal
14. Type of clock
20. Fruity desserts
21. Bear cave
23. To the back of the boat
25. Social grace
27. Doing nothing
29. Steps
30. Give notice
31. Departure
32. Frees
33. Bungle
34. Give up
35. Precinct
37. Unfavorable
38. Alone
41. Floating
45. Frog's cousin
47. Trailing plant
49. Compact
51. Indian's abode
53. ___ tube
54. Memo taker
55. Twelve dozen
56. ___ tie
57. Similar
58. "Truth or ___"
59. Soap-making substances
61. Defrost
62. Wiggly swimmers
65. ___ tide
66. Work by Shelley

1	2	3	4	■	■	5	6	7	8	■	9	10	11	12
13				■	14					■	15			
16				■	17					■	18			
19			■	20					■	21				
22			23			■	■	24	25		■	■	■	■
■	■	■	26			27	■	■	28		29	30	31	32
33	34	35			■	36	37	38		■	39			
40				■	41					■	42			
43				■	44				■	45				
46				47		■	■	48	49			■	■	■
■	■	■	■	50		51	■	■	52			53	54	55
56	57	58	59		■	60	61	62			■	63		
64				■	65					■	66			
67				■	68					■	69			
70				■	71				■	■	72			

PUZZLE 435

ACROSS

1. Shopper's aid
5. "___ It Romantic?"
9. Lights-out signal
13. Brainchild
14. Impassive
16. Spanish jug
17. Wool-eating insect
18. Mother
19. Horse color
20. Tartan design
22. Stitch again
24. Individual
25. "___ Before Bedtime"
27. Disagree
29. Clothes whitener
32. Achiever
33. Voyage segment
34. Feel pain
37. Plunders
41. Electric fish
42. Embarrassed
44. Mauna ___
45. Wood nymph
47. At the top of
48. Race in neutral
49. Flat bell
51. Gas-pump number
54. Make bare
57. Snowy abode
59. Kanga's kid
60. Unevenly notched
62. Greek letter
66. Dish
68. Cap's brim
70. Excursion
71. On the Pacific
72. Evade
73. Fairy-tale brute
74. Dull person
75. Leak
76. Cast

DOWN

1. Wilted
2. Folk hero
3. Bristle
4. Gauguin's island
5. Theory
6. Quarterback Bart ___
7. Records
8. Connections
9. Rocky hill
10. Unsociable
11. Aircraft
12. More sensible
15. Belief
21. Bear's home
23. Manipulate
26. Eastern rulers
28. To's companion
29. Ran, as dye
30. Rude look
31. "The ___ Duckling"
32. Audition tape
35. Locomotive sound
36. Luck
38. Soup vegetable
39. Adolescent
40. Put aside
42. Sun-dried brick
43. Organic compound
46. In history
50. Daring
52. Murmur fondly
53. Indian drum
54. "___ Cowboy"
55. Big slipknot
56. Oarsman
57. Edition
58. Crystal-lined stone
61. Certain paints
63. Consequently
64. "Brown Eyed ___"
65. Emulated
67. Lass's mate
69. D.C. figure

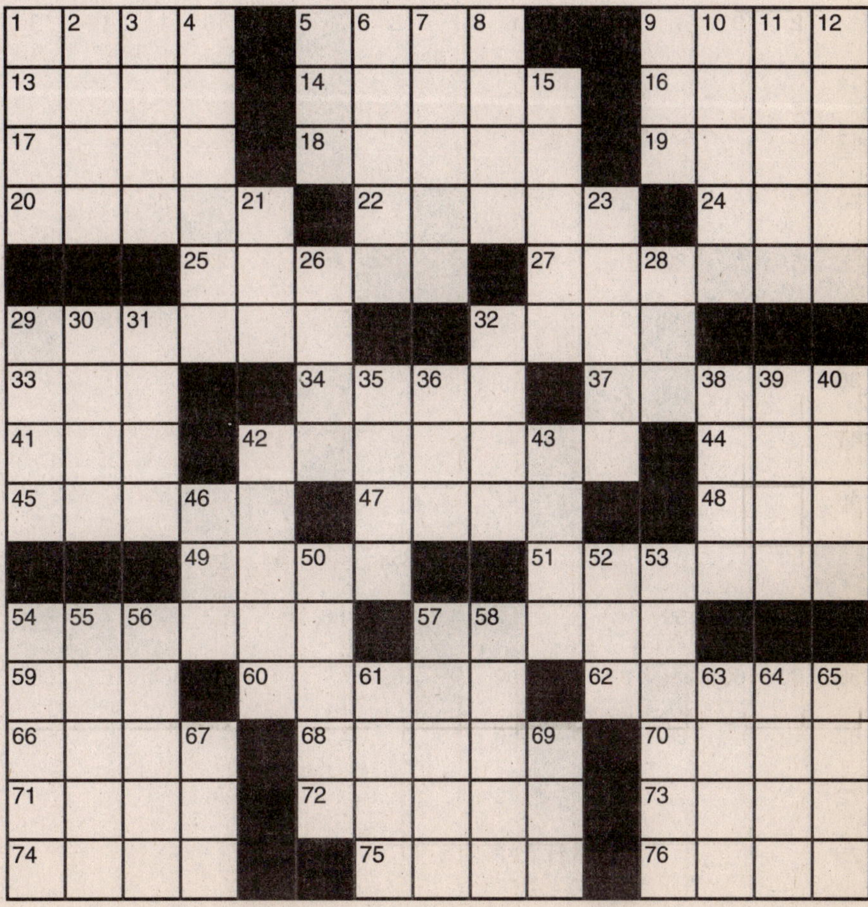

PUZZLE 436

ACROSS

1. Election
5. Contend (with)
9. Stop
14. Increases
15. Submit
16. Had
17. Ages in history
18. Not yup
19. Allotted
20. Painter's board
22. Polish
24. Heavens
25. Guinness's title
26. Family
28. Taproom
31. Turf
33. Overlay
36. Tangy refresher
37. Olympic event
39. Caught congers
41. University of Florida player
44. Jazz instrument
45. Impel
46. Kind of tire
47. Deuce topper
49. Crossed letter
50. Of poor quality
52. Scooped out
54. Tall tree
55. Tell a fib
56. Tourist's need
58. Ventilate
61. Resort
63. Urge
67. Tonto's horse
69. Type of skirt
71. Sounded, as a bell
72. Search party
73. Birthmark
74. Gulp
75. Show scorn
76. Unique chap
77. Tolkien creatures

DOWN

1. Mondale or Agnew
2. Southern veggie
3. Wild duck
4. Sibilant sounds
5. Dominate
6. Woodwind
7. Energy
8. Observer
9. Mixed
10. Fleecy mama
11. Hill builders
12. Hide-and-___
13. Circular current
21. Scale notes
23. Guitar's cousin
27. ___-do-well
28. Captures
29. Modify
30. Cover with pitch again
32. Powdery
33. Provoked
34. Nobility
35. Frolic
38. Needlefish
40. Regard
42. ___ hygiene
43. Opposer
48. More delicious
51. In the know
53. Cavity
57. Pucker
58. Deadly serpents
59. Saintly picture
60. Fragrant blossom
62. Bullets, to a GI
63. At leisure
64. Yard
65. Temper tantrum
66. Souffle items
68. Operate
70. Charged atom

PUZZLE 437

ACROSS

1. Frying vessels
5. Tiff
9. Potato holders
14. "___ the Roof"
15. Long walk
16. Wading bird
17. Food list
18. Harness strap
19. Fend off
20. College teacher, for short
21. Footed vase
22. Ferret's kin
23. Breeze maker
25. Green soup
26. Perched
29. Go downhill
31. Rear ___ (Navy rank)
36. Metallic sound
38. Guzzle
40. Snout
41. Female voice
42. Fierce look
43. Destiny
44. Lightning ___
45. Angry fury
46. Failure
47. Add sugar to
49. "Live and Let ___"
51. Give it a shot
52. Cardinal's color
53. "To ___, With Love"
55. Tennis bat
59. Certainly!
61. Frosted
65. Stadium
66. Hawaiian feast
67. Volcano's flow
68. Aviator
69. Otherwise
70. ___ out (barely made)
71. Like some pretzels
72. Feat
73. Desires

DOWN

1. Woman's shoe
2. Rich Little, e.g.
3. Forbidden thing
4. Tobacco product
5. "Honey, I ___ the Kids"
6. Dock
7. Similar
8. Toe count
9. Yell
10. Sector
11. Baseball hats
12. Leg hinge
13. Vend
22. Pie piece
24. Inquire
25. Coupled
26. Cut coverers
27. Permit
28. Book's name
30. "Gilligan's ___"
32. Data
33. ___ beef
34. Fall bloomer
35. Suspicious
37. Brief letter
39. Shake the tail
42. Welcome
46. Floral necklace
48. Peace pact
50. Distributed
54. Life of ___
55. Hits sharply
56. Vocal solo
57. Biology unit
58. Tangle
59. Santa's time
60. Slacken
62. Bar of soap
63. Uniform
64. Moms' mates
66. Went first

1	2	3	4	■	5	6	7	8	■	9	10	11	12	13
14				■	15				■	16				
17				■	18				■	19				
20				■	21			■	22					
■	■	■	23	24		■	■	25			■	■	■	■
26	27	28	■	29		30	■	31			32	33	34	35
36			37		■	38	39			■	40			
41				■	42					■	43			
44				■	45				■	46				
47				48			■	49	50		■	51		
■	■	■	■	52			■	■	53		54	■	■	■
55	56	57	58			■	59	60		■	61	62	63	64
65					■	66				■	67			
68					■	69				■	70			
71					■	72				■	73			

PUZZLE 438

FLOWER POWER

The answers to this petaled puzzle will go in a curve from the number on the outside to the center of the flower. Each number in the flower will have two 5-letter answers. One goes in a clockwise direction and the second in a counterclockwise direction. We have entered two answers to help you begin.

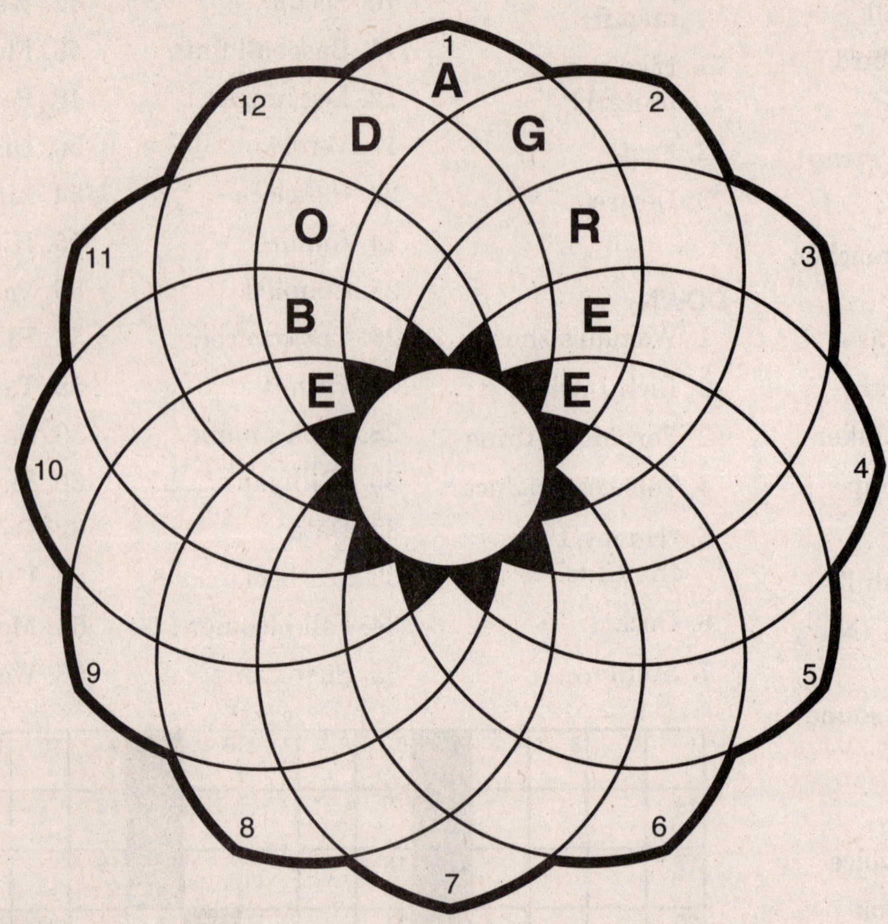

CLOCKWISE

1. Approve
2. Check for fraud
3. Flush
4. Cancel
5. Mitt
6. Courageous
7. Practical joke
8. Derrick
9. Skate across
10. Examine
11. Grill
12. J. ___ Hoover

COUNTERCLOCKWISE

1. Brick house
2. Prize marble
3. Of the country
4. Apple squeezings
5. Bottled being?
6. Dynamite
7. Writings
8. Yearn
9. Solemn
10. Smoothing tool
11. Edge
12. Wear away

PUZZLE 439

ACROSS

1. Tiff
5. Scratch
8. Woeful sigh
12. Zoomed
13. Bus fare
15. Something owed
16. Sheltered
17. Animated
18. Gamble
19. Pound
20. Refuses
22. Fawn's mother
23. ___-been
25. Before, in a poem
26. Lobe's location
27. Stallions' mates
30. Swear
32. Allow to be used
34. Ma that baas
35. Beach vessel
37. Unhealthy
38. Gone
40. Royal rule
42. Tibetan priest
46. Pose a question
48. Flue
50. Hawaiian specialty
51. Waiter's handout
53. 747, e.g.
54. Exterior
56. Male descendant
57. Not amateur
59. Picnic intruder
60. School of whales
61. Seasoned
64. Disguise
68. Spring flower
70. Trite
71. Woodwind
72. Lease payment
73. Bushel parts
74. Hog's food
75. Tense
76. Rules to follow
77. Pitched item

DOWN

1. Pierce
2. Barber's sign
3. Neighborhood
4. Cut molars
5. Beauty spot
6. Related
7. Go over
8. State further
9. Heavy
10. Overseas
11. Guide
13. Boys
14. ___-do-well
21. Persuade
24. Egyptian cobra
27. Torme or Gibson
28. Dazzle
29. Ump's relative
30. Contend
31. Green shade
33. Pipe joint
36. Genesis ship
37. Country hotel
39. Turn brown
41. Obtain
43. Quick to learn
44. Larry, Curly, and ___
45. Tire input
47. Dines
49. 2,000 pounds
51. Anchored
52. Conclusion
53. Startled
55. Ultimate
56. Church topper
58. Coarse file
59. Lemon drinks
62. Tortilla dish
63. Antlered animals
65. Sound
66. By and by
67. Stored
69. Messy home

PUZZLE 440

ACROSS

1. Headliners
6. Spoken
10. If not
14. Holland export
15. Flock
16. One billion years
17. Close by
18. Rubber check
20. Body movement
22. Envision
23. Golfer's goal
24. Expert
25. Like some tree trunks
27. Abates
31. Lunchtime
33. Mr. Ed's morsel
34. Turkey wattle
36. Small amounts
40. Utilizes
42. Interlace
43. Butter replacement
44. Printed mistake
45. Attach
47. "Against ___ Odds"
48. Untanned hide
50. Tiered
52. Muscular contraction
55. Those elected
56. Badge material
57. Bother
60. Farmer's ride
64. Being
67. Bea Arthur TV role
68. "As ___ Goes By"
69. Gloomy
70. Earth's path
71. ___ belt
72. Pipe section
73. Astronaut's milieu

DOWN

1. Male deer
2. Adjust
3. Pub orders
4. Cowboys' needs
5. Tidied
6. Double-reed instrument
7. Vroom
8. Wide sts.
9. Ancient instrument
10. Lobe's locale
11. Makes like a frog
12. Couches
13. Admission
19. Test model
21. Urban ___
26. Cognizant of
27. Oaf
28. Casual
29. Gait
30. Cleaned the floor
31. Seedless-orange type
32. Like alfresco dining
35. Race unit
37. With wings
38. Remove
39. Auctioneer's word
41. Dips in liquid
46. Large generators
49. Give off
51. Steep slope
52. Lets it stand
53. Sprite
54. Soul
58. Warren Beatty film
59. Tie
60. School session
61. Trombone's kin
62. Lyrical
63. Neural network
65. Prepare for diners
66. Stage prompt

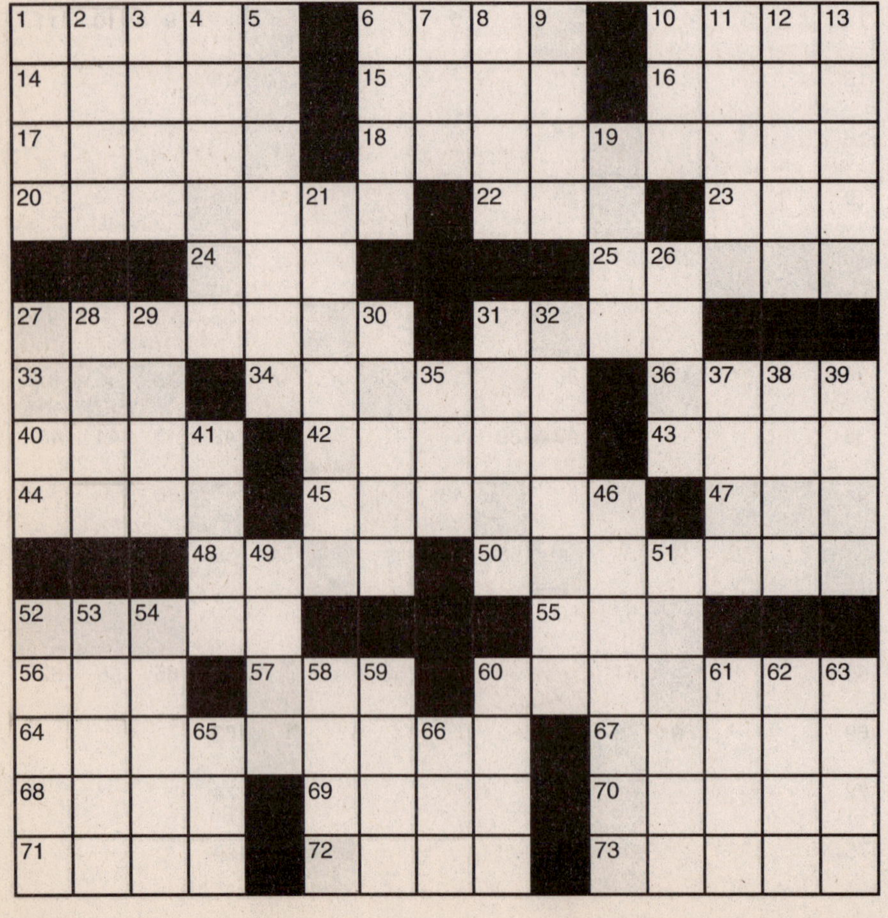

PUZZLE 441

ACROSS

1. Festival
5. Head front
9. Winter illness
12. Certain exam
13. Freshman's cap
15. Rushed
16. Bullets, for short
17. Outsiders
18. "Bonnie ___ Clyde"
19. Mistake in print
20. Rummy or mill
21. Gravy, e.g.
23. Releases
25. More melancholy
26. Atlantic fish
29. Santa's helper
30. BLT spread
31. Humiliates
33. Madden
34. Guns an engine
38. Faithful
39. Tend a baby
40. Legal
41. Confusion
42. Not very bright
43. Conditional release
44. Blooper
46. ___ room
47. Attach by stitches
48. Protect
51. Hankered
53. Unpolished
54. Electrified atom
55. Devours
59. Rescue
60. Spin
63. Came to rest
64. Commanded
65. Showed sleepiness
66. Folk wisdom
67. Look inquisitively
68. Provisions
69. Swarm

DOWN

1. Billy or nanny
2. Military branch
3. Reading light
4. Distant
5. Creed
6. Showers
7. Individual
8. Break the tape
9. Fake
10. Jousting spear
11. Below
13. Rolls with holes
14. Composition
22. Worshiper
24. Fishing-pole part
25. Clinton's instrument
26. Tranquil
27. Woodwind instrument
28. Dennis and Doris
30. Matched
32. Talked back
33. Pep
35. Ids' kin
36. Wretchedly bad
37. Fret
39. Small swallow
40. Delicate fabric
42. Loud uproar
43. Wrote
45. Wary
46. Rose up against
48. Skin on the head
49. Weeper
50. Reddish
51. Spinet or grand
52. Handed out
56. Century plant
57. Radial or spare
58. Bloom holder
61. Blockhead
62. Tango number

PUZZLE 442

ACROSS

1. Yummy smell
6. Tops
10. Hamelin's rodents
14. Operated anew
15. Monster
16. Neutral shade
17. Big deal
18. Lunchtime, often
19. Unattached
20. Pretension
22. Boulevard
24. Witch
26. Had a little lamb
28. Meadow muncher
29. Aspiration
30. Bikini piece
31. Dancing place
34. Ball caller
35. Belch
37. Chafes
39. Rate
40. Personal quirk
41. Ill will
43. Salon aid
44. Encircle
46. Albacore
48. Division of history
49. Hurl
51. Kraal
52. Dingy
53. Shad beginnings
54. Hang low
55. Snaky letter
56. African adventure
59. Hammer part
61. Steep rock
62. Dance instruction
65. Book of maps
69. Deputy
70. Ship's bottom
71. Bias
72. Bulk
73. Automobile part
74. Kind of bear

DOWN

1. "Roses ___ red . . ."
2. Clergy mem.
3. Mineral
4. Get along
5. Naysayer
6. Build
7. In the past
8. Money player
9. Felt
10. Revitalize
11. 43,560 square feet
12. Redwood, e.g.
13. Beef fat
21. Synagogue official
23. Thrice less once
24. Four-base hits
25. Request
27. Jug handle
29. Fit of anger
32. Jazz players
33. Sung dramas
36. GI's grenade
38. Snuff Puff
40. Choir voice
42. Stove
45. Desert illusions
47. Increases
50. Japanese entertainer
52. Soft
56. Sting
57. Battle song?
58. Trends
60. Ninety-degree direction
63. Prom wear
64. Pipe type
66. Youngster
67. Plus
68. Farm coop

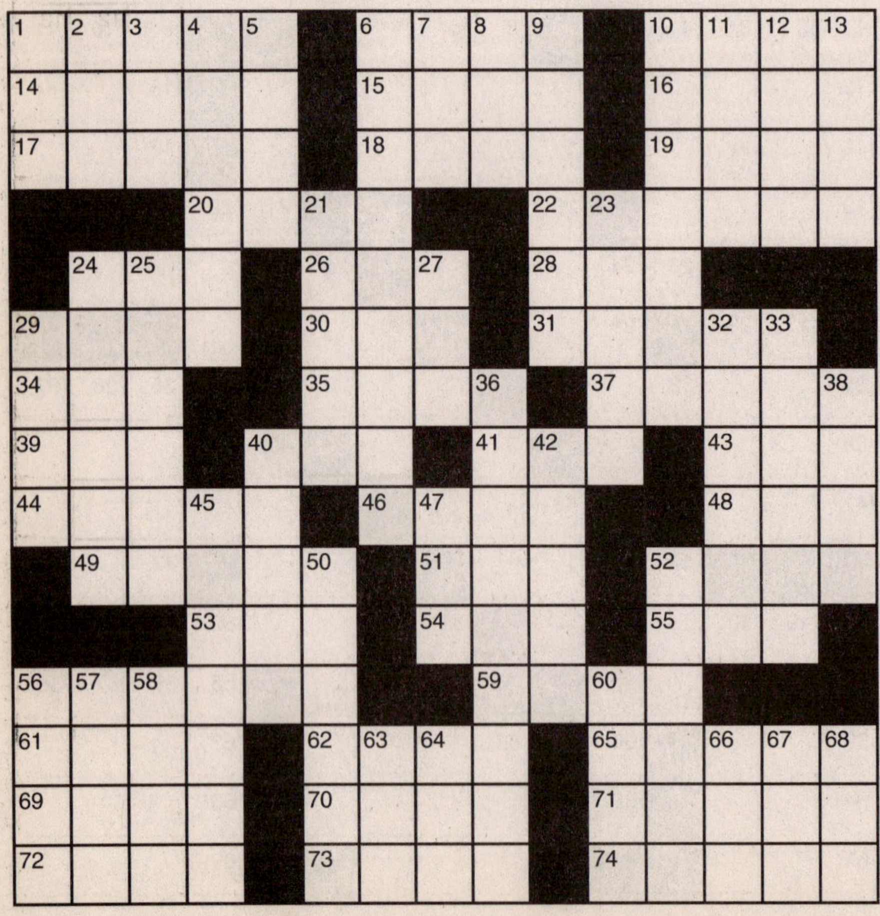

PUZZLE 443

ACROSS

1. Knitting rib
5. Nut
10. Ewe's young
14. Leaf-stem angle
15. Hawaiian porch
16. La Scala specialty
17. Look to be
18. Attraction
20. Luxurious
22. Encrypter
23. Baby bug
24. Bar rocks
26. Affected
28. Monkey
31. Legend
35. Ph.D. exam
37. Eternity
38. Jungle
42. Boot bottom
43. Beauty marks
45. Opponent
46. Coast or Indies
47. Night stalker
48. Phrased
50. Winter melon
53. Unclose, to a poet
54. List in a book
57. Keatsian vase
58. By way of
59. Observers
63. Soaked
68. Burn up
71. Shampoo additive
72. Old English letters
73. Cherub
74. Type of duck
75. Fake
76. Pays attention to
77. Opposite of buy

DOWN

1. Bee's kin
2. Skating maneuver
3. Stead
4. Stately trees
5. Pub order
6. Call off
7. Atop
8. Sudden attack
9. Agreeable
10. Run away quickly
11. "___ We All?"
12. Short skirts
13. Crazy
19. Of an epoch
21. Music system
25. Not unusual
27. Steel reinforcement
28. Basilica part
29. Malayan boat
30. Long fish
32. Actress McGillis
33. Little piggy
34. Reply
36. Oblivion
39. Dismantle
40. Footfall
41. Animal skin
44. Have a debt
49. Holds the deed to
51. Yoked team
52. Cleaned the furniture
54. Clinging vines
55. Crucial inning
56. Country cottage, to Yeltsin
60. Slangy assent
61. Coastal flier
62. Boil over
64. Horse feed
65. Musical club
66. Soccer score
67. Shriek
69. Suffix with critic or real
70. Chicago transports

PUZZLE 444

ACROSS

1. Clip's partner
5. Luxury hotels
9. Raised poodles, e.g.
13. Sixty minutes
14. Melting snow
15. Attract
16. Till
17. Sound judgment
19. Military cafeteria
20. Be beholden to
21. Orals
22. Shoulder enhancer
24. Trimmed
27. Curvy letters
30. Bakes
33. Dapples
35. Hog fat
36. Greek letter
38. Pie
39. Possibly
41. Declared
42. Hit the slopes
43. Bound
44. Tame
46. Decadent
48. Plummets
49. ___ Fisher Hall
51. Regularly, to a poet
52. Clergyman
55. Hen fruit
57. Restaurant bills
61. Painted kitchen utensils
64. Leave the stage
65. Heavy reading?
66. Eagle's nest
67. Annoy
68. Seashore material
69. Arc
70. Did in (the dragon)

DOWN

1. Friend
2. Unaccompanied
3. Umps' calls
4. Search for gold
5. Not busy
6. Thick soup
7. Stubborn animal
8. Feminine pronoun
9. Overcharges
10. Skedaddles
11. Formerly, of old
12. Ruby and Sandra
14. Having footwear on
18. Lieu
23. Request
25. Lackluster
26. Pierced
27. Salamanders
28. Quench
29. Letter stroke
31. Lag behind
32. Carny worker
34. Struck
35. Caustic substance
37. Some poems
40. One who mimics
41. Strews about
43. Embankment
45. Not in tune
47. Raised crops
50. Have a yen
51. Type of molding
52. Cats and gerbils
53. Small forest-buffalo
54. "___ Yankees"
56. Network
58. Leaf's angle
59. Ill temper
60. Hearty dish
62. Hunting dog
63. Diminutive

PUZZLE 445

ACROSS

1. Carpenters' tools
5. Run like mad
9. Venomous serpents
13. Type of exam
14. Statues of gods
16. Rotated
17. Dog's name
18. Dimwitted
19. Roll-call reply
20. Sample, as food
22. Intense
24. So-so grade
25. Quickness
28. Yard cleaner
30. Mary Richards's office
33. Morse code symbol
34. In times past
35. Daze
37. Write with acid
41. Word with neither
42. Stags and bucks
43. The lady's
45. Strong beer
46. Confused
48. Long step
50. ___ and order
51. Destroy the interior of
53. Green gems
55. Is painful
58. Moth-repelling wood
59. "Now I ___ me . . ."
60. Anxious
63. Kinder
67. Command to a child
69. Bowed
72. Baking ingredient
73. Diamond team
74. Linger
75. Throw off
76. Biting bug
77. Printer's term
78. Solidifies

DOWN

1. Gentle
2. Soprano's solo
3. Rolls of cash
4. Slow-moving animals
5. Cast off
6. Fruit quencher
7. Blame
8. Differently
9. Volcanic dust
10. Very little bit
11. Blender button
12. Nasty smile
15. Interview
21. Dry land
23. Master
26. Most tender
27. Salute
29. Grabbed a bite
30. Grandma
31. Self-images
32. Became frayed
33. Transferred, as land
36. Ring
38. "Walking ___"
39. Garbed
40. Chops
44. Operated anew
47. Birthday-candle count
49. Adapt for a new purpose
52. Function
54. Happens
55. Beside
56. Log structure
57. Laughing ___
61. Family member
62. Alum
64. Arrive
65. Prepare for publication
66. Some rodents
68. Up until now
70. Building extension
71. Coloring

PUZZLE 446

ACROSS

1. Unhappy
4. Read quickly
8. ’60s coiffure
12. Pottery oven
16. Dorothy’s dog
17. Last name in spydom
18. Lobster’s relative
19. Gen. Robt. ___
20. Mechanical
22. Mexican food
23. Bird’s home
24. Actress Lupino
25. Pencil utensil
27. Poor
29. Hot off the press
30. Complete: pref.
31. Cry of pain
33. “The Old ___ Bucket”
37. Corner
39. Scallion’s kin
41. Have title to
43. Dined
44. Dangle
47. Son ___ gun!
48. Conducted
49. Edward’s nickname
50. One kind of beehive
53. Fruity drink
54. Literary output
56. Scrape
57. Puzzling question
59. Much
63. Majors and Meriwether
64. Bridge length
66. Thin bit of smoke
68. Stream
69. Ye ___ Tea Shoppe
70. Followed orders
72. Contradict
74. Sketches
77. Alcoholic brew
78. Like sandpaper
79. Andy Capp’s wife
82. Have unpaid bills
83. Night stalker
84. “High ___”
85. Curtsey
86. Sea, in Paris
87. Result
89. Cut
93. Magazine edition
95. Put on the payroll
97. Cathedral part
100. Train stop: abbr.
101. TV’s “___ Buddies”
103. Gave up dessert
105. Dino, to Fred
106. Politician Sonny ___
109. Young dogs
111. Bachman-Turner ___
113. Sphere
114. Customer
115. Actress Harper
116. Mine finds
117. Derision cry
118. Hero’s shop
119. Feed the kitty
120. Perfect number

DOWN

1. At a higher volume
2. City in Ontario
3. Flirt with
4. Stock unit
5. Itemize
6. Gotten up
7. Good-natured
8. Part of a play
9. French coin
10. Preakness contestants
11. Bassoon’s cousin
12. Nairobi’s site
13. ___ du Diable
14. Guitarist Paul
15. High-wire precaution
16. Contaminate
21. Gathered
26. Applied shingles to
28. Reed or Douglas
32. Actress Merkel
34. Comics’ Krazy ___
35. Summer on the Seine
36. Actor Beatty
38. Put into words
40. Antiseptic element
42. Lived
45. Do arithmetic
46. Votes against
50. Heavenly headgear
51. Adam’s son
52. Wrathful
53. Saudis, e.g.
54. Pass by
55. Chattering
58. Broods (on)

60. Plunder

61. Banish

62. Card above a deuce

65. Strong person

67. Jumping stick

71. Showed sleepiness

73. NFL player

75. "___ and Juliet"

76. Wonderment

79. Nat. security police

80. ___ Angeles

81. Sounds of pain

83. Above, in poems

84. Opposite of sloppiest

88. Not level

PUZZLE 446

90. Seek to attain

91. Producer Spielberg

92. Despises

94. WWII craft

96. Urge

98. Poet's product

99. Actor Byrnes

102. Potato

104. Tiny bit

106. Humbug!

107. Spanish gold

108. Recent: pref.

110. ___ Lanka

112. Spoil

PUZZLE 447

ACROSS

1. Tiff
5. Like an omelet
9. Hit sharply
13. Per
14. Gives out sparingly
16. Crown of light
17. Money, to Sophia
18. Big
19. "Let us sing ___ the Lord"
20. Lack of restrictions
22. Porter
24. Billions of years
25. Seniors
26. Lingerie item
29. Carry
30. Celebrity
31. Auburn
33. Valuable stone
34. Lightning and curtain
38. Expert
39. Stuff
40. Tea choice
41. Pull apart
42. Jimmy
43. "___ Bovary"
44. Wriggly
46. Howl deeply
47. Itch
48. Tropical fruit
51. Ponder
52. Eludes
53. Predecessor
58. Lone
59. Craze
61. John XXIII, for one
62. Cake level
63. Enthusiasm
64. Ripened
65. Betting factor
66. Mimicking bird
67. Forbidden thing

DOWN

1. Ego
2. Shoe grouping
3. Farm unit
4. "Of ___ I Sing"
5. Barely defeat
6. Piercing
7. Secluded valleys
8. Not nay
9. Trembled
10. Jouster's weapon
11. Place of worship
12. ___ out (tires)
15. Brook
21. Rent again
23. Type of wood
26. Misbehaving child
27. Uncultured
28. To the ocean
30. Sustained
32. Butter knives
33. Jolly
35. All right
36. Curved roof
37. Espied
39. Crooked
40. Check endorser
42. Blood part
43. Lash enhancer
45. Needle feature
46. Toe ailment
48. Pasta topping
49. Shun
50. Turned white
51. Actor Patinkin
54. Extend over
55. For takeout
56. Diner sign
57. Accomplish again
60. Shirt sleeve

1	2	3	4	■	5	6	7	8	■	■	9	10	11	12
13				■	14				15	■	16			
17				■	18					■	19			
20				21				■	22	23				
■	■	■	■	24				■	25					
26	27	28	■	29			■	30				■	■	■
31			32			■	33			■	34	35	36	37
38					■	39			■	40				
41				■	42			■	43					
■	■	■	44	45			■	46			■	47		
48	49	50				■	51				■	■	■	■
52						■	53				54	55	56	57
58				■	59	60				■	61			
62				■	63					■	64			
65				■	■	66				■	67			

PUZZLE 448

ACROSS

1. Cliff projection
5. Flock papas
9. Big rig
13. Loony
14. Marry secretly
16. Cattle
17. Merit
18. Hinder
19. Tablet
20. Halt
22. Deuce beater
24. Witness
25. Rowboat blades
27. Group of eight
29. Future frog
33. Spirit
35. Above
36. Cinch
38. Woe!
42. Unaccompanied
43. Walking pole
44. Glassy mineral
45. Do the butterfly
46. Polynesian dance
47. Hammerhead end
48. School for the college bound
50. Portion
53. China item
56. Considerate
57. Fortune
58. Reject
61. Arrange
66. Excited
68. Songlike poem
70. Single time
71. Zilch
72. Forked out
73. Sheriff's badge
74. Leg part
75. Acorn producers
76. Bugle

DOWN

1. Musical sign
2. Racket
3. Realty unit
4. Not here
5. Start a card game again
6. Tavern brew
7. Sheds
8. Shadowbox
9. Soak
10. Be
11. Riot
12. Bayou
15. Needle hole
21. Animal park
23. Second person
26. Relax
28. Vises
29. Fling
30. Affirm
31. Sub shop
32. On time
33. Spiced sausage
34. Choose
37. Naught
39. In ___ of (instead of)
40. Scorer on a serve
41. Right-minded
43. That woman
49. Race in neutral
51. Makes into a statute
52. Total (up)
53. Board
54. Use a computer
55. Do penance
56. 1988 Olympics site
59. Some railways
60. Mistake in print
62. Tease
63. "Do ___ others . . ."
64. Imperfection
65. Gull-like bird
67. Golly!
69. Writing liquid

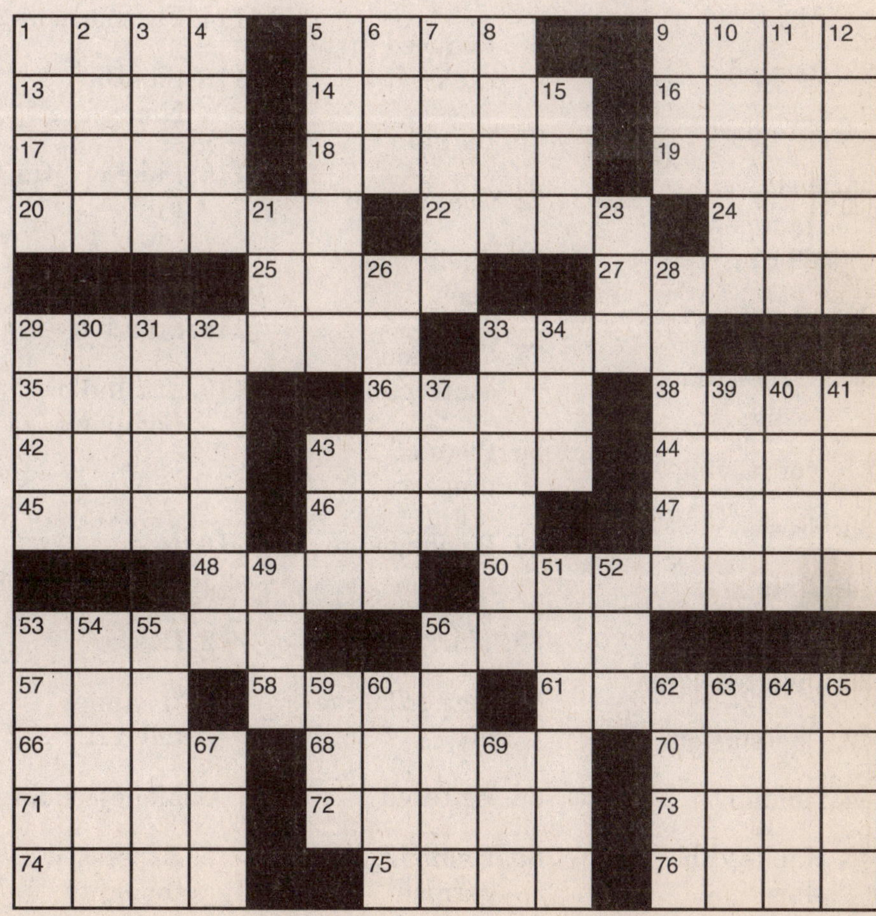

PUZZLE 449

MUSICALS

ACROSS

1. Clean with a mop
5. Resistance units
9. Prepare, as a salad
13. Wallow
17. Filmdom's Kedrova
18. Bucket
19. Hindu queen
20. Columnist Chase
21. Z ___ zebra
22. Native South American
23. Related
24. Kite part
25. Rodgers/ Hammerstein offering
28. Avocation
30. Earlier than, to Keats
31. Not moving
33. Frost
34. Blatant pretense
38. Inverted carets
40. Compulsions
44. Holdup
45. Kander/Ebb show
48. Ivan and Nicholas
49. Join forces with
50. Chilling
52. Mexican Mrs.
53. Wring
54. Dreary
56. Apathetically
58. Gives in
60. Dillydally
62. Snooze
65. Kathie ___ Gifford
66. Reduced in rank
70. Bargain
72. Coal wagon
76. Shelley, for one
77. Common contraction
80. Piece of property
82. Be obliged to pay
83. Thick
84. Lerner/Loewe hit
86. Agitated
88. Hamburger garnish
89. Of an epoch
90. Leading lady
92. Drs.
94. Swap
97. Broke bread
98. Jetsam's partner
102. Willson work
107. Mythical prankster
108. Fancy gold fabric
110. Supportive beam
111. "Jane ___"
112. Batman portrayer West
113. R&B's Redding
114. Furthermore
115. Sleuth Nancy ___
116. Luke of "Kung Fu"
117. Subsequent
118. Scorch
119. ___ India Company

DOWN

1. Narrow board
2. Desire
3. "I cannot tell ___"
4. Moneylenders
5. Expressed thoughts
6. Dangle
7. Isinglasses
8. Bias
9. Campers
10. Furniture wood
11. Quick cut
12. Egyptian peninsula
13. Coward operetta
14. Jai ___
15. Dieter's milk
16. Curly greens
26. Wrathful
27. Stellar soprano
29. Sink, as a vessel
32. Groucho's gaze
34. African country
35. Descendant
36. Radames's love
37. Unbleached color
39. Celebrity
41. Put on weight
42. Once, once
43. JFF sights, once
46. Suffers
47. Dinner gong
51. Brink
55. Donnelly/ Romberg opus
57. "___, Giorgio"

PUZZLE 449

59. Ms. Macpherson
61. Is present at
63. And others
64. Acapulco coin
66. Flightless bird
67. Ancient garden
68. Small: pref.
69. Gaming cubes
71. Nick and Nora's pooch
73. Shade of pink
74. Inspires with fear
75. New York nine
78. Tangy
79. Brainiest
81. ___-frutti
85. Biblical king
87. Come before
91. Twin of Pollux
93. Parlor
95. French painter
96. Author Zola
98. Kind of jacket
99. Metallic vein
100. All right!
101. Better half
103. Major or minor
104. "___ Breckinridge"
105. Mars
106. Eft
109. Combine

PUZZLE 450

ACROSS

1. Restrain
5. Hearty meal
9. Flecks
13. Adrift
14. Pack animal
15. Be next to
16. Couple
17. Having a roof overhang
18. Ear part
19. Easter ___ hunt
20. Gobi transport
21. Jump over
22. Leased
24. Full of information
27. Garden pest
29. Scottish headwear
30. Chump
33. Pastrami purveyor
36. Macadamia, e.g.
38. Not obvious
40. With speed
42. Direct
44. Blue and yellow result
45. Drainpipes
47. Tuna container
49. Unpaid
50. "___ So Fine"
51. Breeze
53. Circle
55. Moving about
57. Family members
61. Lower leg front
64. Falsehoods
66. Paul Bunyan's tool
67. Social grace
68. Tax inspection
69. Smirk
70. Strong brews
71. Drizzly
72. Slippery fellows
73. Like a horror film
74. Curdle
75. Corner

DOWN

1. Adventure
2. Customary practice
3. Royal authority
4. Cocktail lounge
5. Edible mollusk
6. Shelter
7. Breakfast entree
8. Money roll
9. Waste time
10. Reed instrument
11. Oompah horn
12. Stride
14. Heavy
20. Average mark
23. Two times
25. Used to be
26. Conceited
28. Make into a knight
30. Mulligan or beef
31. To the sheltered side
32. Hang fire
33. Quick race
34. Dueling device
35. Decrees
37. Muscle spasm
39. Out of money
41. Periods in history
43. Father, informally
46. Use a throne
48. Ripe old age
52. Ceremony
54. Sib
55. Restless
56. Audio medium
58. Nurturer
59. Banish
60. Hearing or taste
61. Forest dweller
62. Angel's hat
63. Cake froster
65. Dryer fluff
68. Curvature
69. Acquire

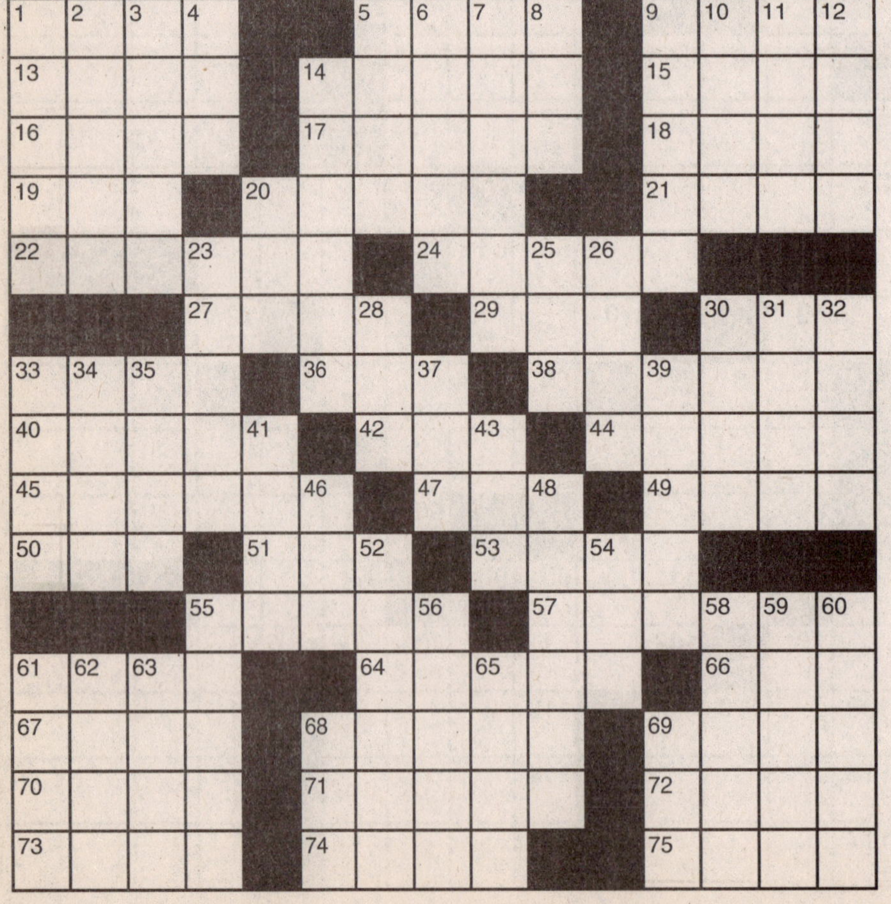

PUZZLE 451

ACROSS

1. Sandpiper
6. Essence
10. Deteriorated
14. Navigational aid
15. Not in favor of
16. Dirk's kin
17. Coral reef
18. Religious
20. Twice five
21. Confident
23. Watch secretly
24. Vinegar bottle
25. Society entrant
27. Marred
30. Zigzag ski race
33. Breakfast dish
34. Pop-singer Bobby ___
35. Assert
37. Sorrow
38. Slangy yes
39. Pen
40. Humdinger
41. Third letter
42. Made into leather
43. Japanese performer
45. Basics
46. Ram's dam
47. Impoverished
48. Dads
51. Counselor
53. Half of a bikini
56. Servant
58. Of a fatty acid
60. Calm
61. Sunburn soother
62. Comedian Milton ___
63. Current units
64. Tear apart
65. ___ on (encouraged)

DOWN

1. Thin strip
2. Musical sound
3. Ferrous element
4. Sidekick
5. Photographer's gadget
6. Gossiped
7. Computer data
8. Excite
9. With fatigue
10. Moistened
11. Grand work
12. Gather crops
13. Slippery
19. Thought
22. Hard fat
24. Measure of heat
26. Flattery
27. Extinct bird
28. Between
29. Confused fight
30. Fool
31. Like sheep
32. Fare measure
34. Expected
36. Crimson and scarlet
38. Pro vote
39. Togs
41. English cheese
42. Quaker pronoun
44. Graceful water bird
45. Quizzed
47. Sheer curtain fabric
48. Tropical rodent
49. Teensy particle
50. Halt
52. Hollow
53. Glacier piece
54. Vex
55. Did better than a B on
57. Chicago railways
59. Support

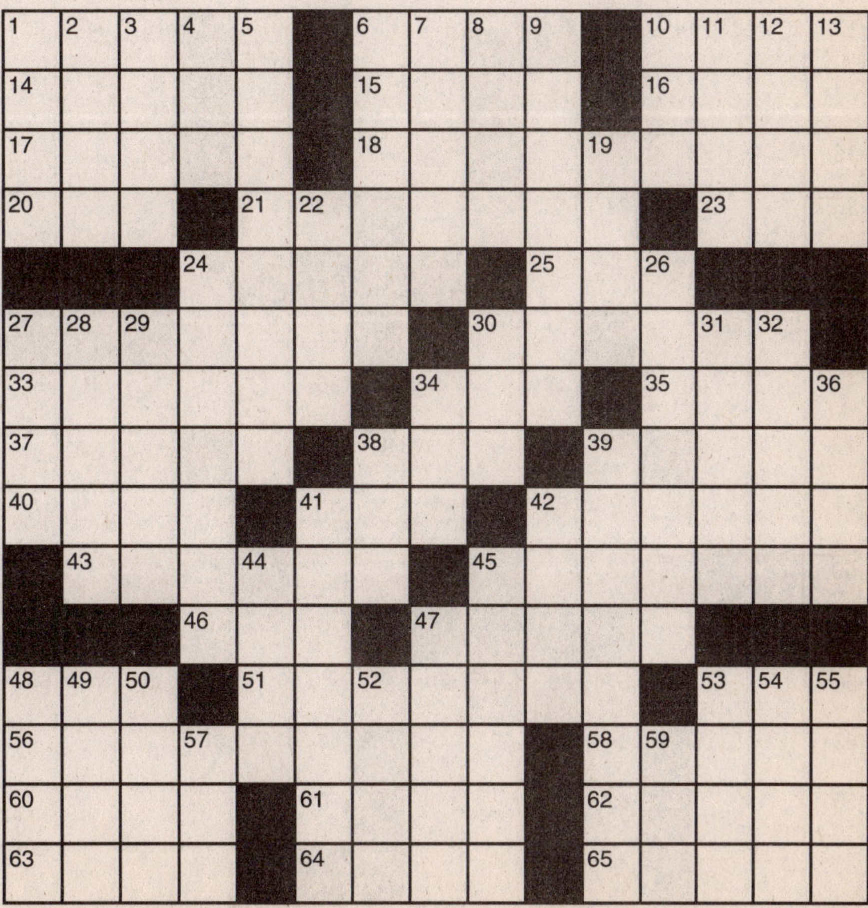

PUZZLE 452

ACROSS

1. Breakfast drink
6. Excitements
10. Stubborn animal
13. Once more
15. Roast
16. Couple
17. Packed away
18. Old harp
19. Skier's line
20. Cargo weight
21. Adorable
23. Respect
25. Craving
26. Like summertime tea
27. Female singer
30. Circle portion
32. Card-player's offer
34. "The ___ King"
35. Moreover
36. With eagerness
40. Certain sprite
41. Room for books
43. Vote for
44. Photographer's workplace
46. Self-image
47. Wood for shipbuilding
48. Still, in verse
49. Block a stream
50. Dangerous snakes
51. Southern bread
54. Substitute worker
56. Piled on
59. Give out
60. Recreation spot
63. Type measures
64. New Zealand fruit
66. Hosted
68. Skillful
69. On an ___ keel
70. Wandered
71. Old pronoun
72. Unpaid bill
73. Makes like a top

DOWN

1. Tease
2. "Do ___ others . . ."
3. Object of devotion
4. Milk source
5. Standing
6. Having talent
7. 24-hour period
8. Gumbo vegetable
9. Plant
10. Top floor
11. Took an oath
12. Planted
14. Instruction
22. Beat
24. Skirt length
25. Positively charged particle
27. Brewed drinks
28. Rhythm
29. Bean curd
31. Removed the center of
32. Forecaster's device
33. Climbing plant
37. Hues
38. Ballerina's jump
39. Babbles
41. Be less than truthful
42. Marble stone
45. Exploit
47. Faucet
51. Skirt fold
52. Vitality
53. Mean
55. Written reminders
57. ___ out (barely made)
58. Plunge into water
59. Julep flavor
60. Highway vehicle
61. Hammer end
62. Inserts
65. Spider's snare
67. Baseball headwear

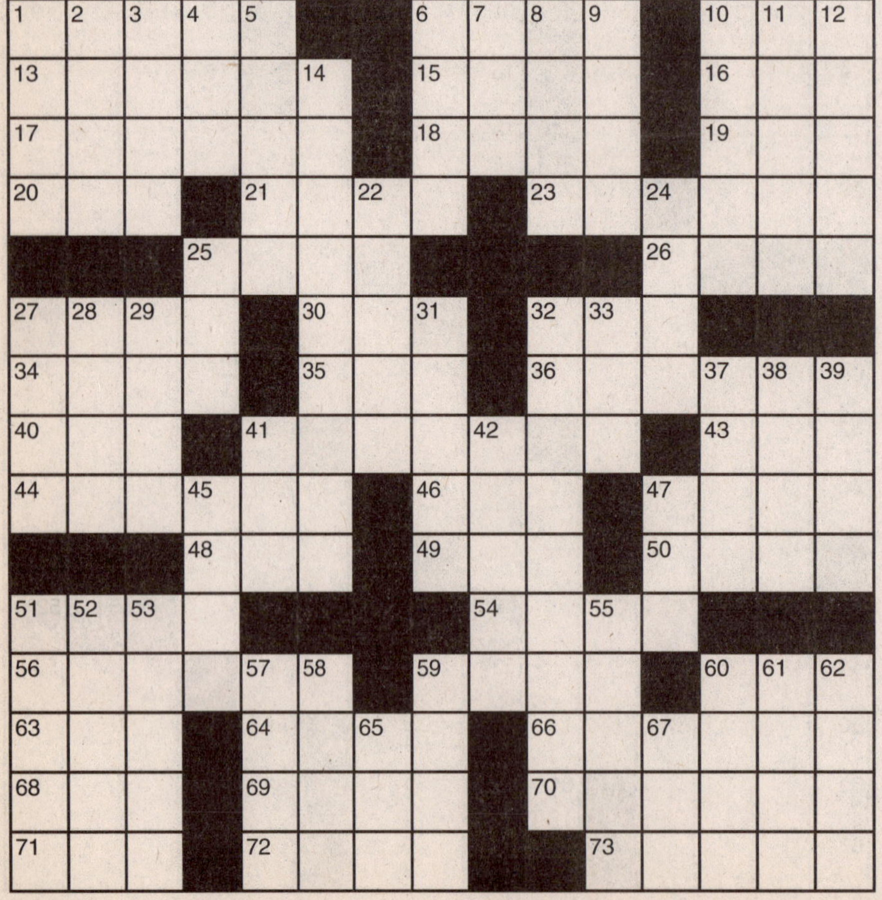

PUZZLE 453

ACROSS

1. Burn
5. Wharf rodent
8. ___ and polish
12. In the past
13. Attack
15. Effortless
16. Anxious
17. Lariat
18. Cow product
19. Angler's need
20. Young boy
21. Novice
23. Procedure
25. Await judgment
26. Garden tool
28. Leftover piece
33. Cued
36. Fables
37. Bakers' needs
38. Shake, as a tail
40. Ear parts
41. Sherry or port
42. Small sofa
44. Melting snow
46. Argue
47. Applied
49. Most adorable
53. Frozen dessert
57. Afternoon snooze
58. Basketball's contents
59. Soda flavor
60. Ingested
62. Fictional monster
63. With competence
64. Hurry
65. Out of the wind
66. Chief
67. Barnyard fowl
68. G-men

DOWN

1. Takes wing
2. Delegate
3. Sour compounds
4. Bright color
5. ___ one's lips
6. Horse's relative
7. Experimenter
8. Large truck
9. Distress
10. Capri, e.g.
11. Tot
13. Accused
14. Tattered
20. Young adults
22. TV spots
24. Threads
25. Biked
27. Dawn droplets
29. Storage spot
30. Lounging wear
31. Telephone code
32. Annoyance
33. Aisles
34. Sermon topic
35. Food list
39. Lump
40. Slow down
43. Empty
45. Center
46. Unleash
48. Witnesses
50. National symbol
51. Fathered
52. Maple and pine
53. Wound covering
54. Tramp
55. Wings
56. Light beams
57. Type of colorful sign
61. Foot digit
62. Clumsy person

1	2	3	4			5	6	7			8	9	10	11
12					13				14		15			
16					17						18			
19				20				21		22				
23			24				25							
			26			27				28	29	30	31	32
33	34	35									36			
37						38		39		40				
41							42		43					
44				45		46								
				47	48				49			50	51	52
53	54	55	56					57				58		
59					60		61				62			
63					64						65			
66						67					68			

PUZZLE 454

ACROSS

1. Fawn's father
5. Buddhist monk
9. Flooded
14. Poi ingredient
15. Of an age
16. Extremely impressive
17. Colorado Indians
18. Called
20. Opera singer
22. ___-do-well
23. Moistens, poetically
24. Hunch
26. Doctrine
28. Jogger
30. Challenge
34. Obtained
35. Angered
38. Preliminary part
39. Not at home
40. Frying pan
42. Playing marble
43. Vertically
45. Small duck
46. No ___, ands, or buts
47. Oil-well rig
49. Pass into law
52. Large African antelope
53. Seed cover
54. Sate
57. Tuber
60. Shriek
64. Uproar
67. Large wading bird
68. Small landmass
69. Peddle
70. Verve
71. Stage
72. Informed
73. Editor's mark

DOWN

1. Theater receipt
2. Cheerio
3. God of war
4. Loose talk
5. Type of serve
6. Bullring
7. Bull or ram
8. Not windward
9. Light gray
10. Lumberjacks
11. Teen woe
12. Distort
13. Brick holders
19. Stiffly neat
21. Song of praise
25. Actor Estrada
27. ___ and polish
28. Watchmaker's lens
29. River creature
30. Dormant
31. Garret
32. Special skill
33. Words of inquiry
34. Incite
36. Hazard
37. Dutch ___ disease
40. Fruit peel
41. Wide-spouted pitcher
44. Preppy socks
48. Sidewalk border
50. Pointed end
51. Related
53. Ring-shaped reef
54. China flaw
55. Abundant
56. Stewpot
58. Baking chamber
59. Muffin topper
61. Apt
62. Irani coin
63. Medieval peasant
65. Supped
66. Shopworn

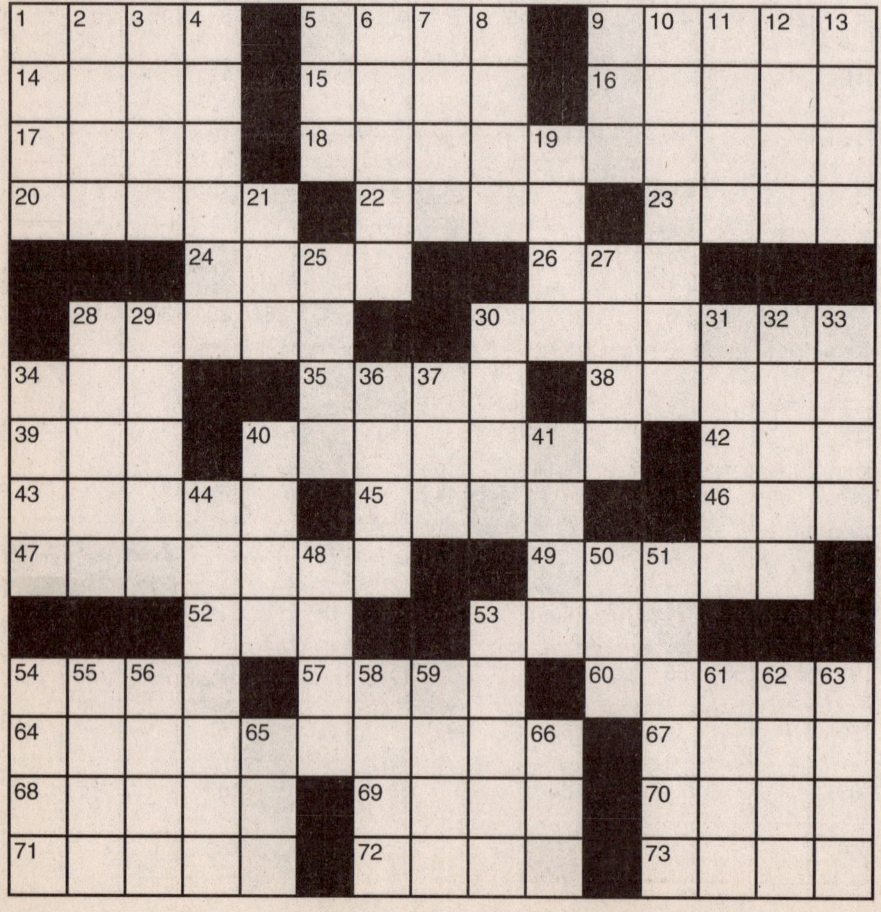

PUZZLE 455

ACROSS

1. Eccentric disks
5. Pod legume
8. Top-grade recipient
12. Biscuit topper
13. Tiny insect
15. Deal
16. GI's supper
17. Blue dyes
18. Shade source
19. See
21. Bambino
22. Seeing red
23. Drink cooler
25. Sogginess
27. Supplant
32. Work units
33. Conscious of
34. Blood part
36. NBA player, e.g.
39. Paper currency
41. Viper
42. Arrogant
44. Feminine pronoun
45. Peasants' cooperatives
48. Destroy
49. "La donna e mobile," e.g.
51. Pale purple
53. Cleaner additive
56. Evergreen plant
57. Opinion sample
58. British title
60. Smaller amount
65. Seed protection
66. Mandate
68. Guitar device
69. Staff
70. Song and dance show
71. Without moisture
72. Watcher
73. Ribbed fabric
74. Asian staple

DOWN

1. Curry
2. Captain's direction
3. Lacework
4. Middling
5. Bowling target
6. Amend a manuscript
7. Radiant
8. Pretending
9. Exchange letters
10. Dueling weapons
11. Clarinets, e.g.
13. Zany
14. Regard highly
20. "___ Abner"
24. Acclaim
26. Booby ___
27. Makeshift bed
28. Foot part
29. Make sleeker
30. Hawaiian dish
31. Picasso's prop
35. Spread out
37. Impertinent
38. Polecat's defense
40. Sharp ache
43. Stand for office
46. Lifter
47. Slender
50. Derby or coaster
52. Fleecy one
53. With speed
54. Tropical eel
55. Supporter
59. Split
61. Wound reminder
62. Delhi dress
63. "Beowulf," e.g.
64. Went by streetcar
67. Eight ounces

PUZZLE 456

ACROSS

1. Vestments
5. Certain haircuts
9. At a distance
13. Fatigue
14. Apportion
16. Overly inquisitive
17. Tense
18. African felines
19. Dealer's tip
20. Roadside stop
21. Farm tool
22. Sock part
24. Cows and steers, e.g.
26. Make a web
28. Baby's food
31. Little bit
33. Neat
35. Skillfully
37. Sheet of cotton
39. Active one
40. TV's "Green ___"
41. Baden-Baden, e.g.
42. Dote on
43. Blacken
44. Golf stroke
45. Fissure
46. Sloppier
48. Arch type
50. Serpentine curve
51. Relinquish
53. Hesitant
57. Boxer Max ___
59. Craving
61. Male or female
62. Elliptical
64. Arabian rulers
66. Lollapalooza
67. OK
68. Elude
69. Dry
70. Lose color
71. Borscht ingredient
72. Group of computer bits

DOWN

1. Garret
2. Woody vine
3. Full impact
4. Become firm
5. "Giselle," e.g.
6. Hodgepodge
7. Punches
8. Cain, to Adam
9. Start the pot
10. Never-failing
11. Inquire
12. Bar drink
15. Jeans partner
21. Tactics
23. Terminus
25. Floor installers
27. Veggie for French fries
29. Vigilant
30. Bonfire
32. Ridiculous
34. Whirlpools
35. Dull pains
36. Trumpet-and-trombone group
38. Suitable
40. Apex
42. Don't exist
44. Stared intently
47. Rink surface
49. Gore
52. Delete
54. Excessive interest
55. Ignited again
56. Ooze out
58. Out of the wind
60. Impel
62. Amiss
63. Through
65. Gang of criminals
66. Experiment site

1	2	3	4	■	5	6	7	8	■	■	9	10	11	12
13				■	14				15	■	16			
17				■	18					■	19			
20			■	21				■	22	23			■	■
24			25			■	26	27			■	28	29	30
■	■	■	31			32	■	33			34			
■	35	36			■	37	38			■	39			
40					■	41			■	42				
43				■	44				■	45				■
46				47			■	48	49			■	■	■
50			■	51			52	■	53			54	55	56
■	■	57	58			■	59	60			■	61		
62	63			■	64	65				■	66			
67				■	68					■	69			
70				■	■	71				■	72			

CODEWORD

PUZZLE 457

Codeword is a special crossword puzzle in which conventional clues are omitted. Instead, answer words in the diagram are represented by numbers. Each number represents a different letter of the alphabet, and all of the letters of the alphabet are used. When you are sure of a letter, put it in the code key chart and cross it off in the Alphabet Box. A group of letters has been inserted to start you off.

1	2	3	4	5	6	7	8	9	10	11	12	13
14	15	16	17	18	19 T	20	21	22	23	24 A	25	26 E

24	8	11		5	24	18		23	15	16		23	7	19
10	7	7		24	5	26		26	1	24		26	12	7
19	7	19		11	15	5	7	19	26	18		20	5	21
7	1	24	5		25	15	24			12	24 A	19 T	26 E	20
1	26	19	24	11	26		13	26	25	26	1			
	18	7	22	26				11	7	20	19	8	24	17
			26	1	26		16	15	18		20	15	18	26
11	24	5			6	2	24	10	14			18	26	4
24	20	26	24		2	1	17		24	20	11			
20	3	15	17	18	15	12				11	24	10	19	
			19	26	11	26	26		4	24	5	1	2	20
3	24	25	26	17			5	21	26		8	24	9	15
7	1	26		19	7	13	13	26	26	20		21	26	19
11	15	26		26	4	26		24	11	26		7	18	26
26	24	1		18	26	26		1	21	26		17	7	18

Alphabet Box

A B C D E F G H I J K L M N O P Q R S T U V W X Y Z

PUZZLE 458

ACROSS

1. Deep wound
5. Young women
9. Picnic crasher
12. Domesticate
16. Not pro
17. Gaucho's rope
19. Regard
20. Of a time
21. Slide
22. Fielding muff
23. TV's Dawber
24. Zeros
25. Shirt part
27. Smidgen
29. Row
31. Pro vote
32. Flawless
34. Desert creature
37. Sings happily
38. Mild cigar
39. "___ Drives Me Crazy"
42. Parisian ocean
45. Peggy or Spike
46. Naval clerk
47. Mazel ___!
48. Rd.
49. Keystone's place
51. Nick's dog
52. Harsh light
54. Clear condensation
56. Elephants' ivories
58. Russian range
59. "___ Got to Be Me"
60. Min. part
61. Salamander
64. Felix, e.g.
65. Road marker
67. "Knight ___"
69. Unwieldy ships
72. Sung drama
74. Frost
76. Santa's time
78. Snakelike swimmer
79. Rowing blade
80. Vast plain
82. Passing grade
83. Judgment ___
84. Tissue layer
85. Waffle topper
86. Trademarks
88. Serrated
89. Mountain ridge
90. Length of life
93. "Moonlight ___"
97. Facts
99. Haven
101. Roasting chamber
102. Apprehend
105. Kinder
107. Mishmash
108. Sand hill
109. Likewise
110. Placed on a cay
111. Roster
112. Diving duck
113. Heavens
114. His and ___
115. Jeans patch site

DOWN

1. Vaporous
2. Lower-limb joint
3. Pigpens
4. Conceal
5. More acquisitive
6. EPA's concern
7. Lasso
8. Bar seats
9. Egypt's snake
10. Teaching org.
11. Painting technique
12. Care for
13. Moistureless
14. Shopper's mecca
15. Choice word
18. Craft
26. Small town
28. Opened
30. Beside
33. Chooses by vote
35. Tons
36. Nursery cry
39. Frightened
40. Circle dance
41. Daring Knievel
42. Crazy
43. Night before
44. Processing plant
46. Chatty ox?
50. Color shade
53. Maui event
55. Ended
57. Threw away
62. Comic Tina ___
63. Plod
64. Cheddars and Bries
65. Farm structure
66. October's gem
68. Anger
70. Large parrot
71. Tricky
73. Black-ink item
74. Main character
75. Grand work
77. Acrobats' garments
81. Cruel despots
86. Somewhat tardy
87. Soothsayer
90. Exhausted
91. Appearance
92. Express feeling
93. Puts down grass
94. Egg
95. Hawaiian goose
96. Freshly
98. Cuckoo
100. Yellow center
103. Hunky-dory
104. Tarzan's kid
106. Racket end

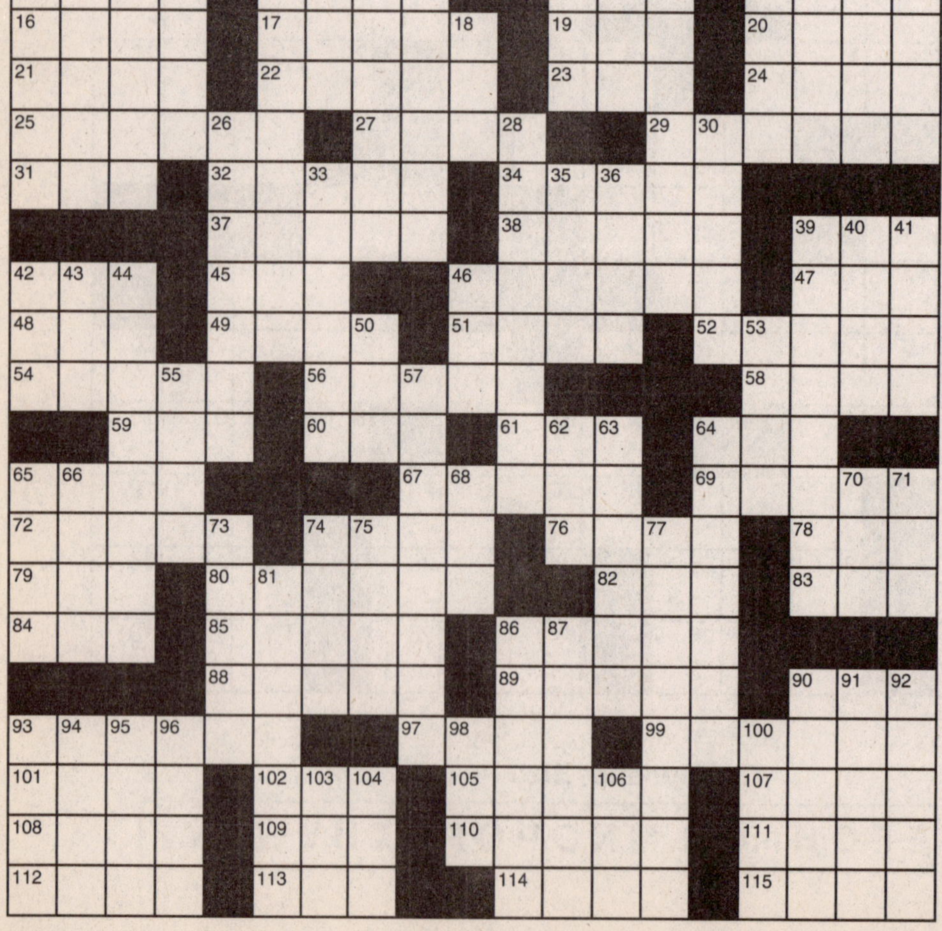

PUZZLE 459

ACROSS

1. Big birds
5. Clock a race
9. Imitating
14. Similar
15. Follow
16. "M*A*S*H" clerk
17. Small bug
18. Telegraph
19. Hag
20. Marvelous things
23. Cabbage salad
24. Squirt
26. Average mark
28. Tornado warnings
30. Be astride
35. Trudge
36. Astaire hit
38. Conger, e.g.
39. Shred
40. Critiques
41. Scoundrel
42. King's better
43. Arouse
44. Out of harm's way
45. Yarn
47. Over there
49. Above, to Keats
50. Supply
51. Work crew
54. Kitchen alcove
59. Motto
61. Industrial fuel
62. Moves with speed
66. Scrooge, e.g.
67. Lyric works
68. Of an age
69. Intent look
70. Capone's nemesis
71. Refute

DOWN

1. Santa's helper
2. Kind of acad.
3. Luau strings
4. Marine plant
5. Hamlet
6. Lat. footnote
7. No more than
8. Voyeur
9. Curved line
10. Analyzed grammatically
11. Revered one
12. Sten movie
13. Developed
21. Personal
22. Lean
24. Sand
25. Push forward
27. Gobbles up
28. No-fat Jack
29. Caretaker
30. Large nail
31. Biblical pronoun
32. Ten years
33. Paged, as through a book
34. Church leader
37. Egg-shaped
40. Evaluate
44. Went ahchoo
46. Lumberjack
48. Frequently, in verse
51. Legs
52. Door to ore
53. Astronaut's org.
55. Holy image
56. Knot
57. Stretches
58. Ms. Trueheart
60. Before of yore
63. Great anger
64. Cooking vessel
65. Wily

Puzzler

PUZZLE 460

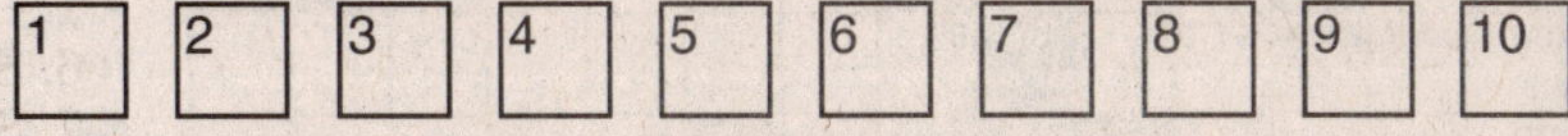

I am a word of ten letters.

My 8, 1, 9, 7, 6 is a seat.

My 3, 1, 2 is bashful.

My 10, 5, 9, 3, 1 is a dog lead.

My 8, 9, 6, 4 is a small wagon.

My 8, 7, 4, 2 is a metropolis.

My 8, 9, 3, 4, 10, 5 is a stronghold.

My 10, 2, 6, 5 is a stringed instrument.

PUZZLE 461

ACROSS

1. Waffle topper
5. Utter loudly
9. Dogma
12. Patrick, e.g.
17. Tempo
18. Chalet part
19. It comes after pi
20. Mr. Doubleday
21. Malt dryer
22. Float ingredient
24. Paris's river
25. Joins
27. He's on first
28. Imprint firmly
30. Fit to a ____
31. Fish beginnings
32. Gender
33. Sesame paste
35. College money managers
39. Southern boy, once
41. Citrus cooler
44. Braggart's problem
45. Like shish kebab
48. Named
49. Crow
51. Awesome!
52. Musical platter
54. Jet ____
55. Side-by-side likeness
57. Distance down
58. Heap of wood
59. Overhead light bulb?
60. Toothed cutter
61. Relieve
63. Hawk, e.g.
66. Wandering pet
68. Of a major blood vessel
72. Had a bagel
73. 11th grader
74. ____ Lanka
75. Skylit courtyards
76. Italian ice cream
79. Fiascos
82. ____ and outs
83. Ruins
85. Not act.
86. Volunteers
88. Dissertations
90. Estuary
92. "Top ____"
93. Snow-crossing slat
95. Urge
96. H.R.H.'s fliers
97. Set on fire
101. Married women
103. Single turn
106. 43,560 square feet
107. Aware
108. Ms. Peron
109. Irish river
110. Utensil
111. Beaks
112. Down yards
113. Poor grades
114. Odds and ____

DOWN

1. Bassoon's cousin
2. Not fatty
3. West's opposite
4. River mammals
5. Frenzied
6. "7 Faces of Dr. ____"
7. States openly
8. Restricted an animal
9. Fierce rage
10. Piece of paper
11. Human
12. Japanese dish
13. The Rail Splitter
14. Originally
15. Maui goose
16. Nest location
23. Prizefighter
26. Cooked in an oven
29. Gossip
34. After taxes
35. Beseeches
36. Homely
37. What they didn't have at the inn
38. Notched
40. Apply morning moisture
42. "____ Abby"
43. Trim
46. Path
47. Party food
50. In a group of
53. Antiseptic
56. Most irritable
57. Light time
58. Sassy
60. Less wacky
62. Aquatic snail
63. Pouches
64. List member
65. Kinfolk
67. ____ herring
68. Circle section
69. Pupil surrounder
70. "____ She Sweet?"
71. Young girl
74. Supplied to excess
77. Cinder
78. Single-deity believers
80. Yogi ____
81. Car motors
84. Undercover
87. Native
89. Push comes to this
91. Burning
93. ____ dive
94. Wt. unit
98. Marilyn, e.g.
99. Traipsed
100. Squiggly swimmers
102. Bard's before
104. Hosiery color
105. Pair half

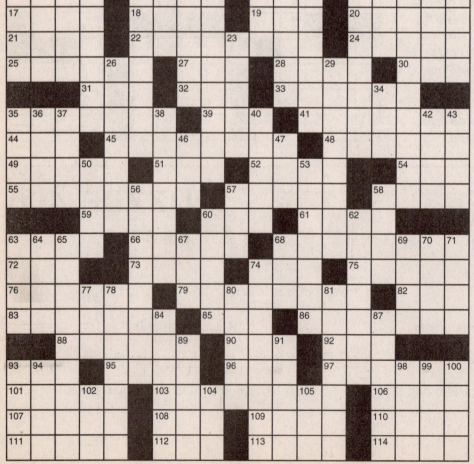

DOUBLE TROUBLE

PUZZLE 462

Not really double trouble, but double fun! Solve this puzzle as you would a regular crossword, except place one, two, or three letters in each box. The number of letters in each answer is shown in parentheses after its clue.

ACROSS

1. Deposited (4)
3. Relocate (4)
5. College official (4)
7. Release air from (7)
10. Hindrance (10)
12. Metal flask (7)
14. Essential (5)
15. Metric measure (10)
17. Doubtful (7)
19. Model (4)
21. Shirt size (5)
22. Most plain (6)
23. Inscribed slab (5)
25. Question (11)
28. Gutsy (4)
29. Pulpit (7)
31. Mosaic piece (4)
32. Last course (7)
34. Fervid (6)
35. Blob (4)
36. Paddy plant (4)
37. Smear (4)
38. Clot (3)
39. Swap goods (6)
40. Excitable (8)
42. Mania (5)
43. Bring back (8)
45. Smoke (4)
46. Bouquet (9)
49. Minus (4)
50. Stair post (5)
52. So (4)
53. Ebb ____ (4)
54. Progressive (7)
55. Inactive (9)
58. Man's hat (6)
60. Gullet (6)
62. Explain away (11)
65. Blood vessel (6)
66. Zoomed (4)
67. Experiment (4)
68. Suit item (4)

DOWN

1. Wilted (4)
2. ____-de-camp (4)
3. Instant (6)
4. Publicize (9)
5. Carafe (8)
6. Initial stake (4)
7. Cunning (7)
8. Apartment (4)
9. Greenish blue (4)
11. Chop finely (4)
13. Withstand (6)
16. Combine (5)
18. Cabaret (6)
19. Main idea (5)
20. Oracle (4)
22. Twaddle (10)
23. German pastry (7)
24. Component (7)
26. Barbecue spit (10)
27. Tempest (4)
28. Employer (4)
30. Astronomer (9)
32. Insincere (9)
33. Vat (3)
35. Sleeping pad (8)
36. Hazard (4)
39. Cask (6)
41. Hour (4)
42. Rugged cliff (4)
44. Wooden facing (6)
46. Thwart (9)
47. Opposed (4)
48. Relinquish (4)
51. Riches (6)
52. Formerly (4)
54. Book collection (7)
55. Tranquilize (6)
56. Creative person (6)
57. Hither and ____ (3)
58. Phobia (4)
59. Lavish affection (4)
61. Chopper blade (5)
63. Dynamic (5)
64. Relish (4)

1	2	■	3	4	■	5	6	■	■	7	8	9
10		11			■	12		13	■	14		
■	■	15			16		■	17	18		■	■
19	20	■	■	21		■	22			■	23	24
25		26	27		■	28		■	29	30		
■	■	31		■	32			33	■	34		
■	35		■	36		■	37		■	38		■
39			■	40		41		■	42		■	■
43			44	■	45		■	46			47	48
49		■	50	51		■	52		■	■	53	
■	■	54			■	55			56	57	■	■
58	59		■	60	61		■	62			63	64
65			■	■	66		■	67		■	68	

PUZZLE 463 BRICK BY BRICK

Rearrange this stack of bricks to form a crossword puzzle. The clues will help you fit the bricks into their correct places. Row 1 has been filled in for you. Use the bricks to fill in the remaining spaces.

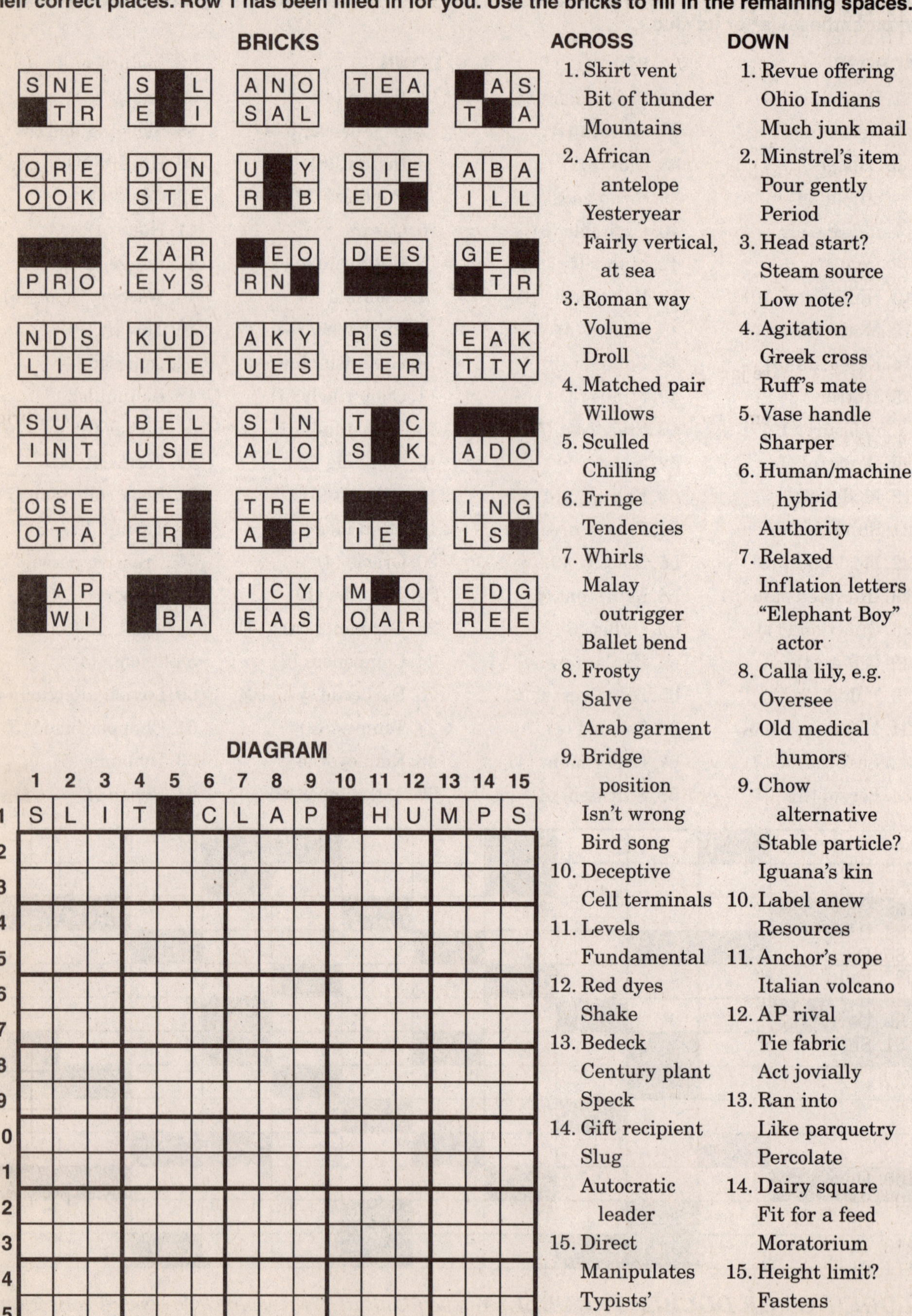

ACROSS

1. Skirt vent
   Bit of thunder
   Mountains
2. African antelope
   Yesteryear
   Fairly vertical, at sea
3. Roman way
   Volume
   Droll
4. Matched pair
   Willows
5. Sculled
   Chilling
6. Fringe
   Tendencies
7. Whirls
   Malay outrigger
   Ballet bend
8. Frosty
   Salve
   Arab garment
9. Bridge position
   Isn't wrong
   Bird song
10. Deceptive
    Cell terminals
11. Levels
    Fundamental
12. Red dyes
    Shake
13. Bedeck
    Century plant
    Speck
14. Gift recipient
    Slug
    Autocratic leader
15. Direct
    Manipulates
    Typists' targets

DOWN

1. Revue offering
   Ohio Indians
   Much junk mail
2. Minstrel's item
   Pour gently
   Period
3. Head start?
   Steam source
   Low note?
4. Agitation
   Greek cross
   Ruff's mate
5. Vase handle
   Sharper
6. Human/machine hybrid
   Authority
7. Relaxed
   Inflation letters
   "Elephant Boy" actor
8. Calla lily, e.g.
   Oversee
   Old medical humors
9. Chow alternative
   Stable particle?
   Iguana's kin
10. Label anew
    Resources
11. Anchor's rope
    Italian volcano
12. AP rival
    Tie fabric
    Act jovially
13. Ran into
    Like parquetry
    Percolate
14. Dairy square
    Fit for a feed
    Moratorium
15. Height limit?
    Fastens
    Sound receivers

PUZZLE 464

• BOYS' CLUB •

ACROSS

1. Gain
5. Find fault
9. Train for a match
13. Feel sore
17. Killer whale
18. Stench
19. Cipher
20. Mr. Coward
21. Mellows
22. ____ Linda
23. Defeat soundly
24. Pupil's site
25. Frank Loesser musical, with "The"
28. Venture
29. Emmet
30. Prior to, in verse
31. Radial, for one
33. In arrears
37. Earthenware jar
39. Paged
43. October's gem
44. Id's kin
46. With it
48. Plants
49. Window ledge
50. Part of RFD
53. Gab
55. Jeer
56. Reconnoiterer
58. Spud
60. Drive back
62. The "S" in WYSIWYG
64. Inamorato
66. WWII soldiers
67. Not gods
71. Waiters' handouts
73. Embarrass
77. Wing-shaped
78. Weep loudly
80. Guns N' ____
82. Healing plant
83. Pseudonym
85. Dunce
87. Faucet
88. In the offing
89. Devilfish
91. Sheikdom of song
94. Vipers
96. Zounds!
98. Pitcher's stat
99. "Chances ____"
100. Uncultivated
103. Song by the Chiffons
110. Dutch cheese
111. Clutched
112. Incline
113. Palindromic model
114. Diva Gluck
115. City on the Humboldt
116. Famed canal
117. Skipjack
118. Sharp
119. Curtail
120. Forest creature
121. Burn

DOWN

1. Go from pillar to post
2. Hence
3. Does well on
4. Bygone
5. It won't hold water
6. Take as one's own
7. Play
8. Orison
9. Shrill sound
10. Kitty
11. Mature
12. Sell (for)
13. Oscar Wilde play
14. Mrs. Dithers
15. He has it coming
16. Besides
26. Chinese dynasty
27. Companion of to
32. TKO caller
33. October 16th honoree
34. Grand
35. Righteous radiance
36. Ray Bradbury tale, with "The"
37. Reef material
38. Crucial
40. Lead down the garden path
41. Greek Cupid
42. Escort
45. Clean, as a fish
47. Average
51. Director Egoyan
52. Recliner activator
54. Beer barrel
57. Steeped drink
59. Vegas alternative
61. Ms. Zadora
63. Subways' kin
65. Out of practice
67. Sir's companion
68. Spanish stew
69. Type of downfall
70. Michigan's ____ Canals
72. Ocean
74. Sheltered
75. Skyrocket
76. Towel marking
79. Ewe said it!
81. Diamond
84. Hang loosely
86. License
90. Pane holders
92. Cunning
93. Washed
95. Agnus ____
97. Pondered
99. Jane Curtin sitcom role
100. Powerless
101. At rest
102. Metallic fabric
104. Sommer of film
105. Billion ender
106. Brooklyn team
107. Bonding agent
108. Forearm bone
109. 1040, e.g.

PUZZLE 465 WORDSWORTH

Fill in each row and column of the Wordsworth diagram with at least two words. The number of words in a row or column is indicated by the number of clues. Words are not separated by extra squares, so all the squares will be filled in when the diagram is completed.

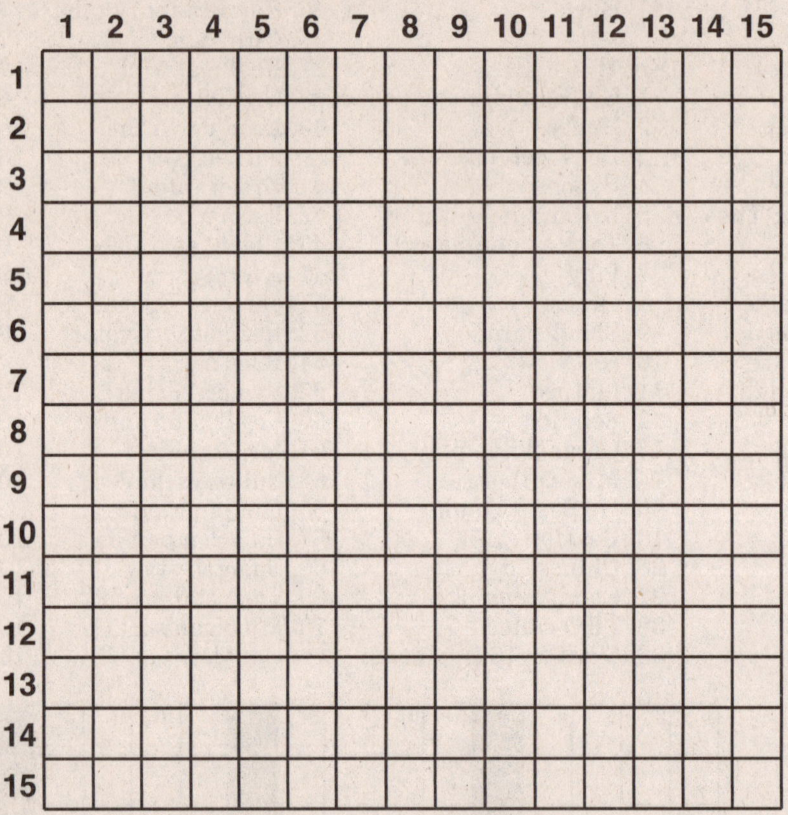

ACROSS

1. Minotaur's realm • Yoga positions
2. See eye to eye • Roman emperor • Cancel
3. Penthouse feature • Cartoon beagle • Pen
4. Joy • Tumult
5. Homer's neighbor • Andes native • Santa has one • Generation
6. Bay deepener • Box material
7. Stand • Drop off • Henley crewman • Oklahoma city
8. Lariat • Neanderthal
9. Serve wine • Dawn • Julia of films
10. Some voices • Utah city • Airs
11. Believe • Cool quaff • Pain in the neck • Guzzle
12. Pub • Bikini top • Scratch • "Splash" actress
13. Implant • Bluish green • Designer Karan
14. Bond's school • Carte du jour • First mate? • NYC station
15. Double-check • Calm • Informant

DOWN

1. Fragrant herb • Walk softly • Bock ____
2. Like a gymnast • Arctic explorer • Corrida cheer • Opening bet
3. Cabbage • Jacob's twin • Fright
4. Conifer • Neap, e.g. • Brass instrument
5. Pine product • Tumbler • Perfume
6. Jury's decision • Debriefed
7. It's a gas • Oak source • Staffs again
8. Wandering minstrel • Not clear
9. "Nighthawks" painter • Pointed arch • Sorry one
10. Some • Possessed • Too • Trim
11. Drain pipe • Chum • Take in • Yemen port
12. Taj Mahal site • John or Jane • Sedate • No way!
13. Unaffected • Author Seton • Usain Bolt, e.g.
14. Flower oil • Ceremony • Siam governess
15. Date • Cheryl or Diane • Pachyderm

PUZZLE 466

• WHAT THE DICKENS?! •

ACROSS

1. Get outta here!
6. Norwegian saint
10. Short-straw chooser
15. Dill seed
19. Midway alternative
20. Request payment
21. Carpet fiber
22. Point to
23. Betsy Trotwood's nephew
26. Workout result
27. Flabbergast
28. Deep resentment
29. Spud
30. Boston neighbor
32. For example
33. Young fowl
36. Serengeti rulers
37. Smiling
40. Dancer's partner
41. In perfect condition
43. Let loose
44. Alternate
45. Bit of information
47. Gotcha!
50. Surveyor's map
51. Kind of campaign
52. Mississippi harbor
54. Sushi choice
55. Blubbers
56. Skier's obstacle
57. In a sec
58. Summer on the Seine
59. Stage signal
60. Two-tiered galley
61. Skim
62. Eared seal
64. Antipodes
65. Column style
67. Suggest
69. Thais and Laotians
71. Ginza sash
72. USSR organization
75. Fixed procedure
76. Posse's rope
77. Plumbing problem
78. July sign
79. Like Nolte in Beverly Hills
82. Sidestep
84. Splitsville?
85. Sioux speaker
86. Starts fishing
87. Island with pineapple plantations
88. Root vegetable
89. Small band
91. Snappy comeback
92. Grand canyon?
93. Frodo's home
95. Christmas
98. ____ Miss
99. Soap base
101. Librarian's stamp
102. Good buddy
103. Ems, e.g.
106. Semi ending
107. Little Nell's domain
112. It should be even
113. Steam bath
114. Sassy one
115. Hold
116. Ultimatum word
117. Representative
118. Place for a beret
119. Held the title

DOWN

1. Cracker variety
2. Tobacco plug
3. Illegal party
4. Actress Meyers
5. Help diffuse
6. Reedy instrument
7. Pitcher spout
8. Matterhorn, e.g.
9. The "she" in "Murder, She Wrote"
10. Cam moving a valve, e.g.
11. Wicker willow
12. Cubic measure
13. Architectural add-on
14. Funnyman Foxx
15. Maine National Park
16. He thrashed Wackford Squeers
17. "____ Frome"
18. Is abundant
24. Emulate Niobe
25. Fall guy?
31. Tree resin
32. Temper tantrum
33. "Gremlins" actress
34. Workplace gp.
35. Amy of the Marshalsea
37. 100 paise
38. Channel
39. Carton and Darnay's story
40. Firm name never realized
42. Made a ditch
45. Genoa magistrates
46. Jack-in-the-pulpit's family
48. Stove canopy
49. Ms. Heche
51. Turn
52. Sweaters?
53. "____ Ha'i"
55. Slash mark?
56. "When We Were Six" author
60. Toot one's horn
61. Hold on tight
63. Child over twelve
64. Reverent
66. Last writes
67. Catholic booklet
68. Shoe filler
70. Chimney black
73. Pool filler
74. Oafs
77. Bridget Jones's book
80. Tops
81. Collar
82. Moliere, e.g.
83. Snarl
84. Country cousin
87. Fulcrum's bar
88. Hunt shout
90. Dodona had one
91. Custom
93. Place for a baseball card
94. Hailey novel
96. Total
97. ____-Arica (South America region)
98. Grain
100. Throw a party
102. Corncob, e.g.
103. Avoid like the plague
104. Affectation
105. Parroted
108. Sung poem
109. Three Dog Night hit
110. Take a load off
111. Seed

PUZZLE 467

• REF'S CALL •

ACROSS

1. Cookie container
4. "____ Kapital"
7. Raggedy-doll name
10. Styptic agent
12. Baseball plate
13. Corp. bigwig
14. Short skirt
15. Novelists' plans
17. Wiser, perhaps
19. Adversary
20. Chopin work
22. Superlative suffix
23. Creative creation
24. Freshly
27. WWII agcy.
30. Where agua flows
31. Judges
33. Shortwave user
35. Veldt antelope
37. Game missile
38. Spanish wave
39. FDR's org.
41. Sprung up
43. Shovel
46. French impressionist
48. Done in
50. Chimney coating
53. GI mailing address
54. Smidgeon
55. Bluefin
56. Jack of clubs
57. Drive obliquely
58. Decade

DOWN

1. Difficult situation
2. Derby winner Ben ____
3. Leave in the lurch
4. Sullen
5. Qty.
6. Palindromic tennis star
7. Teen's spot
8. Insecticide
9. Inquisitive
11. Balmy
12. Plaster-mixing tool
16. Fascinated by
18. Very costly
20. Pitcher part
21. Neat, to a Brit
22. Washstand standard
25. Zip
26. Letter from Greece
28. Type of gunfight
29. Maglie and Mineo
32. Ollie's cohort
34. Capp's Daisy ____
36. Dismantle
40. Overhaul
42. Musical symbol
43. It may be soft
44. Butterfly stage
45. Bohr's bit
46. Brisbane buddy
47. Not ____ rule
49. Adhesive
51. United
52. Treat hides

PUZZLE 468

• SPORTING WORDS •

ACROSS

1. Peer Gynt's mother
4. Handled hook
8. Deadly snakes
12. Uno plus uno
13. Marine hue
14. Screenwriter's need
15. Baseball move
17. Tall story
18. Word before crazy or fry
19. Mid-month days
21. Unruly hair
22. Icicle hanger
24. Peculiar
26. Bid
29. Activist's impetus
32. Cole or Katherine Anne
33. Transgressed
34. Dress feathers
35. Heaped
36. Geological division
37. Agatha's contemporary
38. Sacred chest
40. Yard event
42. Strikes with force
46. Nuisance
48. Hockey move
50. Some time ago
51. Half, from the Greeks
52. Danish astronomer Roemer
53. Dive position
54. Celtic
55. Bow wood

DOWN

1. Appends
2. Ilk
3. Actor Morales
4. Shoot the breeze
5. Shaking
6. Bankrolled
7. Kismet
8. Prone
9. Basketball move
10. Kind of shirt
11. Stage
16. Receptionist
20. Gathering
23. Sporting sites
25. The Rockettes, e.g.
26. Ant.
27. Pro
28. Soccer move
30. Bishopric
31. Hall-of-Famer Roush
33. Rivulets
35. Vendor
38. Each
39. Delhi princess
41. Wimbledon winner
43. Seaman's shout
44. Infiltrator
45. Hobo's meal
47. Maiden-name indicator
49. 12th part of an anna

CODEWORD

PUZZLE 469

Instructions for solving Codeword puzzles are given on page 39.

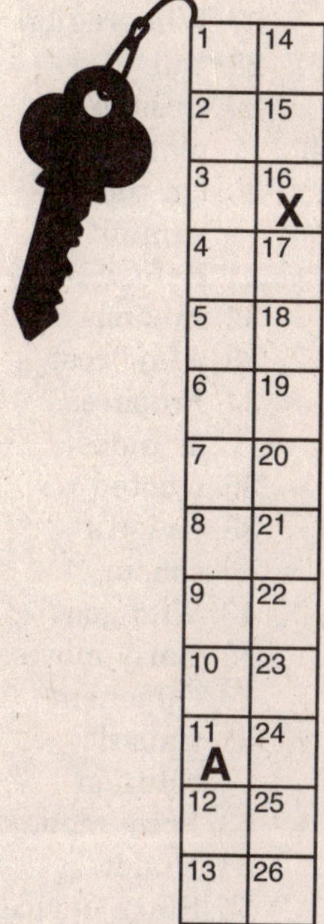

6	11	26	23	21	8	19		10	9	19	11	17
11		23		8		11		11		16		8
22	2	11	9	11		20	11	14	19	24	24	19
5		5		22		19		23		26		
11	18	24		15	11	26	25	23	26	11	15	
	22		4		1		2		11		23	
24	11 A	16 X	2		19	22	12		5	19	20	23
	2		19		11		12		1		8	
	9	23	3	11	17	11	13	5		19	22	15
		18		26		9		18		22		23
18	11	24	24	19	26	9		26	19	6	8	5
11		2		24		11		11		23		19
7	11	7	1	19		22	11	13	11	3	11	13

~~A~~ N
B O
C P
D Q
E R
F S
G T
H U
I V
J W
K ~~X~~
L Y
M Z

CODEWORD

PUZZLE 470

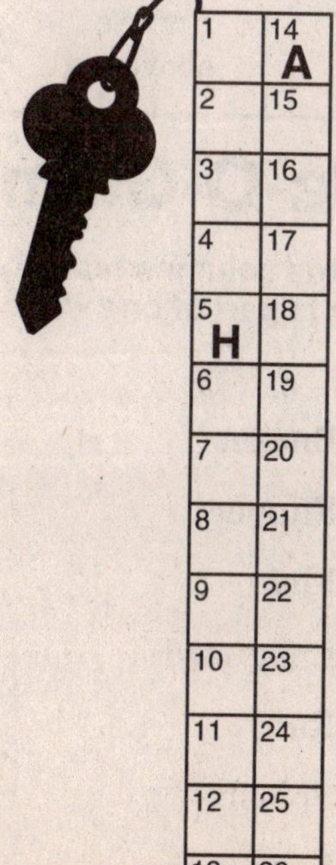

17	24	15	16	14	26	12				19	24	26
14		14		21		26		6		5 H		5
13	14	22	12	16		5	20	26	21	14 A	19	12
12		20		24		24		20		19		26
6	11	1	14	23		21	10	14	16	24	8	14
	1		18		19		20		20		1	
21	20	21	20	20	8		20	8	18	14	16	23
	26		19		24		25		12		6	
25	14	3	12	6	26	22		15	13	12	12	7
20		14		7		20		13		4		14
26	14	15	13	12	14	1		24	25	7	13	22
24		20		18		8		26		12		12
9	24	26				2	14	10	12	13	13	12

~~A~~ N
B O
C P
D Q
E R
F S
G T
~~H~~ U
I V
J W
K X
L Y
M Z

PUZZLE 471

ACROSS

1. Blow gently
5. Spur
9. Menial worker
13. Big sandwich
14. Renovated
16. Quite wicked
17. Abadan's country
18. Worn unevenly
19. Tableland
20. Unique
22. For men and women
24. Gumshoe
25. Fellow
26. Cooler cooler
27. Appropriate
28. Little bird
29. Rotten
32. Newts
35. Back talk?
37. Make one's day
39. Phooey's kin
40. Charged particle
41. City on the Thames
42. Guardian spirits
44. Dolls, e.g.
46. Catch sight of
47. Positive response
48. Road-runner's remark
50. Type
52. Outcome
53. Thickness
54. Pasture call
57. First-class
61. Oddest
63. Sale stipulation
64. Express grief
66. Came to earth
67. Pride of lions?
68. Leavening agent
69. Musical conclusion
70. Brings to court
71. Deli loaves
72. Wide-mouthed jug

DOWN

1. Bridge forerunner
2. High nest
3. Former French coin
4. Chinese association
5. Bishop, e.g.
6. Aired again
7. Olfactory trigger
8. Put down, in slang
9. Truck trailer
10. Holiday precursors
11. Levitate
12. Linen source
15. Tennis tie
21. He may cry foul
23. Maui goose
26. Twist of fate
27. Wine region
28. Yell
29. Goes to the plate
30. On the summit
31. Refuse
32. Anxious
33. At no cost
34. Prepares, as hides
36. Quoted
38. Onion's cousin
43. Wild goat
45. Early movies
49. Opponent
51. Caustic solution
53. Prize money
54. Under
55. Stage device
56. Perfume oil
57. River structures
58. Jacob's twin
59. Fishing filament
60. Functions
61. Pier
62. Meet event
65. Byron's above

PUZZLE 472

Slide-O-Gram

Place the seven words into the diagram, one word for each row, so that one of the columns reading down will spell out a 7-letter word that is related to the others. Each given letter is part of one word.

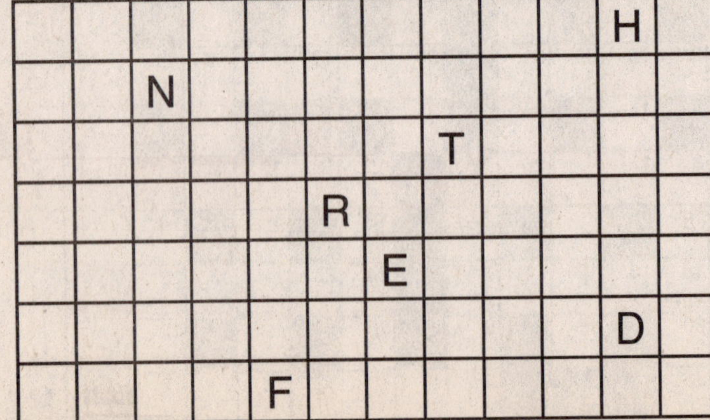

Bucket

Flippers

Float

Lifeguard

Raft

Splash

Suntan

PUZZLE 473

• PART OF SPEECH •

ACROSS

1. Soaking spots
5. Hit
8. Bar bill
11. Convent superior
17. Speech impediment
18. Penny prez
19. High note
20. Have no stomach for
21. Europe's tallest volcano
22. Wise guy?
24. "Just Married" rattler
25. Start of a quip
28. Mideast nation
29. So far
30. Chemistry branch
34. Takes off
38. Laugh and a half
40. Plato's last letter
41. More of the quip
46. Pledge
47. Imagine that!
48. Campaign tactic
49. Funny brothers
52. Shakespeare's flower
54. Decreases?
57. Say with certainty
58. More of the quip
65. Turow memoir
66. "Enigma Variations" composer
67. Ginger ale, e.g.
68. Be a couch potato
72. Toss out
75. Stimpy's pal
76. Here, in Le Havre
77. More of the quip
81. Fish dish
84. Othello, e.g.
85. Dictation taker
86. Consumed
88. Butter?
90. Chilling
94. End of the quip
99. 1994 Nobel winner
102. Make Mickey move
103. Immediately
104. Take out
105. Actor Erwin
106. Odie's owner
107. Marilyn Monroe's mark
108. Hang glider, e.g.
109. Piper's son
110. Quick to learn
111. Agatha's contemporary

DOWN

1. Scads
2. Short but not sweet
3. "Lou Grant" actor
4. Sporting dog
5. Wild party
6. Hautboy
7. Soccer legend
8. Painting technique
9. Like a century plant
10. Judge's seat
11. Temple table
12. Oingo ___ ('80s band)
13. Weight class
14. List extender
15. ___ Na Na
16. D.C. figure
23. Moron prefix
26. Heads for the runway
27. Symbolic pole
31. Word from a literary bird
32. Mr. Sikorsky
33. Raven calls
35. Noun ender
36. Possessive pronoun
37. Rubberneck
39. Exclamations
41. Yikes!
42. Campbell of "Scream"
43. Guy with rocks in his head?
44. Deteriorate
45. Zoo sound
50. '30s dam project
51. They're always on edge
53. Lineup number
55. Stanley Cup org.
56. "Like a Rock" singer
59. Appraise
60. Mideast flier
61. Blows up
62. Type of mill
63. Arabian Sea gulf
64. Emulate Dennis Miller
68. Clamping tool
69. Country at 0° lat.
70. Rhythm
71. "The Name of the Rose" author
73. Fidel's aide, once
74. Creed
78. Blue Jays' home
79. Radioactive element
80. Alas!
82. Young cow
83. Natural
87. Complete
89. Production co. with kitten logo
91. Helicopter part
92. As a whole
93. A Lauder
95. Troupe group
96. Hindu title
97. Crowning
98. Nickel fraction
99. Clio nominees
100. Vintage car
101. Like

PUZZLE 474

• VICE VERSA •

ACROSS

1. Cartwright son
5. Part of QED
9. Male gender, briefly
13. Shakespearean soliloquy starters
17. Weathercock
18. Forfeit
19. Kruger of "These Three"
20. Football's Dickerson
21. Innovation
22. Suffrage
23. Not below?
25. Not a revolution?
28. Musical clef
29. August sign
30. Morsel
31. Bother
33. Actress with a "Tootsie" role
35. Cowpoke's horse group
39. Block house
41. Evening repast
45. Spirit
46. ___ Therese (Quebec isl.)
47. Brazil, for one
49. Dwelling
50. Organic compound
52. Apiece
53. Uninteresting
55. "Exodus" author
56. Texas symbol
58. Dictatorial
59. "___ a man . . ."
60. Posterior
61. Bleed, like colors
62. Convince
64. Yemeni, e.g.
67. Target disk
69. Hospital employee
73. Inspector Clouseau's servant
74. Swiss painter
75. Tiny measurement
76. Floor worker
77. James and Jones
79. Sprite
80. Early hrs.
81. Longest river
82. Paucity
84. Medicinal herb
86. Erich and George
88. Go-getter
90. Clinker
91. Coin of Peru
92. ___ de deux
95. Ginnie ___ (government bonds)
97. Not surface dirt?
103. Not depressed?
106. Mogul
107. Peut-___ (perhaps, in Paris)
108. Encumbrance
109. Salver
110. Legal term
111. RR listings
112. Receivers, at times
113. Table d'___
114. ___-do-well
115. The majority

DOWN

1. Fervent
2. Wainscot
3. From scratch
4. Penurious
5. Oak Ridge Boys hit
6. Come home to ___
7. Turin's neighbor
8. Youth
9. ___ Tse-tung
10. Edison's middle name
11. Process ore
12. Carried
13. Kickoff prop
14. Evangelist Roberts
15. Swallow the bait
16. Repeat
24. Water wheel
26. Poet McKuen
27. Baseball's Hodges
32. Big Ben's site
34. Not a barn?
35. Actual
36. Patron saint of sailors
37. Central
38. Not excessive?
39. Way to Rome
40. Belonging to us
42. Cliff's buddy
43. Mrs. Ernie Kovacs
44. Take five
46. Glitter
48. Mortarboard hangers
51. Compass dir.
54. Unopposed rounds
57. Mission
58. Except
61. Reduced, as sail
63. Turned on the neon
64. Got an "A" on
65. Judge
66. Tropical ant
68. Adult elvers
69. "Green Mansions" girl
70. Famous essayist
71. "Gimme a Break" star Carter
72. Very, in Versailles
75. Lute's cousin
78. Opening
83. "The Cloister and the ___"
85. Protrusion
86. Oklahoma native
87. New Haven tree
89. Updated out-of-date style
91. Emporium
92. Whine
93. Hear ___ drop
94. Molt
96. Government location
98. Fork feature
99. Look as if
100. Physicist Stern
101. 401(k) relatives
102. In order to avoid
104. Printers' widths
105. Anil or eosin

PUZZLE 475

• MEET THE BEATLES •

ACROSS

1. Party dress?
5. Brown or Robinson, e.g.
8. Lab gel
12. Insignificant
16. Word on a Kazakhstan map
17. Sailing vessel
18. Dell
19. Voracious
20. Director Jordan
21. Mjolnir's wielder
22. Mild oath
23. Swanky car
24. Sail away
26. A long time
28. Fit for a king
30. Lennon/ McCartney composition
34. Engine type
37. "Ben-Hur" director
38. Also-rans
40. Hoopla
41. ____ Alto
43. Eskers
45. Feudal slave
46. Soupcon
48. Knoll
50. Model, shortly
53. Boston-to-Savannah dir.
54. Pittsburgh river
55. Adlai's running mate
58. Say good-bye
60. Harrison composition
66. Site of Shannon Airport
67. Eleve's place
68. Lass
70. Sevres soul
73. Quay kin
75. She was born free
77. S-shaped molding
78. Verne captain
80. Tender-hearted
83. Latin verb
85. Break bread
86. Surpassed
89. "____ de lune"
91. Jumps
93. Lennon/ McCartney composition
96. Point of view
97. Narrow inlet
98. Derivations
102. Surfeit
104. End of the line
106. Merry tune
108. Music halls
109. Duet
110. Buffalo's county
111. Osiris sis
112. Me
113. Crescents
114. "Atlas Shrugged" author
115. ____, amas, amat
116. Harvard rival

DOWN

1. Zest
2. Popular dunker
3. Walking rhythm
4. Admixtures
5. Taj ____
6. Grande or Bravo
7. Odd
8. Park and Madison
9. Vaudeville bit
10. Smoke signal?
11. Begin a new game
12. Uneasy feeling
13. Villainy
14. Border
15. Tokyo, to shoguns
17. First-class
25. Percolate
27. Cold capital
29. Miracle-____
31. Flint's neighbor
32. Tack
33. Marine predators
34. Board groove
35. The Gem State
36. Red dye
39. Give a darn?
42. Indebted deed holders
44. Quell
47. Putter's target
49. French infinitive
51. Big boy
52. Conjunctions
56. Catchall abbr.
57. MacNelly comic strip
59. Fast-food order
61. Yelp
62. "Exodus" hero
63. ____ Queen
64. African river
65. Remarkable
69. Certain serves
70. Emmet
71. Cat call
72. Categorical
74. Fabulous birds
76. Classifies
79. Intros
81. Made eyes at
82. Cab
84. Place for a thimble
87. Siamese twin
88. "The Gong Show" regular
90. Roma's country
92. Cargo-laden ship
94. Stiller's partner
95. Manuscript page
99. Fancy
100. Foster film
101. Out of harm's way
102. Belgian resort town
103. Swiss flower
105. Peccadillo
107. Theory

PUZZLE 476 CRYPTIC CROSSWORD

British-style or Cryptic Crosswords are a great challenge for crossword fans. Each clue contains either a definition or direct reference to the answer as well as a play on words. The numbers in parentheses indicate the number of letters in the answer words.

ACROSS

1. Pagans cook chickens (8)
5. Wrongly praise old empire (6)
9. Dear agent trained dog (5,4)
11. Bit player appears in next race (5)
12. Liquid and fluid, not oil (6)
13. Guys score using brainpower (8)
15. Has to feel pain from facial hair (8)
16. I'm repeatedly backing Ms. Rogers (4)
19. Egyptian king keeping one tense (4)
20. Salt found in uncovered sea creature (8)
23. Octet has OK vision (8)
24. Give weapons to a district attorney's fleet (6)
27. Ahead of time, like a nobleman? (5)
28. Fed bananas in our shed (9)
29. A large tree of the mountains (6)
30. "Indian is timid," author Rice said (8)

DOWN

1. Embrace Tarzan actor in a big way (6)
2. A male spy (5)
3. Garden sprinkler traps you in growing room (8)
4. Reportedly be acquainted with a man of the Bible (4)
6. Steven organized activities (6)
7. A shooter of apples in place with revolver? (9)
8. Ms. Nin possesses awfully sly judgment (8)
10. Pachyderm flying the plane (8)
14. Damage a thong, mostly, in long race (8)
15. Pest-catcher traveling map routes (9)
17. Create ET, alien, and so forth (2,6)
18. Shortage hurt urban area (8)
21. Fifty-one near an African (6)
22. Knife part name (6)
25. Pale woman in article (5)
26. Pity Babe (4)

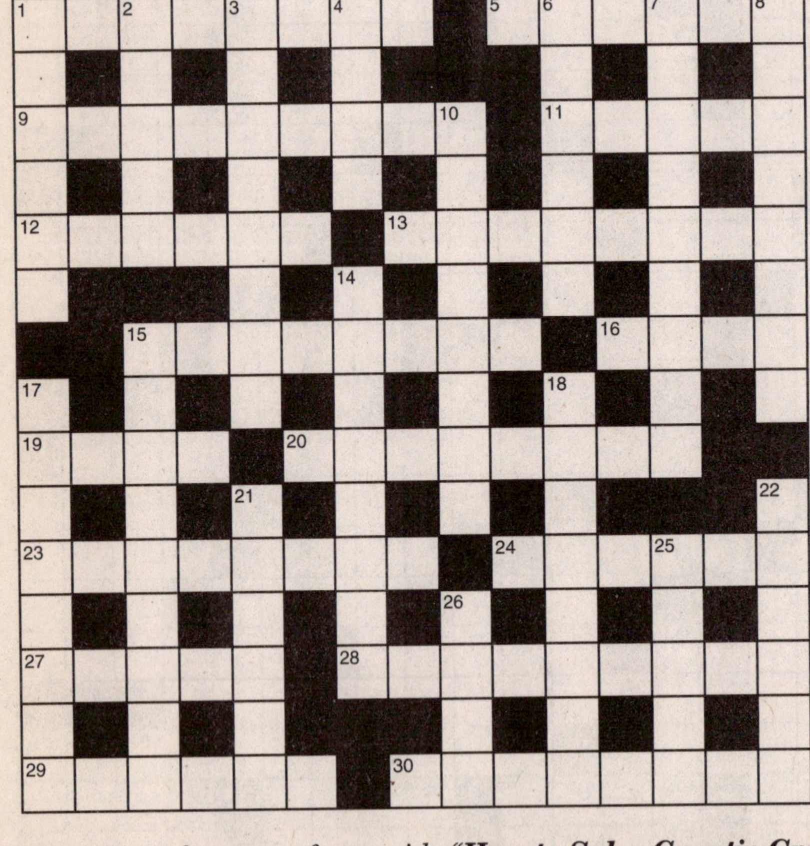

*To receive a free copy of our guide, "**How to Solve Cryptic Crosswords**," send a self-addressed, business-sized, stamped envelope to Cryptic Clues, Penny Press, 6 Prowitt Street, Norwalk, CT 06855-1220 or visit the Puzzler's Corner section of our website at **PennyDellPuzzles.com**.*

PUZZLE 477

• LINKED WITH THUGS •

ACROSS

1. Chutzpa
5. Vaulted recess
9. Bar bills
13. Secured
19. Continent
20. Spiral
21. Earthen pot
22. Athwart
23. Herder's staff
26. Knobby
27. Colonist
28. Ginza buy
29. Facile
30. Puerile
33. Louts
35. Least original
38. Chemical suffix
39. Frigid
40. West Indian shrub
41. Box-off. sign
42. Mex. miss
43. Diplomat St.-John ____
45. Ms. Post
46. Certain star
48. Ciao
49. Isaac's son
50. Gather
52. Kneecap
54. Commotions
56. Sections
58. Kind of conifer
61. Minnow, e.g.
63. Like some columns
64. Roof structure
65. Sigma follower
66. Fairy-tale girl
70. Kook
71. Slender hound
73. Dancer Castle
74. Be agreeable to
76. Region of Israel
77. Belt's site
78. Most melancholy
80. Sneaker features
82. Windblown soil-deposit
83. Some infusions
87. Apiece
89. Actress Turner
90. Facet
92. Cabinet
93. "Desire Under the ____"
95. OR figures
96. Woolen caps
97. Dried alfalfa
99. Surface measure
100. Dives
102. Water or cracker
103. ____ woodpecker
105. Roughneck
106. Maiden
107. Showering
109. Stew
111. Slot machine
116. Heavy hammer
117. PIN-accessed devices
118. Decorative case
119. Emerald Isle
120. Learned
121. "____ of Heaven"
122. Cheek
123. Hied

DOWN

1. Talk idly
2. Light gray
3. Golf ball's position
4. Slip-up
5. Of vinegar
6. Stout
7. Edge
8. If not
9. Rocky pinnacle
10. With indifference
11. Daubs
12. H.H. Munro
13. Marsh tree
14. Dome openings
15. Spheres of influence
16. Unethical capitalists
17. Compass dir.
18. Hosp. staple
24. Skater Sonja ____
25. A.J. or Kevin
30. Gibe
31. Applies
32. Ballerina Zorina
34. Trouble
35. Steps lively
36. Hog haven
37. ____ kwon do
40. Japanese divers
41. Weightlifting feat
44. Muslim mystic
45. Auction ending
47. Refers
50. Verdant
51. Marquis, e.g.
52. Prude
53. Complete circuit
55. Solve
56. Gist
57. Poet Bradstreet
59. Lead
60. Boater, e.g.
61. Home free
62. Muddle
63. Roman date
64. Nat and Natalie
65. Thrash
67. Lariats
68. Spring flower
69. Major work
72. Yo!
75. Aleutian island
77. Travels
78. Foreman
79. Shelter
81. Regretted
82. "Algiers" star
84. Coup d'____
85. Land tract
86. Molt
87. Zip
88. Angled addition
90. Early astronomer
91. Owned
92. Spotted ____
94. Head coverings
97. Readers of the Vedas
98. Defendants' stories
101. Overcharge
102. Ana or Clara
103. Famous sculpture
104. "Moonlighting" role
106. Prod
108. City in Iowa
109. Bib. edition
110. Beer's kin
112. Onager
113. Go-with for crudites
114. Choler
115. Nugent of rock

PUZZLE 478

• FISCAL FOLKS •

ACROSS

1. Prevents
6. Ancient Athens region
12. Rhythmic beat
19. Hopelessly conventional one
20. Refrain
21. Charge for cargo
22. Habit
23. Diners
24. Air-supplying apparatus
25. He's impersonated every U.S. President from 1960 on
27. PBS journalist
29. Clear the slate
30. Fridge forays
32. Teeth holders
33. Highland negative
34. Not morn
35. Facts and figures
36. Gas containers
38. Web-footed mammal
40. Wear down
42. Not as good
43. Removed
44. Spacecraft segment
46. Where Quechua is spoken
47. Expeditions
51. Caress
52. Role for Frankie Muniz
55. Penny
56. Beast of Borden?
57. Cartwright son
58. Be ready for
59. Sound return
60. Observance
61. Knitted
62. Tangy drinks
63. 2004, e.g.
64. Paper weight?
65. Passive
67. ___ out (just makes)
68. Like a gymnast
69. Cartesian word
70. "Rhoda" regular
72. Garlic units
73. Smaller
75. Does not stay
76. Refrigerated
77. Call it quits
78. Kicks off
80. Fit for footwear
81. "The Bells of St. ___"
84. Saw logs
85. Pub offerings
86. Feminine pronoun
89. Singer DiFranco
90. Station wagon, e.g.
91. Textile fiber
93. Pago Pago locale
95. Activist responsible for warning labels on albums
99. 25th Century hero
101. Mercantile establishment
102. Kind of tax
104. Rub off
105. Organizer
106. "Pretty in Pink" actor
107. Stared intently
108. Smoothly
109. Minarets
110. Locket keepsake

DOWN

1. Knight's attendant
2. "Under the ___ Sun"
3. Vows
4. Common man
5. Teamster's rig
6. Synthetic material
7. Muse of comedy
8. Lugged
9. Outrage
10. Edge
11. Allocates
12. Sacred songs
13. Objects
14. Matador's foe
15. Not in
16. Invention protection
17. Greek marketplaces
18. More succinct
19. Landslide debris
26. Exchange
28. The third Gospel
31. Yarn
35. Former Kansas senator
37. Honeymoon destination
38. Fool
39. "Growing Pains" actress
40. "Two Tickets to Paradise" singer
41. Dominate
42. Gets hitched
43. Observes Ramadan
44. "Tartuffe" writer
45. Not in the wings
46. Phony ones
47. They may be friendly
48. Get
49. Breathed in
50. Shops
51. Domesticated polecat
52. Salem assembly?
53. Comes alive
54. 2000 Green Party candidate
57. Respect
61. Telegraphed
66. Calvin's Hobbes, e.g.
67. December 24 and 31
68. Soothing plant
71. Recluse
72. Murmurs
74. Those elected
76. Effrontery
78. Aware of
79. Most in need
80. Deli devices
81. Partners for paters
82. Cracker shape
83. Small wave
84. Sweet
85. Court jester, for one
86. Blurs
87. Multitude
88. Let up
90. Prospero's helper
92. Stomach
93. Levelheaded
94. See eye to eye
96. Gondolier's need
97. Mr. Estrada
98. Large-scale show
100. Absorbed
103. Crow call

PUZZLE 479

CAMOUFLAGE

The answers to the clues can be found in the diagram, but they have been camouflaged. Their letters are in correct order, but sometimes are separated by extra letters that have been inserted throughout the diagram. You must black out all the extra letters. Each of the remaining letters will be used in a word reading across and a word reading down. Solve ACROSS and DOWN together to determine the correct letters where there is a choice. The number of answer words in a row or column is indicated by the number of clues.

	1	2	3	4	5	6	7	8	9	10	11	12	13	14	15
1	I	S	E	C	C	T	A	B	L	T	H	E	R	R	M
2	S	O	C	N	T	I	N	C	A	R	L	D	E	O	R
3	I	N	D	R	O	L	M	A	S	K	K	E	S	P	A
4	S	M	I	O	L	E	D	E	T	E	A	N	C	S	E
5	R	E	T	A	G	I	I	N	H	E	A	G	T	E	D
6	E	G	R	I	N	S	T	E	E	P	L	E	A	S	E
7	N	A	S	S	T	E	Y	A	R	E	E	V	I	E	E
8	S	I	S	L	O	N	T	S	E	C	R	E	T	A	M
9	S	L	A	I	V	E	F	I	F	A	I	T	L	S	Y
10	C	L	I	N	E	N	D	R	A	N	G	E	E	L	S
11	S	P	N	O	R	T	I	F	C	A	O	N	C	S	T
12	P	O	W	A	W	E	R	A	E	R	O	S	I	E	B
13	A	C	T	O	M	R	E	N	T	O	R	A	L	E	P
14	A	P	O	S	E	T	S	R	S	U	B	L	K	E	Y
15	N	E	M	E	T	H	S	E	N	E	G	A	T	T	E

ACROSS

1. Faction • Tailor
2. Of sound • Zeal
3. Fan's hero • Constructs
4. Road measure • Jittery
5. Remember • Vehement
6. Sponsorship • Ball peg • Satisfy
7. Brackish • Pass a rope through
8. Coin taker • Munch portrayal
9. Toil • Flops
10. Flax fabric • Varies
11. Derisive noise • Holy images
12. Authority • Lofty home
13. Dashed • Fin. neighbor • High peak
14. Choir recess • Sullen
15. Seine • Install

DOWN

1. Temptresses • Bridge
2. Any • Fast gait
3. Redacts • Peter or Paul
4. Polish place • Knotted loop
5. Male foal • Done • Moisten
6. Mosaic pieces • Go in
7. Friendship • Wears out
8. Staves • Managed
9. Soap foam • Confronts
10. Ash, e.g. • Praline nut • Cad
11. Curly greens • Austerity
12. Paradise • Equal • ____ carte
13. Hackneyed • Type
14. Garden blooms • Advantage
15. Atone for • Watch covertly

PUZZLE 480

• ON LOCATION •

ACROSS

1. ___ Kadiddlehopper
5. Shadowbox
9. Clutch
14. Residence
19. Split
20. Vigorous
21. Major vessel
22. Confronts
23. Consistent
24. Ladd or Thicke
25. New Orleans jazz route
27. Sassy
28. Suit pieces
30. Back and ___
31. Nude
32. Locomotives
34. Buck or Jesse
36. Ballpark event
38. Crazy bird?
39. Lawn cutter
41. Spur
42. Graceful waterfowl
44. Encrypted
45. Splotches
47. James Van ___ Beek
50. Smidgen
51. John Brown's raid site
54. Arrived
55. Mellowed
57. Nuisance
58. Onion's cousin
59. Boston skater
60. Opposes
62. Food bits
65. Trinket
66. Ghanaian river
68. Tire filler
69. Witch-trial town
71. Flimsy
74. Nabbed
77. Glass spheres
81. Scarlett or Suellen
82. Bride
83. Richard ___ of "Empire"
85. Shoe bottom
86. Flight journals
87. City by the Bay
91. Hula accompaniment
92. Caustic material
93. Forehead hair
94. Yokels
95. Curt
97. Glen
98. ___ Streep
99. Mud and mince
100. Passionate
103. Slides
105. Record holders
108. Boat
109. Correct
111. Gladden
114. Dryer fuzz
115. Lake Champlain fort
118. Dazzled
119. Movie feline
120. Unmoving
121. Stares at
122. Ditty
123. Heavy stick
124. Compass point
125. ___ corgi
126. Wild plum
127. Informal shirts

DOWN

1. Thin pancake
2. Energize
3. Swampy Florida region
4. Cite
5. With stubble removed
6. Blanches
7. Sad cry
8. Budget item
9. Truck section
10. Laceless footwear
11. Fiery felony
12. Arouses
13. Huff and puff
14. Nautical rear
15. Like some wire
16. Bounding main
17. Green-tractor name
18. Fragrant chemical
26. "Get ___"
29. Planter
33. Snack
35. Marries
37. Not neg.
39. Cleaning tools
40. American playwright
41. Ham or bacon
42. Night light
43. Salary
44. Summit
45. Drip
46. Squeeze
47. Smear
48. Author Zola
49. Mr. Lacoste
52. Skillfully
53. Burst of flame
54. Specks of bread
56. Pearl gatherers
59. Boxer Max ___
61. Marsh rail
63. Escapade
64. Tatter
65. Voice-maker Mel ___
67. Serving perfectly
70. Stockpile
71. Voting place
72. Naval greeting
73. Book leaf
75. Switch positions
76. Phony duck
78. Kentucky Derby locale
79. Antlered animals
80. Search for
82. Diminish
84. Young lady
87. Seasoned
88. Still asleep
89. Vikings
90. Theater award
93. Forbid
96. Put into office again
97. Banish
98. Tiny insects
99. Vow
100. Sean or Mackenzie
101. Thick-skinned mammal
102. Kitchen utensil
103. Twilled fabric
104. Small hill
105. Dictation taker
106. Develop
107. Punctures
110. Cat comment
112. Damsel
113. Mil. truant
116. Utmost
117. Blond shade

PUZZLE 481

STATE CAPITALS

ACROSS

1. State in India
6. ___ peeve
9. Scotch serving
13. Tailed amphibian
17. Thick-skinned animal, shortly
18. Chop
19. Hawaiian staple
20. Scope
21. Hawk's weapon
22. Pave
23. Landed
24. Strike
25. It is on the Winooski River
28. Clothing puckers
30. Polite guy
31. In the style of
33. Ms. Tyler of films
34. Compatibility
38. In reserve
40. Somersault and twist
44. Dialect
45. Type of closet
46. Wide-awake
47. Compact
48. Leather strip
50. Photography locale
52. Nasty smile
53. Resounded
54. Exclude
55. Irish, of old
56. "Forever ___"
58. Salary
60. Old Queens stadium
64. Beg
65. Filly feature
66. Role player
71. Sincere
73. ___ down (reduced)
74. Scold
75. Undoes
76. Delete
78. ___ transit
79. Meadow cry
80. Puts on powder
81. Goes by
83. Swee' ___ (Popeye's son)
85. Native of: suff.
86. Gouda's kin
87. Classifies
91. It is a port of entry
96. Brad
97. Matador's adversary
99. Ancient lang.
100. ___-foot oil
102. Against: pref.
103. Cupid
104. Testifier's words
105. Metallic
106. Kicking stands
107. Budget item
108. "___ the ramparts . . ."
109. New York city

DOWN

1. Museum offering
2. Counterfeit
3. Missile housing
4. By-and-by
5. It is a center for cotton sales
6. Inventor's claim
7. Glorify
8. Polo of "Meet the Parents"
9. Black bird
10. Holbrook or Prince
11. Init.
12. Demolish
13. It is a recording center
14. Perry's creator
15. Become tattered
16. Draws off
26. ___ capita
27. Abating
29. Pool or wave
32. Sweet drink
34. Frees of
35. Yemen port
36. Maine tree
37. Stance
38. Together (with)
39. Busy
41. Swerve
42. Goofs
43. Optic problem
48. Reliable
49. Slugger Aaron
51. "People ___ Funny"
54. Spoiler
57. UN group
58. Goods

PUZZLE 481

59. It has canneries

60. Balkan native

61. Drag

62. Cleveland lake

63. It was named for a queen

65. Learn well

67. Roughen

68. Pointers

69. Garfield's pal

70. Stoplight colors

72. Fragrant compound

73. Travel document

77. Parisian street

81. Text reviser

82. Certain child

84. Flower extract

86. Give the slip to

87. Medical sch. course

88. Reasonable

89. Position

90. A few

92. Potpourri

93. A Diamond

94. Bamboo stem

95. Kin of Vesuvius

98. Baseball's Swoboda

101. Antonym's opp.

PUZZLE 482

ACROSS

1. Skier's need
5. Skillful
8. Thick slice
12. Pine
13. Proper order
15. Oriental weight
16. Egg-shaped
17. Cigar by-product
18. Million ender
19. Rapid gait
21. By way of
22. Garden flower
23. Pale
25. Map feature
26. Flicker
30. Piped instrument
32. Assistant
33. Actor Lowe
34. Morsel
39. Adult
41. Completely
42. Like some pretzels
43. Obscure
44. Brood
45. Strange
47. Not those
48. Clip
52. Say yes
54. Certain bills
55. Commotion
56. Jerked
61. Pants problem?
62. Nearby
64. Remove fasteners
65. Lower joint
66. Rationed
67. African nation
68. Dumbo's wings
69. Cover with color
70. Plant stalk

DOWN

1. Urban pollution
2. Bossa ___
3. October gem
4. It holds water
5. Equip with weapons
6. Adage
7. "___ Care of Business"
8. Sully
9. Dens
10. Eagle's home
11. Fortunate
13. Horned vipers
14. Team cheer
20. Hardwood
24. Circular band
25. F, of JFK: abbr.
26. Valises
27. Milan moola, once
28. Rocker Billy ___
29. Ex-Congressman Gingrich
31. Powerful particle
33. Impolite
35. Hurry off
36. "___ Velvet"
37. Ailments
38. Tot
40. Poetic contraction
41. Row of seats
43. Self-respect
46. Elevated
47. Boston ___ Party
48. Pointed stick
49. Red hair tint
50. Come into
51. Beasts of burden
53. Spotted
55. Beaver's creation
57. Pecans and filberts
58. Tie
59. "The River's ___"
60. Adverse fate
63. Poor grade

1	2	3	4	■	■	5	6	7	■	■	8	9	10	11
12				■	13				14	■	15			
16				■	17					■	18			
19				20		■	21			■	22			
■	■	■	■	23		24			■	25				
26	27	28	29		■	30			31		■	■	■	■
32				■	33			■	34		35	36	37	38
39				40			■	41						
42						■	43			■	44			
■	■	■	■	45		46			■	47				
48	49	50	51		■	52			53		■	■	■	■
54				■	55			■	56		57	58	59	60
61				■	62			63		■	64			
65				■	66					■	67			
68				■	■	69			■	■	70			

PUZZLE 483

ACROSS

1. Carpet type
5. Diaphanous
9. Leered
14. Kibbutz dance
15. Winglike parts
16. Vicuna's kin
17. Dislikes
19. Deficit
20. Steep hemp
21. Irish river
22. Pure
23. Gloomy, in literature
25. Novelist Greene
27. School vehicle
29. Position
30. Legal matter
33. "___ Bovary"
36. Unite
37. Regatta, e.g.
38. Mine shipments
39. River nymph
41. Engage
42. Enjoy a banquet
43. Tavern
44. Haven
46. Vocalize
47. Cry of disapproval
48. Aries
49. Folk-dance attire
52. Quizzes
56. Burdens
59. Slick
61. ___ Beta Kappa
62. Vocally
63. Play host
65. Flinch
66. Slangy refusals
67. Teen affliction
68. Ranch animal
69. Let it stand
70. Untidy heap

DOWN

1. Fragment
2. Linger
3. Alpine ridge
4. Long fish
5. Lion's place
6. Beside
7. Chair mender
8. Affirmative reply
9. Trite
10. Sparkle
11. Black retrievers, for short
12. Radiate
13. "Blind ___"
18. Antitoxin
22. Sharp cheese
24. Demean
26. Out of port
28. Elders
30. Banister
31. Beige
32. Look
33. Unconventional ones
34. "Don Giovanni" solo
35. Disavow
36. Triumph
37. ___ or reason
40. Presently
45. Woodland deity
47. Notebook
49. Tennis score
50. Mr. Chips's portrayer
51. Agile
53. Room
54. Dilutes
55. Trigonometry functions
56. Decrees
57. Touched ground
58. "She ___ Him Wrong"
60. For fear that
63. Printers' measures
64. ___-o'-shanter

1	2	3	4	■	5	6	7	8	■	9	10	11	12	13
14				■	15				■	16				
17				18					■	19				
20			■	21				■	22					
23			24		■	25		26				■	■	■
■	■	■	27		28	■	■	29			■	30	31	32
33	34	35				■	36			■	37			
38				■	39	40				■	41			
42				■	43			■	44	45				
46			■	47			■	■	48			■	■	■
■	■	■	49				50	51	■	52		53	54	55
56	57	58				■	59		60		■	61		
62					■	63					64			
65					■	66				■	67			
68					■	69				■	70			

PUZZLE 484

ACROSS

1. Globes
5. Yearn
9. Flutters
14. Hair divider
15. Allow to be borrowed
16. Porch
17. Group of three
18. Discharge
19. Happen
20. Utah lily
21. Inventor Howe
23. "___ a Small World"
24. Gone by
27. Ascended
29. Curve
32. Experimenter
34. Some toothpastes
37. Unlock again
39. Passe
40. Lined up
41. Anglo-Saxon laborer
42. Woodland deity
44. Pedestal shaft
45. Gives silent consent
46. "___ Always Loved You"
47. Pearl's mom?
49. Nerd's kin
50. Two-tiered galley
52. Zone or table
53. Bucks
55. Colorful salamander
57. Female pronoun
59. Certain rays
61. Smell
65. Pound component
67. Long-legged wader
69. Baseball-team number
70. Singing voices
71. Earthen pot
72. Scheme
73. Starchy adhesive
74. Extreme poverty
75. Twine

DOWN

1. Chooses
2. Barely cooked
3. Ship's jail
4. Condescend
5. Bubbly brew
6. Night-sky sights
7. Greet
8. Completely
9. Dental string
10. Natural resin
11. Burn up
12. Without slack
13. Lancelot and Launfal
22. Landing field
25. Corroded
26. Sane
28. Mild oaths
29. "___ We All"
30. Seed again
31. Food flavorings
33. Hauler
35. Olive green
36. Cutlass
38. Basil sauce
43. Pilot's interest
48. Type of evergreen
51. Store, as fodder
54. Overweight
56. Invigorating
57. Serial drama
58. Island dance
60. Qualified
62. Bauble
63. Lulu
64. Enjoy a book
66. Folding bed
68. Feeling low

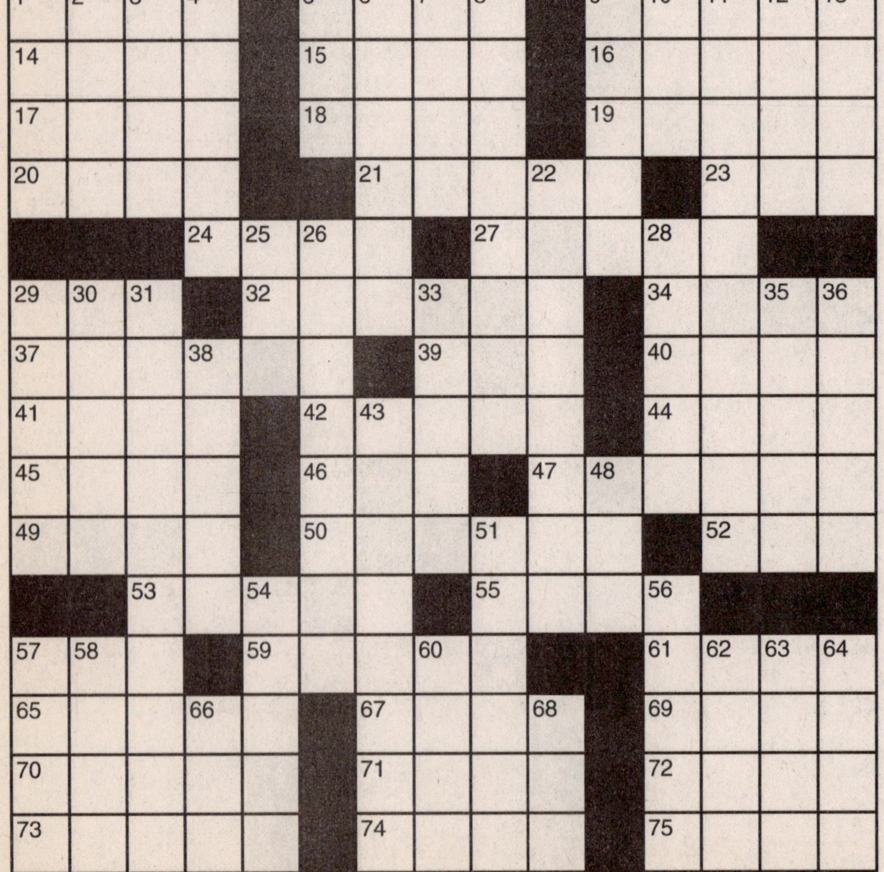

PUZZLE 485

ACROSS

1. Index
5. Question starter
9. Mas' mates
12. Urge
13. Participates
15. Great anger
16. Back end
17. Powerful
18. Curved line
19. Unexpected attack
21. Mark or street
22. "___ Without My Daughter"
23. Pelts
25. Arm joints
27. Gin drink
30. At a loss
31. Cream or pick
32. Breadth
34. Defeat soundly
38. Tested
40. ___ ton soup
41. Avoid
42. Circus structure
43. Tiny
45. Shipboard diary
46. Fireside talk
48. Antennas
50. Crocheted blanket
53. Ordinary
54. Bathing-suit top
55. Vulgar
57. Shooting star
61. Stable morsel
62. Procession
64. Throb
65. Compete
66. Cut
67. Facial feature
68. Subways' cousins
69. Gush out
70. Blow, as a horn

DOWN

1. Turkish currency
2. News flash
3. Wound cover
4. Shove
5. Reporter's query
6. Detests
7. District
8. Most uptight
9. Stevie Wonder's instrument
10. Cupid's weapon
11. Factions
13. Huge Egyptian statue
14. Mode
20. Slalomed
24. Simpleton
26. Cry
27. Catcher's glove
28. Land measure
29. Bridle strap
30. Yearly
33. Long, long time
35. Hawaiian dance
36. Fan favorite
37. Dowels
39. Engrave
41. Spooky
43. Instruction books
44. Grouped
47. Dwells (on)
49. Unbroken
50. Superior to
51. Delicate
52. Entrances
53. Calmness
56. Dribble
58. Mountain feedback
59. Buckeye State
60. Tenant's fee
63. Lawn moisture

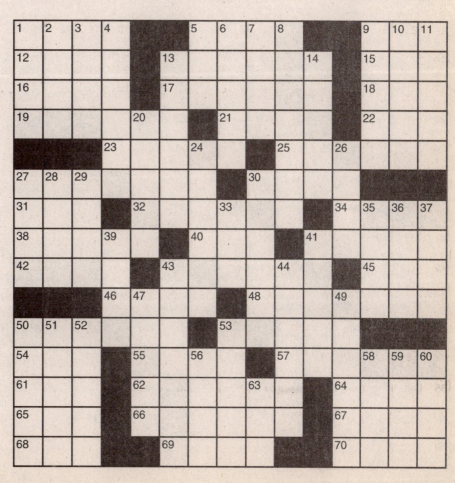

1	2	3	4	■	■	5	6	7	8	■	■	9	10	11
12				■	13					14	■	15		
16				■	17						■	18		
19				20		■	21				■	22		
■	■	■	23			24		■	25		26			
27	28	29					■	30				■	■	■
31			■	32			33			■	34	35	36	37
38			39		■	40			■	41				
42				■	43				44		■	45		
■	■	■	46	47			■	48			49			
50	51	52				■	53					■	■	■
54			■	55		56		■	57			58	59	60
61			■	62				63		■	64			
65			■	66						■	67			
68			■	■	69				■	■	70			

PUZZLE 486

ACROSS

1. Ring out
6. Electrical units, for short
10. Censors
14. Not the express
15. Stable baby
16. Single part
17. Prophetic signs
18. Dominate
19. Leisurely
20. Arrests
21. Roofing goo
22. Snaky fish
24. Arrogance
25. Mineral deposit
26. Rag
30. Overstep
32. Fast aircraft
33. Anger
34. Coat sleeve
35. Harmful
36. Blue
37. Spread
40. Vitality
41. Frothy
42. Ramble
43. Likewise
44. Triangular sail
45. Baking measure
46. Cleave
47. Pay
50. ___ of Liberty
52. GI's bullets
53. Work a row
55. Cackler
56. Tennis shot
57. Hairpieces
58. With competence
61. Berserk
63. Less
64. Out of
65. Departed
66. Esteem greatly
67. Use a camcorder
68. Water jug
69. Pauses

DOWN

1. Exact duplicate
2. Respect
3. Antique fridge
4. Fortifies
5. Raised RRs
6. Scared
7. Express grief
8. Confidant
9. Rained pellets
10. Constructed
11. ___ how!
12. Naught
13. Porker's home
21. Abound
23. Nosh
25. Excessively
27. Even
28. Periods of history
29. Depend
31. Peaceful
32. Bread spread
35. Short life story
36. Brass instrument
37. Rainbows
38. Mope
39. Dad
40. Affirm
41. Farm tower
43. "I Was a ___ Werewolf"
44. Door part
46. Tinge
47. Outdoor cooker
48. Horned animals, for short
49. Custardlike food
51. Kitchen herb
52. Unattended
54. Roadway hazards
57. Spacious
58. Ship's stern
59. Car protector
60. Prune
62. Cut down
63. Blemish

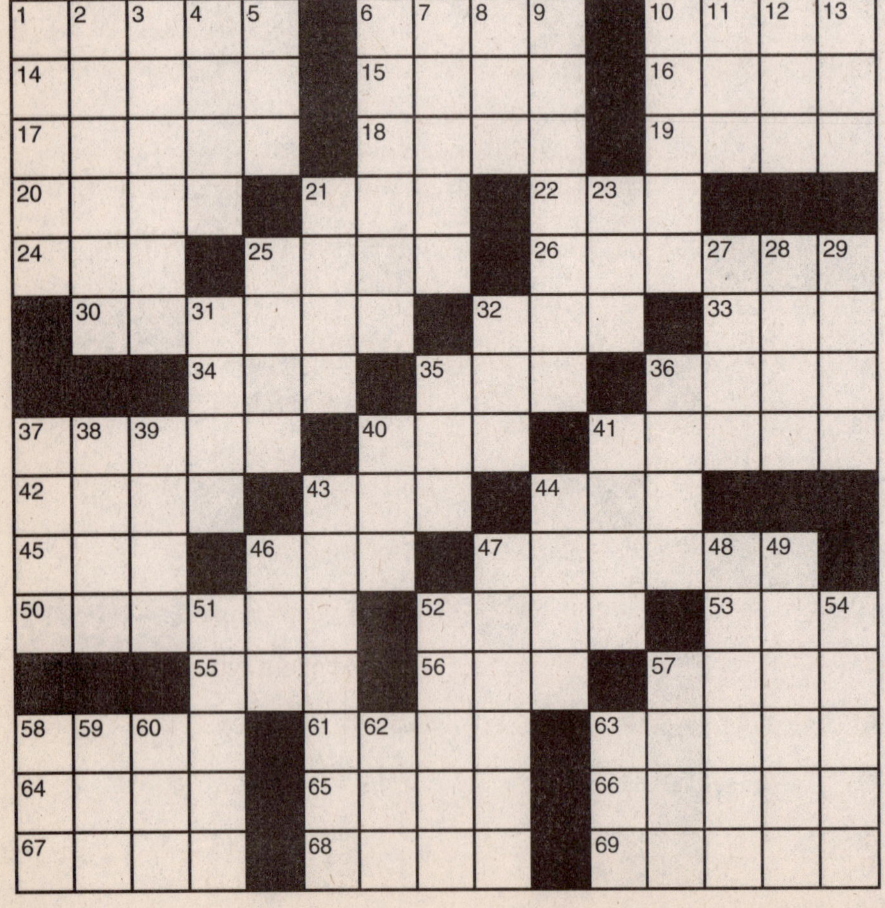

FLOWER POWER

PUZZLE 487

The answers to this petaled puzzle will go in a curve from the number on the outside to the center of the flower. Each number in the flower will have two 5-letter answers. One goes in a clockwise direction and the second in a counterclockwise direction. We have entered two answers to help you begin.

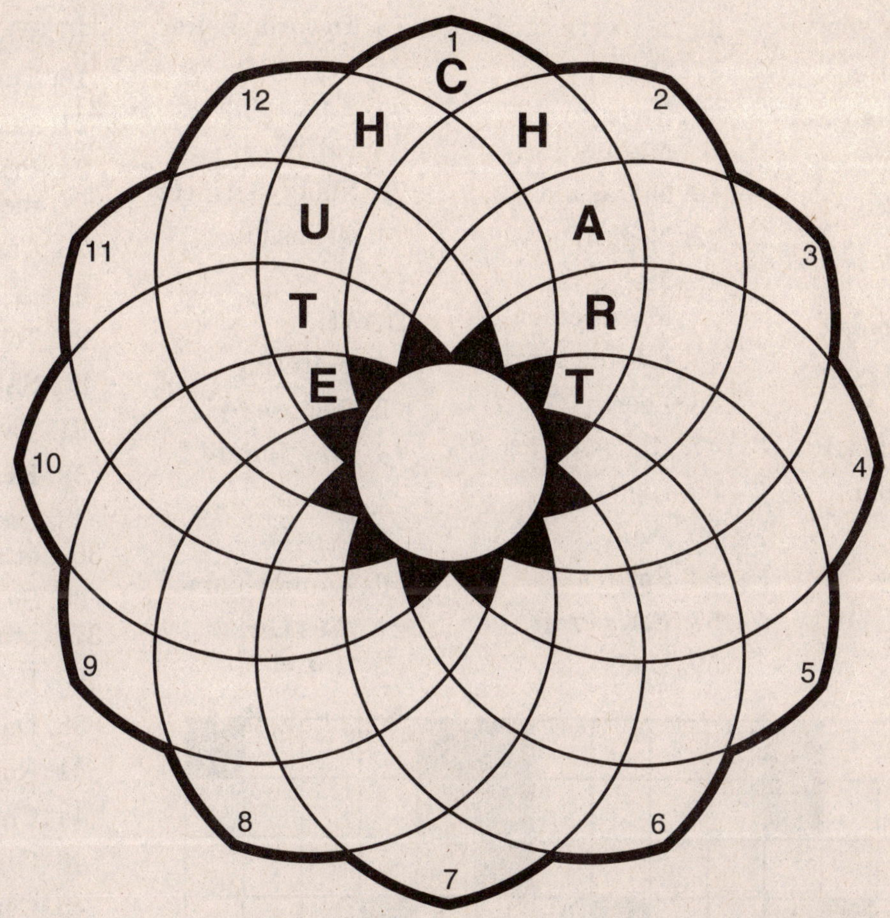

CLOCKWISE

1. Map
2. Sorehead
3. What love is
4. Secreting organ
5. Bread ingredient
6. Power
7. Vital fluid
8. Stroll
9. Mistreat
10. Important vessel
11. Injury
12. Gripe

COUNTERCLOCKWISE

1. Slide
2. Dishes
3. Tattoo, western style
4. Fierce stare
5. Spark producer
6. Metallic sound
7. Flaxen-haired
8. Above a whisper
9. Romance
10. Monastery head
11. Was willing
12. ___ for wear

PUZZLE 488

TUNING UP

ACROSS

1. Swiss peak
4. Border
8. Snaky letter
11. Edgar Allan ___
12. Seed cover
13. Tuck, e.g.
15. "___ of sixpence . . ."
17. Slow, in music
18. Compass point: abbr.
19. Broker, shortly
20. Depot: abbr.
22. Obtain
23. Concur
25. Costa ___
27. Bulk
30. Mr. Arlen
32. TV alien et al.
35. ___ vera
37. Travel
39. River, to Manuel
40. Not as old
42. Negative
43. Ms. Macpherson
45. Editing mark
46. Leer
47. Glides on ice
50. Big truck
52. Walk
53. Sprites
57. E.T.'s craft?
59. Dads
61. Prone
63. Self-regard
64. Ago
66. Romantic tunes
69. Bicker
70. Toward shelter
71. Regret
72. Adjectival suffix
73. Slangy suspect
74. Crimson

DOWN

1. Imitating
2. Recluse
3. Mrs. Bundy
4. Leisure
5. Let fall
6. Rummy game
7. "Les Girls" star et al.
8. Before, to Keats
9. Musical fun
10. Glut
13. Talent
14. Decay
15. Water body
16. Turf
21. ___-la-la
24. Print measures
26. Camp bed
28. ___ Diego
29. Toboggans
30. Shoe parts
31. Twofold
32. Exist
33. Diamond gal et al.
34. Seeger products
36. Be in arrears
38. Deli bread
41. Ruff's mate
44. Chow down
46. Grease
48. Conical home
49. Wetlands group: abbr.
51. Citi Field players
54. Event locale
55. ___ on (encouraged)
56. Mayday!
57. "Surfin' ___"
58. Blaze
60. Smack
61. State firmly
62. Chick's sound
65. Prompt
67. Bullfight cheer
68. Hockey great

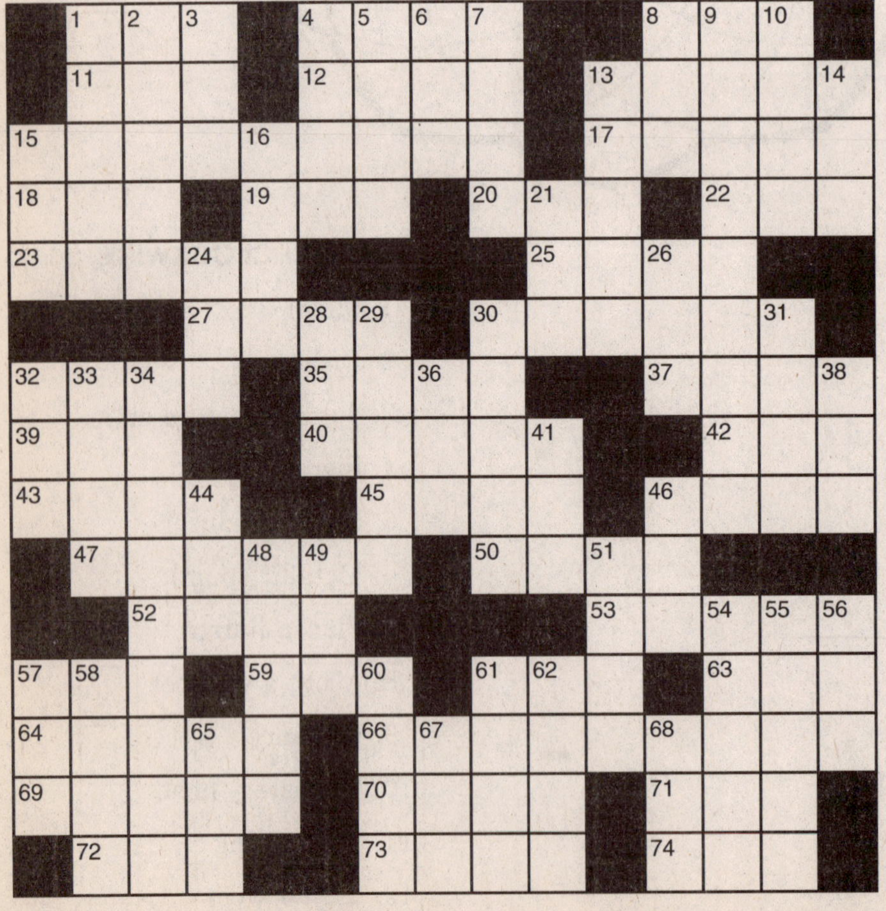

PUZZLE 489

FIRST-NAME BASIS

ACROSS

1. Spa feature
5. Letter afterthought
8. Interrupt
12. Water in a rio
13. Snail-paced
14. Realtor's sign
16. Lost traction
17. Verdi opera
18. Author Zola
19. Toy for Pendergrass?
21. Chew the scenery
22. Bungler's aid
23. John or Tyne
25. Ethereal
28. Delight
32. Balkan natives
36. Pawn
38. "Exodus" author
39. Attribute
40. Edible Japanese plant
41. Cheater
42. Indigo
43. Writing on the wall
44. Autocrats
45. Canary hue
47. Carson's successor
49. Santa's season
51. Florida export
56. Choose
59. Hair clips for Darin?
62. Water sources
63. Football shape
64. Laborer
65. Result
66. ___ majesty
67. Crown
68. Bankruptcy cause
69. Madden
70. Remick and Marvin

DOWN

1. Stick with this
2. Girl watcher
3. Pen name of Louise de la Ramee
4. Alan and Cheryl
5. Ballet movement
6. Faro card
7. Lawn
8. "Remington ___"
9. Arms for Hilfiger?
10. Melange
11. Trapper's trophy
13. British sword
15. One-fourth of a foot?
20. High riser?
24. Noah's command
26. Baba au ___
27. Tyrolienne
29. Sector
30. Mythomaniac
31. Mukluk wearers: abbr.
32. Pause briefly
33. Marine flier
34. Amtrak travel
35. Ocean disco?
37. Traffic barrier
41. Fabrication
43. Night person
46. Start
48. Peer
50. Italian commune
52. Dismay
53. Wednesday, to Fester
54. Troll
55. Serfs of yore
56. Kid's mom
57. Give temporarily
58. If not
60. Finito
61. Sunbathe

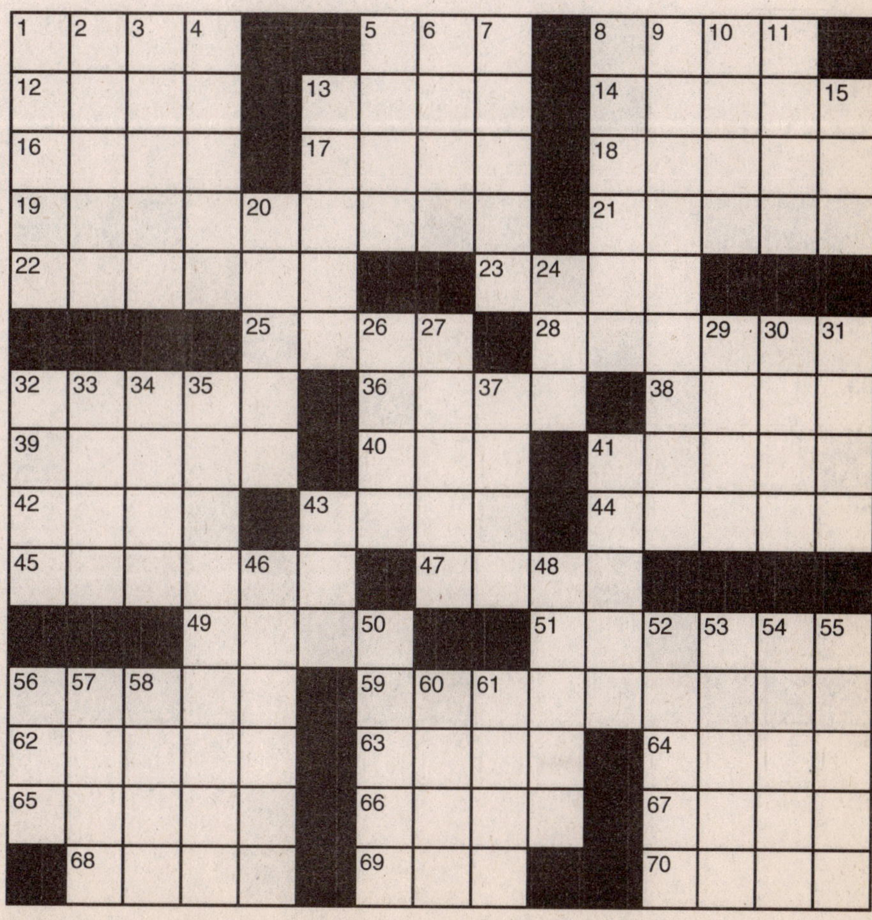

PUZZLE 490

MOVIE SPEAK

ACROSS

1. Comic Johnson
5. Modify
10. Friend
14. Downpour
15. Cozy corner
16. New York school
17. Hackman gabber
20. Yoko ___
21. Legal fig.
22. Steeple
25. Biblical book
27. Youth org.
30. Harmony
31. Felt poorly
32. Spoken
33. Pale gray
34. Flowed out
35. Battery post
36. Bacon babbler
40. Healed
41. Mowry and Carrere
42. Luau garland
44. Mayberry lad
45. Wrench
47. Imprint
48. Fast jet, shortly
49. Wharves
50. Equine
51. Pairs
52. Singer Davis
53. Travolta chatter
61. "___ Ha'i"
62. Jetson son
63. "Thirteen" role
64. Plant stalk
65. Relaxes
66. Pup ___

DOWN

1. Mr. Carney
2. Hooray!
3. Even score
4. Once more
5. ___ Domini
6. Mult.'s reverse
7. King beater
8. Word group
9. Checked
10. Metropolis
11. ___ polloi
12. Numero ___
13. Grown boy
18. Single item
19. ___ glance
22. RR depot
23. Workout exercises
24. Come into
25. Raced
26. Elder
27. Oven section
28. Depresses
29. Ginger ___
31. Ring great
32. Actress Munson
34. Wicked
35. Donkey
37. Envision
38. Boo
39. Feast
40. Lettuce type
43. Devoted suffix
45. Shrivel
46. Repair shoes
47. Agenda
49. Chapel bench
50. Mr. Linden
51. Scan
52. Aprils' followers
53. Wt. units
54. Stable grain
55. Bravo!
56. Jrs., soon
57. Kid
58. "___ Gotta Be Me"
59. Noted diarist
60. Comprehend

PUZZLE 491

AT THE BARBER SHOP

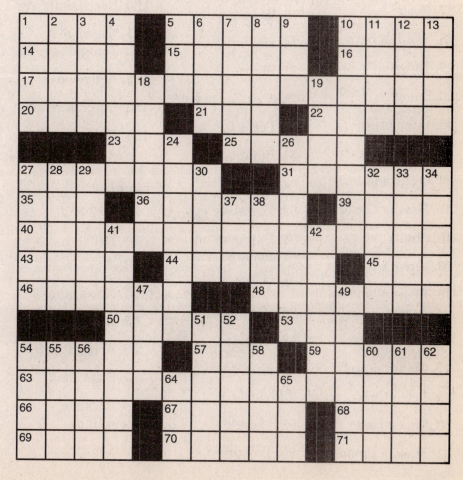

ACROSS

1. Steady gait
5. Jet
10. Nick's wife
14. Jazzy Anita ___
15. Adjust again
16. Effigy
17. Detailed approach, to a barber
20. American inventor
21. ___ Lancelot
22. Gumbo veggies
23. Noted time
25. Russian moola
27. Nautical hatch
31. Alleviates
35. NYC subway line
36. Sanctions
39. Mr. Morales
40. Relax, to a barber
43. Zenith
44. Third sign
45. Opposite of SSW
46. Juan's wrap
48. Clairvoyance
50. Ore deposits
53. Menlo Park monogram
54. Desert garden
57. Delay
59. Air current
63. Unpleasant encounter, to a barber
66. Nastase of tennis
67. Farewell
68. Pinch
69. Preschoolers
70. Star in Cygnus
71. Middle of middle?

DOWN

1. Raised bed
2. Garfield's pal
3. Skillets
4. Lace hole
5. Not con
6. Summer signs
7. Moving about
8. Indian statesman
9. Hot saison
10. ___-and-dimed
11. Aroma
12. Gypsies
13. Priest's robes
18. Plaid
19. Toy baby
24. Claimed
26. Helmet
27. Eliot's Marner
28. Wrinkly paper
29. Speak
30. Otherwise
32. All together
33. Silent shouts
34. Math ratios
37. Unit of resistance
38. Stray
41. Wood sorrels
42. A capital of Saudi Arabia
47. Elegant
49. Sea nymph
51. Slur over
52. Luxury fabric
54. Newspaper item, for short
55. Woody's boy
56. Spades, e.g.
58. Bombay butter
60. Congo lily
61. Kismet
62. "___ brillig . . ."
64. Stuff
65. Vat

1	2	3	4		5	6	7	8	9		10	11	12	13
14					15						16			
17				18						19				
20						21				22				
			23		24		25		26					
27	28	29				30			31			32	33	34
35				36			37	38			39			
40			41							42				
43					44							45		
46				47				48			49			
			50			51	52		53					
54	55	56				57		58		59		60	61	62
63					64				65					
66					67						68			
69					70						71			

PUZZLE 492

FRUITFUL PHRASES

ACROSS

1. "Mask" star
5. Parcel of land
9. Wiesbaden's site
14. Zest source
18. Leaf part
19. Speck
20. Musical Merman
21. Insignia
22. Fats Domino hit lyric
25. Bailiwicks
26. Gobi, e.g.
27. Born
28. Sandy's bark
29. Tangles
30. Some
31. Submerged
33. Campus lawn
34. O'Hare letters
37. Having flavor
40. Shafts
43. Violin's kin
45. Plowed land, to Juan
46. Dinnerware
47. Aviation prefix
49. From Cork
50. Shoestring
51. Mesabi product
52. Gather the family
54. Finale
55. Remove
57. Ant
59. Actor Flynn
60. Not NNW
61. Ad ___ (pertinent)
62. Miseries
63. Hive
64. Poitier film
69. Compositions
72. Revise
73. Women's ___
74. Dress
77. Sharp
78. TV's Kramden
79. Perfect
81. Regret
82. Fray
83. ___ Miss
84. Bateman or Robards
86. Vexed
88. View starter
89. Tanker
91. Muslim council
92. Yields
93. Mangle
95. Ventures
96. French father
97. Christiana, today
98. Blokes
100. Mule of song
102. Friday's boss
105. Very warm
106. Anthem poet
109. Gum arabic
113. Half note, in music
114. Massachusetts resort
117. Marble markings
118. Writer Horatio ___
119. Lap pup, for short
120. Bacchanals' cry
121. "Need You Tonight" group
122. Active ones
123. Belgian river
124. Cub rooms

DOWN

1. Bumpkin
2. Whet
3. Flows back
4. News stories
5. Reverence
6. Arced throw
7. Solar disk
8. Package weight
9. Yo!
10. Film's Hawke
11. Goof off
12. Ego
13. Pipe joint
14. Procession
15. Fulda feeder
16. Even, in Paris
17. Fewer
21. Small tropical nation
23. Footed vase
24. Dwell
29. "Peter ___"
32. Beery/Powell film
33. Noiseless
34. Cleveland Indians?
35. Gulls' relatives
36. Tolerate
37. Spicy sausage
38. Macaws
39. Tempo
40. Flail about
41. Petrarch's lady
42. Malaga mister
44. Spring blooms in D.C.
46. Prancer's pal
48. Depend
53. Gray or Moran
56. "Bad Behaviour" star et al.
58. "___ Oncle"
63. Japan's site
64. Swiss river

PUZZLE 492

65. Base coat
66. Lounger
67. Bite
68. Verdugo and Valova
69. Wild West name
70. Cliff
71. Separate
74. Commerce
75. External
76. Honkers
78. Birling contest
79. Elbe tributary
80. Capitol feature
85. Largest state
87. Shown again
90. Bit of land
94. Red dyes
98. Ravine
99. Say
100. More rational
101. Expert
102. 906, to Cato
103. Nothing, to Lili
104. Computer system acronym
105. Ring of light
107. Catch sight of
108. Actor Montand
110. Grotto
111. Wrought ___
112. Sweet drinks
114. Angry
115. Sixty-min. periods
116. Mamie's hubby

PUZZLE 493

PRODUCTIVE PLANT PRODUCTS

ACROSS

1. Beget
5. Fictional captain
9. Piece of land
13. Man or boy
17. Zounds!
18. Jeer
19. Brand identifier
20. Biblical prophet
21. Chinese parsley
23. Gravy thickener
25. High-pitched voice
26. Specify distinctly
28. Shampoo procedure
29. For fear that
31. Ditty
32. Imposter
33. Take in or let out
36. Artifice
38. Diamond feature
39. Kiwi's kin
40. Travel agent's offering
42. Current
45. Cleric's vestment
48. Contented sound
50. Moved on
52. Hotel freebie
53. Court argument
54. Disco light
56. Sorority member
58. Distance runner
59. Gather
61. Corporate VIP
62. Certain Europeans
64. Keyboard instrument
66. Manufacturers
69. Formally accepts
72. Winged diver
73. Satisfy
74. Poses for a portrait
76. Clock reading
77. Secluded room
78. Job functions
80. Part of CD
82. Middling grade
83. Days gone by
84. Scoundrel
86. Tip over
88. Experts
91. Oaf
93. Pasternak heroine
95. Pertaining to birds
96. Review writer
98. Fodder grass
102. Beverage flavoring
104. Herbal-tea plant
106. Eartha ___ of song
107. Rave
108. Magician's expression
109. Peron and Gabor
110. Do in, as a dragon
111. Has birthdays
112. Extend over
113. Quantities, in radiology

DOWN

1. Cult
2. Franken-stein's aide
3. Very uncommon
4. Fit for food
5. Choreogra-pher DeMille
6. Concealed
7. Retired
8. "The Green ___"
9. Evident
10. Actor Greene
11. Giant
12. Overly
13. Of the water
14. Surrounded by
15. Baggy
16. Fragrant compound
22. Ready for action
24. Arm joint
27. Engine's need
30. Authentic
32. Grate
33. Bandstand equipment
34. Boor
35. Aromatic herb
37. Coffee vessels
38. Smokey and Yogi
41. Has debts
43. John Jacob and Mary
44. Foot part
45. Pimento
46. Grant's opponent
47. Cocktail lounge
49. Holiday or candle
51. Stir to laughter
53. Move around a center
55. Outlaw

PUZZLE 493

57. Visualize

58. Like a wet hen

60. Strike down

63. Scottish girl

64. Antique

65. Mass of spawn

67. Clay, today

68. Flank

70. Feds

71. Kernel

73. Ermine and mink

75. Cultivate, as land

78. Italian lady

79. Vaccine

81. Unusual object

83. Foamy

85. Proclamations

87. Golfer Arnold ___

88. Disguises

89. Benefit

90. Panorama

91. Stretch (the neck)

92. Tabulates

94. Capital of Jordan

96. Rocky cliff

97. English fellow

99. Endure

100. Western-villain actor

101. Hardy character

103. Monk's title

105. Hayward film

PUZZLE 494

ELTON JOHN SONGS

ACROSS

1. Abound
5. Cain's brother
9. Fountain order
13. Old Glory, e.g.
17. Actress Nazimova
18. Gaucho's gear
19. Sp. smell
20. Small stream
21. MGM symbol
22. "___ Lake"
23. Granny
24. Nobelist Stern
25. 1987 hit
29. Truck type
30. Tiptop
31. Dine
32. Official stamp
34. Explosive letters
35. Pollock piece
36. Officiated
40. Bert Parks, e.g.
43. Bowler's target
44. "___ and Let Die"
45. Partly open
46. Follower of Feb.
47. Jug handle
48. Fastener
49. Epoch
50. Not as tall
53. Rhythmic element
54. Seedling
56. Like a cucumber
57. Detach
58. Juvenile
59. Repent
61. Dissuade
62. Strait
65. Lass's mate
66. Foe
67. Green ___ Packers
68. Pension-plan abbr.
69. Moistureless
71. Cyclist Knievel
72. Not near
73. Clean with a broom
75. Willy Loman, e.g.
77. Martini base
78. Saratoga Springs, e.g.
79. Actress Sommer
80. "Norma ___"
81. Actress Young
82. "Tell ___ About It"
84. 1983 hit
91. Proton's place
93. Heifer's home
94. College head
95. Author Hunter
96. Ancient Peruvian
97. Baseball's Cabell
98. ___ the Red
99. Pro ___
100. Leaf collector
101. Neural network
102. Seldom seen
103. Crystallized water

DOWN

1. Fine powder
2. Director Kazan
3. North Carolina college
4. Decree
5. Part of AWOL
6. Hunting knife
7. Panache
8. Camping light
9. French painter
10. What there ought to be
11. Actress Anderson
12. Relocate
13. To's partner
14. 1980 hit
15. Palo ___, California
16. Luster
26. Like a certain ranger
27. Ten-gallon ___
28. Poor grade
33. Macaw
35. Football filler
36. Kitchen gizmo
37. Continually
38. Make money
39. Shucks!
40. Ambulance letters
41. ___-jongg
42. 1972 hit
43. Equal
44. Procrastinator's motto
47. Electric ___
48. Flat
51. Howard or Perlman
52. Tic-tac-___
53. Iridium, e.g.
54. Princess poker

PUZZLE 494

55. Author Deighton
57. VII
58. Quaker pronoun
59. Sorrowful word
60. O'Hara home
61. Met star
62. Daytona entry
63. Sooner than, in verse
64. Race circuit
66. Recall
67. Interdiction
70. Eastern U.S. state
72. Baseballer in the grass
73. Duration
74. Roams
76. Take part in a biathlon
77. Maiden
78. Medium's meeting
80. Flush with water
81. Riser
82. Kojak's lack
83. Sicilian volcano
85. Lucid
86. Horse's gait
87. Italian evening
88. ___ the Terrible
89. Alliance acronym
90. Chew (on)
92. Ms. West

PUZZLE 495

CREATURE FEATURE

ACROSS

1. Foretell
5. Gibson and Torme
9. Choir singer
13. Yearning
17. Bur, e.g.
18. Certain ox
19. Bound
20. Clog or loafer
21. Has an unhappy existence
24. Simple
25. Ms. Barkin
26. Seine
27. Strive
29. Rogue
30. Contest
33. Tans
36. Disney musical
38. Far down
41. Burger bread
43. Eagle type
45. Golf strokes
48. Fire residue
49. Faulty auto
51. Travels
53. Terrible
54. Marginal
56. "___ in a Blue Dress"
58. Legend
60. First named
61. "Grand ___"
63. Rent again
65. Contributed
67. Pep
69. Make merry
71. Stylish
72. Taco cheese
75. Mister, to Miguel
77. Blockade
80. "2001" computer
81. Sputter
83. Thorny blooms
85. Roe source
86. Kegs' contents
88. Oklahoma city
90. Of a kidney
92. Breakfasted
93. Used a lasso
95. Consider
97. Withered
98. Part of a royal flush
99. Red deer
101. Costly
103. Airplane part
105. Ms. Lupino
107. Orange tuber
109. Tatter
111. Jeweled crown
115. ___ and rave
117. Be patient!
122. Informed of
123. Toast spread
124. Bona fide
125. Cloth fuzz
126. Wasp's home
127. Verge
128. Look
129. Ms. Thompson

DOWN

1. Bundle hay
2. City on the Oka
3. Tuner
4. Born first
5. Pasture cry
6. Goal
7. Diving bird
8. Wise ones
9. Each and every
10. Island gift
11. 27th president
12. "Carmen," e.g.
13. Doctrine
14. Dr. Seuss book
15. Dithers' wife
16. Notice
22. Growl
23. Ticket part
28. Sharp bark
31. Female pupil
32. "___ Gantry"
34. Henpeck
35. Coin taker
37. Failure
38. Bind firmly
39. Norway's capital
40. Unwanted possessions
42. Devotee
44. Air or heat
46. Elm, e.g.
47. Spring seller
50. Frasier's brother
52. Sty food
55. Merge
57. Pry bar
59. Son of Seth
62. Boys
64. Domingo, e.g.

PUZZLE 495

66. Sales term
68. Neck section
70. Is bested
72. Blacken with flame
73. Light ring
74. Husk
76. Restore
78. Turnstile
79. Perfect locale
82. Tethered
84. Hindu garb
87. Bering, e.g.
89. One-fourth of a yard?
91. Slowly, in music
94. Desertlike
96. Queen of Scots
100. Nevada lake
102. Mob scenes
104. Young ladies
105. Pressing tool
106. Hamlet, e.g.
108. Sculpt
110. Absolute
112. Pakistan's site
113. Shred
114. Cinema pooch
116. Toddler
118. Lamb cut
119. John or Jane
120. Wish otherwise
121. Dress bottom

PUZZLE 496

COLORFUL TALES

ACROSS

1. Find fault
5. Tool sets
9. ___ -Magnon
12. Island near Java
16. Befuddled
17. Sunday reply
18. Bamboozled
19. Poison ___
20. Grey's "Riders of ___"
23. Track
24. Calm
25. Model Macpherson
26. Easy gallop
27. Desire
28. "Star ___"
29. Muck
30. Fountain treats
33. Expanded
34. Erte's style
38. Oy!
39. Mall court
40. Snazzy
42. Swarm
43. Slurp
44. South African coin
45. Union general
46. Beach resort
47. Antagonistic
49. Brook
50. Pocketbook
51. Hawthorne novel, with "The"
55. Actress Miles
58. Eliel's son
59. Collars
63. Anytime
64. Need a pickle
66. Pat dry
67. Phone cut-in
68. Curly's pal
69. Top-grade
70. Chimney's dirt
71. Misfortune
72. Antique writing table items
75. Bridge
76. Fencing move
77. Submit
78. Comic Sahl
79. Geologic time
80. Flash floods
83. ___ Copley
84. Scottish port
88. "___ Bulba"
89. William Henry Hudson novel
92. Aristocracy
93. Dawn goddess
94. Ms. Lollobrigida
95. Correct copy
96. Go for Baroque
97. Visual sense
98. ___ doute
99. Pop

DOWN

1. Broadway hit
2. Tennis legend
3. Critic Rex ___
4. Smoothie fruits
5. Allen or Black
6. Brat
7. Address book no.
8. Scoffed
9. Sidewalk crayon
10. Fad
11. Pindaric poem
12. Incinerated
13. Amo, amas, ___
14. Chantilly, e.g.
15. Bakery worker
19. Commence
21. Western Indians
22. Struck down
26. Mythical enchantress
28. Stomped
29. Damsel
30. Part of C.O.D.
31. Hodgepodge
32. Pool circuits
33. Hopeless case
35. Mideast title
36. Adult scrods
37. Hautboy
39. White House dog
40. Casals's instrument
41. Sound
44. Like Croesus
45. Corner joint
46. Tempt
48. Bygone leader
49. Pass a rope through
50. Sassy
52. Slant
53. Accipiter's weapon

54. Jog

55. Round before the final

56. River to the Severn

57. Emit fumes

60. Musician Getz

61. Sharp flavor

62. "Graf ___"

64. Actress Phoebe

65. Bright

66. Yawl, e.g.

70. Coils

71. Carrot lovers

73. Latke need

74. Corpulent

75. Sensitive

76. Costello et al.

PUZZLE 496

78. 75th Attorney General

79. May Oliver and Best

80. Lob ending

81. Blanched

82. Like the Atacama

83. Priam's city

85. Bird of yore

86. Oklahoma town

87. This, in Toledo

89. Middle of night?

90. Frank's ex

91. ___-Margret

PUZZLE 497

ACROSS

1. Mulberry's cousins
5. Ravi's item
10. Actions
15. La Scala solo
19. Younger Guthrie
20. Florida city
21. Flynn of films
22. Sharp taste
23. "One O'Clock Jump" composer
25. A.k.a. Baby Snooks
27. Chemical suffix
28. Biddies
29. ___ up (admit)
30. Frog genus
31. Museo offering
32. Lumber source
33. Bridge trick
35. Miles off
38. Earth's neighbor
39. Heightens
43. This place
44. "Call Me Madam" Tony winner
48. Roman 502
49. Mine contents
50. God of thunder
51. Of flight
52. Yemen port
53. Accomplished
54. Electric razor
56. Photo finishes?
57. Gumshoe
58. Hughes's "Spruce Goose," e.g.
60. External
62. Redshank
63. Point of view
64. Softened
65. Morality
67. Admission proof
68. More vile
69. Spanish dance
72. Sting
73. By oneself
75. More like Felix
77. Recent: pref.
78. Mercyhurst College site
79. Franco or Peter
80. Ms. West et al.
81. Actaeon's fate
82. Conflict
83. Gracie Allen's partner
87. Ripped
88. Grammar school items
91. Prayers
92. Recall subjects
93. Feels pain
94. Feds
95. Hemingway sobriquet
98. Heroic story
100. Chinese noodles
101. Ballet dancer Moiseyev
102. Fitting
105. "Showboat" composer
108. "Night and Day" composer
111. Table spread
112. Tenant's document
113. A Castle
114. Biblical weed
115. Verve
116. Gluts
117. Throws off
118. Swordplay item

DOWN

1. Stand before
2. Press
3. Mucilage
4. Beaver, to Ward
5. Like a judge
6. "___ Help Myself"
7. Demi follower
8. Legendary Baba
9. Scottish explorer
10. Football chant
11. Clean the slate
12. Directional endings
13. Scottish river
14. Slick
15. "The Lady Is ___"
16. Downpour
17. Early Peruvian
18. Ripen
24. ___ she blows!
26. Scottish hillside
29. Steadfast
32. Norton, to Ralph
33. Begin
34. Gauze weaves
35. Osprey's abode
36. Ginger Rogers's partner, often
37. Roman bronze
38. Member of la famille
39. Besmirch
40. "Whoopee" actor
41. Wednesday, to Fester
42. Go down
43. Coal scuttles
44. Patriot Allen
45. Burmese diplomat
46. Hoisted
47. Evaluated
52. Wing it verbally
54. Thick piece
55. Awaken
56. Rigid
59. Primp
61. Colorado Indian
62. Trout species
64. Estate residence
65. Devoured
66. Curl

PUZZLE 497

67. Junkyard fodder
68. Golfer Julius ___
69. German river
70. Comes closer
71. Venetian ruler
72. Bastes
73. Backer
74. Nasty looks
76. Flightless birds
81. Train dep.
84. Urchins
85. Tied
86. Crenshaw or Hogan
89. Small pond
90. "The Informer" author
92. Dear, to Luigi
94. To the point
95. Heaps
96. Ten percenter
97. John Paul II et al.
98. Vend
99. Region
100. Protein source
102. Nipa palm
103. Title for Marquette
104. Logger's target
105. Java
106. Spanish articles
107. New Zealand parrot
108. Armed forces VIP
109. Danish money
110. Hwy. choice

PUZZLE 498

ACROSS

1. Summon
5. Ricki's rival
10. Tokyo, formerly
13. Lithe
19. Swabby's greeting
20. Baseball's Pee Wee ___
21. Writer Fleming
22. More open
23. "Kachina Doll" painter
26. Bumpy
27. Rulers
28. Rearward
29. Shoat's home
30. Comic Philips
31. Everything
32. Illustrator ___-de Tirtoff
34. Seaweed
36. Motes
40. "Red Balloon" painter
43. Yodeler's home
47. Empties
48. Gambol
49. Retired
50. Legume
51. LPs
52. Costa ___
53. No-see-um
54. Winged
55. Wood strip
56. Persian king
57. Fly
58. More intimate
59. Word in a threat
60. Strike
61. Out of control
62. Most profound
63. "Madonna of the Rocks" painter
67. "Smiley's People" author
70. Chatters
71. Play a part
72. Wine stopper
76. Exact satisfaction for
77. Scup
78. Prompts
79. ___ Gemayel
80. Freight
81. Make like Greg Lemond
82. Magic stick
83. Kenyan national park
84. Plimpton book
85. Columnist Bombeck
86. Jacket slit
87. Nut
88. "Kiss from a Rose" singer
89. "Landscapes" painter
91. Vampires' targets
92. Butter substitute
94. "The Morning Watch" author
95. Panama or Leghorn, e.g.
96. Hot tub
99. Yuck!
100. Rocker Brian ___
101. Innkeeper
106. Fate
108. "Le Parc Monceau" painter
111. Time of the glaciers
112. An avis lays them
113. Assemble
114. Feels rotten
115. Used a rink
116. Voice master Blanc
117. Journalist Lesley ___
118. Bulk

DOWN

1. Zoo pen
2. Attention-getter
3. Pilot's stunt
4. Stringed instrument
5. Baltimore nine
6. Oysters' gems
7. Antique cars
8. Grill
9. "___ Haw"
10. French tower designer
11. Confused
12. Single
13. Browned
14. House siding
15. Before, before
16. Happening as we speak
17. Abound
18. Inventor Rubik
24. Rye and corn
25. Enjoy enthusiastically
29. Trapshooting
32. Period
33. Incarnation of Vishnu
35. "Mandolin and Guitar" painter
36. Confuse
37. Struggle
38. Kilns for drying hops
39. "The Last Judgment" painter
41. Native Hawaiian
42. Angle iron
44. Contract
45. Appetizers
46. Dog in"Hagar the Horrible"
48. Lariat
52. German river
53. Merchandise
54. Guinness of films
56. Ocean's edge
57. Hazy
58. Small change

PUZZLE 498

61. Proverb
62. Minced
64. Therefore
65. Japanese inn
66. Brag
67. Fastens
68. Avoid
69. Ceramic's raw material
73. Nebraska metropolis
74. Rosie's fastener
75. Understands
77. Fine cotton
78. Hiawatha's conveyance
81. Creek
82. "___ No Angels"
83. Sharper
85. Bailed out
86. Strength
87. Personal property
90. Handbook
91. In spite of
93. Faithful
96. Tackles moguls
97. Choose
98. On the Pacific
100. Roof part
101. Greek Juno
102. Neeson of "Rob Roy"
103. Hip bones
104. Wings
105. Betsy or Diana
107. Cushion
108. May celebrant
109. Contingencies
110. Camp bunk

PUZZLE 499

ACROSS

1. Wharf
5. German dam
9. Wegg of "Our Mutual Friend"
14. Impertinence
18. Opening wager
19. Actress ___ Anderson
20. Gladiator's center
21. "I cannot tell ___"
22. Mitch Miller's forte
24. "Hiawatha" poet
26. Serious
27. Lindbergh, e.g.
30. Pirates manager
31. Bryophyte
34. Activist
35. Comedienne O'Donnell
36. Gooselike
40. Catty
42. Lycra's kin
46. Cry from the stands
47. Prince William's school
48. "The Kingfish"
51. ___ pro nobis
52. Through
54. You were: Lat.
56. Net
57. Diarist of note
58. XY people
60. Chew the scenery
63. Dress down
65. Bible bk.
66. Kindred
68. African antelope
70. Vane dir.
71. Foxy
72. Advantage
73. Eagles album, with "The"
76. Think nothing ___
78. Wages
80. Part of ATV
82. Honkers
83. Handrail supports
86. Springfield's st.
87. Archibald ___ (Cary Grant)
90. Petrol measure
92. Actor Novarro
93. 1970s rock gp.
94. Attempts
96. Bede of fiction
98. Pintail duck
99. Bo's number
100. Hastily
103. Bank holding
105. Lamb's mom
106. Point of view
108. Roast host
109. Bring about
111. Deli denizen
114. ___ avis
116. FDR's mother
117. 1982 Masters champ
120. Least adorned
122. Recorded movie
126. Civil War's "Old Pete"
128. Raiders' great
131. Mrs. Shakespeare
132. Esther of "Good Times"
133. Latin abbr.
134. Sandusky sight
135. Brandy fruit-flavor
136. Operatic delights
137. Strait
138. Miami's county

DOWN

1. "Horseman, ___ By"
2. Monogram ltr.
3. Sicilian spewer
4. Government
5. Building add-on
6. "Da ___ Ron Ron"
7. Italian province
8. Stiff
9. Fixed wages
10. Steel's base
11. Novelist Deighton
12. Part of WASP
13. Money vaults
14. Ship's kitchen
15. Actress Nazimova
16. Oz visitor
17. Indecent
23. Dote on
25. Watching
28. ___ Hashanah
29. Diner's dish list
32. Venue
33. Saw wood
35. Fragment of a martyr
36. Fragrance
37. Nautical
38. "Cheers" star
39. Oil-based paint
41. Alters the hue of
43. Leggy
44. Bay window
45. Mary Poppins, e.g.
49. Yoko's kin
50. Composer Riddle
53. Director Wallace ___
55. Alone
59. "Love Story" author
61. Strong taste
62. Star Georgia ___
64. Postpone
67. Cross out
69. Eins plus zwei

74. Tennis org.

75. Compass pointer

77. "___ a Shoplifter"

78. Vatican attraction

79. Cowboy Rex ___

81. Superman's mom

84. Lerner's partner

85. Rude look

88. Autumn beverage

89. Tiller

91. Monsoons

95. Plato's teacher

97. Byte beginning

100. Cures

101. Close by

102. Richard of "Yanks"

104. Chutzpah

107. Bookkeeper's book

110. Caught in the act

112. Aquarium fish

PUZZLE 499

113. Fallacy

115. Gray

117. Sharp rebuke

118. Pitch

119. Palindromic name

120. Composer Bartok

121. Schlep

123. Dickens's ___ Spenlow

124. City west of Tulsa

125. Architect's curve

127. Biblical high priest

129. WWII enlistee

130. Sort

PUZZLE 500

ACROSS

1. Sort of, for starters
5. Camp bed
8. Wound reminder
12. Hue
13. Relocate
14. Tribe leaders
17. Appetizer
18. Purport
19. Climbing rose
21. Moderate
22. Rasputin's advisee
23. Immerse
24. Artist's prop
26. Ogle
27. Elapse
28. Taxi
29. South American mammal
30. Feminine pronoun
31. Resided
33. Whitest
35. Urban pall
36. Calif.'s neighbor
38. Bounded section
39. Exist
40. Brewed drink
42. Printer's measures
43. Homage
45. Position
47. Prepare fish
49. Recording
51. Wind up
52. Gave a rubdown to
55. Total
58. Grass
60. Circus employee
62. Dubbed
64. Chamber
66. Donny's sister
68. Finals
71. Dollar division
72. "M*A*S*H" locale
74. Beginning
76. Message
78. Heavy weight
79. Having no magnitude
82. Ewe's mate
84. Mr. Donahue
86. Moor
87. Well-founded
89. Indian tribe
93. Wet earth
96. Bother
97. ___ Vegas
98. Vend
100. Male deer
101. Uplifting inventor?
103. Wrap
105. Silvery fish
107. Night preceding
108. German bread
110. Be in debt
111. Blemish
112. Pungent
114. Family car
115. Keats's ceramic
116. Tournament format
117. Swell
118. Keeps
120. Smooth
121. Sport spikes
122. Abdicate
123. Jacket slit
124. Prevention measure?
125. Damage allowance
126. As well as
127. "Little Women" role

DOWN

1. Asdic
2. Excited
3. Brood
4. Exasperation
5. Musical finales
6. Above
7. Ms. Leoni
8. Correspondent
9. Fellow
10. Purpose
11. Yank's foe
12. Nightclub
13. Exaggerate
15. Flutters
16. Italian bread seed
17. Provides food
20. Military mission, shortly
22. Stories
23. Roy's spouse
25. Hangs back
26. Oxford, e.g.
27. Part of rpm
28. Joker
29. Book of maps
32. Peag
33. Chinese "bear"
34. Anatomical pouches
37. Procure
41. Panache
44. Sup
46. Pays to play
47. Kitchen wrap
48. Mild expletive
50. Historic time
52. Tex-___ cooking
53. Give off
54. Sample, for short
55. Noah's boat
56. Fate
57. Dumb girl
59. First yr. collegian
61. Iron or copper, e.g.
63. Study

PUZZLE 500

65. Netting

67. Political electees

69. Clever remark

70. Casual walk

73. Addled

75. Scratch out

77. Long time

80. Filled with cargo

81. Harrow's rival

83. Squandered

85. Affirmative

87. Flower jar

88. Monster

90. Say again

91. Ship cranes

92. Grew older

93. Stone covering

94. Complete

95. Electron tubes

97. Mower's pride

99. Rent

102. Candidate lineup

104. Girdle

106. Natural ability

109. Make into law

111. Disburse money

113. Craig T. Nelson sitcom

115. Wavy, in heraldry

116. Kiln

117. Cerulean

119. Comparative suffix

120. Gabor sister

121. Corn holder

PUZZLE 501

Diagramless crosswords are solved by using the clues and their numbers to fill in the answer words and the arrangement of black squares. Insert the number of each clue with the first letter of its answer, across and down. Fill in a black square at the end of each answer. Every black square must have a corresponding black square on the opposite side of the diagram to form a diagonally symmetrical pattern. Puzzles 501 and 502 have been started for you.

ACROSS
1. Use poor judgment
4. Wooden pin
7. Fast jet
10. Sign of triumph
11. Previously
12. ____ or never
13. Rascal
14. Filch
15. Beer's bitter kin
16. Fragrant shrub
18. On the loose
19. Fashions
21. Doze
22. Andean animal
24. Certain hairdo
27. Man, e.g.
31. Gush
32. Mock
33. Drum lightly
34. Cold-weather ailment
36. Darken
37. "Look ____ ye leap"
38. Ventilate
39. Excitement
40. Paint-the-town color
41. Ruff's mate
42. Males

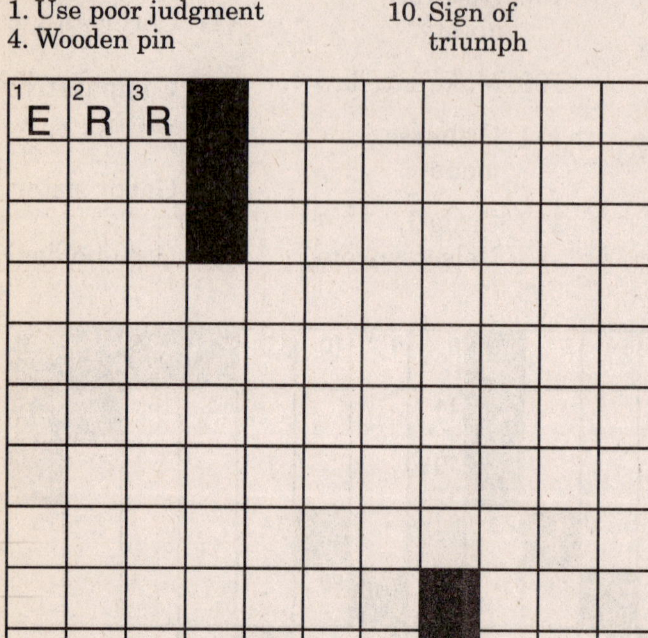

DOWN
1. Wrongs
2. Make payment
3. Answer
4. Lot
5. Kind of maniac
6. Mass
7. Capture
8. Shoe parts
9. Peep
17. Consent to
18. Border
20. American uncle
23. Fully developed
24. Following
25. Emergency signal
26. Made like a cowboy
28. Polite address
29. Apart
30. Defective car
34. Distant
35. Let sleeping dogs ____

PUZZLE 502

ACROSS
1. Cried
5. Coastal flier
9. At any time
10. Freshwater catch
11. Misfortune
12. Curacao's neighbor
13. Sailor
15. Stretch
16. Central European
18. Villa d'____
19. Set
22. Chopped
24. Pass on
26. ____ and yang
27. Native of Peru
31. Quick to the helm
32. Banqueted
34. Hindu ascetics
35. Intense
37. Small amount
40. Sat
41. Greek war god
42. Water pitcher
43. Onion's relative

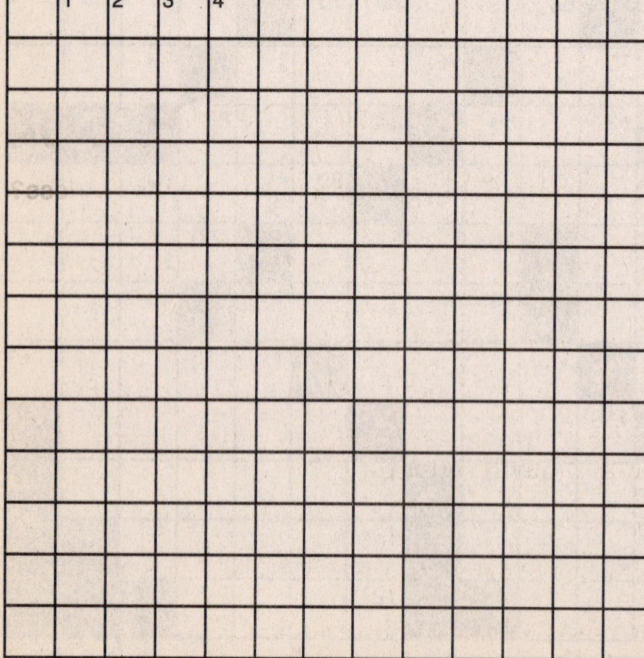

DOWN
1. Gossamer snare
2. Ms. Gabor
3. Wistful
4. Corners
5. Straying
6. More cylindrical
7. Heart of the matter
8. Airport abbr.
10. Gentles
14. Consumed
15. Daybreak
16. Bashful
17. Island floral ring
19. Delighted
20. Corn spike
21. Caustic substance
23. Spread
25. Ugly sight
28. Less messy
29. Crusted
30. Do ____ say . . .
33. Ordeal
35. Gorilla, e.g.
36. Milk producer
38. Informal shirt
39. Inquire

PUZZLE 503

ACROSS

1. Furthermore
5. Verdi opera
9. Soda flavoring
10. Injury memento
11. Prepare to publish
12. Honey factory
13. Dissuade
15. Nairobi's country
16. Emptiness
19. Jib or spinnaker
20. Continental currency
21. Put a stop to
25. "Jane ____"
26. Golf hazard
27. Carney's former costar
30. Church singing group
32. Fruit pastries
36. Crazy bird?
37. ____ parmigiana
38. Basilica nook
39. Author Ferber
40. Hammerhead part
41. Found's companion

DOWN

1. Hit a hole in one
2. Vein of ore
3. Narrow gash
4. Like a hot cereal
5. Pallid
6. Cupcake topper
7. Frontiersman Crockett
8. Field of study
14. Trellis creepers
15. Metric mile
17. Tightly drawn
18. Give a job to
22. "____ Breckinridge"
23. Historic ages
24. Railroad station
27. Gander's mate
28. Type of closet
29. Bellybutton
30. Thunder noise
31. Famous diamond
33. Modernize
34. Browns in the sun
35. Strip of wood

Starting box on page 562

Mystery Word PUZZLE 504

There is a six-letter Mystery Word hidden in the diagram. Can you find it in four minutes or less?

Z	S	Q	E	U	I
C	T	Y	H	E	N
A	K	O	L	M	B
W	U	G	R	V	X
N	P	S	J	I	U
B	G	C	K	F	T

My first letter appears in the first column and the sixth row, but not the third row.

My second appears in both diagonals.

My third appears in the second row and in one corner.

My fourth is from the second half of the alphabet and appears in the fourth column.

My fifth appears more times than any other letter.

My last letter appears in both the second and third columns.

Mystery Word: ___ ___ ___ ___ ___ ___

PUZZLE 505

ACROSS

1. Tack on
4. Towel monogram
7. Observes
9. Shake to-and-fro
12. Soft drink
13. Chaos
15. Slippery
16. Globe
17. Pickle herb
18. Energy
19. Skin problem
20. Baggy
22. Large nail
24. Lend a hand
25. Sure!
26. Supports
29. Small particles
33. Commotion
34. Prune
35. Station
38. African carnivore
40. Refrain starter
42. Spanish day
43. Storage spot
45. Showery month
48. Complimentary
49. KO counter
51. Midnight's opposite
53. "____ Gantry"
54. Santa's staffer
55. Pounce
57. "Since You've ____ Gone"
58. Blue yonder
59. Feed the kitty
60. Flower plot
61. Still

Starting box on page 562

DOWN

1. Fireplace remnant
2. "____ Poets Society"
3. Wicked person
4. Singer Lena ____
5. Inactive
6. Dejected
8. Recital piece
9. Dried
10. Expert
11. ____ moth
12. Anklet
14. ____-and-dagger
16. Midsection
21. Relative, for short
23. ____ soup (dense fog)
26. Naughty
27. Citrus refresher
28. Officer
30. Mexican "Rah!"
31. Sun.'s follower
32. Sauna locale
36. River creature
37. Start for pod or dent
38. ____-hop
39. Tall stories
41. Units of farmland
42. Like a cartoon duck
43. Ready for combat
44. Promgoer
46. The Corn State
47. Demented
48. Take flight
50. Antlered animal
52. Reminder
53. Taper off
56. Special favorite

PUZZLE 506

Say That Again?

Five well-known quotations or phrases have been reworded below, but the original meanings have been kept. Can you identify the originals?

Example: *Lack of awareness brings elation.* (**Answer:** *Ignorance is bliss.*)

1. Anything that ascends is required to descend.
2. Males are unable to subsist on leavened food exclusively.
3. Extraordinary phenomena are not about to discontinue at any time.
4. Firsthand knowledge often turns out to be the most excellent instructor.
5. It can be expected to have dual opinions in the matter of each possible inquiry.

PUZZLE 507

ACROSS
1. Female sibling, briefly
4. ____, skip, and jump
7. Kind of exam
9. Actors' parts
11. Bodies of knowledge
13. Business greeter
15. Genre
16. King's better
17. Long sandwiches
20. "____ Hard" (Willis film)
21. Begged
22. Impressionist painter
23. Bike rider
25. Mishandle
26. ____ conditioning
27. Protrude
28. Charge with an offense
32. Nippers
35. Blessings
36. Red ____
37. Nocturnal bird
39. James Brown's music
40. Curse
41. Letter after cee
42. Make dizzy
47. Silent Marx
48. Frighten
49. Club payments
50. Acquire
51. Compass pt.

DOWN
1. Flew unaccompanied
2. Do a laundry chore
3. Bombay dress
4. Gretzky's sport
5. Shout for a matador
6. Gusto
8. School exercise
9. Souvenir
10. More trite
12. Smarted
13. Dispose (of)
14. Bakery employee
18. Barbara ____ Geddes
19. Fr. holy woman
21. Ballet move
22. Trumpeter's device
24. Mama ____ Elliot
25. Cigar end
27. Having bad luck
28. Belly muscles, shortly
29. Dove's comment
30. Cold symptom
31. Disburden
32. Has-____ (former star)
33. Gnawing mammal
34. What a workout works up
36. Select
38. Rock's ____ Zeppelin
43. Factual
44. Unsealed
45. Hang low
46. Shade

Starting box on page 562

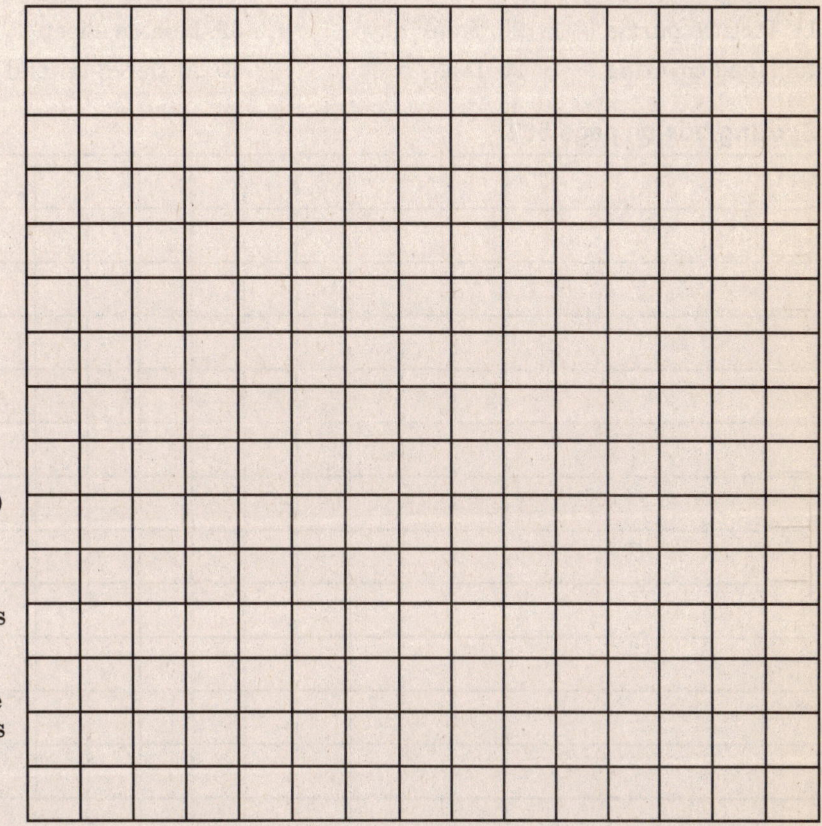

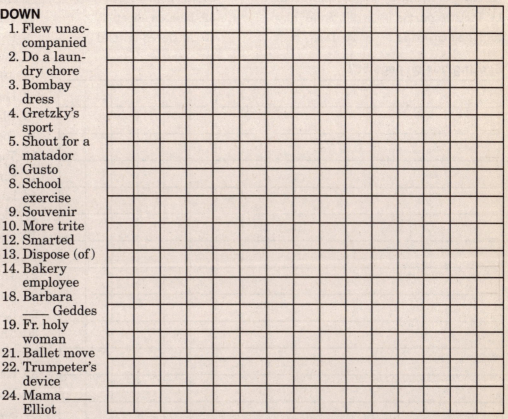

Picture Pairs

PUZZLE 508

Some of these designs match up as pairs, and some designs have no mates. Can you discover the designs that do not match in three minutes or less?

PUZZLE 509

ACROSS

1. Beyond's partner
6. A, E, I, O, or U
7. Sea eagles
8. Kind of drum
11. Picture puzzle
15. Head covering
16. Fire residue
17. Violent anger
18. Coral formation
20. Plant part
22. Light source
25. Small bay
26. Dog's pest
27. Humorist George ___
28. Linger
29. Uncommon
31. Fork prong
32. Sight organs
33. Colony insects
34. Halt
37. Serpent's tooth
39. Female sheep
40. Antlered animal
41. Royal
44. Tibia and fibula
46. Cellist's need
48. Love
49. Warps

DOWN

1. Allege
2. Diameter
3. Possess
4. Swerve
5. Additional
8. Humiliation
9. Old horse
10. Dined
12. Taproom
13. Employ
14. Ledge
17. Worships
19. Descending
20. Frighten
21. This date
23. Intended
24. Book leaves
30. Chemical compound
31. Propane containers
35. Have bills
36. Wooden nail
37. Swamp
38. Strong beer
42. Steed breed
43. Ore vein
44. Feathered friend
45. Individuals
47. Male offspring

Starting box on page 562

PUZZLE 510 Keyword

To find the Keyword, fill in the blanks in words 1 through 10 with the correct missing letters. Transfer those letters to the correspondingly numbered squares in the diagram. Approach with care—this puzzle is not as simple as it first appears.

1	2	3	4	5	6	7	8	9	10

1. ___ O R S E
2. C R A N ___
3. S T O ___ K
4. L ___ V E R
5. P L A I ___
6. S P ___ L L
7. G R E E ___
8. D ___ N C E
9. C O V E ___
10. J U I C ___

PUZZLE 511

ACROSS
1. Prized marble
6. Dreamy
7. Member of Cong.
10. Serrated
11. Maui strings, shortly
12. Eagle's home
13. Easily bent
18. Designate
22. Quality
23. Rope loop
24. Earthen pot
25. Vast plain
26. Profit
27. Introverted
29. Goulash
33. Dash
34. Former Turkish title
35. Yearning
37. "About a ___"
38. Make a selection
41. Bits of land
46. Boring
47. Master
48. Certain fisherman
50. Appoints
52. Indoor-sports buildings
54. Hold it!
57. Card game
58. Baby grand, e.g.
59. Play division
60. Tender spots
61. Motionless

DOWN
1. Mass reply
2. Author Vidal
3. Honker
4. Moment
5. Hurricane center
7. Brood
8. Supplement
9. Succeeding
13. Liberate
14. Strong metal
15. Hay collection
16. Happy tunes
17. Flight info.
19. Sturgeon delicacy
20. Cleaning tool
21. It bit Cleo
25. Coordination
27. Indian title
28. Simple dwelling
30. Checks
31. Sense of self
32. Method
36. Full of gaps
39. Date tree
40. Now and ___
41. Rick's love
42. Relative, for short
43. Floral necklace
44. Future finch
45. Stress
46. Entreat
49. Sitar music
50. "___ No Sunshine"
51. Ogle
53. Attack!
55. Dilly
56. Sentry's station
58. Fraternity letter

Starting box on page 562

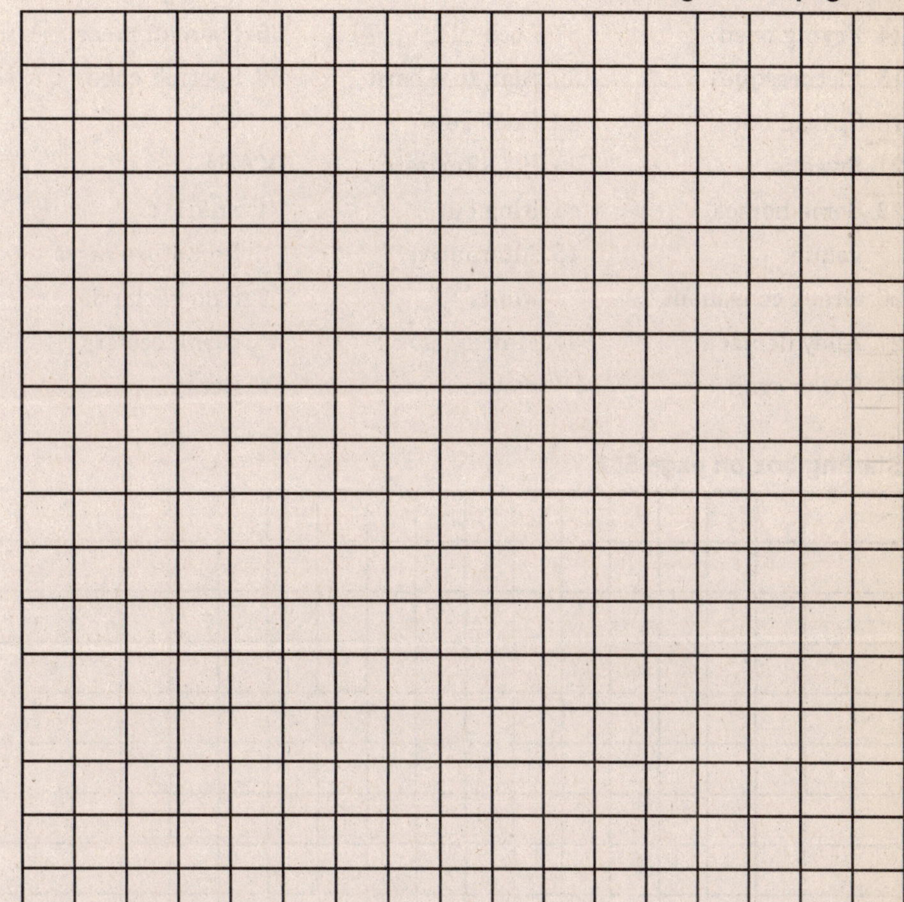

Blockbuilders

PUZZLE 512

Fit the letter blocks into the diagram to spell out the name of a famous person.

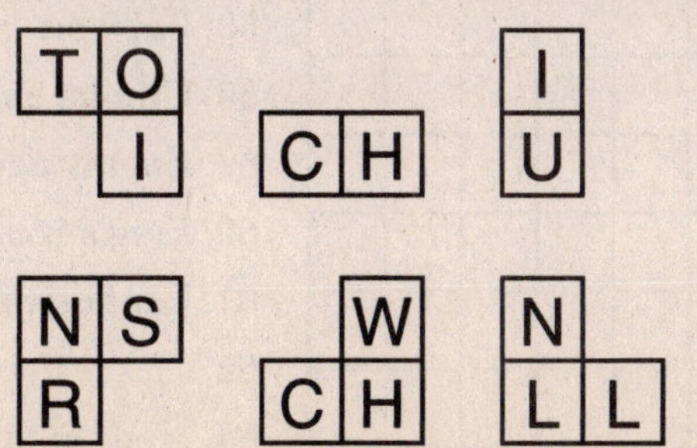

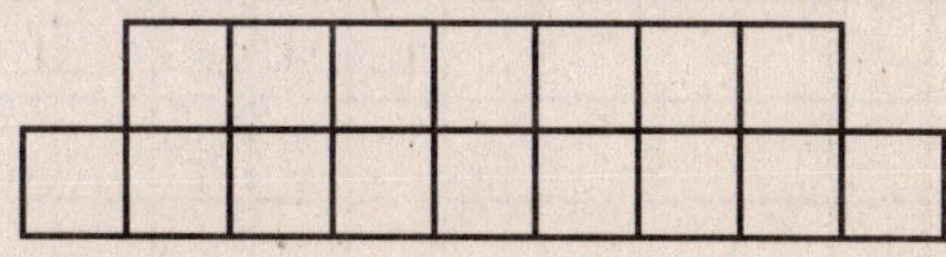

PUZZLE 513

ACROSS

1. Colloid
4. Surmise
6. Furloughs
10. Railroad rail
11. Twig
13. Morse-code click
14. Frying need
15. Picturesque
18. Spread out
21. Sweetie
22. Some horses' venue
26. Greek consonant
27. Alley denizen
28. Shine again
29. Clinging vine
31. Arid
32. Eternally, poetically
33. Hera's mate
35. Select
36. Certain sib
37. Loch ____
39. Ajar, to a bard
42. Conforms
43. It's after zeta
44. Ring out
46. Alternative words
47. Man ____ mouse
49. Japanese entree
51. Reel holder
52. Flower organ
54. Shuns
56. Still, in verse
57. Rural hotel
58. Anxious feeling
61. ____ up (enlightened)
63. Bank patron
65. Football measures
66. Spotted cube

DOWN

1. Snarl
2. Immature newt
3. Hilo garlands
4. Drink coolers
5. Decay
6. Fruitless
7. Lively
8. Cold and damp
9. Surgical souvenir
10. Delightful region
12. Wood knot
15. Infield position
16. Show up
17. Gas-guzzler
18. Coltrane's ax
19. Smart kid
20. Affectionate parrots
23. Third in a series
24. Wool-giving mama
25. Strife
27. Wigwam's kin
30. Tentlike dwellings
31. Male scion
34. Mayday letters
38. Asian wrap
39. Electrical unit
40. Apple seed
41. Cassowary's cousin
42. Caterer's concern
44. Animation unit
45. Eventful time
48. Befuddled
49. Trace of color
50. Dispatch boat
51. Husk
53. Baby-sit
55. Unique chap
59. Enemy agent
60. Frog's relative
61. Expansive
62. ____ a living!
64. Madras mister

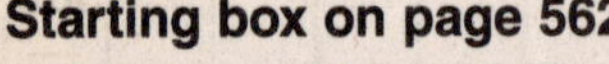
Starting box on page 562

PUZZLE 514

ACROSS

1. Chest muscles, informally
5. Arrests
9. Cleo's biter
12. Indian territory
13. Concept
14. Capture
16. Made from plants
17. Capricorn
18. Made amends
19. Trouble
20. Fossil fuel
21. Drive-____
22. Chevy Chase film
25. Beard of grass
26. Gala
27. Banyan, e.g.
28. Concurs
30. Pens
32. Mexicali Mrs.
34. Born as
35. English surgeon
37. Sob
40. Portent
42. Perm place
43. Pump, e.g.
44. Mastered
45. Meal tidbit
46. Diving bird
47. A Gershwin
48. Complain
51. Yard section
52. Wire measures
54. Cereal grain
55. Sword fight
56. Withhold
57. Schemes
59. Stags
60. Stroll
61. Forest denizen
62. Heed
64. Annexes
65. Proprietor
68. Shuttle org.
69. Sci. class
70. Command to the troops
71. Former fast flyer
72. Steaming
75. More current
77. Geronimo, e.g.
79. Agitate
82. Peel
83. French resort city
85. Judge's milieu
88. Withered
89. Bar none
90. Bank-acct. deposit
91. Thunder
92. Confront
93. Taste
95. Playing marble
96. Dash
97. Grunt
98. Curvy turn
99. Sicilian peak
100. Kett of comics

DOWN

1. ____ annum
2. Pasta shape
3. Unit in a retail empire
4. Window ledge
5. Worker's education alternative
6. Worship
7. Suitor
8. Convened
9. Battery poles
10. Carpenter's tool
11. Quarry
12. Singer Shannon
14. Earp's badge
15. Begley and Asner
16. Backpack
18. Emote
19. Lot unit
21. Golf gizmo
23. Closet items
24. Schedule
25. Nepal's locale
26. Conifer
29. Chicago trains
31. Camp abode
33. ____ rule
36. Sow chow
38. Cheer
39. Itch
41. Coldly
43. ____ gin
48. Gunk
49. Skate
50. Part of TGIF
51. Bonds
52. Pittsburgh facility
53. Readies for printing
55. Candidate, at times
56. Famed surrealist
57. Source of electricity
58. Ms. Horne
59. Osaka's island
60. Spider's net
61. Love excessively
63. Orange tuber
66. Jacob's twin
67. Agt.
70. Reverence
71. Glasgow guy
73. Scents
74. Misgivings
76. Before, before
78. Teen's bane
80. Wight or Skye
81. Grant's foe
82. Pie nut
84. Mete
86. Refrain start
87. Tremendous
88. Tar
89. Church area
90. Addamses' cousin
92. Rate
94. Sky Altar

Starting box on page 562

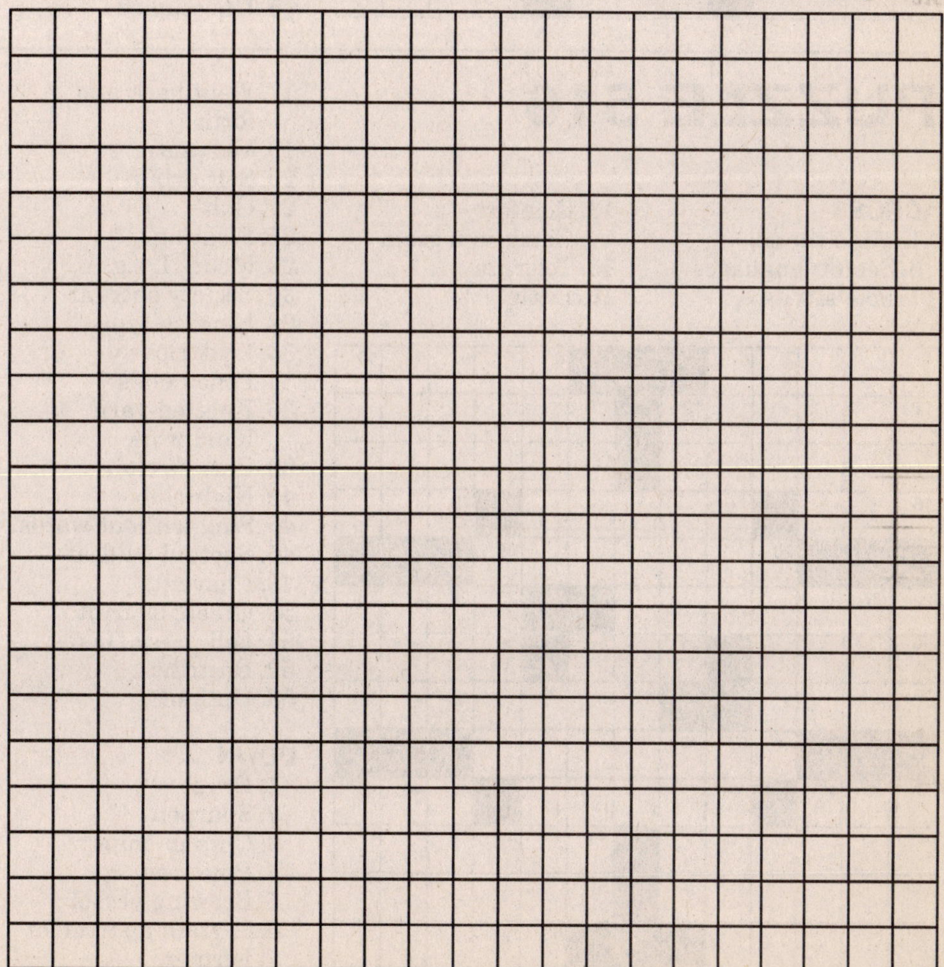

PUZZLE 515

ACROSS
1. Slice off
5. Subside
8. Outrages
12. Effigy
13. Disfigure
14. Remove from print
15. Appearance
16. Expert, for short
17. Pack away
18. Noah's craft
19. Sirloin, e.g.
21. Act like
22. Scrappy
24. Festively arrayed
26. Darling
27. Lower
28. Fund
30. Remit in advance
32. Lyre's cousin
35. Fixed beforehand
36. Terrific
38. Sought office
39. Daybreak
41. Rush
42. Wise about
44. Totally awesome!
45. Chinese dynasty
46. Wound memento
47. 19th letter
48. Whale of a movie
49. Squiggly swimmers
50. Utter
51. Existed

DOWN
1. Rice dish
2. Loved
3. Newcomer
4. Forest animal
5. Unoccupied
6. Nude
7. Widen
8. Freud's concerns
9. Second shooting
10. Gretna Green groom?
11. Fastened with thread
19. Murray/Ramis film
20. Hamburger topping
23. Burglars' targets
25. Inexpensive
27. Anti's answer
29. Temperaments
30. Strut
31. Tenant's residence
33. Employ again
34. Heir to the throne
35. Ordinary language
36. Frothy
37. Inaugurated
40. Spaceflight agcy.
43. Hospital surg. areas
45. Throng

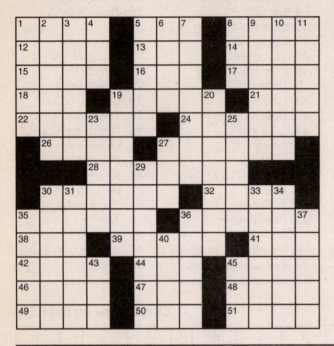

PUZZLE 516

ACROSS
1. Mine tunnel
6. Secret languages
11. Polo steeds
13. Comfort
14. Catch in a scam
15. Tolerate
16. Little
17. Went back and forth
19. Vagrant
20. Soft drink
22. Gab
25. Floating
29. Model T, e.g.
30. Society entrant
32. Herring type
33. Look closely
34. Pencil ends
36. Knotted-yarn handiwork
39. Casey's club
42. Nightclub
43. Sing without words
46. Spotted wildcat
48. I have it!
50. Green, as fruit
51. Fell in icy flakes
52. Doctrine
53. Uptight

DOWN
1. Erupt
2. Sharpen
3. Chip in chips
4. Pine tree
5. Brewing vessel
6. Certain apartment
7. Former
8. Paint
9. Hosiery shade
10. Pretend to be
12. Shoveled
13. Dribble
18. Occupations
20. Blizzard
21. Outdated
22. Headwear
23. Color tone
24. Dined
26. That girl
27. Listening organ
28. Product pitches
31. Brackets
35. Sum
37. Pass into law
38. Quote
39. Boxing match
40. Skin problem
41. Gull-like bird
43. Rough-cut
44. Lanai music-makers
45. Fashioned
47. Let sleeping dogs ____
49. Salmon beginnings

PUZZLE 517

• DOUBLE-TALK •

ACROSS

1. ____ and gown
4. "Evening Shade" role
7. Hooray, in Spain
8. Windy mo.
9. Castle ditch
11. "What's My ____?"
12. Hook's assistant
14. Fruit drink
16. Ginger cookie
19. ____-or-miss
20. Monotonous hum
22. "Rock of ____"
24. Painter's stand
27. Soon
29. Rose essence
32. Mr. Baba
33. Lessen
35. Indonesian island
37. Period of note
38. Tiny amount
39. ____ carte
40. Frying vessel
41. Diaper fastener
42. Coral barriers
44. "La ____" (Lou Diamond Phillips film)
46. Gamble
47. Vote of no
48. Ernie and Gomer
50. Keats, for one
52. Las' followers
53. Yank's foe
55. One ____ million
56. Afternoon brew
58. ____ was saying
59. Heavy hammer
61. Sick as ____
62. House addition
63. Spokes
65. Unnamed person
69. Roomy
71. Actress Joyce
73. Trembled
74. Actress Farrow
75. Saved
77. Hockey-idol Bobby ____
78. Sharpen
79. Breezy
81. "____ Over Miami"
83. Map abbr.
84. Inclined
85. ____ good to be true
86. Summer shirt

DOWN

1. Halley's ____
2. ____ vera
3. Jacket or pod
4. Pierre's pal
5. Moving vehicles
6. Sports locale
10. Scarlett's home
11. Make a loan
12. That girl
13. Over a long distance
15. Comic Rickles
17. Repeatedly
18. Stroke
20. Color
21. ____ and flow
23. Gradually
24. Have a snack
25. Winged
26. Next to each other
27. Young men's org.
28. Jabber
30. Formal solo
31. Raced
34. Capone and Jolson
36. Bio class
43. Long, skinny fish
45. ____ tai (cocktail)
48. Famous tower's site
49. "The Old Man and the ____"
50. Yoko ____
51. Tattle
52. Sailor
54. Student's transport
55. Knot-tying words
57. Ginger ____
60. ____ Angeles
61. Query
64. Kind
66. Nautical greeting
67. Neither's companion
68. Frosh's home
70. Actress West
72. Separated
74. ____ Carlo
76. A Jackson brother
78. "____ and Glory"
80. Vintage car
82. Mare's morsel

PUZZLE 518

ACROSS

1. Hero shop
5. White heron
10. Muscle strain
14. Desktop image
15. Trumpet blast
16. Donkey sound
17. Not open
18. British peer
19. Drill
20. Encrypted
22. Cherry-colored
23. Fancy pitcher
24. Heavy twine
26. See
29. Wild pony
32. Quicken
36. Hilo garlands
37. Indication
41. Is, pluralized
42. Unwell
43. Roads
44. Like sashimi
45. Baked dessert
46. Egg entree
47. Party giver
48. Discord
50. Makes jubilant
52. Confessed
54. Say the rosary
55. Fruity drinks
58. Dentist's org.
60. Actress Hilary ____
64. Maui cookout
65. Witch's spell
67. Steam appliance
68. Lay concrete on
69. Striped stone
70. Sunday drive
71. Snow glider
72. Lead or zinc
73. Comfort

DOWN

1. Plate
2. Canyon's answer
3. Deafening
4. Hospital employees
5. Recede
6. Fierce look
7. Burger order
8. Wear away
9. X, to some
10. Monasteries
11. Black bird
12. Bunny's kin
13. Ogler
21. Sneezy's roommate
25. Letter carriers
27. Fall to pieces
28. Bosom buddies
29. Glitches
30. Ignited again
31. Edmonton skater
33. Mystical card
34. Remove remarks
35. Small amphibians
38. Great anger
39. Hair goo
40. Formerly called
43. Settee
47. Out of control
49. Distributed
51. Spanish article
53. Estimate
54. Ziti, e.g.
55. Swiss mountains
56. Twofold
57. Edge of a roof
59. Dang!
61. Opera tune
62. Dozes
63. On bended ____
65. Type of shaft
66. Long fish

1	2	3	4	■	5	6	7	8	9	■	10	11	12	13
14				■	15					■	16			
17				■	18					■	19			
20				21	■	22			■	■	23			
■	■	■	24		25		■	26	27	28		■	■	■
29	30	31				■	■	■	32			33	34	35
36				■	37	38	39	40			■	41		
42			■	43							■	44		
45			■	46						■	47			
48			49			■	■	■	50	51				
■	■	■	52			53	■	54				■	■	■
55	56	57		■	■	58	59		■	60		61	62	63
64				■	65				66	■	67			
68				■	69					■	70			
71				■	72					■	73			

PUZZLE 519

Tie-In

Place a 3-letter word on the dashes to complete a word on the left and to begin another word on the right. For example, HEN between EART and NA would complete EARTHEN and begin HENNA.

BI __ __ __ ATA

SU __ __ __ IOD

TRAN __ __ __ UATE

NIM __ __ __ TER

AN __ __ __ KLE

MAN __ __ __ NDUM

OBT __ __ __ FUL

FISH __ __ __ TLE

SUN __ __ __ ERAL

BES __ __ __ ARD

PUZZLE 520

ACROSS

1. Flatfish
5. As well
9. Several
13. Gamete
14. Brief brawl
16. Ardent
17. Bargained
19. Extend credit
20. Film's Garbo
21. Guard
22. Black, as pen fluid
23. Flow back
25. Bow freshener
27. College treasurer
30. Costly
33. Solar body
34. Narrate
38. Husky
40. ____-tac-toe
41. Comic Ray and others
42. "Scent ____ Woman"
43. Pipe joint
44. Response
45. Sickly
46. College official
48. Skirmish
51. Hurricane, e.g.
55. Cul-de-____
56. Contract
59. Droplet
61. Measure of gold
65. Killer whale
66. Make penniless
68. Huckleberry ____
69. Chip dip
70. Crate
71. Sock parts
72. Lemon skin
73. This, in Toledo

DOWN

1. Melody
2. Finished
3. Racing sled
4. Ham
5. Greek letter
6. Petal
7. Articulate
8. Exec's clerk
9. Eyewash solution
10. Cook's prop
11. Luxury fur
12. Singer Arnold
15. Bookie's quote
18. Labels
24. Red ____ (Snoopy's foe)
26. The ____ of March
27. Construct
28. Aunt's mate
29. Deep-sleep times
31. Seething
32. Firearm
33. Sault ____ Marie
35. Regulation
36. Dill herb
37. Doughnut shape
39. Maiden
41. Holler
47. Tilted
49. Benefit
50. Hard to find
52. Kimono sashes
53. Chart again
54. Sap producer
56. Tip, as a cap
57. Well-known canal
58. Pimples
60. Potion portion
62. Inlets
63. Atdt.
64. Quaker word
67. Actor Kilmer

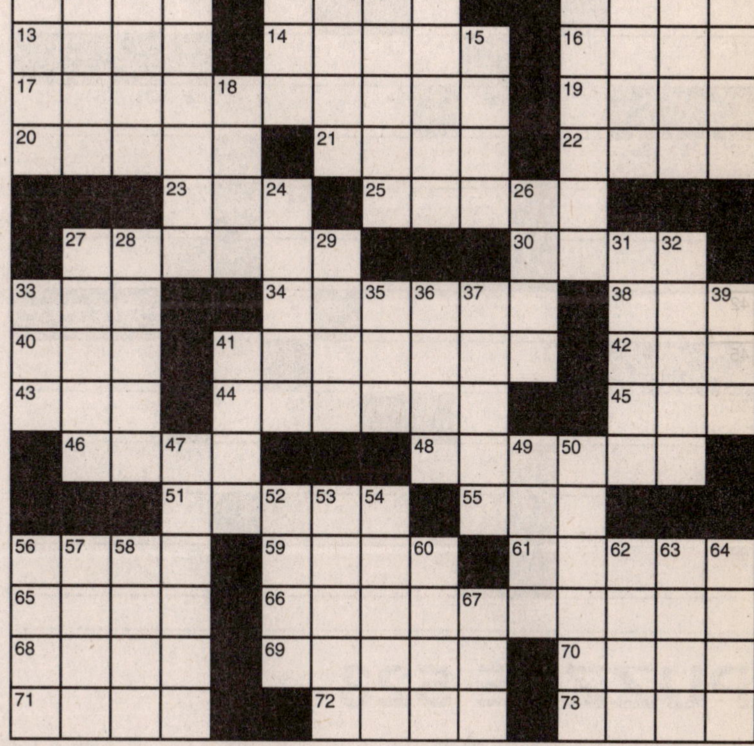

Rapid Reader PUZZLE 521

Eleven 5-letter words appear backward in these lines of letters. Can you find them all in four minutes or less? Underline each word as you find it, as we have done with the first word, BRAVE.

H T R O W E R I V E R C E V A R B U L B

Y G R I L L E C X E D N I C O N W O R C

D I U Q K C I L F E M U S I C I M S O C

T O B O R L E I P S P E S A H C N I H T

I N G N I W S L A Y R P S V O O L G I R

PUZZLE 522

ACROSS
1. Has to
5. Basilica recess
9. Knock down
13. Poker beginning
14. Manhandles
16. Arab bigwig
17. Slimmest
19. Electrical units, shortly
20. Can metal
21. Pen filler
22. Nearly
24. Curbs
26. Lofty abode
29. Opera division
31. Belittle
36. Breathe hard
39. Pearly gem
41. Zenith
42. "Aida" feature
43. Desert havens
45. Coloring
46. Depend
47. Unclothed
48. Concludes
49. Rope-dancer
52. Armed clash
54. Caught congers
56. Church song
60. Captured
64. Before, to Keats
66. Regret bitterly
67. Land amid water
68. Youthful
72. Bopper
73. Gaucho's tool
74. A single time
75. Cuts lumber
76. Alum
77. Slangy refusals

DOWN
1. Spars
2. Dark
3. Shorthand pro
4. Decimal base
5. So be it!
6. Heavy jacket
7. Take to court
8. City railroads
9. Quantity of paper
10. Bullets, briefly
11. Darts
12. Formerly, formerly
15. Solemn
18. Record
23. Hawaiian keepsake
25. Tropical fruit
27. Manuscript smudge
28. Made angry
30. Moreover
32. Provides food for
33. Atop
34. Loan
35. Alimony payers
36. Clothes
37. District
38. Window bottom
40. Door part
44. Ply the needle
50. Named at birth
51. Fragrant tree
53. Orangutans, e.g.
55. River-mouth plain
57. Sports complex
58. Noonday meal
59. Doles
60. Baby bugs
61. Offshore
62. Huffed and puffed
63. Kingsley and Vereen
65. Decipher
69. Excavate
70. Rowing blade
71. Pro and ____

PUZZLE 523

Sunrays

Form 4-letter words using only the nine letters in the center of the diagram. Do not repeat a letter within a word. Place your words into the rays of the diagram so that no two words that are next to each other share a letter.

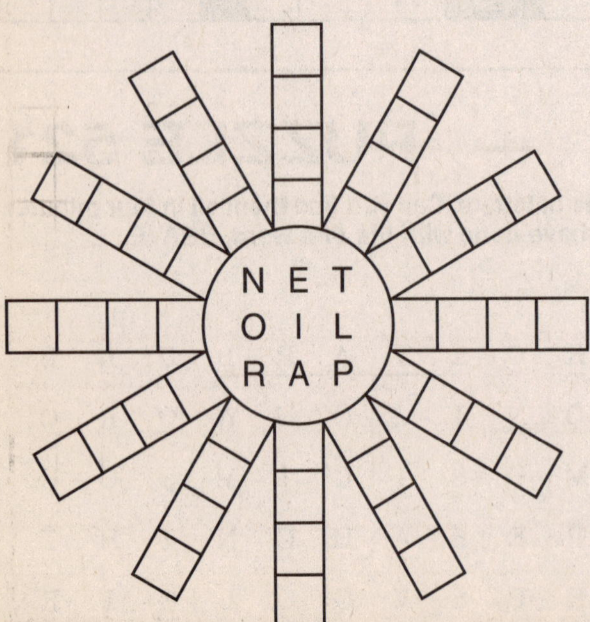

BRICK BY BRICK

PUZZLE 524

Rearrange this stack of bricks to form a crossword puzzle. The clues will help you fit the bricks into their correct places. Row 1 has been filled in for you. Use the bricks to fill in the remaining spaces.

ACROSS

1. Mongrel
   Flat-topped hills
   Grayish brown
2. Eastern title
   Salt's halt
   Put in
3. Thickness
   Slender snake
   Layers
4. Ocular cover
   Facilitate
   Kick stand?
5. Freshly
   Dad
6. Kismet
   Couples
   Upsilon's follower
7. Audacity
   Corridors
8. Given by mouth
   Spicy fare
   Cry mournfully
9. Pepsin, e.g.
   Baloney
10. Make blue?
    Series ending
    Bump into
11. Switch
    College group
12. Shakespeare's luck
    Head
    Phony
13. Crazies
    Influence
    It'll never fly
14. Public
    Kingdom's value?
    Flagstick
15. Grouchy
    Mount
    Insidious

DOWN

1. Matador's lure
   Nailed on a slant
   Destiny
2. Unsightly
   Frondlike
   Flung
3. Last name in comedy
   Flabbergast
   Deck tops?
4. Recently
   Good loser
5. Sailor
   Tend a lawn
   Porker's pad
6. Skirt
   Block party?
7. Baglike part
   Accompanying
   Geologic divisions
8. Floating
   Hitching
   Splotch
9. Narrow band
   Veg out
   Vein yield
10. Realm
    Show thriftiness
11. Pirate's stick
    Inflation letters
    Stung
12. Redacts
    Candy
13. ____ fixe
    Flat surface
    Band boosters
14. "Sommersby" star
    Bad job?
    Drudge
15. Both Begleys
    Key
    Goofy

BRICKS

E R S U T ■	■ H A L O C	R T ■ T Y ■	■ O M S W A	I T E T Y ■
E G A P ■ F	T E ■ E R I	■ F A T E M	P I N S L Y	■ M E R A T
L I D A N E	P ■ N O S ■	O V E T E S	H I L ■ N O	H O R S T E
P H I L E S	E E ■ ■ ■ ■	■ A D ■ T I	S E ■ E D ■	L ■ C Y M E
M S ■ A I S	■ A V ■ R A	A T Z M O A	O B ■ C L O	O R A E N Z
A I L N S E	D ■ T O P S	D E D E R S	I ■ W N S E	E T ■ ■ ■ ■
E Y E ■ ■ ■	D Y E ■ ■ ■	A G A P L Y	■ A I W ■ P	A S T C E R

DIAGRAM

	1	2	3	4	5	6	7	8	9	10	11	12	13	14	15
1	C	U	R	■	M	E	S	A	S	■	B	E	I	G	E
2															
3															
4															
5															
6															
7															
8															
9															
10															
11															
12															
13															
14															
15															

PUZZLE 525

ACROSS

1. Calendar entry
5. Search over
10. Glacier piece, shortly
14. Large wading bird
15. Mount
16. Not shut
17. Let off steam
18. Host
19. Opera singer
20. Threshold
21. More than prompt
23. Mutt
24. Arab chief
27. Artist's prop
29. Universal
32. Boxers do it
34. Deal a blow
35. Hoister
38. Tool boxes
42. Bitter brew
43. Removed
45. Peace officer
46. Write with a keyboard
48. Midday nap
49. "___ American Cousin"
50. Power unit
52. Score number
54. Exposes
57. Talking bird
58. Long, long ___
59. Slip away from
63. Youngsters
67. Near
69. Make a speech
71. Model
72. Kind of adhesive
73. Monsters
74. Forbidden thing
75. Appear
76. Leans
77. Cultivated

DOWN

1. Disreputable bar
2. Sleeping
3. Ringing sound
4. Praise
5. Feminine pronoun
6. Promising person
7. Killer whale
8. Client
9. Folk dance
10. Physique, for short
11. Long poems
12. Variety show
13. Twist
22. Indeed!
25. Bland
26. Coldest
28. Noah's transport
29. Chew the fat
30. Greasy
31. Staircase part
32. Disappears, as the sun
33. Lovely
36. Dart
37. Summer shirt
39. Saintly picture
40. Publicize
41. Nimble
44. Sunrise
47. Fleecy mother
51. Wall Street organization: abbr.
53. Snacking
54. Pounds
55. Limber
56. Scoundrel
57. Allotted
60. Winnings
61. Push along
62. Mend with stitches
64. Perfume
65. Sound pitch
66. Sluggish
68. Alter a skirt
70. Dangerous curve

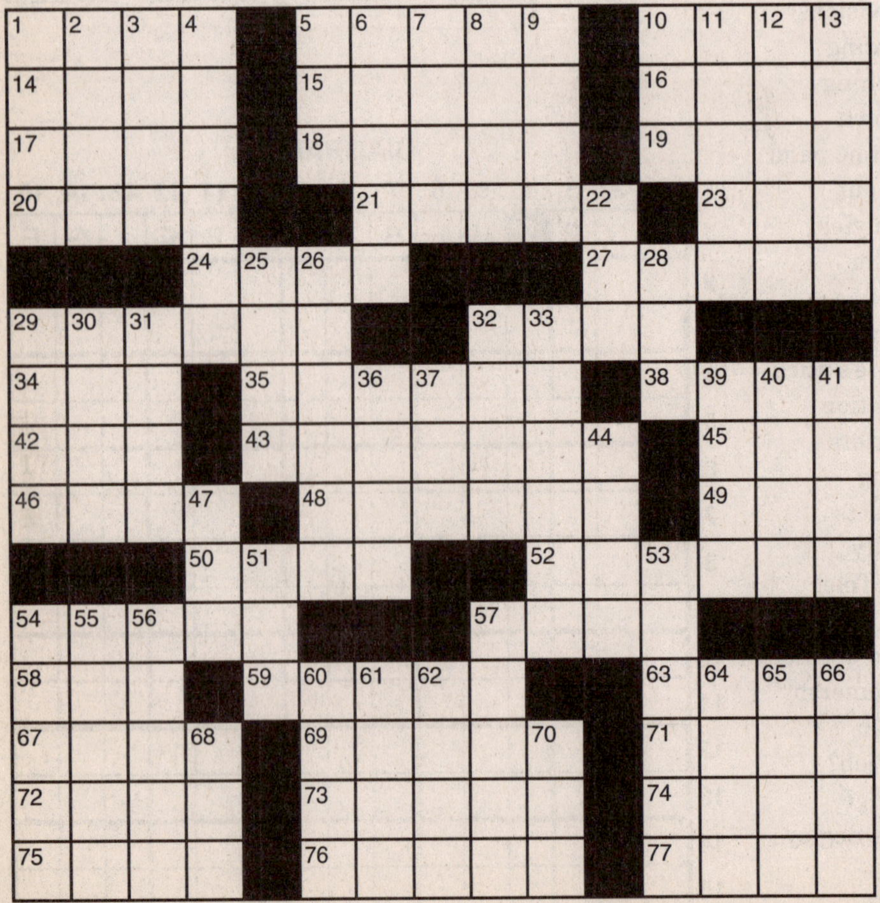

PUZZLE 526

ACROSS

1. Slippery
4. Fathers
9. ". . . maids all in ___"
13. Miner's lode
14. Subtract
15. Choir wear
16. Commandment word
17. Presser
18. Anchor
19. Pigs
21. Fan
23. Sea mammal
27. ___ conditioner
28. Eye feature
31. Historic age
32. Stashes
35. Underscore
36. They don't need dress codes
38. ___ ringer
40. Chop
41. Needle's cousin
42. In times past
43. Seven-card ___
45. RBIs, e.g.
47. Alum
48. Stainless ___
50. Letter after ess
51. Too
52. Cry of contempt
53. Build
55. Canopies
59. Long-legged bird
63. Remain
64. Each
68. Lumberjack's tool
69. Certain parasites
70. ___-minded
71. Comprehend
72. Toboggan
73. Ship section
74. Printers' measures

DOWN

1. Charged particles
2. Brag
3. Sherpa sighting
4. ___ se
5. Confusion
6. Wordplay
7. Scored a hole in one
8. Stripes
9. With a protective covering
10. Ginseng, e.g.
11. Certain woodwind
12. "You ___ Meant for Me"
14. Girth control
20. Organ of smell
22. Scramble (for)
24. Half of twenty
25. Explode, like Etna
26. Glow
28. Sicknesses
29. Mob scenes
30. Data
33. Oyster's prize
34. Epics
37. Jot down
39. Extinct bird
44. Opposite of credited
45. Mottoes
46. Understand
47. Fence door
49. Eternity
54. ___ the fat
55. Boring tools
56. Sob
57. Friendly
58. Quarrel
60. Seethe
61. Yoke of ___
62. Fishermen's tools
65. Great fury
66. Prove human
67. Cheat

1	2	3	■	■	4	5	6	7	8	■	9	10	11	12
13			■	14						■	15			
16			■	17						■	18			
19			20		■	■	■	21		22				
■	■	■	23		24	25	26	■	27			■	■	■
28	29	30		■	31			■	32			33	34	■
35				■	36			37		■	38			39
40			■	■	■	41			■	■	■	42		
43			44	■	45				46	■	47			
■	48			49		■	50			■	51			
■	■	■	52			■	53			54		■	■	■
55	56	57				58	■	■	■	59		60	61	62
63				■	64		65	66	67		■	68		
69				■	70						■	71		
72				■	73					■	■	74		

PUZZLE 527

ACROSS

1. Shoe grouping
5. Outside pitch
9. Locates
14. Summit
15. Place
16. Broken
17. Agts.
18. Certain exam
19. Foolish
20. Mistakes
22. Couple
24. Wallop
25. Is obligated to
26. Interfere
28. Heidi's peak
30. Angler's catch
32. Geese formation
33. Scoundrel
36. Complaint
38. Longish skirt
40. Conscious
42. White heron
44. Disturb
45. Craze
46. Mosaic-maker
47. Inspires with fear
49. RBI, e.g.
50. Pig's home
51. Personal
53. Grab
55. Etna's output
56. Summer quaff
57. Two-masted vessel
59. Ship's bottom
62. Name
65. Fools
68. Merger
70. Map out
72. Doubtless
73. Shorthand pro
74. Small dent
75. Type of sword
76. Watered
77. Chooses
78. Smell nasty

DOWN

1. Trim
2. Scorer on a serve
3. Poorly
4. Plant again
5. Bloom
6. Make known
7. Soft metal
8. Humdinger
9. Enjoy Stowe
10. Purple flower
11. Whitish gem
12. Albacore, e.g.
13. Footfall
21. Family rm.
23. Unlock, in poems
27. Paper amount
28. Assists a felon
29. Legal
31. Parlor piece
32. Fox's mate
33. Certain melon
34. Opera highlights
35. "___ Becomes Her"
37. Charge
39. Morning dampness
41. Had been
43. Stomped on
48. Proverbs
52. Combine
54. Corrupt
56. "Home ___"
58. More knowing
59. Quiet down
60. Till
61. Reclines
63. Hairstyle
64. Radar indicator
66. Poplar, e.g.
67. Search for
69. Beckon
71. Aardvark's prey

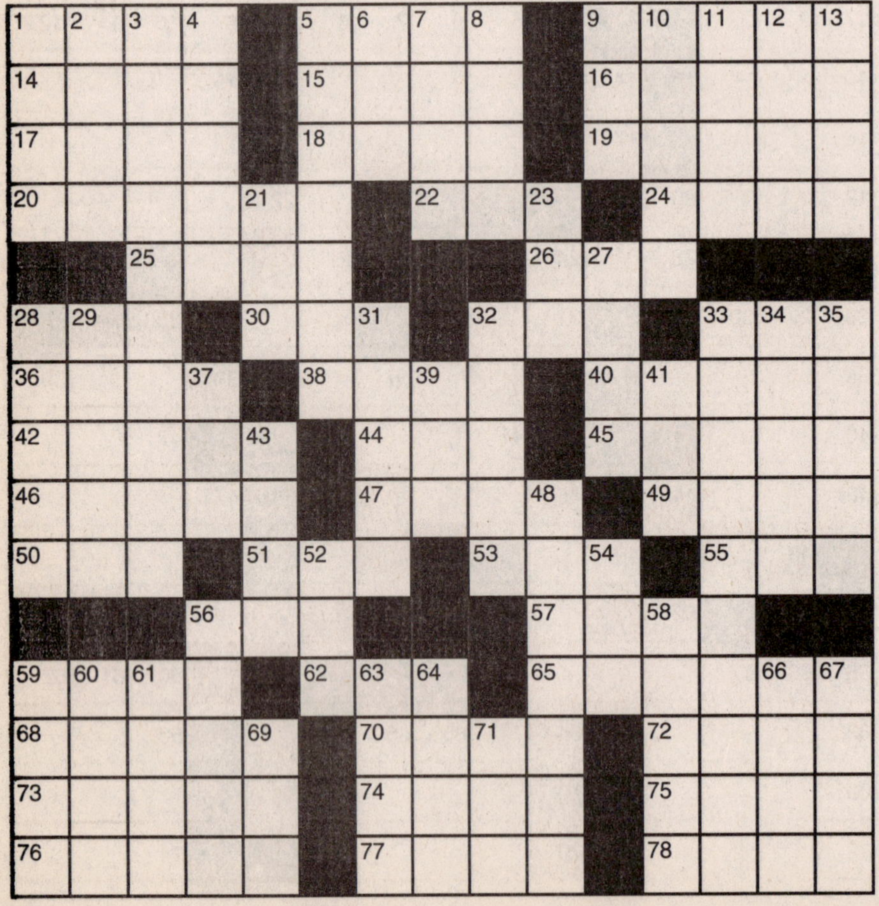

PUZZLE 528

ACROSS

1. Pinna part
5. Opposer
9. Long cut
14. Big monkeys
15. Beef, e.g.
16. Television sound
17. Little bits
18. Has title to
19. Knot
20. High rollers?
21. Beer container
22. Hassled
23. Protector
26. Pajama topper
28. Poetic twilights
29. Modifies
32. Freud topic
34. "The ___ Cometh"
35. Scream
36. Lawn moisture
39. Mako's milieu
40. Wished for
42. Lime drink
43. Total
44. Metallic rocks
45. Alteration
47. Critic's pick?
48. Put a label on
49. Cheery
53. PBS science show
56. Game prop
57. Going by bus
59. The total amount
61. Scamper
64. ___ and beyond
65. Berg
66. Tiger's warning?
67. Nice hat
68. Finger jewelry
69. Winter Olympics event
70. Tundra vehicles
71. Some poems
72. Computer operator

DOWN

1. Past curfew
2. Pearly stone
3. Comforter
4. Snaky letter
5. Frenzied
6. More up-to-date
7. Latin dance
8. "___ My Party"
9. Tale
10. Sudden forward thrust
11. Saying
12. Temptress
13. Clinches
22. Slight
24. Direct at a target
25. Church official
27. Red qualifier
29. Traveler's permit
30. Mastered
31. Sheet music?
33. Dated
35. Positive answer
36. Perilous
37. On ___ (tense)
38. Obnoxious plant
41. President's no
46. Important time
49. Clutches
50. Slander
51. Cherish
52. Submerged
54. Legitimate
55. Isolated
58. Fishing tools
60. Chair supports
62. Beg
63. ___-do-well
65. Certain do
66. Winter shot

1	2	3	4	■	5	6	7	8	■	9	10	11	12	13
14				■	15				■	16				
17				■	18				■	19				
20			■	■	21			■	22					
■	■	23	24	25	■	26		27		■	28			
29	30				31	■	■	32		33	■	■	■	■
34						■	35				■	36	37	38
39			■	40		41					■	42		
43			■	44				■	45		46			
■	■	■	■	47			■	■	48					
49	50	51	52	■	53		54	55	■	56			■	■
57				58		■	59		60	■	■	61	62	63
64					■	65				■	66			
67					■	68				■	69			
70					■	71				■	72			

PUZZLE 529

ACROSS

1. Cave sound
5. Tool housing
9. Jewel weight
14. Puff
15. Metric measure
16. Demean
17. Abundant
19. Prevent
20. Shopping binge
21. Not moving
23. Celtics or Hawks
24. Took flight
26. Downspout feeders
28. Picnic carrier
31. Equipment
32. Practice
35. Tease
36. Incline
38. Neither sold nor given
40. Caper
42. Believe it or ___!
44. Throw
45. In a profound way
47. Baby beagle
49. Rich source of ore
50. Make a mistake
51. Ump's call
53. Starts
55. Geographer's volume
57. A ___ in a poke
58. Rooster's feature
61. Imprint with acid
63. Irritates greatly
67. Sun-dried brick
69. Poisonous mushroom
71. Travels
72. Flow slowly
73. Wise about
74. Quarries
75. Untie
76. Musical pause

DOWN

1. ___ and flows
2. Dull sound
3. Clock cycle
4. Possession
5. Alpine slider
6. 45 player
7. Avoid capture
8. 100 pennies
9. Boor
10. Assists
11. Charge
12. On the ocean
13. Cycle
18. Tropical wood
22. Wickedness
25. Butterfly catcher's need
27. Personality parts
28. Silly mistake
29. Type of flower
30. Small container
32. Joining
33. Passes along
34. "The Razor's ___"
35. Green mineral
37. Father
39. Swamp dweller
41. Thicken
43. Old ship
46. ___ log
48. Energy
52. Skin design
54. Jazz bookings
55. Certain convent
56. Reporter's tidbit
58. Criticize
59. Garlic feature
60. Chess action
62. Fog
64. Solo
65. Loads
66. Coin taker
68. 19th letter
70. Informal room

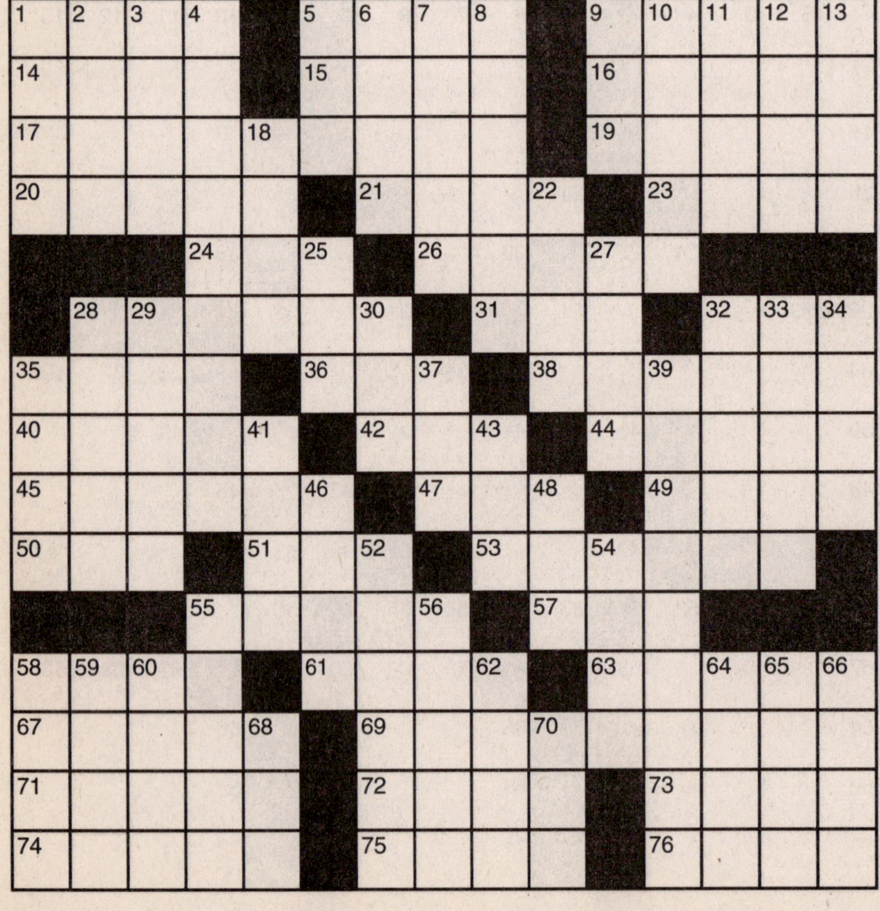

PUZZLE 530

ACROSS

1. Angels' hats
6. Chemists' lairs
10. Soften
14. Flee to marry
15. Nimbus
16. Yow!
17. Playing marble
18. Dilemma
19. Cheerful club?
20. Took flight
21. Jingle
23. Cook in an oven
24. ___ room (family room)
25. 18-wheeler
27. Safari helper
30. Leakey site
31. By way of
34. Egg on
35. Failure
37. Adoring
39. Clothing
41. Grovel
43. Wash off
44. Ogled
46. Crumple
48. Stare
49. Do arithmetic
50. Feel poorly
52. Minimum
54. Cocky
56. Mister
57. Cease, to a sailor
61. Places to pierce
63. Share of profits
66. Electrify
67. Frozen mass
68. Domicile
70. Opposed to aweather
71. Remains
72. Dined
73. Words of assent
74. Certain poems
75. Gown or frock

DOWN

1. Find out
2. Aquatic plant
3. Advance money
4. Settle upon
5. Sower
6. Ultimate
7. Cousins' moms
8. Heehawed
9. Buckle
10. Diner directive
11. Type of hoop
12. Crackerjacks
13. Hone
22. Decorated
23. Harshness
24. Airport device
26. Diameter measure
27. Wearied
28. Having hearing organs
29. Massage
31. Trailing plants
32. Map feature
33. Golden ___ (retiree)
34. Ritzy business
36. Dawn droplets
38. Asp
40. It also rises
42. Sal, e.g.
45. Darken
47. Quantity
51. Soothed
53. Hoped
55. Gander's mate
57. Not here
58. Horrid
59. Territory
60. Watches
62. Plays the horses
63. Like a button
64. Applications
65. Wallet items
67. To and ___
69. Thole insert

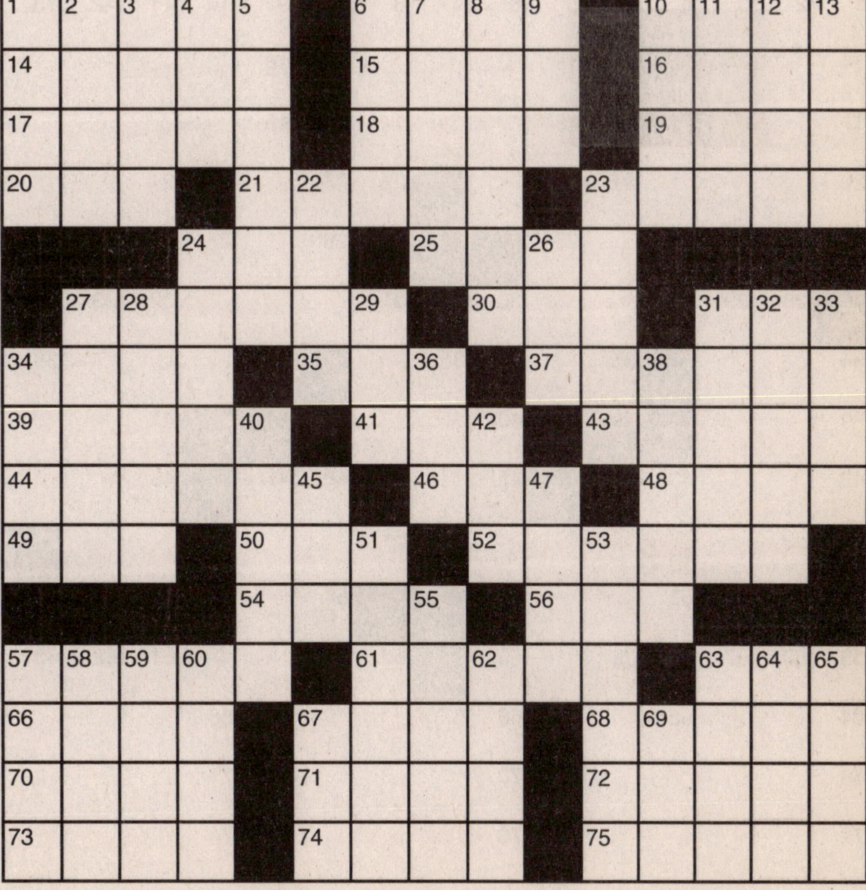

PUZZLE 531

ACROSS

1. Burn
5. Dozes off
9. Goblet
14. Poor excuse
15. October gem
16. R2D2, e.g.
17. Eager
18. Kill, as a bill
19. Mistreat
20. Interfered
22. Summer shade
24. Kid's spinner
25. Moray, e.g.
26. Right this minute
28. Washington body
31. Loafers
34. Guy's date
35. Clothing fabric
37. Conform
39. Get older
40. Country hotel
41. Fawn's ma
42. Treaties
45. Wee
48. Electrified particle
49. Marble figure
51. Logic
53. Vitality
54. Right you ___!
55. Not fore
58. Mule's kin
60. Directed
64. Assert
66. Salary
68. Similar
69. Therefore
70. Woes
71. Like
72. Garden tool
73. Gather
74. Sprinkles

DOWN

1. Shut loudly
2. Roofline detail
3. Surrounded by
4. Blush
5. Newness
6. Impersonated
7. Touch
8. Mailbox opening
9. Breakfast food
10. High tennis shot
11. Border on
12. All right
13. Degree
21. Not fat
23. Furthermore
27. Marry
28. Tales
29. Vote into office
30. Gentry
31. Private
32. Ham operator's item
33. Eating utensil
34. Crack
36. Dollar
38. Bo Derek's number
43. Knock lightly
44. Soft-shell clam
46. Closest
47. House surroundings
50. Elevator directions
52. Teetertotter
55. Be sore
56. Bolted
57. Sharp flavor
59. Do the breaststroke
60. Make goo-goo eyes at
61. Gather, as leaves
62. Give out
63. Home rooms
65. Freezer accumulation
67. Ginger ___

THREE-D CROSSWORD

PUZZLE 532

Here's a crossword with a third dimension! The direction in which you enter the Across and Down answers depends upon the face of the cube. As you solve this puzzle, you'll see that some of the answers from one face continue on another face of the cube.

ACROSS

1. In what way
4. More difficult
7. Ms. Gardner
8. Tropical lizard
9. Marry
10. Required
11. Work dough
13. Barracks
16. Lima's country
19. Singer Lily ___
20. Bounded section
21. MacGraw and namesakes
22. Fibber
23. Actor Eastwood
24. June honoree
25. Trailer truck
26. Author Hermann ___
27. Chemical suffix
28. Client
30. Speeder spotter
32. Picture border
35. Hornet
37. Director Howard
38. Snake
41. Scheme
45. Actress Arden
46. Expunge
47. Pompeii covering
48. Morning moisture
49. Raves
50. Quiz

DOWN

1. Bird of prey
2. Toaster ___
3. Walk through water
4. Indian
5. Grow older
6. Regret
12. Fish tank
14. Native American
15. Caster
16. Buddies
17. Canal of song
18. Quantity of paper
29. Cut
31. Orchard product
32. Wilma's husband
33. Wander
34. Once more
35. "Batman" actor
36. God of war
39. Director Miller
40. Frying need
42. Careless
43. Eggs
44. Flat hat

PUZZLE 533

ACROSS

1. Made less tense
6. Took the wheel
11. Honor
13. Journey
14. Shed
15. Diner patrons
16. Hang loosely
17. Awry
19. Cereal grain

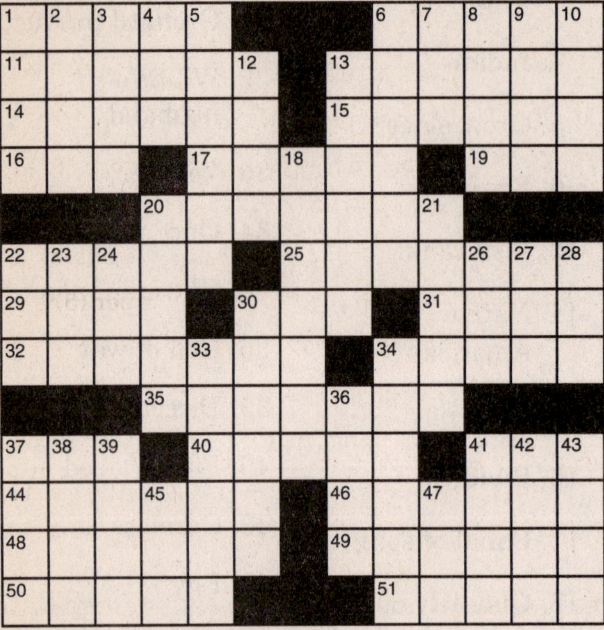

20. Went to see
22. One more time
25. Flourishes
29. Small boat
30. Cube or chest
31. Metric weight
32. Place for mascara
34. Whirls
35. Asserts without proof
37. Printers' measures
40. With glass sections
41. Frequently, to a poet
44. Fiddle
46. Puzzle
48. Away from the shore
49. Leave stranded
50. Rock shelf
51. Ancient instruments

DOWN

1. Snakelike fishes
2. On the briny
3. Antlered deer
4. Still, in verse
5. Apprehend
6. Where lingerie is stored
7. Deserter
8. Completed
9. Considerably
10. Different
12. Lichen's kin
13. Cut one's molars
18. Chef's domain
20. Country home
21. Levees
22. Naval agreement
23. Chipper
24. Fear
26. Compete
27. Architectural add-on
28. Mayday!
30. Maui, for one
33. Of downhill skiing
34. Repeat-a-call button
36. Wheat ___
37. Harmful
38. Excavate
39. Already purchased
41. Bloodhound's trail
42. Arctic floater
43. Decades
45. Fail to keep up
47. Remove moisture from

PUZZLE 534

ACROSS

1. Celebrity
5. Young society entrants
9. Preserves
12. Ashen
13. Cockeyed
14. Big fuss
15. Comparable
16. 1994 or 1492
17. Governed
18. Narrated again
20. Brass horn
22. Hospital section
24. School attendee
27. People without chairs
31. Modernize
32. Pecan, e.g.
33. Pleasure craft
35. Hide ___ hair
36. Poker word
38. Orange flower
40. Couples
42. Sense
43. Basks in the sun
45. Injustices
49. Winter ailment
51. Glazed
53. String tie
54. Lend support
55. Cartoon chipmunk
56. Eager
57. Maiden-name indicator
58. Arab chieftain
59. Chemists' workshops

DOWN

1. Sail pole
2. Remove
3. Touched ground
4. Fame
5. Waking vision
6. Pasture mother
7. Misbehaving child
8. Maple product
9. Hot green pepper
10. Summer quencher
11. In fashion
19. Godiva's title
21. Prickly seed covering
23. Kind of coffee
25. Cherished one
26. Master
27. Crisp cookie
28. Food fish
29. Disposition
30. Sharper
34. Bleacher feature
37. Noted period
39. Worldwide
41. Sarcastic
44. Con game
46. PBS science show
47. Smooth-tongued
48. Puts down turf
49. Loyal admirer
50. Commit perjury
52. Yalie

DOUBLE TROUBLE PUZZLE 535

Not really double trouble, but double fun! Solve this puzzle as you would a regular crossword, except place one, two, or three letters in each box. The number of letters in each answer is shown in parentheses after its clue.

ACROSS

1. Contemptible sort (5)
4. Trash (6)
7. Note (4)
9. Go to (6)
10. Moxie (5)
11. Well-being (6)
12. At hand (4)
13. Press (4)
14. Banter (8)
16. Foul smell (6)
18. Set (3)
19. Chance meeting, e.g. (11)
23. Cement chunk (4)
25. Aplenty (6)
27. Contests (5)
28. One admits one (6)
29. Near or Far (4)
30. Audacity (10)
32. Major work (4)
33. Chaste (6)
35. In secret (9)
37. Call out (3)
38. Burden (4)
40. Type of gear (6)
41. Stirred up (5)
43. Appearance (6)
44. Serenity (5)
45. Its days are numbered (8)
46. Impede (5)

DOWN

1. Wrap with bands (6)
2. Curiosity (8)
3. Cessation (3)
4. Fail to follow suit (6)
5. Bear hair (3)
6. Extreme (6)
7. Brawl (5)
8. Garment varmint (4)
11. Substantial (6)
13. Sea creature (6)
15. Royal digs (6)
17. Concert extra (6)
20. Stogie (5)
21. Evil spirit (5)
22. Lark's lair (4)
23. Ingenious (5)
24. Drive the getaway car (4)
25. Earth goddess (4)
26. Forfeited (4)
28. Assignation (5)
30. Gushing (8)
31. All (5)
32. Choice (6)
34. Designate (8)
35. Heating unit (7)
36. Songlike (7)
37. Aromatic tree (5)
39. Common viper (5)
40. Water main (4)
42. Extend credit (4)
43. Grow dim (4)

1	2	3	■	4	5	6	■	■	7	8
9			■	10			■	11		
12		■	13		■	14	15			■
■	16	17		■	■	■	18		■	■
■	■	19		20	21	22		■	23	24
25	26		■	27			■	28		
29		■	30				31		■	■
■	■	32		■	■	■	33		34	■
■	35			36	■	37		■	38	39
40			■	41	42		■	43		
44		■	■	45			■	46		

Crackers PUZZLE 536

Test your safecracking skills by rotating the four lettered dials until a common 8-letter word can be read across the middle of the dials.

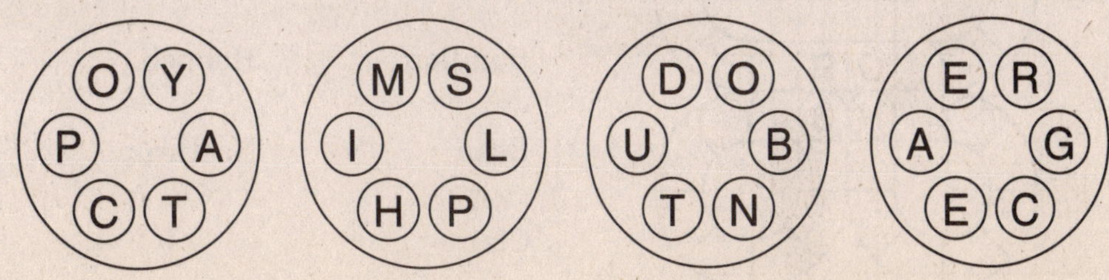

PUZZLE 537

ACROSS
1. French money, once
6. Light brown
10. Hats
14. Related to sound
15. Jump
16. Border
17. One of the senses
18. Does needlepoint
19. Heavy wind
20. Employs
22. Certain fly
24. Andes pack animal
27. Swerve, at sea
28. Snaky creature
29. Turning to the right
30. Hurting
31. Warning sign
32. Perceptive
34. Drain
37. Tentlike dwellings
39. Triumph
40. Flying machine
42. Diction follower
43. Coins
46. Sculpture, e.g.
47. Skater's milieu
48. Lend a hand
50. Perform
53. Belly muscles, briefly
54. Ms. Spacek
55. Flat TV
57. Angler's desire
59. Lively
60. Chief cook
62. Haste
67. Tardy
68. Twice a quarter
69. "____ & Cash"
70. Formerly, formerly
71. Lazily
72. Fire crime

DOWN
1. Sols' preceders
2. Jamaican product
3. Citrus quencher
4. Naught
5. Pillar
6. Besides
7. Mediocre grades
8. Damp and cold
9. Presumptuous fellow
10. Canary's home
11. Diminish
12. Regular beat
13. Durable metal
21. Legend
23. Whisk
24. Ring-tailed primate
25. Suspicious
26. "____ That a Shame"
27. Adolescent
29. Famed Spanish painter
30. Reek
33. Graceful birds
34. Indian garments
35. Restless
36. Gnat, e.g.
38. Vamoose
41. Girl
44. Brazier
45. Atlantic coast
49. Nap, in Mexico
50. Pie fruit
51. Obvious
52. Bakery items
56. Manuscript mark
57. Pepper type
58. Not certain
61. "It ____ to Be You"
63. Golf goal
64. Printers' concerns
65. Self-image
66. Comic Rickles

1	2	3	4	5	■	6	7	8	9	■	10	11	12	13
14					■	15				■	16			
17					■	18				■	19			
■	■	■	■	20	21			■	22	23				
■	24	25	26			■	■	27			■	28		
29						■	30				■	■	■	■
31				■	32	33					■	34	35	36
37				38	■	39			■	40	41			
42			■	43	44				45	■	46			
■	■	■	■	47				■	48	49				
50	51	52	■	53			■	■	54					■
55			56			■	57	58			■	■	■	■
59				■	60	61			■	62	63	64	65	66
67				■	68				■	69				
70				■	71				■	72				

PUZZLE 538

Lucky Clover

Fit the seven words into the four-leaf clover. Each word starts in a circle and may go in any direction. Words sometimes overlap.

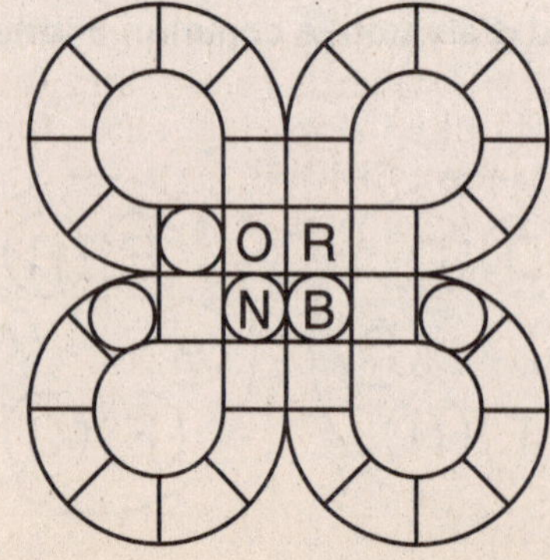

Bequeath
Bouillon
Bran
Clan
Correction
Hobnob
Nocturnal

PUZZLE 539

ACROSS

1. A la ____
5. Warms
10. Jokes
14. Imitates
15. Drawn from a keg
16. Work without ____
17. Hairstyling aids
18. Stale
19. Body of knowledge
20. Outrage
21. Prevalent
22. More lucid
23. Golfer's aide
25. Long (for)
28. Property measure
30. Green
31. See you!
34. Educate
37. Rogue
40. High point
41. Pilfer
42. Some are shocking
43. Pedestrian's lane
45. Soup scoop
46. "____ Gang"
47. Meal starter
48. Singe
50. Changed colors
52. Harvest tool
56. Greek vowel
60. Black
62. Towel marking
63. Portrayal
64. Acquiesce
66. Advanced, as money
67. Certain molding
68. Smile scornfully
69. Hence
70. Pact
71. Contented sounds
72. Low in pitch

DOWN

1. Merlin's craft
2. "Aida," e.g.
3. Removed from print
4. Sharp curve
5. Cozier
6. Slangy sufficiency
7. Uncertain
8. Tit for ____
9. Secret agent
10. Glitzy party
11. Author unknown, for short
12. "Pretty Woman" actor
13. Gang ending
21. Wealthy
22. Sutured
24. Minnows
26. Makes like a frog
27. Carry
29. Manor lands
31. Raised beagles, e.g.
32. Shout
33. Choice word
34. Tex-Mex treat
35. Very light beige
36. Cupid
38. Animation unit
39. Term of endearment
41. Persuade
44. Carbonated beverage
45. Frilly
49. Glacial ridges
51. Worse
53. Not here
54. Joint
55. Prohibit, legally
56. Yankees' slugger, briefly
57. Theater section
58. Prayer
59. Cad
61. Never, in poetry
64. Type of snake
65. Wildebeest
66. Commanded

1	2	3	4	■	5	6	7	8	9	■	10	11	12	13
14				■	15					■	16			
17				■	18					■	19			
20			■	21				■	■	22				
23			24			■	25	26	27		■	■	■	■
■	■	■	28			29	■	30			■	31	32	33
34	35	36			■	37	38				39			
40				■	41					■	42			
43				44					■	45				
46			■	47			■	48	49			■	■	■
■	■	■	■	50			51	■	52			53	54	55
56	57	58	59		■	■	60	61			■	62		
63				■	64	65				■	66			
67				■	68					■	69			
70				■	71					■	72			

Zip It

PUZZLE 540

The letters of six common words are listed below, but we've separated the odd letters (first, third, and fifth) from the even letters (second, fourth, and sixth). Without scrambling the order of the letters in the 3-letter groups, determine which two groups, when zipped together, form each of the answer words. For example, CRL and ICE zipped together form CIRCLE.

CRU EAR ETY GNL ______ ______

ICS IER LNA OAE ______ ______

ONT RPI SNE VYG ______ ______

PUZZLE 541

FULL CIRCLE

To complete this circular puzzle fill in the answers to the AROUND clues in a clockwise direction. For the RADIAL clues move from the outside to the inside.

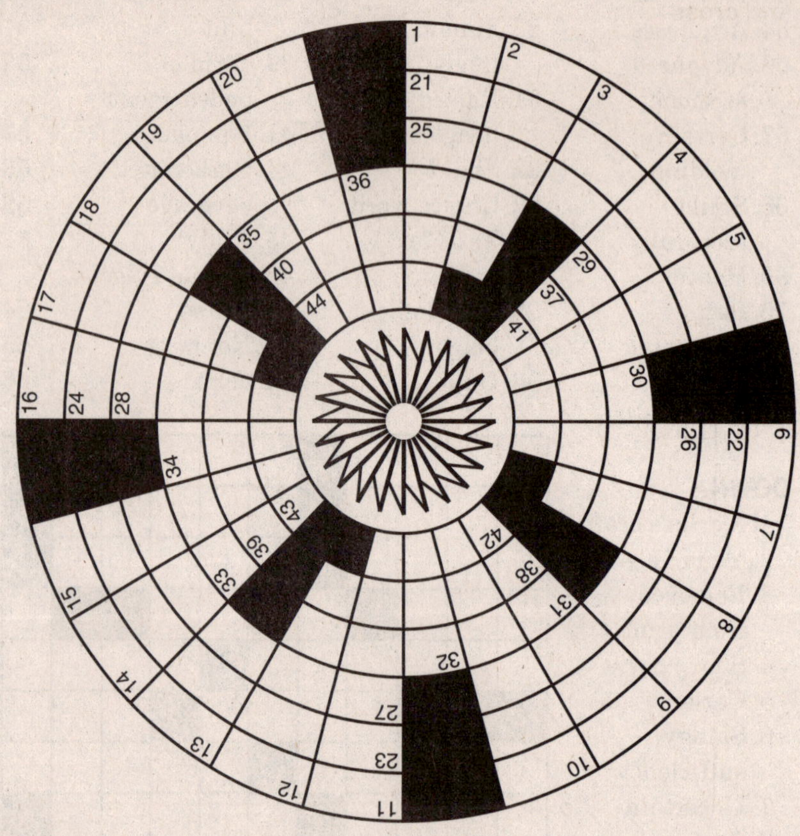

AROUND (Clockwise)

1. Basilica features
6. Pear-shaped instrument
11. Set up
16. The City of Light
21. Papal cape
22. Rub out
23. Kitchen gadget
24. Yawning
25. Roasting fowl
26. Hand trucks
27. ____ alia
28. Blew one's top
29. Sat
31. Great reviews
33. Gold measure
35. Annapolis student
37. Undermine
38. Skirt cut
39. Chopin work
40. Observe Yom Kippur
41. Palm fruit
42. Show the way
43. Deserve
44. Copper coin

RADIAL (Out to in)

1. Museum guide
2. Speechify
3. Navigator's need
4. Fled to wed
5. Foreign address?
6. Withdraw
7. Muslim decree
8. Old salt
9. Stellar
10. Certain value
11. Pal
12. Washer cycle
13. Volstead, e.g.
14. Less assertive
15. Corrections list
16. Rose Bowl event
17. Quartz variety
18. Lurid newspaper
19. Old-fashioned remedy
20. Composed
30. Tippler
32. By way of
34. Wagon track
36. Put on

CODEWORD

PUZZLE 542

Codeword is a special crossword puzzle in which conventional clues are omitted. Instead, answer words in the diagram are represented by numbers. Each number represents a different letter of the alphabet, and all of the letters of the alphabet are used. When you are sure of a letter, put it in the code key chart and cross it off in the alphabet box. A group of letters has been inserted to start you off.

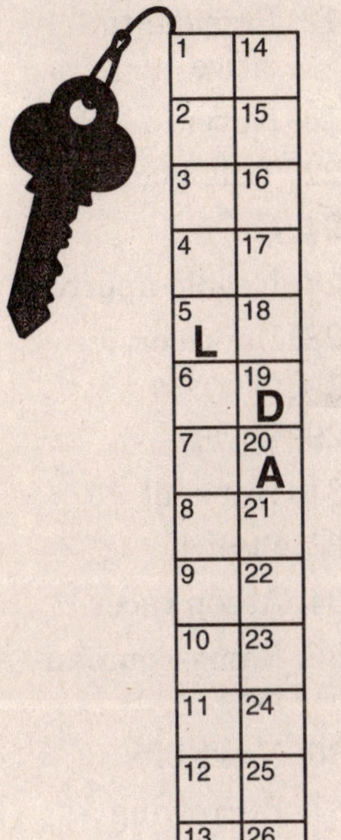

1	14
2	15
3	16
4	17
5 L	18
6	19 D
7	20 A
8	21
9	22
10	23
11	24
12	25
13	26

9	20	11	20	25	■	■	■	10	20	13	2	26
8	2	20	5	8	14	■	13	26	7	3	26	5
19	26	9	8	19	26	■	24	9	3	18	26	13
■	■	■	4	26	26	■	16	26	20	■	■	■
26	20	9	18	■	13	12	8	■	■	26	6	26
15	9	8	13	12	■	21	18	26	■	6	8	23
15	8	18	■	8	23	20	4	26	■	20	17	26
26	13	13	■	18	8	5	■	5 L	20 A	19 D	26	18
19	26	26	■	■	2	20	15	■	1	26	18	19
■	■	■	21	3	2	■	26	5	1	■	■	■
21	24	24	21	13	26	■	19	8	26	13	26	5
1	9	21	22	26	18	■	13	26	14	3	9	26
2	16	24	26	19	■	■	■	13	2	26	26	19

~~A~~	N
B	O
C	P
~~D~~	Q
E	R
F	S
G	T
H	U
I	V
J	W
K	X
~~L~~	Y
M	Z

CODEWORD

PUZZLE 543

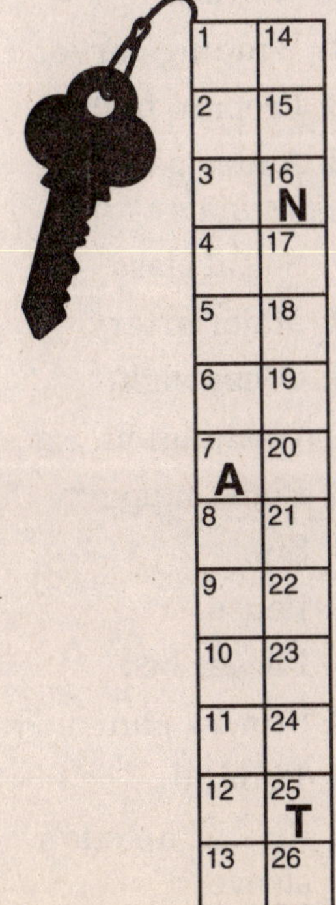

1	14
2	15
3	16 N
4	17
5	18
6	19
7 A	20
8	21
9	22
10	23
11	24
12	25 T
13	26

15	23	21	■	22	4	7	12	■	18	11	25	3
7	18	24	■	4	14	8	24	■	7	14	24	7
1	24	25	■	7	16	24	18	■	5	14	7	2
19	14	7	16	15	■	■	■	1	24	11	■	■
■	■	■	23	13	7	2	■	24	12	8	24	14
10	24	6	25	■	1	23	16	8	■	7	12	24
23	18	16	■	■	24	13	24	■	■	25	11	26
16	24	24	■	20	24	24	6	■	6	24	25	6
24	14	7	6	24	■	6	25	23	26	■	■	■
■	■	13	11	25	■	■	■	17	7	9	23	14
7	26	24	5	■	7 A	16 N	25 T	11	■	23	21	11
18	11	14	24	■	14	11	23	25	■	18	24	25
1	24	6	6	■	24	5	24	6	■	1	2	24

~~A~~	~~N~~
B	O
C	P
D	Q
E	R
F	S
G	~~T~~
H	U
I	V
J	W
K	X
L	Y
M	Z

PUZZLE 544

ACROSS

1. Plus factor
6. "___ So Cold"
10. Sacred image
14. Angry stare
15. Mend
16. PBS science series
17. Type of prisoner
18. Atop
19. Frost
20. "___ to Billy Joe"
21. Cut the grass
23. Stinky
25. "The Way We ___"
27. Under the ___
30. Thataway
32. Nook
36. Obstruct
39. Gear
41. Melt
42. Foot appendage
43. Wilted
46. Strong rage
47. Alternative word
49. Bro or sis
50. Sister's daughters
52. Uniformed maid
54. Easter flowers
56. Adapt for new use
58. Cutting tools
62. Digestion need
65. Venomous reptile
67. Cookie grain
68. Legitimate
69. Did the crawl
72. Immature insect stage
74. Wiggly ones
75. Dress for Caesar
76. Eight musicians
77. Beer ingredient
78. ___ out (barely manages)
79. Kid

DOWN

1. Luminous
2. Slip
3. Less hazardous
4. Sooner than, to a bard
5. Span of time
6. Displayed
7. Coop resident
8. Stop for lunch
9. Wade
10. Acquire
11. Unexcited
12. Presidential office
13. Never
22. Title holders
24. Guys
26. Needle aperture
28. Dance or exercise
29. Voyage
31. Unusual
33. Stylish
34. Aesop racer
35. Rams' companions
36. News bit
37. Burrowing rodent
38. Bother
40. Bottled spirits
44. Slick
45. Metal mold
48. Weirdest
51. Winding curve
53. Prepare to drag
55. Andes pack animals
57. Social class
59. Major artery
60. Ocean sight
61. Washington, e.g.
62. Plant support
63. Site
64. Pause
66. Flower bed
70. Stir-fry pan
71. 18 or 30
73. An ___ up one's sleeve

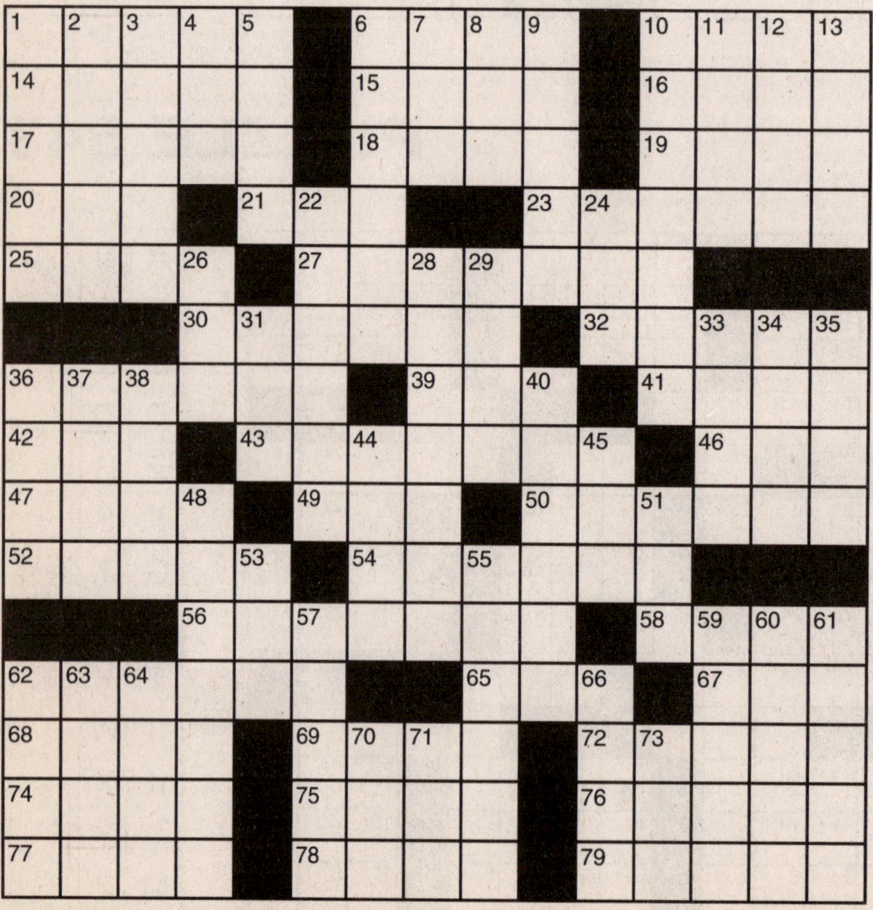

PUZZLE 545

ACROSS

1. Backs of necks
6. Hole punchers
10. Not new
13. Minded
15. Grub
16. Preschooler?
17. Like freezing rain
18. Golf-course half
19. Title
20. Sargasso spawner
21. Come to light
23. That thing's
24. Rich vein
26. Wingspread
28. Leg front
30. Carp at
33. Broadway hit
36. Noisily
38. Ump's relative
40. Faithful
41. Totality
42. Sang a Swiss song
45. Rural hotel
46. Where to go buy-buy
48. She's taken a vow
49. Billfold
51. Speak to God
52. Flit about
54. Ms. Britt et al.
55. Cause of hives?
58. Was sorry for
60. Fitness club
62. Wanders off
65. In what way
68. Abed
69. Music category
70. Plenty
73. Pair
74. "Aida" solo
75. Not often
76. I topic
77. Urges
78. Positive answers

DOWN

1. Smoke detector
2. Adept
3. Banana skin
4. Cyclops's singleton
5. Pair
6. Skin problem
7. Buzz
8. Aches
9. Chimney ___
10. Usually
11. Oaf
12. Southern belles
14. Hid the gray
22. Grown boys
24. Hinged cover
25. Single
27. Take steps
28. From the sun
29. Uproar
31. Combat zone
32. Shaving-cream type
34. Loony ___
35. Dispatched
36. Light fixture
37. Farther
39. "Chosen" quantity
43. Excavated
44. Woman of distinction
47. Caustic material
50. Fellow
53. Towel off
56. Prose paper
57. Retail outlet
59. Purchaser
60. Profile view
61. Spark or ear
63. Spoil
64. Sad cry
65. Tones
66. Peer
67. Reporters' inquiries
71. Vote of no
72. Mine output

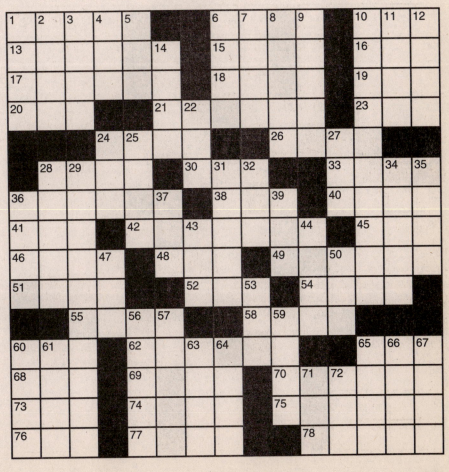

PUZZLE 546

ACROSS

1. Chief
6. ___ and flows
10. In the know about
14. Separate
15. Winter garment
16. Flow
17. Small body of land
18. Sharpen
19. Poker term
20. Small mark
21. Chaos
23. Green with envy
25. Apple dessert
26. Not young
27. English-muffin features
31. Piece of parsley
36. Bathroom item
37. Loony
38. Unkinder
39. First-aid ___
41. Sink
42. Chimpanzees
43. Seeing
45. Pains in the neck
47. Disregarding
48. Large decorative vase
50. Uneven
51. Pilot's place
55. City trains
56. Seeing red
59. Baker
60. Facts
62. Type of glue
64. Built
65. Cut with scissors
66. Scary
67. Whistled
68. Fidgety
69. Put on clothing

DOWN

1. Marian, e.g.
2. Plus
3. Shock
4. Half of two
5. Lawyer's fee
6. Mimic
7. Half a blunder
8. Guitars' kin
9. Wool or guitar
10. Milky stone
11. Taboo
12. Ballet skirt
13. Mine rocks
22. Auto imperfection
24. Radio spots
25. Most colorless
27. Auto type
28. Gets a lift
29. Bug
30. Regarding
32. Tranquil
33. Violinist's need
34. Cake covering
35. Large bell
36. Booby ___
40. Coal measurement
41. Food for Tweety
44. Screwdriver, e.g.
46. Dine in the evening
47. Have in mind
49. Wash lightly
51. Brush's counterpart
52. Circles kin
53. Relinquish
54. Recognized
55. See
56. Oliver's wish
57. Pivot line
58. Coloring agents
61. Falsehood?
63. By means of

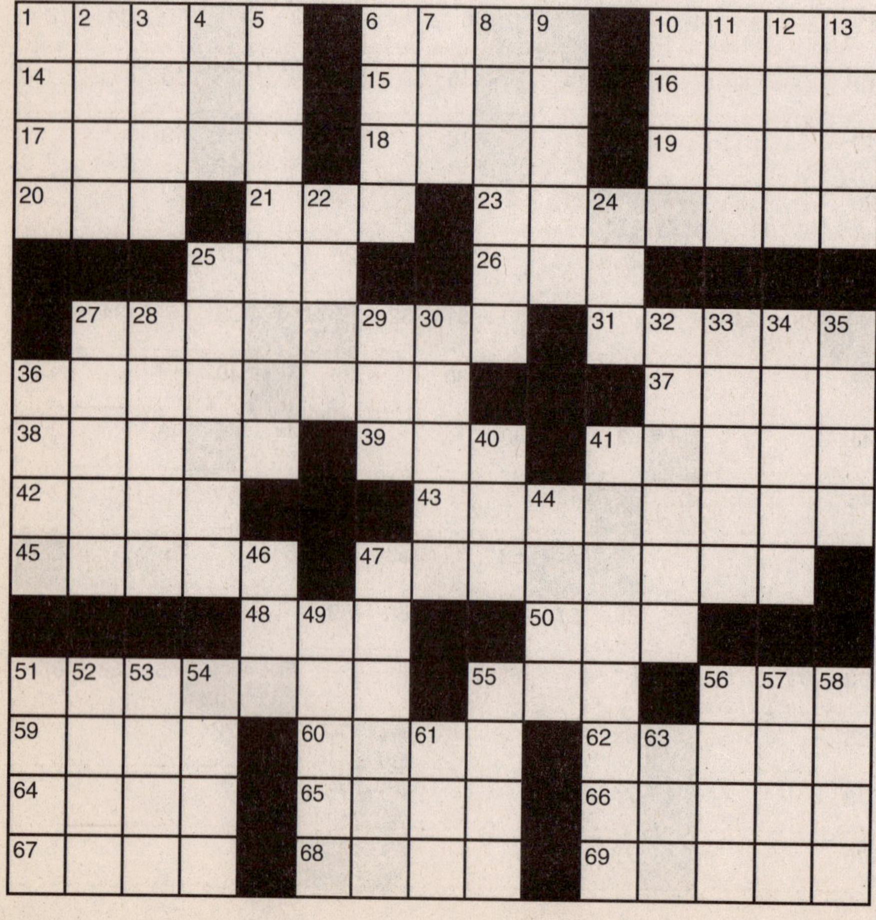

PUZZLE 547

ACROSS

1. Ore's yield
6. Excited
10. Substitute
14. Come about
15. Track
16. Wind
17. Wine-bottle stoppers
18. Reign
19. Went by taxi
20. Fruity drink
21. Unexpected slide
23. Blooming shrub
25. Gets hitched
27. Clinging vine
28. Cut down
29. Swiftness
31. Earth science
35. Made smaller
38. Physique, for short
39. Hiss!
40. Daft
41. Apron front
42. Rocky
44. Electrical unit, shortly
45. Trendy
46. Precede
47. Work unit, for many
50. Grandmother
51. Auction ending
52. Hard to see
53. Brunch or lunch
57. Paths between buildings
60. Served perfectly
62. Perjure oneself
63. Dime, e.g.
64. Hither
66. Admire greatly
68. Hurried
69. Becomes more ripe
70. Squeegee
71. Leading performer
72. Mislaid
73. Wanting

DOWN

1. Large parrot
2. Gnaw away
3. Weary
4. Request
5. Minus
6. Show up
7. Showy
8. Frying liquid
9. Shone
10. Scribble
11. Ram's coat
12. Military helper
13. Urgent request
22. Punt
24. Animal park
26. Reach across
30. Whichever
31. Lump
32. A woodwind
33. Flat bell
34. Stringed toy
35. Deli side order
36. Catcher's plate
37. Heavy cord
38. Offer
41. Young man
42. ___ of a gun
43. London streetcar
45. Sheriff
46. Glory
48. More alert
49. Algerian title, once
50. Friendliest
52. Takes a chance
54. Marry in secret
55. Expressed publicly
56. Apprehensive
57. Behaves
58. Booty
59. Italian money, once
61. Early light
65. Power trip
67. Dotted cube

PUZZLE 548

OVERLAPS

Place the answer to each clue into the diagram beginning at the corresponding number. Words will overlap with other words.

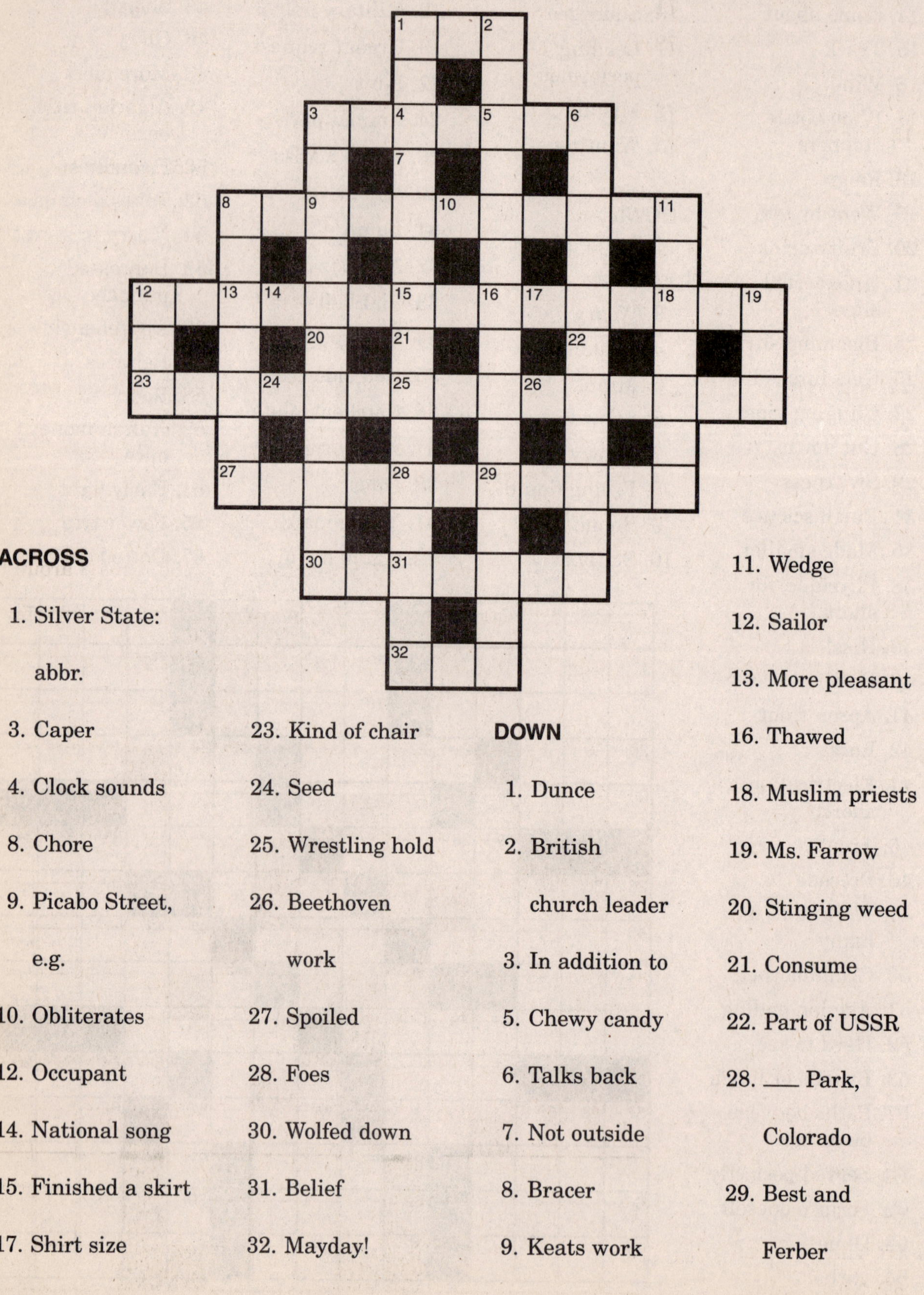

ACROSS

1. Silver State: abbr.
3. Caper
4. Clock sounds
8. Chore
9. Picabo Street, e.g.
10. Obliterates
12. Occupant
14. National song
15. Finished a skirt
17. Shirt size
23. Kind of chair
24. Seed
25. Wrestling hold
26. Beethoven work
27. Spoiled
28. Foes
30. Wolfed down
31. Belief
32. Mayday!

DOWN

1. Dunce
2. British church leader
3. In addition to
5. Chewy candy
6. Talks back
7. Not outside
8. Bracer
9. Keats work
11. Wedge
12. Sailor
13. More pleasant
16. Thawed
18. Muslim priests
19. Ms. Farrow
20. Stinging weed
21. Consume
22. Part of USSR
28. ___ Park, Colorado
29. Best and Ferber

PUZZLE 549

ACROSS

1. Volcanic dust
4. Use a bookie
7. Some tides
12. Maui meal
13. Repaired Venus de Milo?
15. Creepy
16. Swiss height
17. Library no-no
18. Jot down
19. Mushroom topper
20. Staggers
22. Interrogate
23. Eaten away
25. Learned
27. Scheme
29. Categorized
33. Walk heavily
36. Murky
38. Stadium sound
39. Badger
41. Change the subject?
43. Cat's prey
44. Freed
46. Periodical, for short
48. Look narrowly
49. Cuddle
50. Song
52. They sometimes leap
55. Monument
59. Faux ___
62. Coffee dregs
64. Wood chopper
65. Yummy smell
67. Nasal sound
68. Public vehicle
69. Helmsman
70. Representative
71. Poetic tribute
72. Brick house
73. Babble
74. Bad start

DOWN

1. Swiftly
2. ___ system
3. Nile animal, shortly
4. Pondered
5. Expel
6. Samples
7. Brokaw's setting
8. Poet's eternity
9. Elaborate melody
10. Peach leftovers
11. Investigate
13. Paid to play
14. Regard
21. Impetuous
24. Self-respect
26. State policeman
28. Help
30. Not false
31. Lessen
32. Colorist
33. Avoid
34. Forsaken
35. Ins' opposites
37. It's the word!
40. Representative
42. Go up to the plate
45. Loved one
47. Chewy candy
51. Vicious
53. Suitor's gift
54. Cheerful
56. Skewered meat
57. Ooze
58. Witness again
59. Mama's spouse
60. Desert condition
61. Go it alone
63. ___ Scotia
66. Crowd around

PUZZLE 550

ACROSS

1. Marble
4. Slash
8. Lion's noise
12. Last of the log
13. Like a cat's back, at times
15. Wedding-gown shade
16. Large parrot
17. Two-tiered galley
18. ___ off (mad)
19. Fit to consume
21. Scold
23. Like old bread
25. Hermit
26. Find
29. Frightened
32. Has another birthday
33. Get a touchdown
34. Quilting party
37. Final practices
41. No's counterpart
42. Fermented beverages
43. Sand or speed
44. Dormant
45. Snort
47. Chemical compound
51. Worse
53. Workers' walkout
55. Pertaining to the shore
59. Declared
60. In back of
63. Molokai instrument
64. Beach flier
65. Entities
66. Storage area
67. Oracle
68. Relay-race portions
69. Nanny has three

DOWN

1. Conquer
2. Out of port
3. Come again?
4. Automobile feature
5. Landed
6. Female pronoun
7. Bottom edge
8. Of an earlier time
9. Pacific, e.g.
10. Sharp ridge
11. More disrespectful
13. Monastery leader
14. Society miss
20. Hoard
22. Firstborn
24. Sailed
26. Countess or duchess
27. Horrible monster
28. High notes
30. Sorrows
31. Noted period
33. Retail
34. Cow's house
35. Dash
36. Catch a glimpse of
38. Sneer
39. Cool!
40. Arouses
45. Injustices
46. ___ or tails
47. Road curves
48. Intent look
49. Threefold
50. Kind of down
52. Cake topping
54. Wane
56. Boob ___
57. Comparable
58. Contact ___
61. Sushi fish
62. Rush

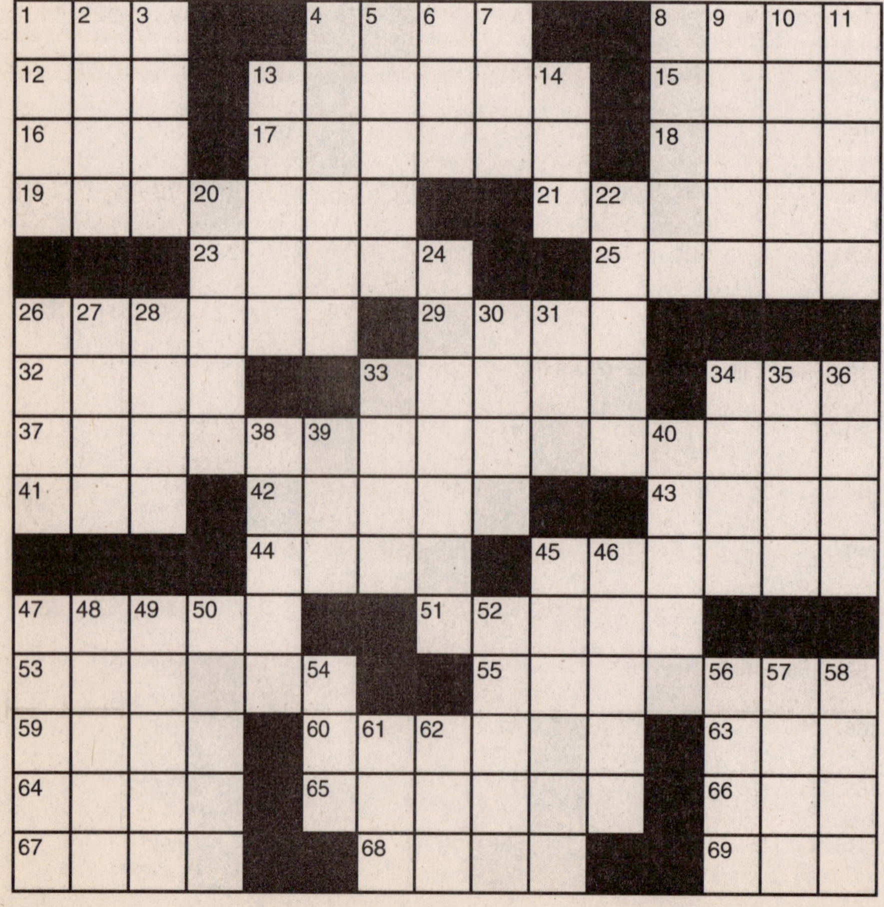

PUZZLE 551

ACROSS

1. ___ but goodie
6. RBI or ERA
10. So-so grades
14. Spoof
15. Dry with a cloth
16. Stare rudely at
17. Sponge
19. Shed feathers
20. Hen's product
21. Hue
22. Broom's wet kin
24. Plant again
27. Every one
30. Of the nose
33. Sagittarius
35. G-men
37. Pact
39. Cab
40. That guy
41. Alpine warbler
44. Trouser part
45. Elderly
47. Interrogates
48. Clumsy boats
50. Shrill scream
52. Grimy
54. Kind
55. Welcomer
59. Jimmy
61. That woman
63. Hewing tool
64. Meany
67. Report-card entry
71. Flow
72. Dog's bark
73. Nosed (out)
74. Weight units
75. Colorful salamander
76. Winter fabrics

DOWN

1. Propose
2. Expansive
3. Sediment
4. Frozen water
5. Moray or electric
6. Influence
7. Moon's pull
8. Tarzan's friend
9. Word
10. ___ disc
11. Conceit
12. House wing
13. Adjust
18. Gambler's concern
23. "___ the fields . . ."
25. Rearmost part
26. Elementary
28. Blackboard crayon
29. Spells
31. Puts two and two together
32. Onions' kin
33. Tavern beverage
34. Outfit
35. Struggle
36. Kind of board
38. As well
40. Possesses
42. Acorn-bearing tree
43. Part of APR
46. Soup spoons
49. Bread or cereal grain
51. At any time, in verse
53. Bird of ill ___
56. Dance for two
57. Surpass others
58. Marsh grasses
60. Show boredom
61. Store away
62. Weight
64. Elect
65. Thick substance
66. Make tracks
68. Finger's opposite
69. Mountain moisture
70. Fuss

1	2	3	4	5	■	6	7	8	9	■	10	11	12	13
14					■	15				■	16			
17					18					■	19			
20			■	■	21			■	22	23		■	■	■
24			25	26		■	■	■	■	27		28	29	■
■	■	■	30			31	32	■	33					34
■	35	36			■	37		38		■	39			
40			■	41	42					43	■	44		
45			46	■	47				■	48	49			■
50				51		■	52		53			■	■	■
■	54				■	■	■	■	55			56	57	58
■	■	■	59		60	■	61	62		■	■	63		
64	65	66		■	67	68				69	70			
71				■	72				■	73				
74				■	75				■	76				

PUZZLE 552

FLOWER POWER

The answers to this petaled puzzle will go in a curve from the number on the outside to the center of the flower. Each number in the flower will have two 5-letter answers. One goes in a clockwise direction and the second in a counterclockwise direction. We have entered two answers to help you begin.

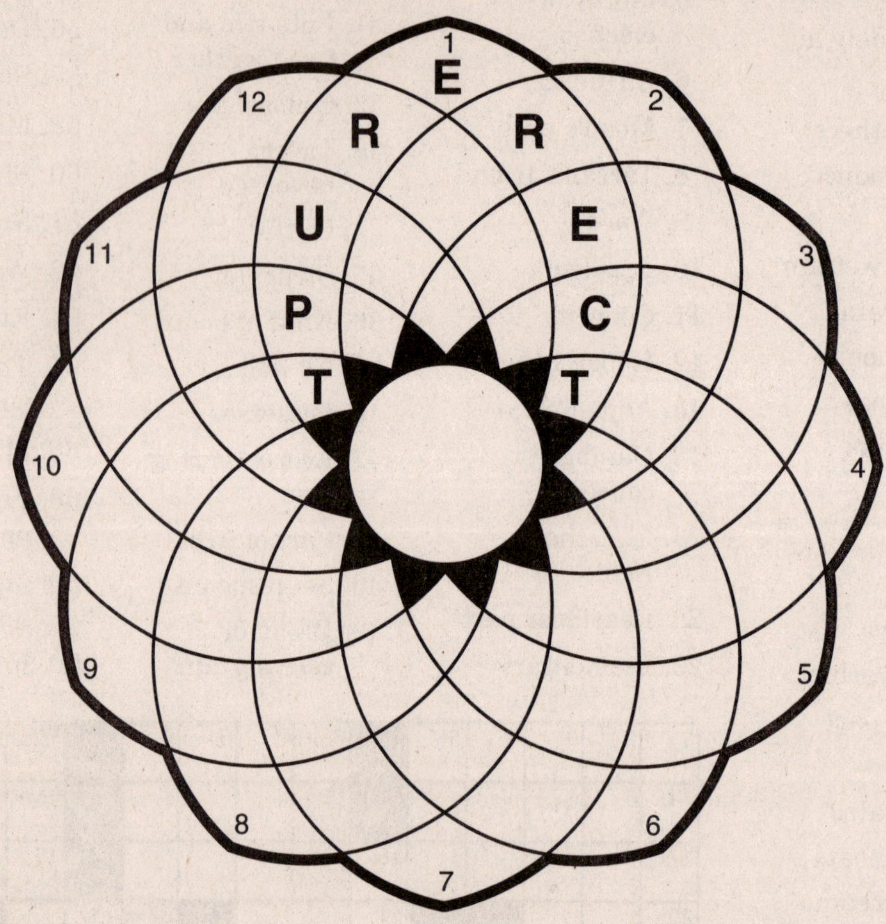

CLOCKWISE

1. Construct
2. Licorice-like seed
3. Teed off
4. Nobel Prize category
5. Fortify
6. Charley horse
7. Took a stab at
8. Gather
9. Piece of bedding
10. Crinkly cloth
11. Have confidence in
12. Squawk

COUNTERCLOCKWISE

1. Spew forth
2. Meet the day
3. Clumsy
4. Cost
5. Beauty's beau
6. Shipping box
7. Copy
8. Prayer before meals
9. Ooze
10. Baby bird's comment
11. Groovy pattern
12. Kermit's color

PUZZLE 553

ACROSS

1. Yellow fruit
7. Joined the choir
11. Grassy layer
14. Avoids
15. Kingston, e.g.
16. Grounded bird
17. Electors
18. Refs' kin
19. Bachelors
20. Approval word
21. Peddle
23. Fishing net
25. Greek cheese
26. Unbiased
28. Pros
30. Where strikes are called
34. Puzzled
35. Bundle
36. Off the deep ___
38. Petty quarrels
40. Altar promise
41. Bog down
43. That guy's
44. Highly impressed
46. Small rodents
47. Bleeped out
50. Candle part
51. Sailor's hail
52. Almost closed
54. Cuban dance
57. Stench
58. Frame border
61. Part of "to be"
62. Stretch wide
65. Obstruct
67. Sunday seat
68. Dueling blade
69. Shorthand experts, shortly
70. Road bend
71. Middle middle?
72. Shove

DOWN

1. Flock
2. Burn reliever
3. Phooey!
4. Citrus drink
5. Stage fright
6. Plus factor
7. Cuff fastener
8. Coat sleeve
9. Playful bite
10. Talked trash
11. Trucker's rig
12. Prognostic
13. Sandy mound
22. Snare
24. Stage
25. Heroic act
26. Defect
27. Everybody
28. Savory jelly
29. Quit
31. Domicile
32. Antique
33. Talent
34. Powdery residue
37. Color fabric
39. Strutted
40. Extremely
42. Arab bigwig
45. Pursue
48. Bug
49. Family member
50. Gentle heat
53. Beam
54. Hatteras or Cod
55. Assay specimens
56. Hot tip
57. Small bills
58. Bill of fare
59. Commotions
60. Explore
63. Band member?
64. Like Willie Winkie
66. Each

PUZZLE 554

ACROSS

1. Wanes
5. Running circuits
9. Wall art
14. Wisecrack
15. On a rampage
16. Materialized
17. Golden-rule word
18. Uh-uh
19. Bumbling
20. Cake decorator
21. Fenced
23. He rings twice?
25. Poet's before
26. Life story, briefly
29. Illustrious
32. Flue
35. No longer is
36. Food thickener
37. Presented
38. Hackneyed
40. Completed
41. Ginger drinks
42. That girl
43. Cast a ballot
44. Besides
48. Eccentric
49. "___ the ramparts . . ."
50. First-throw pair of sixes
55. Court cases
57. Bard of ___
58. Refute
62. U.K. subject
63. Not a soul
64. Uneven
65. Theater section
66. Moon's-pull result
67. Document
68. Widemouthed pitcher
69. Garlic feature

DOWN

1. Supply
2. Con game
3. Takes the lure
4. Curling or lacrosse
5. Four-wheeled carriage
6. Quantity
7. Bishop of Rome
8. Of the bones
9. Lass
10. Large coffeepot
11. Red deer
12. Venomous snake
13. Tennis call
22. Cancel
24. Clever comment
26. Biased one
27. Foolish
28. Fairy-tale brute
30. Throng
31. Pedestal part
32. Appreciate
33. ___ which way
34. Bird's retreat
37. Fisherman's hook
38. Like some hosiery
39. Dreadful
43. Annoy
45. Spicier
46. Accommodate
47. List of names
51. Long-poem division
52. Bypass
53. Musical piece
54. Grimace
56. In line
58. Twilled fabric
59. Historical period
60. Jazz type
61. Practice

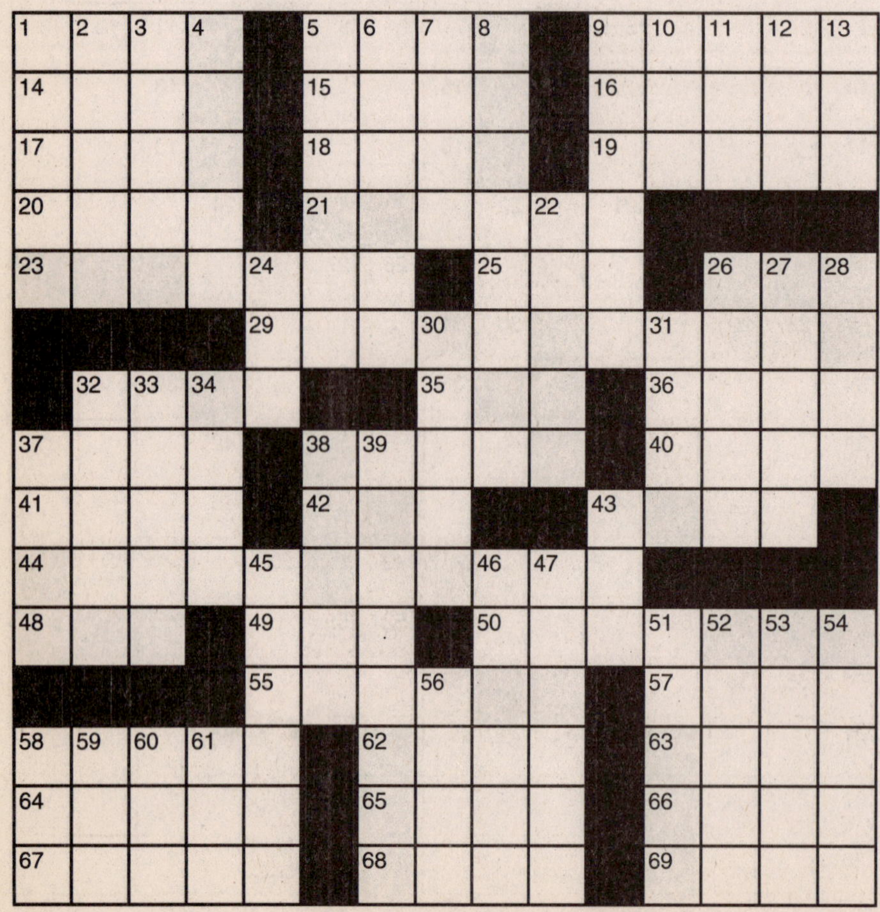

PUZZLE 555

ACROSS

1. Satisfy
5. Chemist's weight
9. Sour compound
13. Inkling
14. Speak in public
15. Valuable vein
16. Willing
17. Entertained with drink
18. Tawny big cat
19. "___ So Shy"
20. Faxed
21. Resides
23. Act toward
25. Spread out
27. Excavated
29. Free time
33. Tranquil
36. Go without food
37. Forbid
38. Paper-towel layer
39. African mammal, for short
41. Frozen dessert
42. Utilize
43. Discharge
44. Coats with a dull finish
47. Lose hope
49. Drop the ball
50. With a skin problem
52. Legendary stories
56. Latin dance
59. Blue bloom
62. Disintegrate
63. Agitate
64. Subway-fare coin
66. Capitol roof
67. Skunk feature
68. Fencing swords
69. Atop
70. Mediocre grades
71. Student's furniture
72. Gull's smaller cousin

DOWN

1. Conflict
2. Lazy person
3. Tenant contract
4. Lass's mate
5. ___ and bear it
6. Speaks wildly
7. Took in food
8. Interfering
9. Narrow thoroughfares
10. Wind
11. False god
12. Libraries
14. Be beholden to
20. Astound
22. Delay
24. Citrus beverage
26. Organize
28. Developed
30. Single thing
31. Chinese staple
32. 24th letters
33. Potato
34. Further
35. Distilled spirits
36. Proper
40. Give a job to
43. Per
45. Up in ___
46. Hear legally
48. Gait setters
51. Embankments
53. Treasure stash
54. Babe Ruth specialty
55. Harsh
56. Gator's cousin
57. Cover up
58. Soothing plant
60. Stench
61. Winners
65. Unclose, poetically
66. Polka ___

1	2	3	4	■	■	5	6	7	8	■	9	10	11	12
13				■	14					■	15			
16				■	17					■	18			
19			■	20				■	21	22				
23			24		■	■	25	26				■	■	■
■	■	■	27		28	■	■	29				30	31	32
33	34	35				■	36				■	37		
38			■	■	39	40				■	■	41		
42			■	43				■	44	45	46			
47			48				■	■	49			■	■	■
■	■	■	50				51	■	■	52		53	54	55
56	57	58				■	59	60	61		■	62		
63				■	64	65				■	66			
67				■	68					■	69			
70				■	71				■	■	72			

PUZZLE 556

STRIKE UP THE BAND

ACROSS

1. Pant
5. Corn-ear cores
9. JFK sights, once
13. China item
17. Oy!
18. Effigy
19. Hilo feast
20. Till
21. Vaccines
22. Gold-rush town
23. Cravings
24. Pitchers' stats
25. Christmas chimes?
28. Least tanned
30. Mother
31. Trifle
32. Actress Moore
33. Hairy cousin?
36. Pad
39. Tangle up
43. Umbra
45. Youngster
46. In the thick of
48. Smirk
49. Skirt length
50. Kind of tent
51. Pesky insect
52. Hold together
53. Suppressor
55. Swell
56. Offers for sale
57. Distant
58. Ruckus
59. Took first prize
60. Clogs or pumps
63. Slacken
64. California city
68. Harken
69. Dobbin's morsels
70. Eavesdrop
71. Sole
72. Davis Cup winner
73. Granny
74. Motorists' gp.
75. Hollywood honor
76. Spooky
78. Capture
80. Preholiday night
81. Pulls behind
82. Sink or bend
83. Sheep's cry
85. Actors' remarks
88. Tiny Tim tune?
93. Inadequate
94. Short skirt
96. Ms. Gray
97. Walk aimlessly
99. "Swan Lake" costume
100. Parched
101. Skin
102. City in Norway
103. Close noisily
104. King Cole et al.
105. Glimpses
106. Deficiency

DOWN

1. Pump buy
2. Saloon orders
3. Hindu garb
4. Hymn
5. Movie house
6. Funk
7. Explosive device
8. Rained ice
9. Sneakily
10. Petitions
11. Cure hides
12. Hang
13. Plucky tune?
14. Regarding
15. RR depots
16. Party giver
26. Cast a ballot
27. Parcel
29. Morning hrs.
32. Goddess, e.g.
33. Theories
34. Not this
35. Hack
37. Smear
38. Circuit
40. In order
41. Skating enclosure
42. Purposes
44. Ringo's favorite song?
46. Building addition
47. Fashioned
50. Miles ___ hour
51. Social events
54. Refrain syllables
55. Silt deposit
56. Darlin'
58. Malicious
59. Method

PUZZLE 556

60. Persian ruler

61. "For ___ jolly good . . ."

62. Diamond Head's site

63. Streets

64. Box lightly

65. Story starter

66. Central European

67. Australian lake

70. Perched

73. Cronkite, e.g.

74. Fishermen

75. Iridescent gem

77. Tip of Italy

78. Perrier, par exemple

79. Revises

82. Slides

84. Composer Copland

85. Rental props.

86. Inner being

87. Particle

88. Division

89. American Indian

90. String of people

91. Portion

92. Bulldogs' school

95. Savings-plan inits.

98. Trendy

PUZZLE 557

• DAD'S DAY •

ACROSS

1. Beatty film
5. Mao ____-tung
8. Peach center
11. Nimble
13. LAX posting
14. It's a miner matter
15. Fops
17. Corral
18. Murmur fondly
19. Dancer's jump
21. Rub dry
24. Function
26. Workout site
28. Hubbub
29. N.Y. hours
30. Fable teller
32. Democrat's opp.
33. Ceases
35. Actress Gabor
36. Syrup flavor
38. Acorn source
39. Shocking swimmer
40. Caustic stuff
41. LPs' successors
42. Bookie's concerns
43. British blackjack
45. Spinning toy
47. NFL player
49. Warhol, for one
54. Cul-de-____
55. D.C.'s country
56. Floor coverings
57. Squid squirt
58. Cozy room
59. Audience action

DOWN

1. Seance response
2. Freudian term
3. Quick swim
4. Toast portion
5. Herbal beverage
6. Panache
7. Soothe
8. Bagel option
9. Wrath
10. Bo's number
12. Rocker Brian ____
16. Knight fight
20. Ripen
21. Heat up
22. Flawless
23. Nonsense!
25. Arose
27. Relocated
29. Wind dir.
30. Inquire
31. Buddies
34. Ziti or linguine
37. Celestial lion
41. Selected
42. Certain nerve
44. Tater
46. Bit for Fido
47. Greek letter
48. Sprinted
50. Skillet
51. Under the weather
52. Pirate's domain
53. Recipe amt.

PUZZLE 558

• TAKE DIRECTIONS •

ACROSS

1. Adams and Ameche
5. Blonde shade
8. Bundle of bills
11. Concept
12. Society-page word
13. Actor Ron ____
14. Polaris
17. Date
18. Severe trial
19. River swimmer
21. Cribbage term
23. Essence
24. Motor fuel
27. Luxury resorts
29. Seasoned sailor?
32. Biblical book
34. Increase
35. Place for a banjo?
36. Actor Newman
37. Valley
39. Actor Kercheval
40. "Barney" fan
42. Female ruff
43. Theater guide
45. Wine server
50. Waiter's reward
51. New York waterway
54. Hayward film
55. ____ Lanka
56. Equipment
57. Chop down
58. Gel
59. Special skills

DOWN

1. Flintstones' pet
2. Aroma
3. Geek
4. Fill completely
5. Colony dweller
6. Baltic, e.g.
7. Wading bird
8. Jordan River region
9. Out of the wind
10. Hair colorist
15. Writer Andersen
16. Inclined
20. Walrus tooth
22. Cupcake maker
24. Mountain pass
25. Doctor's gp.
26. Lefty
28. Pick out
30. Actor Majors
31. Hamilton bill
33. Blackthorn
38. "King ____"
41. Ringlet
43. Provo's locale
44. ____ Dish
46. Latvia capital
47. Affirm
48. Accomplishment
49. Blunders
52. How ____ you?
53. Make a lap

FOUR-MOST

PUZZLE 559

The 4-letter entries in this crossword puzzle are listed separately and are in alphabetical order. Use the answers to the numbered clues to help you determine where each 4-letter entry goes in the diagram.

4 LETTERS

ALAS
ALEE
ALPS
AREA
ARIA
ARID
AURA
BEAR
EGGS
EPOS
ERGO
GORE
INCH
IRON
KILO
LADY
LARK
LOVE
LUAU
LURE
NULL
OOZE
ORZO
PAIN
PALE
PLAY
POOR
RALE
RASP
SAGE
SEEN
SEND
SLAB
SLID
SPAN
UNIT

ACROSS

5. Boring routine
13. Quinine water
17. "Au revoir!"
20. Take-home amount
21. Monkey (with)
25. Decimal unit
26. Camp craft
28. Cutting remark
32. O'Hare est.
33. Impaired vision
35. Placate
39. "The ____ Incident"
42. Sleep soundly?
44. Far-out
46. Game marble
47. Knickknack stand
49. Young eel
51. Chew the fat
53. Self-centered person
57. Permitted
63. Methuselah's father
67. Stage offering
70. Not ne'er

DOWN

4. Unexpected
5. Cowboy exhibition
7. Attachment
13. Citrus fruit
14. Prettier
24. Filch
25. Fortuneteller's card
26. Building-site machine
27. Specialized jargon
28. Dark fur
29. North Sea bird
30. Strike
31. Crushing tooth
32. Beast of burden
34. Community outside a city
36. Fray
38. Sports fig.
40. Encircle
45. Completely
48. Restaurant patron
50. Springlike
52. Happen again
64. Named, before marriage

1	2	3	4	■	■	5	6	7	■	■	8	9	10	11
12				■	13				14	■	15			
16				■	17					■	18			
19				■	20			■	21	22				
■	■	■	23	24			■	25			■	■	■	■
■	26	27				■	28				29	30	31	■
32			■	33		34			■	35				36
37			38	■	39				40	■	41			
42				43	■	44				45	■	46		
■	47				48			■	49		50			■
■	■	■	■	51			■	52				■	■	■
53	54	55	56			■	57			■	58	59	60	61
62				■	63	64				■	65			
66				■	67					■	68			
69				■	■	70			■	■	71			

PUZZLE 560

• COLLEGE DAYS •

ACROSS

1. Indifferent
6. Sacks
10. LPs' speeds
14. OK
15. Ike's ex
16. New York canal
17. College courses
19. Lone
20. Compass pt.
21. Snout
22. Favor
24. Pattern
26. Strike out
28. Scottish loch
30. Give out again
33. Smokes
36. Whip up
38. Draft org.
39. Buckeye State
40. Trims
41. Water-testers
42. Freight weight
43. Mattress cover
44. Type of code
45. More disreputable
47. Catch sight of
49. Four-wheeled carriage
51. Shine
55. Looked narrowly
57. Rain heavily
59. Savings-plan inits.
60. Cab
61. College project
64. Jacob's twin
65. Stagger
66. Weird
67. X-ray quantities
68. Coll. admission tests
69. Demolishes, in London

DOWN

1. Sparked over a gap
2. Adult nit
3. Fairy-tale monsters
4. Above, to Keats
5. Edges
6. AC letters
7. Was ill
8. Wildebeest
9. Novices' embroideries
10. Readjusts
11. College teacher
12. Travel unit
13. Prophet
18. Dupes
23. Restraint
25. News bits
27. Explodes
29. Eyeball's outer covering
31. Expends
32. Latin being
33. Containers
34. Whoops!
35. College ender?
37. Hasten
40. English cheeses
41. Wee ones
43. ____ qua non
44. One who grieves
46. Persian king
48. Promote
50. Overturn
52. Layers
53. Comedian Kovacs
54. Charges
55. Winged suffix
56. Life of Riley
58. Lubricates
62. Ocean
63. ____ culpa

1	2	3	4	5	■	6	7	8	9	■	10	11	12	13
14					■	15				■	16			
17					18					■	19			
20			■	21				■	22	23				
24			25			■	26	27					■	■
■	■	■	28			29	■	30					31	32
33	34	35			■	36	37				■	38		
39				■	40					■	41			
42			■	43					■	44				
45			46				■	47	48			■	■	■
■	■	49					50	■	51			52	53	54
55	56					■	57	58			■	59		
60				■	61	62					63			
64				■	65				■	66				
67				■	68				■	69				

PUZZLE 561

Dial-A-Grams

These messages are in a number code based on the familiar telephone dial. Each number represents one of the letters shown with it on the dial. You must decide which one. A number is not necessarily the same letter each time.

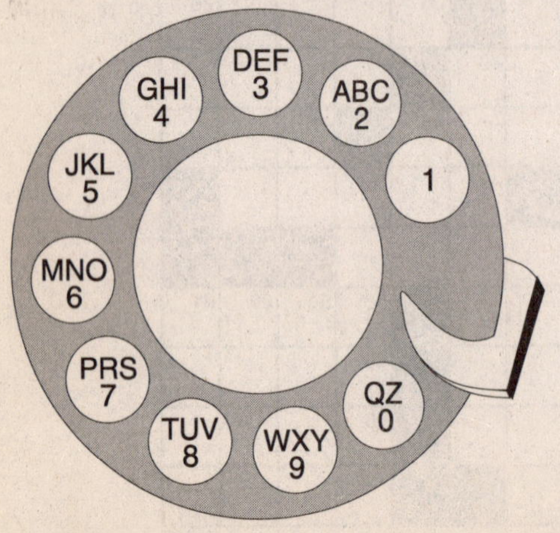

A. 663-4253 86 84733-3687847 63 843 4328 5677 9687 2639 7833377 9436 968 46 688 4686 843 2653 47 288742882253 86 668 9327464 2 428.

B. 2724463337, 2 628436284 2426 46 2624368 473323, 46836833 2 663-737766 35382867 87464 76737 263 7855397.

DOUBLE TROUBLE

PUZZLE 562

Not really double trouble, but double fun! Solve this puzzle as you would a regular crossword, EXCEPT place one, two, or three letters in each box. The number of letters in each answer is shown in parentheses after its clue.

ACROSS

1. Use profanity (5)
4. Comes into sight (7)
7. Sweetheart (8)
8. Rain-gear fabric (7)
10. Cruel (4)
11. Necklace ornament (7)
13. Certain anesthetic (5)
15. Wasp-inflicted wound (5)
17. Flower stalk (4)
18. Burn (4)
19. Valuable possession (5)
21. Bears' lairs (4)
23. Scathing, as satire (6)
24. Grocery or drug (5)
26. In that place (5)
28. Request for insurance reparation (5)
30. Rates of speed, as in music (6)
32. Causing covetousness (8)
35. Whirl (4)
37. Walk with long steps (6)
39. Show to a chair (4)
40. Cause to be delayed (4)
41. Group of seven (6)
43. More adorable (5)
44. Quality of being cherished (8)
46. Wave tops (6)
48. Ventured (5)
49. Crier's output (4)

DOWN

1. Remedy (4)
2. Incline (5)
3. 2, 4, 6, etc. (5)
4. Business engagement (11)
5. Men of rank (5)
6. Quick drawing (6)
7. Errant students (7)
9. Reside in (7)
10. Buttes' cousins (5)
12. Went steady (5)
14. Going astray (6)
16. Swallow (6)
20. Tribal symbol (5)
22. Luster (5)
25. Seized for nonpayment (11)
27. Edit (6)
28. Schoolroom group (5)
29. Collapse toward the middle (7)
31. Comic ____ (funny-paper feature) (5)
33. Bead-and-rod calculation device (6)
34. Epistle (6)
36. Held to one's heart, as thoughts (6)
38. Act like a sleuth (6)
42. Arboretum feature (4)
45. In close proximity (4)
47. Lead player (4)

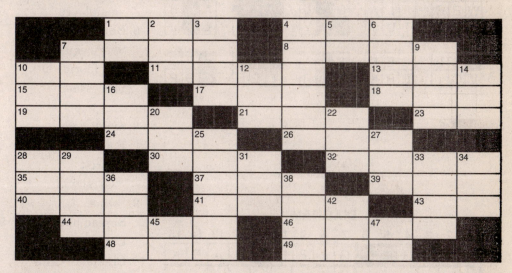

■	■	1	2	3	■	4	5	6	■	■
■	7				■	8			9	■
10		■	11		12		■	13		14
15		16	■	17			■	18		
19			20	■	21		22	■	23	
■	■	24		25	■	26		27	■	■
28	29	■	30		31	■	32		33	34
35		36	■	37		38	■	39		
40			■	41			42	■	43	
■	44		45		■	46		47		■
■	■	48			■	49			■	■

Circle Sums

PUZZLE 563

Each circle, lettered A through H, has its own number value from 1 to 9. No two circles have the same value. The numbers shown in the diagram are the sums of the circles that overlap at those points. For example, 5 is the sum of circles B and C. Can you find the value of each circle?

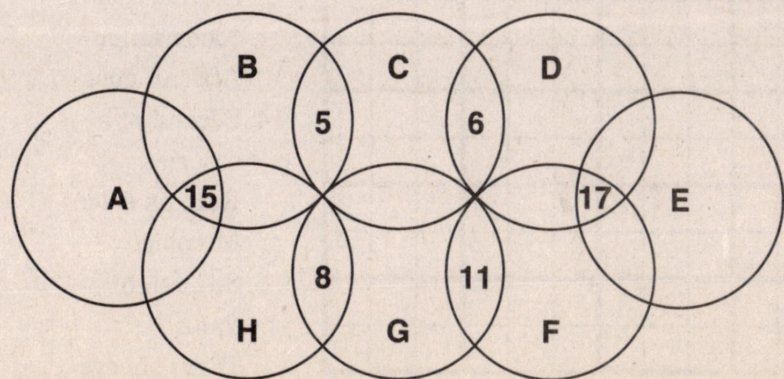

PUZZLE 564 BRICK BY BRICK

Rearrange this stack of bricks to form a crossword puzzle. The clues will help you fit the bricks into their correct places. Row 1 has been filled in for you. Use the bricks to fill in the remaining spaces.

BRICKS

DIAGRAM

	1	2	3	4	5	6	7	8	9	10	11	12	13	14	15
1	E	C	R	U			G	L	E	N		P	A	R	K
2															
3															
4															
5															
6															
7															
8															
9															
10															
11															
12															
13															
14															
15															

ACROSS

1. Very light beige
   Narrow valley
   Public land
2. Spanish dessert
   Knit
   Not fer
3. Bishop Desmond ____
   Mass of metal
   Marathon
4. Looks at
   "Star ____"
   Ship operators
5. Theater employee
6. Blind part
   Share equally
7. Silk fabric
   Succession
   ____ trip
8. Small hotel
   Fueled
   Lyricist Gershwin
9. Swine
   Spread out
   Channel
10. Chocolate drink
    Dawn direction
11. Photocopiers, at times
12. Lion's pad
    Nerdy type
    Large volume
13. Sunburn balm
    Flood foiler
    African goat
14. Second of a series
    Run, as colors
    Misplace
15. Shut tight
    Yank
    Team cheers

DOWN

1. Salamanders
   CEO, e.g.
   Chemists' rooms, shortly
2. Hint
   ____ boom
   To shelter
3. Fixed charge
   Slang
   Jot
4. Rare
   Cornflakes, e.g.
5. Child by marriage
6. Including
   October gem
   JFK's successor
7. Family
   Bird that hoots
   Ms. Astaire
8. Tavern option
   Peggy or Stephen
   Fido's friend
9. Summon
   Towel off
   Athens native
10. Angler's tool
    "Of ____ I Sing"
    Made do
11. Later
12. Package
    Viciously
13. Petri-dish gel
    Hides
    Wind instrument
14. Grain
    White heron
    Flat hill
15. Understood
    Stable bit
    Former mates

PUZZLE 565

ACROSS
1. Jumble
5. Coin taker
9. Consequently
13. Aware of
14. Tennis site
16. Las Vegas light
17. Christmas plant
19. Little brook
20. Mug handle
21. Winners
22. Crisp fabric
24. Prior to
25. Dance noisily
26. Tension
29. Superiority
33. Stand in good ____
34. Looking at
36. Right this minute
37. Recover
38. Lendl and Boesky
39. Charter
40. Slip up
41. Adversary
42. Certain fisherman
43. Gloom
45. Soothed
47. Accomplishment
48. Quick drink
49. Clairvoyant
53. Dock rodent
54. Tango requirement
57. Sunburn reliever
58. Utterly
61. Sightsee
62. Slack
63. Make warm
64. Towel word
65. The Bee ____
66. Longings

DOWN
1. Expectancy
2. Small buffalo
3. Rouse
4. Sweetie
5. Public tantrums
6. Oodles
7. Baseball call
8. Musical combo
9. Caught up
10. Harness piece
11. Medal color
12. Single
15. Plaids
18. Fathered
23. Posse
24. Epochal
26. Cordwood measure
27. "____ on My Pillow"
28. Disconnect
29. Imitation leather
30. Doddering
31. Wounded with a tusk
32. Jug
33. Tool site
35. Colorful tuber
38. Monogram letter
39. Benefit
41. Every
42. Upper crust
44. Racetrack horses
46. Customary ways
49. Bicycle route
50. Blackthorn fruit
51. "Paint ____ Wagon"
52. Wooden shoe
53. American Beauty, e.g.
54. Biblical pronoun
55. Withdraw
56. Food scraps
59. Digit
60. "____ kingdom come . . ."

Hexagon Match

PUZZLE 566

Place the seven words into the hexagons so that each letter will match the letter in the adjacent hexagon. All the words will read in a clockwise direction. One letter has been entered to get you started.

ADRIFT
DOLLOP
ENDEAR
IMPALA
OVERDO
POODLE
RODENT

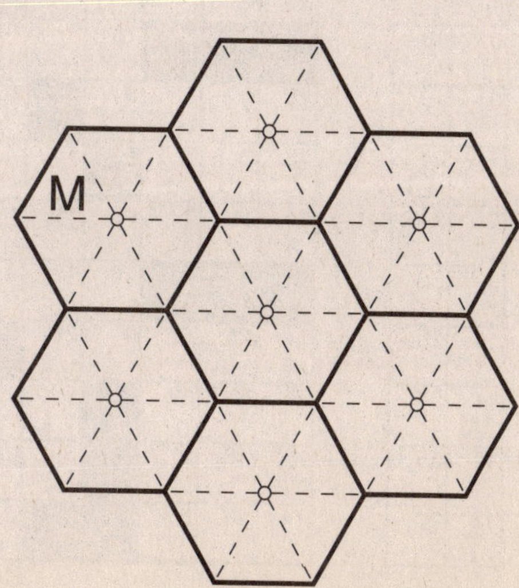

PUZZLE 567

CODEWORD

Codeword is a special crossword puzzle in which conventional clues are omitted. Instead, answer words in the diagram are represented by numbers. Each number represents a different letter of the alphabet, and all of the letters of the alphabet are used. When you are sure of a letter, put it in the code key chart and cross it off in the alphabet box. A group of letters has been inserted to start you off.

1	14
2 A	15 T
3	16
4	17
5	18 N
6	19
7	20
8	21
9	22
10	23
11	24
12	25
13	26

2 A	18 N	15 T	14	23		19	2	9		2	24	17
15	14	2	9	2		17	9	2		24	17	11
17	20	8	17	24		2	14	12		24	2	26
				23	5	13	2	19		17	25	17
19	13	9	17	2	13			24	2	4	17	9
16	9	2	24		16	26	24	17	11			
16	18	15	16		15	17	17		16	8	17	18
			8	23	2	24	12		19	2	10	17
7	2	22	17	15			16	12	17	24	17	15
17	26	16		2	9	17	18	2				
15	9	4		18	16	9		12	2	6	16	9
22	17	17		3	2	26		2	1	2	9	17
21	17	9		2	11	23		23	17	1	17	11

~~A~~	~~N~~
B	O
C	P
D	Q
E	R
F	S
G	~~T~~
H	U
I	V
J	W
K	X
L	Y
M	Z

PUZZLE 568

CODEWORD

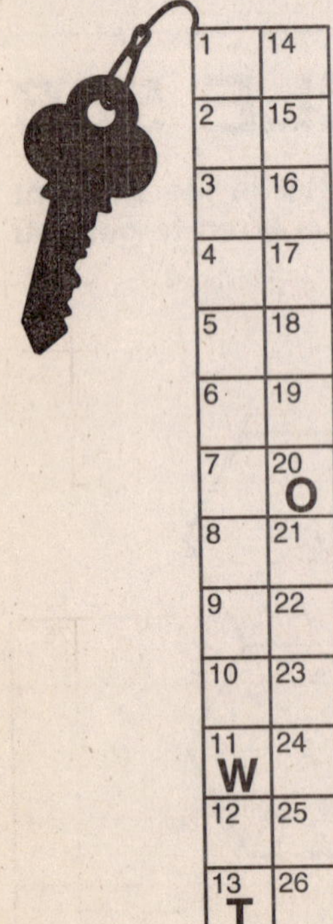

1	14
2	15
3	16
4	17
5	18
6	19
7	20 O
8	21
9	22
10	23
11 W	24
12	25
13 T	26

16	7	26			7	12	20			7	16	3
1	6	3		5	2	6	10	12		23	6	13
3	1	3		7	2	13	3	1		7	1	16
11	7	2	13	24				3	7	1	13	18
			18	3	14		13	7	22			
15	5	5	8		13 T	11 W	20 O	14	20	21	3	14
13	3	7		18	7	15	1	8		7	12	3
14	3	1	19	7	10	13	14		3	22	12	3
			15	10	9		20	1	17			
14	25	6	7	22				3	17	20	10	8
26	6	12		2	20	16	7	2		17	20	7
7	15	2		3	26	20	4	8		20	6	1
14	13	8			3	11	3			3	10	22

A	N
B	~~O~~
C	P
D	Q
E	R
F	S
G	~~T~~
H	U
I	V
J	~~W~~
K	X
L	Y
M	Z

PUZZLE 569

• MAN'S BEST FRIEND •

ACROSS

1. Taxi
4. Sphere
7. Existed
10. Elderly
12. Sailor
13. Shopping vehicle
14. Peel
15. Garret
17. Take apart
18. French sword
19. "The ____ Boat"
21. Back of the neck
24. Biblical place
25. Midas's golden puppy?
27. Hamlet's noble pet?
29. Swerve
30. Back talk
31. Feathery plant
32. Retain
34. School gp.
36. Matterhorn, e.g.
39. Pampered Parisian pooches?
43. Bean Town hound?
47. Prone
48. Pitcher's stat
49. French soul
50. New Deal org.
51. Joe Cocker's canine?
53. Male pooch?
55. Boxer Muhammad ____
56. Chow down
57. Novelist Stoker
61. Frosted
64. Actor Rickman
66. Horse's gait
67. Silent sled-pullers?
72. Dalai Lama's pet?
77. Touched down
78. Lunch, e.g.
79. Em, to Dorothy
80. Smack
81. Bakery product
82. Fearful
84. "Kiss Me ____"
85. Prophetic sign
86. Soup container
87. Agitate
88. Indicate yes
89. Needle hole
90. "Livin' ____ Prayer"

DOWN

1. Antic
2. Open-mouthed
3. French cap
4. "Tarka the ____"
5. Rodent
6. Carry along
7. Actress Hendrix
8. "Our Miss Brooks" star
9. Pebble
11. Bambi, e.g.
13. Prompted
15. Declare positively
16. Sedans
19. Ogle
20. Kiln
22. Pike's discovery
23. Relaxation
26. "____ Waited So Long"
28. Mao ____-tung
31. Fashion craze
33. Golf norm
34. Momma's partner
35. Sum
37. Actress Lavin
38. H. Ross ____
39. Ballet step
40. Flower necklace
41. Before, of yore
42. Actor Mineo
43. Typewriter key
44. Flightless bird
45. Family mem.
46. Dustcloth
52. Penpoint
54. Conducted
58. Lamb's dad
59. Grad
60. Spouse
61. Iraq's neighbor
62. Price
63. Airport info
65. Not messy
66. Thunk
67. Georgia town
68. Texas shrine
69. Cared for
70. Egyptian sun god
71. Pie piece
72. Singer Frankie ____
73. Inquires
74. Greek philosopher
75. Silky fabric
76. "Carmen," e.g.
83. Merry month

PUZZLE 570

ACROSS

1. With 5 Across, links instructor
5. See 1 Across
8. Celebration
12. Organic compound
13. Glistened
15. Iridescent stone
16. Central point
17. Clan symbol
18. Computer problem
19. Treacheries
21. Tropical trees
23. Compensate
24. Flock's perch
25. Check for the id
27. Foretell
28. That lady
31. Intimidates
34. Flushed
36. Ambiance
37. Quartz variety
39. Highway
40. Highway clearer
42. Fondly
44. Alts.
45. Not quite round
46. Sugary suffix
47. Tablet
48. Conquered
50. Sharp bend
54. Court cases
59. Gumbo need
60. Practice piece
62. Marsh bird
63. Nonclerical
64. Fathered
65. Sta. postings
66. Category
67. Auction ending
68. Year portions

DOWN

1. Bloke
2. ____ about
3. Mine vein
4. Kennel pest
5. False
6. Decays
7. Wallet bill
8. Ducks and geese
9. Heroic verse
10. Fictional plantation
11. Shade providers
13. Plato's porch
14. Enclosed
20. Leopard marking
22. Dumbstruck
24. Bard
25. Continental coins
26. Chew steadily
27. Bar disorder
28. Nocturnal noise
29. Make better
30. Rotary flow
31. Dart
32. Female relative
33. Saves
35. Historic ages
38. Spur on
41. Catholic leader
43. Vast periods
48. Fishing boot
49. Unpaid
50. Dimwit
51. Authorize
52. Grasp
53. Ornamental fabric
54. Entice
55. Manipulated
56. Greek vowel
57. Cafeteria server
58. Mouth off
61. Connection

PUZZLE 571

Categories

For each of the Categories listed, can you think of a word or phrase beginning with each letter on the left? Count one point for each correct answer. A score of 15 is good and 21 is excellent.

	BEATLES SONG	BIRD	U.S. CITY	FLOWER	ACTRESS
T					
H					
R					
O					
W					

PUZZLE 572

ACROSS

1. Speck
5. Mavens
9. ____ David
13. Attended
14. Had the nerve
16. Jai ____
17. Unbarred
18. Speak pompously
19. Agreeable
20. Fabric scrap
21. Infuriates
22. Repartee
24. Passed
26. Church section
27. Archaic
28. Happens to
31. Exactly similar
34. Submerged
35. Moving truck
37. Swiftness
38. Loathed
39. Rickey fruit
40. ____ out a living
41. More wan
42. Beef cut
43. Inheritances
45. Prohibition
46. Crescents
47. Ebbs
51. Affection
54. Metalware
55. Thump
56. Healing plant
57. Register
59. Knight's aide
60. Top-billed
61. Put out
62. Minister's word
63. Whale herds
64. Dampens
65. Three feet

DOWN

1. Point total
2. Type of cross
3. Greek letter
4. Toe count
5. Worshiped
6. Worried
7. Stats for Dodgers
8. Put in place
9. Preserved
10. Dismounted
11. Spiked club
12. Marina sight
15. Argued formally
21. Emerald ____
23. Raring to go
25. Prod
26. In no case
28. Nibbles
29. Morally bad
30. Matching
31. Jungle creature
32. TV's Ricki ____
33. Frosts
34. Valleys
36. Angling tool
38. Devised
39. Sales pitch
41. Segment
42. Turn toward
44. Circus workers
45. Southern damsels
47. Rule the ____
48. Serious play
49. Zealous
50. Fork over
51. Yellow jacket
52. Choir singer
53. Turnpike
54. Bona fide
58. Immediately
59. Wages

Changaword

PUZZLE 573

Can you change the top word into the bottom word in each column in the number of steps indicated in parentheses? Change only one letter at a time and do not change the order of the letters. Proper names, slang, and obsolete words are not allowed.

1. LAMP (4 steps)	2. WIRE (5 steps)	3. WATT (6 steps)	4. BLOW (7 steps)
CORD	VOLT	BULB	FUSE

PUZZLE 574

CRYPTIC CROSSWORD

British-style or Cryptic Crosswords are a great challenge for crossword fans. Each clue contains either a definition or direct reference to the answer as well as a play on words. The numbers in parentheses indicate the number of letters in the answer words.

ACROSS

1. Cook traps good mollusk (9)
6. Suggest putting one in mail (5)
9. In the middle of morning, pal gives initial word (7)
10. Refuse outfit, period (7)
11. Sloppy stuff reversed my bridge hand (5)
12. A health resort sent back sweetener for veggie (9)
13. Mr. Torme: Repugnant and nice sounding (9)
16. Loser taking gym class cheated (5)
18. Will object with pained shout (5)
19. Cheese stored in baroque fortress (9)
21. Southeastern story with a message is not fixed, perhaps (9)
24. Listen to benefit for pioneer (5)
25. American League fan is everywhere (3,4)
26. Make a mistake in row with dog (7)
27. Cross set in concrete turns less rigid (5)
28. Trick layers with stone (9)

DOWN

1. Ancestor also entering weight (7)
2. Confused, ran after "Get lost!" (9)
3. Small broken urn next to Cobb (5)
4. Display a gloomy hairdo (9)
5. Unearth dog I'd raised (3,2)
6. Detach crest from bird (9)
7. Vocalized about Latin jargon (5)
8. Upcoming final course is hairy (7)
14. Pilot keeps hold, going with the current (9)
15. Isolate fortune-teller going around search (9)
17. Goading Utah city ruler (9)
18. Not oddly, Dennis and April get tangled up (7)
20. Hero met bad proposition (7)
22. Hear groups of sheep in flowers (5)
23. Drills tires (5)
24. Registered nurse inside, though overly tanned (5)

PUZZLE 575

• PETITE FOUR •

ACROSS
1. Flit
5. Profuse
11. Buster
14. "In the Valley of ____"
15. Hebrew prophet
16. Schubert's "The ____ King"
17. Don Ho hit
19. Become grayer
20. Eastern cartoon
21. "____ and Meek"
22. Understood
23. Puts new bottoms on
26. "Xanadu" band
28. Kids' teams
34. See red?
37. Flynn of flicks
38. Cause to smile
39. It may have lines
41. Mansard features
43. Like birds
44. Pickling medium
46. Hardware pros
48. Deficient
49. Tidy sum
52. Simile center
53. Slim
57. Shankar on sitar
60. Former airline letters
63. "Germinal" author
64. Jackie's O
65. Butter cookies
68. Get a move on
69. Composed
70. Snick's partner
71. Maxim
72. Compact
73. Stag

DOWN
1. Remove gunk from
2. Dress cut
3. Asian queens
4. Aromatic compound
5. Romanian coin
6. Clerical garment
7. Emotional sense
8. Man, e.g.
9. Israeli bill
10. Is ill with
11. Noodle
12. Thirst
13. Tooted
18. Refute
22. It's no bear
24. To be, for mon ami
25. Sphere beginning
27. Protective shelter
29. Flame
30. Decides
31. Lasses
32. Colorado neighbor
33. Strange, strangely
34. Sun and moon
35. Computer pest
36. Literary alias
40. Chou ____
42. Synagogue
45. Drill bits?
47. Mean mien
50. Reverend
51. Tangle
54. Forest goddess
55. Senior
56. Alley button
57. Stadium sounds
58. Domingo offering
59. Opinion
61. Deteriorated
62. Bailiwick
65. Former jet
66. Explosive initials
67. Ottoman title

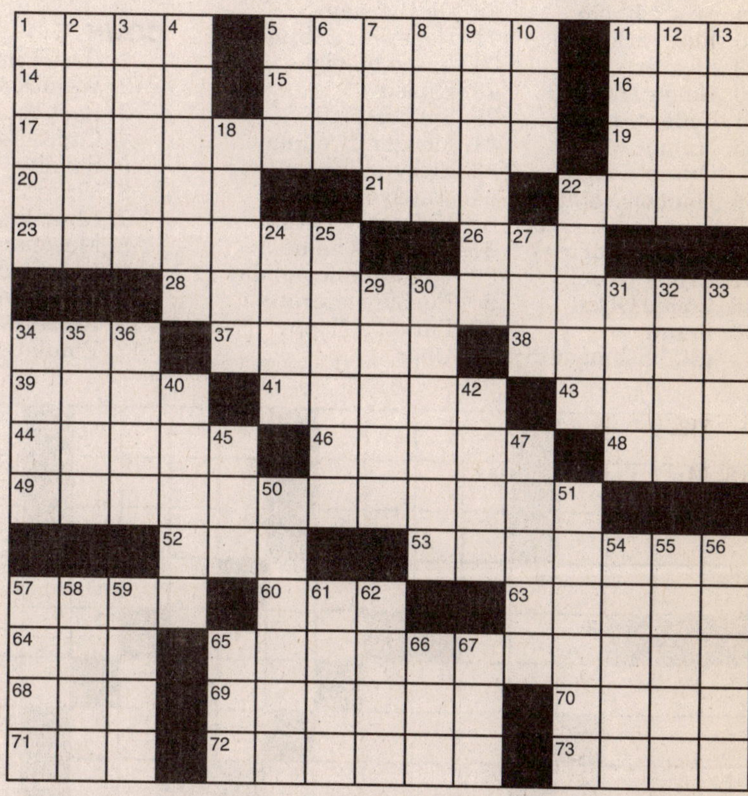

Top to Bottom

PUZZLE 576

Place the letters given below each diagram into the squares to form eight 4-letter words reading from top to bottom from square to connected square. The top letter is the first letter of all eight words, each letter in the second row is the second letter of four words, and so on.

Example:

B / A U / R L R / E K L N

Bare, Bark, Balk, Ball, Bulk, Bull, Burl, Burn.

1.

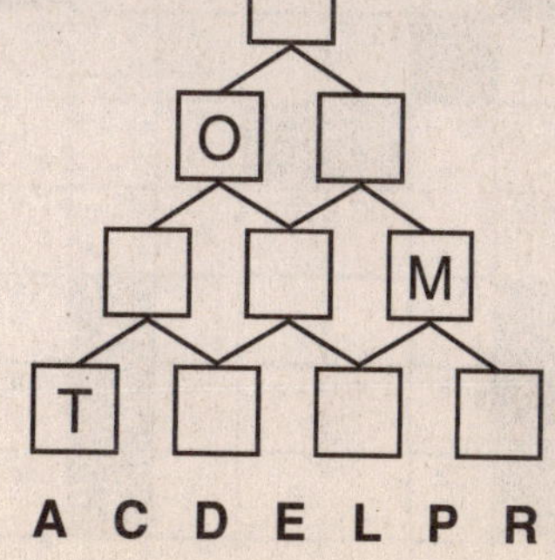

A C D E L P R

2.

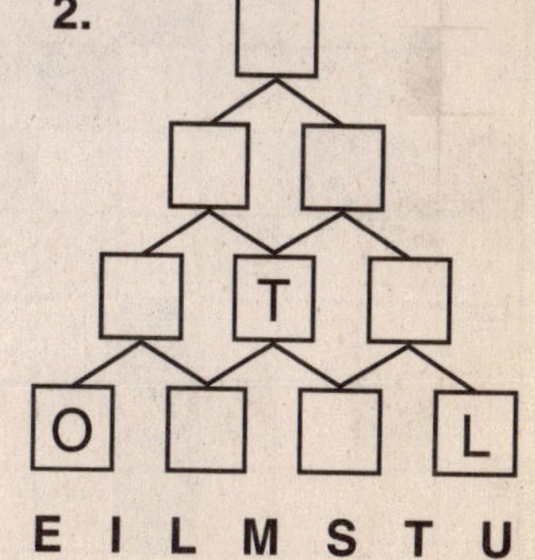

E I L M S T U

PUZZLE 577

• FRUIT BOWL •

ACROSS

1. Spot's dinner?
5. Place for a figurehead
9. Frogner Park's locale
13. Joyous
17. Kind of deck
18. Legends
19. Sheriff's badge
20. One, to Klaus
21. Sicilian spouter
22. Busy as ____
23. Actress Gilbert
24. Mrs. Chaplin
25. Firecracker
28. Motherly
30. Golfer Kite
31. Toiletry item
33. Humpty Dumpty, e.g.
34. Diamond State
39. Jennifer ____ of "Dirty Dancing"
41. Crude vessel
45. Comic Olsen
46. Retail establishment
48. It has a waxed coat
50. Staff officer
51. Character in "Macbeth"
53. Pandora's box contents
55. Wind dir.
56. Glass section
57. First name in photography
59. Glory
61. Not specific
63. Iowa college
65. Buenos ____
67. Social function
68. On the way
72. Honey ____ (bird)
74. Based on eight
78. Espied
79. Sphere
81. Meager dwelling
83. Storytelling dance
84. Watch over
85. Helmer of fiction
87. Gurkha's home
89. Palindromic holiday
90. Pueblo material
92. Put on a floppy
94. Oner
96. Popular ISP
98. Patola
100. Veldt antelope
101. "I'll Be Around" singers
105. Thyroid cartilage
111. Ballet dancer Spessivtzeva
112. Invalid
114. Part of QED
115. Natatorium
116. Cow's hurdle
117. Think-tank outflow
118. ____ Domini
119. She, to Pedro
120. Miss Kett of comics
121. Dork
122. Without much fat
123. Sheepskin leather

DOWN

1. Cartel initials
2. Vocalist David Lee ____
3. Rapper ____-Loc
4. Capital of Laconia
5. Sandbox buddy
6. Virginia senator
7. Chocolate cookie
8. Musician Ted ____
9. CIA predecessor
10. Oater event
11. Byron work
12. Emulate Churchill
13. Ty Cobb's nickname
14. English emblem
15. "Black Beauty" author Sewell
16. Negotiate
26. Aisles
27. Swamp
29. Psyche part
32. Exists
34. Picasso model Maar
35. Zebulun's son
36. Minus
37. Traipse
38. Heath
40. Yin's partner
42. Perjurer
43. Mrs. Garrett (Charlotte Rae role)
44. Folk dance
47. J.R.'s mother
49. Sports competition
52. Straight man
54. Opera's Caldwell
58. Actor/bodybuilder Ferrigno
60. Montana river
62. Prefix for modern
64. School on the Thames
66. Hills of Rome number
68. This, in Toledo
69. Shortcoming
70. Las Vegas rival
71. Piccadilly Circus statue
73. "____ Man"
75. Bishop Desmond ____
76. Pianist Templeton
77. Wood strip
80. More bold
82. Poet Hughes
86. Topaz hummingbird
88. Laptev Sea feeder
91. Month of Sundays
93. Period of note
95. Sing for your ____
97. "Deathtrap" playwright
99. Flawless
101. Indefinite amount
102. Intrigue
103. "____ a Name" (Croce song)
104. Went by howdah
106. "Judith" composer
107. Polynesian force
108. Game of chukkers
109. "Copacabana" girl
110. Enthusiasm
113. Lemmon/Danson film

PUZZLE 578

• RAINBOW •

ACROSS

1. Actor Sandler
5. Lallygag
9. Persian king
13. Hindu philosophy
17. Wrongdoing
18. Inactive
19. Prince Charles's sport
20. Homeric
21. Radiate
22. Sow's mate
23. Diva's solo
24. Wash
25. Misleading clue
28. Sauntered
30. 100 square meters
31. Times past
33. Couple
34. Issued
39. Gentle
41. More than once
45. Nemesis
46. Sour
48. Macadamize
50. Machete's kin
51. Mr. Linkletter
52. Kitchen tools
54. Never used
55. Bond's school
56. Whinny
58. Nonprofessionals
60. Sportscast features
62. Dustcloth
64. Challenges
66. Helios, to Ovid
67. Chirped
71. Valleys
73. Harplike instruments
77. Tennis term
78. Currently
80. Gratify
82. Cortes's quest
83. Islamic nation
84. Designer Piccone
86. Expectorate
87. Send
88. Turkish title
90. Son of Seth
92. Drooled
94. Frequently, in verse
96. Clobber
98. Young louse
99. Liquidate gradually
103. Alan Ladd film, with "The"
109. Principal
110. Mrs. Copperfield
112. Poker move
113. Rowboat need
114. Fashion magazine
115. Dark brews
116. Silent
117. Faucet problem
118. Cozy home
119. Striplings
120. Flightless birds
121. Back talk

DOWN

1. Assert
2. Ten cents
3. Etching fluid
4. Firedamp gas
5. Opera text
6. Stench
7. Jai ____
8. Frondlike
9. Health haven
10. Cossack, e.g.
11. Dismounted
12. Stash
13. Coward
14. Milky gem
15. Donate
16. Served perfectly
26. Memorable period
27. Obtained
29. Not at home
32. Seance sound
34. Israeli Abba ____
35. Stallion's mate
36. Naysayer
37. Viscount's superior
38. Fear
40. Always
42. Smidgen
43. Satiate
44. Billions of years
47. Group of three
49. Lambs' dams
52. Fellow
53. Belt
57. Kato's employer
59. Hollers
61. Rod
63. Krupa or Kelly
65. Oozes
67. Shear
68. Israeli dance
69. Gabor and Peron
70. Hawk's opposite
72. Jib, e.g.
74. Bellow
75. Canal of song
76. Vended
79. Roamed
81. Seatless riders
85. Likewise not
87. Modes
89. Sternward
91. U-boat
93. By means of
95. Basin or wave
97. Find fault with
99. Prayer ender
100. Cob or drake
101. Bribes
102. French novelist
104. "E pluribus ____"
105. "____, Brute?"
106. Dr. Zhivago's flame
107. Eye part
108. Pit vipers
111. Burro

PUZZLE 579

• THE CLAUS'S LAMENT •

ACROSS

1. Tibet's neighbor
6. Thrust
10. French friends
14. Viola da ____
19. Rare violin
20. Rain hard
21. Defy
22. Heep of fiction
23. Start of verse
27. ____-tzu
28. "____, meany, miney, . . ."
29. Punctuation mark
30. "Let ____ Gay" (Crothers play)
31. Comic Johnson
32. Dijon dog
33. Turn right!
34. B'way sign
37. Spurious wings
40. Roof support
41. Tolkien creature
42. Tie the knot
43. Station
44. Restaurateur Toots ____
45. Scottish waterfall
47. December 31, e.g.
48. More verse
54. Greek portico
55. Tinge
56. Papal vestment
57. Knockoff
59. Walking aid
60. Fern seed
61. Least sanguine
62. Chuckling sound
65. 18-wheeler
66. Helicopters
67. Marsh
68. Vintage car
69. One
71. Palindromic title
72. Trade center
73. Sidled
74. Swedish star Marta ____
75. Smooth
76. Wise ____ owl
80. More verse
84. Dunk
85. Affected manner
86. Age
87. Babble
88. GI's hangout
89. Rainbow
90. Less wild
92. Piano type
93. Chop
94. Claudette's key
95. Senator Specter
96. Chafe
97. Kitchen add-on
99. Phony moniker
100. Vocal solo
101. Garden plot
104. Last part of verse
109. Spotless
110. Skater's milieu
111. "Kiss Me, ____"
112. Buffalo player
113. Central group
114. Hungarian politician Imre ____
115. Good golly!
116. Live coal

DOWN

1. Brad, e.g.
2. Jane Austen novel
3. Half a Samoan town?
4. Broke bread
5. Learned people
6. Quill, e.g.
7. Stylish
8. Summer mo.
9. Pamphlet
10. Confuses
11. Bricklayer
12. Islamic nation
13. Rorqual
14. Gore
15. Bedouin
16. Military ship
17. Sosa's stick
18. Eureka!
24. French noggin
25. Superman's girlfriend
26. Governess
31. Don Ho's hello
32. British tenant farm
33. Lamp dweller
35. Gearshift choice
36. "____ to Joy"
37. Ms. Rehan et al.
38. Pre-Easter period
39. Hairstyle
40. Biblical pronoun
44. Big Band music
45. Falsifiers
46. Unemployed
49. Sedate
50. Uppermost voice
51. Forster's "____ With a View"
52. Research money
53. Minister's subj.
58. Palindromic Indian
59. Doctrine
60. Aligned (with)
61. Hidden
62. Shade
63. Upright
64. Dynamic
66. Mr. Burghoff et al.
67. Eucharistic vestment
70. Mystery-writer Josephine ____
71. Jay ____ of "Picture Perfect"
72. City official
74. Doubly
75. Dutch painter Jan ____
76. Showery month
77. Bridge
78. Der ____ (Adenauer)
79. Russian refusal
81. Cotton Club's site
82. Junior
83. Hand clapping
84. Derisive interjection
89. Play opener
90. Puzzling
91. Kirghizia's ____ Mountains
92. Levantine ketch
95. Parallel to
96. Avarice
98. Russian despot
99. "Heat of the Moment" band
100. Nora's pooch
101. Mast support
102. Raison d'____
103. Color changer
104. Regulatory agcy.
105. Coinage suffix
106. Coastal flier
107. Fall behind
108. Butter?

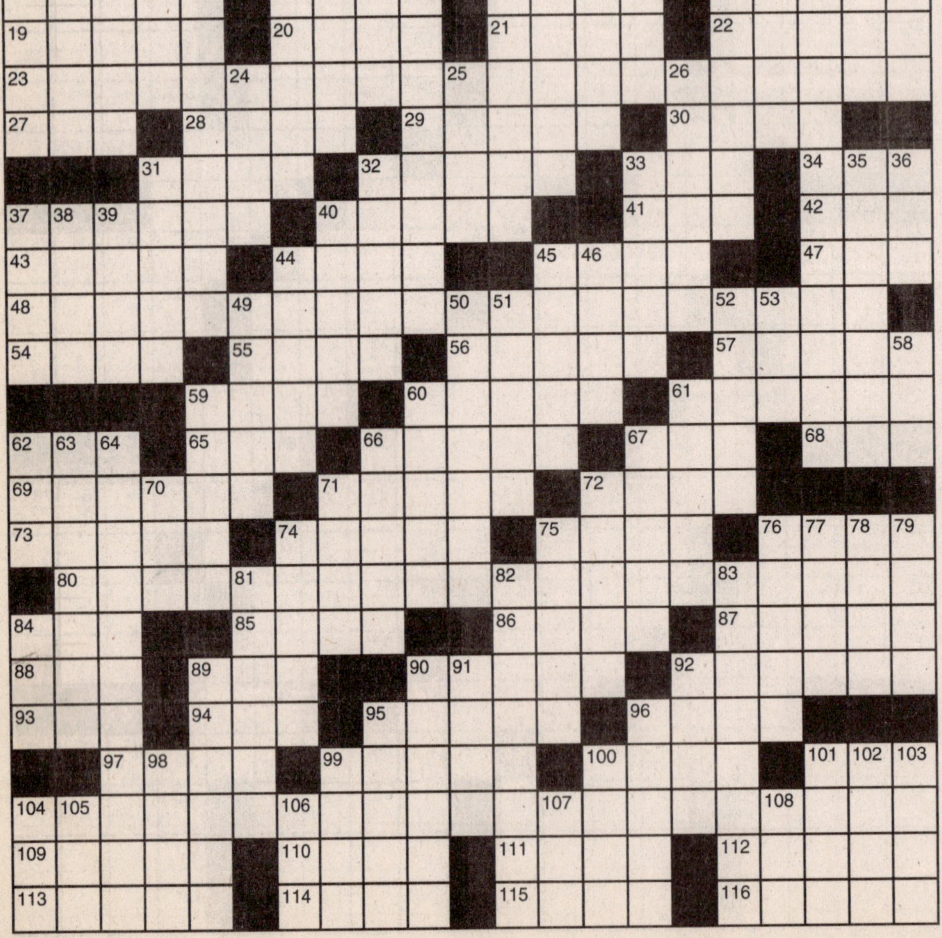

PUZZLE 580

• THAT'S USING THE NOGGIN •

ACROSS

1. Famous cookie maker
5. Social event
9. Kind of race
13. Touched down
17. Actress Remini
18. Gave up
19. Nappy material
20. Actress Thompson
21. Indian relics
23. Prep school boss
25. Hyde Park buggies
26. In good health
27. Spike and Bruce
28. Commences
29. Frank's ex
31. Give notice
33. With, to Pierre
34. Comic Carvey
36. Press for payment
37. Wild attempt
41. Picnic drink
42. Stay cool
47. Actress Thurman
48. Damage
49. Snare
50. Prefix for sun
51. NFL players
52. "The Dukes of Hazzard" role
54. Rex Reed, e.g.
57. Feeling poorly
58. Goddess of love
59. "____, Nanette"
60. Biddy
61. Lodgings, slangily
63. Blue or green
64. Having handles
66. Thesaurus guy
67. Wise lawmaker
68. Queried
69. Verve
70. Adult boy
71. Sample
74. Yearned
75. Bee chaser?
77. Kind of card
79. Tennis star Arthur ____
80. Tinted
81. Nonchalant
83. Cato's way
84. Hasten
85. Timetable info
86. Panic
90. Finale
91. Ancient Asian
93. Autumn mo.
94. Spanish parlor
95. Dear me!
97. Pool table item
99. Coq au ____
100. Was concerned
102. Develop
104. Diamond feature
107. Hanker for
108. Stars
111. Bathing nozzle
116. Egg on
117. Graf's former rival
118. English nobles
119. Funny Johnson
120. Certain shorebirds
121. Harem rooms
122. Meadow mamas
123. Excuse type

DOWN

1. In the manner of
2. French sea
3. Boat paddle
4. Quaint little store
5. Regards
6. Maris and Rehan
7. A Kennedy
8. McMahon et al.
9. Fight for two
10. Authentic
11. Remark further
12. Sparkler
13. Valuable things
14. Tardy
15. March 15, e.g.
16. Sticky substance
18. Detective Charlie ____
19. That girl
22. Destroy
24. Boxing great
26. Diminish
28. Out of the comfort zone
29. Pass a bill
30. Moving vehicle
31. Small game bird
32. Loosen
33. "A Bell for ____"
35. Shade of blond
36. Farmer's place?
38. Flatter with success
39. Love affair
40. Deep voice
41. Prayer closer
43. Carved
44. Bobbled
45. Hurt
46. Bank job?
51. Jai alai ball
53. Drenched
55. Elvis, to some
56. Groucho's prop
58. Hi-fi sound
62. Cowboy Autry
63. Against
65. Debtor's shade?
66. Pee Wee ____
67. Rani's wear
68. Sharp
70. Closet nuisance
72. Leg fronts
73. Set the ball up
74. Attention getter?
75. Timepiece
76. Sunrise direction
78. Certain Italian
81. Political group
82. Dawn deity
87. Church part
88. Inventor Whitney
89. Challenger
92. Wears away
96. "____ Weapon"
98. Hole punch
100. Hooded garments
101. Blvds.
102. Actor Richard ____
103. Fury
104. Mr. Lugosi
105. Land measures
106. Draft org.
107. Apple's center
108. "Ben-____"
109. Bar lead-in?
110. Beatty of films
111. Observe
112. Hem's partner
113. Age of note
114. Money mach.
115. Low grade

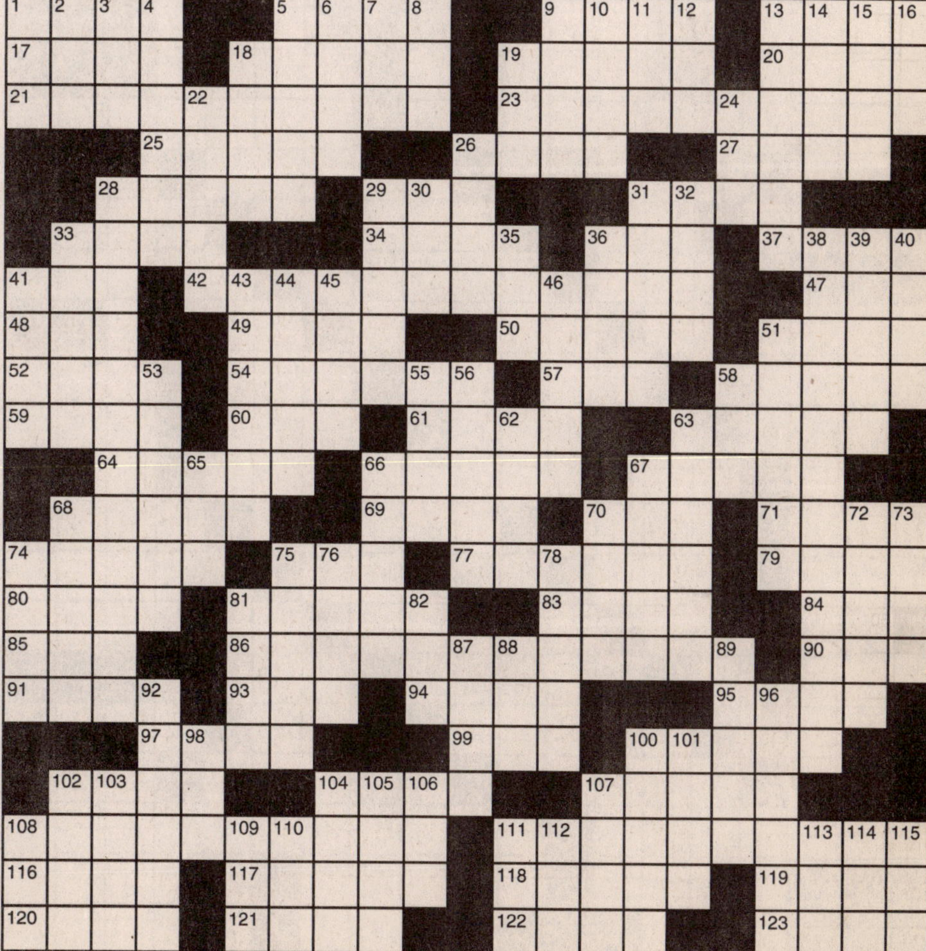

PUZZLE 581

• POSSESSIVES •

ACROSS

1. Desert beast
6. Ignore
10. "The Karate ____"
13. Muscat native
14. Certain Japanese-Americans
16. Heart
17. He can probably pay it
19. Heavenly arc
23. Tokyo, once
24. Not a giver
25. Posts
27. Mr. Lincoln
28. Menial worker
30. Sure!
31. Alabama city
32. Black, in verse
33. Outback bounders
35. Remove
36. Tinkered (with)
37. Scattered
40. Phantom
41. Fish limbs
42. Cross
43. Gleamed
44. Chewing ____
45. Sis's sibling
48. Captures
49. Boutique
50. Arid
51. Awesome!
52. Buddy, sarcastically
53. The badge merits trust
55. WSW's opposite
56. Pierre's pal
57. Tow behind
58. Less wild
59. Rogues
60. Sound recording
61. Tolkien tree creature
62. Buddies
63. Low female voices
64. Don't strike!
66. Carried
67. Hindu deity
68. Volunteer
70. Laconian laborer
71. Coll. terms
72. Jogging gait
73. Under
74. ____ loss
75. British stroller
79. Chinese truth
80. Empire
81. Speak in public
83. Eureka!
84. Exiled person
86. One more than expected
89. Sts.
90. Egglike
91. Flawless
92. Wager
93. Votes for
94. ____ bear

DOWN

1. Carbon fuels
2. Organic compound
3. Lord's property
4. Univ. course
5. Directory
6. Cobra and python
7. Dancer Gregory ____
8. WWII ally
9. New prefix
10. Australian critter
11. Camera feature
12. Lion's lair
15. Submerge
16. Kink
18. Silky fabric
20. More fragrant than expected
21. Slender woodwind
22. Make (one's way)
26. Got down
29. Worries
31. Length depends on the pitcher
32. Geologic age
34. Have debts
35. Brief film
36. Kitchen gadget
37. "Arabian Nights" sailor
38. "____ Center"
39. Not so lucky for the bunny
40. Demon
41. Frenzy
43. Stocky
44. Heredity units
46. Hit-or-miss
47. Texas town
49. Meager
50. French waterway
53. Very steep
54. Hang around
59. Necklace part
62. Sri Lankan city
63. Upper limb
65. Asian holiday
66. Chime
67. Defeats
68. Sarge's dog
69. German wife
70. Warms
71. Gazes
73. Assail
74. Rugged ridge
76. Demolished
77. In front
78. Macho
80. Talk wildly
81. All right!
82. Blue-pencil
85. Taxi
87. Frank's ex
88. Lyric poem

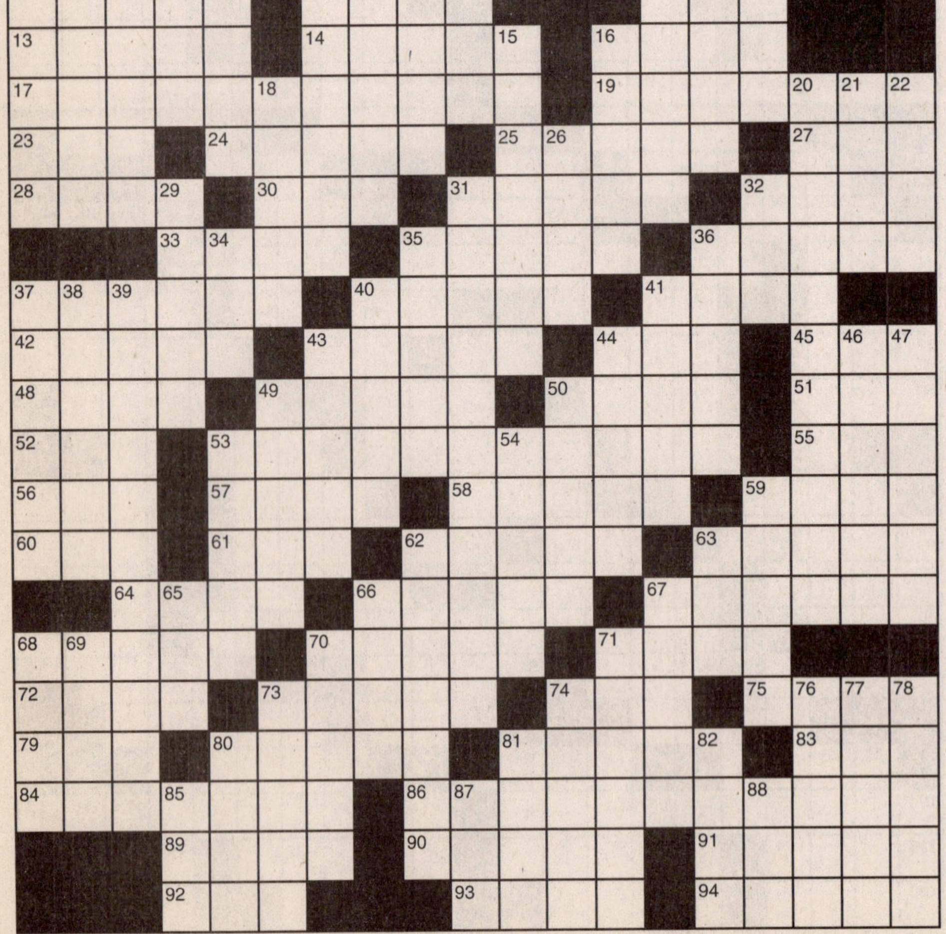

PUZZLE 582

• BE ATTUNED •

ACROSS

1. Control
5. Rouse
9. Buffoon
13. Attention-attractor
17. A Great Lake
18. Heronlike bird
19. Lazily
20. Newspaper section, briefly
21. Creek
22. Church benches
23. Pretty close
24. Radiate
25. "Show Boat" song
28. Movie watchers
30. Defective bomb
31. Aquatic mammal
33. Bird's crop
34. Trend
37. Lion's share
40. "____ Grit"
42. Jacob's eighth son
45. "People ____ Funny"
46. Poison ____
48. Powder ingredient
50. Leander's love
51. Easter flower
53. Certain Delhi drum
55. E.T.'s ships
57. "____ Lobo"
58. Grenoble good-bye
60. Turnpikes
62. Adorn
64. "The Fantasticks" melody
68. St. Francis of ____
71. Texas shrine
72. Political group
76. Touch-me-____
77. Tarzan's pals
80. Push aside
82. Drill
83. Hard trip
85. Broth, e.g.
87. Gives off coherent light
89. Ferber's "So ____"
90. Connery and Penn
92. "Hud" costar
94. Musical pause
95. Hen's pride?
96. Speechless
98. Wild plum
100. Tip of Italy
102. Wastebaskets
105. "Guys and Dolls" ditty
111. Stench
112. Noah's scout
114. Burrow
115. Continental currency
116. Russian river
117. Blue-pencil
118. Arkin or Ladd
119. Cultivated
120. Distribute
121. Water barriers
122. Hardy character
123. Sailboat

DOWN

1. Duration
2. Diva's delight
3. Moo juice
4. Sniggled
5. Destroyed completely
6. Biblical brother
7. New Zealand fruit
8. Double curves
9. Painting, for one
10. Shelley offering
11. Norse king
12. Verse
13. Laundry cycle
14. "West Side Story" ballad
15. Blend
16. Babes
26. Tramps
27. Spot's doc
29. Generation
32. Hawaiian feast
34. FDR's terrier
35. Desertlike
36. Sub shop
38. Agent 86
39. Forbidden
41. Pixie
43. Stoltz or Roberts
44. Chess castle
47. Nurse Barton
49. The Georgia Peach
52. Abominable Snowman
54. An Astaire
56. Dribble
59. Major or Minor
61. Pint-size
63. Dingy
65. Kennel sounds
66. Imprison
67. Bullwinkle, e.g.
68. Picnic pests
69. Hurting
70. "Pajama Game" standard
73. Judge's garb
74. Math subject
75. Safecracker
78. Chunk of eternity
79. Grafton and Lyon
81. Oaters
84. Finger joint
86. Straw beds
88. Greek portico
91. RR depot
93. Comic Costello
97. Completed
99. Brilliance
101. Sad poem
102. Philodendron's family name
103. Parched
104. Soft drink
106. Curly greens
107. Prejudice
108. Distinctive air
109. Sleuth Nancy ____
110. Wail
113. Verve

PUZZLE 583

• FIRST-PRIZE FILMS •

ACROSS

1. "____ in a Gilded Cage"
6. Indian state
11. Porridge of rhyme
16. Hiawatha's craft
17. Oregon city
19. Concede
20. 1978 Oscar-winner
22. Lunar valley
23. On-board budget class
24. Business abbr.
25. Subsequently
26. Stout's Wolfe
27. Imitate
29. Covered with liquid
31. Sergeant Friday's requests
34. Interview question
35. 6/6/44
36. Geologic division
39. Old English letters
40. Monastic official
42. Lends a hand
43. Understanding
44. Guido's high note
45. 1944 Oscar-winner
47. Contended
48. Most grimy
50. Charged particle
51. A Darling child
52. Steaming
53. Tenet
54. Adhere
56. Fishing lure
58. 1040 gp.
59. Mystique
62. Compassion
63. 1964 Oscar-winner
66. Fairy queen
67. Kaline and Smith
68. Complaint
69. Windy City terminal
70. Banquet
71. ____ Speedwagon
72. Parisian landing field
73. Unused
74. Synthetic fabric
75. Furbelow
77. Miranda or Quensel
78. Luau staple
80. Atrocious
82. Hold deed to
84. Memory-jogger
88. Up the ante
89. 1961 Oscar-winner
92. Clothes-drying frame
93. Audio systems
94. Shire of "The Godfather"
95. Consecrate
96. Sprout
97. Type of wrench

DOWN

1. Variety show segments
2. Thai coin
3. Curare's kin
4. Mice and squirrels
5. Plow pioneer and family
6. Tennis great
7. Senator Symington
8. Arlo, to Woody
9. Auerbach of "The Jack Benny Show"
10. Bearing
11. Augments
12. Inventor Howe
13. 1949 Oscar-winner
14. Cobbler's save?
15. Washstand item
17. Golden Fleece seeking ship
18. Pastoral district of Greece
21. Pinna
27. Very eager
28. Authorizations
30. Watercourse
31. Nourish
32. King of the Huns
33. 1981 Oscar-winner
34. "____ She Sweet?"
35. Break of day
37. Surgeon Walter ____
38. One of a famous radio duo
40. Coffeehouse performer
41. Hillock
45. Composer Carlo Menotti
46. Day, in Hebrew
47. ____, vini, vici
49. Priam's city
51. Sinewy
53. Babylonian war god
54. Scorch
55. Fill a hold
56. Vessel's upper deck
57. Nap
58. Tentative
59. Talon
60. Chess term
61. Fourth person
63. European blackbird
64. Lemon and canary
65. Mother of Zeus
68. Double ____
70. Type of attack
74. Grain beard
76. Stratagems
77. Map with a map
78. Spreads hay
79. French soul
80. Mideast native
81. Ululate
83. Dampens
84. Laugh-a-minute
85. Word of endearment
86. Fort ____, Ontario
87. "Sleepless in Seattle" star
90. Chorus lead-in
91. Sun. homily

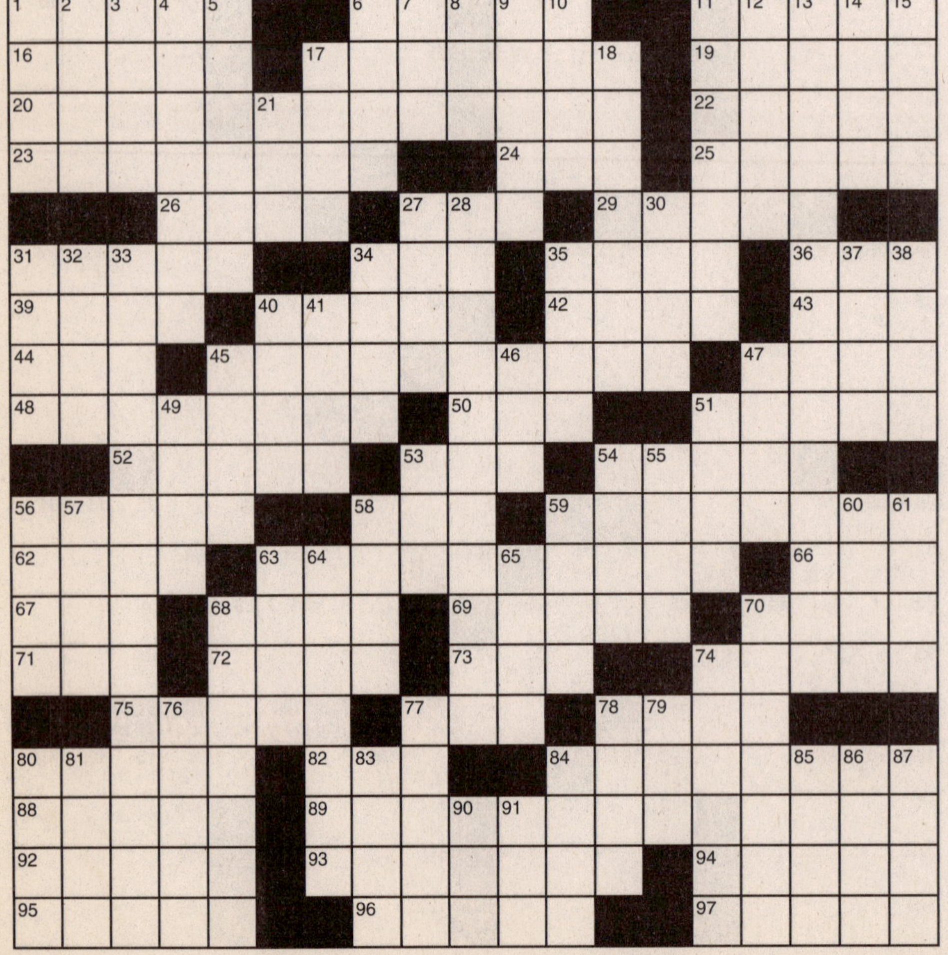

PUZZLE 584

• PUPS WITH PASSPORTS •

ACROSS

1. Catcher's glove
5. Defeat
9. Thin tuft
13. "____ La Douce"
17. Realty parcel
18. Release
19. Tennis's Arthur ____
20. Meander
21. Labor
22. Compos mentis
23. Blunder
24. "Othello" villain
25. Pickwick pup?
28. "Lou Grant" actor
29. Law-enforcement agcy.
30. "The Bells" author
31. Nonsense!
33. Harry
37. Day-____ (fluorescent)
38. Front
42. Zodiac sign
43. Nice street
44. False god
45. French river
46. Vega, e.g.
47. Draw a bead
48. Misrepresent
49. Rents
50. Katherine ____ of "Soap"
52. Russian co-op
53. Dylan's "____ for You"
54. Ancient verb
55. Category
56. Japanese drama
57. Black
60. Lustrous
61. Confronts
65. Telescope feature
66. In the future
67. Freudian concept
68. Idaho's neighbor
69. Airspeed unit
70. Foreman
71. Exist
72. Plumber's aid
73. Pittsburgh eleven
75. Pindaric product
76. Forced
77. Trapper's trophy
78. Plus
79. Boater, e.g.
80. Wood shaper
83. Popigay pup?
90. Phrase of understanding
91. Egyptian sun god
92. Oklahoma town
93. No part
94. Fabricator
95. Single
96. Location
97. Belmonts' front man
98. 0.9144 meter
99. Boom
100. Rustle
101. Spheres

DOWN

1. Companion
2. Holy image
3. Math branch
4. Relate
5. "Children of a ____ God"
6. Normandy beach
7. Anger, envy, etc.
8. Skyline silhouette
9. Squander
10. Land amid water
11. It's often tucked in
12. Vigor
13. Pettigo pup?
14. Speckled horse
15. Sorcerer
16. Love, in Madrid
26. March date
27. Additionally
28. I Kings name
32. Heraldic band
33. Party
34. Comedian Johnson
35. Use a rotary phone
36. Paderborn pup?
37. Viscid exudation
38. Bargain offerings
39. Demeanor
40. Concerning
41. Robin's roost
43. Unburden
44. Seamstress Ross
47. Pangolin's snack
48. Ranch stamp
51. Jazz's Kid ____
52. Assumed name
53. Avery Brundage's org.
55. Board game
56. Sgt., e.g.
57. O'Neill's trees
58. Tempo
59. Back then
60. Pitcher's neighbor
61. Mature
62. Without women
63. Movie shot
64. Cast off
66. First victim
67. Sooner than
71. Speech
72. Clockmaker Thomas
74. Shelter
75. Undivided
76. Stray
78. Li'l ____
79. Part of Hispaniola
80. Mrs. Munster
81. The East
82. Rend
84. New Rochelle school
85. What's ____ for me?
86. Efface
87. Evening: Fr.
88. Round handle
89. Cravings
91. Hirt, Capone, et al.

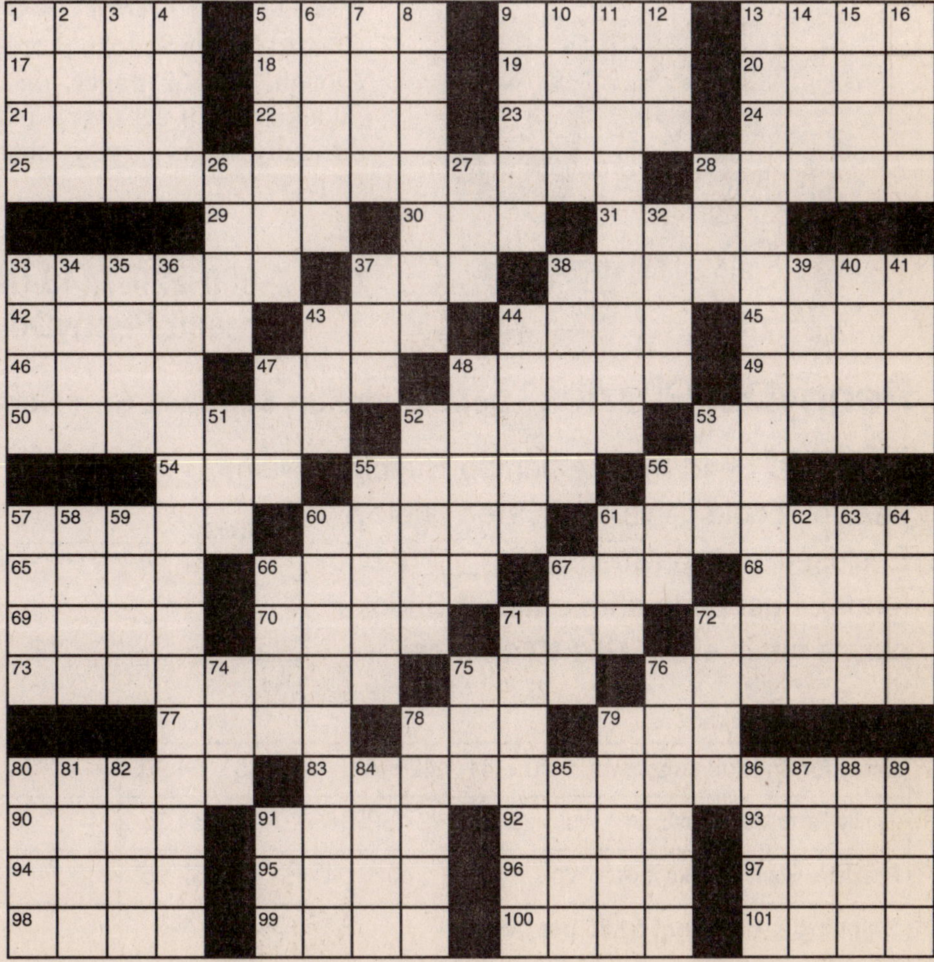

PUZZLE 1

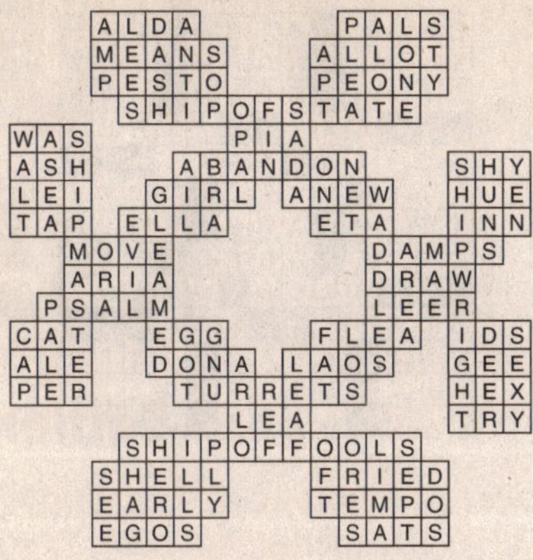

PUZZLE 2

TACT STAT BRA
ACHY PALE RIG
SNAP RUIN OPE
KEROSENE WED
CATNIPS
BEAMED SNEEZE
ARSON FARES
REPAID MISSES
INCISOR
ERR STUMBLED
POI EMUS LAVA
EON WADS ICER
EMS ELSE PENT

PUZZLE 3

ASH PLEA VOTE
SPA EENS IDOL
PAL SITE LETS
STOUT RAIL
SODA SAGAS
ACHE OPAL AGO
CLOSED REELED
TIE GOBI CARS
SPRIG EACH
SYNC OOZED
FOGS EARN EMU
LUAU AMID SIT
URGE REDO TRY

PUZZLE 4

WHET GAPS OFFS
EACH ALOHA FORE
LIRE NENES FRET
TRUMPERY PLATES
EFT CHILI
GADS SLAM SOB
SORROW COLOSSAL
TUBA INAPT LITE
AGITATOR SHAMED
BET CHEF UPON
RINDS FUR
LOANER DISTRICT
ETTA ALIBI OOZE
ETON WOVEN STAR
SORE BERG EARN

PUZZLE 5

Real friends walk in when the rest of the world walks out.

WORD LIST: 1. Rewrite, 2. Sulked, 3. Handsaw, 4. Forklift, 5. Halloween, 6. Northwest.

PUZZLE 6

ACME KID ARTS
NOUN INLET PEAL
TOSS MILER RIPE
SKI FIG IRONED
CLOTH UPON
NAVIGATOR ASPS
ICIEST AGED ETC
CODS ONSET ARIA
ERE TREE EBBING
NOVA ASTROLOGY
ERST UNWED
SCRIPT NIL IAN
PAIL ORBIT ACRE
ANTE PEONY RAGE
REED DOG CLOD

PUZZLE 7

Hilltop, Lampoon, Scrappy, Upright, Improve, Blooper.

BONUS WORD: Publish

PUZZLE 8

ORCA ANNIE TEA
LOAN BEATER REC
DART SEVERE ELM
INDIGO AMID AYE
ESS ORAL ERRS
BOBS TRYOUTS
ACHE ESPY TRUE
MOOT DEARS TENT
MITT TRAM ERAS
OFFENDS NOON
ODOR STOW SAT
PRO SOAP TEETHE
RAT ENRICH DEER
ORE DECREE GEAR
FED SHEER EDDY

PUZZLE 9

1. Field hockey, 2. Table tennis, 3. Bungee jumping, 4. Relay race, 5. Water polo, 6. Bull riding, 7. Beach volleyball, 8. Demolition derby.

PUZZLE 10

SIP LAMA LUTE
HOE AFAR AKIN
ATE DRUM WEED
HARM ALIGN
ARISEN RAD
DARTED SATINY
EXITS WROTE
LESSON BEATER
ILK REMEDY
STIES SCAB
PEST GRID OWE
AREA HIDE LEG
DRAB STEW ADS

PUZZLE 11

POPS STAT BYE
AXLE ARCH ROE
SEEM DINOSAUR
SNAIL PENT
ADO GRAMP
PAW CADS OVER
RIOTED IMPOSE
ODOR ALGA WHY
MELEE ANY
ESPY OWNER
BLOSSOMS EELY
EEN EPEE BASE
DIE SENT SPAS

PUZZLE 12

JAW APE ZAG IRE
AGA BIT ERR MIL
GORILLA BOA PAL
SEA QUAVER
OPAL FLU REMORA
VIDEO AID LIVER
AND DISPEL RETE
ESS BUY
CZAR MIRAGE SAG
OATEN EAT PROXY
OPTION KEA IDEM
ENTICE ELF
OHM ICE PROFFER
RIP CHI AIR AWE
APT EEL WEE SEC

1-Z, 2-S, 3-N, 4-V, 5-I, 6-L, 7-Q, 8-F, 9-H, 10-X, 11-Y, 12-O, 13-W, 14-U, 15-D, 16-A, 17-T, 18-B, 19-R, 20-K, 21-M, 22-G, 23-J, 24-C, 25-E, 26-P.

PUZZLE 13

1. Eyesore, Banjo, Wig; 2. Sidecar, Image, Hug; 3. College, Axiom, Pie; 4. Display, Agree, Vee; 5. Midyear, Theft, Ump; 6. Sausage, Panel, Inn.

PUZZLE 14

IDEA MAS MOPE
BONG UMP ILIA
INTO SPANGLES
STANDEE ERASE
NYE REBA
HAG FRET TWIT
OBLATE OBERON
PEEL EDNA ANT
RULE SIN
SAFER AVENGES
TRIANGLE ALSO
LARD OER PEAR
OBEY ORA TRUE

PUZZLE 15

IMP ACHE MEN
NEAT FLAX YEA
FAIRYTALE SLY
OLDIE WORST
EAT TEETH
DRUG TREE
NEW GAL YAM
AREA SODA
BASIC PER
TRADE AROMA
SHE DIMENOVEL
OUR EVIL WERE
PEN TERM NEE

PUZZLE 19

PAT MOTH COPE
ACE IDEA AWES
SHE CENT BETS
TENOR EEL
BOIL LEROY
DELI CUFF EGO
EXIT EAR SILK
BAR TRUE KNEE
SMEAR SEMI
BYE AMUSE
MAYO ATOP SAD
EYER SOUL EGG
NEWT TOTE RAY

PUZZLE 23

DASH ATOM PAW
EXPO WORE ICE
BEAU REED ERE
STY AIRED
SCREW FALL
LIE OVAL LIFE
ITEM IRE SOLD
DELE AGED TAG
SOLO IMAGE
SUSHI AGO
ONE LEAN UNTO
ADE EMIT NAIL
ROD DUDE DYED

PUZZLE 16

CROP FOAL ATOM
HEIR LOGOS RENO
ALLY OZONE TACO
MAE ERE EAR FED
PYRAMID TOTO
DUD DISTURBS
HIPS ACID EXTRA
IRE EVE WAR
FORMS DEAR YOGA
INTRUDED EKE
ASEA SMEARED
ALI TIN COG ADO
FUND REFER URGE
ALEE YARNS SEAR
RUDE TOTE ERRS

PUZZLE 20

AWE BATS ANEW
WHY AREA LOGO
ROE LEAP IRON
YARDS SPA
EARN ESSAY
DOTE IOTA ERE
EXAM CUE MAIL
SEX PENS ORAL
KNIFE STIR
IRK DELAY
REAR NAIL AXE
ERRS OGLE VIA
FACT BOLD ASH

PUZZLE 24

DATA OWNS ASS
ACID NAIL SPA
DECO TYPO PIG
PRO PASTE
SANTA SPEW
WOO PAPA EACH
ANT JIG DUE
PEER ANEW ERE
OGRE EASEL
EMCEE EBB
COO ROSY LESS
HOE MAKE EMIT
ODD STIR RUBY

PUZZLE 17

AGES BEAU ADD
COLA OLDS BEE
TOFU ALOE ELM
NIT RADIO
LILAC COST
ODE YELP ETCH
ALE DOE WOE
FERN GUNK ORE
EYED EASED
FORTE EGG
APE ASEA ROLE
TAP RUNS EWES
ELS NEST ENDS

PUZZLE 21

ASH AWAY DASH
SHE SOSO IDEA
EAR INKY TOWS
AHEAD OFT
DEAR ROBOT
AWLS MEMO APE
LEI EMU RAN
DAM UNIT GELS
ORALS TERN
YEN OUNCE
PAIR UNTO ALE
ACRE DOOM GAL
TEES EWES SPY

PUZZLE 25

SASS TOO BRAM
CLAP PADRE LENO
ABLY ENDED EATS
BUS FAT EYELET
SMALL REINED
AUBURN ASIDE
ADDS EMENDS RAW
SIESTA ATTIRE
SKY ANTLER ASKS
NESTS EARNER
OTTAWA VAULT
PAPAYA SHE BOO
USES ISSUE LOOT
LINT LEERY EASE
PASS AWE ITEM

PUZZLE 18

STEP PALM SKI
TOLL ARIA HIS
YOKE DEEM ELL
ADS BASTE
CACTI DOS
ASH PINE POLL
LEI RUM DUO
LAND KNOW DAD
YES ISSUE
LAPEL GNU
ERE EDGE ITCH
FEE COIN TRUE
TAR TENT EYES

PUZZLE 22

HEM VETS AWAY
APE IRON LATE
TIS NANA IDEA
SCALY GOB
ALP AIDED
SEND LIST RAY
AXE EARTH USE
SPA KNEE AGED
HORDE MID
ASK NERVE
LAIR IMPS EEL
OGLE CARE DIM
GOLD KNOT ONS

PUZZLE 26

SLOPE CROC ABED
LORIS HIGH DOPE
ACNES OLEO ALOE
BOA SEEM GASP
MOOSE PSI
CLEARINGS TODO
HANKER AHOY ASS
APT EAVED YIP
RIA IDLE DODDER
SLAM BLUEBERRY
OPA TRINE
STAR SLIM ASP
WRIT HILO CAMEO
AURA ELKS AGENT
MESS SYST TARTS

PUZZLE 27

ACHY SAFE LIVE
THEE SPILL EVIL
LILT WALES AYES
ALPINE SELF
SIS EARTH AIDE
STORY PEELS
LUG TYPE SLIP
OBOES EAT STATE
BORN SHOE YEW
EAGLE MOURN
TEAK UNDID WAS
REFS ESCORT
FLAG ACORN AMMO
RACE CLEAT KEEP
OWED TERM ENDS

PUZZLE 28

CLEF GEED AGAR
AUTO AVAIL RUNE
SAHL LEVEL DRAT
TUSK ERE AROUSE
SIN DINER
LOO GAG NOG ASH
ORLON OFF IGLOO
RADII POI MOGUL
ATILT HER ETAPE
NEE ICE MEN ESS
MOORS ATE
DOMINO UPS EDIT
OBIT LANAI RACE
NENE SINCE IRON
EYER DYER EENS

PUZZLE 29

BALSA COME INFO
ALIAS OPAL NEAR
BENCHPRESS SOME
YET INNS DUNES
PACE NIL
RICES ASBESTOS
ADOPT TUNA LOG
PEA UPRISES DUE
TAT TOIL THESE
LIBERATE EARED
ELK NERD
ESSAY SAGA ZOO
RATS MEDITATING
GRIT AGIN DATER
OARS ROTE SPIRE

PUZZLE 30

CRAM TONS SCALP
LEVY WHAT AUDIO
OMEN EMIR GRIME
GARAGE LIL STEM
SIS ADS PIPE
NETS CASTE SAD
APPAL TAHITI
HOUR EMOTE OXEN
ABSORB HERON
DIE ABEAM DEAD
OGLE PRO ZAG
HERB ERG ORDAIN
OCHER ILIA ALSO
EROSE EENS TEEM
RUSES REST EASE

PUZZLE 31

DAUB DEAF LAMPS
ALSO UPDO EMILY
BEER DEER NYLON
APSE ERG OWE
TAXI GETS
SOU CELLOPHANE
ORB AREA ESCORT
FEUD AORTA SOME
ARROWS GALL SIN
ONTHEHOUSE END
SORE VASE
ASH PSI ONYX
SCOOP FAME ICON
PANNE EYES NAPE
SNEER RENT GREW

PUZZLE 32

COOP SPAD PESTO
OKRA ARTE ANWAR
CADS VOLE CLIMB
OPE AFAR AMPS
AIRLINES SAC
ANTS UNEVEN
FEIGN SPICY EMU
OAR PERCH TIN
USE REDYE SLOTS
LESSOR STAY
LOP SKEWERED
SEMI SCAN OER
PROVE LUTE ABLY
ASTER ABET REEL
STERE PASS EDDY

PUZZLE 33

STALE PAL ADORN
CORAL LIE CAMEO
ATOMS ARE TREED
RAM ASTER ENDS
FLAB WIDENED
RUIN DIN ELK
MERINGUE PARDON
RAIDS MOM MINCE
ESTEEM NAMESAKE
DEE EAT RILE
ANDIRON NAGS
CLAP PHOTO NIA
RADAR TIN VITAL
IVORY ONE EVENT
BASTE POD RESTS

PUZZLE 34

	F	R		O		T	H	U		L	N	A
D	I		N		E	R	A	S	H		E	N
W	A		I		T	E	R		O		A	T
		A	C		E		D	H		E	R	
E	N	D		U	R	E		E	R			E
	C	I		S		T	E	R	N	E	B	B
L		O		T	N	I	N		N		Y	
L	E		E	W	A		Y	C	A	K		E
H	E	R		A	L	D		I		S	L	E
	B	A	L		L		A	D	R	O	O	T
A	E	R	I		A		L	E	R		R	
L	E		E	R		Y			O	W		L
T		E		M	P		E	R	W		E	E

PUZZLE 35

OAF GASH TAPE
LIE LUTE OVAL
ELEVATES TINS
IRON EDGE
SWEDE CRAM
LICE SHED ROE
ASHORE IDLING
WHO OMEN LOCO
STIR MATES
TALC ATOM
ARIA ISOLATES
PEEL MEND ORE
SAND PREY NEW

PUZZLE 36

AWLS ELS MOWN
CROC NAH AURA
TYPO VIA TRAP
WEIRD ASPS
SUP RESOLD
TRIPOD WOODSY
OGLED WROTE
WEEDED LESSEN
EDITOR EMS
BOPS SISSY
ABUT MAS OVER
BOLA ARE LAVA
YELL LAS KNEW

PUZZLE 37

SI	L	ENT		RE	AD			HA	ST	Y
TE	ET	ER		SI	MI	LE		VER	AND	A
	HAL	T		DU	RE	SS		S	ING	LE
		AI	SL	E			TR	ACK		
MAT	I	N	EE		UN	LO	AD		A	MID
TE	ND		P	LAT	IT	UD	E		BRI	DE
R	EED		LE	ER	Y		SM	I	DGE	N
		PRE	SS			CH	AN	NEL		
CAS	TE	S		MO	L	AR		A	TOP	
CA	MP	ER		ST	EA	M		STI	P	PLE
DES	ER	VE			SH	ED		C	LE	AT

PUZZLE 38

3-1. Light, 4-2. Koala, 4-6. Kazoo, 7-5. Toast, 9-7. Egypt, 8-10. Hyena, 10-12. Alibi, 13-11. Melon, 13-15. Model, 16-14. Sauna.

OSCAR-WINNING SONG: Talk to the Animals

PUZZLE 39

SALT AFT ACME
ALEE ADORE WHOA
LOAN LOUIS LIPS
SUNDAE NOPE CEE
ADS GRID YANK
BETS CEASE
MICA ELSE HIDER
ODOR DEEMS GEAR
RENEW TWIT HERS
EAGLE TEAS
EYED ISNT PIE
ERA DIPS CEDING
MALE SUSHI REAR
IRES CRUEL ACNE
REDS REP BEET

PUZZLE 40

1. Rob Lowe, 2. Tom Cruise, 3. Meg Ryan, 4. Lucille Ball, 5. Bela Lugosi, 6. Mickey Rooney, 7. Michael Caine, 8. Tom Hanks, 9. Gene Hackman, 10. Anne Hathaway.

PUZZLE 41

CALF INFO OPERA
HULA NEON RACER
AGAS FARE ETHIC
MEN HERESY EONS
PROBER URN
OWN CAKE SAG
ATOM OPAL TETRA
LIMBO OUT EPEES
BRISK SLOG OPAH
SET REEK RID
WAG EVENLY
BABE OSPREY AYE
ELUDE MOAT LIRA
TANGS URGE AVER
ANTES GEAR MESS

PUZZLE 42

Pageboy, Panda, Panther, Partridge, Pastor, Pitchman, Plaintiff, Plankton, Pleasure, Portrait, Presto, Priceless, Primrose, Probable, Proofread, Puppies.

PUZZLE 43

ISSUE HASP ASS
SLATE DONOR CHI
LAGER OUTDO RID
EBON TREADMILL
SAME IDLE
EFFIGY OPAL
CALLER ABLE AHS
HIE NIFTIER LIE
ORE DARE DIVIDE
DADO GAITER
LAMA FELT
ELIMINATE AMID
TIN DOGMA EMOTE
UKE OTHER WIDEN
PER LEAN ENEMY

PUZZLE 44

SHED MEW SOLE
LOVE SEMIS PROS
ARIA HAUNT ANAT
GALLEON ARCADE
SOYA TEEM
FROST VISA EAR
DUEL SPIN DANCE
URGE OAF STUB
ARROW STOW PATS
DYE ECHO AISLE
TBAR RAPT
INTAKE WISHFUL
RAIL ECLAT ALSO
MINS KHAKI ROES
ALGA ICE MERE

PUZZLE 45

PUZZLE 46

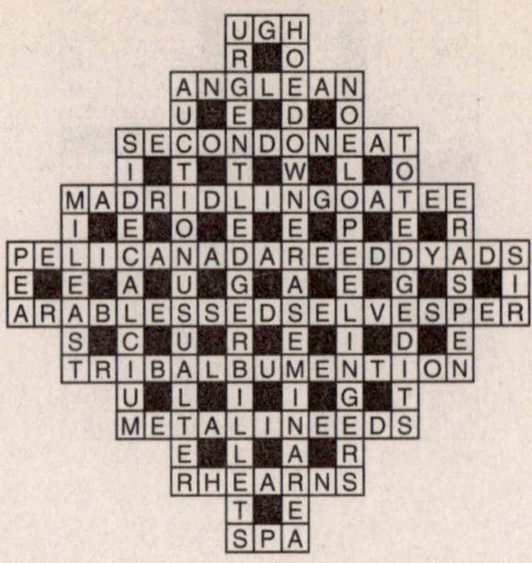

PUZZLE 47

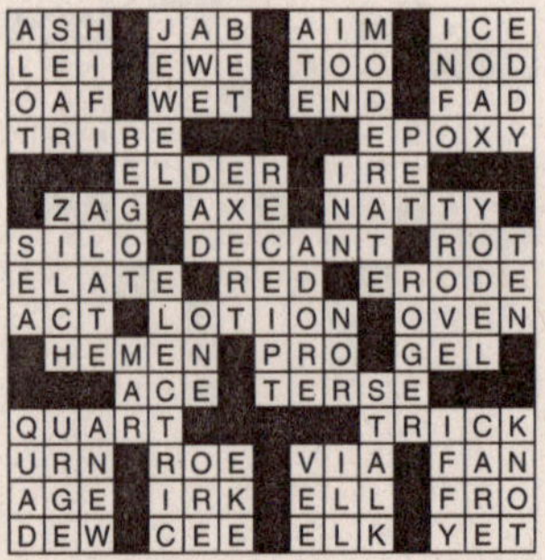

1-Z, 2-D, 3-S, 4-L, 5-N, 6-Y, 7-B, 8-X, 9-A, 10-E, 11-T, 12-G, 13-J, 14-V, 15-W, 16-R, 17-K, 18-U, 19-Q, 20-I, 21-O, 22-M, 23-H, 24-F, 25-C, 26-P.

PUZZLE 48

Discretion is the better part of valor.

WORD LIST: 1. Vital, 2. Trot, 3. Horse, 4. Crate, 5. Dine, 6. Brief, 7. Stop.

PUZZLE 49

PROF GASH SHORT
LAVA RITE LINER
USED AREA EMCEE
SHREWD AVID ELK
OUTLET
CAT OAR SWEAR
AWE LLAMA EASEL
RANGE DAM TRIBE
SITON ERUPT DEN
THOSE SHE ELS
BALERS
BAD ABLY ATTIRE
OPING IRES IDOL
REVUE BIKE ELLS
GRAND ICES DELE

PUZZLE 50

ROMP PAT PITA
ARIA SHRUG IRON
MALL COMBO CENT
PLEA ANY RINSES
TORE MINI
CHIDE GOLFCLUB
AHEAD CELLO ONE
VIAL PANDA BOLL
ILL BASIS PUPIL
DISTASTE FIRST
HITS BRED
POTATO HEY EDIT
AKIN ROUGE NICE
LARK SUGAR EVEN
EYES TEN DART

PUZZLE 51

SWIM BASS ITEMS
LACE EXIT NOVEL
OVEN WERE SPADE
PYRAMID TOT DIP
CUT DETECT
ESSENCE ROPE
TIN CHASER ACTS
CLOTH SEA ALOHA
HOBO FEELER LUG
FALL MASSAGE
DANUBE ROW
OWE OAR INNINGS
LARVA AIDE PELE
LIVER NOES EVEN
STEED GNAT SAND

PUZZLE 52

SLAM SPA SPAT
KIWI TOILS EACH
IRES ADAPT TREE
PEST CAN EATERY
ASK OBESE
PARKA APPEAL
ADHERE RYE BIB
PLY IMPASSE EMU
AIM POT TARTAR
BEAGLE SISSY
BOOTH REV
FROSTY YOU EMIT
LIVE EVENT TODO
OMEN DINES EPEE
WENT MAR DEAD

PUZZLE 53

PUZZLE 54

BEARD BODY STAT
ARGUE ABIE TARE
REATA NIPA ACME
FIT REGION
CADS CABANA TRY
ARIL OMELET
DESIGN SIDE AGE
RECTO WET RIDES
ELS SHOE TYRANT
PONCHO OGRE
VIA EITHER NEER
ANGELS DEW
SALE TWIG ATTAR
ENOL EAVE LOOSE
SEWS DYER LOESS

PUZZLE 55

CACHE ASPS ORCA
ALLOY CHIC FOOT
STARE TUNA TACO
EONS MOTEL SOL
EWERS PORTAL
ERR ELS DELI
PAIRED GOLDFISH
ISLE REC LOPE
CHESTNUT DIETER
TWIN KIN AWE
RANSOM HARKS
AGO BLURT PLOT
JAVA LAMA ALONE
APED EMIT SAVER
HELD REDS STERN

PUZZLE 56

GRIT STAT HANGS
LANE TOTE EQUIP
ENVELOPES RUNNY
AGE ELM TUBA
MEN DEAFENS WAS
STAG SARI PINK
BESTS SCANTY
EFFORTS GOATEES
BLOUSE GENTS
BELT ROOM AYES
SAD AEROSOL NUB
SMOG TWO GEL
GASPE ALONGSIDE
OCEAN NINE ONES
TEXTS SEER NEST

PUZZLE 57

SOAPS MEMO DAB
ANGELS APED EMU
STEREO DILEMMAS
SOD AFFECT OOZE
CZAR IRONED
HOLEY OPENER
ABED SAGE WAD
ROSES VAT FAIRY
MET WAIL KNEE
SALAMI CIGAR
CARING LOAN
ORAL EYELID WHO
MISLABEL LEGION
MAP CRAM STAPLE
ASS TARS SLEDS

PUZZLE 58

LAST ROCS HATER
OLIO ERAL ANILE
GOER CAPO ITEMS
INGEST PEKE
CEE TORS RUDER
ARETES REF
CAROM PANTOMIME
OXIDE ARM PICAS
DEFENSIVE PLANT
ALL PRESTO
SEPIA SHES REE
OGRE REVIEW
AWFUL CABS ISLE
RHINO HIRE LEER
CONDO ODOR ENDS

PUZZLE 59

SIX RAJ SHA MET
IVE OPUS SPED ADA
NAN WRAP HIDE RIN
GNAT INA END AGES
ALL CAL ASTA
NAOMI WELLS TORAH
ONEAL OLSEN OMEGA
GARR ROY YEAR TOM
ABEL EMMA
ADS EDEN CRY NERD
BEAST RENEE EDGAR
ELLIS YIELD DROPS
IDYL GEE ODE
LOVE ASH SAP WAND
EVA KNEE TIRE LEE
NET ACED ELAN ANE
ONE TED SHE NED

PUZZLE 60

AFAR GALS OARS
SORE ELOPE FLAT
SEMI NICER TODO
GET OWED FIR
WRANGLE CUSTOM
HES OER ATOP
ONTO SNOB ERR
ATOM TEASE LOOT
ARE STEM LUGE
NEWT NET SUN
HASSLE TRUSTED
ICE KIDS ABE
THAW GROWL EASE
CORE HUMID DYED
HOST METS YEWS

PUZZLE 61

PETAL UGLY OWES
IVORY PLIE PERT
NONCE HAFT ALGA
UKE STORE ALLOY
PESO ALERTS
DEWS OPENER
ABODE THAN NOVA
SILENCEISGOLDEN
ELLS ORTS FIEND
ALATED EFTS
MADAME TASK
SNAFU ORBED DUN
AIDE VIOL OLDIE
SPIT ELSE REATA
HATE EYED MIXED

PUZZLE 62

TRICK BIBS SHE
EERIE UNLET OAK
ELITE SNEER ATE
MYSELF STEERED
LEATHER
MAS RANI EDITOR
INK EXTRAS NAPE
STIFF ELL ISLET
TIER CRITIC ERR
SCRAWL FADE SAY
MAESTRO
CHEETAH LESSON
LAX EVADE BLAME
ALP REVUE BAKER
WOO REEL SPEND

PUZZLE 63

SHAM CZAR IRE
TOGO TROPIC MAR
AMEN RENTAL MIG
BERG OWE SEDANS
REV ARC
STEREOS ENOUGH
KOALA GARB PLEA
INS LULLABY ANY
WITS MEAT ANTES
ICECAP DEGREES
FUN ANT
ELUDED MAP THAN
GEL NOTICE LYRE
GAL TOILER EPEE
SPY MELD DEAD

PUZZLE 64

BABA HABIT METING
BLOWER OHARA AVENUE
WOOLGATHERER CANCAN
ACTS HUMS GOON AND
NAE STEM DEAN ONCE
ALE HAM TOOTS OATER
POPE EFTS LIRA
FOISTS TATS HAL TAB
INNS JOSH GABS ICE
LIST DALEEVANS POUF
ECU SIRE BIRD ANTI
DEF HES SLAB RUSSET
FIAT HAUL HURT
USING BOLES EEN FLD
NOCK WAFT BIDS OER
FRI AHAB EELS ALMA
OTELLO REDLETTERDAY
LINEAR ASIAN ALIENS
DETAIL UPEND OMAR

PUZZLE 65

ACNE ADOS ATLAS
SHIN LIME GUILT
SITS GREW AGREE
ERR GANG GASP
SPOIL DAWDLE
VEAL HEEDING
SPRYER JILT CAN
TEA CRAZE OVA
ONS CHUG TANNER
ADHERES SERE
SYSTEM ITCHY
SLAP PULL HOE
MOXIE RODE NOVA
EPEES EDGE USER
WELDS PEEK TERN

PUZZLE 66

SMUG SOBS ANIL
TILL REALM LIME
ANTI ENSUE EXAM
GERBIL TRAP EGO
ERA RIG BROADEN
OVERSELL
ODA NENE DAGAMA
BENCH TAG RANIS
INDOOR CRAB IDS
PRESTIGE
FINESSE TEA HIS
AVA ETCH ORIENT
RIME ATOLL CAPE
GEES TOWED OVUM
ODDS ERST NETS

PUZZLE 67

SETS SALT LET
OPAL APPEAL ORE
WERE POTATO CAM
NETWORK NAG ASP
DOE ISLET
REDDEN EDICT
OVER REAM ABED
MILE TULIP ROAR
PLEA ALES VISA
METED OMELET
GRASP PRO
RIM ITS LAWLESS
ADE CRAVAT EXIT
DEN SALINE GALA
ESS MEET SMOG

PUZZLE 68

SLOP JAVA REP
COWL SELECT ERE
AREA PRESTO CUT
BERSERK TAT APT
MAYS EMPTY
ALIAS SEMI
TIN ENAMEL THAW
OATH OGEES TILE
PROA TANNER LOP
SUER ISLET
BATHS DAMP
OPE USE OCEANIC
FIN RAVAGE DIRE
FAT PRISMS ENOL
ONS ILKA DENS

PUZZLE 69

TAR PECAN AJAR
OWE HAVANA ZANY
TAP ENERGY ANTE
ERE NERVE LESS
MELON ELITE
RASP ASHAMED
SHOE OLE RESIDE
LOT SOYBEAN NIL
OUTFIT BYE CITE
BROUGHT ELSE
SNEAK WEDGE
SPAS TAMPA ERA
TAXI STRAIN CAT
OGLE ALERTS ODE
PEER DENTS YEN

PUZZLE 70

HASP AFAR OATS
UNTIL DOSE DROP
BEIGE EXTRADITE
WREN SYRUP DEW
ODE ANTS
WEAN VARY TIDE
AXE CEDE HOYDEN
SIR ANDIRON EVE
PLIERS GORE AIM
SEEK ENDS ALLY
EELS ELM
AFT FACTS APSE
COURTSHIP VENAL
HOBO SERE ARISE
ELSE OWED EPEE

If it's a small world, why is it so expensive to run?

PUZZLE 71

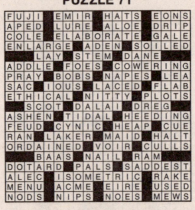

FUJI EMIR HATS EONS
APED LURE ALOE DRIP
COLE ELABORATE GALE
ENLARGE ADEN SOILED
LAY STEM DANE
ADDLE FOES COWERING
PRAY BOBS NAPES LEA
SAC IOUS LACED FLAB
ETHICAL NITTY PLOTS
SCOT DALAI DREG
ASHEN TIDAL HEEDING
FEUD CYNIC HEAP CUE
RAN LAKER MAID HALT
ORDAINED VOIR CULLS
BAAS NAIL RAM
DOTARD PALS SADDEST
ALEC ISOMETRIC RAKE
MENU ACME EIRE USED
NODS NIPS NOES MEWS

PUZZLE 72

TROT HEAT RIOT
EERO ARGO GENRE
EVERGREEN YEARN
SUM ARM
ELTON ABLE PALO
LEA EVE SCARED
FOWL PET ORATE
AFAR YETI
CARTE SOW SPIN
BREEZE AYE ADO
STYX LOGO DRYAD
AIM LOO
CHILL EASYGOING
AURAL GLEN TRIO
BEAT APEX SENT

PUZZLE 73

1. Itemize, 2. Immense, 3. Imitate, 4. Improve, 5. Invoice, 6. Inspire, 7. Involve, 8. Incline, 9. Impinge, 10. Irksome.

10-LETTER WORD: Metropolis

PUZZLE 74

FETA RAM ODES
AXED EKE HERO
CHAS VIM MEAL
TAB ENOL PSI
SLATER SIDLED
EGOIST NAYS
IDEATED
POLE GOADED
BALERS DRYERS
ALE SHED RAP
SLAM OWL LIMO
IOTA NEE YEAR
CREW ERR ERST

PUZZLE 75

ATE SHAM WAFT
SAG NIPA AXLE
HUG ITEM PEON
PITS MAILED
AWLS FONT
CRAMP ATTIRED
HEN SUSHI EMU
ENTRANT CURIE
ILLS ROTS
INCOME MENU
ROOT AWAY TIN
ESNE SOLE ERA
DYER HOED SKY

PUZZLE 76

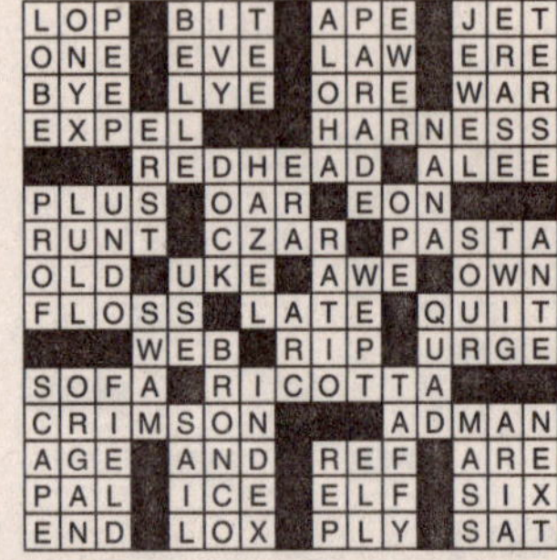

LOP BIT APE JET
ONE EVE LAW ERE
BYE LYE ORE WAR
EXPEL HARNESS
REDHEAD ALEE
PLUS OAR EON
RUNT CZAR PASTA
OLD UKE AWE OWN
FLOSS LATE QUIT
WEB RIP URGE
SOFA RICOTTA
CRIMSON ADMAN
AGE AND REF ARE
PAL ICE ELF SIX
END LOX PLY SAT

1-Q, 2-P, 3-Y, 4-Z, 5-G, 6-H, 7-V, 8-E, 9-T, 10-X, 11-O, 12-B, 13-K, 14-M, 15-D, 16-A, 17-C, 18-L, 19-W, 20-I, 21-J, 22-N, 23-U, 24-S, 25-F, 26-R.

PUZZLE 77

Love is a choice, not simply, or necessarily, a rational choice, but rather a willingness to be present to others without pretense or guile.

PUZZLE 78

LAPEL AMAH ARCH
OKAPI SARI DELI
AEGIS STAB OVEN
FEE THEE ADRIFT
CEE RECENT
FRANC SHE ADO
FLIP KHAKIS LIP
LANE ICE NINE
ERG MANTRA AZAN
EEL EGG NEVER
ESTEEM TRY
STAMEN IRIS SIT
WADI DAME ABATE
ACER UNIT TOWEL
PORK MICE ZONAL

PUZZLE 79

SPAT APT ACHE
LIMO BRIEF CHIN
ITEM RETAR TEND
DYNAMO ALAS AGE
TAUT SNIPPED
BELONGED CEE
EGO HERE GRACE
AGO ATTACHE MAY
MYTHS HIRE ERE
ASK NURTURED
ELEMENT SOON
BEE TEAM INCHED
BARE ALIEN LUAU
EVIL DENSE OGRE
DEEM SIS GENT

PUZZLE 80

```
  554
x   4
-----
 2216
```

PUZZLE 81

MUSE SUMO AREAS
ONCE ASEA GUMBO
CZAR FEATHERBED
HIM EARTHY ARTS
APPEARS POLO
ARI ACHE IDA
ACORN MILER DEN
HAUL COLON REED
ORT ERRED BARRY
YEW LAND PIC
IFFY LADYBUG
RATE OPPOSE EMU
EXTRANEOUS TAPE
ALERT NOPE ORES
REDYE SPED ODDS

PUZZLE 82

1. Old fold, 2. Smile file, 3. Town clown, 4. Near here, 5. Slim limb, 6. Maize craze.

PUZZLE 83

C	AM	PER		DE	C	REE		P	RE	STO
AND	ER	SON		P	ROW	L		AL	CO	VE
LE	I		D	ART	ED		WH	ATE	VER	
	CAN	AP	ES			EXP	OSE			
		PA	K	I	ST	AN		L	EAR	N
FLA	VO	R		TH	AME	S		I	NS	ET
RES	ID	ENT		A	N	E	MO	NE		
			MI	CA			DE	R	BY	
	COM	BI	NED		EXP	E	L		STA	PLE
A	ME	N		F	E	Y		HO	ND	A
QUA	ND	ARY		AME	ND	ED		T	ER	SE

PUZZLE 84

Abbey, Abbot, Adder, Addle, Affix, Alley, Allot, Allow, Alloy, Annex, Annoy, Annul, Apple, Apply, Arrow, Asset, Attic, Baaed, Beech, Beefy, Booed, Boost, Booth, Booty, Booze, Cooed, Ennui, Essay, Goody, Goofy, Goose, Hooka, Hooky, Inner, Issue, Leech, Leery, Loony, Loose, Mooch, Moody, Mooed, Moose, Needy, Noose, Occur, Odder, Offer, Orris, Otter, Reedy, Roomy, Roost, Seedy, Sooty, Teeny, Udder, Upper, Utter, Weedy, Weepy, Weest, Woody, Wooed, Wooer, Woozy.

PUZZLE 85

SPAT IAN AHEM
AURA INA LIME
STICKINTHEMUD
STAIN AER
TOM SHAFT
ASK CAR ISLE
STICKTOGETHER
SODA BEA YAM
NASTY LTS
AVE UNTIE
STICKINGPOINT
ORNE EVE ORDO
PINE DYE PEON

PUZZLE 86

LOOP DRAT GET
OHIO RODE UTE
SOLEMNIZE RUE
TOO RUIN
JULIA METE
AVEC CODIFIED
MEG SATIN SOU
BASSINET MANE
ABEL ROOST
QUAD AAR
URL PERCHANCE
AGO ADAM SEAL
YET NONE SELF

PUZZLE 87

DOG NOR SEW
ILL AWE TEE
ADE PEN ORE
LIAR AVOID
SEMI SMILES
SPIED
PICKAX EASY
AMASS ONCE
CAN TIP TEA
EGO ERE INS
DEE DEW SET

PUZZLE 88

PIE LAB
CENT ACRE
LEACH BEAMS
AID HOME SCAM
LEAD SOL EWE
AURIC DESCENT
CAD DUO
BOHEMIA MIMED
ITA ELF LAMA
GIGS HEAT TIM
SANTA VALET
ROAR OKAY
BID REX

PUZZLE 89

DATA
EVEN
DEPENDS
ALL YAK
RIO PIT
EARS TAR
EAT GOT
TOT EEL
PAD AIL
TIP TENT
MOP NEE
TOM ION
DESCEND
LEAN
TART

PUZZLE 90

1.

3	4	2	9	7	8	5	6	1
6	5	9	1	4	3	7	2	8
8	7	1	2	6	5	9	4	3
7	2	6	4	3	9	8	1	5
1	8	5	7	2	6	3	9	4
4	9	3	8	5	1	6	7	2
2	6	8	3	9	4	1	5	7
5	1	7	6	8	2	4	3	9
9	3	4	5	1	7	2	8	6

2.

2	4	8	7	9	5	6	3	1
9	3	5	2	1	6	8	7	4
1	7	6	8	3	4	2	9	5
5	9	1	6	8	7	4	2	3
6	8	4	5	2	3	7	1	9
3	2	7	9	4	1	5	8	6
4	5	2	3	7	9	1	6	8
8	1	9	4	6	2	3	5	7
7	6	3	1	5	8	9	4	2

PUZZLE 91

ELAM ART
WAGE CRAM VIE
EVENT ROPE DOVE
ANTE EVER ACES
TAP DESERTER
LIME EAT
DENOTED
SCRAM
CHEERIO
TAU GRIM
CONTRITE LOP
LARD EMIT EVEN
ANTS BAKE DETER
TOE AMID RARE
HES SLOT

PUZZLE 92

ACROSS: 1. Lincoln, 2. Kennedy, 3. Madison, 4. Harding, 5. Clinton, 6. Jackson.

DOWN: 1. Taylor, 2. Hoover, 3. Arthur, 4. Pierce, 5. Wilson, 6. Truman, 7. Carter.

QUOTATION: Ideas are a lot like children—our own are wonderful.

PUZZLE 93

DEEP HERE
RAGE AREA
URGE PIER
HYMN LAPELS
WOOS ICY
IOU ONE RIP
SNIFF SAG USE
HIDE ELK BILE
ILL BAY MINER
NEE BAT DAD
GAG TODS
ACTING MICE
BLUR ATOP
LAND GEMS
EYES EASY

PUZZLE 94

1. Chef, 2. Acne, 3. Nice, 4. Chin, 5. Ecru, 6. Lace, 7. Lily, 8. Amen, 9. Tome, 10. Item, 11. Owns, 12. Note.

OUTER RING: Cancellation

THIRD RING: Encirclement

PUZZLE 95

SAPS ANI
WISE DEN
ITALIC SEDATE
MEN ETAS
SPA LOBS
MOA WHIP
EMU DAUB
WIND GHOSTLY
TAIL TRAMP EAST
MILEAGE KEEN
MAAM PEA
SICK AMP
JILT OIL
OVAL PAC
TEPEES DEPUTY
SRI ORES
SAC ERGS

PUZZLE 96

1. Core/Correct, 2. Sane/Spanner, 3. Deep/Develop, 4. Tile/Thimble, 5. Sect/Respect, 6. Lake/Blanket, 7. Cake/Cracker, 8. Slim/Sublime.

PUZZLE 97

SKEW
PAR HALO
OWE PATIO
DEALS CORE
STOA BUNK
ANTE LARRY HUM
GULP AGED ONE
ERMA SOW WIT
HORN STAGE SALT
SIP TAG RICK
EVA VEIN SARI
EEL VILLA NEMO
BOSS ABLY
ARIA MODEL
SOLID ETA
ADEN RIG
PACK

PUZZLE 98

ACMUVW, BEKPTX, DHISYZ, FLNOQR.

PUZZLE 99

SHEDS FACE
ZEALOT DOLOR
OCTAVO CRISIS
POT TEN HAYLOFT
PRAM ERE AURA
SUER DOTE DAWNS
ARID WED CHAP
SEGO ONCE PATINA
HENNA HATH KINSMAN
LEATHERNECK
IDEATED AHOY HEIST
DEACON STOW ANTI
LASH ZOO STOP
ENTER ALPS IRIS
HIND CAP BLOC
AGILITY AXE RAY
PECANS RINSER
SLOMO CANINE
ESNE ELAND

PUZZLE 100

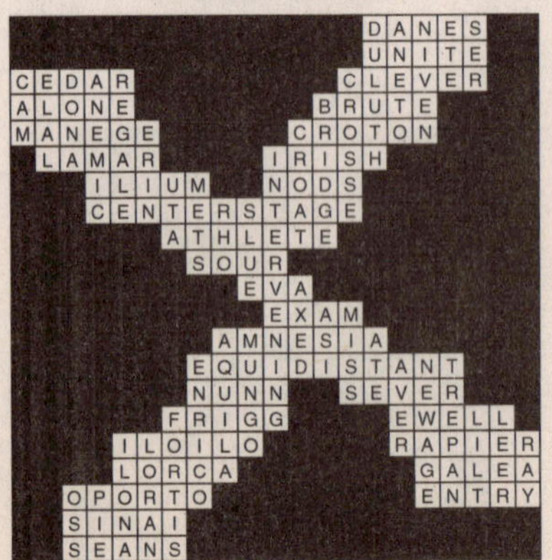

DANES
UNITE
CEDAR CLEVER
ALONE BRUTE
MANEGE CROTON
LAMAR IRISH
ILIUM NODS
CENTERSTAGE
ATHLETE
SOUR
EVA
EXAM
AMNESIA
EQUIDISTANT
NUNN SEVER
FRIGG EWELL
ILOILO RAPIER
LORCA GALEA
OPORTO ENTRY
SINAI
SEANS

PUZZLE 101

FAVA SAGA VALOR
OMEN ODIC EXILE
EMIT BRAT NENES
SONIC ONSET TOT
UNIT KEG
SAP RET WEDLOCK
ARRIVE COD OBOE
GEODE DUO EVERY
ENVY KIT ICEAGE
STOLLEN ALL HID
LAP BOLA
COP UTTER TEMPT
AVOID RITE PILE
GENRE AGAS ILIA
ENDED MESS CEES

PUZZLE 102

DAMP NET ADOBE
IDEA OVA OPENER
ODDS VEX WETTER
DAIS NICE EONS
EXCEL ORCS
SEAMAN OTTER
NAB GLANCED ACE
ONE OSIER PHI
VET RECLINE SON
AWARE ASTERN
EVER GASSY
SHOP YAWN PILE
AERATE HES PEAL
PRAYER YAP EVIL
SALSA STY DENS

PUZZLE 103

SMOG GALA ALMS
PONE RIDER NEAT
LOST EVADE TATA
ALE STEP FINER
TATTOO TONE
ELL POT WEE
FLEXED BERATING
LAVA FUN UPDO
UTENSILS UNLESS
EEN TOO POI
ONER SUPPLY
RESOW OVEN HOE
AVOW CRUET JAVA
CEDE OASES USER
ERAS OPTS TERN

PUZZLE 104

SERA ABED APACE
OWED RALE SINES
DEBS CLAW KNELT
ARE HENS ALE
LOSERS MIRROR
SOLDER FINE
ABIDE ERADICATE
COO DEMERIT TEA
SENSITIVE IOTAS
HEAT RARELY
ADDERS WOOLEN
BUR BEAD TEN
ANODE RAKE AIDE
SCOUR EVEN LOIN
EELER WENT ANTE

PUZZLE 105

SARIS HES SORA
ARETES ISM EVIL
FIASCO GNU DENT
ELL RUSHED UNDO
EBERT GEM
UNSET ROPED PAP
SATE IRE DRAMA
UNAPT AID YELPS
ANTSY TEA SILT
LYE KNELL PINES
BEE ELAND
TOFU BEADED REM
ALIT URN ARROYO
MELT LAD SEEMED
POME ASS STERE

PUZZLE 106

CZAR MARS PAINT
LAVA IDEA ENNUI
ANET LEAF RIFLE
MYRIAD CARS OLD
OPE TRAIT
APTNESS INSECTS
WAR TOP ITALIC
ATOLL BID SLIDE
RELOAD PIC MAN
ENLACER EATABLE
FREES NAG
ULM OPAH ABLAZE
ROOFS POOP EMIR
GILLS ERNE AMPS
ENDUE REES MOST

PUZZLE 107

MAJOR SHAG FLU
ALIBI QUERY LAP
REBID UPPER ADS
ETA OFT
NAPS IDS USABLE
ITALIC KEN DEAR
BERYL MIDI DYE
KEA ITS
TEN LIFT AWARD
AVID ADE TWINER
RETURN ZOO TIDY
POI BOA
PHI FOLIO LLAMA
SEC LIANE BOXER
IRK ELMS SPENT

1-T, 2-A, 3-M, 4-L, 5-Y, 6-N, 7-X, 8-S, 9-F, 10-V, 11-R, 12-K, 13-W, 14-C, 15-G, 16-J, 17-I, 18-H, 19-P, 20-Z, 21-D, 22-U, 23-E, 24-O, 25-B, 26-Q.

PUZZLE 108

ABASH ADDS REST
TEMPO BEEN ECHO
OVERT LAMA IRON
MYNA CEDER NUDE
WAR ALAS
BULLETIN NEAR
MAP LAWN STREET
ASPS MOTEL TREE
STEADY ROIL IVE
EDDY HONEYBEE
DEMO SEE
ANTE ALERT SHOE
WEAN PLAY STANK
LAME LOVE HENCE
SPED EWES EDGED

PUZZLE 109

AWL AMOK MANSE
BIO EXILE OPINE
ESS RETIE TAPIN
THEDA TOP CAPS
ALOE SATE
FIR INSANE BAD
TUNNEL AKIN ACE
END AIMLESS SHE
AGE TEAS EERIER
MIX ESCAPE AND
ANTA ODOR
YARD RAT WEIRD
EDEMA ONION TAR
WIDEN NOONS EGO
STONY INNS MAP

PUZZLE 110

LATHE YEAH ECRU
AMOUR AXLE MOOS
SPIER WILY ELSE
ELL ISNT DARTED
RESENT DADA
AGOG EYELASH
SLIT WAGES DICE
MOD TAP RAW
OGLE SHYER HYMN
GOESAPE RANI
PURR SETTEE
STROKE KEPT RAP
LIEU AVID TEASE
ODES DELI EMCEE
TYKE SENT DUELS

PUZZLE 111

SCAB OBI FOLKS
LOBE RUN NOVENA
OLLA ARK ELATED
EDEMA EELED GEL
LOADED HOLY
AWL GNU ALSO
NOOSES FRECKLES
CRUMB WAN REATA
ENDORSED PAYDAY
TATA JAW ESS
ETRE UNCURL
RHO ARSON SCORN
RIBALD MIL AGUE
ONEWAY MOA LENS
RESEE ARC MEET

PUZZLE 112

WHOM ARC ORCA
HONE ANILS FOAL
IRED CIVET FACT
MARINA AWAY SHE
CECIL NEATER
GELATIN ZAP
IDOL ALPHA ERGO
NIB ERA AND
STEM STOIC ALAE
ICE RIOTERS
PLEXOR MYRRH
AIM BIDE CALLUP
GAPE AURAL EASE
ANTS LARGE TIER
NAYS LYE ERST

PUZZLE 113

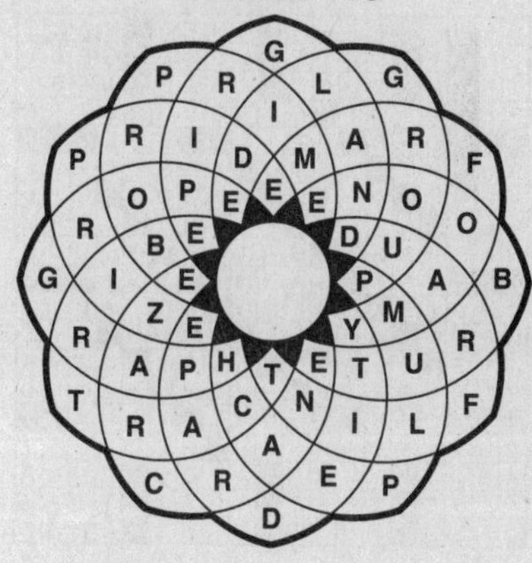

PUZZLE 114

AMPS PRIM EVEN
LURE PRIDE MILE
BLOC RINSE PEAT
SLAT EGG THORNS
OHM SEW
FOREIGN REAR
LIP MENU MERGER
AGE RUMBA ADE
PHRASE BRIG ZIP
TARP SALUTED
TUB ATE
DOMINO RIB MAST
UKES STOOL PIKE
MALT ORATE ONYX
BYTE MYNA STET

PUZZLE 115

SAPOR ETAS DOT
ABODE ALIST EKE
GLIDE MANSE BRA
EEN FROND NATAL
SLEEK EFTS
STEERS TROOPER
PITAS ARBOR LEG
ACTS FLOOD DARE
SKI CALYX DEBUT
SAFARIS MELONS
AGOG POWER
COATI AHEAD AFT
UMP EATER RATIO
TEE SNORT OCEAN
END TIRE PESTS

PUZZLE 116

BASH ASPS APED
ESPY SPEAR CHEW
REAP SIEGE TOLE
GANEF DRAMA TEE
ADES ADSORB
BED CUR BROW
EVOKED AUK ITCH
EIGHT PRY GLARE
PLEA IRK DOLLAR
KENO WOO EBB
RELIEF WAGE
EMU NIGHT YOKED
WENT RAISE DELE
ERGO MINOR APSE
DYER NENE STEM

PUZZLE 117

FLAT ARAB SHAH VALE
LOBE LATE LONE ORAL
IRAN OPEN ABED WEBS
PENDANT ELBOWGREASE
DOME DAYS EEL
PHONY FATE ADHESIVE
EONS WISH BROOD NIL
ROE NASH PRONG ITEM
UPDRAFT GRIME WOODS
APT SAUNA YET
CHOSE CLING NOTABLY
HEMP WHILE ROWS LIE
IRE BEADY COAL MAMA
CONCRETE HUSH FACES
OAK SORE TANK
BELLYDANCER REDDEST
ARID AVER APES ANNA
WIFE YORE NEAT TEAK
LEER SNOW TARS EDGE

PUZZLE 121

PECS ANAS BASSO
ALEE IOTA UNHIP
VILE DOOR RIATA
EDEMA SLICE VAL
DEB FEEL LAGERS
ROTAS FOUR
MEANER DAD AJAR
ALTER DUD SHAME
SKEW WIG STAMPS
ABED THUMB
LAWYER REEF ANY
ORE HEWER FOLIO
AGAVE APSE RAND
NOVEL TREY BYTE
STEED TORE SAHL

PUZZLE 125

ADO SPIN AFAR
PEA STATIC NONE
ELK HASSLE TATA
DISTORT NAILER
ATE OASIS
HUMP EPSOM MEN
OBOE RETIRE AXE
SOLDIER DEDUCTS
TAD SLICED TART
STY LEERS TWAS
WEARY DYE
ACCESS COURAGE
SHOE ENTAIL COG
KELP DOODLE NAG
SWAY ROSY ELS

PUZZLE 118

FOCAL SHAM ABAS
EROSE EARS NONO
RINKS LIES GRAM
NET SULK LEASE
SLAVES UNTIL
CINE OILIEST
DOTE SPINE CAKE
ANI ORC SIN
DENS PREEN GYMS
ORGANIC ADES
VICHY MATTES
PHLOX OVEN RIA
REAR MADE COEDS
EAVE OWES EPEES
PLED PELT RETRY

PUZZLE 122

SPATS LIST DICE
COBRA ACHE IDOL
ALLOW PERM SEAS
BEEP UPSCALE
HAWK NOT
PAYCHECK YACHT
BED NONO FLEE
ADOBE ONS STOWS
RARE GIFT NET
SLEET GALLOPED
WOO TYPE
PEASOUP ELKS
RAMP THAT ALOHA
OVER DELI DECAL
DENY ORES DRONE

PUZZLE 126

MEN DELI HOOT
AYE EXAM URGE
PET LIMP BARE
WATT UNCLES
AROMA FLEA
CARP PASSPORT
IRK BESET RAH
DESSERTS PITA
MESS GREEN
SAFARI LOON
USER SPAN TWO
MEET TIME EON
SASS SEAR DOE

PUZZLE 119

ODAS AND VOLE
LOBE SPEAK AVID
EWER EPODE RAGE
ANTI CAN RHYTHM
FOOL ANI ETA
RAT UNLINED
ONWARD COLESLAW
LOON GIN PACA
LASTCALL SAYING
OBEYING CEE
SAP DIE ROOD
CRAVED FIR RAGA
RILE EROSE ALAI
ISMS DINED WAIT
PEST ADS LETS

PUZZLE 123

SWAG MATE THEN
TOUR BATHE EAVE
OKRA EATEN EVER
WEAN EMIT TEND
OFF CATCH
UNCLASP AHEAD
SARAN REATA BUM
EMU FLORIST ADO
RES AIMER EASEL
STORM STALEST
PEONY RUM
SPAR OILY ATOM
ULNA SNEES NAVE
MOTH ECLAT ALEE
OWES WEDS CENT

PUZZLE 127

CLAM EBBS PEW
RAKE REEK IRE
AVID RETURNED
MANIA PALE
ACHE LLAMA
OAF NODS ICON
ABASES ACCEPT
TUTU ECRU DEE
STEAL LIRA
VETO BLAZE
REHEARSE ARIA
AGO RUES RENT
POP NETS MACS

PUZZLE 120

APHID ABET ALES
REATA SAVE GALA
CAREW KNEESOCKS
STEM ANTE ESS
SMELL HER
PIP IRE REDOUBT
ERE CRAZE APER
KOALA GIN IMPLY
ONCE UPEND ELS
EYESORE GEL RET
TOO HEWED
EGG ZITI EPEE
MARVELING ACORN
ILIA EDGY CONGO
RENT DEEM TRESS

PUZZLE 124

BASS ISNT COMER
ARCH NEER ARETE
NEAR TACO BATHE
CANAPE KOLA ESS
NOR SPORT
VIKING STEAMED
RIM SAT STRIVE
ALPHA BIO STREW
SLEEPS NAG TRY
PALETTE FLESHY
LIONS OAT
ASS TWIN ARROYO
SNAFU GOAT APOD
PAGED MOLE WARD
SPADE APED SHES

PUZZLE 128

ADAM HASP RAT
RAMAR DELTA NILE
IRENE ALLAMERICAN
DEN DILLER DANES
STEN WIT
SAW ASOR DASHING
AMI NUN MOORE NAB
MALONE COWED ADES
LIA JONES CRI
EMIL SALES PLEASE
DOA CONEY RAE NIL
DEMILLE FARM ADO
NEO LORI
TITAN CARESS AES
PETERGRAVES ILLYA
SAAR ODIST MEDES
ILL WENT WASS

PUZZLE 129

STET CLAM RUMPS
EACH AIDE EMAIL
ACRE VEES SPREE
STUFFED ATE ADD
TAR OATS
RAP INK ARTICLE
ABHOR NILS THAN
MOOR CELLO LINT
PUTS HALE FENCE
STOOPED YOU OER
GNAW CRY
APE GYM MELODIC
LUNGE OPAL DICE
PRIOR LOGO EVEN
SECTS TWIT LAST

PUZZLE 130

1. Motif, 2. Nana, 3. Naomi, 4. Amati, 5. Camel, 6. Isuzu, 7. Rhyme, 8. Line.

ANSWER: Nail file

PUZZLE 131

		SE	NA	TE		CON	QUE	ST		
	JU	VEN	I	LE		CO	LL	A	PSE	
RAB	BI		LED	G	E	R		K	UDO	S
B	LAN	CH		RAM	RO	D		E	NY	A
LE	T	AL	ONE		DE	AN	NA		M	INT
		ET	U	DE		CE	N	TER		
ST	AIR		P	LI	ANT		CY	C	LO	NES
EM	P	TOR		CAT	HE	R		EL	A	TE
S	LA	P		E	M	AN	ATE		FE	D
	NE	ED	LE	SS		D	AS	HE	R	
		O	FT	EN		ALL	E	Y		

PUZZLE 132

1. Your aspirations are your possibilities.

2. If you must be blue, at least be bright blue.

PUZZLE 133

SPAN PRO ACRE
ORDO GUILE DOER
LOUD ANNEX ANSA
ASLEEP GOO PETS
RET MESS TAT
TURN INSIST
SAFE ALACK CUE
LIANA FEN HYENA
IDS GAUGE ERGS
DETOUR LORN
VEE YETI ADD
ASHE OPE HARBOR
MOOR LEASE ULNA
MOOD ERROR SEEN
ONTO INN TREK

PUZZLE 134

RACK REAS APPLE
ELAN INFO FLAIR
NONE DRAW TARPS
ANTE GORE ZEST
LEI GEL RAGA
LOO LUSTY TAG
ANEMONES IMPALA
LIVE IDEAL OPAL
SCENIC RUTHLESS
OER CHEST ELS
JEER OAR TAW
ONTO ROMP ARIA
HOOKY ABAS LION
MELEE NOTE GELT
SLEDS DEES ASIS

PUZZLE 135

1. Knit and purl, 2. Hill and dale, 3. Fits and starts, 4. Dog and pony, 5. Body and soul, 6. Bangers and mash.

PUZZLE 136

JOT ESS SPLAT
ERR STOOD QUOTA
TEE PHONE UTTER
AWAIT FLAT
GASH CHERUB SAW
ALOOF EXAM FISH
PENPAL TUB ICKY
PRESIDENT
ISLE GIN RINSER
VEER INCH BELLE
YET DOCTOR SELF
ZONE PHASE
ARROW RAPID PAD
RAYON EMEND EGO
ENEMY PRO ROT

1-I, 2-K, 3-W, 4-X, 5-G, 6-S, 7-E, 8-N, 9-O, 10-Q, 11-L, 12-Y, 13-H, 14-B, 15-T, 16-V, 17-A, 18-J, 19-D, 20-P, 21-Z, 22-F, 23-C, 24-R, 25-M, 26-U.

PUZZLE 137

1-d Biscuits & gravy, 2-i Watson & Crick, 3-h Fear & loathing, 4-g Echo & Narcissus, 5-b Radio & television, 6-j Tracy & Hepburn, 7-f Life & limb, 8-a Time & again, 9-e Simon & Garfunkel, 10-c Stars & Stripes.

PUZZLE 138

STRIP SHOE ACHE
HYENA MUDD SLAY
APING AGOG SORE
HEN OWL RIVETER
IDOLS NIT
SONAR LUGE DAD
DARN SHIP RILE
RUDE TACOS EGOS
ICER VINE MINK
PER AMEN WHITE
ODE GREET
TIMIDLY ARE ROE
ORAL LOUT DRIVE
FILE OGRE EASEL
USED WAND DYERS

PUZZLE 139

TAJ SAGA PUSHY RIGG
EDO IGOR OSTIA ANNA
RONSTADT CHASM SCAB
GEAR FAKER MACAWS
ABLER SURER FETA
LEEK SPLIT WIRELESS
EAU GOALS COOEE ATM
CURRENCY CHORD TREE
URGE BALED DELLA
REALMS FUROR ERASER
ABBES DONEE OBIS
WOAD DAUNT NOBLEMAN
ENS BENNY HAZEL ICE
RYEBREAD METED SNIT
AIRS HINTS GLADS
CLINTS MASSE THOR
RARA KNUTE REMOTELY
AMAN INTER EVAS TAI
MANA NEEDY DENT SOP

PUZZLE 140

BASAL CAMS GOLD
ARTSY ANOA OLEO
BEEKEEPING VEER
KEA VOLT WEARY
ALLUDE SHOER
MYNA RANSOM
ELOPE LODEN TWO
CON AGARS INS
ROE SNAFU BURST
UPROOT BOOR
CREAK IGNITE
OCTET VIAL MIX
WOOL LIONSSHARE
ERGO EAST AUGER
SEAT INKS WEEST

PUZZLE 141

TOIL ABET GAFFE
ULNA LUGE ODIUM
FIST EDGE VERSE
TOTEM GENRE EEN
IRONER ERODED
RAG POT HANG
ERASER GAP LEFT
PITHY TIP REPRO
OLEO OWN MEDIAN
UNDO CUD DYE
FASTED FAMINE
ALL ASHEN PERMS
COURT ONCE EMIT
ENGEL SCAN DACE
TESTY TEND SLAT

PUZZLE 142

CARD SHOW MOST
OLEO HALOS ETUI
DISCRETION DIRE
ENOKI ODA ACER
DEW GLASSFUL
THEM YUP LAC
PETITION SPADE
IRON KIT AMID
EGRET LIBERATE
DOS OFT DUNE
STOUTEST ALB
DATA ORA EERIE
ORAN TENDERNESS
DIRT SEGUE ONTO
OLEA NOON LAST

PUZZLE 143

ORCA SLAM PARKS
NEER PINE OZONE
CELEBRATE DAVIT
ELL EUREKA LETS
PAN LYE
ATINGLE LEASH
SAILS ARROW HES
ORAL STRAY NONO
NOR SLEET SAUCY
NATTY DESPITE
RYE AIL
ACNE REDONE ADS
SLANG PAPERCLIP
PANDA IRES USER
SWAYS CENT ROSY

PUZZLE 144

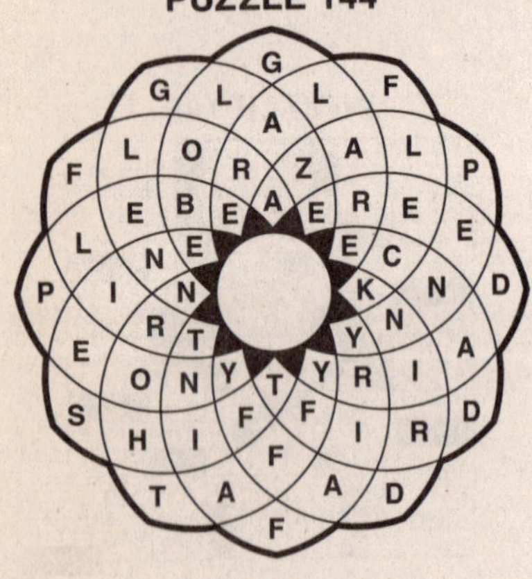

PUZZLE 145

REEF ACHED SORT
EVIL DRAKE TRIO
RAGE MAZES RATE
ADHESIVE TOILED
NET ORES RAP
CLAD FORESTS
SCHOOL FLY HOE
LOANS YOU FLARE
OIL TAG CRIMES
BLOSSOM GOAT
OER DRAM SAW
ENTRAP ROSEBUSH
LAIR ELIOT RAKE
LIMO DELVE EVER
SLEW OGLED WERE

PUZZLE 146

SHELL SPAT LIPS
KOALA LOCH ECRU
ASSAY ANTI VOID
TEEM TEACHINGS
ASHES KEA
WAS POD LENTIL
ACCRUE CAT HOOF
SHRED HUG MATTE
PEAK FAD SENATE
SPIRAL VIA SOT
NET MANLY
TOADSTOOL OPAH
ARIL EVIL OKAPI
MADE SERE VERSE
PLED TREY ADDED

PUZZLE 147

BALD SWIFT OFT
OGEE CHORES PER
GUFF RITUAL PLY
SETA ERAS EARLS
COW THEREAT
RARER SERAPES
ORE AMORAL SIS
SOD LIMITED ILK
EWE RECEDE VIA
CAMERAS CHEAT
PROFESS FOE
HARTS ACME LOLL
OVA AMULET PLIE
NET SALUTE EENS
ERE STEED ROTS

PUZZLE 148

ASCOT TAP AMMO
CLARET HIE GOON
HUMANE ERA EAVE
YES PAWN CANTER
LIRA GOLD
AGAINST OCTAVE
CROC EVOKE APE
MURKY RID RULER
ENT EBBED RUES
TAMALE EARNEST
IRED AXES
ADORNS ILIA TUN
PUPA BAD OPPOSE
SLUG OWE MERGES
ELSE KEA ROAST

PUZZLE 149

TEES AWL PATH
HAVE USHER ACHE
ICED PHOTO LEER
SHRUBS TEASED
CREST ARC
BREATHE TREATS
BRED SARGE SLOT
OUT FRO ONE
SNIT STARE CHAP
STEREO CENTRAL
OAR ESSAY
ASSURE INSIDE
BLAB SLANG TOOL
LOLL TALON ATOM
EPEE BET LAMS

PUZZLE 150

SLAB BACK CHOP
PUPA ARGUE LIAR
AGES SOAPY UNTO
REDHOT TOW ETHS
FREELOAD
PREFAB ARC ASK
SEAR LOP DEGREE
NAVAL NOG SIEGE
OCELOT DAM STEP
WED CHA LETTER
KIELBASA
ZITI ILL SWAMPY
ECHO SUEDE LIRA
SEES TRAYS ENOW
TREK SERE SEWN

PUZZLE 151

ABORT AGAS DOSS
WIRER SOFA ECHO
LLANO KOALABEAR
SELDOM PRAM ALE
PEP MEANER
PARASOL WING
EXAM WIPE DETER
ROGUE GEE SNARE
KNELL HAVE DIAL
EAST IDEALLY
GROTTO LIT
RAW EFTS THATCH
AMNESTIES EXILE
VEER EDGE RERAN
ENDS NEON SLEDS

PUZZLE 152

PANE CHIP DRAW PASS
UFOS AURA ROSE ARIA
MASK REAP EASTEREGG
ARTISTS YEAR CRANE
AMOS PROM NERO
AGLOW FAUN SOLUTION
TOGS GAGS PADS ROE
OBI FIVE LOUSE SIZE
PICCOLO WAND BASED
EXTRAORDINARY
SCALY SUDS OPOSSUM
LOLL SAILS GREW ANY
ODD CLAD PITS EXIT
TEASPOON MESH FROTH
LUTE WART LOOP
OSCAR AHEM MARSHAL
STOVEPIPE ICED IOWA
LAME URSA TONE ONES
ORES BEET SPUN NEST

PUZZLE 153

SABER TEMP ACME
LLANO AXIL PROA
OASIS BALUSTERS
STAGES MEMO ANY
HELM CAP BALM
AREOLE PASSE
ELF UNREST MOLL
RAREBIT CICADAS
SNAP CABANA AYE
TENET SUPERB
CEES SEA ICED
ASH RUST ROLLER
CLIENTELE GLORY
TOSS REEL RETIE
AWES ADDS ETHER

PUZZLE 154

JAVA PARE IMAGE
OXEN APER NEWER
SLAY SPAN SALTS
HELM TAPERED
OPAL ATOMS
AURA LAMB WIPE
LINEN DABS SOD
ERA DEPOSIT HUG
EBB AGER ERASE
KALE GANG NAPE
GENRE ATOP
TADPOLE TOSS
HEART IRON UNTO
EMCEE CARS RYES
MUTED ALEE EXPO

PUZZLE 155

BESS JAMB ERGO BREW
OMIT ERIE SEEP RODE
MILE WING PANE OONA
BROWBEATER STRAWMAN
AIL TOGO ANN
SHORTEST BANG ABODE
TEND RTE DEER AREA
OAT ALMS RAE GNAT
ADOBE GLENN RANGERS
ALL SNOOT LEE
SHOCKED DRAWN ERECT
WALK SOS THEE COY
ARAB STEW ERA CROP
GENRE SPAT DORMOUSE
ERE ADAM MAR
STRANGER BABYBOOMER
TREK ASAP VISA NOTE
AIDE DATE EDEN EROS
BOOR SUET NERD TENT

PUZZLE 159

MACE PADS GEESE
ALAE AGUE ASKER
YARN PEND STEMS
BRO AREA EDIT
EMBODY NAPE
BEAUS LEMURS
ASPIC STILT NEE
COATI EON UDDER
ERG MEDIC NOOSE
SEESAW CHOIR
OLEA DAMASK
DELI SPED LYE
APERY TAXI PONE
DONEE ICES ANON
ASSET RASH CEDE

PUZZLE 163

SPA HIE WAD PET
OUT ION ICE APE
ART DUO GEL VEX
PRIZE WOW TWEET
SERE RAJAH
DEEP FAME ERST
SARAN ASTUTE
EAR PUNGENT BYE
GRAHAM EASEL
GENE BRAT WISH
FRAUD AQUA
VISTA MET CRUMB
ADO MAP AGO EBB
ILL PAL PAN ALE
NEE SHE ELK KEY

1-N, 2-K, 3-E, 4-R, 5-A, 6-Z, 7-H, 8-I, 9-G, 10-L, 11-C, 12-S, 13-X, 14-U, 15-V, 16-Y, 17-F, 18-W, 19-D, 20-B, 21-O, 22-J, 23-T, 24-M, 25-Q, 26-P.

PUZZLE 160

HIFI TOTE BLAH
ELAN TOWEL LIRA
MINT OPENS OMIT
PAGE RAD FABLE
RITZ TOOT
GAFFE SYNC GOB
HAVES APPLIANCE
ONER STRAY NOTE
PERENNIAL WOMEN
EFT OILY JANET
PUTT ZANY
OFTEN COB MAST
LEAS PIANO ISLE
LARK INSET TEAR
ARTY EKED YAWN

PUZZLE 156

EGOS DIRT OMEGA
LAPP OVER BARON
AGAR MYNA INGOT
SALAMI TIP NOPE
EYING LACE
DOS SOLO DORMS
ORCAS AVERSIONS
ORES ERASE STAT
MINSTRELS SMOKE
STEER SERE RET
MEOW NICAD
VERB ROT STURDY
ARILS VANE ROUE
INLET EMIR AMEN
NEEDY NETS LESS

PUZZLE 164

RUST SCAT TRAP GEAR
INCH ALMA BETA ACNE
DIRE FIAT ABOLISHED
ETA FEET WRAP FLOWS
SEPAL NIGH PSI
DEPORT RIPPLE TREE
TRUE UPROARS ARM
ONS ADLIB ALIEN PAS
RITZ EEN EWER OPT
BLOOD FRANC WOUND
POI FLAT ACT PRAY
YAP STAID ETHEL EYE
EWE CRUCIAL ALEE
TERM EXTOLS LLAMAS
AOK PEAL DUNCE
IRISH DAIS BETS TOR
RECOMMEND DINO SLUG
OPEN ALOE EDGE HERO
NODS TINA BEES ERST

PUZZLE 157

PARSE LAMS VEST
ADAMS IMAM ETCH
TODOS SITE LUAU
EPIC UPSTANDING
STOKES SERA
SEW MIRES
SCAMP EAR ERODE
PAPER EGO SEDGE
ARETE DOS ASSES
SEXES YAK
SOAP WEIGHT
PILLOWCASE SLOE
ALOE LUNE STALE
LION ETNA OLDEN
LAND TEEM NEEDY

PUZZLE 161

ACIDS ERGS CALM
RAMIE LOON OLIO
CRAMP LUAU MOLT
HEM ITSELF MEAT
MAR FIASCO
DODO YELPED
AVERT READY ONS
CASEY RAT LAPIN
ELK PEEVE LLANO
ARDENT THAW
GIGOLO AGO
AGOG DOTAGE MOW
SLUR IBEX NEATH
PORE NOSE RETIE
SODS GETS ERECT

PUZZLE 165

FACT AGOG ELAN
EURO PROBE NAVE
ERIN AROOM GNAW
LATENT NEST AIL
EDIE ICILY
TOR ASSESSOR
ALIAS TREE EWER
NEON JAUNT SHOO
GONG ASPS STINT
EIGHTEEN TSE
CHORD MODE
REF SNIP IBISES
ALTA ENACT NAPA
SLEW ACRES GLEN
HONE THEE SEED

PUZZLE 158

SKIDS SEWN SPAR
UNLIT OKRA WALE
POISE WEIR ELAN
SWAMPY SCHEMED
ASEA TOUT
IVY ANDS METAL
ADOS ROE TIRADE
RIG SNAPPED BOA
MOUTHS ORA BORN
SMEAR ATOP EON
MEAN FOAL
SCRAWNY TRIALS
ERAL THEM REDYE
MANE IOTA AVERT
IBIS SWAT YESES

PUZZLE 162

STEAD GRAB CITE
CACTI NULL AROW
ACHES ASEA SIRE
TOO MATH CRISES
INS SKIN
SASSY UNCOOKED
ATLAS GREAT HAY
DRIP BEGET RARE
DAB SANER PIKES
SPIRALED HUMID
ELLS WAS
GROCER BOTH TIA
LIRE ODOR UNITY
OPEN OUST PUREE
BEST MESH STEMS

PUZZLE 166

E W D N N N D N E W E E K K W D K W W N K W N N E
D N E E W K N N D W E D N E N D N D K E D K E K D
D N W W W W E N E W D E N D W W N N E K E E W E N
D E E E D K K N W K W D K K N W E K N D E N N E W
N K N D N E E N W W E D N D E W K E N D E E D W N
W D W W N N W W N E N E K N E E D N N E E E W W D
D N K D W E E K N E D D W N E W E D D K W K N N W

PUZZLE 167

IMPEL CANS EBB SOSO
FARGO OLIO DOE EWER
FROGS MEAL GAL MERE
YEW EVE CAVE IBISES
GRAD ICEDTEA
ALTO LINNET AFT FUR
LEAF VEE SORT TORSO
SAMENESS ETA FEES
OPERA THERMOMETERS
ROO ERA OPT
FILECABINETS CHEAT
ORAL TOO LETHARGY
RISKS INKS ADE SNAP
ESS ITS ATOMIC PESO
TITANIC THIS
EMBLEM BELT ISM DOC
RALE BIO TACO AMEBA
STUN ERR EVEN GAMIN
TEED RET DEES EROSE

PUZZLE 168

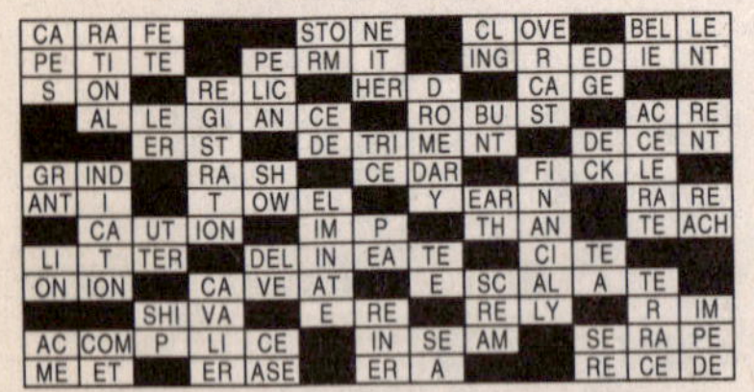

PUZZLE 169

PAPA SCAB JAVA
ORAL STARE EWES
ECRU TORTE WEEP
THEM OPT SHE
NOVA ALAN
ENLIVENS CLERIC
TAI UPDATE RICH
NIB MIGRANT SKI
ALIT POINTY EEN
SEDATE STIPENDS
DODO APEX
POD ALE ALMS
HALO REBID LEAH
AXIL AMAZE TAXI
MEDE MUSE SPIN

PUZZLE 170

COLA DOES DARN DENT
ATOP ERSE ELIA OLEO
STAR NEAL LOOM CLAN
HONOLULULULU EATERY
NOD ETA ALSO
BAT RETIRE SPEARGUN
ALONE EOS SEAS DINO
LISA ANN BEARS ELIS
DESSERT HEART STATE
HEM MALTS FOR
ALIVE CELLO DISOBEY
GOBI DARTS GET IOTA
EVIL OTIS BEL STOOL
REDLIGHT RELISH NNE
ESPY DEL YIN
MANCHA VIVALASVEGAS
AREA THEN TART VAIL
SLOT CORE ETTE ETRE
TONS HEAR DEEM REED

PUZZLE 171

ACED TRACE MEMO
GAME RADAR AMID
ERIS ATONE SILO
STRETCH SCATTER
RATES TIE
SALTS RED DRAPE
CREEKS VOTE NOW
AGAR ARETE RISE
MUD IGOR EVILER
PESTS WEB APERS
OLE DENSE
INSTEAD REENTER
BOAT MACAW ERLE
IDLE EMOTE RASE
SEER SEWER SPED

PUZZLE 172

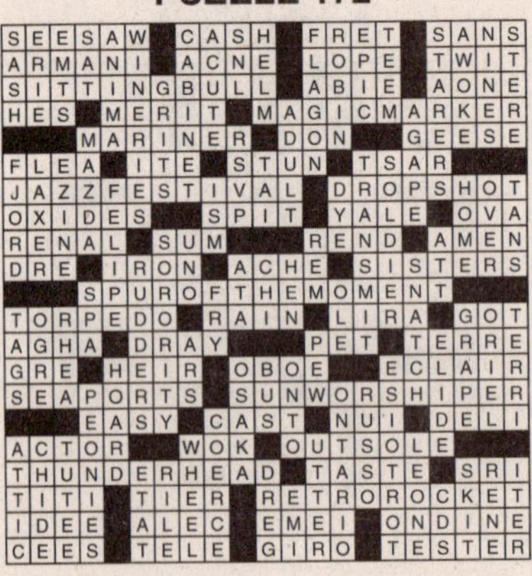

PUZZLE 173

OMEN MESA FAT
AIRE ATON IVY
FIREBRAND RIP
DUE REEVE
CAFES QUEST
AVID FUR TRAM
NOR LAG ULE
EWER EYE SCOT
IOTAS POKES
MARDI GAL
EGO FIREWATER
SUN FOAM CAGY
HAS SUMS EDGE

PUZZLE 174

LAB SEAM ALTO
AGE TRIO SOAR
COLORADO KURT
WAS WEISS
DIMLY DRAWS
IRIS BOON IAN
VAN VALVE AMA
ANN ALEE SNIP
ESTES SHADE
BASIS BOO
AGOG DELAWARE
RUTH AMOK MAR
BEAT DUBS PEN

PUZZLE 175

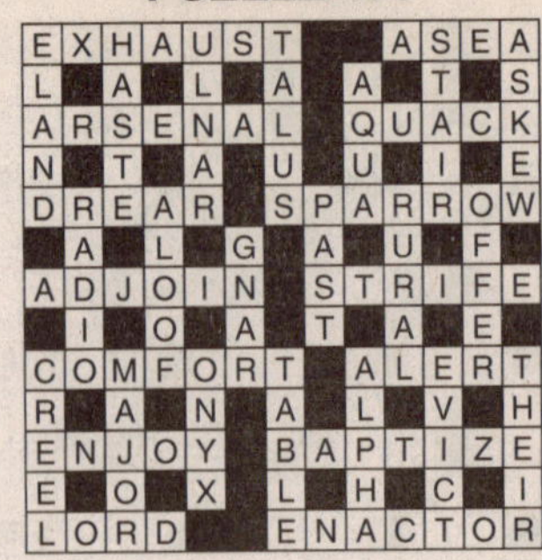

1-W, 2-C, 3-P, 4-G, 5-M, 6-Z, 7-S, 8-Y, 9-V, 10-H, 11-Q, 12-R, 13-A, 14-I, 15-L, 16-F, 17-B, 18-K, 19-D, 20-J, 21-N, 22-U, 23-X, 24-E, 25-O, 26-T.

PUZZLE 176

1-S, 2-M, 3-J, 4-H, 5-F, 6-Q, 7-K, 8-Z, 9-W, 10-B, 11-L, 12-A, 13-N, 14-D, 15-Y, 16-E, 17-U, 18-X, 19-T, 20-I, 21-O, 22-G, 23-R, 24-P, 25-V, 26-C.

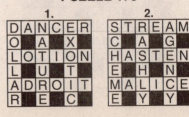

PUZZLE 177

BRAD REAPS JOEL
AARE ADMIT UNDO
STICKTOONESGUNS
SEDAN STEW SAT
DOTS SLAT
PENELOPE EGOISM
ERA LOONS GLEE
COMESTOTHEPOINT
ASEA LEEDS USE
NESTER REDEEMED
SKID PAUL
ION EPEE DEEDS
SWORDOFDAMOCLES
LEVI FEINT TINT
EDAM FRETS SASS

PUZZLE 178

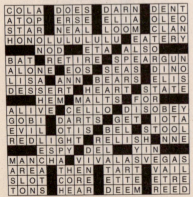

PUZZLE 179

```
STEP STOW TEST CLOD
PAPA HAVE RENO AIDA
AMIR OPAL ALOT TMEN
MACKERELSKY WELFARE
ARES HIND MOI
ALP ASTA DORA USHER
LOUTS RIM RAMS HOME
ECRU CYRUS GEE HUME
CORNER ESPY NATURAL
ARE SIREN RAN
CONCEAL CAME ENTREE
IDEA SAT TEPID EARP
TOMS EDIT NAS WRITE
EROSE SERF LOSE DEE
EAR RUDE TEAM
QUARTET SALMONRIVER
UNTO BOOT DANA DIVA
IDOL ERIE EMIT AVER
DOPE LYLE RACE SANE
```

PUZZLE 180

```
RED PEP MARE BORA
EVEN ALE AGENT IDOL
CAMELLIA SENNA TOTE
ADOBE LET TUN TREE
PEN APE LEG ISLE
SPAR ORAL YARNS
LENO TRIP ROT GROPE
IRATE RESTORE OVAL
TAG ALGA PETAL OATS
BREE SIR CAST
ABEL STEER NENE SKI
TUTU SUPPOSE TAPED
ESTEE PIT ERAT RAGE
TABLE CEDE ROOK
OMIT TAR MOP VAL
BEAN GEE MST ERASE
EARN HADES MAGNOLIA
ESNE TRIPE EVA BIDS
STET SEAL NET DEE
```

PUZZLE 181

```
TOWS SEEP ASK STEM
AMAT PAIR LAIC HERE
RAYE ACNE ASEA EXIT
ERNE SHEPFIELDS BEE
ELAM AIN ETTE
SKEP ART RETAINS
SHIRE FIE BEG CREED
PIN OLD RAG CAKED
ANGRIER MOP WADERS
ADS GLASS ATE
TRAILS LET CROSSED
VERSE CAN GAO AGO
SATIN ACT LIP RAMON
DINETTE MAD ALMS
ESSE SAD ONLY
PAS STANKENTON SKAT
ACHE OTOE EONS TAME
IRAN NAVE SITE AYES
LEWD PAT SLOT RENT
```

PUZZLE 182

```
CHOW PEACECORPS
O R S P A L O O
LOCATIONS EMBER
O H I X H A I E
SKETCHY INNINGS
S S K E U T
ALTOS SCRAPPED
L R U E Y S
BALANCED QUEST
S M C U S E
PIMENTO WHISTLE
A I E T A V R L
RANKS AGGREGATE
S C T S O R I R
EVERYTHING ONUS
```

PUZZLE 183

```
READ ANAT BETAS GAMS
ABRI VEGAS ERODE IMET
GEORGEWASHINGTON NILE
ERATO TITAN SERA SEA
STRING NERVE DETACHED
EERO EARS SEXY
WARRENHARDING ERECT
TAW STOUT ECOLE SUPER
ANEW ARGOT ABODE SOLE
RESET MAD VEST SLY
THOMASJEFFERSON
OAT ERAL WAR WOTAN
SLAB ATLAS TIARA WIVE
LURED TAMPA APART LED
OMEGA HERBERTHOOVER
ALAS NILS SINE
REPTILES TOPSY DISBAR
EVA ILIA OREAD ETUDE
SAIL BENJAMINHARRISON
IDLE INCAS TOOLE GERE
NEST SEERS ROES ESNE
```

PUZZLE 184

```
TACOS EDIT CHIN SCRAG
AROMA RARA LEVA COATI
TINATURNER ALAR AUGER
SASH NOT AARONCOPLAND
ANDREW GET DEE
FAR YES HALT PSI ESTE
ONAGER MORE MAINS CID
BENET MARKTWAIN PRONG
OLDE GIRL RUR CHATTY
FLY ANNS TWIN SLEPT
FIN ZACHARYTAYLOR JAB
ELATE LAOS AIDE OPE
TOWELS TAI OWNS APIS
AIMEE NEILYOUNG TOLET
FLA ALIEN ANTS CALICO
TYNE AND ELOI PAM NEW
NOH ASI ENAMEL
ARTGARFUNKEL ONE EGOS
SARAS ASTI LYLELOVETT
STAGE DEEM DEAL DEARE
NAMES EDDO SANS ARROW
```

PUZZLE 185

```
PRETZELOQUENT
REVIEWERUNNER
UNEASENSITIVE
DENOTEDOVESAN
EWERELINESLIT
NEATESTORTEDO
TARARERNIEDEN
ARESONICEDARS
NILESTEERINSE
ASIDEIDERESET
GOVERNORATITE
EMERGEDINETTE
REDSOLOEDREAM
```

PUZZLE 186

```
AQUA MUSH PSST ITEMS
BUMP INTO RACER LEGAL
LAPS SCOT ORONO LARGO
EISENHOWERWILSON CENT
ENISLE DEMO UTAH
OPTIMAL TENS RIP
SHILOH AERIE AMMO LAS
LINK NIXONTRUMANTAFT
OLE ALERT ADEN EIRE
WHEN COATI BARON
HOOVERJOHNSONFORD
EMERY EATON OILY
COAL SEAT EASEL NAN
HARDINGCOOLIDGE GALE
OTT RIOT RINSE SYNTAX
SAD DATA EPAULET
GAME ETRE NASSER
OTIC ROOSEVELTKENNEDY
FORUM SPITE ARID AURA
ENERO SEGUE MAME GREW
RESET SNIP ODOR SOWN
```

PUZZLE 187

```
TACO SAPS ACID MALL
ASAP TREE ERNE ARIA
LIRA ETON RICE READ
CARLREINER BARNYARD
OLE COMB EAT
FLAMBE KANSAS PYLON
LIMO RAN UGLY LOPE
AMOR SPEAK EOS ERIE
TAKER BELOW TERRIER
YAM LOREN RIM
STEAMED TENOR BOAST
CALM SET ATTIC OBEY
OTIS HERO EPA REAP
TASTE DITTOS NEEDLE
EST SOAP EDS
OVERCOAT JERRYPARIS
WILD NORA ROOM LOGO
LALA GNAW ALDA TOOL
SLAM SEME SEEN OTTO
```

PUZZLE 188

```
SUITS CRIB HAVE
AKRON HULA AGER
PEKOE INKY NUTS
TEMPT ODDEST
EMERY GUYS
FLED RAVE NABOB
RAT URBAN AWOKE
APT PHANTOM BAG
ISLES CELLO BYE
LEECH USED DIET
LOBS EMEND
EXCITE MARES
TRAP LAIC SENSE
CARS LUNE AREEL
HYPE EKED STEWS
```

PUZZLE 189

```
ASPS EGGY HAWS
WHAT ANNES EVIL
LAVA GAUNT RISE
SHERBET RIDDED
ARSENAL
SPELL TOIL AIR
TURKEY EEN MENU
BRIER ERS BARGE
AGED MAN PERIOD
RED PICA ASSET
ATHLETE
INSULT ATTEMPT
DEER EMOTE COLA
LEAN NEWER HOOD
ERRS TERN ODDS
```

PUZZLE 190

```
WOOL GAGA ERGS
RANI EBONY LEAP
ITEM TASTE KALE
THROW CHEAP LAD
AUK RACE
GILLS ENCASES
PARAKEETS SUTRA
EMIR YEN SARI
AUDIE ENERVATED
STEAMER OILED
STIR ETA
PIC TUTOR LEFTY
ALEE PALER LIRE
TINT TWICE MAIL
HATE SOTS STOP
```

PUZZLE 191

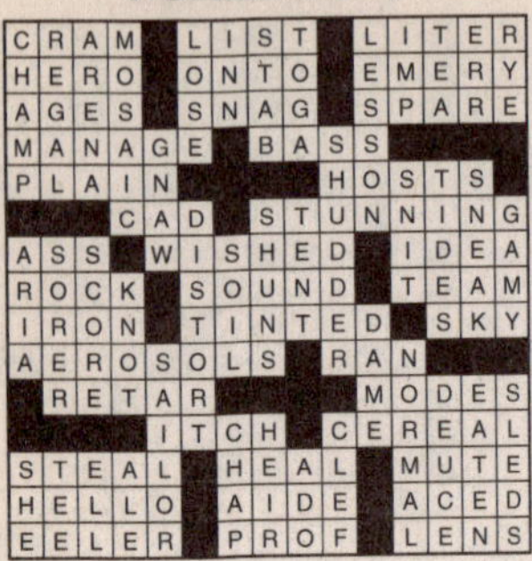

```
CRAM LIST LITER
HERO ONTO EMERY
AGES SNAG SPARE
MANAGE BASS
PLAIN HOSTS
CAD STUNNING
ASS WISHED IDEA
ROCK SOUND TEAM
IRON TINTED SKY
AEROSOLS RAN
RETAR MODES
ITCH CEREAL
STEAL HEAL MUTE
HELLO AIDE ACED
EELER PROF LENS
```

PUZZLE 192

```
CURT ROTS ARID
OLEO ABATE NOSY
ANATOMICAL TALE
LADEN OLDTIMER
REV SLEW
GAD WIZ SOLED
ATE AMIDST ENOW
SLATY NUN DISCO
HALO ICEAGE UKE
STORM GEM ESS
APSE LED
CHEETAHS AORTA
LIMO COTTONWOOD
AKIN TREED SARI
NETS ERNE ERST
```

PUZZLE 193

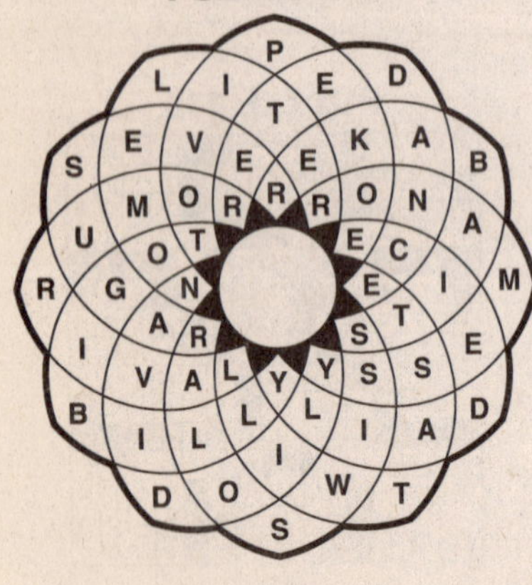

PUZZLE 194

```
REAM GIBB ADOBE
ARLO LOLA LUMEN
FIGURINES DEALT
TEASED AIDE NIE
SPEARCARRIER
METEORS SUMO
EVE SKY BASSES
REEDS SAP NACRE
ENDRUN POI OLE
APIA ONESTEP
MARTINBALSAM
EGO NORN ICEAGE
LANCE UNASHAMED
TIDAL PINT RARE
SNOWY TEAS STEN
```

PUZZLE 195

```
OPERA AJAR SETH
ALLOW RULE ILSA
RUBYKEELER LIAR
SSE WRAY EDVARD
DAIS ACRE
SPIRE FLOURISH
ILIAD DOOR POPI
REAM PARED ENOS
KENO RIDS TRIOS
SPONSORS LOCAL
DUTY POOH
TEEHEE CAST WHO
RAZE GOLDTHREAD
ARIA EVER EERIE
PLOD SAFE DYERS
```

PUZZLE 196

```
BATH LALA ACTED
ELIE EROS BEERY
TOMMYGUNS OLDIE
THESEA GURU DER
EAR ATO MOTHY
CREATES ABA
CABINETS AMIENS
ALINE HAD ORATE
TOLEDO RENDERED
ELM LASSOED
YAWED ITS AGE
ABC ISON ATONED
BALED BOBBYPINS
ENURE EVIL ALIE
DEBAR SANE HEEL
```

PUZZLE 197

```
MADD PITH SECT
ELIE MARIE TREE
LORE AGANA OMIT
THEMORENATURAL
SAC LID STY
THEN TAUT STS
TONE ATOUPEETHE
AVERT HUR RAREE
LESSYOUCAN SEAR
ENS RUSH OGEE
COT PBA TRA
TELLITFROMAWIG
LAVA NORAD DIAL
ETES GRIMY ESTE
EARP SETS NEAT
```

PUZZLE 198

```
SPAR ALA SAME ATOM
HARE PALL THEN DEMO
AVID OSLO RENO EXIT
MISSISSIPPIMULE ATT
ENE GTO EAP ALPS
SOL TESH LATER
CREATE SOAP SWAY
ETNA SHARE SLOE ORE
FIELD ATOLL PASS
TOWER BADGERS TUTOR
YSER EATON SNEVA
AGO WILL ROMAN SPAT
SORT POOR NEGATE
POKER SUET TAT
KNOT GEO OIL LAB
SON COLORADOCOLLEGE
ARID TOME ELAN OVAL
TACO ABET SELA NEIL
ELKS LENS SAL GENE
```

PUZZLE 199

```
ROTS ABES SHOP HORA
ERIC NELL COMA AHEM
BONO GALA ERIN PAPA
TOPUTANENDTO PRES
PAS TATE ROYALS
CREST MAST LADE
RUG TAIL COMANCHE
ONO ELLIS PARA DOOR
ARM LEONA IMAM
MINT ATWITSEND NORA
ORAL AEDES RIG
TIRO SPEE ELLEN BIN
ESCORTED SAID UTE
SEAR RATS INGOT
ESTEEM STUN STE
CARE MAKEENDSMEET
OVEN ELAN EINE DRAG
LEAD ROTO AREA LACE
ESTS SEER LEER EPEE
```

PUZZLE 200

```
AMID ISMS APT CLAW
MAGI SHOO DROP ROSA
EROS TERN AERO UNIT
SCRAWLING GAOL NEAT
LEEK SWIM SIC
MAPLE STROBE THREE
ISAO CONEY LAOTIANS
SKYWALKER LESS ERIS
SSS RISE BESET SADE
DAM CAN ROT
CARE AMBER SLIP CHA
OLAV TARE SPACESHIP
ETCETERA AWASH PARE
DOYLE ECLAIR RITES
ONO EARN ATON
LAMP ILLS DASHBOARD
ALEE LIES LITE FLEA
POOR YETI ENOS FLIT
PEWS USE SURE SYNE
```

PUZZLE 201

```
SHOE DATA FORD ISLE
TILL EMUS ELIE DUEL
EDGE LULU NOLL AGES
PEACHESANDCREAM AKA
TATE DOE WEAR
ORE BEG FLAGRANT
AMORE ORR ALAR ENOS
LEI USA SNAKE DNA
ILLNESS BLOKE MISER
AIRE SLADE HARP
DONNA STOKE PARKING
ADD SPIRE CAM COO
RIVE TINE DAY SHEBA
KNITTING BET LOO
NEAL PEA GADS
SHE MEATANDPOTATOES
LOGE TRES POOH ESTA
OVAL TILT ASSE SLAM
PERK OLLA NEER SOLE
```

PUZZLE 202

```
GRAD ALAS AMES SLAG
AIDE TURN LILT HOBO
FLEA ONTO ALMA OVER
FENCINGSWORD RARELY
ODE MUM SWIT
CLONE COAT SEARCHER
LUM AGAIN SPAR IOTA
ORES ELL BEETS RUNS
GENERAL ALIAS SCRAP
CAR CRANK LOU
TAROT SHINE CABINET
IRON FLASK BOK TILE
LEAD EASE ARIES KIN
LAMBASTE ELAN TREAT
ACTS AMA BEE
BRUNEI ALUMINUMWRAP
ROSA VETO OREL AONE
AMEN ARON DIAL RATE
TARA LAME ESPY DRIP
```

PUZZLE 203

SLOPE LEHAR CLOG JAIL
HOMER ENEMY HEAL OILY
ICONS BARBEROFSEVILLE
MOOR DAM OSAKA EIN
OPENER KEY CESAR
EAUDECOLOGNE CURARE
RUT ARN MEA OATEN MTN
GRITTY BOSTONCREAMPIE
SALEM WELT BITE ALEE
SENORITA PET MASTER
ASIDE PAY KOREA
HANSOM ARC TOREADOR
SORT AMMO CHIS WOKEN
PLASTEROFPARIS VIRAGO
ALB HAKIM PER DIT PAR
ROLLER DRESDENCHINA
SWEET EGO TETCHY
AIR BIRDS FEE PSST
BRUSSELSSPROUTS ANITA
YOKE DEEM ISLET MOLAR
EWES DINO POURS ASTRO

PUZZLE 204

PUZZLE 205

PUZZLE 206

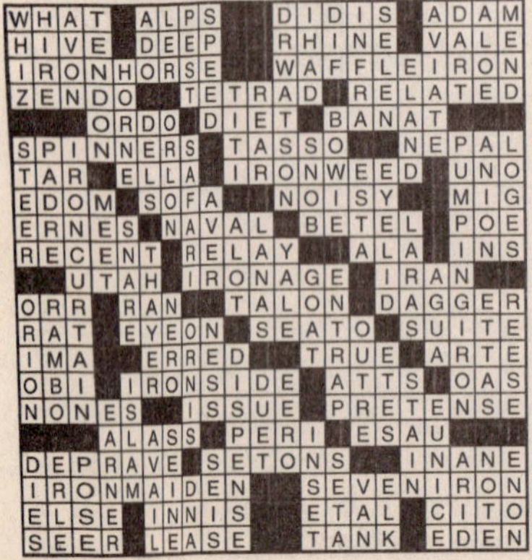

PUZZLE 207

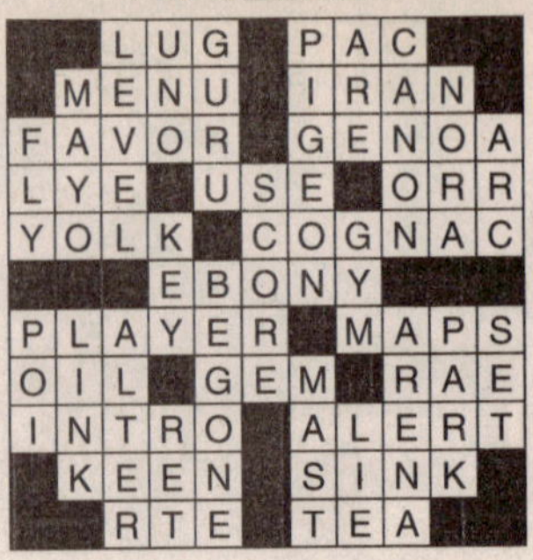

LUG PAC
MENU IRAN
FAVOR GENOA
LYE USE ORR
YOLK COGNAC
EBONY
PLAYER MAPS
OIL GEM RAE
INTRO ALERT
KEEN SINK
RTE TEA

PUZZLE 208

PUZZLE 209

PUZZLE 210

A. 1. Impart, 2. Praise, 3. Retail, 4. Spirit, 5. Diesel, 6. Ignite, 7. Nuclei, 8. Siesta.

BONUS WORD: Patience

B: 1. Gamble, 2. Spigot, 3. Ranger, 4. Resign, 5. Rating, 6. Agreed, 7. Grease, 8. Belong.

BONUS WORD: Minstrel

PUZZLE 211

PUZZLE 212

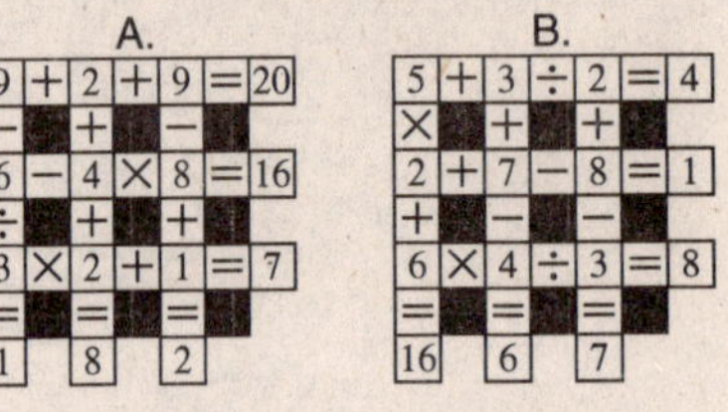

PUZZLE 213

PUZZLE 214

1. Push, 2. Hock, 3. Kelp, 4. Pair, 5. Roam, 6. Mute, 7. Echo, 8. Onus, 9. Spud, 10. Drab, 11. Bold, 12. Dusk, 13. Knot, 14. Tome, 15. Emir, 16. Rind.

7-LETTER WORD: Humdrum

PUZZLE 215

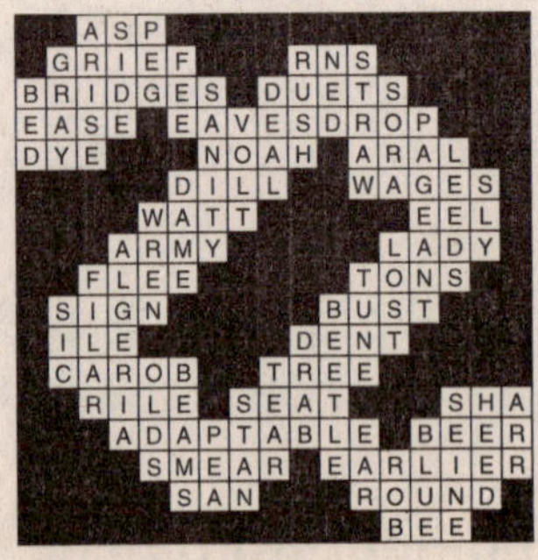

PUZZLE 216

Bingo, Oblige, Gibbon, Giblets, Breaking.

PUZZLE 217

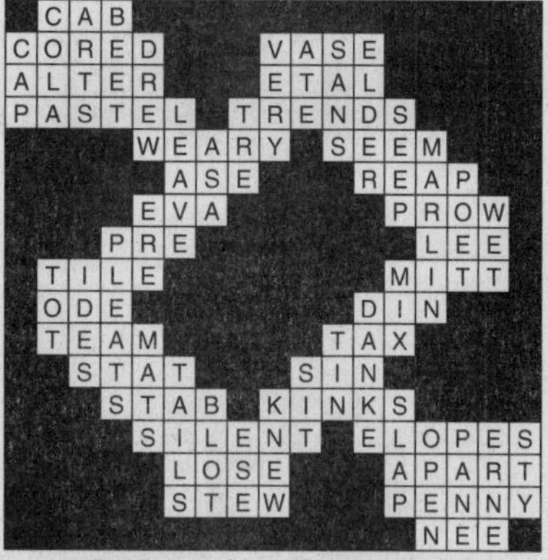

PUZZLE 218

BATHER

PUZZLE 219

PUZZLE 220

PUZZLE 221

R	I	B		W	E	D	S		S	W	A	T
A	D	O		A	R	I	A		C	A	S	H
G	O	O	D	D	E	A	L		A	R	E	A
E	L	S	E			P	O	S	T	M	A	N
			S	E	R	E	N	E				
S	E	M	I	N	A	R		T	I	T	L	E
H	E	A	R	T	Y		A	T	T	A	I	N
E	N	T	E	R		B	R	E	A	D	E	D
				E	N	A	M	E	L			
G	A	L	L	E	O	N			I	R	K	S
A	L	E	E		I	N	N	O	C	E	N	T
S	T	A	T		S	E	A	R		V	I	A
H	O	P	S		E	D	G	E		S	T	Y

PUZZLE 222

A	F	T		W	A	V	E		S	T	U	D
N	I	A		E	R	A	S		P	O	N	E
D	E	C		E	R	R	S		A	N	T	I
E	S	T			A	Y	E	S		S	I	C
S	T	I	C	K	Y		S	T	R	I	D	E
	A	C	H	I	E	R		E	E	L	Y	
			I	N	D	O	O	R	S			
	V	I	E	D		T	R	E	A	T	S	
C	O	N	F	E	R		D	O	W	E	L	S
L	O	G		R	A	R	E			N	O	T
I	D	E	A		C	A	R	P		T	W	O
M	O	S	S		E	V	E	R		E	L	K
B	O	T	H		R	E	D	O		D	Y	E

PUZZLE 223

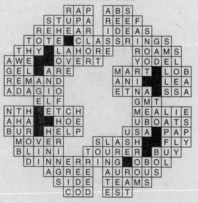

						R	A	P		A	B	S						
				S	T	U	P	A		R	E	E	F					
			R	E	H	E	A	R		I	D	E	A	S				
		T	O	T	E		C	L	A	S	S	R	I	N	G	S		
	T	H	Y		L	A	H	O	R	E			R	O	A	M	S	
A	W	E		O	V	E	R	T					Y	O	D	E	L	
G	E	L		A	R	E					M	A	R	T		L	O	B
R	E	M	A	N	D						A	N	I			L	E	A
A	D	A	G	I	O						E	T	N	A		S	S	A
			E	L	F								G	M	T			
N	T	H		E	T	C	H						M	E	A	L	I	E
A	H	A		H	O	E							U	B	O	A	T	S
B	U	R		H	E	L	P					U	S	A		P	A	P
	M	O	V	E	R				S	L	A	S	H			F	L	Y
	B	L	I	N	I			T	O	U	R	E	R		B	U	Y	
		D	I	N	N	E	R	R	I	N	G		O	B	O	L		
				A	G	R	E	E		A	U	R	O	U	S			
					S	I	D	E		T	E	A	M	S				
						C	O	D		E	S	T						

PUZZLE 224

V	A	S	E		B	A	I	L		S	E	C	T	S
I	C	O	N		R	I	C	E		I	G	L	O	O
E	M	I	R		A	D	E	S		T	O	A	D	S
R	E	L	I	E	V	E		S	H	E		T	O	O
			C	L	A	S	P		I	S	N	T		
	A	C	H	E	D		A	C	E		E	E	L	S
P	R	O		C	O	B	R	A			A	R	I	A
E	G	R	E	T		R	A	P		S	T	I	N	K
A	U	R	A			I	D	E	A	L		N	E	E
T	E	E	S		A	G	E		R	E	I	G	N	
		S	Y	N	C		D	R	O	P	S			
S	O	P		I	T	S		O	U	T	L	A	W	S
A	B	O	D	E		C	A	P	S		A	L	I	T
S	O	N	I	C		A	L	E	E		N	O	N	E
H	E	D	G	E		N	E	R	D		D	E	E	M

PUZZLE 225

The longer we carry a grudge, the heavier it becomes.

PUZZLE 226

A	N	I	M	A		A	R	C	S		E	B	B	S
C	O	D	A	S		P	O	L	E		D	R	O	P
E	V	E	N	S		H	O	A	X		G	A	G	A
S	A	S	H		S	I	T	S		R	E	W	E	T
			A	V	I	D		S	P	A		L	Y	E
E	T	H	N	I	C		S	M	O	G				
T	H	E	D	A		E	M	A	N	A	T	I	O	N
C	E	L	L		E	L	I	T	E		H	A	H	A
H	Y	P	E	R	B	O	L	E		R	E	M	I	T
				N	A	P	E		T	U	R	B	O	S
C	A	W		A	Y	E		T	I	N	E			
A	B	E	T	S		M	A	U	L		F	A	C	T
N	I	L	E		W	E	L	L		M	O	C	H	A
A	D	D	S		A	N	T	I		E	R	R	O	R
L	E	S	T		S	T	O	P		W	E	E	P	S

PUZZLE 227

War, Was, Wax, Web, Wed, Wet, Wig, Win, Wit.

PUZZLE 228

A	W	A	I	T		S	E	W	S		G	A	L	L
R	O	N	D	O		E	X	A	M		E	L	I	E
C	R	E	S	T		M	I	N	I		L	E	N	A
H	E	W		E	D	I	T	E	D		A	X	O	N
			E	M	U				G	A	T			
P	E	A	L		A	P	T		E	L	I	D	E	
A	M	P	S		D	U	R	I	N	G		R	A	D
G	O	R	E	S		R	A	N		A	B	A	T	E
E	T	O		A	D	R	I	F	T		E	P	E	E
	E	N	E	M	Y		T	O	O		E	E	N	S
			F	E	N				M	E	R			
C	A	L	F		A	P	E	M	E	N		T	O	W
O	B	O	E		M	A	Y	O		D	I	O	D	E
B	L	O	C		I	C	E	D		E	R	G	O	T
S	E	N	T		C	E	D	E		R	E	A	R	S

PUZZLE 229

1. Trample, 2. Ottoman, 3. Witness, 4. Earthly, 5. Gelatin, 6. Magnate, 7. Minaret.

PLACE: Montana

PUZZLE 230

SERA ANIS COD
AVER IRONIC EDO
GEAR DIRNDL RIG
ARMORED SEE ENE
YEA CRAM
BLOATS TAKEOFF
PEA CELLAR ONER
ABBOT YAP ANILE
LOOP DEWIER ALT
SPRAYER NEBULA
ALOE LON
AFT UPS TERRACE
ROO REHEAR OLLA
OUR SNORTS BEAR
WRY SENS EENS

PUZZLE 231

BLOT SEC MORN
AUTO SCRUB ECHO
RAIL CORER LEIS
NUCLEAR OCTANE
ELECTOR NOD
TREBLE LIKED
YORE SMOG WEANS
PANIC ASH SINEW
OMEGA YETI STOA
ERGOT NAMING
RUT PERSIST
ATOMIC NEEDLED
NINE KAPPA RIDE
CLAN ODEUM URGE
HELD OPT BAYS

PUZZLE 232

COPS ATOP BETAS
AWRY WORE ELOPE
MEAN AMEN CLONE
PSYCHIC ASTER
ETA OHM HAS
ROGUE TEPEES
AGENDA GAR HEAD
SLAP SIGHT ABBA
HERE TOE ZEROED
GRINDS BENDS
BAN ORS MOB
ALARM OBSERVE
SITUP WAKE LEER
EVADE ODES MATS
DELED NODE SLOT

PUZZLE 233

STAB GORY SHOD
LIRE EPEES LIME
UNDERNEATH AGIN
EGO AINT EIGHTY
SERENE ABET
DISC ARSENAL
ANTI ACNE SOLO
SORT SMEAR SUIT
KNEE TEEN ANTS
SEEDIER ACHY
CLAM HASSLE
GROVEL AFAR TUX
LARA ATMOSPHERE
ALAS REBUT ONER
DELE YORE TORT

PUZZLE 234

APOD SOL SLAW
LOGO UPPER POPE
BURG SIEGE ROSE
STEEPER SEDATED
AIRED NUN
SMIRK ILLEGAL
KEN EMBROIL COD
URN IOTAS OWE
AGE ANOINTS REF
EREMITE CANDY
DEB RETAR
PETUNIA NABBING
ODIC KIOSK ODOR
OGLE ENDUE ROPE
LYES TAE SLEW

PUZZLE 235

PRO TICS UPON
LED AERATE NOPE
OLD LEERED CREW
TIEPIN GAG LENT
SCRUB BOLERO
LIEU EGGED
URAL PLASMA APE
SIR DIGITAL REF
ELK ICEMAN OBEY
DESKS NERD
ECHOED HOSED
HALT ELM CIRCLE
ALIT RIBBON RUB
SEAL OVERDO IDA
HERE ERAS PER

PUZZLE 236

TRESS ASKS ADDS
OUNCE POET WRIT
ADORN ASEA LAVA
DELI PRONTO MAR
BELT URBANE
EUREKA ROTOR
ANI ENGAGE INKY
TIMED OIL AMINO
STEW MELEES PEW
EYERS SPRAWL
RINSED APSE
ODE NICELY PORT
AIRY CALL MANIA
ROVE AMMO ASCOT
SMEW LEST STETS

PUZZLE 237

SAGA BUGS TWO
OVEN NARROW HAG
FELT IGNORE AIL
ASSIGN WRESTLE
CREW TYPO
VISA ASH SPA
LEG SHIP SPOOKS
OIL PETUNIA IRK
GLOSSY RANG SOY
SOP STY OMEN
ITCH SODA
ENSNARE WARDEN
MOP PARCEL ROPE
USE STRESS EDIT
SEW EYES DOCS

PUZZLE 238

ANTI LAVA ARENA
SEAR ARID LOPER
SINK TROD ALERT
EGG KEEL REEDY
THOSE SALEM
KNIT UNSCREW
OPTION INS RIME
DAME FUNGI ACID
EVER ARK GIVERS
SENSING ONCE
STENO EDICT
STILL ODDS MOW
COCOA COLA SARI
ADORN USER AGES
BONED REST PEST

PUZZLE 239

HER JAMB RAKED
AXE ODORS OLIVE
RIG ISLET TOWEL
SLAIN TART FIRE
HELMET KARAT
PROP WAX MUD
MOVE PUN MISERY
ABIDE TIC SINGE
LEVERS BOY CUED
LYE RAG DECK
ISSUE SALAMI
MAIN HAVE NEWER
ACRES VIDEO ADO
SHIRK ALGAE SIN
TESTY SETS HAY

PUZZLE 240

AFAR PER POTS
RODE ADE EVIL
CROC TIP PARE
USHER PLED
EXTRA ICY
ARI LASSO PRO
RAM ALIAS LAW
LYE MAPLE ORE
FIB LOWED
EZRA ADULT
NEER MEN THAI
DRAG ALI EARN
SOLO NET RYES

PUZZLE 241

ESS PLEA ALIT
LEI LORD LODE
KANGAROO ISLE
EYED EATEN
RODE EELS
EGOS ADDS ARC
ELDEST GERBIL
LEO LOBE ALSO
GAME DYED
STRIP HIFI
ARIA NATIONAL
SIGN OVEN AGE
HOST GEMS POT

PUZZLE 242

ROYAL COAST
ARENAS RAPIER
DESIST ENTREE
STUCCO SKY
LOSE BOOED
INN ROSEBUD
STOP ARK BONE
TOBACCO ADE
RHODA ATOP
GAR ERECTS
UNEVEN RAISES
STEAKS ENDURE
HEFTY GENRE

PUZZLE 246

1. Pasty, Paste, Passe, Posse, Poise, Noise.

2. Homer, Hover, Hovel, Novel, Navel, Naval.

3. Droop, Drool, Droll, Drill, Trill, Twill.

4. Forty, Forte, Forge, Gorge, Gouge, Gauge.

PUZZLE 250

HAIKU G QUOTA
E N SNAFU V N
ADDLE Z INERT
R E WELT R I
TOXIC SLAG
UNIFY A E
KABOB D UNPIN
I O EASEL
LORE EQUIP
L E BAWL B A
JUDGE I PROXY
O O VILLA A E
YUMMY D LITHE

1-V, 2-F, 3-J, 4-A, 5-D, 6-E, 7-Y, 8-M, 9-Z, 10-H, 11-W, 12-T, 13-U, 14-K, 15-L, 16-B, 17-O, 18-I, 19-N, 20-Q, 21-G, 22-S, 23-R, 24-P, 25-C, 26-X.

PUZZLE 247

RATE TARE OWLS
ARIL CAPON VEIL
SOBS ONSET EAVE
PSI WADE EARNED
SEAMILE ARID
ICEMAN LORAN
STALKS BOSS HIE
CUD CLANK ODE
ANI TEAS ERASER
RATIO CHOWED
NOSY RESERVE
WEALTH HART EON
RACE APACE MAID
ISNT WORLD IDLE
TEES LIME DYER

PUZZLE 243

	STA	SH		VA	LU	E			SC	AN
PO	MM	EL		ST	RE	TCH		SP	ROU	T
INT	ER	VE	NE			ES	TR	A	NGE	
			WEL	CO	ME		AI	DE		
LA	TE	ST		HE	AD	LI	NE		ST	AFF
TH	R	EAD	BA	RE		TH	E	REF	OR	E
ER	ROR		SE	NT	IN	EL		ER	E	CT
		CO	ME		FO	Y	ER			
	MO	ME	NT	UM			GO	LI	AT	H
CLO	U	DY		BRA	VA	DO		AB	L	AZE
SE	ND			GE	N	ES		LE	AS	

PUZZLE 251

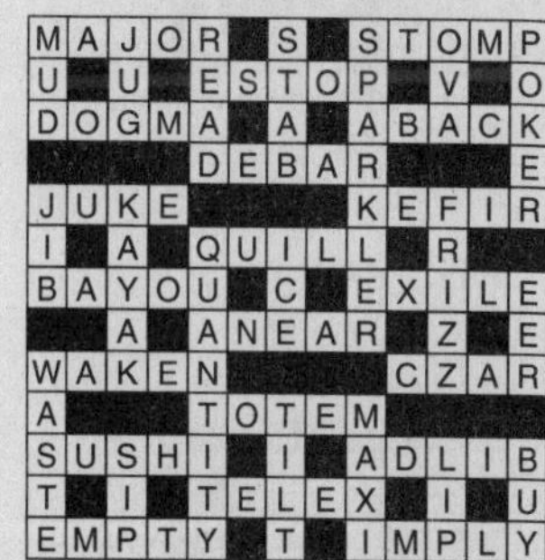
MAJOR S STOMP
U U ESTOP V O
DOGMA A ABACK
DEBAR E
JUKE KEFIR
I A QUILL R
BAYOU C EXILE
A ANEAR Z E
WAKEN CZAR
A TOTEM
SUSHI I ADLIB
T I TELEX I U
EMPTY T IMPLY

1-P, 2-G, 3-I, 4-N, 5-R, 6-Z, 7-M, 8-A, 9-X, 10-K, 11-U, 12-V, 13-T, 14-E, 15-H, 16-J, 17-L, 18-Q, 19-Y, 20-C, 21-O, 22-B, 23-S, 24-W, 25-D, 26-F.

PUZZLE 248

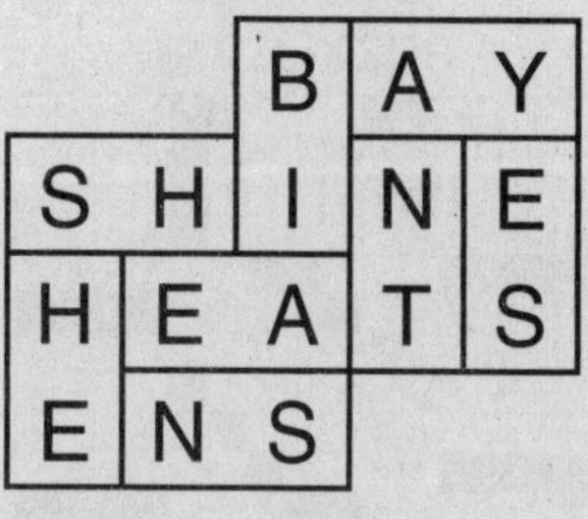

PUZZLE 244

80 women.

PUZZLE 249

PUZZLE 245

STAY VAPOR CARP
HARE ALIVE HEIR
OCCASIONAL ERNE
OOH ONTO EFFIGY
ISLE NINE ESS
FATTEST ODE
IDEA TEED TASTE
NECK SKI SHOE
ESTER TENT SOIL
OWE EAGERLY
SEC LORD LUTE
CAREEN OVER LAM
ASEA DIMINUTIVE
TEDS EVENT ANET
SLOT REDOS MERE

PUZZLE 252

DAD EGOS ACTS
ERR SORROW WHAT
SEA UNABLE LIMA
KABOB DIVAS LEG
PUP TELEVISE
CENTRAL TWO
ACE BLEACH LAPS
SHAMS ASH STILL
TOTE ENSIGN DUO
SIX COOLEST
SENATORS OWE
PRO STEAD MISSY
LOSE IGUANA TOO
IDEA CANNON ELK
TEST LAST WOE

PUZZLE 253

ARM PURE ABED
FOE ARRIVE GORE
TEE DANDER OXEN
KNOW NAG
FREE NUTMEG ART
RISEN PIE ENSUE
OPT ASSERT OPEN
EPIC MOLD
SHOO PAPAYA REF
HENNA LEI DWELL
EWE STEADY ALLY
UKE EASE
STAR SLOGAN AGO
THUG TOWARD SEA
YOKE TERN ELK

PUZZLE 254

HULA SWAM CLAPS
ODES ARIA ROGUE
LOST CENT EXULT
ENTER STRAP ELS
REST ONTO
GANGPLANK URGE
TAG EYED HAZARD
HERON ROW NORAD
OLEATE PHIS ENA
USER AFTERWARD
SAVE REEK
APT MERGE RISEN
CAROB RAVE MORE
TRIAL EPEE BUST
STOKE TERN OPTS

PUZZLE 255

STEM HISS SEED
LOCO ADLIB ALEE
AURA TIARA TILE
WRUNG OBEY ITEM
ACTS OWNERS
STROLL HUE
LOAM ACHE THREW
ANTE WHARF YORE
TEENY ASEA DUNE
EAT DIETED
SHREWD KEEL
KEEN ORAL LOYAL
AIDE RERUN VETO
TRIM EVADE ATOP
ESPY STET LIME

PUZZLE 256

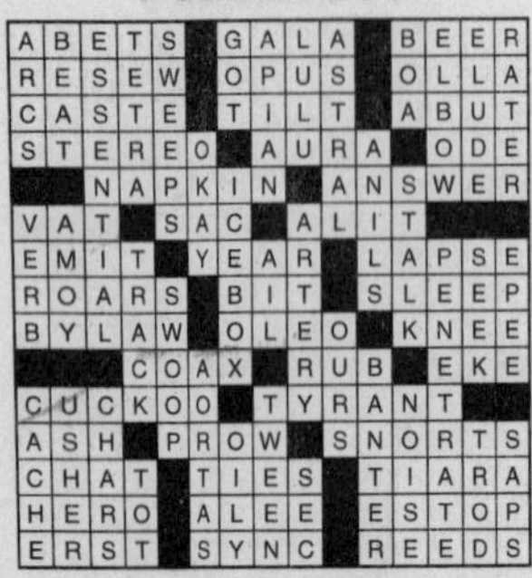

ABETS GALA BEER
RESEW OPUS OLLA
CASTE TILT ABUT
STEREO AURA ODE
NAPKIN ANSWER
VAT SAC ALIT
EMIT YEAR LAPSE
ROARS BIT SLEEP
BYLAW OLEO KNEE
COAX RUB EKE
CUCKOO TYRANT
ASH PROW SNORTS
CHAT TIES TIARA
HERO ALEE ESTOP
ERST SYNC REEDS

PUZZLE 257

MAST PUGS ACMES
ULNA ASEA RHINO
SOAR SELL DONOR
INKPOT APOSTLE
CEE PUT MIRE
CERAMIC RAW
ENTIRELY AFLAME
REATA ERR LONER
GAMEST REDEFINE
OPE ASHIEST
SOLO NTH APT
INSTALL OYSTER
MOLAR ECRU POKE
ADAGE MOOR ANON
METED NEWS DEED

PUZZLE 258

PUZZLE 259

CHAP CHI SKAT
LOLL ARENA UNDO
AUTO MUFTI MOON
PROPRIETOR ACRE
ANT PICKED
ADAGIO CROC
MORON THEREFORE
PLEA CRUST IBEX
SEALPOINT TRITE
AMOK SASSES
ADSORB AWL
WEEP ATTRACTIVE
ALIT THORN ACID
RAZE SAGAS SONG
DYED WAN KNEE

PUZZLE 260

ASEA TWO STEP
BEAD SHADE HOME
ONTO TOKEN REIN
USE PARE TWISTS
TERRAIN GRIN
ERR BLANKETS
ABLE ELOPE PIE
DRILL MAR SMILE
DAM ITCHY ACED
SNATCHES NOD
HIRE POWERED
TOMATO VAIN ADE
AKIN WHETS EGGS
LACK NUTTY GEEK
LYES TOY ODDS

PUZZLE 261

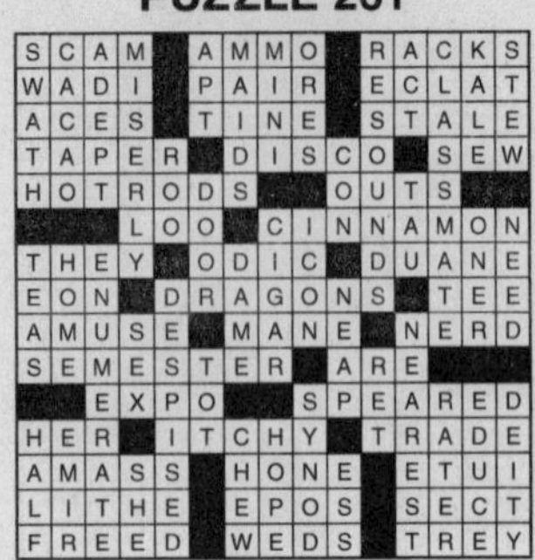

SCAM AMMO RACKS
WADI PAIR ECLAT
ACES TINE STALE
TAPER DISCO SEW
HOTRODS OUTS
LOO CINNAMON
THEY ODIC DUANE
EON DRAGONS TEE
AMUSE MANE NERD
SEMESTER ARE
EXPO SPEARED
HER ITCHY TRADE
AMASS HONE ETUI
LITHE EPOS SECT
FREED WEDS TREY

PUZZLE 262

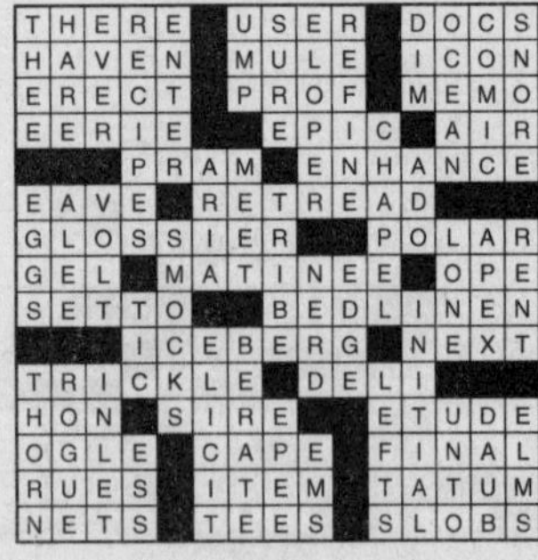

THERE USER DOCS
HAVEN MULE ICON
ERECT PROF MEMO
EERIE EPIC AIR
PRAM ENHANCE
EAVE RETREAD
GLOSSIER POLAR
GEL MATINEE OPE
SETTO BEDLINEN
ICEBERG NEXT
TRICKLE DELI
HON SIRE ETUDE
OGLE CAPE FINAL
RUES ITEM TATUM
NETS TEES SLOBS

PUZZLE 263

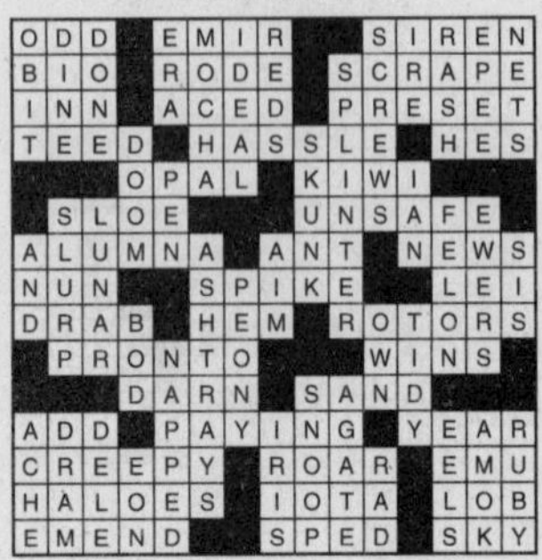

ODD EMIR SIREN
BIO RODE SCRAPE
INN ACED PRESET
TEED HASSLE HES
OPAL KIWI
SLOE UNSAFE
ALUMNA ANT NEWS
NUN SPIKE LEI
DRAB HEM ROTORS
PRONTO WINS
DARN SAND
ADD PAYING YEAR
CREEPY ROAR EMU
HALOES IOTA LOB
EMEND SPED SKY

PUZZLE 264

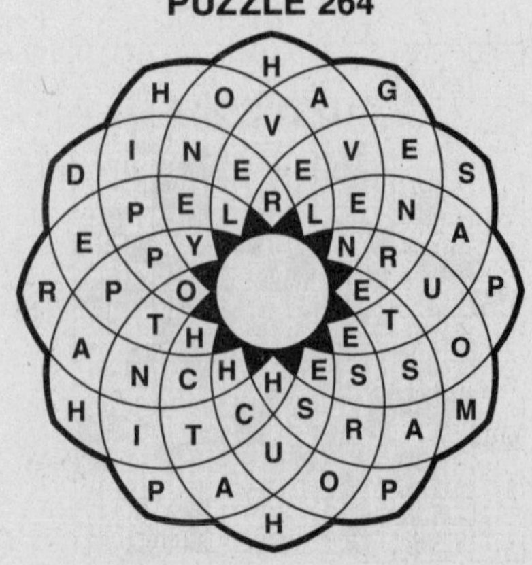

PUZZLE 265

PORES AGE DAB
OPERA CLONE ERE
DECAL READY URN
SILO TEE CAD
GAS NEWT ABBEYS
NUTMEG RURAL
ARIA SEEN LESS
WALLS LET LATHE
SLIT STOW COED
CAMEO ECHOED
CINEMA PURR PRY
HOE MID SEEP
ITS ELOPE ARBOR
MAT REDID MEANY
ESS DOG SPREE

PUZZLE 266

STAMP CALF AFT
ARGUED ALOE LIE
SIESTA PELE INS
HOSE WHEEL BAT
DODO EASILY
DOS ALL EDIT
INTERESTS RAGED
STEM STATE GAVE
COPED ENERGETIC
REAR ERA ELK
SPRYER MAYS
LEI COAST TACO
ION BAWL ICEMAN
ENS IDEA CANINE
RYE BEDS BODES

PUZZLE 267

TYPED SALE TILL
BORER ELAN ALAE
AGORA WEND TINT
RAP BONSAI TADS
RASP INFO
OTIC ELS GLOSS
WHET RACK USHER
NET ATRIA ORE
STOAT SOLO BOIL
ARROW DOR IFFY
BRIM TOOL
FOCI ZODIAC YAM
ABUT AXIS HIPPO
METE RILL ERIES
EYER DELE REEDS

PUZZLE 268

BATH PUPS SAGA SLAB
IDEA ATOP THAN PIKE
TEEN NASA RAIN OKIE
ONTHEDOUBLE RENT
ISAIAH EDD SHEA
NAT MEET DEFT USHER
TUT ERRED LEAST OLA
ECHO SILER EPI OUST
REEVE ELMER ELAPSES
DIVA SUGAR KNEE
EARNEST RIGEL TRACT
ALOE EAR SENOR AFAR
SAP CARES SEVER IRE
ENOCH EPOS EELY ROE
FEAT UKE EASELS
DUAL INANINSTANT
ASHE MIND TAOS OLEA
TEAR ELKE ELLE REEL
ARTY REAR REED KEEP

PUZZLE 269

TOPE RATE STRIP
ADAM OMIT PASTE
CORP BANC ARTEL
ORDERINTHECOURT
REND SET
FAROS ANET SCAR
ABORT ASEA ALE
CLOSEORDERDRILL
EES DREI AERIE
SRTA INRE GHOST
SUE MLII
INAPPLEPIEORDER
TULIP ALGA IOTA
AMORE TORS NONE
LAGER STET GRAS

PUZZLE 270

BOCA SCARP CHIP
AVER AUGUR RODE
BALTIMOREORIOLE
ALT COMA TAMPER
CIAO POKE
WARREN HAZE HAL
ARIAS TOGO COSI
SEATTLESEAHAWKS
TALE ONES ARTEL
ESS ACED STRODE
SCAT ACRE
DESALT SLOE AGE
STLOUISCARDINAL
ONAN ORATE ROTS
SAVE NAMED KNEE

PUZZLE 271

WEB NOW JAR
AXE EDITS UNO
SIT WISHY DEL
THESUPERBOWL
GYM FIT
MILO STAUNCH
PIE COS APE
HIGHBOY RYAN
EON ABE
PLAYOFFGAMES
HOP SEARS YAP
IRS TRIES ENE
LEE LEO DEN

PUZZLE 272

HIS ATE ALAS
ETO SLOB NILE
MOA ALTO JEER
PIGEONHOUSE
SAY IOU
COAL ETA ELS
PIGEONBERRIES
OLE LOB ANTE
TIO WON
PIGEONWINGS
ARIA DOLL INK
CABS ARTY LEA
KNEE YES TON

PUZZLE 273

ELEMENTARYSCHOOL
LAXAMOUREATHORDE
ANTECOREFREELAID
TERSEKENIDEALLOG
IRATELEANIPPYCUE
OAFROUNDERAERASE
NILOUTDODIGNASAL
FLUBREADISLEWELD
ASTEROIDSHORTAGE
LIEGEUSESEWERWAS
SNAPSTARUNTOEAST
EDGECREWEDITMICA
CURTIARAHUBTOTAL
OCEANGINORIELELM
PEELDEEDDEARODDS

PUZZLE 274

AMOS AMAT RUSES
DEBT PERU ENTRE
ODOR PAIR STAIN
LIEUTENANT INKS
FASTENS PARED
TAD MILE AMP
EMBERS EKED REA
DOOR LEE DDAY
NOW BEET WRESTS
AGE ORAS ROT
RAYON GEORGIA
BIBS SITUATIONS
AMINO NEST TONI
BARES GASH USED
ANDRE SKYE SERE

PUZZLE 275

A: 1. March, 2. Chill, 3. Learn, 4. Remit, 5. Ideal, 6. Alien, 7. Elate, 8. Tramp.

B: 1. Arch, 2. Hill, 3. Earn, 4. Emit, 5. Deal, 6. Lien, 7. Late, 8. Ramp.

PUZZLE 276

GR	ID	■	■	■	GU	STO	■	RE	PA	ST
ABS	OL	VE	■	BA	FF	LE	■	LI	NE	AR
■	■	TO	WE	R	■	■	BRA	SH	■	■
RU	SE	■	AL	TER	NA	TI	VE	■	RE	SIN
ST	REN	G	TH	■	VI	M	■	S	MU	G
■	DI	RE	■	EA	G	ER	■	MI	NER	■
MO	P	ED	■	SE	AT	■	COL	LE	A	GUE
DE	ITY	■	CO	L	OR	FU	L	■	TE	ST
■	■	SP	URT	■	■	TI	AR	A	■	■
S	HA	RE	■	W	HO	LE	■	CHE	RI	SH
IN	STE	AD	■	ING	OT	■	■	■	LE	AVE

PUZZLE 277

Agree, Eager, Lager, Regal, Royal, Loyal, Alloy, Allot, Share, Swear, Curse, Verse.

PUZZLE 278

PAST SCAR VALE
ALLY AIOLI IRAS
COUP PREEMINENT
STRESSED CONDO
CENSURE ASP
SALSA NUDE
CLAIM COAL AWED
AGIN COUPE SARI
BARE HART WEDGE
WOOS ALIST
ASK UPTIGHT
FOALS NAUTICAL
OBLITERATE SORA
REEL SYNOD LICK
ERST PEER ELSE

PUZZLE 279

PAAR SPASM THAW
OLLA TONTO RUSE
RIGHTRITEWRIGHT
ETA RISE OBEYS
TAPE FACE
STRIVE OINK LOP
ORATE ADEN RONA
FAILLEFILEPHIAL
ACNE STUD EERIE
SKY ITEM ARTERY
ACER OMIT
STAGE OPUS PEA
HAIRSHARESHERRS
OLDE THERE PONE
ELEE SALAD IDEA

PUZZLE 280

1. Lave, Late, Vise; 2. Stag, Sang, Tang; 3. Rote, Rope, Peer; 4. Came, Name, Mole; 5. Norm, Wore, Worm; 6. Deal, Salt, Alto; 7. Nail, Nine, Lane; 8. Sell, Silo, Sill.

PUZZLE 281

HEW ALE STORE
YEA TUX ERROR
ELS OAT QUEEN
NET PURSUE
AREA ATE VIE
LESSON INS
AZALEA OCEANS
RIG RUDDER
EGO ICE EBBS
KNEELS ALA
OLDIE DIM NOR
FEATS EMU JOG
TIMES DOG ODE

1-L, 2-V, 3-G, 4-Y, 5-M, 6-N, 7-C, 8-Q, 9-Z, 10-W, 11-H, 12-J, 13-E, 14-F, 15-S, 16-A, 17-R, 18-U, 19-K, 20-I, 21-X, 22-B, 23-P, 24-T, 25-O, 26-D.

PUZZLE 282

OAF SLOT MEMO
FIE LAIR AVOW
FLEXIBLE CEDE
RES ASH
SEAR ESCORT
LACY AQUA ERA
OUR SPURN TON
GNU TRAY SALT
ASSAIL EARL
ARC JAW
ZAPS OPOSSUMS
IDES TAKE MAP
PONY SLED PRY

1-X, 2-L, 3-D, 4-N, 5-S, 6-H, 7-B, 8-I, 9-R, 10-A, 11-Q, 12-K, 13-P, 14-O, 15-W, 16-J, 17-F, 18-Z, 19-G, 20-Y, 21-V, 22-E, 23-U, 24-C, 25-T, 26-M.

PUZZLE 283

SCOW INFO PETAL
ALAE VIEW ATRIA
HAKE OPALESCENT
IRED RAT SHEETS
BONSAI SAT
PESETA ERAS
AMP OSPREY RICK
BOARD ION NACRE
EDGE REDONE HEW
TEED ARENAS
OHM UTOPIA
GOALIE LOG RASP
UNDERNEATH RUTS
SCENE EMIT ISLE
TESTS LACY SEES

PUZZLE 284

EGG OSLO VERGES HALL
LAIC RHEA AVIATE ELIA
LOLL LOAF CAPTAINEASY
ALLEYOOP DUDES EDITS
MOPS TRUER SLUE
POSER POEMS AWARDED
RHINE CLOGS PRIMA LID
OATS FOALS JOEPALOOKA
ERA TOPI PUPAE SPED
MARYWORTH ASPS ACCESS
AIDA UNITE ASIA
ADAPTS ANON DICKTRACY
MALO EDGES CHEE GOO
BUCKROGERS DRIED BANK
ONO EARLY PEALS BEIGE
TRACHEA LOBBY ULNAS
GOUT CARTE ITZA
TONER SHUTS KRAZYKAT
BRENDASTARR LION ENVY
ACED SPIREA EENY DIOR
RAMA HARDLY ELSA TWO

PUZZLE 285

JOVE DOLTS AFAR
AVID EROSE NANA
NISI SEPARATING
UNICYCLERIDER
SETTER SEA YOU
SAILS SMALLS
SPA SEOUL WIDE
TIGHTROPEWALKER
AXIS KEVIN ENS
RITTER RINGO
KEA REG DEBRIS
TRAPEZEARTIST
QUIETENING ANTI
TROD ARNIE ISLE
SINS LEEDS NEED

PUZZLE 286

PAPA ABYSS CREW
ULAN LOATH OOZE
BURG BARREDBARD
SMELT SNEER MAS
SEAN STEW
AMP LANDS GAFFE
CUEQUEUE IRIS
CLAUS NIB ATILT
RARE SAILSALE
ANSER SMALL RYE
NOTE LOAF
SEA LUNAR YURTS
NAVALNAVEL GYRO
OVID ATONE HEIR
BEDS SEWED TROT

PUZZLE 287

CHAT RAFT SILO
LENO EPEE PROD
ERNO VIED ROBE
MOONSEED MANOR
ARC FAT
CRO TIE DER COD
RESCUE SUNSTONE
OCCUR OED USUAL
STARNOSE SPECIE
SIR IRE MAI HRS
ANT ATA
AROSE SKYLIGHT
LAIC GEER DRAY
ARLO ETUI EARP
NEST LAPD AMIE

PUZZLE 288

METAL SHEA LAME
ADOBE HUNS IVAN
INDEXCARDS TART
LAOTIAN SALTINE
CREW YELLER
NEURON REESE
ALPINE ODD JEDI
EBON RUT ODES
SANG AUG SCHISM
BAUGH MANTIS
REPENT TRAP
EQUATOR ILLWILL
PURR MIDDLEAGES
RISE ALOE TREAT
OVER TENS SETHS

PUZZLE 289

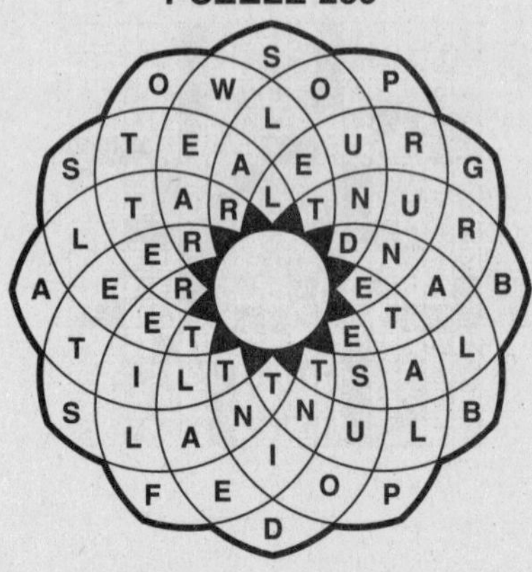

PUZZLE 290

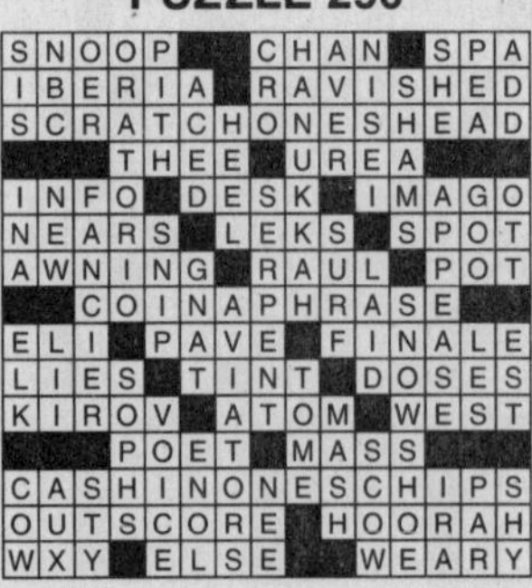

SNOOP CHAN SPA
IBERIA RAVISHED
SCRATCHONESHEAD
THEE UREA
INFO DESK IMAGO
NEARS LEKS SPOT
AWNING RAUL POT
COINAPHRASE
ELI PAVE FINALE
LIES TINT DOSES
KIROV ATOM WEST
POET MASS
CASHINONESCHIPS
OUTSCORE HOORAH
WXY ELSE WEARY

PUZZLE 291

1. Leonard Bernstein, 2. Zubin Mehta, 3. John Williams, 4. Leopold Stokowski, 5. Seiji Ozawa, 6. Robert Shaw.

PUZZLE 292

SWAB GRAB AMPS EDAM
KILO LONE DEEM LOPE
ATOM IOTA ODEA LESS
THEBATTERY INSPIRES
ART DARE HIS
CRESCENT PAVE AILED
LILT RARE WAVE SOLE
USA TYPING LEW LOSE
BENCH EATEN REBATED
EAR DELAY RON
SCANNER RIVEN ADAPT
PACT NIT DESERT VIE
AVER ECRU LENO CONE
MEDAL EASE SEESAWED
LEA MEGA NIP
CLAPTRAP GRANTSTOMB
AURA BELT OREG OBEY
STIR OREO MORE ROLE
TEAK RODE ANON SETS

PUZZLE 293

WICK LARD SOAP ACTS
AGRA ALIE EDGE ROOT
SLOT MINN LIEN MODE
TOWERINGINFERNO LOW
EON ONE MAI YEAH
SPA TSAR ROAMS
TETHER HAIR KNEE
INCA EAGER AMEN DNA
WOOLS TAMES BELL
OWLET EDITION ROUTE
ORES TENSE DUKES
PAR MIRE MULES VEEP
EROS TENT SORTER
RIFLE DERN ETE
MYRA ERR OAT LOT
ONO ABSENCEOFMALICE
MONA OMIT BITE OVER
AVES RENO USER BEAR
RAYS TEEN TENS ORNE

PUZZLE 294

RACE LOBS ODIC MOPS
OLLA AHOY LAVA OLEO
AGAR DIOR DRAM TIER
MAMMYYOKUM KNEEHOLE
AOL PAGE ORE
ETERNIZE DANA ARSON
PERK KELP REDO LUGE
IAN BESTIR DIG OREO
CREME TONER TRODDEN
OAF NOSED EWE
SHAMMED NEARS ESTER
LOAM TON TRIADS IVE
AWRY EGOS METE EDEN
TEETH ENOS DECADENT
RID SNAP ALI
ESCAPADE MOMSMABLEY
BLOC RANG SOUP LORE
BOCK ELSA ETRE EVIL
SEAS DEED REED SEEP

PUZZLE 295

PAC REP
STUPOR HEROIC
HUSTLE ENROLL
ITS LES ART RIA
GNU SILT DEAN AMA
SOD UKE ERI LOP BUY
PRISSY EEE DOSAGE
AGGIE BANQUET WAKEN
ESS SRI NIT PER
HIS ETH
ALA EEL RAY OJO
TRUCE REUNION GUAVA
ORNERY MEN SERMON
ROC GAR BET PIE BID
WHO REDE REAP COD
EGG MAR OAR FIR
ORATOR SENATE
NEGATE ENTREE
ERE THO

PUZZLE 296

CHEF TYPE DAD
LONE HORN ERR
ANTE EGOS ERA
NOR CRAB JAW
GRAHAM ESSAYS
SPIRAL TOYS
PELICAN
DOPE POTATO
FEDORA MURALS
RAD MOBS MIL
ERE ABBA GAVE
TIS SLIT ALEE
SET PETS DESK

PUZZLE 297

EBB GLUM DAMP
YEA LANE EMIR
EER OMIT LOCO
BABES BIKED
AWES EWE
RILE EXIT OWE
ISLAND LAPPED
AHS AGED LEND
BYE ARTY
ABETS REDYE
LAMA LIEU TON
AKIN YENS TRE
SETS ERST ARE

PUZZLE 298

LISP GRAB SCOLD
ESTE NANA HUMOR
SNIT UPON OPERA
STRUM AVE NEW
NAPE NITE
WHITEN AERIAL
WHOA EVES ENDOW
ION GLIMPSE MOI
NOOSE RULE CAST
PRONTO IMMUNE
PEEN TIER
SAG RAM TRAMP
KOALA EDIT EMIR
INLET NAME NOTE
PEASE TYPE TREY

PUZZLE 299

1. He digs it, 2. Garden hose, 3. With its needles, 4. Flypaper, 5. Snaps.

PUZZLE 300

SCAB SASH SPIN
HALO INLET HIDE
AKIN NOISY OLLA
GETS CAT PEELER
ATE STAB ORS
EASIER ELBOW
DUN RECAP ACNE
GROAN HIE STAIR
YAWL AMEBA SPA
BLESS ANNEAL
ETA NUMB NEE
SALADS AND BOON
TILL HEROS UNTO
OGEE ILONA LEIS
PADS KNOW ARCH

PUZZLE 301

JOHN SINGER SARGENT

PUZZLE 302

FLINT EGGS ASKS
RADII BEAU CLAP
EMOTE BARN HALE
EEL PIER DAYBED
RIND SIC
PRANK SCAN LEG
SEEK STALE ANY
NAVEL CAP DATER
ACE EERIE MEMO
GEL FRAN DAIRY
TAM FOND
ABBEYS SICK SSW
MIRA UTES LLAMA
ODOR RUNT EASEL
SEWN ENDS TWEET

PUZZLE 303

7 9	3	7 2
7	4 1 6 8	9
4 2	5	4 6

PUZZLE 304

THAWS VOICE
HEROIC VEERED
ENMESH ERRING
ESS TESTS STY
SERIOUS
TANTRUM STREW
ALOE BIT RARE
GERMS LIMITED
SODAPOP
BRA AORTA FAN
REVOKE ONSALE
ADORER PEELER
TOWER DELED

PUZZLE 305

GUT SORT HOPS
ASH EPEE IDOL
PER MALE NOSE
ICILY GREW
ATLAS OBOE
CALL SNAP SKI
EXEMPT BEATEN
SIR EELY REEK
CAPE LIENS
FISH SMEAR
ANTI ASEA ILL
STAN ROMP NEE
TOGA KNOT GIN

PUZZLE 306

JIB REC SOB APT
ADO AGO PIE TRY
ILL TOM END LIP
LEASE PUCK LAZE
TROLLS POSED
AQUA MET VOW
LURK EXITED ASP
SAGE LEMON FOAL
ODE RESALE INFO
JET TEE SEED
PILAF HURRAH
AROW LAMA LYRIC
SKI SIS TWO IRE
TEN OAT EON TOE
ADS PRY DOE ENS

1-X, 2-I, 3-V, 4-H, 5-T, 6-Q, 7-S, 8-W, 9-O, 10-C, 11-B, 12-J, 13-F, 14-Y, 15-K, 16-D, 17-N, 18-U, 19-G, 20-A, 21-L, 22-R, 23-E, 24-Z, 25-M, 26-P.

PUZZLE 307

Scale, Rhapsody, Symphony, Score, Melody, Composer, Orchestra.

8TH COLUMN DOWN: Concert

PUZZLE 308

ALL TELE BIN
VII REAR ALTO
OFFCOLOR LAST
WETLY SPAS
USE ONTOP
ANTE LEEK ORE
VIA ASSAY FEE
ELK DEPT AFOR
REEVE SAN
SENT STORE
SOOT OFFSIDES
INFO SOLE DOT
REF SEAT SSS

PUZZLE 309

MEAT FAN TOT
ATHOS APE HUH
SCARECROW ESE
SWAM ATTY
ALMOND TAXI
IOU RAVENS
MIN SPINE MAP
SCREAM ANA
HOED AMENDS
FAKE ARIA
ALI BRICKROAD
LON OAR ELIDE
LES AMS SLEW

PUZZLE 310

OLLA BETA AMUSE
ROAN ALUM REPEL
EPIC NENE CLOCK
SERIF GAB ANTS
ELLA AMEN
CANYON ADITS
BUNT ACE IGNITE
ERG IDEALLY DEN
GELATI RIB OARS
SEVEN GOBBLE
ERGO AXIL
STUN MOM DINGO
LONGS EWES GALA
ORIEL GENT EVES
ENTRY ARTY DENT

PUZZLE 311

HEAL AWL BOIL
ACRE DEE ANTI
WHOA SET ZEST
SOWS PUMA
EBB PIANOS
LOB ION GRIME
OAR TOOTH CEE
START RUT END
ESTEEM BYE
BRIG DRAW
MENU ALE GAME
AMOK MEN EKED
DUDE INS DENS

PUZZLE 312

OFT ROMP SAGA
ALE ORAL ICER
TEA MERE GEEK
SALSA ASH
ANY ITCHY
CLAY ODOR HUE
LOW LID ILL
ADE EKED OPAL
MEDIA SUN
STY PEARL
ODES ALAS PEA
LULU RIDE ELM
DELE NEST DYE

PUZZLE 313

STAR STY SALE
PIPE ERE PLAY
YETI MAN RICE
GRIM BITER
HYENA LUG
OER MAMAS ACT
MAR VIM IRE
ESS RIDER DOS
COD EJECT
UPSET SOFA
NAIL SIR PUPS
DILL ERA ASEA
ONTO EEL NERD

PUZZLE 314

OBOE SPAS TEE
PRIM WEPT RAY
TALC ANTE IVE
EBB NAMER
ROMEO TOY
ERE ASHY EVIL
VAN SPIKE ARE
SLUG USED SON
EAR GLENS
SCALP BEE
CAW IDEA EASE
AGE NUNS CLAN
RED GODS HEWS

PUZZLE 315

PROF AWES ODD
LIVE SOLO ROE
OPAL SELF APE
DELTA ABLER
CLASSY
DEW RENT EAST
OOH EAGER CEE
SNOB PLEA EWE
INTERN
CARGO GRIND
ONE BALD ODOR
LED LIEU TONE
TWO EDGE SLEW

PUZZLE 316

ACTS TEAR HEP
LOOP ARIA EAR
POOR LAMB ERE
INK BADLY
BINGO HIT
ROE TOFU EAST
ITS ILL PAR
MATH LULU EGO
ICY SPRAT
THEME OER
WAY AFAR OBOE
ALE SOLE ORAL
SOD EELS FARM

PUZZLE 317

LAB VOID WERE
ERA INTO OVAL
TEA NEST REPS
SASSY EEL
ILL ODDLY
STUN OPEN YOU
HAS SAY ELL
AXE ISLE IDLE
DISCO DOC
AND LEARN
SMOG AMID LEI
PURE TORE TAN
AGED APER ODE

PUZZLE 318

```
WATT#FLAT#ACT
ALOE#AIDE#ROE
GLOP#DEEM#EAR
###EKE##PSALM
AGREE##MOP###
BOA#PAPA#ACHE
URN#TRACY#REV
TYKE#IDEA#ERE
###BAD##NEWER
ALIBI##SKY###
FIN#LANE#ICED
ARK#EDIT#NAME
RAY#DOTS#GRUB
```

PUZZLE 319

```
THEN#BEAU#SPITE
YOYO#IRIS#EARED
PREP#DUDE#ALONG
ENDED#PERM#ANTE
####APT##EAT###
#STAIR#PEACEFUL
ELAPSÉ#OGLE#ONE
DIKE#TAROT#AXIS
ICE#PERK#INLETS
TENDENCY#MOLDY#
###ITS##YEN####
TRAM#EXPO#ESSAY
HARPO#RIDE#HALO
ANKLE#ALEE#OVAL
WISER#YELL#DESK
```

PUZZLE 320

```
HORA#ACRE#EPICS
EBON#BROW#LOGIC
NOVITIATE#SALVO
SEE#ADVERB#COIL
###TREE##UPHOLD
AFOOT#NELLS####
MIMOSA#DELI#ONS
IVE##BEIGE##MOP
DEN#CROC#TAHINI
####HUNTS#SITON
MADCAP##EDIT###
EMIR#TIPPED#RHO
TIMID#TRAPEZOID
EDEMA#COLT#ABLE
RESEW#HASH#PETS
```

PUZZLE 321

```
WIMP##BOP##BODE
AREA#TEALS#IRON
GILL#HERON#SAND
ESTATE##TURTLES
###CAMPS#BAR###
#DUEL#ION#MOTEL
DIP#CANDID#SEMI
ITS#SIT#CUD#EEL
STEP#ROCKER#TRY
HOTEL#SUE#ACHY#
###NAB#BLAME###
ASHAMED##FALLEN
REEL#GUAVA#LOVE
MEAT#SAWER#ABES
SPRY##LET##REST
```

PUZZLE 322

```
ALIT##PEST#GLAD
NONO#HENCE#EASE
TOFU#ARSON#ACHE
STORMY##OSPREYS
####ESCAPEE####
EYE#STAB##AFAR#
RAM#HARD#CRATED
ACES#CLOTH#NOVA
SHRUNK#MEAL#MUD
#TYPO##EXPO#SEA
####SLANTED####
BAYLEAF##RECITE
AREA#MICRO#ORAL
GILD#BRUIN#LINK
SAPS#SEEM##ASKS
```

PUZZLE 323

```
SPAS#FED##RIFLE
LILT#OWE#SOCIAL
ONER#REF#WEEVIL
BESIDE#TEE#REDS
###FIST#NAB####
#DEEPER#CRAFTS#
TIN#LEASH#DRAMA
INTRO#PEA#GOMER
SERUM#DANCE#ELK
#DYNAMO#THRUST#
####TOO#SEEN###
CLOD#IRE#ADRIFT
RAVELS#CAT#IDEA
OMELET#HIE#PLED
CARET##ODD#EELS
```

PUZZLE 324

```
ACRES#UMPS#POPE
SHOAT#NAIL#AWAY
PASTA#PREY#RETE
STY#TSETSE#ADES
###FUNGI#SAD###
#SALSA#NETWORKS
DULY#FAIL#EXERT
OAT#YUP#KID#HOE
EVADE#EBON#CENT
SERENADE#EDEMA#
###ESS#AERIE###
ROMP#CARATS#SPA
EPEE#ORES#OCCUR
TAMS#TIRE#WHACK
SHOT#SASS#NARES
```

PUZZLE 325

```
FAVA#SHOP##JAPE
LIEU#WADED#AGIN
ADIT#ENDER#NOGS
TENURED#WADI###
###MOT##EMOTER#
#PINOCHLE#MONEY
BAN#FOUL#BERATE
LID##REATA##MIL
UNISON#MICA#EEL
REGAL#TANKFULS#
#DOMINO##WAR###
###POUR#BARBERS
IDOL#DEFER#AREA
TIDE#ERRED#NAIL
SEED##OOPS#ESNE
```

PUZZLE 326

```
ICIER#SHIM#CHAT
NOBLE#AIDE#RAGE
FRILL#NEST#ALES
ONS#ASK##EFFORT
###APE##BOUT###
#BONSAI#URN#PRO
PRATE#MAR##FLAW
RAKED#PIE#FLARE
ACED##ERA#OOZED
YEN#DUD#UPROAR#
###HERE##OER###
SEWING##PIC#SSE
OVAL#ECHO#ASHEN
SELL#NEER#SHIED
ONLY#TEXT#TENDS
```

PUZZLE 327

```
BLED#HALL##TART
LIVE#ALOOF#ODOR
ARIA#REUSE#WAGE
BALLAD#SILL#PUN
###SIT#ENLISTED
WED#LOG#GENT###
EVES#PAS#DEEDED
REALM#SAP#SPRAY
ENDEAR#YEA#SAVE
###EGOS#ADD#BED
HOSPITAL#HIT###
ANT#COLA#EDITED
LIED#RATER#DIKE
TONE#SMILE#AMEN
SNOB##INKS#LESS
```

PUZZLE 328

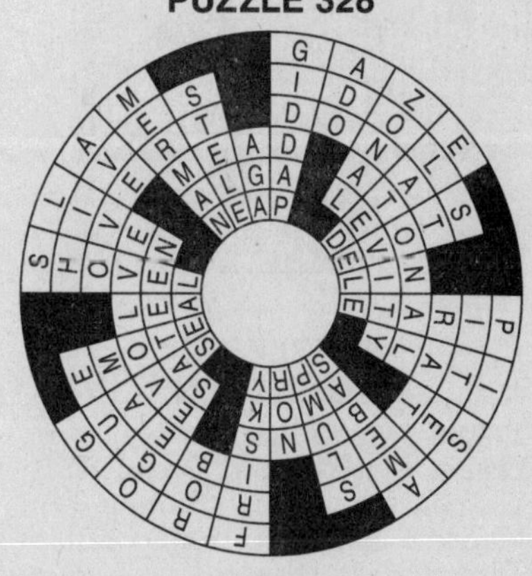

PUZZLE 329

```
CUBA#TAR#ACME
OPEC#UKE#SHIN
ARCH#TIS#HOLD
TOO##ONTO#ODE
SOMBER#FUSSED
#TERN#GUTTER#
###ALFALFA###
#CAVIAR#ILLS#
ALMOST#STEAKS
LOP#THAW##DAM
USES#ERE#ALTO
MERE#RIP#PEEK
STEW#SAT#EDDY
```

PUZZLE 330

S	H	E	S		S	T	O	W		D	O	S
L	O	A	N		H	O	P	E		O	U	T
O	N	C	E		E	Y	E	R		W	R	Y
B	E	H	A	V	E		N	E	O	N		
			K	A	P	P	A		A	B	E	D
V	I	N	Y	L		R	I	C	K	E	T	Y
A	D	O		O	P	E	R	A		A	C	E
S	O	B	E	R	L	Y		B	A	T	H	S
E	L	L	S		A	S	P	I	C			
		E	S	P	Y		U	N	C	U	R	L
H	A	M		A	F	A	R		E	R	I	E
O	W	E		T	U	G	S		S	A	G	A
P	E	N		S	L	O	E		S	L	A	P

PUZZLE 331

DE	C	LAI	M				ST	A	F	F
AD	O	R	A	BLE		ME	A	ND	ER	ING
BEA	RD		RE	MI	T	TA	NCE		RE	E
T	IA	RA		SH	OA	LS		MIS	TE	R
	L	U	SH	E	ST		GR	IN	D	
		CO	AT	S		R	EE	F		
	C	US	TER		ST	EVE	D	OR	E	
HO	L	LY		GL	A	RE		MED	A	L
NE	AP		M	A	GE	N	TA		SI	EVE
S	TR	A	INE	D		T	R	AV	E	L
T	AP	PE	D				T	A	ST	ED

PUZZLE 332

1. Detouring, 2. Abolished.

PUZZLE 333

S	O	D	S		O	B	O	E			S	A	S	H
A	L	I	T		P	A	L	M	S		A	N	T	E
N	E	N	E		T	R	I	P	E		F	O	U	R
D	O	G	M	A		R	O	L	L		E	N	D	S
				B	R	O		O	A	F	S			
	T	A	K	E	A	W	A	Y		A	T	B	A	T
G	A	I	E	T	Y		R	E	A	D		E	W	E
L	I	M	N		E	M	E	E	R		A	L	A	E
A	G	E		I	D	E	A		I	N	F	I	R	M
D	A	R	E	R		C	L	O	S	E	T	E	D	
			M	E	S	H		S	E	A				
C	R	I	B		H	A	L	T		R	O	D	E	O
H	E	R	O		A	N	I	L	E		D	I	V	A
A	P	O	D		W	I	R	E	R		O	R	E	S
P	O	N	Y			C	A	R	E		R	E	N	T

PUZZLE 334

1. Agate, Opal, Jade, Ruby; 2. Stew, Braise, Fry, Bake; 3. Dress, Shirt, Vest, Jacket; 4. Moor, Swamp, Fen, Marsh; 5. Skill, Art, Trade, Craft; 6. Thread, Baste, Sew, Stitch; 7. Pace, Tempo, Speed, Race; 8. Retain, Save, Hold, Keep.

PUZZLE 335

A	G	A	R		O	R	A	L		A	B	E	A	M
R	U	L	E		G	E	N	E		D	R	A	M	A
B	A	L	L	E	R	I	N	A		D	O	V	E	S
O	V	A		D	E	N	U	D	E		W	E	N	T
R	A	Y	E	D			L	E	M	O	N			
			S	Y	N	C		R	U	E		A	F	T
H	A	L	T		I	R	E	S		R	A	C	E	R
A	L	O	E		L	E	T	H	E		D	E	L	E
W	E	I	R	D		P	A	I	L		I	D	L	E
K	E	N		O	D	E		P	L	I	E			
			S	N	I	P	E			C	U	F	F	S
S	L	I	P		M	A	D	A	M	E		L	E	I
H	O	S	E	D		P	E	D	E	S	T	A	L	S
O	G	L	E	R		E	M	I	R		I	R	I	S
W	E	E	D	Y		R	A	T	E		S	E	X	Y

PUZZLE 336

ACCRUE: The people who run a ship.

PUZZLE 337

D	I	S	H		E	D	G	E	S		A	S	P	S
A	R	I	A		R	E	A	L	M		P	L	O	P
M	O	Z	Z	A	R	E	L	L	A		P	I	K	E
S	N	E	E	R					S	E	A	T	E	D
			S	E	R	A		C	H	A	R			
S	P	A			O	L	L	A		R	E	A	P	
U	R	N		S	L	I	E	R		F	L	O	A	T
R	I	G		P	L	A	T	E	A	U		R	C	A
E	M	E	E	R		S	H	E	L	L		T	E	L
	O	L	E	O		E	E	N	S			A	R	K
			R	U	N	S		S	O	U	R			
P	E	T	I	T	E					T	I	L	T	S
A	L	E	E		S	C	O	O	P	E	D	O	U	T
P	A	T	S		T	E	R	R	A		E	R	N	E
A	N	E	T		S	L	O	T	S		R	E	A	M

PUZZLE 338

M	O	O	C	H		B	A	R	S		U	S	S	R
I	G	L	O	O		A	L	I	T		M	A	K	O
E	L	E	N	I		S	A	B	O	T	A	G	E	D
N	E	O	N		R	E	S	A	L	E		O	W	E
			I	V	E			L	E	E				
	F	R	E	E	L	O	A	D		D	O	F	F	S
F	E	E		E	Y	E	R				F	L	E	E
A	L	D	E	R		R	O	W		S	T	O	R	E
S	L	I	T				A	I	D	E		R	A	D
T	A	P	E	R		A	R	T	E	R	I	A	L	
				O	D	D			E	F	T			
S	T	Y		B	E	D	L	A	M		C	R	O	P
P	R	O	P	E	L	L	E	R		S	H	O	R	E
A	U	R	A		T	E	A	M		P	E	A	C	E
M	E	E	T		A	S	P	S		A	D	M	A	N

PUZZLE 339

COLORS: Crocus, Peach, Cocoa, Lavender, Black.

ONE-WORD FILM TITLES: Witness, Elizabeth, Casablanca, Arthur, Boardwalk.

LIQUIDS: Molasses, Broth, Soda, Water, Ink.

WORLD CAPITALS: Paris, Phnom Penh, Ottawa, Dakar, Bangkok.

BIRDS: Ibis, Finch, Myna, Warbler, Hawk.

PUZZLE 340

M	A	N	T	R	A		I	G	N	O	R	E		O	L	D
A	B	A	S	E	S		R	O	A	M	E	R		N	E	E
S	E	P	A	L	S		A	D	V	I	S	E		T	E	N
S	T	E	R	E	O	S		S	A	T	E		P	O	R	T
			S	T	R	U	D	E	L		A	G	E			
S	A	G		S	T	E	R	N		B	L	E	N	D	E	R
A	M	E	N				E	D	D	Y		A	D	O	R	E
R	E	N	O		S	P	A		E	W	E	R		R	E	M
C	R	E	W		A	I	M		C	A	W		A	M	M	O
A	I	R		E	P	E	E		A	Y	E		H	A	I	R
S	C	A	L	P		C	R	O	P				A	N	T	S
M	A	L	A	I	S	E		R	O	A	R	S		T	E	E
			I	C	E		F	I	D	G	E	T	S			
S	C	A	R		D	E	L	E		O	P	U	L	E	N	T
A	L	L		S	A	R	O	N	G		A	D	A	G	I	O
G	A	S		I	N	N	A	T	E		S	I	M	I	L	E
A	D	O		T	S	E	T	S	E		T	O	S	S	E	S

PUZZLE 341

V	E	T		F	L	U		R	A	T		T	A	N
A	G	O		O	A	K		A	D	O		O	R	E
C	O	M	P	U	T	E		I	V	Y		P	O	W
			O	N	E		U	S	E		S	A	M	E
F	J	O	R	D	S		P	E	R		C	Z	A	R
R	A	R	E		H	I	D		B	R	A			
O	D	D	S		O	D	O	R		E	R	R	S	
G	E	E		A	W	L		A	D	D		O	N	S
	D	R	A	M		E	D	G	Y		Q	U	I	P
			S	P	A		Y	E	N		U	N	T	O
H	A	C	K		D	E	E		A	M	I	D	S	T
O	W	E	S		J	A	R		M	I	L			
T	A	D		F	O	R		S	I	X	T	E	E	N
E	K	E		O	I	L		A	T	E		E	R	A
L	E	D		E	N	S		W	E	D		L	E	G

1-B, 2-F, 3-V, 4-Q, 5-D, 6-E, 7-K, 8-L, 9-U, 10-H, 11-I, 12-O, 13-T, 14-W, 15-X, 16-J, 17-S, 18-M, 19-P, 20-Z, 21-G, 22-R, 23-N, 24-Y, 25-A, 26-C.

PUZZLE 342

1. Tradition is a guide and not a jailer. (W. Somerset Maugham)

2. If bread is the first necessity of life, recreation is a close second. (Edward Bellamy)

PUZZLE 343

S	A	P	S			S	T	A	Y		P	A	S	S
A	L	O	E		S	T	I	L	E		L	I	L	T
R	O	L	E		H	U	L	L	A	B	A	L	O	O
I	N	K		S	E	N	T			U	N	S	E	W
S	E	A	P	O	R	T	S		T	O	E			
			O	U	R	S		P	A	Y	R	O	L	L
W	H	I	N	N	Y		J	I	B			B	O	O
H	O	S	E	D		H	A	G		S	P	O	T	S
O	W	N			A	I	M		B	L	U	E	S	T
M	E	T	E	O	R	S		G	R	I	T			
			D	A	M		G	R	O	T	T	O	E	S
S	P	L	I	T			R	A	T	S		Z	A	P
T	O	O	T	H	B	R	U	S	H		S	O	S	O
U	P	D	O		R	U	M	P	S		O	N	E	R
B	E	E	R		A	M	P	S			P	E	S	T

PUZZLE 344

P	R	O	D		W	O	R	S	T		B	L	A	B
L	O	G	O		A	P	A	C	E		R	O	B	E
O	A	R	S		R	E	C	E	P	T	A	C	L	E
D	R	E	A	M			K	N	E	E		H	E	N
			G	U	R	U		T	E	N	D			
	H	E	E	D	I	N	G			T	A	G	S	
F	O	X			V	I	A		S	H	I	R	T	S
O	U	T	S		A	T	I	L	T		S	O	U	P
E	N	R	O	L	L		L	E	I			A	N	Y
	D	A	D	A			Y	E	L	L	I	N	G	
			A	R	C	S		K	E	E	N			
R	O	W		G	U	T	S			T	H	U	M	B
A	B	O	V	E	B	O	A	R	D		A	S	E	A
H	I	R	E		E	R	R	O	R		L	E	A	D
S	T	E	T		D	E	I	T	Y		E	R	N	E

PUZZLE 345

A	N	Y		A	M	P		A	G	E		A	P	E
D	U	E		S	I	R		P	O	P		C	R	Y
O	B	S	C	E	N	E		T	I	E		C	E	E
			H	A	T	S			N	E	A	R	E	R
I	C	E	R			T	A	N	G		N	U	N	S
M	A	X	I		B	O	L	O		A	D	E	S	
P	R	I	S	S	Y		E	V	E	R				
S	E	T		A	T	T	R	A	C	T		T	W	O
				F	E	A	T		H	Y	P	H	E	N
	E	A	V	E		K	E	N	O		R	O	P	E
S	A	V	E		C	E	D	E			O	U	T	S
W	R	I	T	E	R			C	H	I	P			
E	N	D		G	O	T		T	A	S	S	E	L	S
E	E	L		G	O	O		A	L	L		W	O	O
T	R	Y		S	K	Y		R	O	E		E	B	B

PUZZLE 346

```
SETS■■SAC■■SLAB
PLEA■SCRUB■POUR
LILT■HOMER■ECRU
ATE■HER■■AFLOAT
YEP■ASEA■ILL■■■
■■HEN■■SOSO■VAT
SCOLD■THREW■EGO
TANKS■HIE■EDGES
UKE■TREES■RUERS
BED■AIMS■■PET■■
■■■INN■TORO■APT
AWARDS■■LET■TAR
LANK■ERODE■TIDE
MITE■DOWEL■WORK
SLID■■TEN■■ONES
```

PUZZLE 347

```
SHOAL■■TAP■EPIC
EAGLES■ETA■VICE
ERRATA■MOT■EPEE
PEER■LAPPS■REDS
■■■MEOW■■YAM■■■
■RESPONSE■DOSS■
ION■SNITS■ARCED
SWAMI■NIP■PEONY
METAL■GLOAT■ODE
■DECO■STUDENTS■
■■■ANY■■SORE■■■
SCAR■OLDER■SPAS
HALO■KOI■ENTICE
UNTO■EGG■DIETER
NEON■DOS■■TRADE
```

PUZZLE 348

```
GAPS■■BEER■■SHE
ROUT■BRACED■TEN
ANTI■AUTHOR■RAD
DETRACT■ORE■IVE
■■■■UKE■■DAPPER
RAVENS■THEME■■■
AGENT■DOER■NODS
NOTES■OWL■SCRAP
IGOR■SLED■TIARA
■■■GLUER■TILLER
CRAYON■■AIL■■■■
EER■ALL■PELICAN
DUO■NAILER■COKE
ESS■SMEARS■EDIT
SEE■■PUPS■■DENS
```

PUZZLE 349

```
SPA■BIB■AMP■DOT
TAN■ARE■SEE■EGO
ACT■LET■SAP■FLU
BEEFS■ABED■EYER
■■■LAM■ATOLL■■■
CAPE■ITS■WISED■
ALEE■DOSE■EELER
BOA■LID■MEN■ACE
SORRY■OMIT■STOP
■FLORA■ARC■HERS
■■■BETSY■HUE■■■
DIME■TOOL■PSALM
ADE■SIC■ODE■VIA
YEN■ARK■CAN■IMP
SAD■YES■ODD■SOS
```

PUZZLE 350

```
AFT■■PAIL■CASTE
BIO■BAYOU■ALIEN
ELM■ARENA■METED
DEBARK■■USE■EMS
■■■SEAT■■POP■■■
RASP■SALSA■ARCS
OPT■■■MINI■WARP
BERG■OAKEN■STAR
ORAL■GLEE■■■ICE
TYPO■REDRY■JOKE
■■■WOE■■SOFA■■■
ELF■ASK■■GOBBLE
VILER■ENSUE■AIL
EVOKE■PEERS■INS
REWED■TEXT■■TEE
```

PUZZLE 351

```
ALSO■■SOLD■SORE
VAIN■ALLOY■TRAM
APES■DODGE■EGGS
ITS■LOP■■■BRA■■
LOT■USES■SINNER
■PAIL■■CRAB■IVY
■■■CURTAILS■ZEE
HARE■EARNS■PENS
ARE■IRRIGATE■■■
WED■DUPE■■RAVE■
SADDEN■RIPE■ANT
■■ERA■■■DAY■LAW
PANE■BAYOU■JIBE
AGES■ATOLL■ISLE
RODS■TENS■■BEET
```

PUZZLE 352

```
WOK■■DEAD■■ECHO
EKE■PERMIT■NOON
ERE■ELAPSE■JANE
PALACES■CAROLER
■■■CAGES■SOY■■■
■ARENA■PRESENCE
BRA■■TRIO■IDIOM
URN■HEARTEN■GNU
DOGMA■MIST■■HES
SWEETEST■EMITS■
■■■SEX■SORER■■■
AMASSED■INTENSE
SARI■COLLIE■UKE
KNEE■SLEETS■NIL
SEAR■■EDDY■■SPY
```

PUZZLE 353

```
BART■SPA■LAP■LONE
OBOE■TIL■ENE■AMID
ABLE■AGAINST■MANE
TEETER■NASA■CAREN
■■■HATS■NERVES■■■
TOWERING■SAID■SEA
ELI■SNOUT■■NAVIES
NELL■GONE■■TRILLS
■■LAW■PSALM■SEE■■
ANIMAL■■COAL■SNAG
LIABLE■■HIRED■CIA
LAM■TASK■SLEEPERS
■■■DERMAL■OGLE■■■
ANGER■AREA■RITTER
RILE■GRANDMA■ERIE
ICED■ITT■DON■RARE
DEES■NYE■SET■SPED
```

PUZZLE 354

```
ARCS■BOLD■BASTE
JILT■AWAY■ESTOP
ACER■REIN■RHINO
REWORK■NAPE■RES
■■■LEEK■MOT■■■■
■GOLDENROD■ACRE
PEA■EPEE■SAILOR
ANKLE■WIG■CROWS
DREAMT■GNAT■WET
SEND■RUNAROUND■
■■■■PIP■WORN■■■
ITS■ROBE■USABLE
COATI■ETAS■GOES
ETNAS■ACNE■ELAN
SEDUM■THIS■DOSE
```

PUZZLE 355

```
BABY■■TAPS■■LOG
OBOE■THREAT■EGO
WONT■HAIRDO■ALL
LUG■DATA■■TONED
STOLEN■SCREW■■■
■■■INKS■AIMLESS
TEDDY■PITS■SALE
OAR■■ALONE■■SUE
GRAD■MINI■DYERS
ANGELIC■PARE■■■
■■■CIDER■ROAMED
ALTOS■■HUMP■AXE
DUO■PRAISE■TYPE
EAR■SIGNED■ABED
SUN■■MOOS■■GELS
```

PUZZLE 356

```
SWEEP■CAD■SCAMP
HALVE■ALI■EASEL
ADDER■CIA■AMPLY
PEERS■TAMALE■■■
ERR■IBISES■LOSS
■■■ESE■■TSP■SAL
PALATE■VETO■CUE
SWORE■HER■INANE
HAP■NEAT■ANORAK
ARE■TRY■■MSG■■■
WEST■ARCHIE■SOB
■■■SALINE■TWIRL
POLKA■DON■TINGE
GREER■ETC■INCAS
ABIDE■SEE■AGENT
```

PUZZLE 357

```
SCALP■TUBA■PEST
COCOA■ORAL■ALTO
ALIGN■UNTO■PERT
TAD■COP■HEN■CEE
■■■PAVE■■■ACTED
PARAKEETS■MOST■
ERASER■OUTER■■■
WEPT■DARER■SPAS
■■■ODORS■AWEIGH
■SPRY■COMMITTEE
CHOSE■■■OPTS■■■
AIL■RIB■ASH■HAG
RELY■TEEN■EBONY
GLEE■CARE■REHEM
ODDS■HUED■STOWS
```

PUZZLE 358

LEG CASA SPED BABA
RENO APTS HARI ARON
ONTO PEEP ALMS IRAN
USE ERE ADMIRAL
SERVER PAR NOISIER
ESSAY ELM REBS NAE
NET SPADE ELECTS
PANELIST DECADES
IDO ELY JAPAN TAOS
TAROT RAE OPT FALSE
AMMO UPSET INA OLE
PROPOSE ACCUSTOM
GOSSIP RERAN OCT
ANS PEST ILE EAGLE
PATTERN ETC STYLED
SNEAKER DUO IDS
GALA TRIO DONA EDGE
AGER TENN ATIP KEEL
GOES ADDS BETS ERR

PUZZLE 359

LATE PLED TOWNS
APER AIDE ONION
SPAR LOIN TEMPO
ELL ENTICE PEW
RESULT ARM
NOTABLY CANT
FAREWELL CORER
ALIVE EEL RAISE
COPED SEPARATE
TEEN NATIONS
SOW SKETCH
BOW AROMAS WOE
OVALS KALE DIVA
DEGAS EROS ICER
ENEMY NETS NERD

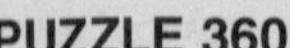

PUZZLE 360

SODS HAGS PLOY
ABET LEMON RIPE
SOLO ELABORATES
SEER NIT WAY
ISSUE SPEAR
PHEW MUCH DRAG
AROSE ROOT CRY
CUR AWL PEA HEM
INN READ TRESS
DEEM AGES EAST
STALK STERN
NIL PUG CLAP
WHITE ICING HAUL
RULE NUTTY ECRU
YELL GEES REAM

PUZZLE 361

BRONCO GAD SOFA
LINEAR ADE IBIS
OCTAVE SHEEPISH
CHORE POPE THY
RAT CELL
CALENDAR RELAY
OPAL OPUS RADON
VIXEN INN SMOKE
ENEMY RIOT AREA
GRILL COARSEST
SOOT PRO
OWE NAIL CLEAT
MODESTLY AKIMBO
EVIL HER SERIES
NETS ERE STARTS

PUZZLE 362

EFT POD SIS FLU
ROE OVA UMP RES
ERA OAT EPISODE
TILLER ANT
EARL OAR ROLL
EYELID OPT OBOE
LEE DOGMA ALIBI
GORE RILL
ORIEL SUTRA SAT
PERI ASP KETTLE
EVES MOD HOPE
HEP ORATOR
CLEANER ARE AGO
OIL ORE GIN GAR
GEM LET ADD EBB

PUZZLE 363

DARES DUB CLOD
ARENAS EKE HIKE
MEDDLE LET ACRE
PAS SEMI PLEAD
MADE WEE
DATA ENCHANTED
ORATOR HARP RUM
WINED HIT ABASE
NAY DEAL BLASTS
SATELLITE LESS
ASS USED
TRYST AGED SHY
HOST LEI TIPTOE
EPEE OWN SCROLL
NERD GET TOWEL

PUZZLE 364

ENAT NETER EPRI
LARA DMITA NAET
ATEL EILVS TEES
RESSPURE HEERCS
EARNS EAT
TEAMSED EDR NAE
ETRARD ONCDENSE
RAYT EET IESV
ESDERTED APTROR
SES GEG TSERILE
TAE ERTSE
TRASYS ESIDRENT
NANA PORES AKTE
ETET LOSSF TEIM
AESE EMSSY EPAS

PUZZLE 365

AGES POND CABS SPCA
FADE ALOE ELAN PROP
ALUM TERMINATE RENT
RECITES ACTS ARISES
ANON ONES SKATE
ALTAR LIDS CLEVERLY
POOR LOSS SHARE VIE
SIR RARE FLOPS FERN
ENSLAVE PEARS MIDAS
AGA CRANE BIG
FORTE MOIST PERSIST
AMAH DEPOT AUTO NEO
SAD PETER EBBS SCAN
TRIBUTES DYES BERRY
AIRED FRET VICE
TITLES GRAB SATRAPS
WOOL TELEGRAMS ESAU
INRE ERIE OBOE TERR
NEST DABS WAGS ESTE

PUZZLE 366

WAFT HEAD CHUB
ALOE ACRE FLARE
STUN SHIP ROUGE
PORES OAT OGLE
TWO HEW
SAW IRON KNAVE
HUE FELINE GELD
ADAPT ICE DONOR
GIVE MOHAIR OPE
TENSE ERNE MEW
AND NAG
HOWL IMP MATCH
PEDAL VIAL FIRE
IRONY ANTE FEAR
TORE NEED EDGE

Never argue with a fool; people might not know the difference.

PUZZLE 367

TH/E S/TA/RS

PUZZLE 368

INTO SHY SLAW
REAP WOE EACH
EDGE ATTORNEY
RAND PIERS
SEPAL OREO
ERE SAGA USER
EGGNOG CASTLE
DOSE ODES ASP
WAGE HAYES
SISSY LIEU
ENAMELED GALE
ACNE ATE EVEL
THEN PEA REEF

PUZZLE 369

ODE BARE ACME
KID ANEW BOAR
ADD LIVE BOYS
YOYOS ERNE
LAIR ISTLE
ISLE BEEP RAM
STOOGE TAHITI
MAG AXON APER
SNEER CAST
APSE LEASE
FROG ALTO MUD
ABLE GOES PIG
TIER ETCH STY

PUZZLE 370

SAP BEG ZAP GAD
AGA ERR IVY ANA
HOT ANI GEL FOR
IRE CEE NONFAT
BANJO FLAUNT
ANT APE HAFT
LAID AQUA GAR
ACRE MUNCH KOLA
RHO IDEA UGLY
KENO FEE WED
POETRY SUPER
ATTEND OAT LEA
MAR SOW USE URN
AXE ERA NEE GIG
HIT TAX GAM SEE

1-D, 2-T, 3-Z, 4-U, 5-N, 6-W, 7-V, 8-E, 9-L, 10-F, 11-B, 12-H, 13-Q, 14-R, 15-X, 16-A, 17-P, 18-I, 19-Y, 20-S, 21-C, 22-O, 23-M, 24-G, 25-K, 26-J.

PUZZLE 371

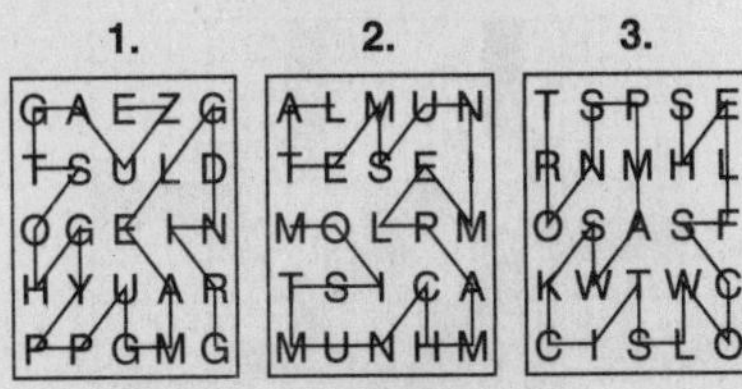

PUZZLE 372

AGA SCRAP BLOT
RUM TOUPEE EURO
ERE RAGTAG FLAG
SUNLIT GHOULS
AVIAN HAG
RETE RIPER PIP
LADEN CREAMSODA
EMUS RAVED PULI
FICTIONAL ALLEN
TEE SCENE BETS
ILK ADORE
SOIREE LANDED
OLLA RANCID AYE
PELT SLEEVE MEW
HOSE TWEED PRY

PUZZLE 373

SAND ASTER STOP
OBOE VIOLA PAPA
RAINFOREST AXEL
ESS ACED IODINE
SHY TAN POPE
LED FAST LID
REDO OBEY SPICE
EPIC ALE OMEN
VENOM GLEE LOST
SEE ASEA TOO
HAUL SEW LIT
SOLEMN ACRE AGE
EKED DEPENDABLE
CRAG ARENA LOON
TAKE EASEL PROS

PUZZLE 374

1. Rigor, 2. Legal, 3. Widow, 4. Hunch, 5. Eagle, 6. Outdo, 7. Going, 8. Civic, 9. Yummy, 10. Tacit, 11. Druid, 12. Kiosk.

PUZZLE 375

SHIP PEP SKIN
LOLL BASIC CEDE
ABLY UPPER ONER
YOU FRAY ABROAD
SPINY OBOE
ACTOR ASK DRIBS
SHRIMP PRAY DOC
SEA AHEAD ERA
EAT FLEA SHINER
STEAL FRO ENTRY
SECT KHAKI
AZALEA LAIR FIR
ROLE BRAYS SIRE
KNEE SAVES HEEL
SEEP GAD EDDY

PUZZLE 376

1. Bedeck, Indeed, Modern; 2. Cocoon, Alcove, Recoup; 3. Afraid, Forage, Herald; 4. Lately, Intent, Meteor.

BONUS WORD: Decorate

PUZZLE 377

GAR TH BA CON NO IR
LIC EN SED QUI N CE RES T ATE
A PAR T DE L ET ION
AT TES TE D CA D ET
LA LA ON BOA RD TER MI TE
S C ALD ST IN T LE A ST
OIL ER S A HEM S RO E
TON SI LS MI SN OM ER
BEG OTT E N BLI TH E
MAR IN ER GL A ND ER A SE
DI NER E YE QUA VER

PUZZLE 378

Edith and Philip are hosting Oliver and his wife, and Ray and his wife are hosting Fay and Ted, so Quincy must be hosting with Diane for Bertha and Stan. Since Oliver's wife isn't Amy, Carol must be his wife, meaning that Amy is Ray's wife.

In summary:
Bertha and Stan are Diane and Quincy's guests
Carol and Oliver are Edith and Philip's guests
Fay and Ted are Amy and Ray's guests

PUZZLE 379

ASKS OBI REF
ATEN SPIN OLE
RUNAROUND USE
RAPS OWNED
BOGEYS ROADS
ALE MYRRH
NATS WOE NABS
AESOP NOT
TRACK MONDAY
VIOLA RALE
EMU ROUNDSOFF
TIN ARTS TUBA
ODD BOS STIR

PUZZLE 380

END CBS LAHR
GOO HOP CANOE
GROCERY RUINS
ORG ONSET
BAYOU LANDED
ONE BREWER
GNAW AGO YOUR
ATTILA ERE
SLIEST STRIP
STATE CPI
CABIN MAILING
AGONY AIR LEI
BERG ANE LEN

PUZZLE 381

SEA FAD BUT
TAR OWE ASH
EGO ELF SUE
ELM ARIAS
LEAP ICICLE
EATEN
GREENS GLOW
RALLY ERA
OIL WAS ADD
USE ADO VEE
PEN YEW ERR

PUZZLE 382

LAND
PATH OLIO
ELIA SCENE
TALES HARES
ONE CELT
MUG ROAD
STEWARDSHIP
ACES ODE
MATE TET
GLADE AREAS
RAZOR LULL
AVER LESS
BASE

PUZZLE 383

CHAP
ELOPE SAP
BLAMED HUE
SLIME ICING
BEETS AGENT
ALONE BURLY
ALOUD HOTEL GEE
IDOL CANOE GRAY
MOM BABES GOOSE
PARIS CRUST
VALET FLAGS
LEVEL SLICE
ATE ESCAPE
SOD SEAMS
SAME

PUZZLE 384

Rebellion, Rebus, Recapitulate, Reciprocal, Rejuvenation, Remunerate, Renewal, Reorganize, Repercussion, Reversal.

HINT: RE

PUZZLE 385

LIFE
ARM EVANS
HER SEA SECTOR
ORE LATHE URDU
WES ECHO BLEAT
POET RIOT
CHEAP ESSAY TAO
ROCK AXELS TEND
OPT BLESS BREED
EACH MAIN
ELDER OMIT ART
VEIL BEAST GOO
ENGINE LEE EWE
TINES ERR
TEAS

PUZZLE 386

The 0-6 is the Loose Tile.

PUZZLE 387

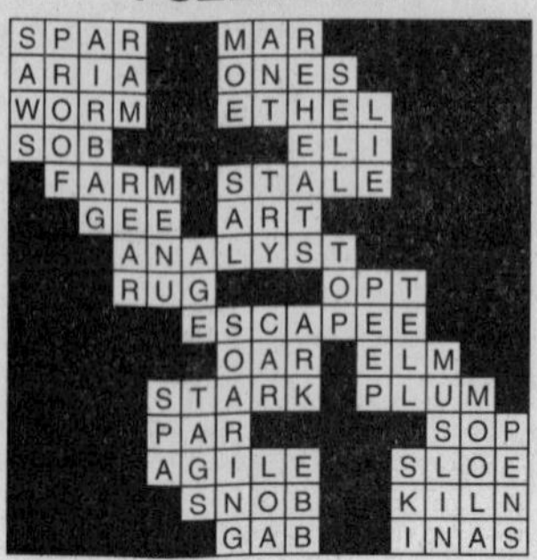
SPAR MAR
ARIA ONES
WORM ETHEL
SOB ELI
FARM STALE
GEE ART
ANALYST
RUG OPT
ESCAPEE
OAR ELM
STARK PLUM
PAR SOP
AGILE SLOE
SNOB KILN
GAB INAS

PUZZLE 388

Way down South where bananas grow,
A grasshopper stepped on an elephant's toe.
The elephant said, with tears in his eyes,
"Pick on somebody your own size."

PUZZLE 389

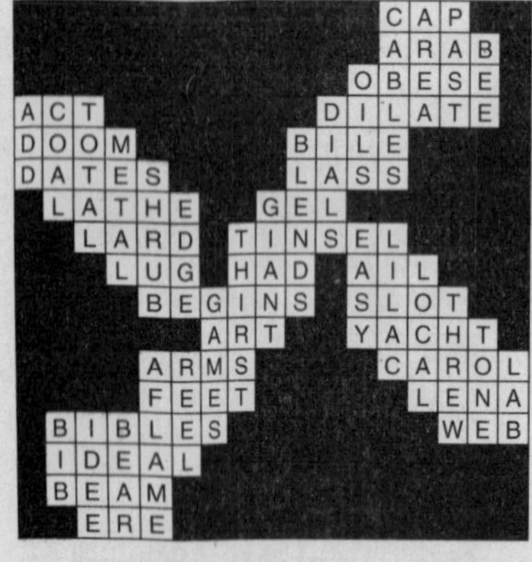
CAP
ARAB
OBESE
ACT DILATE
DOOM BILE
DATES LASS
LATHE GEL
LARD TINSEL
LUG HAD AIL
BEGINS SLOT
ART YACHT
ARMS CAROL
FEET LENA
BIBLES WEB
IDEAL
BEAM
ERE

PUZZLE 390

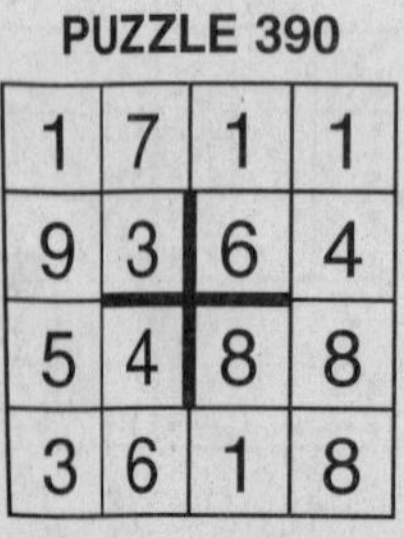

1	7	1	1
9	3	6	4
5	4	8	8
3	6	1	8

PUZZLE 391

SIB CAB
ABET SRI HIE
DEGAS IAN ROME
XEROX ESCAPER
TOLE PLAY RTE
TINFOIL AIR
DOES LEO
NISI BAD
GENAL
BUN SLOE
COS BOLA
ARC SHUDDER
ANA LOAM ERIC
BOXWOOD RIVAL
ACHE AFT EERIE
LAO STY ROMA
ERR LOT

PUZZLE 392

1. Rival, Vista, Steno, Loner.
2. Noisy, Amble, Basil, Money.
3. Range, Limbo, Bagel, Minor.
4. China, Upset, Spice, Haunt.

PUZZLE 393

BATHED SON
ORIOLE NOVICE
TOPPLE RELATOR
HAT ROW LETS
ROB ZEST RET
PACA ABOVE
YOU MUD
SENSOR SPRIT TORE
PIE AWL GARB RIAL
ADAGE HER CUR ELDER
ETAS OWER COY ACE
ROTS SPEAK ALERTS
OFF WED
WORST LEIS
APT BENT TAW
CLOT ORE VET
MONOCLE ABRADE
EYEFUL LOUNGE
SUB TATTED

PUZZLE 394

ALIT ASPS
AROMA PURE
MUDPUPPY PROWL
LARD USUAL DNA
LEARN REL KIEV RAW
ARK MANSE TBA LIRA
CREAMCHEESE UNLOADS
FIG PLOT ASTO
ORR FATES ROB
POTROAST TEDS LOO
OBOE WARP ROIL SELA
DIG LOIS MEATHOOK
SAC ADZES ROO
ATOM ZEES REO
AMERICA CHERRYSTONE
NENE APE EMIRS DEE
TON DART PAS WIDEN
ETA RAISE OHMS
RAVEL PORKCHOP
TOTO ROARS
EWER ARTY

PUZZLE 395

SAKE SWIM BRISK
TUNE NONO LATIN
IDOL ORES UNCLE
NIT COMPASS HOW
TOSSUP TILT
ODES CUE TAG
SPAN DUB GREASE
LILAC NEE YACHT
OPERAS ELL TOYS
WEE POT FUME
ALAS RERUNS
BEG COMPACT BUT
ALIBI ARCH YORE
ISLET LANE EASE
TEDDY EYES STEP

PUZZLE 396

DOOR GODS PLED
ABLE CRUET RAGA
WOLF LISLE EDGY
NEAR ATTEMPT
EAR HEARD
DISCO SPLINTER
LIGHT ALOE DRAY
URN SPLURGE ILL
CEIL OAST PLUMY
ASTONISH ROAMS
STENO ASP
GROMMET TADS
SCAB MOIRE OXEN
AUTO IDEAL PICA
CREW TENS SLOG

PUZZLE 397

MAD LADY HEADS
ICE ASEA GOALIE
DIM MILK RATTAN
IDOL DISBAR OLD
ETE UNDO
SPIES MIO UPS
WHOSE ALL ROOF
EEL NOONDAY IRE
BLAB PRO EASED
FRO PAR NAMER
WOOL ARM
ELF ASSIST ODOR
GALORE SLIP AXE
GNAWED LAVA TEN
SEWED EYED ANT

PUZZLE 398

ILL FIG ASTIR
TOO ALOHA PEACE
EGO TUTOR TIMES
MOTTO AURA ZEST
ELL LADLE
BALLAD YOU OWL
GALL DUO STARRY
UTTER ELF EDGER
SHARED DIM JANE
HER IRE BARONS
INAPT POI
CALM MEAN UNZIP
ARIAS ERECT ADE
BONGO SPARE NEE
SWEEP SPY YAK

PUZZLE 399

SHOD TUTU POPE
TAPE REMIT APED
ALAS APPLE STAG
RELIEVE ENS ICE
SLIER SAUCER
CARTON EMITS
LIE PENCIL ENDS
ARISE ION TROOP
MYNA ENRICH ONE
KEYED RISKED
SPHERE STINT
ERA EBB ASSURED
MOSS RABBI NAVY
INTO ORALS TREE
SEED WERE SEND

PUZZLE 400

OPTS AFAR EBBED
AURA GISH LLAMA
SPAGHETTI MATER
TAP EOSINS ZONE
GAL ROO ENDS
HAZARDS CUED
UNIT ICERS TAM
BONED GAR STALE
SAC RONDO ERAL
MYNA SCRAPED
TACO ETA AUK
AMID SUBTLE POI
RENEW RAILROADS
OBESE ESNE WREN
TASTE SEED LEST

PUZZLE 401

MAP HAS WAY AGO
OPE EVE OWE JAM
NOD MIX KEA AGE
AGA PATE RERAN
DEN TEN INK
ETA OTTER EASE
WAR OLEO DUE
PSALM AUK HAZEL
ALL PURR UMP
TYPO SCAMP TAT
VEE GAS SAD
SQUAB ETCH PIE
OUR OBI TAU ILL
DIG NOR ELF ROT
APE YAK REF ERA

1-W, 2-U, 3-D, 4-R, 5-P, 6-J, 7-T, 8-K, 9-S, 10-C, 11-H, 12-O, 13-Y, 14-E, 15-F, 16-V, 17-M, 18-L, 19-Q, 20-N, 21-B, 22-Z, 23-G, 24-A, 25-X, 26-I.

PUZZLE 402

GRAM ASP SLOB
RULE SPIRE LUAU
ORAL APRON ANTS
PARTICLE ALIGHT
ELM CHESSMEN
DEES NEW DAB
EGOIST WILDFIRE
BOIL TOP AVID
BALLPARK SALADS
STY ADO PURL
WARDROBE ARC
SAFARI ISLANDER
AMID FALSE IOTA
MORE TWEET GRAB
EKED ESS HERS

PUZZLE 403

TEMP GEM SLAM
RAIL TABOO IOTA
UGLY URBAN MOOT
ELL ARDENT IMPS
RESIGNED OIL
NOON CAUSE
THAN VIA KERNEL
YAP LEARNED DAM
PREWAR KAY DOTS
ODDER THEY
ADS PIONEERS
AMOK CAROLS LEI
NAME ALONE BULL
EYES MESAS EDIT
WONT EEL GETS

PUZZLE 404

LAWS IDEA HANG
ECHO TRIAD ANOA
AEON HOSTS ZING
FRAGMENT ALOE
BEE USHER
SLIT REORDER
ALAR EBBING LEI
GONDOLA ZESTFUL
ETA PETTED RISK
HIBACHI BONE
ALTER LIP
SKIS EDITIONS
HULK SEDUM CLOT
IDLE ORLOP AIDE
MUST WAYS LOST

PUZZLE 405

EFTS MUSS HEART
ALOE INCH ALGAE
ROUX STAY CAIRN
ERG ATOM PINNED
DAHLIA PALED
IRK RINSING
PIPE ECHOED DIN
AMEND REM AMEBA
YAP ICEMAN OAST
SMEARED EEL
FELON WATERY
BASICS ERST DUE
OCTET MAAM PUPA
TROLL ETNA ACER
HEADY THIN PEEN

PUZZLE 406

SALE AWAY ABBOT
PLOY MAZE PRIME
ELSE BRAT EATEN
DYES EEL URGENT
OAR ESS
SCARF CACHE ONS
THIEF ASHEN PAL
ROD OFT ORE EMU
EKE RINGO RARER
WED DRILL GRASP
SPA GYM
TARGET MAN OPAL
OCEAN COLA ROBE
UNDID OUST ELLS
RESTS BROS DEES

PUZZLE 407

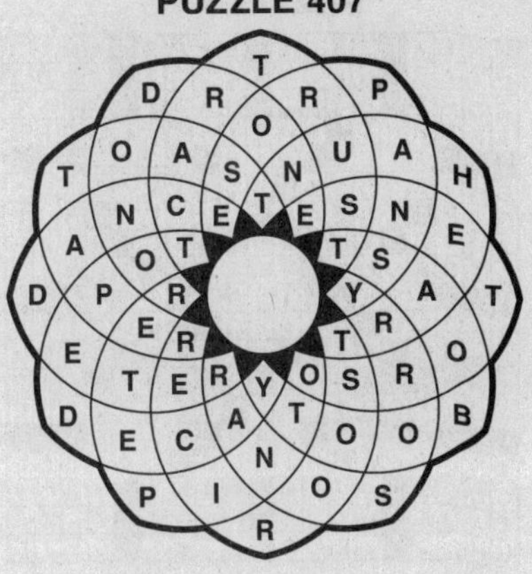

PUZZLE 408

KABOB LAIC STAG
ARENA ORCA LACE
LINER LIEN AURA
EAT GOLD TAMPER
PAP RAG ESS
ESPRITS ETAS
FELON TREASURED
TEEN LAUDS ROSE
SPAGHETTI DRONE
SAVE TWEETED
SOB LED IVY
TREMOR YETI DUO
OLLA AMEN AWASH
ROIL GOAD TOTEM
KNEE EARS EWERS

PUZZLE 409

STRAW LAIR SHOD
POOCH ACNE LOGO
AGATE MEND OURS
NOR EBB AGREE
ILL SON
ECHO ASSENT ATE
SOOT HALVES BIT
SUMAC SEE YOUTH
APE OTHERS ISLE
YES AWAKEN NEER
COY ARK
TRUTH AGE PAL
RANI SELL GAUDY
ACID AGOG ARMOR
METE TOGA LEASE

PUZZLE 410

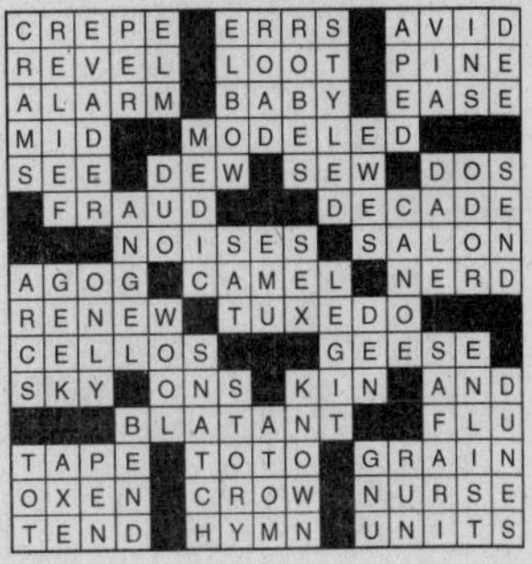

CREPE ERRS AVID
REVEL LOOT PINE
ALARM BABY EASE
MID MODELED
SEE DEW SEW DOS
FRAUD DECADE
NOISES SALON
AGOG CAMEL NERD
RENEW TUXEDO
CELLOS GEESE
SKY ONS KIN AND
BLATANT FLU
TAPE TOTO GRAIN
OXEN CROW NURSE
TEND HYMN UNITS

PUZZLE 411

FRET TACK BARB AMID
LIAR UPON ALOE LODE
ACRE RENO BAWL MOLE
TENANT SWAYS IRONED
TILE NIL TEES
CRESCENT MOTIVATION
OAR KNEAD NOTED ROE
TRIO EMBED OLD RAZE
SECRECY VOILE WANED
ARK WILDS TOM
ANGLE CELLO SHOPPED
LEES FED SLAKE SAGA
ERR RANGE SWIRL PAN
COMFORTERS LEMONADE
ODES MAN DOVE
ANDREW BIDED SETTLE
COOK EVEN PEAT TROY
TAME LINE ALDA EASE
SHED LETS LIST DYED

PUZZLE 412

AGAPE ETHS AJAR
TELEX NEAT MIME
OTARU NAPE OBIS
MAS LEU PARENT
TRIP CADES
DAPPER REBEL
OVOID LONER HON
LOPE RAMIE RACE
EWE LUCID WOMAN
RANKS CHEESE
COMET ETUI
APACHE RET RAP
RETE DADO TRIPE
IRED DRAM LASER
BARE YAWP EGEST

PUZZLE 413

ROAD CROC SPOT
UNDO SHALL NONO
MIME PANDA ALLY
BOA GONG STRAYS
ANNOUNCE PEER
WAGE MET BYE
DESIRE SAD SEAL
EMEND SIT SWARM
LUNG TUX SWORDS
ESS TOP SPAR
AFAR STUNNING
ASTERN MORK GEL
RAIN APART ALSO
CLOD DALES POTS
HENS OWLS TOSS

PUZZLE 414

FOCI ACHE MADE
ALUM SPIEL EWES
DEEP TOTAL THAT
SODA IRED AIDE
STET SPELLER
LASSOS TAT ENS
ICIER SPARE
TEN PAPERER ASP
ERUPT NICHE
SEC DEN RANTER
PRESOAK FILM
RALE ICON ALBS
ISLE SEARS TIRE
TEAM ISSUE EMIR
ERRS STEM SOME

PUZZLE 415

ACTED CODE YAK
BLARE ARENT EKE
LAMES READY TIP
EWE PUP REPAINT
FAN IDES
VALIDATE SKATE
MACARONI SEA
UNITS TAD DATES
LED REDEFINE
ESSAY SANITARY
SECT PER
PREPARE ASS FRO
EEL SORER TILED
ELS TWEAK ERASE
LYE DOTS DEBTS

PUZZLE 416

LACY BOLA DEMOS
AURA RAIL ARENT
STEW AFTERTASTE
TOWN ROE HOT
SCRIPTURE
NAB HONEST MAR
ADE EAST TUTOR
PALMED RESIDE
SPOOK IDEA LED
TWO ACROSS TOO
REGRETTED
SPA WEE ECHO
HORSESENSE LOON
ASKER PEAL VASE
MESAS YEWS EXES

PUZZLE 417

SCUBA APES SOLO
EASES SOLE AWED
CREEP HULA LEAD
TED ICER FLASKS
IRON MAAM
RADIO EARRINGS
MELON INKED IRE
OVAL OTTER BEEN
OUR SPARS PACED
REMOTELY SOWED
NARY SILL
CAMERA RICE BOD
AROW TRIG CARGO
LIRA OATH ADORE
MANY RYES TOWER

PUZZLE 418

BASE BEAM BOMBS
OPTS ERGO IDEAL
ONUS TRIO CELLO
SEN GRANDMA DEB
TAGALONG ARC
BATT CABOOSE
SPLASH GEM VIEW
ELANS RYE GENRE
LEWD GUM WORKER
LANOLIN CAME
NAB SHREDDED
SAW DESPAIR OAR
TROLL NOSE JUTE
EERIE IRES USES
TAMED PEST TENS

PUZZLE 419

WHEY HIFI ECHO
RAVE BATON BROW
ALIT EWERS BORN
POLISH MET ODE
KISS AWAKED
REPAINT NAP
OVEN DUD TIPTOP
BERTS DEB LARVA
ENTICE WIT LIEN
CAN TAILORS
SPASMS FERN
CAP NOR GNAWED
ATOM ABATE ROAR
LIRA REMIT OKRA
POTS EYES WENT

PUZZLE 420

ELLS SCAB GAD
SEEP TACO ATE
STIR UNTO SON
ISNT ZIPPY
BARGE OMEN
ELO MENU COTS
REPAIR TSHIRT
TEES ASEA LIE
ISLE RESOW
QUASI TRIG
URN NATO GALA
AGO GREY ELAN
YEN EKES DEWY

PUZZLE 421

SKY CEDE SKIM
PIE AXON HERO
AWL PANS AREA
DIPLOMA PRODS
UNIT UPS
PACA NEAR ERA
AROUSE PLANED
PER WRAP GEMS
PSI MAKE
GLOOM PROSPER
AURA DEER ICE
TRAP ERNE CHA
EELS BETA SOP

PUZZLE 422

TATE BALI RIIS
ERRS EBAN SENDER
SLEEPLESS TRAILER
TOE ALL ESAU LEE
GALE ACORNS EVE
MARIE SCUM ACRES
IGOR STERES FESS
NEW TEASE IRES
ESTHER SALTED
RENT NATTY DAD
HAIR SMILES MUNI
CANOE ONER BACON
URN SHEREE GENA
PRE IGET IRA TRE
SITTING INTENTION
STATES EASE INTO
EROS SPAR AGES

PUZZLE 423

E	K	E	D		A	P	P	L	E		C	A	D	S
D	E	A	R		C	L	E	A	R		A	L	O	T
I	N	S	I	S	T	E	N	C	E		S	I	L	O
T	O	T	E	M		A	S	K			S	T	E	W
			R	E	P	S		S	A	F	E			
H	A	M		L	A	U	D		N	O	R	T	H	
A	P	E	R	T	U	R	E		T	R	O	W	E	L
L	O	D	E		P	E	A	C	E		L	I	N	E
F	R	I	D	G	E		L	A	N	T	E	R	N	S
	T	A	P	E	R		T	U	N	A		L	A	S
			L	E	S	T		L	A	M	P			
E	R	M	A			B	A	D		P	A	R	K	A
D	E	A	N		C	O	R	R	E	S	P	O	N	D
G	A	T	E		O	N	I	O	N		A	V	I	D
E	R	S	T		B	E	A	N	S		L	E	T	S

PUZZLE 424

1. Babe Ruth, 2. Sally Ride, 3. Eva Peron, 4. Mick Jagger, 5. John Brown, 6. Amy Carter, 7. Glenn Gould, 8. Mary Leakey, 9. Joan Miro, 10. Maxine Waters.

PUZZLE 425

FLA	SK		TA	IN	T	ED		CO	A	CH
GR	IT		PER	V	AD	E		A	FF	AIR
AN	TE	C	ED	ENT		N	EG	L	ECT	
T	R	ACK		OR	AL		AD	E		
		LE	AF		LEV	ER		SCE	P	TER
TA	STE		AR	T	I	ST	IC		LEA	SE
CIT	AD	EL		IDE	A		ING	OT		
		EV	IL		TE	ST		HE	R	D
	HE	A	L	THY		A	SC	R	IB	E
ST	AR	T		M	A	TUR	E		BO	AR
AR	D	OR		E	VID	E	NT		N	EST

PUZZLE 426

Hope is the feeling you have that the feeling you have isn't permanent.

PUZZLE 427

C	R	O	C		I	B	I	S		M	A	S	S	E
L	I	M	O		N	A	D	A		A	L	O	H	A
A	S	E	A		A	C	E	S		N	A	D	I	R
Y	E	N	T	A		K	A	S	H	A		A	N	N
			I	L	K	S			A	G	E			
C	O	T		L	I	L	I		T	E	A	M	S	
R	A	I	D		D	I	N	N	E	R	T	I	M	E
A	T	B	A	T		D	U	O		S	E	N	O	R
W	H	I	T	E	P	E	R	C	H		R	O	T	A
	S	A	U	N	A		E	T	A	S		R	E	S
			M	A	R			U	M	P	S			
B	R	A		C	E	D	E	R		Y	E	A	S	T
R	A	B	B	I		A	C	N	E		P	U	P	A
E	C	L	A	T		S	H	A	Y		A	R	I	D
W	E	E	N	Y		H	O	L	E		L	A	T	S

PUZZLE 428

F	R	A	Y		A	S	P	S			S	E	E	D
R	A	T	E		L	E	A	K	S		L	A	C	E
A	T	O	P		L	I	C	I	T		A	C	H	E
N	I	L		R	E	N	T		A	U	T	H	O	R
C	O	L	L	E	G	E			I	R	E			
			I	V	E		F	E	R	N		B	A	T
A	M	O	K		S	T	O	P		S	L	A	S	H
G	A	M	E			R	O	E			L	I	E	U
E	Y	I	N	G		I	D	E	A		A	L	A	S
R	O	T		A	D	O	S		B	U	M			
			E	G	O			L	A	S	A	G	N	A
B	U	R	E	A	U		L	O	N	E		R	U	M
O	R	A	L		B	L	O	O	D		D	O	D	O
O	G	R	E		T	O	R	S	O		E	W	E	R
S	E	E	R			T	E	E	N		E	L	S	E

PUZZLE 429

1. Curfew, 2. Exotic, 3. Junket, 4. Quiche, 5. Option, 6. Botany, 7. Zealot, 8. Groove, 9. Radish, 10. Esteem.

PUZZLE 430

B	O	D		P	A	P		C	O	B		S	A	G
A	C	E		L	I	E		O	R	E		O	W	E
N	E	E		A	D	E		O	A	F		D	A	M
J	A	M		S	E	R	A			O	K	A	Y	S
O	N	S	E	T			D	O	D	G	E			
			W	E	E		O	V	A		G	Y	R	O
T	A	V	E	R	N		R	E	M			O	A	R
R	O	A	R		M	A	N	N	A		B	U	Z	Z
I	N	N			E	L	M		S	T	E	R	E	O
P	E	E	P		S	E	E		K	E	A			
			A	S	H	E	N			Q	U	A	F	F
E	X	A	L	T			T	H	O	U		P	R	O
A	R	C		R	O	D		O	B	I		P	E	R
V	A	N		A	P	E		N	I	L		L	A	G
E	Y	E		W	E	B		E	T	A		E	K	E

1-X, 2-P, 3-Z, 4-I, 5-M, 6-L, 7-D, 8-K, 9-Q, 10-E, 11-Y, 12-G, 13-W, 14-S, 15-V, 16-O, 17-C, 18-T, 19-F, 20-U, 21-J, 22-H, 23-R, 24-A, 25-N, 26-B.

PUZZLE 431

6-LETTER WORDS: Willow, Pardon, Tongue, Switch, Velour, Glance, Import, Garage.

4-LETTER WORDS: Lord, Swim, Urge, Gait, Glue, Wing, Anon, Race, Poll, Veto, Chow, Part.

PUZZLE 432

C	O	R	P	S		L	I	S	P		C	A	P	E
O	L	E	I	C		E	M	I	R		A	F	A	R
R	E	A	L	E	S	T	A	T	E		R	I	C	O
D	O	M	I	N	O		M	U	S	T	E	R	E	D
			N	E	W	T		P	E	R		E	R	E
S	M	U	G		S	A	C		N	U	B			
E	O	N				P	O	S	T	E	R	I	O	R
M	O	I	S	T		I	V	E		R	O	N	D	O
I	N	T	E	R	P	R	E	T				F	E	D
			A	I	R		T	U	B		T	O	S	S
A	D	S		P	I	P		P	O	P	E			
B	A	C	K	S	E	A	T		L	A	N	C	E	D
A	C	R	E		S	N	A	I	L	S	P	A	C	E
S	H	A	Y		T	E	R	M		T	I	A	R	A
H	A	M	S		S	L	O	P		A	N	N	U	L

PUZZLE 433

PUZZLE 434

E	T	C	H			S	L	A	Y		H	A	R	P
D	E	L	E		A	W	A	R	E		O	B	O	E
G	N	A	W		L	I	M	E	S		E	L	S	E
E	S	S		P	A	G	A	N		D	R	Y	E	R
R	E	P	A	I	R			A	T	E				
			S	E	M	I			A	N	S	W	E	R
F	L	A	T	S		D	I	S	C		T	A	X	I
L	O	R	E		A	L	L	O	T		A	R	I	D
U	S	E	R		S	E	L	L		T	I	N	T	S
B	E	A	N	I	E			O	D	O	R			
				V	A	T			E	A	S	I	N	G
B	A	D	L	Y		E	M	E	N	D		N	O	R
O	K	A	Y		E	P	E	E	S		O	N	T	O
L	I	R	E		B	E	L	L	E		D	E	E	S
O	N	E	S		B	E	T	S			E	R	R	S

PUZZLE 435

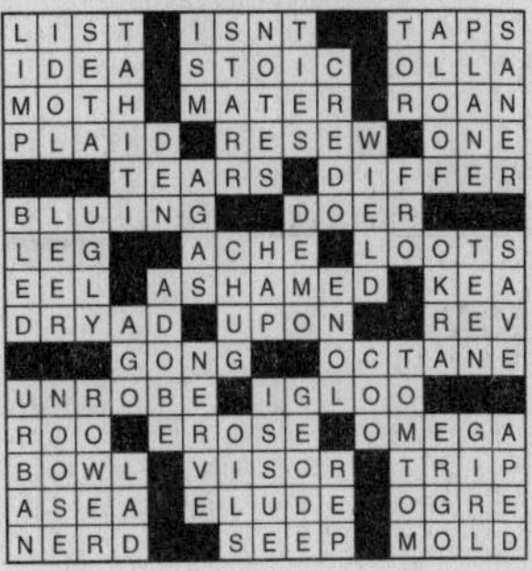

PUZZLE 436

VOTE COPE CEASE
EKES OBEY OWNED
ERAS NOPE METED
PALETTE RUB SKY
SIR KIN
BAR SOD VENEER
ADE LUGE EELED
GATOR SAX DRIVE
SPARE TREY TEE
TRASHY DUG ELM
LIE MAP
AIR SPA IMPULSE
SCOUT MIDI RANG
POSSE MOLE SWIG
SNEER ONER ENTS

PUZZLE 437

PANS SPAT SACKS
UPON HIKE CRANE
MENU REIN REPEL
PROF URN WEASEL
FAN PEA
SAT SKI ADMIRAL
CLINK SWIG NOSE
ALTO GLARE FATE
BOLT RAGE LOSER
SWEETEN DIE TRY
RED SIR
RACKET YES ICED
ARENA LUAU LAVA
PILOT ELSE EKED
SALTY DEED YENS

PUZZLE 438

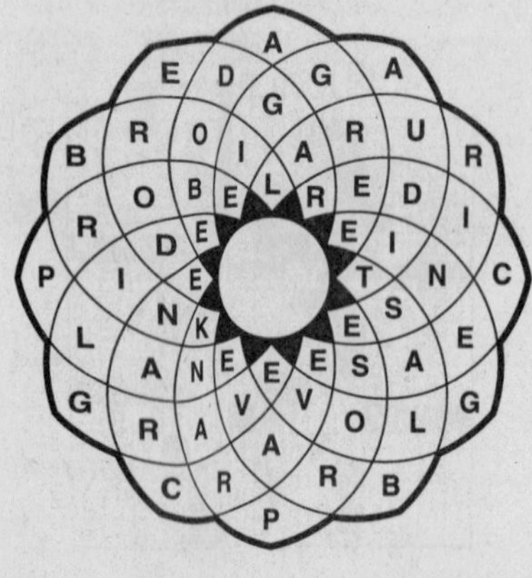

PUZZLE 439

SPAT MAR ALAS
TORE TOKEN DEBT
ALEE ALIVE DARE
BEAT DENIES DOE
HAS ERE EAR
MARES VOW LEND
EWE PAIL ILL
LEFT REIGN LAMA
ASK VENT POI
MENU JET OUTER
SON PRO ANT
POD SALTED MASK
IRIS STALE OBOE
RENT PECKS SLOP
EDGY DOS TENT

PUZZLE 440

STARS ORAL ELSE
TULIP BEVY AEON
ANEAR OVERDRAFT
GESTURE SEE PAR
ACE MOSSY
LESSENS NOON
OAT DEWLAP TADS
USES WEAVE OLEO
TYPO APPEND ALL
PELT LAYERED
SPASM INS
TIN IRK TRACTOR
EXISTENCE MAUDE
TIME DOUR ORBIT
SEAT STEM SPACE

PUZZLE 441

GALA BROW FLU
ORAL BEANIE RAN
AMMO ALIENS AND
TYPO GIN SAUCE
FREES SADDER
COD ELF MAYO
ABASES VEX REVS
LOYAL SIT LEGIT
MESS DIM PAROLE
SLIP REC SEW
SCREEN PINED
CRUDE ION EATS
AID ROTATE ALIT
LED YAWNED LORE
PRY FOOD TEEM

PUZZLE 442

AROMA CAPS RATS
RERAN OGRE ECRU
EVENT NOON FREE
AIRS STREET
HAG ATE EWE
HOPE BRA DISCO
UMP BURP CHAPS
FEE TIC IRE GEL
FRAME TUNA ERA
SLING PEN GRAY
ROE SAG ESS
SAFARI PEEN
CRAG STEP ATLAS
AIDE HULL SLANT
MASS AXLE TEDDY

PUZZLE 443

WALE ACORN LAMB
AXIL LANAI ARIA
SEEM ENTICEMENT
PLUSH CODER NIT
ICE ARTSY
APE FOLKTALE
PRELIM EON BUSH
SOLE MOLES ANTI
EAST OWL WORDED
HONEYDEW OPE
INDEX URN
VIA EYERS SOGGY
INCINERATE ALOE
ETHS ANGEL TEAL
SHAM HEEDS SELL

PUZZLE 444

CLOP SPAS BRED
HOUR SLUSH LURE
UNTO HORSESENSE
MESS OWE TESTS
PAD EDGED
ESSES ROASTS
FLECKS LARD RHO
TART MAYBE SAID
SKI LOPE DOCILE
EFFETE FALLS
AVERY OFT
PADRE EGG TABS
ENAMELWARE EXIT
TOME AERIE RILE
SAND BEND SLEW

PUZZLE 445

SAWS RACE ASPS
ORAL IDOLS SPUN
FIDO DENSE HERE
TASTE DEEP CEE
HASTE RAKER
NEWSROOM DOT
AGO TRANCE ETCH
NOR HES HER ALE
ASEA STRIDE LAW
GUT EMERALDS
ACHES CEDAR
LAY EDGY NICER
OBEY ARCED SODA
NINE DALLY EMIT
GNAT DELE SETS

PUZZLE 446

LOW SCAN AFRO KILN
TOTO HARI CRAB ELEE
AUTOMATIC TACO NEST
IDA ERASER NEEDY
NEW TELE OUCH OAKEN
TRAP ONION OWN ATE
HANG OFA RAN TED
HAIRDO ADE ESSAY
ABRADE RIDDLE ALOT
LEES SPAN WISP POUR
OLDE OBEYED OPPOSE
DRAWS ALE GRITTY
FLO OWE OWL NOON
BOW MER ENSUE GASH
ISSUE HIRE NAVE STA
BOSOM DIETED PET
BONO PUPS OVERDRIVE
AREA USER TESS ORES
HOOT DELI ANTE TEN

PUZZLE 447

SPAT EGGY SLAP
EACH DOLES HALO
LIRE GREAT UNTO
FREEREIN REDCAP
EONS ELDERS
BRA LUG FAME
RUSSET GEM RODS
ADEPT WAD PEKOE
TEAR PRY MADAME
EELY BAY YEN
PAPAYA MUSE
EVADES ANCESTOR
SOLE MANIA POPE
TIER ARDOR AGED
ODDS MYNA NONO

PUZZLE 448

CRAG RAMS SEMI
LOCO ELOPE OXEN
EARN DELAY PILL
FREEZE TREY SEE
OARS OCTET
TADPOLE SOUL
OVER SNAP ALAS
SOLO STILT MICA
SWIM HULA PEEN
PREP MEASURE
PLATE KIND
LOT VETO ADJUST
AGOG LYRIC ONCE
NONE SPENT STAR
KNEE OAKS HORN

PUZZLE 449

SWAB OHMS TOSS BASK
LILA PAIL RANI ILKA
ASIN INCA AKIN TAIL
THEKINGANDI PASTIME
ERE STILL ICE
CHARADE VEES URGES
HEIST CABARET TSARS
AID EERIE SRA TWIST
DRAB DULLY RELENTS
LAG SLEEP LEE
DEMOTED STEAL TRAM
ODIST ITS ASSET OWE
DENSE CAMELOT UPSET
ONION ERAL ACTRESS
MDS TRADE ATE
FLOTSAM THEMUSICMAN
LOKI LAME GIRT EYRE
ADAM OTIS ALSO DREW
KEYE NEXT SEAR EAST

PUZZLE 450

CURB CHOW DOTS
ASEA LLAMA ABUT
PAIR EAVED LOBE
EGG CAMEL LEAP
RENTED NEWSY
WEED TAM SAP
DELI NUT SUBTLE
APACE BID GREEN
SEWERS CAN OWED
HES AIR DISK
ASTIR NIECES
SHIN TALES AXE
TACT AUDIT GRIN
ALES RAINY EELS
GORY CLOT TREE

PUZZLE 451

SNIPE GIST WORE
LORAN ANTI EPEE
ATOLL SPIRITUAL
TEN ASSURED SPY
CRUET DEB
DAMAGED SLALOM
OMELET DAY AVER
DOLOR YUP WRITE
ONER CEE TANNED
GEISHA THREERS
EWE NEEDY
PAS ADVISER BRA
ATTENDANT OLEIC
COOL ALOE BERLE
AMPS REND EGGED

PUZZLE 452

JUICE ADOS ASS
ENCORE BAKE TWO
STOWED LYRE TOW
TON CUTE ADMIRE
ITCH ICED
ALTO ARC BID
LION TOO AVIDLY
ELF LIBRARY YEA
STUDIO EGO TEAK
EEN DAM ASPS
PONE TEMP
LOADED METE SPA
EMS KIWI EMCEED
APT EVEN ROAMED
THY DEBT SPINS

PUZZLE 453

SEAR RAT SPIT
ONCE BESET EASY
AVID LASSO MILK
ROD TAD TRAINEE
SYSTEM PEND
WEEDER SCRAP
REMINDED LORE
OVENS WAG LOBES
WINE LOVESEAT
SLUSH DEBATE
USED CUTEST
SHERBET NAP AIR
COLA EATEN OGRE
ABLY SCOOT ALEE
BOSS HEN FEDS

PUZZLE 454

STAG LAMA AWASH
TARO ERAL SOCKO
UTES TELEPHONED
BASSO NEER DEWS
IDEA ISM
LOPER IMPEACH
GOT IRED INTRO
OUT SKILLET TAW
APEAK SMEW IFS
DERRICK ENACT
GNU ARIL
CLOY ROOT BLARE
HULLABALOO IBIS
ISLET SELL ELAN
PHASE TOLD DELE

PUZZLE 455

CAMS PEA ACER
OLEO MIDGE COPE
MESS ANILS TREE
BEHOLD TOT IRED
ICE WETNESS
DISPLACE ERGS
ONTO PLASMA PRO
SCRIP ASP PROUD
SHE ARTELS UNDO
ARIA LAVENDER
AMMONIA YEW
POLL SIR LESSER
ARIL EDICT CAPO
CANE REVUE ARID
EYER REP RICE

PUZZLE 456

ALBS BOBS AFAR
TIRE ALLOT NOSY
TAUT LIONS TOKE
INN PLOW HEEL
CATTLE SPIN PAP
IOTA ORDERLY
ABLY BATT DOER
ACRES SPA ADORE
CHAR PUTT RIFT
MESSIER OGEE
ESS CEDE UNSURE
BAER LUST SEX
OVAL EMIRS LULU
FINE DODGE ARID
FADE BEET BYTE

PUZZLE 457

AMP LAD JIB JOT
COO ALE ERA EGO
TOT PILOTED SLY
ORAL VIA GATES
RETAPE FEVER
DOZE POSTMAN
ERE BID SIDE
PAL QUACK DEW
ASEA URN ASP
SHINDIG PACT
TEPEE WALRUS
HAVEN LYE MAXI
ORE TOFFEES YET
PIE EWE APE ODE
EAR DEE RYE NOD

1-R, 2-U, 3-H, 4-W, 5-L, 6-Q, 7-O, 8-M, 9-X, 10-C, 11-P, 12-G, 13-F, 14-K, 15-I, 16-B, 17-N, 18-D, 19-T, 20-S, 21-Y, 22-Z, 23-J, 24-A, 25-V, 26-E.

PUZZLE 458

GASH GALS ANT TAME
ANTI RIATA SEE ERAL
SKID ERROR PAM NILS
SLEEVE IOTA PADDLE
YES IDEAL CAMEL
LILTS CLARO SHE
MER LEE YEOMAN TOV
AVE ARCH ASTA GLARE
DEFOG TUSKS URAL
IVE SEC EFT CAT
CONE RIDER HULKS
OPERA HOAR YULE EEL
OAR STEPPE DEE DAY
PLY SYRUP LOGOS
EROSE ARETE AGE
SONATA DATA ASYLUM
OVEN NAB NICER OLIO
DUNE TOO ISLED LIST
SMEW SKY HERS KNEE

PUZZLE 459

EMUS TIME APING
LIKE OBEY RADAR
FLEA WIRE CRONE
WONDERS SLAW
SPEW CEE
SIRENS STRADDLE
PLOD TOPHAT EEL
RIP REVIEWS CAD
ACE AWAKEN SAFE
TALLTALE YONDER
OER FEED
GANG DINETTE
ADAGE COKE ZIPS
MISER ODES ERAL
STARE NESS DENY

PUZZLE 460

HYSTERICAL

PUZZLE 461

OLEO BLAT ISM SAINT
BEAT EAVE RHO ABNER
OAST ROOTBEER SEINE
ENTERS WHO ETCH TEE
ROE SEX TAHINI
BURSARS REB LIMEADE
EGO SKEWERED TITLED
GLOAT RAD DISC LAG
SYMMETRY DEPTH PYRE
IDEA SAW EASE
BIRD STRAY ARTERIAL
ATE TEEN SRI ATRIA
GELATI DEBACLES INS
SMASHES RET ENLISTS
THESES RIA GUN
SKI ITCH RAF IGNITE
WIVES ROTATION ACRE
ALERT EVA ERNE TOOL
NOSES TEN DEES ENDS

PUZZLE 462

L	AID		MO	VE		DE	AN			DE	FLA	TE
IMP	E	DI	ME	NT		CAN	TE	EN		VI	T	AL
		CE	NT	I	ME	TER		DU	BI	OUS		
PO	SE			LA	RGE		BA	RE	ST		ST	ELE
INT	ER	RO	GA	TE		BO	LD		RO	ST	RU	M
		TI	LE		DE	SS	ER	T		AR	D	ENT
	MA	SS		RI	CE		DA	UB		G	EL	
BAR	T	ER		SK	IT	TI	SH		CR	AZE		
RE	TR	IE	VE		FU	ME		FR	AG	R	AN	CE
L	ESS		NE	WE	L		TH	US			TI	DE
		LIB	ER	AL		SED	EN	T	AR	Y		
FE	DO	RA		TH	RO	AT		RA	TI	ON	ALI	ZE
AR	TE	RY			TOR	E		TE	ST		VE	ST

PUZZLE 463

SLIT CLAP HUMPS
KUDU YORE APEAK
ITER BOOK WITTY
TEAM OSIERS
OARED EERIE
EDGING TRENDS
REELS PROA PLIE
ICY ASSUAGE ABA
EAST AINT TRILL
SNEAKY ANODES
TRUES BASAL
EOSINS LOSE
ADORN ALOE IOTA
DONEE BELT CZAR
STEER USES KEYS

PUZZLE 464

REAP CARP SPAR ACHE
ORCA ODOR CODE NOEL
AGES LOMA ROUT IRIS
MOSTHAPPYFELLA DARE
ANT ERE TIRE
BEHIND CROCK LEAFED
OPAL EGO HEP FLORA
SILL RURAL YAK HOOT
SCOUT TATER REPULSE
SEE LOVER GIS
MORTALS MENUS ABASH
ALAR SOB ROSES ALOE
ALIAS OAF TAP NEAR
MANTAS ARABY ADDERS
EGAD ERA ARE
WILD SWEETTALKINGUY
EDAM HELD HILL ELLE
ALMA ELKO ERIE TUNA
KEEN STEM DEER SEAR

PUZZLE 465

LABYRINTHASANAS
AGREENERONEGATE
VIEWSNOOPYWRITE
ELATIONUPHEAVAL
NEDINCABEARDERA
DREDGECARDBOARD
EASELNODOARENID
REATATROGLODYTE
POURSUNRISERAUL
ALTOSPROVOAURAE
DEEMADEPESTGULP
BARBRAMARHANNAH
ENROOTAQUADONNA
ETONMENUEVEPENN
REREADSERENERAT

PUZZLE 466

SCRAM OLAF LOSER ANET
OHARE BILL ISTLE CITE
DAVIDCOPPERFIELD ACHE
AWE IRE TATER DEDHAM
SAY COCKEREL LIONS
RIANT DASHER IDEAL
UNTIE OTHER DATUM AHA
PLAT SMEAR PORTGIBSON
EEL SOBS MOGUL ANON
ETE CUE BIREME GLIDE
OTARY POLES DORIC
OFFER ASIANS OBI KGB
ROTE NOOSE DRIP LEO
DOWNANDOUT SKIRT RENO
OTO CASTS LANAI TUBER
COMBO RETORT ABYSS
SHIRE NATIVITY OLE
POTASH DATER PAL SPA
OTIC OLDCURIOSITYSHOP
KEEL SAUNA SNIP HOUSE
ELSE TYPAL TETE OWNED

PUZZLE 467

JAR DAS ANN
ALUM HOME CEO
MINI OUTLINES
OLDER ENEMY
ETUDE EST
ART ANEW OSS
RIO RATES HAM
GNU DART OLA
NRA AROSE
SPADE MANET
OUTOFGAS SOOT
APO IOTA TUNA
PAM TOE TEN

PUZZLE 468

ASE GAFF ASPS
DOS AQUA PLOT
DRAGBUNT TALE
STIR IDES MOP
EAVE ODD
OFFERED CAUSE
PORTER SINNED
PREEN STACKED
ERA ERLE
ARK SALE RAMS
PAIN SLAPSHOT
ONCE HEMI OLE
PIKE ERSE YEW

PUZZLE 469

BAROQUE KNEAD
A O U A A X U
LIANA GAZETTE
S S L E O R
APT MARJORAM
L V H I A O
TAXI ELF SEGO
I E A F H U
NOWADAYS ELM
P R N P L O
PATTERN REBUS
A I T A A O E
CACHE LAYAWAY

1-H, 2-I, 3-W, 4-V, 5-S, 6-B, 7-C, 8-U, 9-N, 10-K, 11-A, 12-F, 13-Y, 14-Z, 15-M, 16-X, 17-D, 18-P, 19-E, 20-G, 21-Q, 22-L, 23-O, 24-T, 25-J, 26-R.

PUZZLE 470

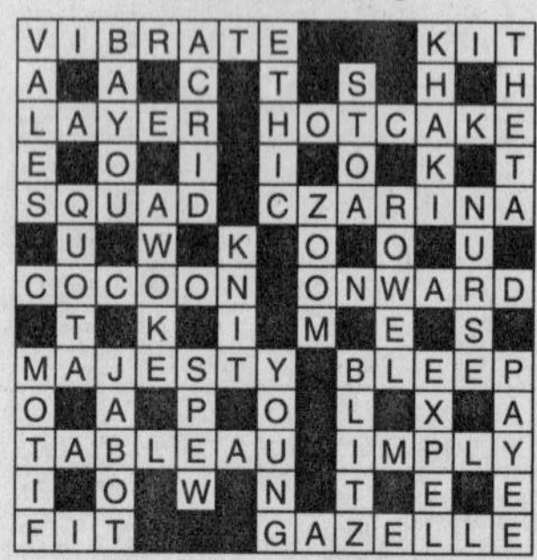

VIBRATE KIT
A A C T S H H
LAYER HOTCAKE
E O I I O K T
SQUAD CZARINA
U W K O O U
COCOON ONWARD
T K I M E S
MAJESTY BLEEP
O A P O L X A
TABLEAU IMPLY
I O W N T E E
FIT GAZELLE

1-U, 2-G, 3-J, 4-X, 5-H, 6-S, 7-P, 8-N, 9-F, 10-Z, 11-Q, 12-E, 13-L, 14-A, 15-B, 16-R, 17-V, 18-W, 19-K, 20-O, 21-C, 22-Y, 23-D, 24-I, 25-M, 26-T.

PUZZLE 471

WAFT PROD SERF
HERO REDID EVIL
IRAN EROSE MESA
SINGULAR UNISEX
TEC MAN ICE
APT WREN BAD
EFTS ECHO ELATE
DRAT ION ETON
GENII TOYS ESPY
YES BEEP ILK
END PLY BAA
DELUXE QUEEREST
ASIS MOURN ALIT
MANE YEAST CODA
SUES RYES EWER

PUZZLE 472

Splash, Suntan, Float, Raft, Bucket, Lifeguard, Flippers.

SIXTH COLUMN DOWN: Snorkel

PUZZLE 473

SPAS BOP TAB ABBESS
LISP ABE ELA LOATHE
ETNA SOLOMON TINCAN
WHENTHEEXPECTANT
SYRIA YET ORGANIC
EXITS RIOT OMEGA
ENGLISHTEACHER VOW
GEE SMEAR SMOTHERS
AVON IRONS AVER
DELIVEREDHERGRAMMAR
ONEL ELGAR SODA
VEGETATE EVICT REN
ICI LECTURESHEWENT
SUSHI MOOR STENO
EATENUP RAM EERIE
INTOCONTRACTIONS
ARAFAT ANIMATE STAT
DELETE STU JON MOLE
SOARER TOM APT ERLE

PUZZLE 474

ADAM ERAT MASC TOBE
VANE LOSE ALMA ERIC
IDEA VOTE OVERNEATH
DOWNRISING ALTO LEO
ORT AIL TERI
REMUDA IGLOO DINNER
ELAN STE NUT ABODE
AMIDE PER DRAB URIS
LONESTAR BOSSY IMET
REAR RUN SELL
ARAB SKEET RESIDENT
CATO KLEE MIL TILER
ETTAS ELF AMS NILE
DEARTH SENNA SEGALS
DOER DUD SOL
PAS MAES BOTTOMSOIL
UPHEARTED LION ETRE
LIEN TRAY INRE ETAS
ENDS HOTE NEER MOST

PUZZLE 475

TOGA MRS AGAR MERE
ARAL SAIC VALE AVID
NEIL THOR EGAD LIMO
GOTOSEA EON REGAL
YELLOWSUBMARINE
DIESEL WYLER LOSERS
ADO PALO OSAR ESNE
DASH RISE DEMO SSW
OHIO ESTES PART
ONLYANORTHERNSONG
EIRE ECOLE GIRL
AME PIER ELSA OGEE
NEMO SOFT ESSE EAT
TOPPED CLAIR STARTS
WHENIMSIXTYFOUR
ANGLE RIA ORIGINS
SATE LAST LILT ODEA
PAIR ERIE ISIS SELF
ARCS RAND AMO YALE

PUZZLE 476

HEATHENS PERSIA
U G O O V A N
GREATDANE EXTRA
E N H H L N E L
LOTION MENTALLY
Y U M P S L S
MUSTACHE MIMI
E O E R A S T S
TAUT BARNACLE
C S L T T A H
EYESIGHT ARMADA
T T B O R C S N
EARLY NOURISHED
R A A T E L
ALPINE CHEYENNE

PUZZLE 477

GALL APSE TABS MOORED
ASIA COIL OLLA ACROSS
SHEPHERDSCROOK NUBBED
SETTLER OBI GLIB
JUVENILE OAFS TRITEST
ASE ICY ANIL SRO SRTA
PERSE EMILY NOVA BYE
ESAU GLEAN PATELLA
FURORS PARTS LARCH
SHINER IONIC CUPOLA
TAU REDRIDINGHOOD NUT
AFGHAN IRENE PLEASE
NEGEV WAIST BLUEST
EYELETS LOESS TEAS
PER LANA PHASE HUTCH
ELMS MDS TAMS HAY ARE
PLUNGES SODA PILEATED
GOON GAL RAINING
RAGOUT ONEARMEDBANDIT
SLEDGE ATMS ETUI EIRE
VERSED DAYS SASS SPED

PUZZLE 478

STOPS ATTICA PITAPAT
SQUARE CHORUS STOWAGE
CUSTOM EATERS AERATOR
RICHLITTLE BILLMOYERS
ERASE RAIDS GUMS NAE
EEN DATA TANKS OTTER
ERODE WORSE FAR
MODULE PERU SAFARIS
FONDLE CODYBANKS CENT
ELSIE HOSS AWAIT ECHO
RITE WOVE ADES YEAR
REAM INERT EKES AGILE
ERGO RONSILVER CLOVES
TEENIER GOES COOLED
END OPENS SHOED
MARYS SNORE ALES SHE
ANI AUTO RAMIE SAMOA
TIPPERGORE BUCKROGERS
EMPORIA EXCISE ABRADE
RALLIER SPADER PEERED
SLEEKLY TOWERS TRESS

PUZZLE 479

SE CTA LT E R
SO N I CAR D OR
I D OLMA KES
MI LE TE N SE
RETA INHEA TED
EG I STEEPLEASE
NAS T Y REEV E
SLO TS CRE AM
SLA VE FAI LS
LINEN RANG E S
S NORTI C ON S
PO WERAER IE
TO REN ORAL P
AP SE SU LK Y
N ET S E A T

PUZZLE 480

CLEM SPAR CLASP ABODE
RIVE HALE AORTA FACES
EVEN ALAN BASINSTREET
PERT VESTS FORTH BARE
ENGINES OWENS OPENER
LOON MOWER PROD
SWANS CODED SPOTS DER
TAD HARPERSFERRY CAME
AGED PEST LEEK BRUIN
RESISTS SCRAPS BAUBLE
VOLTA AIR SALEM
PAPERY COPPED MARBLES
OHARA WIFE EGAN SOLE
LOGS SANFRANCISCO UKE
LYE BANGS BOORS BRISK
DALE MERYL PIES
ARDENT SKIDS SLEEVES
SHIP EMEND ELATE LINT
TICONDEROGA AWED ELSA
INERT OGLES SONG CLUB
NORTH WELSH SLOE TEES

PUZZLE 481

ASSAM PET SHOT NEWT
RHINO AXE TARO AREA
TALON TAR ALIT SLAP
MONTPELIER GATHERS
GENT ALA LIV
RAPPORT ASIDE DIVES
IDIOM LINEN ALERT
DENSE THONG GALLERY
SNEER RANG BAR ERSE
YOUNG WAGES
SHEA ASK MANE ACTOR
EARNEST PARED CHIDE
RUINS ERASE RAPID
BLEAT DUSTS ELAPSES
PEA ESE EDAM
ASSORTS PROVIDENCE
NAIL TORO LAT NEATS
ANTI AMOR IDO TINNY
TEES RENT OER OLEAN

PUZZLE 482

SNOW APT SLAB
MOPE ARRAY TAEL
OVAL SMOKE AIRE
GALLOP VIA IRIS
ASHEN INSET
BLINK ORGAN
AIDE ROB TIDBIT
GROWNUP TOTALLY
SALTED DIM SULK
EERIE THESE
SHEAR AGREE
TENS DIN YANKED
ANTS ASIDE UNDO
KNEE METED TOGO
EARS DYE STEM

PUZZLE 483

PUZZLE 484

ORBS ACHE FLITS
PART LOAN LANAI
TRIO EMIT OCCUR
SEGO ELIAS ITS
PAST RISEN
ARC TESTER GELS
REOPEN OLD AROW
ESNE SATYR DADO
NODS IVE OYSTER
TWIT BIREME END
MOOLA NEWT
SHE BETAS ODOR
OUNCE IBIS NINE
ALTOS OLLA IDEA
PASTE NEED CORD

PUZZLE 485

LIST WHAT PAS
ITCH SHARES IRE
REAR POTENT ARC
AMBUSH EASY NOT
SKINS ELBOWS
MARTINI ASEA
ICE EXTENT WHIP
TRIED WON ELUDE
TENT MINUTE LOG
CHAT AERIALS
AFGHAN PLAIN
BRA RUDE METEOR
OAT PARADE ACHE
VIE SLICED CHIN
ELS SPEW TOOT

PUZZLE 486

CHIME AMPS BANS
LOCAL FOAL UNIT
OMENS RULE IDLY
NABS TAR EEL
EGO VEIN TATTER
EXCEED JET IRE
ARM BAD TEAL
APPLY VIM SUDSY
ROAM TOO JIB
CUP HEW SALARY
STATUE AMMO HOE
HEN LOB WIGS
ABLY AMOK MINUS
FROM GONE ADORE
TAPE EWER RESTS

PUZZLE 487

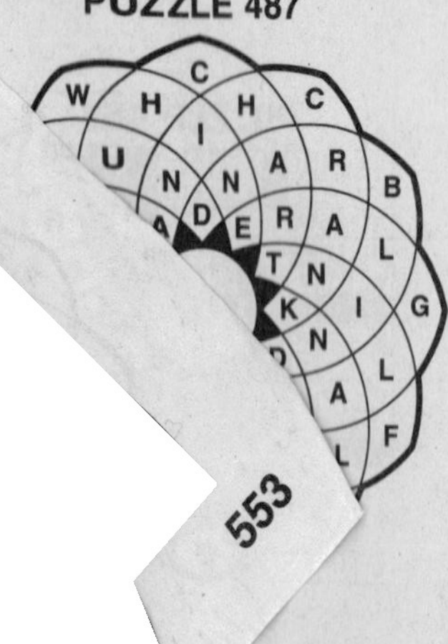

PUZZLE 488

ALP EDGE ESS
POE ARIL FRIAR
SINGASONG LENTO
ENE REP STA GET
AGREE RICA
MASS HAROLD
ALFS ALOE TOUR
RIO NEWER NAY
ELLE DELE OGLE
SKATES SEMI
STEP ELVES
UFO PAS APT EGO
SINCE LOVESONGS
ARGUE ALEE RUE
ESE PERP RED

PUZZLE 489

POOL PSS STOP
AGUA SLOW TOLET
SLID AIDA EMILE
TEDDYBEAR EMOTE
ERASER DALY
AERY REGALE
SERBS HOCK URIS
TRAIT UDO SNEAK
ANIL OMEN TSARS
YELLOW LENO
YULE ORANGE
ELECT BOBBYPINS
WELLS OVAL PEON
ENSUE LESE ACME
DEBT IRK LEES

PUZZLE 490

ARTE ADAPT CHUM
RAIN NICHE IONA
THECONVERSATION
ONO ATTY
SPIRE HOSEA BSA
TUNE AILED ORAL
ASH BLED ANODE
HESAIDSHESAID
CURED TIAS LEI
OPIE WREST DENT
SST PIERS HORSE
SETS MAC
LOOKWHOSTALKING
BALI ELROY EVIE
STEM RESTS TENT

PUZZLE 491

LOPE PLANE NORA
ODAY RESET IDOL
FINETOOTHEDCOMB
TESLA SIR OKRAS
ERA RUBLE
SCUTTLE ALLAYS
IRT ALLOWS ESAI
LETONESHAIRDOWN
APEX GEMINI NNE
SERAPE FEYNESS
LODES TAE
OASIS LAG DRAFT
BRUSHWITHTHELAW
ILIE ADIEU IOTA
TOTS DENEB DEES

PUZZLE 492

CHER PLAT HESSE PEEL
LOBE IOTA ETHEL BADGE
ONBLUEBERRYHILL AREAS
DESERT NEE ARF GNARLS
ANY SANK QUAD
ETAS SAPID TUNNELS
REBEC ARADA CHINA AER
IRISH LACET ORE REUNE
END ERASE EMMET ERROL
SSE REM WOES APIARY
ARAISININTHESUN
ESSAYS EDIT LIB TOG
ACERB RALPH IDEAL RUE
RAVEL OLE JASON IRATE
PRE OILER ULEMA CEDES
PRESSER DARES PERE
OSLO GUYS SAL
CRUSOE HOT KEY ACACIA
MINIM MARTHASVINEYARD
VEINS ALGER PEKE EVOE
INXS DOERS YSER DENS

PUZZLE 493

SIRE AHAB PLOT MALE
EGAD GIBE LOGO AMOS
CORIANDER ARROWROOT
TREBLE DEFINE RINSE
LEST TUNE RINGER
ALTER RUSE BASE
MOA TOUR LATEST ALB
PURR WENT SOAP PLEA
STROBE SISTER MILER
AMASS CEO SLAVS
ORGAN MAKERS ADOPTS
LOON FILL SITS TIME
DEN DUTIES DISC CEE
YORE HEEL UPEND
MAVENS CLOD LARA
AVIAN CRITIC MILLET
SASSAFRAS CHAMOMILE
KITT RANT TADA EVAS
SLAY AGES SPAN REMS

PUZZLE 494

TEEM ABEL MALT FLAG
ALLA BOLA OLOR RILL
LION SWAN NANA OTTO
CANDLEINTHEWIND TOW
AONE EAT SEAL
TNT ART REFEREED
EMCEE PIN LIVE AJAR
MAR EAR LACER ERA
SHORTER METER PLANT
COOL SEVER TEEN
ATONE DETER CHANNEL
LAD RIVAL BAY IRA
ARID EVEL FAR SWEEP
SALESMAN GIN SPA
ELKE RAE SEAN
HER IMSTILLSTANDING
ATOM BARN DEAN EVAN
INCA ENOS ERIC RATA
RAKE RETE RARE SNOW

PUZZLE 495

BODE MELS ALTO ITCH
ARIL ANOA LEAP SHOE
LEADSADOGSLIFE MERE
ELLEN NET TRY CAD
RACE SUNS AIDA
LOW ROLL BALD PUTTS
ASH LEMON GOES DIRE
SLIM DEVIL TALE NEE
HOTEL RELET DONATED
ELAN REVEL POSH
CHEDDAR SENOR SIEGE
HAL SPIT ROSES SHAD
ALES ENID RENAL ATE
ROPED DEEM SERE TEN
HART DEAR WING
IDA YAM RIP TIARA
RANT HOLDYOURHORSES
ONTO OLEO TRUE LINT
NEST EDGE SEEM SADA

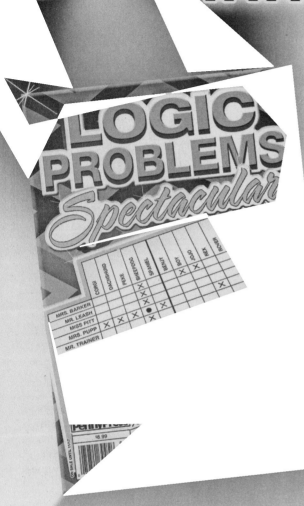

PUZZLE 496

CARP KITS CRO BALI
ASEA AMEN HAD SUMAC
THEPURPLESAGE TRACE
SEDATE ELLE CANTER
YEN TREK MIRE
COLAS GREW ARTDECO
ALAS FOOD CHIC MOB
SIP RAND MEADE LIDO
HOSTILE RILL PURSE
SCARLETLETTER
SARAH EERO ARRESTS
EVER CRAVE BLOT TAP
MOE AONE SOOT BANE
INKPOTS SPAN LUNGE
OBEY MORT EON
SPATES TERI DUNDEE
TARAS GREENMANSIONS
ELITE EOS GINA EDIT
REDO EYE SANS SODA

PUZZLE 497

FIGS SITAR DEEDS ARIA
ARLO OCALA ERROL TANG
COUNTBASIE FANNYBRICE
ENE HENS FESS RANA
ARTE PINE SLAM
AFAR MARS STEEPENS
HERE ETHELMERMAN DII
ORES THOR AERO ADEN
DID SHAVER STATS DICK
SEAPLANE OUTER CLEE
SLANT MUTED ETHIC
STUB BASER SARABAND
SCAM ALONE NEATER NEO
ERIE NERO MAES STAG
WAR GEORGEBURNS TORE
SPELLERS AVES CARS
AILS TMEN PAPA
SAGA MEIN IGOR APT
JEROMEKERN COLEPORTER
OLEO LEASE IRENE TARE
ELAN SATES CASTS EPEE

PUZZLE 498

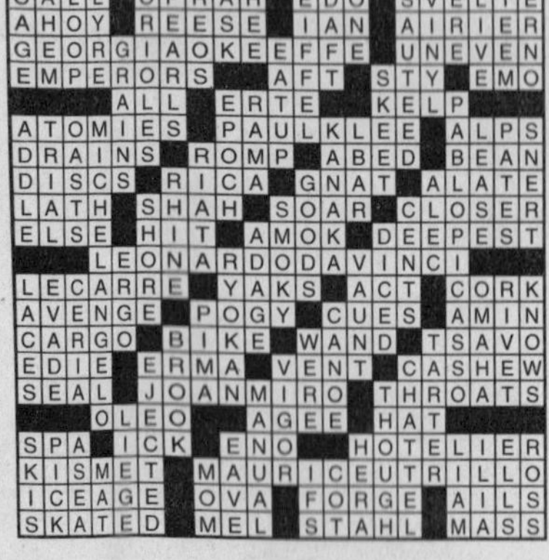

PUZZLE 499

PUZZLE 500

SEMI COT SCAR
COLOR MOVE CHIEFS
CANAPE IDEA RAMBLER
ABATE TSAR DIP EASEL
STARE PASS CAB ALPACA
HER DWELT PALEST SMOG
OREG AREA ARE ALE ENS
ESTEEM STAND SCALE
TAPE END MASSAGED
ADD TURF TAMER NAMED
ROOM MARIE EXAMS DIME
KOREA ONSET NOTE TON
MASSLESS RAM TROY
HEATH VALID ONEIDA
MUD ADO LAS SELL STAG
OTIS ENCASE SMELT EVE
STOLEN OWE SPOT ACRID
SEDAN URN OPEN BLOAT
RETAINS EVEN CLEATS
SECEDE VENT OUNCE
TRET AND BETH

PUZZLE 501

ERR PEG SST
VEE AGO NOW
IMP ROB ALE
LILAC FREE
STYLES REST
LLAMA
AFRO MAMMAL
FLOW TEASE
TAP FLU DIM
ERE AIR ADO
RED REE MEN

PUZZLE 502

WEPT ERNE
EVER TROUT
BANE ARUBA
SEAMAN
DISTEND
SLAV ESTE GEL
HEWED RELAY
YIN INCA YARE
FEASTED
FAKIRS
ACUTE IOTA
POSED ARES
EWER LEEK

PUZZLE 503

PUZZLE 504

CITRUS

PUZZLE 505

ADD HIS
SEES WAG SODA
HAVOC ICY WORLD
DILL PEP ACNE
LOOSE SPIKE
AID YES
BACKS ATOMS
ADO LOP
DEPOT HYENA
TRA DIA
ATTIC APRIL
FREE REF NOON
ELMER ELF SWOOP
BEEN SKY ANTE
BED YET

PUZZLE 506

1. What goes up must come down.
2. Man cannot live by bread alone.
3. Wonders will never cease.
4. Experience is the best teacher.
5. There are two sides to every question.

PUZZLE 507

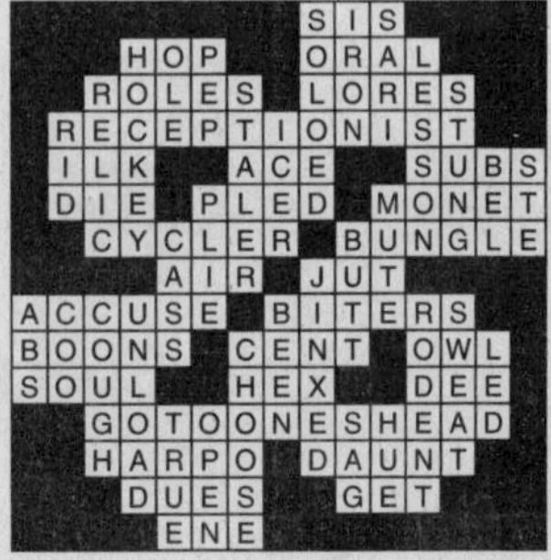

PUZZLE 508

PUZZLE 512

WINSTON CHURCHILL

PUZZLE 513

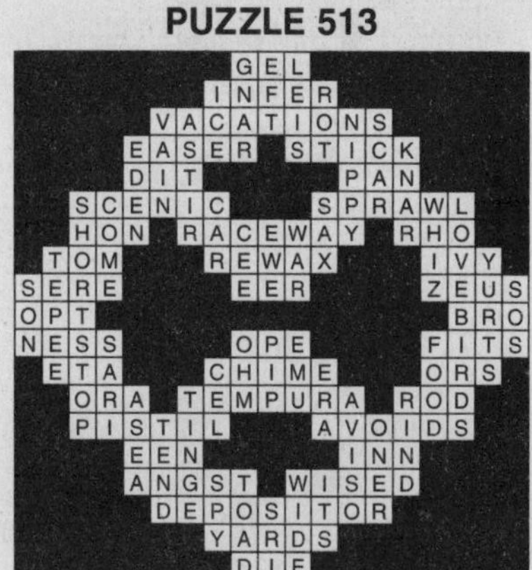

PUZZLE 516

SHAFT CODES
PONIES SOLACE
ENTRAP ENDURE
WEE PACED BUM
SODAPOP
CHATTER ASEA
AUTO DEB SHAD
PEER ERASERS
MACRAME
BAT DISCO HUM
OCELOT EUREKA
UNRIPE SNOWED
TENET TENSE

PUZZLE 509

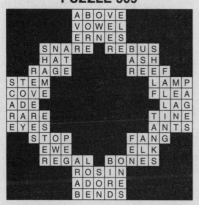

ABOVE
VOWEL
ERNES
SNARE REBUS
HAT ASH
RAGE REEF
STEM LAMP
COVE FLEA
ADE LAG
RARE TINE
EYES ANTS
STOP FANG
EWE ELK
REGAL BONES
ROSIN
ADORE
BENDS

PUZZLE 517

CAP AVA
OLE MAR
MOAT LINE
SMEE ADE SNAP
HIT DRONE AGES
EASEL BYANDBY ATTAR
ALI EASE BALI ERA
TAD ALA PAN PIN
REEFS BAMBA
BET NAY
PYLES ODIST
TIS REB INA TEA
ASI MAUL ADOG ELL
RADII SOANDSO AMPLE
ELLA SHOOK MIA
KEPT ORR HONE
AIRY MOON
RTE APT
TOO TEE

PUZZLE 514

PECS NABS
ASP DELHI IDEA
SNARE HERBAL GOAT
ATONED AIL OIL THRU
CADDYSHACK AWN FETE
TREE AGREES STIES
SRA NEE LISTER CRY
SIGN SALON SHOE
ACED ORT LOON
IRA GRIPE FOOT
MILS OAT DUEL
DENY PLOYS HES
WALK DOE OBEY
ELLS OWNER NASA
BIO ATEASE SST MAD
NEWER APACHE ROIL
PARE PAU COURTHOUSE
SERE ALL INT RUMBLE
FACE PALATE AGATE
ELAN SNORT ESS
ETNA ETTA

PUZZLE 510

HEREDITARY

PUZZLE 518

DELI EGRET ACHE
ICON BLARE BRAY
SHUT BARON BORE
CODED RED EWER
ROPE ESPY
BRONCO HASTEN
LEIS SIGNAL ARE
ILL STREETS RAW
PIE OMELET HOST
STRIFE ELATES
SANG PRAY
ADES ADA SWANK
LUAU CURSE IRON
PAVE AGATE RIDE
SLED METAL EASE

PUZZLE 511

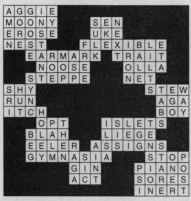

AGGIE
MOONY SEN
EROSE UKE
NEST FLEXIBLE
EARMARK TRAIT
NOOSE OLLA
STEPPE NET
SHY STEW
RUN AGA
ITCH BOY
OPT ISLETS
BLAH LIEGE
EELER ASSIGNS
GYMNASIA STOP
GIN PIANO
ACT SORES
INERT

PUZZLE 515

PARE EBB IRES
IDOL MAR DELE
LOOK PRO STOW
ARK STEAK APE
FEISTY DECKED
DEAR NETHER
FINANCE
PREPAY HARP
PRESET SUPERB
RAN SUNUP HIE
ONTO RAD MING
SCAR ESS ORCA
EELS SAY BEEN

PUZZLE 519

Bison, Sonata; Super, Per
sit, Situate; Nimbus, Bu
Tickle; Manage, Agend
Useful; Fishnet, Nettle
eral; Bestow, Toward.

PUZZLE 520

SOLE PLUS SOME
OVUM SETTO AVID
NEGOTIATED LEND
GRETA FEND INKY
EBB ROSIN
BURSAR DEAR
SUN RELATE BIG
TIC ROMANOS OFA
ELL ANSWER ILL
DEAN TUSSLE
STORM SAC
DEAL BEAD KARAT
ORCA IMPOVERISH
FINN SALSA CASE
FEET PEEL ESTE

PUZZLE 521

Brave, Worth, Crown, Index, Excel, Flick, Chase, Spiel, Robot, Igloo, Swing.

PUZZLE 522

MUST APSE RAZE
ANTE MAULS EMIR
SLENDEREST AMPS
TIN INK ALMOST
STOPS AERIE
ACT RIDICULE
GASP OPAL APEX
ARIA OASES TONE
RELY NUDE ENDS
BALANCER WAR
EELED PSALM
NABBED ERE RUE
ISLE ADOLESCENT
TEEN RIATA ONCE
SAWS GRAD NAHS

PUZZLE 523

Plan, Tore, Pail, Tern, Opal, Tier, Loan, Pert, Nail, Port, Lane, Riot.

PUZZLE 524

PUZZLE 525

DATE SCOUR BERG
IBIS HORSE OPEN
VENT EMCEE DIVA
EDGE EARLY CUR
EMIR EASEL
COSMIC SPAR
HIT LIFTER KITS
ALE DELETED COP
TYPE SIESTA OUR
WATT TWENTY
BARES MYNA
AGO ELUDE TOTS
NIGH ORATE IDOL
GLUE OGRES NONO
SEEM TENDS GREW

PUZZLE 526

ICY PAPAS AROW
ORE DEDUCT ROBE
NOT IRONER MOOR
SWINE DEVOTEE
OTTER AIR
IRIS ERA KEEPS
LINE NUDES DEAD
LOP PIN AGO
STUD STATS GRAD
STEEL TEE ALSO
BOO ERECT
AWNINGS HERON
WAIT APIECE AXE
LICE NARROW GET
SLED STERN ENS

PUZZLE 527

PAIR BALL SPOTS
ACME LIEU KAPUT
REPS ORAL INANE
ERRORS DUO SLAP
OWES PRY
ALP COD VEE CAD
BEEF MIDI AWARE
EGRET VEX MANIA
TILER AWES STAT
STY OWN NAB ASH
ADE YAWL
HULL DUB IDIOTS
UNION PLAN SURE
STENO DING EPEE
HOSED OPTS REEK

PUZZLE 528

LOBE ANTI SLASH
APES MEAT AUDIO
TADS OWNS GNARL
ELS KEG NAGGED
PAD ROBE EENS
VARIES EGO
ICEMAN YELL DEW
SEA COVETED ADE
ADD ORES CHANGE
NIT TAGGED
GLAD NOVA TEE
RIDING ALL RUN
ABOVE FLOE FORE
BERET RING LUGE
SLEDS ODES USER

PUZZLE 529

ECHO SHED CARAT
BLOW KILO ABASE
BOUNTIFUL DETER
SPREE IDLE TEAM
RAN EAVES
BASKET RIG USE
JOSH TIP LOANED
ANTIC NOT SLING
DEEPLY PUP LODE
ERR OUT BEGINS
ATLAS PIG
COMB ETCH GALLS
ADOBE TOADSTOOL
ROVES OOZE ONTO
PREYS OPEN REST

PUZZLE 530

HALOS LABS THAW
ELOPE AURA OUCH
AGATE SNAG GLEE
RAN DITTY ROAST
REC SEMI
BEARER DIG VIA
GOAD DUD LOVING
ARRAY BEG RINSE
LEERED WAD PEER
ADD AIL LOWEST
SMUG SIR
AVAST LOBES CUT
WIRE FLOE HOUSE
ALEE REST EATEN
YEAS ODES DRESS

PUZZLE 531

SEAR NAPS GLASS
LAME OPAL ROBOT
AVID VETO ABUSE
MEDDLED TAN TOP
EEL NOW
SENATE IDLERS
GAL NYLON ADAPT
AGE INN DOE
PACTS TEENY ION
STATUE REASON
PEP ARE
AFT ASS ORDERED
CLAIM WAGE SAME
HENCE ILLS AKIN
EDGER MEET WETS

PUZZLE 532

PUZZLE 533

EASED DROVE
ESTEEM TRAVEL
LEANTO EATERS
SAG ASKEW RYE
VISITED
AGAIN THRIVES
YAWL ICE KILO
EYELASH REELS
ALLEGES
EMS PANED OFT
VIOLIN RIDDLE
INLAND MAROON
LEDGE LYRES

PUZZLE 534

STAR DEBS JAM
PALE AWRY ADO
AKIN YEAR LED
RETOLD TUBA
WARD PUPIL
STANDEES REDO
NUT YACHT NOR
ANTE MARIGOLD
PAIRS FEEL
TANS WRONGS
FLU ICED BOLO
AID DALE AVID
NEE EMIR LABS

PUZZLE 535

SW	IN	E		RE	FU	SE			ME	MO
AT	TE	ND		NE	R	VE		HEA	L	TH
HE	RE		UR	GE		RE	PA	RT	EE	
	ST	EN	CH				LA	Y		
		CO	IN	CI	DE	N	CE		SL	AB
GA	LO	RE		GA	M	ES		T	ICK	ET
EA	ST		EFF	R	ON	T	E	RY		
		OP	US				VE	ST	AL	
	FUR	T	IVE	LY		C	RY		LO	AD
PI	N	ION		RI	L	ED		FA	CA	DE
PE	ACE			CAL	END	AR		DE	TE	R

PUZZLE 536

CYLINDER

PUZZLE 537

FRANC ECRU CAPS
AUDIO LEAP ABUT
SMELL SEWS GALE
USES TSETSE
LLAMA YAW EEL
GEEING SORE
OMEN ASTUTE SAP
YURTS WIN PLANE
ARY CHANGE ARTS
RINK ASSIST
ACT ABS SISSY
PLASMA BITE
PERT CHEF SPEED
LATE HALF TANGO
ERST IDLY ARSON

PUZZLE 538

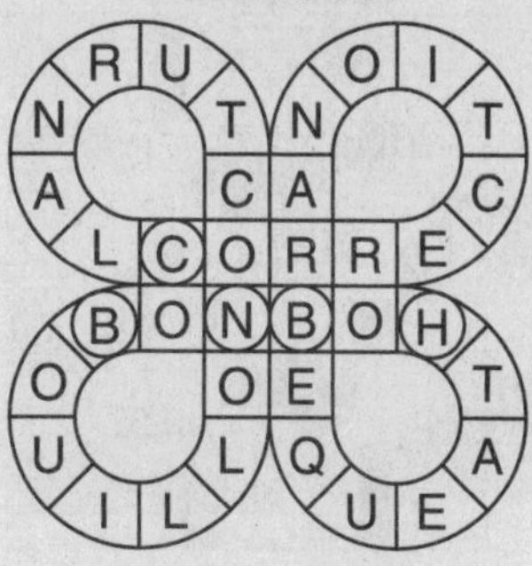

PUZZLE 539

MODE HEATS GAGS
APES ONTAP ANET
GELS MUSTY LORE
IRE RIFE SANER
CADDIE ACHE
ACRE RAW BYE
TEACH SCOUNDREL
ACME STEAL EELS
CROSSWALK LADLE
OUR OAT SEAR
DYED SCYTHE
ALPHA INKY HIS
ROLE AGREE LENT
OGEE SNEER ERGO
DEAL PURRS DEEP

PUZZLE 540

Circus, Gently, Linear, Repair, Sonnet, Voyage.

PUZZLE 541

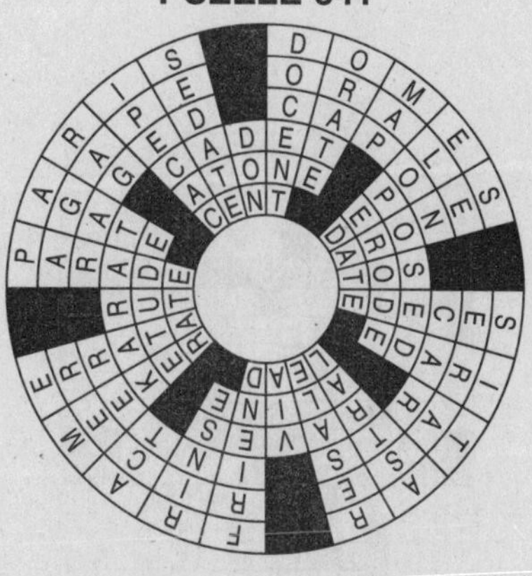

PUZZLE 542

RAJAH WASTE
ITALIC SEQUEL
DERIDE PRUNES
GEE YEA
EARN SKI EVE
BRISK ONE VIM
BIN IMAGE AXE
ESS NIL LADEN
DEE TAB FEND
OUT ELF
OPPOSE DIESEL
FROZEN SECURE
TYPED STEED

1-F, 2-T, 3-U, 4-G, 5-L, 6-V, 7-Q, 8-I, 9-R, 10-W, 11-J, 12-K, 13-S, 14-C, 15-B, 16-Y, 17-X, 18-N, 19-D, 20-A, 21-O, 22-Z, 23-M, 24-P, 25-H, 26-E

PUZZLE 543

COB QUAD WITH
AWE URGE AREA
LET ANEW XRAY
FRANC LEI
OKAY EDGER
ZEST LONG ADE
OWN EKE TIP
NEE VEES SETS
ERASE STOP
KIT MAJOR
APEX ANTI OBI
WIRE RIOT WET
LESS EXES LYE

1-L, 2-Y, 3-H, 4-U, 5-X, 6-S, 7-A, 8-G, 9-J, 10-Z, 11-I, 12-D, 13-K, 14-R, 15-C, 16-N, 17-M, 18-W, 19-F, 20-V, 21-B, 22-Q, 23-O, 24-E, 25-T, 26-P

PUZZLE 544

ASSET SHES ICON
GLARE HEAL NOVA
LIFER ONTO HOAR
ODE MOW SMELLY
WERE WEATHER
YONDER NICHE
IMPEDE RIG THAW
TOE DROOPED IRE
ELSE SIB NIECES
METER LILIES
RECYCLE SAWS
SALIVA ASP OAT
TRUE SWAM LARVA
EELS TOGA OCTET
MALT EKES TEASE

PUZZLE 545

NAPES AWLS OLD
OBEYED CHOW ROE
SLEETY NINE DUB
EEL EMERGE ITS
LODE SPAN
SHIN NAG CATS
LOUDLY REF TRUE
ALL YODELED INN
MALL NUN WALLET
PRAY GAD MAYS
BEES RUED
SPA STRAYS HOW
ILL SOUL ENOUGH
DUO ARIA RARELY
EGO YENS YESES

PUZZLE 546

PUZZLE 547

METAL AGOG SWAP
ARISE RAIL COIL
CORKS RULE RODE
ADE SKID AZALEA
WEDS IVY MOW
PACE GEOLOGY
SHRANK BOD BOO
LOONY BIB STONY
AMP MOD FOREGO
WEEKDAY NANA
EER DIM MEAL
ALLEYS ACED LIE
COIN HERE ADORE
TORE AGES WIPER
STAR LOST NEEDY

PUZZLE 551

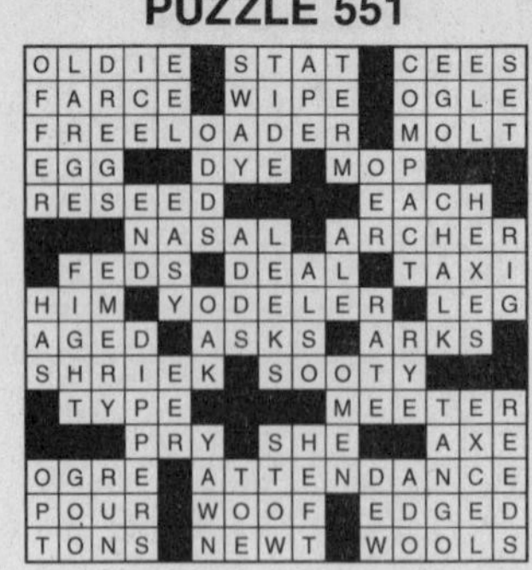

OLDIE STAT CEES
FARCE WIPE OGLE
FREELOADER MOLT
EGG DYE MOP
RESEED EACH
NASAL ARCHER
FEDS DEAL TAXI
HIM YODELER LEG
AGED ASKS ARKS
SHRIEK SOOTY
TYPE MEETER
PRY SHE AXE
OGRE ATTENDANCE
POUR WOOF EDGED
TONS NEWT WOOLS

PUZZLE 555

FILL GRAM ACID
IDEA ORATE LODE
GLAD WINED LION
HES SENT DWELLS
TREAT SPLAY
DUG LEISURE
SERENE FAST NIX
PLY RHINO ICE
USE EMIT MATTES
DESPAIR ERR
ACNED MYTHS
CHACHA IRIS ROT
RILE TOKEN DOME
ODOR EPEES OVER
CEES DESK TERN

PUZZLE 548

NEV
I I
ANTICKS
L W A A
TASKIERASES
O O T A S H
TENANTHEMMEDIUM
A I N I E S M I
ROCKERNELSONATA
E T G T V M
ROTTENEMIES
L S D E
EATENET
E A
SOS

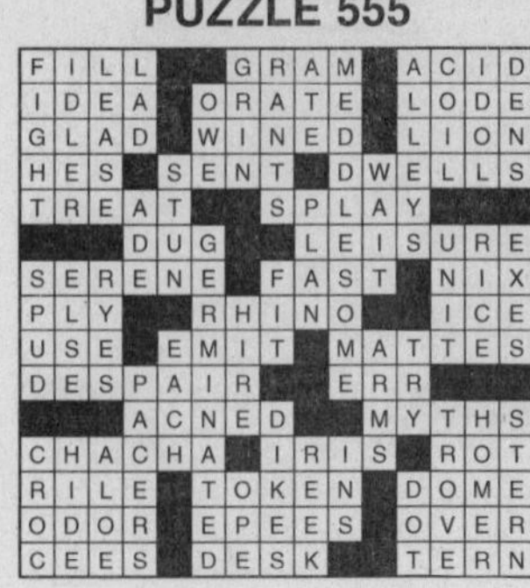

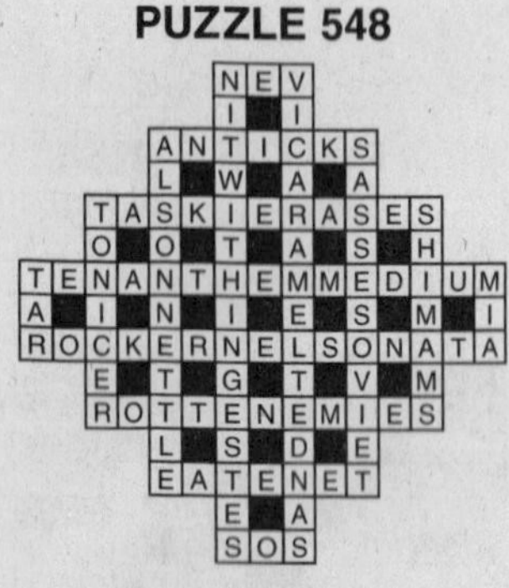

PUZZLE 552

PUZZLE 556

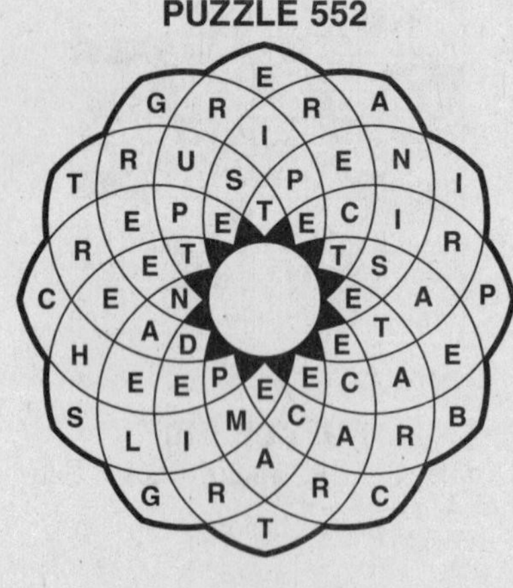

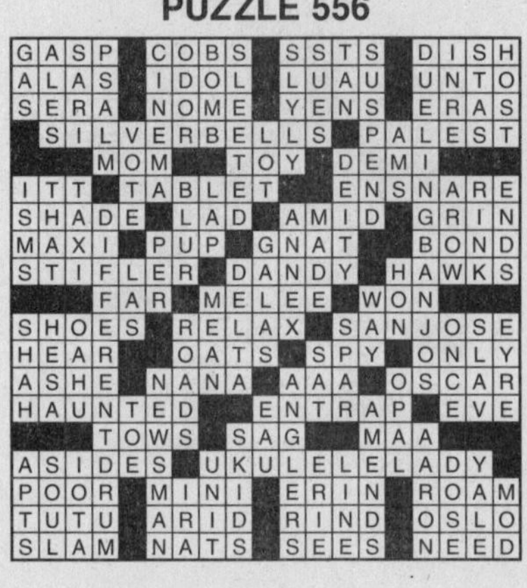

GASP COBS SSTS DISH
ALAS IDOL LUAU UNTO
SERA NOME YENS ERAS
SILVERBELLS PALEST
MOM TOY DEMI
ITT TABLET ENSNARE
SHADE LAD AMID GRIN
MAXI PUP GNAT BOND
STIFLER DANDY HAWKS
FAR MELEE WON
SHOES RELAX SANJOSE
HEAR OATS SPY ONLY
ASHE NANA AAA OSCAR
HAUNTED ENTRAP EVE
TOWS SAG MAA
ASIDES UKULELELADY
POOR MINI ERIN ROAM
TUTU ARID RIND OSLO
SLAM NATS SEES NEED

PUZZLE 549

ASH BET NEAPS
POI ARMED EERIE
ALP NOISE WRITE
CAP TOTTERS ASK
ERODED SMART
IDEA SORTED
SLOG DIM HOORAY
HOUND DUB MOUSE
UNTIED MAG PEER
NESTLE TUNE
YEARS MARKER
PAS GROUNDS AXE
AROMA SNORT BUS
PILOT ENVOY ODE
ADOBE YAP BEE

PUZZLE 553

BANANA SANG SOD
ELUDES TRIO EMU
VOTERS UMPS MEN
YES VEND SEINE
FETA FAIR
ACES BALLPARK
ASEA BALE END
SPATS VOW DELAY
HIS AWED MICE
CENSORED WICK
AHOY AJAR
CONGA ODOR MAT
ARE YAWN IMPEDE
PEW EPEE STENOS
ESS DEES THRUST

PUZZLE 557

REDS TSE PIT
AGILE ETA ORE
POPINJAYS PEN
COO LEAP
WIPE USE GYM
ADO EST AESOP
REP STOPS EVA
MAPLE OAK EEL
LYE CDS ODDS
COSH TOP
PRO POPARTIST
SAC USA TILES
INK DEN CLAP

PUZZLE 550

GASH ROAR
ARCHED ECRU
IREME TEED
E BERATE
Y LONER
WED
RE BEE
RSALS
TRAP
INNY
R
TAL
UKE
BIN
ENS

PUZZLE 554

EBBS LAPS MURAL
QUIP AMOK AROSE
UNTO NOPE INEPT
ICER DUELED
POSTMAN ERE BIO
OUTSTANDING
VENT WAS AGAR
GAVE STALE DONE
ALES HER VOTE
FURTHERMORE
FEY OER BOXCARS
TRIALS AVON
REBUT BRIT NONE
EROSE LOGE TIDE
PAPER EWER ODOR

PUZZLE 558

DONS ASH WAD
IDEA NEE ELY
NORTHSTAR SEE
ORDEAL OTTER
NOB NUB
GAS SPAS SALT
AMOS EKE KNEE
PAUL DELL KEN
TOT REE
USHER CARAFE
TIP EASTRIVER
ADA SRI GEAR
HEW SET ARTS

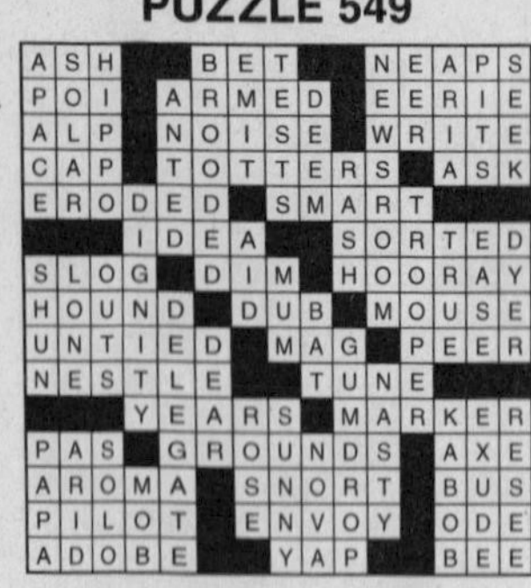

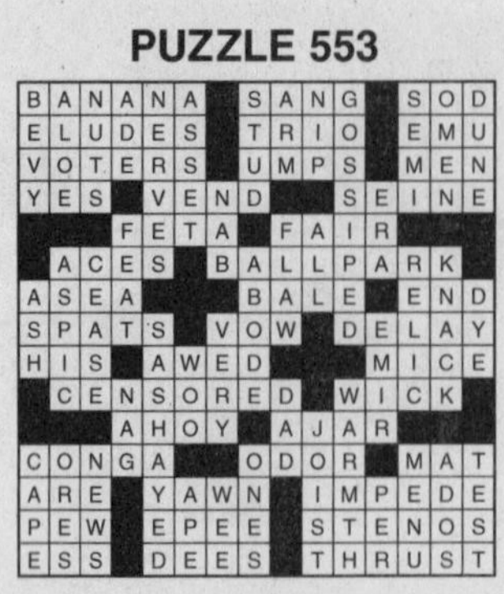

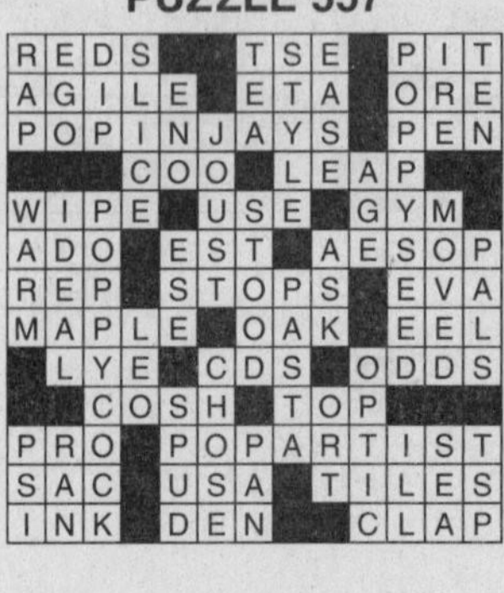

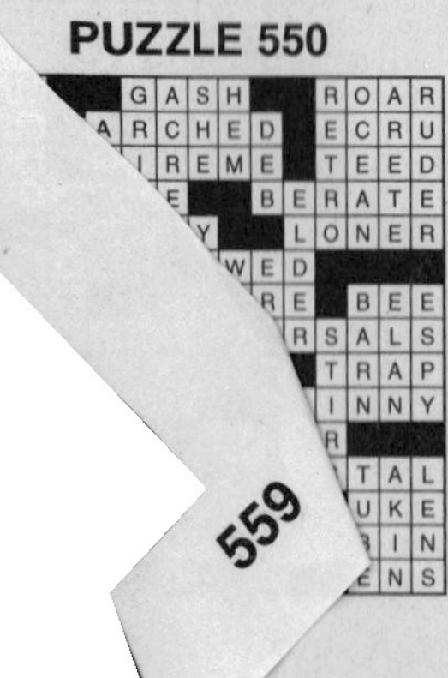

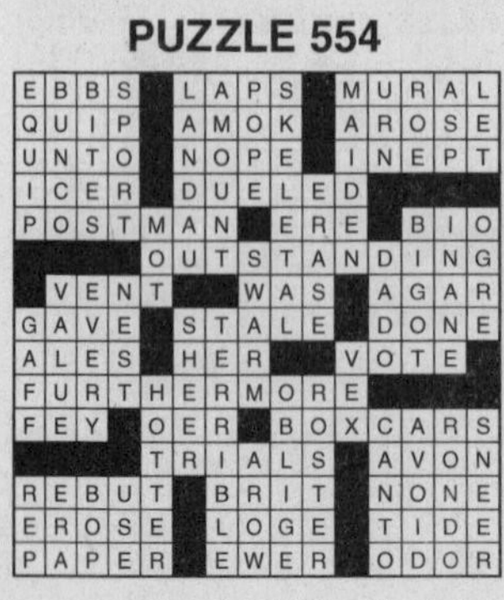

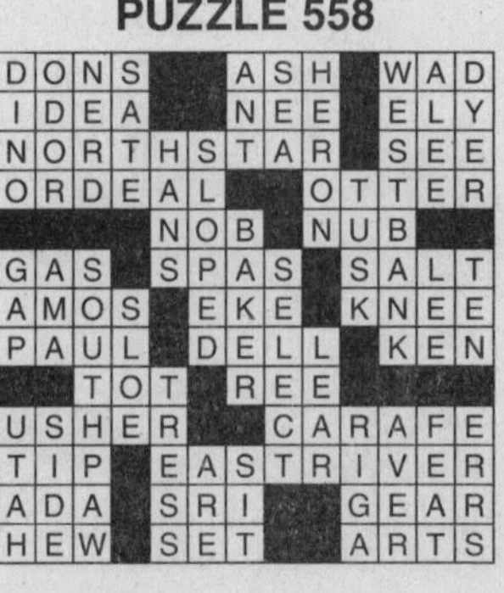

PUZZLE 559

ALPS RUT SLAB
LUAU TONIC PALE
ARID ADIEU AREA
SEND NET TINKER
ERGO TEN
CANOE SARCASM
ARR BLEAR HUMOR
SAGE OXBOW KILO
SNORE ULTRA TAW
ETAGERE ELVER
GAB RALE
EGOIST LET RASP
POOR ENOCH NULL
ORZO REVUE ARIA
SEEN EER LADY

PUZZLE 560

ALOOF BAGS RPMS
ROGER TINA ERIE
CURRICULUM SOLE
ESE NOSE PREFER
DESIGN DELETE
NESS REISSUE
PUFFS CHURN SSS
OHIO CLIPS TOES
TON SHEET MORSE
SHADIER SPOT
LANDAU LUSTER
PEERED POUR IRA
TAXI ASSIGNMENT
ESAU REEL EERIE
REMS SATS RASES

PUZZLE 561

A. One-half to three-fourths of the heat loss your body suffers when you go out into the cold is attributable to not wearing a hat.

B. Archimedes, a mathematician in ancient Greece, invented a one-person elevator using ropes and pulleys.

PUZZLE 562

		CUR	S	E		APP	EAR	S		
	TRU	E	LO	VE		OI	LS	K	IN	
ME	AN		PE	N	DA	NT		ET	H	ER
S	T	ING		S	TE	M		CH	A	R
AS	S	E	T		D	EN	S		BIT	ING
		ST	O	RE		T	HE	RE		
CLA	IM		TEM	PO	S		EN	VI	AB	LE
S	P	IN		S	TRI	DE		SE	A	T
S	LO	W		SE	P	TE	T		CU	TER
	DE	AR	NE	SS		C	RE	ST	S	
		D	AR	ED		T	E	AR		

PUZZLE 563

A-9, B-1, C-4, D-2, E-7, F-8, G-3, H-5.

PUZZLE 564

ECRU GLEN PARK
FLAN WEAVE AGIN
TUTU INGOT RACE
SEES TREK CREW
USHERETTE
SLAT HALVE
VOILE ORDER EGO
INN POWERED IRA
PIG SPLAY INLET
COCOA EAST
ENLARGERS
LAIR DORK TOME
ALOE LEVEE IBEX
BETA BLEED LOSE
SEAL JERK YEAS

PUZZLE 565

HASH SLOT ERGO
ONTO COURT NEON
POINSETTIA RILL
EAR INS ORGANDY
ERE TAP
STRESS VANTAGE
STEAD EYING NOW
HEAL IVANS HIRE
ERR ENEMY EELER
DESPAIR LULLED
ACT SIP
PSYCHIC RAT TWO
ALOE ALTOGETHER
TOUR LOOSE HEAT
HERS GEES YENS

PUZZLE 566

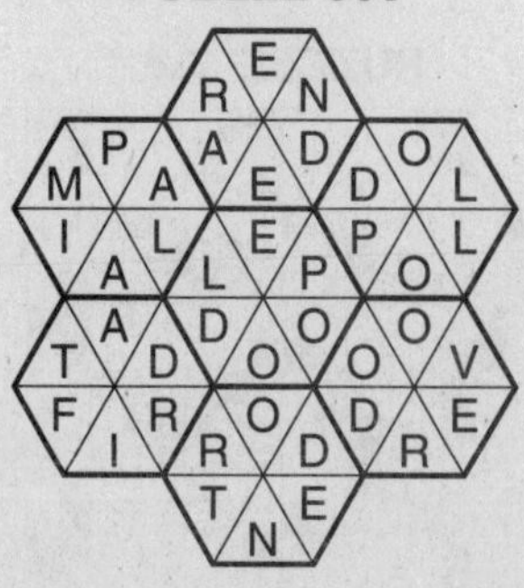

PUZZLE 567

ANTIS BAR ALE
TIARA ERA LED
EXPEL AIM LAG
SQUAB EVE
BUREAU LAYER
ORAL OGLED
ONTO TEE OPEN
PSALM BAKE
FACET OMELET
EGO ARENA
TRY NOR MAJOR
CEE ZAG AWARE
HER ADS SEWED

1-W, 2-A, 3-Z, 4-Y, 5-Q, 6-J, 7-F, 8-P, 9-R, 10-K, 11-D, 12-M, 13-U, 14-I, 15-T, 16-O, 17-E, 18-N, 19-B, 20-X, 21-H, 22-C, 23-S, 24-L, 25-V, 26-G.

PUZZLE 568

CAP AGO ACE
RUE FLUNG JUT
ERE ALTER ARC
WALTZ EARTH
HES TAD
IFFY TWOSOMES
TEA HAIRY AGE
SERVANTS EDGE
INK ORB
SQUAD EBONY
PUG LOCAL BOA
AIL EPOXY OUR
STY EWE END

1-R, 2-L, 3-E, 4-X, 5-F, 6-U, 7-A, 8-Y, 9-K, 10-N, 11-W, 12-G, 13-T, 14-S, 15-I, 16-C, 17-B, 18-H, 19-V, 20-O, 21-M, 22-D, 23-J, 24-Z, 25-Q, 26-P.

PUZZLE 569

CAB ORB WAS
AGED TAR CART
PARE ATTIC UNDO
EPEE LOVE NAPE EDEN
RETRIEVER GREATDANE
VEER SASS
FERN KEEP
PTA ALP
POODLES TERRIER
APT ERA AME NRA
SPANIEL BULLDOG
ALI EAT
BRAM ICED
ALAN TROT
MALAMUTES LHASAAPSO
ALIT MEAL AUNT SLAP
CAKE TIMID KATE
OMEN CAN STIR
NOD EYE ONA

PUZZLE 570

GOLF PRO FETE
ENOL SHONE OPAL
NODE TOTEM WORM
TREASONS BALSAS
PAY PEW
EGO BODE SHE
DAUNTS REDDENED
AURA AGATE ROAD
SNOWPLOW DEARLY
HTS OVAL OSE
PAD WON
DOGLEG LAWSUITS
OKRA ETUDE SORA
LAIC SIRED ETAS
TYPE EER DAYS

PUZZLE 571

SONG: Ticket to Ride, Here Comes the Sun, Rocky Raccoon, Octopus's Garden, We Can Work It Out.

BIRD: Toucan, Heron, Rhea, Osprey, Wren.

CITY: Tulsa, Honolulu, Richmond, Omaha, Wichita.

FLOWER: Tulip, Hibiscus, Rose, Orchid, Wisteria.

ACTRESS: (Charlize) Theron, (Audrey) Hepburn, (Winona) Ryder, (Lena) Olin, (Kate) Winslet.

PUZZLE 572

SPOT ACES CAMP
CAME DARED ALAI
OPEN ORATE NICE
RAG IRES BANTER
ELAPSED NAVE
OLD BETIDES
ALIKE DIVED VAN
PACE HATED LIME
EKE PALER FILET
ESTATES BAN
ARCS RECEDES
WARMTH TOLE RAP
ALOE ENROL PAGE
STAR DOUSE AMEN
PODS WETS YARD

PUZZLE 573

1. Lamp, Camp, Carp, Card, Cord.
2. Wire, Mire, Mile, Mole, Molt, Volt.
3. Watt, Wait, Bait, Bail, Ball, Bull, Bulb.
4. Blow, Blot, Boot, Moot, Most, Must, Muse, Fuse.

PUZZLE 574

GASTROPOD POSIT
R C U O I A L R
ACRONYM GARBAGE
N A T P U T N S
DUMMY ASPARAGUS
A B D I E
MELODIOUS DUPED
E O U E G R
ENDOW ROQUEFORT
N N U V H
SEPARABLE BOONE
N H I O S U K O
ALLOVER TERRIER
R O E E E N N E
LAXER STRATAGEM

PUZZLE 575

DART LAVISH BUB
ELAH ELISHA ERL
TINYBUBBLES AGE
ANIME EEK KNEW
RESOLES ELO
LITTLELEAGUE
OWE ERROL ELATE
ROLE EAVES ALAR
BRINE TECHS SHY
SMALLFORTUNE
ASA SLENDER
RAVI TWA EMILE
ARI SHORTBREADS
HIE SERENE SNEE
SAW TREATY HART

PUZZLE 576

1. Colt, Cold, Cord, Core, Card, Care, Came, Camp.
2. Miso, Mist, Mitt, Mite, Mutt, Mute, Mule, Mull.

PUZZLE 577

ORTS PROW OSLO GLAD
POOP LORE STAR EINE
ETNA ABEE SARA OONA
CHERRYBOMB MATERNAL
TOM SOAP EGG
DELAWARE GREY OILER
OLE STORE EDAM AIDE
ROSS EVILS ENE PANE
ANSEL ECLAT GENERAL
COE AIRES TEA
ENROUTE EATER OCTAL
SEEN ORB HOVEL HULA
TEND NORA NEPAL TET
ADOBE SAVE NONESUCH
AOL SARI GNU
SPINNERS ADAMSAPPLE
OLGA VOID ERAT POOL
MOON IDEA ANNO ELLA
ETTA NERD LEAN ROAN

PUZZLE 578

ADAM LOAF SHAH YOGA
VICE IDLE POLO EPIC
EMIT BOAR ARIA LAVE
REDHERRING STROLLED
ARE YORE DUO
EMANATED TAME TWICE
BANE TART PAVE BOLO
ART CORERS NEW ETON
NEIGH LAITY REPLAYS
RAG DARES SOL
CHEEPED DALES LYRES
LOVE NOW PLEASE ORO
IRAN EVAN SPIT MAIL
PASHA ENOS SLAVERED
OFT DRUB NIT
AMORTIZE BLUEDAHLIA
MAIN DORA ANTE OARS
ELLE ALES MUTE DRIP
NEST LADS EMUS SASS

PUZZLE 579

NEPAL STAB AMIS GAMBA
AMATI POUR DARE URIAH
IMGETTINGOLDSAIDSANTA
LAO EENY COLON USBE
ARTE CHIEN GEE SRO
ALULAE TRUSS ENT WED
DEPOT SHOR LINN EVE
ANDHISWIFESAIDIAGREE
STOA TINT ORALE REPRO
CANE SPORE PALEST
HEH RIG GIROS FEN REO
UNITED MADAM MART
EDGED TOREN SAND ASAN
WHYOHWHYDONTYOUAPPLY
DIP AIRS AEON PRATE
USO ARC TAMER SPINET
HEW CLE ARLEN GALL
ETTE ALIAS ARIA BED
FORSOMESOCIALSECURITY
CLEAN RINK KATE SABRE
CADRE NAGY EGAD EMBER

PUZZLE 580

AMOS DATE DRAG ALIT
LEAH CEDED SUEDE SADA
ARROWHEADS HEADMASTER
PRAMS WELL LEES
OPENS AVA QUIT
AVEC DANA DUN STAB
ADE KEEPONESHEAD UMA
MAR TRAP HELIO PROS
ENOS CRITIC ILL VENUS
NONO HEN DIGS COLOR
EARED ROGET SOLON
ASKED ELAN MAN TEST
ACHED CEE REPORT ASHE
HUED BLASE ITER HIE
ETA LOSEONESHEAD END
MEDE OCT SALA ALAS
RACK VIN CARED
GROW BASE COVET
HEADLINERS SHOWERHEAD
URGE SELES EARLS ARTE
REES ODAS EWES LAME

PUZZLE 581

CAMEL SHUN KID
OMANI NISEI CORE
KINGSRANSOM RAINBOW
EDO TAKER MAILS ABE
SERF YES SELMA EBON
ROOS STRIP TOYED
STREWN GHOST FINS
IRATE SHONE GUM BRO
NABS STORE SERE RAD
BUB SCOUTSHONOR ENE
AMI HAUL TAMER CADS
DAT ENT CHUMS ALTOS
STET BORNE BRAHMA
OFFER HELOT SEMS
TROT BELOW ATA PRAM
TAO REALM ORATE AHA
OUTCAST BAKERSDOZEN
AVES OVATE IDEAL
BET AYES TEDDY

PUZZLE 582

TAME WAKE FOOL PSST
ERIE IBIS IDLY ROTO
RILL PEWS NEAR EMIT
MAKEBELIEVE VIEWERS
DUD SEAL CRAW
FAD MOST TRUE ASHER
ARE SUMAC TALC HERO
LILY TABLA UFOS RIO
ADIEU ROADS BEDECK
TRYTOREMEMBER
ASSISI ALAMO PARTY
NOT APES ELBOW BORE
TREK SOUP LASES BIG
SEANS NEAL REST EGG
MUTE SLOE TOE
ASHCANS LUCKBEALADY
REEK DOVE LAIR EURO
URAL EDIT ALAN GREW
METE DAMS TESS YAWL

PUZZLE 583

ABIRD ASSAM PEASE
CANOE ASTORIA ALLOW
THEDEERHUNTER RILLE
STEERAGE INC LATER
NERO APE AWASH
FACTS AGE DDAY ERA
ETHS PRIOR AIDS KEN
ELA GOINGMYWAY VIED
DIRTIEST ION WENDY
IRATE ISM CLING
SPOON IRS CHARISMA
PITY MYFAIRLADY MAB
ALS BEEF OHARE FETE
REO ORLY NEW ARNEL
FRILL ISA TARO
AWFUL OWN REMINDER
RAISE WESTSIDESTORY
AIRER STEREOS TALIA
BLESS START ALLEN

PUZZLE 584

MITT LOSS WISP IRMA
ACRE EMIT ASHE ROAM
TOIL SANE SLIP IAGO
ENGLISHSETTER ASNER
DEA POE TOSH
BADGER GLO STRAWMAN
ARIES RUE BAAL OISE
STAR AIM BELIE LETS
HELMOND ARTEL IFNOT
ART CLASS NOH
EBONY SHINY ACCOSTS
LENS AHEAD EGO UTAH
MACH BOSS ARE SNAKE
STEELERS ODE WEDGED
PELT AND HAT
LATHE SIBERIANHUSKY
ISEE ATON ENID NONE
LIAR LONE SITE DION
YARD SPAR STIR ORBS

DIAGRAMLESS STARTING BOXES

Puzzle 89 starts in box 3
Puzzle 91 starts in box 1
Puzzle 93 starts in box 7
Puzzle 95 starts in box 6
Puzzle 97 starts in box 14
Puzzle 99 starts in box 6
Puzzle 100 starts in box 15
Puzzle 209 starts in box 1
Puzzle 211 starts in box 6
Puzzle 213 starts in box 9
Puzzle 215 starts in box 3
Puzzle 217 starts in box 2
Puzzle 219 starts in box 2
Puzzle 220 starts in box 6
Puzzle 383 starts in box 7
Puzzle 385 starts in box 9
Puzzle 387 starts in box 1
Puzzle 391 starts in box 1
Puzzle 393 starts in box 1
Puzzle 394 starts in box 7
Puzzle 503 starts in box 1
Puzzle 505 starts in box 1
Puzzle 507 starts in box 9
Puzzle 509 starts in box 7
Puzzle 511 starts in box 1